CRIMINAL PROCEDURE

For my parents and Lidia Janus

CRIMINAL PROCEDURE

MATTHEW LIPPMAN
University of Illinois at Chicago

Los Angeles | London | New Delhi
Singapore | Washington DC

For information:

SAGE Publications, Inc.
2455 Teller Road
Thousand Oaks, California 91320
E-mail: order@sagepub.com

SAGE Publications Ltd.
1 Oliver's Yard
55 City Road
London EC1Y 1SP
United Kingdom

SAGE Publications India Pvt. Ltd.
B 1/I 1 Mohan Cooperative Industrial Area
Mathura Road, New Delhi 110 044
India

SAGE Publications Asia-Pacific Pte. Ltd.
33 Pekin Street #02-01
Far East Square
Singapore 048763

Printed in the United States of America

Library of Congress Cataloging-in-Publication Data

Lippman, Matthew Ross, 1948–
Criminal procedure/Matthew Lippman.
p. cm.
Includes bibliographical references and index.
ISBN 978-1-4129-8130-9 (pbk.: alk. paper)
1. Criminal procedure—United States. I. Title.

KF9619.85.L57 2011
345.73'05—dc22 2009031776

Printed on acid-free paper

10 11 12 13 14 10 9 8 7 6 5 4 3 2 1

Acquiring Editor: Jerry Westby
Assistant Editor: Leah Mori
Editorial Assistant: Eve Oettinger
Production Editor: Sarah K. Quesenberry
Copy Editors: Cate Huisman, Chase Exon
Typesetter: C&M Digitals (P) Ltd.
Proofreader: Scott Oney
Indexer: Michael Ferreira
Cover Designer: Candice Harman

Brief Contents

Detailed Contents

Preface

I have been fascinated by criminal procedure since I was first introduced to the subject in law school. Criminal procedure has continued to inspire me over the two decades that I have taught the course. Writing this text has been a labor of love, and I hope it conveys my passion toward this intellectually challenging field. I tell students that there are good reasons to study criminal procedure:

The American tradition. Criminal procedure provides an introduction to various provisions of the U.S. Constitution and Bill of Rights and involves a discussion of the values and legal judgments that are the foundation of American democracy.

Professional preparation. Anyone who aspires to a career in criminal justice should understand the rules that regulate areas such as interrogations, searches and seizures, and street encounters. Police officers, in particular, apply the rules of criminal procedure on a daily basis.

Academic preparation. The study of criminal procedure helps to develop logical and critical thinking and analytical reading.

Public policy. Criminal procedure addresses issues that are at the heart of the public policy debate in criminal justice, including capital punishment and the limits of police powers.

The study of the law. Reading Supreme Court cases in the field of criminal procedure introduces students to the leading cases in the history of the Court and provides an opportunity to read the actual judgments of some of the greatest jurists in U.S. history.

The text is organized around the theme of balancing the need to detect, investigate, prosecute, and punish crime against the constitutional commitment to protecting the rights and liberties of individuals. The text illustrates how this balance is constantly being adjusted to meet the challenges that confront society. This is a particularly interesting time to be examining the striking of this delicate balance. We have a Supreme Court that includes several recently appointed judges who are introducing new perspectives and points of view that are already impacting the law of criminal procedure. The courts also are confronting novel challenges in areas such as science and technology, terrorism, immigration, and human and narcotics trafficking.

Chapter Organization

The book provides comprehensive essays that introduce each topic with edited versions of the *leading cases* on criminal procedure. Essays typically are followed by *Legal Equations* that summarize the law. The case method provides students with concrete examples and illustrations and thereby facilitates learning and teaching. Reading cases also exposes students to the actual documents that have shaped the American criminal justice system. *Questions for Discussion* follow each case. Instructors can find additional important cases on the *study Web site*. The chapters also feature a number of *You Decide* problems that ask students to apply the law to actual cases.

Each chapter is introduced by an *opening vignette* drawn from a case in the chapter. This is followed by a *chapter outline*. At the end of the chapter, students will find a *Chapter Summary, Chapter Review Questions,* and *Legal Terminology*. Contemporary developments in the law are illustrated by a feature titled *Criminal Procedure in the News*. Students may want to further explore issues in each chapter by exploring *Criminal Procedure on the Web*. The study site, **http://www.sagepub.com/lippmancp**, contains a variety of features, including a summary of the *Leading Cases* discussed in each chapter.

Organization of the Text

The text provides comprehensive coverage of criminal procedure and includes chapters on the structure of the judicial process, the sources and constitutional development of criminal procedure, criminal investigation, remedies for violations of constitutional rights, the pretrial and trial process, sentencing and appeals, and counterterrorism. Although a standard organizational framework is used, instructors may prefer a different approach, and the book is designed to allow teachers to assign chapters in accordance with their own approach to the subject. The book is suitable for a one-semester or two-semester sequence on criminal procedure.

The fifteen chapters of the book may be divided into six sections:

1. ***The criminal justice process and the sources of criminal procedure.*** Chapter 1 discusses the structure of the criminal justice process and is followed by an appendix on the reading of criminal cases. Chapter 2 covers the sources of criminal procedure and the Fourteenth Amendment Due Process Clause incorporation doctrine.
2. ***Searches and seizures.*** Chapter 3 discusses the Fourth Amendment and the legal tests for search and seizure. Chapter 4 covers stop and frisk, and Chapter 5 discusses arrests. Chapter 6 focuses on searches of property, and Chapter 7 covers administrative and special-needs searches.
3. ***Interrogations, lineups, and identifications.*** This section introduces two other investigative methods: interrogations in Chapter 8 and lineups and identifications in Chapter 9.
4. ***Remedies for constitutional violations.*** Chapter 10 covers the exclusionary rule, and Chapter 11 discusses civil and criminal and administrative remedies.
5. ***The pretrial and trial process, sentencing, and appeals.*** Chapter 12 addresses the pretrial process, including prosecutorial discretion, bail, and the right to counsel. Chapter 13 covers preliminary hearings, grand and petit juries, and the trial process. Chapter 14 discusses sentencing, appeals, and habeas corpus.
6. ***Counterterrorism.*** Chapter 15 discusses the challenge of adjusting criminal procedure to meet the threat of international and domestic terrorism.

Acknowledgments

I am hopeful that the textbook conveys my passion and enthusiasm for the teaching of criminal procedure and that the book contributes to the teaching and learning of this most fascinating and vital topic. The book has been the product of the efforts and commitment of countless individuals who deserve much of the credit.

I greatly benefited from reviewers who as noted made valuable contributions to the manuscript. Their comments displayed an impressive insight and commitment to the educational process.

Don Bardel, Bemidji State University

Beth Bjerregaard, University of North Carolina at Charlotte

Gayle Tonvig Carper, Western Illinois University

Kathleen M. Contrino, Buffalo State College

John Edward Coratti, Lamar State College

Kathleen Dunn, Roger Williams University

Peter English, California State University, Fresno

Peter Fenton, Kennesaw State University

Jainta M. Gau, California State University San Bernardino

Michael C. Gizzi, Illinois State University

Donald Haley, Tidewater Community College

Susan Jacobs, University of Nebraska, Omaha

Soraya K. Kawucha, University of North Texas

Ray Kessler, Sul Ross State University

Keith Logan, Kutztown University

Mark Marsolais, Northern Kentucky University

John Milliken, Tri-State University

Kerry Muehlenbeck, Mesa Community College

Chiyere Ogbonna-McGruder, Austin Peay State University

Robert W. Peetz, Midland College

Karen S. Price, Stephen F. Austin State University

Judith Revels, University of North Florida; Florida Community College Jacksonville; Columbia College; Saint Leo University

Mark A. Stelter, Montgomery County Community College

Kelli Styron, Tarleton State University

John Viola, San Francisco State University

Segrest Neal Wailes, Jackson State University

Harrison Watts, Cameron University

The people at SAGE are among the most skilled professionals that an author is likely to encounter. An author is fortunate to publish with SAGE, a publisher that is committed to quality books. The Publisher, Jerry Westby, provided intelligent suggestions and expert direction and in my opinion is unmatched in the field. Denise Simon certainly has no equal as a Developmental Editor. Associate Editor Leah Mori was responsible for organizing a myriad of details associated with the publication of the manuscript. I would also like to thank all the expert professionals at SAGE in production and design who contributed their talents, particularly Senior Project Editor Sarah Quesenberry who coordinated the publication of this lengthy manuscript. The text was immensely improved by the meticulous copyediting of Cate Huisman and Chase Exon. Daniel Hepworth at the University of Illinois at Chicago deserves full credit for his efficient and effective work on the study site.

At the University of Illinois at Chicago, I must mention colleagues Greg Matoesian, Jess Maghan, John Hagedorn, Lisa Frohmann, Beth Richie, the late Gordon Misner, Laurie Schaffner, Dagmar Lorenz, and Dennis Rosenbaum. A great debt of gratitude, of course, is owed to my students, who constantly provide new and creative insights.

I am fortunate to have loyal friends who have provided inspiration and encouragement. These include my dear friends, Wayne Kerstetter, Deborah Allen-Baber, and Agata Fijalkowski, Sharon Savinski, Mindie Lazarus-Black, Kris Clark, the late Leanne Lobravico, Sean McConville, Sheldon Rosing, Bryan Burke, Bill Lane, Ken Janda, Annamarie Pastore, Dennis Judd, Oneida Meranto, Robin Wagner, Jennifer Woodard, and Dr. Peter Ivanovic. I also must thank Ralph and Isadora Semsker and their entire family. Dr. Mary Hallberg has continued to be an important source of support in my life throughout the writing of the text, and the late Lidia Janus remains my true north and inspiration and the love of my life.

I have two members of my family living in Chicago. My sister, Dr. Jessica Lippman, and niece, Professor Amelia Barrett, remain a source of encouragement and generous assistance. Finally, the book is dedicated to my parents, Mr. and Mrs. S.G. Lippman, who provided me with a love of learning. My late father, S.G. Lippman, practiced law for 70 years in the service of the most vulnerable members of society. He believed that law was the highest calling and never turned away a person in need. Law, for him, was a passionate calling to pursue justice and an endless source of discussion, debate, and fascination.

1 An Introduction to Criminal Procedure

Core Concepts and Summary Statements

Introduction

There are good personal and professional reasons to study criminal procedure.

Criminal Law and Criminal Procedure

Criminal procedure influences the enforcement of the criminal law.

Balancing Security and Rights

Criminal procedure strikes a balance between the interests in investigating and detecting crime and in convicting criminals on the one hand and the interest in protecting the right of individuals to be free from intrusions into their privacy and liberty on the other hand.

The Objectives of Criminal Procedure

Criminal procedure seeks to achieve a number of other important objectives. These goals include accuracy, efficiency, public respect, fairness, equality, effective legal representation, popular participation, and allowance for appeals. These all are part of the overall goal, which is "justice."

The Criminal Justice Process

A. A criminal felony case in the federal criminal justice system progresses through a number of stages. The first step is a criminal investigation, and the last step is a petition for postconviction relief.

B. This lengthy procedural process protects individuals against unjustified detention, arrest, prosecution, and conviction.

The Sources of the Law of Criminal Procedure

The sources of criminal procedure include the U.S. Constitution, judicial decisions, state constitutions, the common law tradition, legislative statutes, court rules, agency regulations, and model codes.

The Structure of the Federal and State Court Systems

A. The United States has a federal system of government in which the U.S. Constitution divides powers between the federal government and the fifty state governments. There are parallel judicial systems: Federal courts address those issues that the U.S. Constitution reserves to the federal government, while state courts address issues that are reserved to the states.

B. The federal judicial system is based on a pyramid. At the lowest level are ninety-four district courts. Appeals as a matter of right may be taken to the federal circuit courts of appeals. The U.S. Supreme Court has the discretion to hear appeals as the "court of last resort."

C. State courts also are organized in the form of a pyramid. Prosecutions originate in courts of original jurisdiction, and appeals are made to intermediate appellate courts. Each state's supreme court may grant a discretionary appeal.

Precedent

Courts follow *stare decisis,* which means that once a court has established a legal principle, this rule constitutes a precedent that will be followed by courts in future cases that involve the same legal issue.

Judicial Philosophy

Supreme Court justices and other appellate court judges at times may disagree in deciding a case. These disagreements in many cases are based on divisions in regard to federalism, the role of precedent, bright-line rules, the proper scope of governmental power, differing approaches to interpreting the Constitution, the separation of powers, and the value of achieving a consensus.

Law in Action and Law on the Books

There is a difference between the law established in cases and in statutes and the enforcement of the law.

Introduction

Criminal procedure may seem like a topic that has little relationship to your life and experience. However, anyone who has been stopped by the police, searched, questioned, arrested, or prosecuted for even a minor crime likely has wondered about whether his or her rights were violated and whether the police acted in a lawful fashion. The answer can be found in the body of law that falls under the category of criminal procedure. There are good reasons to study criminal procedure:

- ***Practical usefulness.*** The study of criminal procedure helps you to understand your rights on the street and in court.
- ***Professional usefulness.*** Anyone who plans a career in the criminal justice system should know about criminal procedure.
- ***Understanding of Constitution.*** Judicial decisions on criminal procedure help you to understand various provisions of the U.S. Constitution and the principles of American democracy.
- ***Insight into judicial decisions.*** Judicial decisions on criminal procedure provide insight into how judges decide cases.
- ***Comprehension of public policy.*** Criminal procedure is an arena where important issues are debated and decided.

Criminal Law and Criminal Procedure

Substantive criminal law defines the factual elements of criminal offenses. To convict a defendant, the prosecutor is required to prove the required criminal intent and criminal act and resulting harm beyond a reasonable doubt. A conviction for robbery, for example, requires the prosecutor to establish the intentional, forcible taking of property from the person or presence of another with the intent to permanently deprive the person of the property. Criminal procedure, on the other hand, addresses the procedures involved in the investigation, detection, and prosecution of criminal offenses. In the case of a robbery, this may entail the interrogation of suspects, identifications of suspects by eyewitnesses, searches for weapons and for items belonging to the victim, and the arrest and prosecution of the perpetrator of the crime.

The enforcement of the criminal law is influenced by criminal procedure. Criminal procedure regulates the authority of the police to stop and search individuals, interrogate suspects, and conduct lineups. Strict standards for searches, interrogations, and lineups may interfere with the ability of the police to investigate crimes and to arrest perpetrators. Prosecutors likely find it easier to obtain criminal convictions in the five states that permit juries to convict defendants based on nonunanimous verdicts rather than on the basis of unanimous verdicts.

Balancing Security and Rights

The American system of criminal procedure reflects a faith that fair procedures will result in accurate results. The system can appear to be broken when individuals who appear to be guilty rely on legal technicalities to gain their freedom. There nonetheless is a strong belief that individual freedom is best protected by detailed rules and procedures. We have chosen to create a criminal justice system in which individuals in power are required to follow the law rather than a system in which those in power are free to act as they see fit. The requirement that the police in most cases are required to obtain a search warrant before entering your home protects you against the police conducting searches because they have a hunch or intuition that drugs are stored in your apartment.

Of course, a system of criminal procedure that places too many legal barriers in the way of the police and prosecutors will frustrate the arrest and conviction of the guilty, while a system that places too few barriers in the path of the police may lead to coerced confessions, unnecessary searches, and false convictions. In the United States, there is an effort to create a system of criminal procedure that strikes a balance between the interests of society in investigating and detecting crime and in convicting criminals on the one hand and the interest in protecting the right of individuals to be free from intrusions into their privacy and liberty on the other hand. The balance between security and rights historically has varied depending on historical events. In times of war and other threats to national security, the stress has been placed on the safety and security of society. At other times the pendulum has swung toward protecting the interests of criminal suspects.

The Objectives of Criminal Procedure

In addition to balancing security against the interest of the individual, the American criminal justice system seeks to achieve a range of other objectives. Most of these values reflect the essential principles of American democracy. Keep these goals in mind as you read the textbook and think about the issues presented in each chapter:

- ***Accuracy.*** The innocent should be protected from unjust convictions, and the guilty should be convicted.
- ***Efficiency.*** The criminal justice system should process cases in a reasonable period of time so that individuals do not have the threat of prosecution hanging over them.
- ***Respect.*** The dignity of defendants and victims should be respected.
- ***Fairness.*** Individuals should view the criminal justice process as fair.
- ***Equality.*** The same quality of justice should be provided to both the rich and the poor and to various ethnic and racial groups.
- ***Adversarial.*** Defendants should have the opportunity to be represented by lawyers at crucial points in the criminal justice process.
- ***Participation.*** There is a strong commitment to participation by citizens on juries.
- ***Appeals.*** An individual's freedom should not depend on the decision of a single judge or jury. Appeals are provided to insure that defendants' convictions are reached in a lawful fashion.
- ***Justice.*** These goals together form a criminal justice system whose procedures and results aim to provide justice for defendants and victims and to help insure a just society.

The Criminal Justice Process

A criminal felony in the federal criminal justice system progresses through a number of stages that are outlined below. We will be exploring each phase in depth in the text. Keep in mind that this process is somewhat different in the federal criminal justice system than it is in state systems (see Figure 1.1). The striking feature of the criminal justice process is the number of procedures that exist to protect individuals against an unjustified detention, arrest, prosecution, or conviction. Individuals may be weeded out of the system because there is a lack of evidence that they committed a crime, or because a police officer, prosecutor, or judge or jury exercises his or her **discretion** and decides that there is little social interest in continuing to subject an individual to the criminal justice process. The police may decide not to arrest an individual, a prosecutor may decide not to file a charge or to file a less serious charge or to enter into a plea bargain, the jury may acquit a defendant, or a judge may determine that the offender merits a lenient sentence.

Criminal investigation. The criminal investigation phase involves detecting and investigating criminal offenses. The questions for the police are, first, to determine whether

Figure 1.1 Criminal Justice Flow Chart

What is the sequence of events in the criminal justice system?

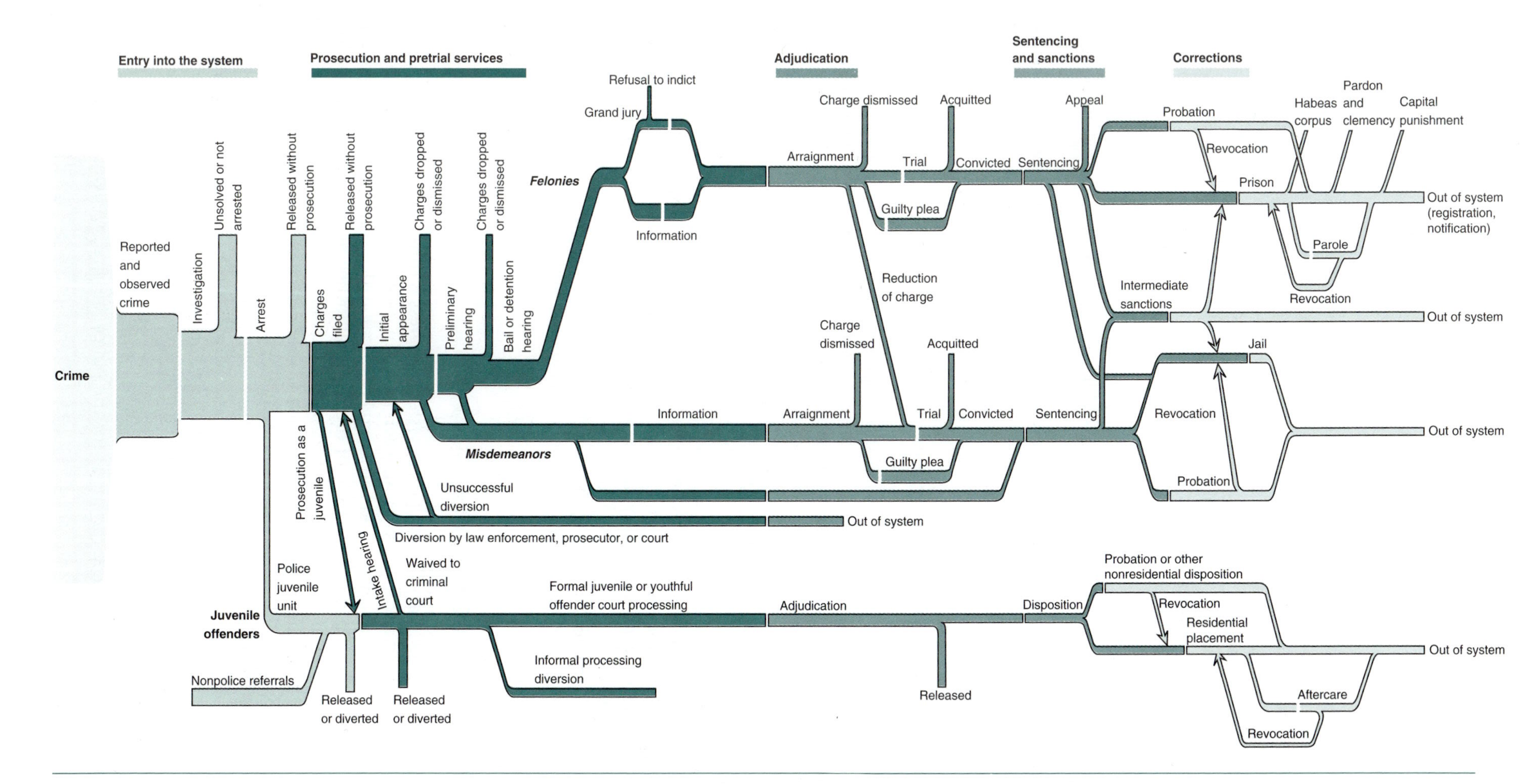

Source: Department of Justice.

Note: This chart gives a simplified view of caseflow through the criminal justice system. Procedures vary among jurisdictions. The weights of the lines are not intended to show actual size of caseloads.

a crime has been committed and, second, to identify who committed the crime. The police may receive reports of a crime from a victim or from an informant, or they may discover ongoing criminal activity and arrest an alleged offender at the scene of the crime. This book will discuss three important methods of criminal investigation: searches and seizures of persons and property based on warrants and warrantless searches and seizures of persons and property (Chapters 3, 4, 5, 6, and 7), interrogations (Chapter 8), and eyewitness identifications along with various methods of physical identification, such as fingerprints and DNA (Chapter 9).

Arrest. Once the police have established that there is probable cause to believe that a crime has been committed and that there is probable cause to believe that a suspect has committed a crime, they are authorized to execute an arrest of an individual and to place him or her in custody. The police may seize a suspect without a warrant or obtain an arrest warrant from a judicial official. A suspect may be searched at the time of his or her arrest (Chapters 5 and 6).

Postarrest. An individual who has been subjected to a custodial arrest will be booked at the police station or jail. This phase involves recording information regarding the arrestee and taking a mug shot and fingerprints. An individual may be subjected to an inventory of his or her possessions (Chapters 5, 6, and 12).

Postarrest investigation. Following an individual's arrest, the police may continue to engage in investigative activities designed to gather evidence of the suspect's guilt (Chapters 3 through 9).

The criminal charge. Prosecutors have the discretion to formally charge suspects with criminal offenses or to decide not to file formal charges and release suspects from custody. Prosecutors who decide to pursue cases file complaints that describe the alleged crimes and the relevant sections of the criminal code. Suspects are then brought for their first appearance before a **magistrate** (a lawyer appointed by a district court judge for an eight-year term) and are informed of the charges against them and of their rights to silence and counsel. Lawyers are appointed for indigents, and bail is fixed. In the case of a warrantless arrest, the first appearance often is combined with a ***Gerstein* hearing** to determine whether there was probable cause to arrest and to detain the suspect (Chapter 12).

Pretrial. The next step in some jurisdictions is a preliminary hearing at which a magistrate determines whether there is probable cause to believe that the defendant committed the crime charged in the complaint. The prosecutor presents witnesses who may be cross-examined by the defense. This allows the defense to learn what some of the evidence is that will be relied on by the prosecution. The defense also may file a motion for discovery, which is a court order requiring the prosecution to turn over information, such as the results of physical examinations or scientific tests, to the defense. A determination that probable cause is lacking results in the magistrate dismissing the case. In the majority of states, a determination of probable cause to support the charge results in the prosecutor filing an **information** with the clerk of the court and the case being bound over for trial. In the federal system and in a minority of states, the case is bound over from the preliminary hearing to a grand jury. A finding of probable cause by the grand jury results in the issuance of an **indictment** against the defendant. Keep in mind that a prosecutor may decide to dismiss the complaint by filing a motion of *nolle prosequi* (Chapter 13).

The next step is the arraignment, at which individuals are informed of the charges against them, advised of their rights, and asked to enter a plea. At this point, plea negotiations between the defense attorney and prosecution may become more heated, as both sides recognize that the case is headed for trial (Chapter 13).

Pretrial motions. The defense attorney may file various pretrial motions. These include a motion to dismiss the charges on the grounds that the defendant already has been prosecuted for the crime or has been denied a speedy trial, a motion to change the location of the trial, or a motion to exclude unlawfully seized evidence from the trial (Chapter 13).

Trial. The accused is guaranteed a trial before a jury in the case of serious offenses. A jury trial may be waived where the defendant pleads guilty or would prefer to stand trial before a judge. A jury generally is composed of twelve persons, although six-person juries are used in some states for less serious felonies and for misdemeanors. Most states require unanimous verdicts despite the fact that nonunanimous verdicts are permitted under the U.S. Constitution (Chapter 14).

Sentencing. Following a criminal conviction, the judge holds a sentencing hearing and establishes the defendant's punishment. There are various types of punishments available to the judge, including incarceration, fines, and probation. States have adopted a variety of approaches to sentencing that provide trial court judges with varying degrees of discretion or flexibility (Chapter 14).

Appeal. A defendant has the right to file an appeal to a higher court. The U.S. Supreme Court and state supreme courts generally possess the discretion to hear a second appeal (Chapter 14).

Postconviction. Individuals who have been convicted and have exhausted their appeals or who have failed to pursue their appeals may file a motion for postconviction relief in the form of a writ of habeas corpus, claiming that the appeals courts committed an error (Chapter 14).

Criminal procedure defines the steps to be followed by the police, prosecutors, defense attorneys, judges, and jurors at each stage in the criminal justice process and also addresses the rights of criminal suspects and defendants. Various sources, outlined in the next section, help to define the procedures that must be followed by criminal justice officials and the rights of individuals in the criminal justice process.

Sources of the Law of Criminal Procedure

The law regarding criminal procedure may be found by consulting various sources.

U.S. Constitution. The U.S. Constitution is the supreme law of the land and is the central source of criminal procedure. You can find issues of criminal procedure referenced in a number of provisions of the Constitution, including the Fourth, Fifth, Sixth, Eighth, and Fourteenth Amendments. These provisions, as we shall see, regulate the conduct of the federal government as well as the fifty states and the District of Columbia.

Judicial decisions. The provisions of the U.S. Constitution are broadly phrased, and their meaning is interpreted and explained by the courts. The U.S. Supreme Court has the final word on the meaning of the text; for example, this court determines what is meant by "unreasonable searches and seizures" in the Fourth Amendment. The Court cannot review every case and rule on every issue. In those instances in which the Supreme Court has not addressed an issue, we look to other courts to understand the meaning of the text of the Constitution. Keep in mind that the study of criminal procedure focuses primarily on the decisions of the U.S. Supreme Court and other federal appeals and state supreme courts.

State constitutions. State constitutions all contain provisions addressing criminal procedure that are similar to the provisions of the U.S. Constitution. The U.S. Supreme Court has the last word on the meaning of the protections that are shared by the U.S. and state constitutions. A state supreme court, however, is free to interpret a provision of its state constitution to provide greater protections than are required by the U.S. Supreme Court. For example, several state supreme courts have held that their state constitutions require that individuals be provided with an attorney during interrogations under circumstances in which the U.S. Supreme Court has held that the federal Constitution does not require that an individual be provided with a lawyer.

Common law. In interpreting the meaning of constitutional phrases such as "cruel and unusual punishment," judges look to the meaning of these terms in the English **common law,** which formed the primary basis of American law and justice in the seventeenth and eighteenth centuries.

Legislative statutes. The U.S. Congress and the fifty state legislatures have passed laws that regulate various aspects of criminal procedure. Federal statutes, for example, provide a detailed description of the requirements for obtaining a warrant and for wiretapping a suspect's phone. Federal and state laws also address jury service and jury selection.

Court rules. The U.S. Congress has authorized the U.S. Supreme Court to formulate **Federal Rules of Criminal Procedure** that provide detailed procedures for the federal criminal justice process; these cover actions from the initial filing of a complaint to the verdict phase of the trial. These rules incorporate the judgments of the U.S. Supreme Court and provide a "road map" that precisely describes how a case is to proceed from the pretrial stage to and through the trial stages. Roughly two-thirds of the states have comprehensive codes drafted by their state supreme courts that regulate criminal procedure. Federal and state courts often adopt their own local rules on how a case is to proceed.

Agency regulations. Law enforcement agencies have their own internal regulations. Police regulations typically address issues such as the conduct of interrogations and the employment of deadly force. These provisions usually are based on the requirements of the U.S. Constitution. The conduct of prosecutors may be controlled by agency guidelines that regulate the policies to be followed in charging individuals with crimes or in plea bargaining. A violation of internal regulations may result in internal disciplinary punishments.

Model codes. The American Law Institute—a group of judges, lawyers, and law enforcement professionals—has drafted a *Model Code of Pre-Arraignment Procedure* to help set standards for street encounters between the police and citizens prior to a formal arrest. This investigative phase of the criminal procedure process is not addressed in the Federal Rules of Criminal Procedure or in state rules of criminal procedure. The American Bar Association's Section on Criminal Justice also publishes suggested standards that address various criminal procedure issues.

Our study of criminal procedure primarily will involve reading federal and state legal decisions. The next section discusses the structure of federal and state courts. The appendix to Chapter 1 introduces you to the process for reading a legal case.

The Structure of the Federal and State Court Systems

The U.S. has a federal system of government in which the Constitution divides powers between the federal government and the fifty state governments. As a result, there are parallel judicial systems. Federal courts address those issues that the U.S. Constitution reserves to the federal government, while state courts address issues that are reserved to the states. Federal courts, for example, have exclusive jurisdiction over prosecutions for treason, piracy, and counterfeiting. Most common law crimes are matters of state jurisdiction. These include murder, robbery, rape, and most property offenses. A state supreme court has the final word on the meaning of a state constitution or state statutes, and the U.S. Supreme Court has no authority to tell a state how to interpret matters of state concern.

The U.S. Supreme Court has recognized the **concurrent jurisdiction** or joint authority of federal and state courts over certain areas, such as claims under federal civil rights law that a law enforcement official has violated an individual's civil rights. This means that an action may be filed in either a state or a federal court.

At a later point in the text we will discuss the fact that because the federal government and a state government are separate sovereign entities, an individual may be prosecuted for the same crime in both a federal and a state court. For example, Terry Nichols was convicted in federal court of involvement in the bombing of the federal building in Oklahoma City and was given life imprisonment. He later was tried in Oklahoma for the same offense and was convicted of 161 counts of murder and was sentenced to 161 life sentences. An individual also can be prosecuted in two states so long as some part of the crime was committed in each state jurisdiction.

The Federal Judicial System

Article III, Section 1 of the U.S. Constitution provides that the judicial power of the United States shall be vested in one Supreme Court and in such "inferior Courts as the Congress may establish."

The federal judicial system is based on a pyramid (see Figure 1.2). At the lowest level are ninety-four district courts. These are federal trial courts of general jurisdiction that hear every

Figure 1.2 Federal Court Hierarchy

Supreme Court

- Highest court in the federal system
- Nine justices, meeting in Washington, D.C.
- Appeals jurisdiction through *certiorari* process
- Limited original jurisdiction over some cases

Courts of Appeal

- Intermediate level in the federal system
- 12 regional "circuit" courts, including D.C. circuit
- No original jurisdiction; strictly appellate

District Courts

- Lowest level in the federal system
- 94 judicial districts in 50 states and territories
- No appellate jurisdiction
- Original jurisdiction over most cases

Sources: Administrative Office of the U.S. Courts; Supreme Court Photo: © 2009 Jupiterimages Corporation; Court of Appeals Photo, © iStock photo.com/David Lewis; District Courts Photo: Public domain.

type of case. District courts are the workhouse of the federal system and are the venue for prosecutions of federal crimes. A single judge presides over the trial. There is at least one judicial district in each state. In larger states with multiple districts, the district courts are divided into geographic divisions (e.g., Eastern District and Western District). There also are judicial districts in the District of Columbia, in the Commonwealth of Puerto Rico, and for the territories of the Virgin Islands, Guam, and the Northern Mariana Islands. Appeals to district courts may be taken from the U.S. Tax Court and from various federal agencies, such as the Federal Communications Commission.

One or more U.S. magistrate judges are assigned to each district court. A magistrate judge is authorized to issue search warrants, conduct preliminary hearings, and rule on pretrial motions submitted by lawyers. Magistrates also may conduct trials for **misdemeanors** (crimes carrying criminal penalties of less than a year in prison) with the approval of the defendant.

The ninety-four district courts, in turn, are organized into twelve regional circuits (see Figure 1.3). Appeals may be taken from district courts to the court of appeals in each circuit. The eleven regional circuit courts of appeals have jurisdiction over district courts in a geographical region. The Fifth Circuit Court of Appeals, for example, covers Texas, Mississippi, and Louisiana. The Tenth Circuit encompasses Colorado, Kansas, New Mexico, Oklahoma, Utah, and Wyoming. The District of Columbia Court of Appeals hears appeals from cases

Figure 1.3 Map of Federal Court of Appeals

Geographic Boundaries

of United States Courts of Appeals and United States District Courts

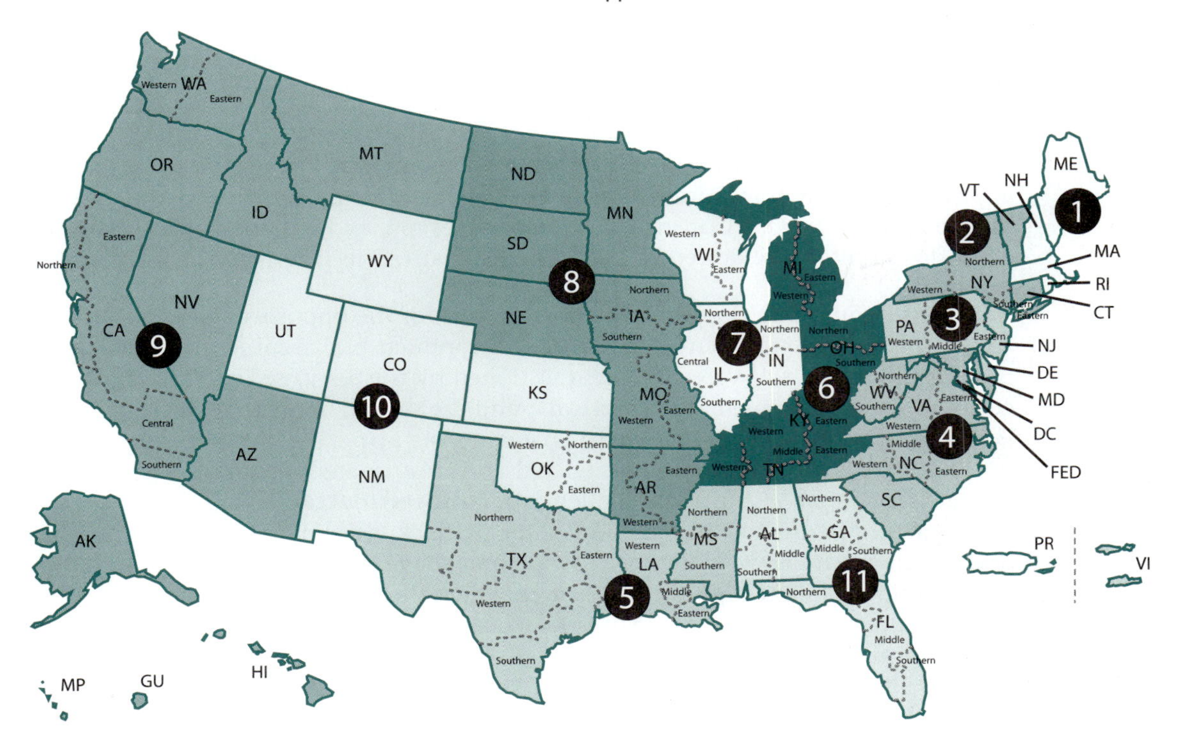

Source: Curtis D. Edmonds, J.D. The Center for Assistive Technology and Environmental Access, Georgia Institute of Technology (GT) College of Architecture (COA), catea@coa.gatech.edu.

involving federal agencies. A thirteenth federal circuit court of appeals has jurisdiction over the Federal Circuit in Washington, D.C., and has nationwide jurisdiction over patent and copyright cases and other specialized appeals involving federal law.

Circuit courts of appeals sit in three-judge panels. In certain important cases, all of the judges in the circuit will sit **en banc.** The decisions of a court of appeals are binding on district courts within the court's circuit. In the event that an appeal is not taken from a district court decision, the district court decision will be final. The number of judges in each circuit varies depending on the size of the circuit. The Ninth Circuit, which includes California, has twenty-eight judges, while the First Circuit in New England has six. Courts of appeals tend to have differing levels of respect and influence within the legal community based on the reputation of the judges on the circuit. One measure of the importance of a circuit is the frequency with which the circuit court's decisions are affirmed by the U.S. Supreme Court.

The U.S. Supreme Court sits at the top of the hierarchy of federal and state courts. It is called the "court of last resort," because there is no appeal from a decision of the Supreme Court. The Supreme Court decision sets the **precedent** and is the binding authority on every state and every federal court in the United States on the meaning of the U.S. Constitution and on the meaning of a federal law. In other words, any court in the country that hears a case involving an issue on which the Supreme Court has ruled is required to follow the Supreme Court's judgment. Precedent is based on the judicial practice of following previous opinions or ***stare decisis,*** which literally translates as "to stand by precedent and to stand by settled points."

The Supreme Court consists of a chief justice and eight associate justices. The Court reviews a relatively limited number of cases. In an active year, the Supreme Court may rule on 150 of the 7,000 cases it is asked to consider. These cases generally tend to focus on issues in which different federal circuit courts of appeals have made different decisions or on significant issues that demand attention. There are two primary ways for a case to reach the Supreme Court.

- **Original jurisdiction.** The Court has **original jurisdiction** over disputes between the federal government and a state, between states, and in cases involving foreign ministers or ambassadors. Conflicts between states have arisen in cases of boundary disputes in which states disagree over which state has a right to water or to natural resources. These types of cases are extremely rare.

- **Writ of certiorari.** The Court may take an appeal from the decision of a court of appeals. The Supreme Court also will review state supreme court decisions that are decided on the basis of the U.S. Constitution. Four judges must vote to grant **certiorari** for a lower court decision to be reviewed by the Supreme Court. This is termed the **rule of four**.

The U.S. Supreme Court requires the lawyers for the opposing sides of a case to submit a **brief** or a written argument. The Court also conducts oral arguments, in which the lawyers present their points of view and are questioned by the justices. The party appealing a lower court judgment is termed the **appellant,** and the second name in the title of a case typically is the party against whom the appeal is filed, or the **appellee**.

Individuals who have been convicted and incarcerated and have exhausted their state appeals may file a constitutional challenge or **collateral attack** against their conviction. The first name in the title of the case on collateral attack is the name of the inmate bringing the case, or the **petitioner**, while the second name, or **respondent,** typically is that of the warden or individual in charge of the prison in which the petitioner is incarcerated. These habeas corpus actions typically originate in federal district courts and are appealed to the federal court of appeals and to the U.S. Supreme Court. In a collateral attack, an inmate bringing the action files a petition for habeas corpus review, requesting a court to issue an order requiring the state to demonstrate that the petitioner is lawfully incarcerated. The ability of a petitioner to compel the state to demonstrate that he or she has been lawfully detained is one of the most important safeguards for individual liberty and is guaranteed in Article I, Section 9, Clause 2 of the U.S. Constitution.

Five of the nine Supreme Court justices are required to agree if they are to issue a **majority opinion**. This is a decision that will constitute a legal precedent. A justice may agree with the majority and want to write a **concurring opinion** that expresses his or her own view. A justice, for example, may agree with the majority decision but base his or her decision on a different reason. In some cases, four justices may agree and, along with various concurring opinions from other justices, constitute a majority. In this instance, there is a **plurality opinion,** and no single majority opinion. A justice who disagrees with the majority may draft a **dissenting opinion** that may be joined by other justices who also disagree with the majority decision. In some instances, a justice may disagree with some aspects of a majority decision while concurring with other parts of the decision. There are examples of dissenting opinions that many years later attract a majority of the justices and come to be recognized as the "law of the land." A fifth type of decision is termed a **per curiam** decision. This is an opinion of the entire court without any single judge being identified as the author.

Supreme Court justices and other federal judges are appointed by the U.S. president with the approval of the U.S. Senate, and they have lifetime appointments so long as they maintain "good behavior." The thinking is that this protects judges from political influence and pressure. There is a question whether Supreme Court justices should have limited tenure, rather than a lifetime appointment, to insure that there is a turnover on the Court. The notion that an unelected judge should hold a powerful court appointment for many years strikes some commentators as inconsistent with democratic principles.

You should also be aware that there are a number of specialized federal courts with jurisdiction that is limited to narrow questions. Two special courts are the U.S. Court of Claims, which considers suits against the government, and the Court of International Trade, which sits in New York and decides international trade disputes and tariff claims. There are also a number of other "non–Article III" courts. These are courts that the framers of the Constitution did not provide for in Article III of the U.S. Constitution and that have been created by Congress. These courts include the U.S. Tax Court, bankruptcy courts, the U.S. Court of Military Appeals and Court of Veterans' Appeals, and the courts of administrative law judges who decide the cases of individuals who appeal an administrative agency's denial of benefits (e.g., a claim for social security benefits).

State Judicial Systems

There is significant variation among the states in the structure of their state court systems. Most follow the general structure outlined below. The organization of California courts in Figure 1.4 illustrates how one state arranges its judicial system. You may want to compare this with the structure of the judicial system in your state.

Prosecutions are first initiated or originate in **courts of original jurisdiction.** There are two types of courts in which a criminal prosecution may originate. First, there are trial **courts of limited jurisdiction**. These local courts are commonly called municipal courts, police courts, or magistrate's courts. The courts prosecute misdemeanors and in some instances specified felonies. Judges in municipal courts also hear traffic offenses, set bail, and conduct preliminary hearings in felony cases. In most instances, judges preside over criminal cases in these courts without a jury. A case in which a judge sits without a jury is termed a **bench trial**. Most jurisdictions also have specialized courts of limited jurisdiction to hear particular types of cases. These include juvenile courts, traffic courts, family or domestic courts, small claims courts, and courts that hear offenses against local ordinances.

Trial **courts of general jurisdiction** hear more serious criminal and civil cases. In some states, courts of general jurisdiction have jurisdiction over criminal appeals from courts of limited jurisdiction. This typically entails a **trial *de novo*,** which means that a completely new trial is conducted that may involve the same witnesses, evidence, and legal arguments that formed the basis of the first trial. These courts of general jurisdiction commonly are referred to as circuit courts, district courts, or courts of common pleas and have jurisdiction over cases that arise in a specific county or region of the state. New York curiously names its court of general jurisdiction the supreme court.

Figure 1.4 California State Court System

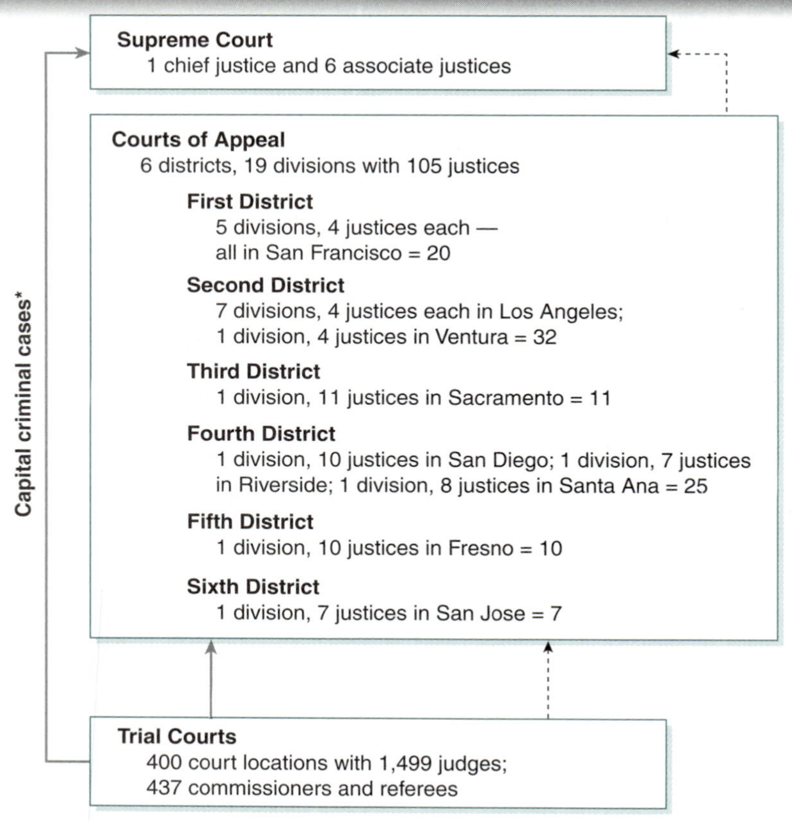

* Death penalty cases are automatically appealed from the superior court directly to the Supreme Court.

(Judgeship numbers are current as of February 2001) —— Line of Appeal ----- Line of Discretionary Review

Two types of courts

California has two types of courts: 58 trial courts, one in each county, and appellate courts. Trial courts are the superior courts; appellate courts are the six districts of the Courts of Appeal and the California Supreme Court. In the trial courts, a judge and sometimes a jury hear witnesses' testimony and other evidence and decide cases by applying the relevant law to the relevant facts. In the appellate courts, people who are not satisfied with a trial court decision appeal cases to judges. The California courts serve nearly 34 million people.

Trial courts. In June 1998, California voters approved Proposition 220, a constitutional amendment that permitted the judges in each county to merge their superior and municipal courts into a "unified," or single, superior court. As of February 2001, all of California's 58 counties have voted to unify their trial courts.

Superior courts now have trial jurisdiction over all criminal cases including felonies, misdemeanors, and traffic matters. They also have jurisdiction over all civil cases, including family law, probate, juvenile, and general civil matters. Nearly 8.8 million cases were filed in the trial courts at some 400 court locations throughout the state during 1998–1999. Appeals in limited civil cases (where $25,000 or less is at issue) and misdemeanors are heard by the appellate division of the superior court. When a small claims case is appealed, a superior court judge decides the case.

Appellate courts

Supreme Court: The state's highest court, the Supreme Court, may grant review of cases decided by the courts of appeal. Certain other cases, such as death penalty appeals and disciplinary cases involving judges and attorneys, are appealed directly to this court. At least four of the seven justices must agree on decisions of the court. The court's decisions are binding on all other state courts.

Courts of Appeals: Panels of three justices hear appeals from superior courts, except in death penalty cases, which are appealed automatically to the Supreme Court. The courts of appeal determine whether a trial court committed legal error in handling the cases that are presented on appeal.

Source: Superior Court of California, County of Glenn (2009). *Structure of California Court System,* http://www.glenncourt.ca.gov/general_info/teachers/structure.html

Appeals from courts of general jurisdiction are taken in forty of the fifty states to **intermediate appellate courts**. An appeal as a matter of right may be filed to an intermediate court, which typically sits in panels of two or three judges. The court usually decides the case based on the transcript or written record of the trial from the lower court. The appeals court does not hear witnesses or consider new evidence.

The Supreme Court is the court of last resort in a state system and has the final word on the meaning of local ordinances, state statutes, and the state constitution. (Note that New York is different and refers to its court of last resort as the Court of Appeals.) A **discretionary appeal** may be available from an intermediate court. This means that the Supreme Court is not required to review the decision of a lower court and will do so at its discretion. In those states that do not have intermediate appellate courts, appeals may be directly taken from trial courts to the state supreme court. State supreme courts function in a similar fashion to the U.S. Supreme Court and hear every type of case. The U.S. Supreme Court has no authority to tell a state supreme court how to interpret the meaning of its state constitution.

State court judges are selected using a variety of procedures. Some states elect judges in a partisan election in which judges run under the label of a political party, while other states hold nonpartisan elections in which judges are not identified as belonging to a political party. In other states, judges are elected by the state legislature. A fourth approach is appointment by the governor with the consent of the legislature. The so-called Missouri Plan provides for appointment by the governor, and following a judge's initial period of judicial service, the electorate is asked whether to retain or to reject the judge's continuation in office. A minority of states provide for the lifetime appointment of judges. Most states limit the length of the judge's term in office. In many states different procedures are used for different courts. There is a continuing debate over whether judges should be elected or appointed based on merit and qualifications.

Precedent

We have seen that courts follow *stare decisis,* which means that once a court has established a legal principle, this rule constitutes a precedent that will be followed by courts in future cases that involve the same legal issue. The advantage of precedent is that courts do not have to reinvent the wheel each time that they confront an issue and, instead, are able to rely on the opinion of other judges. A judgment that is based on precedent and the existing law also takes on credibility and is likely to be respected and followed. Precedent is merely the method that all of us rely on when undertaking a new challenge: We ask how other people went about doing the same task.

Courts have different degrees of authority in terms of precedent. As noted, U.S. Supreme Court decisions constitute precedent for all other courts in interpreting the U.S. Constitution and federal laws. Circuit courts of appeals, U.S. district courts, and state courts are bound by Supreme Court precedent. Circuit courts of appeals and state supreme courts establish binding precedents within their territorial jurisdictions. In other words, a state supreme court decision constitutes precedent for all courts within the state.

What if there is no precedent? A case that presents an issue that a court has never previously decided is termed a case of **first impression.** In these instances, a court will look to see how other courts have decided the issue. These other court decisions do not constitute precedent, but they are viewed as **persuasive authority,** or cases to be considered in reaching a decision. For example, a federal court of appeals will look to see how other courts of appeals have decided an issue and will view these decisions as persuasive authority rather than as **binding authority.**

A decision of the Supreme Court of California has binding authority on all lower courts in California. The decision of a lower level California court that fails to follow precedent likely will be appealed and reversed by the Supreme Court of California. The decisions of the Supreme Court of California do not have binding authority on courts outside of California, but they may be consulted as persuasive authority. Courts are viewed as carrying different degrees of status within the legal world in regard to their persuasive authority. For example, the Second Circuit of Federal Appeals in New York is viewed as particularly knowledgeable on financial matters, because the judges are experienced in deciding cases involving Wall Street, banking, and finance.

Courts are reluctant to overturn precedents, although this does occur on rare occasions. A court may avoid a precedent by distinguishing the facts of the case that they are deciding from the facts involved in the case that constitutes a precedent.

Judicial Philosophy

U.S. Supreme Court decisions are the central source for interpreting the U.S. constitutional provisions addressing criminal procedure. These decisions cover areas ranging from searches and seizures to interrogations and the right to a lawyer at trial. The Supreme Court's approach to criminal procedure historically has undergone significant shifts. These changes in the Supreme Court's approach have reflected transformations in popular attitudes toward crime and criminals and in most instances also reflect the appointment of new justices to the bench. Scholars tend to refer to the name of the chief justice as a shorthand for describing the shifting philosophy of the Supreme Court. The liberal Warren Court (Chief Justice Earl Warren, 1953–1969), for example, soon gave way to the more conservative Burger Court (Chief Justice Warren Burger, 1969–1986) which, in turn, was succeeded by the even more conservative Rehnquist Court (Chief Justice William Rehnquist, 1986–2005). The legacy of the current court, headed by Chief Justice John Roberts, remains to be decided.

Keep in mind that the use of the labels *liberal* and *conservative* to describe justices may not be fully accurate in every instance. A liberal justice who believes in individual liberty also may be tough on crime, and a conservative justice who opposes abortion also may be an absolutist when it comes to freedom of speech. There are other issues where a justice's point of view is not easily categorized as either liberal or conservative. History also has demonstrated that justices have changed their philosophy while serving on the Court. There are several areas of disagreement between Supreme Court justices that may help you in understanding why they may take differing approaches to deciding a case:

Federalism. Some justices stress that states should be free to follow their own approach to criminal procedure, and the justices are reluctant to reverse the decisions of state supreme courts. This "states' rights" approach is contrasted with the view of those justices that believe that it is best to have the same system of criminal procedure in the federal courts and in all fifty states.

Precedent. Justices differ in their willingness to deviate from prevailing precedent.

Bright-line rules. Justices may view their decisions as opportunities to establish general rules to guide the police and lower courts. Other justices limit their decisions to the specific facts of the case before them and do not formulate general rules.

Police power. Some justices have greater trust in the police and are willing to expand police powers, while others favor tighter legal controls on the police.

State of mind. A related question is whether to use an objective or a subjective standard in evaluating the conduct of the police and other criminal justice professionals. In evaluating whether a police officer stopped a motorist based on the driver's gender or race, justices favoring police powers rely on an objective standard in evaluating the lawfulness of an arrest. The only issue is whether there was an objective basis for stopping and arresting the motorist. Justices who are skeptical in regard to police powers may rely on a subjective standard and ask whether the police officer intended to enforce the law in a discriminatory fashion.

Interpretation. In interpreting the U.S. Constitution, **originalist** justices are guided by the intent of the framers of the documents. Justices who believe in **contextualism** tend to interpret the Constitution in a broad fashion and argue that the Constitution is a dynamic, "living" document that should be interpreted to meet the current needs of society.

Separation of powers. There are justices who are reluctant to hold unconstitutional the decisions of the elected executive and congressional branches of government. Other justices are more willing to hold that the executive and legislative branches acted in an unconstitutional fashion.

Consensus. Some justices make an effort to create a consensus and to reach a single majority decision, while other justices are more willing to dissent from the other justices on the Court.

Psychology. Justices are only human, and their decisions in some instances may be influenced by their individual experiences and background.

Justices who favor a judiciary that intervenes to set public policy and to combat social problems are categorized as favoring **judicial activism**. In contrast, justices who believe that the courts should play a limited role and who believe that public policy decisions are to be made by elected officials are viewed as favoring **judicial restraint.**

Law in Action and Law on the Books

As you read the cases in the text, keep in mind that although the American criminal justice system affords defendants a long list of rights and protections, there is a difference between *law on the books* and *law in action*. Defendants may choose to plead guilty, waive their constitutional right to challenge an unlawful search, or waive their right to be tried before a jury. Defense attorneys may not vigorously defend their clients. Prosecutors may choose to charge some defendants with criminal offenses while dropping the charges against other defendants charged with the same crime. There also is the unfortunate fact that the police and other criminal justice professionals may abuse their authority and discriminate against minorities, women, or young people or may fail to abide by the letter of the law. Keep in mind that the exercise of discretion is not necessarily a bad thing. A police officer's decision not to arrest a juvenile, or a prosecutor's decision to offer a light sentence to a first-time offender in return for a guilty plea, may be a way of achieving "justice."

Chapter Summary

The American system of criminal procedure reflects a faith that fair procedures will result in accurate results. Of course, a system of criminal procedure that places too many legal barriers in the way of the police and prosecutors will frustrate the arrest and conviction of the guilty, while a system that places too few barriers in the way of the police may lead to coerced confessions, unwarranted searches, and false convictions. In the United States, there is an effort to create a system of criminal procedure that strikes a balance between the interests of society in investigating and detecting crime and in convicting criminals on the one hand and the interest in protecting the right of individuals to be free from intrusions into their privacy and liberty on the other hand. Criminal procedure also seeks to achieve a range of other objectives, including accuracy, efficiency, public respect, fairness, and equality, all of which together promote the ultimate goal, which is to insure justice.

A criminal felony in the federal criminal justice system progresses through a number of stages. A case may begin with a police investigation and may not conclude until the individual's claim for postconviction relief is exhausted. A striking feature of the criminal justice process is the number of procedures that exist to protect individuals against unjustified detention, arrest, prosecution, and conviction.

There are various sources that set forth the responsibility of criminal justice officials and the rights of individuals in the criminal justice process. These include the relevant provisions of the U.S. Constitution, judicial decisions, state constitutions, the common law, legislative statutes, rules of criminal procedure, agency regulations, and model codes.

The United States has a federal system of government in which the U.S. Constitution divides powers between the federal government and the fifty state governments. As a result, there are parallel judicial systems. Federal courts address those issues that the U.S. Constitution reserves to the federal government, while state courts address issues that are reserved to the states. The federal judicial system is based on a pyramid. At the lowest level are ninety-four district courts. District courts are the workhouse of the federal system and are the venue for prosecutions of federal crimes. The ninety-four district courts, in turn, are organized into eleven regional circuits. There is also a Circuit Court of Appeals for the District of Columbia. A thirteenth U.S. court of appeals is the Federal Circuit in Washington, D.C. Appeals may be taken from district courts to the court of appeals in each circuit. The U.S. Supreme Court sits at the top of the hierarchy of federal courts and may grant certiorari and hear discretionary appeals from circuit courts. The Supreme Court is called the "court of last resort," because there is no appeal from a decision of the Court. A Supreme Court decision sets precedent and has binding authority on every state and every federal court in the United States with respect to the meaning of the U.S. Constitution and on the meaning of federal laws.

There is significant variation in the structure of state court systems. Prosecutions are first initiated in courts of original jurisdiction. In courts of limited jurisdiction, misdemeanors and specified felonies are prosecuted. In trial courts of general jurisdiction, more serious criminal and civil cases are heard. In some states, courts of general jurisdiction have jurisdiction over criminal appeals from courts of limited jurisdiction. Appeals from courts of general jurisdiction are taken in most states to intermediate appellate courts. The state supreme courts are the courts of last resort in each state and have the final word on the meaning of local ordinances, state statutes, and the state constitution. A discretionary appeal is available from intermediate courts to the state supreme court.

Courts have different degrees of authority in terms of precedent. As noted, U.S. Supreme Court decisions constitute precedent for all other courts in interpreting the U.S. Constitution and federal laws. Circuit courts of appeals, district courts, and state courts are bound by U.S. Supreme Court precedent. Circuit courts of appeals and state supreme courts establish binding precedents within their territorial jurisdictions. In those instances in which there is no precedent, an appellate court may look to other coequal courts for persuasive authority.

U.S. Supreme Court decisions are the central source for interpreting the federal constitutional provisions addressing criminal procedure. These decisions cover areas ranging from searches and seizures to interrogations and the right to a lawyer at trial. The Supreme Court's approach to criminal procedure historically has undergone significant shifts. These changes in the Supreme Court's approach have reflected transformations in popular attitudes toward crime and criminals, and in most instances they also reflect the appointment of new justices to the Court. Scholars tend to refer to the name of the chief justice as a shorthand for describing the shifting philosophy of the Supreme Court. There are several areas of disagreement among U.S. Supreme Court justices that account for the differences in their views. These include issues of federalism, the role of precedent, the scope of governmental power, and philosophies of constitutional interpretation.

As you read the textbook, remain aware that while we primarily are concerned with "law on the books," these procedures are not always followed by "law in action."

Chapter Review Questions

1. How does criminal procedure affect the enforcement of criminal law?
2. Discuss the balance between security and rights in criminal procedure.
3. What values does the system of criminal procedure seek to achieve?
4. Outline the steps in the criminal justice system.
5. Describe the organization of the federal and state judicial systems.
6. What is the role of precedent in judicial decision making?
7. Is there a difference between law on the books and law in action?

Legal Terminology

appellant
appellee
bench trial
binding authority
brief
certiorari
collateral attack
common law
concurrent jurisdiction
concurring opinion
contextualism
courts of general jurisdiction
courts of limited jurisdiction
courts of original jurisdiction
discretion
discretionary appeal
dissenting opinion
en banc
Federal Rules of Criminal Procedure
first impression
Gerstein hearing
indictment
information
intermediate appeal late courts
judicial activism
judicial restraint
magistrate
majority opinion
misdemeanor
original jurisdiction
originalist
per curiam
persuasive authority
petitioner
plurality opinion
precedent
respondent
rule of four
stare decisis
trial *de novo*

Criminal Procedure on the Web

Log on to the Web-based student study site at **http://www.sagepub.com/lippmancp** to assist you in completing the Criminal Procedure on the Web exercises, as well as for additional features such as leading cases, podcasts, self-quizzes, and audio/video links.

1. Take a virtual tour of the U.S. Supreme Court.
2. Look up the court structure in the state in which you live.
3. Learn how to brief a case.

Bibliography

Joshua Dressler and Alan C. Michaels, *Understanding Criminal Procedure: Investigation,* vol. 1, 4th ed. (Newark, NJ: LexisNexis, 2006), pp. 1–20. A summary of the major steps in the criminal justice process with a discussion of judicial decision making in criminal procedure cases.

Wayne R. LaFave, Gerald H. Israel, and Nancy J. King, *Criminal Procedure,* 4th ed. (St. Paul, MN: West Publishing, 2004), pp. 2–42. A summary of the criminal justice system and a discussion of the objectives of the criminal justice system.

Anthony Lewis, *Gideon's Trumpet* (New York: Vintage, 1983). An absorbing account of the famous case of *Gideon v. Wainwright* that traces the judicial process from the trial court through to the decision of the U.S. Supreme Court.

Russell L. Weaver, Leslie W. Abramson, John M. Burkoff, and Catherine Hancock, *Principles of Criminal Procedure* (St. Paul, MN: West Publishing, 2004), pp. 2–17. A clear summary of the criminal justice process from criminal investigation to habeas corpus.

Appendix

Reading and Briefing Cases

Introduction

A unique aspect of studying criminal procedure is that you have the opportunity to read actual court decisions. Reading cases likely will be a new experience, and although you may encounter some initial frustrations, in my experience students fairly quickly master the techniques of legal analysis.

The case method was introduced in 1870 by Harvard law professor Christopher Columbus Langdell and is the primary method of instruction in nearly all American law schools. This approach is based on the insight that students most effectively learn the law when they study actual cases. Langdell encouraged instructors to employ a question and answer classroom technique termed the **Socratic method.** The most challenging aspect of this approach involves posing hypothetical or fictitious examples that require students to apply the case material to new factual situations.

The study of cases assists you to

- understand the principles of criminal procedure.
- improve your skills in critical reading and thinking.
- acquaint yourself with legal vocabulary and procedures.
- appreciate how judges make decisions.
- learn to apply the law to the facts.

The cases in this textbook have been edited to highlight the most important points. Some nonessential material has been omitted to assist you in reading and understanding the material. You may want to read the entire, unedited case in the library or online.

The Structure of Cases

In law school, students are taught to divide a case into two parts, an *introduction* and a *judicial opinion.* These two sections have several component parts, which you should keep in mind.

Introduction

The initial portion of a case is divided into title, citation, and identification of the judge.

Title. Cases are identified by the names of the parties involved in the litigation. At the trial level, this typically involves the prosecuting authority, either a city, a county, a state, or the federal government followed by "versus" and the name of the defendant. On appeal, the introduction is slightly different. The first name refers to the appellant who is bringing the appeal, and the second to the appellee who is defending against the appeal. On a collateral attack, remember that the parties are termed petitioners and respondents. You will notice that judicial decisions in some cases utilize a shorthand version of a case and only refer to one of the parties, much like calling someone by his or her first or last name.

Citation. Immediately following the names, you will find the citation, which directs you to the book or **legal reporter** where you can find the case in a law library. Cases also increasingly are available online. The standard form for citations of cases, statutes, and law journals is contained in *The Bluebook* published by the Harvard Law Review Association.

Judge. The name of the judge who wrote the opinion typically appears at the beginning of the case. An opinion written by a respected judge may prove particularly influential with other courts. The respect accorded to a judge's decisions may be diminished by the fact that his or her decisions frequently are reversed by appellate courts.

Outline. The full, unedited cases in legal reporters typically begin with a list of numbered paragraphs or **head notes** that outline the main legal points in the case. There also is a summary of the case and of the decisions of other courts that have heard the case. These outlines have been omitted from the edited cases reprinted in the text.

Judicial Opinions

The judge's legal discussion is referred to as the opinion, judgment, or decision. Students are taught to divide the opinion into history, facts, law, and reasoning. These component parts are not always neatly distinguished, and you may have to organize the material in your mind as you read the case.

- ***History.*** The initial portion of a case typically provides a summary of the decisions of the lower courts that previously considered the case and the statutes involved.
- ***Facts.*** Each case is based on a set of facts that present a question to be answered by the judge. This question, for instance, may involve whether the police were required to read the defendant his or her Miranda rights. This question is termed the *issue.*
- ***Law.*** The judge then applies the legal rule to the facts and reaches a **holding** or decision.

The **reasoning** is the explanation offered by the judge for the holding. Judges also often include comments and observations (in Latin *obiter dicta* or comments from the bench) on a wide range of legal and factual concerns that provide important background, but which may not be central to the holding. These comments may range from legal history to a discussion of a judge's philosophy of punishment.

As noted in Chapter 1, judges typically rely on *precedents* or the holdings of other courts. Precedent is an application of the principle of *stare decisis,* which literally translates as "to stand by precedent and to stand by settled points." The court may follow a precedent or point out that the case at hand is *distinguished* from the precedent and calls for a different rule.

Appellate courts typically are composed of a multiple-judge panel consisting of three or more judges, depending on the level of the court. The judges typically meet and vote on a case and issue a *majority opinion,* which is recognized as the holding in the case. Judges in the majority may choose to write a *concurring opinion* supporting the majority, which typically is based on slightly different grounds. On occasion, a majority of judges agree on the outcome of a case, but are unable to reach a consensus on the reasoning. In these instances there typically is a *plurality opinion* as well as one or more *concurring opinions.* In cases in which a court issues a plurality opinion, the decisions of the various judges in the majority must be closely examined to determine the precise holding of the case.

A judge in the minority has the discretion to write a *dissenting opinion.* Other judges in the minority also may issue separate opinions or join the dissenting opinion of another judge. In those instances in which a court is closely divided, the dissenting opinion with the passage of time may come to reflect the view of a majority of the members of the court. The dissent also may influence the majority opinion. The judges in the majority may feel compelled to answer the claims of the dissent or to compromise in order to attract judges who may be sympathetic to the dissent.

A *per curiam* opinion, as noted, is a brief opinion written by an entire appellate court in which no judge is identified as the author.

In reading the edited cases reprinted in this text, you will notice that the cases are divided into various sections. This has been done to help you in understanding the court's judgment. The facts of the case and the issue to be decided by the court are typically followed by the court's reasoning or justification and holding or decision. A number of questions appear at the end of the case to help you understand the opinion.

Briefing a Case

Your instructor may ask you to *brief* or summarize the main points of the cases reprinted in the text. A student brief is a concise, shorthand, written description of the case and is intended to assist you in understanding and organizing the material and in preparing for class and examinations. A brief generally includes several standard features. These, of course, are only broad guidelines, and there are differing opinions on the proper form of a brief. Keep in mind that a particular case that you are reading also may not be easily reduced to a standard format. You should ask your instructor how he or she would like you to brief the assigned cases.

A general outline of a brief is as follows:

1. ***The name of the case and the year the case was decided.*** The name of the case will help you in organizing your class notes. Including the year of decision places the case in historical context and alerts you to the fact that an older decision may have been revised in light of modern circumstances.

2. ***The state or federal court deciding the case and the judge writing the decision.*** This will assist you in determining the place of the court in the judicial hierarchy and whether the decision constitutes a precedent to be followed by lower-level courts.

3. ***Facts.*** Write down the relevant facts. You should think of this as a story that has a factual beginning and conclusion. The best approach is to put the facts into your own words.

4. ***Determine the issue that the court is addressing in the case.*** This customarily is in the form of a question in the brief and typically is introduced by the word "whether." For instance, the issue might be "whether the police may search a home without a search warrant where the occupant freely and voluntarily consents to the search."

5. ***Holding.*** Write down the legal principle formulated by the court to answer the question posed by the issue. This requires only a statement; for example, "The police may conduct a search of a home based on the occupant's free and voluntary consent to the search. The consent may not be the product of duress or coercion, express or implied. In this case, the court held that the search was constitutional, because the occupant voluntarily consented to the search."

6. ***Reasoning.*** State the reasons that the court provides for the holding. Note the precedents that the court cites and relies on in reaching its decision. Ask yourself whether the court's reasoning is logical and persuasive. Consider how a change in the facts may result in a judgment that consent was not given voluntarily.

7. ***Disposition.*** An appellate court may affirm and uphold the decision of a lower court or reverse the lower court's judgment. The appellate court may reverse the lower court's decision and remand or return the case for additional judicial action. You will want to pay attention to the sentence received by the defendant. Take the time to understand the precise impact of the court decision.

8. ***Concurring and dissenting opinions.*** Note the arguments offered by judges in concurring and dissenting opinions.
9. ***Public policy and psychology.*** Consider the impact of the judgment on society and the criminal justice system. In considering a court decision, do not overlook the psychological, social, and political factors that may have affected the judges' decision.
10. ***Personal opinion.*** Sketch your own judicial opinion, and note whether you agree with the holding of the case and the reasoning of the court.

Approaching the Case

You most likely will develop a personal approach to reading and briefing cases. There are some points that you might keep in mind:

Skim the case to develop a sense of the issue, facts, and holding of the case.

Read the case slowly a second time. You may find it helpful in the beginning to read the case out loud and to write notes in the margin.

Write down the relevant facts in your own words.

Identify the relevant facts, issue, reasoning, and holding. You should not merely mechanically copy the language of the case. Most instructors suggest that you express the material in your own words in order to improve your understanding. You should pay careful attention to the legal language. For instance, there is a significant difference between a legal test that states that consent is involuntary in those instances in which a defendant "reasonably believes" that the police are coercing him or her to consent and a legal test that states that consent is considered involuntary where a defendant "personally believes" that she or he is being attacked. The first is an objective test measured by a "reasonable person" and the second a "subjective test" measured by the defendant's personal perception. You should incorporate legal terminology into your brief. The law, like tennis or music, possesses a distinctive vocabulary that is used to express and communicate ideas.

Consult the glossary in the text or a law dictionary for the definition of unfamiliar legal terms, and write down questions that you may have concerning the case.

The brief should be precise and limited to essential points. You should bring the brief to class, and compare your analysis to the view of your instructor. Modify the brief to reflect the class discussion, and provide space for insights developed in class.

Each case commonly is thought of as "standing for a legal proposition." Some instructors suggest that you write the legal rule contained in the case as a "banner" across the first page of the brief.

Consider why the case is included in the textbook and how the case fits into the general topic covered in the chapter. Remain an active and critical learner, and think about the material you are reading. You also should consider how the case relates to what you learned earlier in the course. Bring a critical perspective to reading the case, and resist mechanically accepting the court's judgment. Keep in mind that there are at least two parties involved in a case, each of whom may have a persuasive argument. Most important, briefing is a learning tool and should not be so time-consuming that you fail to spend time understanding and reflecting on the material.

Consider how the case may relate to other areas you have studied. The court's decision may be based on one of several possible legal rules. Thinking broadly about a case will help you integrate and understand criminal law.

Outline the material. Some instructors may suggest that you develop an outline of the material covered in class. This then can be used to assist you in preparing for the examinations.

Apply the legal rule to hypothetical situations that you develop. This will help you understand the law and identify aspects of the decision that may be unclear.

Legal Citations

The name of each case is followed by a set of numbers and alphabetical abbreviations. These abbreviations refer to various *legal reporters* in which the cases are published. This is useful in the event that you want to read an unedited version in the library. An increasing number of cases also are available online. The rules of citation are fairly technical and are only of immediate concern to practicing attorneys. The discussion below presents the standard approach followed by lawyers. Those of you interested in additional detail should consult *The Bluebook: A Uniform System of Citation* (2005).

The first number you encounter is the volume in which the case appears. This is followed by the abbreviation of the reporter and by the page number and year of the decision. State cases are available in "regional reporters" that contain appellate decisions of courts in various geographic areas of the United States. These volumes are cited in accordance with standard abbreviations: Atlantic (A.), North East (N.E.), Pacific (P.), South East (S.E.), S. (South), and South West (S.W.). The large number of cases decided has necessitated the organization of these reporters into various "series" (e.g., P.2d and P.3d).

Individual states also have their own reporter systems containing the decisions of intermediate appellate courts and state supreme courts. For example, decisions of the Nebraska Supreme Court appear in the *Northwest Reporter* (N.W. or N.W.2d) as well as in the *Nebraska Reports* (Neb.). The decisions of the Nebraska Court of Appeals are reprinted in *Nebraska Court of Appeals Reports* (Neb. Ct. App.). These decisions usually are cited to the *Northwest Reporter,* for example, "*Nebraska v. Metzger,* 319 N.W.2d 459 (Neb. 1982)." New York and California cases appear in state and regional reporters as well as in their own national reporter.

The federal court reporters reprint the published opinions of federal trial as well as appellate courts. District court (trial) opinions appear in the *Federal Supplement Reporter* (F. Supp.), and appellate court opinions are reprinted in the *Federal Reporter* (F.), both of which are printed in several series (F. Supp. 2d; F.2d and F.3d). These citations also provide the name of the federal court that decided the case. The Second Court of Appeals in New York, for instance, is cited as "*United States v. MacDonald,* 531 F.2d 196 (2nd Cir. 1976)." The standard citation for U.S. Supreme Court decisions is the *United States Report* (U.S.). For example, *Papachristou v. Jacksonville,* 405 U.S. 156 (1971). This is the official version issued by the U.S. Supreme Court; the decisions also are available in two privately published reporters, the *Supreme Court Reporter* (S. Ct.) and *Lawyer's Edition* (L. Ed.).

There is a growing trend for cases to appear online on commercial electronic databases. States also are beginning to adopt public-domain citation formats for newly decided cases that appear on state court Web pages. These are cited in accordance with the rules established by each state's judiciary. The standard format includes the case name, the year of the decision, the state's two-digit postal code, the abbreviation of the court in the event that this is not a state supreme court decision, the number assigned to the case, and the paragraph number. A parallel citation to the relevant regional reporter also is provided. The *Bluebook* provides an example of this format: "*Gregory v. Class,* 1998 SD 106, ¶ 3, 54 N.D. 873, 875."

Legal Terminology

appellate courts
head notes
holding
legal reporter
obiter dicta
reasoning
Socratic method

Bibliography

Editors of the Columbia Law Review, the Harvard Law Review, the University of Pennsylvania Law Review, and the Yale Law Journal, *The Bluebook: A Uniform System of Citation,* 18th ed. (Cambridge, MA: The Harvard Law Review Association, 2005).

2 The Sources of Criminal Procedure

Did the police pumping of Rochin's stomach for drugs "shock the conscience"?

When asked, "Whose stuff is this?" Rochin seized the capsules and put them in his mouth. A struggle ensued, in the course of which the three officers "jumped upon him" and attempted to extract the capsules. The force they applied proved unavailing against Rochin's resistance. He was handcuffed and taken to a hospital. At the direction of one of the officers, a doctor forced an emetic solution through a tube into Rochin's stomach against his will. This "stomach pumping" produced vomiting. In the vomited matter were found two capsules, which proved to contain morphine.

Core Concepts and Summary Statements

Introduction

A. The law of criminal procedure provides a road map that guides the police in the detection and investigation of crime and the detention of suspects and provides directions to defense attorneys, prosecutors, and judges in the prosecution and punishment of offenders and in the appeal of verdicts.

B. The U.S. Constitution is the primary source of the law of criminal procedure. The Constitution establishes the powers of the three branches of federal government, allocates responsibilities between the states and the federal government, and sets forth the fundamental rights and liberties of individuals.

C. The Constitution is difficult to amend, and as a result, it would be extraordinarily difficult for a government to "change the rules of the game" and alter the system of government.

D. The last half of the twentieth century has witnessed the nationalization or "constitutionalization" of the law of criminal procedure. The U.S. Supreme Court has held that most of the provisions of the Bill of Rights of the U.S. Constitution are incorporated into the Fourteenth Amendment applicable to the states. As a result, individuals generally enjoy the same rights in the federal criminal justice system and in the criminal justice systems of the fifty states.

The Sources of Criminal Procedure

There are several significant sources of the law of criminal procedure. These include the U.S. Constitution, the U.S. Supreme Court, state constitutions and courts, federal and state statutes, rules of criminal procedure, the American Law Institute's *Model Code of Pre-Arraignment Procedure,* and the judicial decisions of federal and state courts.

The U.S. Constitution

A. The original Constitution of 1788 includes four provisions that address criminal procedure.

B. The first ten amendments comprising the Bill of Rights were added to the Constitution in 1791. The first eight amendments to the Constitution include fifteen provisions addressing criminal procedure.

The U.S. Supreme Court

A. In 1803, in *Marbury v. Madison,* the U.S. Supreme Court asserted the authority of judicial review, the right to define the meaning of the Constitution, and the right to hold unconstitutional federal and state and local laws that do not conform to the requirements of the Constitution.

B. The Supreme Court is the chief interpreter of the meaning of the Constitution, and the Court's judgments bind all other courts, the president, Congress, state officials, and every individual in the criminal justice system.

State Constitutions and Court Decisions

A. The fifty state constitutions include a "declaration of rights."

B. The interpretation of state constitutions is a matter for state courts. The rule is that a state may not provide a defendant with less protection than the corresponding federal provision. A state, however, may provide a defendant with more protection.

Federal and State Statutes

State legislatures and the U.S. Congress have passed laws addressing criminal procedure. Statutes can be very important for defining a defendant's rights in the criminal justice system. The federal statutes, for instance, include provisions on the requirements of speedy trial, witness protection, and postconviction DNA testing.

Rules of Criminal Procedure

A. The Federal Rules of Criminal Procedure detail the steps that are to be followed in the criminal justice process in the federal system from the filing of a complaint through a verdict and sentencing in district court.

B. State courts generally have comprehensive rules of procedure that follow the example of the Federal Rules. Roughly one-third of state constitutions provide that the rules of procedure drawn up by judges are more important than (or take precedence over) the laws passed by the state legislature.

A Model Code of Pretrial Procedure

The American Law Institute's nonbinding *Model Code of Pre-Arraignment Procedure* (1975) addresses pretrial investigations and has been cited by judges in deciding criminal procedure issues.

The Development of Due Process

The last half of the twentieth century witnessed the nationalization or what legal scholars refer to as the "constitutionalization" of criminal procedure. This involves interpreting the Fourteenth Amendment Due Process Clause to extend most of the protections in the Bill of Rights to the states.

The Fourteenth Amendment

A. In 1833, The U.S. Supreme Court in *Barron v. Mayor & City Council of Baltimore* ruled that the Bill of Rights limited the federal government and did not apply to state and local governments.

B. Criminal justice was viewed as a local matter. This system of "states' rights" ultimately did not survive the Civil War. In 1868, Congress passed the Fourteenth Amendment. In 1873, in the *Slaughter-House Cases,* the Supreme Court rejected the argument that the Privileges and Immunities Clause of the Fourteenth Amendment extended the Bill of Rights to citizens of the states. Individuals now looked to the Due Process Clause of the Fourteenth Amendment to secure their rights against state governments.

C. The Supreme Court has adopted three approaches to determining the protections extended by the Fourteenth Amendment to state governments: fundamental fairness, total incorporation, and selective incorporation.

The Due Process Clause

A. Judges favoring the total incorporation approach argue that the rights that are considered fundamental to American democracy are set forth in the Bill of Rights and, accordingly, are incorporated into the Due Process Clause of the Fourteenth Amendment.

B. The fundamental fairness approach leaves the states free to conduct criminal trials so long as the procedures are consistent with fundamental fairness.

C. The selective incorporation approach argues that the provisions in the Bill of Rights that are fundamental to liberty are incorporated into the Due Process Clause.

D. The "selective incorporation plus" approach argues that the fundamental rights in the Bill of Rights along with other fundamental rights outside the Bill of Rights are incorporated into the Bill of Rights.

Fundamental Fairness

A. The Supreme Court developed the due process fundamental fairness test in a series of cases between 1884 and 1908. Lawyers and their clients, however, were continually disappointed over the Supreme Court's refusal to recognize that rights protected by the Bill of Rights are protected by the Fourteenth Amendment.

B. In 1932, in *Powell v. Alabama,* the Supreme Court recognized that the right to a lawyer in a criminal case is fundamental and is protected by the Due Process Clause of the Fourteenth Amendment. This was followed in 1936 by *Brown v. Mississippi* in which the Supreme Court held that confessions had been extracted from three African American defendants through "physical torture" and that "the use of confessions thus obtained as the basis for conviction and sentence was a clear denial of due process."

Total Incorporation

A. Justice Hugo Black was the Supreme Court's foremost proponent of total incorporation. In 1947, Justice Black fully articulated his theory in his dissenting opinion in *Adamson v. California.* This theory has never attracted a majority of the judges.

B. Justice William O. Douglas articulated a total incorporation plus theory.

Selective Incorporation

A. In the 1960s, a majority of the judges, rather than embracing total incorporation, endorsed a selective incorporation approach, first articulated by Justice William Brennan. This theory is based on the view that the Due Process Clause incorporates the entire provision of various amendments that comprise the Bill of Rights and applies to the states to the same extent as to the federal government ("jot-for-jot and case-for-case").

B. The Court also has failed to incorporate five provisions of the Bill of Rights into the Fourteenth Amendment. A state is free to pass a law or include a provision in its constitution that extends the protections of these five provisions to its citizens.

Equal Protection

A. The Fourteenth Amendment guarantees individuals equal protection of the law in addition to providing that no state shall deprive any person of liberty or property without due process of law. In 1954, the Supreme Court declared in *Bolling v. Sharpe* that the Fifth Amendment Due Process Clause imposes an identical obligation on the federal government to insure the equal protection of the law.

B. The sense that we are being treated equally is essential to our respect for the law. One area where equal protection claims arise is a prosecutor's decision to charge and prosecute an individual with a criminal offense. A claim of discriminatory or selective prosecution and request that a court dismiss a prosecution must overcome the presumption of regularity by presenting clear and convincing evidence of a discriminatory impact and discriminatory intent.

The Impact of Supreme Court Decisions

A. Supreme Court decisions establishing a "new rule" are retroactive and are binding precedent on all future cases, cases currently at trial, and cases on appeal. Judgments establishing a new rule do not apply to cases on habeas corpus review. The Supreme Court reserves the right to make a decision fully retroactive.
B. Supreme Court decisions inevitably raise issues that then must be addressed in future judgments.
C. Court decisions often are not immediately or fully implemented by the police, prosecutors, or judges.

Two Models of Criminal Procedure

Herbert Packer proposed two ways of thinking about criminal procedure: the Crime Control Model and the Due Process Model. The Supreme Court, in general, seeks to find a balance between these two perspectives.

Why Criminal Procedure Matters

A. The lesson of "procedural justice" is that people will support and respect the criminal justice system regardless of the outcome of a case so long as they believe that the procedures are fair and objectively applied and that decision makers are acting with integrity and treating people with respect.
B. Fair procedures tend to result in more accurate results.

Introduction

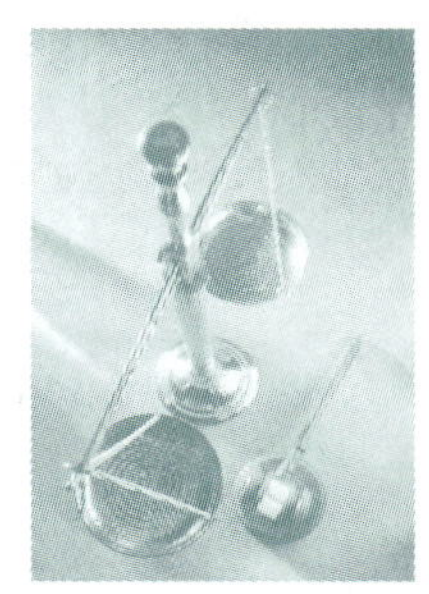

The law of criminal procedure provides a map that guides the police in the detection and investigation of crime and the detention of suspects and provides directions to defense attorneys, prosecutors, and judges in the prosecution and punishment of offenders and in the appeal of verdicts. The list below gives you some idea of the broad range of topics that are covered by the law of criminal procedure.

- Informants
- Stops and frisks of individuals
- Searches and arrests of individuals
- Searches and seizures of automobiles
- Search warrants and searches of homes
- Right to a criminal defense
- Interrogations
- Lineups
- Pretrial proceedings
- Trials
- Appeals

As the first order of business in this chapter, we will discuss the primary sources of the law of criminal procedure listed below (see also Table 2.1).

- U.S. Constitution
- U.S. Supreme Court
- State constitutions and court decisions
- Federal and state statutes
- Rules of criminal procedure
- A model code of pretrial procedure

The primary source of criminal procedure is the U.S. Constitution. The framers of the Constitution experienced the tyranny of British colonial rule and were reluctant to give too much power to the newly established federal government. The colonists under British rule were subjected to warrantless searches, detentions without trial, the quartering of soldiers in homes, and criminal prosecutions for criticizing the government. The framers responded to these repressive policies by creating a **constitutional political system.** The U.S. Constitution is the supreme law of the land and lists the structure and powers of the president (executive), Congress (legislature), and judges (judiciary) and allocates responsibilities between federal and state governments. The **Bill of Rights,** or the first ten amendments to the Constitution, was added to protect individual rights and liberties. The Constitution is intentionally difficult to amend. This prevents a government from coming into power and changing the rules of the game by passing a law that, for instance, states that you do not have a right to an attorney or right to a jury trial in a prosecution for a serious criminal offense. The American colonists' concern with individual rights is indicated by the fact that the Constitution was accepted by several state legislatures only on the condition that a Bill of Rights would be incorporated into the document.

The last half of the twentieth century has witnessed the nationalization or "constitutionalization" of the law of criminal procedure. The U.S. Supreme Court has held that most of the provisions of the Bill of Rights of the U.S. Constitution are incorporated into the Fourteenth Amendment applicable to the states. This has meant that both federal and state governments are required to provide the same basic rights to criminal defendants. The result

Table 2.1 Where to Find the Law of Criminal Procedure
U.S. Constitution. This is the "supreme law of the land" and the primary source of criminal procedure.
U.S. Supreme Court. The Court applies the provisions of the U.S. Constitution to cases that are before the Court. These decisions are binding on courts throughout the land and explain what procedures are required to satisfy the Constitution.
U.S. Courts of Appeals and District Courts. These courts decide cases within their own geographical region. They are required to follow the rulings of the U.S. Supreme Court. In those instances in which the Supreme Court has not ruled, the decisions of each federal court of appeals is binding within its jurisdiction. Federal courts of appeals may look to one another's judgments in arriving at a decision.
State constitutions. Each state has a constitution that contains a list of rights that parallel those provided in the Bill of Rights to the U.S. Constitution.
State courts. The decisions of a state supreme court are binding precedent for all other courts within the state. State courts interpret the provisions of their constitutions. State courts must interpret their constitutions to provide the same protections as the U.S. Supreme Court has held are required under the U.S. Constitution. They are free to recognize greater protections than are required by the U.S. Constitution.
Federal statutes. These are laws passed by Congress that address criminal procedure, such as funding for the analysis of DNA evidence in federal and state court.
State statutes. These are laws passed by state legislatures that address criminal procedure, such as whether cameras are permitted in the courtroom. Local towns and cities also may pass local ordinances or rules of procedure in local courts that address criminal procedure.
Federal Rules of Criminal Procedure. These are comprehensive rules adopted by federal judges and approved by Congress that detail the required steps in federal criminal procedure.
State rules of criminal procedure. These are the rules that set forth the required criminal procedures in the states. In some states, these rules are enacted by the legislature, and in other states, by the judiciary.
Model code of criminal procedure. The American Law Institute, a private group of lawyers and professors, formulated a set of suggested rules regarding pretrial interactions between the police and citizens. Judges occasionally rely on the Model Code in their decisions. There are other documents that courts look to at times, such as the U.S. Justice Department's manual regulating the conduct of prosecutors, ethical guidelines established by bar associations for the conduct of lawyers, and internal police regulations regarding the conduct of law enforcement officers.

is that defendants generally enjoy the same protections in both federal and state criminal justice systems.

In this chapter, following a discussion of the sources of criminal procedure, we will examine the nationalization of the Bill of Rights and the incorporation of rights into the Due Process Clause of the Fourteenth Amendment. We then examine equal protection of the law. The chapter concludes with a discussion of the impact of Supreme Court decisions.

The Sources of Criminal Procedure

As we have seen, the law of criminal procedure details the steps that the government is required to follow in investigating, detecting, prosecuting, and punishing crime and in criminal appeals. This is distinguished from criminal law, which defines the content of the rules whose violation results in penal responsibility. Some commentators compare this to a sporting event. Criminal law defines the points you receive for a goal. Criminal procedure comprises the rules that tell us how we move the ball up the court or field. As a first step, we will examine the fundamental sources of criminal procedure listed below.

- U.S. Constitution
- U.S. Supreme Court
- State constitution and state court decisions
- Federal and state statutes
- Rules of criminal procedure
- A model code of pretrial procedure
- Federal and state court judicial decisions

The U.S. Constitution

The Constitution and the Bill of Rights (the first ten amendments), which was included in the document at the insistence of the legislatures of New York, Virginia, and other states, each includes provisions regarding criminal procedure.

The original Constitution of 1788 includes four provisions that address criminal procedure.

1. ***Habeas corpus.*** Article I, Section Nine limits the ability of Congress to suspend the "Privilege of the Writ of Habeas Corpus." This guarantees individuals the right to go before a court and require the government to explain why they are incarcerated.

2. ***Ex post facto laws.*** Article I, Section Nine also prohibits Congress from adopting bills of attainder (legislative acts punishing a specific individual without a trial) and ex post facto laws (criminalizing an act that was legal when committed).

3. ***Jury trials.*** Article III, Section Two provides that all crimes shall be tried before a jury and that such trials shall be held in the state where the crime has been committed.

4. ***Treason.*** Article III, Section Four states that treason consists of levying war against the United States. A conviction requires the testimony of two witnesses to the same overt act or a confession in open court.

The first ten amendments comprising the Bill of Rights were added to the Constitution in 1791. The first eight amendments to the Constitution include fifteen provisions addressing criminal procedure. As we shall see, most of the provisions that originally applied only to the federal government have been interpreted as applying to state governments as well. The U.S. Supreme Court is the final authority on the meaning of the provisions of the Constitution and the Bill of Rights (see Table 2.2).

Table 2.2 Criminal Procedure Provisions in the Bill of Rights

Fourth Amendment
Unreasonable searches and seizures
Warrants
The right of the people to be secure in their persons, houses, papers, and effects, against unreasonable searches and seizures, shall not be violated, and no Warrants shall issue, but upon probable cause, supported by Oath or affirmation, and particularly describing the place to be searched, and the persons or things to be seized.
Fifth Amendment
Indictment by grand jury
Prohibition against double jeopardy
Right against self-incrimination
Due process of law
No person shall be held to answer for a capital, or otherwise infamous crime, unless on a presentment or indictment of a Grand Jury, except in cases arising in the land or naval forces, or in the Militia, when in actual service in time of War or public danger; nor shall any person be subject for the same offence to be twice put in jeopardy of life or limb; nor shall be compelled in any criminal case to be a witness against himself, or be deprived of life, liberty, or property, without due process of law; nor shall private property be taken for public use, without just compensation.
Sixth Amendment
Speedy and public trial
Impartial jury
Informed charge
Confrontation with witnesses
Obtaining witnesses
Assistance of a lawyer
In all criminal prosecutions, the accused shall enjoy the right to a speedy and public trial, by an impartial jury of the State and district wherein the crime shall have been committed, which district shall have been previously ascertained by law, and to be informed of the nature and cause of the accusation; to be confronted with the witness against him; to have compulsory process for obtaining witnesses in his favor, and to have the Assistance of Counsel for his defence.
Eighth Amendment
Excessive bail
Excessive fines
Cruel and unusual punishment
Excessive bail shall not be required, nor excessive fines imposed, nor cruel and unusual punishments inflicted.

The U.S. Supreme Court

Article VI of the U.S. Constitution, the **Supremacy Clause,** specifically states that the Constitution and the laws passed by Congress are the supreme law of the land and trump any state laws or court decisions that address the same issue. Article VI reads as follows:

> This constitution, and the laws of the United States which shall be made in pursuance thereof... shall be the supreme Law of the Land; and the judges in every state shall be bound thereby, anything in the constitution or laws of any state to the contrary notwithstanding.

The U.S. Constitution is the supreme law of the land, and federal and state laws must conform to the constitutional standard. Alexander Hamilton in the *Federalist Papers* observed that the Constitution is the "standard...for the laws" and that where there is a conflict, the laws "ought to give place to the constitution." The constitutional requirements, however, are not always clear from the text of the document. The Sixth Amendment's provision for "assistance in all criminal prosecutions," for instances, does not tell us whether the federal government and the states must appoint lawyers to represent the indigent and poor during police lineups and does not tell us whether a lawyer must be provided free of charge to defendants undertaking an appeal following a conviction.

In 1803, in *Marbury v. Madison,* the U.S. Supreme Court claimed the authority of **judicial review,** the right to define the meaning of the Constitution and to throw out federal, state, and local laws as unconstitutional that do not conform to the Constitution. *Marbury* is a complicated case to disentangle, and at this point, you merely should appreciate that the lasting significance of this famous case is Justice John Marshall's proclamation that "an act that is repugnant to the Constitution is void" and that "[i]t is emphatically the province and duty of the judicial department to say what the law is" (*Marbury v. Madison,* 5 U.S. [1 Cranch] 137 [1803]).

In two later cases, *Martin v. Hunter's Lessee* and *Cohen v. Virginia,* the Supreme Court explicitly asserted the authority to review whether state laws and court decisions are consistent with the Constitution (*Martin v. Hunter's Lessee,* 14 U.S. [1 Wheat.] 304 [1816]); *Cohen v. Virginia,* 19 U.S. [6 Wheat.] 264 [1821]). In 1958, the Supreme Court affirmed this authority in the famous civil rights case of *Cooper v. Aaron.* In *Cooper,* the Supreme Court ordered Arkansas to desegregate the Little Rock school system and reminded local officials that the Constitution is the supreme law of the land and that *Marbury v. Madison* "declared the basic principle that the federal judiciary is supreme in the exposition of the law of the Constitution, and that principle has ever since been respected by this Court and the Country as a permanent and indispensable feature of our constitutional system.... Every state legislator and executive and judicial officer is solemnly committed by oath...to support this Constitution" (*Cooper v. Aaron,* 358 U.S. 1, 18 [1958]).

As the chief interpreter of the meaning of the Constitution, the Supreme Court's judgments bind all state and federal judges, the president, Congress, state officials, and every official in the criminal justice system. Justice Robert Jackson observed that "we are not final because we are infallible, but we are infallible...because we are final" (*Brown v. Allen,* 344 U.S. 443, 540 [1953]). The Supreme Court cannot review every state and federal criminal case that raises a constitutional question. The Court takes a limited number of cases each term and tends to address those issues in which there is a disagreement among federal appellate courts over the constitutionality of a specific practice or where an issue is particularly important. This results in the vast number of criminal procedure cases being decided by lower federal and state courts. In many instances, these courts merely follow Supreme Court precedent. In other cases, we may find that there is no controlling Supreme Court judgment on an issue and that, in order to determine the law, we must look to various federal circuit court decisions and state supreme court judgments. In this instance, each court establishes the law for its own jurisdiction until the Supreme Court rules on the issue.

On several occasions, the Supreme Court has relied on what it terms its **supervisory authority** over the administration of justice in the federal courts to impose standards that are not required by the U.S. Constitution. This is based on the Supreme Court's authority to maintain "civilized standards of procedure and evidence" in the practice of the federal courts. In *McNabb,* the Supreme Court held that federal agents had blatantly disregarded the requirements of a congressional statute. The Court invoked its supervisory authority and held that although federal agents had not violated the Constitution, permitting the trial court to consider the resulting confession would make the judiciary "accomplices in willful disobedience of the law" (*McNabb v. United States,* 318 U.S. 332 [1943]).

State Constitutions and Court Decisions

Each of the fifty states has a constitution, and virtually all of these constitutions contain a "declaration of rights." In most cases, the provisions are the same as the criminal procedure provisions in the Bill of Rights to the U.S. Constitution. In some instances, state constitutions have provided for additional rights or have clarified the meaning of particular rights. Alaska, Florida, and Illinois, along with other states, recognize the rights of crime victims to confer with prosecutors and to attend trials. In another example, New York makes it explicit that the freedom from unreasonable searches and seizures includes the freedom from the unreasonable interception of telephonic and telegraphic communications.

The interpretation of state constitutions is a matter for state courts. The decisions of state supreme courts are binding on all lower state courts. The rule is that a state provision may not provide a defendant with less protection than the corresponding federal provision. A state, however, may provide a defendant with more protection. In 1977, Supreme Court Justice William Brennan called on state supreme courts to provide defendants with more rights than what he viewed as the increasingly conservative and "law and order"–oriented U.S. Supreme Court. In a 1989 study, Justice Robert Utter of the Washington Supreme Court found 450 published state court opinions that interpreted state constitutions as "going beyond federal constitutional guarantees." Most of these decisions were handed down in Alaska, California, Florida, and Massachusetts. In reaction to this trend, California, Florida, and several other states have amended their constitutions to instruct state court judges that their constitutions' criminal procedure provisions shall be interpreted in "conformity" with the decisions of the U.S. Supreme Court and are not to provide greater protections to individuals.

As you read the text, you will see that in some instances, state courts continue to engage in what has been called the **new judicial federalism.** The important point to keep in mind is that defendants possess the same rights under both the constitutions of the fifty states and the Bill of Rights to the U.S. Constitution. The next section discusses federal and state laws as a source of the law of criminal procedure.

Federal and State Statutes

State legislatures and the U.S. Congress have added to constitutional provisions by passing laws regarding criminal procedure. In state statutes, you can usually find these laws grouped together under the title of the "code of criminal procedure." Roughly one-third of the states follow the example of North Carolina, Ohio, and Utah and have detailed laws that describe procedures to be followed at virtually every step in the criminal process. Roughly ten states have brief statutory codes of criminal procedure that cover a limited number of topics of special concern. A New York law, for instance, provides that judges presiding over "widely publicized or sensational cases" may limit extrajudicial statements by lawyers, defendants, and witnesses and other individuals involved in a trial. Another provision describes the procedures that a court is required to employ in removing an unruly spectator from the courtroom. A third New York statute prohibits the televising or radio transmission of trials and specifies the permissible location of photographers and cameras outside the courtroom. A Virginia law establishes standards for requesting the DNA analysis of biological material by an individual who has been convicted of a crime. A Michigan statute discusses the procedure for extraditing offenders to other states for trial. The remaining states follow the pattern in Massachusetts and have "codes of criminal procedure" that cover two or three areas in depth as well topics of special concern. The interpretation of state statutes is the exclusive concern of state courts, while federal courts are charged with the interpretation of federal statutes.

Statutes can be very important for defining a defendant's rights in the criminal justice system and should not be overlooked. Federal statutes, for instance, include provisions on the requirements of speedy trial, witness protection, and postconviction DNA testing. The Supreme Court may find that a state or federal statute deprives defendants of their constitutional rights and may rule that the statute is unconstitutional. For example, it is doubtful whether the Supreme Court would approve of a law that provided the FBI or state police with the authority to detain individuals indefinitely without probable cause that the individual committed a crime. In the next section, we will see that a full description of state and federal criminal procedure typically can be found in the rules of criminal procedure.

Rules of Criminal Procedure

The Federal Rules of Criminal Procedure detail the steps in the criminal justice process in the federal system from the filing of a complaint through a verdict and sentencing in district court. This includes topics such as the grand jury, motions that must be filed prior to trial, jury instructions and verdicts, and posttrial motions to reconsider sentencing. The Federal Rules are discussed and regularly amended by the Judicial Conference of United States Courts, which is a regular meeting of federal judges. These federal judges, in turn, send their proposals to the Chief Justice of the U.S. Supreme Court. He or she then transmits the rules to Congress and the rules take effect unless amended or vetoed.

The Supreme Court has held that these rules have the force of law and that a federal court has no authority to disregard the requirements of the rules in regard to matters such as the time in which a defendant is required to file various motions or the prohibition on televising trials or providing the media with electronic recordings of trials.

State courts generally also have comprehensive rules of procedure that follow the example of the Federal Rules. Roughly one-third of state constitutions provide that the rules of procedure drawn up by judges are more important than (or take precedence over) laws passed by the state legislature.

A Model Code of Pretrial Procedure

In 1923, a group of prestigious academics, judges, and lawyers formed the privately organized and funded American Law Institute (ALI). These individuals shared a concern that the states dramatically varied in their definitions of crimes and legal procedures. The ALI members drafted a series of model statutes that they hoped would be adopted by state legislatures. The ALI's *Model Code of Pre-Arraignment Procedure* (1975) addresses pretrial police investigations and has been cited by judges grappling with criminal procedure issues. The Supreme Court, for example, referred to the code in a case involving the permissible length of a police investigatory stop of a suspect. An example of the forward-looking nature of the *Model Code* is the document's call for the taping of police interrogations.

In some judicial decisions, you may see that judges refer to administrative procedures developed by government agencies or local police departments or bar associations. One of the most influential manuals is the United States Attorney's *Manual of the Department of Justice*. The manual sets forth the policy of the Justice Department at every stage of the criminal justice process, including grand juries, the filing of criminal charges, plea bargaining, and sentencing. A violation of these internal guidelines might result in a prosecutor's being subject to some form of administrative discipline, such as loss of pay or suspension. A judge may consult these guidelines in determining whether a prosecutor has violated his or her professional responsibilities and should be disciplined by the court. Courts may look at the ethical rules established by state bar associations to determine whether a criminal verdict should be thrown out based on a defense attorney's ineffective representation at trial. In some instances, judges also may consult internal police regulations to assist in determining whether an officer acted reasonably in carrying out his or her responsibilities. The American Bar Association has adopted a set of *Standards for Criminal Justice,* which suggests reforms that might be made to various criminal justice procedures.

The next section examines the incorporation of the Bill of Rights into the Fourteenth Amendment Due Process Clause and the nationalization of the law of criminal procedure.

The Development of Due Process

Nationalization

The last half of the twentieth century witnessed the *nationalization* or what law professors refer to as the **constitutionalization** of criminal procedure. This involved interpreting the

Fourteenth Amendment **Due Process Clause** to extend most of the protections of the Bill of Rights to the states. There now is a single standard of criminal procedure that all levels of government must satisfy. You may be prosecuted in Indiana, in Iowa, or in the federal system and your rights are fundamentally the same. This *constitutionalization* or development of a single standard that applies to the federal government as well as to the states marked a true revolution in the law.

The question of the nationalization of criminal procedure remains a topic of lively debate and disagreement. The development of consistent procedures is intended to insure uniform and fair treatment for individuals wherever they live and whatever their backgrounds. On the other hand, there is strong argument that the states should be left free to experiment and to develop their own criminal procedures. The procedures that may be appropriate for federal agents investigating fraud, environmental crime, or corporate abuse are far removed from the daily demands confronting a police officer on the beat in a major city or officers in a small department with a tight budget. Supreme Court judges sitting in Washington, D.C., with little or no experience in local government or in law enforcement may be ill-equipped to be telling the police in Detroit or Los Angeles how to conduct an interrogation or lineup, and the court's well-intentioned decisions may result in "handcuffing" the police and in frustrating police investigations. Observers of the Supreme Court predict that in the next few years, we are likely to see a renewed debate among the Supreme Court justices over whether each state should be required to follow uniform procedures or whether states should be provided with greater flexibility in their criminal procedures. The Supreme Court, for instance, might hold that the Fifth Amendment does not require states to tape interrogations and that the states may decide for themselves whether to adopt this practice. We now turn our attention to the process of incorporating the Bill of Rights into the Due Process Clause of the Fourteenth Amendment.

The Fourteenth Amendment

In 1833, the U.S. Supreme Court in *Barron v. Mayor & City Council of Baltimore* ruled that the Bill of Rights limited the federal government and did not apply to state and local governments. Justice John Marshall wrote that the "constitution was ordained and established by the people of the United States for themselves for their own government, and not for the government of the individual states." He observed that if the framers had intended for the Bill of Rights to apply to the states, "they would have declared this purpose in plain and intelligible language" (*Barron v. Mayor & City Council of Baltimore,* 32 U.S. [7 Pet.] 243, 247, 250 [1833]).

Professor Erwin Chemerinsky observed that if the Bill of Rights applies only to the federal government, the state and local governments "then are free to infringe even the most precious liberties" and to "violate basic constitutional rights" (Chemerinsky, 2002, p. 472). On the other hand, the *Barron* decision represents the widespread belief in the nineteenth century that the federal government should not intrude into the affairs of state governments and that the citizens of each state should be left free to determine what rights and liberties they wish to preserve and to protect. Criminal justice, in particular, was viewed as a local matter.

This system of states' rights did not fully survive the Civil War. Slavery in the states of the former Confederacy would no longer be tolerated, and former African American slaves were to enjoy the full rights of citizenship. The **Fourteenth Amendment** was added to the Constitution in 1868 in order to guarantee equal treatment and opportunity for African Americans. The Amendment reads as follows:

> All persons born or naturalized in the United States, and subject to the jurisdiction thereof, are citizens of the United States and of the state wherein they reside. No state shall make or enforce any law which shall abridge the privileges and immunities of citizens of the United States nor shall any state deprive any person of life, liberty, or property without due process of law; nor deny to any person within its jurisdiction the equal protection of the laws.

The first sentence recognized that African Americans are citizens of the United States and of the state in which they reside. The purpose was to reverse the Supreme Court's 1857 decision *Scott v. Sandford,* which held that African American slaves were not eligible to become U.S. citizens (*Dred Scott v. Sandford,* 60 U.S. [19 How.] 393 [1857]). Several judges argued that the debates in Congress over the Fourteenth Amendment indicated that the amendment's prohibition on a state's passing a law that abridges "the privileges and immunities of citizens of the United States" was shorthand that was intended to extend the protections of the federal Bill of Rights to the states. What good was citizenship unless African Americans were protected against the violation of their rights by both federal and state governments. This theory, however, was rejected by the Supreme Court in the *Slaughter-House Cases*. Justice Miller held that the Privileges or Immunities Clause was not intended to extend the Bill of Rights to state citizens. Extending the Bill of Rights to the states would establish the Supreme Court as "a perpetual censor upon all legislation of the States, on the civil rights of their own citizens, with authority to nullify such as it did not approve as consistent with those rights. . . . We are convinced that no such results were intended" (*Slaughter-House Cases,* 83 U.S. [16 Wall.] 36 [1873]). Individuals now looked to the Due Process Clause of the Fourteenth Amendment to secure their rights against state governments.

The twentieth century witnessed continued efforts by defendants to extend the protection of the Bill of Rights to the states. Professor Lawrence Friedman, in his book *Crime and Punishment in American History,* notes that with the dawn of the mid-twentieth century, there was an increasing call for fairer procedures in state courts. Lawyers now argued that the Due Process Clause of the Fourteenth Amendment, which applied to the states, included various provisions of the Bill of Rights to the U.S. Constitution. The Supreme Court employed one of three approaches to this argument.

- ***Fundamental fairness.*** The Supreme Court decides on a case-by-case basis whether rights are fundamental to the concept of ordered liberty and therefore apply to the states.
- ***Total incorporation and total incorporation plus.*** The entire Bill of Rights applies to the states. Total incorporation plus includes additional rights not in the Bill of Rights along with the entire Bill of Rights.
- ***Selective incorporation.*** Particular rights in the Bill of Rights apply to the states. Selective incorporation plus includes additional rights not in the Bill of Rights along with the particular rights in the Bill of Rights.

The Due Process Clause

There are strong arguments that the individuals who drafted the Bill of Rights intended that the Due Process Clause incorporate the Bill of Rights and extend these protections to state governments. Judges favoring the **total incorporation** approach argue that these rights were viewed as fundamental by the drafters of the U.S. Constitution and clearly were intended to be guaranteed to African American citizens by the congressional sponsors of the Fourteenth Amendment.

A second approach contends that the Due Process Clause left states free to conduct criminal trials so long as the procedures are consistent with **fundamental fairness.** This leaves states with the flexibility to prosecute individuals without being bound to apply the same procedures as the federal government. There is no indication according to individuals favoring this *freestanding due process* approach that the Fourteenth Amendment incorporates the Bill of Rights. After all, the drafters of the Fourteenth Amendment could have expressly stated that the Amendment incorporates the Bill of Rights if this is what they intended. The Fourteenth Amendment employs broad language like "due process of law" to provide flexibility to state governments and to allow the states to adjust their procedures to meet changing conditions. Proponents of fundamental fairness point out that the Fifth Amendment also contains the language that "[n]o person shall be denied life, liberty, or property without due process of law," and if this language were meant to incorporate the entire Bill of Rights, it would have been unnecessary to include the Bill of Rights in the Constitution. On the other hand, critics of fundamental fairness point out that the drafters of the Fourteenth Amendment could have used the term *fundamental fairness* rather than *due process* if this was their intent.

Other judges favored **selective incorporation.** They argue that only those provisions of the Bill of Rights that are essential to liberty are incorporated into the Fourteenth Amendment. States are otherwise free to structure their criminal procedures. A small number of judges advocated **selective incorporation plus** and contended that there are rights that are not part of the Bill of Rights that also applied to the states. The challenge confronting the selective incorporation approach is to identify what parts of the Bill of Rights are essential.

Keep these points in mind as you read about the Supreme Court's gradual incorporation of the Bill of Rights into the Due Process Clause of the Fourteenth Amendment.

Fundamental Fairness

The Supreme Court developed the fundamental fairness test in a series of cases between 1884 and 1908. Lawyers and their clients were continually disappointed over the next forty years by the Supreme Court's reluctance to recognize that the rights protected by the Bill of Rights were protected by the Fourteenth Amendment.

The fundamental fairness test was first established by the U.S. Supreme Court in 1884 in *Hurtado v. California*. Jose Hurtado had been charged with homicide based on an information (i.e., a document signed by a prosecutor charging an individual with a crime) filed by a prosecutor, and subsequently, he was convicted and sentenced to death. Hurtado claimed that the prosecutor had denied Hurtado's due process rights by disregarding the Fifth Amendment's requirement of indictment (called a "presentment" in England) before a grand jury for a "capital or otherwise infamous crime." The Supreme Court rejected Hurtado's claim and held that the ancient institution of the grand jury was not essential to the preservation of "liberty and justice." States were free to design their own criminal procedures "within the limits of those fundamental principles of liberty and justice which lie at the base of all our civil and political institutions, and the greatest security for which resides in the right of the people to make their own laws, and alter them at their pleasure."

The Supreme Court stressed that the information filed by the prosecutor in California was subject to review in a hearing conducted by a magistrate. At any rate, whether a defendant is brought to trial as a result of an information filed by a prosecutor or an indictment issued by a grand jury is not fundamental to a fair prosecution because the defendant's guilt ultimately is determined by the evidence presented at a criminal trial. The important point is that although the Supreme Court rejected Hurtado's claim, the Court opened the door for defense lawyers to argue in the future that their clients had been denied a right that was a "fundamental principle of liberty and justice" that was embodied in the Fourteenth Amendment (*Hurtado v. California,*110 U.S. 516, 535 [1884]).

Twining v. New Jersey is a second leading case in the development of the fundamental fairness test. In *Twining,* the U.S. Supreme Court rejected Twining's claim that his due process rights had been violated by the trial judge's instruction that the jury could consider the defendant's failure to testify at his trial in determining his guilt or innocence. There was little question that this instruction in a federal trial would be considered to be in violation of the Fifth Amendment right against self-incrimination. The Supreme Court, however, held that the right against self-incrimination at trial was not "an immutable principle of justice which is the inalienable possession of every citizen of a free government." The people of New Jersey were free to change the law in the event that they found the judge's instruction to be fundamentally unfair.

The Supreme Court in *Twining* encouraged lawyers to continue to bring cases claiming that various protections contained within the Bill of Rights were included in the Due Process Clause of the Fourteenth Amendment when it observed that it is "possible that some of the personal rights safeguarded by the first eight amendments against national action may also be safeguarded against state action, because a denial of them would be a denial of due process of law." The Court stressed that these rights are protected "not because those rights are enumerated in the first eight amendments, but because they are of such a nature that they are included in the conception of due process" (*Twining v. New Jersey,* 211 U.S. 78, 99, 113 [1908]).

The world was beginning to change. President Woodrow Wilson had led America into a European conflict in World War I and had proclaimed in his famous "Fourteen Points" that he aspired to bring liberty, freedom, and the rule of law to all the peoples of the world. In Wilson's speech, he called for the formation of a League of Nations to settle international disputes through negotiation and understanding rather than through war. This American commitment to liberty and justice was in stark contrast to the newly developing European fascist movements in Italy, Germany, and Spain, which illustrated the dangers posed to democracy by mob rule, racism, and intolerance.

The Supreme Court took a small step toward recognizing that the Fourteenth Amendment protected individuals against abuse by state authorities in *Moore v. Dempsey.* In *Moore,* a meeting of African American farmers to discuss discriminatory practices in Phillips County, Arkansas, was attacked by white residents. One of the attackers was killed during the exchange of gunfire. Seventy-nine African Americans were prosecuted and convicted, and twelve received the death sentence. In the prosecutions, African Americans were excluded from the juries, the judges rushed through the trials, and threatening mobs surrounded the courthouse. The Supreme Court, based on the totality of the circumstances, held that the murder convictions of five of the defendants violated due process. The Court stressed that it was compelled to intervene to correct the trial court's verdict given that the "whole proceeding" had been a "mask" in which lawyers, judge, and jury had been "swept to the fatal end by an irresistible wave of public opinion" and the Arkansas appellate courts had failed to correct the "wrongful sentence of death" (*Moore v. Dempsey,* 261 U.S. 86, 91 [1923]).

Moore was followed in 1932 by the famous case of *Powell v. Alabama.* The Supreme Court held in *Powell* that the failure of the trial court to insure that indigent, illiterate, and youthful African American defendants confronting the death penalty in a hostile community were represented by an "effective" lawyer constituted a violation of due process of law under the Fourteenth Amendment. The judgment stressed that "this is so... not because [this right is] enumerated in the first eight Amendments, but because [it is of] such a nature that [it is] included in the 'conception of due process of law'" (*Powell v. Alabama,* 287 U.S. 45, 67–68 [1932]).

In *Powell,* five Caucasian homeless men reported that they had been attacked and thrown off a freight train by a group of African Americans. The sheriff deputized every man who owned a firearm, and as the train pulled into Painted Rock, Alabama, the forty-two cars were searched, and the sheriff seized nine African Americans between thirteen and twenty years of age as well as two Caucasian females. The two women were dressed in men's caps and overalls. One of the women, Ruby Bates, informed a member of the posse that the African American suspects had raped her along with her companion, Victoria Price.

The nine "Scottsboro Boys" were brought to trial on April 6, 1932, twelve days following their arrest. The courthouse was ringed by armed national guardsmen to protect the defendants from the angry crowd, which at times numbered several thousand. Judge Alfred E. Hawkins initially appointed the entire local bar to represent the defendants at their arraignment. On the morning of the trial, Judge Alfred E. Hawkins named Stephen R. Roddy to represent the defendants. Roddy was a semi-alcoholic Tennessee lawyer who had been sent to observe the trial by the defendants' families. He protested that he was unfamiliar with Alabama law, and Judge Hawkins responded by appointing a local seventy-year-old senile lawyer, Milo Moody, to assist him. Roddy was given roughly thirty minutes to meet with his clients before the opening of the trial. He immediately filed an unsuccessful motion to change the location of the proceedings to insure his clients a fair trial, which he argued was impossible given the inflammatory newspaper coverage and threatened lynching of his clients. The trial opened on a Monday, and by Thursday, eight of the defendants had been convicted and sentenced to death. The jury divided over whether thirteen-year-old Roy Wright should receive a death sentence or life imprisonment, and Judge Hawkins declared a mistrial in his case. The Alabama Supreme Court affirmed the verdicts.

By the time that the case came before the U.S. Supreme Court, the Scottsboro Boys had become the central cause for political progressives and civil rights activists in the United States and in Europe. The Supreme Court focused on the single issue of denial of counsel. Justice Arthur Sutherland, citing *Twining,* held that the defendants had been deprived of legal representation in violation of the Due Process Clause of the Fourteenth Amendment. Sutherland based his judgment on the lack of time provided to the defendants "to retain a lawyer" as well as the trial judge's appointment of a "less than competent attorney."

The Supreme Court avoided criticism that they were assuming the role of a "super legislator" by narrowly limiting the judgment to the specific facts that confronted the Scottsboro Boys. Justice Sutherland stressed that the trial court's failure to provide the defendants with "reasonable time and opportunity to secure counsel was a clear denial of due process" in light of the "ignorance and illiteracy of the defendants, their youth, the circumstances of public hostility, the imprisonment and . . . the fact that their friends and families were . . . in other states . . . and above all that they stood in deadly peril of their lives." The trial court's obligation to provide a lawyer to defendants confronting capital punishment was not satisfied by an "assignment at such time or under such circumstances as to preclude the giving of effective aid in the preparation and trial." This ruling, according to Justice Sutherland, was based on "'certain immutable principles of justice which inhere in the very idea of free government which no member of the Union may disregard'" (*Powell,* 287 U.S. at 70).

Powell was followed by several cases in which the Supreme Court overturned the convictions of young African American defendants whose confessions had been obtained through abusive and coercive interrogations by Southern police officers. The Court condemned these practices as reminiscent of the totalitarian policies of Nazi Germany and as having no place in a democratic society. In *Brown v. Mississippi,* which is discussed in Chapter 8, confessions were extracted from three African American defendants through "physical torture." The Supreme Court held that it "would be difficult to conceive of methods more revolting to the sense of justice than those taken to procure the confessions . . . and the use of confessions thus obtained as the basis for conviction and sentence was a clear denial of due process" (*Brown v. Mississippi,* 297 U.S. 278, 285 [1936]).

In summary, although *Hurtado* and *Twining* affirmed the respective defendants' convictions, these cases established that the Due Process Clause of the Fourteenth Amendment protected individuals against practices that are contrary to the "immutable principles of liberty and justice." The Supreme Court held that due process had been violated and overturned convictions when confronted with poor, rural, African American defendants who had been subjected to "sham judicial hearings," who had been denied access to effective counsel in a capital punishment case, or whose confessions had been extracted through physical coercion. Keep the following four points in mind in regard to the fundamental rights approach to the Fourteenth Amendment Due Process Clause.

- ***Fundamental rights.*** The Due Process Clause prohibits state criminal procedures and police practices that violate fundamental rights. Justice Felix Frankfurter observed that the Fourteenth Amendment "neither comprehends the specific provisions by which the founders deemed it appropriate to restrict the federal government nor is it confined to them. The Due Process Clause . . . has an independent potency" (*Adamson v. California,* 332 U.S. 46, 66 [1952]).
- ***Bill of Rights.*** The Due Process Clause protects rights because they are fundamental, not because they are in the Bill of Rights.
- ***Legal test.*** The Supreme Court has employed various tests to determine whether a right is fundamental. In 1937, in *Palko v. Connecticut,* the Supreme Court held that the right against double jeopardy was not violated by a Connecticut law that authorized the state to retry a defendant in the event of a successful appeal of a criminal conviction. The Court held that rights are fundamental only if they are of the "very essence of the scheme of ordered liberty," if "'a fair and enlightened system of justice would be impossible without them,'" or if they are based on "'principle[s] of justice so rooted in

the traditions and conscience of our people as to be ranked as fundamental'" (*Palko v. Connecticut,* 302 U.S. 319, 325 [1937]).

- ***Procedures.*** States are free to establish criminal procedures that do not violate fundamental rights protected under the Due Process Clause of the Fourteenth Amendment. The Supreme Court noted that in those instances in which it holds that a state law does not violate due process, the law may be changed through the democratic process.

The first case reprinted in this chapter, *Rochin v. California,* challenged the Supreme Court to determine whether due process prohibited the police from pumping out Rochin's stomach in order to seize capsules of narcotics. It would seem fundamental to the scheme of ordered liberty that the police should be prohibited from forcibly extracting the capsules. In *Rochin,* Justice Felix Frankfurter relied on *Palko v. Connecticut* to establish the famous "shock-the-conscience test" for determining fundamental fairness under the Fourteenth Amendment. Do you agree with Justice Frankfurter that the police violated Rochin's right to due process of law? Were other means of obtaining the evidence available to the police?

You can find Brown v. Mississippi *on the study site, http://www.sagepub.com/lippmancp.*

Did the police's pumping of Rochin's stomach for drugs "shock the conscience" and violate due process of law?

Rochin v. California, *342 U.S. 165 (1952), Frankfurter, J.*

Issue

The Supreme Court is asked to decide whether the petitioner's conviction has been obtained by methods that offend the due process of law.

Facts

Having "some information that [the petitioner here] was selling narcotics," three deputy sheriffs of the County of Los Angeles, on the morning of July 1, 1949, made for the two-story dwelling house in which Rochin lived with his mother, common law wife, brothers, and sisters. Finding the outside door open, the sheriffs entered and then forced open the door to Rochin's room on the second floor. Inside they found petitioner sitting partly dressed on the side of the bed, upon which his wife was lying. On a "night stand" beside the bed, the deputies spied two capsules. When asked, "Whose stuff is this?" Rochin seized the capsules and put them in his mouth. A struggle ensued, in the course of which the three officers "jumped upon him" and attempted to extract the capsules. The force they applied proved unavailing against Rochin's resistance. He was handcuffed and taken to a hospital. At the direction of one of the officers, a doctor forced an emetic solution through a tube into Rochin's stomach against his will. This "stomach pumping" produced vomiting. In the vomited matter were found two capsules, which proved to contain morphine.

Rochin was brought to trial before a California Superior Court, sitting without a jury, on the charge of possessing "a preparation of morphine" in violation of the California Health and Safety Code, 1947, section 11.500. Rochin was convicted and sentenced to sixty days' imprisonment. The chief evidence against him was the two capsules. They were admitted over petitioner's objection, although the means of obtaining them was frankly set forth in the testimony by one of the deputies, substantially as here narrated.

On appeal, the District Court of Appeal affirmed the conviction, despite the finding that the officers "were guilty of unlawfully breaking into and entering defendant's room and were guilty of unlawfully assaulting and battering defendant while in the room," and "were guilty of unlawfully assaulting, battering, torturing and falsely imprisoning the defendant at the . . . hospital." . . . The Supreme Court of California denied without opinion Rochin's petition for a hearing. . . . This Court granted certiorari, because a serious question is raised as to the limitations which the Due Process Clause of the Fourteenth Amendment imposes on the conduct of criminal proceedings by the States.

Reasoning

In our federal system, the administration of criminal justice is predominantly committed to the care of the States. . . . In reviewing a State criminal conviction under a claim of right guaranteed by the Due Process Clause of the Fourteenth Amendment, from which is derived the most far-reaching and most frequent federal basis of challenging State criminal justice, "we must be deeply mindful of the responsibilities of the States for the enforcement of criminal laws, and exercise with due humility our merely negative function in subjecting convictions from state courts to the very narrow scrutiny which the Due Process Clause of the Fourteenth Amendment authorizes." Due process of law, "itself a historical product," is not to be turned into a destructive dogma against the States in the administration of their systems of criminal justice.

However, this Court too has its responsibility. Regard for the requirements of the Due Process Clause "inescapably imposes upon this Court an exercise of judgment upon the whole course of the proceedings [resulting in a conviction] in order to ascertain whether they offend those canons of decency and fairness which express the notions of justice of English-speaking peoples even toward those charged with the most heinous offenses." These standards of justice are not authoritatively formulated anywhere as though they were specifics. Due process of law is a summarized constitutional guarantee of respect for those personal immunities which, as Mr. Justice Cardozo twice wrote for the Court, are "so rooted in the traditions and conscience of our people as to be ranked as fundamental," or are "implicit in the concept of ordered liberty."

The Court's function in the observance of this settled conception of the Due Process Clause does not leave us without adequate guides in subjecting State criminal procedures to constitutional judgment. In dealing not with the machinery of government but with human rights, the absence of formal exactitude, or want of fixity of meaning, is not an unusual or even regrettable attribute of constitutional provisions. Words, being symbols, do not speak without a gloss. On the one hand, the gloss may be the deposit of history, whereby a term gains technical content. Thus, the requirements of the Sixth and Seventh Amendments for trial by jury in the federal courts have a rigid meaning. No changes or chances can alter the content of the verbal symbol of "jury"—a body of twelve men who must reach a unanimous conclusion if the verdict is to go against the defendant. On the other hand, the gloss of some of the verbal symbols of the Constitution does not give them a fixed technical content. It exacts a continuing process of application.

When the gloss has thus not been fixed but is a function of the process of judgment, the judgment is bound to fall differently at different times and differently at the same time through different judges. Even more specific provisions, such as the guaranty of freedom of speech and the detailed protection against unreasonable searches and seizures, have inevitably evoked as sharp divisions in this Court as the least specific and most comprehensive protection of liberties, the Due Process Clause.

The vague contours of the Due Process Clause do not leave judges at large. We may not draw on our merely personal and private notions and disregard the limits that bind judges in their judicial function. Even though the concept of due process of law is not final and fixed, these limits are derived from considerations that are fused in the whole nature of our judicial process. These are considerations deeply rooted in reason and in the compelling traditions of the legal profession. The Due Process Clause places upon this Court the duty of exercising a judgment, within the narrow confines of judicial power in reviewing State convictions, upon interests of society pushing in opposite directions.

Due process of law thus conceived is not to be derided as resort to a revival of "natural law." To believe that this judicial exercise of judgment could be avoided by freezing "due process of law" at some fixed stage of time or thought is to suggest that the most important aspect of constitutional adjudication is a function for inanimate machines and not for judges, for whom the independence safeguarded by Article III of the Constitution was designed and who are presumably guided by established standards of judicial behavior. Even cybernetics has not yet made that haughty claim. To practice the requisite detachment and to achieve sufficient objectivity no doubt demands of judges the habit of self-discipline and self-criticism, incertitude that one's own views are incontestable and alert tolerance toward views not shared. But these are precisely the presuppositions of our judicial process. They are precisely the qualities society has a right to expect from those entrusted with ultimate judicial power.

Restraints on our jurisdiction are self-imposed only in the sense that there is from our decisions no immediate appeal short of impeachment or constitutional amendment. But that does not make due process of law a matter of judicial caprice. The faculties of the Due Process Clause may be indefinite and vague, but the mode of their ascertainment is not self-willed. In each case, "due process of law" requires an evaluation based on a disinterested inquiry pursued in the spirit of science, on a balanced order of facts exactly and fairly stated, on the detached consideration of conflicting claims, on a judgment not *ad hoc* and episodic but duly mindful of reconciling the needs both of continuity and of change in a progressive society.

Holding

Applying these general considerations to the circumstances of the present case, we are compelled to conclude that the proceedings by which this conviction was obtained do more than offend some fastidious squeamishness or private sentimentalism about combating crime too energetically. This is conduct that shocks the conscience. Illegally breaking into the privacy of the petitioner, the struggle to open his mouth and remove what was there, the forcible extraction of his stomach's contents—this course of proceeding by agents of government to obtain evidence is bound to offend even hardened sensibilities. They are methods too close to the rack and the screw to permit of constitutional differentiation.

It has long since ceased to be true that due process of law is heedless of the means by which otherwise relevant and credible evidence is obtained. This was not true even before the series of recent cases enforced the constitutional principle that the States may not base convictions upon confessions, however much verified, obtained by coercion. These decisions are not arbitrary exceptions to the comprehensive right of States to fashion their own rules of evidence for criminal trials. They are not sports in our constitutional law but applications of a general principle. They are only instances of the general requirement that States in their prosecutions respect certain decencies of civilized conduct. Due process of law, as a historic and generative principle, precludes defining, and thereby confining, these standards of conduct more precisely than to say that convictions cannot be brought about by methods that offend "a sense of justice." It would be a stultification of the responsibility which the course of constitutional history has cast upon this Court to hold that in order to convict a man, the police cannot extract by force what is in his mind but can extract what is in his stomach.

To attempt in this case to distinguish what lawyers call "real evidence" from verbal evidence is to ignore the reasons for excluding coerced confessions. Use of involuntary verbal confessions in State criminal trials is constitutionally obnoxious not only because of their unreliability. They are inadmissible under the Due Process Clause even though statements contained in them may be independently established as true. Coerced confessions offend the community's sense of fair play and decency. So here, to sanction the brutal conduct which naturally enough was condemned by the court whose judgment is before us, would be to afford brutality the cloak of law. Nothing would be more calculated to discredit law and thereby to brutalize the temper of a society....

Concurring, *Black, J.*

Adamson v. California, 332 U.S. 46, 68–123 (1961), sets out reasons for my belief that state as well as federal courts and law enforcement officers must obey the Fifth Amendment's command that "No person... shall be compelled in any criminal case to be a witness against himself." I think a person is compelled to be a witness against himself not only when he is compelled to testify, but also when as here, incriminating evidence is forcibly taken from him by a contrivance of modern science. In the view of a majority of the Court, however, the Fifth Amendment imposes no restraint of any kind on the states. They nevertheless hold that California's use of this evidence violated the Due Process Clause of the Fourteenth Amendment. Since they hold as I do in this case, I regret my inability to accept their interpretation without protest. But I believe that faithful adherence to the specific guarantees in the Bill of Rights insures a more permanent protection of individual liberty than that which can be afforded by the nebulous standards stated by the majority.

What the majority hold is that the Due Process Clause empowers this Court to nullify any State law if its application "shocks the conscience," offends "a sense of justice," or runs counter to the "decencies of civilized conduct." The majority emphasize that these statements do not refer to their own consciences or to their senses of justice and decency. For we are told that "we may not draw on our merely personal and private notions"; our judgment must be grounded on "considerations deeply rooted in reason and in the compelling traditions of the legal profession." We are further admonished to measure the validity of state practices, not by our reason, or by the traditions of the legal profession, but by "the community's sense of fair play and decency"; by the "traditions and conscience of our people"; or by "those canons of decency and fairness which express the notions of justice of English-speaking peoples." These canons are made necessary, it is said, because of "interests of society pushing in opposite directions." If the Due Process Clause does vest this Court with such unlimited power to invalidate laws, I am still in doubt as to why we should consider only the notions of English-speaking peoples to determine what are immutable and fundamental principles of justice. Moreover, one may well ask what avenues of investigation are open to discover "canons" of conduct so universally favored that this Court should write them into the Constitution? All we are told is that the discovery must be made by an "evaluation based on a disinterested inquiry pursued in the spirit of science, on a balanced order of facts."... I long ago concluded that the accordion-like qualities of this philosophy must inevitably imperil all the individual liberty safeguards specifically enumerated in the Bill of Rights. Reflection and recent decisions of this Court sanctioning abridgment of the freedom of speech and press have strengthened this conclusion.

Questions for Discussion

1. Why does Justice Felix Frankfurter conclude that the police violated Rochin's due process rights?
2. Are you persuaded by Justice Frankfurter's argument that the determination of the content of due process is an "objective" rather than a "subjective" process?
3. What other police practices would "shock the conscience"?
4. Justice Frankfurter compares the police conduct in *Rochin* to the involuntary confessions in *Brown v. Mississippi.* He writes that the Supreme Court cannot credibly "hold that in order to convict a man, the police cannot extract by force what is in his mind but can extract what is in his stomach." Do you agree with the judge's comparison?
5. Summarize the view of Justice Hugo Black. What is his criticism of the fundamental fairness test?

Cases and Comments

In *Irvine v. California,* law enforcement agents entered Irvine's home three times without a warrant to install and then to move a microphone. The content of his conversations was relied on to convict him of illegal gambling. Justice Jackson noted that "few police measures have come to our attention that more flagrantly, deliberately, and persistently violated the fundamental principle declared... as a restriction on the Federal Government." Justice Jackson nonetheless affirmed Irvine's criminal conviction. He distinguished the trespass to property and the eavesdropping in *Irvine* from *Rochin,* reasoning that in *Irvine,* there was an absence of "coercion, violence or brutality to the person." Justice Frankfurter, in his dissenting opinion, argued that Justice Jackson misinterpreted the significance of *Rochin* by focusing on the physical coercion employed to extract the narcotics and that Irvine's conviction also should be overturned. He explained that the significance of *Rochin* was that the government must respect "certain decencies of civilized conduct" and may not resort to "any form of skullduggery" to obtain a conviction. Due process is concerned with the "mode in which evidence is obtained," and when evidence is "secured by methods which offend elementary standards of justice, the victim of such methods may invoke the protection of the Fourteenth Amendment." Do you find Justice Jackson's or Justice Frankfurter's analysis of *Rochin* more persuasive? See *Irvine v. California,* 347 U.S. 128 (1954).

2.1 YOU DECIDE

Breithaupt was in an automobile collision in New Mexico in which he was seriously injured and three people died. A nearly empty whiskey bottle was found in the glove compartment. Breithaupt was lying unconscious in the hospital emergency room when a state patrolman smelled alcohol on his breath. At the request of the patrolman, a doctor used a hypodermic needle to draw a blood sample that indicated that Breithaupt had a blood alcohol content of .17 percent. An expert witness testified at trial that the blood test indicated that Breithaupt was inebriated at the time of the accident, and Breithaupt was convicted of involuntary manslaughter. Breithaupt relied on the precedent of *Rochin v. California* and claimed that the blood test was improperly admitted at trial. How would you rule? See *Breithaupt v. Abram,* 352 U.S. 432 (1957).

You can find the answer by referring to the study site, http://www.sagepub.com/lippmancp.

Total Incorporation

The fundamental fairness doctrine continued to hold sway in the Supreme Court until the 1960s. Justice Hugo Black was one of the most prominent critics of fundamental fairness. In 1947, Justice Black, in his dissenting opinion in *Adamson v. California,* explained that he had studied the history of the Fourteenth Amendment and that the intent of the drafters of the amendment was to totally incorporate and to protect the principles contained within the Bill of Rights (*Adamson v. California,* 332 U.S. 46 [1947]). Justice Black made the following points in his criticism of the fundamental fairness approach.

- ***Decision making.*** Fundamental fairness does not provide definite standards to determine the rights that are protected by the Fourteenth Amendment Due Process Clause.
- ***Bill of Rights.*** The Bill of Rights includes the rights that the founders struggled to achieve and believed were essential to liberty and freedom. The Fourteenth Amendment is intended to make these rights available to individuals in their relations with state governments.
- ***Textual language.*** The drafters of the Fourteenth Amendment would have used the phrase "rights essential to liberty and justice" if this were their intent.

Justice Black concluded by expressing doubts whether his fellow judges were "wise enough to improve on the Bill of Rights.... To hold that this Court can determine what, if any, provisions of the Bill of Rights will be enforced, and if so to what degree, is to frustrate the great design of the written Constitution" (89–90). Justice Black's "total incorporation" approach never succeeded in attracting a majority of the Supreme Court. Justices Frank Murphy, Wiley Rutledge, and William O. Douglas at various times went so far as to endorse a **total incorporation plus** approach, which extended the Bill of Rights to the states along with additional rights, such as the right to a clean environment and health care. As observed by Justice Frank Murphy in his dissent in *Adamson,* "the specific guarantees of the Bill of Rights should be carried over intact into the . . . Fourteenth Amendment. But I am not prepared to say that the latter is entirely and necessarily limited by the Bill of Rights. Occasions may arise where a proceeding falls so far short of . . . fundamental standards of procedure as to warrant constitutional condemnation in terms of a lack of due process despite the absence of a specific provision in the Bill of Rights" (124). The total incorporation approach is straightforward and involves three simple steps.

- ***Due process.*** Due process is shorthand for the Bill of Rights.
- ***Bill of Rights.*** Identify the rights protected by the Bill of Rights.
- ***Incorporation.*** These rights are incorporated into the Fourteenth Amendment and must be followed by the states to the same extent that the rights are followed by the federal government.

Critics of total incorporation asked Justice Black to explain why the drafters of the Fourteenth Amendment did not explicitly state that their intent was to extend the protections of the Bill of Rights to the states. The total incorporation approach, although never endorsed by a majority of the U.S. Supreme Court, nevertheless is important for making a strong case for extending most of the rights available to defendants in the federal system to defendants in the fifty state criminal procedure systems.

Selective Incorporation

By 1962, the U.S. Supreme Court included five judges who favored incorporation and who provided the votes that resulted in the Supreme Court's adopting the incorporation doctrine. The majority of judges, rather than embracing total incorporation, endorsed a *selective incorporation* approach, first articulated by Justice William Brennan. Justice Brennan wrote the majority opinion in *Malloy v. Hogan* incorporating the Fifth Amendment right against self-incrimination into the Fourteenth Amendment. Justice Brennan "rejected the notion that the Fourteenth Amendment applies to the States only a watered-down . . . version of the individual guarantees of the Bill of Rights. . . . It would be incongruous to have different standards determine the validity of a claim of privilege . . . depending on whether the claim was asserted in a state or federal court. Therefore, the same standards must determine whether an accused's silence in either a federal or state proceeding is justified" (*Malloy v. Hogan,* 378 U.S. 1, 10 [1964]).

The elements of the selective incorporation approach may be easily summarized.

- ***Fundamental rights.*** The Fourteenth Amendment incorporates those provisions of the Bill of Rights that are "fundamental principles of liberty and justice which lie at the base of all our [American] civil and political institutions." The entire amendment rather than a single portion of the amendment is incorporated into the Fourteenth Amendment ("jot-for-jot and case-for-case").
- ***Application.*** The amendment that is incorporated is applicable to the same extent to both state and federal governments. Justice William O. Douglas characterized this as "coextensive coverage."
- ***Federalism.*** States are free to design their own systems of criminal procedures in those areas that are not incorporated into the Fourteenth Amendment.

The U.S. Supreme Court has incorporated a number of the fundamental rights included in the Bill of Rights into the Fourteenth Amendment Due Process Clause. The rights that are incorporated are listed in Table 2.3. The Court has not incorporated the following five provisions of the Bill of Rights into the Fourteenth Amendment, and therefore, a state is free to adopt a law or include a provision in its constitution that extends these five protections to its citizens.

- ***Second Amendment.*** Right to keep and bear arms.
- ***Third Amendment.*** Prohibition against quartering soldiers without consent of the owner.
- ***Fifth Amendment.*** Right to indictment by a grand jury for capital or infamous crimes.
- ***Seventh Amendment.*** Right to trial in civil law cases.
- ***Eighth Amendment.*** Prohibition against excessive bail and fines.

The next case on the study site is *Duncan v. Louisiana* (391 U.S. 145, 148–158 [1968]), which incorporated the Sixth Amendment right to a jury trial into the Fourteenth Amendment. Justice Byron "Whizzer" White wrote the majority opinion and relied on the selective incorporation doctrine to hold that trial by jury in criminal cases is "fundamental to the American scheme of justice" and that the Fourteenth Amendment "guarantees a right of jury trial in all criminal cases which…would come within the Sixth Amendment guarantee." Justice White noted that by the

Table 2.3 Bill of Rights Provisions Related to Criminal Procedure Incorporated Into the Fourteenth Amendment

First Amendment
Fiske v. Kansas, 274 U.S. 380 (1927) [freedom of speech]
Fourth Amendment
Wolf v. Colorado, 338 U.S. 25 (1949) [unreasonable searches and seizures] *Mapp v.Ohio*, 367 U.S. 643 (1961) [exclusionary rule]
Fifth Amendment
Malloy v. Hogan, 378 U.S. 1 (1964) [compelled self-incrimination] *Benton v. Maryland*, 395 U.S. 784 (1969) [double jeopardy]
Sixth Amendment
Gideon v. Wainwright, 372 U.S. 335 (1963) [right to counsel] *Klopfer v. North Carolina*, 386 U.S. 213 (1967) [speedy trial] *In re Oliver*, 333 U.S. 257 (1948) [public trial] *Pointer v. Texas*, 380 U.S. 400 (1965) [right to confront witnesses] *Duncan v. Louisiana*, 391 U.S. 145 (1968) [impartial jury] *Washington v. Texas*, 388 U.S. 14 (1967) [right to compulsory process for obtaining favorable witnesses at trial]
Eighth Amendment
Robinson v. California, 370 U.S. 660 (1962) (cruel and unusual punishment)

time the U.S. Constitution had been drafted, the jury trial had been in existence in England for several centuries. The jury was part of the legal system of the American colonies and then was incorporated into the constitutions of the new states and included in the Sixth Amendment. Justice White concluded by noting that the jury continued to be an important feature of federal and state criminal justice systems and provided as a check on the abuse of power. He stressed that while a criminal justice process that is "fair and equitable but used no juries is easy to imagine," the jury is "fundamental" to the organization and philosophy of the American criminal justice system. Justice Black, in his concurring opinion, remained steadfast in his advocacy of total incorporation, while Justice Harlan provided a passionate defense of fundamental fairness (*Duncan v. Louisiana,* 391 U.S. 145 [1968]). *Duncan* provides the opportunity to review your understanding of the relationship between the Fourteenth Amendment Due Process Clause and the Bill of Rights as we turn our attention to the important topic of equal protection under the law.

Equal Protection

The U.S. Constitution originally did not provide for the equal protection of the laws. Professor Erwin Chemerinsky observed that this should not be surprising given that African Americans were enslaved and women were subject to discrimination. Slavery, in fact, was formally embedded in the legal system. Article I, Section 2 of the U.S. Constitution provides for the apportionment of the House of Representatives based on the "whole number of free persons" as well as three-fifths of the slaves. This was reinforced by Article IV, Section 2, the "Fugitive Slave Clause," which requires the return of a slave escaping into a state that does not recognize slavery (Chemerinsky, 2002, p. 642).

In 1865, immediately following the Civil War, Congress enacted and the States ratified the Thirteenth Amendment, which prohibits slavery and involuntary servitude. Three years later, as we have seen, Congress approved the Fourteenth Amendment. Section 1 guarantees individuals equal protection of the law in addition to providing that no state shall deprive any person of liberty or property without due process of law. In 1954, the U.S. Supreme Court declared in *Bolling v. Sharpe* that the Fifth Amendment Due Process Clause imposes an identical obligation of equal protection of the law on the federal government and explained that "discrimination may be so unjustifiable as to be violative of due process" (*Bolling v. Sharpe,* 347 U.S. 497 [1954]).

The Equal Protection Clause is of the utmost importance. The sense that we are being treated fairly and equally is essential for maintaining our respect for the law and support for the political system. Yet every day, the police, prosecutors, and judges make decisions treating people differently in regard to arrests, criminal charges, bail, and sentencing. We generally accept these decisions because we have confidence that the judgments are fair and reasonable. Individuals who believe that they have been discriminated against may ask a court to determine whether they have been denied equal treatment under the law.

One area of legal challenge involves the decision of a prosecutor to charge an individual with a criminal offense. Would it violate equal protection for a prosecutor to charge one teenager involved in a drag race with reckless driving while deciding not to bring charges against the other driver? Courts generally follow a **presumption of regularity.** Prosecutors are expected to use "judgment and common sense" in filing criminal charges, and courts will not second-guess a prosecutor's decision. Judges recognize that prosecutors are in the best position to evaluate a defendant's role in a crime, criminal record, willingness to cooperate, and expressions of remorse and other factors (*Wayte v. United States,* 470 U.S. 598, 607–608 [1985]).

Prosecutors' discretion, however, is not unlimited. The Supreme Court noted in *Oyler v. Boles* that the Equal Protection Clause prohibits prosecutors from making decisions to prosecute that are "deliberately based upon an unjustifiable standard such as race, religion, [or] other arbitrary classification" (*Oyler v. Boyles,* 368 U.S. 448, 456 [1962]).

In *Yick Wo v. Hopkins,* the U.S. Supreme Court held that focusing prosecutions on the Chinese community for violations of a San Francisco ordinance regulating laundries violated the Fourteenth Amendment. The Court noted that the ordinance was being applied "with a mind so unequal and oppressive as to amount to a practical denial by the state of... equal protection of the law.... Though the law itself be fair on its face, and impartial in appearance, yet, if it is applied and administered by public authority with an evil eye and an unequal hand... the denial of equal justice is... within the prohibition of the constitution" (*Yick Wo v. Hopkins,* 118 U.S. 356 [1886]).

A defendant's claim of discriminatory or **selective prosecution** and request that a court dismiss a prosecution on the grounds of equal protection of the law must overcome the presumption of regularity by presenting clear and convincing evidence of a discriminatory impact and discriminatory intent.

- ***Discriminatory impact.*** Equal enforcement of a law focuses on whether individuals of a group or groups and nonmembers of these groups have violated the same law but have not been prosecuted to the same extent.
- ***Discriminatory intent.*** The prosecutor intentionally or purposefully singles out and targets members of the group for prosecution.

Courts will subject classifications based on race, religion, ethnicity, or national origin or the exercise of First Amendment rights to *strict scrutiny.* These categories in almost every instance are irrelevant to the enforcement of the criminal law. For example, a prosecutor would have a difficult time explaining why he or she brought most prosecutions for speeding against members of a particular religious group who recently moved into the community. On the other hand, it may make sense to direct prosecutions against young drivers who statistics indicate pose a significant threat to safety or who commit more driving violations than other drivers. The following are three frequently noted examples of successful claims of selective prosecution.

- ***Census questions.*** Four individuals were prosecuted in Hawaii for failing to complete their census forms. The individuals were members of a census resistance movement and openly protested the census on the grounds that it constituted an invasion of privacy (*United States v. Steele,* 461 F.2d 1148 [9th Cir. 1972]).
- ***Housing codes.*** A landlord convicted of violating a housing law was allowed to show that she was singled out for prosecution because she had disclosed corruption in the Department of Buildings in New York (*People v. Walker,* 200 N.E.2d 779 [1964]).
- ***Sunday sales.*** The defendant was permitted to argue that he was the only store owner prosecuted for selling items that were prohibited from being sold on Sunday. He alleged that he was singled out because he had a discount drug store that threatened the economic livelihood of other storeowners in the area (*People v. Utica Daw's Drug Company,* 224 N.Y.S.2d 128 [1962]).

The next case in the text is *United States v. Armstrong.* The respondents were indicted on charges of conspiring to possess with intent to distribute and conspiring to distribute more than fifty grams of cocaine base (crack), and using firearms in connection with drug trafficking. The defendants filed a motion for discovery (a legal action asking for the court to order the opposing side, in this instance the U.S. Attorney, to turn over information). This allegation was based on the claim that the defendants were being subjected to "selective prosecution" in violation of equal protection of the law because they are African Americans. The respondents primarily relied on an affidavit by a "Paralegal Specialist" employed by the Federal Public Defender Service who stated that in his experience, every individual against whom similar charges had been filed during 1991 was African American. The affidavit was supported by other documents, including a "study" of crack-cocaine cases processed by the Federal Public Defender during 1991 that indicated that all of the defendants charged with conspiracy to possess or to distribute crack cocaine were African Americans. The respondents anticipated that the U.S.

Attorney's files would reveal a pattern of prosecuting African Americans for charges relating to crack cocaine while dropping or plea-bargaining the same charges against Caucasians.

The U.S. Supreme Court held that a defendant seeking discovery in a selective-prosecution claim based on race must demonstrate that the prosecution had a discriminatory effect and that it was motivated by a discriminatory purpose. The claimant is required to present "some evidence" (a "credible showing") that "similarly situated individuals of a different race were not prosecuted." As you read *Armstrong,* consider whether the claimants presented "some evidence tending to show the existence of the essential elements of a selective-prosecution claim." A second question is whether Justice John Paul Stevens, in his dissenting opinion, is correct in arguing that the respondent's discovery request should be granted based on the "severity of the imposed penalties and the troubling racial patterns of enforcement" that raise a question concerning the "fairness of charging practices for crack offenses" (*United States v. Armstrong,* 517 U.S. 456 [1996]).

Criminal Procedure in the News

The argument for incorporating the central provisions of the Bill of Rights into the Fourteenth Amendment was significantly strengthened by the civil rights movement of the 1960s. A country committed to liberty and justice could not accept that individuals protesting segregation were being attacked by police dogs and water hoses. The tenor of times is illustrated by the "Mississippi Burning" case, later the subject of a Hollywood film.

In April 1964, hundreds of college students descended on Mississippi as part of the "Mississippi Summer Project" sponsored by a coalition of civil rights organizations headed by the Congress of Racial Equality. This was an effort to defy these still largely segregated societies by registering African American voters. Mississippi was to be the center of this effort. This was a state that Martin Luther King had referred to as a land "sweltering with the heat of injustice" and the "heat of oppression." A newspaper in Meridian, Mississippi, warned local residents against the arrival of "beatniks," "outside agitators," "wild-eyed left-wing nuts, the unshaven and unwashed trash, and the just plain stupid or ignorant or misled."

Meridian in Neshoba County was the site of intense resistance to the civil rights workers. Sam Bowers, the Imperial Wizard of the White Knights of the racial supremacist Ku Klux Kan of Mississippi, proclaimed that it was time to implement mass resistance and to start by eliminating the "Jew-Boy," Michael Schwerner, a recent college graduate who had been active in registering voters in Meridian. Civil rights workers in Mississippi were warned by the U.S. Department of Justice that they could not look to local law enforcement for protection. In Meridian, for example, both Sheriff Lawrence Rainey and his deputy Cecil Price were suspected of membership in the Ku Klux Klan.

On June 20, 1964, Schwerner (age twenty-four) along with fellow New York civil rights worker James Goodman (age twenty) and James Chaney (age twenty-one), an African American from Meridian, were warned by residents that they had been targeted by the Klan. As the three drove out of town, they were arrested and jailed by Officer Cecil Price for speeding and suspected involvement in the arson of the Mount Zion Church, which in fact had been burned down in April by the Klan in retribution for the congregation's involvement in civil rights activity. The three civil rights workers were released from jail on the evening of June 21 and subsequently were pulled over by Price as they approached the county line and were placed in his squad car.

The station wagon in which the three young men had been traveling was set ablaze. Price and two carloads of Klan members then traveled down a dirt road where Schwerner, Goodman, and Chaney were shot to death at point-blank range by Wayne Roberts, a twenty-six-year-old dishonorably discharged marine. The bodies were taken to a dam at the 353-acre Old Jolly Farm, owned by businessman Olen Burrage. A tractor was used to cover the bodies with tons of dirt. Burrage reportedly had earlier proclaimed at a Klan meeting that he had a "dam that'll hold a hundred of them." According to trial testimony, Bowers later remarked that this was the "first time that Christians had planned and carried out the execution of a Jew."

Civil rights workers alerted John Doar, the U.S. Justice Department's representative in Mississippi, who immediately intervened. The FBI responded by opening its first office in Mississippi, and on August 4, the FBI located the bodies based on information provided in return for a $30,000 reward. The interrogation of Klan members yielded additional information, and on December 4, several Klan members were arrested for conspiring to deprive Schwerner, Chaney, and Goodman of their civil rights under law. Federal Judge William Harold Cox dismissed all but two of the indictments, a step that might be expected from a federal judge who openly described civil rights workers in his courtroom as "a bunch of chimpanzees." In March 1966, the U.S. Supreme Court in *United States v. Price* reversed Cox and reinstated the indictments on the grounds that the defendants had conspired with Deputy Sheriff Price to employ the power of Mississippi to deprive Schwerner, Goodman, and Chaney of their right to life in violation of the Fourteenth Amendment Due Process Clause. The unanimous Court noted that there was a strong federal interest in the "establishment and vindication of fundamental rights" in those instances in which these rights had been grossly abused by State officials (*United States v. Price,* 383 U.S. 787 [1966]).

The trial of the eighteen defendants opened on October 7, 1967. The U.S. prosecutor relied on three Klan informants, including James Jordan who testified that he had witnessed the killing. In rebuttal, various local residents testified that they had seen the defendants in town at the time of the killing. Prosecutor John Doar in his closing remarks alleged that the young civil rights workers had been killed in a "cold-blooded" conspiracy and that Cecil Price had employed the "machinery of law, his office, his power, his authority, his badge, his uniform, his police car, his police gun...to capture and kill." After deliberating for several days, the jury reached a compromise verdict. Seven men including Price, Bowers, Wayne Roberts, and other defendants from Lauderdale County were convicted. Eight men, most of whom were from Neshoba County, were acquitted, including Sheriff Lawrence Rainey and Olen Burrage. The jury was unable to reach a verdict in the case of three defendants, including Edgar Ray Killen. These were the first convictions in Mississippi history for the murder of a civil rights worker. Judge Cox sentenced two defendants to ten years, two defendants to six years, and three defendants received four years. Cox later allegedly remarked, "They killed one n_____, one Jew , and a white man—I gave them all what I thought they deserved."

In 1999, Mississippi Attorney General Michael Moore announced that he hoped to change "some of those old stereotypes" and reopened the investigation of the Mississippi Burning case. On January 6, 2005, Mississippi charged Baptist preacher Edgar Ray Killen with murder. Killen had escaped conviction in the earlier prosecution when a single juror refused to vote to convict him, and nothing that had occurred over the past forty years had changed Killen's view that the struggle against the civil rights workers in the 1960s was a "holy crusade." Killen's attitude is illustrated by an incident during the 1967 trial. At Killen's request, one of the defense lawyers asked a prosecution witness whether, together with Schwerner, he had tried to "get young Negro males to sign statements that they would rape one white woman a week during the hot summer of 1964 here in Mississippi." Federal officials had long viewed Killen as central to the conspiracy and believed that he had met with Price and had agreed to contact and direct the Klansmen involved in the killings.

The jury of eight whites and four blacks, seven women and five men, deadlocked and compromised by convicting Killen of manslaughter rather than intentional murder. In sentencing Killen to three consecutive twenty-year terms, Mississippi Judge Marcus Gordon pronounced that "I have taken into consideration that there are three lives in this case and that the three lives should be absolutely respected." The formerly prosegregationist *Jackson Clarion-Ledger* proclaimed that the verdicts were a "fitting...ending to the long search for justice in the case."

Some experts view the 1967 Mississippi Burning case as a turning point in the civil rights movement that inspired decision makers in Washington, D.C., to enact legislation providing for equal rights and an end to racial segregation in the South. The events of the "Mississippi summer" also undoubtedly helped to persuade the Supreme Court of the need to extend the protections of the Bill of Rights to citizens of the fifty states. Between 1989 and 2005, twenty-one individuals in the South were convicted of having murdered civil rights workers in the 1960s. Most notable was the conviction of Bryron De La Beckwith in Mississippi for the June 1963 assassination of Medgar Evers, state field secretary for the National Association for the Advancement of Colored People, and the conviction of Imperial Wizard Sam Bowers for the 1966 firebombing of the home of a local civil rights leader in Hattiesburg, Mississippi. In August 2007, former Klansman James Seale was sentenced to three life terms for his role in the 1964 kidnapping and murder of two African American teenagers in Mississippi. The federal judge in announcing the sentence characterized the crime as "unspeakable because only monsters could inflict this." The U.S. Congress recently responded by creating a "cold-case" unit in the Justice Department to pursue civil rights murders. There currently are an estimated one hundred cases under investigation.

Note that Killen's prosecution was not "double jeopardy" because the second trial was for a different crime and was brought on behalf of the state rather than the federal government. Do you agree with prosecuting Edgar Ray Killen and other alleged killers after more than three decades had passed following their crimes? What does the Mississippi Burning trial tell us about "procedural justice"?

Did the respondents present some evidence of the discriminatory enforcement of drug laws?

United States v. Armstrong, 517 U.S. 456 (1996), Rehnquist, C.J.

Issue

In this case, we consider the showing necessary for a defendant to be entitled to discovery on a claim that the prosecuting attorney singled him out for prosecution on the basis of his race. We conclude that respondents failed to satisfy the threshold showing: They failed to show that the Government declined to prosecute similarly situated suspects of other races.

Facts

In April 1992, respondents were indicted in the United States District Court for the Central District of California on charges of conspiring to possess with intent to distribute more than 50 grams of cocaine base (crack) and conspiring to distribute the same, in violation of 21 U.S.C. §§ 841 and 846 (1988 ed. and Supp. IV), and federal firearms offenses. For three months prior to the indictment, agents of the Federal Bureau of Alcohol, Tobacco, and Firearms and the Narcotics Division of the Inglewood, California, Police Department had infiltrated a suspected crack distribution ring by using three confidential informants. On seven separate occasions during this period, the informants had bought a total of 124.3 grams of crack from respondents and witnessed respondents carrying firearms during the sales. The agents searched the hotel room in which the sales were transacted, arrested respondents Armstrong and Hampton in the room, and found more crack and a loaded gun. The agents later arrested the other respondents as part of the ring.

In response to the indictment, respondents filed a motion for discovery or for dismissal of the indictment, alleging that they were selected for federal prosecution because they are black. In support of their motion, they offered only an affidavit by a "Paralegal Specialist," employed by the Office of the Federal Public Defender representing one of the respondents. The only allegation in the affidavit was that, in every one of the twenty-four § 841 or § 846 cases closed by the office during 1991, the defendant was black. Accompanying the affidavit was a "study" listing the twenty-four defendants, their race, whether they were prosecuted for dealing cocaine as well as crack, and the status of each case.

The district court granted the motion. It ordered the Government (1) to provide a list of all cases from the last three years in which the Government charged both cocaine and firearms offenses, (2) to identify the race of the defendants in those cases, (3) to identify what levels of law enforcement were involved in the investigations of those cases, and (4) to explain its criteria for deciding to prosecute those defendants for federal cocaine offenses.

The Government moved for reconsideration of the district court's discovery order. With this motion, it submitted affidavits and other evidence to explain why it had chosen to prosecute respondents and why respondents' study did not support the inference that the Government was singling out blacks for cocaine prosecution. The federal and local agents participating in the case alleged in affidavits that race played no role in their investigation. An Assistant United States Attorney explained in an affidavit that the decision to prosecute met the general criteria for prosecution, because there was over 100 grams of cocaine base involved, over twice the threshold necessary for a ten year mandatory minimum sentence; there were multiple sales involving multiple defendants, thereby indicating a fairly substantial crack cocaine ring;...there were multiple federal firearms violations intertwined with the narcotics trafficking; the overall evidence in the case was extremely strong, including audio and videotapes of defendants;...and several of the defendants had criminal histories including narcotics and firearms violations.

The Government also submitted sections of a published 1989 Drug Enforcement Administration report which concluded that "large-scale, interstate trafficking networks controlled by Jamaicans, Haitians and Black street gangs dominate the manufacture and distribution of crack." In response, one of respondents' attorneys submitted an affidavit alleging that an intake coordinator at a drug treatment center had told her that there are "an equal number of Caucasian users and dealers to minority users and dealers." Respondents also submitted an affidavit from a criminal defense attorney alleging that in his experience, many nonblacks are prosecuted in state court for crack offenses, and a newspaper article reporting that federal "crack criminals...are being punished far more severely than if they had been caught with powder cocaine, and almost every single one of them is black." The district court denied the motion for reconsideration. When the Government indicated it would not comply with the court's discovery order, the court dismissed the case.

A divided three-judge panel of the Court of Appeals for the Ninth Circuit reversed, holding that because of the proof requirements for a selective-prosecution claim, defendants must "provide a colorable basis for believing that 'others similarly situated have not been prosecuted'" to obtain discovery. The court of appeals voted to rehear the case en banc, and the en banc panel affirmed the district court's order of dismissal, holding that "a defendant is not required to demonstrate that the government has failed to prosecute others who are similarly situated." We granted certiorari to determine the appropriate standard for discovery for a selective-prosecution claim.

Reasoning

A selective-prosecution claim is not a defense on the merits to the criminal charge itself, but an independent assertion that the prosecutor has brought the charge for reasons forbidden by the Constitution. Our cases delineating the necessary elements to prove a claim of selective prosecution have taken great pains to explain that the standard is a demanding one. These cases afford a "background presumption" that the showing necessary to obtain discovery should itself be a significant barrier to the litigation of insubstantial claims.

A selective-prosecution claim asks a court to exercise judicial power over a "special province" of the Executive. The Attorney General and United States Attorneys retain "'broad discretion'" to enforce the Nation's criminal laws. They have this latitude because they are designated by statute as the President's delegates to help him discharge his constitutional responsibility to "take Care that the Laws be faithfully executed." U.S. Constitution, Article II, Section 3. As a result, "the presumption of regularity supports" their prosecutorial decisions, and "in the absence of clear evidence to the contrary, courts presume that they have properly discharged their official duties." In the ordinary case, "so long as the prosecutor has probable cause to believe that the accused committed an offense defined by statute, the decision whether or not to prosecute, and what charge to file or bring before a grand jury, generally rests entirely in his discretion."

A prosecutor's discretion is "subject to constitutional constraints." One of these constraints, imposed by the equal protection component of the Due Process Clause of the Fifth Amendment, is that the decision whether to prosecute may not be based on "an unjustifiable standard such as race, religion, or other arbitrary classification." A defendant may demonstrate that the administration of a criminal law is "directed so exclusively against a particular class of persons...with a mind so unequal and oppressive" that the system of prosecution amounts to "a practical denial" of equal protection of the law.

In order to dispel the presumption that a prosecutor has not violated equal protection, a criminal defendant must present "clear evidence to the contrary." We explained in *Wayte v. United States* why courts are "properly hesitant to examine the decision whether to prosecute." Judicial deference to the decisions of these executive officers rests in part on an assessment of the relative competence of prosecutors and courts. "Such factors as the strength of the case, the prosecution's general deterrence value, the Government's enforcement priorities, and the case's relationship to the Government's overall enforcement plan are not readily susceptible to the kind of analysis the courts are competent to undertake." It also stems from a concern not to unnecessarily impair the performance of a core executive constitutional function. "Examining the basis of a prosecution delays the criminal proceeding, threatens to chill law enforcement by subjecting the prosecutor's motives and decision making to outside inquiry, and may undermine prosecutorial effectiveness by revealing the Government's enforcement policy."

The requirements for a selective-prosecution claim draw on "ordinary equal protection standards." The claimant must demonstrate that the federal prosecutorial policy "had a discriminatory effect and that it was motivated by a discriminatory purpose." To establish a discriminatory effect in a race case, the claimant must show that similarly situated individuals of a different race were not prosecuted.... The similarly situated requirement does not make a selective-prosecution claim impossible to prove. In *Yick Wo,* an ordinance adopted by San Francisco prohibited the operation of laundries in wooden buildings. The plaintiff in error successfully demonstrated that the ordinance was applied against Chinese nationals but not against other laundry-shop operators. The authorities had denied the applications of 200 Chinese subjects for permits to operate shops in wooden buildings, but granted the applications of 80 individuals who were not Chinese subjects to operate laundries in wooden buildings "under similar conditions."

Having reviewed the requirements to prove a selective-prosecution claim, we turn to the showing necessary to obtain discovery in support of such a claim. If discovery is ordered, the Government must assemble from its own files documents which might corroborate or refute the defendant's claim. Discovery thus imposes many of the costs present when the Government must respond to a prima facie case of selective prosecution. It will divert prosecutors' resources and may disclose the Government's prosecutorial strategy. The justifications for a rigorous standard for the elements of a selective-prosecution claim thus require a correspondingly rigorous standard for discovery in aid of such a claim.

The courts of appeals "require some evidence tending to show the existence of the essential elements of the defense," discriminatory effect and discriminatory intent. In this case, we consider what evidence constitutes "some evidence tending to show the existence" of the discriminatory effect element.... The vast majority of the courts of appeals require the defendant to produce some evidence that similarly situated defendants of other races could have been prosecuted, but were not, and this requirement is consistent with our equal protection case law. As the three-judge panel explained, "'selective prosecution' implies that a selection has taken place."

The court of appeals reached its decision that a defendant may establish a colorable claim for a discriminatory effect without evidence that the Government failed to prosecute others who are similarly situated to the defendant. The court of appeals reached this decision in part because it started "with the presumption that people of *all* races commit *all* types of crimes—not with the premise that any type of crime is the exclusive province of any particular racial or ethnic group." It cited no authority for this proposition, which seems contradicted by the most recent statistics of the United States Sentencing Commission. Those statistics show: More than 90 percent of the persons sentenced in 1994 for crack cocaine trafficking were black; 93.4 percent of convicted LSD dealers were white; and 91 percent of those convicted for pornography or prostitution were white. Presumptions at war with presumably reliable statistics have no proper place in the analysis of this issue.

The court of appeals also expressed concern about the "evidentiary obstacles defendants face." But all of its sister circuits that have confronted the issue have required that defendants produce some evidence of differential treatment of similarly situated members of other races or protected classes. In the present case, if the claim of selective prosecution were well founded, it should not have been an insuperable task to prove that persons of other races were being treated differently than respondents. For instance, respondents could have investigated whether similarly situated persons of other races were prosecuted by the State of California and were known to federal law enforcement officers but were not prosecuted in federal court. We think the required threshold—a credible showing of different treatment of similarly situated persons—adequately balances the Government's interest in vigorous prosecution and the defendant's interest in avoiding selective prosecution.

Holding

In the case before us, respondents' "study" did not constitute "some evidence tending to show the existence of the essential elements of a selective-prosecution claim." The study failed to identify individuals who were not black and could have been prosecuted for the offenses for which respondents were charged but were not so prosecuted. This omission was not remedied by respondents' evidence in opposition to the Government's motion for reconsideration. The newspaper article, which discussed the discriminatory effect of federal drug sentencing laws, was not relevant to an allegation of discrimination in decisions to prosecute. Respondents' affidavits, which recounted one attorney's conversation with a drug treatment center employee and the experience of another attorney defending drug prosecutions in state court, recounted hearsay and reported personal conclusions based on anecdotal evidence. The judgment of the court of appeals is therefore reversed, and the case is remanded for proceedings consistent with this opinion.

Dissenting, *Stevens, J.*

Federal prosecutors are respected members of a respected profession. Despite an occasional misstep, the excellence of their work abundantly justifies the presumption that "they have properly discharged their official duties." Nevertheless, the possibility that political or racial animosity may infect a decision to institute criminal proceedings cannot be ignored. For that reason, it has long been settled that the prosecutor's broad discretion to determine when criminal charges should be filed is not completely unbridled. As the Court notes, however, the scope of judicial review of particular exercises of that discretion is not fully defined.

The United States Attorney for the Central District of California is a member and an officer of the bar of that district court. As such, she has a duty to the judges of that Court to maintain the standards of the profession in the performance of her official functions. If a district judge has reason to suspect that she, or a member of her staff, has singled out particular defendants for prosecution on the basis of their race, it is surely appropriate for the judge to determine whether there is a factual basis for such a concern. . . .

The Court correctly concludes that in this case, the facts presented to the district court in support of respondents' claim that they had been singled out for prosecution because of their race were not sufficient to prove that defense. Moreover, I agree with the Court that their showing was not strong enough to give them a right to discovery. . . . Like Chief Judge Wallace of the court of appeals, however, I am persuaded that the district judge did not abuse her discretion when she concluded that the factual showing was sufficiently disturbing to require some response from the United States Attorney's Office. Perhaps the discovery order was broader than necessary, but I cannot agree with the Court's apparent conclusion that no inquiry was permissible.

The district judge's order should be evaluated in light of three circumstances that underscore the need for judicial vigilance over certain types of drug prosecutions. First, the Anti-Drug Act of 1986 and subsequent legislation established a regime of extremely high penalties for the possession and distribution of so-called "crack" cocaine. Those provisions treat 1 gram of crack as the equivalent of 100 grams of powder cocaine. The distribution of 50 grams of crack is thus punishable by the same mandatory minimum sentence of 10 years in prison that applies to the distribution of 5,000 grams of powder cocaine. The Sentencing Guidelines extend this ratio to penalty levels above the mandatory minimums: For any given quantity of crack, the guideline range is the same as if the offense had involved 100 times that amount in powder cocaine. These penalties result in sentences for crack offenders that average three to eight times longer than sentences for comparable powder offenders.

Second, the disparity between the treatment of crack cocaine and powder cocaine is matched by the disparity between the severity of the punishment imposed by federal law and that imposed by state law for the same conduct. For a variety of reasons, often including the absence of mandatory minimums, the existence of parole, and lower baseline penalties, terms of imprisonment for drug offenses tend to be substantially lower in state systems than in the federal system. The difference is especially marked in the case of crack offenses. The majority of States draw no distinction between types of cocaine in their penalty schemes; of those that do, none has established as stark a differential as the Federal Government. For example, if respondent Hampton is found guilty, his federal sentence might be as long as a mandatory life term. Had he been tried in state court, his sentence could have been as short as 12 years, less work time credits of half that amount.

Finally, it is undisputed that the brunt of the elevated federal penalties falls heavily on blacks. While 65 percent of the persons who have used crack are white, in 1993, they represented only 4 percent of the federal offenders convicted of trafficking in crack. Eighty-eight percent of such defendants were black. During the first 18 months of full guideline implementation, the sentencing disparity between black and white defendants grew from preguideline levels: Blacks on average received sentences over 40 percent longer than whites. Those figures represent a major threat to the integrity of federal sentencing reform, whose main purpose was the elimination of disparity (especially racial) in sentencing. The Sentencing Commission acknowledges that the heightened crack penalties are a "primary cause of the growing disparity between sentences for Black and White federal defendants."

The extraordinary severity of the imposed penalties and the troubling racial patterns of enforcement give rise to a special concern about the fairness of charging practices for crack offenses. Evidence tending to prove that black defendants charged with distribution of crack in the Central District of California are prosecuted in federal court, whereas members of other races charged with similar offenses are prosecuted in state court, warrants close scrutiny by the federal judges in that district. In my view, the district judge, who has sat on both the federal and the state benches in Los Angeles, acted well within her discretion to call for the development of facts that would demonstrate what standards, if any, governed the choice of forum where similarly situated offenders are prosecuted.

Respondents submitted a study showing that of all cases involving crack offenses that were closed by the Federal Public Defender's Office in 1991, twenty-four out of twenty-four involved black defendants. To supplement this evidence, they submitted affidavits from two of the attorneys in the defense team. The first reported a statement from an intake coordinator at a local drug treatment center that in his experience, an equal number of crack users and dealers were Caucasian as belonged to minorities. The second was from David R. Reed, counsel for respondent Armstrong. Reed was both an active court-appointed attorney in the Central District of California and one of the directors of the leading association of criminal defense lawyers who practice before the Los Angeles County courts. Reed stated that he did not recall "ever handling a [crack] cocaine case involving non-black defendants" in federal court, nor had he even heard of one. He further stated that "there are many crack cocaine sales cases prosecuted in state court that do involve racial groups other than blacks."

The majority discounts the probative value of the affidavits, claiming that they recounted "hearsay" and reported "personal conclusions based on anecdotal evidence." But the Reed affidavit plainly contained more than mere hearsay; Reed offered information based on his own extensive experience in both federal and state courts. Given the breadth of his background, he was well qualified to compare the practices of federal and state prosecutors. In any event, the Government never objected to the admission of either affidavit on hearsay or any other grounds. It was certainly within the district court's discretion to credit the affidavits of two members of the bar of that court, at least one of whom had presumably acquired a reputation by his frequent appearances there, and both of whose statements were made on pains of perjury.

The criticism that the affidavits were based on "anecdotal evidence" is also unpersuasive. I thought it was agreed that defendants do not need to prepare sophisticated statistical studies in order to receive mere discovery in cases like this one. Certainly, evidence based on a drug counselor's personal observations or on an attorney's practice in two sets of courts, state and federal, can "'tend to show the existence'" of a selective prosecution.

Even if respondents failed to carry their burden of showing that there were individuals who were not black but who could have been prosecuted in federal court for the same offenses, it does not follow that the district court abused its discretion in ordering discovery. There can be no doubt that such individuals exist, and indeed the Government has never denied the same. In those circumstances, I fail to see why the district court was unable to take judicial notice of this obvious fact and demand information from the Government's files to support or refute respondents' evidence. The presumption that some whites are prosecuted in state court is not "contradicted" by the statistics the majority cites, which show only that high percentages of blacks are convicted of certain federal crimes, while high percentages of whites are convicted of other federal crimes. Those figures are entirely consistent with the allegation of selective prosecution. The relevant comparison, rather, would be with the percentages of blacks and whites who commit those crimes. But, as discussed above, in the case of crack, far greater numbers of whites are believed guilty of using the substance. The district judge, therefore, was entitled to find the evidence before her significant and to require some explanation from the Government.

Also telling was the Government's response to respondent's evidentiary showing. It submitted a list of more than 3,500 defendants who had been charged with federal narcotics violations over the past three years. It also offered the names of 11 nonblack defendants whom it had prosecuted for crack offenses. All 11, however, were members of other racial or ethnic minorities.... As another court has said, "Statistics are not of course, the whole answer, but nothing is as emphatic as zero...."

In sum, I agree with the Sentencing Commission that "while the exercise of discretion by prosecutors and investigators has an impact on sentences in almost all cases to some extent, because of the 100-to-1 quantity ratio and federal mandatory minimum penalties, discretionary decisions in cocaine cases often have dramatic effects."

The severity of the penalty heightens both the danger of arbitrary enforcement and the need for careful scrutiny of any colorable claim of discriminatory enforcement. In this case, the evidence was sufficiently disturbing to persuade the district judge to order discovery that might help explain the conspicuous racial pattern of cases before her court. I cannot accept the majority's conclusion that the district judge either exceeded her power or abused her discretion when she did so. I therefore respectfully dissent.

Questions for Discussion

1. What is the holding of the case?
2. Did the respondents demonstrate "some evidence" of a discriminatory impact and of a discriminatory intent? What additional evidence would the respondents have to present to meet the "some evidence" standard? List the type of data that the respondents anticipate that the government files would reveal regarding prosecutions for crack cocaine.
3. Summarize Justice Stevens's argument. Do you agree with him that the facts are "sufficiently disturbing to require that the government explain its charging practices for crack offenses"?
4. What is the best argument in support of the respondents' claim? What is the best argument for the government in arguing that the respondents have failed to make a credible case of racial discrimination in charging practices?

Cases and Comments

Equal Protection and the Death Penalty. In *United States v. Bass,* defendant John Bass was charged with the intentional firearm killing of two individuals. The U.S. Attorney filed a notice to seek the death penalty. Bass requested discovery regarding the federal government's capital punishment charging policies. The Sixth Circuit Court of Appeals affirmed the discovery order of the District Court of the Eastern District of Michigan.

In support of his request for discovery, Bass presented data regarding "white" and "black" prisoners contained in *The Federal Death Penalty System: A Statistical Survey* (1988–2000). The Sixth Circuit found that the evidence constituted "some evidence" of a discriminatory impact.

Bass highlighted the following statistics. Caucasians comprise a majority of all federal prisoners and are only one-fifth of those charged with death-eligible offenses. The United States charges African Americans with a death-eligible offense more than twice as often as it charges Caucasians. In addition, fourteen of the seventeen defendants charged with death-eligible crimes in the Eastern District of Michigan are African American, and three are Hispanic. Among death-eligible defendants, the United States enters into plea bargains with Caucasians almost twice as often as it does with African Americans. (The United States entered into a plea bargain with forty-eight percent of the Caucasian defendants against whom it sought the death penalty, compared with twenty-five percent of similarly situated African American defendants. The federal government entered into plea agreements with twenty-eight percent of Latino and twenty-five percent of other nonwhite defendants.) In the "few non-death-eligible offense categories" in which African Americans constituted a higher percentage of total offenders sentenced than Caucasians, "none reflected a statistical disparity comparable to the disparity reflected by the survey for death-eligible charges."

Bass also noted that both U.S. Attorney General Janet Reno and Deputy Attorney General Eric Holder commented after reviewing the federal study that they were concerned that African Americans and Latinos were overrepresented in "those cases presented for consideration of the death penalty, and those cases where the defendant is actually sentenced to death." Deputy Attorney General Holder indicated that further study was required to determine whether race was involved in the decision to seek the death penalty.

The Sixth Circuit Court of Appeals determined that the plea-bargaining statistic identifies a "pool of similarly situated defendants—those whose crimes share sufficient aggravating factors that the United States chose to pursue the death penalty against each of them." The appellate court found it significant that the U.S. government enters into plea bargains with one in two Caucasians in this category of offenders, while it enters into plea bargains with one in four African Americans. The court of appeals held that based on this evidence, the district court "did not abuse its discretion in finding that the statistical disparities are, at the least, some evidence tending to show the death penalty protocol's discriminatory effect warranting discovery."

As for discriminatory intent, the appellate court pointed out that the racial disparities identified by Bass in death penalty charging do not occur in any non-death-eligible federal offenses. "Therefore, they suggest that a defendant's race does play a role during the death penalty protocol." The court also noted that the U.S. Department of Justice had concluded that the statistics indicate sufficient evidence of discrimination to justify further exploration. The circuit court of appeals accordingly ruled that Bass had presented "some evidence" of a discriminatory intent.

The U.S. Supreme Court in a *per curiam* decision limited its discussion to the evidence supporting a discriminatory effect. The Court ruled that the defendant failed to make a "credible showing" that "similarly situated individuals of a different race were not prosecuted." The Sixth Circuit had concluded that Bass met this standard based on nationwide statistics that U.S. prosecutors plea-bargain more frequently with Caucasians charged with death penalty offenses than with African Americans. "Even assuming that the *Armstrong* requirement can be satisfied by a nationwide showing... raw statistics regarding overall charges say nothing about charges brought against similarly situated defendants." The statistics in regard to plea bargains "are even less relevant, since respondent was offered a plea bargain but declined it." The Court concluded that under *Armstrong,* because Bass "failed to submit relevant evidence that similarly situated persons were treated differently, he was not entitled to discovery." What type of evidence would have satisfied the Supreme Court's standard? Do you agree with the Supreme Court's decision? See *United States v. Bass,* 266 F.3d 532 (6th Cir. 2001), 536 U.S. 862 (2002).

The Impact of Supreme Court Decisions

The U.S. Supreme Court for a number of years largely ignored the issue of **retroactivity of judicial decisions** or the impact of a decision announcing a "new rule" on other cases. *New rule* is defined as a procedural requirement that the Court heretofore had not required. An example would be the Supreme Court's holding in *Gideon v. Wainwright* that the Sixth Amendment right to counsel is applicable to the states through the Due Process Clause of the Fourteenth Amendment and that states are required to provide legal representation to indigents charged with a felony. Gideon had been denied counsel at his trial, and the Supreme Court accordingly reversed his conviction. The question is whether individuals who were convicted prior to the decision in *Gideon* should be provided with a new trial.

As the Supreme Court became actively involved in criminal procedure decisions, judges became concerned that a decision announcing a new rule on interrogations, lineups, searches and seizures, or other areas would permit every person in federal or state "custody" (in prison or on probation or parole) whose conviction was obtained under the "old rule" to file a writ of habeas corpus challenging his or her conviction. Many of these individuals had been convicted years ago, and a retrial was not always practical: Witnesses likely would prove difficult to locate, memories may have faded, and records likely would have disappeared. The criminal justice system also could not absorb an avalanche of new trials and appeals.

This is a philosophical as well as a practical question. A Supreme Court ruling might be viewed as a statement of the law as it always existed, in which case individuals in custody should be authorized to rely on the new rule in challenging their convictions. The problem is that this would "open wide the courthouse door" to a cascade of appeals. The Supreme Court in a series of cases wisely decided that courts should follow the "rule that existed at the time of the final decision" and that the new rule would not be available on a habeas corpus review.

The Supreme Court recognized at the same time that it would be unfair to benefit the individual before the Court whose case had resulted in the new ruling while denying this same benefit to individuals whose cases raised the same issue and were currently at trial or on appeal.

In brief, the Supreme Court applies the new rule to cases that are "pending" and denies the new rule to cases that are "final." The rule of retroactivity is summarized below:

- ***Trial.*** The new rule applies to cases that have not yet been brought to trial and to trials that are currently being conducted.
- ***Appeals.*** The new rule applies to cases that are on direct appeal or about to be appealed.
- ***Habeas corpus.*** The new rule is not available to individuals in cases where the judgments have become "final" before the new judgment is issued. These are the

individuals who have exhausted their appeals as a matter of right and now must rely on habeas corpus review of the constitutionality of their conviction.

The Supreme Court reserves the right to make a judgment fully retroactive in a small handful of what are considered "watershed" judgments.

Another impact of a Supreme Court decision is that a host of questions inevitably arises in lower courts that requires the Supreme Court to explain its opinion. In 1966, in *Miranda v. Arizona,* the Supreme Court held that prior to interrogating a suspect who is in custody, the police are required to provide the suspect with the three-part *Miranda* warning. Over the past three decades, the Supreme Court has issued decisions in over thirty-five cases interpreting the requirements of *Miranda* that address questions such as the definition of *custody,* how the rights are to be read, and the standard for waiving and invoking the *Miranda* rights.

A Supreme Court judgment is intended to impact the enforcement of the criminal law. The fact is that the Court cannot "wave a magic wand" after it issues a decision and immediately change the behavior of thousands of police officers, prosecutors, and judges.

As a result, decisions often are not fully implemented, even after a number of years. A second aspect of the impact of a Supreme Court decision is that the judgment may have "unanticipated consequences." The Supreme Court believed that informing suspects of their rights would encourage individuals to assert their Fifth Amendment right against self-incrimination. Professor Gerald N. Rosenberg, in his study of the impact of Supreme Court decisions, found that the *Miranda* rights have had virtually no impact on the frequency of confessions. Professor Rosenberg recounts several factors that have limited the impact of *Miranda* and of the decisions explaining the *Miranda* judgment (Rosenberg, 1991, pp. 324–329).

- A number of police officers continue to resist *Miranda* and give the warnings in a way that discourages individuals from asserting their rights.
- The police are not always able to keep track of the new Supreme Court decisions that are issued regarding interrogations.
- Some suspects feel a "social or moral obligation" to speak or may believe that the prosecutor may reduce their charges if they are cooperative.
- Defendants do not always understand the *Miranda* rights and, for instance, do not comprehend why they should remain silent.
- Suspects may have a great deal of incorrect information. They may believe that only written confessions are admissible in evidence at the trial and that they are free to talk to the police without their statement being used against them at trial.

We have now completed our discussion of the sources of criminal procedure, the incorporation debate, and equal protection. The remainder of the chapter briefly discusses two perspectives that you may find useful in thinking about the material in the text. The first perspective is to appreciate that Supreme Court criminal procedure decisions generally attempt to balance the investigation and punishment of crime with the protection of the rights of suspects. The second perspective to keep in mind is that criminal procedure matters: *How* we achieve results is as important as *what* results we achieve.

Two Models of Criminal Procedure

We want a system of criminal procedure to provide relatively quick and accurate verdicts through fair procedures that treat individuals with respect and without discrimination.

- ***Efficiency.*** There should be a brief period of time between arrest, indictment, trial, and conviction. The verdict should be relatively quickly affirmed or overturned on appeal.
- ***Accuracy.*** The criminal process should reach accurate results and not lead to the conviction of the innocent.

- ***Fairness.*** Suspects should be protected against abuse, corruption, mistreatment, and human error.
- ***Equality.*** Individuals should be treated the same regardless of race, religion, ethnicity, or income.

These goals often fit uneasily with one another. The speedy and efficient prosecution of cases may be in conflict with detailed procedures and lengthy appellate reviews of verdicts. The tension between the various goals of criminal procedure is nicely illustrated by the work of Herbert Packer.

Packer constructed two "models of criminal procedures" or theoretical approaches to criminal procedure. These models illustrate the difference between a criminal justice system that is based on "crime control" and a criminal justice system that is based on "due process." Clearly, no system completely fits either of these two models.The *Crime Control Model* is based on the premise that the repression of crime is one of the most important functions of government. The emphasis is on the rapid arrest, screening, charging, and acquittal or conviction and sentencing of the guilty and limiting the appeals process in order to remove antisocial individuals from society.

The police under the Crime Control Model are able to conduct investigations without being slowed by complicated technical requirements for interrogations and searches or by the right of defendants to ask for the assistance of lawyers. The criminal justice system is an assembly line in which the goal is for suspects to have their cases dismissed or to plead guilty and for police and prosecutors to move on to the next case rather than to spend time establishing guilt or innocence at trial or responding to appeals. In summary, the Crime Control Model has several characteristics:

- ***Purpose.*** The prevention and punishment of crime is the single most important function of the criminal justice system.
- ***Informal procedures.*** There is stress on speed and efficiency, and the police and other criminal justice professionals should not be weighed down by technical procedures.
- ***Determination of guilt.*** Emphasis is placed on the ability of the police and prosecutors to separate the guilty from the innocent rather than look to the courts to determine guilt or innocence.

The Crime Control Model can be contrasted with the *Due Process Model.* While recognizing the importance of preventing and punishing crime, the Due Process Model stresses the importance of protecting suspects against the power of police, prosecutors, and judges. Detailed procedures are viewed as the best protection against human error, mistreatment, corruption, and false convictions. Speed and efficiency are sacrificed in order to protect individual "rights," to provide equal treatment, and most important, to insure reliable results. The Due Process Model is an obstacle course; the Crime Control Model is an assembly line.

The Due Process Model relies on trial and appellate courts to determine guilt and innocence. Trials and multilevel appeals safeguard against witnesses with faulty memories, inaccurate identifications at lineups, coerced or false confessions, and inaccurate laboratory reports. The credo is that it is "better that nine guilty people go free than a single innocent individual is convicted." The Due Process Model is summarized below:

- ***Purpose.*** There is a concern with the prevention and punishment of crime that is accompanied by an equal concern with detailed procedures that protect individual rights in the criminal justice process.
- ***Formal procedures.*** The police and other criminal justice personnel are required to follow detailed procedures that sacrifice speed in the interest of protecting individual rights and insuring reliable results.
- ***Determination of guilt.*** Guilt or innocence is determined at a formal trial, and verdicts are subject to lengthy appeals. The judicial process is a check against human error, corruption, and falsehoods that may lead to inaccurate results.

The American system of criminal justice does not fully embrace either the Crime Control or the Due Process Model. The U.S. Supreme Court is constantly attempting to balance the need to efficiently prevent and to punish crime with the constitutional commitment to protecting the rights of the individual. Keep the Court's search for balance in mind as you read the text, and ask yourself whether in a given instance the Supreme Court is tilting too far toward crime control or too far toward due process. The last section of the chapter stresses the importance that criminal procedure plays in maintaining respect and support for the law.

Why Criminal Procedure Matters

Most of us would agree that the goal of detaining, convicting, and punishing the guilty should be the primary function of the criminal justice system. It may be less apparent why we are concerned with *how* we arrive at a conviction or punishment. Psychologist Tom Tyler has pioneered research on *procedural justice* and has found that confidence in the criminal justice system is based primarily on whether people believe that "just procedures" are being employed rather than on the outcome of the case. Tyler identifies four factors that are crucial in determining whether people perceive that fair procedures are being employed (Tyler, 2006).

- ***Voice.*** Both sides are able to tell their side of the story.
- ***Neutrality.*** Decisions are based on rules that are applied in the same fashion in each case and are not the result of personal opinions or prejudice. Confidence is increased when officials explain their decisions to the public.
- ***Respect.*** Individuals are treated with respect and politeness.
- ***Trust.*** Criminal justice professionals are honest and dedicated to doing a good job.

The lesson of Tyler's work is that no matter our race, religion, ethnicity, income, or age, we will support and respect the criminal justice system regardless of the outcome so long as we believe that the process is fair. Social scientists use the word *legitimate* to summarize feelings of respect and support for an institution. We will continue to view criminal justice as legitimate so long as we have trials in which individuals are able to voice their views, decisions are determined by objective rules that are applied in a uniform fashion by dedicated professionals, and the criminal justice system continues to treat people with respect and concern. An important point to keep in mind is that fair procedures are likely to result in correct outcomes. As you read the remainder of the text, keep in mind that *how* we reach a result may be as important as *what* result is achieved by the criminal justice system.

Chapter Summary

The founders of the United States adopted a written constitution in which the powers of the various branches of the federal government and the rights and liberties of individuals were explicitly articulated. The document is difficult to amend, and it is extremely complicated for any government to come to power and to change the rules of the game by assuming dictatorial powers or by severely limiting the individual liberties and freedoms contained in the Bill of Rights.

The U.S. Constitution and the Bill of Rights are the primary sources of criminal procedure. These provisions, in turn, are interpreted by the U.S. Supreme Court. The Court's decisions interpreting the Constitution are binding on lower federal and state courts. State constitutions have provisions that protect rights that parallel the provisions of the Bill of Rights. State courts are required to interpret these provisions to provide at least the same protections as are contained in the Bill of Rights. Other sources of criminal procedure include federal and state statutes, federal and state rules of criminal procedure, the American Law Institute's *Model Code of Pre-Arraignment Procedure,* and the judgments of state and federal courts.

The last half of the twentieth century has witnessed the nationalization of criminal procedure. This involves the extension of the protections of the Bill of Rights in the U.S. Constitution to the States. Today, we have a fairly uniform system in which the rights of individuals in the criminal justice system generally are the same whether they are in the federal system or are located in one of the fifty states. This has been accomplished by interpreting the Fourteenth Amendment Due Process Clause to incorporate all but five of the provisions of the Bill of Rights. Judges have relied on one of three approaches in interpreting the Fourteenth Amendment.

- ***Fundamental fairness.*** The Due Process Clause permits States to structure their criminal justice systems however they choose so long as the procedures are consistent with those rights and liberties that are fundamental to a system of ordered liberty.
- ***Selective incorporation.*** Those portions of the Bill of Rights are incorporated into the Fourteenth Amendment that are considered to be fundamental principles of liberty and justice that provide a foundation for our American civil and political institutions.
- ***Total incorporation.*** The Bill of Rights contains those liberties and freedoms that the framers viewed as essential to democracy, and the entire Bill of Rights is incorporated into the Fourteenth Amendment.

A few judges, at times, have endorsed a selective plus or total incorporation plus approach.

Equal protection of the law, which is guaranteed by both the Fifth and the Fourteenth Amendments, is a particularly important right. It is a fundamental principle that all people should be treated equally, regardless of race, religion, or ethnicity. An individual challenging his or her criminal prosecution on equal protection grounds must overcome the presumption of regularity and establish a discriminatory impact and intent.

Supreme Court decisions establishing a "new rule" apply retroactively to future cases as well as to cases presently at trial and cases on appeal. A new rule does not apply to cases in which all appeals have been exhausted and which are on habeas corpus review. A Supreme Court judgment also may raise a number of questions that must be addressed by the Court in other decisions. The fact that the Supreme Court issues a judgment does not automatically mean that these rights will be fully implemented.

As you read the remainder of the text, keep Herbert Packer's two models of criminal procedure in mind and analyze how the Supreme Court balances the Crime Control with the Due Process Model. Finally, do not lose sight of the fact that as Tom Tyler documents in his studies of procedural justice, *how* we reach a result may be as important as *what* result is achieved by the criminal justice system.

Chapter Review Questions

1. Describe the reasons for creating a constitutional political system in the United States. What provisions regarding criminal procedure are included in the body of the Constitution? Give some examples of the rights contained in the Bill of Rights.
2. Discuss the importance of the U.S. Constitution and the Supreme Court as sources of criminal procedure. Describe the role of state courts and state constitutions as a source of criminal procedure.
3. What is meant by nationalization or "constitutionalization" of criminal procedure?
4. Explain the difference between various approaches to determining the "fundamental rights" that the Fourteenth Amendment extends to the states: fundamental fairness, total incorporation, and selective incorporation.
5. What provisions of the Bill of Rights are incorporated into the Fourteenth Amendment? What provisions of the Bill of Rights are not incorporated into the Fourteenth Amendment?
6. Discuss equal protection, the presumption of regularity, and prosecutorial discretion in charging criminal defendants with a criminal offense.
7. What is the rule regarding the retroactivity of Supreme Court judgments?
8. Distinguish between the Crime Control Model and the Due Process Model of criminal procedure. Why is "procedural justice" important?

Legal Terminology

Bill of Rights
constitutional political system
constitutionalization
Due Process Clause
Fourteenth Amendment
fundamental fairness
judicial review
new judicial federalism
presumption of regularity

retroactivity
selective incorporation
selective incorporation plus
selective prosecution
supervisory authority
Supremacy Clause
total incorporation
total incorporation plus

Criminal Procedure on the Web

Log on to the Web-based student study site at **http://www.sagepub.com/lippmancp** to assist you in completing the Criminal Procedure on the Web exercises, as well as for additional features such as leading cases, podcasts, self-quizzes, and audio/video links.

1. Learn more about incorporation.
2. Read about the contemporary prosecutions of individuals alleged to be responsible for crimes against civil rights workers and African Americans during the 1960s.
3. Find out more about the trial of the "Scottsboro Boys."
4. Consider whether a high-speed police pursuit in which a police officer's recklessness led to the death of a passenger on a motorcycle that was being pursued "shocks the conscience."
5. Read more about the crack and powder cocaine controversy and criminal sentencing.

Bibliography

Erin Chemerinsky, *Constitutional Law Principle and Policies,* 2nd ed. (New York: Aspen Publishers, 2002), pp. 1–228. An introduction to the development of the Constitution and to the role of the Supreme Court in the American constitutional system.

Joshua Dressler and Alan C. Michaels, *Understanding Criminal Procedure: Investigtion,* vol. 1, 4th ed. (Newark, NJ: LexisNexis, 2006), pp. 21–49. A good overview of the evolution of the Supreme Court's incorporation decisions accompanied by a discussion of some major themes that characterize the Supreme Court's judgments in criminal procedure.

Alexander Hamilton, Federalist 81, 481, 482 in Alexander Hamilton, James Madison, and John Jay, *The Federalist Papers.* New American Library: New York, 1961 [1788].

Michael J. Klarman, "*Powell v. Alabama:* The Supreme Court Confronts 'Legal Lynchings,'" in Carol S. Streiker, ed., *Criminal Procedure Stories* (New York: Foundation Press, 2008), pp. 1–44. An account of *Powell v. Alabama* and the other prosecutions of African Americans in the South that inspired the Supreme Court to incorporate various provisions of the Bill of Rights into the Fourteenth Amendment.

Wayne R. LaFave, Jerold H. Israel, and Nancy King, *Criminal Procedure,* 4th ed. (St. Paul, MN: West Publishing, 2004), pp. 43–101. A comprehensive discussion of the Supreme Court's decisions relevant to the incorporation of the Bill of Rights into the Fourteenth Amendment.

Herbert Packer, *The Limits of the Criminal Sanction* (Stanford, CA: Stanford University Press, 1968), pp. 149–248. A discussion of the Crime Control Model and Due Process Model of criminal procedure and the application of the models to various stages of the criminal justice process. Packer concludes that the formal description of the criminal justice process in most countries is close to the Due Process Model, while the actual functioning of the criminal justice system approximates the Crime Control Model.

Gerald N. Rosenberg, *The Hollow Hope: Can Courts Bring About Social Change?* (Chicago: University of Chicago Press, 1991). An argument that political movement rather than judicial decisions brings about social change. The book reviews the literature on the impact of Supreme Court decisions in the areas of civil rights, women's rights, the environment, reapportionment, and criminal law.

Tom R. Tyler, *Why People Obey the Law* (Princeton, NJ: Princeton University Press, 2006). An elaboration on procedural justice with a discussion of the relevant literature.

Russell L. Weaver, Leslie W. Abramson, John M. Burkoff, and Catherine Hancock, *Principles of Criminal Procedure* (St. Paul, MN: West Publishing, 2004), pp. 18–31. An excellent introduction to the law of incorporation and retroactivity.

3 Searches and Seizures

Did the police require a warrant to search Greenwood's garbage?

On April 6, 1984, [Police Officer] Stracner asked the neighborhood's regular trash collector to pick up the plastic garbage bags that Greenwood had left on the curb in front of his house and to turn the bags over to her without mixing their contents with garbage from other houses. The trash collector cleaned his truck bin of other refuse, collected the garbage bags from the street in front of Greenwood's house, and turned the bags over to Stracner. The officer searched through the rubbish and found items indicative of narcotics use. She recited the information that she had gleaned from the trash search in an affidavit in support of a warrant to search Greenwood's home. Police officers encountered both respondents at the house later that day when they arrived to execute the warrant. The police discovered quantities of cocaine and hashish during their search of the house. Respondents were arrested on felony narcotics charges.

Core Concepts and Summary Statements

Introduction

A. The Fourth Amendment protects persons, houses, papers, and effects.

B. The amendment has two clauses. The first prohibits unreasonable searches and seizures, and the second requires that warrants are to be based on probable cause. The Supreme Court has stated that there is a preference for searches and seizures to be based on warrants founded on probable cause while recognizing that in some instances it is reasonable to carry out warrantless searches and seizures.

C. The police may search for various types of objects: instrumentalities used to commit a crime, contraband, evidence of criminal activity, and conversations recorded during electronic surveillance.

The Historical Background of the Fourth Amendment

A. The Fourth Amendment was drafted to protect individuals against the type of broad searches and seizures carried out by British authorities in the American colonies through reliance on general warrants and writs of assistance.

B. The Fourth Amendment was intended to abolish general warrants and writs of assistance by prohibiting "unreasonable" searches and seizures and providing that "no warrants shall issue, but upon probable cause, supported by oath or affirmation, and particularly describing the place to be searched and the person or things to be seized.

C. The Supreme Court has expressed a preference for searches founded on a warrant based on probable cause that is specific as to where and when the police may search and what the police may search for and seize.

Searches

A. In 1967, in *Katz v. United States,* the Supreme Court adopted Justice Brandeis's dissent in *Olmstead. Katz* rejected the property-rights or trespassory approach and adopted an expectation-of-privacy test for the application of the Fourth Amendment.

B. Justice John Marshall Harlan in his concurring opinion in *Katz* established a two-part test to determine whether an individual has an "expectation of privacy" that is protected by the Fourth Amendment. An individual must exhibit a subjective expectation of privacy that society recognizes as reasonable.

C. An expectation of privacy is unreasonable for those objects and areas that an individual knowingly exposes to the public and in those instances in which information is turned over to a third party.

Informants and Electronic Eavesdropping

There is no constitutionally protected expectation of privacy in conversations with an informant or undercover officer even when conducted in the home. An individual assumes the risk that the person with whom he or she is communicating may be a government agent or informant.

Plain View

Plain view is an exception to the Fourth Amendment warrant requirement that allows the police to seize an item without a search warrant under two conditions. First, the police officer must be lawfully positioned or "have a right to be where he or she is situated." Second, the police officer must have probable cause to seize the object. The probable cause must be immediately apparent on seeing the object.

Open Fields, Curtilage, and the Home

Open fields have no expectation of privacy, and the police do not require a warrant for a search. Curtilage, in contrast to open fields, retains an expectation of privacy and is the site of the "intimate activity" associated with the "sanctity of man's [or woman's] home and the privacies of life" and therefore is considered part of the home itself. Whether land is considered an open field is based on a number of factors.

The Curtilage and Aerial Surveillance

The general rule is that a warrant is required for both the home and the curtilage. In a series of cases, the Supreme Court has held that the police may conduct warrantless aerial surveillance of the curtilage.

Technology and the Home

The Supreme Court has held that the Fourth Amendment prohibits technological surveillance of the home in those instances in which the information obtained through technological means could otherwise have been obtained only by being physically present in the home itself.

Public Places and Private Businesses

The police may seize items in plain view that they observe in public places, streets, parks, and monuments. Public places also include private businesses that are open to the public. A warrant is required to enter portions of the business that are not open to the public, such as "employee only work areas" and employee offices.

Abandoned Property

Abandoned property has no expectation of privacy, and the police are not required to possess probable cause or to obtain a warrant. In determining whether property is intentionally abandoned, courts rely on the totality of the circumstances and consider where property is found, the condition of the property, and the type of property along with other factors.

Seizures of Persons

A. There are two types of seizures that trigger Fourth Amendment protections: physical seizures of suspects and "show of authority" seizures. In show of authority seizures, police officers restrain individuals through the display of official authority without the use of actual physical force that results in an individual's submission.

B. The Supreme Court has recognized a third category of police–citizen interactions that are referred to as "encounters." These are noncoercive and voluntary contacts between the police and citizens that do not constitute Fourth Amendment seizures. The Court has noted that not all street contacts between citizens and the police constitute seizures. This permits the police to question individuals on the street without violating the Fourth Amendment.

C. The line between seizures and encounters may not always be crystal clear. This requires an analysis of the totality of circumstances, including the number of officers, whether they are armed, and whether they indicate that the individual is not free to leave.

D. *United States v. Mendenhall* held that show of authority seizures require acts that would indicate to reasonable persons that they are not free to leave. *California v. Hodari* modified this test by also requiring that the individual actually submit to the demonstration of authority.

Introduction

The investigation and prosecution of crime requires the collection of evidence of criminal activity. This may be physical evidence (e.g., a gun) or testimonial evidence (e.g., an eyewitness account). A criminal investigation may prove relatively uncomplicated. Eyewitnesses may identify the perpetrator, investigators might find forensic evidence at the crime scene, or a suspect may decide to turn himself or herself in to the police. In most instances, however, these types of evidence are unavailable. Eyewitnesses may be reluctant to come forward or to talk, the forensic evidence may point to a number of yet-to-be-identified individuals, and suspects may disappear or refuse to cooperate with the police. In these situations, the police typically turn to other methods of collecting evidence. These include the following:

- ***Searches and seizures.*** The police may search and seize evidence from automobiles, homes, luggage, and other locations so long as they comply with the Fourth Amendment (Chapters 3–7).
- ***Interrogations.*** The Fifth and Sixth Amendments permit the police to question suspects (Chapter 8).

- ***Identifications***. Eyewitnesses and victims may be asked to identify suspects from lineups, showups, or photographs employing procedures that meet the requirements of the Fifth and Sixth Amendments (Chapter 9).

In this chapter, we begin our discussion of Fourth Amendment searches and seizures. The primary purpose of searches and seizures is to collect evidence that will assist law enforcement in the investigation of unlawful activity. These searches and seizures may involve various types of evidence (*Warden v. Hayden,* 387 U.S. 294 [1967]):

- ***Instrumentalities of crime***. Items used to carry out a crime, such as firearms.
- ***Fruits of a crime***. Money stolen from a bank, jewelry taken from a home, a wallet taken during a robbery, or computers stolen from a store.
- ***Contraband***. Unlawful drugs and other prohibited substances.
- ***Evidence of criminal activity***. Clothes with gunpowder stains, bloody clothes, or DNA that link a suspect to a crime.
- ***Incriminating statements***. Statements overheard during electronic surveillance.

The Fourth Amendment to the U.S. Constitution addresses searches and seizures and reads as follows:

> The right of the people to be secure in their persons, houses, papers, and effects, against unreasonable searches and seizures, shall not be violated, and no Warrants shall issue, but upon probable cause, supported by Oath or affirmation, and particularly describing the place to be searched, and the persons or things to be seized.

The Fourth Amendment is directed at searches and seizures by the government and does not restrict searches and seizures by private individuals. The amendment protects individuals against "unreasonable" governmental searches and seizures in four constitutionally protected areas:

- ***Persons.*** This protects individuals against unreasonable detentions and unreasonable searches of their persons.
- ***Houses.*** Homes encompass all residences, dwellings attached to the residence, and areas immediately surrounding the home as well as areas of commercial businesses that are not open to the public.
- ***Papers.*** Letters, diaries, and business records are protected.
- ***Effects.*** Effects include personal possessions such as automobiles, clothing, and firearms.

The Fourth Amendment tells the police that they may search for and seize evidence of unlawful activity involving a person, house, paper, or effect so long as these searches and seizures follow the dictates of the Fourth Amendment. As we shall see in the next few chapters, the U.S. Supreme Court has devoted well over one hundred cases and thousands of pages to interpreting the requirements of the fifty-three words that compose the Fourth Amendment. In undertaking this task the Supreme Court has struggled to balance the social interest in conducting searches and seizures to investigate unlawful activity against the interest of individuals in being free from governmental interference in their personal lives.

There are three steps in analyzing a Fourth Amendment **search** or seizure that we will be discussing in the textbook.

- ***Definition.*** Did the government engage in a search or seizure as defined in the Fourth Amendment? (Chapter 3)
- ***Reasonableness.*** Was the search or seizure reasonable, that is, lawfully conducted? (Chapters 4–7)
- ***Exclusion from evidence.*** If the search or seizure was unreasonable, does the exclusionary rule require that the object(s) seized be excluded from evidence? Or may the item be introduced at trial? (Chapter 10)

In this chapter we define and discuss Fourth Amendment searches and seizures of individuals. Why is this important to consider? As technology advances, the Supreme Court undoubtedly will be asked to determine whether various types of intrusions constitute Fourth Amendment searches and seizures that require the police to obtain a warrant based on **probable cause** from a magistrate or judge, or whether the intrusions do not constitute Fourth Amendment searches and seizures and may be undertaken by the police without the approval of a judicial official. Consider whether the police should be required to obtain a warrant before directing individuals to donate DNA samples or prior to monitoring e-mail activity or search engines or cell phones or before examining databases that contain personal information.

We first turn our attention to the definition of searches and then discuss the definition of seizures of individuals. Ask yourself whether you agree with the Supreme Court decisions discussed in this chapter. Pay particular attention to the court's effort to balance the need for the police to investigate crime against the protection of the individual interest in privacy.

The Historical Background of the Fourth Amendment

The Fourth Amendment was included in the Bill of Rights to protect individuals against the types of far-reaching searches and seizures conducted by British authorities in the American colonies. A particular source of anger was the use of **general warrants** and **writs of assistance** to search homes, businesses, and warehouses for goods that had been smuggled into the country to avoid paying the exorbitant customs duties imposed by the British. Searches also were used to seize able-bodied young men who were forced into the Royal Navy.

The general warrant was issued by a judge or government official and authorized searches anywhere, at any time, and for anything. The writ of assistance was a form of general warrant that authorized an official of the English Crown to compel police officers and citizens to assist in a search. These documents, once authorized, were legally effective for the life of the sovereign and did not expire until six months following the sovereign's death.

In 1761, in the *Writs of Assistance* case, sixty-three Boston merchants unsuccessfully challenged the legal authority of the Massachusetts Superior Court to issue writs of assistance. The superior court found that the English Parliament had granted Massachusetts colonial judges the authority to issue writs of assistance. Attorney James Otis in a celebrated argument proclaimed that the writ was a practice as "destructive of English liberty and the fundamental principles of law, that ever was found in an English law-book." He went on to note that "one of the most essential branches of English liberty is the freedom of one's house.... A man's house is his castle.... This writ, if it should be declared legal, would totally annihilate this privilege."

A number of the colonial state legislatures responded by prohibiting general warrants. The Virginia Declaration of Rights in 1776 proclaimed that "general warrants... are grievous and oppressive, and ought not to be granted." Both English and American colonial courts slowly began to declare "illegal and void" search warrants that authorized "all persons and places throughout the world to be searched" and insisted that local magistrates issue warrants only when there was probable cause that contraband was located in a "particular place or places" (*Frisbie v. Butler,* Kirby 213 [Conn. 1787]).

The Fourth Amendment reflected the tenor of the times and was intended to abolish general warrants and writs of assistance by prohibiting "unreasonable" searches and seizures and providing that "no warrants shall issue, but upon probable cause, supported by oath or affirmation, and particularly describing the place to be searched and the person or things to be seized." In other words, a warrant requires the government to present evidence to a magistrate or judge that shows probable cause that evidence or contraband is located in a specific location at a particular time. A general warrant would be unreasonable under this standard.

The Supreme Court, while expressing a preference that searches be conducted based on a warrant founded on probable cause, has recognized that it is "reasonable" in various instances for the police to conduct a search and make a seizure without a warrant. Examples are "special needs" searches that are intended to protect the public safety rather than to collect evidence of a crime. These searches to do not greatly intrude on an individual's privacy while they protect the public safety. They include searches at airports or at the border between the United States and Mexico or the United States and Canada (discussed in Chapter 7).

Searches

Expectation of Privacy

In *Boyd v. United States,* the U.S. Supreme Court adopted a **property rights** or **trespassory approach** to the Fourth Amendment. The property rights theory protected individuals against physical intrusions or trespasses against their persons, houses, papers, and effects.

- ***Physical intrusions.*** For an intrusion to occur, there must be an actual physical entry into the home or physical examination of an individual or his or her papers or possessions.
- ***Scope of protection.*** Persons, houses, papers, and effects are protected.

Justice Hugo Black captured the essence of the property rights approach when he proclaimed that the Fourth Amendment was "aimed directly at the abhorrent practice of breaking in, ransacking and searching homes and other buildings and seizing people's personal belongings without warrants issued by magistrates" (*Katz v. United States,* 389 U.S. 347, 367 [1967]).

The famous 1928 case of *Olmstead v. United States* starkly presents the limitations of the property rights approach. Olmstead was convicted of conspiracy to unlawfully import, possess, and sell liquor. The central evidence that was relied on at trial was gathered through warrantless wiretaps of the office and home phones of Olmstead and his coconspirators. The U.S. Supreme Court, by a 5–4 vote, rejected Olmstead's contention that the close to 800 pages of notes gathered from the wiretaps had been obtained in violation of his Fourth Amendment rights.

The majority decision rested on two conclusions. First, the conversations that were heard by federal agents were transmitted across telephone wires and did not involve the search and seizure of a "physical object." Second, the wiretaps were attached to phone lines outside the home and did not involve a physical intrusion into the home. The Supreme Court reasoned that the language of the Fourth Amendment "cannot be extended or expanded to include the telephone wires reaching to the whole world from the defendant's home or office. The intervening wires are not part of his house or office any more than are the highways along which they are stretched."

In what was to prove an important dissent, Justice Louis Brandeis argued that the Fourth Amendment must be interpreted in light of changing circumstances. He argued that "the makers of our Constitution . . . conferred as against the government, the right to be let alone—the most comprehensive of rights and the right most valued by civilized men" and so "every unjustifiable intrusion upon the privacy of the individual, by whatever means employed, must be deemed a violation of the Fourth Amendment" (*Olmstead v. United States,* 277 U.S. 438, 465, 478 [1928]). In 1942, in *Goldman v. United States,* the Supreme Court followed the precedent established in *Olmstead* and affirmed that the installation of a detectaphone on the outside wall of an adjoining office for purposes of monitoring a conversation did not violate the Fourth Amendment (316 U.S. 129 [1942]).

In 1967, in *Katz v. United States,* which is the next edited case reprinted in the text, the Supreme Court adopted Justice Brandeis's viewpoint and overruled *Olmstead.* In *Katz,* the Supreme Court rejected the trespassory approach and adopted an **expectation of privacy** test for the application of the Fourth Amendment. The FBI, acting without a search warrant, had attached microphones to the outside of a clear glass enclosed telephone booth and recorded Katz's placing of interstate gambling bets and receipt of wagering information.

The Supreme Court rejected the "trespass doctrine as no longer controlling" and held that the Fourth Amendment "protects people, not places. What a person knowingly exposes to the public... is not a subject of Fourth Amendment protection. But what he seeks to preserve as private, even in an area accessible to the public, may be constitutionally protected." In this instance, the government was determined to have violated the privacy of the telephone booth on which Katz justifiably relied. The fact that the government did not seize a "material object" or "penetrate the wall of the booth" did not remove the search from Fourth Amendment protection (*Katz v. United States,* 389 U.S. 347, 351 [1967]).

Justice John Marshall Harlan in his concurring opinion in *Katz* established a two-part test for a Fourth Amendment expectation of privacy that has been followed by the U.S. Supreme Court (353).

- ***Subjective.*** An individual exhibits a personal expectation of privacy.
- ***Objective.*** Society recognizes this expectation as reasonable.

Justice Harlan illustrated the test by noting that people retain an expectation of privacy in the home, while they do not retain an expectation of privacy in their public words or public actions.

In reading *Katz v. United States,* pay attention to the difference between the trespassory approach and the expectation of privacy approach established in *Katz.* Would *Katz* have been decided the same way under the trespassory approach? Does the Court provide a clear definition of when an individual possesses a reasonable expectation of privacy?

Did Katz have an expectation of privacy in the content of his conversations?

Katz v. United States, 389 U.S. 347 (1967), Stewart, J.

Facts

In February of 1965, the appellant was seen placing calls from a bank of three public telephone booths during certain hours and on an almost daily basis. He was never observed in any other telephone booth.

In the period of February 19 to February 25, 1965, at set hours, special agents of the Federal Bureau of Investigation (FBI) placed microphones on the tops of two of the public telephone booths normally used by the appellant. The other phone was placed out of order by the telephone company. The microphones were attached to the outside of the telephone booths with tape. There was no physical penetration inside of the booths. The microphones were activated only while the appellant was approaching and actually in the booth. Wires led from the microphones to a wire recorder on top of one of the booths. Thus the FBI obtained a record of the appellant's end of a series of telephone calls.

A study of the transcripts of the recordings made of the appellant's end of the conversations revealed that the conversations had to do with the placing of bets and the obtaining of gambling information by the appellant.

On February 23, 1965, FBI Agent Allen Frei rented a room next to the appellant's apartment residence. He listened to conversations through the common wall without the aid of any electronic device. He overheard the appellant's end of a series of telephone conversations and took notes on them. These notes and the tapes made from the telephone booth recordings were the basis of a search warrant, which was obtained to search the appellant's apartment. The search warrant called for bookmaking records and wagering paraphernalia, including but not limited to bet slips, betting markers, run-down sheets, schedule sheets indicating the lines, adding machines, money, telephones, and telephone address listings. The articles seized are all related to the categories described in the warrant.

During the conversations overheard by Agent Frei, the appellant made numerous comments to the effect that "I have Northwestern minus 7," and "Oregon plus 3." Also, there was a statement by the appellant such as, "Don't worry about the line. I have phoned Boston three times about it today."

At the trial, evidence was introduced to show that from February 19 to February 25, 1965, inclusive, the appellant placed calls from two telephone booths located in the 8200 block of Sunset Boulevard in Los Angeles. The conversations were overheard and recorded every day except February 22. The transcripts of the recordings and the normal business records of the telephone company were used to determine that the calls went to Boston, Massachusetts, and Miami, Florida.

From all of the evidence in the case, the court found the volume of business being done by the appellant indicated that it was not a casual incidental occupation of the appellant. The court found that he was engaged in the business of betting or wagering at the time the telephone conversations were transmitted and recorded. The petitioner was convicted in the District Court for the Southern District of California under an eight-count indictment charging him with transmitting wagering information by telephone from Los Angeles to Miami and Boston, in violation of a federal statute. At trial the Government was permitted, over the petitioner's objection, to introduce evidence of the petitioner's end of telephone conversations, overheard by FBI agents who had attached an electronic listening and recording device to the outside of the public telephone booth from which he had placed his calls. In affirming his conviction, the Court of Appeals rejected the contention that the recordings had been obtained in violation of the Fourth Amendment, because "there was no physical entrance into the area occupied by [the petitioner]."

Issue

We granted certiorari in order to consider the constitutional questions thus presented. Was the warrantless surveillance of Katz's conversation a violation of the Fourth Amendment, despite the fact that the Government did not physically penetrate the telephone booth? Are Katz's conversations entitled to Fourth Amendment protection? Because of the misleading way the issues have been formulated, the parties have attached great significance to the characterization of the telephone booth from which the petitioner placed his calls. The petitioner has strenuously argued that the booth was a "constitutionally protected area." The Government has maintained with equal vigor that it was not. But this effort to decide whether or not a given "area," viewed in the abstract, is constitutionally protected deflects attention from the problem presented by this case.

Reasoning

The Fourth Amendment protects people, not places. What a person knowingly exposes to the public, even in his own home or office, is not a subject of Fourth Amendment protection. But what he seeks to preserve as private, even in an area accessible to the public, may be constitutionally protected.

The Government stresses the fact that the telephone booth from which the petitioner made his calls was constructed partly of glass, so that he was as visible after he entered it as he would have been if he had remained outside. But what he sought to exclude when he entered the booth was not the intruding eye—it was the uninvited ear. He did not shed his right to do so simply because he made his calls from a place where he might be seen. No less than an individual in a business office or in a friend's apartment, a person in a telephone booth may rely upon the protection of the Fourth Amendment. One who occupies it, shuts the door behind him, and pays the toll that permits him to place a call is surely entitled to assume that the words he utters into the mouthpiece will not be broadcast to the world. To read the Constitution more narrowly is to ignore the vital role that the public telephone has come to play in private communication.

The Government contends, however, that the activities of its agents in this case should not be tested by Fourth Amendment requirements, for the surveillance technique they employed involved no physical penetration of the telephone booth from which the petitioner placed his calls. It is true that the absence of such penetration was at one time thought to foreclose further Fourth Amendment inquiry, for that Amendment was thought to limit only searches and seizures of tangible property. But "the premise that property interests control the right of the Government to search and seize has been discredited." Thus, although a closely divided Court supposed in *Olmstead* that surveillance without any trespass and without the seizure of any material object fell outside the ambit of the Constitution, we have since departed from the narrow view on which that decision rested. Indeed, we have expressly held that the Fourth Amendment governs not only the seizure of tangible items, but extends as well to the recording of oral statements, overheard without any "technical trespass under...local property law." Once this much is acknowledged, and once it is recognized that the Fourth Amendment protects people—and not simply "areas"—against unreasonable searches and seizures, it becomes clear that the reach of that Amendment cannot turn upon the presence or absence of a physical intrusion into any given enclosure.

We conclude that the underpinnings of *Olmstead* have been so eroded by our subsequent decisions that the "trespass" doctrine there enunciated can no longer be regarded as controlling. The Government's activities in electronically listening to and recording the petitioner's words violated the privacy upon which he justifiably relied while using the telephone booth and thus constituted a "search and seizure" within the meaning of the Fourth Amendment. The fact that the electronic device employed to achieve that end did not happen to penetrate the wall of the booth can have no constitutional significance.

Holding

The question remaining for decision, then, is whether the search and seizure conducted in this case complied with constitutional standards....It is clear that this surveillance was so narrowly circumscribed that a duly authorized magistrate, properly notified of the need for such investigation, specifically informed of the basis on which it was to proceed, and clearly apprised of the precise intrusion it would entail, could constitutionally have authorized, with appropriate safeguards, the very limited search and seizure that the Government asserts in fact took place. Only last Term we sustained the validity of such an authorization, holding that, under sufficiently "precise and discriminate circumstances," a federal court may empower Government agents to employ a concealed electronic device "for the narrow and particularized purpose of ascertaining the truth of the... allegations" of a "detailed factual affidavit alleging the commission of a specific criminal offense...." It is apparent that the agents in this case acted with restraint. Yet the inescapable fact is that this restraint was imposed by the agents themselves, not by a judicial officer. They were not required, before commencing the search, to present their estimate of probable cause for detached scrutiny by a neutral magistrate. They were not compelled, during the conduct of the search itself, to observe precise limits established in advance by a specific court order. Nor were they directed, after the search had been completed, to notify the authorizing magistrate in detail of all that had been seized.... Searches conducted without warrants have been held unlawful "notwithstanding facts unquestionably showing probable cause." The Constitution requires "that the deliberate, impartial judgment of a judicial officer... be interposed between the citizen and the police.... Over and again this Court has emphasized that the mandate of the [Fourth] Amendment requires adherence to judicial processes," and that searches conducted outside the judicial process, without prior approval by judge or magistrate, are per se unreasonable under the Fourth Amendment—subject only to a few specifically established and well-delineated exceptions.

These considerations do not vanish when the search in question is transferred from the setting of a home, an office, or a hotel room to that of a telephone booth. Wherever a man may be, he is entitled to know that he will remain free from unreasonable searches and seizures. The Government agents here ignored "the procedure of antecedent justification... that is central to the Fourth Amendment," a procedure that we hold to be a constitutional precondition of the kind of electronic surveillance involved in this case. Because the surveillance here failed to meet that condition, and because it led to the petitioner's conviction, the judgment must be reversed.

Concurring, *Harlan, J.*

As the Court's opinion states, "the Fourth Amendment protects people, not places." The question, however, is what protection it affords to those people. Generally, as here, the answer to that question requires reference to a "place." My understanding of the rule that has emerged from prior decisions is that there is a twofold requirement, first that a person have exhibited an actual (subjective) expectation of privacy and, second, that the expectation be one that society is prepared to recognize as "reasonable." Thus a man's home is, for most purposes, a place where he expects privacy, but objects, activities, or statements that he exposes to the "plain view" of outsiders are not "protected," because no intention to keep them to himself has been exhibited. On the other hand, conversations in the open would not be protected against being overheard, for the expectation of privacy under the circumstances would be unreasonable.

The critical fact in this case is that "one who occupies it [a telephone booth], shuts the door behind him, and pays the toll that permits him to place a call is surely entitled to assume" that his conversation is not being intercepted. The point is not that the booth is "accessible to the public" at other times, but that it is a temporarily private place whose momentary occupants' expectations of freedom from intrusion are recognized as reasonable.

Dissenting, *Black, J.*

If I could agree with the Court that eavesdropping carried on by electronic means (equivalent to wiretapping) constitutes a "search" or "seizure," I would be happy to join the Court's opinion.... My basic objection is twofold: (1) I do not believe that the words of the amendment will bear the meaning given them by today's decision, and (2) I do not believe that it is the proper role of this Court to rewrite the amendment in order "to bring it into harmony with the times" and thus reach a result that many people believe to be desirable.

While I realize that an argument based on the meaning of words lacks the scope, and no doubt the appeal, of broad policy discussions and philosophical discourses on such nebulous subjects as privacy, for me the language of the amendment is the crucial place to look in construing a written document such as our Constitution. The first clause protects "persons, houses, papers, and effects, against unreasonable searches and seizures...." These words connote the idea of tangible things with size, form, and weight, things capable of being searched, seized, or both. The second clause of the amendment still further establishes its framers' purpose to limit its protection to tangible things by providing that no warrants shall issue but those "particularly describing the place to be searched, and the persons or things to be seized." A conversation overheard by eavesdropping, whether by plain snooping or wiretapping, is not tangible and, under the normally accepted meanings of the words, can neither be searched nor seized.

In addition the language of the second clause indicates that the amendment refers not only to something tangible so it can be seized but to something already in existence so it can be described. Yet the Court's interpretation would have the amendment apply to overhearing future conversations which by their very nature are nonexistent until they take place. How can one "describe" a future conversation, and, if one cannot, how can a magistrate issue a warrant to eavesdrop on one in the future? It is argued that information showing what is expected to be said is sufficient to limit the boundaries of what later can be admitted into evidence; but does such general information really meet the specific language of the amendment, which says "particularly describing"? Rather than using language in a completely artificial way, I must conclude that the Fourth Amendment simply does not apply to eavesdropping.

Tapping telephone wires, of course, was an unknown possibility at the time the Fourth Amendment was adopted. But eavesdropping (and wiretapping is nothing more than eavesdropping by telephone) was ...recognized, "an ancient practice which at common law was condemned as a nuisance. In those days the eavesdropper listened by naked ear under the eaves of houses or their windows, or beyond their walls seeking out private discourse." There can be no doubt that the framers were aware of this practice, and if they had desired to outlaw or restrict the use of evidence obtained by eavesdropping, I believe that they would have used the appropriate language to do so in the Fourth Amendment. They certainly would not have left such a task to the ingenuity of language-stretching judges. No one, it seems to me, can read the debates on the Bill of Rights without reaching the conclusion that its framers and critics well knew the meaning of the words they used, what they would be understood to mean by others, their scope, and their limitations. Under these circumstances it strikes me as a charge against their scholarship, their common sense, and their candor to give to the Fourth Amendment's language the eavesdropping meaning the Court imputes to it today.

The first case to reach this Court that actually involved a clear-cut test of the Fourth Amendment's applicability to eavesdropping through a wiretap was, of course, *Olmstead.* In holding that the interception of private telephone conversations by means of wiretapping was not a violation of the Fourth Amendment, this Court, speaking through Mr. Chief Justice Taft, examined the language of the amendment and found, just as I do now, that the words could not be stretched to encompass overheard conversations.

Goldman v. United States is another example of this Court's traditional refusal to consider eavesdropping as being covered by the Fourth Amendment. There federal agents used a detectaphone, which was placed on the wall of an adjoining room, to listen to the conversation a defendant carried on in his private office and intended to be confined within the four walls of the room. This Court, referring to *Olmstead,* found no Fourth Amendment violation.

While my reading of the *Olmstead* and *Goldman* cases convinces me that they were decided on the basis of the inapplicability of the wording of the Fourth Amendment to eavesdropping, and not on any trespass basis, this is not to say that unauthorized intrusion has not played an important role in search and seizure cases.... "The Court has in the past sustained instances of 'electronic eavesdropping', against constitutional challenge when devices have been used to enable Government agents to overhear conversations that would have been beyond the reach of the human. It has been insisted only that the electronic device not be planted by an unlawful physical invasion of a constitutionally protected area."

In interpreting the Bill of Rights, I willingly go as far as a liberal construction of the language takes me, but I simply cannot in good conscience give a meaning to words that they have never before been thought to have and that they certainly do not have in common ordinary usage. I will not distort the words of the amendment in order to "keep the Constitution up to date" or "to bring it into harmony with the times." It was never meant that this Court have such power, which in effect would make us a continuously functioning constitutional convention.

With this decision the Court has completed, I hope, its rewriting of the Fourth Amendment, which started only recently when the Court began referring incessantly to the Fourth Amendment not so much as a law against unreasonable searches and seizures as one to protect an individual's privacy. By clever word juggling, the Court finds it plausible to argue that language aimed specifically at searches and seizures of things that can be searched and seized may, to protect privacy, be applied to eavesdropped evidence of conversations that can neither be searched nor seized. Few things happen to an individual that do not affect his privacy in one way or another. Thus, by arbitrarily substituting the Court's language, designed to protect privacy, for the Constitution's language, designed to protect against unreasonable searches and seizures, the Court has made the Fourth Amendment its vehicle for holding all laws violative of the Constitution which offend the Court's broadest concept of privacy. As I said in *Griswold v. Connecticut,* 381 U.S. 479, "The Court talks about a constitutional 'right of privacy' as though there is some constitutional provision or provisions forbidding any law ever to be passed which might abridge the 'privacy' of individuals. But there is not." I made clear in that dissent my fear of the dangers involved when this Court uses the "broad, abstract and ambiguous concept" of "privacy" as a "comprehensive substitute for the Fourth Amendment's guarantee against 'unreasonable searches and seizures.'"

The Fourth Amendment protects privacy only to the extent that it prohibits unreasonable searches and seizures of "persons, houses, papers, and effects." No general right is created by the amendment so as to give this Court the unlimited power to hold unconstitutional everything that affects privacy. Certainly the framers, well acquainted as they were with the excesses of governmental power, did not intend to grant this Court such omnipotent lawmaking authority as that. The history of governments proves that it is dangerous to freedom to repose such powers in courts.

Questions for Discussion

1. Why did the Supreme Court hold that the FBI's surveillance of Katz's conversation in the telephone booth violated the Fourth Amendment?
2. How does the rule established in *Katz* differ from the Supreme Court's holding in *Olmstead*?
3. Do you find the majority decision or Justice Black's dissent more persuasive?
4. ***Problems in policing.*** *Katz* requires that law enforcement obtain a warrant before engaging in the electronic surveillance of a phone conversation. The information that the police gathered from monitoring Katz's phone conversations was used to obtain a search warrant to search Katz's apartment for "wagering paraphernalia." Would the Supreme Court's decision that the FBI violated Katz's Fourth Amendment rights have been different had Katz left the door to the telephone booth open? Made the call from an unenclosed telephone booth? If an FBI agent overheard the call while standing outside the closed telephone booth? What if a sign on the telephone booth warned Katz that "all calls may be monitored"?

Cases and Comments

1. ***Pen Register.*** Patricia McDonough was robbed in Baltimore, Maryland, on March 5, 1976. She provided the police with a description of the robber and of a 1975 Monte Carlo automobile that she observed near the scene of the crime. Following the robbery, McDonough began receiving threatening and obscene phone calls from a male who identified himself as the robber. Roughly two weeks after the robbery, the police spotted a man who fit the description given by McDonough driving a 1975 Monte Carlo. The police traced the license plate number to Michael Lee Smith. The next day, the police requested the phone company to place a pen register at its central offices to record the numbers dialed from the telephone at Smith's home. They did not obtain a warrant. The pen register revealed that on March 17, Smith called McDonough's home. The police relied on this information to obtain a search warrant to search Smith's home. The search revealed a phone book with a page turned down to the name and number of Patricia McDonough. Smith filed an unsuccessful motion to suppress "all fruits derived from the pen register" and was convicted of robbery and sentenced to six years in prison.

The U.S. Supreme Court distinguished *Smith* from *Katz*. In contrast to the contents of a telephone conversation, the Court held that an individual does not have a subjective expectation of privacy in the numbers dialed. He or she is aware that all numbers are conveyed to the phone company and that the phone company maintains records of all phone calls for billing and other legitimate business purposes.

Society at any rate is not prepared to recognize that an expectation of privacy in the numbers dialed is reasonable. By using the phone voluntarily, Smith conveyed the information to the phone company and "assumed the risk" that the company would reveal the information to the police. The fact that the phone company customarily does not record the numbers of local calls was not controlling; the information was voluntarily conveyed to the phone company, which had the capacity to record the numbers dialed and to turn the numbers dialed over to the police.

Justice Stewart, in dissent, argued that there is a legitimate expectation of privacy in the numbers dialed. He noted that the pen register, by revealing the numbers dialed, indicates the person and places dialed and "reveals the most intimate details of a person's life." Justice Marshall dismissed the argument that an individual assumes the risk that the information he or she transmits to the phone company will be revealed to the police. He noted that the phone is a necessity of life, and an individual who uses the phone has no alternative other than to transmit the numbers dialed to the police. The issue is not "the risks an individual can be pressured to accept when imparting information to third parties, but on the risks he should be forced to assume in a free and open society."

Do you agree that the police should have access without a warrant to the numbers dialed from a telephone? The Supreme Courts of Colorado, Hawaii, Idaho, New Jersey, Pennsylvania, and Washington have found that their state constitutions provide greater protection than the Fourth Amendment and prohibit the warrantless use of pen registers (*Smith v. Maryland,* 442 U.S. 735 [1979]).

2. ***Bank Records and E-Mail.*** In 1976, in *United States v. Miller,* the Alcohol, Tobacco and Firearms Bureau opened an investigation of Miller and several coconspirators who subsequently were charged and convicted of various federal offenses for manufacturing and selling whiskey without paying the required federal tax. Grand jury subpoenas requesting Miller's financial records were presented to the Citizens & Southern National Bank at Warner Robins and to the Bank of Byron. The banks, without informing Miller, showed microfilm records to a federal agent and turned over checks, deposit slips, financial statements, and monthly statements. Copies of the checks were introduced at trial. Miller claimed that the government had engaged in an unlawful search and seizure of his records in violation of the Fourth Amendment.

The U.S. Supreme Court held that Miller did not have a reasonable expectation of privacy in the financial records. The records "contain . . . information voluntarily conveyed to the banks and exposed to their employees in the ordinary course of business. . . . The depositor takes the risk in revealing his affairs to another, that the information will be conveyed by that person to the government." The Supreme Court noted that it had held on numerous occasions that the Fourth Amendment does not "prohibit the obtaining of information revealed to a third party and conveyed by him to Government authorities, even if the information is revealed on the assumption that it will be used only for a limited purpose and the confidence placed in a third party will be betrayed." See *United States v. Miller,* 425 U.S. 435 (1976).

Katz, Smith, and *Miller* were relied on by the Sixth Circuit Court of Appeals in 2007 in *Warshak v. United States* in deciding whether Steven Warshak possessed an expectation of privacy in the content of his personal e-mail account. Warshak and his company, Berkeley Premium Nutraceuticals, were the subject of a criminal investigation involving mail and wire fraud, money laundering, and other federal offenses. The U.S. government obtained a court order directing Internet service provider (ISP) NuVox Communications to give government agents information involving Warshak's e-mail account. This included the "contents of wire or electronic communication (not in electronic storage unless greater than 181 days) that were placed or stored in directories or files owned or controlled: by Warshak; and...all Log files and backup tapes."

The Sixth Circuit Court of Appeals held that while Warshak assumed the risk that the recipient of a communication will reveal the contents of e-mails, Warshak maintained an expectation of privacy in regard to his ISP. The ISP was not expected to "access the e-mails in the normal course of business," and Warshak maintained an expectation of privacy in the content of these communications. Otherwise, phone conversations would

> never be protected, merely because the telephone company can access them; letters would never be protected, by virtue of the Postal Service's ability to access them; the contents of shared safe deposit boxes or storage lockers would never be protected, by virtue of the bank or storage company's ability to access them.

"Compelled disclosure of subscriber information and related records" are "records of the service provider as well, and may be accessed by...employees in the normal course of their employment," and access to these records "likely creates no Fourth Amendment problems." However, there is a heightened expectation of privacy in regard to the contents of e-mail communications:

> Like telephone conversations, simply because the phone company or the ISP could access the contents of e-mails and phone calls, the privacy expectation in the content of either is not diminished because there is a societal expectation that the ISP or the phone company will not do so as a matter of course.

E-mail is an "ever-increasing mode of private communication, and protecting shared communications through this medium is as important to Fourth Amendment principles today as protecting telephone conversations has been in the past." The ISP's right to access e-mails under the user agreement is reserved for "extraordinary circumstances." The outcome may be different where a user agreement calls for regular auditing, inspection, or monitoring of e-mails. The fact that e-mails may be scanned for pornography or a virus was not considered by the Sixth Circuit Court of Appeals to "invade an individual's content-based privacy interest in the e-mails and has little bearing on his expectation of privacy in the content." This is analogous to the post office screening packages for drugs or explosives, which does not expose the content of written communications.

Do you agree with the decision in *Warshak*? See *Warshak v. United States,* No. 06-00357 (S.D. Ohio, 2007).

3.1 YOU DECIDE

Plainclothes Los Angeles Police Officer Richard Aldahal and two other plainclothes officers observed defendant Leroy Triggs enter a men's room in Arroyo Seco Park. Ten minutes later, David Crockett was observed entering the same men's room. The three officers entered a plumbing access area between the men's room and women's room that provided a vantage point to observe activity in the restrooms. Officer Aldahal was able to position himself in such a fashion that he was able look through vents down into the doorless toilet stalls. He spotted Triggs and Crockett engaged in unlawful oral copulation. Triggs was convicted and placed on probation under the condition that he serve thirty days in the county jail. Officer Aldahal testified at trial that he had entered the plumbing access area roughly fifty times in the past to observe activity in the men's room. Did Triggs possess a reasonable expectation of privacy? Was this an unlawful, warrantless search under the Fourth Amendment? What if there were doors on the stalls that the suspects had closed? See *People v. Triggs,* 506 P.2d 232 (Cal. 1973).

You can learn what the court decided by referring to the study site, http://www.sagepub.com/lippmancp.

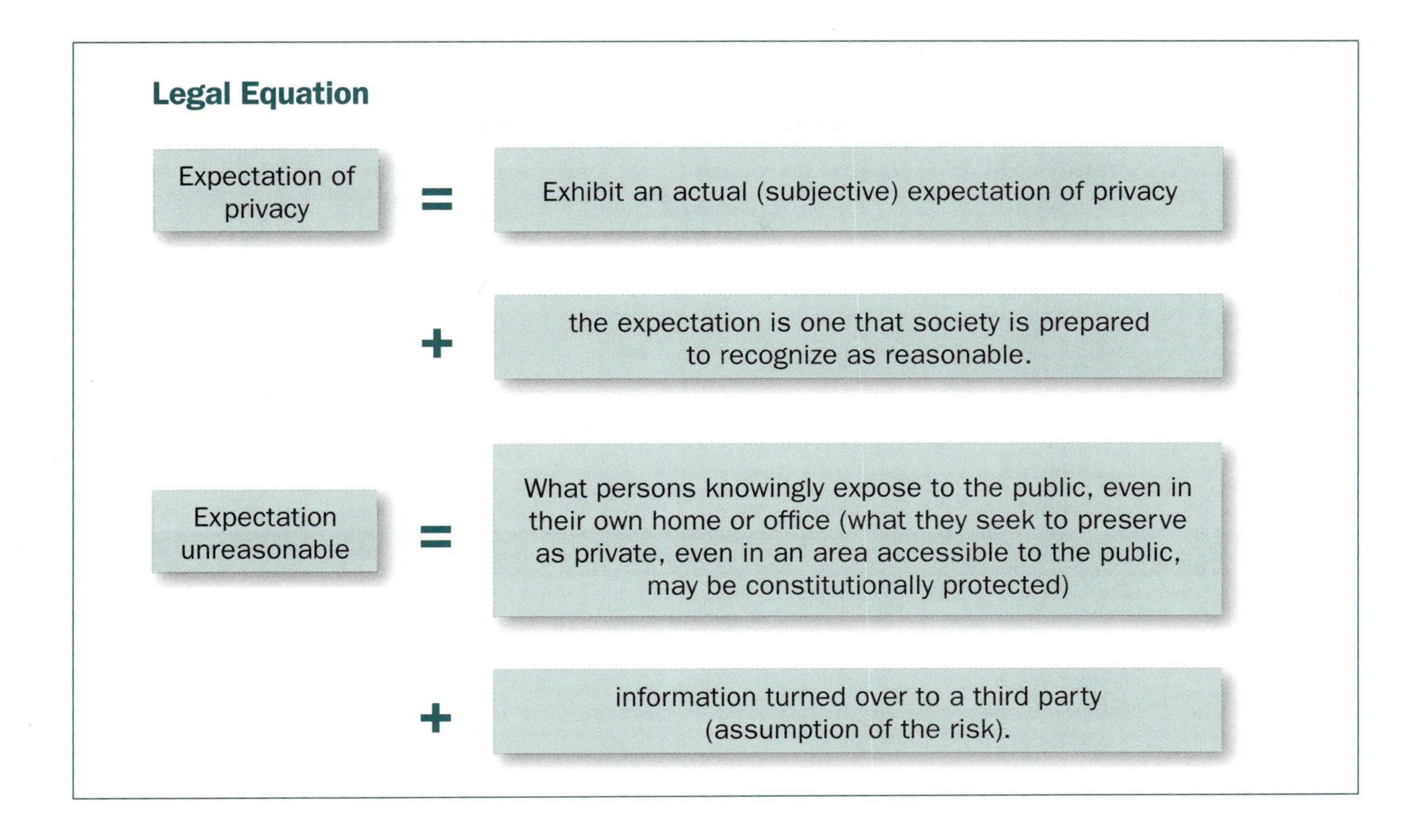

Informants and Electronic Eavesdropping

In *Katz* the government electronically monitored a conversation without the consent of either of the participants. The Supreme Court recognized that Katz had a subjective as well as a reasonable expectation of privacy in the content of his phone calls and held that a reasonable search under the Fourth Amendment required that the government obtain a warrant based on probable cause. The U.S. Supreme Court has taken a different approach to the so-called false friend cases in which a suspect talks to an individual without knowing that he or she is an undercover government agent or informant. In a second type of false friend scenario, the agent or informant is wired and the conversation is recorded or directly transmitted to the police at a remote location. The Supreme Court has held in both situations that the suspect has no reasonable expectation of privacy under the Fourth Amendment that has been violated. He or she *assumes the risk* that the conversation may not remain confidential and will be communicated to the police (Dressler & Michaels, 2006, pp. 84–88).

In *Hoffa v. United States,* Edward Partin, a local Teamsters Union official and government informant, visited the hotel room of Teamsters national president Jimmy Hoffa, who was standing trial for union-related corruption. Partin reportedly overheard conversations in which Hoffa conspired to bribe jurors; Partin later testified as the government's central witness at Hoffa's prosecution for jury tampering. The Supreme Court held that although the hotel room was a "constitutionally protected area," Hoffa was

> not relying on the security of the hotel room; he was relying upon his misplaced confidence that Partin would not reveal his wrongdoing.... [Nothing in the] Fourth Amendment protects a wrongdoer's misplaced belief that a person to whom he voluntarily confides his wrongdoing will not reveal it. (*Hoffa v. United States,* 385 U.S. 293, 302–303 [1996])

The Supreme Court reached the same conclusion in *Lewis v. United States*. Lewis invited undercover agent Cass over to his home on two occasions to sell Cass marijuana. The Supreme Court held that when the home is converted into a commercial center, it is entitled to no greater protection than if the commercial activities were carried on in a "store, garage, car or on the street." Cass during his visits did not "see, hear, or take anything that was not contemplated, and in fact intended, by [Lewis] as a necessary part of his illegal business" (*Lewis v. United States,* 385 U.S. 206, 210–211 [1966]).

Would it make a difference that an informant was wired with an electronic device that recorded the conversation? In *United States v. White,* the informant was wired with a radio transmitter that relayed the conversation to government agents. The Supreme Court continued to follow a "risk analysis" and held that

> if the conduct and revelations of an agent operating without electronic equipment do not invade the defendant's constitutionally justifiable expectations of privacy, neither does a simultaneous recording of the same conversations made... from transmissions received from the agent to whom the defendant is talking and whose trustworthiness the defendant necessarily risks. (*United States v. White,* 401 U.S. 745, 751 [1971])

In summary, we *assume the risk* that the person with whom we are communicating may be working as a government agent or informant. There is no constitutionally protected expectation of privacy in conversations that we engage in with other individuals. It makes no difference whether the other individual is an informant or a government agent who

- immediately reports the contents of the conversation to the police and writes down his or her conversation.
- records the conversation using electronic equipment.
- transmits the conversation to police officers who are monitoring the conversation.

Justice Harlan, in his dissent in *United States v. White,* complained that the Supreme Court's embrace of risk analysis and warrantless surveillance of conversations threatened the trust and security that makes people comfortable with freely talking to one another (787).

Do you agree with the Supreme Court that White assumed the risk that his conversation would be directly transmitted to law enforcement authorities? Should the Court distinguish between conversations in the home and conversations in public? In the next sections, we briefly review the requirements for a plain view search and seizure and discuss the relationship between plain view and the expectation of privacy in the areas surrounding the home and in the home.

You can find United States v. White *on the study site, http://www.sagepub.com/lippmancp.*

Plain View

Plain view is an exception to the Fourth Amendment warrant requirement; it allows the police to seize an item without a search warrant under two conditions:

- ***Legally situated.*** The police officer is lawfully positioned: He or she "has a right to be where he or she is situated."
- ***Probable cause.*** The police officer has probable cause to believe that the object is evidence of criminal activity. The probable cause must be immediately apparent upon observing the item.

We will be discussing plain view searches in greater detail later in the text. At the moment it is sufficient that you understand that an officer who sees an unlawful object or object connected to unlawful activity may seize the object without a warrant. The individual, by exposing the object to "plain view," has lost his or her expectation of privacy with respect to the item. The police, for example, may lawfully stop an individual for a traffic violation and spot and seize drugs or an open bottle of alcohol in plain view on the back seat. An officer searching a house for drugs may encounter and seize unlawful child pornography.

In *Arizona v. Hicks,* the police responded to a gunshot and entered a rundown apartment without a warrant. The officers saw a brand-new stereo unit; one of the officers moved the unit, read the serial numbers, and called headquarters, which confirmed that the stereo had been stolen. The Supreme Court agreed with Hicks that this was not a plain view search. The officers were "lawfully situated," but it was not "immediately apparent" that the stereo was stolen, because the officer was forced to move the unit and to call headquarters to determine whether it had been stolen (*Arizona v. Hicks,* 480 U.S. 321 [1987]). The Supreme Court also has recognized a "plain feel" doctrine when an officer patting down a suspect concludes that he or she has encountered narcotics, and other courts have recognized a "plain smell" doctrine when an officer smells narcotics or alcohol in an automobile. In 2008, a Virginia Court of Appeals noted that an

> individual, after all, has no privacy interest in his odors. He cannot broadcast an unusual odor (particularly one associated with illegal drugs) and reasonably expect everyone he comes into contact with, including police officers, to take no notice of it. [We therefore agree with the accepted view that] there is no "reasonable expectation of privacy" from lawfully positioned agents "with inquisitive nostrils." (*Bunch v. Commonwealth,* 658 S.E.2d 724 [Va. App. 2008])

The next section on open fields and curtilage provides a good example of how the police rely on plain view. We then explore whether the police may rely on technology to enhance their ability to conduct plain view searches and seizures.

Expectation of Privacy

The U.S. Supreme Court has divided the home and the land surrounding the home into three separate categories with differing degrees of expectation of privacy and Fourth Amendment protection.

- ***Open fields.*** This includees land distant from the home, which the police may enter without probable cause or a warrant.
- ***Home.*** The physical structure of the dwelling-house is accorded full and complete protection under the Fourth Amendment, and to enter it, the police in most instances require a search warrant founded on probable cause.
- ***Curtilage.*** The area immediately surrounding the home is considered part of the dwelling-house. Curtilage has no expectation of privacy from aerial surveillance.

There are three other categories of property that we will discuss in this chapter. Each lacks an expectation of privacy under the Fourth Amendment.

- ***Public property.*** This land is generally open to the public, and a warrant is not required for the police to seize property.
- ***Commercial property.*** The police may enter and seize items without a warrant from stores and businesses that are open to the public. A warrant is required to enter those areas reserved for employees.
- ***Abandoned property.*** Property that is intentionally abandoned has no expectation of privacy and may be seized by the police without a warrant.

Open Fields

In *Oliver v. United States,* Kentucky State Police investigated reports that Thornton and Oliver were raising marijuana on Oliver's farm. The police drove past Oliver's house to a locked gate with a "No Trespassing" sign, followed a path around one side of the fence, and walked down the path until they discovered a field of marijuana over a mile from Oliver's home. "No Trespassing" signs were posted along the path, and the marijuana field was surrounded by woods, fences, and embankments and was not visible from any location accessible to the public. The U.S. Supreme Court held that the Fourth Amendment protection of "persons, houses, places and effects" from unreasonable searches and seizures is not intended to protect open fields. Open fields consequently possess no expectation of privacy, and the Kentucky police acted reasonably in entering and seizing the marijuana without a search warrant.

The Supreme Court explained that there are good reasons why **open fields** are not provided with Fourth Amendment protection and lack an expectation of privacy (*Oliver v. United States,* 466 U.S. 170 [1984]).

- ***Purpose.*** The Fourth Amendment is intended to protect "intimate" activities. There is no interest in protecting the type of activities that typically take place in open fields, such as the cultivation of crops.
- ***Access.*** Open fields are more accessible to the public than are houses or offices and are easily monitored from aircraft.

The Supreme Court also held that Oliver did not have an expectation of privacy in the open field despite the warnings to trespassers and efforts to conceal the marijuana plants. The Court explained that declaring that open fields lacked an expectation of privacy despite the "no trespassing" signs avoided placing the police in the position of having to decide on a case-by-case basis whether a particular open field merited Fourth Amendment protection.

Curtilage is the area immediate surrounding the home. Curtilage, in contrast to open fields, is the site of the "intimate activity" associated with the "sanctity of a man's [or woman's] home and the privacies of life" and therefore is considered part of the home itself. The Supreme Court noted that people use their decks, porches, and backyards to barbecue, socialize, and engage in recreation and other activities that are closely identified with the enjoyment of the home.

As a practical matter, how can a police officer distinguish curtilage from open fields? In *Dunn v. United States,* the Supreme Court listed four factors that are to be considered (*Dunn v. United States,* 480 U.S. 294 [1987]).

- ***Distance.*** Whether the area is distant or close to the area of the home
- ***Enclosure.*** Whether the area is within an enclosure surrounding the home
- ***Function.*** Whether the area is used for activities that normally are part of the home activities
- ***Protection.*** Whether an effort is made to protect the area from observation

These are general guidelines. The essential question is whether the area is "so intimately tied to the house itself" that it should be accorded Fourth Amendment protection. One federal judge accurately described the division between curtilage and open fields as an "imaginary boundary line between privacy and accessibility to the public" (*United States v. Redmon,* 138 F.3d 1109, 1112 [7th Cir. 1998]).

In *Dunn,* the U.S. Supreme Court held that a barn was part of open fields rather than the curtilage and that the federal officer who discovered a crystal meth laboratory did not require a search warrant to look into the barn. The barn was outside the fence surrounding the home and was fifty yards from the fence and sixty yards from the house, and Dunn had not taken sufficient steps to protect the inside of the barn from observation. Aerial photographs and chemical odors from the barn indicated that it was not being used for intimate activities associated with the home.

A number of state supreme courts, including those of Mississippi, Montana, New York, Tennessee, Vermont, and Washington, have interpreted their state constitutions to provide protection for open fields in those instances in which signs and fencing indicate that an individual possesses an expectation of privacy. These state courts have explained that the central question is whether an individual's expectation of privacy is reasonable rather than whether the land is separate and apart from the home or curtilage or whether the land is used for "intimate activities" associated with the home.

Which approach do you believe makes more sense? Does it make sense that individuals lack a reasonable expectation of privacy in land that they own?

You can find Oliver v. United States *on the study site, http://www.sagepub.com/lippmancp.*

Curtilage and Aerial Surveillance

Curtilage is viewed as part of the home and has a high expectation of privacy. The general rule is that a warrant is required for a search of the home and the curtilage. However, in this section we shall see that the curtilage does not receive the same degree of protection as the home itself. The U.S. Supreme Court held, in the two cases discussed below, that the warrantless, aerial surveillance of the curtilage does not violate an individual's expectation of privacy.

In *California v. Ciraolo,* the police received information from an informant that Ciraolo was growing marijuana in his backyard. Ciraolo had surrounded his yard with a six-foot outer fence and a ten-foot inner fence that prevented the police from investigating the tip. The police refused to be discouraged; two trained narcotics investigators flew a plane within navigable airspace at 1,000 feet, observed marijuana plants in Ciraolo's backyard, took a photograph, obtained a search warrant, and seized the plants. Ciraolo claimed that the police had violated his reasonable expectation of privacy.

The U.S. Supreme Court held that in an age in which air travel is "routine," it is unreasonable for Ciraolo to expect that his marijuana plants are constitutionally protected from plain view observation with the naked eye from an altitude of 1,000 feet. Ciraolo did not possess a reasonable expectation of privacy, and the police officers were not required to obtain a warrant to conduct aerial surveillance (*California v. Ciraolo,* 476 U.S. 207, 215 [1986]).

The Supreme Court's holding in *Ciraolo* was relied on as precedent by the Supreme Court in *Florida v. Riley.* The police were unable to verify an informant's tip from the street that Riley was growing marijuana in the greenhouse ten to twenty feet behind his mobile home. Two of the four sides of the greenhouse were enclosed, and the top of the greenhouse was partially covered by corrugated roofing panels. An officer circled over the greenhouse in a helicopter flying at 400 feet and was able to see though a slit in the roof and through the open sides of the greenhouse; he identified what he believed were marijuana plants. The officer obtained a warrant, and a search of the greenhouse resulted in the seizure of marijuana plants. The Supreme Court stressed that the helicopter was flying at a legal altitude, and the Court found "nothing" to "suggest that helicopters flying at 400 feet are sufficiently rare in this country to lend substance to respondent's claim that he reasonably anticipated that his greenhouse would not be subject to observation from that altitude" (*Florida v. Riley,* 488 U.S. 445, 452 [1989]).

Dow Chemical Company v. United States is a third case involving aerial surveillance. Although it involved an industrial plant, the case is significant for its discussion of visual enhancement technology. In *Dow,* the Environmental Protection Agency relied on aerial surveillance using a standard precision aerial camera to determine whether Dow's 2,000-acre chemical plant was in compliance with governmental regulations. The Supreme Court held that the "mere fact that human vision is enhanced somewhat, at least to the degree here, does not give rise to constitutional problems." In other words, the camera only clarified what was already visible to the naked eye. Keep in mind that the Supreme Court noted that Dow's plant fell somewhere in between open fields and curtilage and did not deserve the same expectation of privacy as the home (*Dow Chemical Company v. United States,* 476 U.S. 227, 238–239 [1986]).

In summary, the Supreme Court held that despite the fact that curtilage is part of the home and despite efforts to insulate the curtilage from plain view, the curtilage has no expectation of privacy from aerial surveillance, even, it appears, as in *Dow,* where the surveillance is assisted by technology. Do you agree with the Supreme Court's judgments on aerial surveillance? Could Ciraolo and Riley reasonably have anticipated that their curtilage would be subject to aerial surveillance? Would a ruling that warrantless aerial surveillance of the curtilage violates individuals' Fourth Amendment rights handcuff the police? Keep in mind that although aerial surveillance may result in the detection of contraband, the police still require a warrant to enter the curtilage and seize the contraband or other evidence.

You can find Florida v. Riley *on the study site, http://www.sagepub.com/lippmancp.*

Technology and the Home

Search warrants and arrest warrants generally are required to enter into the home, which has the highest expectation of privacy. In *Kyllo v. United States,* the next case in the text, the U.S. Supreme Court confronted the question of whether the police may employ a thermal-imaging device without a warrant to measure the heat emanating from a home. The theory behind the use of thermal imaging is that an unusually high degree of warmth provides probable cause that heat lamps are being used inside the home to grow marijuana.

As we have seen, the Supreme Court has upheld the employment of recording devices, aerial overflights, and photographic technology to enhance surveillance. In the decades to come, we are likely to see new and even more powerful technological techniques of criminal investigation. The Supreme Court has adopted two general rules in regard to police reliance on technology:

- ***Plain view.*** Technology may be used without a search warrant to enhance observation of an area or object already in plain view (open fields, curtilage).
- ***Home.*** The physical structure of the home possesses a high expectation of privacy. Technology may not be used without a warrant founded on probable cause to engage in the surveillance of the interior of the home in order to detect activity that otherwise would not be revealed without physically entering the home.

An example of the use of technology to enhance surveillance of an object in plain view is *Texas v. Brown.* In *Brown,* the Supreme Court ruled that the use of a flashlight to "illuminate a darkened area" in the interior of an automobile does not constitute a Fourth Amendment search (*Texas v. Brown,* 460 U.S. 730 [1983]). In another example, the Supreme Court upheld the use of a beeper installed in a five-gallon drum of chloroform to track the movements of an automobile driven by a suspect in an illegal narcotics ring. The Court reasoned that the defendant's movements on the public roadways also were being tracked through aerial surveillance and that the beeper revealed no information that was not already available to the general public or to the police. The Supreme Court observed that "nothing in the Fourth Amendment prohibit[s] the police from augmenting the sensory faculties bestowed upon them at birth with such enhancement as science and technology afforded them in this case" (*United States v. Knotts,* 460 U.S. 276 [1983])(rule 1).

On the other hand, the Supreme Court drew the line at continuing to electronically monitor a beeper in a can of ether once the can was taken into a home. The purpose was to verify that the can remained inside a home thought to be the site of an illegal narcotics laboratory while the police obtained a search warrant. The Court reasoned that the government may not physically enter the home (without a warrant) to insure that the ether is inside, and the result is the same where the government secretly "employs an electronic device to obtain information that it could not have obtained by observation from outside the . . . house" (*United States v. Karo,* 468 U.S. 705 [1984]) (rule 2).

In 2001, in *Kyllo v. United States,* the U.S. Supreme Court was asked to rule on whether the warrantless use of a thermal-imaging device to measure infrared radiation that emanates from a house constitutes a search. The scan from the device, when combined with other information, provided probable cause to support a warrant to search Kyllo's home, and the search resulted in the seizure of more than one hundred marijuana plants. Consider the cases we have discussed, and ask yourself whether Kyllo had a subjective expectation of privacy that would be considered objectively reasonable under the Fourth Amendment. Did the federal agents require a warrant before using the thermal-imaging device?

Does the use of a thermal-imaging device constitute the search of a home?

Kyllo v. United States, 533 U.S. 27 (2001), Scalia, J.

Issue

This case presents the question of whether the use of a thermal-imaging device aimed at a private home from a public street to detect relative amounts of heat within the home constitutes a "search" within the meaning of the Fourth Amendment.

Facts

In 1991 Agent William Elliott of the U.S. Department of the Interior came to suspect that marijuana was being grown in the home belonging to petitioner Danny Kyllo, part of a triplex on Rhododendron Drive in Florence, Oregon. Indoor marijuana growth typically requires high-intensity lamps. In order to determine whether an amount of heat was emanating from petitioner's home consistent with the use of such lamps, at 3:20 A.M. on January 16, 1992, Agent Elliott and Dan Haas used an Agema Thermovision 210 thermal imager to scan the triplex. Thermal imagers detect infrared radiation, which virtually all objects emit but which is not visible to the naked eye. The imager converts radiation into images based on relative warmth—black is cool, white is hot, shades of gray connote relative differences; in that respect, it operates somewhat like a video camera showing heat images.

The scan of Kyllo's home took only a few minutes and was performed from the passenger seat of Agent Elliott's vehicle across the street from the front of the house and also from the street in back of the house. The scan showed that the roof over the garage and a side wall of petitioner's home were relatively hot compared to the rest of the home and substantially warmer than neighboring homes in the triplex. Agent Elliott concluded that petitioner was using halide lights to grow marijuana in his house, which indeed he was. Based on tips from informants, utility bills, and the thermal imaging, a federal magistrate judge issued a warrant authorizing a search of petitioner's home, and the agents found an indoor growing operation involving more than one hundred plants. Petitioner was indicted on one count of manufacturing marijuana, in violation of 21 U.S.C. § 841(a)(1). He unsuccessfully moved to suppress the evidence seized from his home and then entered a conditional guilty plea.

The Court of Appeals for the Ninth Circuit remanded the case for an evidentiary hearing regarding the intrusiveness of thermal imaging. On remand . . . the district court upheld the validity of the warrant that relied in part upon the thermal imaging and reaffirmed its denial of the motion to suppress. The court of appeals . . . held that petitioner had shown no subjective expectation of privacy, because he had made no attempt to conceal the heat escaping from his home, and even if he had, there was no objectively reasonable expectation of privacy because the imager "did not expose any intimate details of Kyllo's life," only "amorphous 'hot spots' on the roof and exterior wall." We granted certiorari.

Reasoning

At the very core of the Fourth Amendment "stands the right of a man to retreat into his own home and there be free from unreasonable governmental intrusion." With few exceptions, the question of whether a warrantless search of a home is reasonable and hence constitutional must be answered no. On the other hand, the antecedent question of whether or not a Fourth Amendment "search" has occurred is not so simple under our precedent. . . . As Justice Harlan's oft-quoted concurrence described it, a Fourth Amendment search occurs when the Government violates a subjective expectation of privacy that society recognizes as reasonable. We have subsequently applied this principle to hold that a Fourth Amendment search does not occur—even when the explicitly protected location of a house is concerned—unless "the individual manifested a subjective expectation of privacy in the object of the challenged search," and "society [is] willing to recognize that expectation as reasonable." We have applied this test in holding that it is not a search for the police to use a pen register at the phone company to determine what numbers were dialed in a private home, and we have applied the test on two different occasions in holding that aerial surveillance of private homes and surrounding areas does not constitute a search.

The present case involves officers on a public street engaged in more than naked-eye surveillance of a home. We have previously reserved judgment as to how much technological enhancement of ordinary perception from such a vantage point, if any, is too much. While we upheld enhanced aerial photography of an industrial complex in *Dow Chemical,* we noted that we found it "important that this is not an area immediately adjacent to a private home, where privacy expectations are most heightened."

It would be foolish to contend that the degree of privacy secured to citizens by the Fourth Amendment has been entirely unaffected by the advance of technology. For example, as the cases discussed above make clear, the technology enabling human flight has exposed to public view (and hence, we have said, to official observation) uncovered portions of the house and its curtilage that once were private. The question we confront today is what limits there are upon this power of technology to shrink the realm of guaranteed privacy.

Holding

The *Katz* test—whether the individual has an expectation of privacy that society is prepared to recognize as reasonable—has often been criticized as...subjective and unpredictable. While it may be difficult to refine *Katz* when the search of areas such as telephone booths, automobiles, or even the curtilage and uncovered portions of residences are at issue, in the case of the search of the interior of homes—the prototypical and hence most commonly litigated area of protected privacy—there is a ready criterion, with roots deep in the common law, of the minimal expectation of privacy that exists, and that is acknowledged to be reasonable. To withdraw protection of this minimum expectation would be to permit police technology to erode the privacy guaranteed by the Fourth Amendment. We think that obtaining by sense-enhancing technology any information regarding the interior of the home that could not otherwise have been obtained without physical "intrusion into a constitutionally protected area," constitutes a search—at least where (as here) the technology in question is not in general public use. This assures preservation of that degree of privacy against Government that existed when the Fourth Amendment was adopted. On the basis of this criterion, the information obtained by the thermal imager in this case was the product of a search.

The Government maintains, however, that the thermal imaging must be upheld, because it detected "only heat radiating from the external surface of the house.... We rejected such a mechanical interpretation of the Fourth Amendment in *Katz,* where the eavesdropping device picked up only sound waves that reached the exterior of the phone booth. Reversing that approach would leave the homeowner at the mercy of advancing technology—including imaging technology—that could discern all human activity in the home. While the technology used in the present case was relatively crude, the rule we adopt must take account of more sophisticated systems that are already in use or in development.

The Government also contends that the thermal imaging was constitutional, because it did not "detect private activities occurring in private areas."...The Fourth Amendment's protection of the home has never been tied to measurement of the quality or quantity of information obtained. In *Silverman,* for example, we made clear that any physical invasion of the structure of the home, "by even a fraction of an inch," was too much, and there is certainly no exception to the warrant requirement for the officer who barely cracks open the front door and sees nothing but the nonintimate rug on the vestibule floor. In the home, our cases show, all details are intimate details, because the entire area is held safe from prying Government eyes. Thus, in *Karo,* the only thing detected was a can of ether in the home; and in *Arizona v. Hicks,* the only thing detected by a physical search that went beyond what officers lawfully present could observe in plain view was the registration number of a phonograph turntable. These were intimate details, because they were details of the home, just as was the detail of how warm—or even how relatively warm—Kyllo was heating his residence.

We have said that the Fourth Amendment draws "a firm line at the entrance to the house." That line, we think, must be not only firm but also bright—which requires clear specification of those methods of surveillance that require a warrant. While it is certainly possible to conclude from the videotape of the thermal imaging that occurred in this case that no "significant" compromise of the homeowner's privacy has occurred, we must take the long view, from the original meaning of the Fourth Amendment forward.

Where, as here, the Government uses a device that is not in general public use, to explore details of the home that would previously have been unknowable without physical intrusion, the surveillance is a "search" and is presumptively unreasonable without a warrant. Since we hold the Thermovision imaging to have been an unlawful search, it will remain for the district court to determine whether, without the evidence it provided, the search warrant issued in this case was supported by probable cause—and if not, whether there is any other basis for supporting admission of the evidence that the search pursuant to the warrant produced.

The judgment of the court of appeals is reversed; the case is remanded for further proceedings consistent with this opinion.

Dissenting, *Stevens, J.*, joined by *Rehnquist, C.J.*, *O'Connor, J.*, and *Kennedy, J.*

There is, in my judgment, a distinction of constitutional magnitude between "through-the-wall surveillance" that gives the observer or listener direct access to information in a private area, on the one hand, and the thought processes used to draw inferences from information in the public domain, on the other hand. The Court has crafted a rule that purports to deal with direct observations of the inside of the home, but the case before us merely involves indirect deductions from "off-the-wall" surveillance, that is, observations of the exterior of the home. Those observations were made with a fairly primitive thermal imager that gathered data exposed on the outside of petitioner's home but did not invade any constitutionally protected interest in privacy. Moreover, I believe that the supposedly "bright-line" rule the Court has created in response to its concerns about future technological developments is unnecessary, unwise, and inconsistent with the Fourth Amendment.

There is no need for the Court to craft a new rule to decide this case, as it is controlled by established principles from our Fourth Amendment jurisprudence. One of those core principles, of course, is that "searches and seizures inside a home without a warrant are presumptively unreasonable." But it is equally well settled that searches and seizures of property in plain view are presumptively reasonable. Whether that property is residential or commercial, the basic principle is the same: "What a person knowingly exposes to the public, even in his own home or office, is not a subject of Fourth Amendment protection." That is the principle implicated here.

Indeed, the ordinary use of the senses might enable a neighbor or passerby to notice the heat emanating from a building, particularly if it is vented, as was the case here. Additionally, any member of the public might notice that one part of a house is warmer than another part or a nearby building if, for example, rainwater evaporates or snow melts at different rates across its surfaces. Such use of the senses would not convert into an unreasonable search if, instead, an adjoining neighbor allowed an officer onto her property to verify her perceptions with a sensitive thermometer. Nor, in my view, does such observation become an unreasonable search if made from a distance with the aid of a device that merely discloses that the exterior of one house, or one area of the house, is much warmer than another. Nothing more occurred in this case.

The notion that heat emissions from the outside of a dwelling is a private matter implicating the protections of the Fourth Amendment (the text of which guarantees the right of people "to be secure *in* their . . . houses" against unreasonable searches and seizures [emphasis added] is not only unprecedented but also quite difficult to take seriously. Heat waves, like aromas that are generated in a kitchen, or in a laboratory or opium den, enter the public domain if and when they leave a building. A subjective expectation that they would remain private is not only implausible but also surely not "one that society is prepared to recognize as 'reasonable.'"

There is a strong public interest in avoiding constitutional litigation over the monitoring of emissions from homes, and over the inferences drawn from such monitoring. Just as "the police cannot reasonably be expected to avert their eyes from evidence of criminal activity that could have been observed by any member of the public," so too public officials should not have to avert their senses or their equipment from detecting emissions in the public domain such as excessive heat, traces of smoke, suspicious odors, odorless gases, airborne particulates, or radioactive emissions, any of which could identify hazards to the community. In my judgment, monitoring such emissions with "sense-enhancing technology," and drawing useful conclusions from such monitoring, is an entirely reasonable public service.

On the other hand, the countervailing privacy interest is at best trivial. After all, homes generally are insulated to keep heat in, rather than to prevent the detection of heat going out, and it does not seem to me that society will suffer from a rule requiring the rare homeowner who both intends to engage in uncommon activities that produce extraordinary amounts of heat and who wishes to conceal such activity. The interest in concealing the heat escaping from one's house pales in significance to "the chief evil against which the wording of the Fourth Amendment is directed," the "physical entry of the home," and it is hard to believe that it is an interest the framers sought to protect in our Constitution.

Because what was involved in this case was nothing more than drawing inferences from off-the-wall surveillance, rather than any "through-the-wall" surveillance, the officers' conduct did not amount to a search and was perfectly reasonable. Despite the Court's attempt to draw a line that is "not only firm but also bright," the contours of its new rule are uncertain, because its protection apparently dissipates as soon as the relevant technology is "in general public use." Yet how much use is general public use is not even hinted at by the Court's opinion, which makes the somewhat doubtful assumption that the thermal imager used in this case does not satisfy that criterion. In any event, putting aside its lack of clarity, this criterion is somewhat perverse, because it seems likely that the threat to privacy will grow, rather than recede, as the use of intrusive equipment becomes more readily available.

Although the Court is properly and commendably concerned about the threats to privacy that may flow from advances in the technology available to the law enforcement profession, it has unfortunately failed to heed the tried and true counsel of judicial restraint. Instead of concentrating on the rather mundane issue that is actually presented by the case before it, the Court has endeavored to craft an all-encompassing rule for the future. It would be far wiser to give legislators an unimpeded opportunity to grapple with these emerging issues rather than to shackle them with prematurely devised constitutional constraints.

Questions for Discussion

1. What is the holding in *Kyllo*? Explain the significance of the fact that the thermal-imaging device is not in "general use."
2. Discuss the relationship between the Supreme Court rulings in *White, Ciraolo,* and *Riley* with those in *Dow* and *Kyllo.*
3. Summarize the argument of the dissent. Do you find the majority opinion or the dissenting opinion more persuasive?

Criminal Procedure in the News

Law enforcement increasingly is employing dogs to detect whether narcotics and explosives are being carried into subways, airports, and train stations. Dogs also are used to detect prohibited foods, plants, and fruits that are brought into the United States and to uncover land mines in war zones; it is even claimed that some dogs are able to detect cancer in patients. Dogs are currently employed at over seventy-three ports of entry into the United States and are described as much more efficient than humans in detecting contraband in vehicles and large shipping containers.

You might have wondered whether the Fourth Amendment permits the use of dogs to "search" for contraband. In 1983 in *United States v. Place* (462 U.S. 696), Drug Enforcement Agency officers at Miami International Airport tipped off agents at New York's La Guardia Airport that their suspicions had been aroused by passenger Raymond Place. Agents in New York monitored Place's movements at La Guardia and also found his behavior suspicious. The agents approached Place and informed him that they suspected that he was carrying narcotics. Place refused to consent to a search of his baggage, and the agents removed the bags to John F. Kennedy airport where a trained narcotics dog indicated that one of the bags contained unlawful narcotics. Based on the dog's reaction, a federal magistrate issued a search warrant, and the agents discovered 1,125 grams of cocaine in the bag. Place appealed and argued that the dog sniff constituted an unlawful, warrantless search of his luggage and that the resulting search warrant had been based on evidence that had been obtained in an unconstitutional search of his bag.

The U.S. Supreme Court held that a canine sniff is "one of a kind." The Court was aware of no other investigative procedure that is so "limited" both in the manner in which the information is obtained and in the "content" of the information revealed. The sniff discloses only the presence or absence of narcotics and does not require agents to search through a suspect's belongings. The Supreme Court accordingly ruled that the exposure of luggage to a trained narcotics dog does not constitute a "search" within the meaning of the Fourth Amendment. Subsequently, in 2005, in *Illinois v. Caballes,* the Supreme Court held that the use of a narcotics dog during a lawful traffic stop does not infringe on the driver's Fourth Amendment rights (543 U.S. 405).

In summary, *Place* and *Caballes* stand for the proposition that law enforcement personnel are not required to obtain a warrant based on probable cause to use dogs to search containers, automobiles, and other property, because dog sniffs are not a Fourth Amendment search. Federal and state courts remain divided over whether dogs may be lawfully employed without a warrant to search persons.

Law enforcement as a result is relatively free to employ trained narcotics and bomb sniffing dogs. The Transportation Security Agency is spending roughly $2.7 million to train and certify roughly thirty German shepherds, Belgian Malinoises, and Labrador retrievers and their handlers for explosive detection in the nation's subways. Dogs' noses have been estimated to be between 100 and 10,000 times more sensitive than the human nose, depending on the scent. They are able to detect small amounts of certain substances and are able to single out a specific substance even when it is surrounded by other odors.

Despite the deserved praise and regard for our canine friends, some law enforcement officers have noted that dogs are not quite as effective as we might want to believe. In his dissent in *Caballes,* Justice David Souter noted that the "infallible" dog is largely a "legal fiction." He noted that errors by handlers and dogs combined to create a rate of false positives in artificial testing situations of between twelve and one-half and sixty percent. The most comprehensive study of the accuracy of dogs was undertaken in the Australian state of New South Wales, where Sydney is located. A study of the use of trained narcotics dogs over a two-year period by the New South Wales Ombudsman found that drug dogs are accurate between twenty-five and thirty percent of the time. Only slightly more than one percent of the "positive sniffs" resulted in the seizure of a significant amount of marijuana ("one in every 526 positive sniffs"). In most instances the police uncovered a small amount of drugs to be used for personal use. The

Ombudsman concluded that there is "little evidence" to support the argument that drug detection dogs "deter drug use, reduce drug-related crime or increase perceptions of public safety. Further, criticisms of the cost-effectiveness of general drug detection operations appear well-founded." In other words, most people stopped in New South Wales either were completely innocent or possessed only small amounts of drugs.

There are several explanations as to why dogs may not be as useful as we have been led to believe.

Training. There are instances in which trainers have falsely represented the capacity of dogs that they have sold to governmental agencies. Dogs also typically are trained for specific chemicals and are unable to detect other compounds. There are some explosives that are so unstable and so likely to ignite that dogs cannot be trained to detect them.

Effectiveness. Dogs may indicate the presence of a chemical when an individual is not actually in possession of a prohibited substance but has indirectly come in contact with a narcotic or explosive. In their desire to please their handler and to receive a reward, dogs may respond to a smell that is similar to one that they have been trained to detect. Dogs function at a high level in a quiet and contained environment. They can become distracted and confused by noise and people.

Fatigue. Dogs are no different than other creatures. They are likely to grow bored and tired and typically are in need of rest after thirty minutes of intense work.

The Russians claim to have overcome the weakness of existing breeds by creating the Sulimov, which is a combination of reindeer herding hound, fox terrier, and spitz dog. Forty Sulimovs are currently employed in Russian airports, and it is claimed that these dogs are able to detect twelve different chemical components that are used in explosives.

In the coming years, efforts likely will be made to replace dogs with a new generation of more accurate technology. We nevertheless likely will see continuing efforts to harness the unique abilities of animals to counter crime. Some researchers have claimed that nonstinging wasps encapsulated in a plastic container and connected to a laptop computer have proven to be easily trained and highly accurate.

Public Places and Private Businesses

The police may seize items that they observe in public places, streets, parks, and monuments. Public places also include private businesses that are open to the public. A search warrant is required for the police to enter portions of a business that are not open to the public, such as employee-only work areas and employee offices. In *Maryland v. Macon,* a nonuniformed police detective entered a store and paid for a magazine. He later returned and arrested the clerk for distributing obscene material. The U.S. Supreme Court held that the officer's entering the bookstore and examining the material that was "intentionally exposed to all who frequent the place of business did not infringe a legitimate expectation of privacy and hence did not constitute a search within the meaning of the Fourth Amendment" (*Maryland v. Macon,* 472 U.S. 463, 469 [1985]).

Abandoned Property

Abandoned property is the last type of property that we will discuss. Abandoned property is property that an individual intends to abandon and physically abandons. An individual has no expectation of privacy in abandoned property, and the property has no Fourth Amendment protection. As a result, the police are not required to obtain a warrant to examine and take control of the property. Property typically does not carry a sign indicating that it is abandoned. Judges rely on the totality of the circumstances and consider where the property is found, the condition of the property, and the type of property along with other factors. For example, an old and worn-out suitcase found in a dumpster clearly has been abandoned. A different conclusion might be reached if the bag is a new and very expensive leather purse that reportedly has been stolen.

In most instances, the question whether property is abandoned is straightforward. In *Hester v. United States,* Hester fled from government revenue agents and dropped a jug and a jar, and an agent later uncovered a bottle; all three containers held unlawfully manufactured moonshine whiskey. The Supreme Court ruled that the containers had been abandoned and lacked an expectation of privacy and that there had been no Fourth Amendment seizure (*Hester v. United States,* 265 U.S. 57, 58 [1924]). In *Abel v. United States,* the petitioner was found to have voluntarily abandoned items that he left behind in the trash can of his hotel room, and the Supreme Court held that there was "nothing unlawful in the Government's appropriation of such abandoned property" (*Abel v. United States,* 362 U.S. 217, 241 [1960]).

In the next case, *California v. Greenwood,* the U.S. Supreme Court was asked to decide whether the petitioners retained an expectation of privacy in sealed garbage bags that a local ordinance required to be placed on the side of the road outside of the curtilage. The police received information that Greenwood was linked to drug trafficking and asked the regular trash collector to pick up the garbage bags that Greenwood had left on the curb in front of his house and to turn the contents over to the police. On two occasions, the police recovered narcotics paraphernalia from Greenwood's garbage; these provided the basis to obtain search warrants for the home, and the search resulted in the seizure of unlawful narcotics. The petitioners moved to suppress the introduction of the narcotics at trial based on the fact that they retained an expectation of privacy in the trash. They argued that their expectation was that the garbage collector would pick up and mingle the trash with other garbage and deposit the debris in the garbage dump. It was not anticipated that the trash would be turned over to the police and examined.

Garbage reveals the most intimate aspects of an individual's life, and most people do not expect that it will be examined by the police. On the other hand, garbage that is left at the curb arguably has been abandoned and may be examined by anyone who happens to walk down the street. In reading *Greenwood,* consider whether the police should be required to obtain a search warrant to search and seize material from the trash. Pay particular attention to the Supreme Court's discussion of whether Greenwood retained an expectation of privacy in the garbage.

Did the police require a warrant to search Greenwood's trash?

California v. Greenwood, *486 U.S. 35 (1988), White, J.*

Issue

The issue here is whether the Fourth Amendment prohibits the warrantless search and seizure of garbage left for collection outside the curtilage of a home. We conclude, in accordance with the vast majority of lower courts that have addressed the issue, that it does not.

Facts

In early 1984, investigator Jenny Stracner of the Laguna Beach Police Department received information indicating that respondent Greenwood might be engaged in narcotics trafficking. Stracner learned that a criminal suspect had informed a federal drug enforcement agent in February 1984 that a truck filled with illegal drugs was en route to the Laguna Beach address at which Greenwood resided. In addition, a neighbor complained of heavy vehicular traffic late at night in front of Greenwood's single-family home. The neighbor reported that the vehicles remained at Greenwood's house for only a few minutes. Stracner sought to investigate this information by conducting a surveillance of Greenwood's home. She observed several vehicles make brief stops at the house during the late night and early morning hours, and she followed a truck from the house to a residence that had previously been under investigation as a narcotics-trafficking location.

On April 6, 1984, Stracner asked the neighborhood's regular trash collector to pick up the plastic garbage bags that Greenwood had left on the curb in front of his house and to turn the bags over to her without mixing their contents with garbage from other houses. The trash collector cleaned his truck bin of other refuse, collected the garbage bags from the street in front of Greenwood's house, and turned the bags over to Stracner. The officer searched through the rubbish and found items indicative of narcotics use. She recited the information that she had gleaned from the trash search in an affidavit in support of a warrant to search Greenwood's home.

Police officers encountered both respondents at the house later that day when they arrived to execute the warrant. The police discovered quantities of cocaine and hashish during their search of the house. Respondents were arrested on felony narcotics charges. They subsequently posted bail.

The police continued to receive reports of many late night visitors to the Greenwood house. On May 4, investigator Robert Rahaeuser obtained Greenwood's garbage from the regular trash collector in the same manner as had Stracner. The garbage again contained evidence of narcotics use. Rahaeuser secured another search warrant for Greenwood's home based on the information from the second trash search. The police found more narcotics and evidence of narcotics trafficking when they executed the warrant. Greenwood was again arrested.

The superior court dismissed the charges against respondents.... The court of appeal affirmed.... The California Supreme Court denied the State's petition for review of the decision of the court of appeals. We granted certiorari.

Reasoning

The warrantless search and seizure of the garbage bags left at the curb outside the Greenwood house would violate the Fourth Amendment only if respondents manifested a subjective expectation of privacy in their garbage that society accepts as objectively reasonable. Respondents do not disagree with this standard. They assert, however, that they had, and exhibited, an expectation of privacy with respect to the trash that was searched by the police: The trash, which was placed on the street for collection at a fixed time, was contained in opaque plastic bags, which the garbage collector was expected to pick up, mingle with the trash of others, and deposit at the garbage dump. The trash was only temporarily on the street, and there was little likelihood that it would be inspected by anyone.

It may well be that respondents did not expect that the contents of their garbage bags would become known to the police or other members of the public. An expectation of privacy does not give rise to Fourth Amendment protection, however, unless society is prepared to accept that expectation as objectively reasonable. Here, we conclude that respondents exposed their garbage to the public sufficiently to defeat their claim to Fourth Amendment protection. It is common knowledge that plastic garbage bags left on or at the side of a public street are readily accessible to animals, children, scavengers, snoops, and other members of the public. Moreover, respondents placed their refuse at the curb for the express purpose of conveying it to a third party, the trash collector, who might himself have sorted through respondents' trash or permitted others, such as the police, to do so. Accordingly, having deposited their garbage "in an area particularly suited for public inspection and, in a manner of speaking, public consumption, for the express purpose of having strangers take it," respondents could have had no reasonable expectation of privacy in the inculpatory items that they discarded.

Furthermore, as we have held, the police cannot reasonably be expected to avert their eyes from evidence of criminal activity that could have been observed by any member of the public. Hence, "what a person knowingly exposes to the public, even in his own home or office, is not a subject of Fourth Amendment protection."

Holding

Our conclusion that society would not accept as reasonable respondents' claim to an expectation of privacy in trash left for collection in an area accessible to the public is reinforced by the unanimous rejection of similar claims by the federal courts of appeals. In *United States v. Thornton* (746 F.2d 39, 49 [1984]), the court observed that "the overwhelming weight of authority rejects the proposition that a reasonable expectation of privacy exists with respect to trash discarded outside the home and the curtilage thereof." In addition, of those state appellate courts that have considered the issue, the vast majority have held that the police may conduct warrantless searches and seizures of garbage discarded in public areas. The judgment of the California Court of Appeal is therefore reversed, and this case is remanded for further proceedings not inconsistent with this opinion.

Dissenting, *Brennan, J.*, joined by *Marshall, J.*

Every week for two months, and at least once more a month later, the Laguna Beach police clawed through the trash that respondent Greenwood left in opaque, sealed bags on the curb outside his home. Complete strangers minutely scrutinized their bounty, undoubtedly dredging up intimate details of Greenwood's private life and habits. The intrusions proceeded without a warrant, and no court before or since has concluded that the police acted on probable cause to believe Greenwood was engaged in any criminal activity.

The framers of the Fourth Amendment understood that "unreasonable searches" of "paper[s] and effects"—no less than "unreasonable searches" of "person[s] and houses"—infringe privacy.... So long as a package is "closed against inspection," the Fourth Amendment protects its contents, "wherever they may be," and the police must obtain a warrant to search it just "as is required when papers are subjected to search in one's own household."... In *Robbins v. California* (453 U.S. 420 [1921]), for example, Justice Stewart, writing for a plurality of four, pronounced that "unless the container is such that its contents may be said to be in plain view, those contents are fully protected by the Fourth Amendment," and he soundly rejected any distinction for Fourth Amendment purposes among various opaque, sealed containers:

> Even if one wished to import such a distinction into the Fourth Amendment, it is difficult if not impossible to perceive any objective criteria by which that task might be accomplished. What one person may put into a suitcase, another may put into a paper bag....And...no court, no constable, no citizen, can sensibly be asked to distinguish the relative "privacy interests" in a closed suitcase, briefcase, portfolio, duffel bag, or box.

More recently, in *United States v. Ross* (456 U.S. 798 [1982]), the Court, relying on the "virtually unanimous agreement in *Robbins*... that a constitutional distinction between 'worthy' and 'unworthy' containers would be improper," held that a distinction among "paper bags, locked trunks, lunch buckets, and orange crates" would be inconsistent with "the central purpose of the Fourth Amendment.... A traveler who carries a toothbrush and a few articles of clothing in a paper bag or knotted scarf [may] claim an equal right to conceal his possessions from official inspection as the sophisticated executive with the locked attaché case."

Our precedent, therefore, leaves no room to doubt that had respondents been carrying their personal effects in opaque, sealed plastic bags—identical to the ones they placed on the curb—their privacy would have been protected from warrantless police intrusion. So far as Fourth Amendment protection is concerned, opaque plastic bags are every bit as worthy as "packages wrapped in green opaque plastic" and "double-locked footlocker[s]."

Respondents deserve no less protection just because Greenwood used the bags to discard rather than to transport his personal effects. Their contents are not inherently any less private, and Greenwood's decision to discard them, at least in the manner in which he did, does not diminish his expectation of privacy.

A trash bag, like any of the above mentioned containers, "is a common repository for one's personal effects" and, even more than many of them, is "therefore... inevitably associated with the expectation of privacy." "Almost every human activity ultimately manifests itself in waste products...." A single bag of trash testifies eloquently to the eating, reading, and recreational habits of the person who produced it. A search of trash, like a search of the bedroom, can relate intimate details about sexual practices, health, and personal hygiene. Like rifling through desk drawers or intercepting phone calls, rummaging through trash can divulge the target's financial and professional status, political affiliations and inclinations, private thoughts, personal relationships, and romantic interests. It cannot be doubted that a sealed trash bag harbors telling evidence of the "intimate activity associated with the 'sanctity of a man's home and the privacies of life,'" which the Fourth Amendment is designed to protect.... In evaluating the reasonableness of Greenwood's expectation that his sealed trash bags would not be invaded, the Court has held that we must look to "understandings that are recognized and permitted by society." Most of us, I believe, would be incensed to discover a meddler—whether a neighbor, a reporter, or a detective—scrutinizing our sealed trash containers to discover some detail of our personal lives.

Beyond a generalized expectation of privacy, many municipalities, whether for reasons of privacy, sanitation, or both, reinforce confidence in the integrity of sealed trash containers by "prohibit[ing] anyone, except authorized employees of the Town..., to rummage into, pick up, collect, move or otherwise interfere with articles or materials placed on... any public street for collection." That is not to deny that isolated intrusions into opaque, sealed trash containers occur. When, acting on their own, "animals, children, scavengers, snoops, [or] other members of the public," actually rummage through a bag of trash and expose its contents to plain view, "police cannot reasonably be expected to avert their eyes from evidence of criminal activity that could have been observed by any member of the public."

Had Greenwood flaunted his intimate activity by strewing his trash all over the curb for all to see, or had some nongovernmental intruder invaded his privacy and done the same, I could accept the Court's conclusion that an expectation of privacy would have been unreasonable. Similarly, had police searching the city dump run across incriminating evidence that, despite commingling with the trash of others, still retained its identity as Greenwood's, we would have a different case. But all that Greenwood "exposed... to the public" were the exteriors of several opaque, sealed containers. Until the bags were opened by police, they hid their contents from the public's view every bit as much as did Chadwick's double-locked footlocker and Robbins's green, plastic wrapping. Faithful application of the warrant requirement does not require police to "avert their eyes from evidence of criminal activity that could have been observed by any member of the public." Rather, it only requires them to adhere to norms of privacy that members of the public plainly acknowledge.

The mere possibility that unwelcome meddlers might open and rummage through the containers does not negate the expectation of privacy in their contents any more than the possibility of a burglary negates an expectation of privacy in the home, or the possibility of a private intrusion negates an expectation of privacy in an unopened package, or the possibility that an operator will listen in on a telephone conversation negates an expectation of privacy in the words spoken on the telephone. "What a person... seeks to preserve as private, even in an area accessible to the public, may be constitutionally protected."

Nor is it dispositive that "respondents placed their refuse at the curb for the express purpose of conveying it to a third party,... who might himself have sorted through respondents' trash or permitted others, such as the police, to do so." In the first place, Greenwood can hardly be faulted for leaving trash on his curb when a county ordinance commanded him to do so. Orange County Code § 4-3-45(a) (1986) requires that each resident must "remov[e] from the premises at least once each week" all "solid waste created, produced or accumulated in or about [his] dwelling house") and prohibit him from disposing of it in any other way. (Orange County Code § 3-3-85 [1988]: Burning trash is unlawful.) Unlike other circumstances in which privacy is compromised, in these circumstances, Greenwood could not "avoid exposing personal belongings... by simply leaving them at home." More important, even the voluntary relinquishment of possession or control over an effect does not necessarily amount to a relinquishment of a privacy expectation in it. Were it otherwise, a letter or package would lose all Fourth Amendment protection when placed in a mailbox or other depository with the "express purpose" of entrusting it to the postal officer or a private carrier; those bailees are just as likely as trash collectors (and certainly have greater incentive) to "sor[t] through" the personal effects entrusted to them, "or permi[t] others, such as police to do so." Yet, it has been clear for at least 110 years that the possibility of such an intrusion does not justify a warrantless search by police in the first instance.

In holding that the warrantless search of Greenwood's trash was consistent with the Fourth Amendment, the Court paints a grim picture of our society. It depicts a society in which local authorities may command their citizens to dispose of their personal effects in the manner least protective of the "sanctity of [the] home and the privacies of life," and then monitor them arbitrarily and without judicial oversight—a society that is not prepared to recognize as reasonable an individual's expectation of privacy in the most private of personal effects sealed in an opaque container and disposed of in a manner designed to commingle it imminently and inextricably with the trash of others. The American society with which I am familiar "chooses to dwell in reasonable security and freedom from surveillance," and is more dedicated to individual liberty and more sensitive to intrusions on the sanctity of the home than the Court is willing to acknowledge.

Questions for Discussion

1. What is the holding in *Greenwood*? What are the facts that the Supreme Court relied on to establish that Greenwood lacked an expectation of privacy in the garbage?
2. Did Greenwood abandon his trash? Did he intend to convey his garbage to the police?
3. Would the Supreme Court in *Greenwood* have reached the same result in the event that the police directly collected the garbage bags? How would the Supreme Court have ruled if the garbage had been left in the curtilage? Could the police have lawfully searched the trash bags without a warrant in a situation in which Greenwood was about to catch a plane, had used the garbage bags for his clothes, and had left the garbage bags on the curb while he went in the house to make a phone call?
4. Summarize the dissent. Do you agree with the majority or with the dissenting opinion?
5. ***Problems in policing.*** What is the legal test for determining whether an item possesses a reasonable expectation of privacy? Why is it important for the police to understand the concept of expectation of privacy?

Cases and Comments

1. ***State Courts.*** The supreme courts of Hawaii, New Hampshire, New Jersey, Vermont, and Washington all have interpreted their state constitutions to provide an expectation of privacy in garbage. In the New Jersey case of *State v. Hempele,* the police in response to an informant's tip seized white plastic bags from a garbage can and brought the bags to police headquarters, where the police detected traces of marijuana, cocaine, and methamphetamine in them. The police obtained a search warrant and uncovered narcotics and drug paraphernalia in Hempele's home. The New Jersey Supreme Court did not address the significance of the fact that the garbage was situated inside Hempele's property line or that the garbage had been seized by the police rather than by the garbage company. The court held that the legal test followed in New Jersey was whether Hempele possessed an objectively reasonable expectation of privacy in the content of the opaque garbage bags. The court held that most people reasonably expect that their garbage will remain free from arbitrary seizures. Garbage contains sensitive information such as discarded bank statements, pharmaceutical bottles, receipts, and financial records. The Fourth Amendment does not distinguish between "worthy" and "unworthy" containers, and garbage bags have the same expectation of privacy as a purse or luggage.

The fact that dogs or children or the poor might rummage through the garbage did not mean that Hempele lacked a reasonable expectation of privacy against the police. The Fourth Amendment is intended to safeguard individuals against unreasonable governmental searches and seizures and "there is a difference between a homeless person searching for food and clothes, and an officer of the State scrutinizing the contents of a garbage bag for incriminating materials." Only governmental searches may lead to criminal liability.

Hempele may have intended to turn his garbage over to a third party trash company, but the only information conveyed to the company was the number, type, and weight of the bags. He was not transmitting information about the contents of the bags. The expectation was that the trash company would deposit the contents at a garbage dump where Hempele's trash would be commingled with other garbage.

The New Jersey Supreme Court analogized the trash bags to a letter left in the mailbox to be picked up by an employee of the post office. The letter is conveyed to the post office for delivery, and there is no expectation that the contents of the letter will be seized by the police. In addition, the fact that individuals discard an item does not mean that their intent is to surrender an expectation of privacy. You might throw away a letter with the reasonable belief that it will not be read by another individual. It is reasonable for individuals to believe that the garbage that they are required to bag and deposit will remain private and will not be subject to seizure by the police. The New Jersey Supreme Court concluded by observing that law enforcement officers are free to search garbage so long as this is based on a search warrant based on probable cause. See *State v. Hempele,* 576 A.2d 793 (N.J. 1990).

2. ***Luggage.*** Steven Bond was a passenger on a Greyhound bus that was stopped at a border patrol checkpoint in Sierra Blanca, Texas. Agent Cesar Cantu checked the immigration status of the passengers, and as he walked toward the front of the bus, he squeezed the soft luggage that passengers had placed in the overhead storage space above the seats. He squeezed a green canvas bag and detected that it contained a brick-like object. Bond admitted that he owned the bag and consented for Cantu to open the bag. Cantu discovered a "brick" of methamphetamine wrapped in duct tape and rolled into a pair of pants. Bond was convicted of conspiracy to possess methamphetamine and possession with intent to distribute methamphetamine. Bond appealed on the grounds that Agent Cantu had improperly squeezed his bag. The government responded that the bag was exposed to the public and lacked an expectation of privacy.

The U.S. Supreme Court held that Bond had indicated a subjective expectation of privacy by placing his belongings in a closed bag in the overhead bin. Was this expectation of privacy reasonable? The Court recognized that when a passenger places a bag in the overhead bin, he or she reasonably expects "that other passengers or bus employees may move it for one reason or another." However, an individual does not "expect that other passengers or bus employees will, as a matter of course, feel the bag in an exploratory manner. But this is exactly what the agent did here." The Court accordingly held that Cantu's "physical manipulation" of Bond's bag violated the Fourth Amendment.

Justices Breyer and Scalia in dissent argued that Agent Cantu had followed a standard procedure at the border in squeezing Bond's bag and that individuals traveling today would reasonably expect that their bags would be pushed and prodded. Breyer and Scalia stressed that the court's decision would have the unfortunate result of deterring border patrol agents from handling luggage in the investigation of narcotics and other contraband. Would the Supreme Court have ruled differently in the event that Bond had placed his bag in the baggage carriage under the bus? See *Bond v. United States,* 529 U.S. 334 (2000).

3.2 YOU DECIDE

Alan Scott was suspected by the Internal Revenue Service (IRS) of involvement in a plan to defraud the government through the filing of false income tax returns. IRS agents seized garbage bags from the front of Scott's home. They discovered various shredded documents. The agents methodically reconstructed the documents, which provided the probable cause required to obtain a search warrant. The warrant resulted in the search and seizure of additional documents that formed the basis of a forty-seven count indictment. Scott moved to suppress the reconstructed documents. As a judge, how would you rule in this case? See *United States v. Scott,* 975 F.2d 927 (1st Cir. 1992).

You can learn what the court decided by referring to the study site, http://www.sagepub.com/lippmancp.

3.3 YOU DECIDE

On October 17, 2003, Detective Tracey Keegan of the Bucyrus, Ohio, Police Department investigated a burglary at Kinn Brothers Plumbing and Heating. He was informed that several furnaces, a central air conditioner, hot water heaters, sinks, and faucets along with other goods had been stolen. Detective Keegan followed tire tracks leading from Kinn Brothers to a windowless building, owned by Joel Buzzard, that was used as a garage. "A wooden double door at the entrance of the garage was secured by a lock in the middle of the door, but the door was 'weathered,' 'warped' and loose fitting." Detective Keegan testified that when he approached the garage door, he could see a furnace by looking through the crack between the double doors. The police then asked the co-owner of Kinn Brothers to look into the garage to determine whether the furnace was one that had been stolen from his business. The officer enhanced the owner's view by pulling on the locked double door to enlarge the crack in the door. The opening was then approximately one-quarter of an inch. The owner looked through the crack and identified the furnace as one that had been stolen from his business. The police secured a warrant to search the garage and Buzzard's nearby home. The search resulted in the seizure of two furnaces, a central air conditioner, sump pumps, plumbing fixtures, and various other items that belonged to Kinn Brothers. The value of the goods recovered was almost $20,000. Buzzard claimed that the warrant was based on an unlawful "plain view" search. How would you decide this case? See *State v. Buzzard,* 112 Ohio St. 3d 451 (Ohio, 2007).

You can learn what the court decided by referring to the study site, http://www.sagepub.com/lippmancp.

Seizures of Persons

The drafters of the U.S. Constitution were concerned with protecting persons as well as their houses, papers, and effects from unreasonable searches and seizures. A Fourth Amendment seizure occurs when a law enforcement officer detains an individual and restricts his or her freedom of movement. You may want to consult Table 3.1 as you read this section to help you understand the material.

Table 3.1 The Fourth Amendment and Searches and Seizures of Persons

Standard of Justification	*Requirements*	*Scope of Search*
Probable cause.	Reasonable person would conclude that individual has committed a crime.	Full body search for weapons/evidence.
Reasonable suspicion.	Reasonable person would believe that a crime has been or is about to be committed.	Frisk for weapons.
Encounter.	No justification required.	None/may ask for consent.

The U.S. Constitution is intended to promote individual freedom and limits that freedom only to the extent required to protect the safety and security of society. Fourth Amendment seizures follow a simple formula that we will develop in detail in the next few chapters. The greater the interference with an individual's freedom, the greater the factual burden that must be satisfied by the police to justify the stop. An arrest of an individual that may result in the person's being taken into custody, and the accompanying search incident to an arrest for weapons or contraband, requires probable cause. In contrast, a brief investigative stop of an individual may be based on the less demanding standard of reasonable suspicion and permits only the protective frisk of an individual's outer clothing for weapons.

The Supreme Court has recognized a third category of police–citizen interactions that law professors refer to as **encounters**. These are noncoercive and voluntary contacts between the police and citizens that are not regulated by the Fourth Amendment. The Court has observed that not all street contacts between citizens and the police constitute a seizure. There are any number of casual interactions on the street or in a park or in a restaurant that do not restrain an individual's freedom of movement. The Supreme Court has stressed that the police should be free to carry out investigations by briefly questioning individuals in public about suspected criminal activity. In *United States v. Mendenhall* the Court observed that "characterizing every street encounter between a citizen and the police as a 'seizure' . . . would impose wholly unrealistic restrictions upon a wide variety of legitimate law enforcement practices" (446 U.S. 544, 554 [1980]).

Courts analyze the totality of the circumstances to distinguish a **seizure** from an encounter. The distinction at times can be unclear. Consider whether Sylvia Mendenhall's interaction with federal agents was a seizure or an encounter. In *United States v. Mendenhall,* two federal drug agents approached Sylvia Mendenhall in the concourse of the airport in Detroit. They identified themselves and asked to examine her driver's license and airline ticket. The ticket was issued in the name of "Annette Ford." The agents noticed that Mendenhall appeared "shaken" and "nervous" and had difficulty speaking. The agents returned Mendenhall's identification and ticket, and she agreed to accompany them to an office fifty feet from where they were standing. Once inside the office she consented to a body search, which resulted in the seizure of heroin.

The Supreme Court held that this was not a Fourth Amendment seizure. As a result, the officers were not required to establish either probable cause (as would be required if they were to arrest her) or reasonable suspicion (as would be required to stop and frisk her) to justify their decision to approach Mendenhall. Mendenhall had not been seized

> simply by reason of the fact that the agents approached her, asked her if she would show them her ticket and identification and posed a few questions.... Otherwise inoffensive contact between a member of the public and the police cannot, as a matter of law, amount to a seizure of that person.

Examples of circumstances that might indicate a seizure would be the

> threatening presence of several officers, the display of a weapon by an officer, some physical touching... or the use of language or tone of voice indicating that compliance... might be compelled.

The fact that the agents returned Mendenhall's identification and ticket before asking her to accompany them to the office likely was a central consideration in the Supreme Court's analysis.

The lesson is that the police must remain aware of the distinction between seizures and encounters. Note that the federal agents had no firm facts to justify approaching Mendenhall and that if the Supreme Court had ruled that their interaction with Mendenhall constituted a seizure, this would have meant that she had been unlawfully detained, and the drugs would have been inadmissible as the "fruit" of her illegal seizure (*United States v. Mendenhall,* 446 U.S. 544, 553 [1980]).

The recognition that not every contact between a police officer and a citizen is a seizure is consistent with the recommendation of the American Law Institute's *Model Code of Pre-Arraignment Procedure,* which in section 110.1 provides that a law enforcement officer may request an individual to voluntarily

> respond to questions, to appear at a police station, or to comply with any other reasonable request... [and that] compliance with a request... shall not be regarded as involuntary or coerced solely on the ground that such request was made by one known to be a law enforcement officer.

When is an individual seized under the Fourth Amendment? There are two types of seizures: a **physical seizure** of a suspect, and a **show of authority seizure** in which police officers restrain individuals through the display of official authority without the use of actual physical force. Remember that a seizure requires a showing of either probable cause or reasonable suspicion.

- ***Physical seizures.*** A law enforcement officer intentionally takes physical hold of a suspect with the intent to prevent the individual from leaving.
- ***Show of authority seizures.*** Law enforcement officers demonstrate their authority by directing an individual to halt, displaying their weapons, blocking the suspect's movement, or other conduct that would lead a reasonable person not to feel free to leave or otherwise to terminate the encounter. The suspect must actually submit to the demonstration of authority.

In summary, an individual is seized once he or she is physically restrained or once a law enforcement officer acts in a way that would result in a reasonable person not feeling free to leave or to terminate the encounter. In the latter case, the individual must actually submit to the officer's demonstration of authority. As noted, the distinction between a seizure and an encounter is not always crystal clear. Consider the following cases in which the Supreme Court has held that there was no Fourth Amendment seizure.

Factory sweeps. Immigrant and Naturalization Service agents carrying walkie-talkies entered a plant, blocked the exits, and asked workers questions regarding their legal status. The sweep lasted between one and two hours. The Supreme Court noted that the workers were free to move around the plant and that their freedom of movement was restricted by their voluntary commitment to their job rather than by the federal agents (*Immigration and Naturalization Service v. Delgado,* 466 U.S. 210 [1984]).

Bus sweeps. Two sheriff's deputies, one of whom was openly armed, boarded a crowded interstate bus during a stop to pick up passengers and approached Bostick, who was sitting in the back of the bus. The agents asked Bostick a few questions and requested permission to search his luggage. They did not threaten him or display their weapons. Bostick consented and the search revealed illegal narcotics. The Supreme Court held that the question, in light the totality of the circumstances, was whether a reasonable (innocent) person would feel free to decline the officer's request or otherwise terminate the encounter (*Florida v. Bostick,* 501 U.S. 429 [1991]). See also *United States v. Drayton,* 536 U.S. 194 (2002).

Vehicle surveillance. Four officers in a squad car observed a man exit his automobile and approach Michael Chesternut. Chesternut appeared surprised to see the squad car and fled. The officers accelerated and drove alongside Chesternut for a short distance. The officers observed Chesternut discard four packages; one of the officers discovered that these contained unlawful narcotics. The officers did not activate the siren or flashers on their squad car, display weapons, or block Chesternut's movements. The Supreme Court held that Chesternut could not have reasonably concluded that the officers' "mere presence was so intimidating that the particular police conduct as a whole and within the setting of all of the surrounding circumstances" had "in some way restrained his liberty so that he was not free to leave" (*Michigan v. Chesternut,* 486 U.S. 567 [1988]).

The next case in the textbook, *California v. Hodari,* established the legal test for a Fourth Amendment show of force seizure. Four or five juveniles fled as they saw an unmarked police car approach. Officer Jerry Pertoso gave chase, and Hodari claimed that he did not see Pertoso until "he saw Officer Pertoso running towards him." Hodari immediately tossed away what appeared to be a small rock and was tackled, handcuffed, and arrested. The discarded rock was determined to be crack cocaine. Hodari claimed that Officer Pertoso engaged in an unreasonable seizure (lacking reasonable suspicion or probable cause) when he confronted Hodari and that the narcotics should be excluded from evidence as the fruit of the unlawful seizure. The government, on the other hand, argued that Hodari abandoned the drugs and that this provided probable cause to tackle and to seize (arrest) Hodari. In other words, the government's theory was that it was only when Hodari was tackled that he was seized by the officer. Which approach makes more sense? As you read *Hodari,* note how the court's judgment adds an additional requirement to the rule established in *Mendenhall.*

Was Hodari seized when he dropped the drugs?

California v. Hodari, 499 U.S. 821 (1999), Scalia, J.

Facts

Late one evening in April 1988, Officers Brian McColgin and Jerry Pertoso were on patrol in a high-crime area of Oakland, California. They were dressed in street clothes but wearing jackets with "Police" embossed on both front and back. In their unmarked car, they proceeded west on Foothill Boulevard and turned south onto Sixty-Third Avenue. As they rounded the corner, they saw four or five youths huddled around a small red car parked at the curb. When the youths saw the officers' car approaching, they apparently panicked and took flight. The respondent here, Hodari D., and one companion ran west through an alley; the others fled south. The red car also headed south at a high rate of speed.

The officers were suspicious and gave chase. McColgin remained in the car and continued south on Sixty-Third Avenue; Pertoso left the car, ran back north along Sixty-Third, then west on Foothill Boulevard, and turned south on Sixty-Second Avenue. Hodari, meanwhile, emerged from the alley onto Sixty-Second and ran north. Looking behind as he ran, he did not turn and see Pertoso until the officer was almost upon him, whereupon he tossed away what appeared to be a small rock. A moment later, Pertoso tackled Hodari, handcuffed him, and radioed for assistance. Hodari was found to be carrying $130 in cash and a pager, and the rock he had discarded was found to be crack cocaine.

In the juvenile proceeding brought against him, Hodari moved to suppress the evidence relating to the cocaine. The court denied the motion without opinion. The California Court of Appeal reversed, holding that Hodari had been "seized" when he saw Officer Pertoso running toward him, that this seizure was unreasonable under the Fourth Amendment, and that the evidence of cocaine had to be suppressed as the fruit of that illegal seizure. The California Supreme Court denied the State's application for review. We granted certiorari.

Issue

As this case comes to us, the only issue presented is whether, at the time he dropped the drugs, Hodari had been "seized" within the meaning of the Fourth Amendment. If so, respondent argues, the drugs were the fruit of that seizure, and the evidence concerning them was properly excluded. If not, the drugs were abandoned by Hodari and lawfully recovered by the police, and the evidence should have been admitted. (In addition, of course, Pertoso's seeing the rock of cocaine, at least if he recognized it as such, would provide reasonable suspicion for the unquestioned seizure that occurred when he tackled Hodari.)

California conceded that Officer Pertoso did not have the "reasonable suspicion" required to justify stopping Hodari and that it would be unreasonable to stop, for brief inquiry, young men who scatter in panic upon the mere sighting of the police.

We have long understood that the Fourth Amendment's protection against "unreasonable...seizures" includes seizure of the person....The present case...does not involve the application of any physical force; Hodari was untouched by Officer Pertoso at the time he discarded the cocaine. His defense relies instead upon the proposition that a seizure occurs "when the officer, by means of physical force or show of authority, has in some way restrained the liberty of a citizen." Hodari contends (and we accept as true for purposes of this decision) that Pertoso's pursuit qualified as a show of authority when Pertoso called upon Hodari to halt. The narrow question before us is whether, with respect to a show of authority as with respect to application of physical force, a seizure occurs even though the subject does not yield. We hold that it does not.

Reasoning

The language of the Fourth Amendment, of course, cannot sustain respondent's contention. The word "seizure" readily bears the meaning of a laying on of hands or application of physical force to restrain movement, even when it is ultimately unsuccessful. ("She seized the purse-snatcher, but he broke out of her grasp.") It does not remotely apply, however, to the prospect of a policeman yelling "Stop, in the name of the law!" at a fleeing form that continues to flee. That is no seizure....An arrest requires either physical force...or, where that is absent, submission to the assertion of authority.

Mere words will not constitute an arrest, while, on the other hand, no actual, physical touching is essential. The apparent inconsistency in the two parts of this statement is explained by the fact that an assertion of authority and purpose to arrest followed by submission of the arrestee constitutes an arrest. There can be no arrest without either touching or submission.

Respondent contends that his position is sustained by the so-called *Mendenhall* test, formulated by Justice Stewart's opinion in *United States v. Mendenhall* and adopted by the Court in later cases. *Mendenhall* states a necessary, but not a sufficient, condition for seizure—or, more precisely, for seizure effected through a "show of authority." *Mendenhall* establishes that the test of a show of authority is an objective one: not whether the citizen perceived that he was being ordered to restrict his movement but whether the officer's words and actions would have conveyed that to a reasonable person. Application of this objective test was the basis for our decision in the other case principally relied upon by respondent, *Chesternut,* where we concluded that the police cruiser's slow following of the defendant did not convey the message that he was not free to disregard the police and go about his business. We did not address in *Chesternut,* however, the question whether, if the *Mendenhall* test was met—if the message that the defendant was not free to leave had been conveyed—a Fourth Amendment seizure would have occurred.

Quite relevant to the present case, however, was our decision in *Brower v. Inyo County* (489 U.S. 593, 596 [1989]). In that case, police cars with flashing lights had chased the decedent for 20 miles—surely an adequate show of authority—but he did not stop until his fatal crash into a police-erected blockade. The issue was whether his death could be held to be the consequence of an unreasonable seizure in violation of the Fourth Amendment. We did not even consider the possibility that a seizure could have occurred during the course of the chase because, as we explained, that show of authority did not cause the decedent to stop.

Holding

In sum, assuming that Pertoso's pursuit in the present case constituted a show of authority enjoining Hodari to halt, because Hodari did not comply with that injunction, he was not seized until he was tackled. The cocaine abandoned while he was running was in this case not the fruit of a seizure, and his motion to exclude evidence of it was properly denied. We reverse the decision of the California Court of Appeal, and remand for further proceedings not inconsistent with this opinion.

Dissenting, *Stevens, J.*, joined by *Marshall, J.*

The Court's narrow construction of the word "seizure" represents a significant, and in my view, unfortunate, departure from prior case law construing the Fourth Amendment. Almost a quarter of a century ago, in two landmark cases—one broadening the protection of individual privacy, and the other broadening the powers of law enforcement officers—we rejected the method of Fourth Amendment analysis that today's majority endorses. In particular, the Court now adopts a definition of "seizure" that is unfaithful to a long line of Fourth Amendment cases. Even if the Court were defining seizure for the first time, which it is not, the definition that it chooses today is profoundly unwise. In its decision, the Court assumes, without so acknowledging, that a police officer may now fire his weapon at an innocent citizen and not implicate the Fourth Amendment—as long as he misses his target.

For the purposes of decision, the following propositions are not in dispute. First, when Officer Pertoso began his pursuit of respondent, the officer did not have a lawful basis for either stopping or arresting respondent. Second, the officer's chase amounted to a show of authority as soon as respondent saw the officer nearly upon him. Third, the act of discarding the rock of cocaine was the direct consequence of the show of authority. Fourth, as the Court correctly demonstrates, no arrest occurred until the officer tackled respondent. Thus, the Court is quite right in concluding that the abandonment of the rock was not the fruit of an arrest.

In *United States v. Mendenhall*, the Court "adhered to the view that a person is 'seized' only when, by means of physical force or a show of authority, his freedom of movement is restrained." The Court looked to whether the citizen who is questioned "remains free to disregard the questions and walk away," and if she is able to do so, then "there has been no intrusion upon that person's liberty or privacy" that would require some "particularized and objective justification" under the Constitution. The test for a "seizure," as formulated by the Court in *Mendenhall,* was whether, "in view of all of the circumstances surrounding the incident, a reasonable person would have believed that he was not free to leave." Examples of seizures include

> the threatening presence of several officers, the display of a weapon by an officer, some physical touching of the person of the citizen, or the use of language or tone of voice indicating that compliance with the officer's request might be compelled.

The Court's unwillingness today to adhere to the "reasonable person" standard, as formulated by Justice Stewart in *Mendenhall,* marks an unnecessary departure from Fourth Amendment case law.

The Court today draws the novel conclusion that even though no seizure can occur unless the *Mendenhall* reasonable person standard is met, the fact that the standard has been met does not necessarily mean that a seizure has occurred. *Mendenhall*

> states a necessary, but not a sufficient condition for seizure. . . . Whatever else one may think of today's decision, it unquestionably represents a departure from earlier Fourth Amendment case law. . . . Moreover, by narrowing the definition of the term seizure . . . the Court has significantly limited the protection provided to the ordinary citizen by the Fourth Amendment.

Because the facts of this case are somewhat unusual, it is appropriate to note that the same issue would arise if the show of force took the form of a command to "freeze," a warning shot, or the sound of sirens accompanied by a patrol car's flashing lights. In any of these situations, there may be a significant time interval between the initiation of the officer's show of force and the complete submission by the citizen. At least on the facts of this case, the Court concludes that the timing of the seizure is governed by the citizen's reaction, rather than by the officer's conduct. One consequence of this conclusion is that the point at which the interaction between citizen and police officer becomes a seizure occurs not when a reasonable citizen believes he or she is no longer free to go, but, rather, only after the officer exercises control over the citizen.

It is too early to know the consequences of the Court's holding. If carried to its logical conclusion, it will encourage unlawful displays of force that will frighten countless innocent citizens into surrendering whatever privacy rights they may still have. . . . The Court today defines a seizure as commencing not with egregious police conduct, but rather with submission by the citizen. Thus, it both delays the point at which "the Fourth Amendment becomes relevant" to an encounter and limits the range of encounters that will come under the heading of "seizure." Today's qualification of the Fourth Amendment means that innocent citizens may remain "secure in their persons . . . against unreasonable searches and seizures" only at the discretion of the police.

Some sacrifice of freedom always accompanies an expansion in the executive's unreviewable law enforcement powers. A court more sensitive to the purposes of the Fourth Amendment would insist on greater rewards to society before decreeing the sacrifice it makes today. Former Yale law professor Alexander Bickel presciently wrote that "many actions of government have two aspects: their immediate, necessarily intended, practical effects, and their perhaps unintended or unappreciated bearing on values we hold to have more general and permanent interest." The Court's immediate concern with containing criminal activity poses a substantial, though unintended, threat to values that are fundamental and enduring.

Questions for Discussion

1. What is the issue in *Hodari*? Explain the holding of the Supreme Court.
2. How does the holding in *Hodari* modify the rule in *Mendenhall*? Explain how *Hodari* requires both an objective and subjective test for a show of authority seizure. Would an action that constitutes a seizure under the *Hodari* standard also constitute a seizure under the *Mendenhall* standard?
3. Why do Justices Stevens and Marshall write that the judgment "poses a substantial, though unintended, threat to values that are fundamental and enduring"?
4. ***Problems in policing.*** Explain the two tests for a seizure under the Fourth Amendment. In those instances in which a police officer may lack reasonable suspicion or probable cause to stop an individual, describe how a police officer is required to conduct himself or herself when interacting with a suspect.

Cases and Comments

State Law. Connecticut, Massachusetts, Minnesota, New Jersey, New York, Pennsylvania, and Washington State do not follow *Hodari* and continue to adhere to the *Mendenhall* test. In 1998, in *State v. Young,* the Washington State Supreme Court held that the test for a seizure under Article I, Section 7 of the Washington constitution is a "purely objective one, looking to the actions of the law enforcement officer, thus rejecting the test for seizure under the Fourth Amendment articulated by the United States Supreme Court in *California v. Hodari.*"

Deputy Sheriff Robert Carpenter was working in an area with a high incidence of narcotics activity. He stopped and exited his patrol car and approached Kevin Young, whom he did not recognize as living in the neighborhood, and engaged in what the officer described as a "social contact." Officer Carpenter returned to his patrol car and asked for a criminal records check, because he did not know Young. The check revealed that Young had prior narcotics arrests. Carpenter drove away while looking in his rear view mirror. Carpenter saw Young out in the middle of the street. The officer testified that "it appeared to me that he was looking to see if I was leaving the area."

Carpenter drove out of Young's view and then turned his vehicle around and headed back up toward Young. He spotted Young walking at a quick pace. Carpenter accelerated and shined his patrol vehicle spotlight on Young when Young was three or four feet from a tree. Carpenter saw Young walk behind the tree, crouch down, and toss an object the size of a small package near the tree. Young continued walking away from the tree at a fast pace. After he moved a distance from the tree he "stopped running and began walking. Carpenter stopped his patrol car" close to the tree, exited the vehicle, and "asked Young to stop." Then he retrieved the object Young had tossed, which was a charred can that contained a rock-like substance that appeared to be crack cocaine. Carpenter later testified he believed that Young was trying to "dispose of some type of contraband, narcotics or something, that he didn't want me to find on his possession at the time, and I believed that his actions were suspicious enough for me to check what that was."

Young was arrested and charged with the unlawful manufacture of a controlled substance. The evidence was suppressed. The trial court reasoned that Young was stopped at the point that he was illuminated by the spotlight, that at that point Carpenter had no reason to suspect Young was involved in criminal activity, and that Carpenter's detention of Young was unlawful. As a result, the drugs should be excluded from evidence as the result of an unreasonable seizure. The Washington prosecutor appealed on the grounds that, based on the *Hodari* test, there was no seizure under the Fourth Amendment, because Young did not "yield when the spotlight illuminated him." Absent a seizure, Young's discarding the contraband was voluntary and the deputy's recovery of it lawful.

The Washington Supreme Court held that it would continue to follow *Mendenhall* rather than *Hodari* on the grounds that Article I, Section 7 of the Washington State Constitution establishes a high standard for the protection of the privacy of individual citizens. The court held that the focus should be on the conduct of the police rather than on the state of mind and reaction of the citizen to the police conduct. An objective approach that focuses on police conduct provides law enforcement with definite standards to determine whether their conduct constitutes a Fourth Amendment seizure. The Washington Supreme Court applied the *Mendenhall* test and held that Carpenter's shining his spotlight did not constitute the required level of intrusiveness to qualify as a seizure. Carpenter did not activate his siren or emergency lights, he did not draw his weapon, and his squad car did not come screeching to a halt near Young. Shining the light only revealed what was already in plain view.

> The spotlight did not amount to such a show of authority a reasonable person would have believed he or she was not free to leave, not free . . . to keep on walking or continue with whatever activity he or she was then engaged in, until some positive command from Carpenter issued.

Shining the spotlight was a necessary tool to illuminate the scene, and to label this a seizure would unduly handicap the police. Judge Alexander dissented from the judgment of the Washington Supreme Court and argued that Carpenter's turning his car around to confront Young combined with shining the spotlight clearly communicated that the officer was demanding that Young "stop." Judge Alexander analogized shining the spotlight on Young under these circumstances to flashing the vehicle's police lights. The judge expressed concern that placing the bar for a seizure "so high" would permit the police to stop and question citizens without violating the Fourth Amendment. See *Commonwealth v. Young,* 957 P.2d 681 (Wash. 1998).

3.4 YOU DECIDE

Four Buffalo, New York, police officers were patrolling in an unmarked car on June 11, 2002, in search of Kenneth Foster-Brown, who was wanted for dealing drugs. All four officers had encountered Foster-Brown in the past. He was described as an African American male who was five feet eight inches tall and who weighed 145 pounds. Defendant Swindle also is an African American and is six feet one inch tall and at the time weighed 215 pounds.

The officers observed a black Pontiac Bonneville, a type of car that Foster-Brown had previously been seen "near," but had never been known to drive. The officers observed the automobile halting in front of a known drug house that Foster-Brown had frequented in the past. The officers watched an African American male exit the Bonneville, enter the house, leave a short time later, and drive away. The officers were uncertain whether the driver was Foster-Brown.

In fact, the man in the Bonneville was Swindle. The officers followed in their car, and within a minute activated their police lights and ordered Swindle to pull over. Swindle disregarded the order to stop and kept driving. While being pursued, Swindle violated two traffic laws by crossing a double yellow lane divider and driving the wrong way on a one-way street. Swindle also threw a plastic bag out of the car window. The bag was found to contain 33 smaller bags of crack cocaine. Swindle eventually pulled over and then fled on foot. The police apprehended him and placed him under arrest. He was charged with unlawful possession of a controlled substance.

At what point was Swindle seized? Why is it significant when Swindle was seized? See *United States v. Swindle,* 407 F.3d 562 (2nd Cir. 2005).

You can learn what the court decided by referring to the study site, http://www.sagepub.com/lippmancp.

3.5 YOU DECIDE

Two officers of the Washington, D.C., Police Department were driving in an unmarked car in a "high narcotics area." The officers pulled into a parking lot and saw a parked car with two occupants. Johnson was sitting on the passenger's side, and another person was on the driver's side. The officers saw a young woman leaning into the passenger's window who handed Johnson an unidentified object. The officers approached the car, and the woman began to walk away. Officer Michael Fulton saw Johnson make what Fulton described as a "shoving down" motion, leading him to believe that Johnson might be armed. Fulton drew his gun, advised his fellow officer to do the same, and shouted, "Let me see your hands." Johnson did not comply and made "a couple of more shoving motions down" before raising his hands. Fulton reached into the car and felt large, hard objects in Johnson's pocket which he believed to be rocks of crack cocaine. He removed a plastic bag from the pocket that was found to contain 18 rocks of crack cocaine that, together with another rock found in Johnson's clothing, totaled 72 grams.

At what point was Johnson seized? Why is it significant when Johnson was seized? See *United States v. Johnson,* 212 F.3d 1313 (D.C. Cir. 2000).

You can learn what the court decided by referring to the study site, http://www.sagepub.com/lippmancp.

Chapter Summary

The Fourth Amendment was intended to protect individuals against the type of dragnet searches and seizures that were carried out by British colonial authorities through the use of general warrants and writs of assistance. The Fourth Amendment effectively abolishes general warrants and writs of assistance by prohibiting unreasonable searches and seizures and by providing that no warrant shall issue but upon probable cause, particularly describing the place to be searched and the person or things to be seized. The Supreme Court, while expressing a preference for warrants, has recognized that it is reasonable in certain limited circumstances for the police to conduct warrantless searches.

The Supreme Court initially adopted a property rights or trespassory approach to the Fourth Amendment. This protected individuals against physical intrusions or trespasses into their persons, houses, papers, and effects. In 1967, in *Katz v. United States,* the Supreme Court rejected a property rights or trespassory approach and adopted a privacy test for application of the Fourth Amendment. Justice John Harlan in his important concurring opinion in *Katz* established the test for an expectation of privacy. The question is whether an individual exhibits a personal (subjective) expectation of privacy and whether society (objectively) recognizes this expectation as reasonable. An individual is considered to lack a reasonable expectation of privacy in those instances in which he or she turns information over to a third party or where an object or area is accessible to the public.

Commentators question whether the privacy-based approach has increased Fourth Amendment protections. For example, an individual "assumes the risk" that conversations with a government informant in and outside of the home will be overheard or recorded or transmitted to law enforcement authorities. Plain view permits the police to seize items in open fields and to conduct aerial surveillance of curtilage. There also is no expectation of privacy in public areas, in commercial businesses open to the public, or in abandoned objects and trash.

The Supreme Court did draw a firm line of protection at the home in *Kyllo v. United States.* The Court held that the government may not employ heat-sensing technology to obtain information regarding the interior of the home that could not otherwise have been obtained without physical intrusion into the dwelling.

Fourth Amendment seizures of individuals must be based on factual grounds that constitute either probable cause or reasonable suspicion. A seizure may be accomplished by a physical restraint by a show of authority. The show of authority must lead a reasonable person to believe that he or she is not free to leave or to refuse to cooperate, and the individual must actually submit to police authority. The Supreme Court has recognized that not every interaction between the police and citizens constitutes a seizure. The police may engage in informal contacts or encounters without being required to meet the probable cause or reasonable suspicion standard. This provides the police with the flexibility to engage in criminal investigations without being required to satisfy the probable cause or reasonable suspicion requirements of the Fourth Amendment. The line between an encounter and a seizure at times may be difficult to determine. The police run the risk that an encounter will be viewed by a court as constituting a seizure and that any evidence that is uncovered will be excluded on the grounds that the police unreasonably detained a suspect.

In summary, in this chapter we reviewed the requirements for a Fourth Amendment search and a Fourth Amendment seizure. The Supreme Court has struck a balance in Fourth Amendment searches and seizures between the need for the police to detect and investigate crime and individuals' expectation of privacy. Individuals have full Fourth Amendment protection in those areas, such as the home, that have an expectation of privacy that society views as reasonable. On the other hand, areas and objects in plain view do not enjoy an expectation of privacy, and the police are not required to obtain a warrant. These areas generally are accessible to the public or in the case of information or objects have been turned over to a third party. The Supreme Court requires the police to justify seizures on either probable cause or reasonable suspicion. The police, however, may engage in encounters and may question suspects so long as the suspect feels free to leave or to decline to cooperate with the police.

In the next chapters we discuss the requirements for a reasonable search under the Fourth Amendment. Chapter 4 covers reasonable suspicion "stops and frisks," and in the following three chapters, we explore probable cause seizures and searches and "special needs" searches. We complete our coverage of the Fourth Amendment in Chapter 10 with a discussion of the exclusionary rule.

Chapter Review Questions

1. How did the use of general warrants and writs of assistance by British colonial authorities influence the drafting of the text of the Fourth Amendment?
2. Distinguish the property rights or trespassory approach to the Fourth Amendment from the expectation of privacy approach. Which in theory provides individuals with greater protection?
3. What is the legal test for the expectation of privacy established in *Katz v. United States*?
4. Define plain view "searches" and seizures. Describe the relationship between plain view and expectation of privacy.
5. Discuss the expectation of privacy in relation to pen registers, the electronic monitoring of conversations, and trash.

6. Distinguish open fields from curtilage. Why is this significant?
7. What is the importance of the Supreme Court judgment in *Kyllo v. United States*?
8. Describe the difference between physical seizures and show of authority seizures.
9. How do seizures differ from encounters? Why is this distinction significant?
10. What is the holding in *Hodari*? How does this modify the test in *Mendenhall*?

Legal Terminology

abandoned property
curtilage
encounters
expectation of privacy
general warrants
open fields
physical seizure
plain view
probable cause
property rights approach
search
seizure
show of authority seizure
trespassory approach
writs of assistance

Criminal Procedure on the Web

Log on to the Web-based student study site at **http://www.sagepub.com/lippmancp** to assist you in completing the Criminal Procedure on the Web exercises, as well as for additional features such as leading cases, podcasts, self-quizzes, and audio/video links.

1. Read about the threat of contemporary technology to personal privacy and civil liberties.
2. Look at some recent developments and training tips regarding police dogs.
3. See what the FBI Law Enforcement Bulletin has to say about *California v. Greenwood*.

Bibliography

Robert M. Bloom and Mark S. Brodin, *Criminal Procedure: Examples and Explanations,* 4th ed. (New York: Aspen, 2000), pp. 23–44, 74–92. A useful summary with examples and review questions.

Joshua Dressler and Alan C. Michaels, *Understanding Criminal Procedure: Investigation,* vol. 1, 4th ed. (Newark, NJ: LexisNexis, 2006), pp. 69–119. An excellent discussion of searches and seizures with reference to the leading cases.

Wayne R. LaFave, Jerold H. Israel, and Nancy J. King, *Criminal Procedure,* 4th ed. (St. Paul, MN: West Publishing, 2004), pp. 127–141, 217–219. A brief but comprehensive review of searches and seizures with citations to the leading cases.

Donald A. Sklansky, "*Katz v. United States:* The Limits of Aphorism," in *Criminal Procedure Stories,* Carol S. Streiker, Ed. (New York: Foundation, 2006), pp. 223–260. A history of *Katz v. United States* with a discussion of developments in the law of electronic surveillance.

4 Stop and Frisk

Was the stop and frisk of Wardlow lawful?

On September 9, 1995, Officers Nolan and Harvey were working as uniformed officers in the special operations section of the Chicago Police Department. The officers were driving the last car of a four-car caravan converging on an area known for heavy narcotics trafficking in order to investigate drug transactions.... Officer Nolan observed respondent Wardlow standing next to the building holding an opaque bag. Respondent looked in the direction of the officers and fled. Nolan and Harvey turned their car southbound, watched him as he ran through the gangway and an alley, and eventually cornered him on the street. Nolan then exited his car and stopped respondent. Nolan immediately conducted a protective pat-down search for weapons because in his experience it was common for there to be weapons in the near vicinity of narcotics transactions. During the frisk, Officer Nolan squeezed the bag respondent was carrying and felt a heavy, hard object similar to the shape of a gun. The officer then opened the bag and discovered a .38-caliber handgun with five live rounds of ammunition. The officers arrested Wardlow.

Core Concepts and Summary Statements

Introduction

A. In *Terry v. Ohio,* the Supreme Court held that the Fourth Amendment Reasonableness Clause should be interpreted to provide for police stops and frisks without warrants or probable cause.

B. The Court held that stops and frisks under the Fourth Amendment Reasonableness Clause are based on an objective weighing and balancing of the interest in crime detection and investigation against the limited intrusion on individual liberty.

C. These stops are distinguished from custodial arrests by their narrow investigative purpose and limited intrusion on individual liberty and therefore may be based on the lesser standard of reasonable suspicion rather than probable cause. *Terry* took the additional step of holding that officers are entitled to conduct frisks to protect themselves in those instances in which they possess reasonable grounds to believe that the suspect is armed and presently dangerous.

Reasonable Suspicion

A. The police officer, in justifying the intrusion, must present specific and articulable facts that, together with rational inferences drawn from those facts, reasonably suggest that an individual has committed a crime or is about to commit a crime.

B. This is an objective test, and the facts are to be evaluated based on the totality of the circumstances in light of the officer's experience.

C. The Supreme Court has recognized that "articulating what reasonable suspicion means is not possible." It is a "fluid concept" that must be evaluated in a "particular context." Several factors, in combination with other factors, have been held to be relevant to the determination of reasonable suspicion. These include a pattern of activity indicative of criminal conduct, the time of day, whether the suspect is observed in a high-crime area and is known by the police officer to have a criminal record, whether the suspect is nervous or uncooperative or flees from the police, and whether the police officer has experience in making arrests for this type of activity.

Informants and Hearsay

A. The judge asks whether the informant is known to the police and how the informant obtained the information. An informant with firsthand knowledge of criminal activity should be able to provide detailed information.

B. A tip that cannot be supported on these grounds may be relied on where corroborated in essential details by the police. Most important is the police determination that the informant was able to predict a suspect's future conduct.

C. The judge strikes a balance. In those instances in which an informant is not known to the police, the court may require that the informant provide detailed information. A tip from an informant who is not known to a police officer may be strengthened by police corroboration as well as by the fact that the informant came forward personally and that a state criminal statute punishes intentionally "false criminal reports."

Drug Courier Profiles

A. Law enforcement officials have developed profiles to assist in detecting and investigating individuals who may be engaged in criminal conduct. The first profiles were developed to detect trafficking in illegal narcotics.
B. Courts generally do not give special weight to the claim that an individual fits a "profile" and, instead, merely ask whether the combination of the factors identified in the profile constitutes reasonable suspicion that a suspect is engaged in criminal conduct.

Race and Reasonable Suspicion

A. The police may not stop an individual when the only reason for his or her seizure is race, ethnicity, gender, religion, or other protected descriptive characteristic.
B. An individual may not be stopped based on "incongruity" or the fact that he or she "does not belong in a neighborhood."
C. Race, ethnicity, or some other objective characteristic may be considered as one of several factors that together support a finding of reasonable suspicion that crime may be afoot.

The Scope and Duration of a *Terry* Stop

A. A *Terry* stop and frisk is a limited intrusion to investigate and to detect crime. It is a basic constitutional principle that law enforcement officers may interfere with an individual's freedom and privacy only to the extent required to accomplish their purpose. A *Terry* stop is subject to legal challenge in those instances in which a suspect is treated as if he or she has been subjected to a probable cause arrest rather than to a reasonable suspicion stop. This inquiry typically focuses on three areas.
B. A *Terry* stop does not permit the involuntary and significant movement of a suspect unless required by reasons of safety and security. A suspect detained on reasonable suspicion generally cannot be removed to police headquarters.
C. A *Terry* stop must be for a limited duration. A suspect cannot be subjected to a lengthy interrogation.
D. In determining whether the police have carried out the *Terry* stop and frisk in a reasonable manner, courts inquire whether the investigative methods employed were the least intrusive means reasonably available to verify or to dispel the officer's suspicions in a brief period of time. A suspect ordinarily may not be detained by force or threat of force, handcuffed, or locked in a patrol car.

Frisks

A. The Supreme Court in *Terry v. Ohio* recognized that American criminals have a "long tradition of armed violence" and that a number of law enforcement officers are killed and wounded each year in the line of duty. The Court accordingly ruled that where "nothing in the initial stages of the encounter serves to dispel [an officer's] reasonable fear for his own or others' safety, he is entitled for the protection of himself and others in the area to conduct a carefully limited search of the outer clothing of such persons in an attempt to discover weapons which might be used to assault him."
B. In 1983, in *Michigan v. Long,* the Supreme Court extended *Terry* frisks to the passenger compartment of automobiles in those instances in which a police officer possesses a reasonable fear for his or her safety.
C. In *Minnesota v. Dickerson,* the Supreme Court affirmed the limited right of a police officer conducting a frisk to seize illegal narcotics. The officer must have immediate probable cause to believe that the items he or she encounters are illegal narcotics.

Introduction

The text of the Fourth Amendment appears to indicate that a seizure and search of an individual must be based on a warrant founded on probable cause. In 1968, in *Terry v. Ohio,* the U.S. Supreme Court confronted the issue whether individuals may be lawfully stopped and frisked under the Fourth Amendment based on reasonable suspicion. The practice of stopping, interrogating, and frisking individuals without probable cause had been part of the arsenal of local and state law enforcement officers for decades. Reliance on this tactic increased in the late 1960s in reaction to demonstrations over civil rights, the Vietnam War, protests against conditions on college campuses, a rising crime rate, and violent confrontations between police and various self-proclaimed radical groups. States like New York passed statutes explicitly authorizing the police to "stop any person" who is reasonably suspected of engaging or being about to engage in criminal activity and to carry out a search to protect "life or limb" (N.Y. Code Crim. Proc. 180-a [1964]). In 1967, the Presidential Commission on Law Enforcement and the Administration of Justice recommended that in view of the rising crime rate, the state legislatures of the fifty states should provide the police with the clear authority to stop, frisk, and question individuals on a standard of less than probable cause.

Civil libertarians objected that in the past, seizures of individuals on less than probable cause had been employed to harass the homeless, minorities, and political activists.

Law enforcement authorities responded that it would be unreasonable to tell the officer on the beat that he or she is prohibited from stopping an individual who the officer suspects is engaged in criminal activity or about to commit a crime or who the officer suspects has recently completed a crime. On the other hand, Justice William Douglas warned that abandoning the probable cause standard was a step down a "totalitarian path" and that the "hydraulic pressure" of events would lead to the evaporation of civil liberties.

The Supreme Court in the past had resisted efforts to weaken Fourth Amendment protections and had held that a "reasonable search" under the Fourth Amendment required a warrant founded on probable cause or on probable cause in those instances in which time did not permit the police to obtain a warrant (*Henry v. United States*, 361 U.S. 98 [1959]). *Terry v. Ohio* broke new ground and employed a balancing test to establish that brief investigative stops of individuals may be based on reasonable suspicion. The Court explained that field interrogations are essential for investigating and detecting street crimes. These stops are distinguished from custodial arrests by their narrow investigative purpose and limited intrusion on individual liberty and therefore may be based on the lesser standard of reasonable suspicion rather than probable cause. *Terry* took the additional step of holding that an officer is entitled to conduct a frisk to protect himself or herself in those instances in which he or she possesses reasonable grounds to believe that a suspect is armed and presently dangerous. The central holding of *Terry* is summarized below.

- ***Reasonable suspicion and warrant clauses.*** The Fourth Amendment prohibition against "unreasonable searches and seizures" and the Fourth Amendment provision that no warrants shall issue but upon probable cause should no longer be interpreted to mean that searches not based on a warrant founded on probable cause are unreasonable and unlawful under the Fourth Amendment. The Reasonableness Clause authorizes the police to conduct investigative stops and frisks based on reasonable suspicion.
- ***Balancing.*** The *Terry* reasonable suspicion standard for stops and frisks is based on balancing the interest in swift action by an officer on the beat to detect, investigate, and prevent crime against the slight intrusion on the privacy of the individual citizen.

In this chapter, we cover the following topics in reviewing the law of stop and frisk.

- ***Reasonable suspicion.*** Individuals may be seized (stopped) based on reasonable suspicion.
- ***Informants and hearsay.*** The police may rely on informants and hearsay to reach a conclusion that there is reasonable suspicion to stop an individual.
- ***Race and reasonable suspicion.*** A stop may not be based solely on race, ethnicity, or religion. These characteristics may constitute one factor that, along with other factors, constitutes reasonable suspicion.
- ***The scope and duration of a* Terry *stop.*** *Terry* stops are limited in the permissible movement of a suspect and in duration and purpose.
- ***Automobiles and* Terry *stops.*** The police may direct the driver and passengers to exit an automobile during an investigative stop.
- ***Frisks.*** The police may conduct a frisk of a suspect's outer clothing for weapons. This has been extended to passenger compartments and to frisks for drugs.

Reasonable Suspicion

The Balancing Test

Terry v. Ohio was the first case in which the Supreme Court approved a search and seizure of an individual in a criminal case under the Fourth Amendment based on reasonable suspicion.

Chief Justice Earl Warren writing for the majority in *Terry* held that a police officer may in "appropriate circumstances" approach a suspect to investigate possible criminal behavior despite the fact that the officer does not have probable cause to make an arrest. The standard for these investigative stops is **reasonable suspicion**.

The reasonable suspicion standard was derived by *balancing* the need for swift action by an officer to investigate and to detect crime against the modest intrusion on individual privacy. The Supreme Court reasoned that requiring an officer to wait until he or she has developed probable cause would place society at risk. A suspect's interest in being free from unreasonable searches and seizures is adequately protected by requiring that the facts relied on by the police officer are to be judged against the objective standard of whether the facts available to the officer at the moment of the seizure "warrant a man of reasonable caution in the belief that the action taken was appropriate." As we shall see in the next section, Justice Warren applied this reasonable suspicion test to determine the lawfulness of the **stop and frisk** of the suspects in *Terry*.

Reasonable Suspicion and *Terry v. Ohio*

Plainclothes detective Martin McFadden, a thirty-nine-year veteran of the Cleveland, Ohio, police department, observed Chilton and Terry standing on the corner of the downtown streets of Huron Road and Euclid Avenue. The men took turns walking southwest on Huron, looking in a store window, and then returning to the street corner. Each of the men repeated this routine roughly five or six times. At one point, they were joined by a third man, Katz. Katz then left and walked west on Euclid Avenue. He thereafter was joined by Chilton and Terry. At this point, McFadden confronted the three men and asked their names. The men "mumbled something," and McFadden patted down the outside of their clothing and discovered a revolver in Terry's pocket and a revolver in the outer pocket of Chilton's overcoat. McFadden later explained that he had concluded that the three men were "casing a job, a stick-up."

Justice Warren stressed that McFadden observed the three men engage in a "series of acts," each of which may have been "innocent in itself, but which taken together warranted further investigation." He noted that "[i]t would have been poor police work indeed for an officer of thirty years' experience in the detection of thievery from stores in the same neighborhood to have failed to investigate this behavior."

We all likely would agree that McFadden reasonably concluded that although the three men were acting legally, they may have been planning a crime. However, we might get a different result by changing the facts. For instance, we might ask how many times Chilton and Terry would have to walk past the store to arouse reasonable suspicion. The case does not discuss whether McFadden took the race or appearance of the men into consideration. Would McFadden's decision be less persuasive had he approached a group of well-dressed businessmen or individuals who he knew lived in the neighborhood?

The Reasonable Suspicion Determination

The Supreme Court provided guidance in *Terry* for the methodology to use in determining reasonable suspicion in future cases. Keep in mind that each situation confronting the police is different and that the facts that give rise to reasonable suspicion cannot be "reduced to a neat set of legal rules." The determination of reasonable suspicion is a **case-by-case determination.**

Articulable suspicion. A police officer, in justifying an intrusion, must present *specific and articulable facts* that, together with rational inferences drawn from those facts, reasonably suggest that an individual has committed a crime or is about to commit a crime. This is termed **articulable suspicion.**

Objective standard. The facts are to be judged in accordance with a *reasonable person* standard and not based on what the officer (subjectively) believed. Police officers may not rely on a hunch, generalization, or stereotype. This would open the door to discrimination and to the evaporation of individuals' right to be free from unreasonable searches and seizures under the Fourth Amendment.

Experience and expertise. The facts are to be interpreted in light of an *officer's experience and training.* McFadden was a thirty-nine-year veteran of the police and was aware that the store that the three men were "casing" had been the target of recent robberies.

Informants. As discussed later in the chapter, reasonable suspicion may be based on information from a reliable informant or on information from an anonymous **informant** who provides information that is corroborated (found to be correct) by law enforcement officers (*Alabama v. White,* 496 U.S. 325 [1990]).

Totality of the circumstances. The entire factual situation is to be taken into account in determining whether there is reasonable suspicion. Courts consider factors such as whether the suspect is calm or nervous, whether the suspect is observed in a high-crime area, the time of day, the number of arrests for a particular type of crime made in the vicinity by the officer in the past, the suspect's willingness to cooperate with the police, and whether the suspect's pattern of behavior suggests that he or she may be engaged in criminal conduct. The evidence "must be seen and weighed not in terms of library analysis by scholars, but as understood by those versed in the field of law enforcement" (*United States v. Cortez,* 449 U.S. 411, 418 [1981]).

Probabilities. Reasonable suspicion is based on probabilities rather than certainties. The Supreme Court, in *United States v. Arvizu,* observed that while each of the factors relied on by the police officer viewed individually "undoubtedly [were] susceptible to innocent explanation. . . [t]aken together. . . they sufficed to form a particularized and objective basis for. . . stopping the vehicle, making the stop reasonable within the meaning of the Fourth Amendment" (*United States v. Arvizu,* 534 U.S. 266, 277–278 [2002]).

Probable cause and reasonable suspicion. The Supreme Court has clarified that probable cause means "a fair probability that contraband or evidence of a crime will be found." The reasonable suspicion standard, in contrast, is "less demanding" than probable cause and requires "at least a minimal level of objective justification for making the stop. . . . The officer must be able to articulate more than. . . unparticularized suspicion or [a] 'hunch' of criminal activity" (*Illinois v. Wardlow,* 528 U.S. 119 [2000]).

Facts Constituting Reasonable Suspicion

Judges have found reasonable suspicion to justify a *Terry* stop in a variety of situations. This determination often is like a "puzzle" in which the officer must connect a number of innocent acts together to determine whether there is reasonable suspicion to justify a Fourth Amendment seizure. The Supreme Court has recognized that "articulating what reasonable suspicion means is not possible." It is a "fluid concept" that must be evaluated in a "particular context" (*Ornelas v. United States,* 517 U.S. 690, 694 [1996]). The following are some of the factors that in combination with other factors have been held to constitute reasonable suspicion.

- ***Criminal activity.*** Acts that may indicate criminal activity such as casing a store as in *Terry* or an exchange of money on the street.
- ***Time.*** Acts that take place at a time of day in which criminal activity is likely to occur. This may involve loading an unmarked van at a warehouse late at night.
- ***Location.*** A high-crime area or an area that is characterized by a particular type of criminal conduct.
- ***Criminal record.*** Police officer awareness of the individual's arrest record or record of criminal involvement.
- ***Evasion.*** Fleeing from or evading the police.
- ***Noncooperation.*** Noncooperation when approached or questioned.
- ***Nervous.*** Acting nervous during the encounter with police.
- ***Experience.*** Police officer's experience in making arrests for the type of activity.

Consider some cases in which courts found that the police possessed reasonable suspicion to stop a suspect. Can you identify the factors that the police relied on in finding reasonable suspicion?

- The suspect smelled strongly of the illegal narcotic PCP, the suspect appeared nervous, the area was widely known for heavy drug trafficking, and the officers knew that drug traffickers would hide PCP in or near apartment complex dumpsters. One of the officers had made eighty-five PCP-related arrests in the apartment complex (*U.S. v. Foster,* 376 F.3d 577 [6th Cir. 2004]).
- An officer observed an illegally parked vehicle, and an individual emerged from a restaurant, glanced at the officer, hurried to the vehicle, and started to drive away. After being stopped by the police officer for a parking violation, the driver gave the officer an expired as well as a valid driver's license. The suspect was sweating and nervous and evasive when asked direct questions. Although it was late April, the driver wore a thick down coat with a hole in the inseam that the officer concluded could be used to conceal drugs. In addition, feathers were falling out of a hole in the coat's lining that the officer believed might be designed to hide a weapon. A frisk revealed a weapon and narcotics (*State v. DeValle,* 2006 Conn. Super. LEXIS 484 [Super. Ct. Conn. 2006]).
- Uniformed officers John Prilla and Ronald Absten were in a convenience store. Prilla remarked that a customer appeared to be carrying a firearm in the right front pocket of his three-quarter-length leather jacket. Absten then made his own assessment based on Bureau of Alcohol, Tobacco, and Firearms training on identifying armed individuals and types of firearms. He detected the outline of a small handgun in the defendant's right pocket and observed that the pocket hung lower than its opposite pocket, indicating that it contained a weighty object. The defendant was described as carrying the gun in a manner that differed from individuals who are accustomed to possessing a licensed firearm. The suspect also looked nervously over his shoulder at the officers and continually placed his hand on his pocket. Absten had made arrests of individuals in the past who carried illegal firearms in their jackets or pants. The defendant exited the store, and the officers directed him to raise his hands above his head and to place them on his head. The officers then conducted a frisk and discovered a firearm (*Commonwealth v. Stevenson,* 894 A.2d 759 [Sup. Ct. Pa. 2006]).
- Border patrol agent Rudy Sanchez was patrolling the Texas–Mexican border and stopped a vehicle that he suspected to be and, in fact, was carrying illegal immigrants. Sanchez, who was an experienced agent, observed Quintanta-Garcia driving the type of SUV with tinted windows that was favored by smugglers. Quintanta-Garcia was speeding and noticeably slowed his automobile when he spotted Sanchez's patrol car. This particular highway was favored by smugglers because there was no permanent checkpoint. Sanchez was particularly alert because smugglers had learned to cross the border in the early afternoon when there were fewer agents deployed. Quintanta-Garcia's vehicle carried Mexican license plates and had entered the United States in an area that was primarily frequented by domestic American drivers (*United States v. Quintanta-Garcia,* 343 F.3d 1266 [10th Cir. 2003]).

As you read *Terry,* the next case in the textbook, pay attention to the reasoning of the Supreme Court in finding legal support in the Fourth Amendment for detentions based on reasonable suspicion rather than probable cause. You also should note the policy considerations underlying the judgment. The second part of the *Terry* decision discusses frisks, which we will discuss at the end of the chapter.

Some critics contend that *Terry* has provided the police with too much discretion to stop individuals and that, as a result, a significant number of innocent individuals are seized by the police. In the alternative, you might take the position that *Terry* stops rarely inconvenience the relatively small number of individuals who are detained and that the police should be accorded an even greater degree of authority to detain individuals (*Brown v. Texas,* 443 U.S. 47 [1979]).

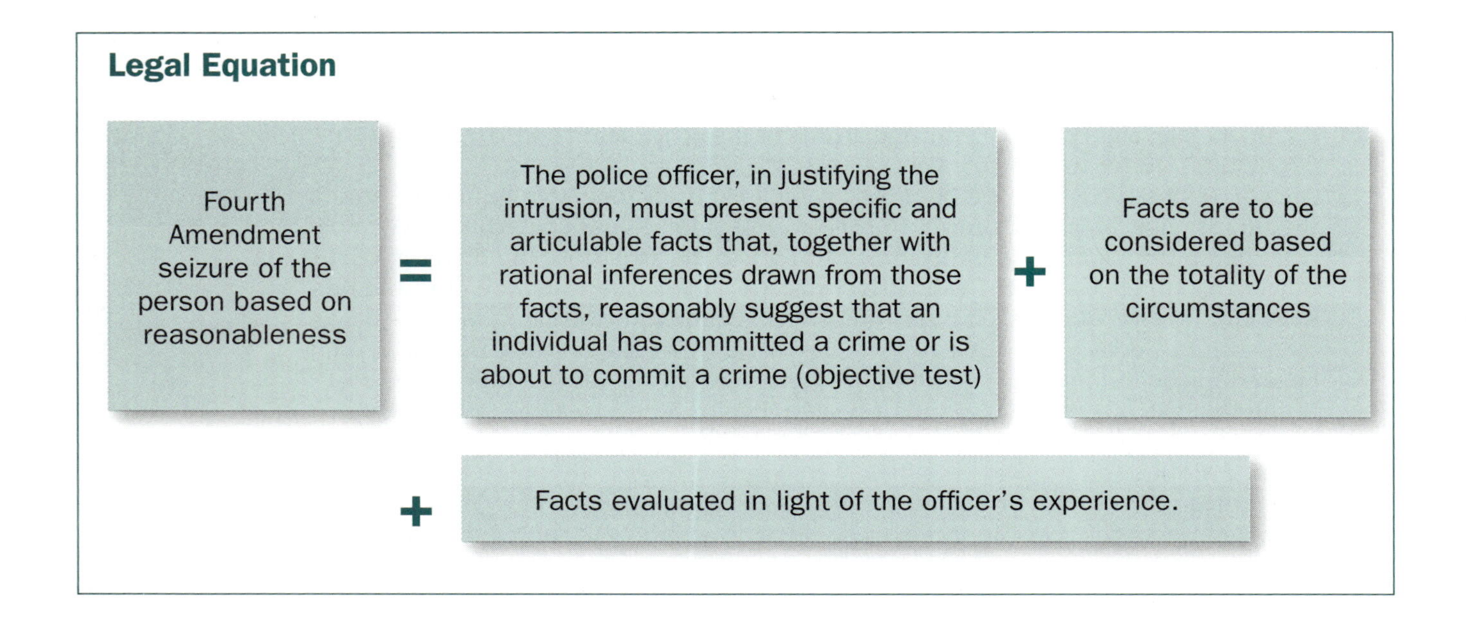

Was McFadden's stop and frisk of Terry justified under the Fourth Amendment?

Terry v. Ohio, 392 U.S. 1 (1968), Warren, J.

Facts

Petitioner Terry was convicted of carrying a concealed weapon and sentenced to the statutorily prescribed term of one to three years in the penitentiary. Following the denial of a pretrial motion to suppress, the prosecution introduced into evidence two revolvers and a number of bullets seized from Terry and co-defendant Richard Chilton, by Cleveland Police Detective Martin McFadden. At the hearing on the motion to suppress this evidence, Officer McFadden testified that while he was patrolling in plain clothes in downtown Cleveland at approximately 2:30 in the afternoon of October 31, 1963, his attention was attracted by two men, Chilton and Terry, standing on the corner of Huron Road and Euclid Avenue. He had never seen the two men before, and he was unable to say precisely what first drew his eye to them. However, he testified that he had been a policeman for thirty-nine years and a detective for thirty-five and that he had been assigned to patrol this vicinity of downtown Cleveland for shoplifters and pickpockets for thirty years. He explained that he had developed routine habits of observation over the years and that he would "stand and watch people or walk and watch people at many intervals of the day." He added, "Now, in this case when I looked over they didn't look right to me at the time."

His interest aroused, Officer McFadden took up a post of observation in the entrance to a store 300 to 400 feet away from the two men. "I get more purpose to watch them when I seen their movements," he testified. He saw one of the men leave the other one and walk southwest on Huron Road, past some stores. The man paused for a moment and looked in a store window, then walked on a short distance, turned around and walked back toward the corner, pausing once again to look in the same store window. He rejoined his companion at the corner, and the two conferred briefly. Then the second man went through the same series of motions, strolling down Huron Road, looking in the same window, walking on a short distance, turning back, peering in the store window again, and returning to confer with the first man at the corner. The two men repeated this ritual alternately between five and six times apiece—in all, roughly a dozen trips. At one point, while the two were standing together on the corner, a third man approached them and engaged them briefly in conversation. This man then left the two others and walked west on Euclid Avenue. Chilton and Terry resumed their measured pacing, peering, and conferring. After this had gone on for 10 to 12 minutes, the two men walked off together, heading west on Euclid Avenue, following the path taken earlier by the third man.

By this time, Officer McFadden had become thoroughly suspicious. He testified that after observing their elaborately casual and oft-repeated reconnaissance of the store window on Huron Road, he suspected the two men of "casing a job, a stick-up" and that he considered it his duty as a police officer to investigate further. He added that he feared "they may have a gun." Thus, Officer McFadden followed Chilton and Terry and saw them stop in front of Zucker's store to talk to the same man who had conferred with them earlier on the street corner. Deciding that the situation was ripe for direct action, Officer McFadden approached the three men, identified himself as a police officer and asked for their names. At this point, his knowledge was confined to what he had observed. He was not acquainted with any of the three men by name or by sight, and he had received no information concerning them from any other source. When the men "mumbled something" in response to his inquiries, Officer McFadden grabbed petitioner Terry, spun him around so that they were facing the other two, with Terry between McFadden and the others, and patted down the outside of his clothing. In the left breast pocket of Terry's overcoat, Officer McFadden felt a pistol. He reached inside the overcoat pocket but was unable to remove the gun. At this point, keeping Terry between himself and the others, the officer ordered all three men to enter Zucker's store. As they went in, he removed Terry's overcoat completely, removed a .38-caliber revolver from the pocket and ordered all three men to face the wall with their hands raised. Officer McFadden proceeded to pat down the outer clothing of Chilton and the third man, Katz. He discovered another revolver in the outer pocket of Chilton's overcoat, but no weapons were found on Katz. The officer testified that he only patted the men down to see whether they had weapons and that he did not put his hands beneath the outer garments of either Terry or Chilton until he felt their guns. So far as appears from the record, he never placed his hands beneath Katz's outer garments. Officer McFadden seized Chilton's gun, asked the proprietor of the store to call a police wagon, and took all three men to the station, where Chilton and Terry were formally charged with carrying concealed weapons.

Issue

Unquestionably, petitioner was entitled to the protection of the Fourth Amendment as he walked down the street in Cleveland. The question is whether in all the circumstances of this on-the-street encounter, his right to personal security was violated by an unreasonable search and seizure. We would be less than candid if we did not acknowledge that this question thrusts to the fore difficult and troublesome issues regarding a sensitive area of police activity—issues which have never before been squarely presented to this Court. Reflective of the tensions involved are the practical and constitutional arguments pressed with great vigor on both sides of the public debate over the power of the police to "stop and frisk"—as it is sometimes euphemistically termed—suspicious persons.

On the one hand, it is frequently argued that in dealing with the rapidly unfolding and often dangerous situations on city streets, the police are in need of an escalating set of flexible responses, graduated in relation to the amount of information they possess. For this purpose, it is urged that distinctions should be made between a "stop" and an "arrest" (or a "seizure" of a person), and between a "frisk" and a "search." Thus, it is argued, the police should be allowed to "stop" a person and detain him briefly for questioning upon suspicion that he may be connected with criminal activity. Upon suspicion that the person may be armed, the police should have the power to "frisk" him for weapons. If the "stop" and the "frisk" give rise to probable cause to believe that the suspect has committed a crime, then the police should be empowered to make a formal "arrest," and a full incident "search" of the person. This scheme is justified in part upon the notion that a "stop" and a "frisk" amount to a mere "minor inconvenience and petty indignity," which can properly be imposed upon the citizen in the interest of effective law enforcement on the basis of a police officer's suspicion.

On the other side, the argument is made that the authority of the police must be strictly circumscribed by the law of arrest and search as it has developed to date in the traditional jurisprudence of the Fourth Amendment.... Acquiescence by the courts in the compulsion inherent in the field interrogation practices at issue here, it is urged, would constitute an abdication of judicial control over, and indeed an encouragement of, substantial interference with liberty and personal security by police officers whose judgment is necessarily colored by their primary involvement in "the often competitive enterprise of ferreting out crime." This, it is argued, can only serve to exacerbate police–community tensions in the crowded centers of our Nation's cities.

Reasoning

In this context, we approach the issues in this case mindful of the limitations of the judicial function in controlling the myriad daily situations in which policemen and citizens confront each other on the street. The State has characterized the issue here as "the right of a police officer . . . to make an on-the-street stop, interrogate and pat down for weapons (known in street vernacular as 'stop and frisk')." But this is only partly accurate. For the issue is not the abstract propriety of the police conduct, but the admissibility against petitioner of the evidence uncovered by the search and seizure. Ever since its inception, the rule excluding evidence seized in violation of the Fourth Amendment has been recognized as a principal mode of discouraging lawless police conduct. Thus, its major thrust is a deterrent one, and experience has taught that it is the only effective deterrent to police misconduct in the criminal context and that, without it, the constitutional guarantee against unreasonable searches and seizures would be a mere "form of words." The rule also serves another vital function—"the imperative of judicial integrity." Courts which sit under our Constitution cannot and will not be made party to lawless invasions of the constitutional rights of citizens by permitting unhindered governmental use of the fruits of such invasions. Thus, in our system, evidentiary rulings provide the context in which the judicial process of inclusion and exclusion approves some conduct as comporting with constitutional guarantees and disapproves other actions by state agents. A ruling admitting evidence in a criminal trial, we recognize, has the necessary effect of legitimizing the conduct which produced the evidence, while an application of the exclusionary rule withholds the constitutional imprimatur.

The exclusionary rule has its limitations, however, as a tool of judicial control.... Doubtless, some police "field interrogation" conduct violates the Fourth Amendment. But a stern refusal by this Court to condone such activity does not necessarily render it responsive to the exclusionary rule. Regardless of how effective the rule may be where obtaining convictions is an important objective of the police, it is powerless to deter invasions of constitutionally guaranteed rights where the police either have no interest in prosecuting or are willing to forgo successful prosecution in the interest of serving some other goal.... The wholesale harassment by certain elements of the police community, of which minority groups, particularly Negroes, frequently complain, will not be stopped by the exclusion of any evidence from any criminal trial. Under our decision, courts still retain their traditional responsibility to guard against police conduct which is overbearing or harassing, or which trenches upon personal security without the objective evidentiary justification which the Constitution requires. When such conduct is identified, it must be condemned by the judiciary and its fruits must be excluded from evidence in criminal trials....

Our first task is to establish at what point in this encounter the Fourth Amendment becomes relevant. That is, we must decide whether and when Officer McFadden "seized" Terry and whether and when he conducted a "search." There is some suggestion in the use of such terms as *stop* and *frisk* that such police conduct is outside the purview of the Fourth Amendment because neither action rises to the level of a "search" or "seizure" within the meaning of the Constitution. We emphatically reject this notion. It is quite plain that the Fourth Amendment governs "seizures" of the person which do not eventuate in a trip to the station house and prosecution for crime—"arrests" in traditional terminology. It must be recognized that whenever a police officer accosts an individual and restrains his freedom to walk away, he has "seized" that person. And it is nothing less than sheer torture of the English language to suggest that a careful exploration of the outer surfaces of a person's clothing all over his or her body in an attempt to find weapons is not a "search." Moreover, it is simply fantastic to urge that such a procedure performed in public by a policeman while the citizen stands helpless, perhaps facing a wall with his hands raised, is a "petty indignity." It is a serious intrusion upon the sanctity of the person, which may inflict great indignity and arouse strong resentment, and it is not to be undertaken lightly.... We therefore reject the notion that the Fourth Amendment does not come into play at all as a limitation upon police conduct if the officers stop short of something called a "technical arrest" or a "full-blown search."

In this case, there can be no question, then, that Officer McFadden "seized" petitioner and subjected him to a "search" when he took hold of him and patted down the outer surfaces of his clothing. We must decide whether at that point it was reasonable for Officer McFadden to have interfered with petitioner's personal security as he did. And, in determining whether the seizure and search were "unreasonable," our inquiry is a dual one—whether the officer's action was justified at its inception and whether it was reasonably related in scope to the circumstances which justified the interference in the first place.

If this case involved police conduct subject to the Warrant Clause of the Fourth Amendment, we would have to ascertain whether "probable cause" existed to justify the search and seizure which took place. However, that is not the case. We do not retreat from our holdings that the police must, whenever practicable, obtain advance judicial approval of searches and seizures through the warrant procedure or that, in most instances, failure to comply with the warrant requirement can only be excused by exigent circumstances. But we deal here with an entire rubric of police conduct—necessarily swift action predicated upon the on-the-spot observations of the officer on the beat—which historically has not been, and as a practical matter could not be, subjected to the warrant procedure. Instead, the conduct involved in this case must be tested by the Fourth Amendment's general proscription against unreasonable searches and seizures.

Nonetheless, the notions which underlie both the warrant procedure and the requirement of probable cause remain fully relevant in this context. In order to assess the reasonableness of Officer McFadden's conduct as a general proposition, it is necessary "first to focus upon the governmental interest which allegedly justifies official intrusion upon the constitutionally protected interests of the private citizen," for there is "no ready test for determining reasonableness other than by balancing the need to search [or seize] against the invasion which the search [or seizure] entails." And, in justifying the particular intrusion, the police officer must be able to point to specific and articulable facts which, taken together with rational inferences from those facts, reasonably warrant that intrusion. The scheme of the Fourth Amendment becomes meaningful only when it is assured that at some point, the conduct of those charged with enforcing the laws can be subjected to the more detached, neutral scrutiny of a judge who must evaluate the reasonableness of a particular search or seizure in light of the particular circumstances. And, in making that assessment, it is imperative that the facts be judged against an objective standard: Would the facts available to the officer at the moment of the seizure or the search "warrant a man of reasonable caution in the belief" that the action taken was appropriate? Anything less would invite intrusions upon constitutionally guaranteed rights based on nothing more substantial than inarticulate hunches, a result this Court has consistently refused to sanction. And simple "'good faith on the part of the arresting officer is not enough.'... If subjective good faith alone were the test, the protections of the Fourth Amendment would evaporate, and the people would be 'secure in their persons, houses, papers, and effects,' only in the discretion of the police."

Applying these principles to this case, we consider first the nature and extent of the governmental interests involved. One general interest is of course that of effective crime prevention and detection; it is this interest which underlies the recognition that a police officer may in appropriate circumstances and in an appropriate manner approach a person for purposes of investigating possibly criminal behavior even though there is no probable cause to make an arrest. It was this legitimate investigative function Officer McFadden was discharging when he decided to approach petitioner and his companions. He had observed Terry, Chilton, and Katz go through a series of acts, each of them perhaps innocent in itself, but which taken together warranted further investigation. There is nothing unusual in two men standing together on a street corner, perhaps waiting for someone. Nor is there anything suspicious about people in such circumstances strolling up and down the street, singly or in pairs. Store windows, moreover, are made to be looked in. But the story is quite different where, as here, two men hover about a street corner for an extended period of time, at the end of which it becomes apparent that they are not waiting for anyone or anything; where these men pace alternately along an identical route, pausing to stare in the same store window roughly twenty-four times; where each completion of this route is followed immediately by a conference between the two men on the corner; where they are joined in one of these conferences by a third man who leaves swiftly; and where the two men finally follow the third and rejoin him a couple of blocks away. It would have been poor police work indeed for an officer of thirty years' experience in the detection of thievery from stores in this same neighborhood to have failed to investigate this behavior further.

The crux of this case, however, is not the propriety of Officer McFadden's taking steps to investigate petitioner's suspicious behavior, but rather, whether there was justification for McFadden's invasion of Terry's personal security by searching him for weapons in the course of that investigation. We are now concerned with more than the governmental interest in investigating crime; in addition, there is the more immediate interest of the police officer in taking steps to assure himself that the person with whom he is dealing is not armed with a weapon that could unexpectedly and fatally be used against him. Certainly it would be unreasonable to require that police officers take unnecessary risks in the performance of their duties. American criminals have a long tradition of armed violence, and every year in this country, many law enforcement officers are killed in the line of duty, and thousands more are wounded. Virtually all of these deaths and a substantial portion of the injuries are inflicted with guns and knives.

In view of these facts, we cannot blind ourselves to the need for law enforcement officers to protect themselves and other prospective victims of violence in situations where they may lack probable cause for an arrest. When an officer is justified in believing that the individual whose suspicious behavior he is investigating at close range is armed and presently dangerous to the officer or to others, it would appear to be clearly unreasonable to deny the officer the power to take necessary measures to determine whether the person is in fact carrying a weapon and to neutralize the threat of physical harm.

We must still consider, however, the nature and quality of the intrusion on individual rights which must be accepted if police officers are to be conceded the right to search for weapons in situations where probable cause to arrest for crime is lacking. Even a limited search of the outer clothing for weapons constitutes a severe, though brief, intrusion upon cherished personal security, and it must surely be an annoying, frightening, and perhaps humiliating experience.... A search for weapons in the absence of probable cause to arrest... must, like any other search, be strictly circumscribed by the exigencies which justify its initiation. Thus, it must be limited to that which is necessary for the discovery of weapons, which might be used to harm the officer or others nearby, and may realistically be characterized as something less than a "full" search, even though it remains a serious intrusion.

Our evaluation of the proper balance that has to be struck in this type of case leads us to conclude that there must be a narrowly drawn authority to permit a reasonable search for weapons for the protection of the police officer, where he has reason to believe that he is dealing with an armed and dangerous individual, regardless of whether he has probable cause to arrest the individual for a crime. The officer need not be absolutely certain that the individual is armed; the issue is whether a reasonably prudent man in the circumstances would be warranted in the belief that his safety or that of others was in danger. And in determining whether the officer acted reasonably in such circumstances, due weight must be given, not to his inchoate and unparticularized suspicion or "hunch," but to the specific reasonable inferences which he is entitled to draw from the facts in light of his experience.

We must now examine the conduct of Officer McFadden in this case to determine whether his search and seizure of petitioner were reasonable, both at their inception and as conducted. He had observed Terry, together with Chilton and another man, acting in a manner he took to be preface to a "stick-up." We think on the facts and circumstances Officer McFadden detailed before the trial judge, a reasonably prudent man would have been warranted in believing petitioner was armed and thus presented a threat to the officer's safety while he was investigating his suspicious behavior. The actions of Terry and Chilton were consistent with McFadden's hypothesis that these men were contemplating a daylight robbery—which, it is reasonable to assume, would be likely to involve the use of weapons—and nothing in their conduct from the time he first noticed them until the time he confronted them and identified himself as a police officer gave him sufficient reason to negate that hypothesis. Although the trio had departed the original scene, there was nothing to indicate abandonment of an intent to commit a robbery at some point. Thus, when Officer McFadden approached the three men gathered before the display window at Zucker's store, he had observed enough to make it quite reasonable to fear that they were armed; and nothing in their response to his hailing them, identifying himself as a police officer, and asking their names served to dispel that reasonable belief. We cannot say his decision at that point to seize Terry and pat his clothing for weapons was the product of a volatile or inventive imagination, or was undertaken simply as an act of harassment; the record evidences the tempered act of a policeman who in the course of an investigation had to make a quick decision as to how to protect himself and others from possible danger, and took limited steps to do so.... Officer McFadden confined his search strictly to what was minimally necessary to learn whether the men were armed and to disarm them once he discovered the weapons. He did not conduct a general exploratory search for whatever evidence of criminal activity he might find.

Holding

We conclude that the revolver seized from Terry was properly admitted in evidence against him. At the time he seized petitioner and searched him for weapons, Officer McFadden had reasonable grounds to believe that petitioner was armed and dangerous, and it was necessary for the protection of himself and others to take swift measures to discover the true facts and neutralize the threat of harm if it materialized. The policeman carefully restricted his search to what was appropriate to the discovery of the particular items which he sought. Each case of this sort will, of course, have to be decided on its own facts. We merely hold today that where a police officer observes unusual conduct which leads him reasonably to conclude in light of his experience that criminal activity may be afoot and that the persons with whom he is dealing may be armed and presently dangerous, where in the course of investigating this behavior he identifies himself as a policeman and makes reasonable inquiries, and where nothing in the initial stages of the encounter serves to dispel his reasonable fear for his own or others' safety, he is entitled for the protection of himself and others in the area to conduct a carefully limited search of the outer clothing of such persons in an attempt to discover weapons which might be used to assault him. Such a search is a reasonable search under the Fourth Amendment, and any weapons seized may properly be introduced in evidence against the person from whom they were taken.

Dissenting, *Douglas, J.*

The infringement on personal liberty of any "seizure" of a person can only be "reasonable" under the Fourth Amendment if we require the police to possess "probable cause" before they seize him. Only that line draws a meaningful distinction between an officer's mere inkling and the presence of facts within the officer's personal knowledge which would convince a reasonable man that the person seized has committed, is omitting, or is about to commit a particular crime.... Until the Fourth Amendment... is rewritten, the person and the effects of the individual are beyond the reach of all government agencies until there are reasonable grounds to believe (probable cause) that a criminal venture has been launched or is about to be launched.

There have been powerful hydraulic pressures throughout our history that bear heavily on the Court to water down constitutional guarantees and give the police the upper hand. That hydraulic pressure has probably never been greater than it is today.

Yet if the individual is no longer to be sovereign, if the police can pick him up whenever they do not like the cut of his jib, if they can "seize" and "search" him in their discretion, we enter a new regime. The decision to enter it should be made only after a full debate by the people of this country.

Questions for Discussion

1. Discuss the importance of the Supreme Court decision in *Terry v. Ohio*.
2. Why did the Supreme Court state that the ruling in *Terry* would not prevent police harassment of minority groups?
3. What is the significance of the Supreme Court's holding that stops and frisks fall within the Fourth Amendment?
4. Discuss the various factors that the Supreme Court weighed and balanced in concluding that stops and frisks were reasonable seizures and searches under the Fourth Amendment.
5. When may a police officer subject a suspect to a frisk? Why is an officer limited to a frisk for weapons and not authorized to conduct a full search?
6. What would be the consequences of adopting Justice Douglas's approach to the Fourth Amendment?
7. Are judges able to effectively supervise the police to insure that they follow the standards established in *Terry*?
8. ***Problems in policing.*** What are the factors that Officer McFadden considered in determining that there was reasonable suspicion to stop and frisk the three suspects? Do you agree that there was reasonable suspicion to seize the suspects? What other factors should alert a law enforcement officer that "crime is afoot"? List some factors that a police officer should consider in determining whether to conduct a frisk for weapons.

The next case in the text, *State v. Wardlow,* raises the issue of whether "unprovoked flight" from the police constitutes reasonable suspicion to seize an individual. The decision illustrates the type of factual analysis that courts undertake in determining whether there is reasonable suspicion. Do you agree with the dissent that the fact that Wardlow is an African American is relevant to the question whether there was reasonable suspicion?

Did Wardlow's fleeing from the police constitute reasonable suspicion?

State v. Wardlow, 528 U.S. 119 (2000), Rehnquist, C.J.

Facts

On September 9, 1995, Officers Nolan and Harvey were working as uniformed officers in the special operations section of the Chicago Police Department. The officers were driving the last car of a four-car caravan converging on an area known for heavy narcotics trafficking in order to investigate drug transactions. The officers were traveling together because they expected to find a crowd of people in the area, including lookouts and customers.

As the caravan passed 4035 West Van Buren, Officer Nolan observed respondent Wardlow standing next to the building holding an opaque bag. Respondent looked in the direction of the officers and fled. Nolan and Harvey turned their car southbound, watched him as he ran through the gangway and an alley, and eventually cornered him on the street. Nolan then exited his car and stopped respondent. He immediately conducted a protective pat-down search for weapons because in his experience it was common for there to be weapons in the near vicinity of narcotics transactions. During the frisk, Officer Nolan squeezed the bag respondent was carrying and felt a heavy, hard object similar to the shape of a gun. The officer then opened the bag and discovered a .38-caliber handgun with five live rounds of ammunition. The officers arrested Wardlow.

The Illinois trial court denied respondent's motion to suppress, finding the gun was recovered during a lawful stop and frisk. Following a stipulated bench trial, Wardlow was convicted of unlawful use of a weapon by a felon. The Illinois Appellate Court reversed Wardlow's conviction, concluding that the gun should have been suppressed because Officer Nolan did not have reasonable suspicion sufficient to justify an investigative stop pursuant to *Terry v. Ohio.* The Illinois Supreme Court agreed. While rejecting the appellate court's conclusion that Wardlow was not in a high crime area, the Illinois Supreme Court determined that sudden flight in such an area does not create a reasonable suspicion justifying a *Terry* stop. The court explained that although police have the right to approach individuals and ask questions, the individual has no obligation to respond. The person may decline to answer and simply go on his or her way, and the refusal to respond, alone, does not provide a legitimate basis for an investigative stop. The court then determined that flight may simply be an exercise of this right to "go on one's way" and, thus, could not constitute reasonable suspicion justifying a *Terry* stop.

The Illinois Supreme Court also rejected the argument that flight combined with the fact that it occurred in a high crime area supported a finding of reasonable suspicion because the "high crime area" factor was not sufficient standing alone to justify a *Terry* stop. Finding no independently suspicious circumstances to support an investigatory detention, the court held that the stop and subsequent arrest violated the Fourth Amendment.

Issue

The state courts have differed on whether unprovoked flight is sufficient grounds to constitute reasonable suspicion. This case, involving a brief encounter between a citizen and a police officer on a public street, is governed by the analysis we first applied in *Terry.* We granted certiorari solely on the question of whether the initial stop was supported by reasonable suspicion. Therefore, we express no opinion as to the lawfulness of the frisk independently of the stop.

Reasoning

Nolan and Harvey were among eight officers in a four-car caravan that was converging on an area known for heavy narcotics trafficking, and the officers anticipated encountering a large number of people in the area, including drug customers and individuals serving as lookouts. It was in this context that Officer Nolan decided to investigate Wardlow after observing him flee. An individual's presence in an area of expected criminal activity, standing alone, is not enough to support a reasonable, particularized suspicion that the person is committing a crime. But officers are not required to ignore the relevant characteristics of a location in determining whether the circumstances are sufficiently suspicious to warrant further investigation. Accordingly, we have previously noted the fact that the stop occurred in a "high crime area" among the relevant contextual considerations in a *Terry* analysis.

In this case, moreover, it was not merely respondent's presence in an area of heavy narcotics trafficking that aroused the officers' suspicion but his unprovoked flight upon noticing the police. Our cases have also recognized that nervous, evasive behavior is a pertinent factor in determining reasonable suspicion. Headlong flight—wherever it occurs—is the consummate act of evasion: It is not necessarily indicative of wrongdoing, but it is certainly suggestive of such. In reviewing the propriety of an officer's conduct, courts do not have available empirical studies dealing with inferences drawn from suspicious behavior, and we cannot reasonably demand scientific certainty from judges or law enforcement officers where none exists. Thus, the determination of reasonable suspicion must be based on commonsense judgments and inferences about human behavior. We conclude Officer Nolan was justified in suspecting that Wardlow was involved in criminal activity and, therefore, in investigating further.

When an officer, without reasonable suspicion or probable cause, approaches an individual, the individual has a right to ignore the police and go about his business. And any "refusal to cooperate, without more, does not furnish the minimal level of objective justification needed for a detention or seizure." But unprovoked flight is simply not a mere refusal to cooperate. Flight, by its very nature, is not "going about one's business"; in fact, it is just the opposite. Allowing officers confronted with such flight to stop the fugitive and investigate further is quite consistent with the individual's right to go about his business or to stay put and remain silent in the face of police questioning.

Respondent . . . also argue[s] that there are innocent reasons for flight from police and that, therefore, flight is not necessarily indicative of ongoing criminal activity. This fact is undoubtedly true, but does not establish a violation of the Fourth Amendment. Even in *Terry*, the conduct justifying the stop was ambiguous and susceptible of an innocent explanation. The officer observed two individuals pacing back and forth in front of a store, peering into the window and periodically conferring. All of this conduct was by itself lawful, but it also suggested that the individuals were casing the store for a planned robbery. *Terry* recognized that the officers could detain the individuals to resolve the ambiguity. In allowing such detentions, *Terry* accepts the risk that officers may stop innocent people. Indeed, the Fourth Amendment accepts that risk in connection with more drastic police action; persons arrested and detained on probable cause to believe they have committed a crime may turn out to be innocent. The *Terry* stop is a far more minimal intrusion, simply allowing the officer to briefly investigate further. If the officer does not learn facts rising to the level of probable cause, the individual must be allowed to go on his way. But in this case the officers found respondent in possession of a handgun, and arrested him for violation of an Illinois firearms statute. No question of the propriety of the arrest itself is before us.

The judgment of the Supreme Court of Illinois is reversed, and the cause is remanded for further proceedings not inconsistent with this opinion.

Concurring in part and dissenting in part, *Stevens, J.*, joined by *Souter, J.*, *Ginsburg, J.*, and *Breyer, J.*

It is a matter of common knowledge that men who are entirely innocent do sometimes fly from the scene of a crime through fear of being apprehended as the guilty parties, or from an unwillingness to appear as witnesses. Nor is it true as an accepted axiom of criminal law that "the wicked flee when no man pursueth, but the righteous are as bold as a lion." Innocent men sometimes hesitate to confront a jury—not necessarily because they fear that the jury will not protect them, but because they do not wish their names to appear in connection with criminal acts, are humiliated at being obliged to incur the popular odium of an arrest and trial, or because they do not wish to be put to the annoyance or expense of defending themselves. In addition to these concerns, a reasonable person may conclude that an officer's sudden appearance indicates nearby criminal activity. And where there is criminal activity, there is also a substantial element of danger—either from the criminal or from a confrontation between the criminal and the police. These considerations can lead to an innocent and understandable desire to quit the vicinity with all speed.

Among some citizens, particularly minorities and those residing in high crime areas, there is also the possibility that the fleeing person is entirely innocent but, with or without justification, believes that contact with the police can itself be dangerous, apart from any criminal activity associated with the officer's sudden presence. For such a person, unprovoked flight is neither "aberrant" nor "abnormal." Moreover, these concerns and fears are known to the police officers themselves and are validated by law enforcement investigations into their own practices. Accordingly, the evidence supporting the reasonableness of these beliefs is too pervasive to be dismissed as random or rare and too persuasive to be disparaged as inconclusive or insufficient. In any event, just as we do not require "scientific certainty" for our commonsense conclusion that unprovoked flight can sometimes indicate suspicious motives, neither do we require scientific certainty to conclude that unprovoked flight can occur for other, innocent reasons.

Taking into account these and other innocent motivations for unprovoked flight leads me to reject Illinois' requested *per se* rule in favor of adhering to a totality-of-the-circumstances test. This conclusion does not, as Illinois suggests, "establish a separate *Terry* analysis based on the individual characteristics of the person seized." My rejection of a *per se* rule, of course, applies to members of all races.

It is true, as Illinois points out, that *Terry* approved of the stop-and-frisk procedure notwithstanding "the wholesale harassment by certain elements of the police community, of which minority groups, particularly Negroes, frequently complain." But in this passage, *Terry* simply held that such concerns would not preclude the use of the stop-and-frisk procedure altogether. Nowhere did *Terry* suggest that such concerns cannot inform a court's assessment of whether reasonable suspicion sufficient to justify a particular stop existed.

The probative force of the inferences to be drawn from flight is a function of the varied circumstances in which it occurs. Sometimes those inferences are entirely consistent with the presumption of innocence, sometimes they justify further investigation, and sometimes they justify an immediate stop and search for weapons. These considerations have led us to avoid categorical rules concerning a person's flight and the presumptions to be drawn therefrom: "Unprovoked flight," in short, describes a category of activity too broad and varied to permit a *per se* reasonable inference regarding the motivation for the activity. While the innocent explanations surely do not establish that the Fourth Amendment is always violated whenever someone is stopped solely on the basis of an unprovoked flight, neither do the suspicious motivations establish that the Fourth Amendment is never violated when a *Terry* stop is predicated on that fact alone. For these reasons, the Court is surely correct in refusing to embrace either *per se* rule advocated by the parties. The totality of the circumstances, as always, must dictate the result.

Guided by that totality-of-the-circumstances test, the Court concludes that Officer Nolan had reasonable suspicion to stop respondent. In this respect, my view differs from the Court's. The entire justification for the stop is articulated in the brief testimony of Officer Nolan. Some facts are perfectly clear; others are not. This factual insufficiency leads me to conclude that the Court's judgment is mistaken.

Respondent Wardlow was arrested a few minutes after noon on September 9, 1995. Nolan was part of an eight-officer, four-car caravan patrol team. The officers were headed for "one of the areas in the 11th District [of Chicago] that's high [in] narcotics traffic." The reason why four cars were in the caravan was that "normally in these different areas there's an enormous amount of people, sometimes lookouts, customers." Officer Nolan testified that he was in uniform on that day, but he did not recall whether he was driving a marked or an unmarked car.

Officer Nolan and his partner were in the last of the four patrol cars that "were all caravaning eastbound down Van Buren." Nolan first observed respondent "in front of 4035 West Van Buren." Wardlow "looked in our direction and began fleeing." Nolan then "began driving southbound down the street observing [respondent] running through the gangway and the alley southbound," and observed that Wardlow was carrying a white, opaque bag under his arm. After the car turned south and intercepted respondent as he "ran right towards us," Officer Nolan stopped him and conducted a "protective search," which revealed that the bag under respondent's arm contained a loaded handgun.

This terse testimony is most noticeable for what it fails to reveal. Though asked whether he was in a marked or unmarked car, Officer Nolan could not recall the answer. He was not asked whether any of the other three cars in the caravan were marked, or whether any of the other seven officers were in uniform. Though he explained that the size of the caravan was because "normally in these different areas there's an enormous amount of people, sometimes lookouts, customers," Officer Nolan did not testify as to whether anyone besides Wardlow was nearby 4035 West Van Buren. Nor is it clear that that address was the intended destination of the caravan. As the Appellate Court of Illinois interpreted the record, "it appears that the officers were simply driving by, on their way to some unidentified location, when they noticed defendant standing at 4035 West Van Buren." Officer Nolan's testimony also does not reveal how fast the officers were driving. It does not indicate whether he saw respondent notice the other patrol cars. And it does not say whether the caravan, or any part of it, had already passed Wardlow by before he began to run.

Indeed, the appellate court thought the record was even "too vague to support the inference that . . . defendant's flight was related to his expectation of police focus on him." Presumably, respondent did not react to the first three cars, and we cannot even be sure that he recognized the occupants of the fourth as police officers. The adverse inference is based entirely on the officer's statement, "He looked in our direction and began fleeing."

No other factors sufficiently support a finding of reasonable suspicion. Though respondent was carrying a white, opaque bag under his arm, there is nothing at all suspicious about that. Certainly the time of day—shortly after noon—does not support Illinois' argument. Nor were the officers "responding to any call or report of suspicious activity in the area." Officer Nolan did testify that he expected to find "an enormous amount of people," including drug customers or lookouts, and the Court points out that "it was in this context that Officer Nolan decided to investigate Wardlow after observing him flee." This observation, in my view, lends insufficient weight to the reasonable suspicion analysis; indeed, in light of the absence of testimony that anyone else was nearby when respondent began to run, this observation points in the opposite direction.

The State, along with the majority of the Court, relies as well on the assumption that this flight occurred in a high crime area. Even if that assumption is accurate, it is insufficient because even in a high crime neighborhood, unprovoked flight does not invariably lead to reasonable suspicion. On the contrary, because many factors providing innocent motivations for unprovoked flight are concentrated in high crime areas, the character of the neighborhood arguably makes an inference of guilt less appropriate, rather than more so. Like unprovoked flight itself, presence in a high crime neighborhood is a fact too generic and susceptible to innocent explanation to satisfy the reasonable suspicion inquiry.

It is the State's burden to articulate facts sufficient to support reasonable suspicion. In my judgment, Illinois has failed to discharge that burden. I am not persuaded that the mere fact that someone standing on a sidewalk looked in the direction of a passing car before starting to run is sufficient to justify a forcible stop and frisk.

Questions for Discussion

1. What was the decision of the Illinois Supreme Court? Why did the U.S. Supreme Court reverse this judgment?
2. Did the U.S. Supreme Court consider factors other than flight in determining whether there was reasonable suspicion to stop Wardlow?
3. Summarize the dissenting argument of Justice Stevens. Would you vote with the majority or with the dissenting judges?
4. ***Problems in policing.*** As a police officer, what factors in combination with flight would you consider to justify stopping a suspect?

4.1 YOU DECIDE

Officers Bickerton and Conway spotted defendant DePeiza walking along the sidewalk while holding his cell phone with his left hand and talking. DePeiza's right arm was stiff and pressed to his side. Based on their experience and training, the officers concluded that his manner of walking was characteristic of individuals carrying a firearm and that additional investigation was required. They activated their vehicle's blue lights and pulled their unmarked automobile alongside DePeiza. Bickerton asked DePeiza if he was from the area, where he was coming from, and where he was going.

The officers were in plain clothes and displayed their badges at chest level. DePeiza explained that he lived in New York and was visiting his family in a Boston suburb. He attempted to shield his right side from view throughout the conversation, avoided eye contact, and nervously shifted his weight from side to side. Bickerton exited the police vehicle, and the defendant voluntarily produced his license, which Conway checked on the computer. The two officers observed that the right pocket of DePeiza's jacket was tilted to the side, indicating that it held a weighty object. Bickerton twice attempted to frisk DePeiza, who on both occasions moved to avoid the search. Bickerton grabbed the defendant's right jacket pocket and felt the handle of a gun. Bickerton removed an unlicensed firearm. The confrontation between the police and DePeiza took place in an area characterized by gun violence. The Massachusetts Court of Appeal held that a "stop" occurred when the officers declared their intent to frisk the defendant. Did the officers have reasonable suspicion to stop DePeiza. See *Commonwealth v. DePeiza,* 848 N.E.3d 429 (Mass. App. Ct. 2007).

You can find the answer by referring to the study site, http://www.sagepub.com/lippmancp.

Informants and Hearsay

Reasonable suspicion may be based on a police officer's direct observations or on information from an **informant,** victim, eyewitness, or police bulletin. Information that is obtained in this "secondhand fashion," rather than through a police officer's direct observation, is a *hearsay report.* The classic example is a bloody victim who flags down a squad car and describes the identity of his or her attacker. In other circumstances, the police understandably may have less confidence in hearsay information. Consider a police officer who is informed by an anonymous phone caller that there is an individual wearing a baseball cap selling narcotics on a street corner across from an elementary school. Would it make a difference if the caller stated that the alleged "drug dealer" is armed?

In *Adams v. Williams,* Sergeant John Connolly was on patrol in a high-crime area of Bridgeport, Connecticut. Sergeant Connolly was approached by an individual "known to Connolly who reported that an individual in a nearby vehicle possessed narcotics and was carrying a gun at his waist." Connolly tapped on the window of the automobile and requested that Williams, the driver, open the door of the vehicle. Williams reacted by rolling down the window, and Connolly immediately reached into the car and removed a loaded revolver from Williams's waist (*Adams v. Williams,* 407 U.S. 143, 144–145 [1972]).

The U.S. Supreme Court confronted the question whether reasonable suspicion may be based on the hearsay report of an informant. The Court held that the tip possessed sufficient *"indicia of reliability"* to justify Connolly's acting on the informant's tip. The informant was known to the officer and had provided information in the past. The informant also came forward personally to provide information that was immediately verifiable at the scene. This was particularly important because Connecticut law provided that it was a crime to make a "false complaint."

The Supreme Court stressed that Connolly properly relied on a *credible informant* and that the police also may justifiably rely on information provided by the victim of a street crime. However, "[s]ome tips, completely lacking in indicia of reliability, would either warrant no police response or require further investigation before a forcible stop of a suspect would be authorized." The Court cautioned that while the informant's unverified tip in *Williams* would have been insufficient to establish probable cause for a narcotics arrest or search warrant, the information carried enough indicia of reliability to justify the officer's investigative stop of Williams (146–147).

The Supreme Court observed in *Adams v. Williams* that the informant's tip was "stronger" than "an anonymous telephone tip." This raises the question whether the police may rely on an **anonymous tip.** This was the precise issue that confronted the court in *Alabama v. White*. Officer Davis of the Montgomery, Alabama, police received an anonymous phone call stating that Vanessa White would be leaving 235-C Lynwood Terrace Apartments in a brown Plymouth station wagon with the right tail light lens broken, that she would be going to Dobey's Motel, and that she would be in possession of roughly an ounce of cocaine inside a brown attaché case. Officers Davis and Reynolds immediately placed Lynwood Terrace under surveillance and observed White leave the 235 building without a briefcase and enter a station wagon. They followed White as she headed toward the Dobey Motel and pulled her over before she reached her destination. The officers seized a locked brown attaché case that was in the automobile, received consent to open the case, and found marijuana. Did the police have reasonable suspicion to stop White (*Alabama v. White,* 496 U.S. 325, 327 [1990])?

The Supreme Court observed in *White* that *Adams v. Williams* established that reasonable suspicion is a "less demanding standard than probable cause" and may be based on less complete and less reliable information than is required for probable cause. The Supreme Court applied a totality-of-the-circumstances test that stressed two critical considerations. First, is the informant reliable (trustworthy), and second, what is the "basis of [his or her] knowledge"? In this instance, the police knew nothing about the informant, and there was no basis to determine whether the anonymous tip satisfied either of these considerations (330).

The Supreme Court nevertheless ruled that the police possessed reasonable suspicion to stop White based on their corroboration of the facts provided by the informant. On the one hand, the police were unable to verify the name of the woman leaving the building, the apartment from which she left, or whether she was carrying a brown attaché case. On the other hand, the informant made a number of accurate predictions. This included the building from which the defendant left, the general time of departure, the type of automobile, and the driver's apparent destination. The Court, in particular, stressed that "because only a small number of people are generally privy to an individual's itinerary, it is reasonable for police to believe that a person with access to such information is likely to also have access to reliable information about that individual's illegal activities." The Supreme Court held that although this is a "close case," under the totality of the circumstances, the anonymous tip, as corroborated by the police, exhibited sufficient indicia of reliability (332).

Justices Stevens, Brennan, and Marshall objected that an anonymous neighbor with a grudge could have provided the information relied on by the police. An unethical police officer also could fabricate the existence of an anonymous informant and falsely claim that he or she was able to corroborate the informant's account. The decision, in the view of the dissenting judges, undermines and "makes a mockery" of the protections accorded to individuals under the Fourth Amendment (333). Would you have voted with the majority or with the dissenting judges? Do you believe that courts should approve police reliance on informants whose identity and background is unknown to the police?

In summary, the Supreme Court in *Adams v. Williams* and in *Alabama v. White* established that a police officer under certain circumstances may rely on an informant's tip to establish reasonable suspicion.

- ***Reliability.*** The judge asks whether the informant is known to the officer and considers whether the informant has been accurate in the past. The court will consider whether there is a statute that makes it a crime to make a false complaint and whether the informant personally approached the police.
- ***Basis of knowledge.*** The judge also asks how the informant has obtained the information. An informant with firsthand knowledge of criminal activity should be able to provide detailed information.
- ***Police corroboration.*** A tip that lacks these two indicia of reliability may be relied on where corroborated in essential details by the police. Most important is the informant's ability to predict a suspect's future conduct.
- ***Totality of the circumstances.*** The judge strikes a balance. The less reliable the informant, the more a court may insist that the informant is in the position to provide detailed information. A tip that is thought to lack the indicia of reliability may be strengthened by police corroboration, by the fact that the informant came forward personally, and by a criminal statute that punishes intentionally "false criminal reports."

In 1984, in *United States v. Hensley,* the Supreme Court decided an additional case that approved of police reliance on hearsay. The Court held that Kentucky police were justified in stopping an individual based on a "wanted bulletin" issued by police in Ohio so long as the officers issuing the bulletin themselves possessed facts supporting a *Terry* stop. Relying on a "wanted bulletin" is similar to basing a stop on hearsay information from an informant (*United States v. Hensley,* 469 U.S. 221 [1985]).

You will find *Florida v. J.L.* on the study site. In this case, the Supreme Court is asked to determine whether the police are justified in relying on an anonymous tip that a suspect reportedly is in possession of a firearm. What if the police receive an anonymous tip that one of several individuals on a street corner is about to ignite a terrorist bomb in the downtown area of a major city? Are the police required to passively wait to determine whether there is an explosion, or is there a "firearms exception" that justifies the police in taking immediate action?

You can find Alabama v. White *and* Florida v. J.L. *on the study site, http://www.sagepub.com/lippmancp.*

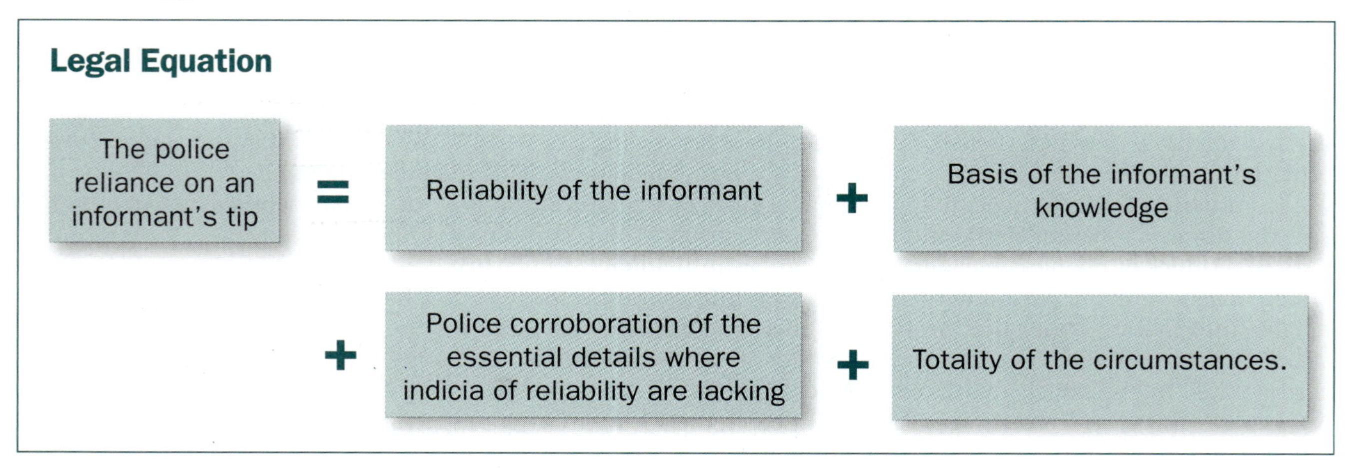

4.2 YOU DECIDE

California Highway Patrol Officer Julian Irigoyen received a police dispatch based on an anonymous tip that reported that a driver who possibly may be intoxicated was "weaving all over the roadway." The vehicle was described as a 1980s model blue van traveling northbound on Highway 99 at Airport Drive, north of Bakersfield. Officer Irigoyen was headed southbound three to four miles north of that location, with only one entry/exit ramp between his position and the reported location of the van. Officer Irigoyen positioned himself on the shoulder of northbound Highway 99 and waited for the vehicle to pass. Officer Irigoyen spotted a blue van traveling roughly fifty miles per hour within three or four minutes. He activated his patrol car lights and stopped the van to investigate whether the driver was intoxicated. Officer Irigoyen did not observe the van weaving, speeding, or otherwise violating any traffic regulations. Susan Wells, the driver of the car, was described by Officer Irigoyen as having constricted pupils and a dry mouth. Officer Irigoyen asked Wells to exit the vehicle and reported that she was becoming increasingly nervous. He concluded that Wells was under the influence of illegal drugs, requested her to undertake field sobriety tests, and soon thereafter, placed her under arrest for driving under the influence. Wells later tested positive for illegal narcotics. Considering the totality of the circumstances, do you think Officer Irigoyen was justified in stopping Wells? See *People v. Wells*, 136 P.3d 801 (Cal. 2006). The decisions of state and federal courts in regard to whether an anonymous report of reckless driving provides sufficient indicia of reliability to justify a stop are discussed in *U.S. v. Wheat*, 278 F.3d 722 (8th Cir. 2001).

You can find the answer by referring to the study site, http://www.sagepub.com/lippmancp.

Drug Courier Profiles

Law enforcement officers have developed profiles to assist in detecting and investigating criminal conduct. An officer relying on a profile compares an individual's actions to the behavior pattern in the profile. A match between an individual's pattern of activity and the profile is thought to provide reasonable suspicion.

Profiles typically are based on an analysis of the behavior of individuals who have been arrested in the past for crimes such as air hijacking and illegal immigration. The first profiles were developed to detect trafficking in illegal narcotics. Primary credit is given to Drug Enforcement Agent Paul J. Markonni in Atlanta. He identified seven primary characteristics and four secondary characteristics that comprise the "Markonni drug courier profile" (*United States v. Elmore,* 595 F.2d 1036, 1039 [5th Cir. 1979]).

The seven primary characteristics of the Markonni drug profile are (1) arriving from or departing to an identified source city; (2) carrying little or no luggage or large quantities of empty suitcases; (3) having an unusual itinerary, such as a rapid turnaround time for a very lengthy airplane trip; (4) using an alias; (5) carrying an unusually large amount of currency; (6) purchasing airline tickets with small denominations of currency; and (7) displaying unusual nervousness. The secondary characteristics are (1) almost exclusively using public transportation, particularly taxicabs, in departing from the airport; (2) immediately making a telephone call after deplaning; (3) leaving a false or fictitious call-back telephone number with the airline; and (4) excessively frequent travel to source or distribution cities.

The difficulty, of course, is that innocent individuals may display several of these characteristics. Some critics complain that the focus on source or distribution cities tends to single out certain ethnic and racial minorities. On the other hand, profiles merely recognize that we rely on past experience to make judgments on a daily basis. In the case of drug courier profiles, there is an indication that the profiles are reasonably accurate. Data from the Detroit Airport, cited by Justice Lewis Powell Jr. in a 1980 Supreme Court decision, indicate that during a period of eighteen months, Drug Enforcement Administration (DEA) agents relying on a drug courier profile searched 141 persons in 96 encounters, and a controlled substance was discovered in 77 of those encounters, leading to the arrest of 122 persons (*United States v. Mendenhall,* 446 U.S. 544, 562 [1980]).

Courts have avoided weighing in on the debate over the accuracy of profiles and generally do not give particular weight to the claim that an individual fits a "profile." Judges, instead, ask whether the combination of the factors identified in the profile constitutes reasonable suspicion. In some instances, courts have found reasonable suspicion where law enforcement agents have supplemented the profile with additional observations.

The U.S. Supreme Court in *Reid v. Georgia* held that law enforcement officers in seizing and questioning Reid improperly relied on a **drug courier profile** (*Reid v. Georgia,* 448 U.S. 438, 440–441 [1980]).

The U.S. Supreme Court considered whether the DEA agent had reasonable grounds to suspect Reid of wrongdoing. The Court considered that Reid arrived in Atlanta from the known drug distribution center of Fort Lauderdale in the early morning, a time when law enforcement at the airport is understaffed. The DEA agent also relied on the facts that Reid and his companion apparently attempted to conceal the fact that they were traveling together and that they carried all their belongings in shoulder bags. The Supreme Court ruled that only the observation that Reid preceded his companion and occasionally looked backward focused on Reid's "particular conduct." The DEA agent's conclusion that they were concealing that they were traveling together was little more than a "hunch" and was not a substantial enough basis to justify a *Terry* stop. The other factors "describe a very large category of presumably innocent travelers, who would be subject to virtually random seizures were the Court to conclude as little foundation as there was...could justify a seizure" (441). Are you troubled by the fact that the Supreme Court substituted its judgment for the accurate conclusion of trained law enforcement agents that the totality of the circumstances indicated that Reid was engaged in drug smuggling?

In *Florida v. Royer,* the Supreme Court found reasonable suspicion where the police went beyond the drug profile and learned that Royer was traveling under an assumed name. Royer was observed in Miami International Airport by plainclothes narcotics detectives. The detectives concluded that Royer fit the drug courier profile in that he was traveling from a major drug distribution city and had purchased a one-way ticket to New York in cash with small bills. The police discovered after approaching Royer that his plane ticket was issued to a name that did not match the name on his driver's license. He also appeared to be nervous when conversing with the detectives (*Florida v. Royer,* 460 U.S. 491, 493–494 [1983]). The Supreme Court held that "when the officers discovered that Royer was traveling under an assumed name, this fact, and the facts already known to the officers...were adequate grounds for suspecting Royer of carrying drugs and for temporarily detaining him...while they attempted to verify or dispel their suspicions" (501).

As you can see, the determination of whether an officer possesses reasonable suspicion is more of an art than a science. In *Royer,* the Supreme Court held that Royer's use of an assumed name when combined with a combination of factors provided law enforcement officers with reasonable suspicion to stop Royer. In contrast, in *Reid,* the police officer could not point to specific acts that indicated that the suspect may be engaged in illegal activity. The Supreme Court determined that most of the factors relied on by the officer were characteristic of a large number of innocent individuals and that the totality of circumstances listed in the profile did not provide law enforcement officers with reasonable suspicion to stop Reid.

Three points emerge concerning reliance on profiles.

- ***Reasonable suspicion.*** Courts will examine profiles to determine whether the factors constitute reasonable suspicion.
- ***Suspect's conduct.*** Reasonable suspicion must be based on evidence of an individual's specific action or actions, which in combination with other factors indicate that criminal conduct may be afoot.
- ***Nonsuspicious conduct.*** A pattern of conduct that is innocent or characteristic of a large number of individuals may contribute to a finding of reasonable suspicion based on the totality of the circumstances. These facts alone are not sufficient to constitute reasonable suspicion.

The next case on the study site is the 1989 case of *United States v. Sokolow.* Andrew Sokolow was stopped by DEA agents at Honolulu International Airport based on the fact that he fit a drug courier profile. DEA agents subsequently discovered 1,063 grams of cocaine in his carry-on luggage. In reading *Sokolow,* consider whether the Supreme Court in this judgment appears willing to recognize that law enforcement officers may rely on drug courier profiles to find reasonable suspicion. You also will be interested in comparing the analysis in the majority and dissenting opinions and whether you agree with the dissent that the Supreme Court's decision is inconsistent with *Reid* and *Royer.*

You can find Reid v. Georgia *and* United States v. Sokolow *on the study site, http://www.sagepub.com/lippmancp.*

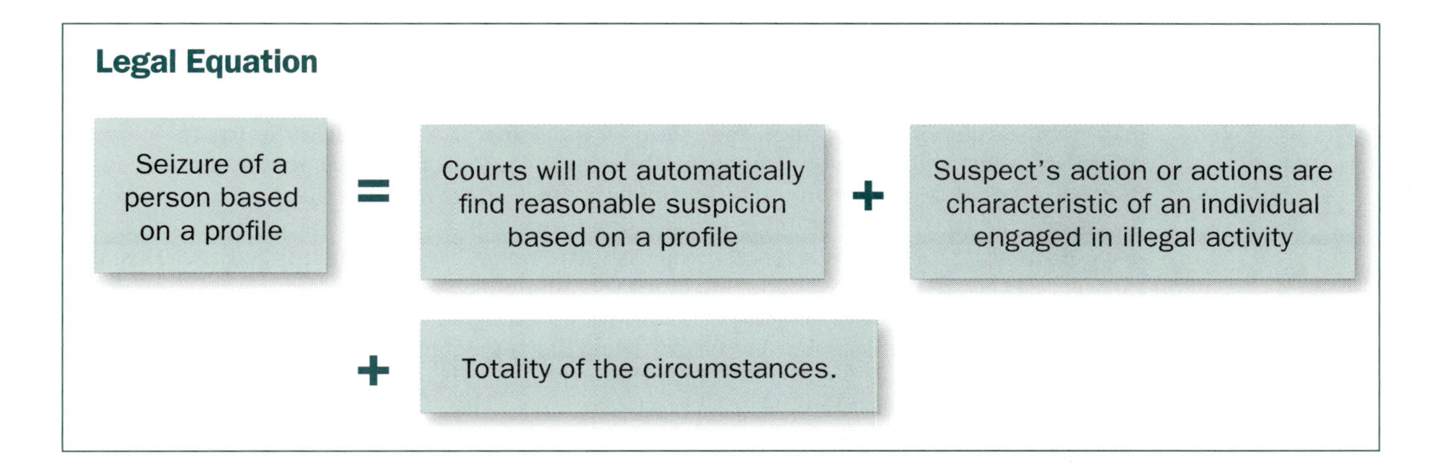

Race and Reasonable Suspicion

The claim is made that the police and law enforcement officials engage in **racial profiling** or stopping individuals because of their race, ethnicity, gender, or other characteristic rather than because of their actions. This practice would be contrary to the Fifth and Fourteenth Amendments to the U.S. Constitution, which entitles individuals to equal protection of the law and makes it unlawful to discriminate against individuals based on their race, ethnicity, gender, or religion. But may a police officer consider race along with an individual's conduct in determining reasonable suspicion? At present, there is an ongoing debate over whether it is lawful to consider an individual's ethnicity or religion in determining whether there is reasonable suspicion that an individual is engaged in terrorism.

Consider *Brown v. City of Oneonta.* Shortly before 2:00 A.M., a male broke into a house outside Oneonta, New York, and attacked a seventy-seven-year-old woman with a knife. The victim was not able to identify her assailant but, during the struggle, saw his hand and forearm and reported that he was an African American. She told the police that he cut his hand with the knife during the scuffle and that he must have been young because of the speed with which he crossed the room. The police proceeded to contact African American male students at the nearby State University of New York College at Oneonta. They failed to find the burglar and initiated a sweep in which they stopped and questioned every African American on the streets of Oneonta and inspected their hands for knife wounds. In justifying this tactic, the police stressed that Oneonta had a small African American population. Do you believe that the police acted in a constitutional fashion (*Brown v. City of Oneonta,* 221 F.3d 329 [2d Cir. 1999])?

There are a number of general points to keep in mind concerning whether the police may consider race in initiating a *Terry* stop.

Sole factor. An individual may not be stopped when the only reason for his or her seizure is his or her race, ethnicity, gender, religion, or other descriptive characteristic. In *United States v. Jones,* an anonymous caller reported to a police dispatcher at 1:13 A.M. that several African American males were drinking at a certain intersection and causing a disturbance. Officer Hart did not find anyone on the corner and, as he was driving out of the neighborhood, encountered and stopped four African American males driving into the area, one of whom subsequently was arrested for drug possession. The Fourth Circuit Court of Appeals concluded that Officer Hart had stopped the men because of their race and that this did not constitute reasonable suspicion to detain the four African American men (*United States v. Jones,* 242 F.3d 215, 218 [4th Cir. 2001]).

Incongruity. An individual may not be stopped based on the fact that he or she "does not belong in a neighborhood." The Washington Supreme Court noted "racial incongruity . . . should never constitute a finding of reasonable suspicion of criminal behavior. Distinctions between citizens solely because of their ancestry are odious to a free people whose institutions are grounded upon the doctrine of equality" (*State v. Barber,* 823 P.2d 1068 [Wash. 1992]).

Identifications. Race may be considered as a factor in determining whether there is reasonable suspicion. The police, for example, may stop an individual who fits the description of a suspect where the totality of the circumstances leads the police to reasonably believe that the individual is the offender. In *United States v. Bautista,* the Ninth Circuit Court of Appeals noted that "[r]ace or color alone is not a sufficient basis for making an investigatory stop. However, race can be a relevant factor." The police in *Bautista* stopped two Hispanic suspects who were the only "people in sight who matched the description of the robbers" as either Iranian or Hispanic. The suspects also were encountered on a likely escape route one-half mile from the bank and a few blocks from the suspected getaway car. The defendants' light and dry clothes were suspicious given that there had been a steady rain (*United States v. Bautista,* 684 F.2d 1286, 1289 [9th Cir. 1982]).

Profiles. Race, ethnicity, or some other description may be considered as one of several factors in a profile. In *United States v. Weaver,* Drug Enforcement Agent Hicks and two local detectives saw Weaver exit a plane from Los Angeles. Hicks focused on Weaver because he was "aware that a number of young roughly dressed black males from street gangs in Los Angeles frequently brought cocaine into Kansas City . . . and that walking quickly towards a taxicab was a common characteristic of narcotics couriers at the airport." Weaver also did not check his luggage, appeared nervous, and did not have any identification or a copy of his ticket. The Eighth Circuit Court of Appeals ruled that a stop based solely on race would be unconstitutional. However, in this case, race was "coupled with other factors." The appellate court stressed that Hicks had knowledge, based upon his own experience and intelligence reports, that "young male members of black Los Angeles gangs were flooding the Kansas City area with cocaine" (*United States v. Weaver,* 966 F.2d 391, 394 [8th Cir. 1992]).

The next case in the text, *State v. Barber,* raises the issues of "incongruity" and the constitutionality of relying on race in making a reasonable suspicion stop. In reading *Barber,* consider whether race played a role in the police officer's decision to stop the defendants.

United States v. Weaver *is available on the study site, http://www.sagepub.com/lippmancp.*

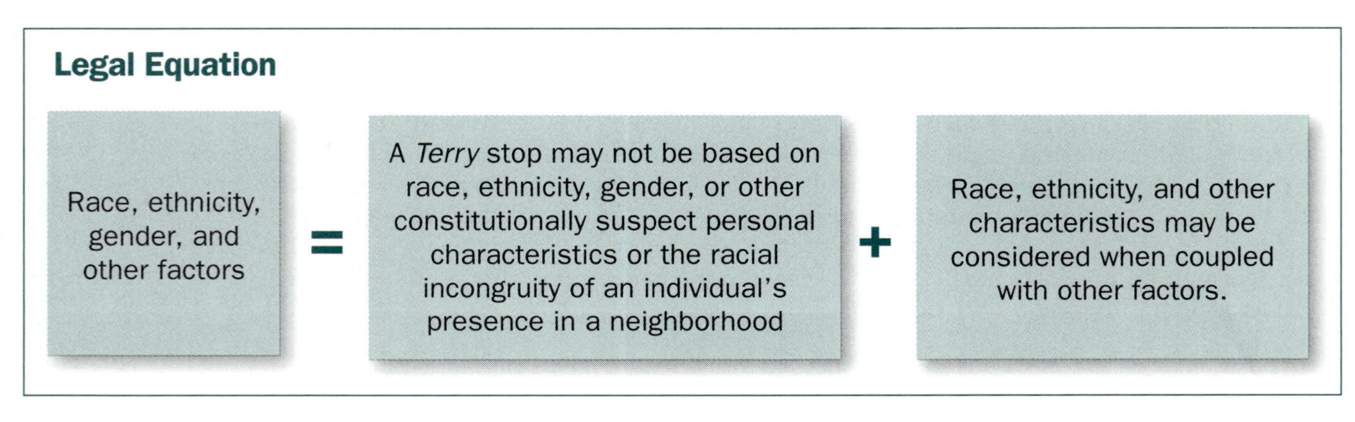

Legal Equation

Race, ethnicity, gender, and other factors	=	A *Terry* stop may not be based on race, ethnicity, gender, or other constitutionally suspect personal characteristics or the racial incongruity of an individual's presence in a neighborhood	+	Race, ethnicity, and other characteristics may be considered when coupled with other factors.

Were these individuals stopped because of their race?

State v. Barber, 823 P.2d 1068 (1992), Andersen, J.

Issue

At issue in this case is whether racial incongruity, i.e., a person of any race being allegedly "out of place" in a particular geographic area, can ever constitute a finding of reasonable suspicion of criminal behavior; we hold that it cannot.

Facts

On the evening in question, a police officer observed three young men walking along the 13300 block of Northeast Eighth Street in Bellevue, Washington. One of the three was carrying a bundle wrapped in a blanket, another a brown paper bag, and the third (the defendant, Darron W. Barber) a duffel bag. The bags appeared to be filled with objects of some kind. After the officer drove past, he continued to observe the three, then made a U-turn, drove back, stopped, and began questioning them. As was to develop, the three men were burglars carrying loot taken in a recent residential burglary.

The defendant, Darron W. Barber, was very shortly thereafter arrested and charged with burglary in the second degree and possession of stolen property in the second degree. In the trial court, he challenged the legality of the officer stopping him as well as the legality of his arrest, and moved to suppress the evidence seized by the police at the time of the arrest.

At the suppression hearing before the trial court, testimony was taken. Pursuant to the Superior Court Criminal Rules, the trial court entered findings of fact and conclusions of law. Therein the trial court detailed the facts of the case and the conclusions it drew therefrom, and denied defendant's motion to suppress. To understand this case, it is first necessary to have the trial court's findings and conclusions before us. They are as follows:

1. On May 25, 1987, at approximately 8:00 P.M., Officer Jim Hershey of the Bellevue Police Department was on patrol in Bellevue in King County, Washington. At that time, he was heading westbound on Northeast Eighth Street in the 13300 block in his patrol vehicle. Officer Hershey is black.

2. As he proceeded down the hillside, Officer Hershey's attention was drawn to three black males walking westbound on the north shoulder of the roadway. Each of the three was carrying a package of some sort. One of the males was carrying a multicolored blanket which appeared to be covering a large bundle. Another of the males was carrying a large blue duffel bag which appeared to be filled with objects. The third male was carrying a brown paper bag. As he drove past the three, they noticed Officer Hershey and began glancing at him and each other.

3. Upon passing the three males, Officer Hershey kept an eye on them through his rearview mirror. The three continued to glance at him and then at each other. Through his mirror, Officer Hershey then observed the male carrying the blanketed bundle heave the bundle into some brush just off the shoulder of the roadway. When thrown, the contents of the blanket appeared to be of substantial weight, as the bundle did not fall very far into the brush despite what appeared to be a fair amount of exertion by the male throwing the bundle.

4. Beside the fact that the male's act constituted littering, Officer Hershey regarded that act and his observations up to that point as unusual and suspicious. Further, it had been his experience on the previous occasions that when a person is carrying a bundle within a blanket on a street, the items covered are usually the fruits of a recent burglary.

5. At that point, Officer Hershey made a U-turn and contacted the three males approximately 40 to 50 yards west of where the male had thrown the bundle into the brush. It was Officer Hershey's intention to investigate these three males' suspicious activities further. He patted down each of the males for weapons and found none. He then advised each of the males of his *Miranda* warnings. Each said he understood those rights. It was Officer Hershey's opinion that the three males were not under arrest at that time.

6. By this time, the males who had been carrying the duffel bag and the brown paper bag had placed those packages on the ground. The brown paper bag sat opened, and in plain view, Officer Hershey observed two telephones and two cartons of Kool cigarettes.

7. The male who had been carrying the duffel bag was identified as defendant Darron Barber. Defendant stated he did not wish to answer any of Officer Hershey's questions, and made movements as if he was going to leave the scene. Concerned as to his ability to investigate the situation further if any or all of the three males fled, Officer Hershey then handcuffed defendant to keep him at the scene. Given that defendant stated he did not wish to talk

to Officer Hershey, Officer Hershey asked him no further questions.

8. The male who had been carrying the brown paper bag identified himself as Junior Aron Walker, although his true name was subsequently determined to be Chris Barber, the brother of defendant. Chris Barber agreed to talk to Officer Hershey and told him that he and his "friend" Darron had met Kim Anderson, the third male, at the bus stop up the street. He further stated that Anderson had told them that he was moving, and asked them to help him carry his property.
9. Officer Hershey then spoke separately with the third male who had thrown the bundle into the brush, identified as Kim Anderson. Anderson told Officer Hershey a different version of recent events. He stated that he had met up with the other two males at the bus stop and that they had told him that they were moving and that they had asked him to help them carry their load. When asked why he threw the bundle into the brush, Anderson told Officer Hershey that he did not know what Officer Hershey was talking about.
10. To make sure none of the three males took off with either of the two packages still in front of Officer Hershey, Officer Hershey placed the open paper bag and duffel bag on top of his patrol car's hood. He patted down the duffel bag for weapons when he moved it, and felt what he immediately recognized to be, from his experience, electronic equipment.
11. At this point, approximately three minutes after Officer Hershey had first contacted the three males, other police officers began arriving in response to an earlier summons by Officer Hershey. Among those arriving was Officer T. Simonton. At Officer Hershey's request, Officer Simonton immediately checked the area where Anderson had thrown the bundle into the brush and found a videocassette recorder wrapped in an afghan blanket.
12. Another officer who had arrived, Lt. Vestal, informed Officer Hershey that approximately one-half hour earlier, he had seen the defendant and the individual later identified as Chris Barber at the bus stop on the north side of Northeast Eighth Street just west of the west entrance to the Foothills Apartments (13700 block of Northeast Eighth Street). With that information, Officer Simonton then immediately drove to that bus stop, approximately four blocks away, and put his tracking dog to work in that area.
13. The dog immediately responded to a strong scent in the brush, and began tracking northbound to the south parking area of Foothills Apartments. The dog continued to the southwest corner of the apartments contained in Building C-4, and showed some interest in the corner apartment's west balcony. The dog then continued northbound past the balcony and responded to very strong scents in some bushes between the corner balcony and the next balcony to the north, of Apartment #103. The dog then directed Officer Simonton to a wall of the building directly below a sliding glass window. Officer Simonton then noticed the screen for that window was lying in the bushes.
14. As he was removing the dog from the bushes, Officer Simonton was contacted by the resident of an apartment in the building, one Dean Bakken. Bakken advised Officer Simonton that his apartment had recently been broken into, and that items were missing. He further told the officer that among the items missing were his Hitachi VCR, telephones, other electronic equipment, and a multicolored afghan.
15. Officer Simonton then radioed the information relating to the burglary and the items stolen to Officer Hershey. The officers at the scene confirmed that the VCR which had been found in the brush was manufactured by Hitachi. At that point, Officer Hershey and the other officers at the scene detaining the defendant and the other two males believed they had probable cause to arrest the three males for possession of stolen property. Accordingly, the three males were then arrested. No more than ten to fifteen minutes had passed between the time of the initial stop by Officer Hershey and the time of the three males' arrests.
16. Incident to the arrests at the scene, Officer Hershey and the other officers searched the three males and opened the duffel bag which had been carried by defendant. All of the items which had been reported stolen by Bakken were found either on the three males, in the open paper bag, or in the opened duffel bag. If the duffel bag had not been opened at the scene, its entire contents would have become visible to the officers once they had arrived at the police station and inventoried the bag's contents, given Bellevue police's inventory procedures.

Following the trial court's ruling adverse to the defendant on his motion to suppress evidence, the facts—including police reports—were stipulated to by the defendant and the case was submitted to the trial court for decision based on those facts. These facts included the following: at the time the defendant was stopped, he was carrying loot taken in a very recent Bellevue residential burglary; police fingerprint experts lifted defendant's palm print from inside the burglarized premises; and the defendant had other property in his possession which proved to have been stolen elsewhere. Based on the stipulated facts and evidence, the trial court found the defendant guilty of the crimes of burglary in the second degree and possession of stolen property in the second degree, then entered judgment and sentence accordingly.

Following his conviction in the trial court, defendant appealed to the court of appeals. That court, in a very short unpublished opinion, reversed defendant's convictions on the basis that the initial stop by the police officer was unlawful; that court did not, however, discuss the racial incongruity issue. The Prosecuting Attorney for King County thereupon petitioned this court for discretionary review; we granted the petition.

Reasoning

The case involves the often difficult question of when a police officer, absent probable cause to arrest, is legally justified in stopping and questioning a citizen. The leading case in this area of the law is, of course, *Terry v. Ohio*. The difficulty here is that on the central "legality of the initial stop" issue, the trial court's findings do not tell us precisely what "specific and articulable facts . . . , taken together with rational inferences from those facts, reasonably warrant that intrusion." Was Officer Hershey's initial stop of defendant and his companions based on a well-founded suspicion of criminal activity based upon specific and articulable facts?

Thus . . . the crucial finding of the trial court on this issue is entirely conclusory and fails to inform us what "specific and articulable facts" the trial court felt justified the investigative or "*Terry*-type" stop of the defendant and his companions. A principal purpose of requiring such findings is to facilitate appellate review of the trial court's decision regarding the suppression motion. The trial court's failure to set out in its findings what specific and articulable facts it relied on leaves the parties to argue widely divergent views of why the stop was made, as they did in the court of appeals and again in this court.

The findings that were entered by the trial court basically constitute a narrative account of what occurred at the scene of the investigatory stop and the subsequent investigation and arrest, but nowhere point to what "specific and articulable facts" reasonably support a suspicion that criminal activity was afoot. The problem in this case is that the absence of such particularized findings does not permit us to determine whether the stop was based on legally permissible and adequate reasons or whether it was based on a perceived racial incongruity between the suspects and the locale in which they were stopped. The defendant and his two companions, who were stopped by the police officer, were black and were walking in a predominantly white neighborhood at the time they were stopped.

The defendant argued that the reason the officer made the investigative stop of the defendant and his companions is that they were blacks in a predominantly white neighborhood, and that the stop was thus illegal. There is testimony in the record that arguably supports this view. There is also testimony in the record, however, that arguably supports a contrary view. This includes the following: (1) one of the three persons walking along the Bellevue street at approximately 8 P.M. was carrying a large blanket-covered bundle; (2) as the officer drove past them in his marked police patrol car, they noticed the officer and began glancing at him and at each other; (3) after the officer had passed the group, he continued observing them through his rearview mirror, and they continued to glance at him and at each other; (4) the officer then saw the one carrying the blanketed bundle heave the bundle into brush off the shoulder of the roadway; (5) the contents of the blanket appeared to the officer to be of substantial weight, since the bundle did not fall very far into the brush despite what appeared to have been a fair amount of exertion by the person throwing the bundle; (6) the acts of the person throwing the bundle constituted at least littering; (7) to this police officer (of some ten years' experience), when a person is carrying a bundle within a blanket on a street at night, the items covered are usually the fruits of a recent burglary; and (8) according to uncontroverted testimony at the suppression hearing, when seen by the officer, the defendant was walking out in the street in violation of law. In short, the testimony given at the suppression hearing is conflicting on a critical factual issue.

It is the law that racial incongruity, i.e., a person of any race being allegedly "out of place" in a particular geographic area, should never constitute a finding of reasonable suspicion of criminal behavior. Distinctions between citizens solely because of their ancestry are odious to a free people whose institutions are founded upon the doctrine of equality. Race or color alone is not a sufficient basis for making an investigatory stop. However, race can be a relevant factor. Appearance, including race and other physical attributes of a suspect, may be relevant in forming a suspicion of criminal activity; racial incongruity, however, is never relevant in forming such a suspicion.

Holding

In reading the trial court's findings and conclusions entered following the suppression hearing in this case, it is at once apparent that the trial court's only reference to race was its observation that both the defendants and the Bellevue police officer who arrested them were black. That statement alone, however, does not indicate that the trial judge found that racial incongruity was a factor which supported the *Terry* stop. So that the basis for the trial court's decision in this case may be clarified, the court of appeals should be reversed and the case remanded to the trial court to make additional findings of fact as to the following: Eliminating any consideration of racial incongruity whatsoever, were there facts to support a legally justified and well-founded suspicion of criminal activity at the time the arresting officer stopped the defendant and his companions? If such facts do exist, the trial court is required to specify them. In requesting such specification, we are not abdicating our responsibility (as the dissenting opinion suggests); we are remanding this case so that the trial court, as the trier of fact (as is its function) may make the factual determinations necessary to assess the legal validity of the investigative stop.

Further response to the dissent is necessary. First, the dissent declares that the *Terry* stop in this case was based on a police officer's assumption that "three black men walking in Bellevue must be up to no good" and therefore was unlawful. The dissent overlooks the fact that, in examining the legal validity of a *Terry* stop, the police officer's assumptions are irrelevant and not to be taken into account by the trial court in its redetermination. As our opinion makes clear, it is well-established law, federal and state, that the facts surrounding an investigative stop must be judged against an objective standard: Would the facts available to the officer at the moment of the seizure or the search "warrant a [person] of reasonable caution in the belief" that the action taken was appropriate? Under the terms of our remand, the trial court is required to reexamine the facts surrounding the investigative stop in this case against this objective standard. If the facts that the trial court relies upon include any reference to racial incongruity, the *Terry* stop was unlawful. If, however, the trial court cites objective facts that support a legally justified and well-founded suspicion of criminal activity—i.e., one based on facts that make no reference to racial incongruity—then the *Terry* stop was valid and the motion to suppress was properly denied.

Dissenting, *Dolliver, J.*

The majority makes the forthright declaration that "racial incongruity...should never constitute a finding of reasonable suspicion" justifying an investigative stop. While I agree with and applaud this statement, as far as it goes, I nonetheless cannot sign the majority opinion and therefore dissent.

The evidence shows that, but for the race of the defendants, Officer Hershey would not have slowed down to look at them twice. As he testified, when he saw them, he "became suspicious. It was unusual to see three black guys carrying items, walking, at least in that part of the city." When asked to explain his statement—given a chance to deny that his suspicion was merely a racially motivated hunch—Officer Hershey stated that, based on his experience, "the whole circumstance" (which at that point consisted of three black men walking together on a street in Bellevue on an evening in late spring, one carrying a gym bag, one a brown paper bag, and one an item wrapped in a blanket) "[n]ormally" meant "a crime had just been committed...."

This type of assumption by a police officer is simply unacceptable. The fact that Officer Hershey is black does not make it more acceptable, nor does the fact that, in this case, Officer Hershey's hunch turned out to be correct. Everything that happened and everything Officer Hershey saw after he initially decided three black men walking in Bellevue must be up to no good are tainted by that decision, and this court should say so.

The majority's holding would allow *Terry* stops if there are sufficient "facts to support a legally justified and well-founded suspicion of criminal activity at the time" of the stop, regardless of whether the initiating factor in the sequence of events leading up to the stop was solely based upon racial incongruity. I strongly disagree with this test.

The court has consistently applied the exclusionary rule where it has deemed it necessary to deter police misconduct and preserve the dignity of the judiciary. The same mandates should be applied here.

Racial incongruity overhangs this entire case like a noxious pall, and it will not be eliminated by the test set forth by the majority anymore than all the perfumes of Arabia would sweeten the little hand of Lady Macbeth.

Some might argue that adopting my view would merely encourage police officers not to tell the truth, unlike Officer Hershey who, to his great credit, did. Human nature being what it is, this gloomy view may have some force. There is, however, another more important characteristic of human nature which must be considered. If appropriate conduct is practiced, even hypocritically at first, the conduct will eventually become the belief. Put another way, the mask will become the face. I would hold that if racial incongruity, alone, initiates the sequence of events leading to an investigative stop—as I am convinced it does here—then the conviction must be overturned. I think this court should do no less.

Questions for Discussion

1. What factors did Officer Hershey testify led him to stop the defendants?
2. How did the majority and dissenting opinions differ on the role of race in the stop of the defendants? Which opinion do you find more persuasive?
3. What is the rule proposed by Judge Dolliver? Do you believe that this rule would prove workable?
4. ***Problems in policing.*** Summarize the circumstances under which a police officer may consider a suspect's race or ethnicity in making a *Terry* stop.

4.3 YOU DECIDE

Officer David Mathison was an eighteen-month veteran of the St. Paul, Minnesota, Police Department. He was working with the vice unit when he spotted Stephen D. Uber, a Caucasian, at 2:15 A.M. Mathison once again saw Uber's pickup truck at 2:45 A.M. Mathison radioed in the license plate number and learned that the vehicle was registered to a person in Moundsview, Minnesota, a predominantly Caucasian suburb. After checking the registration of the automobile, Mathison made a decision to stop Uber because he thought that Uber was "engaging in suspicious criminal activity relative to prostitution." Mathison stated that he did not observe Uber drive in an erratic or unlawful fashion and did not observe Uber circle the block, stop, or pick up anyone. Mathison testified that the Summit–University area is a "mixed neighborhood" well known for prostitution and that Uber demonstrated various characteristics that typify a person looking for prostitutes. These characteristics include there being one person in a car, late at night, which is observed in the area on multiple occasions in a short period of time, stops frequently, and may pick up a passenger. In addition, Uber had an out-of-the-area address. Was this a lawful *Terry* stop? See *City of St. Paul v. Uber,* 450 N.W.2d 623 (Minn. App. 1990).

You can find the answer by referring to the study site, http://www.sagepub.com/lippmancp.

City of St. Paul v. Uber *is available on the study site, http://www.sagepub.com/lippmancp.*

The Scope and Duration of a *Terry* Stop

A *Terry* stop and frisk is a limited intrusion to investigate and to detect crime. You recall that because *Terry* seizures are for a narrow purpose and involve a limited restraint on freedom, the police are required to satisfy a lesser standard of proof (reasonable suspicion) than is required for an arrest (probable cause). It is a basic constitutional principle that law enforcement officials may interfere with your freedom and privacy only to the extent required to accomplish their purpose. As the Supreme Court observed, *Terry* stops "warrant a limited intrusion on the personal security of the suspect. . . . [A]n investigative detention must be temporary and last no longer than is necessary to effectuate the purpose of the stop" (*Florida v. Royer,* 460 U.S. 491, 500 [1983]). As a result, a *Terry* stop may be challenged as unlawful when a suspect is treated as if he or she is being subjected to a probable cause arrest rather than to a reasonable suspicion stop. This inquiry typically focuses on three areas.

- ***Movement.*** A *Terry* stop does not permit the involuntary and significant movement of a suspect unless required by reasons of safety and security. You cannot be involuntarily transported to police headquarters.
- ***Length of detention.*** A *Terry* stop must be for a limited duration. You cannot be subjected to a lengthy detention or interrogation.
- ***Intrusiveness.*** The police are to employ the "least intrusive" methods reasonably available to them to investigate suspected criminal activity under the circumstances and to interfere as little as possible with an individual's freedom. A suspect ordinarily may not be detained by force, handcuffed, or locked in a patrol car.

In other words, the justification for the stop (e.g., *Terry*) defines the scope (limited movement and intrusiveness) and duration (limited time) of the stop. A probable cause stop, in contrast, permits an arrest that may result in the jailing of an individual for an extended period while awaiting trial. *The question is whether the Terry stop is being conducted in an unreasonable fashion and whether any evidence that is seized is the product of this unlawful seizure.*

Movement

The Supreme Court has held that a *Terry* stop permits only the modest movement of a suspect for the purpose of protecting the safety and security of a suspect or the police.

Terry stops have been held to be unlawful in those instances in which individuals have been removed to a police-dominated location or police headquarters and subjected to treatment resembling a probable cause arrest.

You may recall that we previously discussed *Florida v. Royer* in which two plainclothes detectives stopped Royer in Miami International Airport after determining that he fit a drug courier profile. The U.S. Supreme Court observed that the detectives had impermissibly moved Royer forty feet to an office where Royer consented to a search of his two suitcases that the police had retrieved from the airline. The Supreme Court rejected the agents' explanation that Royer had been moved to the office in order to question him in a securer location. The purpose, in the view of the Court, was to isolate Royer and to gain his consent to a search of his luggage. Royer, as "a practical matter," was under arrest, and "[w]hat had begun as a consensual inquiry in a public place had escalated into an investigatory procedure in a police interrogation room, where the police, unsatisfied with previous explanations, sought to confirm their suspicions" (*Florida v. Royer,* 460 U.S. 491, 502 [1983]).

The U.S. Supreme Court also has condemned removing individuals subjected to *Terry* stops to police headquarters for questioning. For example, in *Dunaway v. New York,* the police detained Dunaway, who they suspected had killed an individual during an attempted robbery, and took him to police headquarters for questioning. He was not formally arrested or charged and confessed to the crime. The Supreme Court held that this type of lengthy and involuntary detention could be justified only by a probable cause arrest and that the police in *Dunaway* had gone far beyond the "narrowly defined intrusions" permitted under *Terry* (*Dunaway v. New York,* 442 U.S. 200 [1979]). In *Kaupp v. Texas,* the seventeen-year-old Kaupp was awakened at three in the morning by several police officers who suspected that Kaupp had been involved in a homicide. Dressed only in his underwear, Kaupp was handcuffed, placed in a patrol car, driven to the scene of the crime, and then taken to police headquarters and questioned. The Supreme Court held that Kaupp's removal and detention were "'in important respects indistinguishable from a traditional arrest' and therefore required probable cause or judicial authorization to be legal" (*Kaupp v. Texas,* 538 U.S. 626, 631 [2003]).

Length of Detention

We have seen that *Terry* stops are brief seizures whose purpose is to detect and to investigate suspected criminal conduct. The U.S. Supreme Court accordingly has held that *Terry* detentions are required to be limited in duration and do not permit the type of lengthy detentions that are characteristic of probable cause custodial arrests. The Supreme Court noted that the length of a detention is an "important factor in determining whether the seizure is so minimally intrusive as to be justifiable on reasonable suspicion" (*United States v. Place,* 462 U.S. 696, 709 [1983]).

In *United States v. Sharpe,* Drug Enforcement Agent Cooke was on patrol near the North Carolina coast, a known center of drug activity. Cooke observed a blue pickup truck driving in tandem with a blue Pontiac Bonneville. Cooke suspected that the vehicles were transporting narcotics and followed the vehicles for roughly twenty miles before radioing state police for assistance. Cooke was joined by a squad car driven by Officer Thrasher. Cooke pulled the Pontiac over based on reasonable suspicion. The pickup continued down the highway roughly one-half mile before being pulled over by State Trooper Thraser. Thrasher radioed Cooke, who arrived twenty minutes later. Cooke opened the back doors of the truck, discovered marijuana, and arrested Savage. Cooke then returned to the Pontiac and arrested both occupants of the vehicle, Sharpe and Davis. Thirty to forty minutes had passed between Cooke's initial stop of the Pontiac and the arrest of Sharpe and Davis (*United States v. Sharpe,* 470 U.S. 675, 677–680 [1984]).

The issue before the Supreme Court was whether Savage had been detained for too lengthy a period under a *Terry* stop and whether Savage's detention therefore constituted the "functional equivalent" of a formal arrest. The Supreme Court held that Cooke acted in a "diligent and reasonable manner" and that there was no "unnecessary delay" in investigating Savage. The Court declined to establish a time limit on *Terry* seizures and held that a twenty-minute stop is not "unreasonable when the police have acted diligently and a suspect's actions contribute to the added delay about which he complains" (686–687).

Sharpe suggests that the permissible time of a *Terry* detention is measured by whether the police carried out their criminal investigation in a reasonable fashion without unreasonable delay. The twenty-minute period should not be thought of as a "bright-line" limit on *Terry* stops. A good example of an overly lengthy seizure is provided in *United States v. Place.* In *Place,* DEA agents detained Place for ninety minutes at La Guardia Airport in New York while they waited for the arrival of a drug dog to examine Place's luggage. The Supreme Court observed that the police had caused this delay by failing to arrange for a drug dog to be present when Place's plane arrived at La Guardia. The Court declined to adopt any outside limit on a *Terry* stop but ruled that the ninety-minute period made the seizure unreasonable (*United States v. Place,* 462 U.S. 696, 709 [1983]).

On the other hand, in *United States v. Montoya de Hernandez,* the Supreme Court upheld the reasonableness of the twenty-four-hour seizure of Montoya de Hernandez at an international border. Customs agents suspected that Montoya de Hernandez had swallowed narcotic-filled balloons that she was smuggling into the United States. Montoya de Hernandez refused an x-ray, and the Court ruled that customs agents had no alternative other than to wait until she discharged the balloons in a bowel movement. The Supreme Court observed that the defendant's detention was "long, uncomfortable, indeed, humiliating; but both its length and its discomfort resulted solely from the method by which she chose to smuggle illicit drugs into this country.... [T]he customs officers were not required by the Fourth Amendment to pass respondent and her 88 cocaine-filled balloons into the interior. Her detention for the period of time necessary to either verify or dispel the suspicion was not unreasonable" (*United States v. Montoya de Hernandez,* 473 U.S. 531, 544 [1985]).

In summary, the Supreme Court has adopted a flexible approach to the length of *Terry* detentions and asks whether the length of the stop is reasonable under the totality of the circumstances. The Court examines whether the police acted in a diligent and responsible fashion in discharging their responsibilities and, in the case of lengthy detentions, examines whether the suspect contributed to the length of the detention. This approach differs from section 110.2 of the American Law Institute's *Model Penal Code of Pre-Arraignment Procedure,* in which a group of respected lawyers, professors, and judges stated that a *Terry* stop may last "for such period as it is reasonably necessary... but in no case for more than twenty minutes." Does it make sense to tell the police that after twenty minutes, they are required to release a criminal suspect? On the other hand, we want to guard against the police employing *Terry* stops to engage in lengthy investigations, interrogations, or various forensic tests.

You can find United States v. Montoya de Hernandez *on the study site, http://www.sagepub.com/lippmancp.*

Investigative Techniques

The Supreme Court also examines whether the investigative techniques employed by the police during a *Terry* stop violate an individual's privacy to a greater extent than is reasonable under the circumstances.

As you recall, in *Florida v. Royer,* the detectives at the airport detained Royer and moved him against his will to a room where he agreed to a search of his luggage. The Supreme Court held that nothing was achieved by moving Royer to the office that could not have been accomplished by questioning him in the airport concourse where he was first detained. The Court suggested that the police could have achieved the same results in a "more expeditious way" by relying on trained drug dogs. In the event that the search by the dogs "proved negative, Royer would have been free to go much earlier and with less likelihood of missing his flight" (*Florida v. Royer,* 460 U.S. 491, 502 [1983]).

Courts have approved intrusive techniques of detention during *Terry* stops when the police reasonably believe that they confront potentially violent suspects and must take precautions for their safety. In determining whether the police have carried out the *Terry* stop and frisk in a reasonable fashion, courts inquire whether the investigative methods employed were the *least intrusive means reasonably available to verify or dispel the officer's suspicion in a short period of time.* In those instances in which a suspect threatens an officer's safety and the police resort to physical force, to displaying a weapon, or to detaining an individual in a squad car, courts examine whether these tactics were necessary under the circumstances.

Judges in these instances consider a number of factors (*United States v. Seelye,* 815 F.2d 48 [8th Cir. 1987]):

- The number of officers and number of suspects
- The nature of the crime and whether there is reason to believe that the suspect is armed
- The need for immediate action for the officer to protect himself or herself
- Threatening behavior by the suspect
- The opportunity for the police to make the stop in a less intrusive fashion

In a drug case, the Minnesota Supreme Court held that the police had acted in a reasonable fashion to protect themselves.

- The police stopped an SUV with several occupants late at night. The officers had received information that the occupants might be armed and that the vehicle might contain a large cache of illegal drugs. The Minnesota Supreme Court held that it was reasonable to approach the SUV with "weapons drawn, removing the occupants from the Blazer, frisking them placing them in the back seat of squad cars and even handcuffing them briefly until it was determined that they were not armed" (*State v. Munson,* 594 N.W.2d 128, 137 [Minn. 1999]).

In another drug case, a federal court of appeals ruled that DEA agents had gone beyond the permissible limits of a *Terry* stop and acted as if they were executing a probable cause arrest rather than a reasonable suspicion stop.

- A car containing two suspected drug dealers was stopped by four DEA agents waiving firearms, and the occupants were handcuffed, placed in the backseats of separate DEA vehicles, transported to a nearby parking lot, read their *Miranda* rights, and questioned by the police. The court of appeals ruled that the police had gone beyond the measures required for their safety by transporting the suspects to another location and questioning them (*United States v. Lopez-Arias,* 344 F.3d 623, 628 [6th Cir. 2003]).

Can you see why the Fourth Circuit Court of Appeals ruled that police acted in an overly intrusive fashion in the case summarized below?

- The suspect entered into a store that was closed, triggered the burglar alarm, and was detained by the police for suspected breaking and entering. The suspect began to walk away and was handcuffed, had his legs kicked apart, was thrown against a wall, and was locked in the patrol car until the owner arrived. The Fourth Circuit Court of Appeals concluded that his freedom was improperly "curtailed to a degree associated with formal arrest" (*Park v. Shiflett,* 250 F.3d 843 [4th Cir. 2001]).

United States v. Sharpe and *Florida v. Royer* on the study site provide you with an opportunity to review what we have discussed regarding the requirement that *Terry* detentions be carried out in a reasonable fashion. The next case in the text is *Hiibel v. Sixth Judicial District.* In *Hiibel,* the Supreme Court confronted the challenge of determining whether the police can require you to present identification during a *Terry* stop. Does this intrude on your liberty to a greater extent than is required to execute a *Terry* stop? *Hiibel* specifically addresses the constitutionality under the Fourth Amendment of so-called **stop-and-identify statutes.**

You can find United States v. Sharpe *and* Florida v. Royer *on the study site, http://www.sagepub.com/lippmancp.*

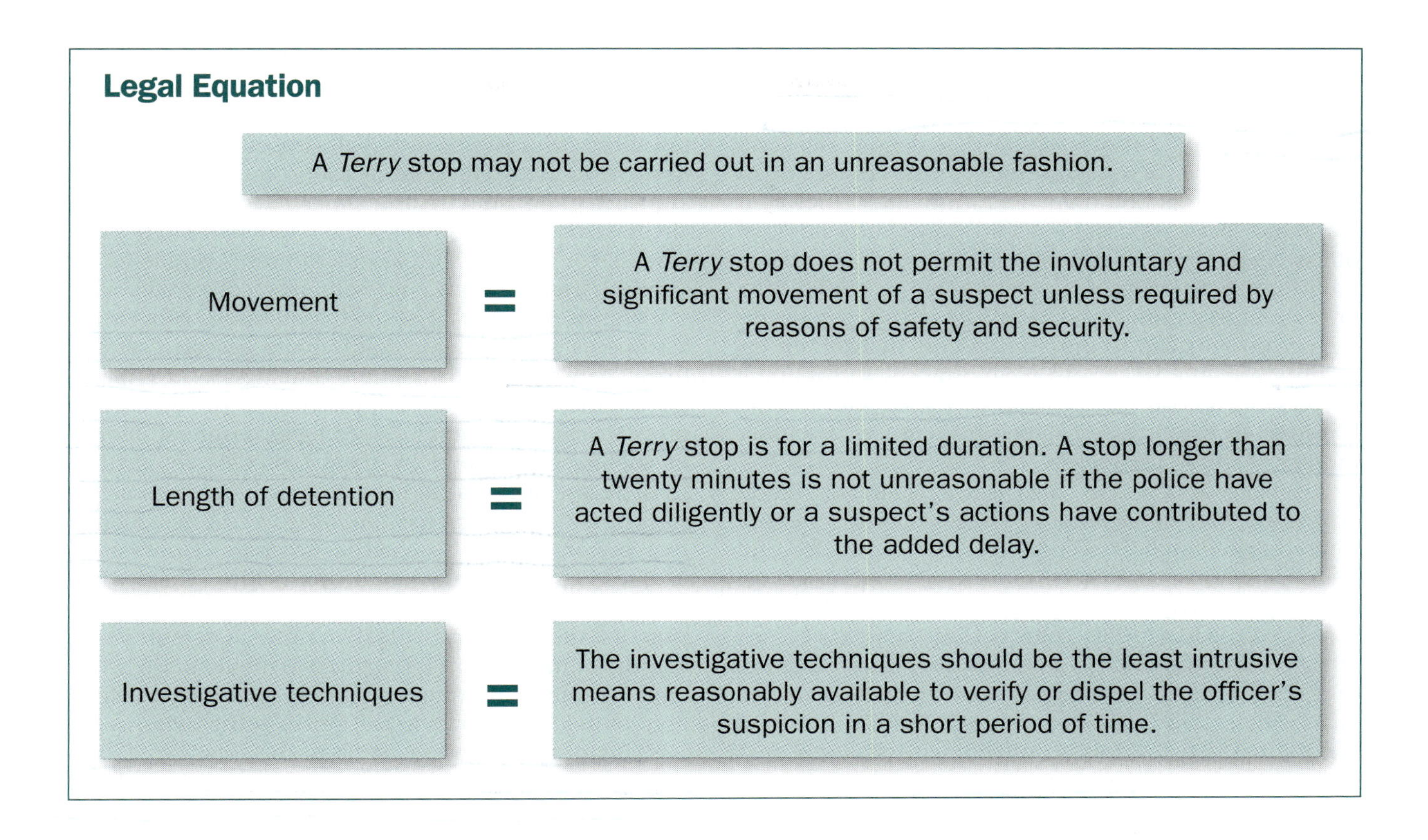

May an officer require an individual to present identification?

Hiibel v. Sixth Judicial District, *542 U.S. 177 (2004), Kennedy, J.*

Issue

The petitioner was arrested and convicted for refusing to identify himself during a stop allowed by *Terry v. Ohio*. He challenges his conviction under the Fourth and Fifth Amendments to the United States Constitution, applicable to the States through the Fourteenth Amendment.

Facts

The sheriff's department in Humboldt County, Nevada, received an afternoon telephone call reporting an assault. The caller reported seeing a man assault a woman in a red and silver GMC truck on Grass Valley Road. Deputy Sheriff Lee Dove was dispatched to investigate. When the officer arrived at the scene, he found the truck parked on the side of the road. A man was standing by the truck, and a young woman was sitting inside it. The officer observed skid marks in the gravel behind the vehicle, leading him to believe it had come to a sudden stop.

The officer approached the man and explained that he was investigating a report of a fight. The man appeared to be intoxicated. The officer asked him if he had "any identification on [him]," which we understand as a request to produce a driver's license or some other form of written identification. The man refused and asked why the officer wanted to see identification. The officer responded that he was conducting an investigation and needed to see some identification. The unidentified man became agitated and insisted he had done nothing wrong. The officer explained that he wanted to find out who the man was and what he was doing there. After continued refusals to comply with the officer's request for identification, the man began to taunt the officer by placing his hands behind his back and telling the officer to arrest him and take him to jail. This routine kept up for several minutes: The officer asked for identification eleven times and was refused each time. After warning the man that he would be arrested if he continued to refuse to comply, the officer placed him under arrest.

We now know that the man arrested on Grass Valley Road is Larry Dudley Hiibel. Hiibel was charged with "willfully resist[ing], delay[ing], or obstruct[ing] a public officer in discharging or attempting to discharge any legal duty of his office" in violation of Nev. Rev. Stat. (NRS) section 199.280 (2003). The government reasoned that Hiibel had obstructed the officer in carrying out his duties under . . . a Nevada statute that defines the legal rights and duties of a police officer in the context of an investigative stop. Section 171.123 provides in relevant part that a "peace officer may detain any person whom the officer encounters under circumstances which reasonably indicate that the person has committed, is committing or is about to commit a crime. . . . The officer may detain the person pursuant to this section only to ascertain his identity and the suspicious circumstances surrounding his presence abroad. Any person so detained shall identify himself, but may not be compelled to answer any other inquiry of any peace officer."

Hiibel was tried in the Justice Court of Union Township. The court agreed that Hiibel's refusal to identify himself as required by section 171.123 "obstructed and delayed Dove as a public officer in attempting to discharge his duty" in violation of section 199.280. Hiibel was convicted and fined $250. The Sixth Judicial District Court affirmed, rejecting Hiibel's argument that the application of section 171.123 to his case violated the Fourth and Fifth Amendments. On review, the Supreme Court of Nevada rejected the Fourth Amendment challenge in a divided opinion. . . . We granted certiorari.

Reasoning

NRS section 171.123(3) is an enactment sometimes referred to as a "stop-and-identify statute." . . . Stop-and-identify statutes often combine elements of traditional vagrancy laws with provisions intended to regulate police behavior in the course of investigatory stops. The statutes vary from state to state, but all permit an officer to ask or require a suspect to disclose his identity. A few states model their statutes on the Uniform Arrest Act, a model code that permits an officer to stop a person reasonably suspected of committing a crime and "demand of him his name, address, business abroad and where he is going." Other statutes are based on the text proposed by the American Law Institute. The provision, originally designated section 250.12, provides that a person who is loitering "under circumstances which justify suspicion that he may be engaged or about to engage in crime commits a violation if he refuses the request of a peace officer that he identify himself and give a reasonably credible account of the lawfulness of his conduct and purposes." In some states, a suspect's refusal to identify himself is a misdemeanor offense or civil violation; in others, it is a factor to be considered in whether the suspect has violated loitering laws. In other states, a suspect may decline to identify himself without penalty. . . .

Hiibel argues that his conviction cannot stand because the officer's conduct violated his Fourth Amendment rights. We disagree.

Beginning with *Terry v. Ohio,* the Court has recognized that a law enforcement officer's reasonable suspicion that a person may be involved in criminal activity permits the officer to stop the person for a brief time and take additional steps to investigate further. To ensure that the resulting seizure is constitutionally reasonable, a *Terry* stop must be limited. The officer's action must be "'justified at its inception, and . . . reasonably related in scope to the circumstances which justified the interference in the first place.'" For example, the seizure cannot continue for an excessive period of time, or resemble a traditional arrest.

Our decisions make clear that questions concerning a suspect's identity are a routine and accepted part of many *Terry* stops. "The ability to briefly stop [a suspect], ask questions, or check identification in the absence of probable cause promotes the strong government interest in solving crimes and bringing offenders to justice." If there are articulable facts supporting a reasonable suspicion that a person has committed a criminal offense, that person may be stopped in order to identify him, to question him briefly, or to detain him briefly while attempting to obtain additional information. "A brief stop of a suspicious individual, in order to determine his identity or to maintain the status quo momentarily while obtaining more information, may be most reasonable in light of the facts known to the officer at the time."

Obtaining a suspect's name in the course of a *Terry* stop serves important government interests. Knowledge of identity may inform an officer that a suspect is wanted for another offense, or has a record of violence or mental disorder. On the other hand, knowing identity may help clear a suspect and allow the police to concentrate their efforts elsewhere. Identity may prove particularly important in cases such as this, where the police are investigating what appears to be a domestic assault. Officers called to investigate domestic disputes need to know whom they are dealing with in order to assess the situation, the threat to their own safety, and possible danger to the potential victim. . . .

The principles of *Terry* permit a State to require a suspect to disclose his name in the course of a *Terry* stop. The reasonableness of a seizure under the Fourth Amendment is determined "by balancing its intrusion on the individual's Fourth Amendment interests against its promotion of legitimate government interests." The Nevada statute satisfies that standard. The request for identity has an immediate relation to the purpose, rationale, and practical demands of a *Terry* stop. The threat of criminal sanction helps ensure that the request for identity does not become a legal nullity. On the other hand, the Nevada statute does not alter the nature of the stop itself: It does not change its duration. A State law requiring a suspect to disclose his name in the course of a valid *Terry* stop is consistent with Fourth Amendment prohibitions against unreasonable searches and seizures.

Petitioner argues that the Nevada statute circumvents the probable cause requirement, in effect allowing an officer to arrest a person for being suspicious. According to petitioner, this creates a risk of arbitrary police conduct that the Fourth Amendment does not permit. Petitioner's concerns are met by the requirement that a *Terry* stop must be justified at its inception and "reasonably related in scope to the circumstances which justified" the initial stop.... Under these principles, an officer may not arrest a suspect for failure to identify himself if the request for identification is not reasonably related to the circumstances justifying the stop.... It is clear in this case that the request for identification was "reasonably related in scope to the circumstances which justified" the stop. The officer's request was a commonsense inquiry, not an effort to obtain an arrest for failure to identify after a *Terry* stop yielded insufficient evidence. The stop, the request, and the State's requirement of a response did not contravene the guarantees of the Fourth Amendment.

Petitioner further contends that his conviction violates the Fifth Amendment's prohibition on compelled self-incrimination. The Fifth Amendment states that "[n]o person... shall be compelled in any criminal case to be a witness against himself."... The Fifth Amendment prohibits only compelled testimony that is incriminating. A claim of Fifth Amendment privilege must establish "'reasonable ground to apprehend danger to the witness from his being compelled to answer.... [T]he danger to be apprehended must be real and appreciable, with reference to the ordinary operation of law in the ordinary course of things—not a danger of an imaginary and unsubstantial character, having reference to some extraordinary and barely possible contingency, so improbable that no reasonable man would suffer it to influence his conduct.'" In this case, petitioner's refusal to disclose his name was not based on any articulated real and appreciable fear that his name would be used to incriminate him, or that it "would furnish a link in the chain of evidence needed to prosecute" him. As best we can tell, petitioner refused to identify himself only because he thought his name was none of the officer's business. Even today, petitioner does not explain how the disclosure of his name could have been used against him in a criminal case. While we recognize petitioner's strong belief that he should not have to disclose his identity, the Fifth Amendment does not override the Nevada Legislature's judgment to the contrary absent a reasonable belief that the disclosure would tend to incriminate him.

The narrow scope of the disclosure requirement is also important. One's identity is, by definition, unique; yet it is, in another sense, a universal characteristic. Answering a request to disclose a name is likely to be so insignificant in the scheme of things as to be incriminating only in unusual circumstances.... Still, a case may arise where there is a substantial allegation that furnishing identity at the time of a stop would have given the police a link in the chain of evidence needed to convict the individual of a separate offense. In that case, the court can then consider whether the privilege applies and, if the Fifth Amendment has been violated, what remedy must follow. We need not resolve those questions here.

Dissenting, *Breyer, J.*, joined by *Souter, J.*, and *Ginsburg, J.*

There are sound reasons rooted in Fifth Amendment considerations for adhering to this Fourth Amendment legal condition circumscribing police authority to stop an individual against his will.... Can a State, in addition to requiring a stopped individual to answer, "What's your name?" also require an answer to, "What's your license number?" or "Where do you live?" Can a police officer, who must know how to make a *Terry* stop, keep track of the constitutional answers? After all, answers to any of these questions may, or may not, incriminate, depending upon the circumstances.

Indeed, as the majority points out, a name itself—even if it is not "Killer Bill" or "Rough 'em up Harry"—will sometimes provide the police with "a link in the chain of evidence needed to convict the individual of a separate offense." The majority reserves judgment about whether compulsion is permissible in such instances. How then is a police officer in the midst of a *Terry* stop to distinguish between the majority's ordinary case and this special case where the majority reserves judgment?...

Questions for Discussion

1. Why does the Supreme Court conclude that asking a person subjected to a *Terry* stop for identification is reasonable under the Fourth Amendment?
2. Did the officer need to know Hiibel's name? Was this request reasonably related to the purpose of the stop? Argue both sides of this question.
3. ***Problems in policing.*** Write a brief paragraph summarizing the limits of a *Terry* stop in terms of movement, duration, and investigative techniques. Under what circumstances may a defendant refuse to identify himself or herself to an officer?

Cases and Comments

Fingerprints and State Law. Davis was convicted of rape and sentenced to life imprisonment. The victim identified her assailant as an African American "youth." Finger and palm prints at the crime scene were the only other available evidence. The Meridian, Mississippi, police took at least twenty-four African American young people to police headquarters for brief questioning and fingerprinting and then released them without charge. Forty or fifty other young people were interrogated at school, on the street, or at police headquarters. Davis was fourteen and occasionally worked in the victim's yard. He was detained and taken to police headquarters for fingerprinting and routine questioning on December 3, 1965, and over the course of the next four days, Davis was interrogated by the police in a car, at his home, or at police headquarters. On December 12, Davis, without consent, was driven ninety miles to Jackson, Mississippi, and confined overnight. He took a lie detector test the same day and confessed. On December 14, Davis was fingerprinted a second time. His prints together with the fingerprints of twenty-three other individuals were sent to FBI headquarters, and the FBI reported that they matched the prints found at the crime scene.

The Supreme Court held that Davis's detention on December 3 was in violation of the temporary seizures authorized by *Terry v. Ohio* under the Fourth Amendment and that he had been subjected to a warrantless seizure that subjected him to the "harassment and ignominy incident to involuntary detention" without probable cause.

The Supreme Court recognized that "because of the unique nature of the fingerprinting process...detentions [for fingerprinting] might, under narrowly defined circumstances, be found to comply with the Fourth Amendment even though there is no probable cause in the traditional sense." See *Davis v. Mississippi,* 394 U.S. 721 (1969).

In *Hayes v. Florida,* the police investigation indicated that Hayes was the primary suspect in a series of burglary-rapes in Punta Gorda, Florida, in 1980. Hayes was detained and taken to the stationhouse for fingerprinting. An officer determined that Hayes's fingerprints matched those at the crime scene, and he was arrested. The U.S. Supreme Court stressed that Hayes was subjected to an involuntary detention without probable cause or a judicial warrant authorizing the detention for the purpose of fingerprinting. The Court recognized that Hayes's detention for fingerprinting violated the Fourth Amendment, despite the fact that this was a much less intrusive invasion of bodily integrity than a lineup or interrogation. The Supreme Court stressed that the "line is crossed when the police, without probable cause or warrant, forcibly remove a person from his home or other place...and transport him to the police station, where he is detained, although briefly for investigative purposes." The Court significantly observed that "[n]one of the foregoing implies that a brief detention in the field for the purpose of fingerprinting, where there is only reasonable suspicion not amounting to probable cause, is necessarily impermissible under the Fourth Amendment....There is...support...for the view that the Fourth Amendment would permit seizures for the purpose of fingerprinting, if there is reasonable suspicion that the suspect has committed a criminal act, if there is a reasonable basis for believing that fingerprinting will establish or negate the suspect's connection with that crime, and if the procedure is carried out with dispatch." The Supreme Court also noted that the Fourth Amendment "might permit the judiciary to authorize the seizure of a person on less than probable cause and his removal to the police station for the purpose of fingerprinting." See *Hayes v. Florida,* 470 U.S. 811 (1985).

In reaction to the decision in *Hayes,* several states, including Arizona, Idaho, Indiana, Iowa, Nebraska, and Utah, passed statutes providing for the limited detention of suspects for fingerprinting and other identification procedures when a judge finds that there is probable cause that a crime has been committed and that there are reasonable grounds to believe that a suspect committed the offense. See *People v. Madson,* 638 P.2d 18 (Colo. 1981).

Automobiles and *Terry* Stops

May law enforcement officers require the driver as well as the passengers in a vehicle that they detain on a traffic stop to exit the automobile? On one hand, this seems to interfere with the liberty of individuals without reasonable suspicion that they pose a danger. On the other hand, an officer should not be required to run the risk that a motorist or passenger has a firearm and to place the officer's life in jeopardy.

In *Pennsylvania v. Mimms,* the Supreme Court ruled that the "legitimate and weighty" interest in protecting the safety of a police officer outweighed the "de minimis" (minor) intrusion on the liberty of the citizen and justified requiring a driver to exit an automobile (*Pennsylvania v. Mimms,* 434 U.S. 106, 108–111 [1977]). In *Maryland v. Wilson,* the Supreme Court extended the ruling in *Mimms* and held that an officer may require a *passenger* to leave a car (*Maryland v. Wilson,* 519 U.S. 408 [1997]).

The dissenting justices in *Wilson* viewed the judgment as an unwarranted extension of *Terry* and argued that a passenger should be ordered out of the automobile only where the officer reasonably believes that the passenger poses a threat. The dissenters argued that approving the automatic removal of an individual from a car imposes a burden on thousands of innocent citizens who may be "offended, embarrassed, and sometimes provoked" by "arbitrary official commands"(420).

In 2009, the Supreme Court issued an opinion in *Arizona v. Johnson.* In *Johnson,* three members of the Arizona police gang task force pulled over an automobile after a license plate check revealed that the vehicle's registration had been suspended. The stop took place in a neighborhood frequented by the Crips street gang. Officer Trevizo observed that Johnson, the passenger in the backseat, was wearing a bandanna that symbolized membership in the Crips, had a police scanner, and told Trevizo that he lived in an area that was a known to be a home of the Crips street gang. Johnson also admitted that he had served time in prison for burglary and had been released roughly a year ago. Trevizo asked Johnson to exit the vehicle and fearing for her safety patted him down and seized a handgun. The U.S. Supreme Court held that the driver as well as passengers in an automobile are "effectively seized" when the vehicle is "pulled over for investigation of a traffic violation." The temporary seizure of the driver and passengers "ordinarily continues, and remains reasonable for the duration of the stop." The Court went on to hold that an officer is free to interrogate and investigate criminal activity on the part of passengers that is unrelated to the purpose of the traffic stop so long as this investigation does not "measurably extend the duration of the stop." The officer also may frisk a passenger or driver when there are reasonable grounds to believe that the passenger or driver is armed and presently dangerous (*Arizona v. Johnson,* 555 U.S. ___ [2008]).

Three state supreme courts have refused to follow the U.S. Supreme Court and have held that the police require reasonable suspicion to order a driver out of an automobile. These state supreme courts have reasoned that their state constitutions provide individuals with greater protections against searches and seizures than the Fourth Amendment to the U.S. Constitution. For instance, the Massachusetts Supreme Court ruled in *Commonwealth v. Gonsalves* that the state constitution requires that a police officer in a "routine traffic stop... have a reasonable belief that the officer's safety, or the safety of others, is in danger before ordering a driver out of a motor vehicle." The Massachusetts court noted that state courts under a federal system must be "strong and independent repositories of authority in order to protect the rights of their citizens" (*Commonwealth v. Gonsalves,* 711 N.E.2d 108, 111, 115 [1999]).

You can find *State v. Sprague* on this book's study site. In *Sprague,* the Vermont Supreme Court considers whether the provision of the Vermont Constitution providing that "the people have a right to hold themselves free from search or seizure" prohibits the police from directing that a passenger exit a vehicle on a traffic stop absent reasonable suspicion. You should compare the reasoning of the court in *Sprague* with the U.S. Supreme Court decisions in *Mimms* and in *Wilson.* Which approach do you find more persuasive?

You can find Pennsylvania v. Mimms, Maryland v. Wilson, *and* Arizona v. Johnson *on the study site, http://www.sagepub.com/lippmancp.*

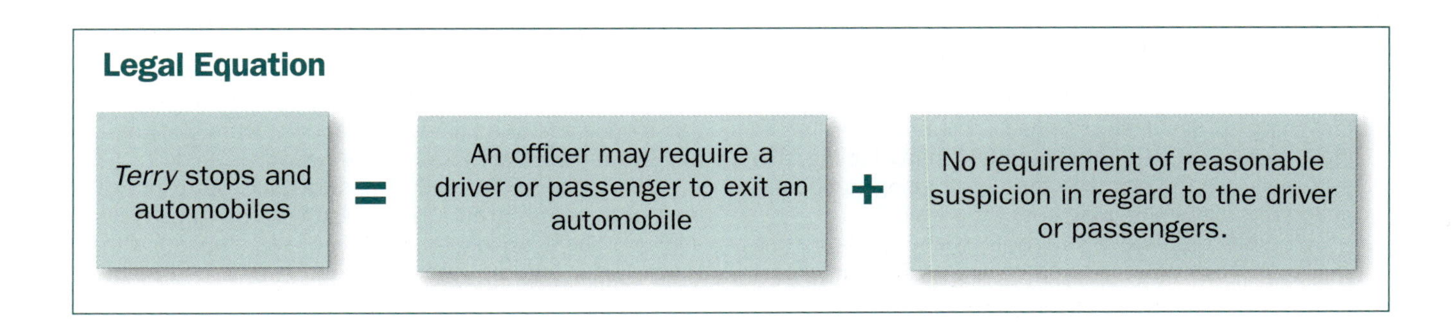

Criminal Procedure in the News

On the evening of February 4, 1999, four plainclothes officers in New York's specially organized Street Crimes Unit were patrolling the Bronx in an unmarked police car in search of a serial rapist. Officers Sean Carroll, Edward McMellon, Kenneth Boss, and Richard Murphy spotted twenty-two-year-old Amadou Diallo at roughly 12:45 A.M. The officers concluded that Diallo fit the description of the serial rapist. The ensuing confrontation resulted in the fatal shooting of Diallo and in the criminal prosecution and ultimate acquittal of four officers.

Amadou Diallo was born in Liberia, West Africa. His father was a businessman, and the family had lived in a number of countries, including Togo, Guinea, Thailand, and Singapore. Amadou possessed a love of reading, music, and dancing and was an avid fan of basketball star Michael Jordan. He attended a string of private schools abroad and, in 1996, immigrated to New York City to pursue his "American dream" of education in computer technology. Amadou initially was employed as a delivery man and then worked six days a week as a street peddler selling gloves, socks, and videotapes. He was a devout Muslim who sent his earnings home to his parents while continuing to foster his educational ambitions. Amadou was returning from getting something to eat when he encountered the police officers.

Officer Carroll would later testify that his attention was drawn to Diallo's suspicious behavior, hiding in the shadows of a vestibule and periodically darting out of the darkness to look up and down the block. Carroll and McMellon testified that they approached Diallo in order to question him, and when they identified themselves as police officers, Diallo fled into the dimly lit vestibule. The officers gave chase. Carroll testified that he did not want Diallo to get inside the building and risk that Diallo would take a resident hostage. Both Carroll and McMellon saw Diallo reach into his pocket with his right hand while opening the door with his left hand. As Diallo turned toward the officers, Carroll cried "gun, he's got a gun," and both officers fired their weapons in what they described as self-defense. McMellon fell off the step leading to the vestibule, and Carroll thought that his partner had been shot. Boss and Murphy saw Diallo standing in the vestibule amid the gunfire and testified that they thought that Diallo was aiming a weapon at them as they rushed to the defense of their fellow officers. Boss testified that "I think, oh my God, I'm going to die. I start firing. . . . I was in the line of fire." Murphy added that "I had this empty feeling, this sick feeling in my stomach that I was going to be hit. I pulled the trigger, jumping out of the way."

The officers fired a total of forty-one shots, hitting Diallo nineteen times. Professor James Fyfe, an expert on police procedures, testified that the officers had followed New York Police Department procedures and had acted properly. Diallo had disregarded an order to halt and had run into the vestibule, and at this point, the police had an obligation to protect the residents of the building.

The trial was moved to Albany, New York, to avoid the taint of pretrial publicity. The prosecution argued that the police had improperly escalated the confrontation and that Diallo was unarmed and apparently was reaching for his wallet. The only other object in his possession was his keys. The prosecution stressed that standing in the vestibule of your home and looking up and down the street is not suspicious behavior and under no circumstances merits the police use of deadly force.

A prosecution expert testified that an analysis of the bullet wounds indicated that Diallo almost immediately had been knocked to the ground and that the officers nevertheless continued firing, allegedly intentionally killing Diallo or killing him with depraved indifference as to whether he lived or died. The defense contended that Diallo had remained standing throughout the police assault. An eyewitness contradicted this version and testified that she heard someone shout "gun" and that Diallo had been shot while on the ground.

The jury deliberated for twenty-three hours over a three-day period before acquitting all four officers of second-degree murder, reckless endangerment, and various lesser included offenses. Large demonstrations against police brutality in New York City led to the arrest of 1,700 individuals. Diallo's parents filed a civil suit against the officers for gross negligence and wrongful death and other civil rights violations, which was settled for three million dollars.

Diallo's death became a source of criticism for individuals who objected to the stop-and-frisk policies of the New York City Police, and thousands of people turned out for his funeral. In June 2000, Bruce Springsteen found himself in the middle of this controversy when he wrote and performed the song "American Skin," in which he addressed the Diallo shooting with the powerful lyrics, "You can get killed just for living in your American skin / 41 shots / 41 shots / 41 shots." Patrick Lynch, president of the Patrolmen's Benevolent Association, wrote a letter to his members calling for a boycott of Springsteen's concerts. Lynch's letter stated, "I consider it an outrage that [Springsteen] would be trying to fatten his wallet by reopening the wounds of this tragic case at a time when police officers and community members are in a healing period."

The officers who shot Amadou Diallo were members of the elite Street Crimes Unit created to rid New York of illegal handguns. The city was flooded with these guns, and the rate of serious crimes and homicides seemed to be escalating out of control. The tactic of the Street Crimes Unit was to conduct widespread stops and frisks in order to confiscate handguns and to deter individuals from carrying firearms. The 138 officers were known as the "commandos" of the New York Police, and their motto was "We Own the Night." The unit's productivity was measured by firearms and drug seizures, and its tactic was to swarm a suspect, often with guns drawn. The plainclothes officers in the Street Crimes Unit were given a great deal of credit for radically shrinking crime statistics.

According to the Washington think tank Cato Foundation, the Street Crimes Unit would stop and frisk individuals regardless of whether they were able to establish reasonable suspicion. In response to the shooting, reforms were introduced to insure that the Amadou Diallo tragedy would not be repeated.

In 1999, New York Attorney General Eliot Spitzer reported that a study of 175,000 stops recorded by the New York City Police over a fifteen-month period revealed a pattern of possible discrimination and stops and frisks that did not meet the reasonable suspicion standard.

Stop and frisk. African Americans were 23 percent more likely to be stopped than Caucasians; Hispanics were 39 percent more likely than Caucasians to be stopped; African Americans were 2.1 times more likely to be stopped for suspicion of committing a violent crime than Caucasians and 2.4 times more likely to be stopped for suspicion of carrying a weapon. Hispanics were 1.7 times more likely to be stopped for suspicion of committing a violent crime than were Caucasians and 2.0 times more likely to be stopped for suspicion of carrying a weapon.

Arrest. The Street Crimes Unit stopped 16.3 African Americans, 14.5 Hispanics, and 9.6 Caucasians for each stop that resulted in an arrest. The New York City Police stopped 9.5 African Americans, 8.8 Hispanics, and 9.6 Caucasians for each stop that resulted in an arrest.

Stops. A study of 10,000 forms filled out by New York City Police on which the officers recorded the factors that caused the police to stop an individual indicated that 15.4 percent did not state facts that satisfied the legal definition of reasonable suspicion. One quarter of the forms did not state sufficient information to permit a determination whether the stop met the legal standard. The Street Crimes Unit failed to state facts to meet the legal definition of reasonable suspicion in 23 percent of the cases. Roughly 16 percent of the stops of African Americans, 14.3 percent of the stops of Hispanics, and 16.6 percent of the stops of Caucasians by New York City Police were not based on facts that constituted reasonable suspicion.

Psychologists Tom Tyler and Cheryl Wakslak of New York University conclude that while African Americans are more likely than other racial groups to believe that racial profiling occurs, racial profiling undermines public support for the police among all racial groups. On the other hand, there is belief among a significant percentage of the population that police officers acting in a neutral and objective fashion may inevitably stop a disproportionate number of minorities, particularly in combating terrorism. What is your view?

Are you persuaded that stop-and-frisk policies contribute to incidents such as the death of Amadou Diallo? Would you limit the authority of the police to conduct stops and frisks? Is the criticism of the police merely "Monday morning quarterbacking" by critics of the police? Consider that in the first three months of 2009, New York City Police officers made 170,000 stops of people on the street, the most for any three-month period since the police began reporting these data. More than 144,000 of the stops were of African Americans or of Hispanics. These stops resulted in the seizure of 924 guns (compared with 886 in 2008), and roughly 10 percent of the stops resulted in arrests.

Frisks

The *Terry* Standard

The Supreme Court in *Terry v. Ohio* recognized that American criminals have a "long tradition of armed violence" and that a number of law enforcement officers are killed and wounded every year in the "line of duty." Most of these fatalities and injuries are inflicted at fairly close range with guns and knifes. The Court accordingly ruled that where "nothing in the initial stages of the encounter serves to dispel [an officer's] reasonable fear for his own or others' safety, he is entitled for the protection of himself and others in the area to conduct a carefully limited search of the outer clothing of such persons in an attempt to discover weapons which might be used to assault him" (30–31). You should keep the following several points in mind.

Weapons. The Supreme Court explained that this carefully limited **frisk** is intended to protect the officer and others in the vicinity and that it must therefore be "confined to an intrusion reasonably designed to discover guns, knives, clubs or other hidden instruments for assault of the police officer."

Reasonableness. The officer need not be absolutely certain that the individual is armed and presently dangerous. The test is whether a reasonably prudent man or woman under the circumstances would believe that his or her safety or the safety of others is at risk. Reasonableness is to be determined based on the facts as interpreted in light of the officer's experience. This is an objective test. An officer may not base a frisk on the officer's subjective fear or apprehension or hunch. The opposite also is true. An officer who lacks fear that a suspect is armed and presently dangerous may conduct a frisk so long as an objective person would believe that the frisk is required.

Scope. The frisk must be directed at the discovery of guns, knives, and other weapons. The officer may reach inside the clothing only when he or she feels an object that is reasonably believed to be a weapon (*Minnesota v. Dickerson,* which is discussed below later extended this rule to narcotics). An officer may remove a container or package and open it if the officer reasonably believes that it may contain a weapon.

Dispel. The frisk does not automatically follow from the stop. A suspect is to be afforded the opportunity to dispel the officer's fear that the suspect is armed and presently dangerous.

The key fact is whether the suspect is reasonably believed to pose a threat. Courts have upheld frisks based on a combination of factors:

- A bulge in the suspect's pocket
- A suspect's reaching into his or her pocket
- The suspect's movements
- The officer's knowledge that the suspect had been involved in violent activity
- The type of criminal activity
- The suspect's presence in a high-crime neighborhood, particularly late at night
- An individual's being is with another individual who is arrested by the police for a serious offense

A cooperative suspect who immediately offers a credible explanation and does not appear to pose a threat may *dispel* (eliminate) an officer's reasonable fear that the suspect is armed and presently dangerous. Despite the fact that the frisk does not automatically follow from the stop, it should be noted that a number of courts have approved "automatic" frisks in the cases of suspected drug trafficking on the grounds that drugs, gangs, and guns are closely connected to one another (see *United States v. Garcia,* 459 F.3d 1059 [10th Cir. 2006]).

On the same day that the Supreme Court decided *Terry,* the Court held in *Sibron v. New York* that the fact that a suspect had been observed talking to known narcotics addicts for a number of hours did not give "rise to reasonable fear of life and limb on the part of the police officer." The Court also ruled that, assuming that there were adequate grounds to search Sibron for weapons, the officer had gone beyond the limits of a *Terry* frisk when he immediately thrust his hand into Sibron's pocket and removed heroin rather than first frisking Sibron's outer clothing and then removing weapons (*Sibron v. New York,* 392 U.S. 40, 63–65 [1968]).

In *Adams v. Williams,* an officer responding to an informant's tip approached a narcotics dealer sitting in his car at 2:15 in the morning. The suspect rolled down his window rather than comply with a request to exit his automobile, and Sergeant Connolly immediately responded by removing a pistol from the suspect's waist, which was precisely where the informant stated that it was located. The Supreme Court held that Connolly had acted to protect himself from an imminent harm and ruled that he had undertaken a "limited intrusion designed to insure his safety" (*Adams v. Williams,* 407 U.S. 143, 147–148 [1972]).

Extending *Terry* Searches to Automobiles

In 1983, in *Michigan v. Long,* the U.S. Supreme Court extended *Terry* frisks to the passenger compartment of automobiles when police officers possess a reasonable fear for their safety. Deputies Lewis and Howell observed a car swerve into a ditch in rural Michigan. The officers stopped to investigate and were met by David Long at the rear of the car. The door on the driver's side of the vehicle was left open. Long, who one of the officers testified "appeared to be under the influence of something," failed to respond to a request to produce his registration and turned and began walking toward the open door of the vehicle. The officers followed Long and spotted a hunting knife on the floorboard of the driver's side of the car. Deputy Howell shined his flashlight into the car, noticed something protruding from under the armrest on the front seat, lifted the armrest, and discovered marijuana (*Michigan v. Long,* 463 U.S. 1032, 1035 [1983]).

How can this search of Long's automobile be justified as a limited *Terry* frisk for weapons? The Supreme Court upheld Deputy Howell's search and explained that the search of the passenger compartment of an automobile is justified in those instances in which an officer possesses a reasonable belief that the suspect is potentially dangerous and may gain immediate control of weapons. The Court stressed that the search must be limited to those areas in which a "weapon may be placed or hidden." In this case, there was the possibility that Long might have broken away from the police and gained access to a weapon. In the event that Long was not arrested, he might have grabbed a weapon after reentering his car. Are you persuaded that Long posed a threat to the officers? Should the Court have required the police to demonstrate that the search was the only alternative available to protect themselves. How would the Supreme Court have ruled in the event that the automobile was locked (1049–1051)?

We also should note the Supreme Court decision in *Maryland v. Buie.* In *Buie,* the police relied on an arrest warrant to arrest Buie in his home for armed robbery. The Court cited *Michigan v. Long* to uphold the right of the police to carry out a protective sweep of a home where there is reasonable suspicion that the sweep is necessary to locate individuals who may pose a threat to the safety and security of the police officers. Buie's co-conspirator had yet to be found, and the police could reasonably have concluded that he was hiding in the basement (*Maryland v. Buie,* 494 U.S. 325, 327–331 [1990]).

Extending *Terry* Searches to Illegal Narcotics

In 1993, in *Minnesota v. Dickerson,* the U.S. Supreme Court upheld the right of a police officer conducting a frisk to seize illegal narcotics. The officer must have immediate probable cause to believe that the items he or she encounters are illegal narcotics.

The Supreme Court explained that a pat down in which a law enforcement officer feels an object that he or she has probable cause to believe is an illegal narcotic is analogous to a plain-view search. The Court explained that the plain-view doctrine permits a law enforcement officer to seize contraband that he or she views during the course of a lawful search. An illustration of plain view is a police officer who while searching a home for drugs encounters and seizes an illegal assault rifle. The "plain-feel" doctrine is based on an officer's touch rather than visual examination. This permits a police officer to seize an object that the officer's physical examination indicates is contraband.

The Supreme Court in *Dickerson* held that "[i]f a police officer lawfully pats down a suspect's outer clothing and feels an object whose contour or mass makes its identity immediately apparent, there has been no invasion of the suspect's privacy beyond that already authorized by the officer's search for weapons; if the object is contraband, its warrantless seizure would be justified by the same practical considerations that inhere in the plain-view context" (*Minnesota v. Dickerson,* 508 U.S. 366, 375 [1993]). Keep in mind that a major limitation on the seizure of illegal narcotics under the **plain-feel doctrine** is that it must be "immediately apparent" (probable cause) to the officer that he or she is feeling illegal narcotics (378).

You can find Michigan v. Long *and* Minnesota v. Dickerson *on the study site, http://www.sagepub.com/lippmancp.*

Legal Equation

A *Terry* frisk	=	Where nothing in the initial stages of the encounter serves to dispel an officer's reasonable fear for his or her own or others' safety
	+	The officer is entitled for the protection of himself or herself and others in the area to conduct a carefully limited search of the outer clothing of such persons
	+	In an attempt to discover weapons that might be used to assault him.
A *Terry* search of the passenger compartment of an automobile	=	The search of the passenger compartment of an automobile is justified in those instances in which an officer possesses a reasonable belief that the suspect is dangerous and may gain immediate control of weapons
	+	The search must be limited to those areas in which a weapon may be placed or hidden in those cases in which the police possess articulable and objectively reasonable belief that the suspect is potentially dangerous.
A *Terry* frisk and the seizure of drugs	=	A police officer who lawfully pats down a suspect's outer clothing
	+	Feels an object whose contour or mass makes its identity as illegal narcotics immediately apparent.

4.4 YOU DECIDE

Officer James Burns of the Minneapolis Police Department and his partner observed a vehicle make a quick left turn from the right lane without signaling. The officers decided to stop the driver for a traffic violation. Burns activated his red lights and saw the driver lean toward the passenger compartment, leading Burns to suspect that the driver was making an effort to conceal something. The driver pulled over and parked. Burns approached the driver, Damon Cortez Richmond, and informed him that he was being stopped for a moving violation. Burns asked Richmond where he was coming from and where he was going. Richmond did not appear to understand the questions and appeared "nervous and fidgety." Burns repeated his questions, and Richmond once again failed to respond.

Richmond was unable to locate his driver's license. At this point, Burns directed Richmond to exit his car and escorted him back to the squad car. Burns testified that he commonly grabs a suspect from the back of the jacket to keep the suspect from fleeing and that as soon as Burns grabbed Richmond's jacket, Richmond inexplicably stuck his arms straight out in front of him. Burns did not know whether Richmond was going to run and instructed Richmond to place his hands on the squad car. Burns began to frisk for weapons, repeated his question concerning Richmond's travel, and again did not receive a response. Richmond took his hands off the squad car and started to reach for his outside left coat pocket. Burns's partner grabbed Richmond's arm and forcibly placed it back on the squad car. "Fearing that Richmond had a weapon in the pocket, Burns stuck his hand into the pocket and immediately recognized a large quantity of cocaine." Burns did not frisk Richmond around his pockets before reaching for the weapon. Burns handcuffed Richmond and placed him under arrest. Was the cocaine legally seized by officer Burns? See *State v. Richmond,* 602 N.W.2d 647 (Ct. App. Minn. 1999).

You can find the answer by referring to the study site, http://www.sagepub.com/lippmancp.

4.5 YOU DECIDE

The Beloit, Wisconsin, police received an anonymous telephone tip that four or five African American males were selling drugs to motorists at a specific intersection. Two officers arrived at the location within thirty minutes and saw a Ford with three other black males seated on the hood of a car. One of the officers approached Lamardus Ford and smelled marijuana. The officer ordered Ford off the car, placed Ford's hands on the hood, and began patting him down. The officer testified that the frisk was routine practice because he was investigating possible drug activity, he had smelled marijuana, and it was his routine practice to conduct frisks during street encounters for safety reasons. During the pat down, the officer felt a large square wad of soft material in Ford's front pants pocket. Ford was asked what it was and replied that it was money. Ford became "jumpy" whenever the officer's hands approached the front of Ford's waist, and Ford even grabbed the officer's hand as it approached that area. Because Ford was not cooperative, the officer took Ford in a "full Nelson" hold to his squad car, where he placed Ford's hands behind his back and handcuffed him. The officer then resumed the pat down. Ford was still jumpy whenever the officer approached the waistband of his boxer shorts, which were visible above Ford's jeans. The officer testified that it is common practice for people to put guns and other contraband down the front of their shorts. The officer asked if he could look inside Ford's shorts. Ford took a step back. The officer responded by pulling out the waistband about one and one-half inches and shined a flashlight into Ford's underwear. The officer discovered plastic bags of marijuana between Ford's thigh and the genitals. The officer removed the bags of marijuana and arrested Ford for possession of a controlled substance. Were the narcotics legally seized by the officer? See *State v. Ford,* 565 N.W.2d 286 (Ct. App. Wisc. 1997).

You can find the answer by referring to the study site, http://www.sagepub.com/lippmancp.

Chapter Summary

In *Terry v. Ohio,* Chief Justice Earl Warren stressed that a police officer may in "appropriate circumstances" approach and seize an individual to investigate possible criminal behavior despite the fact that the officer does not have probable cause to make an arrest. The question asked by a judge in reviewing a police officer's decision to stop an individual is "whether the facts available to the officer at the moment of the intrusion warrant a man or woman of reasonable caution in the belief" that there is reasonable suspicion that a crime has occurred, is under way, or is about to occur.

The Supreme Court stressed that reasonable suspicion is a "less demanding standard than probable cause" and may be based on less complete and less reliable information. In determining whether there is reasonable suspicion, the "totality of the circumstances" are to be taken into account. Judges consider a number of factors, including whether there is a pattern of conduct indicative of criminal activity, the time of day, whether the events occur in a high-crime area, the police officer's knowledge that a suspect has an arrest record or criminal background, flight or evasion or nervousness of the suspect, and the officer's experience in making arrests for this type of activity. The facts are to be interpreted in light of an officer's experience and training. Reasonable suspicion is based on probabilities rather than certainties, and in putting together the pieces of the puzzle that constitute reasonable suspicion, innocent people inevitably may be mistakenly stopped and searched.

Reasonable suspicion also may be based on an informant's tip. An informant is required to be known to the police and to have proven reliable in the past. The court also will ask how the informant has obtained the information. An informant with firsthand knowledge of criminal activity should be able to provide detailed information.

A tip that lacks these indicia of reliability may be relied on where corroborated in essential details by the police. Most important is the informant's demonstrated ability to have predicted a suspect's pattern of activity. The judge strikes a balance. The less reliable the informant, the more a court may insist that the informant is in the position to provide detailed information. A tip that is thought to initially lack the indicia of reliability may be strengthened by police corroboration and by the fact that the informant came forward personally and by a criminal statute that punishes intentionally "false criminal reports."

Law enforcement has developed profiles to detect terrorists, drug couriers, and other offenders. Courts generally do not give particular weight to the claim that an individual fits a "profile" and, instead, ask whether the combination of the factors identified in the profile constitutes reasonable suspicion. In many instances, courts have found reasonable suspicion where law enforcement agents have supplemented the profile with additional observations.

An individual may not be lawfully stopped by the police when the sole reason for his or her seizure is race, ethnicity, gender, religion, or other descriptive characteristic. An individual also may not be stopped based on the fact that he or she "does not belong in a neighborhood." Race, ethnicity, or some other physical characteristic, however, may be considered as one of several factors in a finding of reasonable suspicion.

The Supreme Court has stressed that a *Terry* stop and frisk is a limited intrusion to investigate and to detect crime. Law enforcement officials may interfere with your freedom and privacy only to the extent required to accomplish their purpose. A *Terry* stop is open to constitutional challenge when a suspect is treated as if he or she has been subjected to a probable cause arrest rather than to a reasonable suspicion stop. This inquiry typically focuses on three areas: movement, length of detention, and intrusiveness.

The Supreme Court has introduced some modest flexibility into *Terry* in the case of traffic stops. In *Pennsylvania v. Mimms,* the Supreme Court held that the "legitimate and weighty" interest in protecting the safety of a police officer outweighs the "de minimis" (trivial) intrusion on the liberty of the citizen involved in requiring a driver to leave an automobile. In *Maryland v. Wilson,* the Supreme Court extended the ruling in *Mimms* and held that an officer may require a passenger or passengers to exit a car. Several state supreme courts, however, have rejected the U.S. Supreme Court's rulings and require that law enforcement officers possess reasonable suspicion before directing individuals to vacate a motor vehicle. The Supreme Court also has held that an officer is free to interrogate and investigate criminal activity on the part of passengers that is unrelated to the purpose of the traffic stop so long as this investigation does not "measurably extend the duration of the stop."

The second prong of the judgment in *Terry* addresses the nature and scope of a *Terry* frisk. The Supreme Court in *Terry v. Ohio* recognized that American criminals have a "long tradition of armed violence" and that a number of law enforcement officers are killed and wounded every year in the line of duty. Most of these fatalities and injuries are inflicted at fairly close range with guns and knifes. The Court accordingly ruled that where "nothing in the initial stages of the encounter serves to dispel [an officer's] reasonable fear for his own or others' safety, he is entitled for the protection of himself and others in the area to conduct a carefully limited search of the outer clothing of such persons in an attempt to discover weapons which might be used to assault him." The frisk is not automatic. The suspect must be provided with the opportunity to dispel the officer's reasonable fear for his own or others' safety and security.

In *Michigan v. Long,* the Supreme Court extended *Terry* frisks to the passenger compartment of automobiles. The Court stressed that the search must be limited to those areas in which a "weapon may be placed or hidden" and to those instances in which the police "possess [an] articulable and objectively reasonable belief that the suspect is potentially dangerous and may gain immediate control of weapons." *Minnesota v. Dickerson* affirmed the limited right of a police officer conducting a frisk to seize illegal narcotics. The officer under the "plain-feel" doctrine must have probable cause to believe that the object that he or she encounters is an illegal narcotic.

In summary, in *Terry v. Ohio,* the Supreme Court explicitly balanced the interest in investigating and detecting crime against the intrusion into individual privacy and held that individuals may be subjected to limited seizures based on reasonable suspicion. The Court further ruled that officers may conduct frisks to protect themselves. The Court attempted to insure that these police–citizen interactions would be perceived as fair and neutral by requiring that an officer base his or her decision making on objective facts interpreted in light of his or her experience. This balancing test has been employed by the Court in addressing areas ranging from the removal of the occupants of automobiles to the searches of passenger compartments and intrusions to seize narcotics. *Terry* stops and frisks are based on probabilities and predictions and on occasion may result in interference with the liberty of innocents. We have traded a measure of liberty for safety and security. Do you agree that the appropriate balance has been struck by the Supreme Court in regard to stop and frisk?

Chapter Review Questions

1. What is the relationship between the Reasonableness Clause and Warrant Clause of the Fourth Amendment?
2. Summarize the decision in *Terry v. Ohio.*
3. Discuss the role of reasonableness, objectivity, experience, expertise, probability, and the totality of the circumstances in the determination of reasonable suspicion.
4. What are some of the factors that a police officer may consider in determining whether there is reasonable suspicion to stop an individual?
5. What is the standard adopted by courts to determine whether the police were justified in relying on an informant's tip to determine reasonable suspicion?
6. How are profiles developed? Do courts give particular weight to profiles in determining reasonable suspicion?
7. Under what circumstances may race be considered in determining reasonable suspicion? Is racial profiling ever justified?
8. Discuss the scope and duration of a *Terry* stop in regard to the permissible movement of a suspect, the length of the detention, and the intrusiveness of the stop.
9. What is the legal standard for a *Terry* frisk?
10. May a police officer order a driver or a passenger to exit an automobile? Under what circumstances may an officer frisk a driver or passenger who has exited a vehicle?
11. Discuss the extension of *Terry* frisks to automobile passenger compartments and to drugs.
12. Write a one-page essay for police officers summarizing the law of stops and frisks.

Legal Terminology

anonymous tip
articulable suspicion
case-by-case determination
drug courier profile
frisk
informant
plain-feel doctrine
racial profiling
reasonable suspicion
stop and frisk
stop-and-identify statutes

Criminal Procedure on the Web

Log on to the Web-based student study site at **http://www.sagepub.com/lippmancp** to assist you in completing the Criminal Procedure on the Web exercises, as well as for additional features such as leading cases, podcasts, self-quizzes, and audio/video links.

1. Read about the debate between Supreme Court judges in drafting the decision in *Terry v. Ohio.* What were the major divisions between the judges?
2. Test your knowledge by reading the Federal Law Enforcement Training Center module on stop and frisk for Homeland Security personnel.
3. Examine New York Attorney General Eliot Spitzer's study of stop-and-frisk practices in New York City. What are the major findings of the study?
4. Read the U.S. Department of Justice guidelines on racial profiling. Compare the permissible role of racial profiling in ordinary criminal investigations and in national security investigations.
5. Read the Amnesty International report on racial profiling in the United States. Find the law in your state.

Bibliography

John Q. Barrett, "*Terry v. Ohio:* The Fourth Amendment Reasonableness of Police Stops and Frisks Based on Less Than Probable Cause," in C.S. Streiker, ed., *Criminal Procedure Stories* (New York: Foundation Press, 2006), pp. 295–313. A history of the Supreme Court decision in *Terry v. Ohio.*

Joshua Dressler and Alan C. Michaels, *Understanding Criminal Procedure: Investigation,* vol. 1, 4th ed. (Newark, NJ: LexisNexis, 2006), pp. 109–119. A brief overview of *Terry v. Ohio* and of the law of stop and frisk.

Wayne R. LaFave, Jerald H. Israel, and Nancy J. King, *Criminal Procedure,* 4th ed. (St. Paul, MN: Thomson/West Publishing, 2004), pp. 213–227. A good summary of the law of stop and frisk.

Stephen A. Saltzburg, Daniel J. Capra, and Angela J. Davis, *Basic Criminal Procedure,* 4th ed. (St. Paul, MN: Thomson/West Publishing, 2005), pp. 199–251. A helpful discussion of the primary stop-and-frisk cases decided by the U.S. Supreme Court.

Terry v. Ohio 30 Years Later: A Symposium on the Fourth Amendment, Law Enforcement & Police-Citizen Encounters, *St. John's Law Review,* vol. 72 (Summer–Fall, 1998), pp. 721–1524. A series of articles by legal scholars offering various perspectives on *Terry v. Ohio* and stop and frisk. Portions of the trial transcript are reprinted.

5 Probable Cause and Arrests

Did the police have probable cause to arrest Draper?

On the morning of September 8, Marsh and a Denver police officer went to the Denver Union Station and kept watch over all incoming trains from Chicago, but they did not see anyone fitting the description that Hereford [a Government informant] had given. Repeating the process on the morning of September 9, they saw a person, having the exact physical attributes and wearing the precise clothing described by Hereford, alight from an incoming Chicago train and start walking "fast" toward the exit. He was carrying a tan zipper bag in his right hand and the left was thrust in his raincoat pocket. Marsh, accompanied by the police officer, overtook, stopped, and arrested him. They then searched him and found the two "envelopes containing heroin" clutched in his left hand in his raincoat pocket, and found the syringe in the tan zipper bag. Marsh then took him (petitioner) into custody.

Core Concepts and Summary Statements

Introduction

An arrest is reasonable under the Fourth Amendment when the seizure is supported by probable cause and the arrest is executed or carried out in a reasonable fashion.

Arrests

A. An arrest results in an individual's being taken into custody and is more intrusive than a reasonable suspicion stop.

B. A formal arrest occurs when an officer directly tells a suspect that "you are under arrest." In a de facto arrest, an officer does not directly announce that an individual is under arrest, but a reasonable person would believe based on the totality of the circumstances that he or she is under arrest.

Probable Cause

A. Police officers possess probable cause for an arrest where the facts and circumstances within their knowledge and of which they have reasonably trustworthy information are sufficient to warrant a person of reasonable caution in the belief that an offense has been or is being committed.

B. Probable cause is based on "common sense" and on a practical evaluation of the totality of the facts and cannot be reduced to a set of rules or to a mathematical formula. In making this objective determination, courts recognize that officers have special expertise. Probable cause is based on probabilities rather than certainties.

C. A police officer may rely on his or her five senses in developing probable cause to conduct an arrest. He or she may develop probable cause through sights, sounds, smell, touch, and taste.

D. Probable cause may be based on hearsay or "secondhand information" provided by eyewitnesses, crime victims, or police officers. Hearsay information also may come from informants.

E. The traditional approach for evaluating whether an informant's report constitutes probable cause is the *Aguilar–Spinelli* two-prong test. The U.S. Supreme Court held that probable cause may be based on the hearsay report of an informant so long as the informant satisfies the *veracity prong* and the *basis-of-knowledge prong*.

F. In 1983, in *Illinois v. Gates,* the U.S. Supreme Court modified this test and adopted a "totality of the circumstances" analysis. Various states nonetheless continue to follow the *Aguilar–Spinelli* approach.

Reasonableness and Arrest

The Fourth Amendment, as we have seen, requires that an arrest be based on probable cause. The Fourth Amendment also requires that an arrest be carried out in a reasonable fashion.

Probable Cause, Warrants, and the Courts

A. The Supreme Court has expressed a preference that arrests be based on a warrant issued by a judge or magistrate. This means that the police must appear before a judicial official and establish probable cause to arrest an individual.

B. The warrant procedure establishes that the police have probable cause to arrest an individual.

C. In the case of warrantless arrests, the Fourth Amendment requires that the individual who is experiencing an extended loss of his or her liberty is entitled to a *Gerstein* hearing to determine whether a "reasonable person would believe that the suspect committed the offense."

Arrests and Warrants

Arrests for felonies in public do not require a warrant. Arrests for misdemeanors committed in the presence of a police officer also do not require warrants.

Arrests in the Home

Payton v. New York held that absent consent or exigent circumstances, an arrest warrant founded on probable cause is required to enter a house to arrest an individual.

Exigent Circumstances

A. The U.S. Supreme Court has held that the police may enter a home without an arrest warrant or search warrant when there is probable cause that there are exigent circumstances or a situation of urgency in which the police do not have time to obtain a warrant.

B. Courts have recognized exigent circumstances where there is hot pursuit, a threat to public safety, probable cause of the destruction of evidence, a threat that the suspect may flee, or the need to assist an individual in peril.

Deadly Force and Arrests

A. The common law fleeing-felon rule provides that the police may employ deadly force to apprehend a suspect who flees the police.

B. This was modified in *Tennesse v. Garner. Garner* held that where the suspect poses no immediate threat to the officer or threat to the public, the harm resulting from failing to apprehend him or her does not justify the use of deadly force. Reliance on deadly force to prevent the escape of all felony suspects is constitutionally unreasonable.

Nondeadly Force

A. The police employment of deadly as well as nondeadly force during an arrest, investigative stop, or other seizure is analyzed under the Fourth Amendment reasonableness standard.

B. The question is whether the police officer's actions are objectively reasonable in light of the facts and circumstances.

Misdemeanor Arrests and Citations

In *Atwater v. City of Lago Vista,* the U.S. Supreme Court held that if an officer has probable cause to believe that a suspect has committed even a minor criminal offense in the officer's presence, the officer may, without violating the Fourth Amendment, arrest the offender rather than issue a citation.

Introduction

An arrest is reasonable under the Fourth Amendment when two conditions are satisfied.

- The arrest must be based on *probable cause.* Probable cause may be based on *direct observations* or on *hearsay.*
- The arrest is carried out in a *reasonable fashion.*

Carrying out an arrest in a reasonable fashion involves various requirements that will be discussed in this chapter.

- ***Determination of probable cause.*** An arrest warrant must be issued by a judge or magistrate. A warrantless arrest must be found by a judge or magistrate to have been based on probable cause.
- ***Warrants.*** An *arrest warrant* is not required to arrest individuals in most instances. Absent consent or exigent circumstances, arrests in the home require a warrant.
- ***Physical force.*** The police may employ *reasonable force* to seize a suspect.
- ***Arrests and citations.*** Individuals are subject to *arrest* for both felonies and misdemeanors. There is no requirement that a citation be issued to an individual who has committed a misdemeanor in the presence of an officer.

As you read the chapter, consider how the probable cause standard and the requirement that arrests be carried out in a reasonable fashion balance the individual right to privacy with the responsibility of the police to enforce the law and to arrest individuals.

Arrests

An **arrest** under the Fourth Amendment occurs when an individual is lawfully taken into custody. An arrest is more intrusive than an investigative stop and frisk in several respects.

- ***Place.*** An investigative stop typically involves a brief detention on the street or in a public location. In contrast, an individual who is arrested is detained at the police station or in jail.
- ***Time.*** An investigative stop may last only as long as required to complete the investigation, while an arrest may result in detention for several hours or several days or, in some cases, even longer.
- ***Documentation.*** A stop and frisk is not recorded as part of an individual's criminal history. An arrest is entered into an individual's criminal record.
- ***Searches.*** An investigative stop may be accompanied by a brief interrogation and frisk. A custodial arrest may lead to a full search and to an inventory of an individual's possessions at the police station and to an extended interrogation.
- ***Criminal consequences.*** A stop and frisk results in a brief investigative stop. A custodial arrest may lead to a criminal indictment, trial, and criminal punishment.

How do you know that you have been arrested rather than stopped for a *Terry* investigation? An officer may directly tell you that "you are under arrest." This is a *formal arrest.* A *de facto arrest* occurs when an officer does not directly tell you that you are under arrest but, based on the totality of the circumstances, a reasonable person would conclude that he or she is under arrest. An individual under this objective test would know that he or she is detained when handcuffed, restrained by force or the threat of force, or involuntarily taken to the police station. There are three characteristics of an arrest to keep in mind.

- ***Lawful authority.*** The officer is acting in his or her official capacity as a law enforcement official. Restraint by a private person is kidnapping.
- ***Detention.*** An officer may restrain an individual through a formal statement ("you are under arrest") or through actions that constitute a de facto arrest.
- ***Reasonable person.*** A reasonable person, based on the objective circumstances, would believe that he or she is under arrest.

Probable Cause

As you recall, a stop and frisk is a brief investigative stop and requires reasonable suspicion. An arrest, as we have seen, is more intrusive than a stop and frisk, and courts have held that under the Fourth Amendment reasonableness standard, an arrest requires **probable cause.** Officers possess probable cause for an arrest where the facts and circumstances within their knowledge and of which they have reasonably trustworthy information are sufficient to warrant a person of reasonable caution in the belief that an offense has been or is being committed. Stated somewhat more simply, probable cause requires that a police officer objectively conclude, based on reasonably reliable facts, that a crime has been committed and that the person being arrested has committed the crime (*Carroll v. United States,* 267 U.S. 132, 162 [1925]).

The Supreme Court has stressed on a number of occasions that probable cause is based on "common sense" and on a "practical evaluation of the totality of the facts" and that probable cause cannot be reduced to a set of rules or to a mathematical formula. It is a matter of "probabilities" rather than "certainties." In an effort to clarify the degree of proof that is required for probable cause, the Supreme Court has observed that probable cause is more than reasonable suspicion and less than the beyond-a-reasonable-doubt standard required for a criminal conviction. In making this objective determination, judges recognize that law enforcement officers may possess a special expertise based on their experience on the streets. In *United States v. Ortiz,* the U.S. Supreme Court observed that border patrol officers are entitled to rely on their experience in combating illegal immigration in making a probable cause determination (*United States v. Ortiz,* 422 U.S. 891 [1975]).

The central point is that probable cause is based on facts, and an officer may not rely solely on intuition, opinion, or a hunch. You can think of probable cause to arrest an individual as more than fifty percent likelihood that the particular individual committed a crime.

The U.S. Supreme Court explained that the probable cause standard strikes a balance between the responsibility of law enforcement to investigate crimes and to apprehend offenders and the interest of citizens in protecting their privacy. The Court noted in *Brinegar* that "[r]equiring more would unduly hamper law enforcement. To allow less would be to leave law-abiding citizens at the mercy of the officer's whim or caprice" (*Brinegar v. U.S.,* 338 U.S. 160, 176 [1949]).

In the next sections, we will see that the police may rely on their five senses to establish probable cause. An officer also may rely on hearsay or facts reported by informants to the police officer that the officer does not directly observe himself or herself.

Direct Observations

A police officer may rely on his or her five senses in developing probable cause to arrest an individual. This means that the officer may develop probable cause through sight, sound, smell, touch, and taste. In some instances, the officer may directly observe a crime. In other instances, an officer must piece together a factual jigsaw puzzle. An officer may *hear* a gunshot, *observe* an individual flee, *stop and frisk* the individual, *seize* an unlawful firearm, and *arrest* the individual based on *probable cause.* The police may rely on various types of observations in making a probable cause determination.

- ***Direct observations.*** An officer may directly *observe* an individual engage in criminal conduct or conduct characteristic of an individual who is about to commit a crime or who has committed a crime.
- ***Statements.*** The police may *hear* a suspect make an incriminating remark or confess to a crime.
- ***Seize evidence.*** The police may *collect and analyze* scientific evidence that indicates that a suspect was involved in a crime. This includes DNA, blood, fingerprints, and hair samples.
- ***Smell.*** A police officer may *smell* narcotics or alcohol.

United States v. Humphries illustrates how the police rely on various "senses" in developing probable cause to make an arrest. The officers were patrolling in an area known for drug trafficking and observed a group of men gathered on the street. As the officers pulled their marked squad car onto the block, they saw the defendant pat his waist, an act that the officers interpreted as the defendant's insuring that his firearm was readily accessible. As the officers approached the men, the officers smelled marijuana, and the defendant began to quickly walk away. The officers followed the suspect and smelled an even stronger aroma of marijuana as they closed within five or ten feet. The defendant disregarded the officer's order to halt and went into a house where he was arrested. Can you identify the facts that the Fourth Circuit Court of Appeals found constituted probable cause (*United States v. Humphries,* 372 F.3d 653 [4th Cir. 2004])? The Supreme Court's 1968 judgment in *Peters v. United States* also illustrates how visually observable factors can combine to constitute probable cause. Police officer Lasky heard noises outside the door of his apartment that suggested that someone was trying to enter his apartment. He peered out and saw two men tiptoeing down the hallway whom he had never seen before in the twelve years he had lived in the building. Lasky entered the hallway, and the men fled and were apprehended by Lasky in the stairwell. Peters was unable to explain why he was in the building, and Lasky searched him and found burglar tools. The

U.S. Supreme Court concluded that although Lasky did not actually see the two men attempt to jimmy the lock, it is "difficult to conceive of stronger grounds for an arrest, short of actual eyewitness observation of criminal activity" (*Peters v. United States,* 392 U.S. 40, 66 [1968]).

What if an officer strongly believes there is probable cause but lacks objective facts? In *Beck v. Ohio,* a police officer stopped Beck's automobile and searched Beck based on the fact that the officer recognized Beck and knew that on three previous occasions that he had been arrested and convicted of gambling offenses. The Supreme Court held that the officer's knowledge of Beck's background did not constitute probable cause to arrest Beck for unlawful gambling. The Court stressed that an arrest could not be justified based on such "scant evidence" and that if "these facts constituted probable cause," "anyone with a previous criminal record could be arrested at will." The officer's subjective good faith belief is not in and of itself sufficient to constitute probable cause. "If subjective good faith alone were the test, the protections of the Fourth Amendment would evaporate, and the people would not be 'secure in their persons, houses, papers, and effects'" (*Beck v. Ohio,* 379 U.S. 89, 94, 97 [1964]).

Hearsay

Probable cause also may be based on hearsay or secondhand information that is communicated to the police (hearsay is commonly defined as information that is not derived from the personal knowledge of the witness but from the repetition of what he or she has heard others say). This information may come from eyewitnesses, crime victims, police officers, or informants. Informants typically are individuals who themselves are involved in criminal activity and who cooperate with the police by providing information. The problem with hearsay is that it is difficult to determine whether secondhand information is truthful and accurate. This is because the police officer who appears before the judge did not actually witness the events himself or herself and is reporting the observations of another person. Judges in criminal trials, for this reason, strictly limit the introduction of hearsay evidence (hearsay is discussed in Chapter 13). The police do not have the luxury of deciding whether to rely on hearsay. Law enforcement officers must react immediately to reports of crime and would be criticized for failing to investigate a citizen's complaint that an armed and dangerous individual is in a school parking lot.

In determining whether hearsay provides probable cause, courts follow several simple rules. First, eyewitnesses and victims along with police officers are considered reliable, and their reports are accepted as accurate. Second, informants are presumed to be unreliable, and as a result, the information provided by informants must satisfy strict standards before a judge or magistrate finds that the information constitutes probable cause. The approach of courts to informants is summarized below.

- ***Citizen-informants.*** Eyewitnesses and victims are presumed reliable, and their reports may constitute probable cause. These individuals do not have a motive to distort the truth, and their credibility is enhanced by the fact that they often are interviewed immediately after observing a crime or being victimized by a crime (*Commonwealth v. Carey,* 554 N.E.2d 1199, 1203 [Mass. 1990]).
- ***Police.*** The reports of law enforcement officers are considered credible and may constitute probable cause (*United States v. Ventresca,* 380 U.S. 102 [1965]).
- ***Informants.*** Courts are reluctant to find that the reports of informants constitute probable cause. Informants may have a self-interest in the prosecution of the individuals named in their reports. They may hope that their cooperation and assistance lead to a plea bargain or other benefits. The U.S. Supreme Court accordingly has adopted special requirements that are discussed below for evaluating whether an informant's report constitutes probable cause (*Jones v. United States,* 266 F.2d 924 [D.C. Ct. App. 1959]).

The U.S. Supreme Court has devoted a significant amount of time to the question of informants. An example is *McCray v. Illinois.* In *McCray,* Chicago police arrested McCray based on a tip from a police informant that McCray "was selling narcotics and had narcotics on his person and that he could be found in the vicinity of 47th and Calumet at this particular time." The officers drove the informant to the designated intersection, and the informant pointed to McCray walking at a fast pace between two buildings. Officer Jackson testified that the informant had assisted in the arrest of drug dealers in the past and that the informant had told him that McCray had supplied him with narcotics over the course of the past year. The U.S. Supreme Court concluded that the police possessed probable cause to arrest McCray based on the informant's report that he was in possession of narcotics.

The Court went on to hold that the prosecution is not required to disclose an informant's identity at a probable cause hearing before a judge or even at a trial in which a defendant's guilt or innocence is at stake. Disclosure would discourage informants from assisting the police. The judge has the discretion to require that the government produce an informant to testify in those instances in which the judge questions the informant's existence or in which the judge is persuaded that the defendant must be given the opportunity to cross-examine the informant to establish the defendant's innocence. For example, federal courts have held that the **informant privilege** does not protect an informant from testifying in those cases in which the defendant is charged with selling narcotics to the informant and there are no other prosecution witnesses who observed the sale (*McCray v. Illinois,* 386 U.S. 300 [1975]).

The *Aguilar–Spinelli* Test

The traditional approach for evaluating whether the police may rely on an informant's report to establish probable cause is the so-called ***Aguilar–Spinelli* test**. In 1983, in *Illinois v. Gates,* the U.S. Supreme Court modified this test and adopted a "totality of the circumstances" analysis. Several states nonetheless continue to follow the *Aguilar–Spinelli* approach. The standard that must be met for an informant's tip to constitute probable cause is the same whether the police are relying on an informant to obtain an arrest warrant or to obtain a search warrant.

In *Aguilar v. Texas,* two police officers obtained a warrant from a local justice of the peace. The officers submitted a sworn statement, an **affidavit,** to the justice of the peace, which recounted that they had received "reliable information from a credible person" that Aguilar was engaged in the unlawful sale of narcotics and that the officers "believe that heroin, marijuana, barbituates [*sic*] and other narcotics and narcotic paraphernalia are being kept" at Aguilar's home. A search of Aguilar's home based on the warrant led to the discovery of heroin, and Aguilar was sentenced to twenty years in prison. The U.S. Supreme Court held that the warrant relied on by the police was based on "mere conclusions" and did not provide probable cause to search Aguilar's home. Justice Arthur Goldberg, writing for the majority, held that probable cause may be based on the hearsay report of an informant so long as the *veracity prong* and the *basis-of-knowledge prong* are satisfied by the information in the affidavit. Justice Goldberg stressed that these two requirements are "commonsense conditions" for relying on "secondhand information" (*Aguilar v. Texas,* 378 U.S. 108 [1964]). The two prongs are explained below.

Veracity prong. The police officer is required to demonstrate that he or she has good reason to believe that the informant's information is accurate. How is this accomplished? An informant's credibility is established by highlighting that the informant has provided accurate information in the past. In *McCray v. Illinois,* the informant had provided the police with accurate information that had led to narcotics arrests fifteen or sixteen times over the past year (302). Trustworthiness also may be established by an informant who exposes himself or herself to criminal liability by admitting involvement in illegal activity. In *United States v. Harris,* the informant reported that he had purchased unlawfully produced alcohol from the suspect over the past two years. The U.S. Supreme Court held that this was a sufficient indicator of credibility to support a finding of probable cause. Justice Burger explained that people "do not lightly admit a crime" and "place critical evidence in the hands of the police" and "place themselves at risk of criminal prosecution" (*United States v. Harris,* 403 U.S. 573, 583–584 [1971]).

Basis-of-knowledge prong. The police officer must indicate how the informant obtained knowledge of the criminal activity. Did the informant witness a narcotics sale or purchase narcotics, or is the informant relying on a hearsay report from a friend? The U.S. Supreme Court held that in some instances, detailed information provided to the police may be sufficient because this detail could have been obtained only by someone who witnessed the criminal activity. In *Draper v. United States,* the Supreme Court held that the accurate detail provided by the informant Hereford justified the inference that Hereford obtained the information regarding Draper's possession of three ounces of heroin in a reliable fashion. The Supreme Court pointed to the fact that the information Hereford provided federal narcotic agent Marsh accurately reported the date that Draper's train from Chicago would arrive in Denver and accurately described Draper's "exact physical attributes . . . precise clothing" and the fact that he was carrying a "tan zipper bag" and typically walked at a rapid pace (*Draper v. United States,* 358 U.S. 307 [1959]).

The Supreme Court followed this two-prong test in *Spinelli v. United States* in holding that the informant's tip relied on by the police did not constitute probable cause. The Court stressed that both conditions established in *Aguilar* must be satisfied to constitute probable cause. William Spinelli was convicted of traveling to St. Louis, Missouri, from an adjacent Illinois suburb with the intention of conducting gambling activity. He alleged that the affidavit on which the arrest warrant was based did not constitute probable cause. The affidavit contained a report from an anonymous informant along with the results of an FBI investigation that corroborated the informant's tip. The affidavit contained the following four allegations (*Spinelli v. United States,* 393 U.S. 410 [1969]).

- The FBI had monitored Spinelli's movements for five days, and on four occasions, he crossed a bridge leading from Illinois to St. Louis and entered an apartment house.
- An FBI investigation revealed that the apartment contained two telephones.
- William Spinelli was known to law enforcement agents and to the informant as a bookmaker and gambler.
- The FBI had been informed by a confidential and reliable informant that William Spinelli was accepting wagers and disseminating wagering information through two telephones.

The Supreme Court concluded that the affidavit did not satisfy the two-prong test established in *Aguilar.* First, there was no information supporting the past accuracy of the informant and the veracity prong. What of the basis-of-knowledge prong? The tip does not indicate how the FBI's source obtained the information. It is not "alleged that the informant personally observed Spinelli at work or that he had ever placed a bet with him." In other words, there was not enough detail for the magistrate to conclude that the informant was relying on "something more substantial than a casual rumor." The fact that Spinelli had two telephones was not the type of detailed information that indicates that the informant obtained the information in a reliable fashion. There is nothing unusual about an apartment with two separate telephone lines. The allegation that Spinelli was a "known" gambler and an associate of gamblers is an "unilluminating assertion of suspicion that is entitled to no weight in appraising the magistrate's decision." The Supreme Court in *Spinelli* stressed that the informant's tip may have proved significant had the FBI provided *corroborating information* that more fully supported the informant's tip. For example, the FBI could have bolstered the tip by reporting that there was a significant amount of activity at the apartment or that there was an unusual number of phone calls being made from the two phones. *Spinelli* teaches us that an informant's tip that lacks detail may be enhanced by a police investigation that supplements the information in the tip.

In summary, the *Aguilar–Spinelli* test provides that information obtained from an informant must satisfy both the veracity prong and the basis-of-knowledge prong in order to constitute probable cause. The Supreme Court characterizes this as a "commonsense approach" because these are the two factors that most of us would consider when we decide to rely on information that is provided by another person. Do you believe that the Supreme Court is correct in holding that because the tip in *Spinelli* did not meet the two-prong test, the affidavit did not constitute probable cause?

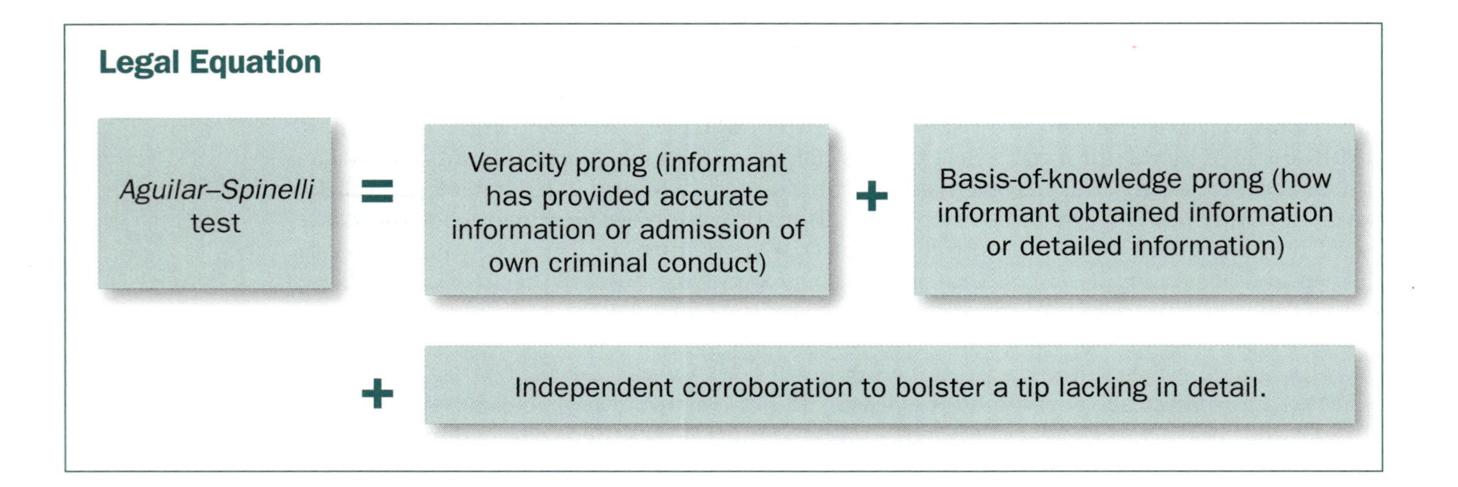

Totality of the Circumstances

Justice Hugo Black was a strong dissenting critic of the *Aguilar–Spinelli* test. Justice Black complained that "[n]othing in our Constitution . . . requires that the facts be established with that degree of certainty and with such elaborate specificity before a policeman can be authorized by a disinterested magistrate" to conduct an arrest or search based on probable cause. This exacting standard threatened to "'make it increasingly easy for criminals to operate'" (429–433). In 1983, in *Illinois v. Gates,* the U.S. Supreme Court adopted Justice Black's point of view and abandoned the *Aguilar–Spinelli* test in favor of a "totality of the circumstances" approach (*Illinois v. Gates,* 462 U.S. 213 [1983]).

In *Gates,* the Bloomingdale, Illinois, Police Department received an anonymous handwritten letter by mail. The letter alleged that two of the town's residents, Sue and Lance Gates, were engaged in selling narcotics. The letter reported that the unlawful enterprise involved Sue's driving their automobile to Florida, where she would leave the car to be loaded with drugs. Sue would fly back after dropping the car off in Florida. Lance would then fly down and drive the car back to Bloomingdale. The letter stated that Sue was driving down to Florida on May 3, 1978, and that when Lance drove the auto back to Bloomingdale the trunk would be loaded with over $100,000 in unlawful narcotics. The letter also stated that the couple had drugs stored in their basement valued at $100,000.

The police verified the Gateses' address and that Lance was scheduled to fly to Florida on May 5. In West Palm Beach, Lance was observed taking a taxi to a motel where Sue was registered. The next morning, Sue and Lance were seen driving their automobile on an interstate used by travelers to the Chicago area. These facts were incorporated into an affidavit, and a judge issued a search warrant for the Gateses' residence and for their automobile. Twenty-two hours after leaving Florida, Lance and Sue returned home. The police seized the automobile and discovered 350 pounds of marijuana in the trunk. A search of the Gateses' home led to the seizure of marijuana, weapons, and other contraband (225–227).

The U.S. Supreme Court found that the informant's letter did not satisfy the *Aguilar–Spinelli* two-prong test. The letter provided "virtually nothing from which one might conclude that its author is either honest or his information reliable; likewise, the letter gives absolutely no indication of the basis for the writer's predictions regarding the Gates' criminal activities." The Supreme Court majority, however, held that the letter satisfied the probable cause standard. The Court explained that the veracity and basis-of-knowledge prongs are not independent requirements both of which must be established. The two prongs are best thought of as "relevant considerations" in evaluating whether a tip satisfies probable cause. In other words, looking at the "totality of the circumstances," the Court concluded that there was probable cause to issue a search warrant. Three aspects of the tip discussed below are important in understanding the Court's conclusion that there is a "substantial basis" to conclude that there was probable cause to search the Gateses' home and car (225–227).

Future action. The Supreme Court was impressed by the fact that the tip contained a range of details including the suspects' "future actions" and that these facts were corroborated by law enforcement.

Type of information. The tip was consistent with law enforcement's knowledge of drug dealing. Florida is a center of drug activity, and the Gateses' predicted pattern of behavior is typical of drug traffickers. An informant with access to this type of detailed information in the view of the Supreme Court likely had "access to reliable information of the Gates' alleged illegal activities," perhaps from the Gateses themselves.

Corroboration. Confidence in the accuracy of the information provided by the informant was bolstered by the fact that the police corroborated a significant number of the details.

The Supreme Court recognized that the tip in *Gates* was not completely accurate and that some of the information could have been based on rumor or speculation. The Court, however, stressed that probable cause requires only a "fair probability that the writer of the anonymous letter had obtained his entire story either from the Gates or someone they trusted. And corroboration of major portions of the letter's predictions provides just this probability" (246).

Why did the Supreme Court adopt the totality-of-the-circumstances test? The Court likely concluded that anonymous tips from informants may not always easily satisfy both prongs of the *Aguilar–Spinelli* test. The entire process simply had become much too technical and demanding. Justices Brennan and Marshal dissented and warned that the totality-of-the-circumstances test left judicial officials with no guidance for determining whether informants' tips constituted probable cause and that, as a result, magistrates were likely to "rubber-stamp" requests from the police. This threatened to "obliterate one of the most fundamental distinctions between our form of government, where officers are under the law, and the police-state, where they are the law" (291).

Several state supreme courts have held that their state constitutions provide greater protection in regard to the use of informants than the U.S. Constitution and have rejected the totality-of-the-circumstances approach. Courts in Alaska, California, Massachusetts, New York, Oregon, Tennessee, Vermont, and Washington have reasoned that *Aguilar–Spinelli* provides definite standards that provide a check on the police, which is lacking under the test established in *Gates* (*People v. Campa,* 686 P.2d 634 [Cal. 1984]; *State v. Jackson,* 688 P.2d 136 [Wash. 1984]).

The next case in the text is *Draper v. United States*. *Draper* typically is cited as an example of an informant's tip that satisfies the probable cause standard. In reading *Draper,* consider why the U.S. Supreme Court held that Hereford's tip combined with the corroborating information observed by DEA agent Marsh constituted probable cause to arrest Draper.

Was there probable cause to arrest Draper?

Draper v. United States, *358 U.S. 307 (1959), Whitaker, J.*

Facts

Petitioner was convicted of knowingly concealing and transporting narcotic drugs in Denver, Colorado.... [H]is conviction was based in part on the use in evidence against him of two "envelopes containing [865 grams of] heroin" and a hypodermic syringe that had been taken from his person, following his arrest, by the arresting officer. Before the trial, he moved to suppress that evidence as having been secured through an unlawful search and seizure. After hearing, the district court found that the arresting officer had probable cause to arrest petitioner without a warrant and that the subsequent search and seizure were therefore incident to a lawful arrest, and overruled the motion to suppress. At the subsequent trial, that evidence was offered and, over petitioner's renewed objection, was received in evidence, and the trial resulted, as we have said, in petitioner's conviction. The court of appeals affirmed the conviction and certiorari was sought on the sole ground that the search and seizure violated the Fourth Amendment and therefore the use of the heroin in evidence vitiated the conviction. We granted the writ to determine that question.

The evidence...established that one Marsh, a federal narcotic agent with 29 years' experience, was stationed at Denver; that one Hereford had been engaged as a "special employee" of the Bureau of Narcotics at Denver for about six months, and from time to time gave information to Marsh regarding violations of the narcotic laws, for which Hereford was paid small sums of money, and that Marsh had always found the information given by Hereford to be accurate and reliable. On September 3, 1956, Hereford told Marsh that James Draper (petitioner) recently had taken up abode at a stated address in Denver and "was peddling narcotics to several addicts" in that city. Four days later, on September 7, Hereford told Marsh "that Draper had gone to Chicago the day before [September 6] by train [and] that he was going to bring back three ounces of heroin [and] that he would return to Denver either on the morning of the 8th of September or the morning of the 9th of September also by train." Hereford also gave Marsh a detailed physical description of Draper and of the clothing he was wearing and said that he would be carrying "a tan zipper bag," and that he habitually "walked real fast."

On the morning of September 8, Marsh and a Denver police officer went to the Denver Union Station and kept watch over all incoming trains from Chicago, but they did not see anyone fitting the description that Hereford had given. Repeating the process on the morning of September 9, they saw a person, having the exact physical attributes and wearing the precise clothing described by Hereford, alight from an incoming Chicago train and start walking "fast" toward the exit. He was carrying a tan zipper bag in his right hand and the left was thrust in his raincoat pocket. Marsh, accompanied by the police officer, overtook, stopped, and arrested him. They then searched him and found the two "envelopes containing heroin" clutched in his left hand in his raincoat pocket, and found the syringe in the tan zipper bag. Marsh then took him (petitioner) into custody. Hereford died four days after the arrest and therefore did not testify at the hearing on the motion.

Issue

The crucial question for us then is whether knowledge of the related facts and circumstances gave Marsh "probable cause" within the meaning of the Fourth Amendment to believe that petitioner had committed or was committing a violation of the narcotic laws. If it did, the arrest, though without a warrant, was lawful, and the subsequent search of petitioner's person and the seizure of the found heroin were validly made incident to a lawful arrest, and therefore the motion to suppress was properly overruled and the heroin was competently received in evidence at the trial.

Reasoning

In *Brinegar v. United States*...the convict contended "that the factors relating to inadmissibility of the [hearsay] evidence [for] purposes of proving guilt at the trial, deprive[d] the evidence as a whole of sufficiency to show probable cause for the search..." But this Court, rejecting that contention, said, "The so-called distinction places a wholly unwarranted emphasis upon the criterion of admissibility in evidence, to prove the accused's guilt, of the facts relied upon to show probable cause. That emphasis, we think, goes much too far in confusing and disregarding the difference between what is required to prove guilt in a criminal case and what is required to show probable cause for arrest or search. It approaches requiring (if it does not in practical effect require) proof sufficient to establish guilt in order to substantiate the existence of probable cause. There is a large difference between the two things to be proved [guilt and probable cause], as well as between the tribunals which determine them, and therefore a like difference in the quanta and modes of proof required to establish them."

Nor can we agree with...the contention that Marsh's information was insufficient to show probable cause...to believe that petitioner had violated or was violating the narcotic laws and to justify his arrest without a warrant. The information given to narcotic agent Marsh by "special employee" Hereford may have been hearsay to Marsh, but coming from one employed for that purpose and whose information had always been found accurate and reliable, it is clear that Marsh would have been derelict in his duties had he not pursued it. And when, in pursuing that information, he saw a man, having the exact physical attributes and wearing the precise clothing and carrying the tan zipper bag that Hereford had described, alight from one of the very trains from the very place stated by Hereford and start to walk at a "fast" pace toward the station exit, Marsh had personally verified every facet of the information given him by Hereford except whether petitioner had accomplished his mission and had the three ounces of heroin on his person or in his bag. And, surely, with every other bit of Hereford's information being thus personally verified, Marsh had "reasonable grounds" to believe that the remaining unverified bit of Hereford's information—that Draper would have the heroin with him—was likewise true.

Holding

"In dealing with probable cause...as the very name implies, we deal with probabilities. These are not technical; they are the factual and practical considerations of everyday life on which reasonable and prudent men, not legal technicians, act." Probable cause exists where "the facts and circumstances within [the arresting officers'] knowledge and of which they had reasonably trustworthy information [are] sufficient in themselves to warrant a man of reasonable caution in the belief that" an offense has been or is being committed. We believe that, under the facts and circumstances here, Marsh had probable cause and reasonable grounds to believe that petitioner was committing a violation of the laws of the United

States relating to narcotic drugs at the time he arrested him. The arrest was therefore lawful, and the subsequent search and seizure, having been made incident to that lawful arrest, were likewise valid. It follows that petitioner's motion to suppress was properly denied and that the seized heroin was competent evidence lawfully received at the trial.

Dissenting, *Douglas, J.*

Decisions under the Fourth Amendment, taken in the long view, have not given the protection to the citizen, which the letter and spirit of the Amendment would seem to require. One reason, I think, is that wherever a culprit is caught red-handed, as in leading Fourth Amendment cases, it is difficult to adopt and enforce a rule that would turn him loose. A rule protective of law-abiding citizens is not apt to flourish where its advocates are usually criminals. Yet the rule we fashion is for the innocent and guilty alike. If the word of the informer on which the present arrest was made is sufficient to make the arrest legal, his word would also protect the police who, acting on it, hauled the innocent citizen off to jail.

Of course, the education we receive from mystery stories and television shows teaches that what happened in this case is efficient police work. The police are tipped off that a man carrying narcotics will step off the morning train. A man meeting the precise description does alight from the train. No warrant for his arrest has been—or, as I see it, could then be—obtained. Yet he is arrested; and narcotics are found in his pocket and a syringe in the bag he carried. This is the familiar pattern of crime detection which has been dinned into public consciousness as the correct and efficient one. It is, however, a distorted reflection of the constitutional system under which we are supposed to live.

The Court is quite correct in saying that proof of "reasonable grounds" for believing a crime was being committed need not be proof admissible at the trial. It could be inferences from suspicious acts, e.g., consort with known peddlers, the surreptitious passing of a package, an intercepted message suggesting criminal activities, or any number of such events coming to the knowledge of the officer. But, if he takes the law into his own hands and does not seek the protection of a warrant, he must act on some evidence known to him. The law goes far to protect the citizen. Even suspicious acts observed by the officers may be as consistent with innocence as with guilt. That is not enough, for even the guilty may not be implicated on suspicion alone. The reason is, as I have said, that the standard set by the Constitution and by the statute is one that will protect both the officer and the citizen. For if the officer acts with "probable cause" or on "reasonable grounds," he is protected even though the citizen is innocent. This important requirement should be strictly enforced, lest the whole process of arrest revert once more to whispered accusations by people. When we lower the guards as we do today, we risk making the role of the informer—odious in our history—once more supreme. I think the correct rule is that "[m]ere suspicion is not enough; there must be circumstances represented to the officers through the testimony of their senses sufficient to justify them in a good-faith belief that the defendant had violated the law."

Here, the officers had no evidence—apart from the mere word of an informer—that petitioner was committing a crime. The fact that petitioner walked fast and carried a tan zipper bag was not evidence of any crime. The officers knew nothing except what they had been told by the informer. If they went to a magistrate to get a warrant of arrest and relied solely on the report of the informer, it is not conceivable to me that one would be granted. For they could not present to the magistrate any of the facts which the informer may have had. They could swear only to the fact that the informer had made the accusation. They could swear to no evidence that lay in their own knowledge. They could present, on information and belief, no facts which the informer disclosed. No magistrate could issue a warrant on the mere word of an officer, without more. We are not justified in lowering the standard when an arrest is made without a warrant and allowing the officers more leeway than we grant the magistrate. With all deference I think we break with tradition when we sustain this arrest.... "[A] search is not to be made legal by what it turns up. In law it is good or bad when it starts and does not change character from its success." In this case it was only after the arrest and search were made that there was a shred of evidence known to the officers that a crime was in the process of being committed.

Questions for Discussion

1. Why did the Supreme Court conclude that there was probable cause to arrest Draper?
2. Did *Draper* establish any general legal principles in regard to informants that are important to keep in mind?
3. Compare and contrast the facts in *Draper* with the facts in *Illinois v. Gates*. Is the claim of probable cause equally as persuasive in each of these cases?
4. Do you agree with Justice Douglas that the information provided by the informant even when corroborated by law enforcement agents did not amount to probable cause? Does Justice Douglas have a point when he claims that the Supreme Court is sacrificing the rule of law in order to make it easier for the police to enforce the criminal law?
5. ***Problems in policing.*** As a police officer, what information should you require before relying on an informant's tip?

Cases and Comments

Probable Cause. A Baltimore County police officer stopped a Nissan Maxima for speeding at 3:16 A.M. There were three occupants in the car: the driver, Donte Partlow, the front-seat passenger, Jermaine Pringle, and the back-seat passenger, Otis Smith. Partlow opened the glove compartment to get the vehicle registration, and the officer observed a bundle of money. A check of the police computer system indicated that Partlow did not have any outstanding violations, and the officer issued Partlow a warning. A second officer arrived and asked and received consent from Partlow to search the automobile. The officer seized $763 in cash and several glassine envelopes containing cocaine that were concealed behind the backseat armrest. Partlow, Pringle, and Smith refused to provide any information regarding the ownership of the money and drugs, and the three were placed under arrest. Pringle subsequently confessed and said that he owned the drugs and that Partlow and Smith were unaware that the narcotics were in the car. He was convicted of cocaine possession and was sentenced to ten years in prison. Pringle appealed and argued that he had been improperly arrested without probable cause and that his confession was therefore invalid. The U.S. Supreme Court explained that probable cause could not be reduced to a mathematical formula and that the various definitions of probable cause all include the common denominator that there must a "reasonable ground to believe that a crime has been committed" and a "reasonable belief that a particular individual committed the crime." The Supreme Court concluded that it is "an entirely reasonable inference from these facts that any or all three of the occupants had knowledge of, and exercised dominion and control over, the cocaine." A reasonable officer could conclude that there was probable cause to believe that Pringle committed the crime of drug possession, either by himself or in conjunction with other individuals. The quantity of money and drugs in the car indicated the possibility that there was a common enterprise to engage in drug dealing and the conspirators were unlikely to invite an innocent outsider who might testify against them to ride in the automobile. Do you agree that there is probable cause to arrest Pringle? See *Maryland v. Pringle,* 540 U.S. 366 (2003).

Compare the facts and holding in *Pringle* with the facts and holding in *United States v. Di Re*. In *Di Re,* Reed informed an employee of the U.S. Price Administration that he had arranged to purchase counterfeit gasoline ration coupons (this was during World War II) from Buttitta. The police tailed Buttitta's car and, at a strategic moment, approached the car and found Reed with two counterfeit coupons in his hand. He stated that he had purchased them from Buttitta. Reed and Buttitta were arrested along with Di Re, who was sitting in the front seat of the car next to Buttitta. Di Re was found to have roughly one hundred counterfeit coupons in an envelope concealed beneath his clothes. Di Re claimed that the police lacked probable cause to arrest him and that the counterfeit coupons were inadmissible because the search was based on what he claimed was his unlawful arrest. The Supreme Court agreed that although Di Re may have witnessed the exchange between Buttitta and Reed, it did not follow that he knew that coupons were exchanged or that he knew that the coupons were counterfeit. When detained by the police, Reed singled out Buttitta as the guilty party. The fact that Di Re accompanied Buttitta to the meeting with Reed did not necessarily indicate that Di Re was involved in the crime. "Presumptions of guilt are not lightly to be indulged from mere meetings." The meeting took place in broad daylight and in plain sight of observers on a public street in a large city, and the passing of the papers between Buttitta and Reed was not an obviously criminal activity. The Supreme Court reversed Di Re's criminal conviction. Why did the Supreme Court reach different results in *Pringle* and in *Di Re?* See *United States v. Di Re,* 332 U.S. 581 (1948).

5.1 YOU DECIDE

Whiskey was stolen from a storage facility in Chicago. The next day, two FBI agents were in the area investigating the theft. They saw Henry and Pierotti leave a tavern and get into an automobile. The agents had been given information of an "undisclosed nature" from Pierotti's employer suggesting that Pierotti was involved with interstate shipments. The tip did not specifically indicate that Pierotti was responsible for any thefts. The agents observed the car drive into an alley and stop. Henry entered a residence and later emerged with several cartons. The same car later was observed parked in front of the tavern. Shortly thereafter, Henry and Pierotti returned to the residence, and Henry once again emerged with cartons. The agents were 300 feet away and could not observe the size, number, or content of the cartons. The agents followed and then stopped the car, and as they approached the vehicle, Henry exclaimed, "It's the G's (FBI)" and "tell them [you] just picked me up." The agents searched the car and seized the cartons. They subsequently learned that the cartons contained stolen radios and placed Henry and Pierotti under arrest. The prosecution conceded that the arrest took place when the FBI agents stopped the defendants' car and restricted Henry and Pierotti's freedom of movement. Was this a valid probable cause arrest? See *Henry v. United States*, 361 U.S. 98 (1959).

You can find the answer by referring to the study site, http://www.sagepub.com/lippmancp.

Reasonableness and Arrests

The Fourth Amendment, as we have seen, requires that arrests be based on probable cause. An arrest also must be carried out in a reasonable fashion. The remainder of the chapter discusses six points regarding the reasonableness requirement.

- ***Warrants.*** There are strict requirements for the issuance of warrants.
- ***Arrests and warrants.*** Arrests, under some circumstances, require arrest warrants.
- ***Arrests in the home.*** Arrest warrants are required for arrests in the home.
- ***Exigent circumstances.*** There is an exigent-circumstances exception to the warrant requirement for arrests in the home.
- ***Arrests and force.*** Officers may use reasonable force in making arrests.
- ***Misdemeanors, citations, and arrests.*** States and localities may authorize arrests for misdemeanors.

Probable Cause, Warrants, and the Courts

The Supreme Court has expressed a preference for arrests to be based on arrest warrants. An **arrest warrant** is issued by a judge, magistrate, or other judicial official acting as a representative of the government and establishes that there is probable cause to arrest a particular individual or individuals. Why this preference for warrants? To obtain a warrant, the police appear before a neutral and detached judge or magistrate and are required to satisfy the judge or magistrate that there is probable cause to arrest an individual. As the Supreme Court observed in *Aquilar v. Texas,* "the informed and deliberate determinations of magistrates empowered to issue warrants . . . are to be preferred over the hurried action of officers . . . who happen to make arrests." The thinking is that an arrest can be an intrusive and demeaning experience and that the liberties of citizens are best protected when the police appear before a public official and are required to present evidence that there is probable cause to make an arrest (*Aguilar v. Texas,* 378 U.S. 108, 111 [1964]).

The Fourth Amendment requires that "no Warrants shall issue but upon probable cause, supported by Oath or affirmation." There are several important constitutional requirements for issuing a warrant under the Fourth Amendment.

Probable cause. There must be a demonstration by the police that there is a "fair probability" that a crime has been committed and that the person named in the warrant committed the crime.

Neutral officials. Probable cause must be established before a neutral and detached official who reviews the request. This typically is a judge or magistrate although the Supreme Court approved the issuance of a misdemeanor warrant by a nonlawyer court clerk who was part of the judicial branch of government. A nonlawyer must have the ability to determine probable cause.

Warrants and affidavits. The warrant must specify with "particularity" the name of the person to be arrested, the time and place of the offense, and the specific crime with which the individual is charged. This must be supported by an affidavit (statement), which typically is sworn under oath by a police officer (**affiant**) who swears to the specific facts and circumstances set forth in the affidavit that constitute the probable cause on which the warrant is based.

Judicial official. A judge or magistrate determines whether there is probable cause to issue a warrant. The warrant process is not an adversarial procedure and usually involves a police officer who presents the warrant and the affidavit to a magistrate or judge. Article 41 of the Federal Rules of Criminal Procedure authorizes officers to phone or radio in a warrant request to a federal magistrate who is authorized to issue the warrant over the phone.

As outlined below, a defendant may challenge the legality of an arrest based on the contention that the warrant was not based on probable cause or that proper procedures were not followed in issuing the warrant.

Probable cause. A warrant may be attacked on the grounds that it was not based on probable cause. An example is the challenge to the warrants in *Aguilar* and *Spinelli.*

Affidavit. The warrant may be overturned on the grounds that the probable cause is based on a knowingly false statement by the affiant (*Franks v. Delaware,* 483 U.S. 154 [1978]).

Procedural irregularity. A warrant may be overturned based on improper procedures. Warrants must be issued by a judge, magistrate, or, in the case of minor misdemeanors, another qualified member of the judicial branch of government. The U.S. Supreme Court has held that a warrant issued by a prosecutor or police officer does not adequately protect the rights of individuals and is invalid (*Coolidge v. New Hampshire,* 403 U.S. 443 [1971]). In *Connally v. Georgia,* the U.S. Supreme Court held that the warrant procedure violated the Fourth Amendment where the warrant had been issued by an unsalaried justice of the peace who received five dollars for each warrant he issued and no payment for warrants that he refused to issue (*Connally v. Georgia,* 429 U.S. 245 [1977]).

What about postarrest challenges to warrantless arrests? The probable cause required for a warrantless arrest must meet the same standard as the probable cause required for an arrest based on a warrant. In *Gerstein v. Pugh,* the Supreme Court held that a police officer's "on-the-scene" assessment of probable cause provides legal justification for the arrest of an individual suspected of a crime. Once the suspect is in custody, the "reasons that justify dispensing with the magistrate's neutral judgment [of probable cause] evaporate." At this point, the Supreme Court ruled that the Fourth Amendment requires that the individual who is experiencing an extended loss of his or her liberty is entitled to a *Gerstein* hearing to determine whether a "reasonable person would believe that the suspect committed the offense" (*Gerstein v. Pugh,* 420 U.S. 103 [1975]). In *County of Riverside v. McLaughlin,* the U.S. Supreme Court held that the Fourth Amendment requires that the *Gerstein* probable cause hearing be conducted within forty-eight hours of an arrest. The hearing may be delayed only by an emergency or other pressing circumstance (*County of Riverside v. McLaughlin,* 500 U.S. 44 [1991]). (We will discuss this in greater detail in Chapter 12.)

Arrests and Warrants

Despite the U.S. Supreme Court's preference for warrants, most arrests take place without warrants. In *United States v. Watson,* the U.S. Supreme Court recognized that under some circumstances, warrants may slow the enforcement of the law. In *Watson,* the Court upheld the warrantless arrest by federal postal inspectors of Watson for possession of stolen credit cards based on an informant's tip. The inspectors relied on a federal statute that authorizes postal inspectors to carry out warrantless arrests for felonies. Watson challenged the warrantless arrest and subsequent search that uncovered the credit cards as a violation of the Fourth Amendment. The Supreme Court held that *warrantless arrests in public* of individuals based on probable cause that they have committed a felony is consistent with the historic practice of the common law as well as with state statutes and state constitutions and therefore is reasonable under the Fourth Amendment. The warrantless arrest of individuals is permissible even when the officers could have obtained a warrant. The U.S. Supreme Court concluded by declaring that it "declined to transform the judicial preference for warrants into a constitutional requirement" when the state and federal governments historically had authorized warrantless public arrests on probable cause (*United States v. Watson,* 423 U.S. 411, 423–424 [1976]).

The Supreme Court has taken a somewhat different approach to arrests for misdemeanors. In *Atwater v. City of Lago Vista,* the Supreme Court answered the question whether it is *constitutionally permissible* for the police to carry out a warrantless arrest for a misdemeanor. Justice David Souter found that the common law and historic practice of the federal government and fifty states for two centuries establish that an arrest for a misdemeanor may be carried out without a warrant only when the offense is "*committed in the officer's presence*" (*Atwater v. City of Lago Vista,* 532 U.S. 318, 327–345 [2001]). The requirement that a misdemeanor take place in an officer's presence has been interpreted to mean that the officer must actually perceive the commission of the misdemeanor with one of the five senses of sight, hearing, touch, taste, or smell, or the individual must admit the crime to the officer. The officer also must carry out the arrest as promptly as possible. The "in-presence standard" is strictly interpreted to require that the officer actually witness every element of the offense. A California court of appeals held that an officer did not satisfy the in-presence standard when he did not actually see a juvenile ingesting paint fumes. The appellate court noted that the "mere fact that Alonzo had paint on his face and an odor of paint and had dropped the sock saturated with paint only shows that at sometime in the past Alonzo had undoubtedly been sniffing, but the time [of the arrest] any sniffing is not established. . . . While the officer may have had reasonable cause to believe that Alonzo had violated penal section 381 [prohibiting ingesting the fumes of paint and other substances] the officer did not have reasonable cause to believe that that misdemeanor took place in his presence" (*People v. Alonzo,* 151 Cal. Rptr. 192, 196 [Cal. App. 1978]).

Atwater establishes that the police may arrest an individual without a warrant for misdemeanors committed in an officer's presence. What about misdemeanors committed outside an officer's presence. A number of lower appellate courts have questioned whether the Fourth Amendment requires warrants for arrests for misdemeanors committed outside an officer's presence. Several state legislatures accordingly have authorized warrantless arrests for various misdemeanors including domestic violence, shoplifting, drunken driving, and violations of hunting and fishing regulations despite the fact that the officer may not have actually witnessed the offense. We shall be returning to *Atwater* later in the chapter when we discuss arrests and citations.

In summary, we have seen that although there is a preference for arrest warrants, arrests for felonies and for misdemeanors may be carried out without warrants. The next sections discuss the warrant requirement and arrests in the home.

- ***Arrests in the home.*** An arrest warrant is required.
- ***Exigent circumstances.*** Warrants are not required for arrests in the home when there are exigent circumstances.

You can find United States v. Watson *on the study site, http://www.sagepub.com/lippmancp.*

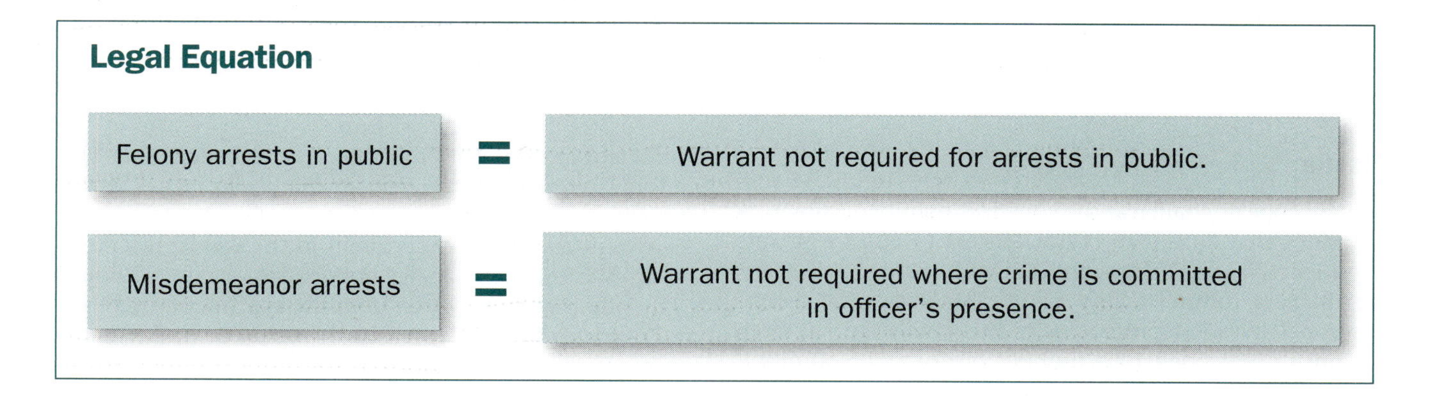

Arrests in the Home

United States v. Watson, as you recall, held that an arrest warrant is not required to arrest an individual for a felony in public. *Watson* left open the question whether a warrant is required to arrest an individual in his or her home. *Payton v. New York* answered this question and held that (1) absent consent or exigent circumstances, (2) an arrest warrant founded on probable cause is required to arrest individuals in the home (3) when there is "reason to believe that the suspect is within" (*Payton v. New York,* 445 U.S. 573, 602–603 [1980]).

The U.S. Supreme Court stressed that the unjustified "physical entry into the home is the chief evil at which the Fourth Amendment is directed" and that the Fourth Amendment draws a firm line of protection at the entrance to an individual's house. The requirement that the arrests in the home must be based on an arrest warrant protects an individual's privacy in the home from searches that are not based on probable cause (586–587).

You may be interested in learning whether an arrest warrant is required when arresting individuals for felonies in some of the scenarios sketched below.

Doorways. A number of courts have held that a defendant who is arrested when he or she opens the door is arrested in his or her home and that a warrant is required. Other courts have ruled that so long as the police remain outside the dwelling when executing the arrest of an individual who is inside the home that the arrest occurs in public and that an arrest warrant is not required (*United States v. Berkowitz,* 927 F.2d 1376 [7th Cir. 1991]). Courts differ on whether an individual who exits his or her residence in response to an order by the police and who then is arrested is considered to have been arrested in the home without a warrant (*United States v. Al-Azzawy,* 784 F.2d 890 [9th Cir. 1985]).

Common hallways. An arrest that is made in the hallway outside the defendant's apartment does not require a warrant (*United States v. Holland,* 755 F.2d 253 [2d Cir. 1985]).

Hotels. An arrest warrant is required to apprehend an individual in a hotel or motel room that he or she has rented (*United States v. Morales,* 737 F.2d 761 [8th Cir. 1984]).

In summary, the Supreme Court held in *Payton v. New York* that if there is sufficient evidence of a citizen's participation in a felony to convince a judicial officer that his or her arrest is justified, it is constitutionally reasonable to require the individual to "open his [or her] doors to the officers of the law" who are armed with an arrest warrant (602–603). In reading *Payton v. New York,* the next case in the text, pay particular attention to the Supreme Court's justification for requiring a warrant for arrests in the home. Why does the dissent believe that the arrest warrant requirement will hamper the police? Do you find the dissent's argument persuasive that requiring a warrant to arrest individuals in the home will interfere with the ability of the police to enforce the criminal law? Which approach is more consistent with individuals' expectation of privacy in the home?

Do the police need a warrant to arrest individuals for felonies in the home?

Payton v. New York, 445 U.S. 573 (1980), Stevens, J.

Issue

These appeals challenge the constitutionality of New York statutes that authorize police officers to enter a private residence without a warrant and with force, if necessary, to make a routine felony arrest. The important constitutional question presented by this challenge has been expressly left open in a number of our prior opinions. In *United States v. Watson,* we upheld a warrantless "midday public arrest," expressly noting that the case did not pose "the still unsettled question . . . 'whether and under what circumstances an officer may enter a suspect's home to make a warrantless arrest.'" The question has been answered in different ways by other appellate courts.

Facts

On January 14, 1970, after two days of intensive investigation, New York detectives had assembled evidence sufficient to establish probable cause to believe that Theodore Payton had murdered the manager of a gas station two days earlier. At about 7:30 A.M. on January 15, six officers went to Payton's apartment in the Bronx, intending to arrest him. They had not obtained a warrant. Although light and music emanated from the apartment, there was no response to their knock on the metal door. They summoned emergency assistance and, about thirty minutes later, used crowbars to break open the door and enter the apartment. No one was there. In plain view, however, was a .30-caliber shell casing that was seized and later admitted into evidence at Payton's murder trial. In due course, Payton surrendered to the police, was indicted for murder, and moved to suppress the evidence taken from his apartment. The trial judge held that the warrantless and forcible entry was authorized by the New York Code of Criminal Procedure and that . . . exigent circumstances justified the officers' failure to announce their purpose before entering the apartment as required by the statute.

He had no occasion, however, to decide whether those circumstances also would have justified the failure to obtain a warrant, because he concluded that the warrantless entry was adequately supported by the statute without regard to the circumstances.

On March 14, 1974, Obie Riddick was arrested for the commission of two armed robberies that had occurred in 1971. He had been identified by the victims in June 1973, and in January 1974, the police had learned his address. They did not obtain a warrant for his arrest. At about noon on March 14, a detective, accompanied by three other officers, knocked on the door of the Queens house where Riddick was living. When his young son opened the door, they could see Riddick sitting in bed covered by a sheet. They entered the house and placed him under arrest. Before permitting him to dress, they opened a chest of drawers two feet from the bed in search of weapons and found narcotics and related paraphernalia. Riddick was subsequently indicted on narcotics charges. At a suppression hearing, the trial judge held that the warrantless entry into his home was authorized by the revised New York statute and that the search of the immediate area was reasonable under *Chimel v. California*.

The New York Court of Appeals, in a single opinion, affirmed the convictions of both Payton and Riddick. The court recognized that the question whether and under what circumstances an officer may enter a suspect's home to make a warrantless arrest had not been settled either by that court or by this Court.

Reasoning

It is familiar history that indiscriminate searches and seizures conducted under the authority of "general warrants" were the immediate evils that motivated the framing and adoption of the Fourth Amendment. Indeed, as originally proposed in the House of Representatives, the draft contained only one clause, which directly imposed limitations on the issuance of warrants but imposed no express restrictions on warrantless searches or seizures. As it was ultimately adopted, however, the Amendment contained two separate clauses, the first protecting the basic right to be free from unreasonable searches and seizures and the second requiring that warrants be particular and supported by probable cause. It is thus perfectly clear that the evil the Amendment was designed to prevent was broader than the abuse of a general warrant. Unreasonable searches or seizures conducted without any warrant at all are condemned by the plain language of the first clause of the Amendment. Almost a century ago, the Court stated in resounding terms that the principles reflected in the Amendment "reached farther than the concrete form" of the specific cases that gave it birth and "apply to all invasions on the part of the government and its employees of the sanctity of a man's home and the privacies of life." Without pausing to consider whether that broad language may require some qualification, it is sufficient to note that the warrantless arrest of a person is a species of seizure required by the Amendment to be reasonable.

The simple language of the Fourth Amendment applies equally to seizures of persons and to seizures of property.... As the Court reiterated just a few years ago, the "physical entry of the home is the chief evil against which the wording of the Fourth Amendment is directed." And we have long adhered to the view that the warrant procedure minimizes the danger of needless intrusions of that sort. It is a "basic principle of Fourth Amendment law" that searches and seizures inside a home without a warrant are presumptively unreasonable. This distinction has equal force when the seizure of a person is involved.... [A]bsent exigent circumstances, a warrantless entry to search for weapons or contraband is unconstitutional even when a felony has been committed and there is probable cause to believe that incriminating evidence will be found within.... [T]he constitutional protection afforded to the individual's interest in the privacy of his own home is equally applicable to a warrantless entry for the purpose of arresting a resident of the house; for it is inherent in such an entry that a search for the suspect may be required before he can be apprehended.... [A]n entry to arrest and an entry to search for and to seize property implicate the same interest in preserving the privacy and the sanctity of the home and justify the same level of constitutional protection.

The critical point is that any differences in the intrusiveness of entries to search and entries to arrest are merely ones of degree rather than kind. The two intrusions share this fundamental characteristic: the breach of the entrance to an individual's home. The Fourth Amendment protects the individual's privacy in a variety of settings. In none is the zone of privacy more clearly defined than when bounded by the unambiguous physical dimensions of an individual's home—a zone that finds its roots in clear and specific constitutional terms: "The right of the people to be secure in their ... houses ... shall not be violated." That language unequivocally establishes the proposition that "[a]t the very core [of the Fourth Amendment] stands the right of a man to retreat into his own home and there be free from unreasonable governmental intrusion." In terms that apply equally to seizures of property and to seizures of persons, the Fourth Amendment has drawn a firm line at the entrance to the house. Absent exigent circumstances, that threshold may not reasonably be crossed without a warrant.

The majority of the States that have taken a position on the question permit warrantless entry into the home to arrest even in the absence of exigent circumstances.... But these current figures reflect a significant decline during the last decade in the number of States permitting warrantless entries for arrest.... A long-standing, widespread practice is not immune from constitutional scrutiny. But neither is it to be lightly brushed aside.... Seven state courts have recently held that warrantless home arrests violate their respective State constitutions.... This is significant because by invoking a state constitutional provision, a state court immunizes its decision from a review by this Court.... In all events, the issue is not one that can be said to have been definitively settled by the common law at the time the Fourth Amendment was adopted. In this case, however, neither history nor this Nation's experience requires us to disregard the overriding respect for the sanctity of the home that has been embedded in our traditions since the origins of the Republic.

The parties have argued at some length about the practical consequences of a warrant requirement as a precondition to a felony arrest in the home. In the absence of any evidence that effective law enforcement has suffered in those States that already have such a requirement, we are inclined to view such arguments with skepticism. More fundamentally, however, such arguments of policy must give way to a constitutional command that we consider to be unequivocal. Finally, we note the State's suggestion that only a search warrant based on probable cause to believe the suspect is at home at a given time can adequately protect the privacy interests at stake, and since such a warrant requirement is manifestly impractical, there need be no warrant of any kind. We find this ingenious argument unpersuasive. It is true that an arrest warrant requirement may afford less protection than a search warrant requirement, but it will suffice to interpose the magistrate's determination of probable cause between the zealous officer and the citizen.

Holding

If there is sufficient evidence of a citizen's participation in a felony to persuade a judicial officer that his arrest is justified, it is constitutionally reasonable to require him to open his doors to the officers of the law. Thus, for Fourth Amendment purposes, an arrest warrant founded on probable cause implicitly carries with it the limited authority to enter a dwelling in which the suspect lives when there is reason to believe the suspect is within. Because no arrest warrant was obtained in either of these cases, the judgments must be reversed and the cases remanded to the New York Court of Appeals for further proceedings not inconsistent with this opinion.

Dissenting, *White, J.*, joined by *Rehnquist, C.J.*

The Court today holds that absent exigent circumstances, officers may never enter a home during the daytime to arrest for a dangerous felony unless they have first obtained a warrant. This hard-and-fast rule, founded on erroneous assumptions concerning the intrusiveness of home arrest entries, finds little or no support in the common law or in the text and history of the Fourth Amendment. I respectfully dissent.

The history of the Fourth Amendment does not support the rule announced today. At the time that Amendment was adopted, the constable possessed broad inherent powers to arrest.... [A]t the time of the Bill of Rights, the warrant functioned as a powerful tool of law enforcement rather than as a protection for the rights of criminal suspects. In fact, it was the abusive use of the warrant power, rather than any excessive zeal in the discharge of peace officers' inherent authority, that precipitated the Fourth Amendment. That Amendment grew out of colonial opposition to the infamous general warrants known as writs of assistance, which empowered customs officers to search at will, and to break open receptacles or packages, wherever they suspected unaccustomed goods to be. The writs did not specify where searches could occur, and they remained effective throughout the sovereign's lifetime. In effect, the writs placed complete discretion in the hands of executing officials. Customs searches of this type were beyond the inherent power of common-law officials and were the subject of court suits when performed by colonial customs agents not acting pursuant to a writ. In sum, the background, text, and legislative history of the Fourth Amendment demonstrate that the purpose was to restrict the abuses that had developed with respect to warrants; the Amendment preserved common-law rules of arrest. Because it was not considered generally unreasonable at common law for officers to break doors to effect a warrantless felony arrest, I do not believe that the Fourth Amendment was intended to outlaw the types of police conduct at issue in the present cases.

Today's decision rests, in large measure, on the premise that warrantless arrest entries constitute a particularly severe invasion of personal privacy.... [A]s Mr. Justice Powell observed in *United States v. Watson,* all arrests involve serious intrusions into an individual's privacy and dignity. Yet we settled in *Watson* that the intrusiveness of a public arrest is not enough to mandate the obtaining of a warrant. The inquiry in the present case, therefore, is whether the incremental intrusiveness that results from an arrest's being made in the dwelling is enough to support an inflexible constitutional rule requiring warrants for such arrests whenever exigent circumstances are not present.

Today's decision ignores the carefully crafted restrictions on the common-law power of arrest entry and thereby overestimates the dangers inherent in that practice. At common law, absent exigent circumstances, entries to arrest could be made only for felony. Even in cases of felony, the officers were required to announce their presence, demand admission, and be refused entry before they were entitled to break doors. Further, it seems generally accepted that entries could be made only during daylight hours. And, in my view, the officer entering to arrest must have reasonable grounds to believe, not only that the arrestee has committed a crime, but also that the person suspected is present in the house at the time of the entry.

These four restrictions on home arrests—felony, knock and announce, daytime, and stringent probable cause—constitute powerful and complementary protections for the privacy interests associated with the home. The felony requirement guards against abusive or arbitrary enforcement and ensures that invasions of the home occur only in case of the most serious crimes. The knock-and-announce and daytime requirements protect individuals against the fear, humiliation, and embarrassment of being roused from their beds in states of partial or complete undress. And these requirements allow the arrestee to surrender at his front door, thereby maintaining his dignity and preventing the officers from entering other rooms of the dwelling. The stringent probable-cause requirement would help ensure against the possibility that the police would enter when the suspect was not home and, in searching for him, frighten members of the family or ransack parts of the house, seizing items in plain view. In short, these requirements, taken together, permit an individual suspected of a serious crime to surrender at the front door of his dwelling and thereby avoid most of the humiliation and indignity that the Court seems to believe necessarily accompany a house arrest entry. Such a front-door arrest, in my view, is no more intrusive on personal privacy than the public warrantless arrests which we found to pass constitutional muster in *Watson*.

All of these limitations on warrantless arrest entries are satisfied on the facts of the present cases. The arrests here were for serious felonies—murder and armed robbery—and both occurred during daylight hours. The authorizing statutes required that the police announce their business and demand entry; neither Payton nor Riddick makes any contention that these statutory requirements were not fulfilled. And it is not argued that the police had no probable cause to believe that both Payton and Riddick were in their dwellings at the time of the entries. Today's decision, therefore, sweeps away any possibility that warrantless home entries might be permitted in some limited situations other than those in which exigent circumstances are present. The Court substitutes, in one sweeping decision, a rigid constitutional rule in place of the common-law approach, evolved over hundreds of years, which achieved a flexible accommodation between the demands of personal privacy and the legitimate needs of law enforcement.

While exaggerating the invasion of personal privacy involved in home arrests, the Court fails to account for the danger that its rule will "severely hamper effective law enforcement." The policeman on his beat must now make subtle discriminations that perplex even judges in their chambers. As Mr. Justice Powell noted, concurring in *United States v. Watson,* police will sometimes delay making an arrest, even after probable cause is established, in order to be sure that they have enough evidence to convict. Then, if they suddenly have to arrest, they run the risk that the subsequent exigency will not excuse their prior failure to obtain a warrant. This problem cannot effectively be cured by obtaining a warrant as soon as probable cause is established because of the chance that the warrant will go stale before the arrest is made.

Further, police officers will often face the difficult task of deciding whether the circumstances are sufficiently exigent to justify their entry to arrest without a warrant. This is a decision that must be made quickly in the most trying of circumstances. If the officers mistakenly decide that the circumstances are exigent, the arrest will be invalid and any evidence seized incident to the arrest or in plain view will be excluded at trial. On the other hand, if the officers mistakenly determine that exigent circumstances are lacking, they may refrain from making the arrest, thus creating the possibility that a dangerous criminal will escape into the community. The police could reduce the likelihood of escape by staking out all possible exits until the circumstances become clearly exigent or a warrant is obtained. But the costs of such a stakeout seem excessive in an era of rising crime and scarce police resources.

The uncertainty inherent in the exigent-circumstances determination burdens the judicial system as well. In the case of searches, exigent circumstances are sufficiently unusual that this Court has determined that the benefits of a warrant outweigh the burdens imposed, including the burdens on the judicial system. In contrast, arrests recurringly involve exigent circumstances, and this Court has heretofore held that a warrant can be dispensed with without undue sacrifice in Fourth Amendment values. The situation should be no different with respect to arrests in the home. Under today's decision, whenever the police have made a warrantless home arrest, there will be the possibility of "endless litigation with respect to the existence of exigent circumstances, whether it was practicable to get a warrant, whether the suspect was about to flee, and the like."

Questions for Discussion

1. What is the holding in *Payton*? How does this differ from the holding in *Watson*?
2. Explain why the Supreme Court holds that an arrest warrant is required to arrest an individual in the home.
3. Examine the factual basis for arresting Obie Riddick. Could the police have obtained an arrest warrant from a magistrate based on the facts that they relied on to support Riddick's arrest? Why was Riddick prosecuted for the possession of unlawful narcotics rather than for armed robbery?
4. What steps would the dissent require the police to follow in arresting individuals in the home? Why does the dissent argue that the warrant requirement will hamper the police in arresting individuals within the home?
5. Do you agree with the majority decision in *Payton*? Is the Supreme Court providing an unnecessary degree of protection to the home?
6. ***Problems in policing.*** Under what circumstances do the police require a warrant to arrest an individual for a felony or for a misdemeanor?

Cases and Comments

Homes of Third Parties. DEA agents entered the home of Gary Steagald with an arrest warrant for Ricky Lyons, a federal fugitive wanted on drug charges. Steagald filed a motion to suppress the cocaine discovered by the agents during the search. The U.S. Supreme Court held that the entry into the home of a "third party" (Steagald) to arrest a suspect (Lyons) requires a search warrant and that an arrest warrant is not sufficient. The Court explained that the purpose of a warrant is to allow a neutral judicial officer to assess whether the police have probable cause to carry out an arrest or conduct a search. The Court stressed that while both warrants require a probable cause determination, they protect different interests. An arrest warrant protects individuals from unreasonable seizures. A search warrant, in contrast, is based on probable cause that the object of a search is located in a specific location and therefore protects an individual's interest in the privacy of his or her dwelling and possessions from an unjustified intrusion by the police. The burden placed on the police by the search warrant requirement is outweighed by the right of presumptively innocent people to be secure in their homes from unjustified forcible intrusions. In this instance, the federal agents knew two days in advance that they planned to search Steagald's home for Lyons and had sufficient time to obtain a search warrant that specified that the agents were authorized to search Steagald's home. The Supreme Court expressed the concern that permitting the police to search the homes of "third parties" based on an arrest warrant would give the police the freedom to search the homes of a suspect's friends, relatives, and acquaintances. See *Steagald v. United States,* 451 U.S. 204 (1981). In determining whether a suspect lives in a dwelling, courts consider the totality of the circumstances. This includes factors such as how long the individual has been continually resident, whether the individual is responsible for the rent and utilities, whether the individual has a key and receives mail at the address, and whether the individual stores his or her clothes and personal items on the premises. See *United States v. Risse,* 83 F.3d 212 (8th Cir. 1996).

Exigent Circumstances

In *Payton v. New York,* the Supreme Court held that arrests inside the home without an arrest warrant are presumptively unreasonable absent **exigent circumstances** or consent. The Court in *Payton* did not define or discuss exigent circumstances. *Exigent* means an urgent need to take action. In *Mincey v. Arizona,* the U.S. Supreme Court pronounced that warrants "are generally required... unless the 'exigencies of the situation' make the needs of law enforcement so compelling that the warrantless search is objectively reasonable under the Fourth Amendment" (*Mincey v. Arizona,* 437 U.S. 385, 393–394 [1978]). In *Warden v. Hayden,* the police arrived at Hayden's residence within minutes after having been informed that Hayden, who the police had probable cause to believe had just robbed the office of a taxicab company, had fled into his home. The U.S. Supreme Court in affirming the legality of the police officers' warrantless entry into Hayden's home noted that "the exigencies of the situation made that course imperative." The Fourth Amendment "does not require police officers to delay in the course of an investigation [if] to do so would gravely endanger their lives or the lives of others. Speed here was essential" (*Warden v. Hayden,* 387 U.S. 294, 298–299 [1967]). The Supreme Court has recognized various emergencies that qualify as exigent circumstances that permit the police to enter a home without a warrant when they have probable cause to justify the entry. The following situations have been held to constitute exigent circumstances.

Hot pursuit. The police are in pursuit of a suspect. In *United States v. Santana,* Santana fled inside her house when the police attempted to arrest her for drug possession. The police pursued her and executed a warrantless arrest within her house. The U.S. Supreme Court held that the police were in hot pursuit and that the narcotics would have been destroyed had the police waited to obtain a warrant. The Court explained that a suspect "may not defeat an arrest which has been set in motion in a public place" by retreating into the home (*United States v. Santana,* 427 U.S. 38, 43 [1976]).

Public safety. The police believe that the public safety is endangered. In *Tyler v. Michigan,* the U.S. Supreme Court approved of the warrantless entry to fight a fire. A "burning building clearly presents an exigency of sufficient proportions to render a warrantless entry 'reasonable.' Indeed, it would defy reason to suppose that firemen must secure a warrant or consent before entering a burning structure to put out the blaze" (*Michigan v. Tyler,* 436 U.S. 499, 509 [1978]).

Destruction of evidence. A failure to act will result in the destruction of evidence. In *Ker v. California,* police officers had probable cause to believe that they observed Ker purchase narcotics and that he was dealing drugs from his apartment. Fearing that Ker was aware that they were following him, the officers hurried to his apartment, obtained the key from the landlord, seized narcotics, and subsequently, arrested Ker. The Supreme Court held that "suspects have no constitutional right to destroy or dispose of evidence, and no basic constitutional guarantees are violated because an officer succeeds in getting to a place where he is entitled to be more quickly than he would had he complied" with the warrant process (*Ker v. California,* 374 U.S. 23, 39 [1963]).

Flight. The suspect may flee the jurisdiction. Federal officers entered a hotel room and arrested Richard Sumpter, a major drug trafficker who was supervising the delivery from California to Detroit of a significant quantity of narcotics. Sumpter dropped his cellular phone on the floor when the federal agents entered his hotel room, and the phone line remained open during the arrest. The officers feared that the individual on the other end of the line had learned of the arrest and would either flee or destroy evidence. As a consequence, the police immediately entered a nearby hotel room and arrested Charles Crehore, a drug courier who worked for Sumpter. The Sixth Circuit Court of Appeals held that "[i]t was not unreasonable for officers to believe Sumpter's companions, who had not yet been arrested, would have been alerted of the arrests through the open phone line, and imminently would have destroyed the evidence or fled the hotel" (*United States v. Gaitan-Acevedo,* 148 F.3d 577 [6th Cir. 1998]).

In the frequently cited case of *United States v. Rubin,* the Third Circuit Court of Appeals indicated that the crucial question in determining whether there are exigent circumstances is whether the police have probable cause to believe that they must act immediately and that they do not have time to secure a warrant (*United States v. Rubin,* 474 F.2d 262 [3d Cir. 1973]). A court's consideration of a claim of exigent circumstances is based on an analysis of the facts that confronted the police at the time of the entry. There is an appreciation that the police must act on the "spur of the moment."

The police, by relying on exigent circumstances, risk that a judge may find that the police mistakenly concluded that there were exigent circumstances justifying entry into the home without an arrest warrant. In *Minnesota v. Olson,* the police apprehended one of two men thought to be responsible for the robbery and murder of a service station attendant. The police shortly thereafter located Olson, the driver of the getaway car, in an upstairs apartment where he was staying as the guest of two women. The police entered the apartment without a warrant and arrested Olson, who subsequently confessed. The U.S. Supreme Court agreed with the Minnesota Supreme Court that the police had unlawfully arrested Olson in the apartment without a warrant. The Court stressed that Olson likely was unarmed because the police had recovered the murder weapon and knew that the two women with the suspect were not in danger and that three or four Minneapolis police squads had surrounded the apartment. The Supreme Court concluded that under the circumstances, there was little likelihood that Olson would have been able to flee and that the police had sufficient time to obtain a warrant (*Minnesota v. Olson,* 495 U.S. 91 [1990]).

Welsh v. Wisconsin is the next case in the text. Welsh drove his car off the road and walked away on foot in what witnesses indicated appeared to be an inebriated condition. The police arrived soon thereafter and arrested Welsh in his home. As you read the decision of the U.S. Supreme Court, ask yourself whether the warrantless entry into Welsh's home was justified based on exigent circumstances. Was there a hot pursuit, a threat to public safety, or a need to preserve evidence? *Welsh* also raises the question whether a warrantless entry into the home is reasonable under the Fourth Amendment when the police have probable cause that an individual has committed a traffic infraction that Wisconsin categorizes as a "noncriminal, civil forfeiture offense." Drunk driving clearly is a serious offense despite the fact that Wisconsin considers it to be a noncriminal violation. In reading *Welsh,* ask yourself whether the Supreme Court's decision provides the police with definite standards for determining exigent circumstances that justify the warrantless entry into a home.

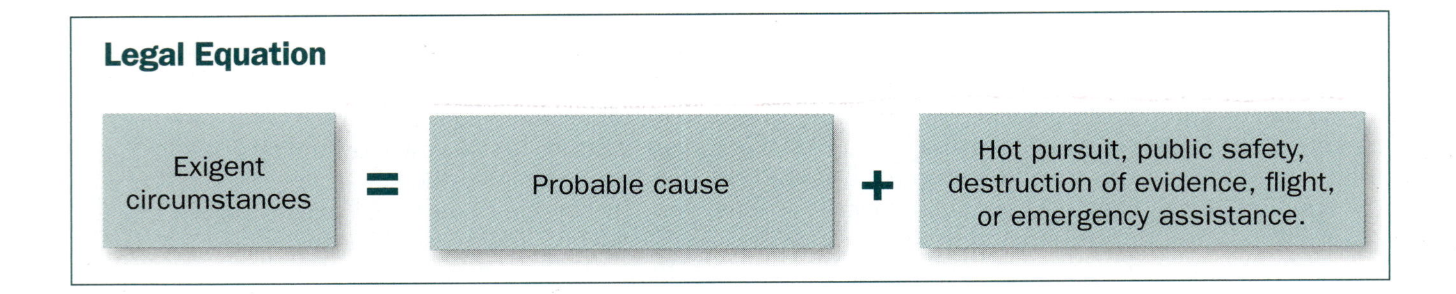

May the police enter a home without a warrant to apprehend a drunk driver under a claim of exigent circumstances?

Welsh v. Wisconsin, 466 U.S. 740 (1984), Brennan, J.

Issue

Payton v. New York, 445 U.S. 573 (1980), held that absent probable cause and exigent circumstances, warrantless arrests in the home are prohibited by the Fourth Amendment. But the Court in that case explicitly refused "to consider the sort of emergency or dangerous situation, described in our cases as 'exigent circumstances,' that would justify a warrantless entry into a home for the purpose of either arrest or search." Certiorari was granted in this case to decide at least one aspect of the unresolved question: whether, and if so under what circumstances, the Fourth Amendment prohibits the police from making a warrantless night entry of a person's home in order to arrest him for a nonjailable traffic offense.

Facts

Shortly before nine o'clock on the rainy night of April 24, 1978, a lone witness, Randy Jablonic, observed a car being driven erratically. After changing speeds and veering from side to side, the car eventually swerved off the road and came to a stop in an open field. No damage to any person or property occurred. Concerned about the driver and fearing that the car would get back on the highway, Jablonic drove his truck up behind the car so as to block it from returning to the road. Another passerby also stopped at the scene, and Jablonic asked her to call the police. Before the police arrived, however, the driver of the car emerged from his vehicle, approached Jablonic's truck, and asked Jablonic for a ride home. Jablonic instead suggested that they wait for assistance in removing or repairing the car. Ignoring Jablonic's suggestion, the driver walked away from the scene.

A few minutes later, the police arrived and questioned Jablonic. He told one officer what he had seen, specifically noting that the driver was either very inebriated or very sick. The officer checked the motor vehicle registration of the abandoned car and learned that it was registered to the petitioner, Edward G. Welsh. In addition, the officer noted that the petitioner's residence was a short distance from the scene and therefore easily within walking distance.

Without securing any type of warrant, the police proceeded to the petitioner's home, arriving about 9:00 P.M. When the petitioner's stepdaughter answered the door, the police gained entry into the house. Proceeding upstairs to the petitioner's bedroom, they found him lying naked in bed. At this point, the petitioner was placed under arrest for driving or operating a motor vehicle while under the influence of an intoxicant, in violation of Wis. Stat. section 346.63(1) (1977). The petitioner was taken to the police station, where he refused to submit to a breath-analysis test.

Separate statutory provisions control the penalty that might be imposed for the substantive offense of driving while intoxicated. At the time in question, the Vehicle Code provided that a first offense for driving while intoxicated was a noncriminal violation subject to a civil forfeiture proceeding for a maximum fine of $200; a second or subsequent offense in the previous five years was a potential misdemeanor that could be punished by imprisonment for up to one year and a maximum fine of $500. Since that time, the State has made only minor amendments to these penalty provisions. Indeed, the statute continues to categorize a first offense as a civil violation that allows for only a monetary forfeiture of no more than $300.

The State filed a criminal complaint against Welsh for driving while intoxicated. The petitioner responded by filing a motion to dismiss the complaint, relying on his contention that the underlying arrest was invalid. After receiving evidence at a hearing on this motion in July 1980, the trial court concluded that the criminal complaint would not be dismissed because the existence of both probable cause and exigent circumstances justified the warrantless arrest.

Contrary to the trial court, the appellate court concluded that the warrantless arrest of the petitioner in his home violated the Fourth Amendment because the State, although demonstrating probable cause to arrest, had not established the existence of exigent circumstances. The petitioner's refusal to submit to a breath test was therefore reasonable. The Supreme Court of Wisconsin in turn reversed the court of appeals, relying on the existence of three factors that it believed constituted exigent circumstances: the need for "hot pursuit" of a suspect, the need to prevent physical harm to the offender and the public, and the need to prevent destruction of evidence. Because of the important Fourth Amendment implications of the decision below, we granted certiorari.

Reasoning

It is axiomatic that the "physical entry of the home is the chief evil against which the wording of the Fourth Amendment is directed." And a principal protection against unnecessary intrusions into private dwellings is the warrant requirement imposed by the Fourth Amendment on agents of the government who seek to enter the home for purposes of search or arrest. It is not surprising, therefore, that the Court has recognized, as "a 'basic principle of Fourth Amendment law[,]' that searches and seizures inside a home without a warrant are presumptively unreasonable."

Consistently with these long-recognized principles, the Court decided in *Payton v. New York* that warrantless felony arrests in the home are prohibited by the Fourth Amendment, absent probable cause and exigent circumstances. At the same time, the Court declined to consider the scope of any exception for exigent circumstances that might justify warrantless home arrests, thereby leaving to the lower courts the initial application of the exigent-circumstances exception. Prior decisions of this Court, however, have emphasized that exceptions to the warrant requirement are "few in number and carefully delineated," and that the police bear a heavy burden when attempting to demonstrate an urgent need that might justify warrantless searches or arrests. Indeed, the Court has recognized only a few such emergency conditions, see, e.g., *United States v. Santana,* 427 U.S. 38, 42–43 (1976) (hot pursuit of a fleeing felon); *Warden v. Hayden,* 387 U.S. 294, 298–299 (1967) (same); *Schmerber v. California,* 384 U.S. 757, 770–771 (1966) (destruction of evidence); *Michigan v. Tyler,* 436 U.S. 499, 509 (1978) (ongoing fire), and has actually applied only the "hot pursuit" doctrine to arrests in the home.

Our hesitation in finding exigent circumstances, especially when warrantless arrests in the home are at issue, is particularly appropriate when the underlying offense for which there is probable cause to arrest is relatively minor. Before agents of the government may invade the sanctity of the home, the burden is on the government to demonstrate exigent circumstances that overcome the presumption of unreasonableness that attaches to all warrantless home entries. When the government's interest is only to arrest for a minor offense, that presumption of unreasonableness is difficult to rebut, and the government usually should be allowed to make such arrests only with a warrant issued upon probable cause by a neutral and detached magistrate.

Consistently with this approach, the lower courts have looked to the nature of the underlying offense as an important factor to be considered in the exigent-circumstances calculus. In a leading federal case defining exigent circumstances, for example, the en banc United States Court of Appeals for the District of Columbia Circuit recognized that the gravity of the underlying offense was a principal factor to be weighed. Without approving all of the factors included in the standard adopted by that court, it is sufficient to note that many other lower courts have also considered the gravity of the offense an important part of their constitutional analysis.... The approach taken in these cases should not be surprising. Indeed, without necessarily approving any of these particular holdings or considering every possible factual situation, we note that it is difficult to conceive of a warrantless home arrest that would not be unreasonable under the Fourth Amendment when the underlying offense is extremely minor.

Holding

We therefore conclude that the commonsense approach utilized by most lower courts is required by the Fourth Amendment prohibition on "unreasonable searches and seizures," and hold that an important factor to be considered when determining whether any exigency exists is the gravity of the underlying offense for which the arrest is being made. Moreover, although no exigency is created simply because there is probable cause to believe that a serious crime has been committed, application of the exigent-circumstances exception in the context of a home entry should rarely be sanctioned when there is probable cause to believe that only a minor offense, such as the kind at issue in this case, has been committed.

Application of this principle to the facts of the present case is relatively straightforward. The petitioner was arrested in the privacy of his own bedroom for a noncriminal, traffic offense. The State attempts to justify the arrest by relying on the hot-pursuit doctrine, on the threat to public safety, and on the need to preserve evidence of the petitioner's blood-alcohol level. On the facts of this case, however, the claim of hot pursuit is unconvincing because there was no immediate or continuous pursuit of the petitioner from the scene of a crime. Moreover, because the petitioner had already arrived home, and had abandoned his car at the scene of the accident, there was little remaining threat to the public safety. Hence, the only potential emergency claimed by the State was the need to ascertain the petitioner's blood-alcohol level.

Even assuming, however, that the underlying facts would support a finding of this exigent circumstance, mere similarity to other cases involving the imminent destruction of evidence is not sufficient. The State of

Wisconsin has chosen to classify the first offense for driving while intoxicated as a noncriminal, civil forfeiture offense for which no imprisonment is possible. This is the best indication of the State's interest in precipitating an arrest, and is one that can be easily identified both by the courts and by officers faced with a decision to arrest. Given this expression of the State's interest, a warrantless home arrest cannot be upheld simply because evidence of the petitioner's blood-alcohol level might have dissipated while the police obtained a warrant. To allow a warrantless home entry on these facts would be to approve unreasonable police behavior that the principles of the Fourth Amendment will not sanction.

Concurring, *Blackmun, J.*

I join the Court's opinion but add a personal observation. I yield to no one in my profound personal concern about the unwillingness of our national consciousness to face up to—and to do something about—the continuing slaughter upon our Nation's highways, a good percentage of which is due to drivers who are drunk or semi-incapacitated because of alcohol or drug ingestion. I have spoken in these Reports to this point before. And it is amazing to me that one of our great States—one which, by its highway signs, proclaims to be diligent and emphatic in its prosecution of the drunken driver—still classifies driving while intoxicated as a civil violation that allows only a money forfeiture of not more than $300 so long as it is a first offense.... But if Wisconsin and other States choose by legislation thus to regulate their penalty structure, there is, unfortunately, nothing in the United States Constitution that says they may not do so.

Dissenting, *White, J.*, joined by *Rehnquist, C.J.*

The gravity of the underlying offense is, I concede, a factor to be considered in determining whether the delay that attends the warrant-issuance process will endanger officers or other persons. The seriousness of the offense with which a suspect may be charged also bears on the likelihood that he will flee and escape apprehension if not arrested immediately. But if, under all the circumstances of a particular case, an officer has probable cause to believe that the delay involved in procuring an arrest warrant will gravely endanger the officer or other persons or will result in the suspect's escape, I perceive no reason to disregard those exigencies on the ground that the offense for which the suspect is sought is a "minor" one.

A warrantless home entry to arrest is no more intrusive when the crime is "minor" than when the suspect is sought in connection with a serious felony.... [N]othing in our previous decisions suggests that the fact that a State has defined an offense as a misdemeanor for a variety of social, cultural, and political reasons necessarily requires the conclusion that warrantless in-home arrests designed to prevent the imminent destruction or removal of evidence of that offense are always impermissible.

A test under which the existence of exigent circumstances turns on the perceived gravity of the crime would significantly hamper law enforcement and burden courts with pointless litigation concerning the nature and gradation of various crimes.... The decision to arrest without a warrant typically is made in the field under less-than-optimal circumstances; officers have neither the time nor the competence to determine whether a particular offense for which warrantless arrests have been authorized by statute is serious enough to justify a warrantless home entry to prevent the imminent destruction or removal of evidence.

[T]he fact that Wisconsin has chosen to punish the first offense for driving under the influence with a fine rather than a prison term does not demand the conclusion that the State's interest in punishing first offenders is insufficiently substantial to justify warrantless in-home arrests under exigent circumstances. As the Supreme Court of Wisconsin observed, "[this] is a model case demonstrating the urgency involved in arresting the suspect in order to preserve evidence of the statutory violation." We have previously recognized that "the percentage of alcohol in the blood begins to diminish shortly after drinking stops, as the body functions to eliminate it from the system." Moreover, a suspect could cast substantial doubt on the validity of a blood or breath test by consuming additional alcohol upon arriving at his home. In light of the promptness with which the officers reached Welsh's house, therefore, I would hold that the need to prevent the imminent and ongoing destruction of evidence of a serious violation of Wisconsin's traffic laws provided an exigent circumstance justifying the warrantless in-home arrest.

Questions for Discussion

1. What is the holding in *Welsh*? Why did the Supreme Court conclude that the police did not have exigent circumstances to enter Welsh's home without an arrest warrant?
2. Discuss the relationship between the Supreme Court's decision in *Welsh* and the Supreme Court's decision in *Payton*.
3. Why does the dissent argue that there was an emergency that justified the warrantless entry into Welsh's home?
4. ***Problems in policing.*** Does the holding in *Welsh* provide the police with a clear rule for the application of the exigent-circumstances exception to the Fourth Amendment warrant requirement? What other offenses are not sufficiently "serious" to justify a warrantless entry into the home to arrest an individual? You can consult the California Supreme Court decision in *People v. Thompson,* 135 P.3d 3 (Cal. 2006), to learn about how state courts have interpreted the "serious offense" limitation on exigent circumstances established in *Welsh*.

Cases and Comments

Emergency-Aid Doctrine. In *Brigham City v. Stuart,* four police officers responded to a call complaining about a loud party. They arrived at the residence at roughly 3:00 A.M. and heard "shouting," "crashing," and "thumping" and entered the backyard. They looked through a screen door and windows and observed four adults attempting to restrain a juvenile. The juvenile broke free and hit one of the adults in the face and drew blood. The other adults pressed the juvenile against a refrigerator with such force that the unit moved across the floor. One of the officers opened the screen door and announced the presence of the police. The men were so involved in the physical confrontation that they did not hear the announcement. The officer then entered the kitchen and again cried out, and the men abandoned the struggle.

The Supreme Court held that "one exigency obviating the requirement of a warrant is the need to assist persons who are seriously injured or threatened with such injury. 'The need to protect or preserve life or avoid serious injury is justification for what would be otherwise illegal absent an exigency or emergency.'" In other words, the **emergency-aid doctrine** authorizes the warrantless entry into a home to provide emergency assistance to an injured occupant or to protect an occupant from imminent harm.

The test is whether the circumstances viewed objectively justify the warrantless entry to render emergency assistance. The fact that the police may have possessed the subjective motivation to make an arrest rather than to render assistance is not relevant to this analysis.

A second important aspect of the decision in *Brigham City* is the Supreme Court's holding that the criminal conduct was sufficiently serious to justify the warrantless entry into the home. The Supreme Court noted that *Welsh* involved an entry to arrest an individual for driving while intoxicated. The only emergency that confronted the officers in *Welsh* was the need to preserve evidence of the suspect's blood-alcohol content. In contrast, the officers in *Brigham* "were confronted with ongoing violence occurring within the home. *Welsh* did not address such a situation." The Supreme Court concluded that the police possessed an "objectively reasonable basis" for believing that the injured adult might be in need of assistance and that the violence was likely to escalate. "Nothing in the Fourth Amendment required [the police] to wait until another blow rendered someone 'unconscious' or 'semi-conscious' or worse before entering" (see *Brigham City v. Stuart,* 547 U.S. 398 [2006]).

You can find Brigham City v. Stuart *on the study site, http://www.sagepub.com/lippmancp.*

5.2 YOU DECIDE

Tyroshia Walker called 911 and reported that Jasper Black had beaten her up that morning in their apartment and that Black was in the possession of a firearm. Walker stated that she was returning to the apartment with her mother to collect her clothing. Walker also stated that they would wait outside the apartment in a white Ford pickup truck for the police. Officer Rodriguez was dispatched to meet Walker, and when Rodriguez arrived, he did not see Walker or the truck. Rodriguez contacted Officer Kikkert, who was already on his way to the apartment, and asked Kikkert to check whether Walker was at the grocery store from which she had made the phone call. Kikkert failed to find Walker at the store. The two officers knocked on the front door of the apartment and received no response. Kikkert discovered an individual who matched Black's physical description in the backyard. The individual identified himself as Jasper Black and acknowledged that he was aware that the police were investigating a domestic violence complaint. Black stated that he had no idea where Walker was at the moment and denied that he lived in the apartment. Kikkert testified that Black appeared agitated and patted Black down for weapons and, with Black's consent, searched his pockets and found a key to the apartment. Rodriguez used the key to enter the apartment and conducted a sweep to check whether anyone was inside. Rodriquez discovered a gun on the bed. He then arrested Black and obtained a warrant to seize the gun. The officers explained that they initially decided to enter the apartment without a warrant because they feared that Walker was badly injured inside the unit. The fact that Black had a firearm made the threat of serious injury to Walker of even greater concern. The dissenting judge noted that Walker had a two-minute drive to the apartment building and that Officer Rodriguez arrived roughly three minutes following Walker's call and that, as a result, there was insufficient time following Walker's arrival for Black to have "force[d] her into the apartment." Was the warrantless entry into the apartment justified by exigent circumstances? See *United States v. Black,* 482 F.3d 1044 (9th Cir. 2007).

You can find the answer by referring to the study site, http://www.sagepub.com/lippmancp.

Deadly Force and Arrests

We have seen that the Fourth Amendment requires probable cause to make an arrest and requires that an arrest be carried out in a reasonable fashion. The U.S. Supreme Court has balanced the interest in individual privacy against the interest in enforcing the criminal law to determine when a warrant is required to arrest an individual. The Court also has employed a balancing test to determine (1) when it is reasonable for the police to use physical force in making an arrest and (2) how much force is reasonable for the police to use under the circumstances.

There are few areas as controversial as the employment of deadly force by police officers who are attempting to apprehend a fleeing suspect. This, in effect, imposes a fatal punishment without trial. The police up until the Fourteenth Century possessed the right to employ deadly force against an individual who the officer reasonably believed had committed a felony. This was the case even in those circumstances in which a felon could have been apprehended without the use of deadly force. The authorization of deadly force was based on the notion that felons were a lawless element whose lives could be taken in order to safeguard the public. This presumption was strengthened by the fact that felons were subject to capital punishment and to the forfeiture of property. Felons were considered to have forfeited their right to life, and the police were merely imposing the punishment that awaited offenders in any event. In contrast, only reasonable force could be applied to apprehend a **misdemeanant.** Misdemeanors were punished by a modest fine or brief imprisonment and were not considered to pose a threat to the community. As a consequence, it was considered inhumane for the police to employ deadly force against individuals responsible for minor violations of the law.

The arming of the police and the **fleeing-felon rule** were reluctantly embraced by the American public, which, while distrustful of governmental power, remained fearful of crime. The common law fleeing-felon rule authorizes the police to use deadly force to apprehend a felon who is fleeing from the police. Some state legislatures attempted to moderate the fleeing-felon rule by adopting the standard that a police officer who reasonably believed that deadly force was required to apprehend a suspect would be held criminally liable in the event that he was shown to have been mistaken.

The judiciary began to seriously reconsider the application of the fleeing-felon rule in the 1980s. Only a small number of felonies remained punishable by death, and offenses in areas such as white-collar crime posed no direct danger to the public. The rule permitting the employment of deadly force against fleeing felons also developed prior to arming the police with firearms in the mid-nineteenth century. Deadly force under the fleeing-felon rule traditionally was employed at close range and rarely was invoked to apprehend a felon who escaped an officer's immediate control. An additional problematic aspect of the fleeing-felon rule was the authorization for private citizens to employ deadly force although private citizens in most states risked criminal liability in the event that they were proven to have been incorrect.

The growing recognition that criminal suspects retained various constitutional rights also introduced a concern with balancing the interests of suspects against the interests of the police and society. In 1986, the U.S. Supreme Court reviewed the fleeing-felon rule in *Tennessee v. Garner,* the next case reprinted in the text. The case was brought under a federal civil rights statute by the family of the deceased who were seeking monetary damages for deprivation of the "rights...secured by the Constitution" (42 U.S.C. § 1983 [discussed in Chapter 11]). The Supreme Court, in an important statement, dismissed Tennessee's contention that so long as the police possess probable cause, the Fourth Amendment has "nothing to say about how that seizure is made." The Court in *Garner* balanced the intrusion on a suspect's privacy interest against the need for the seizure and held that probable cause to seize a suspect did not justify the employment of deadly force in every instance. On the other hand, "[w]here the officer has probable cause to believe that the suspect poses a threat of serious physical harm, either to the officer or to others, it is not constitutionally unreasonable to prevent escape by using deadly force."

We may question whether it is fair to place the fate of a police officer who is charged with the unlawful employment of deadly force in the hands of a judge or jury who may not fully appreciate the pressures confronting an officer who is required to make a split-second decision. On the other hand, some commentators argue that the law is ineffective in controlling the police use of deadly force because the utilization of deadly force in many instances occurs in situations in which there are few witnesses and that the judge and jury typically must rely on the well-rehearsed testimony of the police. Do you think the standard established in *Garner* strikes a fair balance between the interests of the suspect and the interests of society in apprehending felons?

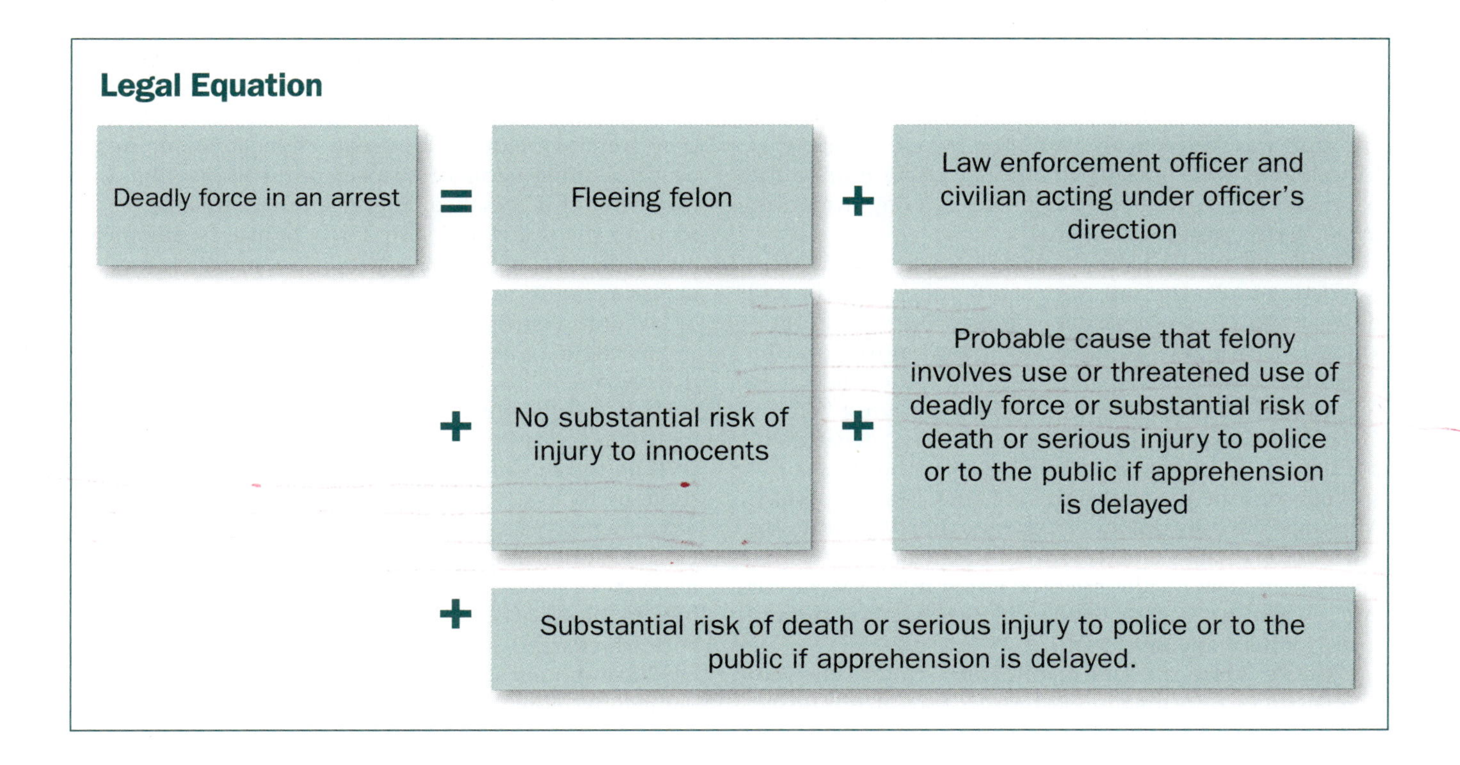

Was the officer justified in killing the burglar?

Tennessee v. Garner, *471 U.S. 1 (1985), White, J.*

Issue

This case requires us to determine the constitutionality of the use of deadly force to prevent the escape of an apparently unarmed suspected felon. We conclude that such force may not be used unless it is necessary to prevent the escape and the officer has probable cause to believe that the suspect poses a significant threat of death or serious physical injury to the officer or others.

Facts

At about 10:45 P.M. on October 3, 1974, Memphis Police Officers Elton Hymon and Leslie Wright were dispatched to answer a "prowler inside call." Upon arriving at the scene, they saw a woman standing on her porch and gesturing toward the adjacent house. She told them she had heard glass breaking and that "they" or "someone" was breaking in next door. While Wright radioed the dispatcher to say that they were on the scene, Hymon went behind the house. He heard a door slam and saw someone run across the backyard. The fleeing suspect, who was appellee-respondent's decedent, Edward Garner, stopped at a six-feet-high chain link fence at the edge of the yard. With the aid of a flashlight, Hymon was able to see Garner's face and hands. He saw no sign of a weapon, and, though not certain, was "reasonably sure" and "figured" that Garner was unarmed. He thought Garner was seventeen or eighteen years old and about 5'5" or 5'7" tall. [In fact, Garner, an eighth-grader, was fifteen. He was 5'4" tall and weighed around 100 or 110 pounds.] While Garner was crouched at the base of the fence, Hymon called out "police, halt" and took a few steps toward him. Garner then began to climb over the fence. Convinced that if Garner made it over the fence, he would elude capture, Hymon shot him. The bullet hit Garner in the back of the head. Garner was taken by ambulance to a hospital, where he died on the operating table. Ten dollars and a purse taken from the house were found on his body....

Garner had rummaged through one room in the house, in which, in the words of the owner, "[all] the stuff was out on the floors, all the drawers was pulled out, and stuff was scattered all over." The owner testified that his valuables were untouched but that, in addition to the purse and the ten dollars, one of his wife's rings was missing. The ring was not recovered....

In using deadly force to prevent the escape, Hymon was acting under the authority of a Tennessee statute and pursuant to Police Department policy. The statute provides that "[if], after notice of the intention to arrest the defendant, he either flee or forcibly resist, the officer may use all the necessary means to effect the arrest." Tenn. Code Ann. section 40-7-108 (1982). The department policy was slightly more restrictive than the statute but still allowed the use of deadly force in cases of burglary. Although the statute does not say so explicitly, Tennessee law forbids the use of deadly force in the arrest of a misdemeanant. The incident was reviewed by the Memphis Police Firearm's Review Board and presented to a grand jury. Neither took any action....

Garner's father then brought this action in the Federal District Court for the Western District of Tennessee, seeking damages under 42 U.S.C. § 1983 for asserted violations of Garner's constitutional rights....After a three-day bench trial, the district court entered judgment for all defendants....[I]t...concluded that Hymon's actions were authorized by the Tennessee statute, which in turn was constitutional. Hymon had employed the only reasonable and practicable means of preventing Garner's escape. Garner had "recklessly and heedlessly attempted to vault over the fence to escape, thereby assuming the risk of being fired upon." The court of appeals reversed....

Reasoning

Whenever an officer restrains the freedom of a person to walk away, he has seized that person....There can be no question that apprehension by the use of deadly force is a seizure subject to the reasonableness requirement of the Fourth Amendment. A police officer may arrest a person if he has probable cause to believe that person committed a crime....Petitioners and appellant argue that if this requirement is satisfied, the Fourth Amendment has nothing to say about how that seizure is made. This submission ignores the many cases in which this Court, by balancing the extent of the intrusion against the need for it, has examined the reasonableness of the manner in which a search or seizure is conducted....

The same balancing process...demonstrates that, notwithstanding probable cause to seize a suspect, an officer may not always do so by killing him. The intrusiveness of a seizure by means of deadly force is unmatched. The suspect's fundamental interest in his own life need not be elaborated upon. The use of deadly force also frustrates the interest of the individual, and of society, in judicial determination of guilt and punishment. Against these interests are ranged governmental interests in effective law enforcement. It is argued that overall violence will be reduced by encouraging the peaceful submission of suspects who know that they may be shot if they flee. Effectiveness in making arrests requires the resort to deadly force, or at least the meaningful threat thereof. "Being able to arrest such individuals is a condition precedent to the state's entire system of law enforcement."...

Without in any way disparaging the importance of these goals, we are not convinced that the use of deadly force is a sufficiently productive means of accomplishing them to justify the killing of nonviolent suspects.... [W]hile the meaningful threat of deadly force might be thought to lead to the arrest of more live suspects by discouraging escape attempts, the presently available evidence does not support this thesis. The fact is that a majority of police departments in this country have forbidden the use of deadly force against nonviolent suspects. If those charged with the enforcement of the criminal law have abjured the use of deadly force in arresting nondangerous felons, there is a substantial basis for doubting that the use of such force is an essential attribute of the arrest power in all felony cases....Petitioners and appellant have not persuaded us that shooting nondangerous fleeing suspects is so vital as to outweigh the suspect's interest in his own life. [The use of punishment to discourage flight has been largely ignored. The Memphis City Code punishes escape with a $50 fine.]

Holding

The use of deadly force to prevent the escape of all felony suspects, whatever the circumstances, is constitutionally unreasonable. It is not better that all felony suspects die than that they escape. Where the suspect poses no immediate threat to the officer and no threat to others, the harm resulting from failing to apprehend him does not justify the use of deadly force to do so. It is no doubt unfortunate when a suspect who is in sight escapes, but the fact that the police arrive a little late or are a little slower afoot does not always justify killing the suspect. A police officer may not seize an unarmed, nondangerous suspect by shooting him dead. The Tennessee statute is unconstitutional insofar as it authorizes the use of deadly force against such fleeing suspects....

It is not, however, unconstitutional on its face. Where the officer has probable cause to believe that the suspect poses a threat of serious physical harm, either to the officer or to others, it is not constitutionally unreasonable to prevent escape by using deadly force. Thus, if the suspect threatens the officer with a weapon or there is probable cause to believe that he has committed a crime involving the infliction or threatened infliction of serious physical harm, deadly force may be used if necessary to prevent escape, and if, where feasible, some warning has been given. As applied in such circumstances, the Tennessee statute would pass constitutional muster....

Officer Hymon could not reasonably have believed that Garner—young, slight, and unarmed—posed any threat. Indeed, Hymon never attempted to justify his actions on any basis other than the need to prevent an escape....The fact that Garner was a suspected burglar could not, without regard to the other circumstances, automatically justify the use of deadly force. Hymon did not have probable cause to believe that Garner, whom he correctly believed to be unarmed, posed any physical danger to himself or others....

While we agree that burglary is a serious crime, we cannot agree that it is so dangerous as automatically to justify the use of deadly force. The FBI classifies burglary as a "property" rather than a "violent" crime. Although the armed burglar would present a different situation, the fact that an unarmed suspect has broken into a dwelling at night does not automatically mean he is physically dangerous. This case demonstrates as much. Statistics demonstrate that burglaries only rarely involve physical violence. During the ten-year period from 1973 to 1982, only 3.8 percent of all burglaries involved violent crime....

We hold that the statute is invalid insofar as it purported to give Hymon the authority to act as he did....

Dissenting, *O'Connor, J.*, joined by *Burger, C.J.*, and *Rehnquist, J.*

The public interest involved in the use of deadly force as a last resort to apprehend a fleeing burglary suspect relates primarily to the serious nature of the crime. Household burglaries not only represent the illegal entry into a person's home, but also "[pose] real risk of serious harm to others." According to recent Department of Justice statistics, "[three-fifths] of all rapes in the home, three-fifths of all home robberies, and about a third of home aggravated and simple assaults are committed by burglars." During the period 1973–1982, 2.8 million such violent crimes were committed in the course of burglaries. Victims of a forcible intrusion into their home by a nighttime prowler will find little consolation in the majority's confident assertion that "burglaries only rarely involve physical violence."...

Admittedly, the events giving rise to this case are in retrospect deeply regrettable. No one can view the death of an unarmed and apparently nonviolent fifteen-year-old without sorrow, much less disapproval....The officer pursued a suspect in the darkened backyard of a house that from all indications had just been burglarized. The police officer was not certain whether the suspect was alone or unarmed; nor did he know what had transpired inside the house. He ordered the suspect to halt, and when the suspect refused to obey and attempted to flee into the night, the officer fired his weapon to prevent escape. The reasonableness of this action for purposes of the Fourth Amendment is not determined by the unfortunate nature of this particular case; instead, the question is whether it is constitutionally impermissible for police officers, as a last resort, to shoot a burglary suspect fleeing the scene of the crime....

I cannot accept the majority's creation of a constitutional right to flight for burglary suspects seeking to avoid capture at the scene of the crime....I respectfully dissent.

Questions for Discussion

1. Did Officer Hymon's shooting of Garner comply with the Tennessee statute? How does the Tennessee statute differ from the Court's holding in *Garner*? Do you believe that the Supreme Court majority places too much emphasis on protecting the fleeing felon?
2. Justice O'Connor writes at one point in her dissent that the Supreme Court majority offers no guidance regarding the factors to be considered in determining whether a suspect poses a significant threat of death or serious bodily harm and does not specify the weapons, ranging from guns to knives to baseball bats, that will justify the officer's employment of deadly force. Is Justice O'Connor correct that the majority's "silence on critical factors in the decision to use deadly force simply invites second-guessing of difficult police decisions that must be made quickly in the most trying of circumstances"?
3. Summarize the facts that Officer Hymon considered in the "split second" in which he decided to fire at the suspect. Was his decision reasonable? What of Justice O'Connor's conclusion that the Supreme Court decision will lead to a large number of cases in which lower courts are forced to "struggle to determine if a police officer's split-second decision to shoot was justified by the danger posed by a particular object and other facts related to the crime"?
4. Is Justice O'Connor correct that the Supreme Court majority unduly minimizes the serious threat posed by burglary? Should the Supreme Court be setting standards for police across the country based on the facts in a single case?
5. ***Problems in policing.*** Provide examples of several situations that you believe would justify the police use of deadly force.

Nondeadly Force

What about police use of nondeadly force? In *Graham v. Connor,* the Supreme Court held that claims of excessive nondeadly force as well as claims of excessive deadly force are to be analyzed under the Fourth Amendment reasonableness standard. The question is whether the use of force to seize an individual is objectively reasonable under the totality of the circumstances (*Graham v. Connor,* 490 U.S. 386 [1989]).

Police Officer Connor observed Graham rushing out of a convenience store. Graham later related that he was suffering a diabetic reaction and was in need of orange juice to counteract the reaction. He explained that he was deterred by the long line in the store from purchasing orange juice, hurriedly left the store, and asked his friend William Berry to drive him to a friend's house. The officer grew suspicious and pulled Graham and William Berry over for investigation. Berry explained to the officer that Graham was suffering from a "sugar reaction." The police arriving at the scene were convinced that Graham was drunk and questioned whether he was suffering from a diabetic reaction. The situation escalated and culminated in four officers' throwing Graham headfirst into the squad car (389–391).

The U.S. Supreme Court held that cases in which the police are alleged to have employed nondeadly excessive force during an arrest, investigative stop, or other seizure are to be analyzed under the Fourth Amendment objective reasonableness standard. The Court stated that the question is whether the police officer's actions are "objectively reasonable in light of the facts and circumstances." The relevant factors to be considered are the seriousness of the offense, the immediacy of the threat posed by the suspect, and whether the suspect is resisting arrest or attempting to escape. In evaluating the officer's response, courts must consider the circumstances confronting the police at the time rather than analyze the situation with the benefit of "20/20 vision of hindsight." The fact that an officer personally believes that nondeadly force is required to seize a suspect is not the determining factor. The question is whether the force is justified under the objective circumstances that confront the officer (396–399).

In reading *Graham v. Connor,* consider whether the Fourth Amendment reasonableness standard strikes the proper balance between the interests of society in the apprehension of criminal suspects and the interest of the individual in being free from the application of force by the police. Should the police be permitted greater freedom to employ nondeadly force than deadly force?

Did the police officers employ excessive force?

Graham v. Connor, 490 U.S. 386 (1989), Rehnquist, C.J.

Issue

This case requires us to decide what constitutional standard governs a free citizen's claim that law enforcement officials used excessive force in the course of making an arrest, investigatory stop, or other "seizure" of his person. We hold that such claims are properly analyzed under the Fourth Amendment's "objective reasonableness" standard, rather than under a substantive due process standard.

On November 12, 1984, Graham, a diabetic, felt the onset of an insulin reaction. He asked a friend, William Berry, to drive him to a nearby convenience store so he could purchase some orange juice to counteract the reaction. Berry agreed, but when Graham entered the store, he saw a number of people ahead of him in the checkout line. Concerned about the delay, he hurried out of the store and asked Berry to drive him to a friend's house instead.

Respondent Connor, an officer of the Charlotte, North Carolina, Police Department, saw Graham hastily enter and leave the store. The officer became suspicious that something was amiss and followed Berry's car. About one-half mile from the store, he made an investigative stop. Although Berry told Connor that Graham was simply suffering from a "sugar reaction," the officer ordered Berry and Graham to wait while he found out what, if anything, had happened at the convenience store. When Officer Connor returned to his patrol car to call for backup assistance, Graham got out of the car, ran around it twice, and finally sat down on the curb, where he passed out briefly.

In the ensuing confusion, a number of other Charlotte police officers arrived on the scene in response to Officer Connor's request for backup. One of the officers rolled Graham over on the sidewalk and cuffed his hands tightly behind his back, ignoring Berry's pleas to get him some sugar. Another officer said, "I've seen a lot of people with sugar diabetes that never acted like this. Ain't nothing wrong with the M.F. but drunk. Lock the S.B. up." Several officers then lifted Graham up from behind, carried him over to Berry's car, and placed him face down on its hood. Regaining consciousness, Graham asked the officers to check in his wallet for a diabetic decal that he carried. In response, one of the officers told him to "shut up" and shoved his face down against the hood of the car. Four officers grabbed Graham and threw him headfirst into the police car. A friend of Graham's brought some orange juice to the car, but the officers refused to let him have it. Finally, Officer Connor received a report that Graham had done nothing wrong at the convenience store, and the officers drove him home and released him.

At some point during his encounter with the police, Graham sustained a broken foot, cuts on his wrists, a bruised forehead, and an injured shoulder; he also claims to have developed a loud ringing in his right ear that continues to this day. He commenced this action under 42 U.S.C. § 1983 against the individual officers involved in the incident, all of whom are respondents here, alleging that they had used excessive force in making the investigatory stop, in violation of "rights secured to him under the Fourteenth Amendment to the United States Constitution and 42 U.S.C. § 1983." The case was tried before a jury. At the close of petitioner's evidence, respondents moved for a directed verdict. In ruling on that motion, the district court considered the following four factors, which it identified as "[t]he factors to be considered in determining when the excessive use of force gives rise to a cause of action under § 1983": (1) the need for the application of force; (2) the relationship between that need and the amount of force that was used; (3) the extent of the injury inflicted; and (4) "[w]hether the force was applied in a good faith effort to maintain and restore discipline or maliciously and sadistically for the very purpose of causing harm." Finding that the amount of force used by the officers was "appropriate under the circumstances," that "[t]here was no discernable injury inflicted," and that the force used "was not applied maliciously or sadistically for the very purpose of causing harm," but in "a good faith effort to maintain or restore order in the face of a potentially explosive situation," the district court granted respondents' motion for a directed verdict. A divided panel of the Court of Appeals for the Fourth Circuit affirmed.... We granted certiorari and now reverse.

Reasoning

Fifteen years ago, in *Johnson v. Glick* (1973), the Court of Appeals for the Second Circuit addressed a § 1983 damages claim filed by a pretrial detainee who claimed that a guard had assaulted him without justification. In evaluating the detainee's claim, Judge Friendly applied neither the Fourth Amendment nor the Eighth, the two most textually obvious sources of constitutional protection against physically abusive governmental conduct. Instead, he looked to "substantive due process," holding that "quite apart from any 'specific' of the Bill of Rights, application of undue force by law enforcement officers deprives a suspect of liberty without due process of law." As support for this proposition, he relied upon our decision in *Rochin v. California* (1952), which used the Due Process Clause to void a state criminal conviction based on evidence obtained by pumping the defendant's stomach. If a police officer's use of force which "shocks the conscience" could justify setting aside a criminal conviction, Judge Friendly reasoned, a correctional officer's use of similarly excessive force must give rise to a due process violation actionable under § 1983. Judge Friendly went on to set forth four factors to guide courts in determining "whether the constitutional line has been crossed" by a particular use of force—the same four factors relied upon by the courts below in this case.

In the years following *Johnson v. Glick,* the vast majority of lower federal courts have applied its four-part "substantive due process" test indiscriminately to all excessive force claims lodged against law enforcement and prison officials under § 1983, without considering whether the particular application of force might implicate a more specific constitutional right governed by a different standard. Indeed, many courts have seemed to assume, as did the courts below in this case, that there is a generic "right" to be free from excessive force, grounded not in any particular constitutional provision but rather in "basic principles of § 1983 jurisprudence."

We reject this notion that all excessive force claims brought under § 1983 are governed by a single generic standard. As we have said many times, § 1983 "is not itself a source of substantive rights," but merely provides "a method for vindicating federal rights elsewhere conferred." In addressing an excessive force claim brought under § 1983, analysis begins by identifying the specific constitutional right allegedly infringed by the challenged application of force. In most instances, that will be either the Fourth Amendment's prohibition against unreasonable seizures of the person or the Eighth Amendment's ban on cruel and unusual punishments, which are the two primary sources of constitutional protection against physically abusive governmental conduct. The validity of the claim must then be judged by reference to the specific constitutional standard which governs that right, rather than to some generalized "excessive force" standard.

Where, as here, the excessive force claim arises in the context of an arrest or investigatory stop of a free citizen, it is most properly characterized as one invoking the protections of the Fourth Amendment, which guarantees citizens the right "to be secure in their persons...against unreasonable...seizures" of the person. This much is clear from our decision in *Tennessee v. Garner.* In *Garner,* we addressed a claim that the use of deadly force to apprehend a fleeing suspect who did not appear to be armed or otherwise dangerous violated the suspect's constitutional rights, notwithstanding the existence of probable cause to arrest. Though the complaint alleged violations of both the Fourth Amendment and the Due Process Clause, we analyzed the constitutionality of the challenged application of force solely by reference to the Fourth Amendment's prohibition against unreasonable seizures of the person, holding that the "reasonableness" of a particular seizure depends not only on when it is made, but also on how it is carried out. Today, we make explicit what was implicit in *Garner*'s analysis, and hold that all claims that law enforcement officers have used excessive force—deadly or not—in the course of an arrest, investigatory stop, or other "seizure" of a free citizen should be analyzed under the Fourth Amendment and its "reasonableness" standard, rather than under a "substantive due process" approach. Because the Fourth Amendment provides an explicit textual source of constitutional protection against this sort of physically intrusive governmental conduct, that Amendment, not the more generalized notion of "substantive due process," must be the guide for analyzing these claims.

Determining whether the force used to effect a particular seizure is "reasonable" under the Fourth Amendment requires a careful balancing of "'the nature and quality of the intrusion on the individual's Fourth Amendment interests'" against the countervailing governmental interests at stake. Fourth Amendment jurisprudence has long recognized that the right to make an arrest or investigatory stop necessarily carries with it the right to use some degree of physical coercion or threat thereof to effect it.... "The test of reasonableness under the Fourth Amendment is not capable of precise definition or mechanical application"; however, its proper application requires careful attention to the facts and circumstances of each particular case, including the severity of the crime at issue, whether the suspect poses an immediate threat to the safety of the officers or others, and whether he is actively resisting arrest or attempting to evade arrest by flight.

The "reasonableness" of a particular use of force must be judged from the perspective of a reasonable officer on the scene, rather than with the 20/20 vision of hindsight. The Fourth Amendment is not violated by an arrest based on probable cause, even though the wrong person is arrested, nor by the mistaken execution of a valid search warrant on the wrong premises. With respect to a claim of excessive force, the same standard of reasonableness at the moment applies: "Not every push or shove, even if it may later seem unnecessary in the peace of a judge's chambers," violates the Fourth Amendment. The calculus of reasonableness must embody allowance for the fact that police officers are often forced to make split-second judgments—in circumstances that are tense, uncertain, and rapidly evolving—about the amount of force that is necessary in a particular situation.

As in other Fourth Amendment contexts, however, the "reasonableness" inquiry in an excessive force case is an objective one: The question is whether the officers' actions are "objectively reasonable" in light of the facts and circumstances confronting them, without regard to their underlying intent or motivation. An officer's evil intentions will not make a Fourth Amendment violation out of an objectively reasonable use of force; nor will an officer's good intentions make an objectively unreasonable use of force constitutional.

Because petitioner's excessive force claim is one arising under the Fourth Amendment, the court of appeals erred in analyzing it under the four-part *Johnson v. Glick* test. That test, which requires consideration of whether the individual officers acted in "good faith" or "maliciously and sadistically for the very purpose of causing harm," is incompatible with a proper Fourth Amendment analysis. We do not agree with the court of appeals' suggestion that the "malicious and sadistic" inquiry is merely another way of describing conduct that is objectively unreasonable under the circumstances. Whatever the empirical correlations between "malicious and sadistic" behavior and objective unreasonableness may be, the fact remains that the "malicious and sadistic" factor puts in issue the subjective motivations of the individual officers, which our prior cases make clear has no bearing on whether a particular seizure is "unreasonable" under the Fourth Amendment. Nor do we agree with the court of appeals' conclusion that because the subjective motivations of the individual officers are of central importance in deciding whether force used against a convicted prisoner violates the Eighth Amendment, it cannot be reversible error to inquire into them in deciding whether force used against a suspect or arrestee violates the Fourth Amendment. Differing standards under the Fourth and Eighth Amendments are hardly surprising: The terms *cruel* and *punishments* clearly suggest some inquiry into subjective state of mind, whereas the term *unreasonable* does not. Moreover, the less protective Eighth Amendment standard applies "only after the State has complied with the constitutional guarantees traditionally associated with criminal prosecutions." The Fourth Amendment inquiry is one of "objective reasonableness" under the circumstances, and subjective concepts like "malice" and "sadism" have no proper place in that inquiry.

Holding

Because the court of appeals reviewed the district court's ruling on the motion for directed verdict under an erroneous view of the governing substantive law, its judgment must be vacated and the case remanded to that court for reconsideration of that issue under the proper Fourth Amendment standard.

Questions for Discussion

1. What is the holding in *Graham v. Connor*?
2. Courts traditionally analyzed claims that the police employed excessive nondeadly force under the Due Process Clause of the Fourteenth Amendment and held that the individuals had the right under the Fourteenth Amendment to be free from the "malicious and sadistic application of force intentionally applied for the very purpose of causing harm." The central consideration, in other words, was whether the officer intended to harm the suspect by employing unnecessary force. Can you explain how the Fourth Amendment reasonableness test in *Graham* modifies the "substantive due process" test established in *Johnson v. Glick*? Explain how these two tests in some instances may lead to different outcomes in a case.
3. Apply the reasonableness standard for excessive force to the facts in *Graham*. Did the officers employ reasonable force?
4. Are judges and juries equipped to evaluate the reasonableness of the application of force by a law enforcement officer?
5. ***Problems in policing.*** What are the factors that a law enforcement officer should weigh and balance in deciding whether to use nondeadly physical force against a suspect? How can an officer determine whether the force is excessive?

Cases and Comments

Hot Pursuit. In 2007, in *Scott v. Harris,* a Georgia county deputy clocked Harris's vehicle traveling at seventy-three miles per hour on a road with a fifty-five-mile-per-hour speed limit. Scott turned on his flashing lights indicating that Harris should stop. Harris, instead, accelerated, and the deputy initiated a high-speed chase. The two sped down two-lane roads at speeds exceeding eighty-five miles per hour. Deputy Timothy Scott heard the radio communication and joined the pursuit. In the middle of the chase, Scott pulled into a parking lot, and Harris was nearly boxed in by several police vehicles. Harris evaded the trap by making a sharp right turn, colliding with Scott's police car, exiting the parking lot, and speeding down the highway. Scott's squad car was the lead police chase vehicle. Six minutes and nearly ten miles following the beginning of the chase, Scott decided to disable Harris's automobile and was given radio authorization to employ a "Precision Intervention Technique" maneuver, which causes the fleeing vehicle to spin to a stop. Scott, instead, applied his push bumper to the rear of Harris's vehicle. Harris lost control of his automobile, which left the roadway, ran down an embankment, overturned, and crashed. Harris was seriously injured and was left a quadriplegic. Harris filed a suit under 42 U.S.C. § 1983 seeking civil damages for Deputy Scott's use of what Harris alleged was excessive force and an unreasonable seizure under the Fourth Amendment.

The U.S. Supreme Court determined that the videotape indicated that Harris's vehicle sped down narrow two-lane roads at "shockingly fast" speeds. This was a "Hollywood-style car chase of the most frightening sort, placing police officers and innocent bystanders alike at great risk of serious injury." Scott conceded that his decision to ram Harris's vehicle constituted a Fourth Amendment seizure, which the Supreme Court defined as the "governmental termination of freedom of movement through means intentionally applied."

The Supreme Court held that the claim that Scott employed excessive force in making a seizure is properly analyzed under the Fourth Amendment's "objective reasonableness" standard. The questions are whether Scott's actions are reasonable and whether they constitute deadly force.

In determining reasonableness, the Court balances the nature and quality of the intrusion on an individual's Fourth Amendment interests against the importance of the governmental interests justifying the intrusion. Thus, "in judging whether Scott's actions were reasonable, we must consider the risk of bodily harm that Scott's actions posed to [Harris] in light of the threat to the public that Scott was trying to eliminate." The Court concluded that Harris "posed an actual and imminent threat to the lives of any pedestrians who might have been present, to other civilian motorists, and to the officers involved in the chase." On the other hand, Scott's actions also "posed a high likelihood of serious injury or death" to Harris—"though not the near certainty of death posed by, say, shooting a fleeing felon in the back of the head."

How should a court weigh the "perhaps lesser probability of injuring or killing numerous bystanders against the perhaps larger probability of injuring or killing a single person"? The Supreme Court placed particular weight on the number of innocent lives that Harris intentionally placed at risk by engaging in a reckless high-speed police chase. Under the circumstances, the Court had "little difficulty in concluding it was reasonable for Scott to take the action that he did."

The Supreme Court rejected the contention that the reasonable course of action was for Scott to abandon the pursuit with the expectation that Harris would no longer fear apprehension and would reduce the speed of his vehicle. "Whereas Scott's action—ramming respondent off the road—was certain to eliminate the risk that respondent posed to the public, ceasing pursuit was not." Harris was equally as likely to have responded to the abandonment of the pursuit by continuing to drive in a reckless fashion as by slowing down. He might have concluded that the police abandonment was a trick and that they planned to intercept his vehicle at a later time. Requiring the police to abandon a pursuit whenever a motorist drives so recklessly that he or she places other people's lives in danger would lead "[e]very fleeing motorist [to] know that escape is within his [or her] grasp, if only he [or she] accelerates to 90 miles per hour, crosses the double-yellow line a few times, and runs a few red lights." The Court, instead, established a "more sensible rule: *A police officer's attempt to terminate a dangerous high-speed car chase that threatens the lives of innocent bystanders does not violate the Fourth Amendment, even when it places the fleeing motorist at risk of serious injury or death.*"

In summary, Harris posed a "substantial and immediate risk of serious physical injury to others." Scott's attempt to terminate the chase by forcing Harris off the road was reasonable. The court cautioned that the facts of a high-speed chase may lead to a different result under different circumstances: "A high-speed chase in a desert in Nevada is, after all, quite different from one that travels through the heart of Las Vegas."

Justice Stevens, in dissent, argued that the videotape indicated that Harris's flight did not pose a risk to the public and that, under the circumstances, the employment of deadly force was unreasonable. He asked what would have happened if the police had decided to abandon the chase. Justice Stevens contends that there is no basis for concluding that an individual will continue to flee once the police call off a pursuit. The police in any event had recorded Harris's license number and could have apprehended him at a later date. Even if Harris would have eluded capture had Officer Scott abandoned the pursuit, "the use of deadly force in this case was no more appropriate than the use of a deadly weapon against a fleeing felon in *Tennessee v. Garner.*" Justice Stevens proposed an alternative test to the standard adopted by the majority of the Court. This test establishes a preference for the police to abandon pursuits rather than engage in high-speed automobile pursuits. "When the immediate danger to the public created by the pursuit is greater than the immediate or potential danger to the public should the suspect remain at large, then the pursuit should be discontinued or terminated.... [P]ursuits should usually be discontinued when the violator's identity has been established to the point that later apprehension can be accomplished without danger to the public." Do you agree with Justice Stevens? The topic of the civil liability of the police is pursued in greater depth in Chapter 11. See *Scott v. Harris,* 550 U.S. 372 (2007).

You can find Scott v. Harris *on the study site, http://www.sagepub.com/lippmancp.*

Criminal Procedure in the News

On September 17, 2007, Senator John Kerry of Massachusetts addressed a town hall meeting at the University of Florida. Kerry, who was the unsuccessful Democratic Party nominee for president in 2004, finished his speech and began answering student questions. The last questioner was twenty-one-year-old Andrew Meyer, a columnist for the student newspaper who was known for his provocative opinions. Meyer, with obvious intensity, asked a series of challenging questions including whether Kerry really had wanted to win the 2004 election, whether Senator Kerry had belonged to the same "secret society" as President Bush when he was at Yale, and why President Bush had not been impeached. Meyer refused to stop talking, and campus police officers took Meyer by the arm, removed him from the microphone, and began to escort him out of the auditorium. Meyer resisted and tried to break away, and the officers forced him to the ground. He yelled at the officers to let him go and shouted, "Don't Tase me, bro," before being "Tasered" and led out of the room. Meyer was charged with resisting an officer and disturbing the peace and spent the night in jail. He later admitted having "lost his cool," wrote three letters of apology, accepted a term of probation, and agreed to pay $150 to charity or to engage in ten hours of community service. The Florida Department of Law Enforcement later issued a report that concluded that the officers had acted in accordance with state guidelines on the use of Tasers and that the reliance on the Taser was preferable to escalating to "hard empty hand strikes, kicks, knees or [the] baton."

The incident in Florida drew attention to the policy of the police in regard to the use of Tasers. The U.S. Justice Department reports that over 180 individuals in the United States have died since 2001 following the application of a Taser by law enforcement personnel. Critics contend that the figure is much higher. The manufacturer cites studies finding that the Taser does not pose a danger and claims that these deaths primarily are attributable to factors such as heart attacks or drug overdoses rather than the Taser. Thousands of police officers have voluntarily subjected themselves to the Taser without incident.

Taser guns (which stands for Thomas A. Swift Electric Rifle) are small pistols that shoot two darts that are connected by electric cables to the gun. The pistol can shoot the darts at a distance of roughly twenty-five feet. Each time the trigger is pulled, the Taser delivers a 50,000-volt electric shock for five seconds. The darts are able to penetrate and to deliver a shock through up to five centimeters of clothing. Tasers also are able to be employed by direct contact ("dry stunning"). The Taser works by overstimulating the nervous system, which causes an uncontrollable contraction of the muscles and physically disables the targeted individual. It is estimated that as many as 100,000 people have been Tasered by law enforcement since 1998. For example, the Seattle, Washington, police report that between January 2003 and June 2004, officers used a Taser on 269 occasions.

The first Taser was developed by a scientist named Jack Cover. The early Taser relied on gunpowder, was classified as a firearm, and was used by between 400 and 500 police departments as a weapon to be deployed in isolated, special circumstances. In the early 1990s, Rick Smith contacted Cover with the idea of developing the Taser as a mass-market, self-defense weapon. Smith had taken this project on as a personal crusade after several of his friends had been killed by an angry motorist. In 1993, Smith and Cover created a corporation, now known as Taser International Inc. The Taser was reengineered to operate with nitrogen propellant rather than gunpowder. In 2000, the company introduced the Advanced Taser (M-26) that disabled individuals in 1.5 seconds in tests and that subsequently became hugely popular with police departments. Texas International generates roughly fifty million dollars per year in revenue from the sale of the Taser.

An estimated 9,500 law enforcement, correctional, and military agencies in forty-three countries employ Taser guns, and over 130,000 Tasers are being used by law enforcement personnel in the United States. More than 100,000 civilians in the United States possess Tasers. The Taser is favored by law enforcement for several reasons.

Safety. The police can immobilize an individual without resorting to severe or deadly force. Disabling an assailant also prevents the escalation of conflicts and limits police injuries and fatalities.

Accountability. The Taser "data port" records the date, time, and duration each time the device is employed. A Taser camera that records the use of the weapon also recently has been made available. This technology insures that the use of the weapon by law enforcement personnel can be reviewed by police authorities.

The U.S. government General Accounting Office, in a study, determined that most police departments regulate the use of Tasers as part of their "force escalation" policy and limit the application of Tasers to suspects who pose a threat to officers or present a threat to other individuals. Departments prohibit the use of Tasers against pregnant women, children, and the mentally challenged and prohibit the use of Tasers in the proximity of bystanders or flammable liquids. Police regulations also generally require that people hit by a Taser in sensitive areas are to be examined by a physician.

Critics contend that the Taser is not as safe as often portrayed and is subject to abuse by police who do not understand that the Taser is a potentially dangerous weapon. There are two main criticisms of Tasers.

Force. Guidelines on the use of force at times are not followed, and the Taser is used against individuals who do not pose a direct threat to the officers. It is alleged that the Taser is relied on in situations where force is unnecessary. The charge is made that Tasers continue to be used against children, pregnant women, and the mentally challenged and against individuals who verbally challenge officers. The allegation is made that Tasers are employed with very little oversight to maintain order in prisons and in schools.

Deaths. The Taser poses a lethal danger to individuals with various types of physical disabilities.

Critics also point out that the Taser is not the answer to every situation. In the Rodney King incident in Los Angeles in 1991, King was able to continue resisting the officers despite being Tasered. In addition, the Taser fires a single shot, and the officer may miss the assailant or the gun may misfire. The potential problems with the reliance on Tasers has led several departments to limit their reliance on the weapon.

The leading case on the use of Tasers is *Draper v. Reynolds,* 369 F.3d 1270 (11th Cir. 2004). In *Draper,* Georgia Deputy Sheriff Clinton Reynolds pulled Allen Draper over for driving his truck with an improperly illuminated tag light. Draper asked Reynolds to stop shining his flashlight at him and was ordered out of the truck. The video camera in Reynolds's squad car recorded Draper shouting at Reynolds. Draper is described by the court as "belligerent, [having] gestured animatedly...[and as] very excited and [speaking] loudly." He accused Reynolds of harassing him and refused to show the officer his proof of insurance and other documents. Draper then proclaimed, "How 'bout you just go ahead and take me to f__ing jail, then, man, you know, because I'm not going to kiss your d__ a__ because you're a police officer." Reynolds requested for a fourth time that Draper retrieve the documents, and Draper reacted by accusing Reynolds of treating him like a child and of disrespecting him. Reynolds asked Draper to cooperate for a fifth time and then discharged a Taser. Reynolds later testified that he felt threatened. Draper was criminally charged and convicted of obstruction of an officer and with an improperly illuminated tag light. Draper later explained that he thought that he had been pulled over because he was an African American.

The Eleventh Circuit Court of Appeals held that Reynolds had acted in a reasonable fashion and that an attempt to arrest Draper without the use of the Taser likely would have resulted in a physical confrontation.

The appellate court recognized that being hit with a Taser is not a "pleasant experience, but that a single shot was proportionate to the need for force and did not result in serious injury." On the other hand, appellate courts have held that the repeated use of a Taser against a suspect who is on the ground and under the physical control of an officer is an unreasonable application of force (*Roberts v. Manigold,* 240 Fed. Appx. 675 [6th Cir. 2007]).

On November 16, 2007, Canadian Royal Mounted Police were called to the Vancouver Airport to subdue Robert Dziekanski, a forty-year-old, newly arrived Polish immigrant who had been detained in the airport for ten hours while his mother, who was a Canadian resident, was making desperate efforts to contact him. Dziekanski did not speak English and, according to witnesses, was highly agitated, threw a computer, and broke a chair but did not directly threaten authorities. The Royal Canadian Mounted Police Tasered and subdued the obviously agitated Dziekanski, who died roughly a minute after being hit by the Taser shots. Dziekanski was the eighteenth individual to die in Canada after being Tasered, and civil liberties groups called for a prohibition on the use of the weapon. Several weeks following Dziekanski's death, the United Nations Committee Against Torture condemned the Taser as a form of torture that creates "extreme pain" and that "in certain cases . . . could also cause death." Taser International responded that the United Nations Committee "is out of touch with the reality that confronts law enforcement officers every day worldwide" and posted a study on its Web site by the United Kingdom Defense Science and Technology Laboratory that concluded that the Taser does not have a lethal impact on the human heart. Taser International points out that virtually every police restraint technique and instrument involves some degree of physical pain. Are critics seizing on isolated incidents in which the weapon has been misused or has resulted in death? Do you believe that use of the Taser is a reasonable application of force under the Fourth Amendment?

Misdemeanor Arrests and Citations

An arrest, as previously noted, results in a considerable restriction on an individual's liberty. As Justice Powell noted in *United States v. Robinson,* a custodial arrest is a "significant intrusion of state power" that severely restricts an individual's freedom and that may prove to be humiliating and degrading. Professor Malcolm Feeley captured this in the title of his book *The Process Is the Punishment.* An individual who is arrested is taken into police custody and may be searched along with the passenger compartment of his or her automobile. The arrestee then can expect to be taken to the police station or to jail. Suspects now enter into a legal process in which they are booked, photographed, fingerprinted, and subjected to an inventory of their possessions. They may be held for as long as forty-eight hours before they must be formally charged with a criminal offense.

An issue of continuing debate is whether an arrest for a minor misdemeanor traffic offense or other minor misdemeanors may be subject to a custodial arrest. The alternative course is for the officer to issue a **citation.** An individual who receives a citation from a police officer is not taken into custody so long as he or she is able to present reliable identification and agrees to appear in court at a later date.

There are good reasons for issuing citations rather than arresting individuals for minor misdemeanors. The argument is that it is unreasonable to subject individuals to the indignity and inconvenience of an arrest for a minor offense. An arrest also consumes the time and energy of the police and of the criminal justice system. Civil libertarians argue that permitting arrests for minor crimes invites the police to profile minorities and to arrest people pretextually for minor offenses who the police suspect are engaged in more serious offenses. The strong case for issuing citations accounts for Justice Stewart's observation in *Guatafson v. Florida* that a "persuasive claim might have been made . . . that the custodial arrest of the petitioner for a minor traffic offense violated [the petitioner's] rights" (*Guatafson v. Florida,* 414 U.S. 260, 266–267 [1973]).

On the other hand, the police understandably do not want to be burdened with the responsibility of distinguishing between offenses that permit an arrest and offenses that require a citation. What standard would we use to distinguish offenses deserving of an arrest from offenses that merit the issuance of a citation in any event? Society benefits when the police are able to arrest and to search and question misdemeanants who very well may be involved in other types of criminal activity. In *People v. Pendleton,* an Illinois appellate court held that the police had properly arrested Pendleton for a failure to display a front license plate and for a failure to produce a valid driver's license. This ruling took on particular significance because as a result of the arrest, the police discovered that Pendleton was a suspect in a rape prosecution, and he subsequently was identified by the victim in a lineup (*People v. Pendleton,* 433 N.E.2d 1076 [Ill. App. 1982]).

How should the balance be struck between these considerations? In 2001, in *Atwater v. Lago Vista,* the Supreme Court was asked to decide whether the Fourth Amendment reasonableness standard permits the police to arrest individuals for a minor criminal offense committed in the officer's presence. In other words, did the Fourth Amendment require the police to issue citations for minor misdemeanors, or could the police continue to arrest violators? Was the same rule to be followed in the case of every misdemeanor?

Gail Atwater was driving her pickup truck with her two young children in the front seat. None of the three was wearing a seat belt. Officer Barton Turak stopped, arrested, and handcuffed Atwater and drove her to the police station. At the station, Atwater was booked, forced to remove and turn her possessions over to the police, photographed, and detained in a jail cell for one hour before being released on a $310 bond. She later pled guilty to a misdemeanor and paid a $50 fine (*Atwater v. City of Lago Vista,* 532 U.S. 318, 323–324 [2001]).

Texas law authorized Officer Turak to arrest Atwater or to issue a citation. Atwater asked the U.S. Supreme Court to hold that the Reasonableness Clause of the Fourth Amendment prohibits a custodial arrest for an offense that is not punishable by jail when there is no immediate need for detention. Justice David Souter conceded that he would have ruled for Atwater if he was required to consider only the facts in her case. Justice Souter, however, held that the police should not be placed in the position of having to distinguish in the heat of the moment between offenses that permit an arrest and offenses that require a citation. For example, this might require the police to determine whether an offense carries a "jail sentence" or a "fine" or to determine whether an arrest is required because the suspect might flee or posed a threat to the police or to the public. The Supreme Court accordingly adopted a "bright-line" rule and held that "[i]f an officer has probable cause to believe that an individual has committed even a very minor criminal offense in his presence, he may without violating the Fourth Amendment arrest the offender" (345–355).

Justice O'Connor, in her dissenting opinion, argued that it is unreasonable to permit the police to arrest an individual for a misdemeanor in every instance. She proposed that when there is probable cause to believe that a fine-only offense has been committed, the police should issue a citation unless there are facts that "reasonably warrant" a full custodial arrest (360–373).

Atwater is significant for allowing states to continue to give police officers the choice whether to arrest individuals for minor misdemeanor offenses. Several state supreme courts have held that their constitutions provide greater protection than the Fourth Amendment and have upheld statutes providing that absent "special circumstances," the police are required to issue citations rather than arrest individuals for misdemeanors. The Supreme Court of Montana, in the frequently cited case of *Montana v. Bauer,* explained that it is unreasonable for a police officer to undertake a custodial arrest and detention for a misdemeanor "in the absence of special circumstances such as a concern for the safety of the offender or the public." The Montana court held that a person stopped for a "non-jailable offense such as . . . a seatbelt infraction should not be subjected to the indignity of an arrest and a police station detention when a simple non-intrusive notice to appear . . . will serve the interests of law enforcement" (*Montana v. Bauer,* 36 P.3d 892 [Mont. 2001]). The Ohio Supreme Court issued a similar ruling in the case of an arrest for jaywalking (*State v. Brown,* 792 N.E.2d 175 [Ohio 2003]). The Nevada Supreme Court, in following these precedents, noted that issuing citations conserves police resources and limits the arbitrary arrest and harassment of minority groups (*State v. Bayard,* 71 P.3d 498 [Nev. 2003]).

In reading *Atwater v. City of Lago Vista,* ask yourself whether it is reasonable to arrest individuals for misdemeanors. Should the police be required to issue a citation for certain misdemeanors? Where would you draw the line?

Was it reasonable to subject Gail Atwater to a custodial arrest for violation of the seat belt law?

Atwater v. City of Lago Vista, 532 U.S. 318 (2001), Souter, J.

Issue

The question is whether the Fourth Amendment forbids a warrantless arrest for a minor criminal offense, such as a misdemeanor seatbelt violation punishable only by a fine. We hold that it does not.

Facts

In Texas, if a car is equipped with safety belts, a front-seat passenger must wear one and the driver must secure any small child riding in front. Tex. Tran. Code Ann. section 545.413(a) (1999). Violation of either provision is "a misdemeanor punishable by a fine not less than $25 or more than $50." Section 545.413(d). Texas law expressly authorizes "[a]ny peace officer [to] arrest without warrant a person found committing a violation" of these seatbelt laws, section 543.001, although it permits police to issue citations in lieu of arrest, sections 543.003–543.005.

In March 1997, Petitioner Gail Atwater was driving her pickup truck in Lago Vista, Texas, with her three-year-old son and five-year-old daughter in the front seat. None of them was wearing a seatbelt. Respondent Bart Turek, a Lago Vista police officer at the time, observed the seatbelt violations and pulled Atwater over. According to Atwater's complaint (the allegations of which we assume to be true for present purposes), Turek approached the truck and "yell[ed]" something to the effect of "[w]e've met before" and "[y]ou're going to jail." He then called for backup and asked to see Atwater's driver's license and insurance documentation, which state law required her to carry. Tex. Tran. Code Ann. sections 521.025, 601.053 (1999). When Atwater told Turek that she did not have the papers because her purse had been stolen the day before, Turek said that he had "heard that story two-hundred times."

Atwater asked to take her "frightened, upset, and crying" children to a friend's house nearby, but Turek told her, "You're not going anywhere." As it turned out, Atwater's friend learned what was going on and soon arrived to take charge of the children. Turek then handcuffed Atwater, placed her in his squad car, and drove her to the local police station, where booking officers had her remove her shoes, jewelry, and eyeglasses, and empty her pockets. Officers took Atwater's "mug shot" and placed her, alone, in a jail cell for about one hour, after which she was taken before a magistrate and released on $310 bond.

Atwater was charged with driving without her seatbelt fastened, failing to secure her children in seatbelts, driving without a license, and failing to provide proof of insurance. She ultimately pleaded no contest to the misdemeanor seatbelt offenses and paid a $50 fine; the other charges were dismissed. Atwater and her husband, petitioner Michael Haas, filed suit in a Texas state court under 42 U.S.C. § 1983 against Turek and respondents City of Lago Vista and Chief of Police Frank Miller. So far as concerns us, petitioners (whom we will simply call Atwater) alleged that respondents (for simplicity, the City) had violated Atwater's Fourth Amendment "right to be free from unreasonable seizure."

Reasoning

The Fourth Amendment safeguards "[t]he right of the people to be secure in their persons, houses, papers, and effects, against unreasonable searches and seizures."

Atwater . . . asks us to mint a new rule of constitutional law on the understanding that when historical practice fails to speak conclusively to a claim grounded on the Fourth Amendment, courts are left to strike a current balance between individual and societal interests by subjecting particular contemporary circumstances to traditional standards of reasonableness. Atwater accordingly argues for a modern arrest rule . . . forbidding custodial arrest, even upon probable cause, when conviction could not ultimately carry any jail time and when the government shows no compelling need for immediate detention.

If we were to derive a rule exclusively to address the uncontested facts of this case, Atwater might well prevail. She was a known and established resident of Lago Vista with no place to hide and no incentive to flee, and common sense says she would almost certainly have buckled up as a condition of driving off with a citation. In her case, the physical incidents of arrest were merely gratuitous humiliations imposed by a police officer who was (at best) exercising extremely poor judgment. Atwater's claim to live free of pointless indignity and confinement clearly outweighs anything the City can raise against it specific to her case.

But we have traditionally recognized that a responsible Fourth Amendment balance is not well served by standards requiring sensitive, case-by-case determinations of government need, lest every discretionary judgment in the field be converted into an occasion for constitutional review. Often enough, the Fourth Amendment has to be applied on the spur (and in the heat) of the moment, and the object in implementing its command of reasonableness is to draw standards sufficiently clear and simple to be applied with a fair prospect of surviving judicial second-guessing months and years after an arrest or search is made. Courts attempting to strike a reasonable Fourth Amendment balance thus credit the government's side with an essential interest in readily administrable rules (Fourth Amendment rules "'ought to be expressed in terms that are readily applicable by the police in the context of the law enforcement activities in which they are necessarily engaged'" and not "'qualified by all sorts of ifs, ands, and buts'").

At first glance, Atwater's argument may seem to respect the values of clarity and simplicity, so far as she claims that the Fourth Amendment generally forbids warrantless arrests for minor crimes not accompanied by violence or some demonstrable threat of it (whether "minor crime" be defined as a fine-only traffic offense, a fine-only offense more generally, or a misdemeanor). But the claim is not ultimately so simple, nor could it be, for complications arise the moment we begin to think about the possible applications of the several criteria Atwater proposes for drawing a line between minor crimes with limited arrest authority and others not so restricted.

One line, she suggests, might be between "jailable" and "fine-only" offenses, between those for which conviction could result in commitment and those for which it could not. The trouble with this distinction, of course, is that an officer on the street might not be able to tell. It is not merely that we cannot expect every police officer to know the details of frequently complex penalty schemes, but that penalties for ostensibly identical conduct can vary on account of facts difficult (if not impossible) to know at the scene of an arrest. Is this the first offense or is the suspect a repeat offender? Is the weight of the marijuana a gram above or a gram below the fine-only line?

But Atwater's refinements would not end there. She represents that if the line were drawn at nonjailable traffic offenses, her proposed limitation should be qualified by a proviso authorizing warrantless arrests where "necessary for enforcement of the traffic laws or when [an] offense would otherwise continue and pose a danger to others on the road." ... Would, for instance, either exception apply to speeding? ... And why, as a constitutional matter, should we assume that only reckless driving will "pose a danger to others on the road" while speeding will not? There is no need for more examples to show that Atwater's general rule and limiting proviso promise very little in the way of administrability.... Atwater's rule therefore would not only place police in an almost impossible spot but would guarantee increased litigation over many of the arrests that would occur. For all these reasons, Atwater's various distinctions between permissible and impermissible arrests for minor crimes strike us as "very unsatisfactory line[s]" to require police officers to draw on a moment's notice.

One may ask, of course, why these difficulties may not be answered by a simple tie breaker for the police to follow in the field: If in doubt, do not arrest.... [W]hatever help the tie breaker might give would come at the price of a systematic disincentive to arrest in situations where even Atwater concedes that arresting would serve an important societal interest. An officer not quite sure that the drugs weighed enough to warrant jail time or not quite certain about a suspect's risk of flight would not arrest, even though it could perfectly well turn out that, in fact, the offense called for incarceration and the defendant was long gone on the day of trial. Multiplied many times over, the costs to society of such underenforcement could easily outweigh the costs to defendants of being needlessly arrested and booked, as Atwater herself acknowledges.

So far as such arrests might be thought to pose a threat to the probable-cause requirement, anyone arrested for a crime without formal process, whether for felony or misdemeanor, is entitled to a magistrate's review of probable cause within forty-eight hours, and there is no reason to think the procedure in this case atypical in giving the suspect a prompt opportunity to request release, see Tex. Tran. Code Ann. section 543.002 (1999) (persons arrested for traffic offenses to be taken "immediately" before a magistrate).

Indeed, when Atwater's counsel was asked at oral argument for any indications of comparably foolish, warrantless misdemeanor arrests, he could offer only one. We are sure that there are others, but just as surely the country is not confronting anything like an epidemic of unnecessary minor-offense arrests. That fact caps the reasons for rejecting Atwater's request for the development of a new and distinct body of constitutional law.

Holding

Accordingly, we confirm today what our prior cases have intimated: The standard of probable cause "applie[s] to all arrests, without the need to 'balance' the interests and circumstances involved in particular situations." If an officer has probable cause to believe that an individual has committed even a very minor criminal offense in his presence, he may, without violating the Fourth Amendment, arrest the offender.

Atwater's arrest satisfied constitutional requirements. There is no dispute that Officer Turek had probable cause to believe that Atwater had committed a crime in his presence. She admits that neither she nor her children were wearing seatbelts, as required by Tex. Tran. Code Ann. section 545.413 (1999). Turek was accordingly authorized (not required, but authorized) to make a custodial arrest without balancing costs and benefits or determining whether or not Atwater's arrest was in some sense necessary.

Nor was the arrest made in an "extraordinary manner, unusually harmful to [her] privacy or ... physical interests." ... Atwater's arrest was surely "humiliating," as she says in her brief, but it was no more "harmful to . . . privacy or . . . physical interests" than the normal custodial arrest. She was handcuffed, placed in a squad car, and taken to the local police station, where officers asked her to remove her shoes, jewelry, and glasses, and to empty her pockets. They then took her photograph and placed her in a cell, alone, for about an hour, after which she was taken before a magistrate, and released on $310 bond. The arrest and booking were inconvenient and embarrassing to Atwater, but not so extraordinary as to violate the Fourth Amendment.

Dissenting, *O'Connor, J.*, joined by *Stevens, J., Ginsburg, J.*, and *Breyer, J.*

The Court recognizes that the arrest of Gail Atwater was a "pointless indignity" that served no discernible state interest, and yet holds that her arrest was constitutionally permissible. Because the Court's position is inconsistent with the explicit guarantee of the Fourth Amendment, I dissent. A full custodial arrest, such as the one to which Ms. Atwater was subjected, is the quintessential seizure. When a full custodial arrest is effected without a warrant, the plain language of the Fourth Amendment requires that the arrest be reasonable.

"The touchstone of our analysis under the Fourth Amendment is always the reasonableness in all the circumstances of the particular governmental invasion of a citizen's personal security. . . . [W]e evaluate the search or seizure under traditional standards of reasonableness by assessing, on the one hand, the degree to which it intrudes upon an individual's privacy and, on the other, the degree to which it is needed for the promotion of legitimate governmental interests." In other words, in determining reasonableness, "each case is to be decided on its own facts and circumstances." . . .

A custodial arrest exacts an obvious toll on an individual's liberty and privacy, even when the period of custody is relatively brief. The arrestee is subject to a full search of her person and confiscation of her possessions. If the arrestee is the occupant of a car, the entire passenger compartment of the car, including packages therein, is subject to search as well. The arrestee may be detained for up to forty-eight hours without having a magistrate determine whether there in fact was probable cause for the arrest. Because people arrested for all types of violent and nonviolent offenses may be housed together awaiting such review, this detention period is potentially dangerous. And once the period of custody is over, the fact of the arrest is a permanent part of the public record.

If the State has decided that a fine, and not imprisonment, is the appropriate punishment for an offense, the State's interest in taking a person suspected of committing that offense into custody is surely limited, at best. This is not to say that the State will never have such an interest. A full custodial arrest may on occasion vindicate legitimate state interests, even if the crime is punishable only by fine. Arrest is the surest way to abate criminal conduct. It may also allow the police to verify the offender's identity and, if the offender poses a flight risk, to ensure her appearance at trial. But when such considerations are not present, a citation or summons may serve the State's remaining law enforcement interests every bit as effectively as an arrest. (Texas Department of Public Safety, Student Handout, Traffic Law Enforcement 1 (1999) defines Citations . . . "Definition—a means of getting violators to court without physical arrest. A citation should be used when it will serve this purpose except when by issuing a citation and releasing the violator, the safety of the public and/or the violator might be imperiled as in the case of D.W.I.").

Because a full custodial arrest is such a severe intrusion on an individual's liberty, its reasonableness hinges on "the degree to which it is needed for the promotion of legitimate governmental interests." In light of the availability of citations to promote a State's interests when a fine-only offense has been committed, I cannot concur in a rule which deems a full custodial arrest to be reasonable in every circumstance. Giving police officers constitutional carte blanche to effect an arrest whenever there is probable cause to believe a fine-only misdemeanor has been committed is irreconcilable with the Fourth Amendment's command that seizures be reasonable. Instead, I would require that when there is probable cause to believe that a fine-only offense has been committed, the police officer should issue a citation unless the officer is "able to point to specific and articulable facts which, taken together with rational inferences from those facts, reasonably warrant [the additional] intrusion" of a full custodial arrest.

The majority insists that a bright-line rule focused on probable cause is necessary to vindicate the State's interest in easily administrable law enforcement rules. . . . While clarity is certainly a value worthy of consideration in our Fourth Amendment jurisprudence, it by no means trumps the values of liberty and privacy at the heart of the Amendment's protections.

There is no question that Officer Turek's actions severely infringed Atwater's liberty and privacy. Turek was loud and accusatory from the moment he approached Atwater's car. Atwater's young children were terrified and hysterical. Yet when Atwater asked Turek to lower his voice because he was scaring the children, he responded by jabbing his finger in Atwater's face and saying, "You're going to jail." Having made the decision to arrest, Turek did not inform Atwater of her right to remain silent. He instead asked for her license and insurance information.

Atwater asked if she could at least take her children to a friend's house down the street before going to the police station. But Turek—who had just castigated Atwater for not caring for her children—refused and said he would take the children into custody as well. Only the intervention of neighborhood children who had witnessed the scene and summoned one of Atwater's friends saved the children from being hauled to jail with their mother.

With the children gone, Officer Turek handcuffed Ms. Atwater with her hands behind her back, placed her in the police car, and drove her to the police station. Ironically, Turek did not secure Atwater in a seatbelt for the drive. At the station, Atwater was forced to remove her shoes, relinquish her possessions, and wait in a holding cell for about an hour. A judge finally informed Atwater of her rights and the charges against her, and released her when she posted bond. Atwater returned to the scene of the arrest, only to find that her car had been towed.

Ms. Atwater ultimately pleaded no contest to violating the seatbelt law and was fined $50. Even though that fine was the maximum penalty for her crime, and even though Officer Turek has never articulated any justification for his actions, the City contends that arresting Atwater was constitutionally reasonable because it advanced two legitimate interests: "the enforcement of child safety laws and encouraging [Atwater] to appear for trial."

It is difficult to see how arresting Atwater served either of these goals any more effectively than the issuance of a citation. With respect to the goal of law enforcement generally, Atwater did not pose a great danger to the community. She had been driving very slowly—approximately fifteen miles per hour—in broad daylight on a residential street that had no other traffic. Nor was she a repeat offender; until that day, she had received one traffic citation in her life—a ticket, more than ten years earlier, for failure to signal a lane change. Although Officer Turek had stopped Atwater approximately three months earlier because he thought that Atwater's son was not wearing a seatbelt, Turek had been mistaken. Moreover, Atwater immediately accepted responsibility and apologized for her conduct. Thus, there was every indication that Atwater would have buckled herself and her children in had she been cited and allowed to leave.

With respect to the related goal of child welfare, the decision to arrest Atwater was nothing short of counterproductive. Atwater's children witnessed Officer Turek yell at their mother and threaten to take them all into custody. Ultimately, they were forced to leave her behind with Turek, knowing that she was being taken to jail. Understandably, the three-year-old boy was "very, very, very traumatized." After the incident, he had to see a child psychologist regularly, who reported that the boy "felt very guilty that he couldn't stop this horrible thing... he was powerless to help his mother or sister." Both of Atwater's children are now terrified at the sight of any police car. According to Atwater, the arrest "just never leaves us. It's a conversation we have every other day, once a week, and it's—it raises its head constantly in our lives."

Citing Atwater surely would have served the children's interests well. It would have taught Atwater to ensure that her children were buckled up in the future. It also would have taught the children an important lesson in accepting responsibility and obeying the law. Arresting Atwater, though, taught the children an entirely different lesson: that "the bad person could just as easily be the policeman as it could be the most horrible person they could imagine." Respondents also contend that the arrest was necessary to ensure Atwater's appearance in court. Atwater, however, was far from a flight risk. A sixteen-year resident of Lago Vista, population 2,486, Atwater was not likely to abscond. Although she was unable to produce her driver's license because it had been stolen, she gave Officer Turek her license number and address. In addition, Officer Turek knew from their previous encounter that Atwater was a local resident.

The City's justifications fall far short of rationalizing the extraordinary intrusion on Gail Atwater and her children. Measuring "the degree to which [Atwater's custodial arrest was] needed for the promotion of legitimate governmental interests," against "the degree to which it intrud[ed] upon [her] privacy," it can hardly be doubted that Turek's actions were disproportionate to Atwater's crime. The majority's assessment that "Atwater's claim to live free of pointless indignity and confinement clearly outweighs anything the City can raise against it specific to her case," is quite correct. In my view, the Fourth Amendment inquiry ends there.

The Court's error, however, does not merely affect the disposition of this case. The per se rule that the Court creates has potentially serious consequences for the everyday lives of Americans. A broad range of conduct falls into the category of fine-only misdemeanors. In Texas alone, for example, disobeying any sort of traffic warning sign is a misdemeanor punishable only by fine, as is failing to pay a highway toll, and driving with expired license plates. Nor are fine-only crimes limited to the traffic context. In several States, for example, littering is a criminal offense punishable only by fine.

My concern lies not with the decision to enact or enforce these laws, but rather with the manner in which they may be enforced. Under today's holding, when a police officer has probable cause to believe that a fine-only misdemeanor offense has occurred, that officer may stop the suspect, issue a citation, and let the person continue on her way. Or if a traffic violation, the officer may stop the car, arrest the driver, search the driver, search the entire passenger compartment of the car including any purse or package inside, and impound the car and inventory all of its contents. Although the Fourth Amendment expressly requires that the latter course be a reasonable and proportional response to the circumstances of the offense, the majority gives officers unfettered discretion to choose that course without articulating a single reason why such action is appropriate.

Such unbounded discretion carries with it grave potential for abuse. The majority takes comfort in the lack of evidence of "an epidemic of unnecessary minor-offense arrests." But the relatively small number of published cases dealing with such arrests proves little and should provide little solace. Indeed, as the recent debate over racial profiling demonstrates all too clearly, a relatively minor traffic infraction may often serve as an excuse for stopping and harassing an individual. After today, the arsenal available to any officer extends to a full arrest and the searches permissible concomitant to that arrest. An officer's subjective motivations for making a traffic stop are not relevant considerations in determining the reasonableness of the stop. But it is precisely because these motivations are beyond our purview that we must vigilantly ensure that officers' poststop actions—which are properly within our reach—comport with the Fourth Amendment's guarantee of reasonableness.

The Court neglects the Fourth Amendment's express command in the name of administrative ease. In so doing, it cloaks the pointless indignity that Gail Atwater suffered with the mantle of reasonableness. I respectfully dissent.

Questions for Discussion

1. What are the facts in *Atwater*? Why does Atwater argue that her arrest was unreasonable under the Fourth Amendment? Explain the holding of the Supreme Court.
2. Discuss why the Supreme Court concludes that the best approach is to authorize arrests for all misdemeanors rather than to distinguish between offenses on the basis of criteria such as whether an offense is "jailable" or "nonjailable."
3. Do you agree with Justice Souter that Atwater's arrest was not conducted in a manner that was unusually "harmful" to Atwater's "privacy or physical interests"?
4. Is it significant that the Supreme Court finds that the decision in *Atwater* will not lead to an "epidemic" of arrests for misdemeanors?
5. What is the legal test proposed by Justice O'Connor? Why do the dissenting judges favor this approach? As a judge, would you support the majority or dissenting opinion?
6. ***Problems in policing.*** Assuming that a statute provides a police officer with a choice whether to issue a citation or to arrest an individual for a misdemeanor, what factors would you consider in making a determination whether to issue a citation or to arrest an individual?

Cases and Comments

Citizen's Arrests. Private citizens are authorized in most states to arrest individuals who the citizens have probable cause to believe have committed a felony or a misdemeanor involving a breach of the peace. The citizen is permitted to use reasonable force to make the arrest. The citizen, however, risks civil and even criminal liability for arresting an individual for an offense that is not included in the state statute regulating citizen arrests or for arresting an individual without probable cause.

5.3 YOU DECIDE

The Washington, D.C., Metropolitan Area Transit Authority (WMATA) was receiving complaints about "bad behavior" by students using the Metrorail. In response, the WMATA embarked on an undercover operation to enforce a "zero-tolerance" policy regarding violations of various ordinances, including a law that makes it unlawful to eat or drink in a Metrorail station. Adults who violate the ordinance typically receive a citation subjecting them to a fine of between $10 and $50.

District of Columbia law does not provide for citations to be issued to individuals under eighteen for nontraffic offenses. A criminal offense under District of Columbia law, such as eating in a Metrorail station, constitutes a juvenile "delinquent act." A minor who has committed a delinquent act may be taken into custody. On October 23, 2000, twelve-year-old Ansche Hedgepeth and a classmate entered a Metrorail station. Ansche removed and ate a French fry from the take-out bag that she was holding. Ansche was detained by a plainclothes Metro Transit Police officer who proceeded to arrest her for eating in the station. The officer handcuffed Ansche, and her backpack was searched and shoelaces removed. Ansche was taken to the District of Columbia Juvenile Processing Center, where she was fingerprinted and processed. Three hours later, Ansche was released to the custody of her mother. Was the arrest of Ansche lawful under *Atwater v. City of Lago Vista?* See *Hedgepeth v. Metropolitan Area Transit Authority,* 386 F.3d 1148 (D.C. App. 2004).

You can find the answer by referring to the study site, http://www.sagepub.com/lippmancp.

Chapter Summary

An arrest satisfies the reasonableness requirement of the Fourth Amendment when the seizure is supported by probable cause and the arrest is executed or carried out in a reasonable fashion.

The first requirement is probable cause. Police officers have probable cause where "the facts and circumstances within their knowledge and of which they had reasonably trustworthy information are sufficient in themselves to warrant a man of reasonable caution in the belief that an offense has been or is being committed." The Supreme Court, in an effort to clarify this standard, has explained that probable cause is more than reasonable suspicion and less than the beyond-a-reasonable-doubt standard required for a criminal conviction. This test balances the responsibility of law enforcement to investigate crimes and to apprehend offenders with the protection of individual privacy.

Probable cause to arrest an individual may be developed through an officer's five senses: sight, sound, smell, touch, and taste. Probable cause also may be based on hearsay, or "secondhand" information from victims, eyewitnesses, police officers, and informants. Courts are particularly cautious in accepting the accuracy of tips from informants. The Supreme Court initially relied on the *Aguilar–Spinelli* two-prong test for informants. The affidavit under this test must establish both the informant's veracity and the informant's basis of knowledge. These requirements proved difficult to satisfy, and in 1983, in *Illinois v. Gates,* the Supreme Court adopted a totality-of-the-circumstances test. The veracity and basis of knowledge prongs under *Gates* are described as relevant considerations in determining whether there is probable cause rather than as separate considerations.

The second requirement is that the arrest must be carried out in a reasonable fashion. The Fourth Amendment provides that "no Warrant shall issue but upon probable cause, supported by Oath or affirmation." The central element that is important in the warrant process is that probable cause must be established in a nonadversarial hearing before a neutral and objective magistrate capable of determining probable cause. The warrant must with "particularity" specify the person to be arrested, the time and place of the offense, and the specific statutory violation. This must be supported by an affidavit swearing to the facts on which the probable cause is based. In *Gerstein v. Pugh,* the U.S. Supreme Court held that a police officer's on-the-scene assessment of probable cause provides legal justification for the arrest of an individual. Once the suspect is taken into custody, the Fourth Amendment requires that a *Gerstein* hearing determine whether a "reasonable person would believe that the suspect committed the offense."

The Supreme Court has expressed a preference for warrants. In *United States v. Watson,* the U.S. Supreme Court nevertheless upheld the warrantless arrest of individuals in public based on probable cause that they had committed a felony. This was permissible even when the officers could have obtained a warrant. The law as to misdemeanors is somewhat different. In *Atwater v. City of Lago Vista,* the U.S. Supreme Court held that the common law and the historic practice of the federal government and the fifty states establish that it is constitutionally permissible under the Fourth Amendment to arrest an individual without a warrant for a misdemeanor when the offense is committed in an officer's presence.

Watson left open the question whether a warrant is required to arrest an individual in his or her home. In *Payton v. New York,* the U.S. Supreme Court held that an arrest warrant founded on probable cause is required to arrest an individual in his or her home when there is "reason to believe that a suspect is within." The Court reasoned that the unreasonable physical entry into the home is the "chief evil at which the Fourth Amendment is directed." There is an exigent-circumstances exception to the warrant requirement in those instances in which the police have probable cause that they are in hot pursuit of a suspect, that there is a threat to public safety, or that there is probable cause that evidence may be destroyed or that a suspect may flee. The Supreme Court recently recognized the exigent circumstance of "emergency aide" as an additional exception to the Fourth Amendment warrant requirement.

In 1985, in *Tennessee v. Garner,* the Supreme Court held that the police may resort to deadly force to apprehend a fleeing felon under the Fourth Amendment where the officer has probable cause to believe that the suspect threatens the officer with a weapon or where there is probable cause to believe that he or she has committed a crime involving the infliction or threatened infliction of serious physical harm. The officer, where feasible, should issue a warning. Four years later, in *Graham v. Connor,* the U.S. Supreme Court held that the exercise of nondeadly force also is to be analyzed under the Fourth Amendment reasonableness standard. In evaluating the officer's response, courts must evaluate the circumstances confronting the police at the time rather than consider the situation with "20/20 hindsight." The relevant facts and circumstances include the severity of the crime, whether the suspect posed an immediate threat to the officers, and whether the suspect was actively resisting or evading arrest.

In Chapter 6, we turn our attention to searches and seizures of property.

Chapter Review Questions

1. Compare and contrast reasonable suspicion and probable cause.
2. Define probable cause and explain the meaning of probable cause in your own words.
3. How does the probable cause standard for arrests balance the privacy interests of the individual against the societal interest in criminal investigation and the apprehension of offenders?
4. Discuss how a police officer's use of his or her "five senses" may constitute probable cause.
5. Compare and contrast the *Aguilar–Spinelli* test with the totality-of-the-circumstances test in *Illinois v. Gates*.
6. How does *Draper v. United States* illustrate the determination of probable cause?
7. Describe the process of issuing a warrant. What information must appear on the face of the warrant? Discuss the purpose of a *Gerstein* hearing.
8. When do arrests for felonies and arrests for misdemeanors require warrants?
9. Compare *Watson v. United States* with *Payton v. New York*.
10. What are exigent circumstances? Discuss the justifications for exigent circumstances.
11. Discuss the significance of *Tennessee v. Garner* and *Graham v. Connor*.
12. What is the difference between an arrest and receiving a citation for a misdemeanor? Explain the Supreme Court's holding in *Atwater v. City of Lago Vista*.

Legal Terminology

affiant
affidavit
Aguilar–Spinelli test
arrest
arrest warrant
citation
emergency-aid doctrine
exigent circumstances
fleeing-felon rule
informant privilege
misdemeanant
probable cause

Criminal Procedure on the Web

Log on to the Web-based student study site at **http://www.sagepub.com/lippmancp** to assist you in completing the Criminal Procedure on the Web exercises, as well as for additional features such as leading cases, podcasts, self-quizzes, and audio/video links.

1. Read about police use of excessive force.
2. Watch a video of Andrew Meyer at the University of Florida Town Hall address by Senator John Kerry.
3. Examine FBI local, state, and federal arrest data.

Bibliography

Joshua Dressler and Alan C. Michaels, *Understanding Criminal Procedure: Investigation,* vol. 1, 4th ed. (Newark, NJ: 2006), pp. 121–166. A clear and concise discussion of probable cause and of the law of arrest.

Gerald H. Israel and Wayne R. LaFave, *Criminal Procedure: Constitutional Limitations in a Nutshell,* 6th ed. (St. Paul, MN: West Publishing, 2001), pp. 88–92, 66–78. A brief introduction to probable cause, arrests, and warrants.

Wayne R. LaFave, Jerold H. Israel, and Nancy J. King, *Criminal Procedure,* 4th ed. (St. Paul, MN: West Publishing, 2004), pp. 141–157, 174–180, 673–676. A comprehensive discussion of probable cause, arrests, and citations.

Stephen A. Saltzburg, Daniel J. Capra, and Angela J. Davis, *Basic Criminal Procedure,* 4th ed. (St. Paul, MN: West Publishing, 2005), pp. 127–148, 180–199. An accessible presentation of the important Supreme Court decisions regarding probable cause, arrests, and exigent circumstances with examples.

Russell L. Weaver, Leslie W. Abramson, John M. Burkoff, and Catherine Hancock, *Principles of Criminal Procedure* (St. Paul, MN: Thomson/West, 2004), pp. 60–72. A straightforward introduction to probable cause, arrests, and warrants.

6 Searches and Seizures of Property

Were the police legally justified in breaking down the door to Richards's hotel room?

Officer Pharo knocked on Richards's door and, responding to the query from inside the room, stated that he was a maintenance man. With the chain still on the door, Richards cracked it open. Although there is some dispute as to what occurred next, Richards acknowledges that when he opened the door he saw the man in uniform standing behind Officer Pharo. He quickly slammed the door closed and, after waiting two or three seconds, the officers began kicking and ramming the door to gain entry to the locked room. At trial, the officers testified that they identified themselves as police while they were kicking the door in. When they finally did break into the room, the officers caught Richards trying to escape through the window. They also found cash and cocaine hidden in plastic bags above the bathroom ceiling tiles.

Core Concepts and Summary Statements

Introduction

A. The Supreme Court has expressed a preference for warrants.
B. The Court has recognized the reasonableness of several types of warrantless searches.

Search Warrants

A. A search warrant is based on probable cause.
B. Probable cause is based on an affidavit submitted by a police officer in support of the warrant.
C. The warrant must particularly state the place to be searched and the objects that are the subject of the search.
D. Within the definition of the place to be searched, the police may search any area in which what they are looking for may be found.

Knock and Announce

A. The police are required under the Fourth Amendment to knock and announce their presence.
B. The police are not required to knock and announce when this will interfere with the enforcement of the criminal law and will prove dangerous or futile or lead to the destruction of evidence.
C. The police are required to wait a reasonable amount of time before forcefully entering the premises.

Warrantless Searches

There are various types of warrantless searches that the Supreme Court has held are reasonable searches under the Fourth Amendment, including consent searches, searches incident to arrests of individuals, probable cause searches of automobiles, and probable cause searches of containers in automobiles. Also considered reasonable are searches of the operator, occupants, and interior of a motor vehicle incident to an arrest of the operator or occupants of that motor vehicle.

Searches Incident to an Arrest

The police may search an arrestee and the area in his or her immediate control.

Searches Incident to an Arrest and the Contemporaneous Requirement

A search incident to an arrest must be contemporaneous with the arrest. This means that the search must be undertaken "immediately before the arrest, at the same time as the arrest, or immediately after the arrest."

Searches of the Area of Immediate Control and Automobiles

A. A search incident to the arrest of a suspect in an automobile may be conducted when the suspect is in a position to gain access to the interior of the vehicle or when it is reasonable to believe that evidence of the offense for which the suspect was arrested might be found in the vehicle.

B. When these justifications are absent, a search of an arrestee's vehicle will be unreasonable, unless police obtain a warrant or show that another exception to the warrant requirement applies.

Misdemeanors and Searches Incident to an Arrest

A misdemeanor arrest permits a search incident to an arrest. There is no requirement that the officer reasonably believe that the suspect is armed or dangerous, or that the offense for which the suspect is arrested is associated with the possession of weapons, or that there is a risk that evidence may be concealed or destroyed.

Pretext Arrests and Searches Incident to an Arrest

A. The question is whether there is probable cause for an arrest. An officer's subjective motivations "play no part in Fourth Amendment analysis" and do not make otherwise lawful conduct "illegal or unconstitutional."
B. The U.S. Constitution prohibits selective enforcement of the law based on considerations such as race, ethnicity, or gender. The basis for objecting to intentionally discriminatory application of the laws is the Equal Protection Clause rather than the Fourth Amendment.

Consent Searches

A. Consent must be voluntary and not the result of duress or coercion express or implied.
B. Whether or not consent is voluntary is to be determined by the totality of the circumstances, and the fact that an individual is aware of the right to refuse is one factor to be taken into consideration.

The Scope of a Consent Search

The standard for "measuring the scope of a suspect's consent under the Fourth Amendment is that of 'objective' reasonableness—what would a reasonable person understand by the exchange between the officer and the suspect."

Withdrawal of Consent

Courts require a clear, unambiguous, and unequivocal act or statement of withdrawal of consent.

Third Party Consent

A. Third party consent may be based on actual or apparent authority.
B. Common authority third party consent requires "mutual use of the property by persons having joint access or control for most purposes."
C. Apparent authority third party consent occurs when a police officer reasonably (but mistakenly) believes that a person has common authority.

Third Party Consent and Co-Occupants

A cotenant wishing to consent to a search has no recognized authority in law or social practice to prevail over a present and objecting cotenant.

Probable Cause Searches of Motor Vehicles

The automobile exceptions to the Fourth Amendment provide that a warrant is not required to search a motor vehicle.

Probable Cause Searches of Containers Within Automobiles

A warrant is not required to search containers within automobiles that may hold the object of the search.

Other Warrantless Searches

Other warrantless searches include those where the object of the search is in plain view, frisks undertaken pursuant to reasonable suspicion stops, and searches undertaken under exigent circumstances.

Inventories

A. At the station house, it is entirely reasonable for police to remove and list or inventory property found on the person or in the possession of an arrested person who is to be jailed.
B. The contents of an impounded motor vehicle also may be inventoried.

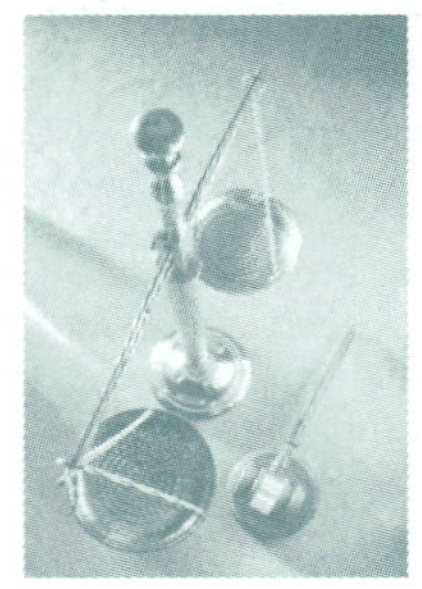

Introduction

The Fourth Amendment's Reasonableness Clause prohibits "unreasonable searches and seizures" and its Warrant Clause proclaims that "no warrants shall issue, but upon probable cause, supported by oath or affirmation, and particularly describing the place to be searched, and the person or things to be seized." Historically, the U.S. Supreme Court has expressed a preference for searches to be conducted with warrants based on probable cause issued by a magistrate or by a judge. The Court has reasoned that the question of whether there is probable cause to justify a search is best answered by a "neutral and detached magistrate" rather than by a police officer "engaged in the often competitive enterprise of ferreting out crime" (*Johnson v. United States,* 333 U.S. 10, 14 [1948]).

In this chapter, we will briefly look at search warrants and at the "knock and announce" rule. The remainder of the chapter is devoted to reviewing warrantless searches. These exceptions to the warrant requirement enable the police to act immediately to detect and investigate crime without the need to obtain a search warrant from a magistrate or judge (*United States v. Harris,* 331 U.S. 145, 162 [1947]). We will review several types of warrantless searches:

- Searches incident to an arrest of a person
- Searches incident to an arrest of a person in a motor vehicle or of a recent occupant of a motor vehicle

- Consent searches
- Probable cause searches of automobiles
- Probable cause searches of containers in automobiles
- Other warrantless searches
- Inventories

In reading this chapter, keep in mind that the Supreme Court once again is engaged in the balancing of interests. In addressing the issue of searches and seizures, the Court is balancing the need to conduct searches to investigate crimes and to seize evidence of crimes against the interest in individual privacy. The warrant process has the benefit of ensuring that a magistrate or judge determines whether the police possess probable cause to search. This provides protection for the privacy of individuals. On the other hand, requiring the police to obtain a warrant before undertaking every search may endanger the police and public, interfere with the investigation and prevention of crime, and prove unreasonably time-consuming. In reading this chapter, consider whether the Supreme Court has struck the proper balance in defining the situations in which police are authorized to conduct warrantless searches. We first turn our attention to search warrants.

Search Warrants

We discussed the arrest warrant process in Chapter 5. Virtually the same process is involved in obtaining a **search warrant**. Chart 6.1 lists some important points to keep in mind in regard to search warrants. This topic can be extremely complex, and you may want to read more on your own. Keep in mind that a warrant must be based on probable cause. The facts supporting probable cause appear in the sworn affidavit submitted by the police officer applying for the search warrant. Most important is the **particularity requirement**. The warrant must set forth the specific address to be searched and the objects that are the subject of the search. These objects define the scope of the search. The police may search wherever these objects are likely to be found. Some important points regarding the warrant process for telephones and for eavesdropping and for electronic devices are summarized in Chart 6.2.

Chart 6.1 Search Warrants

1. **Neutral and detached judicial official.**
   Warrants should be issued by an objective magistrate or judge or individual with the ability to determine probable cause. In *Coolidge v. New Hampshire*, the Supreme Court held that a warrant issued by the attorney general of New Hampshire was invalid. The attorney general was the chief law enforcement officer of the state and was engaged in investigating the murder that was the subject of the search warrant and in preparing the prosecution (*Coolidge v. New Hampshire*, 403 U.S. 443 [1971]).

2. **Affidavit.**
   The warrant must be supported by a sworn affidavit that details the facts and circumstances supporting the warrant.

3. **Probable cause.**
   The affidavit should establish that a crime has been committed and that there are objects relating to the criminal offense in a particular location. The objects should be described with specificity.

4. **Anticipatory warrants.**
   In *United States v. Grubbs*, the U.S. Supreme Court upheld the reasonableness of anticipatory search warrants. These warrants are based on probable cause that an object not yet at a location will have arrived at the time that the warrant is served. Grubbs had ordered a videotape of unlawful child pornography from an undercover postal inspector, and the warrant specified that the search was to be carried out following the arrival of the package (*United States v. Grubbs*, 547 U.S. 90 [2006]).

(Continued)

Chart 6.1 (Continued)

5. **Property and persons subject to search or seizure.**
The Federal Rules of Criminal Procedure, in article 41(c), state that warrants may be issued for evidence of a crime; contraband, fruits of crime, and other illegally possessed items; property designed or intended for use in committing a crime; or for a person to be arrested or a person who is to be lawfully restrained.

6. **The particularity of the location to be searched.**
The warrant must identify the place to be searched with a "reasonable particularity" that removes "any uncertainty" about the premises that are to be searched. The test is whether the description is sufficient "to enable an officer to locate and to identify the premises with reasonable effort and whether there is any reasonable probability another premise may be mistakenly searched that is not the one intended to be searched under the search warrant" (*United States v. Prout,* 526 F.2d 380, 387–388 [5th Cir. 1978]). This typically requires a street address and where relevant an apartment number. The police are not required to be technically accurate in every detail. An accurate physical description of the structure and the surrounding area likely will be determined to be reasonable. The police are required to make reasonable efforts to describe the premises and are not required to achieve the impossible.
In *Maryland v. Garrison,* a search was conducted based on a warrant that authorized the search of the third floor of 2036 Park Avenue. Following the search, the police discovered that there were two apartments rather than a single apartment on the third floor and that they had seized unlawful narcotics from the "wrong" unit. The Supreme Court nonetheless affirmed the constitutionality of the search and explained that the police had taken a number of steps before applying for the warrant to determine the layout of the building. The Court held that the constitutionality of the police conduct must be evaluated "in light of the information available to them [the police] at the time they acted. [Facts] that emerge after the warrant is issued have no bearing on whether or not a warrant was validly issued" (*Maryland v. Garrison,* 480 U.S. 79, 85 [1987]).

7. **Particularity of things to be seized.**
The warrant must describe with particularity the "things" to be seized. In *Marron v. United States,* the Supreme Court explained that this is intended to inform the police of the objects that are to be seized, to insure that the police do not conduct a general or dragnet search throughout the entire home, and to insure that "nothing is left to the discretion of the officers executing the warrant" (*Marron v. United States,* 275 U.S. 192 [1927]). A warrant that authorized the police to seize jewelry rather than the specific items that a store listed as stolen was held to be invalid (*United States v. Blakeney,* 942 F.2d 1010, 1027 [6th Cir. 1991]). A warrant that authorized the seizure in a warehouse of stolen cartons of women's clothing was invalid, because the warrant did not provide identifying information that distinguished stolen cartons from boxes of legally purchased clothing (*United States v. Fuccillo,* 808 F.2d 173, 176–177 [1st Cir. 1987]). In *Groh v. Ramirez,* the failure to particularly describe the items to be seized in the warrant resulted in the U.S. Supreme Court holding that the warrant was "obviously deficient" and that the resultant search and seizure were unconstitutional (*Groh v. Ramirez,* 540 U.S. 551 [2004]).

8. **Staleness.**
A search must be carried out while the evidence is likely to be located at a designated location. This depends on various factors, including the nature of the criminal activity. Drugs are bought and sold relatively quickly, and it would be unreasonable to delay the search. Rule 41(2)(A)(ii) of the Federal Rules of Criminal Procedure requires that all searches must be carried out within ten days. State rules differ on the required time in which a search is to be conducted.

9. **Time of day.**
Most states and the federal government require that search warrants are to be executed during the day absent "reasonable cause" to conduct the search at night. This is because searches at night are more intrusive of personal privacy and increase the likelihood of a violent confrontation.

10. **Scope of the search.**
The area that may be searched is defined by the objects that are the subject of the search. The Supreme Court observed in *United States v. Ross* that the search "generally extends to the entire area in which the object of the search may be found and is not limited by the possibility that separate acts of entry or opening may be required to complete the search." In other words, a warrant for a firearm "provides authority to open closets, chests, drawers, and containers in which the weapon may be found." The police are to remain on the premises as long as it is reasonably necessary to search for the objects of the search and are to avoid unnecessary damage to property (*United States v. Ross,* 456 U.S. 798, 820–821 [1982]).

Chart 6.2 Electronic Surveillance

Title III of the Omnibus Crime Control and Safe Streets Act of 1968. *The requirements for a warrant for telephones and eavesdropping on "oral communications" are set forth in Title III of the Omnibus Crime Control and Safe Streets Act of 1968, 18 U.S.C. §§ 2510–2520. States may employ electronic surveillance by passing implementing legislation. Only twenty-eight states have passed such statutes.*

Electronic Communications Privacy Act of 1986 (ECPA). *Title I of this act amended Title III of the 1968 Omnibus act to provide protection for electronic communications, including cellular telephones, computer-to-computer transmissions, and electronic mail systems. The ECPA also provides protection for "stored wire and electronic communications" such as voice mail and for information held by an internet service provider. Some protections are provided in regard to pen registers, which allow the government to determine the phone numbers a suspect calls and those numbers from which he or she receives calls. A law enforcement official must demonstrate to a judge that the "information likely to be obtained by such installation and use is relevant to an ongoing criminal investigation."*

Communications Assistance for Law Enforcement Act of 1994 (CALEA). *Telephone companies are required to design their digital equipment to facilitate government monitoring of these lines.*

Uniting and Strengthening America by Providing Appropriate Tools Required to Intercept and Obstruct Terrorism Act of 2001 (USA PATRIOT Act). *This act provided various investigative tools to combat terrorism. Electronic surveillance and national security are discussed in Chapter 15. These searches generally are carried out under the Foreign Intelligence and Surveillance Act of 1978 (FISA).*

Applications for warrants. *A judge who is asked to issue a warrant for wiretapping, eavesdropping, or electronic surveillance must determine whether such action is justified based on whether the facts submitted by the applicant satisfy all of the following conditions:*

1. There is probable cause to believe that an individual is committing, has committed, or is about to commit a particular offense that may be the subject of electronic surveillance,
2. there is probable cause to believe that particular communications concerning that offense will be obtained through such interception,
3. normal investigative procedures have been tried or have failed or reasonably appear unlikely to succeed if tried or will prove too dangerous, and
4. there is probable cause to believe that the facilities from which, or the place where, the wire, oral, or electronic communications are to be intercepted are being used, or are about to be used, in connection with the commission of the offense, or are commonly used by the person who is the subject of surveillance.

Warrant contents. *Each order authorizing the interception of any wire, oral, or electronic communication under Title III must include*

1. the identity of the applicant.
2. the identity of the agency authorized to intercept the communication.
3. details of the offense.
4. a particular description of the type of communications to be intercepted and of the types of "facilities" to be used in intercepting the communication.
5. the identity of the individual whose conversation is to be intercepted.
6. the time period of the surveillance. In the event that the surveillance will not automatically terminate when the described communication has been first obtained, facts are to be presented establishing probable cause to believe that additional communications of the same type will occur in the future. The *minimization* requirement provides that wire, oral, or electronic communications shall not be intercepted for any period longer than is necessary to achieve the object of the authorization and, in any event, shall not be approved for longer than thirty days. This period may be extended an additional thirty days.
7. a description of previous applications for surveillance of the same persons, facilities, or places.
8. arrangements for storage of intercepted communications. If possible, these shall be recorded and stored with the court.

Emergency situation or consent. *A court order under federal legislation is not necessary in the event of an emergency situation or in the event that one of the parties consents to the interception.*

The first topic discussed in this chapter is the "knock and announce" rule that the police are required to follow in executing a search and seizure in a home or residence.

Knock and Announce

In 1603, in *Semayne's Case* the English common law courts pronounced that a sheriff in serving an arrest warrant or a search warrant is required to announce his or her presence and purpose for entering a home and wait to be admitted by the occupant. The English court qualified the **knock and announce** rule and held that if a home owner refuses to open his or her door to the King's representative, the sheriff is entitled to break down the door to the home (*Semayne's Case*, 77 Eng. Rep. 194–195 [K.B. 1603]). The common law knock and announce rule was incorporated into the constitutions of the original American states. In 1994, in *Wilson v. Arkansas*, Supreme Court Justice Clarence Thomas held that a reasonable search and seizure under the Fourth Amendment requires that the police follow the long-standing common law principle of knock and announce. Justice Thomas explained that the knock and announce rule is an acknowledgment of the special status of the home as an individual's "castle," which merits heightened protections against governmental intrusions. Three explanations typically are offered for the knock and announce rule (*Wilson v. Arkansas*, 514 U.S. 927 [1995]).

- ***Violence.*** Knock and announce protects against individuals mistakenly believing that their home is being burglarized and acting in self-defense against the "intruders."
- ***Privacy.*** The occupants of the home are able to prepare for the entry of the police and avoid embarrassment.
- ***Destruction of property.*** The police are voluntarily admitted into the home and are not forced to knock down the door and destroy property.

The U.S. Supreme Court followed the common law in cautioning that knock and announce is not a strict requirement and is not required where it interferes with the enforcement of the criminal law. In *Wilson v. Arkansas*, the Supreme Court listed three situations in which knock and announce is not required and in which it is "reasonable" for the police to break down the door to the home.

- ***Physical violence.*** There is a threat of physical violence.
- ***Prison escape.*** A prisoner escapes and flees into the home.
- ***Destruction of evidence.*** There is reason to believe that evidence will be destroyed.

The police are not required to knock and announce when they gain entrance through a trick and misrepresent their identity, and some courts hold that knock and announce is not required where there is an open door.

The Supreme Court judgment in *Wilson* raises a number of questions that the Court addressed in later cases. May the police simply disregard the knock and announce requirement in the case of searches for narcotics because of the risk that the drugs will be destroyed and because of the risk that the drug traffickers will be armed and dangerous? What is the standard that the police must satisfy before they can disregard the knock and announce requirement and forcibly enter a home? How long must police officers wait at the door after knocking and announcing their presence before deciding to forcibly enter a home?

In *Richards v. Wisconsin*, the U.S. Supreme Court answered the first and second questions posed above. In *Richards*, the police obtained a warrant to search Steiney Richards's motel room for drugs and drug paraphernalia. An officer dressed as a maintenance man knocked on the door. Richards cracked open the door, observed a uniformed officer, and, realizing that the police were at the door, slammed it shut. The police waited two or three seconds and then kicked and rammed the door open, entered, and seized drugs and drug paraphernalia. Richards sought to suppress the evidence on the grounds that the police failed to knock and announce their presence prior to breaking down the door (*Richards v. Wisconsin*, 520 U.S. 385, 388–389 [1997]).

In *Richards,* the Wisconsin Supreme Court upheld the search of Richards's motel room and ruled that because drug crimes always create danger and the risk of destruction of evidence, the police may enter without knocking and announcing their presence. The U.S. Supreme Court rejected the Wisconsin court's blanket exception for narcotics offenses for two reasons (393–394):

- ***Overly broad.*** There is no necessity to disregard the knock and announce requirement in every instance of a search for narcotics. For example, the individuals involved in the drug trade may not be in the home at the time that the police serve the warrant.
- ***Other crimes.*** The reasons for a "no knock" entry and search for drug crimes may be applied to a number of other offenses, such as bank robbery. Creating a blanket exception will lead to additional exceptions and to the eventual disappearance of the knock and announce rule.

As for the second question, what is the standard for determining whether the police may dispense with the knock and announce requirement? Justice Stevens held that the reasonableness of a no knock search is based on a determination that the "facts and circumstances of the particular entry justified dispensing with the knock and announce requirement" at the "time that the police entered the hotel room" (394). The Supreme Court held that to justify a no knock entry, the police must have reasonable suspicion that knocking and announcing their presence would be dangerous or futile [serve no purpose] or inhibit the effective investigation of crime by allowing for the destruction of evidence. The Court stated that reasonable suspicion as opposed to probable cause "strikes the right balance." The reasonable suspicion standard was easily satisfied by the fact that Richards knew after opening the door that the police were outside. At this point, it was reasonable for the police to forcibly enter Richards's motel room given the "disposable nature of the drugs" (393). In *United States v. Ramirez,* the Supreme Court upheld a failure to knock and announce and the breaking of a window, because the police had reasonable suspicion that announcing their presence might be dangerous to the police and to individuals in the home (*United States v. Ramirez,* 523 U.S. 65, 71 [1998]). Do you agree with critics that the exceptions to the knock and announce rule established by the Supreme Court's decision in Richards are so broad that they enable the police to disregard the rule in a significant number of criminal investigations?

In 2003, in *United States v. Banks,* the Supreme Court answered the third question and considered how long the police must wait before breaking down the door after knocking and announcing their presence. Too brief a waiting period would make the knock and announce requirement meaningless, while too lengthy a period would risk the destruction of evidence, allow a suspect's escape, or enable individuals inside the home to arm themselves and endanger the police. In *Banks,* the Las Vegas Police and FBI obtained a warrant to search Banks's home for cocaine. The officers loudly announced "police search warrant" and rapped loudly on the door. There was no response, and after waiting fifteen to twenty seconds, the officers broke open the front door with a battering ram. Banks emerged from the shower as the police entered his home. The officers seized weapons, crack cocaine, and other evidence of drug dealing (*United States v. Banks,* 540 U.S. 31, 33 [2003]).

The Supreme Court stated that in the absence of exigent circumstances, the police may forcibly enter a home when the occupant's "failure to admit [the police] fairly suggested a refusal to let them in." This period generally depends on the "size of the establishment." In *Banks,* the Court rejected the argument that the officers had failed to wait a sufficient amount of time before breaking down the door. The test is not how long it would take the suspect to reach the front door, but the time required

> to get rid of the cocaine, which a prudent dealer will keep near a commode or kitchen sink.... And 15 to 20 seconds does not seem an unrealistic guess about the time that someone would need to rid his quarters of cocaine.

The officers served the warrant during the day at a time when individuals would have been up and around and able to quickly dispose of the narcotics.

The Court held that a reasonable time to wait before breaking down a door varies with the circumstances and the police should not damage property absent real suspicion that a failure to act will interfere with the enforcement of the criminal law. The time required for the inhabitants of a home to destroy evidence depends on the nature of the evidence. The Court explained that if the police were seeking a bulky piano, "they may be able to spend more time to make sure they really need the battering ram" (40).

Richards v. Wisconsin is the next case in the textbook. Do you agree with critics that the exceptions to the knock and announce rule in the Supreme Court's judgment reduce the knock and announce rule to a meaningless concept?

You can find Wilson v. Arkansas *on the study site, http://www.sagepub.com/lippmancp.*

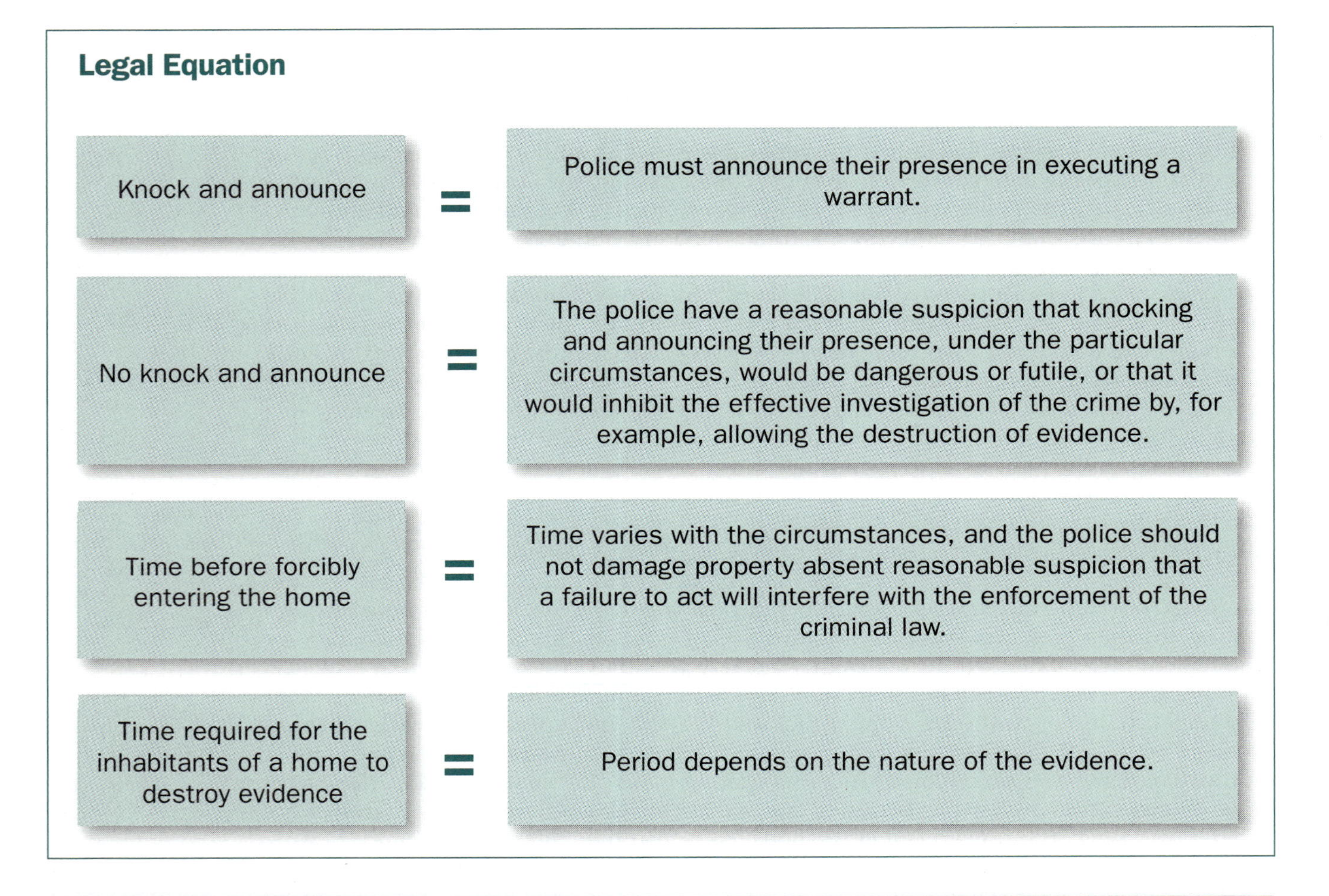

Legal Equation

Knock and announce	=	Police must announce their presence in executing a warrant.
No knock and announce	=	The police have a reasonable suspicion that knocking and announcing their presence, under the particular circumstances, would be dangerous or futile, or that it would inhibit the effective investigation of the crime by, for example, allowing the destruction of evidence.
Time before forcibly entering the home	=	Time varies with the circumstances, and the police should not damage property absent reasonable suspicion that a failure to act will interfere with the enforcement of the criminal law.
Time required for the inhabitants of a home to destroy evidence	=	Period depends on the nature of the evidence.

Were the police required to knock and announce their presence before entering the motel room?

Richards v. Wisconsin, *520 U.S. 385 (1997), Stevens, J.*

Issue

In *Wilson v. Arkansas,* we held that the Fourth Amendment incorporates the common law requirement that police officers entering a dwelling must knock on the door and announce their identity and purpose before attempting forcible entry. At the same time, we recognized that the "flexible requirement of reasonableness should not be read to mandate a rigid rule of announcement that ignores countervailing law enforcement interests," and left "to the lower courts the task of determining the circumstances under which an unannounced entry is reasonable under the Fourth Amendment."

In this case, the Wisconsin Supreme Court concluded that police officers are never required to knock and announce their presence when executing a search warrant in a felony drug investigation. In so doing, it reaffirmed a pre-*Wilson* holding and concluded that *Wilson* did not preclude this per se rule. We disagree with the court's conclusion that the Fourth Amendment permits a blanket exception to the knock and announce requirement for this entire category of criminal activity. But because the evidence presented to support the officers' actions in this case establishes that the decision not to knock and announce was a reasonable one under the circumstances, we affirm the judgment of the Wisconsin court.

Facts

On December 31, 1991, police officers in Madison, Wisconsin, obtained a warrant to search Steiney Richards's hotel room for drugs and related paraphernalia. The search warrant was the culmination of an investigation that had uncovered substantial evidence that Richards was one of several individuals dealing drugs out of hotel rooms in Madison. The police requested a warrant that would have given advance authorization for a no knock entry into the hotel room, but the magistrate explicitly deleted those portions of the warrant.

The officers arrived at the hotel room at 3:40 A.M. Officer Pharo, dressed as a maintenance man, led the team. With him were several plainclothes officers and at least one man in uniform. Officer Pharo knocked on Richards's door and, responding to the query from inside the room, stated that he was a maintenance man. With the chain still on the door, Richards cracked it open. Although there is some dispute as to what occurred next, Richards acknowledges that when he opened the door, he saw the man in uniform standing behind Officer Pharo. He quickly slammed the door closed and, after waiting two or three seconds, the officers began kicking and ramming the door to gain entry to the locked room. At trial, the officers testified that they identified themselves as police while they were kicking the door in. When they finally did break into the room, the officers caught Richards trying to escape through the window. They also found cash and cocaine hidden in plastic bags above the bathroom ceiling tiles.

Richards sought to have the evidence from his hotel room suppressed on the ground that the officers had failed to knock and announce their presence prior to forcing entry into the room. The trial court denied the motion, concluding that the officers could gather from Richards's strange behavior when they first sought entry that he knew they were police officers and that he might try to destroy evidence or to escape. The judge emphasized that the easily disposable nature of the drugs the police were searching for further justified their decision to identify themselves as they crossed the threshold instead of announcing their presence before seeking entry. Richards appealed the decision to the Wisconsin Supreme Court, and that court affirmed.

The Wisconsin Supreme Court did not delve into the events underlying Richards's arrest in any detail but accepted that on December 31, 1991, police executed a search warrant for the motel room of the defendant, seeking evidence of the felonious crime of Possession with Intent to Deliver a Controlled Substance. The court concluded that nothing in *Wilson's* acknowledgment that the knock and announce rule was an element of the Fourth Amendment "reasonableness" requirement would prohibit application of a per se exception to that rule in a category of cases.... In reaching this conclusion, the Wisconsin court found it reasonable—after considering criminal conduct surveys, newspaper articles, and other judicial opinions—to assume that all felony drug crimes will involve "an extremely high risk of serious if not deadly injury to the police as well as the potential for the disposal of drugs by the occupants prior to entry by the police."

Notwithstanding its acknowledgment that in "some cases, police officers will undoubtedly decide that their safety, the safety of others, and the effective execution of the warrant dictate that they knock and announce," the court concluded that exigent circumstances justifying a no knock entry are always present in felony drug cases. Further, the court reasoned that the violation of privacy that occurs when officers who have a search warrant forcibly enter a residence without first announcing their presence is minimal, given that the residents would ultimately be without authority to refuse the police entry. The principal intrusion on individual privacy interests in such a situation, the court concluded, comes from the issuance of the search warrant, not the manner in which it is executed. Accordingly, the court determined that police in Wisconsin do not need specific information about dangerousness, or the possible destruction of drugs in a particular case, in order to dispense with the knock and announce requirement in felony drug cases.

Reasoning

We recognized in Wilson that the knock and announce requirement could give way "under circumstances presenting a threat of physical violence," or "where police officers have reason to believe that evidence would likely be destroyed if advance notice were given." It is indisputable that felony drug investigations may frequently involve both of these circumstances. The question we must resolve is whether this fact justifies dispensing with case by case evaluation of the manner in which a search was executed.

The Wisconsin court explained its blanket exception as necessitated by the special circumstances of today's drug culture, and the State asserted at oral argument that the blanket exception was reasonable in "felony drug cases because of the convergence in a violent and dangerous form of commerce of weapons and the destruction of drugs." But creating exceptions to the knock and announce rule based on the "culture" surrounding a general category of criminal behavior presents at least two serious concerns.

First, the exception contains considerable overgeneralization. For example, while drug investigation frequently does pose special risks to officer safety and the preservation of evidence, not every drug investigation will pose these risks to a substantial degree. For example, a search could be conducted at a time when the only individuals present in a residence have no connection with the drug activity and thus will be unlikely to threaten officers or destroy evidence. Or the police could know that the drugs being searched for were of a type or in a location that made them impossible to destroy quickly. In those situations, the asserted governmental interests in preserving evidence and maintaining safety may not outweigh the individual privacy interests intruded upon by a no knock entry. Wisconsin's blanket rule impermissibly insulates these cases from judicial review.

A second difficulty with permitting a criminal category exception to the knock and announce requirement is that the reasons for creating an exception in one category can, relatively easily, be applied to others. Armed bank robbers, for example, are, by definition, likely to have weapons, and the fruits of their crime may be destroyed without too much difficulty. If a per se exception were allowed for each category of criminal investigation that included a considerable—albeit hypothetical—risk of danger to officers or destruction of evidence, the knock and announce element of the Fourth Amendment's reasonableness requirement would be meaningless.

Thus, the fact that felony drug investigations may frequently present circumstances warranting a no knock entry cannot remove from the neutral scrutiny of a reviewing court the reasonableness of the police decision not to knock and announce in a particular case. Instead, in each case, it is the duty of a court confronted with the question to determine whether the facts and circumstances of the particular entry justified dispensing with the knock and announce requirement.

In order to justify a no knock entry, the police must have a reasonable suspicion that knocking and announcing their presence, under the particular circumstances, would be dangerous or futile, or that it would inhibit the effective investigation of the crime by, for example, allowing the destruction of evidence. This standard—as opposed to a probable cause requirement—strikes the appropriate balance between the legitimate law enforcement concerns at issue in the execution of search warrants and the individual privacy interests affected by no knock entries. This showing is not high, but the police should be required to make it whenever the reasonableness of a no knock entry is challenged.

Holding

Although we reject the Wisconsin court's blanket exception to the knock and announce requirement, we conclude that the officers' no knock entry into Richards's hotel room did not violate the Fourth Amendment. We agree with the trial court, and with Justice Abrahamson, that the circumstances in this case show that the officers had a reasonable suspicion that Richards might destroy evidence if given further opportunity to do so.

The judge who heard testimony at Richards's suppression hearing concluded that it was reasonable for the officers executing the warrant to believe that Richards knew, after opening the door to his hotel room, that the men seeking entry were the police. Once the officers reasonably believed that Richards knew who they were, the court concluded, it was reasonable for them to force entry immediately given the disposable nature of the drugs.

In arguing that the officers' entry was unreasonable, Richards places great emphasis on the fact that the magistrate who signed the search warrant for his hotel room deleted the portions of the proposed warrant that would have given the officers permission to execute a no knock entry. But this fact does not alter the reasonableness of the officers' decision, which must be evaluated as of the time they entered the hotel room. At the time the officers obtained the warrant, they did not have evidence sufficient, in the judgment of the magistrate, to justify a no knock warrant. Of course, the magistrate could not have anticipated in every particular the circumstances that would confront the officers when they arrived at Richards's hotel room. These actual circumstances—petitioner's apparent recognition of the officers combined with the easily disposable nature of the drugs—justified the officers' ultimate decision to enter without first announcing their presence and authority.

Accordingly, although we reject the blanket exception to the knock and announce requirement for felony drug investigations, the judgment of the Wisconsin Supreme Court is affirmed.

Questions for Discussion

1. Can you explain why the U.S. Supreme Court rejects the holding of the Wisconsin Supreme Court?
2. What is the legal standard for determining when the police may disregard the knock and announce principle? Explain this test in your own words.
3. Did the Supreme Court rule that the no knock entry in *Richards* was reasonable? Explain the court's decision.
4. Do you agree with the argument that the legal test established in *Richards* permits the police in most instances to ignore the knock and announce rule when conducting a search for narcotics?
5. ***Problems in policing.*** What does the knock and announce rule require the police to do when executing a warrant? Formulate a hypothetical situation illustrating a situation in which the police would be justified in disregarding the knock and announce principle. Create a hypothetical scenario in which the police would be justified in breaking down the door after knocking and announcing their presence.

Cases and Comments

1. ***Number of Raids.*** Criminologist Peter Kraska of Eastern Kentucky University reports that the number of no knock raids has increased from 3,000 in 1981 to more than 50,000 in 2005 (Jonsson, 2006). In reaction to several "wrong-door" raids in which the police entered the homes of innocent individuals and citizens or the police suffered injury or death, several jurisdictions have decided to require Special Weapons and Tactics (SWAT) teams to meet a higher standard of proof for no knock entries. These cities include Atlanta, Georgia; Modesto, California; New Haven, Connecticut; and Denver, Colorado. This is unlikely to prove to be a national trend given the dangers involved in enforcing narcotics laws against heavily armed drug gangs.

2. ***Detentions and Searches.*** May the police detain individuals on the premises of a house while they conduct a search? In the dispute at issue in *Muehler v. Mena,* police officers Muehler and Brill had reason to believe that Raymond Romero, along with several other members of the West Side Locos street gang, lived at 1363 Patricia Avenue. The officers suspected that Ray Romero, who rented a room from Iris Mena at Patricia Avenue, had been involved in a drive-by shooting and was armed and presently dangerous. Romero and other residents each had their own rooms and shared a common area. The officers obtained a search warrant, and their search resulted in the seizure of a handgun, ammunition, a small amount of marijuana, and gang paraphernalia.

Patricia Mena was asleep at the time that the police executed the warrant. Muehler and Brill feared for their safety during the search and requested that members of a SWAT team accompany them. The police were aware that the gang was composed primarily of illegal immigrants, and they invited Immigration and Nationalization Service agents along on the raid to question any individuals who might be present on the premises. Immediately after entering the house, Mena was detained at gunpoint, handcuffed, and held in the garage together with three individuals who lived in trailers in the rear of Mena's home. Mena claimed that her three-hour detention while handcuffed during the search was unreasonable.

In 1981, in *Michigan v. Summers* (452 U.S. 692 [1981]), the U.S. Supreme Court held that police officers in executing a search warrant may reasonably detain individuals on the premises while conducting a search. The Court reasoned that this modest intrusion on individual privacy was outweighed by the "legitimate law enforcement interests" in preventing flight, minimizing the risk of harm to the police, and ensuring that an occupant is available to assist the police with the search. The police clearly were authorized to detain Mena under the *Summers* precedent, but what of the use of handcuffs? The U.S. Supreme Court held that the officers' use of force to detain Mena in the garage, as well as the detention of the other occupants, was "objectively reasonable." The

> governmental interests . . . are at their maximum when, as here, a warrant authorizes a search for weapons and a wanted gang member resides on the premises. The use of handcuffs "minimizes" the threat of harm to the officers and occupants.

The lengthy detention "does not outweigh the government's continuing safety interests."

In your view, was it "objectively reasonable" to detain Mena with the use of handcuffs? Mena was not a suspect in the shooting, and eighteen police officers were present in her home during the search. An earlier search had located Romero at his mother's house, and he had been arrested for the misdemeanor of marijuana possession and released. See *Muehler v. Mena,* 544 U.S. 93 (2005).

You can find Muehler v. Mena *on the study site, http://www.sagepub.com/lippmancp.*

6.1 YOU DECIDE

The Denver Police Department's SWAT team along with FBI agents stormed into defendant Stewart's residence and seized cocaine and marijuana. The defendant appealed the trial court's dismissal of his motion to suppress. The affidavit accompanying the search warrant noted that "drug dealers usually keep records, receipts, cash and contraband at their residences, and maintain the names of associates." Drug dealers also "commonly possess and carry a firearm during the sale and distribution of cocaine and/or controlled substances." The affidavit stated that an undercover agent on two occasions purchased narcotics from Wiley McClain in Stewart's home.

There was no effort to knock and to announce the presence of law enforcement. The SWAT team used a two-man steel battering ram to break down the front door and threw a full charge stun grenade into the living room, where it detonated with an explosion and a flash. The three occupants were blinded and disoriented for five or ten seconds. None of the three were armed, although a semiautomatic pistol was seized in an upstairs room. The search led to the discovery of considerable amounts of cocaine, crack cocaine, marijuana, and drug related paraphernalia and over $10,000 in cash, and a loaded .45 caliber semiautomatic pistol was found in an upstairs bedroom.

(Continued)

(Continued)

There was no testimony that anyone had seen a firearm, although several months before the entry, the police had been told by a private investigator that an informant had told him that Stewart had been seen with a gun. The police knew that the defendant was "a Jamaican and that some Jamaican drug dealers fortified their houses and most were armed."

Was the entry into Stewart's home lawful? See *United States v. Stewart*, 867 F.2d 581 (10th Cir. 1989).

You can learn what the court decided by referring to the study site, http://www.sagepub.com/lippmancp.

Warrantless Searches

The next section of the chapter discusses warrantless searches. The interest in conducting these searches without warrants is considered to outweigh individuals' privacy interests. As you read about warrantless searches, pay attention to the U.S. Supreme Court's explanation for holding that these warrantless searches are reasonable. The remainder of Chapter 6 covers the following topics:

- Searches incident to an arrest of a person
- Searches incident to an arrest of a person in a motor vehicle or who has exited a motor vehicle
- Misdemeanors and searches incident to an arrest
- Pretext arrests and searches incident to an arrest
- Consent searches
- Probable cause searches of automobiles
- Probable cause searches of containers in automobiles
- Other warrantless searches
- Inventories

Searches Incident to an Arrest

In 1969, in *Chimel v. California,* the U.S. Supreme Court defined the scope (extent) of a **search incident to an arrest**. Chimel was arrested in his home for the burglary of a coin shop. The police proceeded to search the entire house and the garage and seized coins and medals. Chimel claimed that this wide-ranging search could not be justified as a search incident to an arrest. See *Chimel v. California* (395 U.S. 752, 754 [1969]).

The Supreme Court held that when an individual is arrested, it is reasonable for an officer to search the person arrested. This warrantless search has three purposes (763):

- ***Safety.*** To seize weapons that may harm the officer
- ***Resist arrest.*** To seize weapons that may be used to resist arrest or to flee
- ***Evidence.*** To prevent the destruction or concealment of evidence

Once again, the U.S. Supreme Court strikes a balance. The scope of a search incident to an arrest is carefully limited to achieve these three purposes. A police officer may search the person and the area of his or her immediate control for weapons, evidence, or contraband (unlawful objects). Immediate control includes those areas from which an individual may obtain a weapon or destroy contraband. The Supreme Court observed that a gun on a table or in a drawer in front of an individual who is arrested may prove as dangerous to the arresting officer as a firearm concealed in the clothing of the individual who is arrested. The area of immediate control commonly is referred to as the **grab area** or lunging area. The Court held that Chimel was properly arrested, and while the police properly searched Chimel and the area within his immediate control, there is no justification for the police to search rooms other than the room in which the arrest occurred or to search through all the desk drawers or other closed or concealed containers in the room itself. As a result, the Court determined that the coins and medals had been unlawfully seized by the police (763–764).

As you read *Chimel,* consider why the Supreme Court ruled that a search incident to an arrest is limited to the arrestee and to his or her area of immediate control and why the Court did not extend searches incident to an arrest to a broader area or to the entire house. Following *Chimel,* we will look at the requirement that a search must be contemporaneous with the arrest.

Did the police conduct a lawful search incident to an arrest?

Chimel v. California, 395 U.S. 752 (1969), Stewart, J.

Facts

The relevant facts are essentially undisputed. Late in the afternoon of September 13, 1965, three police officers arrived at the Santa Ana, California, home of the petitioner with a warrant authorizing his arrest for the burglary of a coin shop. The officers knocked on the door, identified themselves to the petitioner's wife, and asked if they might come inside. She ushered them into the house, where they waited ten or fifteen minutes until the petitioner returned home from work. When the petitioner entered the house, one of the officers handed him the arrest warrant and asked for permission to "look around." The petitioner objected, but was advised that "on the basis of the lawful arrest," the officers would nonetheless conduct a search. No search warrant had been issued.

Accompanied by the petitioner's wife, the officers then looked through the entire three-bedroom house, including the attic, the garage, and a small workshop. In some rooms the search was relatively cursory. In the master bedroom and sewing room, however, the officers directed the petitioner's wife to open drawers and "to physically move contents of the drawers from side to side so that [they] might view any items that would have come from [the] burglary." After completing the search, they seized numerous items—primarily coins, but also several medals, tokens, and a few other objects. The entire search took between forty-five minutes and an hour.

At the petitioner's subsequent state trial on two charges of burglary, the items taken from his house were admitted into evidence against him over his objection that they had been unconstitutionally seized. He was convicted, and the judgments of conviction were affirmed by both the California Court of Appeal and the California Supreme Court.... The appellate courts [held] that the search of the petitioner's home had been justified, despite the absence of a search warrant, on the ground that it had been incident to a valid arrest. We granted certiorari in order to consider the petitioner's substantial constitutional claims.

Issue

Without deciding the question, we proceed on the hypothesis that the California courts were correct in holding that the arrest of the petitioner was valid under the U.S. Constitution. This brings us directly to the question of whether the warrantless search of the petitioner's entire house can be constitutionally justified as incident to that arrest. The decisions of this Court bearing upon that question have been far from consistent, as even the most cursory review makes evident.

Reasoning

When an arrest is made, it is reasonable for the arresting officer to search the person arrested in order to remove any weapons that the latter might seek to use in order to resist arrest or effect his escape. Otherwise, the officer's safety might well be endangered, and the arrest itself frustrated. In addition, it is entirely reasonable for the arresting officer to search for and seize any evidence on the arrestee's person in order to prevent its concealment or destruction. And the area into which an arrestee might reach in order to grab a weapon or evidentiary items must, of course, be governed by a like rule. A gun on a table or in a drawer in front of one who is arrested can be as dangerous to the arresting officer as one concealed in the clothing of the person arrested. There is ample justification, therefore, for a search of the arrestee's person and the area "within his immediate control"—construing that phrase to mean the area from within which he might gain possession of a weapon or destructible evidence.

There is no comparable justification, however, for routinely searching any room other than that in which an arrest occurs—or, for that matter, for searching through all the desk drawers or other closed or concealed areas in that room itself. Such searches, in the absence of well-recognized exceptions, may be made only under the authority of a search warrant. The "adherence to judicial processes" mandated by the Fourth Amendment requires no less.

It is argued in the present case that it is "reasonable" to search a man's house when he is arrested in it. But that argument is founded on little more than a subjective view regarding the acceptability of certain sorts of police conduct and not on considerations relevant to Fourth Amendment interests. Under such an unconfined analysis, Fourth Amendment protection in this area would approach the evaporation point. It is not easy to explain why, for instance, it is less subjectively "reasonable" to search a man's house when he is arrested on his front lawn—or just down the street—than it is when he happens to be in the house at the time of arrest.

Holding

After arresting a man in his house, to rummage at will among his papers in search of whatever will convict him appears to us to be indistinguishable from what might be done under a general warrant; indeed, the warrant would give more protection, for presumably it must be issued by a magistrate.... Application of sound Fourth Amendment principles to the facts of this case produces a clear result. The search here went far beyond the petitioner's person and the area from within which he might have obtained either a weapon or something that could have been used as evidence against him. There was no constitutional justification, in the absence of a search warrant, for extending the search beyond that area. The scope of the search was, therefore, "unreasonable" under the Fourth and Fourteenth Amendments, and the petitioner's conviction cannot stand.

Dissenting, *White, J.*, joined by *Black, J.*

This case provides a good illustration of my point that it is unreasonable to require police to leave the scene of an arrest in order to obtain a search warrant when they already have probable cause to search and there is a clear danger that the items for which they may reasonably search will be removed before they return with a warrant.... There was doubtless probable cause not only to arrest petitioner but also to search his house. He had obliquely admitted, both to a neighbor and to the owner of the burglarized store, that he had committed the burglary. In light of this and of the fact that the neighbor had seen other admittedly stolen property in petitioner's house, there was surely probable cause on which a warrant could have issued to search the house for the stolen coins. Moreover, had the police simply arrested petitioner, taken him off to the station house, and later returned with a warrant, it seems very likely that petitioner's wife, who in view of petitioner's generally garrulous nature must have known of the robbery, would have removed the coins. For the police to search the house while the evidence they had probable cause to search out and seize was still there cannot be considered unreasonable.

If circumstances so often require the warrantless arrest that the law generally permits it, the typical situation will find the arresting officers lawfully on the premises without arrest or search warrant. Like the majority, I would permit the police to search the person of a suspect and the area under his immediate control either to assure the safety of the officers or to prevent the destruction of evidence. And like the majority, I see nothing in the arrest alone furnishing probable cause for a search of any broader scope. However, where as here the existence of probable cause is independently established and would justify a warrant for a broader search for evidence, I would... permit such a search to be carried out without a warrant... [and permit] the suspect to... immediately seek judicial determination of probable cause in an adversary proceeding, and appropriate redress.

Questions for Discussion

1. What is the holding in *Chimel*?
2. Does the court provide adequate guidance to the police regarding the scope of a search incident to an arrest?
3. What are the main differences between a *Terry* frisk and a search incident to an arrest?
4. Summarize the dissenting opinion of Justice White and Justice Black. Do you agree with their argument that the court should have held that the search of Chimel's home was lawful?
5. ***Problems in policing.*** Write several sentences summarizing the scope of a search incident to an arrest. Distinguish between reasonable suspicion stops and frisks and searches incident to an arrest.

Cases and Comments

1. ***State Law.*** Boise, Idaho, police possessed outstanding misdemeanor warrants for Benjamin LaMay and learned that his brother, Joseph, had rented a hotel room. Three officers proceeded to the hotel room and smelled marijuana when Joseph answered the door. They entered the room and observed seven individuals and drug paraphernalia on a table. Benjamin was lying on the bed. The police moved six of the individuals into the hallway and detained Joseph LaMay in the room. They questioned Joseph in the bathroom and during a protective sweep of the hotel room observed a backpack on the floor about ten inches from where Benjamin's hand had been hanging off the bed when the officers first entered the room.

Benjamin meanwhile was arrested in the hallway, handcuffed, and required to remain seated. An officer guarded Benjamin, who admitted that there was marijuana in a jar under the pillow of the bed. The marijuana from the jar was seized along with cocaine, currency, and Benjamin LaMay's driver's license, all of which were found in the backpack. The prosecution appealed the suppression of the narcotics in the backpack, arguing that the drugs had been seized as part of a lawful search incident to an arrest. The Idaho Supreme Court held that the backpack was fifteen feet from where Benjamin had been arrested and was located in a different room at the time of his arrest. The backpack, according to the Idaho court, "presented no danger . . . [and the evidence was] not in danger of being destroyed [because] Benjamin LaMay was restrained in handcuffs and guarded by an officer in the hallway." The Idaho Supreme Court based its decision on the Fourth Amendment to the U.S. Constitution rather than on the Idaho Constitution and rejected the argument accepted by most other state and federal courts that "a container is considered to be within an arrestee's immediate control where the item was formerly within the defendant's immediate control at the time officers first encountered the defendant."

Would it have been realistic for the police to search Benjamin's backpack at the time that they first encountered him in the bedroom? See *Idaho v. LaMay,* 103 P.3d 448 (Idaho 2004). A contrasting view is presented in *People v. Perry,* 286 N.E.2d 330 (Ill. 1971).

2. ***Immediate Control and Firearms.*** In contrast to the decision in *LaMay,* other courts have broadly interpreted immediate control, particularly when firearms are involved. In the incident at issue in *United States v. Queen,* three FBI agents served an arrest warrant for Ellery Queen at Queen's home; the warrant had been issued after Queen failed to surrender voluntarily to serve a sentence for prior criminal convictions. The agents were aware that Queen had carried a gun in the past and might be armed and dangerous. Agent John Dolan went to the basement of the home and searched a closet for Queen. He determined that Queen was under a blanket in the closet, drew his gun, and ordered Queen: "Put your hands out, palms up." Queen initially displayed only a single arm from beneath the blanket under which he was hiding, and Dolan testified that he believed that Queen was concealing a firearm. Dolan requested help from Agents Dzwilewski and Canady, and while Agent Dolan trained his handgun on Queen, Dzwilewski and Canady patted down Queen and handcuffed him in an area three feet from the closet. Agent Dolan then returned to the closet, from which he seized a revolver, two hollow-point bullets, and four standard bullets.

Queen appealed the dismissal of his motion to suppress the objects that had been seized, contending that with his hands handcuffed behind his back, he could not have twisted away from two armed agents and dived past a third to grab the handgun lying on the closet floor. The government replied that Agent Dolan reasonably believed that any weapon on the floor of the closet was within the grabbing range of Mr. Queen. The Seventh Circuit Court of Appeals held that although the possibility of Queen seizing the weapon was "remote," the court would not "second-guess the agents' on-the-scene determination. This is especially so where, as here, the agents reasonably could have feared for their safety." The court reasoned that custodial arrests are often dangerous, and the police must act decisively and cannot be expected to exercise an exacting judgment in regard to "what is within and what is just beyond the arrestee's grasp." The Seventh Circuit Court of Appeals also noted that Queen's stepson was in the home and that the gun may have placed him in danger. The appellate court noted that searches have been upheld "even when hindsight might suggest that the likelihood of the defendant reaching the area in question was slight."

How would the Idaho Supreme Court have decided this case based on the precedent in *LaMay?* See *United States v. Queen,* 847 F.2d 346 (7th Cir. 1988).

6.2 YOU DECIDE

Detectives Michael Bland and John Centrella were engaged in the undercover investigation of narcotics trafficking in the District of Columbia. An informant assisted them in arranging to purchase two kilograms of cocaine from Judah Lyons, who had flown in from Colorado. Lyons was staying in a local hotel. Centrella and Bland purchased cocaine from Lyons, and immediately thereafter they were joined by four police officers, who arrested and handcuffed Lyons. Lyons was seated on a chair close to the door of the room. One of the police officers systematically searched the room. The officer located an overcoat that Lyons had been wearing earlier in the day in an open closet that was several yards from Lyons. The officer noticed that one side of the coat was unusually heavy, reached into the pocket, and discovered a loaded revolver. From a suitcase at the foot of the bed, the officer seized a shoulder holster, two "speed loaders," ammunition, and financial records. The police did not have a search warrant.

Was the seizure of the weapon in the coat a search incident to an arrest? See *United States v. Lyons,* 706 F.2d 321 (Ct. App. D.C., 1983).

You can learn what the court decided by referring to the study site, http://www.sagepub.com/lippmancp.

Searches Incident to an Arrest and the Contemporaneous Requirement

A search incident to an arrest is required to be **contemporaneous** with the arrest. This means that the search must be undertaken "immediately before the arrest, at the same time as the arrest or immediately after the arrest" (*Rawlings v. Kentucky,* 448 U.S. 98, 111 [1980]). What is the reason for this requirement? It would make no sense to delay the search and give a suspect the opportunity to destroy evidence or to use a weapon against an officer. The Supreme Court accordingly has held that a search that is "remote in time and place" fails to meet the "test of reasonableness under the Fourth Amendment."

In the arrest at issue in *Preston v. United States,* three individuals sitting in car at 3:00 A.M. in the business district of Newport, Kentucky, were arrested for vagrancy. The car was driven to the police station and searched, resulting in the seizure of two pistols. A second search led to the discovery of objects that clearly were meant to be used during a robbery. One of the detainees admitted that the men planned to rob a bank. The U.S. Supreme Court held that the justifications for searches incident to an arrest "are absent where a search is remote in time or place from the arrest. Once an accused is under arrest and in custody, then a search made at another place without a warrant is simply not incident to an arrest." The Court noted that at the time that the car was searched, there was "no danger that any of the men arrested could have used any weapons in the car or could have destroyed any evidence of the crime" (*Preston v. United States,* 376 U.S. 384, 367–368 [1964]). The Supreme Court has upheld the reasonableness of a search incident to an arrest where the police had probable cause to arrest and the arrest followed "quickly on the heels" of the search (*Rawlings v. Kentucky,* 448 U.S. 98, 111 [1980]).

United States v. Edwards is viewed as a significant exception to the contemporaneous requirement. In *Edwards,* the U.S. Supreme Court upheld the warrantless search and seizure of paint chips from Edwards's clothing ten hours after he arrived at the jail as a "normal incident of an arrest." The Court held that the "effects" in Edwards's "immediate possession" may be searched "on the spot at the time of arrest" or "later when the accused arrives at the place of detention, if need be." See *United States v. Edwards* (415 U.S. 800 [1974]).

An example of an application of *Edwards* is *Curd v. City Court of Judsonia.* In *Curd,* the Eighth Circuit Court of Appeals held that searches of the person and articles "immediately associated with the person of the arrestee" are measured by a "flexible constitutional time clock" and may be searched either at "the time of arrest or when the accused arrives at the place of detention." The court noted that a purse, like a wallet, is an object "immediately associated" with the person and accordingly held that the "search of Curd's purse at the station house fifteen minutes after her arrest fell well within the constitutionally acceptable time zone for searches of persons and objects 'immediately associated' with them incident to arrest." Courts have not yet fully defined those objects that are "immediately associated with the person" of an arrestee. See *Curd v. City Court of Judsonia* (141 F.3d 839, 844 [8th Cir. 1998]).

Cases and Comments

1. ***Contemporaneous Searches of Containers.*** In the incident at issue in *United States v. Chadwick,* federal agents in Boston placed Gregory Machado and Bridget Leary under surveillance following the arrival of their train. Machado and Leary removed a footlocker from the train and sat on it in the departure area. A trained drug dog indicated that the footlocker contained narcotics. The suspects then moved the footlocker into the trunk of a car, and the federal agents arrested Machado, Leary, and the driver. The agents took the footlocker to the federal building in Boston, the footlocker was opened without a warrant, and a large amount of marijuana was seized. The search took place ninety minutes following the arrest. After subsequent court proceedings, the Government appealed the suppression of the evidence of possession of marijuana to the U.S. Supreme Court. The Government relied on several arguments, including the contention that opening the footlocker was a lawful search incident to an arrest.

The U.S. Supreme Court stressed that the respondents manifested an expectation of privacy in the double locked footlocker. "No less than one who locks the doors of his home against intruders, one who safeguards his personal possessions in this manner is due the protection of the Fourth Amendment Warrant Clause." The Government claimed that the footlocker was seized contemporaneously with respondents' arrests and was searched as soon as reasonable under the circumstances. The Supreme Court rejected this contention, reasoning that

> once law enforcement officers have reduced luggage or other personal property not immediately associated with the person of the arrestee to their exclusive control, and there is no longer any danger that the arrestee might gain access to the property to seize a weapon or destroy evidence, a search of that property is no longer incident of the arrest.

The Court accordingly held that the footlocker had been removed from the custody of the defendants and that the police required a search warrant to open the luggage. Note that the police lawfully could have opened the footlocker at the time of the arrest as a search incident to an arrest. See *United States v. Chadwick,* 433 U.S. 1 (1977). How do you explain the different outcomes of *Edwards* and *Chadwick?*

Contrast *Chadwick* with *United States v. Fleming.* Chicago police arrested Joseph Rolenc as Rolenc was completing a drug transaction with Edward Fleming on Fleming's front porch. In the struggle with the police, a bag was knocked from Rolenc's hand. Officer Bobko picked up the bag and opened it only after he had handcuffed Rolenc and escorted Rolenc to the street. The bag contained $10,000. Was the bag seized and searched by Bobko within Rolenc's area of immediate control, and was the search contemporaneous with his arrest? The Seventh Circuit determined that the bag was within Rolenc's "grabbing area" when it was first picked up by Bobko.

The lesson from *Chadwick* is that a *Chimel* search may be taken

> too long after the arrest and too far from the arrestee's person . . . but we do not . . . think that a five minute delay between seizing Rolenc's bag and opening it, occasioned by Bobko's handcuffing Rolenc and moving him to the street, decreased Bobko's right to search under *Chimel* principles.

The Seventh Circuit Court of Appeals stressed that "it does not make sense to prescribe a constitutional test that is entirely at odds with safe and sensible police procedures." The Fourth Amendment does not require that a search be "absolutely contemporaneous with the arrest, no matter what the peril to [police] or to bystanders." See *United States v. Fleming,* 677 F.2d 602 (7th Cir. 1999).

6.3 YOU DECIDE

Chris Todd Bleichfeld left Fort Lauderdale, Florida, on a train bound for New York City. An Amtrak officer, Suave, had his suspicions aroused by the fact that Bleichfeld made his reservations two days before departure, did not give a callback number, purchased his ticket with cash a few minutes before the train departed, and switched his sleeping room on the train three times. During a twenty-minute layover in Washington, D.C., Officer Suave engaged Bleichfeld in a conversation and discovered that Bleichfeld had purchased his ticket under his first and middle names, Chris Todd. Suave persuaded Bleichfeld to place his luggage in the corridor of the train and to allow a dog sniff of his luggage.

Detective Vance Beard of the Metropolitan Police Department then boarded the train, and his narcotics dog Axel indicated that drugs were present in two of the three pieces of luggage. Bleichfeld was arrested, handcuffed, and removed from the train along with his bags. The officers waited with Bleichfeld on the platform until the bags were picked up by railroad employees and driven to the security office in Union Station. The bags were placed outside of Bleichfeld's reach in the same room in which Bleichfeld was handcuffed to a chair. The luggage was opened without a warrant, and $635,000 in cash was discovered, which the government then sought to seize as the fruits of unlawful narcotics activity. The time between the arrest and the search was between forty-one and sixty-three minutes.

Was the search of the bags at the security office a search incident to Bleichfeld's arrest? Did the Washington, D.C., police require a search warrant to open the luggage? See *United States v. Six Hundred Thirty-Nine Thousand Five Hundred and Fifty-Eight Dollars,* 955 F.2d 712 (D.C. Ct. App. 1992).

You can learn what the court decided by referring to the study site, http://www.sagepub.com/lippmancp.

Searches of the Area of Immediate Control and Automobiles

In 1981, in *New York v. Belton,* the U.S. Supreme Court defined the scope of a search incident to an arrest of an individual in an automobile. Agent Douglas Nicot pulled a vehicle over for speeding on the New York State Thruway. Officer Nicot smelled burnt marijuana and saw an envelope marked "Supergold" (a brand of marijuana) on the floor of the car. He ordered the driver and passengers out of the automobile and placed them under arrest. Officer Nicot then searched the passenger compartment and found a black leather jacket belonging to Belton, the driver. Nicot unzipped one of the pockets and discovered cocaine, and Belton subsequently was charged with criminal possession of a controlled substance. The question before the Supreme Court was the lawfulness of the seizure of cocaine (*New York v. Belton,* 453 U.S. 454, 455–456 [1981]).

Justice Stewart applied the precedent in *Chimel* and held that articles within the passenger compartment as a rule are within the area in which an individual might "reach in order to grab a weapon or evidentiary item." The Court accordingly held that when officers make lawful custodial arrests of individuals in automobiles, they may as a "contemporaneous incident of that arrest search the passenger compartment of that automobile." Containers within the passenger compartment also are within the grasp of the arrestee and may be searched. The jacket was inside the passenger compartment of the car, and the court held that it was properly searched as an object "within the arrestee's immediate control" (460–462).

In the incident at issue in *Thornton v. United States,* Officer Deion Nichols determined that the license tags on Thornton's automobile had been issued to another vehicle. Thornton drove into a parking lot, and as Thornton exited his vehicle, he was detained by Nichols. Thornton admitted that he was in possession of marijuana and cocaine and was placed under arrest, handcuffed, and secured in the backseat of the patrol car. Nichols then proceeded to search the passenger compartment of Thornton's automobile and discovered a handgun. Thornton sought to suppress the handgun as evidence, contending that the precedent in *Belton* was not applicable, because it is limited to situations in which the suspect is first encountered while inside the passenger compartment of an automobile. The U.S. Supreme Court dismissed this argument and held that *Belton* applies to "recent occupants" who have exited an automobile. "Once an officer determines that there is probable cause to make an arrest, it is reasonable to allow officers to ensure their safety and to preserve evidence by searching the entire passenger compartment" (*Thornton v. United States,* 541 U.S. 615 [2004]).

Justices Scalia, Ginsburg, Stevens, and Breyer dissented from the Supreme Court's ruling in *Thornton.* Scalia and Ginsburg questioned the reasonableness of searching the passenger compartment of an automobile, because there was little risk that an arrestee like Thornton, once handcuffed and placed in a squad car, could gain access to his or her vehicle and seize a weapon. Justice Scalia would limit searches incident to an arrest to "situations in which the car might contain evidence relevant to the crime for which he was arrested."

In *Arizona v. Gant,* the U.S. Supreme Court significantly modified the bright-line rule established in *Belton.* Justice Stevens in his plurality opinion held that

> *Belton* does not authorize a vehicle search incident to a recent occupant's arrest after the arrestee has been secured and cannot access the interior of the vehicle.... We also conclude that circumstances unique to the automobile context justify a search incident to arrest when it is reasonable to believe that evidence of the offense of arrest might be found in the vehicle.

As you read *Gant,* pay attention to the reasons offered by the plurality for modifying *Belton.* Why does the dissent disagree with the plurality opinion?

Did the police lawfully search Gant's automobile?

Arizona v. Gant, 556 U.S. ___ (2009), Stevens, J.

Issue

After Rodney Gant was arrested for driving with a suspended license, handcuffed, and locked in the back of a patrol car, police officers searched his car and discovered cocaine in the pocket of a jacket on the back seat. Gant could not have accessed his car to retrieve weapons or evidence at the time of the search. The court considers whether the Arizona Supreme Court was correct in holding that the "search incident to arrest" exception to the Fourth Amendment's warrant requirement, as defined in *Chimel v. California* and applied to vehicle searches in *New York v. Belton,* did not justify the search in this case.

Facts

On August 25, 1999, acting on an anonymous tip that the residence at 2524 North Walnut Avenue was being used to sell drugs, Tucson police officers Griffith and Reed knocked on the front door and asked to speak to the owner. Gant answered the door and, after identifying himself, stated that he expected the owner to return later. The officers left the residence and conducted a records check, which revealed that Gant's driver's license had been suspended and there was an outstanding warrant for his arrest for driving with a suspended license.

When the officers returned to the house that evening, they found a man near the back of the house and a woman in a car parked in front of it. After a third officer arrived, they arrested the man for providing a false name and the woman for possessing drug paraphernalia. By the time Gant arrived, both arrestees had been handcuffed and secured in separate patrol cars. The officers recognized Gant's car as it entered the driveway, and Officer Griffith confirmed that Gant was the driver by shining a flashlight into the car as it drove by him. Gant parked at the end of the driveway, got out of his car, and shut the door. Griffith, who was about 30 feet away, called to Gant, and they approached each other, meeting ten to twelve feet from Gant's car. Griffith immediately arrested Gant and handcuffed him. Because the other arrestees were secured in the only patrol cars at the scene, Griffith called for backup. When two more officers arrived, they locked Gant in the back seat of their vehicle. After Gant had been placed in the back of a patrol car, two officers searched his car. One of them found a gun, and the other discovered a bag of cocaine in the pocket of a jacket on the back seat.

Gant was charged with two offenses—possession of a narcotic drug for sale and possession of drug paraphernalia (i.e., the plastic bag in which the cocaine was found). He moved to suppress the evidence seized from his car on the ground that the warrantless search violated the Fourth Amendment. Among other things, Gant argued that *Belton* did not authorize the search of his vehicle, because he posed no threat to the officers after he was handcuffed in the patrol car, and because he was arrested for a traffic offense for which no evidence could be found in his vehicle. When asked at the suppression hearing why the search was conducted, Officer Griffith responded, "because the law says we can do it."

The trial court rejected the State's contention that the officers had probable cause when the search began to search Gant's car for contraband, but it denied the motion to suppress. Relying on the fact that the police saw Gant commit the crime of driving without a license and apprehended him only shortly after he exited his car, the court held that the search was permissible as a search incident to arrest. A jury found Gant guilty on both drug counts, and he was sentenced to a three-year term of imprisonment.

The Arizona Supreme Court concluded that the search of Gant's car was unreasonable within the meaning of the Fourth Amendment. The court's opinion discussed at length our decision in *Belton,* which held that police may search the passenger compartment of a vehicle and any containers therein as a contemporaneous incident of an arrest of the vehicle's recent occupant. The court distinguished *Belton* as a case concerning the permissible scope of a vehicle search incident to arrest and concluded that it did not answer "the threshold question whether the police may conduct a search incident to arrest at all once the scene is secure." Relying on our earlier decision in *Chimel,* the court observed that the "search incident to arrest" exception to the warrant requirement is justified by interests in officer safety and evidence preservation. When "the justifications underlying *Chimel* no longer exist because the scene is secure and the arrestee is handcuffed, secured in the back of a patrol car, and under the supervision of an officer," the court concluded, a "warrantless search of the arrestee's car cannot be justified as necessary to protect the officers at the scene or prevent the destruction of evidence." Accordingly, the court held that the search of Gant's car was unreasonable. The dissenting justices would have upheld the search of Gant's car based on their view that "the validity of a *Belton* search . . . clearly does not depend on the presence of the *Chimel* rationales in a particular case."

Reasoning

The chorus that has called for us to revisit *Belton* includes courts, scholars, and members of this Court who have questioned that decision's clarity and its fidelity to Fourth Amendment principles. Consistent with our precedent, our analysis begins, as it should in every case addressing the reasonableness of a warrantless search, with the basic rule that "searches conducted outside the judicial process, without prior approval by judge or magistrate, are *per se* unreasonable under the Fourth Amendment—subject only to a few specifically established and well-delineated exceptions."

Among the exceptions to the warrant requirement is a search incident to a lawful arrest. The exception derives from interests in officer safety and evidence preservation that are typically implicated in arrest situations. In *Chimel,* we held that a search incident to arrest may include only "the arrestee's person and the area 'within his immediate control'—construing that phrase to mean the area from within which he might gain possession of a weapon or destructible evidence." That limitation, which continues to define the boundaries of the exception, ensures that the scope of a search incident to arrest is commensurate with its purposes of protecting arresting officers and safeguarding any evidence of the offense of arrest that an arrestee might conceal or destroy (noting that searches incident to arrest are reasonable "in order to remove any weapons [the arrestee] might seek to use" and "in order to prevent [the] concealment or destruction" of evidence). If there is no possibility that an arrestee could reach into the area that law enforcement officers seek to search, both justifications for the "search incident to arrest" exception are absent, and the rule does not apply.

In *Belton,* we considered *Chimel*'s application to the automobile context. A lone police officer in that case stopped a speeding car in which Belton was one of four occupants. While asking for the driver's license and registration, the officer smelled burnt marijuana and observed an envelope on the car floor marked "Supergold"—a name he associated with marijuana. Thus having probable cause to believe the occupants had committed a drug offense, the officer ordered them out of the vehicle, placed them under arrest, and patted them down. Without handcuffing the arrestees, the officer "split them up into four separate areas of the Thruway . . . so they would not be in physical touching area of each other" and searched the vehicle, including the pocket of a jacket on the back seat, in which he found cocaine.

We held that when an officer lawfully arrests "the occupant of an automobile, he may, as a contemporaneous incident of that arrest, search the passenger compartment of the automobile" and any containers therein. That holding was based in large part on our assumption "that articles inside the relatively narrow compass of the passenger compartment of an automobile are in fact generally, even if not inevitably, within 'the area into which an arrestee might reach.'"

The Arizona Supreme Court read our decision in *Belton* as merely delineating "the proper scope of a search of the interior of an automobile" incident to an arrest. That is, when the passenger compartment is within an arrestee's reaching distance . . . the entire compartment and any containers therein may be reached. On this view of *Belton,* the state court concluded that the search of Gant's car was unreasonable, because Gant clearly could not have accessed his car at the time of the search. It also found that no other exception to the warrant requirement applied in this case. Gant now urges us to adopt the reading of *Belton* followed by the Arizona Supreme Court.

Despite the textual and evidentiary support for the Arizona Supreme Court's reading of *Belton,* our opinion has been widely understood to allow a vehicle search incident to the arrest of a recent occupant even if there is no possibility the arrestee could gain access to the vehicle at the time of the search. This reading may be attributable to Justice Brennan's dissent in *Belton,* in which he characterized the Court's holding as resting on the "fiction . . . that the interior of a car is *always* within the immediate control of an arrestee who has recently been in the car." Under the majority's approach, he argued, "the result would presumably be the same even if [the officer] had handcuffed Belton and his companions in the patrol car" before conducting the search.

Since we decided *Belton,* courts of appeals have given different answers to the question of whether a vehicle must be within an arrestee's reach to justify a vehicle search incident to arrest, but Justice Brennan's reading of the Court's opinion has predominated. As Justice O'Connor observed, "Lower court decisions seem now to treat the ability to search a vehicle incident to the arrest of a recent occupant as a police entitlement rather than as an exception justified by the twin rationales of *Chimel.*" Justice Scalia has similarly noted that although it is improbable that an arrestee could gain access to weapons stored in his vehicle after he has been handcuffed and secured in the back seat of a patrol car, cases allowing a search in "this precise factual scenario . . . are legion." Indeed, some courts have upheld searches under *Belton* "even when . . . the handcuffed arrestee has already left the scene."

Under this broad reading of *Belton,* a vehicle search would be authorized incident to every arrest of a recent occupant notwithstanding that in most cases the vehicle's passenger compartment will not be within the arrestee's reach at the time of the search. To read *Belton* as authorizing a vehicle search incident to every recent occupant's arrest would thus untether the rule from the justifications underlying the *Chimel* exception—a result clearly incompatible with our statement in *Belton* that it "in no way alters the fundamental principles established in the *Chimel* case regarding the basic scope of searches incident to lawful custodial arrests." Accordingly, we reject this reading of *Belton* and hold that the *Chimel* rationale authorizes police to search a vehicle incident to a recent occupant's arrest only when the arrestee is unsecured and within reaching distance of the passenger compartment at the time of the search.

Although it does not follow from *Chimel,* we also conclude that circumstances unique to the vehicle context justify a search incident to a lawful arrest when it is "reasonable to believe evidence relevant to the crime of arrest might be found in the vehicle." In many cases, as when a recent occupant is arrested for a traffic violation, there will be no reasonable basis to believe the vehicle contains relevant evidence. But in others, including *Belton* and *Thornton,* the offense of arrest will supply a basis for searching the passenger compartment of an arrestee's vehicle and any containers therein.

Neither the possibility of access nor the likelihood of discovering offense-related evidence authorized the search in this case. Unlike the situation in *Belton,* which involved a single officer confronted with four unsecured arrestees, the five officers in this case outnumbered the three arrestees, all of whom had been handcuffed and secured in separate patrol cars before the officers searched Gant's car. Under those circumstances, Gant clearly was not within reaching distance of his car at the time of the search. An evidentiary basis for the search was also lacking in this case. Whereas Belton and Thornton were arrested for drug offenses, Gant was arrested for driving with a suspended license—an offense for which police could not expect to find evidence in the passenger compartment of Gant's car. Because police could not reasonably have believed either that Gant could have accessed his car at the time of the search or that evidence of the offense for which he was arrested might have been found therein, the search in this case was unreasonable.

The State does not seriously disagree with the Arizona Supreme Court's conclusion that Gant could not have accessed his vehicle at the time of the search, but it nevertheless asks us to uphold the search of his vehicle under the broad reading of *Belton* discussed above. The State argues that *Belton* searches are reasonable regardless of the possibility of access in a given case, because that expansive rule correctly balances law enforcement interests, including the interest in a bright-line rule, with an arrestee's limited privacy interest in his vehicle.

For several reasons, we reject the State's argument. First, the State seriously undervalues the privacy interests at stake. Although we have recognized that a motorist's privacy interest in his vehicle is less substantial than that in his home, the former interest is nevertheless important and deserving of constitutional protection. It is particularly significant that *Belton* searches authorize police officers to search not just the passenger compartment but every purse, briefcase, or other container within that space. A rule that gives police the power to conduct such a search whenever an individual is caught committing a traffic offense, when there is no basis for believing evidence of the offense might be found in the vehicle, creates a serious and recurring threat to the privacy of individuals. Indeed, the character of that threat implicates the central concern underlying the Fourth Amendment—the concern about giving police officers unbridled discretion to rummage at will among a person's private effects.

At the same time as it undervalues these privacy concerns, the State exaggerates the clarity that its reading of *Belton* provides. Courts that have read *Belton* expansively are at odds regarding how close in time to the arrest and how proximate to the arrestee's vehicle an officer's first contact with the arrestee must be to bring the encounter within *Belton*'s purview and whether a search is reasonable when it commences or continues after the arrestee has been removed from the scene. The rule has thus generated a great deal of uncertainty, particularly for a rule touted as providing a "bright line."

Contrary to the State's suggestion, a broad reading of *Belton* is also unnecessary to protect law enforcement safety and evidentiary interests. Under our view, *Belton* and *Thornton* permit an officer to conduct a vehicle search when an arrestee is within reaching distance of the vehicle or when it is reasonable to believe the vehicle contains evidence of the offense of arrest. Other established exceptions to the warrant requirement authorize a vehicle search under additional circumstances when safety or evidentiary concerns demand. For instance, *Michigan v. Long* permits an officer to search a vehicle's passenger compartment when the officer has reasonable suspicion that an individual, whether or not the arrestee, is "dangerous" and might access the vehicle to "gain immediate control of weapons." If there is probable cause to believe a vehicle contains evidence of criminal activity, *United States v. Ross* authorizes a search of any area of the vehicle in which the evidence might be found.... *Ross* allows searches for evidence relevant to offenses other than the offense of arrest, and the scope of the search authorized is broader. Finally, there may be still other circumstances in which safety or evidentiary interests would justify a search.

These exceptions together ensure that officers may search a vehicle when genuine safety or evidentiary concerns encountered during the arrest of a vehicle's recent occupant justify a search. Construing *Belton* broadly to allow vehicle searches incident to any arrest would serve no purpose except to provide a police entitlement, and it is anathema to the Fourth Amendment to permit a warrantless search on that basis. For these reasons, we are unpersuaded by the State's arguments that a broad reading of *Belton* would meaningfully further law enforcement interests and justify a substantial intrusion on individuals' privacy.

Our dissenting colleagues argue that the doctrine of *stare decisis* requires adherence to a broad reading of *Belton* even though the justifications for searching a vehicle incident to arrest are in most cases absent. The doctrine of *stare decisis* is of course "essential to the respect accorded to the judgments of the Court and to the stability of the law," but it does not compel us to follow a past decision when its rationale no longer withstands "careful analysis." We have never relied on *stare decisis* to justify the continuance of an unconstitutional police practice. And we would be particularly loath to uphold an unconstitutional result in a case that is so easily distinguished from the decisions that arguably compel it. The safety and evidentiary interests that supported the search in *Belton* simply are not present in this case. Indeed, it is hard to imagine two cases that are factually more distinct, as *Belton* involved one officer confronted by four unsecured arrestees suspected of committing a drug offense, and this case involves several officers confronted with a securely detained arrestee apprehended for driving with a suspended license. This case is also distinguishable from *Thornton,* in which the petitioner was arrested for a drug offense. It is thus unsurprising that members of this Court who concurred in the judgments in *Belton* and *Thornton* also concur in the decision in this case.

We do not agree with the contention in Justice Alito's dissent that consideration of police reliance interests requires a different result. Although it appears that the State's reading of *Belton* has been widely taught in police academies and that law enforcement officers have relied on the rule in conducting vehicle searches during the past 28 years, many of these searches were not justified by the reasons underlying the *Chimel* exception. Countless individuals guilty of nothing more serious than a traffic violation have had their constitutional right to the security of their private effects violated as a result. The fact that the law enforcement community may view the State's version of the *Belton* rule as an entitlement does not establish the sort of reliance interest that could outweigh the countervailing interest that all individuals share in having their constitutional rights fully protected. If it is clear that a practice is unlawful, individuals' interests in its discontinuance clearly outweigh any law enforcement entitlement to its becoming embedded in routine police practice.

The experience of the 28 years since we decided *Belton* has shown that the generalization underpinning the broad reading of that decision is unfounded. We now know that articles inside the passenger compartment are rarely "within the area into which an arrestee might reach," and blind adherence to *Belton*'s faulty assumption would authorize myriad unconstitutional searches. The doctrine of *stare decisis* does not require us to approve routine constitutional violations.

Holding

Under *Chimel,* police may search incident to arrest only the space within an arrestee's "immediate control," meaning "the area from within which he might gain possession of a weapon or destructible evidence." The safety and evidentiary justifications underlying *Chimel*'s reaching-distance rule determine *Belton*'s scope. Accordingly, we hold that *Belton* does not authorize a vehicle search incident to a recent occupant's arrest after the arrestee has been secured and cannot access the interior of the vehicle. Consistent with the holding in *Thornton v. United States,* and following the suggestion in Justice Scalia's opinion concurring in the judgment in that case, we also conclude that circumstances unique to the automobile context justify a search incident to arrest when it is reasonable to believe that evidence of the offense of arrest might be found in the vehicle.

Police may search a vehicle incident to a recent occupant's arrest only if the arrestee is within reaching distance of the passenger compartment at the time of the search or it is reasonable to believe the vehicle contains evidence of the offense of arrest. When these justifications are absent, a search of an arrestee's vehicle will be unreasonable unless police obtain a warrant or show that another exception to the warrant requirement applies. The Arizona Supreme Court correctly held that this case involved an unreasonable search. Accordingly, the judgment of the state supreme court is affirmed.

Concurring, *Scalia, J.*

To determine what is an "unreasonable" search within the meaning of the Fourth Amendment, we look first to the historical practices the framers sought to preserve; if those provide inadequate guidance, we apply traditional standards of reasonableness.... Since the historical scope of officers' authority to search vehicles incident to arrest is uncertain, traditional standards of reasonableness govern. It is abundantly clear that those standards do not justify what I take to be the rule set forth in *New York v. Belton* and *Thornton v. United States:* that arresting officers may always search an arrestee's vehicle in order to protect themselves from hidden weapons. When an arrest is made in connection with a roadside stop, police virtually always have a less intrusive and more effective means of ensuring their safety—and a means that is virtually always employed: ordering the arrestee away from the vehicle, patting him down in the open, handcuffing him, and placing him in the squad car. Law enforcement officers face a risk of being shot whenever they pull a car over. But that risk is at its height at the time of the initial confrontation, and it is not at all reduced by allowing a search of the stopped vehicle after the driver has been arrested and placed in the squad car. I observed in *Thornton* that the Government had failed to provide a single instance in which a formerly restrained arrestee escaped to retrieve a weapon from his own vehicle.

Justice Stevens acknowledges that an officer-safety rationale cannot justify all vehicle searches incident to arrest, but asserts that that is not the rule *Belton* and *Thornton* adopted. Justice Stevens would therefore retain the application of *Chimel v. California* in the car-search context but would apply in the future what he believes our cases held in the past: that officers making a roadside stop may search the vehicle so long as the "arrestee is within reaching distance of the passenger compartment at the time of the search." I believe that this standard fails to provide the needed guidance to arresting officers and also leaves much room for manipulation, inviting officers to leave the scene unsecured (at least where dangerous suspects are not involved) in order to conduct a vehicle search.

In my view we should simply abandon the *Belton-Thornton* charade of officer safety and overrule those cases. I would hold that a vehicle search incident to arrest is "reasonable" only when the object of the search is evidence of the crime for which the arrest was made or of another crime that the officer has probable cause to believe occurred. Because respondent was arrested for driving without a license (a crime for which no evidence could be expected to be found in the vehicle), I would hold in the present case that the search was unlawful. No other justice shares my view that application of *Chimel* in this context should be entirely abandoned.

It seems to me unacceptable for the Court to come forth with a 4-to-1-to-4 opinion that leaves the governing rule uncertain. I am therefore confronted with the choice of either leaving the current understanding of *Belton* and *Thornton* in effect or acceding to what seems to me the artificial narrowing of those cases adopted by Justice Stevens. The latter, as I have said, does not provide the degree of certainty I think desirable in this field, but the former opens the field to what I think are plainly unconstitutional searches—which is the greater evil. I therefore join the opinion of the Court.

Dissenting, *Breyer, J.*

The matter, however, is not one of first impression, and that fact makes a substantial difference. The *Belton* rule has been followed not only by this Court in *Thornton v. United States* but also by numerous other courts. Principles of *stare decisis* must apply, and those who wish this Court to change a well-established legal precedent—where, as here, there has been considerable reliance on the legal rule in question—bear a heavy burden. I have not found that burden met. . . .

Dissenting, *Alito, J.*, joined by *Roberts, J.*, *Kennedy, J.*, and *Breyer, J.*

Twenty-eight years ago, in *New York v. Belton,* this Court held that "when a policeman has made a lawful custodial arrest of the occupant of an automobile, he may, as a contemporaneous incident of that arrest, search the passenger compartment of that automobile." Five years ago, in *Thornton v. United States*—a case involving a situation not materially distinguishable from the situation here—the Court not only reaffirmed but extended the holding of *Belton,* making it applicable to recent occupants. Today's decision effectively overrules those important decisions, even though respondent Gant has not asked us to do so. To take the place of the overruled precedents, the Court adopts a new two-part rule under which a police officer who arrests a vehicle occupant or recent occupant may search the passenger compartment if (1) the arrestee is within reaching distance of the vehicle at the time of the search, or (2) the officer has reason to believe that the vehicle contains evidence of the offense of arrest. The first part of this new rule may endanger arresting officers and is truly endorsed by only four justices; Justice Scalia joins solely for the purpose of avoiding a "4-to-1-to-4 opinion." The second part of the new rule is taken from Justice Scalia's separate opinion in *Thornton* without any independent explanation of its origin or justification and is virtually certain to confuse law enforcement officers and judges for some time to come. The Court's decision will cause the suppression of evidence gathered in many searches carried out in good-faith reliance on well-settled case law, and although the Court purports to base its analysis on the landmark decision in *Chimel v. California,* the Court's reasoning undermines *Chimel*. I would follow *Belton,* and I therefore respectfully dissent.

The precise holding in *Belton* could not be clearer. The Court stated unequivocally: "We hold that when a policeman has made a lawful custodial arrest of the occupant of an automobile, he may, as a contemporaneous incident of that arrest, search the passenger compartment of that automobile." Despite this explicit statement, the opinion of the Court in the present case curiously suggests that *Belton* may reasonably be read as adopting a holding that is narrower than the one explicitly set out in the *Belton* opinion, namely, that an officer arresting a vehicle occupant may search the passenger compartment "when the passenger compartment is within an arrestee's reaching distance." According to the Court, the broader reading of *Belton* that has gained wide acceptance "may be attributable to Justice Brennan's dissent." Contrary to the Court's suggestion, however, Justice Brennan's *Belton* dissent did not mischaracterize the Court's holding in that case or cause that holding to be misinterpreted. As noted, the *Belton* Court explicitly stated precisely what it held. In *Thornton,* the Court recognized the scope of *Belton*'s holding. So did Justice Scalia's separate opinion. ("In *[Belton]* we set forth a bright-line rule for arrests of automobile occupants, holding that . . . a search of the whole [passenger] compartment is justified in every case.") . . . This "bright-line rule" has now been interred.

Because the Court has substantially overruled *Belton* and *Thornton,* the Court must explain why its departure from the usual rule of *stare decisis* is justified. I recognize that *stare decisis* is not an "inexorable command" that should be followed unless there is a "special justification" for its abandonment. On the contrary, there are good reasons to continue to adhere to the original precedent of *Belton* and *Thornton.*

The *Belton* rule has been taught to police officers for more than a quarter century. Many searches—almost certainly including more than a few that figure in cases now on appeal—were conducted in scrupulous reliance on that precedent. It is likely that, on the very day when this opinion is announced, numerous vehicle searches will be conducted in good faith by police officers who were taught the *Belton* rule. The opinion of the Court recognizes that "*Belton* has been widely taught in police academies and that law enforcement officers have relied on the rule in conducting vehicle searches during the past 28 years." But for the Court, this seemingly counts for nothing.

Abandonment of the *Belton* rule cannot be justified on the ground that the dangers surrounding the arrest of a vehicle occupant are different today than they were 28 years ago. The Court claims that "we now know that articles inside the passenger compartment are rarely within the area into which an arrestee might reach," but surely it was well known in 1981 that a person who is taken from a vehicle, handcuffed, and placed in the back of a patrol car is unlikely to make it back into his own car to retrieve a weapon or destroy evidence.

The *Belton* rule has not proved to be unworkable. On the contrary, the rule was adopted for the express purpose of providing a test that would be relatively easy for police officers and judges to apply. The first part of the Court's new rule—which permits the search of a vehicle's passenger compartment if it is within an arrestee's reach at the time of the search—reintroduces the same sort of case-by-case, fact-specific decision making that the *Belton* rule was adopted to avoid. As the situation in *Belton* illustrated, there are cases in which it is unclear whether an arrestee could retrieve a weapon or evidence in the passenger compartment of a car.

Even more serious problems will also result from the second part of the Court's new rule, which requires officers making roadside arrests to determine whether there is reason to believe that the vehicle contains evidence of the crime of arrest. What this rule permits in a variety of situations is entirely unclear.

The *Chimel* Court, in an opinion written by Justice Stewart, concluded that there are only two justifications for a warrantless search incident to arrest—officer safety and the preservation of evidence. The Court stated that such a search must be confined to "the arrestee's person" and "the area from within which he might gain possession of a weapon or destructible evidence." Unfortunately, *Chimel* did not say whether "the area from within which [an arrestee] might gain possession of a weapon or destructible evidence" is to be measured at the time of the arrest or at the time of the search, but unless the *Chimel* rule was meant to be a specialty rule, applicable to only a few unusual cases, the Court must have intended for this area to be measured at the time of arrest. This is so because the Court can hardly have failed to appreciate the following two facts. First, in the great majority of cases, an officer making an arrest is able to handcuff the arrestee and remove him to a secure place before conducting a search incident to the arrest. Second, because it is safer for an arresting officer to secure an arrestee before searching, it is likely that this is what arresting officers do in the great majority of cases. Thus, if the area within an arrestee's reach were assessed, not at the time of arrest, but at the time of the search, the *Chimel* rule would rarely come into play.

Moreover, if the applicability of the *Chimel* rule turned on whether an arresting officer chooses to secure an arrestee prior to conducting a search, rather than searching first and securing the arrestee later, the rule would "create a perverse incentive for an arresting officer to prolong the period during which the arrestee is kept in an area where he could pose a danger to the officer." If this is the law, the D.C. Circuit observed,

> the law would truly be, as Mr. Bumble said, "a ass." If the police could lawfully have searched the defendant's grabbing radius at the moment of arrest, he has no legitimate complaint if, the better to protect themselves from him, they first put him outside that radius.

I do not think that this is what the *Chimel* Court intended. Handcuffs were in use in 1969. The ability of arresting officers to secure arrestees before conducting a search—and their incentive to do so—are facts that can hardly have escaped the Court's attention. I therefore believe that the *Chimel* Court intended that its new rule apply in cases in which the arrestee is handcuffed before the search is conducted. . . . Viewing *Chimel* as having focused on the time of arrest, *Belton*'s only new step was to eliminate the need to decide on a case-by-case basis whether a particular person seated in a car actually could have reached the part of the passenger compartment where a weapon or evidence was hidden. For this reason, if we are going to reexamine *Belton,* we should also reexamine the reasoning in *Chimel* on which *Belton* rests.

The second part of the Court's new rule, which the Court takes uncritically from Justice Scalia's separate opinion in *Thornton,* raises doctrinal and practical problems that the Court makes no effort to address. Why, for example, is the standard for this type of evidence-gathering search "reason to believe" rather than probable cause? And why is this type of search restricted to evidence of the offense of arrest? It is true that an arrestee's vehicle is probably more likely to contain evidence of the crime of arrest than of some other crime, but if reason-to-believe is the governing standard for an evidence-gathering search incident to arrest, it is not easy to see why an officer should not be able to search when the officer has reason to believe that the vehicle in question possesses evidence of a crime other than the crime of arrest.

Questions for Discussion

1. Summarize the facts in *Gant.*
2. How does the holding in *Gant* modify the rule established in *Belton?*
3. Explain why Justice Stevens did not follow the precedent established in *Belton.*
4. Why did Justice Alito dissent from the plurality decision? Discuss the significance of whether the reasonableness of a warrantless search of an automobile is based on the time of the arrest or on the time of the search.
5. If you were a member of the Supreme Court, how would you decide *Gant?*
6. ***Problems in policing.*** Apply the holding in *Gant* to the facts in *Belton* and *Thornton.* Would the police be justified in searching the automobile compartments in *Belton* and *Thornton?* Did *Gant* introduce uncertainty into the law of search and seizure?

You can find New York v. Belton *and* United States v. Thornton *on the study site,http://www.sagepub.com/lippmancp.*

Cases and Comments

State Courts. Several state supreme courts have refused to follow *Belton.* In the Pennsylvania case of *Commonwealth v. White,* the police arranged for a confidential informant to purchase cocaine from William White. White drove his automobile into the stakeout area, and six or eight police converged on White's car and took both White and a passenger into custody. White was patted down for weapons and moved a short distance from his car under close control by the police. An officer blocked White's path to the vehicle. Two officers entered the car and seized a marijuana cigarette and a bag of cocaine. The two suspects were handcuffed. The Pennsylvania Supreme Court held that the two individuals had been placed under arrest at the time of the search. The court noted that over the past few years, it increasingly had emphasized the privacy interests inherent in Article 1, Section 8 of the Pennsylvania Constitution that prohibits unreasonable searches and seizures.

In rejecting *Belton,* the Pennsylvania Supreme Court held that "merely arresting someone does not give the police [authority] to search any property belonging to the arrestee." The police may search the arrestee and the area in which the person is detained in order to prevent the arrestee from obtaining weapons or destroying evidence. In this instance, "whatever was contained in the vehicle was not accessible to White, and there is nothing to indicate that there were any exigent reasons, such as danger to the police, which would justify a warrantless search of the car."

Do you agree with the approach of the Pennsylvania Supreme Court? See *Commonwealth v. White,* 669 A.2d 896 (Pa. 1995). A good discussion of searches incident to an arrest of individuals in automobiles is *State v. Bauder,* 934 A.2d 38 (Vt. 2007).

6.4 YOU DECIDE

Korvell Pittman pled guilty to being a felon in possession of a firearm and reserved the right to challenge the denial of his motion to suppress evidence that was seized from his car when he was arrested. A Rock Island, Illinois, police officer on patrol noticed that Pittman's automobile did not have a functioning rear license plate light. The officer turned on his emergency lights, and Pittman pulled over to the side of the road.

As the car stopped, a passenger leapt out of the auto and started running. The police gave chase and located the passenger, Raymond Stinde, in the basement of a house half a block from the car. Stinde was found to have an outstanding arrest warrant. The police arrested him and brought him back to the squad car.

Meanwhile, Pittman, the driver of the car, also had fled, and the police did not immediately find him. The police proceeded to search the glove compartment of the car and discovered shotgun shells. The officers learned from Stinde that there was a shotgun in the trunk. The police towed the car to the police department and located Pittman at his home. Pittman agreed to accompany the police to headquarters. The police used the car keys they had recovered from where Pittman had discarded them at the crime scene to open the trunk, from which they seized a shotgun.

One of the several issues considered by the court was whether the search of the glove compartment was a search incident to an arrest despite the fact that Stinde was "half a block away from the car when he was arrested." See *United States v. Pittman,* 411 F.3d 813 (7th Cir. 2005).

You can learn what the court decided by referring to the study site, http://www.sagepub.com/lippmancp.

Misdemeanors and Searches Incident to an Arrest

May the police conduct a search incident to an arrest for a minor misdemeanor such as driving without a seat belt, as in the *Atwater* case (that we discussed in Chapter 5)? Gail Atwater was not likely to be armed, and there was no evidence linked to the crime that might have been destroyed. The rule is that any arrest permits a search incident to an arrest of the individual who is placed under arrest. In other words, there is no requirement that the officer reasonably believe that the suspect is armed or dangerous or that the offense for which the suspect is arrested is associated with the possession of weapons or that there is a risk that evidence may be concealed or destroyed.

In the incident at issue in *United States v. Robinson,* Officer Richard Jencks stopped Robinson for operating a motor vehicle after Robinson's driver's license had been revoked. Jencks arrested Robinson and then conducted a search incident to the arrest; during the search, Jencks discovered a crumpled cigarette package that contained heroin. Robinson contended that the search of his person was unlawful, because there was no indication that Jencks believed that there was evidence associated with the offense of driving without a license that might be destroyed. The defense attorney challenged the legality of the search on the grounds that Jencks would have been adequately protected by a *Terry* frisk and that a frisk would have the added advantage of minimally intruding on Robinson's privacy. The U.S. Supreme Court upheld the constitutionality of the search and explained that

> it is the...custodial arrest which gives rise to the authority to search, it is of no moment that Jencks did not indicate any subjective fear of [Robinson] or that he did not himself suspect that [Robinson] was armed. (*United States v. Robinson,* 414 U.S. 218, 235 [1973])

In the companion case of *Gustafson v. Florida,* the Supreme Court upheld the lawfulness of an officer's arrest and full search of Gustafson for driving without a license. The Supreme Court noted that Florida law provides a police officer with discretion to arrest the suspect or to issue a citation. The Court relied on the precedent established in *Robinson* and noted that the fact of the arrest provided a justification to search Gustafson despite the facts that the officer did not fear that Gustafson was armed and that there was no basis for believing that the officer would uncover incriminating evidence (*Gustafson v. Florida,* 414 U.S. 260 [1973]).

The Supreme Court decisions in *Robinson* and *Gustafson* establish a **bright-line rule**. The fact of an arrest authorizes a search incident to an arrest regardless of the offense for which a suspect is arrested. Why did the Supreme Court adopt this bright-line approach?

- ***Judicial review.*** The courts do not have the time and resources to review the reasonableness of every search incident to an arrest conducted by the police that may be challenged by a defendant. Each situation involves a complicated factual determination.
- ***Safety.*** Searches incident to an arrest protect the safety of officers. A frisk does not fully safeguard the police.
- ***Evidence.*** Searches incident to an arrest may result in the seizure of evidence of other crimes.
- ***Privacy.*** A search is a modest intrusion on an individual who, once having been subjected to an arrest, already has lost a degree of personal privacy.

Knowles v. Iowa is the next case in the text. An officer pulled over Patrick Knowles for speeding. The arresting officer under Iowa law is provided with the discretion to issue a citation or to arrest an individual stopped for speeding and in either instance to conduct a search incident to an arrest. The officer issued Knowles a citation and carried out a search of the automobile that resulted in the seizure of a bag of marijuana and a "pot pipe." The U.S. Supreme Court examined the historical justifications for a search incident to an arrest and asked whether it was reasonable to conduct a search when an individual is issued a citation. How would you predict that the Supreme Court ruled in *Knowles v. Iowa?*

May the police search a vehicle when they issue a citation?

Knowles v. Iowa, 525 U.S. 113 (1986), Rehnquist, J.

Issue

An Iowa police officer stopped petitioner Knowles for speeding but issued him a citation rather than arresting him. The question presented is whether such a procedure authorizes the officer, consistent with the Fourth Amendment, to conduct a full search of the car.

Facts

Knowles was stopped in Newton, Iowa, after having been clocked driving forty-three miles per hour on a road where the speed limit was twenty-five miles per hour. The police officer issued a citation to Knowles, although under Iowa law he might have arrested him. The officer then conducted a full search of the car, and under the driver's seat he found a bag of marijuana and a "pot pipe." Knowles was then arrested and charged with violation of state laws dealing with controlled substances.

Before trial, Knowles moved to suppress the evidence so obtained. He argued that the search could not be sustained under the "search incident to arrest" exception recognized in *United States v. Robinson,* because he had not been placed under arrest. At the hearing on the motion to suppress, the police officer conceded that he had neither Knowles's consent nor probable cause to conduct the search. He relied on Iowa law dealing with such searches.

Iowa Code Annotated section 321.485(1)(a) provides that Iowa peace officers having cause to believe that a person has violated any traffic or motor vehicle equipment law may arrest the person and immediately take the person before a magistrate. Iowa law also authorizes the far more usual practice of issuing a citation in lieu of arrest or in lieu of continued custody after an initial arrest (Iowa Code Ann. § 805.1(1)). Section 805.1(4) provides that the issuance of a citation in lieu of an arrest "does not affect the officer's authority to conduct an otherwise lawful search." The Iowa Supreme Court has interpreted this provision as providing authority to officers to conduct a full-blown search of an automobile and driver in those cases where police elect not to make a custodial arrest and instead issue a citation—thus, officers may conduct a search incident to citation.

Based on this authority, the trial court denied the motion to suppress and found Knowles guilty. The Iowa Supreme Court...affirmed by a divided vote. The Iowa Supreme Court upheld the constitutionality of the search under a bright-line "search incident to citation" exception to the Fourth Amendment's warrant requirement, reasoning that so long as the arresting officer had probable cause to make a custodial arrest, there need not in fact have been a custodial arrest.

Reasoning

In *Robinson* we noted the two historical rationales for the "search incident to arrest" exception: (1) the need to disarm the suspect in order to take him into custody and (2) the need to preserve evidence for later use at trial. But neither of these underlying rationales for the "search incident to arrest" exception is sufficient to justify the search in the present case.

We have recognized that the first rationale—officer safety—is "both legitimate and weighty." The threat to officer safety from issuing a traffic citation, however, is a good deal less than in the case of a custodial arrest. In *Robinson,* we stated that a custodial arrest involves "danger to an officer" because of "the extended exposure which follows the taking of a suspect into custody and transporting him to the police station." We recognized that "the danger to the police officer flows from the fact of the arrest, and its attendant proximity, stress, and uncertainty, and not from the grounds for arrest." A routine traffic stop, on the other hand, is a relatively brief encounter and "is more analogous to a so-called *Terry* stop...than to a formal arrest." ("Where there is no formal arrest...a person might well be less hostile to the police and less likely to take conspicuous, immediate steps to destroy incriminating evidence.")

This is not to say that the concern for officer safety is absent in the case of a routine traffic stop. It plainly is not. But while the concern for officer safety in this context may justify the "minimal" additional intrusion of ordering a driver and passengers out of the car, it does not by itself justify the often considerably greater intrusion attending a full field-type search. Even without the search authority Iowa urges, officers have other, independent bases to search for weapons and protect themselves from danger. For example, they may order out of a vehicle both the driver and any passengers, perform a pat down of a driver and any passengers upon reasonable suspicion that they may be armed and dangerous, conduct a *Terry* pat down of the passenger compartment of a vehicle upon reasonable suspicion that an occupant is dangerous and may gain immediate control of a weapon, and even conduct a full search of the passenger compartment, including any containers therein, pursuant to a custodial arrest.

Nor has Iowa shown the second justification for the authority to search incident to arrest—the need to discover and preserve evidence. Once Knowles was stopped for speeding and issued a citation, all the evidence necessary to prosecute that offense had been obtained. No further evidence of excessive speed was going to be found either on the person of the offender or in the passenger compartment of the car.

Iowa nevertheless argues that a search incident to citation is justified, because a suspect who is subject to a routine traffic stop may attempt to hide or destroy evidence related to his identity (e.g., a driver's license or vehicle registration) or destroy evidence of another, as yet undetected, crime. As for the destruction of evidence relating to identity, if a police officer is not satisfied with the identification furnished by the driver, this may be a basis for arresting him rather than merely issuing a citation. As for destroying evidence of other crimes, the possibility that an officer would stumble onto evidence wholly unrelated to the speeding offense seems remote.

Holding

In *Robinson,* we held that the authority to conduct a full field search as incident to an arrest was a "bright-line rule," which was based on the concern for officer safety and destruction or loss of evidence, but which did not depend in every case upon the existence of either concern. Here we are asked to extend that "bright-line rule" to a situation where the concern for officer safety is not present to the same extent and the concern for destruction or loss of evidence is not present at all. We decline to do so. The judgment of the Supreme Court of Iowa is reversed, and the cause remanded for further proceedings not inconsistent with this opinion.

Questions for Discussion

1. What is the holding in *Knowles v. Iowa*? Why did the Supreme Court not follow the precedent established in *Robinson*?
2. Are you persuaded that it is unreasonable to authorize the police to search an individual who is issued a citation? Does it make sense that a search would have been lawful had Knowles been arrested, but the search is unlawful because Knowles was issued a citation?
3. What if the officer had arrested and searched Knowles and after failing to find contraband had decided to issue a citation? Would Knowles be successful in contending that the search was unlawful and that the officer had violated his civil rights?
4. ***Problems in policing.*** When an officer has discretion either to arrest an individual or to issue a citation for a traffic offense, what factors should the officer consider in deciding whether to issue a citation or to arrest the driver?

Cases and Comments

1. ***State Law.*** In 1994, in *State v. Pierce,* the New Jersey Supreme Court held that Article 1, paragraph 7 of the New Jersey constitution prohibiting unreasonable searches provides greater protection than the Fourth Amendment to the U.S. Constitution in regard to searches of automobiles incident to arrests. As a consequence, the New Jersey Supreme Court held that "we should not apply the rule of *New York v. Belton* in so far as it purports to authorize vehicular searches...based only on contemporaneous arrests for [all] motor-vehicle violations." In the case at issue, Officer Rette stopped a Ford van owned and operated by codefendant Nicholas Grass for traveling fifty-one miles per hour in a forty-mile-per-hour zone. Defendant Pierce and codefendant Bernardo also were in the vehicle. Rette contacted headquarters and learned that Grass's driver's license had been suspended, ordered Grass to step out of the van, and informed Grass that he was being arrested for driving with a suspended license. Grass was searched, handcuffed, and placed in the rear of the patrol car. Pierce and Bernardo then were ordered out of the van and frisked for weapons. A search of the automobile led to the seizure of an unlicensed revolver loaded with four rounds. A jacket was found to contain trace amounts of cocaine. The three men who had been in the car were arrested and indicted for unlawful possession of a weapon, receiving stolen property (the weapon), and possession of cocaine. Pierce pled guilty to the cocaine charge and appealed the denial of his motion to suppress.

New Jersey authorizes an officer to either issue a summons (citation) or arrest an individual for a traffic offense committed in the officer's presence. The New Jersey Supreme Court noted that driving with a revoked license is a more serious offense than most other traffic offenses punishable under New Jersey law. A license is revoked when an individual has been convicted of serious offense or as a result of an accumulation of offenses that directly implicate the public safety. The first violation is penalized by a fine of $500, a second offense by a fine of $750 and five days in jail, and a third offense by a fine of $1,000 and ten days in jail.

The Supreme Court acknowledged that most states have followed the rule in *Belton.* The Court noted that the *Belton* rule, however, has been modified in several states, including Connecticut, Massachusetts, Nevada, New York, Pennsylvania, Vermont, and Wyoming. The New Jersey judges reasoned that in most cases of arrests for routine traffic violations, a search of the driver of an automobile adequately protects the police. There is no justification for extending a search incident to an arrest to the automobile. Individuals arrested for routine traffic violations rarely pose a threat to harm an officer and, with the possible exception of driving under the influence of alcohol or narcotics, there typically is no evidence linked to the traffic offense in the automobile. The Court reasoned that in arrests for routine traffic violations, the police officer should have the burden of justifying the extension of a search incident to the passenger compartment.

A second objection to applying the rule in *New York v. Belton* is that it provides an incentive for the police to stop individuals for minor traffic offenses in order to conduct searches of the interior of automobiles. After stopping an individual, if an officer observes luggage or containers in the automobile that he or she wants to search, the officer may decide to arrest the individual rather than issue a summons. In such a case, the arrest is made because the officer wants to search the vehicle rather than because an arrest is merited by the seriousness of the offense or by the surrounding circumstances.

Do you agree with the New Jersey Supreme Court? How does the holding of the New Jersey Supreme Court differ from the holding of the U.S. Supreme Court in *Arizona v. Gant?* See *State v. Pierce,* 642 A.2d 947 (N.J. 1994).

2. ***State Law.*** Several states authorize a search incident to an arrest only for *nontraffic offenses* in those instances in which the prosecution meets the burden of establishing that the search was undertaken to protect the officer or to prevent the destruction or concealment of evidence. The Massachusetts legislature passed a law that specifically provides that a

> search conducted incident to an arrest may be made only for the purposes of seizing fruits, instrumentalities, contraband and other evidence of the crime for which the arrest has been made, in order to prevent its destruction or concealment; and removing any weapons that the arrestee might use to resist arrest or effect his escape. Objects seized in violation of this provision shall not be admissible in evidence. (G.L.C. 27 § 1)

State supreme courts in Alaska, Hawaii, Montana, Oregon, Wyoming, and several other states have adopted similar rules, reasoning that their state constitutions provided greater protection than the Fourth Amendment to the U.S. Constitution. See *State v. Hardaway,* 36 P.3d 900 (Mont. 2007).

Pretext Arrests and Searches Incident to an Arrest

In *United States v. Robinson,* discussed in the previous section, Officer Richard Jencks pulled Robinson over based on a prior investigation that indicated that Robinson was driving with a revoked driver's license. A pat down led to the seizure of heroin. Robinson alleged that Jencks was aware that Robinson had two prior drug arrests and had used the traffic stop as a **pretext arrest** to enable Jencks to search for unlawful narcotics. The Supreme Court did not address Robinson's contention that Jencks had engaged in a pretext arrest and in a footnote merely observed that Robinson had been "lawfully arrested for an offense." Justice Marshall, however, insisted in his dissent that "an arrest may not be used as a pretext for a search for evidence" (*United States v. Robinson,* 414 U.S. 218, 220, 248 [1963]).

Thirty-six years later, in *United States v. Whren,* the U.S. Supreme Court provided an answer to the questions of whether a defendant may raise the defense that his or her seizure is the product of a pretext arrest and whether any items seized pursuant to the resulting search should be excluded from evidence. In the case at issue in *Whren,* Michael Whren and James Brown were stopped in Brown's truck for three traffic violations in a "high drug area" in Washington, D.C., by plainclothes vice officers. On approaching the truck, the officers observed two bags of crack cocaine in the truck, and they arrested both Whren and Brown. The two arrestees conceded that there was probable cause to stop them. However, they alleged that the traffic stop was a pretext to investigate their suspected narcotics activity. They also suggested that they had been singled out because they were African Americans. Whren and Brown pointed out that police regulations stated that plainclothes vice officers were to make traffic arrests only in situations posing a threat to public safety.

The Supreme Court held that a police officer may arrest the driver of an automobile based on probable cause that the driver is violating the law and may then conduct a search incident to an arrest. An officer's subjective motivations "play no part in Fourth Amendment analysis" and do not make otherwise lawful conduct "illegal or unconstitutional." The Court stressed that the U.S. Constitution prohibits selective enforcement of the law based on considerations such as race. But the basis for objecting to the intentionally discriminatory application of the laws is the Equal Protection Clause rather than the Fourth Amendment.

In reading *United States v. Whren,* ask yourself whether Whren and Brown were stopped on a pretext arrest and whether you agree with the Supreme Court's decision. Why does the court hold that an officer's "subjective intentions" should not be considered in evaluating the "reasonableness" of an arrest and search? Is the "reasonable officer test" proposed by the defendants a realistic approach to the question of pretext arrests?

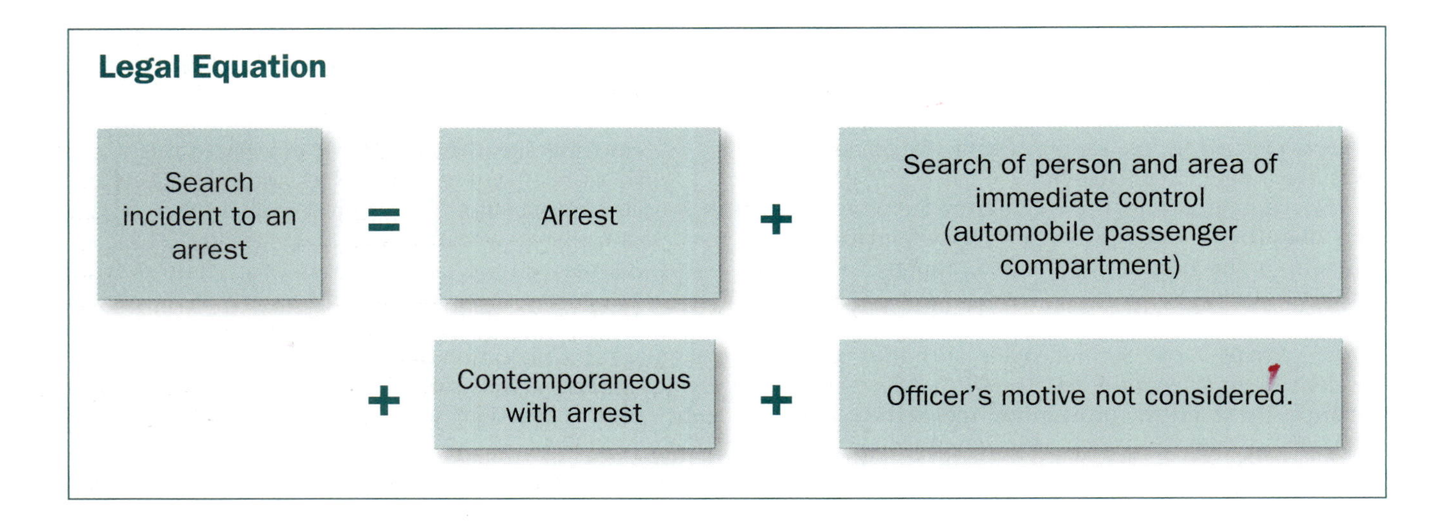

Does the Fourth Amendment prohibit "pretext arrests"?

United States v. Whren, 517 U.S. 806 (1996), Scalia, J.

Issue

In this case we decide whether the temporary detention of a motorist who the police have probable cause to believe has committed a civil traffic violation is inconsistent with the Fourth Amendment's prohibition against unreasonable seizures unless a reasonable officer would have been motivated to stop the car by a desire to enforce the traffic laws.

Facts

On the evening of June 10, 1993, plainclothes vice squad officers of the District of Columbia Metropolitan Police Department were patrolling a "high drug area" of the city in an unmarked car. Their suspicions were aroused when they passed a dark Pathfinder truck with temporary license plates and youthful occupants waiting at a stop sign, the driver looking down into the lap of the passenger at his right. The truck remained stopped at the intersection for what seemed an unusually long time—more than 20 seconds. When the police car executed a U-turn in order to head back toward the truck, the Pathfinder turned suddenly to its right, without signaling, and sped off at an "unreasonable" speed. The policemen followed, and in a short while overtook the Pathfinder when it stopped behind other traffic at a red light. They pulled up alongside, and Officer Ephraim Soto stepped out and approached the driver's door, identifying himself as a police officer and directing the driver, petitioner Brown, to put the vehicle in park. When Soto drew up to the driver's window, he immediately observed two large plastic bags of what appeared to be crack cocaine in petitioner Whren's hands. Petitioners were arrested, and quantities of several types of illegal drugs were retrieved from the vehicle.

Petitioners were charged in a four-count indictment with violating various federal drug laws. At a pretrial suppression hearing, they challenged the legality of the stop and the resulting seizure of the drugs. They argued that the stop had not been justified by probable cause to believe, or even reasonable suspicion, that petitioners were engaged in illegal drug-dealing activity and that Officer Soto's asserted ground for approaching the vehicle—to give the driver a warning concerning traffic violations—was pretextual. The District Court denied the suppression motion, concluding that "the facts of the stop were not controverted," and "there was nothing to really demonstrate that the actions of the officers were contrary to a normal traffic stop." Petitioners were convicted of the counts at issue here. The Court of Appeals affirmed the convictions, holding with respect to the suppression issue that

> regardless of whether a police officer subjectively believes that the occupants of an automobile may be engaging in some other illegal behavior, a traffic stop is permissible as long as a reasonable officer in the same circumstances could have stopped the car for the suspected traffic violation.

Reasoning

An automobile stop is thus subject to the constitutional imperative that it not be "unreasonable" under the circumstances. As a general matter, the decision to stop an automobile is reasonable where the police have probable cause to believe that a traffic violation has occurred. Petitioners accept that Officer Soto had probable cause to believe that various provisions of the District of Columbia traffic code had been violated, including the following:

> "An operator shall . . . give full time and attention to the operation of the vehicle." (18 D.C. Mun. Regs. § 2213.4 [1995])
>
> "No person shall turn any vehicle . . . without giving an appropriate signal." (18 D.C. Mun. Regs. § 2204.3 [1995])
>
> "No person shall drive a vehicle . . . at a speed greater than is reasonable and prudent under the conditions." (D.C. Mun. Regs. § 2200.3 [1995])

They argue, however, that "in the unique context of civil traffic regulations," probable cause is not enough. Since, they contend, the use of automobiles is so heavily and minutely regulated that total compliance with traffic and safety rules is nearly impossible, a police officer will almost invariably be able to catch any given motorist in a technical violation. This creates the temptation to use traffic stops as a means of investigating other law violations, as to which no probable cause or even articulable suspicion exists. Petitioners, who are both black, further contend that police officers might decide which motorists to stop based on decidedly impermissible factors, such as the race of the car's occupants. To avoid this danger, they say, the Fourth Amendment test for traffic stops should not be the normal one (applied by the court of appeals) of whether probable cause existed to justify the stop, but rather whether a police officer, acting reasonably, would have made the stop for the reason given. . . . Petitioners contend that the standard they propose is consistent with disapproval in past cases of police attempts to use valid bases of action against citizens as pretexts for pursuing other investigatory agendas. . . .

Petitioners' difficulty is not simply a lack of affirmative support for their position. Not only have we never held, outside the context of inventory search or administrative inspection, that an officer's motive invalidates objectively justifiable behavior under the Fourth Amendment, but we have repeatedly held and asserted the contrary. In *United States v. Villamonte-Marquez* (462 U.S. 579 [1983]), we held that an otherwise valid warrantless boarding of a vessel by customs officials was not rendered invalid "because the customs officers were accompanied by a Louisiana state policeman, and were following an informant's tip that a vessel in the ship channel was thought to be carrying marihuana." We flatly dismissed the idea that an ulterior motive might serve to strip the agents of their legal justification. In *United States v. Robinson,* we held that a traffic violation arrest (of the sort here) would not be rendered invalid by the fact that it was "a mere pretext for a narcotics search," and that a lawful postarrest search of the person would not be rendered invalid by the fact that it was not motivated by the officer safety concern that justifies such searches. . . . We described *Robinson* as having established that

> the fact that the officer does not have the state of mind which is hypothecated by the reasons which provide the legal justification for the officer's action does not invalidate the action taken as long as the circumstances, viewed objectively, justify that action.

Recognizing that we have been unwilling to entertain Fourth Amendment challenges based on the actual motivations of individual officers, petitioners disavow any intention to make the individual officer's subjective good faith the touchstone of "reasonableness." They insist that the standard they have put forward—whether the officer's conduct deviated materially from usual police practices, so that a reasonable officer in the same circumstances would not have made the stop for the reasons given—is an "objective" one.

But although framed in empirical terms, this approach is plainly and indisputably driven by subjective considerations. Its whole purpose is to prevent the police from doing under the guise of enforcing the traffic code what they would like to do for different reasons. Petitioners' proposed standard may not use the word *pretext,* but it is designed to combat nothing other than the perceived "danger" of the pretextual stop, albeit only indirectly and over the run of cases. Instead of asking whether the individual officer had the proper state of mind, the petitioners would have us ask, in effect, whether (based on general police practices) it is plausible to believe that the officer had the proper state of mind.

Why one would frame a test designed to combat pretext in such fashion that the court cannot take into account actual and admitted pretext is a curiosity that can only be explained by the fact that our cases have foreclosed the more sensible option. If those cases were based only upon the evidentiary difficulty of establishing subjective intent, petitioners' attempt to root out subjective vices through objective means might make sense. But those cases were not based only upon that, or indeed even principally upon that. Their principal basis—which applies equally to attempts to reach subjective intent through ostensibly objective means—is simply that the Fourth Amendment's concern with "reasonableness" allows certain actions to be taken in certain circumstances, whatever the subjective intent. But even if our concern had been only an evidentiary one, petitioners' proposal would by no means assuage it. Indeed, it seems to us somewhat easier to figure out the intent of an individual officer than to plumb the collective consciousness of law enforcement in order to determine whether a "reasonable officer" would have been moved to act upon the traffic violation. While police manuals and standard procedures may sometimes provide objective assistance, ordinarily one would be reduced to speculating about the hypothetical reaction of a hypothetical constable—an exercise that might be called virtual subjectivity.

Moreover, police enforcement practices, even if they could be practicably assessed by a judge, vary from place to place and from time to time. We cannot accept that the search and seizure protections of the Fourth Amendment are so variable, and can be made to turn upon such trivialities. The difficulty is illustrated by petitioners' arguments in this case. Their claim that a reasonable officer would not have made this stop is based largely on District of Columbia police regulations which permit plainclothes officers in unmarked vehicles to enforce traffic laws "only in the case of a violation that is so grave as to pose an immediate threat to the safety of others." This basis of invalidation would not apply in jurisdictions that had a different practice. And it would not have applied even in the District of Columbia, if Officer Soto had been wearing a uniform or patrolling in a marked police cruiser....

In what would appear to be an elaboration on the "reasonable officer" test, petitioners argue that the balancing inherent in any Fourth Amendment inquiry requires us to weigh the governmental and individual interests implicated in a traffic stop such as we have here. That balancing, petitioners claim, does not support investigation of minor traffic infractions by plainclothes police in unmarked vehicles; such investigation only minimally advances the Government's interest in traffic safety and may indeed retard it by producing motorist confusion and alarm—a view said to be supported by the Metropolitan Police Department's own regulations generally prohibiting this practice. And as for the Fourth Amendment interests of the individuals concerned, petitioners point out that our cases acknowledge that even ordinary traffic stops entail "a possibly unsettling show of authority" and that they at best "interfere with freedom of movement, are inconvenient, and consume time" and at worst "may create substantial anxiety." That anxiety is likely to be even more pronounced when the stop is conducted by plainclothes officers in unmarked cars.

It is of course true that in principle every Fourth Amendment case, since it turns upon a "reasonableness" determination, involves a balancing of all relevant factors. With rare exceptions not applicable here, however, the result of that balancing is not in doubt where the search or seizure is based upon probable cause.... Where probable cause has existed, the only cases in which we have found it necessary actually to perform the "balancing" analysis involved searches or seizures conducted in an extraordinary manner that is unusually harmful to an individual's privacy or even physical interests—such as, for example, seizure by means of deadly force (*Tennessee v. Garner,* 471 U.S. 1 [1985]), unannounced entry into a home (*Wilson v. Arkansas,* 514 U.S. 927 [1995]), entry into a home without a warrant (*Welsh v. Wisconsin,* 466 U.S. 740 [1984]), or physical penetration of the body (*Winston v. Lee,* 470 U.S. 753 [1985]). The making of a traffic stop out of uniform does not remotely qualify as such an extreme practice and so is governed by the usual rule that probable cause to believe the law has been broken "outbalances" private interest in avoiding police contact.

Petitioners urge as an extraordinary factor in this case that the "multitude of applicable traffic and equipment regulations" is so large and so difficult to obey perfectly that virtually everyone is guilty of violation, permitting the police to single out almost whomever they wish for a stop. But we are aware of no principle that would allow us to decide at what point a code of law becomes so expansive and so commonly violated that infraction itself can no longer be the ordinary measure of the lawfulness of enforcement. And even if we could identify such exorbitant codes, we do not know by what standard (or what right) we would decide, as petitioners would have us do, which particular provisions are sufficiently important to merit enforcement.

Holding

We think that the case law forecloses any argument that the constitutional reasonableness of traffic stops depends on the actual motivations of the individual officers involved. We of course agree with petitioners that the Constitution prohibits selective enforcement of the law based on considerations such as race. But the constitutional basis for objecting to intentionally discriminatory application of laws is the Equal Protection Clause, not the Fourth Amendment. Subjective intentions play no role in ordinary, probable-cause Fourth Amendment analysis or the run-of-the-mine case, which this surely is. We think there is no realistic alternative to the traditional common law rule that probable cause justifies a search and seizure. Here the district court found that the officers had probable cause to believe that petitioners had violated the traffic code. That rendered the stop reasonable under the Fourth Amendment, the evidence thereby discovered admissible, and the upholding of the convictions by the court of appeals for the District of Columbia Circuit correct.

Questions for Discussion

1. What facts support the claim of Whren and Brown that they were subjected to a pretext arrest?

2. Explain the holding of the Supreme Court. Can you speculate on why the Court decided against considering an officer's subjective motivation in reviewing the reasonableness of an arrest?

3. Why does the Supreme Court dismiss the legal tests proposed by Whren and Brown?

4. The Supreme Court states that an individual who is arrested for a traffic offense may not rely on the defense that the arrest is a pretext and therefore is unreasonable. Should a pretext arrest be unlawful under the Fourth Amendment and result in the exclusion from trial of evidence seized during the search of the individual or of his or her automobile?

5. The Court observes that an individual's remedy for racial discrimination lies in the Equal Protection Clause to the U.S. Constitution. An Equal Protection claim requires a demonstration that an officer's conduct resulted in a discriminatory impact (i.e., similarly situated individuals of a different race were not arrested for the same offense) and that the officer was motivated by a discriminatory intent. What type of evidence would you present to establish a violation of the Equal Protection Clause? Is a violation of the Equal Protection Clause easily established?

6. ***Problems in policing.*** Is it ethical for a police officer to engage in a "pretext arrest"?

Cases and Comments

State Law. In November 1998, Andrew Sullivan pulled into a service station and was informed by Officer Joe Taylor of the Conway, Arkansas, police that he had clocked Sullivan as traveling at forty miles per hour in a thirty-five-mile-per-hour zone. Sullivan opened the door of his automobile in order to locate his registration and proof of insurance, and Officer Taylor noticed a rusting roofing hatchet that was corroding into the carpet of the vehicle. Sullivan was arrested for speeding, for failing to possess a vehicle registration and proof of insurance, for carrying a weapon, and for having an improper tint on the windshield. Officer Taylor further held that the vehicle was unsafe because of a defective speedometer. Another officer arrived and placed Sullivan in the back of his vehicle. Taylor searched Sullivan's car and seized methamphetamine and drug paraphernalia. Taylor later conceded that he had formerly been assigned to the narcotics section of the Conway police force and that he was aware of intelligence indicating Sullivan's involvement in drug activity.

The Arkansas Supreme Court concluded that it is "doubtful" whether Sullivan would have been arrested "simply for traveling forty miles per hour in a thirty-five mile-per-hour zone and possessing a roofing hatchet that had clearly been in his vehicle for quite a long time, given that it was corroding into the carpet." The court affirmed the finding of the trial court that "the search and seizure was pretextual and should be suppressed" (*State v. Sullivan,* 11 S.W.3d 526 [2000]).

The judgment of the Arkansas Supreme Court was reversed by the U.S. Supreme Court, which held that the state court had failed to follow the precedent established in *Whren.* The U.S. Supreme Court explained that the Arkansas judges had improperly interpreted the Fourth Amendment to the U.S. Constitution as prohibiting the introduction into evidence of the narcotics seized as a result of a pretext arrest. The Supreme Court remanded the case to Arkansas for reconsideration in light of the judgment in *Whren* (*Sullivan v. Arkansas,* 532 U.S. 769 [2001]).

The Arkansas Supreme Court then reconsidered *Sullivan* and issued a second judgment. The state court recognized that under *Whren,* "so long as a police officer's actions are objectively reasonable, there is no Fourth Amendment violation even if the police officer's actions are wholly pretextual." However, the Arkansas Supreme Court relied on the Arkansas constitution rather than the U.S. Constitution and held that in interpreting the Arkansas constitution over the past twenty years, the Arkansas Supreme Court had viewed pretext arrests as unreasonable and had not followed the direction of the U.S. Supreme Court. The Arkansas court proceeded to apply a "but for" test to determine whether a pretext arrest had taken place. The court asked, "Would the arrest not have occurred but for the other, typically more serious, crime?" The Arkansas Supreme Court affirmed the judgment of the trial court judge that Officer Taylor had executed a pretext arrest and noted that the "trial court was bothered by the fact that the police officer arrested Sullivan rather than citing him for traffic violations and that the police officer used the roofing hatchet to bolster the case."

Do you agree with the legal test proposed by the Arkansas Supreme Court? Is it significant that Arkansas law authorizes the arrest of an individual who has committed a misdemeanor in an officer's presence? See *State v. Sullivan,* 74 S.W.3d 215 (Ark. 2002).

Criminal Procedure in the News

In 1996, in *Washington v. Lambert,* the Ninth Circuit Court of Appeals reluctantly concluded that "neither society nor our enforcement of the law is yet 'colorblind'" (*Washington v. Lambert,* 98 F.3d 1181, 1187–1188 [9th Cir. 1996]). The racially biased enforcement of the law by the police is thought to be exemplified by the policy of singling out African American and Hispanic drivers for minor traffic offenses. This practice of racial profiling is commonly referred to as "driving while black" and in the case of Hispanics "driving while brown [DWB]." (See *United States v. Jones,* 242 F.3d 215 [4th Cir. 2001].)

It is alleged that stopping individuals for DWB singles out members of minority groups for stops and arrests for relatively minor traffic violations as a pretext for questioning individuals and for searching their persons and vehicles for narcotics, drugs, and evidence of criminal activity. In this practice of stopping individuals for DWB, the police arrest and search minorities for offenses that they generally overlook when committed by individuals who are not members of minority groups.

What is the evidence? Studies made during the 1990s in Maryland, New Jersey, Illinois, Ohio, and other states document the disproportionate stop, arrest, and search of African American drivers by the police. In Maryland, a lawsuit brought by the American Civil Liberties Union against the Maryland State Police was settled when an internal police memo was discovered that advised troopers to be alert to the fact that drug dealers are "predominantly" African American. The memo provided evidence of a policy of encouraging the stop and search of African Americans by the Maryland State Police. The settlement required Maryland to turn data over to the plaintiffs regarding police stops and searches on Interstate 95 north of Baltimore.

An analysis of drivers on Interstate 95 by Temple University Professor Dr. John Lamberth concluded that over ninety percent of drivers on Interstate 95 north of Baltimore disregard speed laws and, as a result, may be justifiably stopped by the police. Roughly three-quarters of these drivers who were breaking the law were found to be Caucasian, and roughly seventeen percent were African American. These data, according to Lamberth, are difficult to reconcile with the fact that between January 1995 and September 1996, the Maryland State Police reported searching 823 motorists on Interstate 95. Six hundred, or 72.9 percent, of the individuals who were searched were African Americans, while 19.7 percent of the individuals who were searched were Caucasian. Lamberth reports that the disparity between these figures is "statistically vast," and the possibility that this result occurred "by chance" is "infinitesimally small." Lamberth concludes that the data indicate "without question a racially discriminatory impact on blacks and other minority motorists from state police behavior along I-95."

In June 1999, President Bill Clinton directed federal agencies to collect data on the race and ethnicity of drivers stopped or searched. In February 2001, President George W. Bush condemned racial profiling as "wrong" and pledged to "end" racial profiling in America. Twenty states presently have laws addressing racial profiling. Some merely mandate training programs, while others call for the voluntary collection of data by local police departments. In 2001, Texas passed a strong Racial Profiling Data Collection Law that requires Texas law enforcement agencies that are engaged in traffic and pedestrian stops to collect "race data" on stops and searches. In the first phase of this program, agencies are required to collect data on stops that result in a ticket or arrest. In the second phase, a locality is provided the option to mount cameras on their squad cars or to submit data on every traffic stop and pedestrian stop. A majority of departments in Texas have responded by installing cameras on their squad cars.

Experts have concluded that in addition to strong reporting requirements, there are various steps that should be taken to limit racial profiling. These include the training of police officers, the recruitment of a diverse police force, the denial of federal funds to departments that engage in racial profiling, and the establishment of local hotlines for victims to report racially motivated pretext stops and searches.

In a September 2002 article in the conservative online *National Review,* Heather MacDonald of the Manhattan Institute challenges the notion that minority drivers are discriminated against by the police and points out that a 2002 survey of 80,000 adults by the Bureau of Justice Statistics found that an identical proportion of African Americans, Hispanics, and Caucasians report being stopped by the police (nine percent). According to MacDonald, "These results demolish the claim that minorities are disproportionately subject to 'pretextual' stops." The difference between the three groups, according to the survey, lies in the fact that 10.2 percent of African Americans, 11.4 percent of Hispanics, and 3.3 percent of Caucasians report that they were subjected to a search following a stop. A second difference is that 2.4 percent of Hispanics, 2.7 percent of African-Americans, and 0.8 percent of Caucasian drivers claimed that force had been threatened or used against them (e.g., pushing, grabbing, or hitting).

MacDonald contends that the differences in the percentages of individuals in various groups who report being subject to a search and who report having been subject to the application of force is explained by the fact that African Americans and Hispanics are "far more likely to be arrested following a stop." African Americans constituted roughly eleven percent of stopped drivers and twenty-four percent of arrested drivers, and Hispanics constituted 9.5 percent of all stopped drivers and 18.4 percent of arrested drivers. Caucasians constituted 76.5 percent of all stopped drivers and 58.5 percent of all arrested drivers. MacDonald concludes that the higher arrest rates for African Americans and Hispanics is due to the fact that these drivers are more likely to have outstanding arrest warrants that turn up when the police run a computer search, more likely to be violating the traffic laws when stopped, or more likely to challenge police officers and provoke a confrontation. MacDonald writes that "these higher arrest rates in turn naturally result in higher search rates.... Moreover, the higher crime rates among blacks and Hispanics mean a greater likelihood that evidence of a crime, such as weapons or drugs, may be in plain view, thereby triggering an arrest and a search."

MacDonald argues in an earlier article that the allegation that the police engage in racial profiling in enforcing traffic laws is based on "junk science." She concludes that the accusation that the police enforce the law in a racially discriminatory fashion damages police–community relations and leads the police to avoid enforcing the law out of a fear that they will be accused of racial profiling. Do you believe that there are police officers who single individuals out for arrest based on race or gender or other factors? Should the police be required to record the race of each individual operating a motor vehicle whom they stop or arrest or search?

Consent Searches

In *Schneckloth v. Bustamonte* (412 U.S. 218 [1973]), the U.S. Supreme Court held that a **consent search** is a reasonable Fourth Amendment search. An individual who consents to a search waives his or her right to privacy under the Fourth Amendment. This provides legal authorization for the police to conduct a search even in those instances in which the police do not have a legal basis to conduct a search of a person or of a container, home, or automobile. The Supreme Court noted that consent searches are part of the standard investigatory technique of law enforcement agencies and that consent in many instances may be the only means of obtaining important and reliable evidence.

Schneckloth held that the legal test for a consent search is that the consent must be voluntary and may not be the result of duress or coercion, express or implied. Voluntariness is to be determined by the totality of the circumstances, and the fact that an individual is aware of the right to refuse consent is one factor to be taken into consideration. The Supreme Court noted that this "voluntary test" balances the need for the police to conduct consent searches against the need to insure that consent is freely given and is not the result of duress or coercion. The Court candidly conceded in *Schneckloth* that informing individuals of the right to refuse consent runs the risk of individuals refusing consent and might interfere with police investigations. The judges also observed that individuals benefit from consent searches, because these searches permit the police to quickly determine guilt or innocence and enable innocent individuals to avoid being the target of a criminal investigation or arrest.

The burden of proof is on the prosecution to establish voluntariness by a preponderance of the evidence (fifty-one percent). There is no single factor that determines voluntariness. In evaluating the totality of the circumstances, courts consider various factors to be significant. The question to ask is whether the totality of the circumstances indicate that the defendant voluntarily consented to the search. Some of the factors typically considered by courts in evaluating voluntariness are listed below (*United States v. Gonzalez-Basulto*, 898 F.2d 1011 [5th Cir. 1990]).

- ***Coercive police procedures.*** Whether there is police psychological pressure or a police dominated atmosphere that may coerce an individual into consenting to a search against his or her will.
- ***Requests for consent.*** Whether there are a number of requests for consent before the individual agrees to the consent. The more requests that are made the less likely it is that there is voluntary consent.
- ***Custody.*** Whether the individual is in custody or physically restrained or handcuffed when he or she is requested to consent to a search. An individual who voluntarily

turns himself or herself in to the police is more likely to have voluntarily cooperated with the police and to have freely consented to a search. A suspect who proposes on his or her own initiative that the police conduct a search also is less likely to have been coerced into a waiver.

- ***Awareness of the right to refuse.*** Whether an individual is informed of his or her right to refuse consent.
- ***Experience in the criminal justice system.*** An individual who has experience in the criminal justice system is less likely to be tricked or coerced into a waiver.
- ***Consent to search form.*** Many police departments provide individuals with a form to sign that indicates that they consent to the search. Did the defendant sign or refuse to sign the consent form? A refusal to sign a form is not considered controlling in those instances in which a defendant verbally agrees to a consent search. The fact that a defendant signed a form that clearly indicated that the defendant possessed the right to refuse consent is strong evidence that the consent was voluntary.
- **Miranda warning.** Individuals in custody who are read the *Miranda* warnings are informed that they are not required to submit to police interrogation, and in many cases when asked to consent to a search they also are informed that any objects seized during a consent search may be used against them. An individual who receives a warning is less likely to have been coerced into a waiver.
- ***Seizure of contraband.*** Defendants in several cases have argued that their consent could not have been voluntary because the police found incriminating evidence in the course of the consent search. Courts, however, generally have held that the fact that the object of the search is well-hidden may indicate that the individual consented because he or she did not expect that it would be discovered.

United States v. Gonzalez-Basulto nicely illustrates how a court weighs and balances the totality of the circumstances. Edilberto Gonzalez and Jose Rodriquez-Minozo were stopped at an immigration checkpoint. Gonzalez, who claimed to be hauling oranges, was asked whether he would consent to opening the trailer attached to his truck for inspection and replied, "No problem." A drug-sniffing dog discovered cocaine in the trailer. The Fifth Circuit Court of Appeals held that Gonzalez's consent was voluntary. The agents did not display weapons or threaten Gonzalez in any fashion. He readily cooperated with the search and was not placed under arrest until the cocaine was discovered. Gonzalez was not well educated, but he clearly understood the federal agent's request. He responded to the request by stating "no problem" and unlocked and opened the trailer doors. The agent admitted that he did not inform Gonzalez of his right to refuse to consent and merely asked for permission to search the trailer. Gonzalez, according to the court, nevertheless appeared to understand the request and did not appear confused. The Fifth Circuit Court of Appeals noted that Gonzalez may well have consented because he believed that the drugs would not be found. The cocaine was well concealed in boxes, and there was limited crawl space in the trailer.

Consider some of the situations in which courts have held that the defendants did not voluntarily consent to a search. These cases illustrate that in determining the voluntariness of a consent, judges engage in a detailed analysis of the facts.

- ***Lack of consent.*** Two juveniles walked past a squad car. The police officer had previously arrested one of the young men for burglary and possession of LSD. The young man "spread his hands out" and proclaimed "I'm clean this time." The officer searched the young man and seized marijuana and amphetamines. The Massachusetts Supreme Court held that the defendant had not consented to the search. A consent must be "unequivocal and specific" (*Commonwealth v. McGrath,* 310 N.E.2d 601 [Mass. 1974]).
- ***Mental disability.*** Clarence Tye lived next door to the victim of a fatal stabbing. A police investigator and a police photographer approached Tye on his porch and, seeing blood on Tye's clothes, requested that Tye give the officer his shoes. The blood

on the shoes was traced to the victim. The Georgia Supreme Court held that Tye had not freely consented to the search. Tye had a low IQ and a predisposition to comply with requests from authority figures. The pressure on Tye to consent was increased by the fact that the interview took place next to an ongoing crime scene investigation at a time when a large number of officers were searching the neighborhood (*State v. Tye,* 580 S.E.2d 528 [Ga. 2003]).

- ***Threats to obtain a warrant.*** The police received an anonymous tip lacking in reliability that two occupants of a hotel room were armed and were selling narcotics. Three armed police officers knocked on the door and asked seventeen-year-old Kane Searcy for consent to search the room. Twenty-year-old Ruth McMorran also was in the room. One officer testified that he "invaded Searcy's space to control the situation," and Searcy then consented to the search. The police informed Searcy that he was not required to consent, and Searcy then changed his mind. The officers next stated that they would remain in the room, while a third officer obtained a search warrant. (The police had no intention of seeking a warrant, and this was a trick.) McMorran responded by consenting to the search, and the police searched for and seized narcotics. The Nevada Supreme Court held that based on the "totality of the circumstances," the consent was involuntary (*McMorran v. Nevada,* 46 P.2d 81 [Nev. 2002]).
- ***False claims of a warrant.*** Four Caucasian law enforcement officers went to the home of sixty-six-year-old Hattie Leah. She met the officers at the front door, and the officers told her that they had a warrant to search the house. Leah responded, "Go ahead." The police discovered a rifle in the kitchen that was introduced in the murder trial of Leah's grandson. The U.S. Supreme Court held that Leah's consent was invalid. The prosecution never presented a warrant in court and justified the search on the grounds of consent. The claim of a warrant "announces, in effect that the occupant has no right to resist the search. The situation is instinct [sic] with coercion. . . . Where there is coercion there cannot be consent" (*Bumper v. North Carolina,* 391 U.S. 543 [1968]).
- ***Coercion.*** Ralph Hatley was arrested for selling narcotics. The police threatened to take his child into custody unless he consented to a search of his automobiles. Hatley consented, and the police seized eight ounces of cocaine. The Ninth Circuit Court of Appeals held that the officers' "manifestly improper behavior rendered defective the signed consent form" (*United States v. Hatley,* 15 F.3d 856 [9th Cir. 1993]).
- ***Trickery.*** The police received a tip from an unnamed informant that narcotics were being sold at an apartment. Two patrolmen knocked on the door and stated that they were investigating a gas leak. The door to the apartment was opened, and the police saw a clear plastic bag containing marijuana and arrested the occupants. The court held that the police misrepresentation prevented the residents from making a fair assessment of whether to consent (*People v. Jefferson,* 350 N.Y.S.2d 3 [N.Y. S. Ct. 1973]).

The Arkansas and Washington State supreme courts have held that the protections in their state constitutions provide greater privacy protection to individuals than is provided by the Fourth Amendment to the U.S. Constitution. They have ruled that their constitutions indicate that in conducting consent searches in the home, the police are required to inform individuals of their right to refuse consent. (Hence, these are called "knock and talk" searches.) These courts have explained that the "knowing and voluntary" standard is an important safeguard for individuals' expectation of privacy in the home (*State v. Ferrier,* 960 P.2d 927 [Wash. 1968]).

The next case in the text is *Schneckloth v. Bustamonte.* In reading *Schneckloth,* ask yourself whether you agree with the U.S. Supreme Court that consent should be based on a "voluntariness test" or whether the police should be required to inform a suspect of his or her right to refuse consent. Other aspects of consent searches are discussed following the *Schneckloth* case.

Did Alcala voluntarily consent to the search?

Schneckloth v. Bustamonte, 412 U.S. 218 (1973), Stewart, J.

Issue

It is well settled under the Fourth and Fourteenth Amendments that a search conducted without a warrant issued upon probable cause is "per se unreasonable . . . subject only to a few specifically established and well-delineated exceptions." The constitutional question in the present case concerns the definition of "consent" in this Fourth and Fourteenth Amendment context. The precise question in this case, then, is what must the prosecution prove to demonstrate that a consent was "voluntarily" given. And upon that question there is a square conflict of views between the state and federal courts that have reviewed the search involved in the case before us. The Court of Appeals for the Ninth Circuit concluded that it is an essential part of the State's initial burden to prove that a person knows he has a right to refuse consent. The California courts have followed the rule that voluntariness is a question of fact to be determined from the totality of all the circumstances and that the state of a defendant's knowledge is only one factor to be taken into account in assessing the voluntariness of a consent.

Facts

While on routine patrol in Sunnyvale, California, at approximately 2:40 in the morning, police officer James Rand stopped an automobile when he observed that one headlight and its license plate light were burned out. Six men were in the vehicle. Joe Alcala and the respondent, Robert Bustamonte, were in the front seat with Joe Gonzales, the driver. Three older men were seated in the rear. When, in response to the policeman's question, Gonzales could not produce a driver's license, Officer Rand asked if any of the other five had any evidence of identification. Only Alcala produced a license, and he explained that the car was his brother's. After the six occupants had stepped out of the car at the officer's request and after two additional policemen had arrived, Officer Rand asked Alcala if he could search the car. Alcala replied, "Sure, go ahead." Prior to the search, no one was threatened with arrest, and, according to Officer Rand's uncontradicted testimony, it "was all very congenial at this time." Gonzales testified that Alcala actually helped in the search of the car, by opening the trunk and glove compartment. In Gonzales's words, "The police officer asked Joe [Alcala], he goes, 'Does the trunk open?' And Joe said, 'Yes.' He went to the car and got the keys and opened up the trunk." Wadded up under the left rear seat, the police officers found three checks that had previously been stolen from a car wash.

Reasoning

The most extensive judicial exposition of the meaning of "voluntariness" has been developed in those cases in which the Court has had to determine the "voluntariness" of a defendant's confession for purposes of the Fourteenth Amendment. . . . This Court's decisions reflect a frank recognition that the Constitution requires the sacrifice of neither security nor liberty. The Due Process Clause does not mandate that the police forgo all questioning, or that they be given carte blanche to extract what they can from a suspect.

> The ultimate test remains that which has been the only clearly established test in Anglo-American courts for two hundred years: the test of voluntariness. Is the confession the product of an essentially free and unconstrained choice by its maker? If it is, if he has willed to confess, it may be used against him. If it is not, if his will has been overborne and his capacity for self-determination critically impaired, the use of his confession offends due process. (412 U.S. 218, 226)

In determining whether a defendant's will was overborne in a particular case, the Court has assessed the totality of all the surrounding circumstances—both the characteristics of the accused and the details of the interrogation. Some of the factors taken into account have included the youth of the accused; the length of detention; the repeated and prolonged nature of the questioning; and the use of physical punishment such as the deprivation of food or sleep. In all of these cases, the Court determined the factual circumstances surrounding the confession, assessed the psychological impact on the accused, and evaluated the legal significance of how the accused reacted.

The significant fact about all of these decisions is that none of them turned on the presence or absence of a single controlling criterion; each reflected a careful scrutiny of all the surrounding circumstances. In none of them did the Court rule that the Due Process Clause required the prosecution to prove as part of its initial burden that the defendant knew he had a right to refuse to answer the questions that were put. While the state of the accused's mind, and the failure of the police to advise the accused of his rights, were certainly factors to be evaluated in assessing the "voluntariness" of an accused's responses, they were not in and of themselves determinative.

Similar considerations lead us to agree with the courts of California that the question whether a consent to a search was in fact "voluntary" or was the product of duress or coercion, express or implied, is a question of fact to be determined from the totality of all the circumstances. While knowledge of the right to refuse consent is one factor to be taken into account, the Government need not establish such knowledge as the sine qua non of an effective consent. As with police questioning, two competing concerns must be accommodated in determining the meaning of a "voluntary" consent—the legitimate need for such searches and the equally important requirement of assuring the absence of coercion.

In situations where the police have some evidence of illicit activity but lack probable cause to arrest or search, a search authorized by a valid consent may be the only means of obtaining important and reliable evidence. In the present case, for example, while the police had reason to stop the car for traffic violations, the State does not contend that there was probable cause to search the vehicle or that the search was incident to a valid arrest of any of the occupants. Yet, the search yielded tangible evidence that served as a basis for a prosecution and provided some assurance that others, wholly innocent of the crime, were not mistakenly brought to trial. And in those cases where there is probable cause to arrest or search but where the police lack a warrant, a consent search may still be valuable. If the search is conducted and proves fruitless, that in itself may convince the police that an arrest with its possible stigma and embarrassment is unnecessary, or that a far more extensive search pursuant to a warrant is not justified. In short, a search pursuant to consent may result in considerably less inconvenience for the subject of the search, and properly conducted, is a constitutionally permissible and wholly legitimate aspect of effective police activity.

But the Fourth and Fourteenth Amendments require that a consent not be coerced.... In examining all the surrounding circumstances to determine if in fact the consent to search was coerced, account must be taken of subtly coercive police questions as well as the possibly vulnerable subjective state of the person who consents. Those searches that are the product of police coercion can thus be filtered out without undermining the continuing validity of consent searches. In sum, there is no reason for us to depart, in the area of consent searches, from the traditional definition of "voluntariness."

The approach of the Court of Appeals for the Ninth Circuit... that the State must affirmatively prove that the subject of the search knew that he had a right to refuse consent, would, in practice, create serious doubt whether consent searches could continue to be conducted. There might be rare cases where it could be proved from the record that a person in fact affirmatively knew of his right to refuse—such as a case where he announced to the police that if he didn't sign the consent form, "you [police] are going to get a search warrant," or a case where by prior experience and training a person had clearly and convincingly demonstrated such knowledge. But more commonly, where there was no evidence of any coercion, explicit or implicit, the prosecution would nevertheless be unable to demonstrate that the subject of the search in fact had known of his right to refuse consent. The very object of the inquiry—the nature of a person's subjective understanding—underlines the difficulty of the prosecution's burden under the rule applied by the court of appeals in this case. Any defendant who was the subject of a search authorized solely by his consent could effectively frustrate the introduction into evidence of the fruits of that search by simply failing to testify that he in fact knew he could refuse to consent. And the near impossibility of meeting this prosecutorial burden suggests why this Court has never accepted any such litmus-paper test of voluntariness.

One alternative that would go far toward proving that the subject of a search did know he had a right to refuse consent would be to advise him of that right before eliciting his consent. That, however, is a suggestion that has been almost universally repudiated by both federal and state courts, and, we think, rightly so. For it would be thoroughly impractical to impose on the normal consent search the detailed requirements of an effective warning. Consent searches are part of the standard investigatory techniques of law enforcement agencies. They normally occur on the highway, or in a person's home or office, and under informal and unstructured conditions. The circumstances that prompt the initial request to search may develop quickly or be a logical extension of investigative police questioning. The police may seek to investigate further suspicious circumstances or to follow up leads developed in questioning persons at the scene of a crime. These situations are a far cry from the structured atmosphere of a trial where, assisted by counsel if he chooses, a defendant is informed of his trial rights. And, while surely a closer question, these situations are still immeasurably far removed from "custodial interrogation" where, in *Miranda v. Arizona* (384 U.S. 436 [1966]), we found that the Constitution required certain now familiar warnings as a prerequisite to police interrogation. Consequently, we cannot accept the position of the court of appeals in this case that proof of knowledge of the right to refuse consent is a necessary prerequisite to demonstrating a "voluntary" consent. Rather, it is only by analyzing all the circumstances of an individual consent that it can be ascertained whether in fact it was voluntary or coerced. It is this careful sifting of the unique facts and circumstances of each case that is evidenced in our prior decisions involving consent searches. Conversely, if under all the circumstances it has appeared that the consent was not given voluntarily—that it was coerced by threats or force, or granted only in submission to a claim of lawful authority—then we have found the consent invalid and the search unreasonable.

Much of what has already been said disposes of the argument that the Court's decision in the *Miranda* case requires the conclusion that knowledge of a right to refuse is an indispensable element of a valid consent. The considerations that informed the Court's holding in *Miranda* are simply inapplicable in the present case. In *Miranda* the Court found that the techniques of police questioning and the nature of custodial surroundings produce an inherently coercive situation. The Court concluded that "unless adequate protective devices are employed to dispel the compulsion inherent in custodial surroundings, no statement obtained from the defendant can truly be the product of his free choice." And at another point the Court noted that

> without proper safeguards the process of in-custody interrogation of persons suspected or accused of crime contains inherently compelling pressures which work to undermine the individual's will to resist and to compel him to speak where he would not otherwise do so freely.

In this case, there is no evidence of any inherently coercive tactics—either from the nature of the police questioning or the environment in which it took place. Indeed, since consent searches will normally occur on a person's own familiar territory, the specter of incommunicado police interrogation in some remote station house is simply inapposite. There is no reason to believe, under circumstances such as are present here, that the response to a policeman's question is presumptively coerced, and there is, therefore, no reason to reject the traditional test for determining the voluntariness of a person's response. *Miranda,* of course, did not reach investigative questioning of a person not in custody, which is most directly analogous to the situation of a consent search, and it assuredly did not indicate that such questioning ought to be deemed inherently coercive.

It is also argued that the failure to require the Government to establish knowledge as a prerequisite to a valid consent will relegate the Fourth Amendment to the special province of "the sophisticated, the knowledgeable and the privileged." We cannot agree. The traditional definition of voluntariness we accept today has always taken into account evidence of minimal schooling, low intelligence, and the lack of any effective warnings to a person of his rights, and the voluntariness of any statement taken under those conditions has been carefully scrutinized to determine whether it was in fact voluntarily given.

Holding

Our decision today is a narrow one. We hold only that when the subject of a search is not in custody and the State attempts to justify a search on the basis of his consent, the Fourth and Fourteenth Amendments require that the State demonstrate that the consent was in fact voluntarily given and not the result of duress or coercion, express or implied. Voluntariness is a question of fact to be determined from all the circumstances, and while the subject's knowledge of a right to refuse is a factor to be taken into account, the prosecution is not required to demonstrate such knowledge as a prerequisite to establishing a voluntary consent. Because the California court followed these principles in affirming the respondent's conviction, and because the Court of Appeals for the Ninth Circuit in remanding for an evidentiary hearing required more, its judgment must be reversed.

Dissenting, *Douglas, J.*

I agree with the court of appeals that "verbal assent" to a search is not enough, that the fact that consent was given to the search does not imply that the suspect knew that the alternative of a refusal existed. As that court stated, "Under many circumstances a reasonable person might read an officer's 'May I' as the courteous expression of a demand backed by force of law."

Dissenting, *Marshall, J.*

Several years ago, Mr. Justice Stewart reminded us that "the Constitution guarantees . . . a society of free choice. Such a society presupposes the capacity of its members to choose. . . ." I would have thought that the capacity to choose necessarily depends upon knowledge that there is a choice to be made. But today the Court reaches the curious result that one can choose to relinquish a constitutional right—the right to be free of unreasonable searches—without knowing that he has the alternative of refusing to accede to a police request to search. I cannot agree, and therefore dissent.

I believe that the Court misstates the true issue in this case. That issue is not, as the Court suggests, whether the police overbore Alcala's will in eliciting his consent, but rather, whether a simple statement of assent to search, without more, should be sufficient to permit the police to search and thus act as a relinquishment of Alcala's constitutional right to exclude the police. This Court has always scrutinized with great care claims that a person has forgone the opportunity to assert constitutional rights. I see no reason to give the claim that a person consented to a search any less rigorous scrutiny. Every case in this Court involving this kind of search has heretofore spoken of consent as a waiver.

If consent to search means that a person has chosen to forgo his right to exclude the police from the place they seek to search, it follows that his consent cannot be considered a meaningful choice unless he knew that he could in fact exclude the police. The Court appears, however, to reject even the modest proposition that, if the subject of a search convinces the trier of fact that he did not know of his right to refuse assent to a police request for permission to search, the search must be held unconstitutional. For it says only that "knowledge of the right to refuse consent is one factor to be taken into account." I find this incomprehensible. I can think of no other situation in which we would say that a person agreed to some course of action if he convinced us that he did not know that there was some other course he might have pursued. I would therefore hold, at a minimum, that the prosecution may not rely on a purported consent to search if the subject of the search did not know that he could refuse to give consent.

The burden on the prosecutor would disappear, of course, if the police, at the time they requested consent to search, also told the subject that he had a right to refuse consent and that his decision to refuse would be respected. The Court's assertions to the contrary notwithstanding, there is nothing impractical about this method of satisfying the prosecution's burden of proof. It must be emphasized that the decision about informing the subject of his rights would lie with the officers seeking consent. If they believed that providing such information would impede their investigation, they might simply ask for consent, taking the risk that at some later date the prosecutor would be unable to prove that the subject knew of his rights or that some other basis for the search existed.

The Court contends that if an officer paused to inform the subject of his rights, the informality of the exchange would be destroyed. I doubt that a simple statement by an officer of an individual's right to refuse consent would do much to alter the informality of the exchange, except to alert the subject to a fact that he surely is entitled to know. (It is not without significance that for many years the agents of the Federal Bureau of Investigation have routinely informed subjects of their right to refuse consent, when they request consent to search.) The reported cases in which the police have informed subjects of their right to refuse consent show, also, that the information can be given without disrupting the casual flow of events. What evidence there is, then, rather strongly suggests that nothing disastrous would happen if the police, before requesting consent, informed the subject that he had a right to refuse consent and that his refusal would be respected.

I must conclude, with some reluctance, that when the Court speaks of practicality, what it really is talking of is the continued ability of the police to capitalize on the ignorance of citizens so as to accomplish by subterfuge what they could not achieve by relying only on the knowing relinquishment of constitutional rights. Of course it would be "practical" for the police to ignore the commands of the Fourth Amendment, if by practicality we mean that more criminals will be apprehended, even though the constitutional rights of innocent people also go by the board. But such a practical advantage is achieved only at the cost of permitting the police to disregard the limitations that the Constitution places on their behavior, a cost that a constitutional democracy cannot long absorb.

I find nothing in the opinion of the Court to dispel my belief that, in such a case, as the Court of Appeals for the Ninth Circuit said, "Under many circumstances a reasonable person might read an officer's 'May I' as the courteous expression of a demand backed by force of law." Consent is ordinarily given as acquiescence in an implicit claim of authority to search. Permitting searches in such circumstances, without any assurance at all that the subject of the search knew that, by his consent, he was relinquishing his constitutional rights, is something that I cannot believe is sanctioned by the Constitution.

The holding today confines the protection of the Fourth Amendment against searches conducted without probable cause to the sophisticated, the knowledgeable, and, I might add, the few. In the final analysis, the Court now sanctions a game of blind man's bluff, in which the police always have the upper hand, for the sake of nothing more than the convenience of the police. But the guarantees of the Fourth Amendment were never intended to shrink before such an ephemeral and changeable interest. The framers of the Fourth Amendment struck the balance against this sort of convenience and in favor of certain basic civil rights. It is not for this Court to restrike that balance because of its own views of the needs of law enforcement officers. I fear that that is the effect of the Court's decision today.

Questions for Discussion

1. What is the legal test for a consent search under the Fourth Amendment?
2. Would the police have had a legal basis for searching the automobile and seizing the stolen checks absent consent? As a judge, would you rule that it is lawful for a police officer to stop a motorist for a minor traffic violation like a burned-out light and then to conduct a consent search for evidence of a more serious crime?
3. Should the Supreme Court require the police to inform an individual of his or her right to refuse consent? Are the critics correct that the decision in *Schneckloth* permits the police to take advantage of a citizen's "ignorance" of the right to refuse consent? Do most interactions between the police and public involve a measure of coercion that intimidates individuals into consenting to the search?
4. Could the criminal justice system function as effectively without consent searches?
5. ***Problems in policing.*** What are some points that a police officer should keep in mind in conducting a consent search?

Cases and Comments

Arrests and Consent Searches. In *United States v. Watson,* the U.S. Supreme Court held that the *Schneckloth* voluntariness test for consent searches applies to individuals under arrest who are in police custody. Watson (discussed in Chapter 5) was arrested by postal inspectors for offenses involving stolen credit cards. A search incident to arrest of Watson did not uncover any stolen credit cards and Watson consented to a search of his automobile. The Supreme Court held that Watson's consent was voluntary and determined that neither is there evidence of an "act or threat of force against Watson" nor is there evidence of promises made to Watson or other "more subtle forms of coercion that might flaw his judgment." Watson was in police custody, but custody "alone" is not "enough in itself" to conclude that there is a coerced consent. The Court stressed that Watson consented while on a public street rather than in a police station. It is true that there is no indication that Watson was aware that he could withhold consent and while this "may be a factor in the overall judgment, [this] is not to be given controlling significance." He was not a "newcomer to the law, mentally deficient, or unable in the face of a custodial arrest to exercise a free choice." Watson also was given the *Miranda* warnings, and was told that whatever was found in his car could be used against him. The Supreme Court concluded that "in these circumstances, to hold that illegal coercion is made out from the fact of arrest and the failure to inform the arrestee that he could withhold consent would be inconsistent with the holding in *Schneckloth* establishing the 'voluntariness standard'" (*United States v. Watson,* 423 U.S. 411 [1976]). The "totality of the circumstances" approach has been extended by lower federal and state supreme courts to consent searches by individuals held in custody in the police station (*United States v. Smith,* 543 F.2d 1141 [5th Cir. 1976]).

The U.S. Supreme Court next addressed arrests and consent searches in *Ohio v. Robinette*. Robinette was clocked at almost twenty-five miles over the speed limit. Deputy Roger Newsome examined Robinette's driver's license and a check of the computerized records indicated that Robinette had no previous traffic violations. Newsome then asked Robinette to exit his vehicle, turned on his mounted video camera, issued a verbal warning to Robinette, and returned Robinette's license. Newsome then asked, "One question before you get gone; are you carrying... any weapons of any kind, drugs, anything like that [in your car]?" Robinette consented to a search of his motor vehicle and Newsome seized illegal narcotics that were in the auto. Newsome had used this same technique for searching automobiles 786 times in a one-year period. Robinette claimed that Newsome had unlawfully detained him after processing the driving offense and that he had been held without probable cause and that the consent search therefore was the product of an unconstitutional seizure. Robinette argued that he should have been told by Newsome that he was free to leave following the return of Robinette's license. The Supreme Court noted that in *Schneckloth* it had held that it would be "impractical to impose on the normal consent search the detailed requirements of an effective warning... [and] so too would it be unrealistic to require police officers to always inform detainees that they are free to go before a consent to search may be deemed voluntary." The Court in *Robinette* held that the question is whether a motorist would feel free to leave and that whether an individual would feel free to leave is a question of fact. In this instance, Robinette's license had been returned and a reasonable person would feel free to leave (*Ohio v. Robinette,* 519 U.S. 33 [1996]). Do you agree that Robinette was aware that he was free to leave?

6.5 YOU DECIDE

Shelby County Sheriff Department officers were told by an informant that a fugitive they were interested in was at a Memphis, Tennessee, address. Pursuant to this tip, officers went to the home of James Ivy, who admitted them. On entering the home, an officer found a small quantity of cocaine, and other officers then were summoned. The officers obtained Ivy's consent to search the house. In a bedroom, they found and seized crack cocaine in a dresser drawer and over $15,000 in cash in a nightstand. They seized a set of scales in another bedroom, and in the kitchen they found several guns in a drawer and a cooking tube with cocaine residue.

The Sixth Circuit Court of Appeals found that Ivy refused to sign the form for roughly ninety minutes before consenting to sign it. Ivy asked what would occur in the event that he refused to consent to a search. Sergeant Jackie Setliff told him that a "search warrant would be sought; that all adults in the house (including Tina Jones) would be arrested and that, since there would be no adults to take care of the child who was also in the house, the child would be taken to the Department of Human Services for care." The police handcuffed Jones to the kitchen table, took Jones's child from her, and only returned the child after Ivy signed the consent form.

Was this a voluntary consent search? See *United States v. Ivy,* 165 F.3d 397 (6th Cir. 1998).

You can learn what the court decided by referring to the study site, http://www.sagepub.com/lippmancp.

The Scope of a Consent Search

How broad is a consent search? May an officer search an entire automobile or home? The U.S. Supreme Court provided a partial answer in *Florida v. Jimeno*. Officer Frank Trujillo overheard Jimeno negotiating what appeared to be a drug transaction, followed Jimeno's car, and pulled Jimeno over for making an illegal turn. Officer Trujillo informed Jimeno that he had grounds to believe that Jimeno was transporting narcotics and asked for permission to search Jimeno's automobile. Jimeno stated that he had nothing to hide and gave Trujillo permission to search the car. Trujillo spotted and opened a brown paper bag on the floorboard and found a kilogram of cocaine in it. Jimeno challenged the search on the grounds that he had not consented to Trujillo opening containers in the auto (*Florida v. Jimeno,* 500 U.S. 248 [1990]).

The Supreme Court held that the standard for "measuring the scope of a suspect's consent under the Fourth Amendment is that of 'objective' reasonableness—what would the typical reasonable person have understood by the exchange between the officer and the suspect?" The Court recognized that Jimeno may not have intended to consent to a search of the brown paper bag, but concluded that it was reasonable for Trujillo to conclude that Jimeno's consent to a search of the automobile for unlawful narcotics included authorization to open bags and containers. In other words, Trujillo reasonably concluded that Jimeno's consent to a search of his automobile for narcotics included consent to open bags and containers (251).

A search that goes beyond the scope of the consent is unlawful. In the case at issue in *United States v. Dichiarinte,* Anthony Dichiarinte was arrested for the sale of narcotics. In response to a question of whether he had narcotics in his home, Dichiarinte responded that "I have never seen narcotics. You guys come over to the house and look, you are welcome to." As the search progressed, one of the agents began to examine and seize various financial records that later proved important in convicting Dichiarinte for evading federal taxes by failing to disclose his drug-related income. The Seventh Circuit Court of Appeals stated that a "consent search is reasonable only if kept within the bounds of the actual consent. . . . The defendant's consent sets the parameters of the agents' conduct at that which would reasonably be necessary to determine whether he had narcotics in his home." In this instance, federal agents read through Dichiarinte's private papers, and this "constituted a greater intrusion into a defendant's privacy than he had authorized" (*United States v. Dichiarinte,* 445 F.2d 126, 131 [7th Cir. 1971]).

In *Dichiarinte,* the agents went beyond the scope of Anthony Dichiarinte's consent. The reasonable scope of a suspect's consent, however, in some cases is not completely clear. In the incident at issue in *United States v. Rodney,* Rodney was approached by a plainclothes police officer, Detective Beard, in a Washington, D.C., bus station and asked if he was carrying drugs. Rodney denied carrying drugs, and when asked for his consent to a body search, he replied "sure" and raised his hands above his head. Detective Beard "placed his hands on Rodney's ankles and, in one sweeping motion, ran them up through the inside of Rodney's legs. As he passed over the crotch area, Beard felt small, rock-like objects." Rodney was placed under arrest, and Beard unzipped Rodney's pants and seized cocaine.

The United States Court of Appeals for the District of Columbia relied on *Jimeno* and held that "a request to conduct a body search for drugs reasonably includes a request to conduct some search of [the crotch] area." Indeed, Sergeant Beard testified that narcotics are seized from the crotch area in roughly seventy-five percent of the cases involving body searches for drugs (*United States v. Rodney,* 956 F.2d 295 [D.C. Cir. 1992]). The court in *Rodney* did indicate that a separate consent would be required to search an individual's body cavities. Other courts have held that separate consent should be required to conduct a search of an individual's genital area. The Eleventh Circuit Court of Appeals, in *United States v. Blake,* held that "it cannot be said that a reasonable individual would understand that a search of one's person would entail [an] officer touching his or her genitals" (*United States v. Blake,* 888 F.2d 795, 800–801 [11th Cir. 1989]). What is your view?

In summary, the Supreme Court has held that consent should be interpreted in accordance with objective reasonableness—what a reasonable person would understand is the extent of the individual's consent. Another challenge confronting the Supreme Court in regard to consent search is the question of whether an individual may withdraw his or her consent.

You can find United States v. Rodney *on the study site, http://www.sagepub.com/lippmancp.*

Withdrawal of Consent

In *Dichiarinte,* Dichiarinte saw the federal agents going through his papers and complained to the agents that he had consented to a search for narcotics and had not consented to a search of his personal financial records. The question is whether the federal agents would have been required to stop the entire search had Dichiarinte withdrawn his consent to the search of his home. The rule is that an individual can withdraw his or her consent or limit the scope of the consent search at any time. Keep in mind that a withdrawal of consent does not affect the items already seized by the police. As noted in *United States v. Lattimore,* "a consent to search is not irrevocable, and thus if a person effectively revokes . . . consent prior to the time that the search is complete, the police may not thereafter search in reliance upon the earlier consent" (*United States v. Lattimore,* 87 F.3d 647, 651 [4th Cir. 1996]).

In general, courts require a clear, unambiguous, and unequivocal act or statement of withdrawal of consent. Individuals who verbally consent and then refuse to sign a consent form are sending a mixed message, and courts have held that such individuals have not unequivocally withdrawn their consent (*United States v. Thompson,* 876 F.2d 1381, 1384 [8th Cir. 1989]). In the incident at issue in *United States v. Fuentes,* federal narcotics agents stopped Juan Fuentes, whom the police suspected of drug activity, as he boarded a flight. Fuentes was observed continually fingering a lump in his right front pants pocket that appeared to be roughly the size of a split softball. Fuentes consented to a search despite the fact that he was informed that he had the right to refuse consent. The officer reached inside Fuentes's right front pocket and felt "a thick rubbery bulge" that the officer believed to be a package of cocaine. As the officer reached into Fuentes's pocket and asked "What's this," Fuentes shouted "No, wait." He tried to push one officer away with one arm and pull his other arm free of the second officer. The Ninth Circuit Court of Appeals affirmed the district court judge's decision that Fuentes had revoked his consent before the officer pulled the cocaine out of Fuentes's pocket and before the officer concluded that it was cocaine.

At what point would the court have determined that it was too late for Fuentes to have withdrawn his consent? (*United States v. Fuentes,* 105 F.3d 487, 489 [9th Cir. 1996]).

Third Party Consent

The last issue regarding consent searches is the complicated area of third party consent. As you read *Schneckloth v. Bustamonte,* you may have asked yourself how Joe Alcala could have had the authority to consent to a police search of his brother's auto. Who in addition to the owner may consent to a search of an automobile? What about a passenger or an individual who has borrowed the car? May consent be given by the mechanic who is repairing the vehicle or by the tow truck driver who is hauling the car to the service station? What of the garage attendant where the automobile is parked? May a car thief who has stolen the car consent to a search of the car? As you can see, the issue of **third party consent** is more complicated than you might have imagined, and the U.S. Supreme Court has attempted to clarify the requirements of consent searches in several decisions.

In *Frazier v. Cupp,* the Supreme Court held that Frazier, by leaving his duffel bag at his cousin Rawls's home and allowing Rawls to jointly use the bag, had "assumed the risk that Rawls would allow someone else [the police] to look inside." Under these circumstances, there was no doubt that Rawls as a joint user of the bag had authority to consent to the search (*Frazier v. Cupp,* 394 U.S. 731, 740 [1969]).

In 1990, in *Illinois v. Rodriguez,* the Supreme Court established the legal standard for third party consent searches. An individual may consent who possesses *common authority* over the premises to be searched. A consent also is valid in those instances in which the police reasonably rely on consent from an individual who, in fact, lacks common authority. In brief, as outlined below, the police may rely on individuals exercising *actual authority* as well as *apparent authority.*

- ***Common authority third party consent***. This requires "mutual use of the property by persons having joint access or control for most purposes." The important point is not ownership. Think about this as frequent and free use of the property. A roommate may consent to a search of all areas of a house that he or she shares with the other coinhabitants. The roommate would not be in a position to consent to a search of his or her coinhabitants' individual bedrooms.
- ***Apparent authority third party consent***. In this instance, police officers reasonably (but mistakenly) believe that a person has common authority. For example, the police may mistakenly but reasonably conclude, based on a roommate's statements, that he or she shares use of an automobile parked in the driveway with the owner and shares possession of a key to the car.

Keep in mind that there are some relationships in which courts have held that individuals do not have common authority as a matter of law and that it is unreasonable for the police to rely on third party consent. The approach of courts to various relationships is outlined in Chart 6.3.

Chart 6.3 Authority for Third Party Consent

Relationship	*Authority to Consent*
Wife–Husband	Either spouse may consent to a search of the home other than those areas under the exclusive control of the other spouse.
Parent–Child	A parent may consent to a search of those areas under the control of a juvenile, such as the juvenile's bedroom. A juvenile may not consent to a search of the home.
Motel Clerk	A motel clerk may not consent to the search of a room that has been rented out.
Landlord–Tenant	A landlord may not consent to the search of a tenant's apartment.
Employer–Employee	An employer may give consent to a search of all areas other than those with a high expectation of privacy, such as a locked desk drawer in an office.
Garage Manager–Customer	An individual who parks his or her car in a garage and leaves the key with the attendant assumes the risk that consent will be given to search the car.
Roommates	Roommates may consent to searches of areas that they share with one another.

In reading *Illinois v. Rodriguez,* ask yourself why the U.S. Supreme Court held that Gail Fischer lacked common authority to consent to police entry into Rodriguez's apartment. Was it nevertheless reasonable for the police to rely on her apparent authority to consent to a search of "our apartment"? The Hawaii and Montana state supreme courts have rejected the doctrine of apparent authority. These courts have held that a search based on the consent of an individual whom the police mistakenly but reasonably believe possesses common authority is a violation of their state constitutions' prohibition on unreasonable searches and seizures. As the Hawaii Supreme Court remarked, "An invasion of privacy is no less of an 'invasion' if the government officials are 'reasonable' in their mistaken belief that the third party possesses the authority to consent" (*State v. Lopez,* 896 P.2d 889, 902 [Haw. 1995]; *State v. McLess,* 994 P.2d 683 [Mont. 2000]). Do you believe that courts should follow the principle of apparent authority?

Did the police reasonably believe that Gail Fischer possessed authority to consent to their entry of Edgar Rodriguez's apartment?

Illinois v. Rodriguez, 497 U.S. 177 (1990), Scalia, J.

Issue

A warrantless entry and search by law enforcement officers does not violate the Fourth Amendment's proscription of "unreasonable searches and seizures" if the officers have obtained the consent of a third party who possesses common authority over the premises. The present case presents [the] issue . . . whether a warrantless entry is valid when based upon the consent of a third party whom the police, at the time of the entry, reasonably believe to possess common authority over the premises, but who in fact does not possess such authority.

Facts

On July 26, 1985, police were summoned to the residence of Dorothy Jackson on South Wolcott in Chicago. They were met by Ms. Jackson's daughter, Gail Fischer, who showed signs of a severe beating. She told the officers that she had been assaulted by respondent Edward Rodriguez earlier that day in an apartment on South California Avenue. Fischer stated that Rodriguez was then asleep in the apartment, and she consented to travel there with the police in order to unlock the door with her key so that the officers could enter and arrest him. During this conversation, Fischer several times referred to the apartment on South California as "our" apartment and said that she had clothes and furniture there. It is unclear whether she indicated that she currently lived at the apartment or only that she used to live there.

The police officers drove to the apartment on South California, accompanied by Fischer. They did not obtain an arrest warrant for Rodriguez, nor did they seek a search warrant for the apartment. At the apartment, Fischer unlocked the door with her key and gave the officers permission to enter. They moved through the door into the living room, where they observed in plain view drug paraphernalia and containers filled with white powder that they believed (correctly, as later analysis showed) to be cocaine. They proceeded to the bedroom, where they found Rodriguez asleep and discovered additional containers of white powder in two open attaché cases. The officers arrested Rodriguez and seized the drugs and related paraphernalia.

Rodriguez was charged with possession of a controlled substance with intent to deliver. He moved to suppress all evidence seized at the time of his arrest, claiming that Fischer had vacated the apartment several weeks earlier and had no authority to consent to the entry. The Cook County Circuit Court granted the motion, holding that at the time she consented to the entry, Fischer did not have common authority over the apartment. The court concluded that Fischer was not a "usual resident" but rather an "infrequent visitor" at the apartment on South California, based upon its findings that Fischer's name was not on the lease, that she did not contribute to the rent, that she was not allowed to invite others to the apartment on her own, that she did not have access to the apartment when respondent was away, and that she had moved some of her possessions from the apartment. The Appellate Court of Illinois affirmed the circuit court in all respects. The Illinois Supreme Court denied the State's petition for leave to appeal.

Reasoning

The Fourth Amendment generally prohibits the warrantless entry of a person's home, whether to make an arrest or to search for specific objects. The prohibition does not apply, however, to situations in which voluntary consent has been obtained, either from the individual whose property is searched or from a third party who possesses common authority over the premises. The State of Illinois contends that that exception applies in the present case.

"Common authority" rests "on mutual use of the property by persons generally having joint access or control for most purposes. . . ." The burden of establishing that common authority exists rests upon the State. On the basis of this record, it is clear that burden was not sustained. The evidence showed that although Fischer, with her two small children, had lived with Rodriguez beginning in December 1984, she had moved out on July 1, 1985, almost a month before the search at issue here, and had gone to live with her mother. She took her and her children's clothing with her, though she left behind some furniture and household effects. During the period after July 1, she sometimes spent the night at Rodriguez's apartment, but never invited her friends there, and never went there herself when he was not home. Her name was not on the lease, nor did she contribute to the rent. She had a key to the apartment, which she said at trial she had taken without Rodriguez's knowledge (though she testified at the preliminary hearing that Rodriguez had given her the key). On these facts the State has not established that, with respect to the South California apartment, Fischer had "joint access or control for most purposes." To the contrary, the appellate court's determination of no common authority over the apartment was obviously correct.

The State contends that, even if Fischer did not in fact have authority to give consent, it suffices to validate the entry that the law enforcement officers reasonably believed she did. Before reaching the merits of that contention, we must consider a jurisdictional objection: that the decision below rests on an adequate and independent state ground. Respondent asserts that the Illinois constitution provides greater protection than is afforded under the Fourth Amendment and that the appellate court relied upon this when it determined that a reasonable belief by the police officers was insufficient.

The fundamental objective that alone validates all unconsented government searches is, of course, the seizure of persons who have committed or are about to commit crimes, or of evidence related to crimes. But "reasonableness," with respect to this necessary element, does not demand that the Government be factually correct in its assessment that that is what a search will produce. In order to satisfy the "reasonableness" requirement of the Fourth Amendment,...what is generally demanded of the many factual determinations that must regularly be made by agents of the Government—whether the magistrate issuing a warrant, the police officer executing a warrant, or the police officer conducting a search or seizure under one of the exceptions to the warrant requirement—is not that they always be correct but that they always be reasonable. As we put it in *Brinegar v. United States* (338 U.S. 160, 176 [1949]),

> Because many situations which confront officers in the course of executing their duties are more or less ambiguous, room must be allowed for some mistakes on their part. But the mistakes must be those of reasonable men, acting on facts leading sensibly to their conclusions of probability.

We see no reason to depart from this general rule with respect to facts bearing upon the authority to consent to a search.... The Constitution is no more violated when officers enter without a warrant because they reasonably (though erroneously) believe that the person who has consented to their entry is a resident of the premises than it is violated when they enter without a warrant because they reasonably (though erroneously) believe they are in pursuit of a violent felon who is about to escape.

Holding

What we hold today does not suggest that law enforcement officers may always accept a person's invitation to enter premises. Even when the invitation is accompanied by an explicit assertion that the person lives there, the surrounding circumstances could conceivably be such that a reasonable person would doubt its truth and not act upon it without further inquiry. As with other factual determinations bearing upon search and seizure, determination of consent to enter must "be judged against an objective standard: Would the facts available to the officer at the moment... 'warrant a man of reasonable caution in the belief' that the consenting party had authority over the premises? If not, then warrantless entry without further inquiry is unlawful, unless authority actually exists. But if so, the search is valid. In the present case, the appellate court found it unnecessary to determine whether the officers reasonably believed that Fischer had the authority to consent, because it ruled as a matter of law that a reasonable belief could not validate the entry. Since we find that ruling to be in error, we remand for consideration of that question. The judgment of the Illinois Appellate Court is reversed, and the case is remanded for further proceedings not inconsistent with this opinion.

Dissenting, *Marshall, J.,* with *Brennan, J.,* and *Stevens, J.*

Our cases demonstrate that third party consent searches are free from constitutional challenge only to the extent that they rest on consent by a party empowered to do so. The majority's conclusion to the contrary ignores the legitimate expectations of privacy on which individuals are entitled to rely. That a person who allows another joint access to his property thereby limits his expectation of privacy does not justify trampling the rights of a person who has not similarly relinquished any of his privacy expectation.

Instead of judging the validity of consent searches, as we have in the past, based on whether a defendant has in fact limited his expectation of privacy, the Court today carves out an additional exception to the warrant requirement for third party consent searches without pausing to consider whether "'the exigencies of the situation' make the needs of law enforcement so compelling that the warrantless search is objectively reasonable under the Fourth Amendment." Where this free-floating creation of "reasonable" exceptions to the warrant requirement will end, now that the Court has departed from the balancing approach that has long been part of our Fourth Amendment jurisprudence, is unclear. But by allowing a person to be subjected to a warrantless search in his home without his consent and without exigency, the majority has taken away some of the liberty that the Fourth Amendment was designed to protect.

Questions for Discussion

1. What is the holding in *Rodriguez*?
2. Why did the Supreme Court hold that Gail Fischer lacked "common access and authority" to the apartment? What facts are crucial in the court's determination that it was reasonable for the police to conclude that Fischer had "common access and authority"?
3. Do you agree with Justice Marshall's criticism of the judgment in *Rodriguez*?
4. Why is the lawfulness of the police entry into Rodriguez's apartment significant in determining the lawfulness of the police seizure of the narcotics?
5. ***Problems in policing.*** List questions that an officer should ask an individual who claims third party authority to consent to the police to enter a house.

Third Party Consent and Co-Occupants

In *United States v. Matlock,* the U.S. Supreme Court held that a co-occupant of a house has the right to consent to a search. Matlock was arrested in the front yard of a house that he lived in along with Gayle Graff, her three-year-old son, her mother, and various members of Graff's extended family. Gayle consented to a search of the bedroom that she "jointly occupied" with Matlock, and the police discovered cash in a diaper bag. The Court upheld the search on the grounds that Gayle exercised "common authority" over the bedroom. Matlock had "assumed the risk" that Gayle might permit the search of the areas that they shared in the home (*United States v. Matlock,* 415 U.S. 164, 171 [1974]).

What would have been the judgment of the U.S. Supreme Court if Matlock had refused consent and Graff had disagreed and had given consent? In 2006, in *Georgia v. Randolph,* the U.S. Supreme Court addressed the issue of whether the police may rely on the consent of one spouse to search a home when the other spouse refuses to consent.

May the police rely on the consent of one spouse when the other spouse refuses to consent to the search?

Georgia v. Randolph, 547 U.S. 103 (2006), Souter, J.

Issue

The Fourth Amendment recognizes a valid warrantless entry and search of premises when police obtain the voluntary consent of an occupant who shares, or is reasonably believed to share, authority over the area in common with a co-occupant who later objects to the use of evidence so obtained. The question here is whether such an evidentiary seizure is likewise lawful with the permission of one occupant when the other, who later seeks to suppress the evidence, is present at the scene and expressly refuses to consent. We hold that, in the circumstances here at issue, a physically present co-occupant's stated refusal to permit entry prevails, rendering the warrantless search unreasonable and invalid as to him.

Facts

Respondent Scott Randolph and his wife, Janet, separated in late May 2001, when she left the marital residence in Americus, Georgia, and went to stay with her parents in Canada, taking their son and some belongings. In July, she returned to the Americus house with the child, though the record does not reveal whether her object was reconciliation or retrieval of remaining possessions.

On the morning of July 6, she complained to the police that after a domestic dispute her husband took their son away, and when officers reached the house, she told them that her husband was a cocaine user whose habit had caused financial troubles. She mentioned the marital problems and said that she and their son had only recently returned after a stay of several weeks with her parents. Shortly after the police arrived, Scott Randolph returned and explained that he had removed the child to a neighbor's house out of concern that his wife might take the boy out of the country again; he denied cocaine use, and countered that it was in fact his wife who abused drugs and alcohol.

One of the officers, Sergeant Murray, went with Janet Randolph to reclaim the child, and when they returned she not only renewed her complaints about her husband's drug use but also volunteered that there were "items of drug evidence" in the house. Sergeant Murray asked Scott Randolph for permission to search the house, which he unequivocally refused.

The sergeant turned to Janet Randolph for consent to search, which she readily gave. She led the officer upstairs to a bedroom that she identified as Scott's, where the sergeant noticed a section of a drinking straw with a powdery residue he suspected was cocaine. He then left the house to get an evidence bag from his car and to call the district attorney's office, which instructed him to stop the search and apply for a warrant. When Sergeant Murray returned to the house, Janet Randolph withdrew her consent. The police took the straw to the police station, along with the Randolphs. After getting a search warrant, they returned to the house and seized further evidence of drug use, on the basis of which Scott Randolph was indicted for possession of cocaine.

He moved to suppress the evidence as the product of a warrantless search of his house unauthorized by his wife's consent over his express refusal. The trial court denied the motion, ruling that Janet Randolph had common authority to consent to the search.

The Court of Appeals of Georgia reversed and was itself sustained by the state supreme court, principally on the ground that "the consent to conduct a warrantless search of a residence given by one occupant is not valid in the face of the refusal of another occupant."

Reasoning

The constant element in assessing Fourth Amendment reasonableness in consent cases . . . is the great significance given to widely shared social expectations, which are . . . influenced by the law of property, but not controlled by its rules. The reasonableness of . . . a [third party] consent search is in significant part a function of commonly held understanding about the authority that coinhabitants may exercise in ways that affect each other's interest. . . . Although we have not dealt directly with the reasonableness of police entry in reliance on consent by one occupant subject to immediate challenge by another, we took a step toward the issue in an earlier case dealing with the Fourth Amendment rights of a social guest arrested at premises the police entered without a warrant and without the benefit of any exception to the warrant requirement. In *Minnesota v. Olson* (495 U.S. 91 [1990]), we held that overnight houseguests have a legitimate expectation of privacy in their temporary quarters, because "it is unlikely that [the host] will admit someone who wants to see or meet with the guest over the objection of the guest." If that customary expectation of courtesy or deference is a foundation of Fourth Amendment rights of a houseguest, it presumably should follow that an inhabitant of shared premises may claim at least as much, and it turns out that the coinhabitant naturally has an even stronger claim.

To begin with, it is fair to say that a caller standing at the door of shared premises would have no confidence that one occupant's invitation was a sufficiently good reason to enter when a fellow tenant stood there saying, "Stay out." Without some very good reason, no sensible person would go inside under those conditions. Fear for the safety of the occupant issuing the invitation, or of someone else inside, would be thought to justify entry, but the justification then would be the personal risk or the threats to life or limb, not the disputed invitation.

The visitor's reticence without some such good reason would show not timidity but a realization that when people living together disagree over the use of their common quarters, a resolution must come through voluntary accommodation, not by appeals to authority. Unless the people living together fall within some recognized hierarchy, like a household of parent and child or barracks housing military personnel of different grades, there is no societal understanding of superior and inferior, a fact reflected in a standard formulation of domestic property law, that "each cotenant . . . has the right to use and enjoy the entire property as if he or she were the sole owner, limited only by the same right in the other cotenants." The want of any recognized superior authority among disagreeing tenants is also reflected in the law's response when the disagreements cannot be resolved. The law does not ask who has the better side of the conflict; it simply provides a right to any cotenant, even the most unreasonable, to obtain a decree partitioning the property (when the relationship is one of co-ownership) and terminating the relationship. And while a decree of partition is not the answer to disagreement among rental tenants, this situation resembles co-ownership in lacking the benefit of any understanding that one or the other rental cotenant has a superior claim to control the use of the quarters they occupy together. In sum, there is no common understanding that one cotenant generally has a right or authority to prevail over the express wishes of another, whether the issue is the color of the curtains or invitations to outsiders.

Since the cotenant wishing to open the door to a third party has no recognized authority in law or social practice to prevail over a present and objecting cotenant, his disputed invitation, without more, gives a police officer no better claim to reasonableness in entering than the officer would have in the absence of any consent at all. Accordingly, in the balancing of competing individual and governmental interests entailed by the bar to unreasonable searches, the cooperative occupant's invitation adds nothing to the Government's side to counter the force of an objecting individual's claim to security against the Government's intrusion into his dwelling place. Since we hold to the "centuries-old principle of respect for the privacy of the home," it is beyond dispute that the home is entitled to special protection as the center of the private lives of our people. We have, after all, lived our whole national history with an understanding of "the ancient adage that a man's home is his castle [to the point that] the poorest man may in his cottage bid defiance to all the forces of the Crown."

Disputed permission is thus no match for this central value of the Fourth Amendment, and the State's other countervailing claims do not add up to outweigh it. Yes, we recognize the consenting tenant's interest as a citizen in bringing criminal activity to light. ("It is no part of the policy underlying the Fourth . . . Amendment to discourage citizens from aiding to the utmost of their ability in the apprehension of criminals.") And we understand a cotenant's legitimate self-interest in siding with the police to deflect suspicion raised by sharing quarters with a criminal. ("The risk of being convicted of possession of drugs one knows are present and has tried to get the other occupant to remove is by no means insignificant." Evidence obtained pursuant to a consent search "may insure that a wholly innocent person is not wrongly charged with a criminal offense.")

But society can often have the benefit of these interests without relying on a theory of consent that ignores an inhabitant's refusal to allow a warrantless search. The cotenant acting on his own initiative may be able to deliver evidence to the police (suspect's wife retrieved his guns from the couple's house and turned them over to the police) and can tell the police what he knows for use of such information before a magistrate in getting a warrant. The reliance on a cotenant's information instead of disputed consent accords with the law's general partiality toward

> police action taken under a warrant [as against] searches and seizures without one. . . . The informed and deliberate determinations of magistrates empowered to issue warrants as to

> what searches and seizures are permissible under the Constitution are to be preferred over the hurried action of officers.

Nor should this established policy of Fourth Amendment law be undermined by the principal dissent's claim that it shields spousal abusers and other violent cotenants who will refuse to allow the police to enter a dwelling when their victims ask the police for help. It is not that the dissent exaggerates violence in the home; we recognize that domestic abuse is a serious problem in the United States.... But this case has no bearing on the capacity of the police to protect domestic victims.

The dissent's argument rests on the failure to distinguish two different issues: when the police may enter without committing a trespass and when the police may enter to search for evidence. No question has been raised, or reasonably could be, about the authority of the police to enter a dwelling to protect a resident from domestic violence; so long as they have good reason to believe such a threat exists, it would be silly to suggest that the police would commit a tort by entering, say, to give a complaining tenant the opportunity to collect belongings and get out safely, or to determine whether violence (or threat of violence) has just occurred or is about to (or soon will) occur, however much a spouse or other cotenant objected. (And since the police would then be lawfully in the premises, there is no question that they could seize any evidence in plain view or take further action supported by any consequent probable cause.) Thus, the question of whether the police might lawfully enter over objection in order to provide any protection that might be reasonable is easily answered yes:

> Even when...two persons quite clearly have equal rights in the place, as where two individuals are sharing an apartment on an equal basis, there may nonetheless sometimes exist a basis for giving greater recognition to the interests of one over the other.... Where the defendant has victimized the third party,...the emergency nature of the situation is such that the third party consent should validate a warrantless search despite defendant's objections.

The undoubted right of the police to enter in order to protect a victim, however, has nothing to do with the question in this case, of whether a search with the consent of one cotenant is good against another standing at the door and expressly refusing consent. None of the cases cited by the dissent support its improbable view that recognizing limits on merely evidentiary searches would compromise the capacity to protect a fearful occupant. In the circumstances of those cases, there is no danger that the fearful occupant will be kept behind the closed door of the house simply because the abusive tenant refuses to consent to a search....

The dissent's red herring aside, we know, of course, that alternatives to disputed consent will not always open the door to search for evidence that the police suspect is inside. The consenting tenant may simply not disclose enough information, or information factual enough, to add up to a showing of probable cause, and there may be no exigency to justify fast action. But nothing in social custom or its reflection in private law argues for placing a higher value on delving into private premises to search for evidence in the face of disputed consent than on requiring clear justification before the Government searches private living quarters over a resident's objection. We therefore hold that a warrantless search of a shared dwelling for evidence over the express refusal of consent by a physically present resident cannot be justified as reasonable based on consent given to the police by another resident.

There are two loose ends, the first being the explanation given in *Matlock* for the constitutional sufficiency of a cotenant's consent to enter and search: It

> rests...on mutual use of the property by persons generally having joint access or control for most purposes, so that it is reasonable to recognize that any of the coinhabitants has the right to permit the inspection in his own right.

If *Matlock*'s cotenant is giving permission "in his own right," how can his "own right" be eliminated by another tenant's objection? The answer appears in the very footnote from which the quoted statement is taken: the "right" to admit the police to which *Matlock* refers is not an enduring and enforceable ownership right as understood by the private law of property but is instead the authority recognized by customary social usage as having a substantial bearing on Fourth Amendment reasonableness in specific circumstances. Thus, to ask whether the consenting tenant has the right to admit the police when a physically present fellow tenant objects is not to question whether some property right may be divested by the mere objection of another. It is, rather, a question of whether customary social understanding accords the consenting tenant authority powerful enough to prevail over the cotenant's objection. The *Matlock* Court did not purport to answer this question, a point made clear by another statement: The Court described the cotenant's consent as good against that of "the absent, nonconsenting" resident.

The second loose end is the significance of *Matlock* and *Rodriguez* after today's decision. Although the *Matlock* defendant was not present with the opportunity to object, he was in a squad car not far away; the *Rodriguez* defendant was actually asleep in the apartment, and the police might have roused him with a knock on the door before they entered with only the consent of an apparent cotenant. If those cases are not to be undercut by today's holding, we have to admit that we are drawing a fine line; if a potential defendant with self-interest in objecting is in fact at the door and objects, the cotenant's permission does not suffice for a reasonable search, whereas the potential objector, nearby but not invited to take part in the threshold colloquy, loses out.

This is the line we draw, and we think the formalism is justified. So long as there is no evidence that the police have removed the potentially objecting tenant from the entrance for the sake of avoiding a possible objection, there is practical value in the simple clarity of complementary rules, one recognizing the cotenant's permission when there is no fellow occupant on hand, the other according dispositive weight to the fellow occupant's contrary indication when he expresses it. For the very reason that *Rodriguez* held it would be unjustifiably impractical to require the police to take affirmative steps to confirm the actual authority of a consenting individual whose authority was apparent, we think it would needlessly limit the capacity of the police to respond to ostensibly legitimate opportunities in the field if we were to hold that reasonableness required the police to take affirmative steps to find a potentially objecting cotenant before acting on the permission they had already received. There is no ready reason to believe that efforts to invite a refusal would make a difference in many cases, whereas every cotenant consent case would turn into a test about the adequacy of the police's efforts to consult with a potential objector. Better to accept the formalism of distinguishing *Matlock* from this case than to impose a requirement, time consuming in the field and in the courtroom, with no apparent systemic justification. The pragmatic decision to accept the simplicity of this line is, moreover, supported by the substantial number of instances in which suspects who are asked for permission to search actually consent, albeit imprudently, a fact that undercuts any argument that the police should try to locate a suspected inhabitant because his denial of consent would be a foregone conclusion.

Holding

This case invites a straightforward application of the rule that a physically present inhabitant's express refusal of consent to a police search is dispositive as to him, regardless of the consent of a fellow occupant. Scott Randolph's refusal is clear, and nothing in the record justifies the search on grounds independent of Janet Randolph's consent. The State does not argue that she gave any indication to the police of a need for protection inside the house that might have justified entry into the portion of the premises where the police found the powdery straw (which, if lawfully seized, could have been used when attempting to establish probable cause for the warrant issued later). Nor does the State claim that the entry and search should be upheld under the rubric of exigent circumstances, owing to some apprehension by the police officers that Scott Randolph would destroy evidence of drug use before any warrant could be obtained.

Dissenting, *Roberts, C.J.*, and *Scalia, J.*

The Court creates constitutional law by surmising what is typical when a social guest encounters an entirely atypical situation. The rule the majority fashions does not implement the high office of the Fourth Amendment to protect privacy but instead provides protection on a random and happenstance basis, protecting, for example, a co-occupant who happens to be at the front door when the other occupant consents to a search, but not one napping or watching television in the next room. And the cost of affording such random protection is great, as demonstrated by the recurring cases in which abused spouses seek to authorize police entry into a home they share with a nonconsenting abuser.

The correct approach to the question presented is clearly mapped out in our precedents: The Fourth Amendment protects privacy. If an individual shares information, papers, or places with another, he assumes the risk that the other person will in turn share access to that information or those papers or places with the Government. And just as an individual who has shared illegal plans or incriminating documents with another cannot interpose an objection when that other person turns the information over to the Government, just because the individual happens to be present at the time, so too someone who shares a place with another cannot interpose an objection when that person decides to grant access to the police, simply because the objecting individual happens to be present. A warrantless search is reasonable if police obtain the voluntary consent of a person authorized to give it. Co-occupants have "assumed the risk that one of their number might permit [a] common area to be searched." Just as Mrs. Randolph could walk upstairs, come down, and turn her husband's cocaine straw over to the police, she can consent to police entry and search of what is, after all, her home, too.

Today's opinion creates an exception to [an] otherwise clear rule: A third party consent search is unreasonable, and therefore constitutionally impermissible, if the co-occupant against whom evidence is obtained was present and objected to the entry and search. This exception is based on what the majority describes as "widely shared social expectations" that "when people living together disagree over the use of their common quarters, a resolution must come through voluntary accommodation." But this fundamental predicate to the majority's analysis gets us nowhere: Does the objecting cotenant accede to the consenting cotenant's wishes, or the other way around? The majority's assumption about voluntary accommodation simply leads to the common stalemate of two gentlemen insisting that the other enter a room first.

Nevertheless, the majority is confident in assuming—confident enough to incorporate its assumption into the Constitution—that an invited social guest who arrives at the door of a shared residence, and is greeted by a disagreeable co-occupant shouting "stay out," would simply go away. The Court observes that "no sensible person would go inside under those conditions," and concludes from this that the inviting co-occupant has no "authority" to insist on getting her way over the wishes of her co-occupant. But it seems equally accurate to say—based on the majority's conclusion that one does not have a right to prevail over the express wishes of his co-occupant—that the objector has no "authority" to insist on getting his way over his co-occupant's wish that her guest be admitted.

The fact is that a wide variety of differing social situations can readily be imagined, giving rise to quite different social expectations. A relative or good friend of one of two feuding roommates might well enter the apartment over the objection of the other roommate. The reason the invitee appeared at the door also affects expectations: A guest who came to celebrate an occupant's birthday, or one who had traveled some distance for a particular reason, might not readily turn away simply because of a roommate's objection. The nature of the place itself is also pertinent: Invitees may react one way if the feuding roommates share one room, differently if there are common areas from which the objecting roommate could readily be expected to absent himself. Altering the numbers might well change the social expectations: Invitees might enter if two of three co-occupants encourage them to do so, over one dissenter.

The possible scenarios are limitless, and slight variations in the fact pattern yield vastly different expectations about whether the invitee might be expected to enter or to go away. Such shifting expectations are not a promising foundation on which to ground a constitutional rule, particularly because the majority has no support for its basic assumption—that an invited guest encountering two disagreeing co-occupants would flee—beyond a hunch about how people would typically act in an atypical situation.

The majority suggests that "widely shared social expectations" are a "constant element in assessing Fourth Amendment reasonableness," but that is not the case; the Fourth Amendment precedents the majority cites refer instead to a "legitimate expectation of privacy." Whatever social expectation the majority seeks to protect, it is not one of privacy. The very predicate giving rise to the question in cases of shared information, papers, containers, or places is that privacy has been shared with another. Our common social expectations may well be that the other person will not, in turn, share what we have shared with them with another—including the police—but that is the risk we take in sharing. If two friends share a locker and one keeps contraband inside, he might trust that his friend will not let others look inside. But by sharing private space, privacy has "already been frustrated" with respect to the lockermate. If two roommates share a computer and one keeps pirated software on a shared drive, he might assume that his roommate will not inform the Government. But that person has given up his privacy with respect to his roommate by saving the software on their shared computer.

A wide variety of often subtle social conventions may shape expectations about how we act when another shares with us what is otherwise private, and those conventions go by a variety of labels—courtesy, good manners, custom, protocol, even honor among thieves. The Constitution, however, protects not these but privacy, and once privacy has been shared, the shared information, documents, or places remain private only at the discretion of the confidant.

In *United States v. White* (401 U.S. 745 (1971), we held that one party to a conversation can consent to government eavesdropping, and statements made by the other party will be admissible at trial. This rule is based on privacy: "Inescapably, one contemplating illegal activities must realize and risk that his companions may be reporting to the police. . . . If he has no doubts, or allays them, or risks what doubt he has, the risk is his." The same analysis applies to the question of whether our privacy can be compromised by those with whom we share common living space. If a person keeps contraband in common areas of his home, he runs the risk that his co-occupants will deliver the contraband to the police. Even in our most private relationships, our observable actions and possessions are private at the discretion of those around us. A husband can request that his wife not tell a jury about contraband that she observed in their home or illegal activity to which she bore witness, but it is she who decides whether to invoke the testimonial marital privilege. The common thread in our decisions upholding searches conducted pursuant to third party consent is an understanding that a person "assume[s] the risk" that those who have access to and control over his shared property might consent to a search. . . .

In *Matlock,* we explained that this assumption of risk is derived from a third party's "joint access or control for most purposes" of shared property. And we concluded that shared use of property makes it "reasonable to recognize that any of the coinhabitants has the right to permit the inspection in his own right." In this sense, the risk assumed by a joint occupant is comparable to the risk assumed by one who reveals private information to another. If a person has incriminating information, he can keep it private in the face of a request from police to share it, because he has that right under the Fifth Amendment. If a person occupies a house with incriminating information in it, he can keep that information private in the face of a request from police to search the house, because he has that right under the Fourth Amendment. But if he shares the information—or the house—with another, that other can grant access to the police in each instance. To the extent a person wants to ensure that his possessions will be subject to a consent search only due to his own consent, he is free to place these items in an area over which others do not share access and control, be it a private room or a locked suitcase under a bed. Mr. Randolph acknowledged this distinction in his motion to suppress, where he differentiated his law office from the rest of the Randolph house by describing it as an area that "was solely in his control and dominion." At a "common area," however, co-occupants with "joint access or control" may consent to an entry and search.

The majority states its rule as follows: "A warrantless search of a shared dwelling for evidence over the express refusal of consent by a physically present resident cannot be justified as reasonable as to him on the basis of consent given to the police by another resident." Just as the source of the majority's rule is not privacy, so too the interest it protects cannot reasonably be described as such. That interest is not protected if a co-owner happens to be absent when the police arrive, or in the backyard gardening, asleep in the next room, or listening to music through earphones so that only his co-occupant hears the knock on the door. That the rule is so random in its application confirms that it bears no real relation to the privacy protected by the Fourth Amendment. What the majority's rule protects is not so much privacy as the good luck of a co-owner who just happens to be present at the door when the police arrive. Usually when the development of Fourth Amendment jurisprudence leads to such arbitrary lines, we take it as a signal that the rules need to be rethought. We should not embrace a rule at the outset that its sponsors appreciate will result in drawing fine, formalistic lines....

Rather than draw such random and happenstance lines—and pretend that the Constitution decreed them—the more reasonable approach is to adopt a rule acknowledging that shared living space entails a limited yielding of privacy to others and that the law historically permits those to whom we have yielded our privacy to in turn cooperate with the Government. Such a rule flows more naturally from our cases concerning Fourth Amendment reasonableness and is logically grounded in the concept of privacy underlying that Amendment. Under the majority's rule, there will be many cases in which a consenting co-occupant's wish to have the police enter is overridden by an objection from another present co-occupant. What does the majority imagine will happen, in a case in which the consenting co-occupant is concerned about the other's criminal activity, once the door clicks shut? The objecting co-occupant may pause briefly to decide whether to destroy any evidence of wrongdoing or to inflict retribution on the consenting co-occupant first, but there can be little doubt that he will attend to both in short order. It is no answer to say that the consenting co-occupant can depart with the police; remember that it is her home, too, and the other co-occupant's very presence, which allowed him to object, may also prevent the consenting co-occupant from doing more than urging the police to enter.

Perhaps the most serious consequence of the majority's rule is its operation in domestic abuse situations, a context in which the present question often arises. While people living together might typically be accommodating to the wishes of their cotenants, requests for police assistance may well come from coinhabitants who are having a disagreement.... Mrs. Randolph did not invite the police to join her for dessert and coffee; the officer's precise purpose in knocking on the door was to assist with a dispute between the Randolphs—one in which Mrs. Randolph felt the need for the protective presence of the police. The majority's rule apparently forbids police from entering to assist with a domestic dispute if the abuser whose behavior prompted the request for police assistance objects. Rather than give effect to a consenting spouse's authority to permit entry into her house to avoid such situations, the majority again alters established Fourth Amendment rules to defend giving veto power to the objecting spouse. In response to the concern that police might be turned away under its rule before entry can be justified based on exigency, the majority creates a new rule: A "good reason" to enter, coupled with one occupant's consent, will ensure that a police officer is "lawfully in the premises."...And apparently a key factor allowing entry with a "good reason" short of exigency is the very consent of one co-occupant the majority finds so inadequate in the first place.

Our third party consent cases have recognized that a person who shares common areas with others "assume[s] the risk that one of their number might permit the common area to be searched." The majority reminds us, in high tones, that a man's home is his castle, but even under the majority's rule, it is not his castle if he happens to be absent, asleep in the keep, or otherwise engaged when the constable arrives at the gate. Then it is his co-owner's castle. And, of course, it is not his castle if he wants to consent to entry, but his co-owner objects. Rather than constitutionalize such an arbitrary rule, we should acknowledge that a decision to share a private place, like a decision to share a secret or a confidential document, necessarily entails the risk that those with whom we share may in turn choose to share—for their own protection or for other reasons—with the police.

Questions for Discussion

1. What is the holding in *Randolph*? Compare and contrast the facts and holdings in *Rodriguez* and *Randolph*. Does *Randolph* establish a rule that is easily followed by the police?
2. Does the majority opinion indicate that there are situations in which it would be reasonable for the police to enter a home without a warrant despite the objections of a co-occupant?
3. Why does Chief Justice Roberts disagree with the majority opinion? Consider his discussion of "social expectations," "assumption of the risk," "joint access and control," and "common areas."
4. Is Chief Justice Roberts correct that the majority opinion places the victims of domestic violence at risk?
5. Is it at all relevant that Janet may have been angry at Scott and that they appear to have had a conflict over the custody of their son? How would the Supreme Court have decided this case if Scott had not been home but had instructed Janet "not to consent to any police search"?
6. ***Problems in policing.*** Write a brief summary of the law of third party consent instructing police officers of the legal rules to keep in mind.

6.6 YOU DECIDE

The Oklahoma City Police Department received a phone call from Dianne Hale that she was being held against her will in a trailer park by two men who had been sexually assaulting her and had threatened her with guns. Officers Culbertson and Wise were dispatched to the trailer, knocked on the door, and were admitted by Hale. Dianne alleged that she had been assaulted for six months, the last two months in the trailer park. Dianne directed the officers to the back of the trailer where they seized guns, ammunition, gun cases, and numerous handcuffs. They then secured a search warrant and seized additional weapons.

May a crime victim like Hale consent to a search of the trailer? See *United States v. McAlpine*, 919 F.2d 1461 (10th Cir. 1990).

You can learn what the court decided by referring to the study site, http://www.sagepub.com/lippmancp.

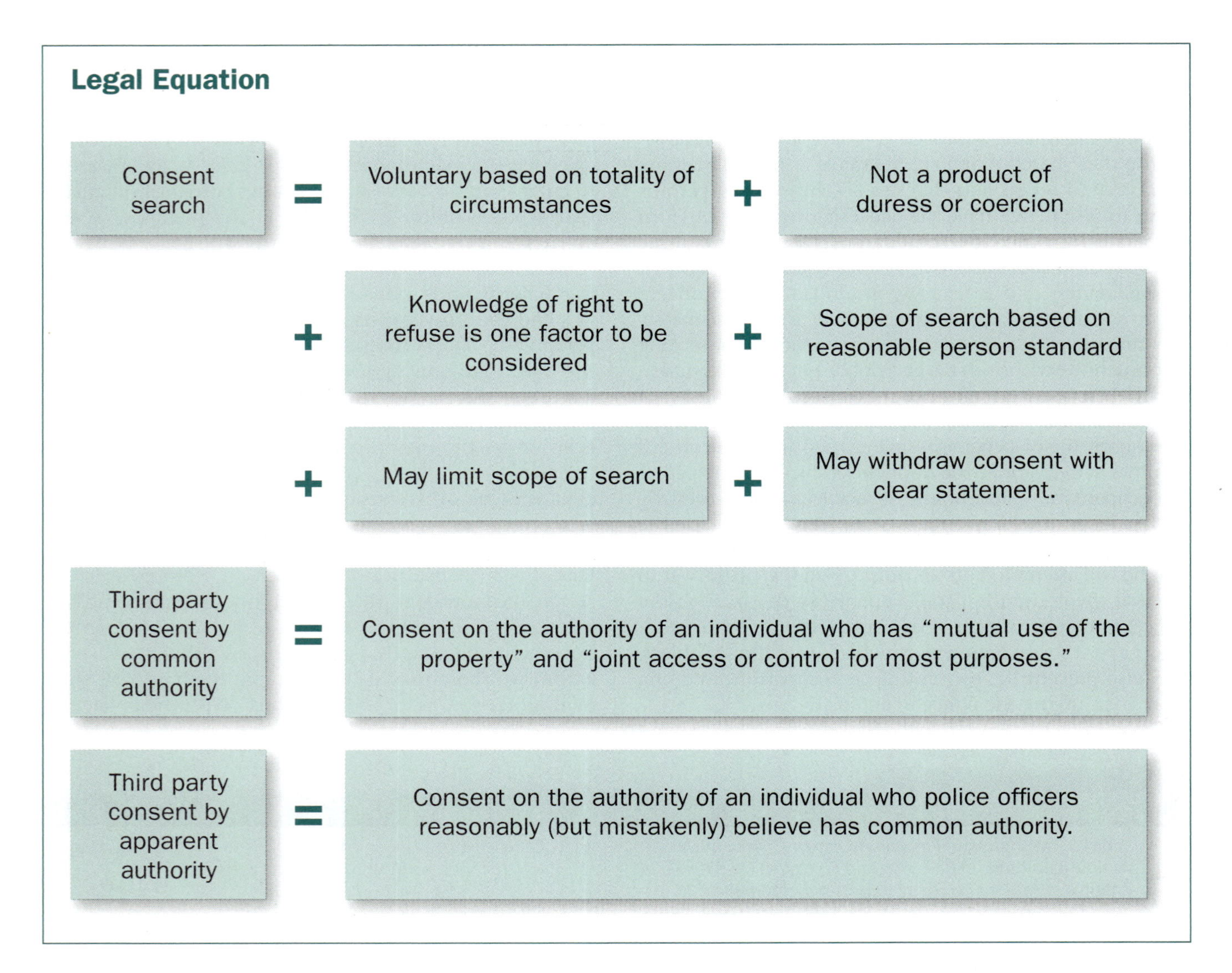

Probable Cause Searches of Motor Vehicles

We have seen that a search incident to an arrest may permit the search of the passenger compartment of a motor vehicle. The police also may conduct a consent search of a car. There is a third type of warrantless search of an automobile. The **automobile exception** to the Fourth Amendment permits the police to conduct warrantless searches of automobiles where there is probable cause to believe that the vehicle contains contraband or evidence related to criminal activity. The U.S. Supreme Court first established the automobile exception in 1925 in *Carroll v. United States.* Defendants Carol and Kin were convicted for unlawfully transporting sixty-eight quarts of alcohol in violation of the National Prohibition Act. They challenged the search of their automobile and the seizure of the bottles of alcohol on the grounds that the federal agents had not obtained a search warrant.

The U.S. Supreme Court observed that the Fourth Amendment freedom from unreasonable searches and seizures historically had been interpreted to distinguish between a "search of a store, dwelling, house, or other structure in respect of which a proper official warrant" based on probable cause must be obtained, and "a search of a ship, motorboat, wagon, or automobile," which may be searched based on probable cause without a warrant. The Court explained that it is not "practicable" to require the police to obtain a search warrant for motor vehicles, because the mobility of the automobile might result in the vehicle disappearing down the highway by the time the federal agents obtained a warrant (*Carroll v. United States,* 267 U.S. 132, 153 [1925]). As the U.S. Supreme Court observed in *Chambers v. Maroney,* "The car is movable, the occupants are alerted, and the car's contents may never be found again if a warrant must be obtained. Hence an immediate search is constitutionally permissible" (*Chambers v. Maroney,* 399 U.S. 42, 51 [1970]).

The explanation in *Carroll* that the mobility of automobiles makes it impractical to require that the police obtain a warrant to search a motor vehicle does not fit each and every situation. Consider a case in which the police stop, seize, and immobilize a motor vehicle and transport the car to the police station. The police, once having taken the automobile into custody, could easily obtain a warrant. In *Texas v. White,* the Supreme Court nevertheless affirmed that

> when police officers have probable cause to believe that there is contraband inside an automobile that has been stopped on the road, the officers may conduct a warrantless search of the vehicle, even after it has been impounded and is in police custody.... The justification to conduct such a warrantless search does not vanish once the car has been immobilized. (*Michigan v. Thomas,* 458 U.S. 259, 261 [1958]; *Texas v. White,* 423 U.S. 67 [1975])

In 1985, in *California v. Carney,* the U.S. Supreme Court held that the automobile exception to the Fourth Amendment warrant requirement is based on the mobility of the vehicle as well as on the vehicle's reduced expectation of privacy. In the events at issue in *Carney,* federal narcotics agents conducted a warrantless search of a motor home parked in a public lot in downtown San Diego. The agents observed marijuana, plastic bags, and a scale used in weighing drugs. A search of the vehicle at the police station led to the seizure of additional marijuana. The Supreme Court explained that while "ready mobility alone" is the original justification for the automobile exception, warrantless searches also are based on the reduced expectation of privacy in an automobile.

> When a vehicle is being used on the highways, or if it is readily capable of such use and is found stationary in a place not regularly used for residential purposes,... the two justifications for the vehicle exception come into play. (*California v. Carney,* 471 U.S. 386, 388, 399 [1985])

The two justifications for the warrantless search of motor vehicles are summarized below.

- ***Mobility.*** The motor vehicle is "obviously readily mobile by the turn of a switch key, if [it is] not actually [already] moving."
- ***Regulation.*** There is a reduced expectation of privacy in a motor vehicle, because the vehicle is subject to a range of "police regulation inapplicable to a fixed dwelling." This includes a license to drive, vehicle registration, and safety and environmental regulations. The Supreme Court in other cases has held that motor vehicles have a reduced

expectation of privacy based on the facts that vehicles travel on public highways, the exterior and interior of autos is easily observable by a plain view search, and individuals rarely store personal belongings in their cars.

The Supreme Court in *Carney* rejected the argument that the fact that a motor home is "capable of functioning as a home" provides the vehicle with a heightened degree of privacy that requires the police to obtain a search warrant. The Court reasoned that the motor home in *Carney* was readily mobile and was clearly being used as a mode of transport. The Supreme Court indicated that a warrant might be required where a motor home is "situated in a way or place that objectively indicates that it is being used as a residence" (393–394).

In reading *California v. Carney,* ask yourself whether you are persuaded by the argument that a motor home possesses "less of an expectation of privacy" than a home. Should the Supreme Court have held that federal agents are required to obtain a search warrant once a motor home has been placed under police custody?

You can find Carroll v. United States *on the study site, http://www.sagepub.com/lippmancp.*

May the police search a motor home without a search warrant?

California v. Carney, 471 U.S. 386 (1985), Burger, C.J.

Issue

We granted certiorari to decide whether law enforcement agents violated the Fourth Amendment when they conducted a warrantless search, based on probable cause, of a fully mobile "motor home" located in a public place.

Facts

On May 31, 1979, Drug Enforcement Agency Agent Robert Williams watched respondent, Charles Carney, approach a youth in downtown San Diego. The youth accompanied Carney to a Dodge Mini Motor Home parked in a nearby lot. Carney and the youth closed the window shades in the motor home, including one across the front window. Agent Williams had previously received uncorroborated information that the same motor home was used by another person who was exchanging marijuana for sex. Williams, with assistance from other agents, kept the motor home under surveillance for the entire one and one-quarter hours that Carney and the youth remained inside. When the youth left the motor home, the agents followed and stopped him. The youth told the agents that he had received marijuana in return for allowing Carney sexual contacts.

At the agents' request, the youth returned to the motor home and knocked on its door; Carney stepped out. The agents identified themselves as law enforcement officers. Without a warrant or consent, one agent entered the motor home and observed marijuana, plastic bags, and a scale of the kind used in weighing drugs on a table. Agent Williams took Carney into custody and took possession of the motor home. A subsequent search of the motor home at the police station revealed additional marijuana in the cupboards and refrigerator.

Respondent was charged with possession of marijuana for sale. At a preliminary hearing, he moved to suppress the evidence discovered in the motor home. The magistrate denied the motion.... The Superior Court also rejected the claim.... Respondent then pleaded *nolo contendere* to the charges against him and was placed on probation for three years.... The California Court of Appeal affirmed.... The California Supreme Court reversed... the conviction.... The California Supreme Court held that the expectations of privacy in a motor home are more like those in a dwelling than in an automobile, because the primary function of motor homes is not to provide transportation but to "provide the occupant with living quarters."

Reasoning

The Fourth Amendment protects the "right of the people to be secure in their persons, houses, papers, and effects against unreasonable searches and seizures." This fundamental right is preserved by a requirement that searches be conducted pursuant to a warrant issued by an independent judicial officer. There are, of course, exceptions to the general rule that a warrant must be secured before a search is undertaken; one is the so-called automobile exception at issue in this case. This exception to the warrant requirement was first set forth by the Court 60 years ago in *Carroll v. United States*. There, the Court recognized that the privacy interests in an automobile are constitutionally protected; however, it held that the ready mobility of the automobile justifies a lesser degree of protection of those interests. The Court rested this exception on a long-recognized distinction between stationary structures and vehicles:

The capacity to be "quickly moved" was clearly the basis of the holding in *Carroll,* and our cases have consistently recognized ready mobility as one of the principal bases of the automobile exception. In *Chambers v. Maroney,* for example, commenting on the rationale for the vehicle exception, we noted that "the opportunity to search is fleeting since a car is readily movable." More recently, in *United States v. Ross* (456 U.S. 798 [1982]), we once again emphasized that "an immediate intrusion is necessary" because of "the nature of an automobile in transit...." The mobility of automobiles, we have observed, "creates circumstances of such exigency that, as a practical necessity, rigorous enforcement of the warrant requirement is impossible."

However, although ready mobility alone was perhaps the original justification for the vehicle exception, our later cases have made clear that ready mobility is not the only basis for the exception. The reasons for the vehicle exception, we have said, are twofold. "Besides the element of mobility, less rigorous warrant requirements govern because the expectation of privacy with respect to one's automobile is significantly less than that relating to one's home or office."

Even in cases where an automobile was not immediately mobile, the lesser expectation of privacy resulting from its use as a readily mobile vehicle justified application of the vehicular exception. In some cases, the configuration of the vehicle contributed to the lower expectations of privacy; for example, we held, in *Cardwell v. Lewis* (417 U.S. 583 [1974]), that because the passenger compartment of a standard automobile is relatively open to plain view, there are lesser expectations of privacy. But even when enclosed "repository" areas have been involved, we have concluded that the lesser expectations of privacy warrant application of the exception. We have applied the exception in the context of a locked car trunk (*Cady v. Dombrowski,* 413 U.S. 433 [1973]), a sealed package in a car trunk (*Ross*), a closed compartment under the dashboard (*Chambers v. Maroney*), the interior of a vehicle's upholstery (*Carroll*), and sealed packages inside a covered pickup truck (*United States v. Johns,* 469 U.S. 478 [1985]).

These reduced expectations of privacy derive not from the fact that the area to be searched is in plain view but from the pervasive regulation of vehicles capable of traveling on the public highways (*Cady v. Dombrowski*). As we explained in *South Dakota v. Opperman* (428 U.S. 364 [1976]), an inventory search case,

> Automobiles, unlike homes, are subjected to pervasive and continuing governmental regulation and controls, including periodic inspection and licensing requirements. As an everyday occurrence, police stop and examine vehicles when license plates or inspection stickers have expired, or if other violations, such as exhaust fumes or excessive noise, are noted, or if headlights or other safety equipment are not in proper working order.

The public is fully aware that it is accorded less privacy in its automobiles because of this compelling governmental need for regulation. Historically, "individuals always [have] been on notice that movable vessels may be stopped and searched on facts giving rise to probable cause that the vehicle contains contraband, without the protection afforded by a magistrate's prior evaluation of those facts." The pervasive schemes of regulation, which necessarily lead to reduced expectations of privacy, and the exigencies attendant to ready mobility justify searches without prior recourse to the authority of a magistrate so long as the overriding standard of probable cause is met.

Holding

When a vehicle is being used on the highways, or if it is readily capable of such use and is found stationary in a place not regularly used for residential purposes—temporary or otherwise—the two justifications for the vehicle exception come into play. First, the vehicle is obviously readily mobile by the turn of an ignition key, if not actually moving. Second, there is a reduced expectation of privacy stemming from its use as a licensed motor vehicle subject to a range of police regulation inapplicable to a fixed dwelling. At least in these circumstances, the overriding societal interests in effective law enforcement justify an immediate search before the vehicle and its occupants become unavailable.

While it is true that respondent's vehicle possessed some, if not many of the attributes of a home, it is equally clear that the vehicle falls clearly within the scope of the exception laid down in *Carroll* and applied in succeeding cases. Like the automobile in *Carroll,* respondent's motor home was readily mobile. Absent the prompt search and seizure, it could readily have been moved beyond the reach of the police. Furthermore, the vehicle was licensed to "operate on public streets; [was] serviced in public places,...and [was] subject to extensive regulation and inspection." And the vehicle was so situated that an objective observer would conclude that it was being used not as a residence, but as a vehicle.

Respondent urges us to distinguish his vehicle from other vehicles within the exception, because it was capable of functioning as a home. In our increasingly mobile society, many vehicles used for transportation can be and are being used not only for transportation but for shelter, i.e., as a "home" or "residence." To distinguish between respondent's motor home and an ordinary sedan for purposes of the vehicle exception would require that we apply the exception depending upon the size of the vehicle and the quality of its appointments. Moreover, to fail to apply the exception to vehicles such as a motor home ignores the fact that a motor home lends itself easily to use as instrument of illicit drug traffic and other illegal activity. . . . We decline today to distinguish between "worthy" and "unworthy" vehicles which are either on the public roads and highways or situated such that it is reasonable to conclude that the vehicle is not being used as a residence.

Our application of the vehicle exception has never turned on the other uses to which a vehicle might be put. The exception has historically turned on the ready mobility of the vehicle and on the presence of the vehicle in a setting that objectively indicates that the vehicle is being used for transportation. These two requirements for application of the exception ensure that law enforcement officials are not unnecessarily hamstrung in their efforts to detect and prosecute criminal activity and that the legitimate privacy interests of the public are protected. Applying the vehicle exception in these circumstances allows the essential purposes served by the exception to be fulfilled, while assuring that the exception will acknowledge legitimate privacy interests.

Dissenting, *Stevens, J.*, with *Brennan, J.*, and *Marshall, J.*

In my opinion, searches of places that regularly accommodate a wide range of private human activity are fundamentally different from searches of automobiles, which primarily serve a public transportation function. Although it may not be a castle, a motor home is usually the functional equivalent of a hotel room, a vacation and retirement home, or a hunting and fishing cabin. These places may be as Spartan as a humble cottage when compared to the most majestic mansion, but the highest and most legitimate expectations of privacy associated with these temporary abodes should command the respect of this Court. In my opinion, a warrantless search of living quarters in a motor home is "presumptively unreasonable absent exigent circumstances."

Questions for Discussion

1. What is the holding in *Carney*?
2. Could the court have reached the same result by basing its decision solely on the mobility of motor vehicles? Why did the Supreme Court hold that a warrantless search was justified despite the fact that the motor home may have been used as a residence?
3. Are you persuaded that a motor home has significantly less expectation of privacy than a stationary home?
4. Is there a social interest in allowing the police to search motor vehicles without warrants?
5. ***Problems in policing.*** Compare and contrast searches incident to an arrest of an individual within a motor vehicle, consent searches of motor vehicles, and probable cause searches of motor vehicles.

Probable Cause Searches of Containers in Automobiles

The U.S. Supreme Court has held that individuals retain a reasonable expectation of privacy in enclosed containers. A container is defined as "any object capable of holding another object" (*New York v. Belton,* 453 U.S. 454, 460 [1981]). Containers include luggage, book bags, knapsacks, boxes, and paper bags. In *United States v. Chadwick* (discussed above), the U.S. Supreme Court held that federal agents should have obtained a warrant before opening a footlocker that they had probable cause to believe contained unlawful narcotics. The Court explained that a warrant is required to open the footlocker, because, in contrast to automobiles, the content of luggage is not "open to public view . . . [and] subject to regular inspections and official scrutiny on a continuing basis. Unlike an automobile, whose primary function is transportation, luggage is intended as a repository of personal effects" (*United States v. Chadwick,* 433 U.S. 1, 13 [1977]). Keep in mind that there is some precedent for the view that there are containers that "communicate their contents by their appearance" and therefore lack a significant expectation of privacy and may be opened without a warrant (e.g., a guitar case) (*Texas v. Brown,* 460 U.S. 730 [1983]).

The Supreme Court has struggled with the question of whether a warrant is required to open containers encountered during the search of an automobile. Clearly, a warrant is required to open luggage that is seized outside of an automobile. Does it make sense for luggage to lose its reasonable expectation of privacy because it is inside an automobile? The

Supreme Court's internal debate over this question has taken a number of twists and turns. The judges now have settled on the sensible rule that a container inside the automobile may be searched without a warrant when there is probable cause to believe that the container houses the object of the search.

Consider the following two scenarios involving containers:

- ***Probable cause limited to container.*** The police have probable cause to believe that there is contraband or criminal evidence inside a container that is within an automobile. For example, the police observe a drug courier place a backpack containing unlawful narcotics in his or her automobile. The police have probable cause to seize and to search the backpack and do not require a search warrant. Their search is limited to the backpack.
- ***Probable cause extends to the vehicle.*** The police have probable cause to believe that there are narcotics somewhere within a motor vehicle. They therefore may search the entire vehicle for narcotics and open, without a warrant, any containers that may house the narcotics.

In *California v. Acevedo,* the police possessed probable cause to believe that a paper bag that Acevedo carried to his automobile contained marijuana. He placed the bag in the trunk of his automobile and drove away. The police stopped the vehicle, opened the trunk, and removed the marijuana from the bag. The Supreme Court held that "if probable cause justifies the search of a lawfully stopped vehicle, it justifies the search of every part of the vehicle and its contents that may conceal the object of the search." The police had probable cause to believe that the paper bag in the automobile's trunk contained marijuana. They therefore were entitled to conduct a warrantless search of the paper bag. On the other hand, the

> facts in the record reveal that the police did not have probable cause to believe that contraband was hidden in any other part of the automobile and a search of the entire vehicle would have been without probable cause and unreasonable under the Fourth Amendment.

Do you believe that it makes sense to hold that the expectation of privacy in a container depends on whether it is inside or outside the automobile? (*California v. Acevedo,* 500 U.S. 565, 570, 580 [1991]).

In *Wyoming v. Houghton,* the next case in the text, a police officer stopped David Young, the driver of an automobile, for speeding and driving with a faulty brake light. The officer developed probable cause to believe that David Young had narcotics in his possession inside the car. In conducting the search, the officer opened a purse that belonged to Sandra Houghton, a female passenger. Did the probable cause to search the vehicle for narcotics extend to a purse belonging to a passenger? Or was the probable cause limited to containers belonging to David Young?

May police officers, in conducting a probable cause search of an automobile, examine a passenger's property?

Wyoming v. Houghton, *526 U.S. 295 (1999), Scalia, J.*

Issue

This case presents the question of whether police officers violate the Fourth Amendment when they search a passenger's personal belongings inside an automobile that they have probable cause to believe contains contraband.

Facts

In the early morning hours of July 23, 1995, a Wyoming Highway Patrol officer stopped an automobile for speeding and driving with a faulty brake light. There were three passengers in the front seat of the car: David Young (the driver), his girlfriend, and respondent. While questioning Young, the officer noticed a hypodermic syringe in Young's shirt pocket. He left the occupants under the supervision of two backup officers as he went to get gloves from his patrol car. Upon his return, he instructed Young to step out of the car and place the syringe on the hood. The officer then asked Young why he had a syringe; with refreshing candor, Young replied that he used it to take drugs.

At this point, the backup officers ordered the two female passengers out of the car and asked them for identification. Respondent falsely identified herself as "Sandra James" and stated that she did not have any identification. Meanwhile, in light of Young's admission, the officer searched the passenger compartment of the car for contraband. On the back seat, he found a purse, which respondent claimed as hers. He removed from the purse a wallet containing respondent's driver's license, identifying her properly as Sandra K. Houghton. When the officer asked her why she had lied about her name, she replied: "In case things went bad."

Continuing his search of the purse, the officer found a brown pouch and a black wallet-type container. Respondent denied that the former was hers and claimed ignorance of how it came to be there; it was found to contain drug paraphernalia and a syringe with 60 cubic centimeters of methamphetamine. Respondent admitted ownership of the black container, which was also found to contain drug paraphernalia and a syringe (which respondent acknowledged was hers) with 10 cubic centimeters of methamphetamine—an amount insufficient to support the felony conviction at issue in this case. The officer also found fresh needle-track marks on respondent's arms. He placed her under arrest.

The State of Wyoming charged respondent with felony possession of methamphetamine in a liquid amount greater than three-tenths of a gram. After a hearing, the trial court denied her motion to suppress all evidence obtained from the purse as the fruit of a violation of the Fourth and Fourteenth Amendments. The Wyoming Supreme Court, by divided vote, reversed the conviction and held that the search of respondent's purse violated the Fourth and Fourteenth Amendments, because the officer "knew or should have known that the purse did not belong to the driver, but to one of the passengers," and because "there was no probable cause to search the passengers' personal effects and no reason to believe that contraband had been placed within the purse."

Reasoning

It is uncontested in the present case that the police officers had probable cause to believe there were illegal drugs in the car.... The framers would have regarded such a search as reasonable in light of legislation enacted by Congress from 1789 through 1799—as well as subsequent legislation from the founding era and beyond—that empowered customs officials to search any ship or vessel without a warrant if they had probable cause to believe that it contained goods subject to duty. Thus in *Carroll v. United States* the Court held that "contraband goods concealed and illegally transported in an automobile or other vehicle may be searched for without a warrant" where probable cause exists.

We have read the historical evidence to show that the framers would have regarded as reasonable (if there was probable cause) the warrantless search of containers within an automobile. In *United States v. Ross,* we upheld as reasonable the warrantless search of a paper bag and leather pouch found in the trunk of Ross's car by officers who had probable cause to believe that the trunk contained drugs.... [We] summarized our holding as follows: "If probable cause justifies the search of a lawfully stopped vehicle, it justifies the search of every part of the vehicle and its contents that may conceal the objects of the search." And our later cases describing *Ross* have characterized it as applying broadly to all containers within a car, without qualification as to ownership. Neither *Ross* itself nor the historical evidence it relied upon admits of a distinction among packages or containers based on ownership. When there is probable cause to search for contraband in a car, it is reasonable for police officers—like customs officials in the founding era—to examine packages and containers without a showing of individualized probable cause for each one. A passenger's personal belongings, just like the driver's belongings or containers attached to the car like a glove compartment, are "in" the car, and the officer has probable cause to search for contraband in the car.

Even if the historical evidence... were thought to be equivocal, we would find that the balancing of the relative interests weighs decidedly in favor of allowing searches of a passenger's belongings. Passengers, no less than drivers, possess a reduced expectation of privacy with regard to the property that they transport in cars, which "travel public thoroughfares," "seldom serve as... the repository of personal effects," are subjected to police stop and examination to enforce "pervasive" governmental controls "as an everyday occurrence," and, finally, are exposed to traffic accidents that may render all their contents open to public scrutiny.

Whereas the passenger's privacy expectations are, as we have described, considerably diminished, the governmental interests at stake are substantial. Effective law enforcement would be appreciably impaired without the ability to search a passenger's personal belongings when there is reason to believe contraband or evidence of criminal wrongdoing is hidden in the car. As in all car-search cases, the "ready mobility" of an automobile creates a risk that the evidence or contraband will be permanently lost while a warrant is obtained. In addition, a car passenger... will often be engaged in a common enterprise with the driver, and have the same interest in concealing the fruits or the evidence of their wrongdoing. A criminal might be able to hide contraband in a passenger's belongings as readily as in other containers in the car,—perhaps even surreptitiously, without the passenger's knowledge or permission. . . .

To be sure, these factors favoring a search will not always be present, but the balancing of interests must be conducted with an eye to the generality of cases. To require that the investigating officer have positive reason to believe that the passenger and driver were engaged in a common enterprise, or positive reason to believe that the driver had time and occasion to conceal the item in the passenger's belongings, surreptitiously or with friendly permission, is to impose requirements so seldom met that a "passenger's property" rule would dramatically reduce the ability to find and seize contraband and evidence of crime.

Of course these requirements would not attach . . . until the police officer knows or has reason to know that the container belongs to a passenger. But once a "passenger's property" exception to car searches became widely known, one would expect passenger-confederates to claim everything as their own. And one would anticipate a bog of litigation—in the form of both civil lawsuits and motions to suppress in criminal trials—involving such questions as whether the officer should have believed a passenger's claim of ownership, whether he should have inferred ownership from various objective factors, whether he had probable cause to believe that the passenger was a confederate, or to believe that the driver might have introduced the contraband into the package with or without the passenger's knowledge. When balancing the competing interests, our determinations of "reasonableness" under the Fourth Amendment must take account of these practical realities. We think they militate in favor of the needs of law enforcement, and against a personal-privacy interest that is ordinarily weak.

Surely Houghton's privacy would have been invaded to the same degree whether she was present or absent when her purse was searched. And surely her presence in the car with the driver provided more, rather than less, reason to believe that the two were in league. It may ordinarily be easier to identify the property as belonging to someone other than the driver when the purported owner is present to identify it—but in the many cases where the car is seized, that identification may occur later, at the station house, and even at the site of the stop one can readily imagine a package clearly marked with the owner's name and phone number, by which the officer can confirm the driver's denial of ownership.

Holding

The sensible rule . . . is that such a package may be searched, whether or not its owner is present as a passenger or otherwise, because it may contain the contraband that the officer has reason to believe is in the car. We hold that police officers with probable cause to search a car may inspect passengers' belongings found in the car that are capable of concealing the object of the search.

Dissenting, *Stevens, J.*, *Souter, J.*, and *Ginsburg, J.*

In all of our prior cases applying the automobile exception to the Fourth Amendment's warrant requirement, either the defendant was the operator of the vehicle and in custody of the object of the search, or no question was raised as to the defendant's ownership or custody—the Court held that the exception to the warrant requirement did not apply. . . . The information prompting the search directly implicated the driver, not the passenger. . . . Nor am I persuaded that the mere spatial association between a passenger and a driver provides an acceptable basis for presuming that they are partners in crime or for ignoring privacy interests in a purse. . . .

Whether or not the Fourth Amendment required a warrant to search Houghton's purse, at the very least the trooper in this case had to have probable cause to believe that her purse contained contraband. The Wyoming Supreme Court concluded that he did not. . . . Finally, in my view, the State's legitimate interest in effective law enforcement does not outweigh the privacy concerns at issue. . . . Certainly the ostensible clarity of the Court's rule is attractive. But that virtue is insufficient justification for its adoption. Moreover, a rule requiring a warrant or individualized probable cause to search passenger belongings is every bit as simple as the Court's rule; it simply protects more privacy. . . . Instead of applying ordinary Fourth Amendment principles to this case, the majority extends the automobile warrant exception to allow searches of passenger belongings based on the driver's misconduct.

Questions for Discussion

1. Outline the facts and holding in *Houghton*.
2. Why does the U.S. Supreme Court argue that the ability of the police to enforce the law would be frustrated without the ability to search containers belonging to passengers (the "passenger property" exception)?
3. What of the argument of the dissent that the police only should be permitted to search a passenger's belongings when there is "individualized" probable cause to believe that a specific container contains contraband?
4. Do you agree with the Supreme Court decision in *Houghton*?
5. ***Problems in policing.*** Summarize the law regarding the probable cause search of containers.

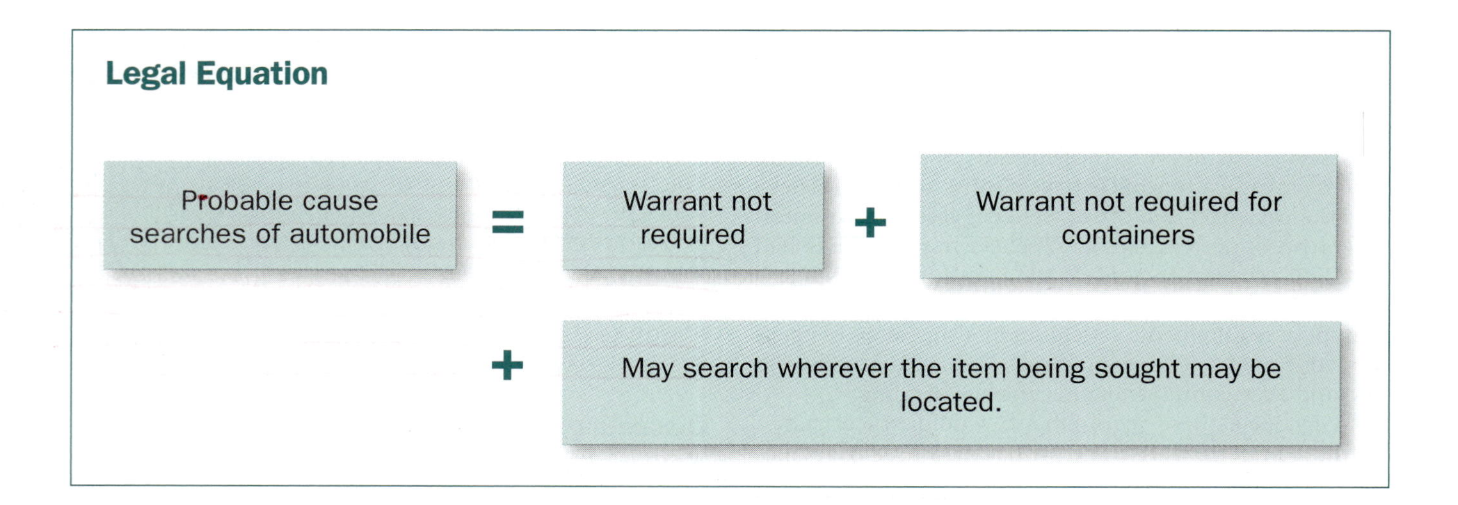

Other Warrantless Searches

We previously discussed three other warrantless searches.

- ***Plain view.*** Most law school texts categorize plain view as a warrantless search. An officer who is legally situated may seize an object that he or she has probable cause to believe constitutes evidence of criminal behavior (*Arizona v. Hicks,* 480 U.S. 321 [1987]) (Chapter 3).
- ***Frisks.*** The police may conduct a frisk of an individual subjected to a reasonable suspicion stop who fails to dispel an officer's reasonable fear that the individual is armed and presently dangerous (*Terry v. Ohio,* 392 U.S. 1 [1968]) (Chapter 4).
- ***Exigent circumstances.*** The police may enter a dwelling without a warrant to prevent the destruction of evidence or in hot pursuit of a fleeing suspect or in response to a threat to the public safety. The scope of a warrantless exigent circumstances search is defined by the object of the search. A search that goes beyond this limited purpose requires a search warrant. The U.S. Supreme Court also has upheld the warrantless seizure of evidence from an individual's person or immediate possession when there is an imminent threat that it may be destroyed. In *Cupp v. Murphy,* the Court held that it was reasonable for the police to scrape an individual's fingernails without a warrant when there was a threat that the individual would destroy evidence relevant to a homicide investigation (*Cupp v. Murphy,* 412 U.S. 291 [1971]) (Chapter 5).

Inventories

We have seen that automobiles are subject to warrantless searches incident to an arrest and to warrantless probable cause searches. Automobiles also may be inventoried.

In an **inventory**, the police record on an inventory form all of the *possessions and clothes* that are with an arrestee at the time he or she is detained. This includes the objects inside an automobile that is impounded. Objects that typically are inventoried include jewelry, cash, keys, credit cards, and various forms of identification. An inventory is a reasonable administrative procedure under the Fourth Amendment; it is intended to achieve four principal purposes. Keep in mind that an inventory is not undertaken to investigate criminal activity.

- ***False claims.*** Deter false claims of theft by the police
- ***Property.*** Protect property against theft by the police

- ***Safety.*** Prevent arrestees from injuring themselves or others using belts, knives, firearms, or other instrumentalities that are smuggled into the jail lockup
- ***Identification.*** Confirm or ascertain an individual's identity

Law school textbooks typically refer to inventories as *inventory searches,* because any unlawful objects that are seized during an inventory may be used against the arrestee. The U.S. Supreme Court has held that the governmental interest in conducting an inventory far outweighs the intrusion on an individual's privacy that is involved in the inventory. The individual already has been arrested, and the inventory does not involve a significant additional intrusion on his or her privacy. The Supreme Court has noted that inventories at the station house allow the police to intrude on individuals' privacy in a way that would be "impractical or embarrassingly intrusive" on the street, such as requiring individuals to turn their clothes over to the police. There are several important aspects of inventories to keep in mind.

- ***Uniformity.*** An inventory search must be a *standardized* or uniform procedure. This means that there are fixed guidelines, and all individuals and objects are treated alike. These guidelines establish matters such as whether suitcases are to be opened and the contents inventoried or whether suitcases are to be sealed rather than opened. The police are to follow a routine procedure in every arrest situation. In other words, the "minister's picnic basket and grandma's knitting bag are opened and inventoried right along with the biker's tool box and the gypsy's satchel" (*State v. Shamblin,* 763 P.2d 425, 428 [Ut. Ct. App. 1988]).
- ***Probable cause.*** There is no requirement that the police have probable cause in order to inventory an object or to open and inventory the contents of a container.
- ***Reasonable procedures.*** The Supreme Court will not second-guess the inventory procedure adopted by a police department as long as the procedure is reasonably designed to protect the police against false allegations of theft, insure safety, and protect a detainee's property.
- ***Criminal investigation.*** An inventory search is unlawful and invalid where it is intended to investigate a crime rather than to inventory an individual's possessions.

The U.S. Supreme Court has approved inventory searches in three separate cases.

- ***Shoulder bag.*** In *Illinois v. Lafayette,* the Court upheld the seizure of amphetamines found in Lafayette's shoulder bag during an inventory at the police station (*Illinois v. Lafayette,* 462 U.S. 640 [1983]).
- ***Automobile.*** In *South Dakota v. Opperman,* the Court affirmed the legality of the warrantless inventory of the contents of Opperman's automobile, which had been towed to the police impound lot (*South Dakota v. Opperman,* 428 U.S. 364 [1976]).
- ***Containers.*** Lee Bertine was arrested for driving while under the influence of alcohol and taken into custody. In *Colorado v. Bertine,* the police were held to have lawfully inventoried the contents of his backpack, which was found to contain narcotics, cocaine paraphernalia, and cash (*Colorado v. Bertine,* 479 U.S. 367 [1987]).

In *Florida v. Wells,* the Supreme Court held that a Florida state police officer had improperly inventoried a locked suitcase in an impounded vehicle, because the Florida Highway Patrol had no established policy and left the decision regarding the objects to be inventoried to the individual officer (*Florida v. Wells,* 495 U.S. 1 [1990]). Inventory searches also have been held to be unlawful where an officer "clearly had an investigatory purpose" (*United States v. Monclavo-Cruz,* 662 F.2d 1285, 1289 [9th Cir. 1980]).

Inventories often are categorized as "special need" searches, because they are undertaken for an administrative purpose and not to investigate a criminal offense. The next chapter in the text discusses other "special needs" searches.

You can find Illinois v. Lafayette *and* South Dakota v. Opperman *on the study site, http://www.sagepub.com/lippmancp.*

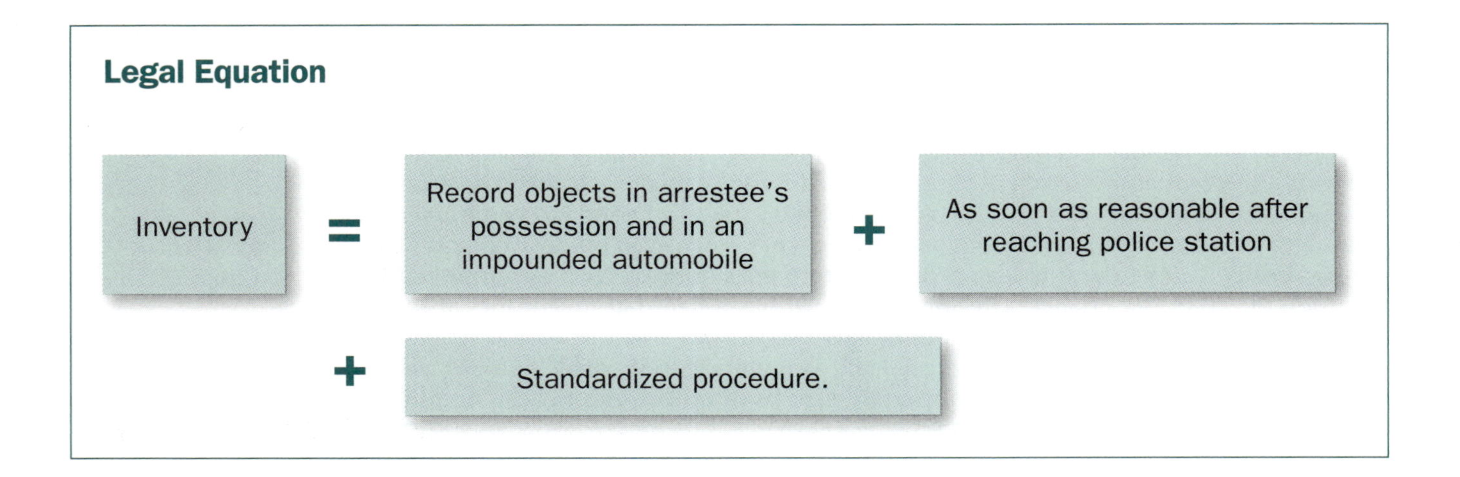

Chapter Summary

The U.S. Supreme Court has held that there is a preference under the Fourth Amendment for searches to be based on warrants founded on probable cause. In the view of the Court, the rights of citizens are more fully protected when the existence of probable cause is determined by a judge rather than by a police officer acting under the pressures of the moment. A magistrate or judge must find that an affidavit provides probable cause to issue a search warrant. The warrant must "particularly" describe the object of the search and the address where there is probable cause to believe that the object is located. The search may extend to any place in a home or structure where the object "may be found." The police are required to knock and announce their presence in executing a warrant. The knock and announce requirement may be disregarded when the facts and circumstances justify an immediate entry. In such cases, the proper balance between the need of the police to investigate crime and the personal privacy of the individual is struck where there is reasonable suspicion that an announcement of the police presence would be dangerous or futile or inhibit the effective investigation of a crime by allowing for the destruction of evidence.

Despite the preference for warrants, the U.S. Supreme Court has recognized the reasonableness under the Fourth Amendment of a number of warrantless searches. Warrantless searches incident to an arrest are reasonable under the Fourth Amendment when an individual is arrested for a felony or even for a minor misdemeanor. Contemporaneous with the arrest, the police may conduct a search for weapons or contraband on the individual's person and in the area under his or her immediate control. This protects the officer and prevents the destruction of evidence. A search incident to an arrest permits the contemporaneous search of the passenger compartment of an automobile and any containers within the passenger compartment. A search of an automobile incident to an arrest may be undertaken when the

> arrestee is within reaching distance of the passenger compartment at the time of the search or it is reasonable to believe the vehicle contains evidence of the offense of arrest. When these justifications are absent, a search of an arrestee's vehicle will be unreasonable unless police obtain a warrant or show that another exception to the warrant requirement applies.

A court will not examine the motivation of an officer who executes an arrest. The only question is whether there is probable cause. A "pretext arrest" accordingly does not constitute a defense to an arrest under the Fourth Amendment. An individual may challenge a pretext arrest as a violation of the Equal Protection Clause of the Fifth and Fourteenth Amendments.

A consent search also is reasonable under the Fourth Amendment. The standard is whether the consent is voluntary and is not the product of duress or coercion, express or implied. The prosecution possesses a heavy burden to establish that a consent is voluntary based on the totality of the circumstances. The scope of a consent search is based on what a reasonable person would understand by the exchange between the individual and the police officer. An individual may limit the scope of his or her consent and may withdraw consent by a clear, unambiguous, and unequivocal statement. The Supreme Court has recognized the reasonableness of a third party's consent when an individual possesses common authority or apparent authority. The Court also has held that there is "no recognized authority in law or social practice" for a third party to consent to a search when a co-occupant is present and refuses to consent.

The automobile exception to the Fourth Amendment warrant requirement permits the police to search a motor vehicle without a warrant. The search may extend to any part of the automobile or container within the automobile where the object of the search may be located. In Chapter 5, we previously discussed other warrantless searches: plain view, frisks pursuant to reasonable suspicion stops, and exigent circumstances.

The last section of Chapter 6 covered inventories. An inventory of an automobile and of a suspect's possessions may be conducted as soon as is reasonable after reaching the station house. An inventory is considered a special needs search, because it is an administrative procedure that is not intended to investigate a crime. In Chapter 7, we discuss other administrative and special needs searches.

Chapter Review Questions

1. Discuss search warrants and the particularity requirement.
2. Define the knock and announce rule. When are the police justified in not adhering to the knock and announce requirement?
3. Discuss the purpose of a search incident to an arrest. Compare and contrast searches incident to arrest with frisks.
4. What is the scope (extent) of a search incident to an arrest? Why is there a contemporaneous requirement for searches incident to an arrest?
5. Define the scope of a police search when they arrest the driver of an automobile on the highway. How does *Thornton* expand the holding in *Belton*?
6. Elaborate on pretext arrests and whether pretext arrests constitute a defense under the Fourth Amendment.
7. What is the legal standard for a consent search?
8. Define the scope of a consent search. May an individual withdraw his or her consent?
9. What is the scope of a probable cause search of an automobile?
10. Discuss the requirements for a third party consent search.
11. Under what circumstances may the police search a container in an automobile without a warrant? Does it matter whether the container is owned by the driver or by a passenger? Is a warrant required when the same container is searched when it is outside the motor vehicle?
12. When may the police conduct an inventory? What are the requirements for an inventory search?

Legal Terminology

automobile exception
bright-line rule
consent search
contemporaneous
grab area
inventory
knock and announce
particularity requirement
pretext arrest
search incident to an arrest
search warrant
third party consent

Criminal Procedure on the Web

Log on to the Web-based student study site at **http://www.sagepub.com/lippmancp** to assist you in completing the Criminal Procedure on the Web exercises, as well as for additional features such as leading cases, podcasts, self-quizzes, and audio/video links.

1. Examine state laws on racial profiling compiled by the Northeastern University Racial Profiling Data Collection Center.
2. You can find a federal search warrant form at a U.S. government Web site.
3. Read a *Christian Science Monitor* article on the cities that are reconsidering the advisability of no knock warrants.
4. A *National Law Journal* article considers third party consent searches and computers.

Bibliography

Jonathan Dressler and Alan C. Michaels, *Understanding Criminal Procedure: Investigation,* vol. 1, 4th ed. (Newark, NJ: LexisNexis, 2006), pp. 167–189, 197–240, 251–276. A comprehensive and easily understood discussion of warrants and warrantless searches.

Patrik Jonsson, "After Atlanta Raid Tragedy, New Scrutiny of Police Tactics." *The Christian Science Monitor* (2006, November 29). Retrieved September 3, 2009, from http://www.csmonitor.com/2006/1129/p03s03-ussc.html. The debate over the wisdom of no-knock police entries into homes.

Wayne R. LaFave, Jerold H. Israel, and Nancy J. King, *Criminal Procedure,* 4th ed. (St. Paul, MN: West Publishing, 2004), pp. 141–211, 249–297. A sophisticated discussion of probable cause, search warrants, and warrantless searches.

Stephen A. Saltzburg, Daniel J. Capra, and Angela J. Davis, *Basic Criminal Procedure,* 4th ed. (St. Paul, MN: West Publishing, 2006), pp. 148–170, 295–349. An outline of the essential cases on warrants and warrantless searches.

Russell L. Weaver, Leslie W. Abramson, John M. Burkoff, and Catherine Hancock, *Principles of Criminal Procedure* (St. Paul, MN: West Publishing, 2004), pp. 60–82, 92–113. A clear and accessible discussion of the basic legal principles regarding warrants and warrantless searches.

7 Inspections and Regulatory Searches

May New York City employ suspicionless container searches to protect the subway system from a terrorist attack?

In 1997, police uncovered a plot to bomb Brooklyn's Atlantic Avenue subway station—a massive commuter hub that joins ten different subway lines and the Long Island Railroad. In 2004, police thwarted another plot to bomb the Herald Square subway station, which networks eight different subway lines in Manhattan. . . . In 2004, terrorists killed over 230 people by using concealed explosives to bomb commuter trains in Madrid and Moscow. On July 7, 2005, terrorists—again using concealed explosives—killed more than 56 people and wounded another 700 individuals by launching a coordinated series of attacks on the London subway and bus systems. Two weeks later, on July 21, 2005, terrorists launched a second but unsuccessful wave of concealed explosive attacks on the London subway system.

Core Concepts and Summary Statements

Introduction

A. Administrative inspections enforce agency rules and regulations in regard to building codes, health, immigration, fire and worker safety, and other matters and require warrants based on a modified probable cause standard.

B. Special-needs searches do not serve the ordinary needs of law enforcement and are not designed to gather evidence or to investigate a crime. These searches typically require reasonable suspicion or do not require any articulable suspicion whatsoever.

Administrative Inspections

A. Government agencies conduct searches of homes, businesses, and factories to check on compliance with governmental regulations. These regulations cover health, fire and worker safety, environmental measures, and housing codes.

B. The Supreme Court held in *Camera v. Municipal Court* that the governmental interest in administrative inspections of the home outweighs an individual's privacy interests and accordingly requires only a modified probable cause standard for the administrative search.

C. In *See v. Seattle,* the Supreme Court approved the inspection of commercial enterprises based on a modified probable cause standard.

D. Probable cause and warrants are not required in the case of "closely regulated businesses." This includes junkyards, automobile dismantlers, liquor dealers, gun stores, and nuclear power plants.

Special-Needs Searches

A. Special-needs searches involve two steps. First, is the search based on special needs beyond the normal needs of law enforcement? Second, the court balances the governmental interest against the intrusion on the individual interest to determine whether the search requires probable cause, requires reasonable suspicion, or may be undertaken without articulable suspicion.

B. Special-needs searches have been relied on for border searches, airport screening, workplace drug testing, school drug testing, physical searches of students, and searches of probationers, parolees, and prisoners.

International Borders

A. Suspicionless stops and searches by "roving patrols" are lawful at the border or at the functional equivalent of the border. Stops outside the narrow confines of the border must be based on reasonable suspicion.

B. The border exception to the Fourth Amendment authorizes warrantless, routine searches at the American border or at its functional equivalent without reasonable suspicion. Routine searches include the search of luggage and persons.

C. Nonroutine border searches entail intrusive searches, such as strip and body-cavity searches or x-rays. These searches intrude on an individual's dignity and privacy and require reasonable suspicion.

Motor Vehicle Checkpoints

A. Stops of automobiles by roving patrols outside the area of the border require reasonable suspicion.
B. Automobiles may be stopped at checkpoints on the U.S.–Mexican border without reasonable suspicion or probable cause in order to protect the territory of the United States.
C. Checkpoints may be employed in the United States in the interests of highway safety. Checkpoints whose primary purpose is to detect ordinary crimes are an unreasonable intrusion on individual privacy.

Airport Screening

Courts have recognized the "special need" to x-ray carry-on baggage for weapons and explosives and to subject passengers to both a preboarding "walk-through screening" and a handheld magnometer "wanding" without reasonable suspicion.

Workplace Drug Testing

The Supreme Court upheld the workplace drug testing of railroad employees following an accident in *Skinner v. Railway Labor Executives' Association.* The government has a strong interest in regulating the conduct of railroad employees involved in "safety-sensitive" activities in order to protect the railroad-traveling public.

Searches in High Schools

A. The Supreme Court held in *New Jersey v. T.L.O.* that the Fourth and Fourteenth Amendments protect students against unreasonable searches and seizures by public school authorities. Reasonableness, however, in the context of student disciplinary investigations is not a matter of probable cause. The reasonable suspicion standard, according to the Supreme Court, relieves school personnel of the burden of learning the "niceties of probable cause" and insures that searches will be carried out in accordance with the "dictates of reason and common sense."
B. In *Vernonia School District 473 v. Acton,* the U.S. Supreme Court upheld the random drug testing of high school athletes.

Probation and Parole

A. In *Griffin v. Wisconsin,* the Supreme Court upheld the constitutionality of the warrantless searches of probationers based on reasonable suspicion that the individual was violating the conditions of his or her probation. The Court explained that the reasonable suspicion standard permits probation officers to intervene at the first signs of trouble rather than wait to develop probable cause.
B. In *United States v. Knights,* the Court upheld the warrantless search of a probationer's home based on reasonable suspicion of criminal activity.

Correctional Institutions

A. In *Hudson v. Palmer,* the U.S. Supreme Court held that inmates have no expectation of privacy in their cells.
B. *Bell v. Wolfish* approved visual cavity inspections of pretrial detainees or inmates returning to the cell block from a contact visit with an individual from outside the institution. These searches were viewed as reasonable because the need to deter the smuggling of weapons, drugs, and other prohibited items outweighed the intrusion into individuals' privacy interests.

Introduction

This chapter discusses administrative searches and "special needs" searches. These two categories of searches have a great deal in common and often are treated as a single type of search in textbooks.

First, they primarily are carried out by public agencies that are not part of the police (although at times the police may be involved).

Second, unlike most other Fourth Amendment searches, they are not aimed at investigating or collecting evidence of a specific crime committed by a specific individual or individuals.

Third, a *strict* probable cause standard is not required. The reasonableness of these searches is based on a balancing of the government's interest in the search against the intrusion on individual rights resulting from the search.

Administrative inspections are conducted by government agencies to determine whether individuals and businesses are following local ordinances regulating areas such as housing and fire codes and health standards. Searches also are carried out by federal investigators in areas regulated by national law, such as mine safety and nuclear power plants. There are some additional points to keep in mind regarding administrative searches.

- Administrative inspections usually are conducted by agency investigators rather than by the police, and a violation of the law typically results in a civil fine. In some cases, a statute also may impose a modest criminal penalty.

- Administrative searches primarily are intended to determine whether standards that protect public safety and welfare are being met. These searches typically do not significantly intrude on individuals' privacy and may be based either on consent or on a warrant supported by modified or relaxed probable cause.
- Administrative inspections of "highly regulated industries" may be carried out without probable cause or a warrant. The rights of individuals are considered to be adequately protected by the comprehensive legal standards that limit the discretion of government investigators.

Special-needs searches do not serve the ordinary needs of law enforcement and are not undertaken to investigate a crime or to gather evidence of a crime. In this chapter, we discuss a number of special-needs searches including border searches, motor vehicle checkpoints, drug testing in the workplace, physical searches and drug testing in schools, and searches of probationers, parolees, and prisoners.

- Special-needs searches are not necessarily conducted by a police officer. They may involve individuals ranging from airport screeners and public school teachers to probation officers.
- Special-needs searches generally are concerned with enforcing regulations that protect the safety and welfare of individuals and of the public rather than with investigating the criminal conduct of a specific individual or group of individuals.
- Special-needs searches do not require a warrant or probable cause. They typically are based on reasonable suspicion and, in some instances, may be carried out without any articulable basis whatsoever.

A central point to keep in mind as you read this chapter is that administrative searches and special-needs searches are different than searches carried out to investigate criminal activity. The courts employ a balancing test under the Reasonableness Clause of the Fourth Amendment to determine the standard governing these searches. The U.S. Supreme Court has held that the government interest in conducting these searches outweighs the resulting intrusion on individual rights, and in most instances, the traditional probable cause and warrant requirements have been found to unduly interfere with the government's ability to undertake these searches. As a result, administrative inspections and special-needs searches are not required to meet a strict probable cause standard.

As you read this chapter, pay particular attention to the balancing approach that is employed by the Supreme Court to determine whether an administrative or special-needs search is reasonable under the Fourth and Fourteenth Amendments. Consider whether the Court strikes the proper balance between the societal interests in conducting the search and the individual interest in privacy. Should the law distinguish between administrative and special-needs searches and searches undertaken to investigate crimes?

Administrative Inspections

Searches of homes and businesses are carried by government administrative agencies as well as by the police. Agencies undertake these **administrative inspections** to insure that individuals and businesses are conforming to a broad range of agency regulations. This includes complying with health regulations by restaurants, adhering to fire codes by bars and clubs, maintaining records by gun dealers, protecting worker safety in factories, and insuring that apartments and homes satisfy housing codes. Another example is the U.S. Citizen and Immigration Services' monitoring of businesses to determine whether they are employing undocumented workers. These searches typically are carried out by administrative investigators, although the police at times may be involved. A violation of an administrative requirement may result in both a civil fine and a criminal conviction. Criminal liability also may result when the administrative violation violates a separate criminal statute. For example, a business may be fined for failing to obey environmental regulations regarding water pollution. The corporation's chemical pollution of the water supply also may violate a separate criminal statute and result in penal punishment.

In the frequently cited case of *Camara v. Municipal Court,* the U.S. Supreme Court held unconstitutional a San Francisco ordinance that authorized fire, health, housing, and other inspectors to enter private residences without a warrant based on probable cause. The Court held that administrative inspections are regulated by the Fourth and Fourteenth Amendments and observed that the failure to require a warrant would leave individuals without protection against administrative intrusions (*Camara v. Municipal Court,* 387 U.S. 523, 534 [1967]).

Camara refused to permit a housing inspector to enter his home without a warrant on three occasions and was subject to a fine and imprisonment. The Court held that administrative inspections for housing code violations are entirely reasonable under the Fourth Amendment. Society, for example, has an interest in insuring that fire escapes, fire alarms, and sprinkler systems are operating properly that clearly outweighs the limited inconvenience caused by an administrative inspection to a resident or to residents of a building (538–539).

The Supreme Court noted that it is virtually impossible to require an agency to establish probable cause that a particular building has a specific defect. Safety hazards such as faulty wiring or a defective elevator often are not even apparent to occupants. The Supreme Court accordingly ruled that it is entirely reasonable to base an administrative warrant to search a house or apartment on a **modified probable cause** standard. This may entail an "area warrant" that authorizes the search of every building of a particular age or design or the search of all homes in an area of the city. A warrant is not required in those instances in which an individual consents to the administrative search (535–538).

In *See v. City of Seattle,* the Supreme Court considered whether a "routine, periodic citywide canvass" to determine whether *commercial buildings* are in compliance with the city fire code may be conducted without a warrant. The owner of a warehouse refused access to a city inspector and was fined $100. The Supreme Court applied the precedent in *Camera* and held that the "businessman, like the occupant of a residence, has a constitutional right to go about his business free from unreasonable official entries upon his private commercial property. The businessman, too, has that right placed in jeopardy if the decision to enter and inspect for violation of regulatory laws can be made and enforced by the inspector in the field without official authority evidenced by a warrant." The Supreme Court also recognized that there is a significant governmental interest in conducting the commercial inspection and held that an inspector may obtain a warrant to search a commercial enterprise on the same modified probable cause standard that applies to residences. The inspector is required to demonstrate only that the business is the type of structure that is subject to inspection (*See v. City of Seattle,* 387 U.S. 541, 543 [1967]).

In 1987, the Supreme Court, in *New York v. Burger,* affirmed the reasonableness of a warrantless search by the police of an automobile junkyard under the **closely regulated business** exception. In *Burger,* the police arrived unannounced at Joseph Burger's automobile junkyard and found that Burger did not have the required license to operate the junkyard or maintain the required records of automobiles and vehicle parts. The officers then carried out an inspection and discovered various stolen vehicles and vehicle parts. Burger was arrested and charged with five counts of possession of stolen property and one count of operating without a license (*New York v. Burger,* 482 U.S. 691 [1987]).

The Supreme Court held that automobile junkyards historically have been subject to numerous administrative regulations and obligations and qualified as closely regulated businesses. Warrantless searches without probable cause of automobile junkyards are justified by the substantial government interest in assisting the police in tracing stolen goods and in deterring "auto dismantlers" from purchasing and selling stolen vehicles and vehicle parts. Burger was aware that his business was subject to periodic inspections, and despite the fact that the police were not required to obtain a warrant, his privacy interest in his heavily regulated business was adequately protected by the New York law that provided that inspections are to be conducted during business hours and are to be limited to an examination of business records and of vehicles and vehicle parts.

The closely regulated business exception has been extended to authorize the warrantless inspection of liquor and gun dealers, the mining industry, racetracks, chemical and nuclear power plants, and railroads. Note that evidence of a crime that is discovered in plain view during an administrative search may be seized by the police. In the event that the police decide to launch a criminal investigation, they must obtain a criminal warrant based on probable cause and can no longer rely on an administrative warrant (*Michigan v. Clifford,* 464 U.S. 287 [1984]).

In the next section of this chapter, we turn our attention to the reasonableness of special-needs searches.

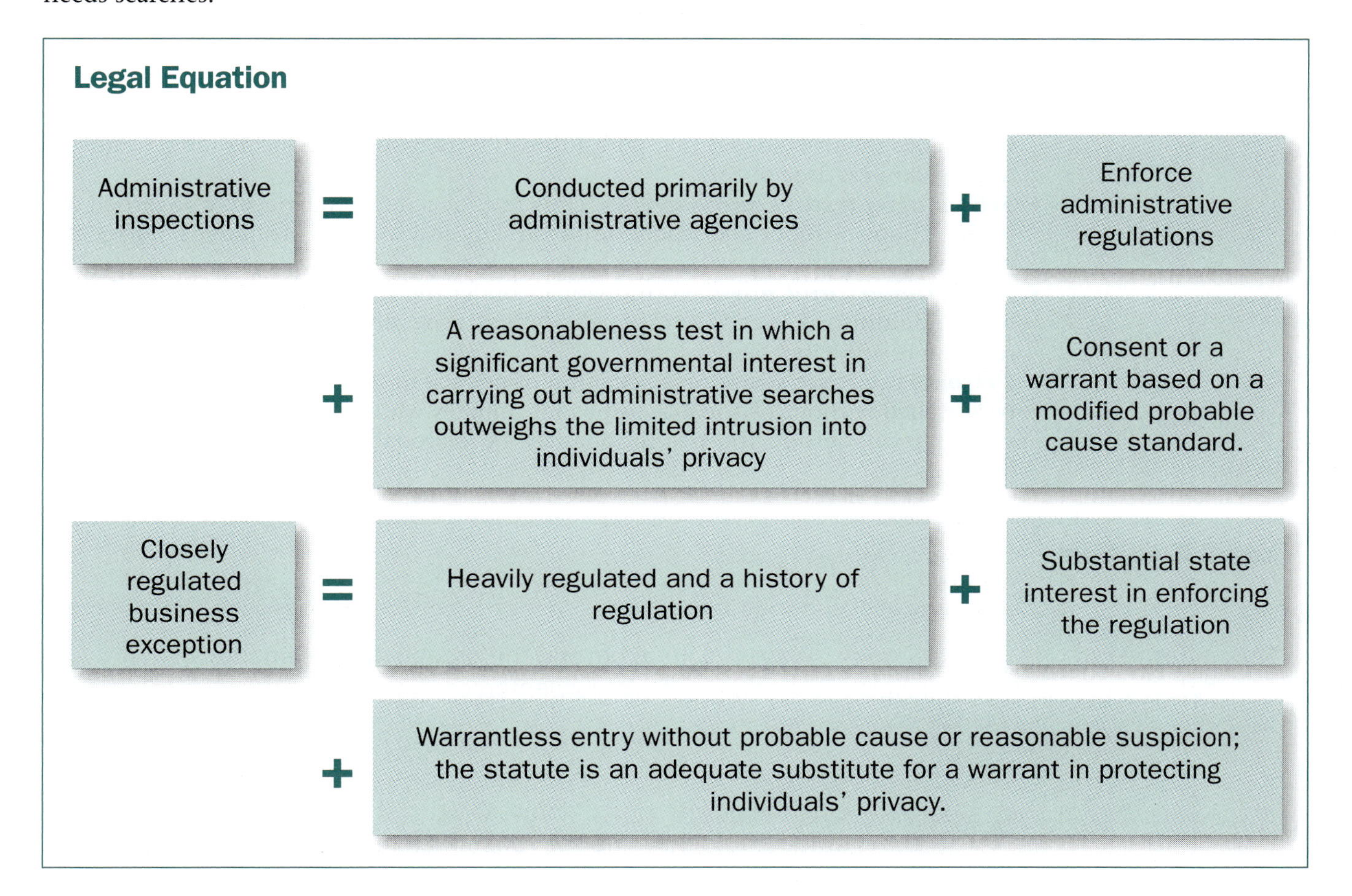

Special-Needs Searches

Special-needs searches do not serve the ordinary needs of law enforcement and are intended to promote the safety and welfare of individuals and of the public. They are not intended to gather evidence of a crime. The reasonableness of these searches is determined by balancing the interests of the government against the privacy rights of the individual, and these searches generally do not require a warrant or probable cause.

The courts employ a two-step analysis in a special-needs search.

The first step is to establish that the search is directed at a special need "beyond the special needs of law enforcement." In other words, the search is not being carried out to investigate a crime.

The second step is to evaluate the reasonableness of the search. The Court asks whether the government interest at stake outweighs the individual privacy interest. In those instances in which the probable cause and/or warrant requirement interferes with the government's achievement of the special need, courts have held that it is reasonable to conduct the search based on the "lesser standard" of reasonable suspicion or without any articulable suspicion whatsoever.

In this chapter, we discuss several special-needs searches. Pay attention to the balancing process undertaken by the courts in considering the reasonableness of these searches.

- ***Border searches.*** Brief and unintrusive routine searches at the U.S. border may be conducted without reasonable suspicion or probable cause. Nonroutine searches require reasonable suspicion.
- ***Automobile checkpoints.*** Automobiles may be briefly stopped at fixed checkpoints in the interests of highway safety.
- ***Airport screening of passengers.*** Airline passengers and their belongings and baggage may be searched without reasonable suspicion.
- ***Workplace drug testing.*** Employees who are on the job during a railroad accident or whose jobs involve dangers that pose a threat to the public may be required to submit to suspicionless drug testing.
- ***School drug testing and searches.*** Drug tests of certain students may be carried out in the schools without reasonable suspicion. Physical searches of students' purses and possessions require reasonable suspicion.
- ***Probationers and parolees.*** Individuals under the supervision of state authorities have a diminished expectation of privacy and generally may be searched based on reasonable suspicion.
- ***Prisoners.*** Prisoners lack an expectation of privacy in their cells, and their cells may be searched without reasonable suspicion. Inmates who have had contact with individuals from outside the institution may be reasonably subjected to body-cavity searches.

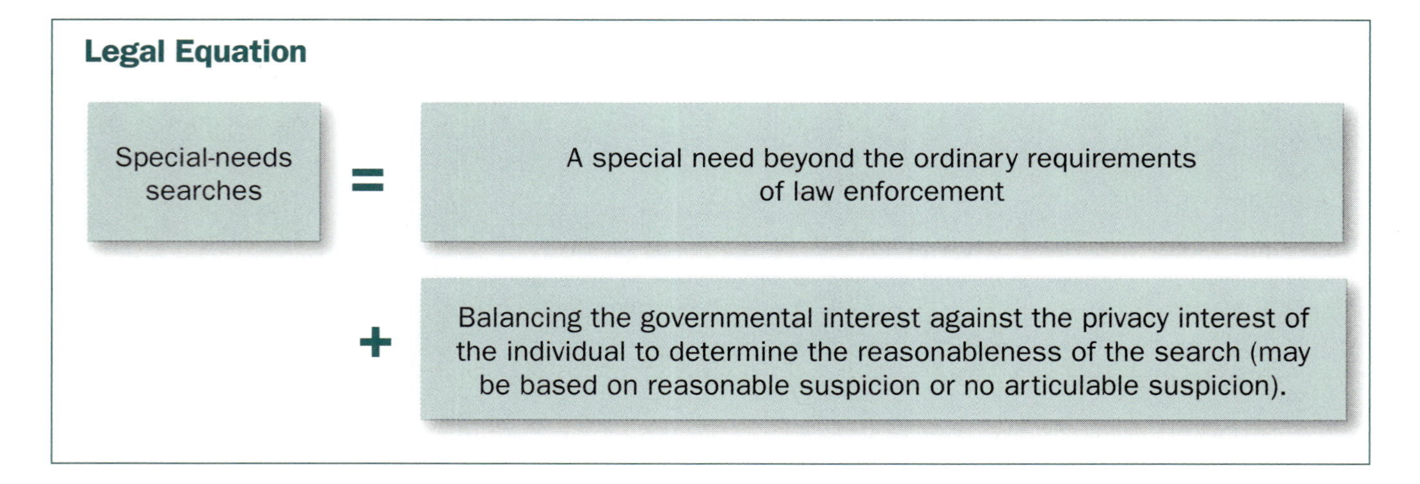

International Borders

The so-called **border exception** to the Fourth Amendment provides that routine searches at the border without reasonable suspicion are reasonable based on the sovereign right of the United States to prevent illegal entry and to protect against the smuggling of illegal drugs and other contraband. This interest outweighs the greatly diminished privacy interest of individuals seeking to enter the United States. Nonroutine searches, however, require reasonable suspicion. The governmental interest in carrying out searches is at its zenith at the international border.

Chief Justice William Rehnquist observed in 1977 that border searches have been considered to be "'reasonable' by the single fact that the person or item in question had entered into our country from outside.... This longstanding recognition that searches at our borders without probable cause and without a warrant are nonetheless 'reasonable' has a history as old as the Fourth Amendment itself." We first discuss the Supreme Court's "roving patrol" cases in which the Court defined the territory that is considered to be within the border area, and then, we examine the law regarding searches at the United States' international borders (*United States v. Ramsey,* 431 U.S. 606, 616, 619 [1977]).

Roving Patrols

In *Almedia-Sanchez v. United States,* the U.S. Supreme Court held that the border extends beyond the intersection between the United States and Mexico. The Court defined the border to include what it termed the *functional equivalent of the border.* This includes a *border station close to the border, the intersection of two highways leading from the border, or the point of arrival of a nonstop flight from a foreign country to the United States.* In *Almedia-Sanchez,* the U.S. Supreme Court ruled that *roving patrol* seizures and searches by the U.S. Border Patrol without reasonable suspicion on a California road that "lies at all points" at least twenty miles north of the Mexican border violated motorists' Fourth Amendment right to be free from unreasonable searches and seizures. The Supreme Court explained that while "roving patrols" are important in apprehending undocumented individuals who evaded border inspection, the random stops in *Almedia-Sanchez* were too far removed from the border and threatened to interfere with the rights of innocent American citizens and residents (*Almeida-Sanchez v. United States,* 413 U.S. 266, 273–274 [1973]). In *United States v. Brignoni-Ponce,* the Supreme Court stressed that "except for the border and its functional equivalent, officers on roving patrol may stop vehicles and question the occupants only if they are aware of specific articulable facts, together with rational inferences from those facts, that reasonably warrant suspicion that the vehicles contain aliens who may be illegally in the country" (*United States v. Brignoni-Ponce,* 433 U.S. 873, 886–887 [1975]).

In brief, suspicionless stops and searches by roving patrols are lawful at the border or at the functional equivalent of the border. Stops outside the narrow confines of the border region must be based on reasonable suspicion. Should the Supreme Court extend the territory that is considered the functional equivalent of the border to assist law enforcement in combating the flow of undocumented workers into the United States? We now examine the law regarding border searches.

Border Searches

Courts have distinguished between **routine border searches** and **nonroutine border searches.** Routine border searches are the typical searches of luggage and persons that you experience at an airport. There is *no requirement of articulable suspicion*. Nonroutine border searches are intrusive searches, such as strip and body-cavity searches or involuntary x-rays. Nonroutine searches intrude on individuals' dignity and privacy and require articulable suspicion.

The Seventh Circuit Court of Appeals explained that routine border searches are distinguished by the fact that they "do not pose a serious invasion of privacy and do not embarrass or offend the average traveler" (*United States v. Johnson,* 991 F.2d 1287, 1291 [7th Cir. 1993]).

The U.S. Supreme Court's decision in *United States v. Manuel Flores-Montano* illustrates the exception for routine border searches. In *United States v. Manuel Flores-Montano,* customs officials seized as much as eighty-one pounds of marijuana from Manuel Flores-Montano's gas tank at the international border. A customs official tapped the gas tank of Flores-Montano's automobile and concluded that it sounded solid and called a mechanic to detach the tank from the car. The mechanic managed to remove the gas tank, a process that consumed roughly sixty minutes. The U.S. Supreme Court ruled that reasonable suspicion is not required for the search of vehicles at the border because these searches are not "highly intrusive" and do not threaten an individual's "dignity and privacy." The Court noted that suspicionless searches of automobile gas tanks were an increasingly important law enforcement tool. During the previous sixty-six months, there had been 18,788 gas-tank drug seizures at the border, which accounted for roughly twenty percent of drug seizures. At what point would a search of a motor vehicle require reasonable suspicion? Would the Supreme Court require reasonable suspicion to drill into the shell of an SUV or to dismantle an engine or exhaust pipes (*United States v. Manuel Flores-Montano,* 541 U.S. 149, 154–156 [2004])?

The difference in intrusiveness between a routine and a nonroutine border search may be somewhat clarified by examining the Supreme Court's decision in *United States v. Montoya de Hernandez.* In *Montoya de Hernandez,* the U.S. Supreme Court approved the detention of Rosa Elvira Montoya de Hernandez on reasonable suspicion that she had swallowed and was smuggling cocaine-filled balloons into the United States. Montoya de Hernandez had arrived at Los Angeles International Airport from Colombia and was told that she would be detained until she either consented to an x-ray or had a bowel movement. The Supreme Court held that the detention of an individual "at a border, beyond the scope of a routine customs search and inspection, is justified . . . if customs agents . . . reasonably suspect that the traveler is smuggling contraband in her alimentary canal" (*United States v. Montoya de Hernandez,* 473 U.S. 531, 541 [1985]).

After sixteen hours, customs officials decided to obtain a court order authorizing a pregnancy test, an x-ray, and a rectal examination. A physician conducted a rectal examination and removed cocaine-filled balloons. *Montoya de Hernandez* was formally arrested and, over the next four days, passed eighty-eight similar balloons (533–536). The Supreme Court held that Montoya de Hernandez's detention was not "unreasonably long. It occurred at the international border, where the Fourth Amendment balance of interests leans heavily to the Government. . . . In the presence of articulable suspicion of smuggling . . . her detention for the period of time necessary to either verify or dispel the suspicion was not unreasonable" (544).

Can you explain how the Court has balanced the protection of our nation's borders against the interests of the individual? Has the Court struck the right balance? The next case in the book, *United States v. Esieke,* asks you to consider at what point the search and seizure of suspected alimentary canal drug smugglers may be unreasonable and whether there should be judicial monitoring of the extended detention of drug smugglers.

You can find United States v. Manuel Flores-Montano *on the study site, http://www.sagepub.com/lippmancp.*

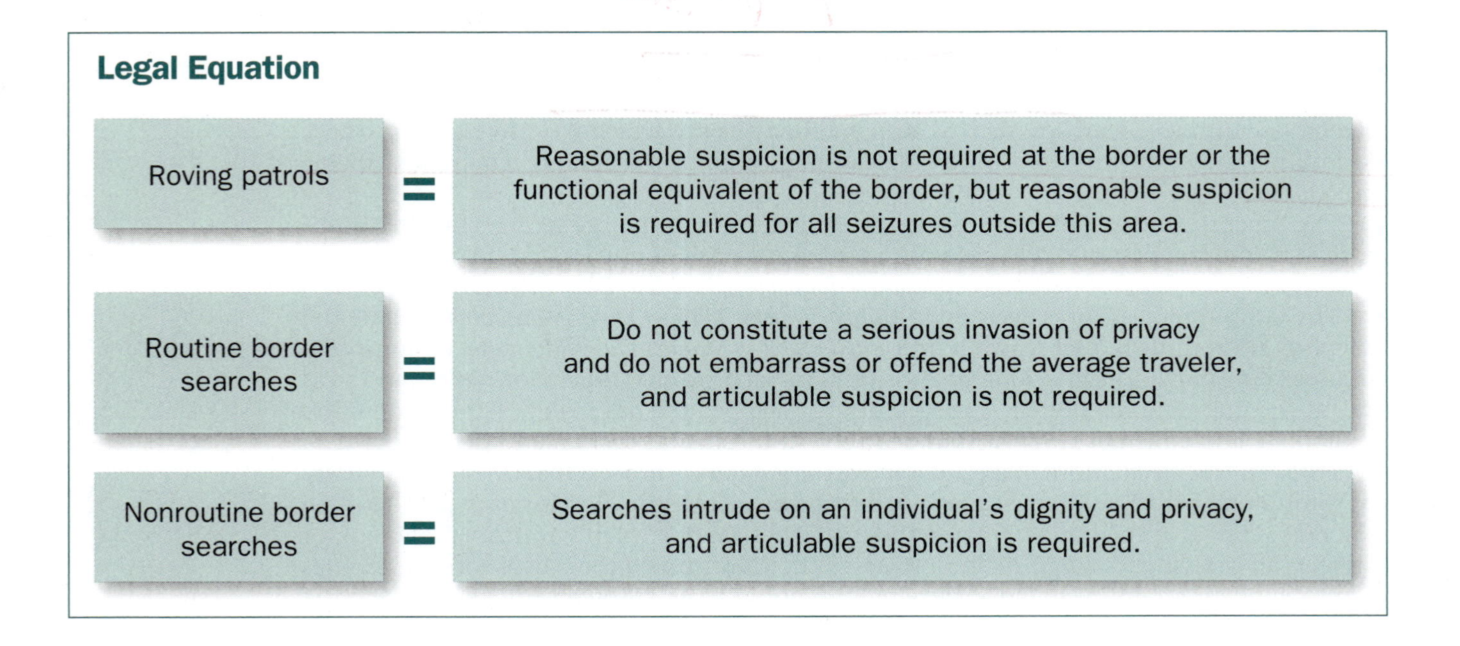

Legal Equation

Roving patrols	=	Reasonable suspicion is not required at the border or the functional equivalent of the border, but reasonable suspicion is required for all seizures outside this area.
Routine border searches	=	Do not constitute a serious invasion of privacy and do not embarrass or offend the average traveler, and articulable suspicion is not required.
Nonroutine border searches	=	Searches intrude on an individual's dignity and privacy, and articulable suspicion is required.

Was the defendant's three-day detention unreasonable?

United States v. Esieke, 940 F.2d 29 (2d Cir. 1991), Altimari, J.

Facts

On the morning of March 10, 1990, defendant-appellant Chico Esieke arrived at John F. Kennedy Airport ("Kennedy Airport") on a flight that originated in Lagos, Nigeria. As Esieke proceeded through the customs area of the International Arrivals Building, he was stopped by Senior Inspector Dwight Powers of the U.S. Customs Service. Inspector Powers identified himself and asked to see Esieke's passport and customs declaration card. According to Powers, Esieke appeared to be very nervous; his hands were shaking and he fumbled about as he attempted to locate and produce the requested documents.

In response to the inspector's questions, Esieke related that he was in the camera sales business and had traveled to Nigeria for approximately six weeks to conduct business. Esieke further stated that he was a Nigerian citizen who resided in Fort Worth, Texas, and possessed a green card. Indeed, Esieke produced a Nigerian passport, which had been issued in Lagos, Nigeria, on March 5, 1990, five days prior to his return to the United States. The passport listed Esieke's occupation as an engineer and indicated that his previous passport had been lost. Additionally, Esieke informed Inspector Powers that, for reasons related to his camera business, he had taken $5,000 with him to Nigeria. However, Esieke subsequently remarked that he had taken only $1,000 on his trip. Esieke also told Powers that he expected to earn $10,000 to $15,000 in the camera business this year.

Inspector Powers accompanied Esieke to the custom's baggage examining area and then turned his attention to Esieke's luggage, which consisted of a small garment bag and a briefcase. Upon examination of the contents of the garment bag, Powers found that Esieke was traveling with few items of clothing. Inside the briefcase, Powers found a billfold, which contained a check imprinted with the name "Chico Food Market." When Powers removed the check from the billfold, Esieke explained that he had neglected to mention that he owned a supermarket. While examining the briefcase, Powers also discovered Esieke's Texas driver's license as well as several photographs of Esieke standing next to and sitting inside a new BMW automobile. Unlike Esieke's other forms of identification, the driver's license included a middle name, "Oruworuowho." After completing the luggage examination, Powers and Esieke moved to a room that was off the main floor of the International Arrivals Building.

As a result of the foregoing, Inspector Powers suspected that Esieke might be an alimentary canal smuggler, that Esieke had swallowed balloons or condoms containing narcotics that would be recovered from Esieke's feces after he had successfully entered the United States. After conferring with his supervisor, Powers conducted a strip search of Esieke, which failed to reveal any contraband. At this point, Powers informed Esieke that he was suspected of carrying narcotics internally and presented Esieke with an x-ray consent form, which Esieke was asked to read. In response, Esieke became extremely angry, threw the form down, and asked to see his lawyer. Powers then explained that if Esieke did not consent to an x-ray, he could be detained for monitored bowel movements. Nevertheless, Esieke refused to be x-rayed, commenting that he had been x-rayed in Dallas and that x-rays were harmful. Powers once again consulted with his supervisor, who ordered Esieke to be held for monitored bowel movements.

Additionally, at some point during the course of these events, Powers ran Esieke's name and date of birth through the Treasury Enforcement Communications System Computer. The computer system revealed that "Esieke Chico Oruworuowho" was suspected of narcotics smuggling. Powers later learned that the alleged smuggling activities had occurred in the Dallas–Fort Worth area.

Inspector Powers informed Esieke that he was going to be detained for monitored bowel movements. Powers handcuffed Esieke and escorted him to a large mobile two-story structure that served as a customs detention facility. Inside the structure, Esieke changed into a hospital gown and was placed on a bed. One of his hands was secured to the bed railing by a handcuff, and his legs were placed in leg irons. There were several other customs detainees held in the facility, and like Esieke, each was handcuffed to a bed. The detainees were permitted to leave their beds only if they needed to use the facility's "potty seat," which consisted of a toilet seat mounted on a receptacle. On such occasions, a customs inspector would escort the detainee to the potty seat and observe as the detainee relieved himself.

During his first day in detention, Esieke failed either to defecate or urinate. The following day, around noontime, Esieke indicated that he wanted to speak with one of the customs inspectors on duty. According to Customs Inspector Michael Snow, Esieke motioned for him to come to his bedside and then stated, "Inspector, I have been here for about a day and a half and I seen [*sic*] other prisoners come in and pass drugs . . . I hadn't [*sic*] admitted this to anyone, but I swallowed sixty-three balloons." In response, Inspector Snow called over his supervisor, Senior Inspector Thomas Falanga. In the presence of both Inspectors Falanga and Snow, Esieke repeated that he had swallowed sixty-three balloons.

Later that afternoon, Esieke moved his bowels for the first time since he had been detained. Upon examination, it was determined that Esieke had passed 24 balloons containing heroin. One of the inspectors then placed Esieke under arrest and informed Esieke of his rights. Over the course of the next day-and-a-half, Esieke, who was still being held in the customs detention facility, passed an additional 39 heroin-filled balloons.

On the morning of March 13, after Esieke passed the final balloon, an agent of the Drug Enforcement Administration (DEA) took custody of Esieke. The DEA agent again read Esieke his rights and drove him to the United States Courthouse for the Eastern District of New York. En route, Esieke questioned the DEA agent about the weight of the drugs he had passed. The agent stated that the gross weight, i.e., the weight of both the drugs and the balloons, was 600 to 700 grams. Esieke then commented that he thought he had swallowed only 300 grams. In response, the agent explained that the net weight is usually several hundred grams lower than the gross weight. During the ride, Esieke also admitted that the "stuff" was supposed to go to Baltimore.

An... indictment was ultimately filed against Esieke, charging him with importing into the United States over 100 grams of heroin... and with possessing with intent to distribute over 100 grams of heroin, in violation of 21 U.S.C. § 841(a)(1).

Issue

On this appeal, as in district court, Esieke primarily argues that his detention was not supported by reasonable suspicion and, therefore, that the products of that detention must be suppressed. In addition, Esieke suggests that extended border detentions violate the Fourth Amendment unless authorized by a judicial officer. We disagree with both contentions.

Reasoning

In *United States v. Montoya de Hernandez,* the Supreme Court considered the unique problems presented by the advent of alimentary canal smuggling. In that case, customs officials at Los Angeles International Airport stopped and questioned respondent Rosa Montoya de Hernandez, who had arrived on a flight from Bogota, Colombia. The officials suspected that Montoya was an alimentary canal smuggler. When she declined to undergo an x-ray examination and could not be placed on a return flight to Colombia, Montoya was detained. After more than sixteen hours, the customs officials obtained a court order authorizing a rectal examination and an involuntary x-ray. The rectal examination resulted in the discovery of the first of eighty-eight cocaine-filled balloons. The district court denied Montoya's motion to suppress the cocaine contained in the balloons, and Montoya was convicted of possession with intent to distribute and of unlawful importation of cocaine. The case was ultimately appealed to the Supreme Court.

Writing on behalf of the Court, the present Chief Justice stressed that consistent with "Congress' power to protect the Nation by stopping and examining persons entering this country, the Fourth Amendment's balance of reasonableness is qualitatively different at the border than in the interior." Chief Justice Rehnquist also emphasized that individuals presenting themselves for entry into the United States have a lesser expectation of privacy at the border than in the interior.

The Supreme Court held that the detention of a traveler at the border, beyond the scope of a routine customs search and inspection, is justified at its inception if customs agents, considering all the facts surrounding the traveler and her trip, reasonably suspect that the traveler is smuggling contraband in her alimentary canal.... Under this standard, officials at the border must have a "particularized and objective basis for suspecting the particular person" of alimentary canal smuggling. In essence, the Court concluded that an extended border detention of a suspected alimentary canal smuggler would not violate the Fourth Amendment, so long as reasonable suspicion supported the decision to detain the suspect. Chief Justice Rehnquist noted that "courts should not indulge in 'unrealistic second-guessing'" and that "'creative judge[s], engaged in 'after the fact' evaluations of police conduct can almost always imagine some alternative means by which the objectives of the police might have been accomplished.'"

More recently, in *United States v. Odofin,* 929 F.2d 56 (2d Cir. 1991), this court rejected a claim that a five-day border detention without judicial authorization was so long as to violate the Fourth Amendment. In that case, appellant Delaney Abi Odofin was detained by customs officials who suspected that he was an alimentary canal drug smuggler. Like Esieke and Montoya, Odofin refused to consent to an x-ray. After five days of detention without a bowel movement, a lawyer for Odofin appeared before a magistrate and argued that the continued detention of Odofin was unreasonable. The magistrate disagreed and permitted the detention to continue. Ultimately, Odofin was held for a total of twenty-four days until he began to pass several balloons containing narcotics. On appeal, we found "no violation of the Fourth Amendment... where the [customs] agents' well-founded suspicion could reasonably be expected to be confirmed or dispelled within twenty-four hours and the postponement beyond that interval was entirely due to conduct of the defendant."

Turning to the present case, we are convinced that a variety of factors provided Inspector Powers with ample justification for initially detaining Esieke. During his encounter with Inspector Powers, Esieke appeared to be excessively nervous. In response to Powers's routine questioning, Esieke provided contradictory information about his employment and the amount of money he had taken to Nigeria. Esieke was travelling from Nigeria, which, according to the government, is a source country for narcotics, and despite a six-week stay, Esieke was travelling with few items of clothing. While in Nigeria, Esieke had reported that his passport was lost and thereby obtained a replacement passport that concealed the frequency and destination of his prior travel. Moreover, a computer search revealed that an individual with Esieke's name and date of birth was suspected of narcotics smuggling. Finally, the customs inspectors' suspicions were enhanced when Esieke belligerently refused to undergo an x-ray that might have conclusively established whether or not he was internally smuggling contraband. Considering the totality of these circumstances, we have no difficulty concluding that the decision to detain Esieke was supported by reasonable suspicion and did not violate the Fourth Amendment.

We are also satisfied that the length of Esieke's detention did not give rise to a Fourth Amendment violation. *Montoya* and *Odofin* clearly instruct that once reasonable suspicion exists to detain a traveler, the detention can continue "for the period of time necessary to either verify or dispel the suspicion." In other words, an otherwise permissible border detention does not run afoul of the Fourth Amendment simply because a detainee's intestinal fortitude leads to an unexpectedly long period of detention. Here, the customs agents initially offered Esieke the option of undergoing an x-ray examination. Once Esieke rejected that alternative, the officials had little choice but to detain him and "wait him out moment-to-moment." Since any undue delay was the consequence of Esieke's own obstinacy, he alone was responsible for the duration of his detention.

Esieke next contends that a border detention must be treated as a quasi-arrest requiring prompt judicial determination of the grounds supporting the officer's decision to seize the detainee. An extended border detention of a suspected alimentary canal smuggler does not implicate the Fourth Amendment's warrant clause and, accordingly, does not require judicial approval. Rather, the Supreme Court has advised that the border "detention of a suspected alimentary canal smuggler . . . is analogous to the detention of a suspected tuberculosis carrier at the border: both are detained until their bodily processes dispel the suspicion that they will introduce a harmful agent into this country." Accordingly, we do not believe that the Fourth Amendment requires us "to draw any line, 'bright' or otherwise, by which time judicial approval for a border detention must be obtained." As explained above, the length of an extended border detention is governed by the detainee's bodily processes, not by a clock.

We now turn to what is the most vexing issue presented by this appeal—whether the conditions of Esieke's detention violated the Fourth Amendment. As stated above, Esieke was held for one-and-one-half days until he had his first bowel movement, and then for another one-and-one-half days until he had expelled all sixty-three balloons from his body. During that time, he was forced to wear leg irons and was handcuffed to a bed. Further, he was not permitted to leave the bed, except in the company of a customs inspector, and then only to use a makeshift toilet. According to Esieke, these conditions demonstrate that his detention violated the Fourth Amendment.

At oral argument, in response to questioning by the court, the Government explained that Esieke was forced to wear handcuffs and leg irons because suspected narcotic smugglers present a potential threat to the customs inspectors as well as to themselves. We certainly agree that law enforcement officials "ha[ve] a right to take reasonable steps to protect [themselves] . . . regardless of whether probable cause to arrest exists." However, the use of handcuffs and leg irons strongly suggests that the detainees pose a very real and imminent threat of physical violence. While we need not decide whether such a risk is actually presented, we do take notice of the fact that the individuals being detained on suspicion of alimentary canal smuggling are subjected to strip searches, are clad solely in hospital gowns, and presumably are in less than peak physical condition. We therefore question whether the risk they pose is as extreme as the Government imagines. Furthermore, it seems to us that the officials responsible for devising the detention procedures utilized at Kennedy Airport have approached their duties with an unwarranted degree of callousness and may have lost sight of the fact that the persons they detain are merely suspects who have not yet been—and may never be—charged with a crime.

With this said, we are nonetheless unpersuaded that the use of handcuffs and leg irons converted an otherwise permissible detention into a detention in violation of the Fourth Amendment. Under both *Montoya* and *Odofin*, it clearly is permissible to detain incommunicado a traveler suspected of alimentary canal smuggling, against his or her will, in the confines of a guarded room, until the person has had a bowel movement. It is doubtful, although barely so, that the use of handcuffs and leg irons during such a border detention dramatically alters the Fourth Amendment analysis.

Holding

While we acknowledge that this is an extremely close case, we believe that the Fourth Amendment is not violated by the type of detention to which Esieke was subjected. Nevertheless, we are seriously troubled by the Government's practice of detaining suspects for fairly extensive periods of time without judicial authorization. Underlying *Montoya* and its progeny is an assumption that natural forces will compel a traveler, who has just completed a long journey by airplane, to move his bowels within a relatively short time of his arrival. Unfortunately, alimentary canal smugglers have proven unusually adept at staving off the call of nature. While the suspected smuggler is clearly responsible for such delay, this fact does not minimize our concern about the potential health hazards posed by allowing this physiological drama to play itself out. Moreover, with all due respect to the U.S. Customs Service, we are deeply distressed by the notion that individuals are being constrained in handcuffs and leg irons for days and possibly weeks based solely on a customs agent's reasonable suspicion. Consequently, we believe that the interests of justice, as well as the potential health risks engendered by the detention of suspected alimentary canal smugglers, necessitate some form of judicial oversight.

At oral argument, the Government informed the court that it is now standard policy in the Eastern District of New York to notify the U.S. Attorney within seventy-two hours when conducting an extended border detention of a suspected alimentary canal smuggler. We do not think this is sufficient. Henceforth, the U.S. Customs Service—or any other governmental agency overseeing such detentions—shall inform the local U.S. Attorney within twenty-four hours of its decision to detain a suspected alimentary canal smuggler. In turn, the U.S. Attorney shall immediately notify a United States Magistrate Judge and detainee's legal counsel (or the Legal Aid Society) of the ongoing detention.

Questions for Discussion

1. Did customs officials have reasonable suspicion to detain Esieke?
2. Do you agree that the conditions of Esieke's detention were reasonable under the Fourth Amendment?
3. Why does the court of appeals hold that the U.S. Attorney should seek judicial approval from a magistrate judge within twenty-four hours of a detention? What is your view?
4. ***Problems in policing.*** Write a paragraph informing customs officials how to proceed when they suspect that an individual entering the country is carrying drugs in his or her alimentary canal. In this paragraph, also list factors that should alert customs agents that there is reasonable suspicion that an individual is an alimentary canal smuggler.

7.1 YOU DECIDE

Gjon Berisha was in the process of boarding an international flight at the Dallas–Fort Worth International Airport. A U.S. Customs inspector stopped Berisha and asked whether he was carrying more than $10,000. Berisha replied that he was carrying only $8,000 and patted a bulge in his front pants pocket. The inspector told Berisha that if he was carrying more than $10,000, he was required to file a U.S. government report. Berisha again replied that he was carrying only $8,000. The inspector observed a bulge in Berisha's other front pants pocket and directed Berisha to accompany him to a secondary detention area. As Berisha began to walk down the concourse, a customs official grabbed Berisha and prevented him from handing $17,000 over to a friend. Do border searches encompass persons exiting as well as persons entering the United States? See *United States v. Berisha*, 925 F.2d 791 (5th Cir. 1991).

You can find the answer by referring to the study site, http://www.sagepub.com/lippmancp.

Roving patrols without reasonable suspicion at the border, as we have seen, have been viewed as a reasonable measure to safeguard the territory of the United States. The next section discusses the reasonableness of motor vehicle checkpoints at the border as well as the use of checkpoints within the interior of the United States to insure the safety of our nation's roadways.

Motor Vehicle Checkpoints

You undoubtedly have been stopped by the police at a **motor vehicle checkpoint** and wondered whether this is legal. How can you be stopped when you have not acted in a suspicious, let alone unlawful, fashion? After all, you have read that the Fourth Amendment prohibits unreasonable seizures that are not based on either reasonable suspicion or probable cause.

In 1979, in *Delaware v. Prouse*, the U.S. Supreme Court ruled that the police may not pull motor vehicles over to "spot check" for drivers' licenses and registration without reasonable suspicion. The Court explained that this practice inevitably would result in a large number of law-abiding drivers being unnecessarily stopped in order to detect a small number of unlicensed drivers. Balancing the costs and benefits of spot checks, it is clear that the modest contribution to "safety possibly resulting from...spot checks cannot justify subjecting...every vehicle...to seizure...at the...discretion of law enforcement officials.... [W]e cannot conceive of any...basis upon which a patrolman could decide that stopping a particular driver for a spot check would be more productive than stopping any other driver." The Supreme Court stressed that the rejection of spot checks does not preclude the development of alternatives that "involve less intrusion or that do not involve the unconstrained exercise of discretion....Questioning of all oncoming traffic at roadblock-type stops is one possible alternative" (*Delaware v. Prouse,* 440 U.S. 648, 659, 663 [1979]).

Three years earlier, the Supreme Court had addressed the constitutionality of fixed automobile checkpoints ("roadblock-type stops") that were mentioned in *Prouse* as an alternative to spot checks. In *United States v. Martinez-Fuerte,* the Border Patrol established an immigration checkpoint on a highway in San Clemente, California, sixty miles north of the Mexican border. Vehicles were halted, drivers briefly questioned, and most then were permitted to continue on their way. A small number of drivers were directed to a secondary inspection area for interrogation. Three individuals challenged their arrest for illegally transporting aliens on the grounds that they had been stopped without reasonable suspicion (*United States v. Martinez-Fuerte,* 428 U.S. 543, 546–547 [1976]).

The Supreme Court balanced the intrusion into the privacy of drivers against the need for checkpoints to combat the flow of undocumented workers into the United States, which the Court noted may total as many as twelve million people. The judges noted that traffic on the highway was too heavy to permit reasonable suspicion stops of individual automobiles and that it was virtually impossible to secure the 2,000-mile border with Mexico without checkpoints on highways that undocumented workers used to enter the United States (552–554).

The Supreme Court concluded that the interest in eliminating illegal entry into the United States far outbalanced the individual interest in being free from stops and questioning at checkpoints without reasonable suspicion. The Court noted that several characteristics of checkpoints reduced the stress and strain experienced by motorists (558–562).

- ***Discretion.*** The locations of fixed checkpoints are selected to effectively combat illegal immigration.
- ***Notice.*** Drivers are informed by signs announcing the checkpoint as they approach the checkpoint and are not taken by surprise.
- ***Public.*** The brief and public stops minimize the stress and fear experienced by motorists.
- ***Uniform.*** Law enforcement authorities stop and inspect every motor vehicle at the checkpoint and do not single out particular automobiles for inspection. This limits the anger and frustration of drivers. The police exercise limited discretion and only refer selected motorists to a secondary inspection area for further investigation.

We have seen that the Supreme Court in *Martinez-Fuerte* approved of checkpoints to detect individuals illegally crossing the Mexican border into the United States. The Supreme Court in *Michigan Department of State Police v. Sitz* next addressed the other permissible purposes for which a roadblock checkpoint may be deployed. In 1986, the Michigan State Police in conjunction with other law enforcement agencies and a university research institute established sobriety checkpoints along state highways (*Michigan Department of State Police v. Sitz,* 496 U.S. 444, 448 [1990]).

The Supreme Court held that the Michigan checkpoints were lawful under the Fourth Amendment. The judges reached this conclusion by balancing Michigan's interest in preventing accidents caused by drunk driving and the effectiveness of sobriety checkpoints in achieving this goal against the intrusion on individual privacy caused by the checkpoints. There was no doubt that drunk driving posed a serious threat to road safety. The Court noted that Americans paid a heavy price for drunk driving that included an annual death toll of 25,000, one million personal injuries, and five billion dollars in property damage. The seriousness of drunk driving in the view of the Court majority far outweighed the "slight" intrusion at checkpoints that is required to detect drunk driving. The Supreme Court stressed that the threat posed by inebriated drivers must be taken as seriously as the illegal immigration that motivated the checkpoints in *Martinez-Fuerte* (451).

Michigan also established that the suspicionless checkpoint program was *reasonably effective*. During the operation of the checkpoint in Saginaw County, 126 vehicles passed through the checkpoint, the average delay per vehicle was twenty-five seconds, and two drivers were arrested for DWI. Experts testified that in other states, sobriety checkpoints resulted in drunken-driving arrests of roughly one percent of all drivers. This compares favorably with data from one of the checkpoints in *Martinez-Fuerte,* which reported that the ratio of aliens detected to vehicles stopped was 0.5 percent (555).

Sitz tipped the balance between the privacy of the driver and the protection of the public in favor of societal safety. Justice Stevens objected that the Court majority failed to examine data comparing the effectiveness of checkpoints in Michigan against traditional law enforcement techniques and neglected to inquire into whether checkpoints lowered the number of holiday fatalities. Do you agree with Justice Stevens that the judgment in *Sitz* gives "no weight to the citizen's interest in freedom from suspicionless unannounced investigative seizures" and, instead, "places a heavy thumb on the law enforcement interest" by considering only the benefits rather than the costs of the checkpoints? On the other hand, can Justice Stevens doubt that public safety is enhanced by checkpoints that deter some people from drinking and driving and that remind the public of the carnage caused by drunk drivers? What would have been the impact on the enforcement of drunk-driving laws of a Supreme Court ruling that sobriety checkpoints were unlawful (473).

The Supreme Court next turned its attention to determining the other law enforcement purposes for which checkpoints might be employed. What about inspections investigating whether individuals were driving with a proper license or were carrying insurance or had an outstanding arrest warrant or owed back taxes? In 2001, in *City of Indianapolis v. Edmond,* the U.S. Supreme Court ruled that checkpoints whose primary purpose is the detection of narcotics are unconstitutional. Motorists in Indianapolis were asked to present a license and registration, and a search was to be conducted only where an officer developed individualized suspicion. The program resulted in an arrest for roughly nine percent of all automobiles stopped between August and November 1998 (*City of Indianapolis v. Edmond,* 531 U.S. 32 [2001]).

The U.S. Supreme Court ruled that "[w]e have never approved a checkpoint program whose primary purpose was to detect evidence of ordinary criminal wrongdoing....[E]ach of the checkpoint programs that we have approved was designed primarily to serve purposes closely related to the problems of policing the border or the necessity of ensuring roadway safety." In other words, the Court declined to suspend the requirement of individualized suspicion where the police employed checkpoints for ordinary law enforcement purposes. The justices were fearful that the use of checkpoints for "the general interest in crime control" would result in the use of suspicionless stops to get around the Fourth Amendment limitations on the seizure of motorists (43–44).

In reading *Indianapolis v. Edmond,* ask yourself whether a distinction should be drawn between automobile checkpoints used for "policing the border" and "ensuring roadway safety" on the one hand and automobile checkpoints used for drug offenses and other "ordinary law enforcement purposes" on the other hand.

You can find United States v. Martinez-Fuerte *and* Michigan Department of State Police v. Sitz *on the study site, http://www.sagepub.com/lippmancp.*

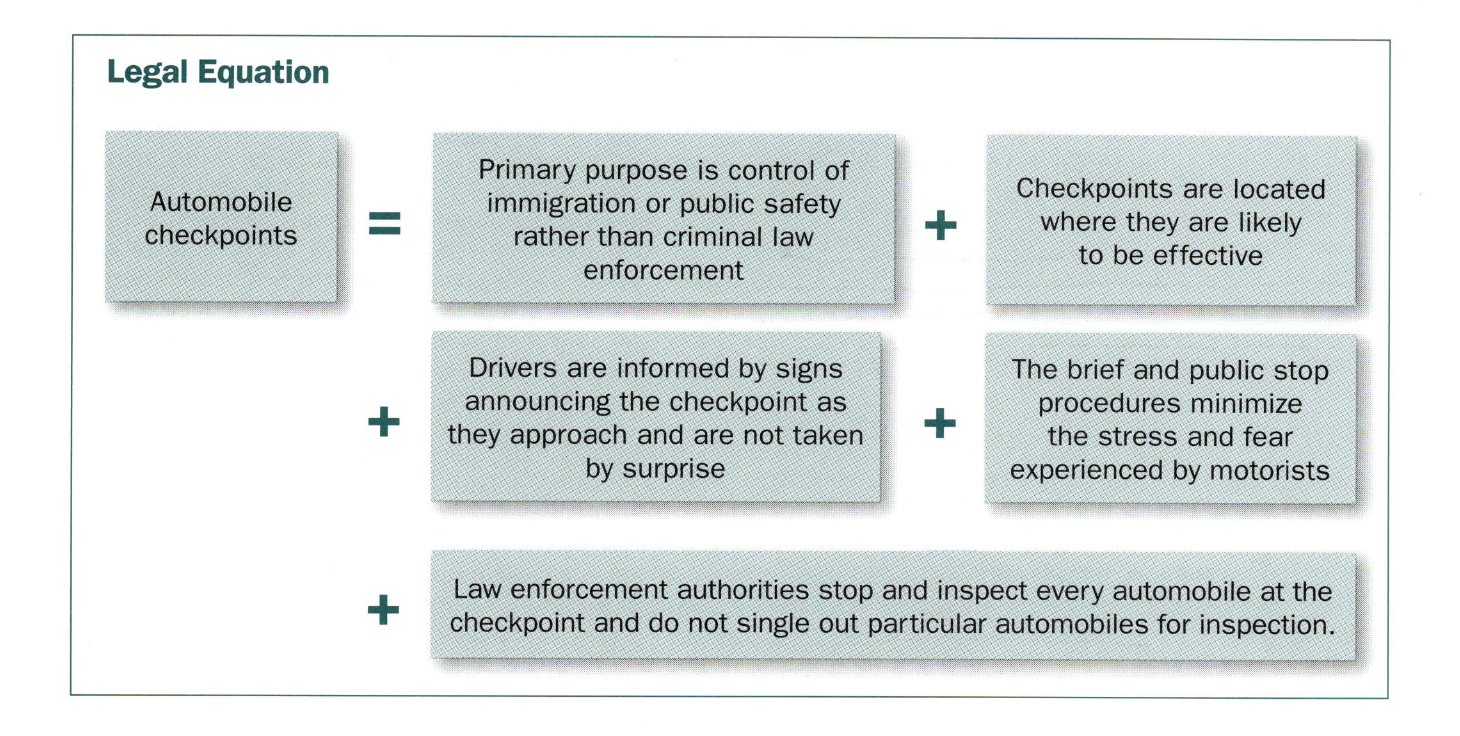

Is it constitutional to use a checkpoint to interdict illegal narcotics?

City of Indianapolis v. Edmond, 531 U.S. 32 (2000), O'Connor, J.

Facts

In August 1998, the City of Indianapolis began to operate vehicle checkpoints on Indianapolis roads in an effort to interdict unlawful drugs. The City conducted six such roadblocks between August and November that year, stopping 1,161 vehicles and arresting 104 motorists. Fifty-five arrests were for drug-related crimes, while forty-nine were for offenses unrelated to drugs. The overall "hit rate" of the program was thus approximately nine percent.

At each checkpoint location, the police stop a predetermined number of vehicles. Approximately thirty officers are stationed at the checkpoint. Pursuant to written directives issued by the chief of police, at least one officer approaches the vehicle, advises the driver that he or she is being stopped briefly at a drug checkpoint, and asks the driver to produce a license and registration. The officer also looks for signs of impairment and conducts an open-view examination of the vehicle from the outside. A narcotics-detection dog walks around the outside of each stopped vehicle.

The directives instruct the officers that they may conduct a search only by consent or based on the appropriate quantum of particularized suspicion. The officers must conduct each stop in the same manner until particularized suspicion develops, and the officers have no discretion to stop any vehicle out of sequence.... [T]he total duration of each stop, absent reasonable suspicion or probable cause, would be five minutes or less.

The affidavit of Indianapolis Police Sergeant Marshall DePew...provides further insight concerning the operation of the checkpoints. According to Sergeant DePew, checkpoint locations are selected weeks in advance based on such considerations as area crime statistics and traffic flow. The checkpoints are generally operated during daylight hours and are identified with lighted signs reading, "NARCOTICS CHECKPOINT MILE AHEAD, NARCOTICS K-9 IN USE, BE PREPARED TO STOP." Once a group of cars has been stopped, other traffic proceeds without interruption until all the stopped cars have been processed or diverted for further processing. Sergeant DePew also stated that the average stop for a vehicle not subject to further processing lasts two to three minutes or less.

Issue

Respondents James Edmond and Joell Palmer were each stopped at a narcotics checkpoint in late September 1998. Respondents then filed a lawsuit on behalf of themselves and the class of all motorists who had been stopped or were subject to being stopped in the future at the Indianapolis drug checkpoints. Respondents claimed that the roadblocks violated the Fourth Amendment of the United States Constitution and the search and seizure provision of the Indiana Constitution. Respondents requested declaratory and injunctive relief for the class, as well as damages and attorney's fees for themselves.

Respondents then moved for a preliminary injunction.... The United States District Court for the Southern District of Indiana ... denied the motion for a preliminary injunction, holding that the checkpoint program did not violate the Fourth Amendment. A divided panel of the United States Court of Appeals for the Seventh Circuit reversed, holding that the checkpoints contravened the Fourth Amendment. The issue is whether a checkpoint intended to control illegal narcotics is constitutional.

Reasoning

The Fourth Amendment requires that searches and seizures be reasonable. A search or seizure is ordinarily unreasonable in the absence of individualized suspicion of wrongdoing. While such suspicion is not an "irreducible" component of reasonableness, we have recognized only limited circumstances in which the usual rule does not apply.... We have ... upheld brief, suspicionless seizures of motorists at a fixed Border Patrol checkpoint designed to intercept illegal aliens and at a sobriety checkpoint aimed at removing drunk drivers from the road. In addition, in *Delaware v. Prouse,* we suggested that a similar type of roadblock with the purpose of verifying drivers' licenses and vehicle registrations would be permissible. In none of these cases, however, did we indicate approval of a checkpoint program whose primary purpose was to detect evidence of ordinary criminal wrongdoing.

In *Martinez-Fuerte,* we entertained Fourth Amendment challenges to stops at two permanent immigration checkpoints located on major United States highways less than 100 miles from the Mexican border.... [W]e found that the balance tipped in favor of the Government's interests in policing the Nation's borders. In so finding, we emphasized the difficulty of effectively containing illegal immigration at the border itself. We also stressed the impracticality of the particularized study of a given car to discern whether it was transporting illegal aliens, as well as the relatively modest degree of intrusion entailed by the stops. In *Sitz,* we evaluated the constitutionality of a Michigan highway sobriety checkpoint program. The *Sitz* checkpoint involved brief suspicionless stops of motorists so that police officers could detect signs of intoxication and remove impaired drivers from the road.... This checkpoint program was clearly aimed at reducing the immediate hazard posed by the presence of drunk drivers on the highways, and there was an obvious connection between the imperative of highway safety and the law enforcement practice at issue. The gravity of the drunk driving problem and the magnitude of the State's interest in getting drunk drivers off the road weighed heavily in our determination that the program was constitutional.

In *Prouse,* we invalidated a discretionary, suspicionless stop for a spot check of a motorist's driver's license and vehicle registration. The officer's conduct in that case was unconstitutional primarily on account of his exercise of "standardless and unconstrained discretion." We nonetheless acknowledged the States' "vital interest in ensuring that only those qualified to do so are permitted to operate motor vehicles, that these vehicles are fit for safe operation, and hence that licensing, registration, and vehicle inspection requirements are being observed." Accordingly, we suggested that "questioning of all oncoming traffic at roadblock-type stops" would be a lawful means of serving this interest in highway safety.

We further indicated in *Prouse* that we considered the purposes of such a hypothetical roadblock to be distinct from a general purpose of investigating crime. The State proffered the additional interests of "the apprehension of stolen motor vehicles and of drivers under the influence of alcohol or narcotics" in its effort to justify the discretionary spot check. We observed in a footnote, however, that "the ... governmental interest in controlling automobile thefts is not distinguishable from the general interest in crime control...."

What principally distinguishes these checkpoints from those we have previously approved is their primary purpose. As petitioners concede, the Indianapolis checkpoint program unquestionably has the primary purpose of interdicting illegal narcotics.... [T]he parties repeatedly refer to the checkpoints as "drug checkpoints" and describe them as "being operated by the City of Indianapolis in an effort to interdict unlawful drugs in Indianapolis."... [B]oth the District Court and the Court of Appeals recognized that the primary purpose of the roadblocks is the interdiction of narcotics.... We have never approved a checkpoint program whose primary purpose was to detect evidence of ordinary criminal wrongdoing. Rather, our checkpoint cases have recognized only limited exceptions to the general rule that a seizure must be accompanied by some measure of individualized suspicion. We suggested in *Prouse* that we would not credit the "general interest in crime control" as justification for a regime of suspicionless stops. Consistent with this suggestion, each of the checkpoint programs that we have approved was designed primarily to serve purposes closely related to the problems of policing the border or the necessity of ensuring roadway safety. Because the primary purpose of the Indianapolis narcotics checkpoint program is to uncover evidence of ordinary criminal wrongdoing, the program contravenes the Fourth Amendment.... [W]ithout drawing the line at roadblocks designed primarily to serve the general interest in crime control, the Fourth Amendment would do little to prevent intrusions through the use of checkpoints from becoming a routine part of American life.

Petitioners also emphasize the severe and intractable nature of the drug problem as justification for the checkpoint program. There is no doubt that traffic in illegal narcotics creates social harms of the first magnitude.... But the gravity of the threat alone cannot be dispositive of questions concerning what means law enforcement officers may employ to pursue a given purpose....We are... reluctant to recognize exceptions to the general rule of individualized suspicion where governmental authorities primarily pursue their general crime control ends.

Nor can the narcotics-interdiction purpose of the checkpoints be rationalized in terms of a highway safety concern similar to that present in *Sitz*. The detection and punishment of almost any criminal offense serves broadly the safety of the community, and our streets would no doubt be safer but for the scourge of illegal drugs. Only with respect to a smaller class of offenses, however, is society confronted with the type of immediate, vehicle-bound threat to life and limb that the sobriety checkpoint in *Sitz* was designed to eliminate.

Petitioners also liken the anticontraband agenda of the Indianapolis checkpoints to the antismuggling purpose of the checkpoints in *Martinez-Fuerte*. Petitioners cite this Court's conclusion in *Martinez-Fuerte* that the flow of traffic was too heavy to permit "particularized study of a given car that would enable it to be identified as a possible carrier of illegal aliens," and claim that this logic has even more force here. The problem with this argument is that the same logic prevails any time a vehicle is employed to conceal contraband or other evidence of a crime. This type of connection to the roadway is very different from the close connection to roadway safety that was present in *Sitz* and *Prouse*. Further, the Indianapolis checkpoints are far removed from the border context that was crucial in *Martinez-Fuerte*. While the difficulty of examining each passing car was an important factor in validating the law enforcement technique employed in *Martinez-Fuerte,* this factor alone cannot justify a regime of suspicionless searches or seizures. Rather, we must look more closely at the nature of the public interests that such a regime is designed principally to serve.

The primary purpose of the Indianapolis narcotics checkpoints is in the end to advance "the general interest in crime control." We decline to suspend the usual requirement of individualized suspicion where the police seek to employ a checkpoint primarily for the ordinary enterprise of investigating crimes. We cannot sanction stops justified only by the generalized and ever-present possibility that interrogation and inspection may reveal that any given motorist has committed some crime.

Of course, there are circumstances that may justify a law enforcement checkpoint where the primary purpose would otherwise, but for some emergency, relate to ordinary crime control. For example, as the court of appeals noted, the Fourth Amendment would almost certainly permit an appropriately tailored roadblock set up to thwart an imminent terrorist attack or to catch a dangerous criminal who is likely to flee by way of a particular route. The exigencies created by these scenarios are far removed from the circumstances under which authorities might simply stop cars as a matter of course to see if there just happens to be a felon leaving the jurisdiction. While we do not limit the purposes that may justify a checkpoint program to any rigid set of categories, we decline to approve a program whose primary purpose is ultimately indistinguishable from the general interest in crime control.

Petitioners argue that the Indianapolis checkpoint program is justified by its lawful secondary purposes of keeping impaired motorists off the road and verifying licenses and registrations. If this were the case, however, law enforcement authorities would be able to establish checkpoints for virtually any purpose so long as they also included a license or sobriety check. For this reason, we examine the available evidence to determine the primary purpose of the checkpoint program. While we recognize the challenges inherent in a purpose inquiry, courts routinely engage in this enterprise in many areas of constitutional jurisprudence as a means of sifting abusive governmental conduct from that which is lawful. As a result, a program driven by an impermissible purpose may be proscribed while a program impelled by licit purposes is permitted, even though the challenged conduct may be outwardly similar....

Holding

When law enforcement authorities pursue primarily general crime control purposes at checkpoints such as here, however, stops can only be justified by some quantum of individualized suspicion. Our holding also does not affect the validity of border searches or searches at places like airports and government buildings, where the need for such measures to ensure public safety can be particularly acute. Nor does our opinion speak to other intrusions aimed primarily at purposes beyond the general interest in crime control. Our holding also does not impair the ability of police officers to act appropriately upon information that they properly learn during a checkpoint stop justified by a lawful primary purpose, even where such action may result in the arrest of a motorist for an offense unrelated to that purpose.... Because the primary purpose of the Indianapolis checkpoint program is ultimately indistinguishable from the general interest in crime control, the checkpoints violate the Fourth Amendment. The judgment of the court of appeals is accordingly affirmed.

Dissenting, *Rehnquist, C.J.,* joined by *Thomas, J.,* and *Scalia, J.*

One's expectation of privacy in an automobile and of freedom in its operation are significantly different from the traditional expectation of privacy and freedom in one's residence. This is because "automobiles, unlike homes, are subjected to pervasive and continuing governmental regulation and controls." The lowered expectation of privacy in one's automobile is coupled with the limited nature of the intrusion: a brief, standardized, nonintrusive seizure. The brief seizure of an automobile can hardly be compared to the intrusive search of the body or the home....

Because of these extrinsic limitations upon roadblock seizures, the Court's newfound non-law-enforcement primary purpose test is both unnecessary to secure Fourth Amendment rights and bound to produce wide-ranging litigation over the "purpose" of any given seizure. Police designing highway roadblocks can never be sure of their validity, since a jury might later determine that a forbidden purpose exists. Roadblock stops identical to the one that we upheld in *Sitz* ten years ago, or to the one that we upheld twenty-four years ago in *Martinez-Fuerte,* may now be challenged on the grounds that they have some concealed forbidden purpose.

Efforts to enforce the law on public highways used by millions of motorists are obviously necessary to our society. The Court's opinion today casts a shadow over what had been assumed, on the basis of *stare decisis,* to be a perfectly lawful activity. Conversely, if the Indianapolis police had assigned a different purpose to their activity here, but in no way changed what was done on the ground to individual motorists, it might well be valid. The Court's non-law-enforcement primary purpose test simply does not serve as a proxy for anything that the Fourth Amendment is, or should be, concerned about in the automobile seizure context....

Questions for Discussion

1. Does the holding in *Edmond* logically follow from the precedents established in *Martinez-Fuerte, Sitz,* and *Prouse*?
2. Why does the Supreme Court resist approving roadblocks intended to further the "general interest in crime control"?
3. Is the interdiction of narcotics unrelated to automobile safety?
4. Under what circumstances would the Supreme Court approve checkpoints that are intended to further the "general interest in crime control"?
5. Summarize the argument of the dissent.
6. ***Problems in policing.*** On what roads may the police establish checkpoints? Describe the types of signs that should be posted to alert the public to the checkpoint. Write a brief set of guidelines instructing the police on the proper procedures at a sobriety checkpoint.

You can find People v. Lidster *on the study site, http://www.sagepub.com/lippmancp.*

Cases and Comments

1. ***Roadblocks.*** On the study site, you will find the U.S. Supreme Court's decision in *People v. Lidster.* In August 1997, the Lombard, Illinois, police established a roadblock and distributed leaflets requesting information regarding a hit-and-run accident. The Illinois Supreme Court ruled that the roadblock violated the Fourth Amendment, explaining that the prohibition against suspicionless seizures "should not give way to the normal needs of law enforcement, be they identified as crime control, criminal investigation or canvassing efforts to obtain information leading to the identification and apprehension of the perpetrator of a crime" (*People v. Lidster,* 779 N.E.2d 855, 861 [Ill. 2001]). In *Lidster,* the U.S. Supreme Court reviewed the decision of the Illinois Supreme Court. Pay particular attention to the Court's discussion of the checkpoint cases that we have previously discussed. Can you predict how the Supreme Court ruled in *Lidster? People v. Lidster,* 540 U.S. 419 (2004).

2. ***State Law.*** The U.S. Supreme Court remanded *Sitz* to the Michigan Supreme Court. The Michigan court ruled that sobriety checkpoints are contrary to the Michigan State Constitution. The Michigan judges noted that "our jurisprudence conclusively demonstrates that, in the context of automobile seizures, we have extended more expansive protection to our citizens than that extended in *Sitz* [by the U.S. Supreme Court]." The judges observed that Michigan courts have never recognized the prerogative of the State to detain individuals "without any level of suspicion whatsoever...for criminal investigatory purposes." The Michigan Supreme Court cautioned that there may be situations such as the apprehension of a fleeing felon in which checkpoints may be constitutional.

Judge James Brickley dissented and argued that advancements in the technological development of easily concealed destructive devices combined with increasing levels of violence and the prospect of international terrorism increased the need for "surveillance-inspection techniques that involve minimum inconveniences and intrusions as a necessary tradeoff for the personal safety and security of the population at large." Judge Brickley stressed that the use of checkpoints does not mean that the reasonable suspicion and probable cause standards cannot continue to be employed in the traditional criminal investigation process. See *Sitz v. Michigan Department of State Police,* 506 N.W.2d 209 (Mich. 1993).

Airport Screening

There likely is no one who has not experienced an **airport screening** before boarding a flight. You might have been annoyed by the fact that you were subjected to a search without any obvious reason. In this section, we will discuss the special needs that justify airport screening without reasonable suspicion or probable cause.

In *United States v. Marquez,* the Ninth Circuit Court of Appeals explained that "[i]t is hard to overestimate the need to search air travelers for weapons and explosives before they are allowed to board the aircraft . . . the potential damage and destruction from air terrorism is . . . enormous" (*United States v. Marquez,* 410 F.3d 612, 618 [9th Cir. 2005]). Courts accordingly have recognized the special need to x-ray and to inspect carry-on and checked baggage for weapons and explosives and to subject individuals to both a preboarding "walk-through screening" and a handheld magnometer "wanding" without reasonable suspicion. Judges have affirmed the right of airport personnel to conduct even more intrusive searches where there is an indication that a passenger may be in possession of a weapon or explosive. For example, an individual may be asked to empty his or her pockets, and security personnel may reach into an individual's pockets in the event that the individual refuses to cooperate with the reasonable requests of screeners. Courts have held that an individual may not avoid the search at this point in the screening process by stating that he or she no longer plans to board the aircraft.

The reasonableness of special-needs airline screening is based on the vital interest in preventing airborne terrorism and in providing for the safety and security of the public that outweighs the inconvenience and invasion of privacy resulting from the search. In finding that a preboarding screening is reasonable, courts have highlighted various factors regarding the search.

- ***Security threat.*** The search is carried out in response to a clear danger and threat to aircraft.
- ***Minimally intrusive.*** X-rays and wanding are directed at the discovery of weapons and explosives and are brief and limited in intrusiveness. More intrusive procedures are used only when there is an indication that a passenger may possess a weapon or explosive.
- ***Effectiveness.*** The mass and random screening of airline passengers prior to boarding an aircraft is reasonably related to the detection and deterrence of air terrorism, and random procedures contribute to deterrence.
- ***Notice.*** Individuals are aware that they will be subjected to screening at the airport and are not surprised by the fact that they are required to submit to screening before boarding an aircraft.
- ***Abuse.*** The possibility of the abuse of passengers is limited by the public nature of airport screening, and because every air passenger is subjected to these procedures, individuals are not made to feel that they are being singled out for embarrassing or humiliating treatment.
- ***Intrusiveness.*** The intrusiveness of the search is strictly limited by the need to combat threats to air safety.
- ***Avoidance.*** To be considered reasonable under the Fourth Amendment, airport screening procedures must permit individuals to avoid a search by deciding not to board the aircraft.

The events of the past several years have made it clear that transportation systems are a major target of terrorists. In 2006, the Second Circuit Court of Appeals considered the constitutionality of the special-needs search of individuals seeking to board the subway system in New York City. Based on the holding of courts in the airport-screening cases, how would you predict the Second Circuit ruled in *MacWade v. Kelly,* the next case in the textbook?

Does New York City have a special need to engage in random, suspicionless searches in order to protect mass transportation facilities from a terrorist attack?

MacWade v. Kelly, 460 F.3d 260 (2d Cir. 2006), Straub, J.

Issue

We consider whether the government may employ random, suspicionless container searches in order to safeguard mass transportation facilities from terrorist attack. The precise issue before us is whether one such search regime, implemented on the New York City subway system, satisfies the special needs exception to the Fourth Amendment's usual requirement of individualized suspicion. We hold that it does.

Facts

Shortly after New York City implemented its search program, plaintiffs-appellants Brendan MacWade, Andrew Schonebaum, Joseph E. Gehring Jr., Partha Banerjee, and Norman Murphy each attempted to enter the subway system. Each plaintiff either submitted to a baggage search and entered the subway or refused the search and consequently was required to exit the subway system. Disturbed by their treatment, they sued defendants-appellees New York City and Police Commissioner Raymond Kelly pursuant to 42 U.S.C. § 1983, asserting that the search regime violated the Fourth and Fourteenth Amendments. They sought a declaratory judgment, preliminary and permanent injunctive relief, and attorney's fees. After a two-day bench trial, the United States District Court for the Southern District of New York (Richard M. Berman, Judge) found the search program constitutional pursuant to the special needs exception and dismissed the complaint with prejudice.

Plaintiffs timely appealed, raising three claims: (1) the special needs doctrine applies only in scenarios where the subject of a search possesses a diminished expectation of privacy, and because subway riders enjoy a full expectation of privacy in their bags, the district court erred in applying the special needs exception here; (2) the district court erred in finding that the search program serves a "special need" in the first instance; and (3) even if the search program serves a special need, the district court erred in balancing the relevant factors because (a) the searches are intrusive, (b) there is no immediate terrorist threat, and (c) the City's evidence fails as a matter of law to establish that the program is effective.

The New York City subway system is a singular component of America's urban infrastructure. The subway is an icon of the city's culture and history, an engine of its colossal economy, a subterranean repository of its art and music, and most often, the place where millions of diverse New Yorkers and visitors stand elbow to elbow as they traverse the metropolis. Quantified, the subway system is staggering. It comprises 26 interconnected train lines and 468 far-flung passenger stations. It operates every hour of every day. On an average weekday, it carries more than 4.7 million passengers, and over the course of a year, it transports approximately 1.4 billion riders. By any measure, the New York City subway system is America's largest and busiest.

Given the subway's enclosed spaces, extraordinary passenger volume, and cultural and economic importance, it is unsurprising—and undisputed—that terrorists view it as a prime target. In fact, terrorists have targeted it before. In 1997, police uncovered a plot to bomb Brooklyn's Atlantic Avenue subway station—a massive commuter hub that joins ten different subway lines and the Long Island Railroad. In 2004, police thwarted another plot to bomb the Herald Square subway station, which networks eight different subway lines in midtown Manhattan.

Other cities have not been so fortunate in protecting their mass transportation systems. In 2004, terrorists killed over 240 people by using concealed explosives to bomb commuter trains in Madrid and Moscow. On July 7, 2005, terrorists—again using concealed explosives—killed more than 56 people and wounded another 700 individuals by launching a coordinated series of attacks on the London subway and bus systems. Two weeks later, on July 21, 2005, terrorists launched a second but unsuccessful wave of concealed explosive attacks on the London subway system.

That same day, the New York City Police Department (NYPD) announced the Container Inspection Program (the "Program") that is the subject of this litigation. The NYPD designed the Program chiefly to deter terrorists from carrying concealed explosives onto the subway system and, to a lesser extent, to uncover any such attempt. Pursuant to the Program, the NYPD establishes daily inspection checkpoints at selected subway facilities. A "checkpoint" consists of a group of uniformed police officers standing at a folding table near the row of turnstiles disgorging onto the train platform. At the table, officers search the bags of a portion of subway riders entering the station.

In order to enhance the Program's deterrent effect, the NYPD selects the checkpoint locations "in a deliberative manner that may appear random, undefined, and unpredictable." In addition to switching checkpoint locations, the NYPD also varies their number, staffing, and scheduling so that the "deployment patterns . . . are constantly shifting." While striving to maintain the veneer of random deployment, the NYPD bases its decisions on a sophisticated host of criteria, such as fluctuations in passenger volume and threat level, overlapping coverage provided by its other counterterrorism initiatives, and available manpower.

The officers assigned to each checkpoint give notice of the searches and make clear that they are voluntary. Close to their table, they display a large poster notifying passengers that "backpacks and other containers [are] subject to inspection." The Metropolitan Transportation Authority, which operates the subway system, makes similar audio announcements in subway stations and on trains. A supervising sergeant at the checkpoint announces through a bullhorn that all persons wishing to enter the station are subject to a container search and those wishing to avoid the search must leave the station. Although declining the search is not by itself a basis for arrest, the police may arrest anyone who refuses to be searched and later attempts to reenter the subway system with the uninspected container.

Officers exercise virtually no discretion in determining whom to search. The supervising sergeant establishes a selection rate, such as every fifth or tenth person, based upon considerations such as the number of officers and the passenger volume at that particular checkpoint. The officers then search individuals in accordance with the established rate only.

Once the officers select a person to search, they limit their search as to scope, method, and duration. As to scope, officers search only those containers large enough to carry an explosive device, which means, for example, that they may not inspect wallets and small purses. Further, once they identify a container of eligible size, they must limit their inspection "to what is minimally necessary to ensure that the...item does not contain an explosive device," which they have been trained to recognize in various forms. They may not intentionally look for other contraband, although if officers incidentally discover such contraband, they may arrest the individual carrying it. Officers may not attempt to read any written or printed material. Nor may they request or record a passenger's personal information, such as his name, address, or demographic data.

The preferred inspection method is to ask the passenger to open his bag and manipulate his possessions himself so that the officer may determine, on a purely visual basis, if the bag contains an explosive device. If necessary, the officer may open the container and manipulate its contents himself. Finally, because officers must conduct the inspection for no "longer than necessary to ensure that the individual is not carrying an explosive device," a typical inspection lasts for a matter of seconds.

Two weeks after the Program commenced, plaintiffs sued to halt it....The bench trial lasted two days. Of the evidence elicited, most relevant to this appeal is the testimony of three defense expert witnesses: David Cohen, the NYPD's Deputy Commissioner for Intelligence; Michael Sheehan, the NYPD's Deputy Commissioner for Counter-Terrorism; and Richard C. Clarke, former Chair of the Counter-Terrorism Security Group of the National Security Council. Because each witness offered nearly identical opinions as to the Program's efficacy, and supported their opinions with nearly identical reasons, we summarize their testimony in one piece. Before doing that, we pause briefly to note the basis of each witness's expertise, as their credentials are essential to understanding why the district court credited their testimony.

Cohen served for thirty-five years in the analysis and operations divisions of the Central Intelligence Agency (CIA). Early in his career, he established the CIA's first terrorism analysis program. When he later became the deputy director of the CIA's Directorate of Operations, he oversaw the CIA's entire analysis program on a daily basis, including its preparation of political, military, and economic assessments for the president and his senior national security advisors. Later, as the director of the Directorate of Operations, he bore responsibility for the agency's worldwide counterterrorism operations. At that time, he created the CIA's Al Qaeda Osama bin Laden unit. In 2002, he joined the NYPD and assumed responsibility for its intelligence programs.

Like Cohen, Sheehan has considerable counterterrorism experience. He began his career as a member of a counterterrorism unit in the U.S. Army's Special Forces. He served under two presidents as the National Security Council's Director of International Programs, and later served as the State Department's Ambassador-at-Large for Counter-Terrorism. In 2003, he joined the NYPD, where he commands its counterterrorism division and its contingent of the FBI joint terrorism task force. In his current post, he bears responsibility for "critical infrastructure protection."

Clarke also possesses substantial counterterrorism experience. For seven years, he served in the Department of State, holding the positions of Assistant Secretary for Politico-Military Affairs and Deputy Assistant Secretary for Intelligence. For the following eleven years, he held a number of positions on the National Security Council, including Chair of its Counter-Terrorism Security Group; National Coordinator for Security, Infrastructure Protection, and Counter-Terrorism; and Special Advisor to four presidents.

The expert testimony established that terrorists "place a premium" on success. Accordingly, they seek out targets that are predictable and vulnerable—traits they ascertain through surveillance and a careful assessment of existing security measures. They also plan their operations carefully: They "rehearse [the attack], they train it, they do dry runs." In light of these priorities, the Al Qaeda Manual advises that terrorists "traveling on a mission" should avoid security "checkpoints along the way."

The witnesses also testified that the Program's flexible and shifting deployment of checkpoints deters a terrorist attack because it introduces the variable of an unplanned checkpoint inspection and thus "throws uncertainty into every aspect of terrorist operations—from planning to implementation." Terrorists "don't want to be in a situation where one of their bombs doesn't go off, because on the day that they chose to go in subway station X, there were police doing searches." That unpredictability deters both a single-bomb attack and an attack consisting of multiple, synchronized bombings, such as those in London and Madrid.

Because the Program deters a terrorist from planning to attack the subway in the first place, the witnesses testified, the fact that a terrorist could decline a search and leave the subway system makes little difference in assessing the Program's efficacy. Similarly, the precise number of checkpoints employed on any given day is relatively unimportant because the critical aspects of the Program are that it is "random" and "routine," the combination of which "creates an incentive for terrorists to choose... an easier target." Finally, the testimony established that each of the City's counterterrorism programs incrementally increases security and that, taken together, the programs "address the broad range of concerns related to terrorist activity" and "have created an environment in New York City that has made it more difficult for terrorists to operate."

[T]he district court issued an opinion in which it concluded that the Program was constitutional pursuant to the special needs exception. In its analysis, the district court determined that the Program served a special need because it aimed to prevent, through deterrence and detection, "a terrorist attack on the subways."... It concluded that the government interest in preventing a terrorist attack on the subway was "of the very highest order."... As to the Program's efficacy, the district court credited the expert testimony of Sheehan, Cohen, and Clarke in concluding that the Program was a "reasonable method of deterring (and detecting) a terrorist bombing" on the subway....

Finally, the district court resolved that the searches were "narrowly tailored and only minimally intrude[] upon privacy interests." Accordingly, the court concluded that on balance, the Program was constitutional, denied plaintiffs' application for declaratory and injunctive relief, and dismissed the complaint with prejudice.

Reasoning

The Fourth Amendment to the Constitution provides that, "The right of the people to be secure in their persons, houses, papers, and effects, against unreasonable searches and seizures, shall not be violated, and no Warrants shall issue, but upon probable cause...." As the Fourth Amendment's text makes clear, the concept of reasonableness is the "touchstone of the constitutionality of a governmental search." "What is reasonable, of course, depends on all of the circumstances surrounding the search or seizure and the nature of the search or seizure itself." As a "general matter," a search is unreasonable unless supported "by a warrant issued upon probable cause." However, "neither a warrant nor probable cause, nor, indeed, any measure of individualized suspicion, is an indispensable component of reasonableness in every circumstance."...

One example of reasonableness is the "special needs exception." This states that "[o]nly in those exceptional circumstances in which special needs, beyond the need for normal law enforcement, make the warrant and probable-cause requirement impracticable, is a court entitled to substitute its balancing of interests for that of the Framers." Both before and after the doctrine's formal denomination, courts have applied it in a variety of contexts relevant here, including random airport searches, highway sobriety checkpoints, and random checkpoint stops near military installation[s].

The doctrine's central aspects are as follows. First, as a threshold matter, the search must "serve as [its] immediate purpose an objective distinct from the ordinary evidence gathering associated with crime investigation." Second, once the government satisfies that threshold requirement, the court determines whether the search is reasonable by balancing several competing considerations. These balancing factors include (1) the weight and immediacy of the government interest; (2) "the nature of the privacy interest allegedly compromised by" the search; (3) "the character of the intrusion imposed" by the search; and (4) the efficacy of the search in advancing the government interest.

We address in turn each of plaintiffs' arguments as delineated in the introduction.

Plaintiffs first raise the purely legal contention that, as a threshold matter, the special needs doctrine applies only where the subject of the search possesses a reduced privacy interest. While it is true that in most special needs cases, the relevant privacy interest is somewhat "limited,"... the Supreme Court never has implied—much less actually held—that a reduced privacy expectation is a *sine qua non* of special needs analysis....

Accordingly, to the extent that the principle needs clarification, we expressly hold that the special needs doctrine does not require, as a threshold matter, that the subject of the search possess a reduced privacy interest. Instead, once the government establishes a special need, the nature of the privacy interest is a factor to be weighed in the balance.

Plaintiffs next maintain that the district court erred in concluding that the Program serves the special need of preventing a terrorist attack on the subway. Plaintiffs contend that the Program's immediate objective is merely to gather evidence for the purpose of enforcing the criminal law.

As a factual matter, we agree with the district court's conclusion that the Program aims to prevent a terrorist attack on the subway. Defendants implemented the Program in response to a string of bombing[s] of trains and subway systems abroad, which indicates that its purpose is to prevent similar occurrences in New York City.

In its particulars, the Program seeks out explosives only: Officers are trained to recognize different explosives, they search only those containers capable of carrying explosive devices, and they may not intentionally search for other contraband, read written or printed material, or request personal information. Additionally, the Program's voluntary nature illuminates its purpose: that an individual may refuse the search provided he leaves the subway establishes that the Program seeks to prevent a terrorist, laden with concealed explosives, from boarding a subway train in the first place.

As a legal matter, courts traditionally have considered special the government's need to "prevent" and "discover... latent or hidden" hazards, in order to ensure the safety of mass transportation mediums, such as trains, airplanes, and highways.... We have no doubt that concealed explosives are a hidden hazard, that the Program's purpose is prophylactic, and that the nation's busiest subway system implicates the public's safety. Accordingly, preventing a terrorist from bombing the subways constitutes a special need that is distinct from ordinary post hoc criminal investigation.... Further, the fact that an officer incidentally may discover a different kind of contraband and arrest its possessor does not alter the Program's intended purpose.

Having concluded that the Program serves a special need, we next balance the factors set forth above to determine whether the search is reasonable and thus constitutional.

Given the "enormous dangers to life and property from terrorists" bombing the subway, "we need not labor the point with respect to need...." As they must, plaintiffs concede that the interest in preventing such an attack is "paramount" but contend that the lack of "any specific threat to the subway system" weakens that interest by depriving it of immediacy. Plaintiffs again overstate the relevance of a specific, extant threat. [N]o express threat or special imminence is required before we may accord great weight to the government's interest in staving off considerable harm....

Pursuant to this standard, the threat in this case is sufficiently immediate. In light of the thwarted plots to bomb New York City's subway system, its continued desirability as a target, and the recent bombings of public transportation systems in Madrid, Moscow, and London, the risk to public safety is substantial and real.... The district court did not err in according this factor substantial weight in support of constitutionality.

Although not a dispositive, threshold consideration, the nature of the privacy interest compromised by the search remains an important balancing factor. Whether an expectation of privacy exists for Fourth Amendment purposes depends upon two questions. "First, we ask whether the individual, by his conduct, has exhibited an actual expectation of privacy...." "Second, we inquire whether the individual's expectation of privacy is one that society is prepared to recognize as reasonable."... As to the first question, a person carrying items in a closed, opaque bag has manifested his subjective expectation of privacy by keeping his belongings from plain view and indicating "that, for whatever reason, [he] prefer[s] to keep [them] close at hand." Further, the Supreme Court has recognized as objectively reasonable a bus rider's expectation that his bag will not be felt "in an exploratory manner" from the outside, let alone opened and its contents visually inspected or physically manipulated. "[T]he Fourth Amendment provides protection to the owner of every container that conceals its contents from plain view." Accordingly, a subway rider who keeps his bags on his person possesses an undiminished expectation of privacy therein. We therefore weigh this factor in favor of plaintiffs.

Although a subway rider enjoys a full privacy expectation in the contents of his baggage, the kind of search at issue here minimally intrudes upon that interest. Several uncontested facts establish that the Program is narrowly tailored to achieve its purpose: (1) passengers receive notice of the searches and may decline to be searched so long as they leave the subway; (2) police search only those containers capable of concealing explosives, inspect eligible containers only to determine whether they contain explosives, inspect the containers visually unless it is necessary to manipulate their contents, and do not read printed or written material or request personal information; (3) a typical search lasts only for a matter of seconds; (4) uniformed personnel conduct the searches out in the open, which reduces the fear and stigma that removal to a hidden area can cause; and (5) police exercise no discretion in selecting whom to search, but rather employ a formula that ensures they do not arbitrarily exercise their authority. Although defendants need not employ "the least intrusive means," to serve the state interest, it appears they have approximated that model. Given the narrow tailoring that the Program achieves, this factor weighs strongly in favor of defendants, as the district court properly concluded.

In considering the "degree to which the seizure advances the public interest," we must remember not to wrest "from politically accountable officials... the decision as to which among reasonable alternative law enforcement techniques should be employed to deal with a serious public danger." That decision is best left to those with "a unique understanding of, and responsibility for, limited public resources, including a finite number of police officers." Accordingly, we ought not conduct a "searching examination of effectiveness." The district court credited the expert testimony of Sheehan, Cohen, and Clarke concerning the Program's deterrent effect. Plaintiffs neither contest their expertise nor directly attack the substance of their testimony. Instead, plaintiffs claim that the Program can have no meaningful deterrent effect because the NYPD employs too few checkpoints. We will not peruse, parse, or extrapolate... data in an attempt to divine how many checkpoints the City ought to deploy in the exercise of its day-to-day police power.

Counterterrorism experts and politically accountable officials have undertaken the delicate and esoteric task of deciding how best to marshal their available resources in light of the conditions prevailing on any given day. We will not—and may not—second-guess the minutiae of their considered decisions.

Undoubtedly, the City could make the Program more effective by applying greater resources, which would result in greater burdens on subway riders. Even so, the existence of such a possibility does not render clearly erroneous the district court's finding of reasonable effectiveness. Further, we note in passing several reasons why it is unwise for us to substitute our judgment for that of experienced, accountable experts and require the commitment of additional resources. First, although it might appear on certain days that a small percentage of subway stations had checkpoints, that group of stations might include, for example, the City's twenty busiest or most vulnerable. Further, the City's other counterterrorism programs might offer protection to seemingly unguarded stations. Moreover, the checkpoint figures on any given day also might reflect a diversion of manpower to another pressing need. Last, too many checkpoints might well disrupt and delay travel to an unacceptable degree. From that vantage, the expert testimony established that terrorists seek predictable and vulnerable targets, and the Program generates uncertainty that frustrates that goal, which, in turn, deters an attack....

Plaintiffs next contend that because defendants' experts could not quantify the Program's deterrent effect, their testimony fails as a matter of law to establish efficacy. The concept of deterrence need not be reduced to a quotient before a court may recognize a search program as effective. Indeed, expressing the phenomena in numeric terms often is impossible because deterrence by definition results in an absence of data.... For that same reason, the absence of a formal study of the Program's deterrent effect does not concern us.

Plaintiffs further claim that the Program is ineffective because police notify passengers of the searches, and passengers are free to walk away and attempt to reenter the subway at another point or time. Yet we always have viewed notice and the opportunity to decline as beneficial aspects of a suspicionless search regime because those features minimize intrusiveness. Striking a search program as ineffective on account of its narrow tailoring would create a most perverse result: Those programs "more pervasive and more invasive of privacy" more likely would satisfy the Fourth Amendment. Importantly, if a would-be bomber declines a search, he must leave the subway or be arrested—an outcome that, for the purpose of preventing subway bombings, we consider reasonably effective, especially since the record establishes that terrorists prize predictability. An unexpected change of plans might well stymie the attack, disrupt the synchronicity of multiple bombings, or at least reduce casualties by forcing the terrorist to detonate in a less populated location.

Finally, plaintiffs claim that since no other city yet has employed a similar search program, New York's must be ineffective. In the first place, plaintiffs' inference is flawed: Other cities must design programs according to their own resources and needs, which, quite apart from the question of efficacy, may not warrant or make possible such an initiative. Further, the upshot of plaintiffs' argument—that a program must be duplicated before it may be constitutional—strikes us as unsustainable. All things considered, the district court properly concluded that the Program is reasonably effective.

Holding

In sum, we hold that the Program is reasonable, and therefore constitutional, because (1) preventing a terrorist attack on the subway is a special need; (2) that need is weighty; (3) the Program is a reasonably effective deterrent; and (4) even though the searches intrude on a full privacy interest, they do so to a minimal degree. We thus affirm the judgment of the district court.

Questions for Discussion

1. How do the subway searches "serve as [their] immediate purpose an objective distinct from the ordinary evidence gathering associated with crime investigation"?
2. Discuss the "balancing factors" considered by the court. These balancing factors include the weight and immediacy of the government interest, "the nature of the privacy interest allegedly compromised" by the search, "the character of the intrusion imposed" by the search, and the effectiveness of the search in advancing the government interests.
3. Can the police achieve the same results by relying on the less intrusive alternatives of police dogs, undercover officers, and chemical detection monitoring devices?
4. As a judge, would you approve of these subway searches being made a permanent feature of travel on the subway?
5. ***Problems in policing.*** Design a constitutionally acceptable strategy for searching individuals boarding the public bus system in a major American city.

7.2 YOU DECIDE

In 2006, the Tampa Sports Authority (TSA) instituted a mandatory, suspicionless frisk policy for National Football League (NFL) games at Raymond James Stadium. This was undertaken by the TSA, a public authority that administers the stadium, in response to an NFL policy requiring pat down searches to safeguard fans from terrorist attacks. The TSA hired a private security company with taxpayer dollars to conduct the searches. "Generally, the pat-down is performed above the patron's waist. If the security personnel observe suspicious bulges, the screener may pat the pockets and instruct the patron to empty them. The screener conducts a visual inspection of the person by asking the person to extend his arms sideward and upward, parallel to the ground, with palms facing up, and then visually inspect[s] the person's wrists and arms for switches, wires, or push-button devices. The screener then conducts a physical inspection by touching, patting, or lightly rubbing the person's torso, around his waist, along the belt line and touches, pats, or lightly rubs the person's back along the spine from the belt line to the collar line." Fans carrying contraband are detained while the police are contacted. An individual who refuses to be patted down may not enter the stadium. Are these frisks reasonable special-needs searches? See *Johnston v. Tampa Bay Sports Authority,* 490 F.2d 820 (11th Cir. Fla. 2007).

You can find the answer by referring to the study site, http://www.sagepub.com/lippmancp.

Criminal Procedure in the News

The activities of the residents of London, England, each day are recorded by roughly 200,000 surveillance cameras, and there are as many as four million surveillance cameras monitoring individuals throughout the United Kingdom. There is a closed-circuit camera for every fourteen people in London, and the average person is seen on 300 cameras a day and is on camera once every five minutes. This so-called Ring of Steel system is able to read the license plates of automobiles and was instrumental in the apprehension of individuals suspected of involvement in the 2007 London car bombings. Roughly seventy-four other countries have followed the United Kingdom and have installed cameras.

Following the attacks of September 11, 2001, a major initiative was undertaken in the United States to install cameras. The cameras are intended to deter crime, to identify offenders, and to facilitate a rapid response to terrorism and crime. Proponents of surveillance systems argue that the September 11 attacks could have been prevented had sophisticated technology been installed, which would have detected and identified the hijackers entering the United States or boarding airlines. Roughly four million cameras now have been installed across the country. You can find cameras monitoring the mass transit system in San Francisco; the airport in Fresno, California; the Pacific Coastline Highway in California; agricultural land in Hawaii; and national monuments in Washington, D.C. There also is a heavy reliance on surveillance cameras in major urban areas such as New York and Chicago. Cameras in Times Square in New York City can swivel in a 360-degree arc, and several are able to zoom in close enough to read a document in a pedestrian's hand. Mayor Richard Daley of Chicago has observed that cameras are the next best thing to posting an officer at every potential "trouble spot." Chicago has roughly 2,250 cameras, and Mayor Daley has stated that he looks forward to 2016 when he hopes to have a camera on every intersection. The most frequent use of cameras in cities and suburbs is to detect drivers who go through stop signs or red lights or who drive in a reckless fashion.

Modern high-definition color cameras are capable of being connected to one another through a network and can track an individual's movements or can be equipped with motion sensors to detect movements in secure areas. The most sophisticated cameras can be designed to single out and focus on any individual who engages in behavior that the camera is programmed to highlight as suspicious. Cameras in the United Kingdom are equipped with microphones to overhear conversations, and many cameras in urban areas in the United States are able to detect gunshots. Proponents of cameras consider facial-recognition technology to be one of the most promising developments. This enables the camera to compare the face of an individual with a database of known offenders or terrorists.

The U.S. Supreme Court has held that there is no right to privacy in what an individual knowingly exposes to the public. Critics nevertheless argue that people have a right to be "left alone" and to be free from constant surveillance. The nightmare scenario is linking a database of driver's license photos and criminal records with surveillance cameras and then employing the cameras to single out individuals for reasons ranging from a failure to pay child support to bank robbery. An archive of surveillance footage may result in an individual being considered a criminal suspect merely because a camera recorded him or her in the company of a suspected terrorist or drug dealer.

Studies differ on the impact of cameras, and opponents are able to cite studies that indicate that cameras have had little impact on crime prevention. These critics argue that good lighting and an increased police presence are more effective than cameras and that cameras divert scarce resources from other more valuable law enforcement strategies. Detroit, Miami, and Oakland, for instance, have found cameras to be relatively ineffective and have abandoned reliance on cameras as a crime-control strategy.

Critics of cameras note that cameras can be vandalized, malfunction, and deliver a poor-quality picture. There reportedly is a tendency for operators to single out "minorities" for surveillance and to focus cameras on sexually attractive individuals. The Washington, D.C., police and other departments also have reportedly abused surveillance technology by employing the cameras to record the identity of political demonstrators.

On the other hand, the experience in Chicago is that cameras have decreased crime, and proponents point out that cameras must be coordinated with other law enforcement techniques to have a truly significant impact. There also is little question that cameras assist in identifying and prosecuting offenders and in curbing police misconduct.

The question remains whether the objections to cameras are exaggerated and reflect a resistance to technological innovation. As Mayor Richard Daley notes, Chicago has every right to secure its streets, sidewalks, and alleys, and there is nothing wrong with cameras so long as they do not interfere with individuals' right to privacy in the home. As a police chief, would you want to devote financial resources to installing cameras in your city or town? Do cameras violate your right to privacy?

Workplace Drug Testing

The abuse of drugs and alcohol by individuals working in the transportation industry whose job performance may threaten the safety of the public is another area that has been the subject of judicial decisions regarding the reasonableness of special-needs searches.

In 1989, in *Skinner v. Railway Labor Executives' Association,* the U.S. Supreme Court upheld the constitutionality of an alcohol and drug-testing program established by the U.S. Federal Railroad Administration (FRA). The FRA concluded that the existing prohibition on the possession or use of alcohol or drugs by railway employees had proven ineffective. Between 1972 and 1983, despite the prohibition on alcohol and drug possession and abuse, the nation's railroads experienced at least twenty-one significant train accidents in which drug or alcohol use was identified as the cause or as a contributing factor. These accidents resulted in twenty-five deaths, sixty-one nonfatal injuries, and property damage amounting to roughly nineteen billion dollars. Alcohol or drug abuse by railroad employees also led to seventeen accidental deaths, numerous injuries, various train accidents, and roughly twenty-eight million dollars in property damage (*Skinner v. Railway Labor Executives' Association,* 489 U.S. 602, 607 [1989]).

Subpart C of the newly instituted FRA regulations required employees involved in a major train accident or an accident that involves death or injury to undergo blood and urine testing at an independent medical facility. Employees who refused to submit to testing were suspended for nine months. Breath or urine tests also may be required under Subpart D when there is a reasonable suspicion that an employee's drug or alcohol use contributed to an accident or to a serious violation of railroad rules or where there is a reasonable suspicion that an employee is under the influence of drugs or alcohol (611).

The Supreme Court in *Skinner* ruled that blood, breath, and urine tests constitute Fourth Amendment searches. Chemical analysis of blood and urine, in addition to revealing narcotics, intrude on an employee's privacy by revealing "a host of private medical facts... including whether he or she is epileptic, pregnant, or diabetic." The issue confronting the U.S. Supreme Court was whether these blood and urine tests may be conducted under the Fourth Amendment without a warrant and without articulable suspicion. The Court held that reasonableness of the blood and urine searches is to be evaluated based on the familiar formula of balancing the intrusion on employees' Fourth Amendment interests against the need to advance "legitimate governmental interests." The Supreme Court had little difficulty deciding that the government interest in safety clearly outweighed the limited intrusion on individual privacy (617–627).

- ***Government interests.*** The government has a strong interest in regulating the conduct of railroad employees involved in "safety-sensitive" activities in order to protect the railroad traveling public.
- ***Intrusiveness.*** Blood and breath tests are minimally intrusive, and employees working in dangerous occupations in the heavily regulated railroad industry possess a diminished expectation of privacy.

The Supreme Court also held that a search warrant would be impractical and unnecessary.

- ***Warrants.*** A warrant requirement for the search of railroad employees would be impractical because evidence of drug or alcohol use likely would disappear before authorities could obtain a warrant. Despite the absence of a warrant, individuals are protected against harassment by regulations that authorize only suspicionless testing under specific circumstances (622).

A reasonable suspicion requirement would impede the government's capacity to protect the public.

- ***Articulable suspicion.*** A program of testing without reasonable suspicion following an accident deters alcohol or drug abuse because employees are aware that the unpredictable nature of railroad accidents means that they may be tested and detected at any time that they are on the job.

In summary, the Supreme Court held that the alcohol and drug-testing scheme established by the FRA carried out without warrants or reasonable suspicion satisfies the reasonableness requirement of the Fourth Amendment (634). The government has a "surpassing safety interest" in drug and alcohol tests following an accident. The tests are modestly intrusive and railroad employees possess minimal expectations of privacy. The regulations clearly limit the circumstances in which a search may be conducted. A requirement of reasonable suspicion and/or a judicial warrant will inhibit the ability to test workers and will diminish the deterrent value of the searches.

Warrantless alcohol and drug tests conducted without reasonable suspicion have been extended to other occupations that place the public at risk or that pose a danger. This includes the police and firefighters, airline pilots, mass transit operators, nuclear power plant employees, and racetrack jockeys. In 1997, the Supreme Court in *Chandler v. Miller* indicated that it would not approve of drug testing in every instance. In *Miller,* the Court rejected a requirement that candidates for public office in Georgia submit to suspicionless testing on the grounds that there was no history of drug abuse among candidates for political office and that elected officials do not present a risk to the public safety. The Court also noted that candidates are closely monitored and observed by the public and that any unusual behavior would quickly become apparent (*Chandler v. Miller,* 520 U.S. 305 [1997]).

Do you agree with Justice Marshall and Justice Brennan's dissent in *Skinner* that in compelling entire railroad crews to submit to "invasive blood and urine tests," the majority of the Supreme Court is permitting Fourth Amendment rights to "fall prey to momentary emergencies" and that, in the long run, these "mass governmental intrusions upon the integrity of the human body" will "reduce the privacy of all citizens" (635, 654).

You can continue to explore the issue of workplace drug testing on the study site. *National Treasury Employees Union v. Von Raab* was decided by the Supreme Court on the same day as *Skinner v. Railway Labor Executives' Association. Von Raab* affirmed the constitutionality of a drug-testing program established by the U.S. Customs Service as a condition of employment for positions involving drug interdiction or enforcement or for positions in which employees carry a firearm or handle "sensitive information." Does the result in *Von Raab* logically follow from the holding of the Supreme Court in *Skinner* (*National Treasury Employees Union v. Von Raab,* 489 U.S. 656 [1989])? The next section discusses the Fourth Amendment rights of high school students, particularly in regard to drug testing.

You can find National Treasury Employees Union v. Von Raab *on the study site, http://www.sagepub.com/lippmancp.*

Searches in High Schools

School officials historically have been viewed as acting *in loco parentis* ("in the place of the parent"). This status as a substitute for absent parents provided schools with complete and unlimited authority over students. In the past forty years, the U.S. Supreme Court modified this approach and recognized that in a democratic society, students are entitled to constitutional rights and protections. The challenge is to strike the appropriate balance between the exercise of students' rights and liberties and the discipline and order that is required for schools to carry out their educational mission. One of the first cases to recognize the rights of students was *Tinker v. Des Moines Independent Community School District* in 1968. In *Tinker,* the Supreme Court held that students were entitled under the First Amendment to wear black armbands to demonstrate their disapproval of the Vietnam War so long as their protest did not cause substantial interference with classroom learning (*Tinker v. Des Moines Independent Community School District,* 393 U.S. 503 [1969]). But, in 2007, in *Morse v. Frederick,* the Court held that the "'special characteristics' of the school environment, and the governmental interest in stopping student drug abuse . . . allow schools to restrict student expression that they reasonably regard as promoting illegal drug use" (*Morse v. Frederick,* 551 U.S. 393 [2007]). A number of cases have addressed the Fourth Amendment right of students to be free from unreasonable searches and seizures.

In *New Jersey v. T.L.O.,* the Supreme Court addressed the special need for disciplinary searches and seizures within high schools. A teacher at Piscataway High School discovered fourteen-year-old T.L.O. smoking together with T.L. in violation of school rules. The two young women were taken to Vice-Principal Choplick's office where T.L. admitted that she was smoking. T.L.O., however, denied that she had been smoking, and Choplick asked T.L.O. to come into his office and demanded to see her purse. The vice-principal opened the purse, found a package of cigarettes, and accused T.L.O. of lying to him. Choplick also noticed a package of cigarette rolling papers, which he associated with marijuana. He proceeded to search the entire purse and discovered a small amount of marijuana, a pipe, a number of plastic bags, a substantial amount of money in one-dollar bills, a list of students who owed T.L.O. money, and two letters that indicated that T.L.O. was involved in dealing marijuana. Choplick contacted T.L.O.'s mother and turned the evidence of T.L.O.'s marijuana use over to the police. T.L.O. confessed to the police, and New Jersey filed delinquency charges against T.L.O. Her lawyer filed a motion to suppress the evidence discovered in her purse as well as the confession (*New Jersey v. T.L.O.,* 469 U.S. 325 [1985]).

Was the evidence seized from T.L.O.'s purse the product of an unlawful search and seizure? The Supreme Court held that the Fourth and Fourteenth Amendment protects students against unreasonable searches and seizures by public school authorities. Reasonableness, however, in the context of special-needs student disciplinary hearings is not automatically a matter of probable cause. Reasonableness instead is determined by balancing the purpose of the search against the degree of intrusion into a student's privacy. On one hand, there is a "substantial interest" of teachers and administrators in maintaining the discipline required to promote learning. On the other hand, students bring books, supplies, keys, money, and personal items to school, and any search inevitably intrudes into their personal privacy (*T.L.O.,* 469 U.S. at 334–338).

In striking this balance, the Supreme Court found that a reasonable suspicion standard enabled school administrators to act relatively quickly to maintain order while providing students a measure of protection (341–343).

Warrants. A probable cause warrant requirement would interfere with the "swift and informal" disciplinary procedures that are required in a school.

Reasonableness. The reasonable suspicion standard, according to the Supreme Court, relieves school personnel of the burden of learning the "niceties of probable cause" and insures that searches will be carried out in accordance with the "dictates of reason and common sense."

Did Choplick satisfy the reasonable suspicion standard? The Supreme Court held that given the allegation that T.L.O. had been smoking, it was reasonable to believe that there were cigarettes in her purse. The cigarettes corroborated the report that she had been smoking, and the discovery of the rolling papers provided reasonable suspicion to search T.L.O.'s purse for marijuana. Consider that under a probable cause standard, the rolling papers may not have provided Vice-Principal Choplick with an adequate basis to search T.L.O's purse for marijuana. This would have resulted in T.L.O.'s avoiding detection for drug use. Do you agree that high school students should be subject to searches without warrants based on reasonable suspicion rather than probable cause? What should be the standard for college students?

In 2009, in *Safford United School District v. Redding,* the U.S. Supreme Court was asked to decide whether school authorities were constitutionally justified in conducting a "strip search" of a high school student suspected of the unauthorized possession of prescription drugs.

Was the strip search of a student suspected of drug possession constitutionally justified?

Safford United School District v. Redding, 557 U.S. ___ (2009), Souter, J.

Issue

The issue here is whether a thirteen-year-old student's Fourth Amendment right was violated when she was subjected to a search of her bra and underpants by school officials acting on reasonable suspicion that she had brought forbidden prescription and over-the-counter drugs to school.

Facts

The events immediately prior to the search in question began in thirteen-year-old Savana Redding's math class at Safford Middle School one October day in 2003. The assistant principal of the school, Kerry Wilson, came into the room and asked Savana to go to his office. There, he showed her a day planner, unzipped and open flat on his desk, in which there were several knives, lighters, a permanent marker, and a cigarette. Wilson asked Savana whether the planner was hers; she said it was, but that a few days before, she had lent it to her friend, Marissa Glines. Savana stated that none of the items in the planner belonged to her. Wilson then showed Savana four white prescription-strength ibuprofen 400-mg pills, and one over-the-counter blue naproxen 200-mg pill, all used for pain and inflammation but banned under school rules without advance permission. He asked Savana if she knew anything about the pills. Savana answered that she did not. Wilson then told Savana that he had received a report that she was giving these pills to fellow students; Savana denied it and agreed to let Wilson search her belongings. Helen Romero, an administrative assistant, came into the office, and together with Wilson, they searched Savana's backpack, finding nothing.

At that point, Wilson instructed Romero to take Savana to the school nurse's office to search her clothes for pills. Romero and the nurse, Peggy Schwallier, asked Savana to remove her jacket, socks, and shoes, leaving her in stretch pants and a T-shirt (both without pockets), which she was then asked to remove. Finally, Savana was told to pull her bra out and to the side and shake it, and to pull out the elastic on her underpants, thus exposing her breasts and pelvic area to some degree. No pills were found. Savana's mother filed suit against Safford Unified School District #1, Wilson, Romero, and Schwallier for conducting a strip search in violation of Savana's Fourth Amendment rights. The District Court for the District of Arizona granted the motion to dismiss the suit on the ground that there was no Fourth Amendment violation, and a panel of the Ninth Circuit affirmed. A closely divided circuit sitting en banc, however, reversed.... [T]he Ninth Circuit held that the strip search was unjustified under the Fourth Amendment test for searches of children by school officials set out in *New Jersey v. T.L.O.*

Reasoning

The Fourth Amendment "right of the people to be secure in their persons...against unreasonable searches and seizures" generally requires a law enforcement officer to have probable cause for conducting a search. "Probable cause exists where 'the facts and circumstances within [an officer's] knowledge and of which [he] had reasonably trustworthy information [are] sufficient in themselves to warrant a man of reasonable caution in the belief that' an offense has been or is being committed." In *T.L.O.*, we recognized that the school setting "requires some modification of the level of suspicion of illicit activity needed to justify a search," and held that for searches by school officials, "a careful balancing of governmental and private interests suggests that the public interest is best served by a Fourth Amendment standard of reasonableness that stops short of probable cause." We have thus applied a standard of reasonable suspicion to determine the legality of a school administrator's search of a student, and have held that a school search "will be permissible in its scope when the measures adopted are reasonably related to the objectives of the search and not excessively intrusive in light of the age and sex of the student and the nature of the infraction." A number of our cases on probable cause have an implicit bearing on the reliable knowledge element of reasonable suspicion, as we have attempted to flesh out the knowledge component by looking to the degree to which known facts imply prohibited conduct, the specificity of the information received, and the reliability of its source. At the end of the day, however, we have realized that these factors cannot rigidly control, and we have come back to saying that the standards are "fluid concepts that take their substantive content from the particular contexts" in which they are being assessed. Perhaps the best that can be said generally about the required knowledge component of probable cause for a law enforcement officer's evidence search is that it raise a "fair probability," or a "substantial chance," of discovering evidence of criminal activity. The lesser standard for school searches could as readily be described as a moderate chance of finding evidence of wrongdoing. In this case, the school's policies strictly prohibit the nonmedical use, possession, or sale of any drug on school grounds, including "'[a]ny prescription or over-the-counter drug, except those for which permission to use in school has been granted pursuant to Board policy.'" A week before Savana was searched, another student, Jordan Romero (no relation of the school's administrative assistant), told the principal and Assistant Principal Wilson that "certain students were bringing drugs and weapons on campus," and that he had been sick after taking some pills that "he got from a classmate." On the morning of October 8, the same boy handed Wilson a white pill that he said Marissa Glines had given him. He told Wilson that students were planning to take the pills at lunch. Wilson learned from Peggy Schwallier, the school nurse, that the pill was ibuprofen 400 mg, available only by prescription. Wilson then called Marissa out of class. Outside the classroom, Marissa's teacher handed Wilson the day planner, found within Marissa's reach, containing various contraband items. Wilson escorted Marissa back to his office. In the presence of Helen Romero, Wilson requested Marissa to turn out her pockets and open her wallet. Marissa produced a blue pill, several white ones, and a razor blade. Wilson asked where the blue pill came from, and Marissa answered, "I guess it slipped in when she gave me the IBU 400s." When Wilson asked whom she meant, Marissa replied, "Savana Redding." Wilson then enquired about the day planner and its contents; Marissa denied knowing anything about them. Wilson did not ask Marissa any follow-up questions to determine whether there was any likelihood that Savana presently had pills: neither asking when Marissa received the pills from Savana nor where Savana might be hiding them. Schwallier did not immediately recognize the blue pill, but information provided through a poison control hotline indicated that the pill was a 200-mg dose of an anti-inflammatory drug, generically called naproxen, available over the counter. At Wilson's direction, Marissa was then subjected to a search of her bra and underpants by Romero and Schwallier, as Savana was later on. The search revealed no additional pills. It was at this juncture that Wilson called Savana into his office and showed her the day planner. Their conversation established that Savana and Marissa were on friendly terms: While she denied knowledge of the contraband, Savana admitted that the day planner was hers and that she had lent it to Marissa. Wilson had other reports of their friendship from staff members, who had identified Savana and Marissa as part of an unusually rowdy group at the school's opening dance in August, during which alcohol and cigarettes were found in the girls' bathroom. Wilson had reason to connect the girls with this contraband, for Wilson knew that Jordan Romero had told the principal that before the dance, he had been at a party at Savana's house where alcohol was served. Marissa's statement that the pills came from Savana was thus sufficiently plausible to warrant suspicion that Savana was involved in pill distribution.

This suspicion of Wilson's was enough to justify a search of Savana's backpack and outer clothing. If a student is reasonably suspected of giving out contraband pills, she is reasonably suspected of carrying them on her person and in the carryall that has become an item of student uniform in most places today. If Wilson's reasonable suspicion of pill distribution were not understood to support searches of outer clothes and backpack, it would not justify any search worth making. And the look into Savana's bag, in her presence and in the relative privacy of Wilson's office, was not excessively intrusive, any more than Romero's subsequent search of her outer clothing. Here it is that the parties part company, with Savana's claim that extending the search at Wilson's behest to the point of making her pull out her underwear was constitutionally unreasonable. The exact label for this final step in the intrusion is not important, though strip search is a fair way to speak of it. Romero and Schwallier directed Savana to remove her clothes down to her underwear, and then "pull out" her bra and the elastic band on her underpants. Although Romero and Schwallier stated that they did not see anything when Savana followed their instructions, we would not define strip search and its Fourth Amendment consequences in a way that would guarantee litigation about who was looking and how much was seen. The very fact of Savana's pulling her underwear away from her body in the presence of the two officials who were able to see her necessarily exposed her breasts and pelvic area to some degree, and both subjective and reasonable societal expectations of personal privacy support the treatment of such a search as categorically distinct, requiring distinct elements of justification on the part of school authorities for going beyond a search of outer clothing and belongings. Savana's subjective expectation of privacy against such a search is inherent in her account of it as embarrassing, frightening, and humiliating. The reasonableness of her expectation (required by the Fourth Amendment standard) is indicated by the consistent experiences of other young people similarly searched, whose adolescent vulnerability intensifies the patent intrusiveness of the exposure. The common reaction of these adolescents simply registers the obviously different meaning of a search exposing the body from the experience of nakedness or near undress in other school circumstances. Changing for gym is getting ready for play; exposing for a search is responding to an accusation reserved for suspected wrongdoers and fairly understood as so degrading that a number of communities have decided that strip searches in schools are never reasonable and have banned them no matter what the facts may be. The indignity of the search does not, of course, outlaw it, but it does implicate the rule of reasonableness as stated in *T.L.O.*, that "the search as actually conducted [be] reasonably related in scope to the circumstances which justified the interference in the first place." The scope will be permissible, that is, when it is "not excessively intrusive in light of the age and sex of the student and the nature of the infraction."

Here, the content of the suspicion failed to match the degree of intrusion. Wilson knew beforehand that the pills were prescription-strength ibuprofen and over-the-counter naproxen, common pain relievers equivalent to two Advil, or one Aleve. He must have been aware of the nature and limited threat of the specific drugs he was searching for, and while just about anything can be taken in quantities that will do real harm, Wilson had no reason to suspect that large amounts of the drugs were being passed around, or that individual students were receiving great numbers of pills.

Nor could Wilson have suspected that Savana was hiding common painkillers in her underwear. Petitioners suggest, as a truth universally acknowledged, that "students . . . hid[e] contraband in or under their clothing," and cite a smattering of cases of students with contraband in their underwear. But when the categorically extreme intrusiveness of a search down to the body of an adolescent requires some justification in suspected facts, general background possibilities fall short; a reasonable search that extensive calls for suspicion that it will pay off. But nondangerous school contraband does not raise the specter of stashes in intimate places, and there is no evidence in the record of any general practice among Safford Middle School students of hiding that sort of thing in underwear; neither Jordan nor Marissa suggested to Wilson that Savana was doing that, and the preceding search of Marissa that Wilson ordered yielded nothing. Wilson never even determined when Marissa had received the pills from Savana; if it had been a few days before, that would weigh heavily against any reasonable conclusion that Savana presently had the pills on her person, much less in her underwear. In sum, what was missing from the suspected facts that pointed to Savana was any indication of danger to the students from the power of the drugs or their quantity, and any reason to suppose that Savana was carrying pills in her underwear. We think that the combination of these deficiencies was fatal to finding the search reasonable.

Holding

In so holding, we mean to cast no ill reflection on the assistant principal, for the record raises no doubt that his motive throughout was to eliminate drugs from his school and protect students from what Jordan Romero had gone through. Parents are known to overreact to protect their children from danger, and a school official with responsibility for safety may tend to do the same. The difference is that the Fourth Amendment places limits on the official, even with the high degree of deference that courts must pay to the educator's professional judgment. We do mean, though, to make it clear that the *T.L.O.* concern to limit a school search to reasonable scope requires the support of reasonable suspicion of danger or of resort to underwear for hiding evidence of wrongdoing before a search can reasonably make the quantum leap from outer clothes and backpacks to exposure of intimate parts. The meaning of such a search, and the degradation its subject may reasonably feel, places a search that intrusive in a category of its own demanding its own specific suspicions.

Concurring in part and dissenting in part, *Ginsburg, J.*

Fellow student Marissa Glines, caught with pills in her pocket, accused Redding of supplying them. Asked where the blue pill among several white pills in Glines's pocket came from, Glines answered, "I guess it slipped in when she gave me the IBU 400s." Asked next "who is she?," Glines responded, "Savana Redding." As the Court observes, no follow-up questions were asked. Wilson did not test Glines's accusation for veracity by asking Glines when did Redding give her the pills, where, for what purpose. Any reasonable search for the pills would have ended when inspection of Redding's backpack and jacket pockets yielded nothing. Wilson had no cause to suspect, based on prior experience at the school or clues in this case, that Redding had hidden pills—containing the equivalent of two Advils or one Aleve—in her underwear or body. To make matters worse, Wilson did not release Redding, to return to class or to go home, after the search. Instead, he made her sit on a chair outside his office for over two hours. At no point did he attempt to call her parent. Abuse of authority of that order should not be shielded by official immunity. In contrast to *T.L.O.*, where a teacher discovered a student smoking in the lavatory, and where the search was confined to the student's purse, the search of Redding involved her body and rested on the bare accusation of another student whose reliability the assistant principal had no reason to trust. The Court's opinion in *T.L.O.* plainly stated the controlling Fourth Amendment law: A search ordered by a school official, even if "justified at its inception," crosses the constitutional boundary if it becomes "excessively intrusive in light of the age and sex of the student and the nature of the infraction."

Here, "the nature of the [supposed] infraction," the slim basis for suspecting Savana Redding, and her "age and sex," establish beyond doubt that Assistant Principal Wilson's order cannot be reconciled with this Court's opinion in *T.L.O.* Wilson's treatment of Redding was abusive, and it was not reasonable for him to believe that the law permitted it.

Concurring in the judgment in part and dissenting in part, *Thomas, J.*

A search of a student is permissible in scope under *T.L.O.* so long as it is objectively reasonable to believe that the area searched could conceal the contraband.... "[I]f a student brought a baseball bat on campus in violation of school policy, a search of that student's shirt pocket would be patently unjustified."... The reasonable suspicion that Redding possessed the pills for distribution purposes did not dissipate simply because the search of her backpack turned up nothing. It was eminently reasonable to conclude that the backpack was empty because Redding was secreting the pills in a place she thought no one would look. Redding would not have been the first person to conceal pills in her undergarments. Nor will she be the last after today's decision, which announces the safest place to secrete contraband in school.

The majority compounds its error by reading the "nature of the infraction" aspect of the *T.L.O.* test as a license to limit searches based on a judge's assessment of a particular school policy. According to the majority, the scope of the search was impermissible because the school official "must have been aware of the nature and limited threat of the specific drugs he was searching for" and because he "had no reason to suspect that large amounts of the drugs were being passed around, or that individual students were receiving great numbers of pills." Thus, in order to locate a rationale for finding a Fourth Amendment violation in this case, the majority retreats from its observation that the school's firm no-drug policy "makes sense, and there is no basis to claim that the search was unreasonable owing to some defect or shortcoming of the rule it was aimed at enforcing." Even accepting the majority's assurances that it is not attacking the rule's reasonableness, it certainly is attacking the rule's importance. This approach directly conflicts with *T.L.O.* in which the Court was "unwilling to adopt a standard under which the legality of a search is dependent upon a judge's evaluation of the relative importance of school rules." Indeed, the Court in *T.L.O.* expressly rejected the proposition that the majority seemingly endorses—that "some rules regarding student conduct are by nature too 'trivial' to justify a search based upon reasonable suspicion."

The majority's decision in this regard also departs from another basic principle of the Fourth Amendment: that law enforcement officials can enforce with the same vigor all rules and regulations irrespective of the perceived importance of any of those rules.... The majority has placed school officials in this "impossible spot" by questioning whether possession of ibuprofen and naproxen causes a severe enough threat to warrant investigation. Had the suspected infraction involved a street drug, the majority implies that it would have approved the scope of the search. In effect, then, the majority has replaced a school rule that draws no distinction among drugs with a new one that does. As a result, a full search of a student's person for prohibited drugs will be permitted only if the Court agrees that the drug in question was sufficiently dangerous. Such a test is unworkable and unsound. School officials cannot be expected to halt searches based on the possibility that a court might later find that the particular infraction at issue is not severe enough to warrant an intrusive investigation.

Judges are not qualified to second-guess the best manner for maintaining quiet and order in the school environment.... Even if this Court were authorized to second-guess the importance of school rules, the Court's assessment of the importance of this district's policy is flawed. It is a crime to possess or use prescription-strength ibuprofen without a prescription. By prohibiting unauthorized prescription drugs on school grounds—and conducting a search to ensure students abide by that prohibition—the school rule here was consistent with a routine provision of the state criminal code. It hardly seems unreasonable for school officials to enforce a rule that, in effect, proscribes conduct that amounts to a crime. Moreover, school districts have valid reasons for punishing the unauthorized possession of prescription drugs on school property as severely as the possession of street drugs; "[t]eenage abuse of over-the-counter and prescription drugs poses an increasingly alarming national crisis." School administrators can reasonably conclude that this high rate of drug abuse is being fueled, at least in part, by the increasing presence of prescription drugs on school campuses. The risks posed by the abuse of these drugs are every bit as serious as the dangers of using a typical street drug.... [S]ince 1999, there has "been a dramatic increase in the number of poisonings and even deaths associated with the abuse of prescription drugs." At least some of these injuries and deaths are likely due to the fact that "[m]ost controlled prescription drug abusers are poly-substance abusers," a habit that is especially likely to result in deadly drug combinations. Furthermore, even if a child is not immediately harmed by the abuse of prescription drugs, research suggests that prescription drugs have become "gateway drugs to other substances of abuse."... If a student with a previously unknown intolerance to ibuprofen or naproxen were to take either drug and become ill, the public outrage would likely be directed toward the school for failing to take steps to prevent the unmonitored use of the drug. In light of the risks involved, a school's decision to establish and enforce a school prohibition on the possession of any unauthorized drug is thus a reasonable judgment.

Questions for Discussion

1. Summarize the facts in *Redding*.
2. Did the Court find that there was reasonable suspicion to search Savana's backpack and outer clothing? Why did the majority rule that the strip search of Savana was unreasonable?
3. Do you agree with the Court that a strip search is "excessively" intrusive and humiliating? What additional facts can you think of that would have justified Vice Principal Wilson in conducting a strip search of Savana?
4. Why does Justice Thomas conclude that the strip search was reasonable? How does Justice Thomas differ from the Court majority in his view of how judges should approach cases involving schoolchildren and adults?

Drug Testing in High Schools

In 1995, the U.S. Supreme Court once again considered the Fourth Amendment rights of high school students in *Vernonia School District 473 v. Acton.* The school district in Vernonia, Oregon, adopted a Student Athlete Drug Policy that authorized random urinalysis drug testing of students participating in athletic programs. The program was initiated in response to a doubling of disciplinary referrals for drug use in the high school between 1988 and 1989 as compared with the early 1980s. Student athletes were considered the "leaders of the drug culture," and their drug use allegedly had impaired their athletic performances and had led to the serious injury of a wrestler (*Vernonia School District 473 v. Acton,* 515 U.S. 646, 648–649 [1995]).

This drug problem persisted despite special classes, outside speakers and presentations, and the use of a dog to detect drugs in the school. District officials grew increasingly frustrated, and the introduction of a Student Athlete Drug Policy was endorsed by parents and the school board. The policy had several central components.

Purpose. The purpose of the policy is to prevent student-athletes from using drugs, to protect their health and safety, and to provide assistance to drug users.

Athletes. Students participating in sports along with their parents are required to sign a form agreeing to the testing. Athletes are to be tested at the beginning of the season, and each week, ten percent of the athletes are to be selected at random for testing.

Drug samples. Students are to provide a urine sample in an empty locker room with their back to an adult monitor. Female students produce samples in an enclosed stall with the monitor standing outside. The products are sent to a laboratory for independent analysis.

Disciplinary punishment. A positive test results in the administration of a second test. In the event that the second test also is positive, the athlete's parents are notified, and the parents and student meet with the school principal, who offers the alternatives of either participating in a six-week assistance program that includes weekly urinalysis or being suspended from the athletic teams for the remainder of the current season and the next season. A second offense automatically results in suspension for the current season and the next season, and a third offense leads to a suspension for the current season and two additional seasons (650–651).

James Acton, a seventh grader, was barred from participating on a sports team because his parents refused to consent to his participation in the drug-testing program. Acton responded by filing a lawsuit alleging that the drug-testing program violated the Fourth Amendment prohibition on unreasonable searches and seizures. The Supreme Court held that the legitimate governmental interest in carrying out drug tests outweighed the modest intrusion on the diminished privacy interests of students. Requiring reasonable suspicion would interfere with the effectiveness of the tests. The Court's reasoning is summarized below (653).

- ***Governmental interest.*** Schools have a duty to protect and to educate children. Drug use is destructive to students, especially those engaged in athletics. Individuals engaged in athletic pursuits are particularly at risk of injury or serious health problems. The Vernonia School District also asserted that the drug problem had reached epidemic proportions among athletes, who generally serve as role models for other students.
- ***Student privacy.*** Students have a diminished expectation of privacy, and athletes have even less of an expectation of privacy than the average student. The Court pointed out that athletes are subjected to a regime of regulation that includes preseason physical examinations, maintenance of a minimum grade point average, and adherence to rules of dress, training, and practice.
- ***Intrusiveness of drug tests.*** The drug tests are conducted in a relatively unintrusive fashion. The tests look only for drugs and do not examine whether an individual is an epileptic, pregnant, or diabetic. The results are disclosed only to a limited number of school authorities and are not distributed to law enforcement.
- ***Suspicionless drug testing.*** Teachers are not trained to make reasonable suspicion determinations of drug use. Parents also would resist basing testing on reasonable suspicion on the grounds that this singles out and embarrasses students and places them in a negative light.

Do you agree with the Supreme Court that it is impractical to employ a reasonable suspicion standard to determine which students should be subjected to drug tests and that the only practical alternative is the suspicionless testing of all students involved in athletics?

In the next case in the text, *Board of Education of Independent School District No. 92 of Pottawatomie County v. Earls,* the U.S. Supreme Court considered the constitutionality of a drug-testing policy that requires all middle and high school students who participate in any of the district's competitive extracurricular activities to submit to urinalysis. Apply the precedent in *Vernonia* and ask yourself whether you would uphold the constitutionality of the drug-testing program in *Pottawatomie.*

Can the board of education require all students participating in extracurricular activities to submit to drug testing?

Board of Education of Independent School District No. 92 of Pottawatomie County v. Earls,
536 U.S. 822 (2002), Thomas, J.

Issue

Student Activities Drug Testing Policy implemented by the Board of Education of Independent School District No. 92 of Pottawatomie County (School District) requires all students who participate in competitive extracurricular activities to submit to drug testing. [The question is whether] this Policy reasonably serves the School District's important interest in detecting and preventing drug use among its students. . . .

Facts

The city of Tecumseh, Oklahoma, is a rural community located approximately forty miles southeast of Oklahoma City. The School District administers all Tecumseh public schools. In the fall of 1998, the School District adopted the Student Activities Drug Testing Policy (Policy), which requires all middle and high school students to consent to drug testing in order to participate in any extracurricular activity. In practice, the Policy has been applied only to competitive extracurricular activities sanctioned by the Oklahoma Secondary Schools Activities Association, such as the Academic Team, Future Farmers of America, Future Homemakers of America, band, choir, cheerleading, and athletics. Under the Policy, students are required to take a drug test before participating in an extracurricular activity, must submit to random drug testing while participating in that activity, and must agree to be tested at any time upon reasonable suspicion. The urinalysis tests are designed to detect only the use of illegal drugs, including amphetamines, marijuana, cocaine, opiates, and barbiturates, not medical conditions or the presence of authorized prescription medications.

At the time of their suit, both respondents attended Tecumseh High School. Respondent Lindsay Earls was a member of the show choir, the marching band, the Academic Team, and the National Honor Society. Respondent Daniel James sought to participate in the Academic Team. Together with their parents, Earls and James brought a legal action against the School District, challenging the Policy.... They alleged that the Policy violates the Fourth Amendment as incorporated by the Fourteenth Amendment.... They also argued that the School District failed to identify a special need for testing students who participate in extracurricular activities, and that the "Drug Testing Policy neither addresses a proven problem nor promises to bring any benefit to students or the school."

[T]he United States District Court for the Western District of Oklahoma rejected respondents' claim that the Policy was unconstitutional and granted judgment to the School District. The court noted that "special needs" exist in the public school context and that, although the School District did "not show a drug problem of epidemic proportions," there was a history of drug abuse starting in 1970 that presented "legitimate cause for concern." ... The United States Court of Appeals for the Tenth Circuit reversed, holding that the Policy violated the Fourth Amendment.... Before imposing a suspicionless drug testing program, the Court of Appeals concluded that a school "must demonstrate that there is some identifiable drug abuse problem among a sufficient number of those subject to the testing, such that testing that group of students will actually redress its drug problem."...

Reasoning

The Fourth Amendment to the United States Constitution protects "the right of the people to be secure in their persons, houses, papers, and effects, against unreasonable searches and seizures." Searches by public school officials, such as the collection of urine samples, implicate Fourth Amendment interests.... We must therefore review the School District's Policy for "reasonableness," which is the touchstone of the constitutionality of a governmental search....

The School District's Policy is not in any way related to the conduct of criminal investigations. Respondents do not contend that the School District requires probable cause before testing students for drug use. Respondents instead argue that drug testing must be based at least on some level of individualized suspicion. It is true that we generally determine the reasonableness of a search by balancing the nature of the intrusion on the individual's privacy against the promotion of legitimate governmental interests. But we have long held that "the Fourth Amendment imposes no irreducible requirement of [individualized] suspicion." "In certain limited circumstances, the Government's need to discover... hidden conditions, or to prevent their development, is sufficiently compelling to justify the intrusion on privacy entailed by conducting such searches without any measure of individualized suspicion." Therefore, in the context of safety and administrative regulations, a search unsupported by probable cause may be reasonable "when 'special needs, beyond the normal need for law enforcement, make the warrant and probable-cause requirement impracticable.'"

Significantly, this Court has previously held that "special needs" inhere in the public school context. While schoolchildren do not shed their constitutional rights when they enter the schoolhouse, "Fourth Amendment rights... are different in public schools than elsewhere; the 'reasonableness' inquiry cannot disregard the schools' custodial and tutelary responsibility for children." In particular, a finding of individualized suspicion may not be necessary when a school conducts drug testing.

In *Vernonia,* this Court held that the suspicionless drug testing of athletes was constitutional. The Court, however, did not simply authorize all school drug testing, but rather conducted a fact-specific balancing of the intrusion on the children's Fourth Amendment rights against the promotion of legitimate governmental interests. Applying the principles of *Vernonia* to the somewhat different facts of this case, we conclude that Tecumseh's Policy is also constitutional.

We first consider the nature of the privacy interest allegedly compromised by the drug testing. As in *Vernonia,* the context of the public school environment serves as the backdrop for the analysis of the privacy interest at stake and the reasonableness of the drug testing policy in general ("Central... is the fact that the subjects of the Policy are (1) children, who (2) have been committed to the temporary custody of the State as schoolmaster"); ("The most significant element in this case is the first we discussed: that the Policy was undertaken in furtherance of the government's responsibilities, under a public school system, as guardian and tutor of children entrusted to its care"); ("When the government acts as guardian and tutor the relevant question is whether the search is one that a reasonable guardian and tutor might undertake").

A student's privacy interest is limited in a public school environment where the State is responsible for maintaining discipline, health, and safety. Schoolchildren are routinely required to submit to physical examinations and vaccinations against disease. Securing order in the school environment sometimes requires that students be subjected to greater controls than those appropriate for adults.

In any event, students who participate in competitive extracurricular activities voluntarily subject themselves to many of the same intrusions on their privacy as do athletes. Some of these clubs and activities require occasional off-campus travel and communal undress. All of them have their own rules and requirements for participating students that do not apply to the student body as a whole. For example, each of the competitive extracurricular activities governed by the Policy must abide by the rules of the Oklahoma Secondary Schools Activities Association, and a faculty sponsor monitors the students for compliance with the various rules dictated by the clubs and activities. This regulation of extracurricular activities further diminishes the expectation of privacy among schoolchildren. ("Somewhat like adults who choose to participate in a closely regulated industry, students who voluntarily participate in school athletics have reason to expect intrusions upon normal rights and privileges, including privacy.") We therefore conclude that the students affected by this Policy have a limited expectation of privacy.

Next, we consider the character of the intrusion imposed by the Policy. Urination is "an excretory function traditionally shielded by great privacy." But the "degree of intrusion" on one's privacy caused by collecting a urine sample "depends upon the manner in which production of the urine sample is monitored." Under the Policy, a faculty monitor waits outside the closed restroom stall for the student to produce a sample and must "listen for the normal sounds of urination in order to guard against tampered specimens and to insure an accurate chain of custody." The monitor then pours the sample into two bottles that are sealed and placed into a mailing pouch along with a consent form signed by the student. This procedure is virtually identical to that reviewed in *Vernonia,* except that it additionally protects privacy by allowing male students to produce their samples behind a closed stall. Given that we considered the method of collection in *Vernonia* a "negligible" intrusion, the method here is even less problematic.

In addition, the Policy clearly requires that the test results be kept in confidential files separate from a student's other educational records and released to school personnel only on a "need to know" basis. Respondents nonetheless contend that the intrusion on students' privacy is significant because the Policy fails to protect effectively against the disclosure of confidential information and, specifically, that the school "has been careless in protecting that information: for example, the Choir teacher looked at students' prescription drug lists and left them where other students could see them." But the choir teacher is someone with a "need to know," because during off-campus trips she needs to know what medications are taken by her students. Even before the Policy was enacted, the choir teacher had access to this information. In any event, there is no allegation that any other student did see such information. This one example of alleged carelessness hardly increases the character of the intrusion.

Moreover, the test results are not turned over to any law enforcement authority. Nor do the test results here lead to the imposition of discipline or have any academic consequences. Rather, the only consequence of a failed drug test is to limit the student's privilege of participating in extracurricular activities. Indeed, a student may test positive for drugs twice and still be allowed to participate in extracurricular activities. After the first positive test, the school contacts the student's parent or guardian for a meeting. The student may continue to participate in the activity if within five days of the meeting the student shows proof of receiving drug counseling and submits to a second drug test in two weeks. For the second positive test, the student is suspended from participation in all extracurricular activities for fourteen days, must complete four hours of substance abuse counseling, and must submit to monthly drug tests. Only after a third positive test will the student be suspended from participating in any extracurricular activity for the remainder of the school year, or eighty-eight school days, whichever is longer.

Given the minimally intrusive nature of the sample collection and the limited uses to which the test results are put, we conclude that the invasion of students' privacy is not significant.

Finally, this Court must consider the nature and immediacy of the government's concerns and the efficacy of the Policy in meeting them. This Court has already articulated in detail the importance of the governmental concern in preventing drug use by schoolchildren. The drug abuse problem among our Nation's youth has hardly abated since *Vernonia* was decided in 1995. In fact, evidence suggests that it has only grown worse. As in *Vernonia,* "the necessity for the State to act is magnified by the fact that this evil is being visited not just upon individuals at large, but upon children for whom it has undertaken a special responsibility of care and direction." The health and safety risks identified in *Vernonia* apply with equal force to Tecumseh's children. Indeed, the nationwide drug epidemic makes the war against drugs a pressing concern in every school.

For instance, the number of twelfth graders using any illicit drug increased from 48.4 percent in 1995 to 53.9 percent in 2001. The number of twelfth graders reporting they had used marijuana jumped from 41.7 percent to 49.0 percent during that same period. Additionally, the School District in this case has presented specific evidence of drug use at Tecumseh schools. Teachers testified that they had seen students who appeared to be under the influence of drugs and that they had heard students speaking openly about using drugs. A drug dog found marijuana cigarettes near the school parking lot. Police officers once found drugs or drug paraphernalia in a car driven by a Future Farmers of America member. And the school board president reported that people in the community were calling the board to discuss the "drug situation." We decline to second-guess the finding of the District Court that "viewing the evidence as a whole, it cannot be reasonably disputed that the [School District] was faced with a 'drug problem' when it adopted the Policy."

Respondents consider the proffered evidence insufficient and argue that there is no "real and immediate interest" to justify a policy of drug testing nonathletes. We have recognized, however, that "[a] demonstrated problem of drug abuse . . . [is] not in all cases necessary to the validity of a testing regime," but that some showing does "shore up an assertion of special need for a suspicionless general search program." The School District has provided sufficient evidence to shore up the need for its drug testing program.

Furthermore, this Court has not required a particularized or pervasive drug problem before allowing the government to conduct suspicionless drug testing. For instance, in *Von Raab,* the Court upheld the drug testing of customs officials on a purely preventive basis, without any documented history of drug use by such officials. In response to the lack of evidence relating to drug use, the Court noted generally that "drug abuse is one of the most serious problems confronting our society today," and that programs to prevent and detect drug use among customs officials could not be deemed unreasonable based on studies that identified on-the-job alcohol and drug use by railroad employees. Likewise, the need to prevent and deter the substantial harm of childhood drug use provides the necessary immediacy for a school testing policy. Indeed, it would make little sense to require a school district to wait for a substantial portion of its students to begin using drugs before it was allowed to institute a drug testing program designed to deter drug use.

We reject the Court of Appeals' novel test that "any district seeking to impose a random suspicionless drug testing policy as a condition to participation in a school activity must demonstrate that there is some identifiable drug abuse problem among a sufficient number of those subject to the testing, such that testing that group of students will actually redress its drug problem." Among other problems, it would be difficult to administer such a test. As we cannot articulate a threshold level of drug use that would suffice to justify a drug testing program for schoolchildren, we refuse to fashion what would in effect be a constitutional quantum of drug use necessary to show a "drug problem."

Respondents are correct that safety factors into the special needs analysis, but the safety interest furthered by drug testing is undoubtedly substantial for all children, athletes and nonathletes alike. We know all too well that drug use carries a variety of health risks for children, including death from overdose. We also reject respondents' argument that drug testing must presumptively be based upon an individualized reasonable suspicion of wrongdoing because such a testing regime would be less intrusive. In this context, the Fourth Amendment does not require a finding of individualized suspicion, and we decline to impose such a requirement on schools attempting to prevent and detect drug use by students. Moreover, we question whether testing based on individualized suspicion in fact would be less intrusive. Such a regime would place an additional burden on public school teachers who are already tasked with the difficult job of maintaining order and discipline. A program of individualized suspicion might unfairly target members of unpopular groups. The fear of lawsuits resulting from such targeted searches may chill enforcement of the program, rendering it ineffective in combating drug use. . . .

Finally, we find that testing students who participate in extracurricular activities is a reasonably effective means of addressing the School District's legitimate concerns in preventing, deterring, and detecting drug use. While in *Vernonia* there might have been a closer fit between the testing of athletes and the trial court's finding that the drug problem was "fueled by the 'role model' effect of athletes' drug use," such a finding was not essential to the holding. *Vernonia* did not require the school to test the group of students most likely to use drugs, but rather considered the constitutionality of the program in the context of the public school's custodial responsibilities. Evaluating the Policy in this context, we conclude that the drug testing of Tecumseh students who participate in extracurricular activities effectively serves the School District's interest in protecting the safety and health of its students.

Holding

Within the limits of the Fourth Amendment, local school boards must assess the desirability of drug testing schoolchildren. In upholding the constitutionality of the Policy, we express no opinion as to its wisdom. Rather, we hold only that Tecumseh's Policy is a reasonable means of furthering the School District's important interest in preventing and deterring drug use among its schoolchildren. . . .

Dissenting, *Ginsburg, J.,* joined by *Stevens, J., O'Connor, J.,* and *Souter, J.*

Seven years ago, in *Vernonia,* this Court determined that a school district's policy of randomly testing the urine of its student athletes for illicit drugs did not violate the Fourth Amendment. In so ruling, the Court emphasized that drug use "increased the risk of sports-related injury" and that Vernonia's athletes were the "leaders" of an aggressive local "drug culture" that had reached "epidemic proportions." Today, the Court relies upon *Vernonia* to permit a school district with a drug problem its superintendent repeatedly described as "not . . . major," to test the urine of an academic team member solely by reason of her participation in a nonathletic, competitive extracurricular activity—participation associated with neither special dangers from, nor particular predilections for, drug use. . . . The particular testing program upheld today is not reasonable, it is capricious, even perverse: Petitioners' policy targets for testing a student population least likely to be at risk from illicit drugs and their damaging effects. I therefore dissent.

A search unsupported by probable cause nevertheless may be consistent with the Fourth Amendment "when special needs, beyond the normal need for law enforcement, make the warrant and probable-cause requirement impracticable. Fourth Amendment rights, no less than First and Fourteenth Amendment rights, are different in public schools than elsewhere; the 'reasonableness' inquiry cannot disregard the schools' custodial and tutelary responsibility for children."

The *Vernonia* Court concluded that a public school district facing a disruptive and explosive drug abuse problem sparked by members of its athletic teams had "special needs" that justified suspicionless testing of district athletes as a condition of their athletic participation. This case presents circumstances dispositively different from those of *Vernonia*. True, as the Court stresses, Tecumseh students participating in competitive extracurricular activities other than athletics share two relevant characteristics with the athletes of *Vernonia*. First, both groups attend public schools. "Our decision in *Vernonia*," the Court states, "depended primarily upon the school's custodial responsibility and authority." Concern for student health and safety is basic to the school's caretaking, and it is undeniable that "drug use carries a variety of health risks for children, including death from overdose."

Those risks, however, are present for all schoolchildren. *Vernonia* cannot be read to endorse invasive and suspicionless drug testing of all students upon any evidence of drug use, solely because drugs jeopardize the life and health of those who use them. Many children, like many adults, engage in dangerous activities on their own time; that the children are enrolled in school scarcely allows government to monitor all such activities. If a student has a reasonable subjective expectation of privacy in the personal items she brings to school, surely she has a similar expectation regarding the chemical composition of her urine. Had the *Vernonia* Court agreed that public school attendance, in and of itself, permitted the State to test each student's blood or urine for drugs, the opinion in *Vernonia* could have saved many words. ("It must not be lost sight of that [the Vernonia School District] program is directed . . . to drug use by school athletes, where the risk of immediate physical harm to the drug user or those with whom he is playing his sport is particularly high.")

The second commonality to which the Court points is the voluntary character of both interscholastic athletics and other competitive extracurricular activities. "By choosing to 'go out for the team,' [school athletes] voluntarily subject themselves to a degree of regulation even higher than that imposed on students generally." Comparably, the Court today observes, "students who participate in competitive extracurricular activities voluntarily subject themselves to" additional rules not applicable to other students.

The comparison is enlightening. While extracurricular activities are "voluntary" in the sense that they are not required for graduation, they are part of the school's educational program; for that reason, the petitioner (hereinafter School District) is justified in expending public resources to make them available. Participation in such activities is a key component of school life, essential in reality for students applying to college, and, for all participants, a significant contributor to the breadth and quality of the educational experience. . . . Voluntary participation in athletics has a distinctly different dimension: Schools regulate student athletes discretely because competitive school sports by their nature require communal undress and, more important, expose students to physical risks that schools have a duty to mitigate. For the very reason that schools cannot offer a program of competitive athletics without intimately affecting the privacy of students, *Vernonia* reasonably analogized school athletes to "adults who choose to participate in a closely regulated industry." Interscholastic athletics similarly require close safety and health regulation; a school's choir, band, and academic team do not.

Enrollment in a public school and election to participate in school activities beyond the bare minimum that the curriculum requires are indeed factors relevant to reasonableness, but they do not on their own justify intrusive, suspicionless searches. *Vernonia*, accordingly, did not rest upon these factors; instead, the Court performed what today's majority aptly describes as a "fact-specific balancing." Balancing of that order, applied to the facts now before the Court, should yield a result other than the one the Court announces today. . . .

Activities of the kind plaintiff-respondent Lindsay Earls pursued—choir, show choir, marching band, and academic team—afford opportunities to gain self-assurance, to "come to know faculty members in a less formal setting than the typical classroom," and to acquire "positive social supports and networks [that] play a critical role in periods of heightened stress." On "occasional out-of-town trips," students like Lindsay Earls "must sleep together in communal settings and use communal bathrooms." But those situations are hardly equivalent to the routine communal undress associated with athletics; the School District itself admits that when such trips occur, "public-like restroom facilities," which presumably include enclosed stalls, are ordinarily available for changing, and that "more modest students" find other ways to maintain their privacy.

After describing school athletes' reduced expectation of privacy, the *Vernonia* Court turned to "the character of the intrusion... complained of." Observing that students produce urine samples in a bathroom stall with a coach or teacher outside, *Vernonia* typed the privacy interests compromised by the process of obtaining samples "negligible." As to the required pretest disclosure of prescription medications taken, the Court assumed that "the School District would have permitted [a student] to provide the requested information in a confidential manner—for example, in a sealed envelope delivered to the testing lab." On that assumption, the Court concluded that Vernonia's athletes faced no significant invasion of privacy. In this case, however, Lindsay Earls and her parents allege that the School District handled personal information collected under the policy carelessly, with little regard for its confidentiality. Information about students' prescription drug use, they assert, was routinely viewed by Lindsay's choir teacher, who left files containing the information unlocked and unsealed, where others, including students, could see them; and test results were given out to all activity sponsors whether or not they had a clear "need to know."...

Finally, the "nature and immediacy of the governmental concern" faced by the Vernonia School District dwarfed that confronting Tecumseh administrators. Vernonia initiated its drug testing policy in response to an alarming situation: "[A] large segment of the student body, particularly those involved in interscholastic athletics, was in a state of rebellion... fueled by alcohol and drug abuse as well as the student[s'] misperceptions about the drug culture." Tecumseh, by contrast, repeatedly reported to the Federal Government during the period leading up to the adoption of the policy that "types of drugs [other than alcohol and tobacco] including controlled dangerous substances, are present [in the schools] but have not identified themselves as major problems at this time."

Not only did the Vernonia and Tecumseh districts confront drug problems of distinctly different magnitudes, they also chose different solutions: Vernonia limited its policy to athletes; Tecumseh indiscriminately subjected to testing all participants in competitive extracurricular activities. Urging that "the safety interest furthered by drug testing is undoubtedly substantial for all children, athletes and nonathletes alike," the Court cuts out an element essential to the *Vernonia* judgment....

The Vernonia district, in sum, had two good reasons for testing athletes: Sports team members faced special health risks and they "were the leaders of the drug culture." No similar reason, and no other tenable justification, explains Tecumseh's decision to target for testing all participants in every competitive extracurricular activity.

Nationwide, students who participate in extracurricular activities are significantly less likely to develop substance abuse problems than are their less-involved peers.... Even if students might be deterred from drug use in order to preserve their extracurricular eligibility, it is at least as likely that other students might forgo their extracurricular involvement in order to avoid detection of their drug use. Tecumseh's policy thus falls short doubly if deterrence is its aim: It invades the privacy of students who need deterrence least, and risks steering students at greatest risk for substance abuse away from extracurricular involvement that potentially may palliate drug problems.

Questions for Discussion

1. Compare and contrast the drug-testing policy adopted by the school districts in Vernonia and in Tecumseh in terms of the individuals who are tested, evidence of a drug problem, the handling of confidential information, and other factors.
2. Summarize the arguments of the majority and of the dissent. Do you agree with the Supreme Court majority that the Tecumseh plan is constitutional? Why does the dissent contend that the Tecumseh plan is unreasonable under the Fourth Amendment?
3. ***Problems in policing.*** You are the local police chief. Design a drug-testing program that includes all students at the local high school that is consistent with the Supreme Court precedents in *Vernonia* and *Pottawatomie*.

7.3 YOU DECIDE

In 1988, the public hospital operated by the Medical University of South Carolina in Charleston became concerned about drug use by female patients who were receiving prenatal care. The hospital began to order drug screens on urine samples from maternity patients who were suspected of using cocaine. A patient who tested positive was referred to the county substance abuse commission for counseling and treatment. This program apparently had a limited impact on the drug abuse problem. The hospital formed a joint task force with the police and other public officials that developed a hospital policy for combating drug abuse. The names of women who tested positive a second time or who missed an appointment with a substance abuse counselor after testing positive were turned over to the police who typically arrested the individuals. Women also were referred to the police who tested positive for illegal narcotics during labor. Women who tested positive were subject to criminal charges ranging from simple possession to child abuse and delivery of narcotics to a person under eighteen years of age, depending on the number of months that they were pregnant. The women were unaware that their test results were being provided to law enforcement. The hospital explained at trial that the ultimate purpose was to protect the "children" by deterring their mothers from using drugs and persuading the women to enter substance abuse treatment programs. As a judge, would you find that this is a constitutionally permissible special-needs search? See *Ferguson v. City of Charleston*, 532 U.S. 67 (2001).

You can find the answer by referring to the study site, http://www.sagepub.com/lippmancp.

Probation and Parole

In 1987, in *Griffin v. Wisconsin,* the U.S. Supreme Court recognized the "special need" to search the apartment of Wisconsin probationer Joseph Griffin. Griffen's apartment was searched by two probation officers and three plainclothes police officers acting on an unauthenticated tip from a police detective that Griffin was or might be in possession of guns. The search uncovered a handgun, and Griffin subsequently was convicted of possession of a weapon by a convicted felon. Wisconsin law provides that probationers are in the legal custody of the State Department of Health and Social Services. The U.S. Supreme Court affirmed the constitutionality under the Fourth Amendment of the State Department of Health and Social Services regulation authorizing probation officers to search the home of probationers when there are "reasonable grounds" to believe that contraband or any other item that a probationer is prohibited from possessing is present (*Griffin v. Wisconsin,* 483 U.S. 868, 870–871, 873 [1987]).

The Supreme Court explained that Wisconsin's operation of its "probation system" presents "'special needs' beyond normal law enforcement that may justify departures from the usual warrant and probable-cause requirements." Probation is a form of criminal punishment imposed by a court following a defendant's plea of guilty or conviction and is one punishment on a continuum of possible punishments available in the criminal justice system. A probationer remains in legal custody of Wisconsin and typically is required to report to a probation officer and satisfy the officer that he or she is satisfying various conditions, which typically include continuing employment and the avoidance of narcotics, excessive alcohol, and gambling. Probationers as well as parolees accordingly enjoy only a "conditional liberty properly dependent on observance of special [probation] restrictions" (874).

These restrictions are designed to rehabilitate offenders and to protect the community (874). Special-needs searches of probationers' homes according to the Supreme Court are required to insure that offenders comply with the conditions of their probation. The reasonable suspicion standard permits probation officers to intervene at the first signs of trouble rather than wait to develop a warrant based on probable cause. The probation officers in *Griffin* under a probable cause standard would not have been able to conduct a search based on the unauthenticated tip that Griffin "had or might have" weapons (878–879).

The judgment in *Griffin* left open the question whether the special need to conduct searches of probationers is limited to searches intended to insure that probationers are adhering to the conditions of their probation or extends to criminal investigations. In other words, do probationers enjoy less protection under the Fourth Amendment than other citizens? The U.S. Supreme Court addressed this question in *United States v. Knights*. Can you predict the Court's answer (*United States v. Knights,* 534 U.S. 112 [2001])?

In *Knights,* Mark James Knights was sentenced to probation for a drug offense. The probation order included the condition that Knights "submit his... person, property, place of residence, vehicle, personal effects to search at any time, with or without a search warrant, warrant of arrest or reasonable cause by any probation officer or law enforcement officer" (115). The judge who sentenced Knights explained that he deliberately imposed this broad search condition to further the state interests in the protection of society and in Knights's rehabilitation. Knights was clearly informed of this condition, which "significantly diminished... [his] expectation of privacy" (117–119).

PG&E electric power company filed a theft of services complaint against Knights for a failure to pay his bill and discontinued his service. Shortly thereafter, a fire at an electric power transformer owned by the company caused $1.5 million in damage; this was the latest in a series of more than thirty acts of vandalism directed against PG&E. Detective Todd Hancock of the Napa Valley, California, County Sheriff's Department noticed that the dates of the vandalism coincided with the dates of Knights's court appearances for theft of PG&E services (115).

Detective Hancock established a surveillance of Knights's apartment and developed reasonable suspicion that Knights was responsible for the vandalism. Hancock was aware of the search provision in Knights's probation order and immediately conducted a warrantless search of Knights's apartment that led to the discovery of a detonation cord, ammunition, liquid chemicals, instruction manuals, electric circuitry, bolt cutters, telephone pole-climbing spurs, drug paraphernalia, and a brass padlock stamped "PG&E." Knights was arrested and charged with conspiracy to commit arson and possession of an unregistered destructive device and for being a felon in possession of ammunition (115).

The order issued by the judge in *Knights* specifically required that Knights submit to a search by "any probation officer or law enforcement officer." The search provision was not limited to searches with a "probationary purpose." Balanced against Knights's diminished expectation of privacy was the fact that the state possessed a number of important interests. Most important was the fact that probationers are more likely than other citizens to violate the law and to possess an incentive to conceal and to dispose of incriminating evidence. They are aware that detection of their criminal activities will almost certainly result in the suspension of their probation and lead to a return to prison. The Supreme Court recognized that searches of probationers' homes had to be immediately and regularly conducted and ruled that "[w]hen an officer has reasonable suspicion that a probationer subject to a search condition is engaged in criminal activity, there is enough likelihood that criminal conduct is occurring that an intrusion on the probationer's significantly diminished privacy interests is reasonable" (120). The Supreme Court stressed that the judgment was based on "ordinary Fourth Amendment analysis" and was not a "special needs" or "administrative" search case.

In summary, in *Knights,* the Supreme Court held that Knights's probationary status combined with the broad search order issued by the trial court reduced Knights's expectation of privacy under the Fourth Amendment. As a result, the Court ruled that a law enforcement officer who possesses reasonable suspicion that a probationer is engaged in criminal activity is entitled to conduct a warrantless search because "there is enough likelihood that criminal conduct is occurring that an intrusion on the probationer's significantly diminished privacy interests is reasonable."

The Supreme Court noted in *Knights* that Detective Hancock possessed reasonable suspicion and that therefore there was no reason to address whether Hancock could have lawfully searched Knights's home without any suspicion whatsoever (122). In 2006, the U.S. Supreme Court took a step toward answering this question in *Samson v. California,* which you will find on the study site. In *Samson,* the U.S. Supreme Court held that California's concerns with recidivism, public safety, and reintegrating parolees clearly outweighed parolees' diminished expectations of privacy and that the suspicionless search of parolees was reasonable under the Fourth Amendment. The question remains whether the holding in *Samson* applies only to parolees or also applies to probationers.

You can find Samson v. California *on the study site, http://www.sagepub.com/lippmancp.*

Correctional Institutions

The traditional view was that a prisoner lost all his or her rights, except what "the law in its humanity accords to him. He is for the time being the slave of the state" (*Ruffin v. Commonwealth,* 62 Va. 790, 796 [1871]). Courts followed a "hands-off doctrine" and refused to review the conditions of confinement in correctional institutions, leaving prison administrators free to establish whatever policies were required. The judiciary gradually abandoned the hands-off doctrine and recognized that while prison officials must be provided with significant discretion to insure institutional safety and security, prisoners indeed retain some rights.

In 1984, in *Hudson v. Palmer,* the U.S. Supreme Court proclaimed that prisoners "are not beyond the reach of the Constitution" and retain those rights that are not "fundamentally inconsistent with imprisonment itself or incompatible with the objectives of incarceration." The "reasonable opportunity" to attend religious worship services, for example, in most instances does not threaten the maintenance of security inside a prison. On the other hand, prisoners reentering the cell block after meeting with visitors may be subjected to full body-cavity searches (*Hudson v. Palmer,* 468 U.S. 517, 523 [1984]).

The issue in *Hudson v. Palmer* was whether the protections of the Fourth Amendment apply within a prison cell. In *Hudson v. Palmer,* Hudson and other officers at a Virginia penal institution conducted a "shakedown" search of Palmer's prison locker and cell for contraband and discovered a ripped pillowcase in a nearby trash can. Palmer was held responsible by a prison disciplinary committee for destroying state property and was fined. Hudson appealed on the grounds that he retained an expectation of privacy in his cell and had a Fourth Amendment right to be free from unreasonable searches and seizures (524).

The Supreme Court stressed that the prison population is composed of involuntarily confined individuals with a demonstrated record of antisocial and often violent criminal activity. There is a clear need to protect inmates and the staff, to inhibit the flow of weapons and drugs, and to frustrate escape plots. These objectives would be "literally impossible to accomplish . . . if inmates retained a right of privacy in their cells." The "only place inmates can conceal weapons, drugs, and other contraband is in their cells." Unlimited access to cells by prison officials "is imperative" if security and internal order are to be maintained. A right of privacy accordingly is "fundamentally incompatible with the close and continual surveillance of inmates and their cells required to ensure institutional security and internal order" (527).

An issue that continues to be controversial is strip searching incarcerated individuals. In *Bell v. Wolfish,* the U.S. Supreme Court approved visual cavity inspections in those instances in which a pretrial detainee or inmate returned to his or her cell block following a contact visit with an individual from outside the institution. These visual cavity searches are reasonable because the need to deter the smuggling of weapons, drugs, and other prohibited items outweighed the intrusion into individuals' privacy interests (*Bell v. Wolfish,* 441 U.S. 520, 558–560 [1979]).

Courts have continued to grapple with whether prisoners may be subjected to body-cavity searches without reasonable suspicion in other circumstances. This was discussed in *Roberts v. Rhode Island,* which you will find on the study site. In 2001, Craig Roberts was arrested for failing to appear for a court hearing. Roberts challenged the constitutionality of the suspicionless strip search and visual body-cavity search that was carried out against Roberts and against all other inmates as part of the "intake procedure" at the Adult Correctional Institution, a facility that housed both pretrial detainees and a general prison population. In reading this case, pay attention to the First Circuit's discussion of *Bell v. Wolfish* and ask yourself whether the First Circuit Court of Appeals has struck the proper balance between institutional security and the Fourth Amendment rights of pretrial detainees (*Roberts v. Rhode Island,* 239 F.3d 107 [1st Cir. 2001]).

You can find Hudson v. Palmer *and* Roberts v. Rhode Island *on the study site, http://www.sagepub.com/lippmancp.*

Chapter Summary

In this chapter, we discussed two categories of searches in which the courts have relaxed the probable cause and warrant requirements. In each instance, the searches primarily are intended to promote the welfare and safety of society rather than to investigate criminal activity.

Administrative inspections. Inspections to enforce administrative requirements involving health, safety, fire, and other matters require warrants based on a "modified probable cause standard." As noted in *Camera v. Municipal Court,* this protects individuals' privacy interests while recognizing the difficulty of developing probable cause to search a specific home or building.

In *New York v. Burger,* the Supreme Court held that warrants and probable cause are not required for "highly regulated" industries that are subject to close and regular inspections. The highly regulated business exception permits warrantless inspections without probable cause of liquor dealers, gun dealers, the mining industry, racetracks, nuclear power plants, and railroads. The detailed statutory regulation of these inspections provides sufficient limitation on these inspections to make a warrant unnecessary.

Special-needs searches. Special-needs searches serve purposes beyond the normal needs of law enforcement. Once a court determines that a search meets a "special need," the court asks whether a search is reasonable by balancing the significance of the government interests against the intrusiveness of the search. This balancing process also considers factors such as whether requiring a warrant based on probable cause or a requirement of reasonable suspicion will impede the effectiveness of the search. The Supreme Court has upheld the reasonableness of suspicionless airport screening and workplace and school drug testing and the suspicionless seizure of automobiles at checkpoints. On the other hand, school searches and seizures and the search of probationers require reasonable suspicion. Border searches are an example of the application of the balancing test. Routine border searches of luggage and persons may be carried out without reasonable suspicion. The Supreme Court has imposed a reasonable suspicion standard for nonroutine searches that intrude on individuals' dignity and privacy, such as strip and body-cavity searches or involuntary x-rays. The reasonable suspicion rather than probable cause standard for nonroutine border searches is a recognition of the interest in protecting America's territorial borders.

In Chapter 8, we shift our attention to interrogations and confessions, which along with searches and seizures constitute one of the central investigative tools available to the police.

Chapter Review Questions

1. Summarize the holding in *Camera v. Municipal Court* and explain the modified probable cause standard.
2. Discuss the closely regulated businesses exception.
3. Outline the requirements for a special-needs search.
4. What is the law regarding roving patrols? Distinguish between routine and nonroutine border searches.
5. List the requirements that must be met for motor vehicle checkpoints.
6. Discuss the special need to conduct airport screening.
7. Outline the rationale for the suspicionless drug testing of railroad employees.
8. What is the law regarding the drug testing of students and the physical searches of students?
9. Explain why governmental officials are legally entitled to conduct searches of probationers based on reasonable suspicion.
10. Summarize the Fourth Amendment rights of prisoners as discussed in the text.

Legal Terminology

administrative inspections
airport screening
border exception
closely regulated business
modified probable cause
motor vehicle checkpoint
nonroutine border searches
routine border searches
special-needs searches

Criminal Procedure on the Web

Log on to the Web-based student study site at **http://www.sagepub.com/lippmancp** to assist you in completing the Criminal Procedure on the Web exercises, as well as for additional features such as leading cases, podcasts, self-quizzes, and audio/video links.

1. Read about the First Amendment rights of students. You also will be interested in a November 5, 2003, incident at Stratford High School in South Carolina in which fourteen police officers were caught by a surveillance camera ordering students to the ground at gunpoint and subjecting them to a search by a drug dog. A federal judge approved a settlement in which the school district and police agreed to pay $1.6 million to the students.
2. Explore prison conditions throughout the world.
3. Research the scope of the drug problem in the United States.
4. Read about the major threats to privacy and consider whether your "right to privacy" is jeopardized.

Bibliography

Joshua Dressler and Alan C. Michaels, *Understanding Criminal Procedure: Investigation,* vol. 1, 4th ed. (Newark, NJ: LexisNexis, 2006), pp. 311–341. An informative discussion of the cases, law, and policy issues covered in this chapter.

Wayne R. LaFave, Jerald H. Israel, and Nancy J. King, *Criminal Procedure* (St. Paul, MN: West Publishing, 2004), pp. 229–249. A comprehensive discussion of inspections and regulatory searches with detailed footnotes.

Robert O'Harrow Jr., *No Place to Hide* (New York: Free Press, 2005). A journalistic account of the contemporary development and application of surveillance technology.

Stephen A. Saltzburg, Daniel J. Capra, and Angela J. Davis, *Basic Criminal Procedure,* 4th ed. (New York: Free Press, 2005), pp. 251–295. A detailed review of the major cases on administrative searches, checkpoints, border searches, and special-needs searches.

8 Interrogations and Confessions

Did the police constitutionally obtain the defendant's confession to murder?

Dr. Jeffrey Metzner, a psychiatrist employed by the state hospital, testified that respondent was suffering from chronic schizophrenia and was in a psychotic state at least as of August 17, 1983, the day before he confessed. Metzner's interviews with respondent revealed that respondent was following the "voice of God." This voice instructed respondent to withdraw money from the bank, to buy an airplane ticket, and to fly from Boston to Denver. When respondent arrived from Boston, God's voice became stronger and told respondent either to confess to the killing or to commit suicide. Reluctantly following the command of the voices, respondent approached Officer Anderson and confessed.

Dr. Metzner testified that, in his expert opinion, respondent was experiencing "command hallucinations." This condition interfered with respondent's "volitional abilities; that is, his ability to make free and rational choices."

Core Concepts and Summary Statements

Introduction

A. Confessions are an efficient method of crime investigation and detection. An admission of responsibility and guilt is an important step toward a defendant's rehabilitation.

B. One risk of relying too heavily on interrogations is coerced and false confessions. The poor and uneducated are likely to be particularly vulnerable to coercion and trickery. Confessions, in effect, result in guilt being determined at the pretrial stage rather than in a trial courtroom presided over by a judge and decided by a jury.

C. The constitutional regulation of interrogations is designed to assure that confessions are the product of fair and regular procedures and are not the result of police coercion.

D. There are three constitutional approaches to regulating confessions: the involuntariness test based on the Due Process Clause of the Fifth Amendment and of the Fourteenth Amendment, the *Miranda* rule that is required under the Fifth Amendment, and the protection accorded under the Sixth Amendment right to counsel.

Due Process

A. The due process test asks whether a confession was voluntary or involuntary. To be admissible in evidence, a confession must have been made freely and voluntarily without compulsion or inducement. It must not be the product of physical or psychological coercion that overcomes the will of an individual to resist. Involuntary confessions are inadmissible in evidence.

B. In determining whether a confession is voluntary, courts apply a "totality-of-the-circumstances" test. Relevant factors include the application of physical abuse or psychological coercion; the time, length, circumstances, and place of the interrogation; and the age and education of the detainee, along with other considerations.

C. At various times, courts have indicated that the due process test is intended to insure reliable confessions, to eliminate offensive police methods, to make certain that confessions are the result of fundamentally fair procedures, and to insure that confessions are the product of a rational and free choice.

D. The due process test is subject to various criticisms. The major criticism is that there is a lack of clear standards and that, as a result, the test fails to provide guidance to the police or courts.

The *McNabb–Mallory* Rule

The Supreme Court sought clearer standards regulating police interrogations. In *McNabb v. United States* (1943) and *Mallory v. United States* (1957), the Court held that federal law enforcement officers were required to bring criminal suspects immediately before a judge. Confessions obtained in violation of this rule were inadmissible in evidence.

Escobedo v. Illinois

In *Escobedo v. Illinois* (1964), the Supreme Court extended the Sixth Amendment right to counsel to interrogations by state as well as federal law enforcement officials. A defendant was to be informed of the right to silence and the right to an attorney prior to interrogation.

The Right Against Self-Incrimination

A. The Self-Incrimination Clause of the Fifth Amendment provides that "[n]o person . . . shall be compelled in any criminal case to be a witness against himself." This right was extended to the states in *Malloy v. Hogan* (1964).
B. The right against self-incrimination reflects the fact that the United States has an adversarial system in which the state has the burden of proving an individual's guilt beyond a reasonable doubt and in which the defendant is not required to take the stand or to offer evidence at trial.
C. The right against self-incrimination extends only to *testimonial* evidence that is incriminating. Testimonial evidence communicates facts, thoughts, and ideas and is incriminating because it may lead to a criminal charge.

Miranda v. Arizona

A. *Miranda v. Arizona* provides that statements of an individual subjected to custodial interrogation by the police may not be introduced into evidence absent procedural safeguards protecting an individual's Fifth Amendment rights. *Miranda* requires that the police warn individuals of their right to remain silent, that anything they say may be used against them, and that they have the right to an attorney appointed or retained.
B. In *Dickerson v. United States* (2000), the Supreme Court ruled that *Miranda* was a "constitutional decision" and that the *Miranda* warnings were required by the Fifth Amendment to protect a defendant's right against self-incrimination. The federal and state law enforcement agents were required as a matter of law to provide criminal suspects the *Miranda* warnings.

Custodial Interrogation

The *Miranda* warnings are triggered by placing an individual in custody and subjecting the individual to interrogation. The *Miranda* decision defines custodial interrogation as "questioning initiated by law enforcement officers after a person has been taken into custody or otherwise deprived of his [or her] freedom of action in any significant way." In determining whether an individual who has not been subjected to custodial arrest is subjected to custodial interrogation, courts ask whether, based on the totality of the circumstances, a reasonable person would believe that he or she was being subjected to a degree of custody consistent with being subjected to custodial arrest.

The Public Safety Exception

In *New York v. Quarles,* the Supreme Court recognized a public safety exception to *Miranda*. This exception permits the police to ask questions reasonably prompted by a reasonable concern with public safety without first advising a suspect of his or her *Miranda* rights.

The *Miranda* Warnings

The three-part *Miranda* warnings inform suspects of their rights and the consequences of waiving these rights. These warnings require the police to inform individuals of the right to remain silence, that anything they say may be used against them, and of the right to an attorney retained or appointed. The *Miranda* judgment specifies that these rights must be recited in "clear and unequivocal terms" and that a suspect must be "clearly informed" of his or her rights.

Invoking the *Miranda* Rights

Following the reading of the *Miranda* rights, the defendant has the opportunity to assert his or her right to a lawyer or right to silence or to waive these rights. The Supreme Court held that an individual intending to "articulate his desire to have counsel present" must express this "sufficiently clearly that a reasonable police officer in the circumstances would understand the statement to be a request for an attorney." This same level of clarity is required for invoking the right to silence.

Waiver

A. The Supreme Court stressed in *Miranda* that the government must meet a "heavy burden" in demonstrating that a suspect voluntarily, knowingly, and intelligently waived his or her rights. According to the *Miranda* decision, a waiver requires an express statement and may not be presumed from the fact that an accused is silent following the warnings.
B. In determining whether a confession was voluntary, a court will examine the totality of the circumstances. The primary focus is on the interrogation techniques employed by the police. The likely impact of these techniques will be evaluated in light of the age, education, background, and other characteristics of the accused; the conditions of the interrogation; and the length of the interrogation and of the detention prior to the reading of the *Miranda* rights.
C. A police officer may not automatically conclude that an individual knowingly and intelligently waived his or her rights. In determining whether a waiver is knowing and intelligent, a court will consider the totality of the circumstances on a case-by-case basis. Courts also will examine a defendant's emotional stability, ability to think clearly during the interrogation, general intelligence, and prior experience with the criminal justice system.
D. In considering whether a juvenile has waived his or her rights, a court inquires into the "juvenile's age, experience, education, background, and intelligence and into whether he [or she] has the capacity to understand the warnings given him [or her], the nature of his [or her] Fifth Amendment rights, and the consequences of waiving those rights."
E. A waiver may be express, a direct affirmative act, or implied from a course of conduct by a defendant indicating that he or she consented to a waiver.

Waiver: Question First and Warn Later

The Supreme Court held that the issue when the police question first and warn later is whether "it would be reasonable to find that in these circumstances the warnings could function 'effectively'" to advise the suspect that he or she "had a real choice about giving an admissible statement."

Waiver Following Invocation of the *Miranda* Rights

A. The Supreme Court has held that the admissibility of statements obtained after a person in custody had decided to remain silent depends on whether his or her right to silence was scrupulously honored by the police.
B. An individual who invokes his or her right to an attorney may waive this right by initiating contact with the police.

Interrogation

In *Rhode Island v. Innis,* the Supreme Court defined interrogation. The Court explained that interrogation entails express questioning or the functional equivalent of direct questioning. Express questions are questions directed to a suspect by the police. The functional equivalents of direct questions are words or actions on the part of the police (other than those normally attendant to arrest and custody) that the police should know are reasonably likely to elicit an incriminating response from the suspect.

Sixth Amendment Right to Counsel: Police Interrogations

A. The Sixth Amendment is applicable to both federal and state governmental agents at or after the time that judicial proceedings have been initiated against an accused—whether by way of formal charge, preliminary hearing, indictment, information, or arraignment. The accused must also have requested or arranged for legal representation.
B. The Sixth Amendment prohibits the government from intentionally eliciting information from an accused. This prohibits interrogations and prohibits creating a situation likely to induce a defendant to make incriminating statements concerning a pending charge without the assistance of counsel. The suspect must voluntarily, knowingly, and intelligently relinquish his or her right to an attorney.

Introduction

Interrogations

The writings of the late Professor Fred Inbau of Northwestern University continue to have a significant influence on the tactics and strategy of police interrogations. Professor Inbau argued throughout his career that detective novels, films, and television had misled the public into believing that the police solve most crimes by relying on scientific evidence or eyewitness testimony. He pointed out that in a significant number of cases, this type of evidence is unavailable and that the police are forced to rely on confessions.

Professor Inbau illustrates the importance of confessions by pointing to the hypothetical example of discovering the dead body of a female who appears to have been the victim of a criminal assault. There is no indication of a forced entry into her home, and the police investigation fails to yield DNA, fingerprints, clothing fibers, or witnesses. Law enforcement officers question everyone who may have had a motive to kill the victim, including the victim's angry former husband and her brother-in-law, who had accumulated large gambling debts and owed the victim money. The brother-in-law eventually tires under skillful police questioning and confesses. This example, according to Inbau, illustrates three important points concerning the importance of confessions (Inbau, 1961):

- Many criminal cases can be solved only through confessions or through information obtained from other individuals.
- Suspects often will not admit their guilt unless subjected to lengthy interrogations by the police.
- Successful police questioning requires sophisticated interrogation techniques that may be considered trickery or manipulative in ordinary police interactions with the public.

Inbau's argument is nicely echoed by Supreme Court Justice Antonin Scalia's remark that "even if I were to concede that an honest confession is a foolish mistake, I would welcome rather than reject it; a rule that foolish mistakes do not count would leave most offenders not only unconvicted but undetected" (*Minnick v. Mississippi,* 498 U.S. 146, 166–167 [1990]). It often is overlooked that in addition to speeding the conviction and punishment of the guilty, confessions can help to exonerate the innocent without subjecting these individuals to the time and expense of a lengthy criminal investigation and trial. There also is the practical consideration that the admission of criminal guilt is an important step in an offender's acceptance of responsibility and commitment to rehabilitation (Dressler & Michaels, 2006, p. 418).

There is no reliable data that clearly establish the percentage of cases in which interrogations play a central role in establishing a defendant's guilt. We can only note that jurors credit confessions with a great deal of importance in the determination of a defendant's guilt or innocence. In summary, confessions play an important role in the criminal justice process for several reasons.

- ***Crime detection.*** Confessions help the police solve crimes where there is an absence of scientific evidence and witnesses.
- ***Accountability.*** Acknowledging guilt is a significant step toward rehabilitation.
- ***Efficiency.*** Confessions facilitate both criminal convictions of the guilty and exoneration of the innocent.

Confessions also present potential challenges and problems for the criminal justice system.

- ***Abuse.*** The police may be tempted to employ physical abuse and psychological coercion to extract confessions. Abusive conduct is encouraged by the practice of incommunicado police interrogation—the carrying out of interrogations in police stations without the presence of defense lawyers or judicial supervision.
- ***Fair procedures.*** A reliance on pretrial confessions to establish a suspect's guilt is contrary to the principle that guilt is to be established beyond a reasonable doubt through the adversarial process in a courtroom.
- ***Reliability.*** There is the danger that a conviction will be based on a false confession.
- ***Inequality.*** Uneducated and disadvantaged suspects and individuals lacking self-confidence may be particularly vulnerable to manipulation and trickery. On the other hand, the wealthy and educated are more likely to possess the self-confidence and understanding to refuse to talk to the police and are more likely to be able to afford a lawyer.

The threat of **false confessions** and convictions has been of particular concern. This calls into question the adequacy of the protections that are made available to defendants in the criminal justice process and is pointed to by critics as illustrating the lack of fairness in the criminal justice process.

False Confessions

Individuals isolated in interrogation rooms have been known to make false confessions, even in instances in which the police did not pressure or manipulate suspects and treated suspects in a balanced and respectful fashion.

On April 19, 1989, a twenty-eight-year-old jogger was viciously attacked and raped in Central Park in New York City. Five African American and Latino teenagers ranging in age from fourteen to sixteen who had been arrested for muggings in the park that night confessed and the following year were convicted in two separate trials. Four of the five made videotaped statements with parents or relatives present. Typical was one young man's description that "Raymond had her arms, and Steve had her legs. He spread it out. And Antron got on top, took her panties off." A second confessed that "I grabbed one arm, some other kid grabbed one arm, and we grabbed her legs and stuff. Then we all took turns getting on her, getting on top of her." One suspect went so far as to reenact how he pulled off her running pants.

The young men claimed in court that they had been pressured into the confessions. The jurors at the two trials nevertheless convicted the defendants. The massive publicity surrounding the case may have influenced the jurors to overlook the inconsistencies in the defendants' accounts and to disregard the fact that only a few hairs on one of the defendants linked the juveniles to the rape. In 2002, Matia Reyes, who was serving over thirty years for murder and four rapes, confessed to the Central Park rape, and his DNA was found to match that of the perpetrator. On December 19, 2002, the convictions of the five men were overturned.

How is this possible? A number of factors in the Central Park Jogger case combined to create the danger of a false confession:

- ***Police bias.*** The police were under intense pressure to solve the crime and quickly concluded that the suspects must be guilty and focused on obtaining confessions.
- ***Age and intelligence.*** Several of the young suspects may have been tricked into confessing. Two had IQs below 90 and may have failed to understand the meaning of a confession.
- ***Misleading remarks and false evidence.*** Some of the young men claimed that they had been told that they would be permitted to go home if they confessed. One suspect reportedly was told that his fingerprints had been found at the crime scene, another was informed that the others had implicated him, and others were told that hairs linked one of the young men to the crime.
- ***Lengthy interrogations.*** The young men confessed after being interrogated for more than twenty-eight hours.

How frequent are false confessions? Professors Steve Drizen and Richard Leo have documented 125 proven false confessions between 1971 and 2002. The good news is that the criminal justice system responded by detecting two-thirds of these confessions prior to trial. On the other hand, forty-four of the defendants were sentenced to at least ten years in prison, and nine of these defendants were sentenced to death. This is not an overwhelming number of false convictions, but even a small number of false convictions are "too many" (Drizen & Leo, 2004). Psychologists tell us that there are three types of false confessors (Kassin & Gudjonsson, 2005):

- ***Voluntary false confessors.*** Suspects provide false confessions out of a desire for publicity or because they feel guilty about a past crime or are mentally challenged.
- ***Compliant false confessors.*** Suspects confess in order to obtain a benefit such as the avoidance of abuse or mistreatment or to receive favorable consideration at sentencing. This might range from a lighter sentence to imprisonment in an institution nearby to an offender's family.
- ***Internalized false confessors.*** Suspects accept the police version of the facts or fail a lie detector test and come to believe that they actually committed the crime.

False confessions are a small percentage of all confessions obtained by the police. These confessions, however, may result in conviction of the innocent and undermine respect for the entire criminal justice system. Consider the case of Eddie Joe Lloyd, a resident of a mental institution, who contacted the police in 1984 with suggestions on how to solve the rape and murder of a sixteen-year-old Michigan girl. The police were convinced that Lloyd was the perpetrator and persuaded the heavily medicated Lloyd that if he confessed, this would lead the real killer to relax and lower his guard and would lead to the killer's apprehension. The police allegedly fed Lloyd information to strengthen the credibility of his confession. Lloyd was pardoned in 2002 after spending seventeen years in prison when a DNA test indicated that he could not have been responsible for the crime.

In the United States, we believe that it is better for ten guilty people to go free than for an innocent individual to be criminally condemned. This is no mere academic concern. A conviction based on a false confession shakes confidence in the integrity of the criminal justice system. Courts have struggled to balance the need for confessions against the need for procedures that will guard against a miscarriage of justice. As you read this chapter, pay particular attention to how the U.S. Supreme Court has attempted to balance these twin concerns.

Three Constitutional Limitations on Police Interrogations

The judiciary has relied on three constitutional provisions to insure that confessions are the product of fair procedures.

Fourteenth Amendment Due Process Clause. As we have seen, there is a danger that the pressures of the interrogation process may lead to false confessions. The poor, uneducated, and mentally challenged are particularly vulnerable to trickery and manipulation. Former Supreme Court Justice Arthur Goldberg observed that history teaches that "a system of criminal law enforcement which comes to depend on the 'confession' will, in the long run, be less reliable and more subject to abuses than a system which depends on extrinsic evidence independently secured through skillful investigation" (*Escobedo v. Illinois,* 378 U.S. 478, 488–489 [1964]).

In the 1930s, the Supreme Court began to rely on the Fourteenth Amendment Due Process Clause to insure that confessions obtained by state law enforcement officials were voluntary and were not the product of psychological or physical abuse. The Due Process Clause provides that "[n]o state shall... deprive any person of life, liberty, or property without due process of law" and continues to be employed by courts to insure that confessions are voluntary. An involuntary confession violates an individual's *liberty* to make a voluntary choice whether to confess and ultimately may lead to imprisonment and to a loss of liberty.

Fifth Amendment Self-Incrimination Clause. Herbert Packer notes that in the American *accusatorial system* of criminal procedure, the burden is on the prosecution to establish guilt beyond a reasonable doubt at trial, and the defendant may not be compelled to testify against himself or herself. This is distinguished from an *inquisitorial system* of criminal procedure in which the defendant does not enjoy the privilege against self-incrimination and must answer questions posed by the judge, who typically interrogates witnesses. The drafters of the U.S. Constitution were familiar with the English **Star Chamber,** a special court established by the English king in the fifteenth century that was charged with prosecuting and punishing political and religious dissidents. This inquisitorial tribunal employed torture and abuse to extract confessions and was authorized to hand out any punishment short of death. The reign of terror was effectively ended by Puritan John Lillburne who, in 1637, defied the chamber's order that he confess to spreading dissident religious views. Lillburne was fined, pilloried, whipped, and imprisoned in leg irons in solitary confinement. Parliament ordered his release in 1640, and the House of Lords subsequently vacated Lillburne's sentence, noting that it was "illegal... unjust... [and] against the liberty of the subject and law of the land" (Levy, 1968, pp. 272–291).

The right against self-incrimination was viewed as sufficiently important that eight of the original American states included provisions that no one may be "compelled to give witness against himself," and the right against self-incrimination subsequently was included in the Fifth Amendment to the U.S. Constitution.

In 1966, in *Miranda v. Arizona,* the U.S. Supreme Court concluded that the inherently coercive environment of incommunicado police interrogation overwhelmed individuals' ability to assert their right against self-incrimination. The Supreme Court responded by interpreting the Self-Incrimination Clause requirement that "[n]o person... shall be compelled in any criminal case to be a witness against himself" to require the police to read individuals the *Miranda* rights prior to police interrogation (*Miranda v. Arizona,* 384 U.S. 436 [1966]).

The Supreme Court later held that the Sixth Amendment right to counsel protects individuals subjected to interrogation following the "initiation of proceedings against them."

Sixth Amendment right to counsel. The U.S. Supreme Court supplemented the *Miranda* judgment in a series of cases that held that once the government has taken formal steps to prosecute an individual, he or she possesses a Sixth Amendment right to counsel. At this point, it is clear that the government is determined to prosecute, and the Supreme

Court ruled that the police are prohibited by the Sixth Amendment from circumventing the trial process and establishing a suspect's guilt through extrajudicial interrogation. The Court explained that the right to an attorney cannot be limited to the trial itself because the denial of access to a lawyer at this early stage of the prosecutorial process may seal the defendant's fate and reduce the trial into a "mere formality" (*Brewer v. Williams,* 430 U.S. 387, 398 [1977]).

Your goal in this chapter should be to learn the strengths and weaknesses and differences between the three constitutional approaches to interrogations. Pay attention to the judiciary's effort to strike a balance between the need for confessions and the rights of suspects. Consider whether the pendulum has swung too far toward law enforcement or has swung too far toward the protection of defendants or whether a proper balance has been struck. One final point: Keep three terms in mind as you read this chapter. The text, at times, uses these terms interchangeably, but they have distinct meanings.

Admissions. An individual admits a fact that tends to establish guilt, such as his or her presence at the shooting scene. An admission when combined with other facts may lead to a criminal conviction.

Confessions. An individual acknowledges the commission of a crime in response to police questioning or may voluntarily approach the police and admit to the crime.

Statements. An oral or written declaration to the police in which an individual may assert his or her innocence.

Due Process

The Voluntariness Test

Between 1936 and 1966, the U.S. Supreme Court held over thirty confessions obtained by state and local police unconstitutional and inadmissible at trial under the **Fourteenth Amendment due process voluntariness test**.

The *voluntariness test* can be traced to the English common law. Eighteenth-century English common law judges declared that confessions were inadmissible into evidence if they had been extracted through the threat or application of force, through a false promise not to prosecute, or through a promise of lenient treatment. Confessions obtained by a threat or promise of favorable treatment were thought to be unreliable and might result in the conviction of innocent individuals. There was no easy method to determine whether a confession was true or false, and English courts employed the shorthand test of asking whether the defendant's statement was voluntary or involuntary (*Rex v. Warickshall,* 168 Eng. Rep. 234, 235 [K.B. 1783]).

In 1884, the U.S. Supreme Court adopted the English rule and announced that as a matter of the law of evidence, confessions were inadmissible in federal courts if obtained by police tactics that were sufficiently coercive such that the assumption that "one who is innocent will not imperil his safety or prejudice his interests by an untrue statement, ceases" (*Hopt v. Utah,* 110 U.S. 574 [1884]).

In 1897, the Supreme Court, in *Bram v. United States,* held that the Fifth Amendment privilege against self-incrimination provides the same protections as the English common law and that the Fifth Amendment prohibits the use of involuntary confessions against defendants. The holding in *Bram* was applicable only to the federal government because it was based on the Fifth Amendment, which the Supreme Court did not declare to be applicable to the states until 1964 in *Malloy v. Hogan* (*Bram v. United States,* 168 U.S. 532 [1897]).

State courts generally also followed the voluntariness test. There, however, was a significant gap between the law on the books and the law in practice. The Wickersham Commission established by President Herbert Hoover to investigate the administration of criminal justice in the United States reported in 1931 that there was widespread use of the **third degree** by the police to extract confessions.

The *third degree* is illustrated by *Beecher v. Alabama,* which was the subject of two decisions by the U.S. Supreme Court. Beecher was fleeing the Tennessee police across an open field when he was shot in the leg. The chief of police jammed a loaded pistol against Beecher's face while another officer pointed a rifle at the side of Beecher's head. The police chief threatened to kill Beecher, who was an African American, unless he confessed to the rape and murder of a "white woman." The other officer then fired his rifle next to Beecher's ear, and Beecher confessed. Beecher was taken to the hospital and received an injection to ease the pain that he was suffering as a result of most of the bone having been blown out of his leg. He then was instructed to sign extradition papers to Alabama or face a "white mob" that was determined to kill him. By the time Beecher arrived in Alabama five days later, his leg had become swollen, and he was in immense pain. He required morphine every four hours, and the leg ultimately was amputated. Two Alabama investigators interrogated Beecher in the prison hospital, and the medical assistant instructed him to cooperate with the authorities. Numb from the morphine, feverish, and in intense pain, Beecher signed two statements. The U.S. Supreme Court overturned Beecher's confession and conviction (*Beecher v. Alabama,* 389 U.S. 35 [1967]). Three months later, Beecher was again prosecuted in Alabama, and an oral confession that he allegedly made to a doctor while under the influence of morphine in the Tennessee hospital was used as the basis for his conviction and death sentence. Should the Supreme Court affirm or reverse Beecher's second conviction? The Supreme Court held that "realistic appraisal of the circumstances of this case compels the conclusion that this petitioner's [confession was] the product of gross coercion. Under the Due Process Clause of the Fourteenth Amendment, no conviction tainted by a confession so obtained can stand" (*Beecher v. Alabama,* 408 U.S. 234, 247 [1972]).

The U.S. Supreme Court's condemnation of the third degree in *Beecher* was based on the precedents established in a series of Supreme Court decisions, beginning with *Brown v. Mississippi* in 1936.

Due Process and State Courts

The Supreme Court held in *Brown v. Mississippi* that the use of confessions at trial that have been obtained through physical coercion violate suspects' fundamental rights and constitute a violation of the Due Process Clause of the Fourteenth Amendment. The Court explained that reliance on unreliable confessions creates the risk that innocent individuals will be condemned to lengthy terms of imprisonment or death (*Brown v. Mississippi,* 297 U.S. 278 [1936]).

In *Brown,* three African American males were convicted of murder in Mississippi solely based on their confessions. Defendant Ellington had been confronted by a deputy sheriff and by a mob of white men who accused him of murder. He denied the crime and was hanged by a rope from the limb of a tree, let down, and then strung up once again. Ellington continued to deny his guilt, and he was tied to a tree, whipped, and then released. He later was arrested and severely whipped while being transported to jail and, when threatened with additional beatings, signed a confession dictated by the sheriff. Defendants Brown and Shields also were arrested, stripped, and beaten with leather straps with inlaid metal buckles. Chief Justice of the U.S. Supreme Court Charles Evans Hughes observed that the trial transcript read "more like pages torn from some medieval account than a record made within the confines of a modern civilization which aspires to an enlightened and constitutional government" (282).

The Supreme Court, in reversing the defendants' convictions, held that the Due Process Clause requires that the treatment of suspects "shall be consistent with the fundamental principles of liberty and justice which lie at the basis of all our civil and political institutions." The Court observed that it would be difficult to conceive of methods "more revolting to the sense of justice than those taken to procure [these] confessions.... The rack and torture chamber may not be substituted for the witness stand" (316).

The Supreme Court in *Brown* concluded that Mississippi authorities had conspired to extract a coerced and untruthful confession. The Court's decision was a clear message that the government bears the burden of establishing individuals' guilt in the courtroom beyond a reasonable doubt and that government authorities may not coerce individuals into involuntarily providing evidence of their own guilt. The cost to the government of police tactics that violate the Due Process Clause is the exclusion of confessions from the prosecutor's case-in-chief at trial.

In 1944, in *Ashcraft v. Tennessee,* the Supreme Court extended the protection of the Due Process Clause to include psychological coercion. Ashcraft confessed to soliciting the murder of his wife after having been detained and subjected to **incommunicado interrogation** for thirty-six hours by teams of police officers and lawyers. The Supreme Court concluded that Ashcraft's confession was the product of a coercive set of circumstances that overwhelmed his ability to exercise a rational choice and observed that the "efficiency of the rack and the thumbscrew" is now matched by equally effective techniques of psychological persuasion (*Ashcraft v. Tennessee,* 322 U.S. 143 [1944]). In *Chambers v. Florida,* the Supreme Court concluded that a group of young African Americans had been subjected to "protracted questioning... calculated to break the stoutest nerves and the strongest resistance.... To permit human lives to be forfeited upon confessions thus obtained would make... due process... a meaningless symbol" (*Chambers v. Florida,* 309 U.S. 227, 238–240 [1948]).

The Supreme Court held that the confessions in *Brown* and *Ashcraft* were the product of police coercion and were in violation of the Due Process Clause. The Court's application of the voluntariness test in these cases prevented innocent individuals from being convicted on the basis of *coerced and false confessions. Reliable* or *trustworthy confessions* are not the only goal of the voluntariness test. In *Blackburn v. Alabama,* the Supreme Court explained that the due process approach is designed to achieve a "complex of values" (*Blackburn v. Alabama,* 361 U.S. 199, 207 [1960]). We now briefly examine three interrelated goals in addition to trustworthiness that the Supreme Court identified as underlying the voluntariness test.

Fundamental Fairness

The Supreme Court pronounced in *Lisenba v. California,* in 1941, that the aim of the voluntariness test is not only to exclude false confessions but also to insure **fundamental fairness** in the methods used to obtain confessions. Justice Owen Roberts noted that it would be contrary to due process to employ threats, promises, or torture in the courtroom to induce an individual to testify against himself and a "case can stand no better if, by resort to the same means, the defendant is induced to confess and his confession is given in evidence" (*Lisenba v. California,* 314 U.S. 219 [1941]). This type of abusive behavior, according to Justice Roberts, undermines respect for the criminal justice system.

Police Methods

The **police methods test** is based on "deep-rooted feeling that the police must obey the law while enforcing the law... in the end life and liberty can be as much endangered from illegal methods used to convict those thought to be criminals as from the actual criminals themselves" (*Spano v. New York,* 360 U.S. 315, 320–321 [1959]).

This approach was first articulated in *Watts v. Indiana* in 1949. In *Watts,* the police interrogated Watts for five consecutive evenings and deprived him of sufficient sleep and food. Watts also was not taken before a judge for a formal charge and was not advised of his constitutional rights, as required under Indiana law. The U.S. Supreme Court ruled that Watts's confession was unconstitutionally obtained and held that the Due Process Clause "bars police procedures which violate the basic notions of our accusatorial mode of prosecuting crime... [and stressed that] brutal methods of law enforcement are essentially self-defeating, whatever may be their effect in a particular case" (*Watts v. Indiana,* 338 U.S. 49, 54 [1949]).

Involuntary Confessions

A fourth purpose behind the due process approach is the exclusion of **involuntary confessions** that result from mental disabilities or drugs administered by the police and are not the product of a *rational intellect and free will.* In *Townsend v. Sain,* defendant Charles Townsend was arrested in connection with a robbery and murder. The nineteen-year-old Townsend had been addicted to narcotics since age fifteen and was under the influence of heroin at the time of his arrest. Townsend complained during his interrogation that he was suffering from withdrawal and asked for a dose of narcotics. A doctor injected Townsend with a combination of phenobarbital and hyoscine. This alleviated Townsend's symptoms, and he agreed to talk to the police, confessed within twenty-five minutes, and signed a statement the next day. Townsend soon thereafter experienced additional discomfort, and he was given a tablet of phenobarbital and again confessed several hours later (*Townsend v. Sain,* 372 U.S. 293 [1963]).

Following Townsend's conviction, it was revealed that the police were unaware that hyoscine possessed the property of truth serum and that the combination of the drugs administered to Townsend adversely affected his ability to think clearly. The U.S. Supreme Court ruled that "[i]t is difficult to imagine a situation in which a confession would be less the product of a free intellect, less voluntary, than when brought about by a drug having the effect of truth serum.... Any questioning by police offices which in fact produces a confession which is not the product of a free intellect renders the confession inadmissible" (308–309).

The Four Purposes of the Voluntariness Test

In summary, the due process voluntariness test is designed to achieve four interrelated purposes.

Trustworthiness. Confessions that result from physical or psychological coercion run the risk that a defendant confessed to avoid or to halt abuse. Statements made under such threats are unreliable and may be false. In *Payne v. Arkansas,* a nineteen-year-old African American defendant accused of murder was subjected to incommunicado interrogation for three days and confessed following the sheriff's threat to turn him over to a white mob. The Supreme Court ruled that the confession was "coerced and did not constitute an 'expression of free choice'" (*Payne v. Arkansas,* 356 U.S. 560, 567 [1958]).

Fundamental fairness. The use of an involuntary confession against a defendant is fundamentally unfair and compromises the integrity of the courtroom. In *White v. Texas,* White, an illiterate African American farmhand, was illegally detained and taken to the home of the brother-in-law of a rape victim. There, he found fifteen or sixteen other African American suspects who also were being illegally detained without charge or access to a lawyer. White then was taken to the jail where he was detained for six or seven days and was removed at night, taken to the woods, and interrogated. He ultimately signed a confession after having been interrogated most of the night. The Supreme Court ruled that due process prohibits condemning an accused to death through such practices (*White v. Texas,* 310 U.S. 530 [1940]).

Offensive police methods. Confessions are in violation of the Due Process Clause are the product of police tactics that are offensive to fundamental values. In *Lynumn v. Illinois,* the defendant confessed after three police officers threatened that she would lose her children unless she cooperated and signed a confession. The Supreme Court observed that isolated and inexperienced defendants had "no reason not to believe that the police had ample power to carry out their threats" (*Lynumn v. Illinois,* 372 U.S. 528, 534 [1963]).

Free will and rational choice. Confessions violate due process if they are the product of drugs administered by the police or of a suspect's psychological disabilities and if they do not result from free will or rational choice. In *Blackburn v. Alabama,* a "mentally incompetent" defendant confessed after having been interrogated for eight or nine hours in a small room filled with police officers. Shortly thereafter, he was evaluated as legally insane. Four years later, Blackburn was declared mentally competent and was prosecuted and convicted of robbery. The Supreme Court held that the chance of Blackburn's four-year-old confession having been the product of "rational choice and free will" was "remote" and that the confession's introduction into evidence was a flagrant abuse of due process (*Blackburn v. Alabama,* 361 U.S. 199, 208 [1960]).

The voluntariness test is based on the controversial proposition that an involuntary confession should be excluded from evidence, regardless of whether the confession is true or false. We outline in the next section the factors considered by judges in determining whether a confession is voluntary or is the product of coercion.

Voluntariness

The Supreme Court has held that to be admissible into evidence, a confession must have been made freely, voluntarily, and without compulsion or inducement of any sort. A confession violates due process and is excluded from evidence that involves the following:

Coercion. The police or government officials subject the defendant to physical or psychological coercion.

Will to resist. The coercion overcomes the will of an individual to resist.

We have seen examples of coercive conduct in the cases discussed in this section. How do courts determine whether there was coercion and whether the coercion overcame a defendant's will to resist? The determination as to whether a confession is involuntary is based on the totality of the circumstances surrounding a confession (*Haynes v. Washington,* 373 U.S. 503, 533–534 [1963]). The prosecution bears the burden of establishing voluntariness by a "preponderance of the evidence" (*Lego v. Twomey,* 404 U.S. 477 [1972]). In evaluating the totality of the circumstances, courts consider a number of factors.

Physical abuse. Physical abuse and threats of abuse by the police or angry crowds.

Psychological abuse and manipulation. Threats, rewards, or trickery inducing a suspect to confess.

Interrogation. The length, time, and place of questioning and the number of police officers involved.

Attorney. A refusal to permit a suspect to consult with an attorney, friends, or family.

Defendant. The age, education, and mental and emotional development of the defendant.

Procedural regularity. A failure by the police to follow proper legal procedures, including the *Miranda* warning.

Necessity. The police are provided greater flexibility in interrogation when attempting to solve a crime or exonerate a defendant than when they already possess evidence of a defendant's guilt.

Spano v. New York illustrates the totality-of-the-circumstances approach to determining whether a confession is voluntary or involuntary. In *Spano,* the U.S. Supreme Court held that the defendant's "will was overborne by official pressure, fatigue and sympathy falsely aroused." The Court's conclusion was based on a number of factors (*Spano v. New York,* 360 U.S. 315, 323 [1959]):

Psychological abuse. The police employed a childhood friend to play on the defendant's sympathy.

Interrogation. The defendant was questioned for eight hours at night by fourteen officers, and his confession was written down by a skilled and aggressive prosecutor.

Attorney. The police disregarded the defendant's refusal to speak on the advice of counsel and ignored his request to contact his lawyer.

Defendant. The defendant was twenty-five years of age and never before had been subjected to custodial arrest or to police interrogation. He had not completed high school and had a psychological disability.

Procedural regularity. The police failed to immediately bring the defendant before a judge and instead subjected him to interrogation.

Necessity. The police already possessed eyewitnesses to the shooting and were engaged in securing the evidence required to convict the defendant rather than in identifying the individual responsible for the crime.

Criticism of the Due Process Test

The due process test is subject to several criticisms.

Standards. There are no clear guidelines for the police concerning what conduct is permissible and what conduct is impermissible.

Evidence. The defendant and the police may offer radically different versions of the defendant's treatment during the interrogation. Judges find it difficult to reconstruct what actually occurred.

Litigation. The lack of definite standards encourages legal appeals and increases the caseloads of state and federal courts.

The Due Process Test Today

Keep in mind as you continue to read this chapter that an involuntary confession violates due process of law and is inadmissible into evidence, even in those instances in which a defendant may have been read his or her *Miranda* rights. Two recent cases illustrate the U.S. Supreme Court's continuing reliance on the due process, voluntariness test:

Mincey v. Arizona. Mincey, while in intensive care in the hospital, was interrogated by a police detective who informed him that he was under arrest for murder. Mincey's requests for a lawyer were disregarded, and the detective continued the interrogation. The suspect was unable to talk because of a tube in his mouth and responded by writing down his answers. The Supreme Court determined that Mincey was "weakened by pain and shock, isolated from family, friends, and legal counsel, and barely conscious, and his will was simply overborne" and that his confession had been obtained in violation of due process of law. The Court stressed that an involuntary confession may not be used at trial for any purpose whatsoever (*Mincey v. Arizona,* 437 U.S. 385, 401–402 [1978]).

Arizona v. Fulminante. Fulminante was incarcerated on federal firearms charges and established a friendship with Sarivola, a paid federal informant who was serving a sixty-day sentence for extortion and posing as an organized crime figure. Sarivola was instructed to obtain information regarding Fulminante's possible involvement in the murder of his young daughter. Sarivola offered to protect Fulminante from the other inmates who allegedly disliked "child killers" on the condition that Fulminante tell him what happened to his daughter. Fulminante admitted sexually assaulting and shooting his daughter in the head. Sarivola later testified at Fulminante's murder trial. The Supreme Court examined the totality of circumstances and concluded that the confession was involuntary. The Court reasoned that Fulminante was a child murderer whose fear of physical retaliation led him to confide in Sarivola. Fulminante, according to the Court, felt particularly susceptible to physical retaliation because he possessed a slight build and, while previously incarcerated, could not cope with the pressures of imprisonment and in the past had been admitted to a psychiatric institution (*Arizona v. Fulminante,* 499 U.S. 279 [1991]).

In the next case in the text, *Colorado v. Connelly,* the U.S. Supreme Court addresses whether the prosecution's use of a confession against a defendant who claimed to have been directed by God to confess constitutes a violation of the Due Process Clause. Do you agree with the decision in *Connelly?*

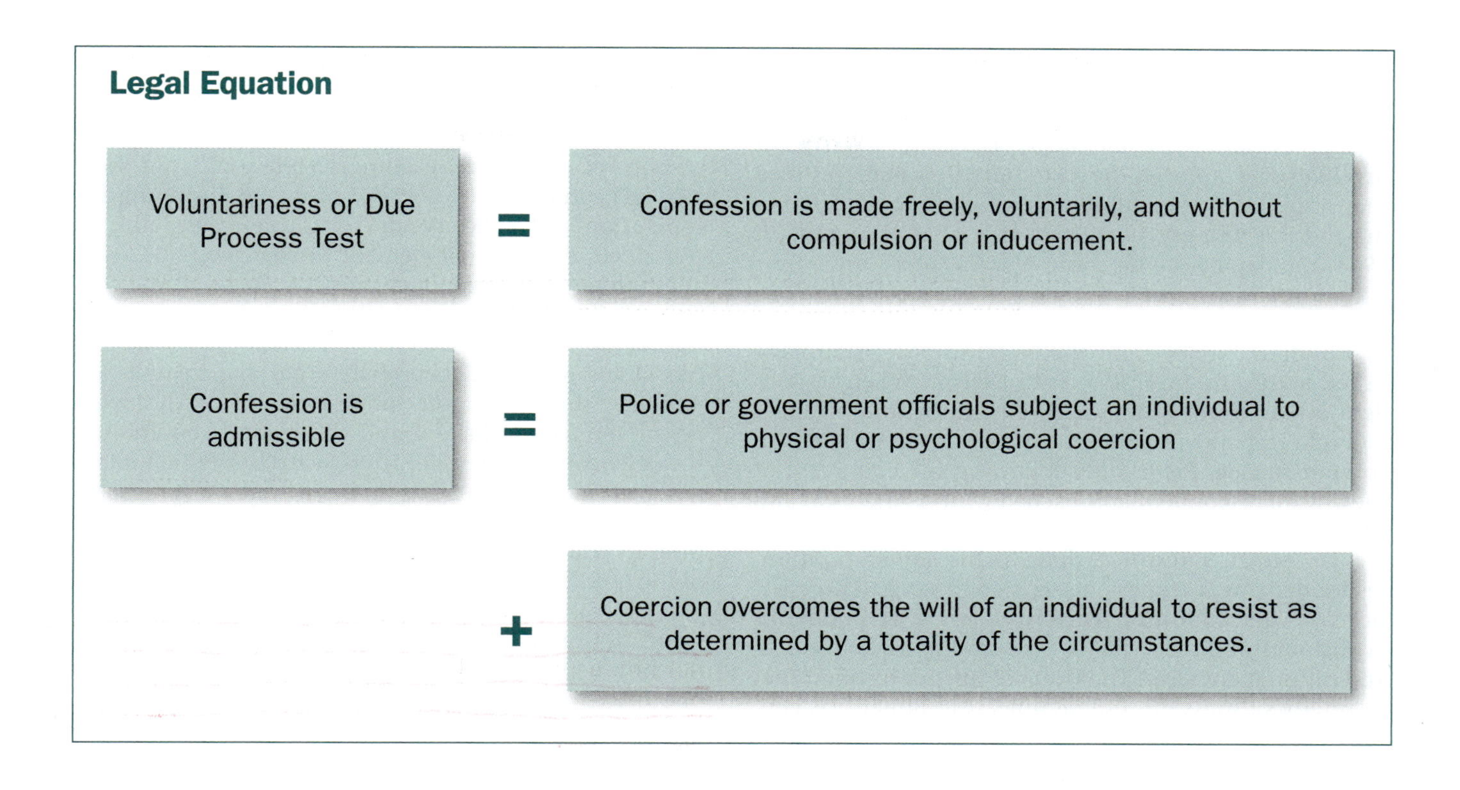

Was the defendant's confession involuntary?

Colorado v. Connelly, 479 U.S. 157 (1986), Rehnquist, C.J.

Facts

On August 18, 1983, Officer Patrick Anderson of the Denver Police Department was in uniform, working in an off-duty capacity in downtown Denver. Respondent Francis Connelly approached Officer Anderson and, without any prompting, stated that he had murdered someone and wanted to talk about it.... Understandably bewildered by this confession, Officer Anderson asked respondent several questions. Connelly denied that he had been drinking, denied that he had been taking any drugs, and stated that, in the past, he had been a patient in several mental hospitals. Officer Anderson again told Connelly that he was under no obligation to say anything. Connelly replied that it was "all right," and that he would talk to Officer Anderson because his conscience had been bothering him. To Officer Anderson, respondent appeared to understand fully the nature of his acts.

Shortly thereafter, Homicide Detective Stephen Antuna arrived. Connelly was again advised of his rights...and Detective Antuna asked him "what he had on his mind." Respondent answered that he had come all the way from Boston to confess to the murder of Mary Ann Junta, a young girl whom he had killed in Denver sometime during November 1982. Respondent was taken to police headquarters, and a search of police records revealed that the body of an unidentified female had been found in April 1983. Respondent openly detailed his story to Detective Antuna and Sergeant Thomas Haney, and readily agreed to take the officers to the scene of the killing. Under Connelly's sole direction, the two officers and respondent proceeded in a police vehicle to the location of the crime. Respondent pointed out the exact location of the murder. Throughout this episode, Detective Antuna perceived no indication whatsoever that respondent was suffering from any kind of mental illness.

Respondent was held overnight. During an interview with the public defender's office the following morning, he became visibly disoriented. He began giving confused answers to questions, and for the first time, stated that "voices" had told him to come to Denver and that he had followed the directions of these voices in confessing. Respondent was sent to a state hospital for evaluation. He was initially found incompetent to assist in his own defense. By March 1984, however, the doctors evaluating respondent determined that he was competent to proceed to trial. At a preliminary hearing, respondent moved to suppress all of his statements. Dr. Jeffrey Metzner, a psychiatrist employed by the state hospital, testified that respondent was suffering from chronic schizophrenia and was in a psychotic state at least as of August 17, 1983, the day before he confessed. Metzner's interviews with respondent revealed that respondent was following the "voice of God." This voice instructed respondent to withdraw money from the bank, to buy an airplane ticket, and to fly from Boston to Denver. When respondent arrived from Boston, God's voice became stronger and told respondent either to confess to the killing or to commit suicide. Reluctantly following the command of the voices, respondent approached Officer Anderson and confessed.

Dr. Metzner testified that, in his expert opinion, respondent was experiencing "command hallucinations." This condition interfered with respondent's "volitional abilities; that is, his ability to make free and rational choices." Dr. Metzner further testified that Connelly's illness did not significantly impair his cognitive abilities. Thus, respondent understood the rights he had when Officer Anderson and Detective Antuna advised him that he need not speak. Dr. Metzner admitted that the "voices" could in reality be Connelly's interpretation of his own guilt, but explained that in his opinion, Connelly's psychosis motivated his confession.

Issue

On the basis of this evidence, the Colorado trial court decided that respondent's statements must be suppressed because they were "involuntary." The court ruled that a confession is admissible only if it is a product of the defendant's rational intellect and "free will." Although the court found that the police had done nothing wrong or coercive in securing respondent's confession, Connelly's illness destroyed his volition and compelled him to confess.... Accordingly, respondent's initial statements and his custodial confession were suppressed. The Colorado Supreme Court affirmed. In that court's view, the proper test for admissibility is whether the statements are "the product of a rational intellect and a free will." Indeed, "the absence of police coercion or duress does not foreclose a finding of involuntariness. One's capacity for rational judgment and free choice may be overborne as much by certain forms of severe mental illness as by external pressure."...

Reasoning

The cases considered by this Court over the fifty years since *Brown v. Mississippi* have focused upon the crucial element of police overreaching. While each confession case has turned on its own set of factors justifying the conclusion that police conduct was oppressive, all have contained a substantial element of coercive police conduct. Absent police conduct causally related to the confession, there is simply no basis for concluding that any state actor has deprived a criminal defendant of due process of law. Respondent correctly notes that as interrogators have turned to more subtle forms of psychological persuasion, courts have found the mental condition of the defendant a more significant factor in the "voluntariness" calculus. But this fact does not justify a conclusion that a defendant's mental condition, by itself and apart from its relation to official coercion, should ever dispose of the inquiry into constitutional "voluntariness."

The difficulty with the approach of the Supreme Court of Colorado is that it fails to recognize the essential link between coercive activity of the State, on the one hand, and a resulting confession by a defendant, on the other. The flaw in respondent's constitutional argument is that it would expand our previous line of "voluntariness" cases into a far-ranging requirement that courts must divine a defendant's motivation for speaking or acting as he did even though there be no claim that governmental conduct coerced his decision.... The most outrageous behavior by a private party seeking to secure evidence against a defendant does not make that evidence inadmissible under the Due Process Clause.... The purpose of excluding evidence seized in violation of the Constitution is to substantially deter future violations of the Constitution.... Only if we were to establish a brand new constitutional right—the right of a criminal defendant to confess to his crime only when totally rational and properly motivated—could respondent's present claim be sustained.... A statement rendered by one in the condition of respondent might be proved to be quite unreliable, but this is a matter to be governed by the evidentiary laws of the forum....

Holding

We hold that coercive police activity is a necessary predicate to the finding that a confession is not "voluntary" within the meaning of the Due Process Clause of the Fourteenth Amendment. We also conclude that the taking of respondent's statements and their admission into evidence constitute no violation of that clause.

Questions for Discussion

1. Summarize the holding of the Supreme Court in *Connelly.*
2. In their dissenting opinions, Justices Brennan and Marshall argued that the use of a mentally challenged person's involuntary confession is contrary to the notion of fundamental fairness embodied in the Due Process Clause. Do you agree with this argument? Is there a justified concern over the truthfulness of Connelly's confession?
3. Is there a difference between the cause of Connelly's confession and the cause of a confession that results from a sense guilt or shame?
4. As a defense lawyer, what argument would you make in your next "confession case" if the Supreme Court had ruled that Connelly's confession was inadmissible on the grounds that God had directed him to confess?
5. The decision in *Connelly* suggests that a judge may exercise his or her discretion and exclude a confession that is unreliable from evidence. As a trial court judge, would you prohibit the prosecution from introducing Connelly's confession at trial?
6. ***Problems in policing.*** As a police officer, how should the due process test influence your tactics in the interrogation of suspects?

8.1 YOU DECIDE

The defendant, Frazier, was arrested and interrogated for slightly over an hour and signed a written confession to murder. Prior to the interrogation, he was informed of his right to an attorney. Frazier then was asked where he was on the night of the homicide. He admitted that he was with his cousin Jerry Lee Rawls. The officer then lied and told Frazier that Rawls had been brought in and had confessed. The officer also sympathetically suggested that the male victim had started the fight by making sexual advances toward Frazier. Frazier then began to talk. He hesitated and stated that he better get a lawyer before proceeding with the interview to avoid getting into even more trouble. The officer replied, "You can't be in any more trouble than you are in now," and the questioning continued. Frazier subsequently signed a written confession. Would you admit the confession into evidence under the due process test? Should limitations be placed on police misrepresentation of the facts during interrogation? What if the police had misrepresented that they had DNA evidence linking Frazier to the killing? See *Frazier v. Cupp,* 394 U.S. 731 (1969).

You can find the answer by referring to the study site, http://www.sagepub.com/lippmancp.

The *McNabb–Mallory* Rule

The police justifiably complained that the due process test left them with limited guidance. How many police could interrogate a defendant? For how long? Could they advise a defendant that they already possessed some evidence suggesting that he or she was guilty? Were they required to allow a defendant to consult with an attorney? Defendants who felt that their confessions had been coerced were forced to spend time and money appealing the introduction of their confessions at trial.

The U.S. Supreme Court responded by attempting to develop clearer guidelines for the police. In *McNabb v. United States* and *Mallory v. United States,* the Court required federal law enforcement officials to immediately bring suspects before a judicial officer. Confessions obtained in violation of this rule were inadmissible in federal court. This "bright-line" rule for the admissibility of confessions ultimately failed to make a significant impact on police practices.

In 1943, in *McNabb,* three residents of the mountains of Appalachia were convicted of murdering a federal revenue agent who was investigating the McNabb family's rumored illegal whiskey operation. The defendants were arrested at night, incarcerated in a barren cell, and questioned continually over the course of two days without being brought before a court to determine whether the evidence justified their detention. The defendants appealed on the grounds that the confessions had been obtained in violation of their Fifth Amendment rights (*McNabb v. United States,* 318 U.S. 332 [1943]).

The Supreme Court relied on its inherent supervisory authority over the federal courts to reverse the defendants' convictions. The Court pointed out that existing congressional statutes explicitly required federal officers to immediately bring arrestees before a magistrate or judge and demonstrate a legal justification for the arrest. Justice Felix Frankfurter held that the defendants' confessions had been secured through "flagrant disregard" of the law and that their convictions "cannot be allowed to stand without making the courts themselves accomplices in willful disobedience to the law." Congress had not explicitly prohibited the introduction into evidence of confessions obtained without first taking defendants before a federal official, but the failure to exclude such statements from evidence would stultify the policy established by Congress (345).

In 1957, in *Mallory v. United States,* the Supreme Court affirmed the decision in *McNabb.* The Court, however, based its decision on Rule 5(a) of the Federal Rules of Criminal Procedure, adopted three years following *McNabb.* Rule 5(a) is binding on federal courts and requires that federal officers making an arrest shall "take the arrested person without unnecessary delay before the nearest available commissioner or before any other nearby officer empowered to commit persons charged with offenses against the laws of the United States." Mallory's confession to a rape charge was obtained after nearly eight hours of interrogation, and only then was he formally charged before a judge. The Supreme Court threw out Mallory's confession and explained that the police may not arrest and interrogate a defendant and then decide whether there is probable cause to charge him or her with a crime (*Mallory v. United States,* 345 U.S. 449 [1943]).

The *McNabb–Mallory* rule focused on the length of delay between an arrest and a suspect's initial appearance before a magistrate. This differed from the due process test that examined whether the totality of the circumstances indicated that a confession had been coerced. Critics of *McNabb–Mallory* objected that the Supreme Court was impeding the conviction of criminals and argued that there was no reason to exclude a voluntary confession merely because the confession had been obtained without promptly presenting a defendant before a federal magistrate. Congress responded by passing the Omnibus Crime Control and Safe Streets Act of 1968, which specifies that a voluntary confession "shall not be inadmissible solely because of delay" in bringing an individual before a judicial official "if such confession was made or given by such person within six hours immediately following his arrest or other detention." The six-hour limitation "shall not apply in any case in which the delay . . . is found . . . to be reasonable considering the means of transportation and the distance to be traveled to the nearest available such magistrate or other officer" (18 U.S.C. § 3501(a), (b)).

The *McNabb–Mallory* decisions today are of greater historical than practical significance. Federal courts generally consider unreasonable delay to be one of several factors to be considered in evaluating the voluntariness of a defendant's confession. The U.S. Supreme Court has now clarified that § 3501 is not required to be followed by the U.S. Constitution and is not applicable to the states (*United States v. Alvarez-Sanchez,* 511 U.S. 350 [1994]). Most state courts, in any event, have refused to follow the *McNabb–Mallory* approach and merely view the failure to present a detainee for arraignment to be one of many factors to be considered in evaluating whether the totality of the circumstances indicate that a confession was coerced.

Escobedo v. Illinois

In 1964, in *Escobedo v. Illinois,* the U.S. Supreme Court took an additional step to clarify police procedures and to protect suspects when it extended the Sixth Amendment right to counsel to individuals subjected to police interrogation by state as well as federal law enforcement officers.

There were indications in several of the earlier cases decided under the Due Process Clause that four members of the Supreme Court viewed access to a lawyer as fundamental to protecting defendants during police interrogation. These justices, although they were unable to attract an additional vote to constitute a majority, would have excluded confessions from evidence in cases in which the police refused to provide a defendant access to a lawyer. Justice William Douglas observed in *Spano v. New York* that the failure to extend the right to a lawyer to pretrial interrogation meant that the "secret trial in the police precincts effectively supplants the public trial guaranteed by the Bill of Rights" (*Spano v. New York,* 360 U.S. 315, 326 [1959]).

Consider two examples of the division between the Supreme Court judges on whether a denial of access to an attorney was a violation of due process that should result in the exclusion of a confession from the prosecution's case-in-chief.

Crooker v. California. The petitioner confessed to murdering his lover and appealed that although he had voluntarily confessed, the police had denied him due process by rejecting his request for a lawyer. A majority of the Supreme Court held that requiring that defendants be provided access to an attorney would have a "devastating effect" on interrogations because the impact would be to "preclude police questioning... until the accused was afforded opportunity to call his attorney." Four judges dissented on the grounds that access to an attorney during pretrial interrogation following an arrest was essential to the protection of a defendant's right at trial (*Crooker v. California,* 357 U.S. 433 [1958]).

Cicenia v. La Gay. Cicenia's lawyer appeared at the police station and was denied access to Cicenia. Cicenia subsequently asked and was denied the opportunity to meet with his lawyer while being questioned by the police. The U.S. Supreme Court affirmed the petitioner's murder conviction and rejected the argument that due process required that local law enforcement officers inform suspects of their constitutional right to confer with an attorney. The dissenting judges, once again, argued for recognition of the due process right of access to a lawyer during pretrial interrogation (*Cicenia v. La Gay,* 357 U.S. 504 [1958]).

Massiah v. United States. *Massiah* was the breakthrough decision that extended the Sixth Amendment right to an attorney to individuals subjected to pretrial interrogation. Massiah and Colson were indicted for violating federal narcotics laws and were released on bail. Colson was persuaded to cooperate with the government and agreed to the installation of a radio transmitter under the front seat of his automobile. He engaged Massiah in a conversation, and at trial, an FBI agent testified regarding the conversation that he had overheard. Justice Potter Stewart held that after Massiah had been indicted and was entitled to a lawyer and to the determination of his guilt before a judge and jury, he had been improperly subjected to an extrajudicial, police-orchestrated proceeding designed to obtain incriminating statements (*Massiah v. United States,* 377 U.S. 201 [1964]).

Massiah provided the foundation for the Supreme Court decision in *Escobedo v. Illinois.* The petitioner, Danny Escobedo, a twenty-two-year-old Hispanic, was arrested for the murder of his brother-in-law. Escobedo was interrogated for fifteen hours, refused to make a statement, and was released on the order of a court. He was rearrested eleven days later, and on the way to police headquarters, Escobedo was told by the police that he had been named by DiGerlando, a suspected accomplice, as "[t]he one who shot" the deceased. Escobedo responded by requesting permission to consult with his lawyer (*Escobedo v. Illinois,* 378 U.S. 478 [1964]).

During Escobedo's interrogation by the police, he repeatedly asked and was denied permission to speak with his lawyer, who he was told "didn't want to see him." In fact, Escobedo's lawyer appeared shortly after Escobedo's arrival at the police headquarters and was denied access to his client. At one point, Escobedo and his lawyer came into eye contact with one another. The police confronted Escobedo, who was handcuffed, kept standing, nervous, and suffering from a lack of sleep, with DiGerlando. Escobedo responded by exclaiming, "I didn't shoot Manuel, you did it." Escobedo then made a series of incriminating remarks, implicating himself in the crime. The Supreme Court of Illinois determined that the refusal to permit Escobedo to see his lawyer did not change the fact that he voluntarily confessed to the murder.

Justice Arthur Goldberg wrote the opinion for the U.S. Supreme Court and held that Escobedo was entitled to be informed of his right to silence and counsel under the Sixth Amendment to the Constitution. As a result, his statement had been unconstitutionally obtained and had been improperly introduced by the prosecution at trial.

The significance of *Escobedo* is that the decision extended the Sixth Amendment right to a lawyer established in *Massiah* to the period prior to indictment. Justice Goldberg reasoned that this was the point at which most confessions were elicited, and a failure to provide access to an attorney at this stage would render legal representation at trial meaningless. Goldberg recognized that any competent lawyer would undoubtedly instruct his or her client not to talk to the police and that affording defendants the right to counsel prior to their formal indictment likely would impede interrogations and prevent the police from gathering the required evidence to prosecute crimes. Justice Goldberg nevertheless explained that the Constitution strikes a balance in favor of the accused's right against self-incrimination when weighed against the interests of society in eliciting a confession. Goldberg went on to observe that history teaches that a criminal justice system that "comes to depend on the 'confession' will, in the long run, be less reliable and more subject to abuses than a system which depends on extrinsic evidence independently secured through skillful investigation" (489).

Escobedo was based on the belief that informing defendants of their right to silence and of their right to the presence of a lawyer would protect suspects against uninformed and involuntary confessions. An attorney undoubtedly would have advised Escobedo that admitting his complicity in the murder would result in criminal liability for the killing.

Two years later, in *Miranda v. Arizona,* the Supreme Court abandoned the Sixth Amendment analysis and extended the Fifth Amendment right against self-incrimination to the interrogation of criminal suspects. The Supreme Court would later look back on *Escobedo* and observe that the decision set the stage for *Miranda*. In 1972, in *Kirby v. Illinois,* Justice Louis Powell explained that the underlying impact of *Escobedo* was "not to vindicate the constitutional right to counsel as such, but, like *Miranda,* to guarantee full effectuation of the privilege against self-incrimination" (*Kirby v. Illinois,* 406 U.S. 682, 689 [1972]). *Miranda v. Arizona* was the next step in the comprehensive constitutional regulation of police interrogations. We first need to understand the Fifth Amendment right against self-incrimination.

The Right Against Self-Incrimination

The Self-Incrimination Clause of the Fifth Amendment to the U.S. Constitution provides that "[n]o person . . . shall be compelled in any criminal case to be a witness against himself." This constitutional right was extended to the states in *Malloy v. Hogan* in which the U.S. Supreme Court held that the Fifth Amendment's prohibition on compulsory self-incrimination is incorporated into the Fourteenth Amendment and is applicable against the states. Justice William Brennan observed that the state and federal governments are "constitutionally compelled to establish guilt by evidence independently and freely secured, and may not, by coercion prove a charge against an accused out of his own mouth" (*Malloy v. Hogan,* 378 U.S. 1, 6 [1964]).

In other words, *you do not have to answer questions that may tend to incriminate you, and your failure to respond cannot be used against you in a criminal proceeding.* Why do we have a right that works to the advantage of guilty individuals by allowing them to withhold evidence from prosecuting authorities? This right was a reaction to procedures in religious courts and in the politically repressive Star Chamber in sixteenth-century England. These tribunals placed the burden on individuals to answer questions and to prove that they were not heretics or political dissidents. Justice Arthur Goldberg provided several reasons for the right against self-incrimination, a right that he stated "reflects many of our fundamental values and most noble aspirations" (*Murphy v. Waterfront Commission,* 378 U.S. 52, 55 [1964]). In considering these points, ask yourself whether we should have a right against self-incrimination.

- ***Cruel trilemma.*** Individuals should not be compelled to choose between "self-accusation, perjury or contempt." The law, in other words, should not place an individual in the position of making the unhappy choice between admitting guilt or denying guilt and facing a perjury charge for false testimony or refusing to speak and being held in contempt of court for failing to cooperate with the judicial process.

- ***Coercion.*** The fear that coercion and force will be used to compel individuals to incriminate themselves.
- ***Adversarial system.*** We have an *adversarial* rather than *inquisitorial* legal system. The accused is not required to establish his or her innocence; the State has the burden of proving guilt beyond a reasonable doubt.
- ***Privacy.*** An individual should not be forced to disclose information to the government.

Information is *incriminating* if there is a "substantial" and "real" threat that the information may lead to a criminal charge or establish a link in the chain of evidence that may result in a criminal prosecution. The U.S. Supreme Court recently dismissed a defendant's challenge to a "stop-and-identify" statute on the grounds that the defendant did not possess "any articulated real and appreciable fear that his name would be used to incriminate him, or that it 'would furnish a link in the chain of evidence needed to prosecute' him.... Answer[ing] a request to disclose a name is likely to be so insignificant... as to be incriminating only in unusual circumstances" (*Hiibel v. Sixth Judicial Court,* 542 U.S. 177 [2004]).

The second point to remember is that the privilege against self-incrimination is violated when the incriminating information is used against an individual in a legal proceeding. In *Chavez v. Martinez,* the defendant was shot by a police officer and was questioned by the officer while he was in intense pain in a hospital. Chavez admitted during the interrogation that he had taken the officer's pistol from his holster and pointed the weapon at him. Chavez filed a civil action for damages against the officer for violating his right against self-incrimination. The Supreme Court ruled that Martinez was never made a "witness" against himself because his statements were never admitted as testimony against him in a criminal case. Nor was he ever placed under oath and exposed to "'the cruel trilemma of self-accusation, perjury or contempt'"(*Chavez v. Martinez,* 538 U.S. 760 [2003]).

The third point is that the requirement that you may not be *compelled* to be a witness against yourself is satisfied when you are *required* to answer questions asked by the government. In *Hoffman v. United States,* the Supreme Court upheld the right of an organized crime figure to refuse to answer questions regarding his employment and associates before a grand jury investigating frauds perpetrated against the government. The Supreme Court observed that the "immediate and potential evils of compulsory self-disclosure transcend any difficulties that the exercise of the privilege may impose on society in the detection and prosecution of crime" (*Hoffman v. United States,* 341 U.S. 479, 485 [1951]). On the other hand, there is no compulsion when a driver arrested for drunk driving is *offered the choice* of either submitting to a simple and relatively painless blood-alcohol test or having his or her refusal to do so used against him or her in court (*South Dakota v. Neville,* 459 U.S. 553 [1983]).

Finally, the prohibition against being compelled to be a witness against oneself is limited to **testimonial evidence,** or evidence that is communicative in character. What does this mean? The Supreme Court explained the testimonial or communicative requirement in *Doe v. United States.* The Court stated that the government is prohibited from compelling you to make a factual statement, forcing you to disclose information that connects you to a criminal offense, or requiring you to share your private thoughts or beliefs with the government. The Supreme Court has noted that the privilege against self-incrimination encompasses trial testimony, oral confessions to the police, and personal documents. On the other hand, there is no privilege against self-incrimination where the government compels you to provide **nontestimonial evidence.** Judges have held that nontestimonial evidence includes voice and handwriting exemplars, fingerprints, participation in a lineup, the police requiring you to try on clothes or to walk in a straight line, hair and urine samples, the withdrawing of blood, the examination of scars and tattoos, and the taking of photos. This evidence may be used against you in a criminal proceeding, and your failure to cooperate in these procedures may be introduced at trial to establish your guilt. You also will be held in contempt of court if you refuse to provide this type of physical or nontestimonial evidence (*Doe v. United States,* 487 U.S. 201 [1988]).

You no doubt have a puzzled look on your face because the line between testimonial or communicative and nontestimonial or physical evidence does not appear to be crystal clear.

You are correct. Consider *Pennsylvania v. Muniz.* Muniz was arrested for driving while intoxicated. He was taken to a "booking center," and his subsequent interrogation by the police was recorded. Muniz was first asked his name, address, height, weight, eye color, date of birth, and current age. His response was slow and slurred. These questions asked for routine information and were not incriminating. The police officer then asked Muniz whether he knew the date of his sixth birthday. Muniz replied, "No, I don't."

Was Muniz's answer to the sixth-birthday question admissible in evidence? The Supreme Court held in a 5-to-4 ruling that this question called for a *testimonial response* that violated Muniz's right against self-incrimination and that his response was inadmissible in evidence. The question confronted Muniz with the unhappy situation of choosing either self-incrimination or perjury. Muniz, according to Justice Brennan, either could admit that he did not know the date of his sixth birthday or could answer untruthfully and report a date of birth that he knew was inaccurate. His answer in either case would indicate that Muniz's mental state was impaired by alcohol. The Supreme Court majority reasoned that either alternative would be the equivalent of Muniz's admitting that he was too intoxicated to answer the question accurately.

Eight justices also held for different reasons that Muniz's slurred speech in answering the booking questions was admissible to establish that he was inebriated. Four of these justices explained that Muniz's slurred speech was nontestimonial and demonstrated Muniz's lack of "muscular coordination" in forming his words and that this related to Muniz's physical act of speaking rather than to the words that he was speaking. As a result, the slurred speech was nontestimonial rather than testimonial evidence, did not violate Muniz's right against self-incrimination, and was properly introduced into evidence. Is this distinction persuasive? (*Pennsylvania v. Muniz,* 496 U.S. 582 [1990]).

The next case in the text, *Schmerber v. California,* asks you to decide whether the courts' distinction between testimonial and nontestimonial evidence makes sense.

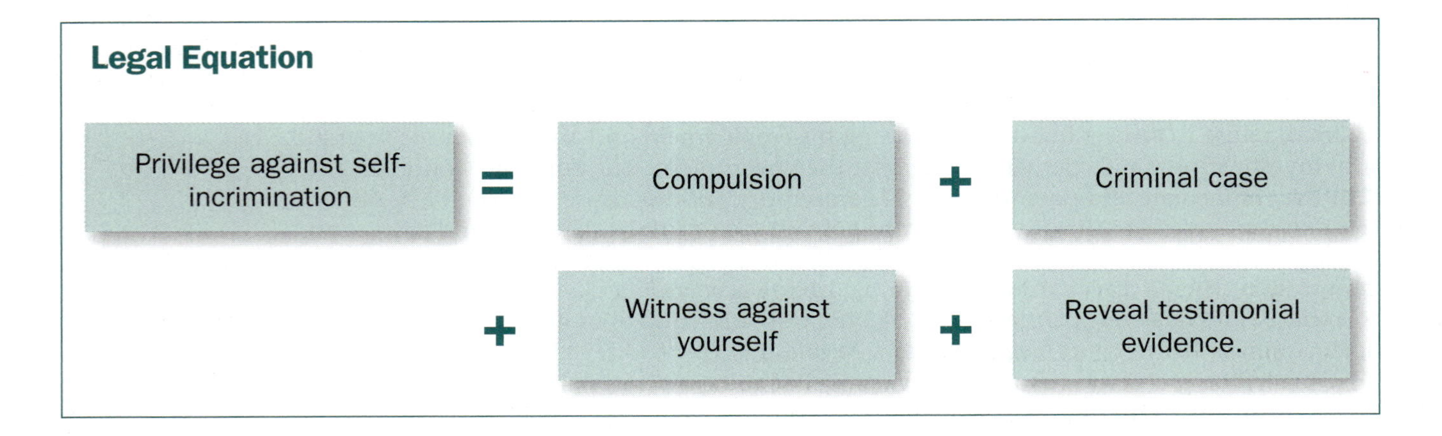

Did the involuntary withdrawal of the petitioner's blood violate his right against self-incrimination?

Schmerber v. California, 384 U.S. 757 (1966), Brennan, J.

Facts

Petitioner was convicted in Los Angeles Municipal Court of the criminal offense of driving an automobile while under the influence of intoxicating liquor.

Petitioner and a companion had been drinking at a tavern and bowling alley. There was evidence showing that petitioner was driving from the bowling alley about midnight November 12, 1964, when the car skidded, crossed the road, and struck a tree. Both petitioner and his companion were injured and taken to a hospital for treatment. He had been arrested at a hospital while receiving treatment for injuries suffered in an accident involving the automobile that he had apparently been driving. At the direction of a police officer, a blood sample was then withdrawn from petitioner's body by a physician at the hospital. The chemical analysis of this sample revealed a percent by weight of alcohol in his blood at the time of the offense which indicated intoxication, and the report of this analysis was admitted in evidence at the trial. Petitioner objected to receipt of this evidence of the analysis on the ground that the blood had been withdrawn despite his refusal, on the advice of his counsel, to consent to the test. He contended that in that circumstance, the withdrawal of the blood and the admission of the analysis in evidence denied him due process of law under the Fourteenth Amendment, as well as specific guarantees of the Bill of Rights secured against the States by that Amendment: his privilege against self-incrimination under the Fifth Amendment; his right to counsel under the Sixth Amendment; and his right not to be subjected to unreasonable searches and seizures in violation of the Fourth Amendment. The Appellate Department of the California Superior Court rejected these contentions and affirmed the conviction.... We affirm.

Issue

Malloy v. Hogan... held that the Fourteenth Amendment secures against state invasion the same privilege that the Fifth Amendment guarantees against federal infringement—the right of a person to remain silent unless he chooses to speak in the unfettered exercise of his own will, and to suffer no penalty... for such silence. We therefore must now decide whether the withdrawal of the blood and admission in evidence of the analysis involved in this case violated petitioner's privilege.

Reasoning

It could not be denied that in requiring petitioner to submit to the withdrawal and chemical analysis of his blood, the State compelled him to submit to an attempt to discover evidence that might be used to prosecute him for a criminal offense. He submitted only after the police officer rejected his objection and directed the physician to proceed. The officer's direction to the physician to administer the test over petitioner's objection constituted compulsion for the purposes of the privilege. The critical question, then, is whether petitioner was thus compelled "to be a witness against himself."

The withdrawal of blood necessarily involves puncturing the skin for extraction, and the percent by weight of alcohol in that blood, as established by chemical analysis, is evidence of criminal guilt. Compelled submission fails on one view to respect the "inviolability of the human personality." Moreover, since it enables the State to rely on evidence forced from the accused, the compulsion violates at least one meaning of the requirement that the State procure the evidence against an accused "by its own independent labors."

However, the privilege has never been given the full scope which the values it helps to protect suggest. History and a long line of authorities in lower courts have consistently limited its protection to situations in which the State seeks to submerge those values by obtaining the evidence against an accused through "the cruel, simple expedient of compelling it from his own mouth.... In sum, the privilege is fulfilled only when the person is guaranteed the right 'to remain silent unless he chooses to speak in the unfettered exercise of his own will.'" The leading case in this Court is *Holt v. United States,* 218 U.S. 245 [1910]. There the question was whether evidence was admissible that the accused, prior to trial and over his protest, put on a blouse that fitted him. It was contended that compelling the accused to submit to the demand that he model the blouse violated the privilege. Mr. Justice Holmes, speaking for the Court, rejected the argument as "based upon an extravagant extension of the Fifth Amendment," and went on to say, "The prohibition of compelling a man in a criminal court to be witness against himself is a prohibition of the use of physical or moral compulsion to extort communications from him, not an exclusion of his body as evidence when it may be material. The objection in principle would forbid a jury to look at a prisoner and compare his features with a photograph in proof."

Both federal and state courts have usually held that it offers no protection against compulsion to submit to fingerprinting, photographing, or measurements, to write or speak for identification, to appear in court, to stand, to assume a stance, to walk, or to make a particular gesture. The distinction which has emerged, often expressed in different ways, is that the privilege is a bar against compelling "communications" or "testimony," but that compulsion which makes a suspect or accused the source of "real or physical evidence" does not violate it.

Holding

In the present case, however, no... problem of application is presented. Not even a shadow of testimonial compulsion upon or enforced communication by the accused was involved either in the extraction or in the chemical analysis. Petitioner's testimonial capacities were in no way implicated; indeed, his participation, except as a donor, was irrelevant to the results of the test, which depend on chemical analysis and on that alone. Since the blood test evidence, although an incriminating product of compulsion, was neither petitioner's testimony nor evidence relating to some communicative act or writing by the petitioner, it was not inadmissible on privilege grounds....

Dissenting, *Black, J.,* joined by *Douglas, J.*

The Court admits that "the State compelled [petitioner] to submit to an attempt to discover evidence [in his blood] that might be [and was] used to prosecute him for a criminal offense." To reach the conclusion that compelling a person to give his blood to help the State convict him is not equivalent to compelling him to be a witness against himself strikes me as quite an extraordinary feat.... It seems to me that the compulsory extraction of petitioner's blood for analysis so that the person who analyzed it could give evidence to convict him had both a "testimonial" and a "communicative nature." The sole purpose of this project which proved to be successful was to obtain "testimony" from some person to prove that petitioner had alcohol in his blood at the time he was arrested. And the purpose of the project was certainly "communicative" in that the analysis of the blood was to supply information to enable a witness to communicate to the court and jury that petitioner was more or less drunk....

How can it reasonably be doubted that the blood test evidence was not in all respects the actual equivalent of "testimony" taken from petitioner when the result of the test was offered as testimony, was considered by the jury as testimony, and the jury's verdict of guilt rests in part on that testimony? The refined, subtle reasoning and balancing process used here to narrow the scope of the Bill of Rights' safeguard against self-incrimination provides a handy instrument for further narrowing of that constitutional protection, as well as others, in the future. Believing with the Framers that these constitutional safeguards broadly construed by independent tribunals of justice provide our best hope for keeping our people free from governmental oppression, I deeply regret the Court's holding....

Questions for Discussion

1. What is the holding of the Supreme Court in *Schmerber*? Is Justice Brennan's decision consistent or inconsistent with the purposes of the privilege against self-incrimination?
2. Summarize the argument of the dissenting judges.
3. How would you rule in this case?
4. Does the extraction of DNA evidence from a suspect in a criminal case violate an individual's right against self-incrimination?
5. ***Problems in policing.*** Explain why it is important to understand the difference between testimonial and nontestimonial evidence in regard to self-incrimination. Give some examples of nontestimonial evidence.

Miranda v. Arizona

In 1966, in *Miranda v. Arizona,* a five-judge majority of the U.S. Supreme Court held that the prosecution may not use statements stemming from the custodial interrogation absent procedural safeguards to protect a defendant's Fifth Amendment privilege against self-incrimination. The Court majority concluded that absent a three-part *Miranda* warning, the "inherently coercive" pressures of police interrogation had been proven to overwhelm individuals' capacity to exercise their right against self-incrimination, and no confession given under these conditions "can truly be the product of a suspect's free choice."

What were these coercive pressures? According to the Court, individuals held in detention were isolated from friends, family, and lawyers in unfamiliar surroundings and were subject to sophisticated psychological tactics, manipulation, and trickery designed to wear down their resistance. The Court pointed to police manuals instructing officers to engage in tactics such as displaying confidence in a suspect's guilt, minimizing the seriousness of the offense, wearing down individuals through continuous interrogation, and using the "Mutt and Jeff" strategy in which one officer berates a suspect and the other gains the suspect's trust by playing the part of his or her protector. The "false lineup" involves placing a suspect in a lineup and using fictitious witnesses to identify the suspect as the perpetrator. In another scenario, fictitious witnesses identify the defendant as the perpetrator of a previously undisclosed serious crime, and the defendant panics and confesses to the offense under investigation.

Before you begin to read the *Miranda* decision, you may find it interesting to learn about Ernesto Miranda, the individual whose name is attached to one of the most important U.S. Supreme Court decisions in recent history. Miranda was in constant trouble as a young man and committed a felony car theft in 1954 while in the eighth grade. This arrest was followed by a string of convictions and brief detentions for burglary, attempted rape and assault, curfew violations, "Peeping Tom" activities, and car theft. In 1959, Miranda was sentenced to a year in prison and, following his release, seemingly settled down and found a regular job, moved in with a woman, and fathered a child. In 1963, Miranda reverted to his previous pattern of criminal behavior and kidnapped and raped eighteen-year-old "Jane Doe." The victim identified him in a lineup, and his car had been seen in the neighborhood of the attack. Miranda confessed in less than two hours and was convicted and sentenced to not less than twenty nor more than thirty years in prison. Miranda's conviction was affirmed by the Arizona Supreme Court, and his lawyers appealed to the U.S. Supreme Court.

In reading *Miranda v. Arizona,* pay attention to the procedural protections the Supreme Court requires that the police provide a suspect. Why are these specific protections required?

Was Miranda's confession admissible at trial?

Miranda v. Arizona, *384 U.S. 436 (1966), Warren, C.J.*

Facts

On March 13, 1963, petitioner, Ernesto Miranda, was arrested at his home and taken in custody to a Phoenix police station. He was there identified by the complaining witness. The police then took him to "Interrogation Room No. 2" of the detective bureau. There, he was questioned by two police officers. The officers admitted at trial that Miranda was not advised that he had a right to have an attorney present. Two hours later, the officers emerged from the interrogation room with a written confession signed by Miranda. At the top of the statement was a typed paragraph stating that the confession was made voluntarily, without threats or promises of immunity, and "with full knowledge of my legal rights, understanding any statement I make may be used against me." At his trial before a jury, the written confession was admitted into evidence over the objection of defense counsel.

Miranda was found guilty of kidnapping and rape. He was sentenced to twenty to thirty years imprisonment on each count, the sentences to run concurrently. On appeal, the Supreme Court of Arizona held that Miranda's constitutional rights were not violated in obtaining the confession and affirmed the conviction.... The Court emphasized the fact that Miranda did not specifically request counsel....

Issue

The constitutional issue we decide... is the admissibility of statements obtained from a defendant questioned while in custody or otherwise deprived of his freedom of action in any significant way. In each of the four cases before the Court, the defendant was questioned by police officers, detectives, or a prosecuting attorney in a room in which he was cut off from the outside world. In none of these cases was the defendant given a full and effective warning of his rights at the outset of the interrogation process. In all the cases, the questioning elicited oral admissions, and in three of them, signed statements as well which were admitted at their trials. They all thus share salient features—incommunicado interrogation of individuals in a police-dominated atmosphere, resulting in self-incriminating statements without full warnings of constitutional rights....

Reasoning

We start here, as we did in *Escobedo,* with the premise that our holding is not an innovation in our jurisprudence, but is an application of principles long recognized and applied in other settings. We have undertaken a thorough reexamination of the *Escobedo* decision and the principles it announced, and we reaffirm it. That case was but an explication of basic rights that are enshrined in our Constitution—that "No person... shall be compelled in any criminal case to be a witness against himself," and that "the accused shall... have the Assistance of Counsel"—rights which were put in jeopardy in that case through official overbearing. These precious rights were fixed in our Constitution only after centuries of persecution and struggle....

An understanding of the nature and setting of this in-custody interrogation is essential to our decisions today. The difficulty in depicting what transpires at such interrogations stems from the fact that in this country they have largely taken place incommunicado. From extensive factual studies undertaken in the early 1930s, including the famous Wickersham Report to Congress by a Presidential Commission, it is clear that police violence and the "third degree" flourished at that time.... [However] we stress that the modern practice of in-custody interrogation is psychologically rather than physically oriented. Interrogation still takes place in privacy.... A valuable source of information about present police practices... may be found in various police manuals and texts which document procedures employed with success in the past, and which recommend various other effective tactics.... [T]he setting prescribed by the manuals and observed in practice becomes clear. In essence, it is this: To be alone with the subject is essential to prevent distraction and to deprive him of any outside support. The aura of confidence in his guilt undermines his will to resist. He merely confirms the preconceived story the police seek to have him describe. Patience and persistence, at times relentless questioning, are employed. To obtain a confession, the interrogator must "patiently maneuver himself or his quarry into a position from which the desired objective may be attained." When normal procedures fail to produce the needed result, the police may resort to deceptive stratagems such as giving false legal advice. It is important to keep the subject off balance, for example, by trading on his insecurity about himself or his surroundings. The police then persuade, trick, or cajole him out of exercising his constitutional rights....

In the cases before us today, given this background, we concern ourselves primarily with this interrogation atmosphere and the evils it can bring. In *Miranda v. Arizona,* the police arrested the defendant and took him to a special interrogation room where they secured a confession. In *Vignera v. New York,* the defendant made oral admissions to the police after interrogation in the afternoon, and then signed an inculpatory statement upon being questioned by an assistant district attorney later the same evening. In *Westover v. United States,* the defendant was handed over to the Federal Bureau of Investigation by local authorities after they had detained and interrogated him for a lengthy period, both at night and the following morning. After some two hours of questioning, the federal officers had obtained signed statements from the defendant. Lastly, in *California v. Stewart,* the local police held the defendant five days in the station and interrogated him on nine separate occasions before they secured his inculpatory statement.... The potentiality for compulsion is forcefully apparent, for example, in *Miranda,* where the indigent Mexican defendant was a seriously disturbed individual with pronounced sexual fantasies, and in *Stewart,* in which the defendant was an indigent Los Angeles Negro who had dropped out of school in the sixth grade. To be sure, the records do not evince overt physical coercion or patent psychological ploys. The fact remains that in none of these cases did the officers undertake to afford appropriate safeguards at the outset of the interrogation to insure that the statements were truly the product of free choice.

It is obvious that such an interrogation environment is created for no purpose other than to subjugate the individual to the will of his examiner. This atmosphere carries its own badge of intimidation. To be sure, this is not physical intimidation, but it is equally destructive of human dignity. The current practice of incommunicado interrogation is at odds with one of our Nation's most cherished principles—that the individual may not be compelled to incriminate himself. Unless adequate protective devices are employed to dispel the compulsion inherent in custodial surroundings, no statement obtained from the defendant can truly be the product of his free choice.

The question in these cases is whether the privilege is fully applicable during a period of custodial interrogation. In this Court, the privilege has consistently been accorded a liberal construction. We are satisfied that all the principles embodied in the privilege apply to informal compulsion exerted by law-enforcement officers during in-custody questioning. An individual swept from familiar surroundings into police custody, surrounded by antagonistic forces, and subjected to the techniques of persuasion... cannot be otherwise than under compulsion to speak. As a practical matter, the compulsion to speak in the isolated setting of the police station may well be greater than in courts or other official investigations, where there are often impartial observers to guard against intimidation or trickery....

Today, then, there can be no doubt that the Fifth Amendment privilege is available outside of criminal court proceedings and serves to protect persons in all settings in which their freedom of action is curtailed in any significant way from being compelled to incriminate themselves. We have concluded that without proper safeguards, the process of in-custody interrogation of persons suspected or accused of crime contains inherently compelling pressures which work to undermine the individual's will to resist and to compel him to speak where he would not otherwise do so freely. In order to combat these pressures and to permit a full opportunity to exercise the privilege against self-incrimination, the accused must be adequately and effectively apprised of his rights and the exercise of those rights must be fully honored.

Holding

At the outset, if a person in custody is to be subjected to interrogation, he must first be informed in clear and unequivocal terms that he has the right to remain silent. For those unaware of the privilege, the warning is needed simply to make them aware of it—the threshold requirement for an intelligent decision as to its exercise. More important, such a warning is an absolute prerequisite in overcoming the inherent pressures of the interrogation atmosphere.... In accord with our decision today, it is impermissible to penalize an individual for exercising his Fifth Amendment privilege when he is under police custodial interrogation. The prosecution may not, therefore, use at trial the fact that he stood mute or claimed his privilege in the face of accusation....

The Fifth Amendment privilege is so fundamental to our system of constitutional rule and the expedient of giving an adequate warning as to the availability of the privilege so simple, we will not pause to inquire in individual cases whether the defendant was aware of his rights without a warning being given.

The warning of the right to remain silent must be accompanied by the explanation that anything said can and will be used against the individual in court. This warning is needed in order to make him aware not only of the privilege, but also of the consequences of forgoing it....

The circumstances surrounding in-custody interrogation can operate very quickly to overbear the will of one merely made aware of his privilege by his interrogators. Therefore, the right to have counsel present at the interrogation is indispensable to the protection of the Fifth Amendment privilege under the system we delineate today. Our aim is to assure that the individual's right to choose between silence and speech remains unfettered throughout the interrogation process.... [T]he need for counsel to protect the Fifth Amendment privilege comprehends not merely a right to consult with counsel prior to questioning, but also to have counsel present during any questioning if the defendant so desires.

The presence of counsel at the interrogation may serve several significant subsidiary functions as well. If the accused decides to talk to his interrogators, the assistance of counsel can mitigate the dangers of untrustworthiness. With a lawyer present, the likelihood that the police will practice coercion is reduced, and if coercion is nevertheless exercised, the lawyer can testify to it in court. The presence of a lawyer can also help to guarantee that the accused gives a fully accurate statement to the police and that the statement is rightly reported by the prosecution at trial.... No effective waiver of the right to counsel during interrogation can be recognized unless specifically made after the warnings we here delineate have been given. The accused who does not know his rights and therefore does not make a request may be the person who most needs counsel.

Accordingly, we hold that an individual held for interrogation must be clearly informed that he has the right to consult with a lawyer and to have the lawyer with him during interrogation under the system for protecting the privilege we delineate today. As with the warnings of the right to remain silent and that anything stated can be used in evidence against him, this warning is an absolute prerequisite to interrogation. No amount of circumstantial evidence that the person may have been aware of this right will suffice to stand in its stead. Only through such a warning is there ascertainable assurance that the accused was aware of this right.

If an individual indicates that he wishes the assistance of counsel before any interrogation occurs, the authorities cannot rationally ignore or deny his request on the basis that the individual does not have or cannot afford a retained attorney.... The need for counsel in order to protect the privilege exists for the indigent as well as the affluent.... While authorities are not required to relieve the accused of his poverty, they have the obligation not to take advantage of indigence in the administration of justice....

In order fully to apprise a person interrogated of the extent of his rights under this system then, it is necessary to warn him not only that he has the right to consult with an attorney, but also that if he is indigent, a lawyer will be appointed to represent him. Without this additional warning, the admonition of the right to consult with counsel would often be understood as meaning only that he can consult with a lawyer if he has one or has the funds to obtain one. The warning of a right to counsel would be hollow if not couched in terms that would convey to the indigent—the person most often subjected to interrogation—the knowledge that he too has a right to have counsel present. As with the warnings of the right to remain silent and of the general right to counsel, only by effective and express explanation to the indigent of this right can there be assurance that he was truly in a position to exercise it.

Once warnings have been given, the subsequent procedure is clear. If the individual indicates in any manner, at any time prior to or during questioning, that he wishes to remain silent, the interrogation must cease. At this point, he has shown that he intends to exercise his Fifth Amendment privilege; any statement taken after the person invokes his privilege cannot be other than the product of compulsion, subtle or otherwise. Without the right to cut off questioning, the setting of in-custody interrogation operates on the individual to overcome free choice in producing a statement after the privilege has been once invoked. If the individual states that he wants an attorney, the interrogation must cease until an attorney is present. At that time, the individual must have an opportunity to confer with the attorney and to have him present during any subsequent questioning. If the individual cannot obtain an attorney and he indicates that he wants one before speaking to police, they must respect his decision to remain silent.

This does not mean, as some have suggested, that each police station must have a "station house lawyer" present at all times to advise prisoners. It does mean, however, that if police propose to interrogate a person, they must make known to him that he is entitled to a lawyer and that if he cannot afford one, a lawyer will be provided for him prior to any interrogation. If authorities conclude that they will not provide counsel during a reasonable period of time in which investigation in the field is carried out, they may refrain from doing so without violating the person's Fifth Amendment privilege so long as they do not question him during that time.

If the interrogation continues without the presence of an attorney and a statement is taken, a heavy burden rests on the government to demonstrate that the defendant knowingly and intelligently waived his privilege against self-incrimination and his right to retained or appointed counsel.... An express statement that the individual is willing to make a statement and does not want an attorney followed closely by a statement could constitute a waiver. But a valid waiver will not be presumed simply from the silence of the accused after warnings are given or simply from the fact that a confession was in fact eventually obtained....

Whatever the testimony of the authorities as to waiver of rights by an accused, the fact of lengthy interrogation or incommunicado incarceration before a statement is made is strong evidence that the accused did not validly waive his rights. In these circumstances, the fact that the individual eventually made a statement is consistent with the conclusion that the compelling influence of the interrogation finally forced him to do so. It is inconsistent with any notion of a voluntary relinquishment of the privilege. Moreover, any evidence that the accused was threatened, tricked, or cajoled into a waiver will, of course, show that the defendant did not voluntarily waive his privilege. The requirement of warnings and waiver of rights is a fundamental with respect to the Fifth Amendment privilege and not simply a preliminary ritual to existing methods of interrogation....

General on-the-scene questioning as to facts surrounding a crime or other general questioning of citizens in the fact-finding process is not affected by our holding. It is an act of responsible citizenship for individuals to give whatever information they may have to aid in law enforcement. In such situations, the compelling atmosphere inherent in the process of in-custody interrogation is not necessarily present.... There is no requirement that police stop a person who enters a police station and states that he wishes to confess to a crime, or a person who calls the police to offer a confession or any other statement he desires to make. Volunteered statements of any kind are not barred by the Fifth Amendment, and their admissibility is not affected by our holding today.

Over the years, the Federal Bureau of Investigation has compiled an exemplary record of effective law enforcement while advising any suspect or arrested person, at the outset of an interview, that he is not required to make a statement, that any statement may be used against him in court, that the individual may obtain the services of an attorney of his own choice and, more recently, that he has a right to free counsel if he is unable to pay.... The practice of the FBI can readily be emulated by state and local enforcement agencies.... The experience in some other countries also suggests that the danger to law enforcement in curbs on interrogation is overplayed.... There appears to have been no marked detrimental effect on criminal law enforcement in these jurisdictions as a result of these rules. Conditions of law enforcement in our country are sufficiently similar to permit reference to this experience as assurance that lawlessness will not result from warning an individual of his rights or allowing him to exercise them....

Dissenting, *Clark, J.*

Rather than employing the arbitrary Fifth Amendment rule which the Court lays down, I would following the more pliable dictates of Due Process Clauses of the Fifth and Fourteenth Amendments which we are accustomed to administering and which... are effective instruments in protecting persons in police custody. In this way, we would not be acting in the dark nor in one full sweep change the traditional rules of custodial interrogation which this Court has for so long recognized as a justifiable and proper tool in balancing individual rights against the rights of society....

Dissenting, *White, J.*, joined by *Harlan, J.*, and *Stewart, J.*

The proposition that the privilege against self-incrimination forbids in custody interrogation without the warnings specified in the majority opinion and without a clear waiver of counsel has no significant support in the history of the privilege or in the language of the Fifth Amendment.... [T]he Court has not discovered or found the law in making today's decision, nor has it derived it from some irrefutable sources; what is has done is to make new law and new public policy....

The obvious underpinning of the Court's decision is a deep-seated distrust of all confessions.... [T]he rule announced today [is] a deliberate calculus to prevent interrogations, to reduce the incidence of confessions and pleas of guilty, and to increase the number of trials.... [I]t is something else again to remove from the ordinary criminal case all those confessions which heretofore have been held to be free and voluntary acts of the accused and to thus establish a new constitutional barrier to the ascertainment of truth by the judicial process. There is... every reason to believe that a good many criminal defendants who otherwise would have been convicted on what this Court has previously thought to be the most satisfactory kind of evidence, will now under this new version of the Fifth Amendment, either not be tried at all or acquitted if the State's evidence, minus the confession, is put to the test of litigation.... [W]here probable cause exists to arrest several suspects... it will often be true that a suspect may be cleared only through the results of interrogation of other suspects. Here too the release of the innocent may be delayed by the Court's rule.

Much of the trouble with the Court's new rule is that it will operate... in all criminal cases, regardless of the severity of the crime or the circumstances involved.... It will slow down the investigation and the apprehension of confederates in those cases where time is of the essence, such as kidnapping, those involving the national security, [and] some organized crime situations....

Questions for Discussion

1. Outline the *Miranda* rule. Explain the purpose of the required warnings.
2. Why did the Supreme Court base *Miranda* on the Fifth rather than the Sixth Amendment?
3. Do the *Miranda* warnings adequately counteract the pressure that the majority describes as inherent in custodial interrogation?
4. Compare and contrast the requirements of the due process voluntariness test and the *Miranda* rule.
5. Are you persuaded by the arguments of the dissent? Is the majority distrustful of confessions as alleged by the defense?
6. Is it realistic to expect defendants to invoke their *Miranda* rights and for the police to fully follow the requirements of the *Miranda* ruling?
7. ***Problems in policing.*** What is required of police officers under the *Miranda* rule?

Cases and Comments

1. ***Miranda.*** Miranda was retried for kidnapping and rape. The twenty-one-year-old Jane Doe testified against him but, on cross-examination, admitted that she was unable to positively identify Miranda as the perpetrator. Miranda's common law wife, however, came forward and testified that Miranda had confided in her that he had committed the kidnapping and rape and that he had asked her to tell Doe that he would marry her if she would drop the charges. Miranda then asked his wife to show Doe their baby daughter and to ask her to drop the charges so that the baby could be with her father. Miranda was once again convicted and was sentenced to serve twenty to thirty years in prison. In 1972, at the age of thirty, Miranda was paroled. He was returned to prison when he was found with a gun and illegal drugs in violation of the terms of his parole. Miranda was released in 1975 and sold autographed "*Miranda* warning cards" to raise money. In January 1976, while drinking and playing cards, he got involved in a bar fight and was stabbed to death. You can read about the *Miranda* case in Liva Baker, *Miranda: Crime, Law, and Politics* (New York: Atheneum, 1983).

2. ***Interrogation Techniques.*** Saul M. Kassin and Gisli H. Gudjonsson are two of the most prominent psychologists working in the area of interrogation and confessions. The two scholars found that a number of suspects waive their *Miranda* rights because of an inability to fully comprehend the warnings. This may result from youth, a lack of intelligence or education, or an inability to understand their rights. Some commentators suggest that individuals who lack confidence or who are inexperienced in the criminal justice process also may a have a difficult time asserting their rights in the presence of the police.

Individuals who waive their rights may confront sophisticated police interrogation tactics. Kassin and Gudjonsson (2005) find that police interrogation techniques result in confessions from roughly forty-two percent of individuals subjected to police interrogation. They write that the police are advised to conduct interrogations in a small, sparsely furnished room in order to isolate the suspect and to make him or her uncomfortable and feel cramped and confined. The police are taught to align themselves with the suspect by justifying or excusing the crime. This, for example, might entail portraying the act as understandable under the circumstances. The police also are instructed to stress that the victim's behavior contributed to the crime and to minimize the seriousness of the suspect's actions. Another tactic is to display a certainty in the suspect's guilt and to immediately interrupt and challenge the suspect's denial of guilt or claim that he or she acted out of self-defense. The police also are instructed to encourage the suspect to unburden his or her guilt and to provide a written or oral account of the crime. Kassin and Gudjonsson observe that although most people confess for a variety of reasons, the most powerful factor is the suspect's belief that the police have evidence implicating him or her in the crime, such as fingerprint, hair, or blood evidence.

Miller v. Fenton is a leading case on police interrogation tactics. Frank Miller was a suspect in the murder and accompanied the police to a state police barracks. He was read and waived his *Miranda* rights. The issue was whether Detective Boyce had employed tactics during the fifty-three-minute interrogation that "were sufficiently manipulative to overbear the will of a person with [the defendant's] characteristics." The majority concluded that Miller's confession was voluntary "under the circumstances."

Miller was thirty-two, had some high school education, and previously had served time in prison. During the interrogation, Boyce falsely told Miller that the deceased was alive, hoping that the possibility that the victim would identify Miller as the assailant would persuade him to confess to the crime and to "cut a deal." Boyce, having met with no success, arranged to receive a phone call during the interrogation and announced with mock surprise that the victim had just died. Boyce, with apparent concern, then sympathetically related that he knew that Miller suffered from mental problems and that Boyce would like to insure that Miller received psychological help. Boyce next stressed that Miller was "not responsible" or a "criminal," that the death must be "eating you up," that "you've got to come forward," and that he wanted to help Miller "unburden his inner tensions." Roughly one hour passed before Miller confessed and collapsed in a robot-like state onto the floor and was taken to the hospital.

The two-judge majority indicated that Boyd's interrogation "did not produce psychological pressure strong enough to overbear the will of a mature, experienced man [like Miller] who was suffering from no mental or physical illness and was interrogated for less than an hour at a police station close to home." Judge Gibbons, in dissent, criticized the majority for adopting a test that asked the court to speculate on the impact of Boyce's "promises and lies" on Miller. Gibbon, instead, argued that that when the police resort to promises of psychological help and assure suspects that they will not be punished, the confession should be ruled inadmissible. Do you agree with the two-judge majority or with Judge Gibbons? See *Miller v. Fenton,* 796 F.2d 598 (3d Cir. 1986).

8.2 YOU DECIDE

Robert L. Brown was charged in a Louisiana court with unlawful possession of heroin. He was convicted and sentenced to ten years in prison. Brown was apprehended when he unsuccessfully attempted to flee from a police raid of a drug house. He was advised that he had a right to speak or remain silent, that anything he said might be used against him, and that he had a right to counsel. During the reading of the *Miranda* warnings, Brown proclaimed, "I know all that." Brown then confessed that he used narcotics and, in fact, had injected earlier in the day.

A federal district court pointed out that Brown was not told that he had the right to have an attorney present if he decided to make a statement and that he was not told that a lawyer would be appointed to represent him in the event that he lacked funds. One of the arresting officers also testified that he did not afford the defendant "any opportunity to procure a lawyer." Did Brown's statement that "I know all that" constitute a waiver of Brown's right to receive the full *Miranda* warnings? Cite language from the *Miranda* decision in support of your answer. See *Brown v. Heyd,* 277 F. Supp. 899 (D.C.E.D. La. 1967).

You can find the answer by referring to the study site, http://www.sagepub.com/lippmancp.

Legal Equation

Fifth Amendment privilege against self-incrimination and police interrogation

The prosecution may not use inculpatory or exculpatory statements stemming from custodial interrogation of the defendant unless it demonstrates use of procedural safeguards effective to secure privilege against self-incrimination

Custodial interrogation is questioning initiated by law enforcement officers after an individual has been taken into custody or deprived of his or her freedom of action in a significant way

Prior to any questions, the suspect must be clearly and unequivocally informed that he or she has the right to remain silent, that any statement he or she makes may be used as evidence against him or her, and that he or she has the right to the presence of an attorney, appointed or retained

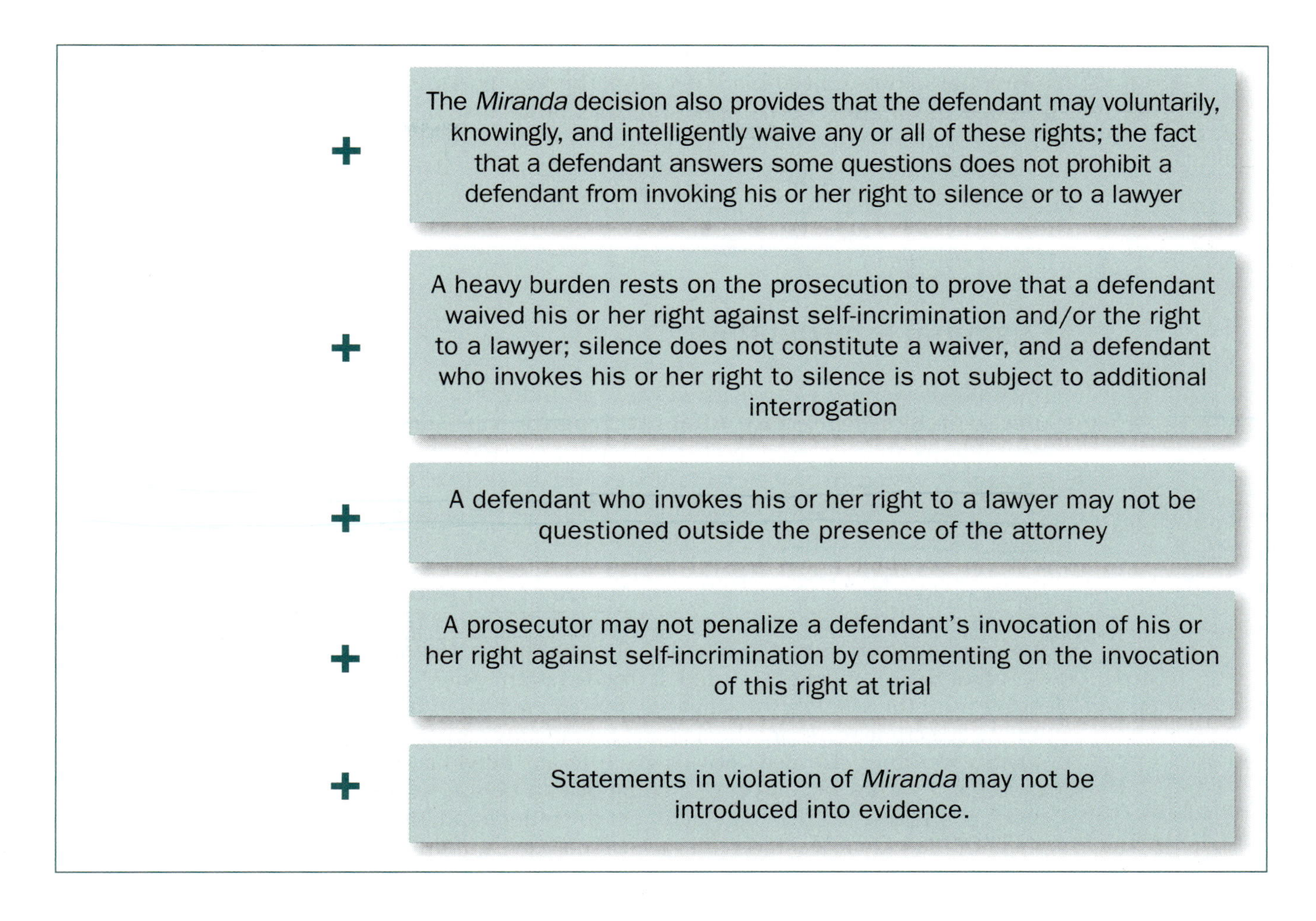

Miranda and the Constitution

Miranda, as we have seen, supplemented the due process voluntariness test by requiring that the police read suspects subjected to custodial interrogation the *Miranda* warnings. The decision in *Miranda* sparked a wave of criticism, and in 1968, the U.S. Congress took the aggressive step of passing legislation that required federal judges to apply the voluntariness test. The Omnibus Crime Control and Safe Streets Act provided that a confession shall be admissible as evidence in federal court if it is "voluntarily given." The Act listed a number of factors that judges were to consider in determining whether a confession was voluntary.

In 2000, in *Dickerson v. United States,* Chief Justice William Rehnquist, who himself had been a constant critic of *Miranda,* held that *Miranda* was a "constitutional decision" that is required by the Fifth Amendment to insure that detainees are able to exercise their right against self-incrimination in the inherently coercive atmosphere of custodial interrogation. This is an important statement because laws passed by Congress are required to conform to the U.S. Constitution, in this instance, the Fifth Amendment. Congress accordingly lacked authority to instruct the judiciary to disregard the requirements of *Miranda* and to rely solely on the voluntariness test. Justice Rehnquist also stressed that *Miranda* has become "embedded in routine police practice to the point where the warnings have become part of our national culture" (*Dickerson v. United States,* 530 U.S. 428 [2000]). We now will examine the central elements of the *Miranda* rule:

- custodial interrogation,
- public safety exception,
- three-part warning,
- invocation of *Miranda* rights,
- interrogation, and
- waiver of and right to counsel.

In reading this chapter, you will see that although the Supreme Court affirmed the constitutional status of the *Miranda* decision, the requirements of *Miranda* are constantly being adjusted in an effort to balance *Miranda*'s protection of suspects against society's interest in obtaining confessions. As you progress through the chapter, ask yourself whether the *Miranda* warnings provide adequate protection for defendants. In the alternative, does *Miranda* handcuff the police? In addition, consider whether the *Miranda* rules are too complex to be easily absorbed by police, lawyers, and judges. We start by examining custodial interrogation.

Custodial Interrogation

The *Miranda* warnings are triggered when an individual is in custody and interrogated. The *Miranda* decision defines **custodial interrogation** as "questioning initiated by law enforcement officers after a person has been taken into custody or otherwise deprived of his [or her] freedom of action in any significant way." In *Beckwith v. United States,* the Supreme Court clarified that a *focus* by law enforcement on an individual is not sufficient to require the reading of the *Miranda* rights. In *Beckwith,* two Internal Revenue Service (IRS) agents interviewed Beckwith for three hours in a private home; the conversation was described by one of the agents as "friendly" and "relaxed." The Supreme Court held that being the focus of an investigation does not involve the inherently coercive pressures that *Miranda* described as inherent in incommunicado custodial interrogation (*Beckwith v. United States,* 425 U.S. 341 [1976]).

What then is meant by custodial interrogation? *Miranda* stated that it is not considered custody and the *Miranda* warnings are not required when the police engage in general questioning at a crime scene or other general investigative questioning of potential witnesses. The *Miranda* warnings also need not be given to an individual who voluntarily enters a police station and wishes to confess to a crime or to a person who voluntarily calls the police to offer a confession or other statement. On the other hand, the *Miranda* warnings are required when an individual is subjected to a custodial arrest and to interrogation. At this point, an individual is under the control of the police and likely will be subjected to incommunicado interrogation in an isolated and unfamiliar environment.

The challenge is to determine at what point, short of being informed that he or she is under custodial arrest, an individual is exposed to pressures that are the "functional equivalent of custodial arrest" and the *Miranda* rights must be read. What if you are walking home and are stopped by the police late at night and they ask what you are doing in the neighborhood? This has important consequences for law enforcement. Requiring *Miranda* warnings whenever an officer comes in contact with a citizen would impede questioning. This might make sense because every citizen interaction with an officer is somewhat intimidating and coercive. On the other hand, requiring a clearly coercive environment before the *Miranda* warnings are required would limit the *Miranda* warnings to a narrow set of circumstances. How does the Supreme Court resolve these considerations? At what point short of a custodial arrest are the *Miranda* warnings required.

The Supreme Court adopted an "objective test" for custodial interrogation that requires judges to evaluate the totality of the circumstances. In *Stansbury v. California,* the Supreme Court held that "the initial determination of custody depends on the objective circumstances of the interrogation, not on the subjective views harbored by either the interrogating officers or the person being questioned" (*Stansbury v. California,* 511 U.S. 318, 323 [1994]).

Custodial interrogation is not based solely on the seriousness of the crime for which you have been stopped and questioned or based simply on the location of the interrogation. Custody is based on whether, in the totality of the circumstances, a reasonable person would believe that he or she is subjected to formal arrest or to police custody to a degree associated with a formal arrest (i.e., the functional equivalent of formal arrest).

Courts typically *ask whether a reasonable person would feel free to leave.* In evaluating the totality of circumstances, judges consider a number of factors. Remember, no single factor is crucial in determining whether a reasonable person would believe that he or she is subject to custodial interrogation (not free to leave). The factors to be considered include the following:

- The number of police officers
- Whether the officer tells the individual that he or she is free to leave or not free to leave
- The length and intensity of the questioning
- Whether the officer employs physical force to restrain the individual
- Whether the stop is in public or in private
- The location of the interrogation
- Whether a reasonable person would believe that the stop would be brief or whether the stop would result in a custodial arrest
- Whether the individual is in familiar or unfamiliar surroundings
- Whether the suspect is permitted to leave following the interrogation

The totality-of-the-circumstances test means that custody is determined on a case-by-case basis. Consider the Supreme Court decisions in the following cases.

Home. In *Orozco v. Texas,* the Supreme Court held that the defendant was subjected to custodial interrogation when four police officers entered his bedroom at 4:00 A.M. to interrogate him regarding a shooting (*Orozco v. Texas,* 394 U.S. 324 [1969]).

Parole interview. Murphy, a probationer, agreed to meet his probation officer regarding his "treatment plan" and, during the meeting, admitted that he had committed a rape and murder. The Supreme Court found that Murphy was familiar both with the surroundings and with his probation officer and that he was not physically restrained and could have left at any time. The possibility that terminating the meeting would lead to revocation of probation, in the view of the Court, was not comparable to the pressure on a criminal suspect who is not free to walk away from interrogation by the police (*Minnesota v. Murphy,* 465 U.S. 420 [1984]).

Police station. In *Oregon v. Mathiason,* Carl Mathiason, a parolee, voluntarily appeared at the police station at the request of an officer. Mathiason confessed after the officer stated that he believed that the suspect was involved in a recent burglary, falsely told Mathiason that his fingerprints had been discovered at the scene of the crime, and explained that truthfulness would possibly be considered in mitigation at sentencing. The Supreme Court determined that there was no custodial interrogation because the defendant voluntarily came to the station house, was informed that he was not under arrest, and left following the interview (*Oregon v. Mathiason,* 429 U.S. 492 [1977]).

Prison. A prison inmate who is interrogated regarding a crime for which he was not incarcerated is considered to be in custody. Courts have recently held that an inmate is in custody for purposes of *Miranda* only when the interrogation is associated with tighter controls and restrictions than an inmate normally experiences in prison (*Mathis v. United States,* 391 U.S. 1 [1968]).

Traffic stop. In *Berkemer v. McCarty,* McCarty was stopped by Highway Patrol Officer Williams who observed McCarty weaving in and out of a lane. Williams observed that McCarty experienced difficulty with his balance when he exited the vehicle and concluded that he would charge him with a traffic arrest and take him into custody. McCarty was unable to successfully complete a field sobriety test and in response to questions admitted that he had consumed several beers and marijuana. McCarty was taken into custody without being read his *Miranda* rights and made several additional incriminating statements. McCarty was subsequently convicted of the first-degree misdemeanor of operating a motor vehicle while under the influence of drugs or alcohol. McCarty appealed and argued that he was in custody when pulled over by Officer Williams and should have been read his *Miranda* rights.

The Supreme Court rejected the argument that the *Miranda* warnings are required only for felonies. The Court nonetheless ruled that McCarty was not in custody when initially required to pull over, ruling that a traffic stop normally does not exert pressures that significantly impair an individual's exercise of his or her Fifth Amendment right against self-incrimination. Traffic stops presumably are brief and public and typically are not police dominated. The Supreme Court also held that between the initial stop and the custodial arrest, McCarty was not subject to constraints "comparable" to formal arrest. During this relatively short period, Williams did not communicate his intent to arrest McCarty, and his unarticulated plan was considered to have little relevance to the question of custody. The relevant inquiry in determining whether an individual is in custody is how a reasonable person in the suspect's situation would understand his or her situation. Would a reasonable person feel free to leave (not in custody), or would a reasonable person feel that his or her freedom of movement was restricted (custody)? In this case, a single police officer asked a limited number of questions and requested that McCarty perform a field sobriety test. The Supreme Court held that McCarty was not subjected to the "functional equivalent of formal arrest" (*Berkemer v. McCarty,* 468 U.S. 420 [1984]).

Apply what you have read to *Yarborough v. Alvarado,* which is the Supreme Court's most recent attempt to outline the factors to be considered in determining whether a defendant is subjected to custodial interrogation. The judgment is important for establishing that in applying the reasonable person standard, an individual's age, experience, and other personal characteristics are not to be considered.

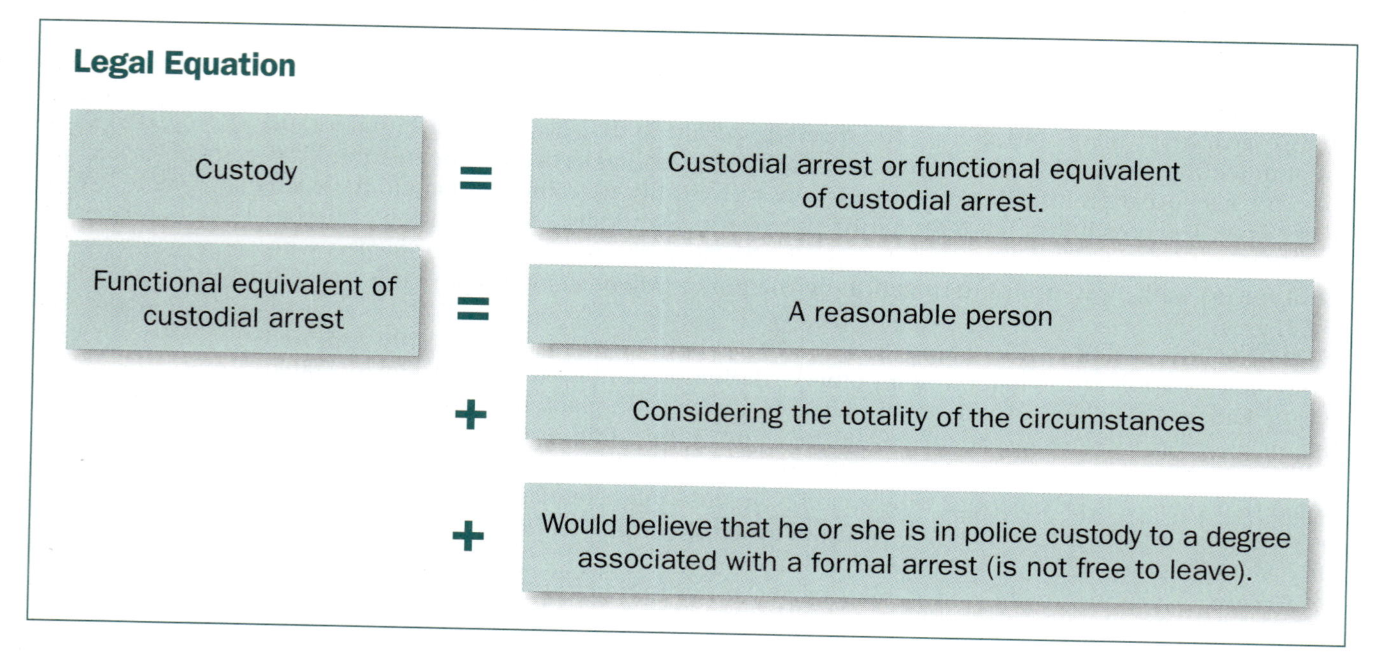

Was Alvarado in custody?

Yarborough v. Alvarado, 541 U.S. 652 (2004), Kennedy, J.

Facts

Paul Soto and respondent Michael Alvarado attempted to steal a truck in the parking lot of a shopping mall in Santa Fe Springs, California. Soto and Alvarado were part of a larger group of teenagers at the mall that night. Soto decided to steal the truck, and Alvarado agreed to help. Soto pulled out a .357 Magnum and approached the driver, Francisco Castaneda, who was standing near the truck emptying trash into a dumpster. Soto demanded money and the ignition keys from Castaneda. Alvarado, then five months short of his eighteenth birthday, approached the passenger side door of the truck and crouched down. When Castaneda refused to comply with Soto's demands, Soto shot Castaneda, killing him. Alvarado then helped hide Soto's gun.

Los Angeles County Sheriff's detective Cheryl Comstock led the investigation into the circumstances of

Castaneda's death. About a month after the shooting, Comstock left word at Alvarado's house and also contacted Alvarado's mother at work with the message that she wished to speak with Alvarado. Alvarado's parents brought him to the Pico Rivera Sheriff's Station to be interviewed around lunchtime. They waited in the lobby while Alvarado went with Comstock to be interviewed. Alvarado contends that his parents asked to be present during the interview but were rebuffed.

Comstock brought Alvarado to a small interview room and began interviewing him at about 12:30 P.M. The interview lasted about two hours and was recorded by Comstock with Alvarado's knowledge. Only Comstock and Alvarado were present. Alvarado was not given a warning under *Miranda v. Arizona.* Comstock began the interview by asking Alvarado to recount the events on the night of the shooting. On that night, Alvarado explained, he had been drinking alcohol at a friend's house with some other friends and acquaintances. After a few hours, part of the group went home and the rest walked to a nearby mall to use its public telephones. In Alvarado's initial telling, that was the end of it. The group went back to the friend's home and "just went to bed." Unpersuaded, Comstock pressed on. . . .

At this point, Alvarado slowly began to change his story. First, he acknowledged being present when the carjacking occurred but claimed that he did not know what happened or who had a gun. When he hesitated to say more, Comstock tried to encourage Alvarado to discuss what happened by appealing to his sense of honesty and the need to bring the man who shot Castaneda to justice. . . . Alvarado then admitted he had helped the other man try to steal the truck by standing near the passenger side door. Next, he admitted that the other man was Paul Soto, that he knew Soto was armed, and that he had helped hide the gun after the murder. Alvarado explained that he had expected Soto to scare the driver with the gun, but that he did not expect Soto to kill anyone. Toward the end of the interview, Comstock twice asked Alvarado if he needed to take a break. Alvarado declined. When the interview was over, Comstock returned with Alvarado to the lobby of the sheriff's station where his parents were waiting. Alvarado's father drove him home.

A few months later, the State of California charged Soto and Alvarado with first-degree murder and attempted robbery. . . . Alvarado moved to suppress his statements from the Comstock interview. The trial court denied the motion on the ground that the interview was noncustodial. . . . The jury convicted Soto and Alvarado of first-degree murder and attempted robbery. The trial judge later reduced Alvarado's conviction to second-degree murder for his comparatively minor role in the offense. The judge sentenced Soto to life in prison and Alvarado to fifteen-years-to-life. . . . The California District Court of Appeals affirmed.

The Court of Appeals for the Ninth Circuit reversed. . . . [T]he Court of Appeals held that the state court erred in failing to account for Alvarado's youth and inexperience when evaluating whether a reasonable person in his position would have felt free to leave. It noted that this Court has considered a suspect's juvenile status when evaluating the voluntariness of confessions and the waiver of the privilege against self-incrimination. . . . In light of the clearly established law considering juvenile status, it was "simply unreasonable to conclude that a reasonable seventeen-year-old, with no prior history of arrest or police interviews, would have felt that he was at liberty to terminate the interrogation and leave."

Issue

The issue before the Supreme Court is whether Alvarado should have been provided with *Miranda* warnings. . . .

Reasoning

Fair-minded jurists could disagree over whether Alvarado was in custody. On one hand, certain facts weigh against a finding that Alvarado was in custody. The police did not transport Alvarado to the station or require him to appear at a particular time. They did not threaten him or suggest he would be placed under arrest. Alvarado's parents remained in the lobby during the interview, suggesting that the interview would be brief. In fact, according to trial counsel for Alvarado, he and his parents were told that the interview was "not going to be long." During the interview, Comstock focused on Soto's crimes rather than Alvarado's. Instead of pressuring Alvarado with the threat of arrest and prosecution, she appealed to his interest in telling the truth and being helpful to a police officer. In addition, Comstock twice asked Alvarado if he wanted to take a break. At the end of the interview, Alvarado went home. All of these objective facts are consistent with an interrogation environment in which a reasonable person would have felt free to terminate the interview and leave. . . .

Other facts point in the opposite direction. Comstock interviewed Alvarado at the police station. The interview lasted two hours. . . . Comstock did not tell Alvarado that he was free to leave. Alvarado was brought to the police station by his legal guardians rather than arriving on his own accord, making the extent of his control over his presence unclear. Counsel for Alvarado alleges that Alvarado's parents asked to be present at the interview but were rebuffed, a fact that—if known to Alvarado—might reasonably have led someone in Alvarado's position to feel more restricted than otherwise. These facts weigh in favor of the view that Alvarado was in custody.

The Ninth Circuit placed considerable reliance on Alvarado's age and inexperience with law enforcement. Our Court has not stated that a suspect's age or experience is relevant to the *Miranda* custody analysis. . . . The objective test furthers "the clarity of *Miranda,* ensuring that the police do not need to make guesses . . . [in] deciding how they may interrogate the suspect." . . .

Holding

These differing indications lead us to hold that the state court's application of our custody standard was reasonable. The court of appeals was nowhere close to the mark when it concluded otherwise. . . .

Dissenting, *Breyer, J.*, joined by *Stevens, J.*, *Souter, J.*, and *Ginsburg, J.*

Would a reasonable person in Alvarado's position have felt free simply to get up and walk out of the small room in the station house at will during his two-hour police interrogation? I ask the reader to put himself, or herself, in Alvarado's circumstances and then answer that question: Alvarado hears from his parents that he is needed for police questioning. His parents take him to the station. On arrival, a police officer separates him from his parents. His parents ask to come along, but the officer says they may not. . . .

The police take Alvarado to a small interrogation room, away from the station's public area. A single officer begins to question him, making clear in the process that the police have evidence that he participated in an attempted carjacking connected with a murder. When he says that he never saw any shooting, the officer suggests that he is lying, while adding that she is "giving [him] the opportunity to tell the truth" and "take care of himself." Toward the end of the questioning, the officer gives him permission to take a bathroom or water break. After two hours, by which time he has admitted he was involved in the attempted theft, knew about the gun, and helped to hide it, the questioning ends. . . . A reasonable person would not have thought he was free simply to pick up and leave. . . . In this case, common sense and an understanding of the law's basic purpose in this area are enough to make clear that Alvarado's age—an objective, widely shared characteristic about which the police plainly knew—is also relevant to the inquiry. Unless one is prepared to pretend that Alvarado is someone he is not, a middle-aged gentleman, well-versed in police practices, it seems to me clear that the California courts made a serious mistake. I agree with the Ninth Circuit's similar conclusions. Consequently, I dissent.

Questions for Discussion

1. What legal test was used by the Supreme Court to determine whether Alvarado was subjected to custodial interrogation? List the facts relied on by the majority in concluding that Alvarado was not subjected to custodial interrogation. Summarize the facts that support the dissenting justices' view that Alvarado was subjected to custodial interrogation.
2. How could you change the facts to result in a majority of the judges holding that Alvarado was subjected to custodial interrogation?
3. The Ninth Circuit Court of Appeals considered what a "reasonable seventeen-year-old with no prior history of arrest or police interviews" would perceive. Explain why the Supreme Court held that the reasonable person standard should not take the suspect's age or background into consideration. Do you agree? What if Alvarado was fifteen years old?
4. How would you rule in this case?
5. ***Problems in policing.*** *Yarborough* illustrates the challenge in applying the totality-of-the-circumstances approach to custody. Write a brief set of guidelines informing police officers how they can lawfully interrogate a suspect at the station house without being required to read the *Miranda* rights. For instance, in some jurisdictions, the police will inform suspects that voluntarily come to police headquarters that they are not under arrest and are free to leave. This reinforces that the interrogation is a voluntary encounter and that the *Miranda* rights are not required to be read. This is often referred to as the *Beheler* warning based on the tactics employed in *California v. Beheler* (463 U.S. 1121 [1983]).
6. *Illinois v. Perkins,* which you will find on the Web site, discusses whether the use of government informants in prison constitutes custodial interrogation. Is the government required to read an inmate his or her *Miranda* rights? See *Illinois v. Perkins,* 496 U.S. 292 (1990).

You will find Illinois v. Perkins *on the study site, http://www.sagepub.com/lippmancp.*

8.3 YOU DECIDE

Mesa shot both his wife and daughter and barricaded himself in a hotel room. FBI agents surrounded the area and called on Mesa through a bullhorn to surrender. Mesa was armed, and the FBI did not know whether he was holding hostages. An FBI "hostage negotiator" and Mesa communicated over a mobile phone for over three hours. In response to questions from the negotiator, Mesa engaged in lengthy descriptions of his life and frustrations and occasionally conversed with the negotiator. Mesa made some incriminating comments during this conversation that were used against him at trial. Should Mesa have been read his *Miranda* rights? See *United States v. Mesa*, 638 F.2d 582 (3d Cir. 1980).

You can find the answer by referring to the study site, http://www.sagepub.com/lippmancp.

The Public Safety Exception

In *New York v. Quarles,* the U.S. Supreme Court recognized a **public safety exception** to *Miranda.* This exception permits the police to ask questions reasonably prompted by a concern with public safety without first advising a suspect of his or her *Miranda* rights. The Supreme Court explained that a reasonable concern with the safety of the police or the public outweighs the interest in protecting a suspect's right against self-incrimination. This "narrow exception" requires that questions be directed at public safety rather than guilt or innocence. Coerced and involuntary statements are not admissible under the public safety rule. Reliance on the public safety exception requires that the following steps be satisfied (*New York v. Quarles,* 467 U.S. 649 [1984]).

- ***Reasonableness.*** There must be a reasonable need to protect the police or the public. The exception does not depend on the officer's subjective motivation.
- ***Threat.*** There must be a reasonable belief that the threat is immediate.
- ***Questions.*** Questions must be prompted by a reasonable concern for public safety and must be directed at public safety rather than guilt or innocence.
- ***Coercion.*** The statements may not be the product of police compulsion that overcomes the suspect's will to resist.

New York v. Quarles broadly defines public safety and offers no clear guidance to lower court judges and the police. A police officer who concludes that there is a threat to public safety and who fails to administer the *Miranda* warnings may find that the trial judge disagrees and orders the confession excluded from evidence. The lack of a clear definition of public safety also runs the risk that courts will broadly interpret the public safety exception. In *United States v. Reyes,* the police arrested a narcotics dealer who an informant reported might be armed. Reyes, when asked by the arresting officer whether he had "anything in his pocket that could harm the officer," responded that he had a gun. The officer removed the firearm and repeated the question. Reyes stated that there were drugs in his car. The federal court of appeals ruled that the officer's question was directed at public safety and that the drugs were properly admitted into evidence at Reyes's trial, but the court warned of the "inherent risk that the public safety exception might be distorted into a general rule" that individuals arrested on narcotics charges could be questioned in every instance prior to reading the *Miranda* rights (*United States v. Reyes,* 353 F.3d 148, 155 [2d Cir. 2003]).

In *United States v. Newton,* police officers received a complaint from Newton's mother that Newton, a parolee, had threatened to kill her and her husband. She reported that Newton was staying in their apartment and reportedly kept a gun in a shoe box by the door. The police entered the apartment and handcuffed Newton without advising him of his *Miranda* rights. An officer asked whether Newton had any contraband in the apartment, and Newton replied, "only what is in the box." The police seized a .22 caliber automatic pistol. The Second Circuit Court of Appeals held that the question fell within the public safety exception based on the officers' knowledge that Newton possessed a gun and had recently threatened to kill two people. Although Newton was handcuffed, his girlfriend was in the apartment and might have handed Newton the gun. The officer's question concerning "contraband" could include material not presenting immediate safety concerns, but the appellate court noted that Newton clearly understood this to include weapons. The Second Circuit stressed that the police could not be expected to closely edit their questions when conducting an arrest (*United States v. Newton,* 369 F.3d 659 [2d Cir. 2004]).

You can find *New York v. Quarles* on the study site. Do the facts in *Quarles* support the claim that the public safety was endangered? Consider the argument of the dissent questioning whether law enforcement requires a public safety exception to *Miranda.* Are questions directed at public safety also relevant for a suspect's guilt or innocence?

Legal Equation

Public safety exception	=	A reasonable need to protect the police or the public
	+	A reasonable belief that the threat is immediate
	+	Questions must be prompted by a reasonable concern for public safety and directed at public safety rather than guilt or innocence
	+	The statements may not be the product of police compulsion that overcomes the suspect's will to resist.

8.4 YOU DECIDE

Carrillo was arrested for selling narcotics and was transported to the detention facility. Before beginning to search Carrillo and prior to reading Carrillo his *Miranda* rights, Officer Weeks asked Carrillo "if he had any drugs or needles on his person." Carrillo responded, "No, I don't use drugs, I sell them." Weeks asked no additional questions. Is Carrillo's response admissible under the public safety exception? See *United States v. Carrillo,* 16 F.3d 1046 (9th Cir. 1994).

You will find the answer by referring to the study site, http://www.sagepub.com/lippmancp.

8.5 YOU DECIDE

John Wayne Dean and his wife kidnapped Ellen, the daughter of a wealthy family, and demanded a ransom. Throughout the negotiation, there was no indication whether the young woman was dead or alive or how she was being treated. Four days later, FBI agents staked out the "drop location." Agent Krahling spotted Dean in the woods, armed with a pistol. Krahling pointed a shotgun at Dean and ordered him to throw down his gun. He then drew his pistol and ordered Dean to lie on the ground. Krahling proceeded to handcuff Dean and holstered his service revolver. In response to a question from Krahling, Dean then revealed where Ellen was being held, and she subsequently was rescued. Does the public safety exception extend to the protection of a single member of the public? See *People v. Dean,* 114 Cal. Rptr. 555 (Cal. App. 1974).

You will find the answer by referring to the study site, http://www.sagepub.com/lippmancp.

The *Miranda* Warnings

The three-part ***Miranda* warnings** inform suspects of their Fifth Amendment rights and the consequences of waiving these rights. These warnings require that the police inform individuals of the right to remain silent, that anything they say may be used against them, and of their right to an attorney, retained or appointed. The *Miranda* judgment specifies that the rights are to be recited in "clear and unequivocal terms" and that a suspect should be "clearly informed" of his or her rights. At this point, you might want to review the Supreme Court's explanation as to why the police are required to read *Miranda* rights to suspects.

These rights may be communicated to a suspect verbally, or a suspect may be asked to read the rights for himself or herself. In practice, the police typically employ both approaches. How should the rights be read to a suspect? As a judge, you might take the position that the rights must be read as set forth in the *Miranda* decision. On the other hand, you might take the position that a suspect's rights can be effectively communicated without using the precise language of the *Miranda* judgment. This would be a practical recognition that an officer in the field may not have access to a *Miranda* card or may inadvertently depart from the required warnings. What are the costs and benefits of these alternative approaches?

The Supreme Court has provided broad guidance to the police on how to recite the *Miranda* warnings. *Miranda is a flexible formula. The test is whether the warnings viewed in their totality convey the essential information to the suspect.*

In 1981, in *California v. Prysock,* Police Sergeant Byrd told the suspect, Randall Prysock, that he had "the right to talk to a lawyer before you are questioned, have him present with you while you are being questioned, and all during the questioning." Prysock then was informed that as a juvenile, he had the right to have his "parents present, which they are." Sergeant Byrd completed the warnings on Randall's right to a lawyer by advising Prysock that "you have the right to have a lawyer appointed to represent you at no cost to yourself." Mrs. Prysock stated that she "didn't understand," inquired if her son "could still have an attorney at a later time if he gave a statement now without one," and agreed that Randall would talk to the Sergeant (*California v. Prysock,* 453 U.S. 355, 356, 357 [1981]).

The outcome of this case centered on the meaning of the term *represent.* Does this mean that a lawyer will be appointed to represent Randall at trial while Randall would have to pay for any attorney before that time? Did Sergeant Byrd contribute to the confusion by giving two separate warnings regarding the right to a lawyer and using the term *represent* rather than the term *consult,* which is the term used in the *Miranda* decision? The U.S. Supreme Court majority ruled that the "rigidity" of *Miranda* does not extend to the precise formulation of the warnings given a criminal defendant. The judges noted that the *Miranda* judgment indicates that "no talismanic incantation" was required to satisfy its strictures. Three dissenting judges argued that Sergeant Byrd's warnings did not adequately inform Prysock of his rights and that "a lawyer appointed to represent you" could reasonably have been understood by Mrs. Prysock to refer to a lawyer at trial.

If Miranda is not a *talismanic incantation,* how much flexibility is permitted? At what point are the rights so inadequately and incoherently read that a suspect is not fully and effectively informed of his or her rights? In *Duckworth v. Eagan,* the defendant was arrested for an attempted murder and was informed that he had the right to the advice and presence of a lawyer, "even if you cannot afford to hire one." Eagan then was told that "we have no way of giving you a lawyer, but one will be appointed for you, if you wish, if and when you go to court." The police officer then stated that Eagan had the right to answer or not to answer questions and that he had "the right to stop answering at any time until you've talked to a lawyer." The Supreme Court pointed out that the "if and when language" merely provided the defendant with the additional information that in Indiana, lawyers are appointed at the defendant's initial appearance in court and that, if he requested an appointed attorney, the police would not question him until a lawyer was present (*Duckworth v. Eagan,* 492 U.S. 195 [1989]).

The Supreme Court stressed that the warnings in their totality satisfied *Miranda* and, most important, that Eagan was informed of his immediate right to a lawyer and right to refuse to answer questions until a lawyer was present. The test was whether the warnings *reasonably conveyed the Miranda rights.* The Supreme Court majority stressed that judges should not closely examine every word of the *Miranda* warnings as if "construing a will or defining the terms of an easement." The four dissenting judges observed that the "if and when you go to court" language would reasonably lead a suspect to believe that a lawyer would not be appointed until "some indeterminate time in the future after questioning." Justice Marshall noted that an unsophisticated suspect might be understandably confused and decide to talk to the police in an "effort to extricate himself from his predicament."

In both *Prysock* and *Duckworth,* the warnings in their totality were held to satisfy the requirements of *Miranda.* On the other hand, warnings that judges have considered to fail to provide the essential information required by the *Miranda* rights or which judges have concluded are misleading have been held to be inadequate. An example of a deficient warning is the statement that the suspect had "the right to talk to an attorney and have him here with you before we ask you any questions." This warning was held to be deficient because it failed to inform the suspect of the right to an attorney during questioning. The same court also rejected as inadequate a verbal warning that "if you decide to answer questions now without an attorney present, you will give up the right to stop answering questions until you speak to an attorney." This distorted the fact that a suspect could stop answering questions at any time (*Brown v. Crosby,* 249 F. Supp. 2d 1285, 1304 [S.D. Fla. 2003]).

In 2001, the Supreme Court unanimously ruled that it would not review the lower court judgment in *Bridgers v. Texas.* Three justices took advantage of this occasion to announce that they would not approve of warnings that failed to fully inform suspects of their *Miranda* rights. The police in *Bridgers* neglected to inform the defendant that he had the right to consult an attorney not only prior to but also during questioning. The three justices wrote that the warnings left out "an essential...element" and warned in the event that this problem "proves to be a recurring one...it may well warrant the Court's attention" (*Bridgers v. Texas,* 532 U.S. 1034 [2001]).

The Supreme Court also has been reluctant to require the police to expand the warnings beyond the three-part warning required in the *Miranda* judgment. In *Colorado v. Spring,* Spring waived his rights presumably thinking that he would be interrogated by federal agents on an illegal gun charge and then was surprised with a question regarding a homicide. The Supreme Court held that Spring's admission that he had "shot [a] guy once" was admissible. The Court explained that Spring had been read his *Miranda* rights and that it was neither trickery nor deception for the police to fail to inform him of the topic of interrogation (*Colorado v. Spring,* 479 U.S. 546 [1987]). The next case in the text, *Moran v. Burbine,* asks whether the police are required to go beyond the warnings required in the *Miranda* judgment and inform a suspect of the availability of an attorney.

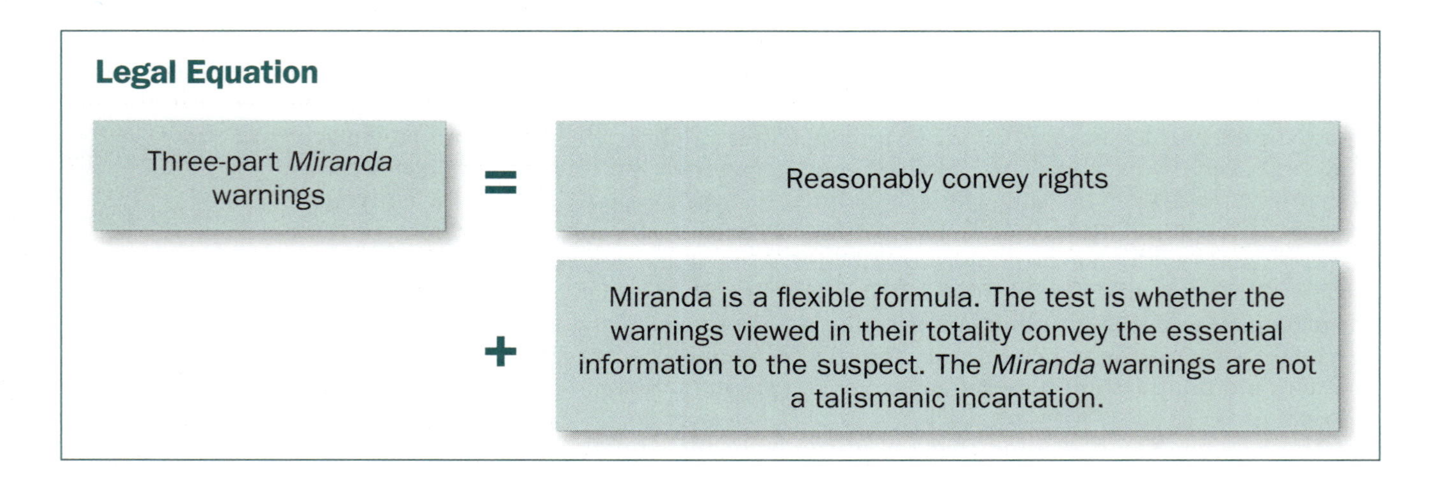

Was Burbine adequately informed of his right to access to a lawyer?

Moran v. Burbine, 475 U.S. 412 (1986), O'Connor, J.

Facts

On the morning of March 3, 1977, Mary Jo Hickey was found unconscious in a factory parking lot in Providence, Rhode Island. Suffering from injuries to her skull apparently inflicted by a metal pipe found at the scene, she was rushed to a nearby hospital. Three weeks later, she died from her wounds.

Several months after her death, the Cranston, Rhode Island, police arrested respondent and two others in connection with a local burglary. Shortly before the arrest, Detective Ferranti of the Cranston police force had learned from a confidential informant that the man responsible for Ms. Hickey's death lived at a certain address and went by the name of "Butch." Upon discovering that respondent lived at that address and was known by that name, Detective Ferranti informed respondent of his *Miranda* rights. When respondent refused to execute a written waiver, Detective Ferranti spoke separately with the two other suspects arrested on the breaking and entering charge and obtained statements further implicating respondent in Ms. Hickey's murder. At approximately 6 P.M., Detective Ferranti telephoned the police in Providence to convey the information he had uncovered. An hour later, three officers from that department arrived at the Cranston headquarters for the purpose of questioning respondent about the murder.

That same evening, at about 7:45 P.M., respondent's sister telephoned the public defender's office to obtain legal assistance for her brother. Her sole concern was the breaking and entering charge, as she was unaware that respondent was then under suspicion for murder. She asked for Richard Casparian, who had been scheduled to meet with respondent earlier that afternoon to discuss another charge unrelated to either the break-in or the murder. As soon as the conversation ended, the attorney who took the call attempted to reach Mr. Casparian. When those efforts were unsuccessful, she telephoned Allegra Munson, another assistant public defender, and told her about respondent's arrest and his sister's subsequent request that the office represent him.

At 8:15 P.M., Ms. Munson telephoned the Cranston police station and asked that her call be transferred to the detective division. A male voice responded with the word "Detectives." Ms. Munson identified herself and asked if Brian Burbine was being held; the person responded affirmatively. Ms. Munson explained to the person that Burbine was represented by attorney Casparian who was not available; she further stated that she would act as Burbine's legal counsel in the event that the police intended to place him in a lineup or question him. The unidentified person told Ms. Munson that the police would not be questioning Burbine or putting him in a lineup and that they were through with him for the night. Ms. Munson was not informed that the Providence Police were at the Cranston police station or that Burbine was a suspect in Mary's murder. At all relevant times, respondent was unaware of his sister's efforts to retain counsel and of the fact and contents of Ms. Munson's telephone conversation.

Less than an hour later, the police brought respondent to an interrogation room and conducted the first of a series of interviews concerning the murder. Prior to each session, respondent was informed of his *Miranda* rights, and on three separate occasions, he signed a written form acknowledging that he understood his right to the presence of an attorney and explicitly indicating that he "[did] not want an attorney called or appointed for [him]" before he gave a statement. Uncontradicted evidence at the suppression hearing indicated that at least twice during the course of the evening, respondent was left in a room where he had access to a telephone, which he apparently declined to use. Eventually, respondent signed three written statements fully admitting to the murder.

Prior to trial, respondent moved to suppress the statements. The court denied the motion, finding that respondent had received the *Miranda* warnings and had "knowingly, intelligently, and voluntarily waived his privilege against self-incrimination [and] his right to counsel." The jury found respondent guilty of murder in the first degree, and he appealed to the Supreme Court of Rhode Island. A divided court rejected his contention that the Fifth and Fourteenth Amendments to the Constitution required the suppression of the inculpatory statements and affirmed the conviction.

Issues

We granted certiorari to decide whether a prearraignment confession preceded by an otherwise valid waiver must be suppressed either because the police misinformed an inquiring attorney about their plans concerning the suspect or because they failed to inform the suspect of the attorney's efforts to reach him.

Reasoning

The record amply supports the state-court findings that the police administered the required warnings, sought to assure that respondent understood his rights, and obtained an express written waiver prior to eliciting each of the three statements. Nor does respondent contest the Rhode Island courts' determination that he at no point requested the presence of a lawyer. He contends instead that the confessions must be suppressed because the police's failure to inform him of the attorney's telephone call deprived him of information essential to his ability to knowingly waive his Fifth Amendment rights. In the alternative, he suggests that to fully protect the Fifth Amendment values served by *Miranda,* we should extend that decision to condemn the conduct of the Providence police....

The purpose of the *Miranda* warnings instead is to dissipate the compulsion inherent in custodial interrogation and, in so doing, guard against abridgment of the suspect's Fifth Amendment rights. Clearly, a rule that focuses on how the police treat an attorney—conduct that has no relevance at all to the degree of compulsion experienced by the defendant during interrogation—would ignore both *Miranda*'s mission and its only source of legitimacy.

Nor are we prepared to adopt a rule requiring that the police inform a suspect of an attorney's efforts to reach him. While such a rule might add marginally to *Miranda*'s goal of dispelling the compulsion inherent in custodial interrogation, overriding practical considerations counsel against its adoption. As we have stressed on numerous occasions, "[one] of the principal advantages" of *Miranda* is the ease and clarity of its application.... We have little doubt that the approach urged by respondent... would have the inevitable consequence of muddying *Miranda*'s otherwise relatively clear waters. The legal questions it would spawn are legion: To what extent should the police be held accountable for knowing that the accused has counsel? Is it enough that someone in the station house knows, or must the interrogating officer himself know of counsel's efforts to contact the suspect? Do counsel's efforts to talk to the suspect concerning one criminal investigation trigger the obligation to inform the defendant before interrogation may proceed on a wholly separate matter?...

Holding

The position urged by respondent would upset this carefully drawn approach in a manner that is both unnecessary for the protection of the Fifth Amendment privilege and injurious to legitimate law enforcement. Because, as *Miranda* holds, full comprehension of the rights to remain silent and request an attorney are sufficient to dispel whatever coercion is inherent in the interrogation process, a rule requiring the police to inform the suspect of an attorney's efforts to contact him would contribute to the protection of the Fifth Amendment privilege only incidentally, if at all. This minimal benefit, however, would come at a substantial cost to society's legitimate and substantial interest in securing admissions of guilt. Indeed, the very premise of the court of appeals was not that awareness of Ms. Munson's phone call would have dissipated the coercion of the interrogation room, but that it might have convinced respondent not to speak at all. Because neither the letter nor purposes of *Miranda* require this additional handicap on otherwise permissible investigatory efforts, we are unwilling to expand the *Miranda* rules to require the police to keep the suspect abreast of the status of his legal representation....

Dissenting, *Stevens, J.,* joined by *Brennan, J.,* and *Marshall, J.*

What is the cost of requiring the police to inform a suspect of his attorney's call? It would decrease the likelihood that custodial interrogation will enable the police to obtain a confession. This is certainly a real cost, but it is the same cost that this Court has repeatedly found necessary to preserve the character of our free society.... Just as the "cost" does not justify taking a suspect into custody or interrogating him without giving him warnings simply because police desire to question him, so too the "cost" does not justify permitting police to withhold from a suspect knowledge of an attorney's communication, even though that communication would have an unquestionable effect on the suspect's exercise of his rights. The "cost" that concerns the Court amounts to nothing more than an acknowledgment that the law enforcement interest in obtaining convictions suffers whenever a suspect exercises the rights that are afforded by our system of criminal justice....

In my view, as a matter of law, the police deception of Munson was tantamount to deception of Burbine himself. It constituted a violation of Burbine's right to have an attorney present during the questioning that began shortly thereafter.... If a lawyer is seen as a nettlesome obstacle to the pursuit of wrongdoers... then the Court's decision today makes a good deal of sense. If a lawyer is seen as an aid to the understanding and protection of constitutional rights... then today's decision makes no sense at all....

Questions for Discussion

1. Why does the Supreme Court hold that the police are not required to inform Burbine of the availability of a lawyer? What problems would requiring this warning create in terms of judicial supervision of the *Miranda* rule?
2. What is your reaction to the Court's holding that the inadvertent or intentional misleading of a lawyer is not relevant in determining whether Burbine's waiver was knowing, voluntary, and intelligent?
3. What if Burbine signed a contract with a lawyer providing that "if I am ever arrested, you are obligated to advise me during any police interrogation"? Would the police be obligated under this contract to inform Burbine that his lawyer was at the police station and ready to assist him under such circumstances?
4. Do you believe that Burbine's waiver was knowing, voluntary, and intelligent in light of the fact that he was not informed of the availability of a public defender?
5. ***Problems in policing.*** Write a policy guideline for the police discussing the reading of the *Miranda* warnings and detailing how the police should treat a lawyer who appears at a police station while a suspect is being subjected to custodial interrogation.

Cases and Comments

Criminal Procedure in the States. Several state supreme courts have rejected the Supreme Court's reasoning in *Burbine* and have held that their state constitutions require the police to inform a defendant of an attorney's immediate availability.

In *People v. McCauley,* the police brought McCauley to the Chicago Area Three police station in connection with a shooting death. Detectives Kocan and Byron advised McCauley of his *Miranda* rights, and he offered an alibi statement. After roughly thirty minutes, the officers told their supervisor that they were leaving to interview witnesses to the shooting. Roughly thirty minutes later, at 7:00 P.M., attorney William O. Walters received a phone call from McCauley's family. Walters phoned a number of police stations, including Area Three, and was informed that the suspect was not there. He nevertheless went to the Area Three station and asked to speak to McCauley. The desk sergeant telephoned upstairs and, at roughly 7:40 P.M., Sergeant Bonke came downstairs and told Walters that he could not speak with McCauley and that McCauley had not asked to speak with a lawyer in any event. They disagreed over whether McCauley's constitutional rights were being violated. Bonke told Walters that McCauley was voluntarily at the station and was not a target of the investigation. Bonke said that he would call Walters if McCauley became a target. Walters waited at the station ten more minutes and left at 8:00 P.M. Bonke disputed much of Walters's testimony.

Detectives Kocan and Byron returned to Area Three between 8:00 P.M. and 8:15 P.M. and told McCauley that his alibi had not been corroborated. Around 10:00 P.M., McCauley was identified in a lineup. An hour later, McCauley was again interrogated and repeated his earlier alibi. At roughly 1:00 A.M., Kocan successfully located the defendant's alibi witnesses and told McCauley that they did not support his story. He was subsequently charged with the shooting.

The Illinois Supreme Court observed that a state is free to interpret its constitution to provide greater protections than are available under the U.S. Constitution. A suspect's right against self-incrimination is guaranteed by the Fifth and Fourteenth Amendments of the U.S. Constitution and by Article I, Section 10 of the Illinois Constitution. The Illinois Supreme Court held that the state constitutional guarantees "simply do not permit police to delude custodial suspects...into falsely believing they are without immediately available legal counsel and to also prevent that counsel from accessing and assisting their clients during the interrogation." This constitutes an interference with the client–attorney relationship and places pressure on the police to extract a confession before the suspect requests or learns of the presence of a lawyer.

The Illinois Supreme Court stressed that "if a defendant is entitled to the benefit of an attorney's assistance and presence during custodial interrogation...certainly fundamental fairness requires that immediately available assistance and presence not be denied by police authorities." The Supreme Court concluded that McCauley had been denied the information required to make a voluntary, knowing, and intelligent waiver and that it was contrary to the American constitutional system to fear the consequences of individuals' exercise of their rights and liberties. Statements made after Walters was denied access to McCauley accordingly should be suppressed. Do you believe that McCauley would have invoked his right to counsel if informed that his family had contacted a lawyer who was available to talk to him. Do you support the approach of the Illinois Supreme Court? See *People v. McCauley,* 163 Ill. 2d 414 (Ill. 1994).

8.6 YOU DECIDE

Connell was charged with theft. He received a verbal *Miranda* warning that provided that "if you cannot afford a lawyer, one may be appointed for you." The written *Miranda* warning provided that if he could not afford a lawyer, "arrangements will be made to obtain one for you in accordance with the law." Did Connell receive adequate *Miranda* warnings? See *United States v. Connell*, 869 F.2d 1349 (9th Cir. 1989).

You can find the answer by referring to the study site, http://www.sagepub.com/lippmancp.

Invoking the *Miranda* Rights

Following the reading of the *Miranda* rights, a defendant may assert his or her right to a lawyer or right to silence or may waive both of these rights. Is it sufficient that a defendant indicates that he or she "might" want a lawyer or "probably" should remain silent? Are the police required to ask the defendant to clarify his or her intent?

In *Davis v. United States,* Davis, a member of the Navy, was suspected of murdering another sailor and, when interviewed by the Naval Investigative Service, initially waived his *Miranda* rights. An hour and a half into the interview, Davis blurted out that "maybe I should talk to a lawyer." One of the agents later testified at trial that we made it clear that we "weren't going to pursue the matter unless we have it clarified is he asking for a lawyer or is he just making a comment about a lawyer." Davis replied, "No, I'm not asking for a lawyer," and then added, "No, I don't want a lawyer." Following a break in the interrogation, the investigators again read Davis his *Miranda* rights, and the interview continued for an additional hour. At this point, Davis asserted, "I think I want a lawyer before I say anything," and the investigators stopped their interrogation (*Davis v. United States,* 512 U.S. 452 [1994]).

Did Davis invoke his right to an attorney when he remarked that "maybe" he should talk to a lawyer? Was he then impermissibly persuaded to continue the interrogation as a result of the investigators' request for clarification? The U.S. Supreme Court held that an individual intending to assert his or her right to have counsel present must articulate this "sufficiently clearly that a reasonable police officer in the circumstances would understand the statement to be a request for an attorney." A rule that required the police to cease questioning following an ambiguous statement by the accused would transform *Miranda* into a "wholly irrational obstacle to interrogations."

In other words, the investigators were free to continue interrogating Davis following his ambiguous statement as to whether he "should talk to a lawyer" They were not required to clarify his intent. In fact, in an effort to clarify a suspect's statement, the police might be accused of influencing the suspect to waive his or her right to an attorney. For example, in *Hart v. A.G.,* a police officer was asked by the suspect about the pros and cons of hiring a lawyer. The Eleventh Circuit Court of Appeals ruled that an officer had discouraged the suspect from invoking his right to an attorney when the officer stated that "I'm going to want to ask you questions and he's [the lawyer] going to tell you can't answer me," but I am telling you that "honesty wouldn't hurt" (*Hart v. A.G.,* 323 F.3d 884 [11th Cir. 2003]).

Justice Souter, writing on behalf of four concurring judges in *Davis,* observed that the Court's ruling in *Davis* would impose a special hardship on the poor and uneducated and on women and minorities. These individuals were particularly likely to feel overwhelmed by the interrogation process and would find it difficult to assert themselves. Justice Souter accordingly favored requiring the police to clarify ambiguous statements that might "reasonably be understood" as expressing a desire for the protection of a lawyer.

In another important ruling, the Supreme Court held in *Fare v. Michael C.* that the right to a lawyer did not encompass a juvenile's request to talk to his probation officer and that the juvenile's confession was properly admitted at his murder trial. The Supreme Court explained that lawyers, rather than probation officers, clergy, or friends, are trained and equipped to protect a suspect's right against self-incrimination (*Fare v. Michael C.,* 442 U.S. 707 [1979]).

Courts also have required suspects invoking their right to silence to invoke this right in a clear and unambiguous fashion. The Seventh Circuit Court of Appeals held that a defendant's statement that he "had nothing to say" was ambiguous because it could be interpreted as either an invocation of silence or an angry response. This was not considered a clear and unambiguous assertion of the right to silence, and the police had properly continued the interrogation (*United States v. Banks,* 78 F.3d 1190, 1198 [7th Cir. 1996]).

You can find Davis v. United States *on the study site, http://www.sagepub.com/lippmancp.*

Legal Equation

Invocation of *Miranda* rights	=	Sufficiently clear that a reasonable police officer would understand that the suspect is asserting a right to a lawyer or to silence.

Waiver

A suspect, of course, may choose to waive his or her *Miranda* right to silence or right to an attorney. The Supreme Court stressed in *Miranda* that the government is required to meet a "heavy burden" in demonstrating that a suspect voluntarily, knowingly, and intelligently waived his or her rights. The *Miranda* judgment stated that a waiver requires an express statement and may not be presumed from the fact that an accused remains silent following the warnings.

What do we mean by a **voluntary, knowing, and intelligent waiver?** In *Moran v. Burbine,* the Supreme Court explained that a waiver inquiry involves a three-step process (475 U.S. 412, 421 [1985]).

Voluntary. The right must be voluntarily relinquished, it must be the product of a free and deliberate choice, and it may not be caused by intimidation, coercion, or deception. *I am doing this because I want to; the police did not make me waive my rights.*

Knowing and intelligent. The waiver must be made with a full awareness both of the nature of the right being abandoned and of the consequences of the decision to abandon the right. A suspect must possess sufficient mental competence to understand the rights and the significance of a waiver. *I know what the Miranda rights mean and what may happen to me if I talk.*

Totality of the circumstances. The determination whether the waiver is voluntary, knowing, and intelligent is based on the totality of the circumstances surrounding the interrogation. *We cannot read your mind, but we can see from the entire situation that the police did not pressure you into waiving your rights, and you seemed to know what you were doing.*

The prosecution is required to establish a *knowing, voluntary, and intelligent waiver* by a *predominance of the evidence* (fifty-one percent). The Supreme Court explained in *Colorado v. Connelly* that holding the prosecution to this relatively modest burden of proof is sufficient to deter illegal behavior on the part of the police (*Colorado v. Connelly,* 479 U.S. 157, 169 [1986]).

Voluntary

The *Miranda* decision noted that evidence that an accused was threatened, tricked, or cajoled (pressured) into a waiver is sufficient to establish that a suspect did not voluntarily waive his or her rights. A waiver also will not be recognized if obtained under coercive circumstances, such as a lengthy interrogation or a lengthy incarceration prior to the confession.

The Supreme Court has equated the test for voluntariness under *Miranda* with the due process voluntariness ("but for") test that we discussed earlier in this chapter. In *Oregon v.*

Elstad, the Supreme Court dismissed the defendant's claim that his confession was involuntary and explained that the defendant had not alleged "coercion of a confession by physical violence or other deliberate means calculated to break the suspect's will" (*Oregon v. Elstad,* 470 U.S. 298, 312 [1985]).

As you recall, in *Colorado v. Connelly,* the Supreme Court ruled that a defendant's confession that was the product of a mental disability was not involuntary for the purposes of *Miranda.* An involuntary confession requires an *"essential link between coercive activity of the State, on the one hand, and a resulting confession by a defendant on the other."* In determining whether a confession is involuntary, a court will evaluate the impact of the police interrogation techniques in light of the totality of the circumstances. The factors to be considered include the following:

- ***Offender.*** The age, education, background, and other characteristics of the accused.
- ***Conditions of interrogation.*** The length of the interrogation or the length of the suspect's detention prior to the reading of the *Miranda* rights.
- ***Interrogation techniques.*** Whether there was the threat or use of coercion, duress, or violence.
- ***Motivation.*** Whether the suspect had a reason to confess such as a desire for a reduced sentence that was not related to the actions of the police.

The question always is whether the totality of circumstances caused the defendant to involuntarily confess. Was his or her will overborne by the totality of the circumstances (*Colorado v. Connelly,* 479 U.S. 157, 166 [1986]).

Judges have generally been reluctant to find involuntary waivers in cases in which the police misrepresented or exaggerated the evidence against a suspect. In *United States v. Velasquez,* the police misrepresented the strength of the case against Velasquez by falsely informing her that a co-conspirator had implicated her in a drug scheme. The Third Circuit Court of Appeals ruled that the educated and experienced suspect had weighed and balanced various factors in deciding whether to waive her rights and that her co-conspirator's alleged confession was only one consideration in her decision. In other words, Velasquez's will and capacity for independent judgment were not overcome by the police officers' misrepresentation; this was only one of many factors in her decision to talk to the police (*United States v. Velasquez,* 885 F.2d 1076, 1086 (3d Cir. 1989). The Second Circuit, in another case, ruled that a defendant's confession was based on his desire to be isolated from society in order to prevent himself from continuing his pattern of uncontrollable violence and that his confession had not been caused by the false representation that his fingerprints had been identified at the crime scene (*Green v. Scully,* 850 F.2d 894 [2d Cir. 1988]).

Knowing and Intelligent

We have seen that a suspect is required to understand the meaning of the *Miranda* rights as well as the consequences of a waiver. Once having read the *Miranda* warnings, may an officer assume that a suspect fully comprehends his or her rights? What if an individual clearly does not understand the rights?

In *Tague v. Louisiana,* the arresting officer testified that he read Tague the *Miranda* warnings, but the officer "could not presently remember what those rights were . . . could not recall whether he asked [Tague] whether he understood the rights as read to him, and 'couldn't say yes or no' whether he rendered any tests to determine whether [Tague] was literate or otherwise capable of understanding his rights." The U.S. Supreme Court concluded that Louisiana had failed to satisfy the heavy burden of establishing that Tague knowingly and intelligently waived his rights before confessing. In other words, a police officer may not automatically assume that an individual knowingly and intelligently waived his or her rights (*Tague v. Louisana,* 444 U.S. 469 [1980]).

What factors are relevant in determining whether a suspect's waiver of *Miranda* is knowing and intelligent? In *Fare v. Michael C.,* the Supreme Court indicated that this is based on the *totality of the circumstances*. Michael was sixteen and a half years of age and the Supreme Court indicated that the proper approach is to inquire into a "juvenile's age, experience, education, background, and intelligence and into whether he [or she] has the capacity to understand the warnings given him [or her], the nature of his [or her] Fifth Amendment rights, and the consequences of waiving those rights." The Court stressed that the police were careful to insure that Michael C. understood his rights and that he clearly indicated a desire to waive them. In addition, there was nothing in Michael's background to indicate that he lacked the capacity to understand his rights. He was a sixteen-and-a-half-year-old juvenile who had significant experience in the criminal justice system, including a history of multiple arrests, internment in a youth camp, and having been on probation for several years. There also was no indication that he lacked the intelligence to understand the *Miranda* rights (*Fare v. Michael C.*, 442 U.S. 707, 725–727 [1979]). Judges also examine a defendant's behavior during interrogation. In *United States v. Gaddy,* the Eleventh Circuit Court of Appeals noted that despite the defendant's addiction to drugs and his mental illness, he was of above-average intelligence, had been involved with the criminal justice system on several occasions in the past, and did not exhibit "'scattered' thinking, 'panicky' behavior," severe depression, or anxiety during his interrogation and that his waiver was knowing and voluntary (*United States v. Gaddy,* 894 F.2d 1307, 1312 [11th Cir. 1990]).

We have already seen in *Colorado v. Spring* and in *Moran v. Burbine* that the Supreme Court has resisted requiring the police to incorporate additional information into the *Miranda* warnings, such as informing defendants of the topic of interrogation or of the availability of an attorney. The Court has stressed that the U.S. Constitution does not require that an individual be informed of all information that might prove useful in arriving at his or her decision, such as the strength of the prosecution's case. The Supreme Court also has recognized that absent this information, a decision to talk might be voluntary but not necessarily the best course to follow (*Colorado v. Spring,* 479 U.S. 564, 577 [1987]). In other words, a voluntary, knowing, and intelligent waiver is not necessarily a wise waiver.

Express and Implied Waiver

A waiver, as we have seen, must be voluntary, knowing, and intelligent. *Miranda* indicated that an "express statement" that the individual is willing to make a statement and does not want an attorney followed closely by a statement constitutes a waiver and that a waiver will not be presumed from silence or "from the fact that a confession was in fact eventually obtained." Have courts continued to require a clear and affirmative statement? Must a defendant sign a waiver form?

A mentally competent defendant who affirmatively waives his or her rights clearly meets the **express waiver** standard. However, the issue of waiver is not always this clear. Consider *North Carolina v. Butler.* Butler was convicted of kidnapping, armed robbery, and felonious assault stemming from the robbery of a service station and the shooting of the attendant. He was arrested and fully advised of his rights. Butler thereafter was taken to the FBI office, and after determining that he had an eleventh-grade education and was able to read, he was given a written *Miranda* warning form to review. Butler stated that he understood his rights and refused to sign the waiver of his right to silence and right to a lawyer at the bottom of the page. The FBI agents assured him that he was not required to speak or to sign the form and asked whether Butler was willing to talk to them. He replied that he would talk to the agents but would not sign the rights waiver form and then proceeded to make incriminating statements. An FBI agent testified at trial that Butler had said "nothing" when advised of his rights and attempted neither to request an attorney or to halt the interrogation (*North Carolina v. Butler,* 441 U.S. 369 [1979]).

The U.S. Supreme Court ruled that the prosecution's burden is "great, but that... in some cases, a waiver can be clearly inferred from the actions and words of the person interrogated." In these instances, the prosecution is required to establish that although there was no affirmative waiver, the suspect nevertheless understood his or her rights and engaged in a "course of conduct indicating waiver" (373). This is an **implied waiver.** Do you believe that Butler fully understood that he was waiving his *Miranda* rights? A similar issue arose in *Connecticut v. Barrett,* which you will find on the study site. Barrett was arrested for sexual assault and indicated that he would not provide a written statement without his lawyer but that he was happy to talk to the police. Was Barrett's confession admissible?

You can find North Carolina v. Butler *and* Connecticut v. Barrett *on the study site, http://www.sagepub.com/lippmancp.*

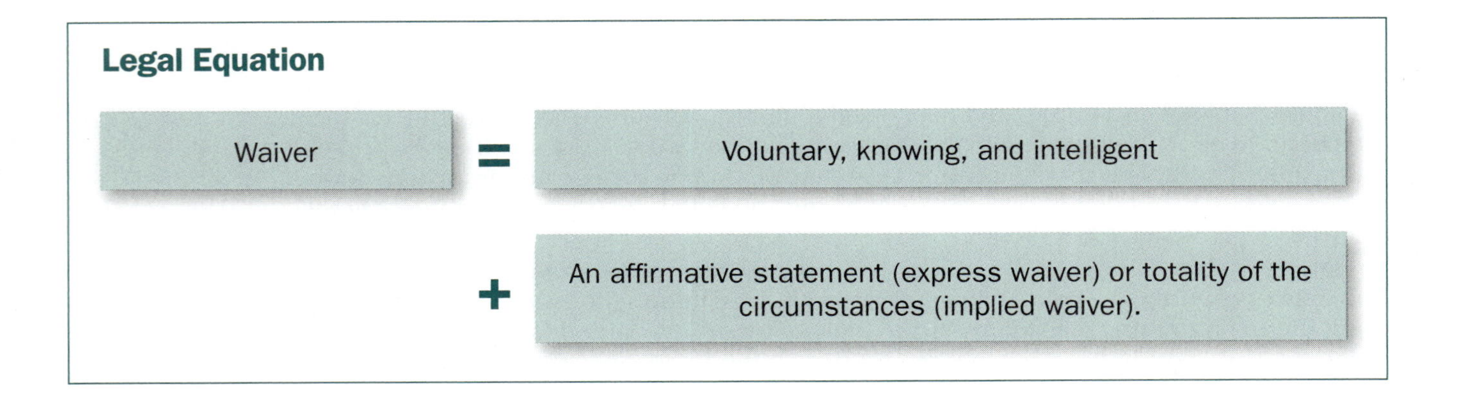

Waiver: Question First and Warn Later

In *Elstad v. Oregon,* the police visited the home of eighteen-year-old Michael James Elstad, briefly and casually interrogated him regarding a burglary, and obtained a voluntary incriminating statement. The officers then arrested Elstad and, at police headquarters, read Elstad his *Miranda* rights and obtained a detailed confession. The U.S. Supreme Court had no difficulty in ruling that the first confession was inadmissible because the officers had failed to read Elstad his *Miranda* rights. What of the second confession? Elstad clearly must have believed that there was little reason not to continue talking to the police after having already "let the cat out of the bag" concerning his guilt. It would seem only fair to require the police to inform Elstad that in considering whether to invoke his *Miranda* rights, he should be aware that his first confession was inadmissible.

The U.S. Supreme Court held that the unlawful character of Elstad's first voluntary confession did not automatically taint his second voluntary confession and ruled that a "suspect who has once responded to unwarned yet uncoercive questioning is not thereby disabled from waiving his rights and confessing after he has been given the requisite *Miranda* warnings." The Supreme Court found that the *Miranda* warnings cured the taint of the initial confession and that warning a suspect that his or her first confession was inadmissible was neither "practicable nor constitutionally necessary." The police, according to the majority, were sufficiently deterred from failing to give the *Miranda* warning by excluding the first confession. Justices Brennan and Marshall in dissent criticized what they viewed as the Supreme Court's growing impatience with constitutional rights and condemned their fellow justices for increasingly viewing civil liberties as impediments to combating crimes (*Oregon v. Elstad,* 470 U.S. 298, 312 [1985]).

Following *Elstad,* a number of police departments adopted a policy of interrogating suspects in "successive, unwarned and warned phases." The Supreme Court reacted to this tactic in *Missouri v. Seibert* by reconsidering the judgment in *Elstad.* Patrice Seibert's twelve-year-old son, Jonathan, had cerebral palsy and died in his sleep. Fearing charges of neglect because of the bedsores on Jonathan's body, Seibert entered into a plan with her sons and some of their friends to incinerate Jonathan's body in the family's mobile home. They intentionally left

Donald Rector, a mentally challenged teenager who lived with the Seiberts, in the home to give the impression that he was looking after Jonathan at the time of the fire.

Five days later, Seibert was arrested at the hospital where Donald was being treated for burns. She was taken to the police station and left alone in the interrogation room for fifteen to twenty minutes. Officer Hanrahan then followed orders and neglected to give Seibert the *Miranda* warnings prior to the thirty- to forty-minute interrogation. Seibert ultimately confessed to her crime and was given a twenty-minute break. Officer Hanrahan then turned on the tape recorder, indicated that they should continue their conversation, and gave Seibert the *Miranda* warnings, and Seibert waived her rights. Hanrahan initiated the questioning by confronting Seibert with her prewarning statements, and she immediately admitted that the plan was for Donald "to die in his sleep" (*Missouri v. Seibert,* 542 U.S. 600 [2004]).

The Supreme Court stated that the issue when the police **question first and warn later** is whether "it would be reasonable to find that in these circumstances the warnings could function 'effectively'" to advise the suspect that he or she "had a real choice about giving an admissible statement." In other words, when a suspect is warned that "anything you say may be used against you," will he or she understand that the first confession is inadmissible and cannot be introduced into evidence to establish his or her guilt and that the defendant may find that it is in his or her self-interest to invoke the right to silence or the right to an attorney (613–614)?

The Supreme Court pointed out that in *Elstad,* one of the arresting officers likely was confused as to whether the suspect was in custodial interrogation and committed the "oversight" of casually remarking that he believed that Elstad was involved in the burglary. Elstad then confirmed that he was at the crime scene. The living-room conversation in *Elstad* was corrected at the police station when another officer read Elstad the *Miranda* warnings before undertaking a systematic interrogation. The Supreme Court noted that a reasonable person would view the station-house interrogation by a separate police officer as "a markedly different experience from the short conversation at home" (614).

In *Seibert,* the plurality of the Supreme Court concluded that the facts challenge the "efficacy of the *Miranda* warnings to the point that a reasonable person in the suspect's shoes would not have understood them to convey a message that she retained a choice about continuing to talk." In contrast to the casual, inadvertent, and brief questioning in *Elstad,* the facts in *Seibert* reveal a police strategy intended to undermine the *Miranda* warnings. Both the unwarned interrogation and the warned interrogation took place in the station house and were conducted by the same officer. The first interrogation was systematic, exhaustive, and conducted with psychological skill, and the officer did nothing to inform Seibert that the first confession could not be used against her. Officer Hanrahan gave the impression that the second interrogation was a continuation of the earlier questioning when he noted that he had been talking to Seibert about "what happened" (616–617). As you read *Missouri v. Seibert* on the study site, consider whether you agree with the Supreme Court decision.

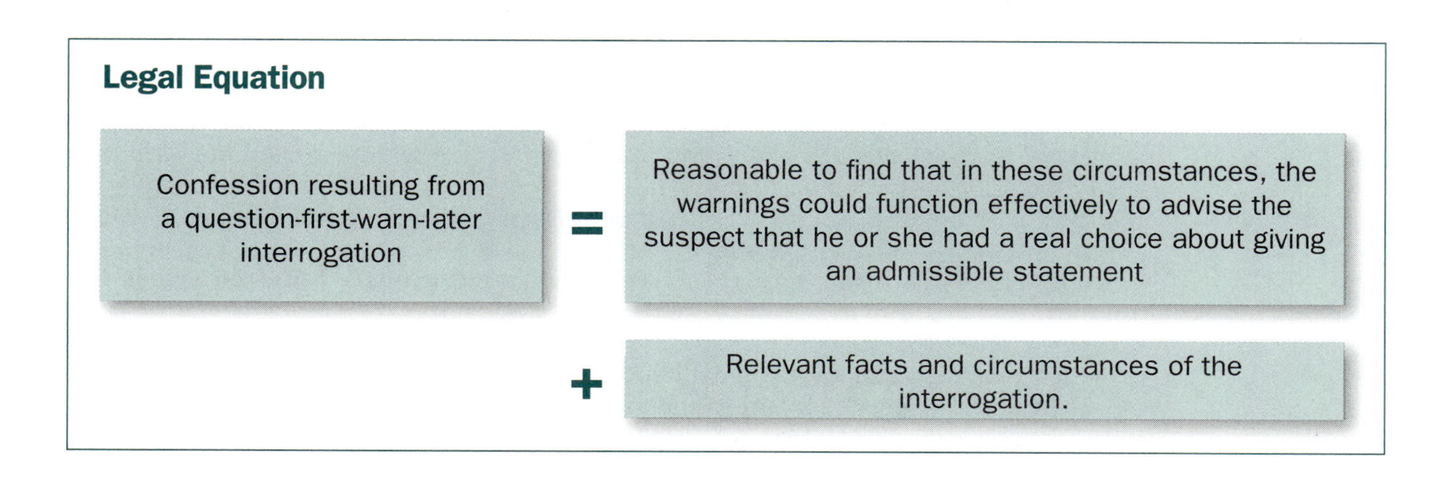

8.7 YOU DECIDE

Alexander Texidor was arrested by federal authorities for the unlawful purchase of firearms and agreed to provide the FBI with information concerning other individuals involved in the illicit trade in firearms. This led to the arrest of Luis Gonzalez-Lauzan Sr. on January 8, 2002. On January 28, 2002, Texidor was murdered and Senior and his son, Gonzalez-Lauzan Jr., and two other individuals were indicted for the murder in September 2002. Gonzalez-Lauzan Jr. was in prison on unrelated charges prior to the indictment when he was questioned by state and federal authorities in the interview room of the courthouse regarding Texidor's murder. The three officers made a decision not to administer the *Miranda* warnings and spent between two and a half and three hours talking to Gonzalez-Lauzan Jr. The officers explained that they were working on a murder investigation and believed that Gonzalez-Lauzan Jr. was involved. The officers instructed Gonzalez-Lauzan Jr. that "we are not asking you any questions. We don't want you to say anything. We just have something to say to you and we ask that you listen to it so that you can understand where we are coming from." The officers described the evidence linking Gonzalez-Lauzan Jr. to the killing in detail and instructed him several times merely to listen when he occasionally interjected and denied involvement. After roughly two and a half hours, Gonzalez-Lauzan Jr. interrupted and exclaimed that "okay, you got me." Gonzalez-Lauzan Jr. was then immediately read his *Miranda* rights and signed a form agreeing to waive his rights. He admitted that he instructed the co-conspirators to teach Texidor a lesson, that he had provided the murder weapon, and that he had been present at the killing. Is Gonzalez-Lauzan Jr.'s confession admissible? See *United States v. Gonzalez-Lauzan Jr.*, 437 F.3d 1128 (11th Cir. 2006). See also *Hairston v. United States*, 905 A.2d 765 (D.C. 2006).

You can find the answer by referring to the study site, http://www.sagepub.com/lippmancp.

Waiver Following Invocation of the *Miranda* Rights

Once an individual invokes his or her *Miranda* rights, are the police prohibited from questioning him or her again? On one hand, the police clearly are obligated to respect a suspect's desire to invoke his or her *Miranda* rights. On the other hand, the police may desire to confront a suspect with new evidence or to question a suspect concerning an unrelated offense. How does the Supreme Court balance these competing interests?

The Supreme Court has established one legal test in those instances in which a defendant invokes his or her right to silence and another legal test in those instances in which a defendant invokes his or her right to an attorney. In this section, we will describe the two legal tests and explain the reason for the Court's reliance on separate tests. We first turn to the approach employed when a suspect invokes his or her right to silence.

In *Michigan v. Mosley,* Mosley was arrested in connection with two robberies. He was read his *Miranda* rights and invoked his right to silence, and the robbery detective ceased questioning. The detective then took Mosley to the cell block. Two hours later, Mosley was moved to the homicide bureau for questioning about "an unrelated holdup murder." He once again was advised of his rights and this time waived them and made an incriminating statement. Mosley later appealed that his second interrogation for murder was unlawful and pointed out that *Miranda* clearly stated that if an individual indicates at any time that he wishes to remain silent, the interrogation must cease. Did this mean that the police interrogation of Mosley for the homicide was a violation of his right against self-incrimination (*Michigan v. Mosley,* 423 U.S. 96 [1975])?

The U.S. Supreme Court ruled that the Detroit police acted in lawful fashion. The legal test for whether a statement obtained after a person in custody decides to remain silent depends on whether his or her right to silence was **scrupulously honored.** What does this mean?

- The police immediately ceased questioning.
- The police suspended interrogation for a significant period.
- The police provided a fresh set of *Miranda* warnings.
- The second interrogation focused on a crime different in *time, nature, and place.*

The Supreme Court stressed that the critical consideration is whether the police respected Mosley's "right to cut off questioning." This was not a situation in which the police failed to honor a decision to terminate questioning by refusing to discontinue the interrogation or by engaging in repeated efforts to wear down Mosley's resistance and pressure him to change his mind.

The dissent pointed out that Mosley initially did not want to talk about the robberies and argued that the police had taken advantage of the coercive environment of Mosley's incommunicado detention to extract a confession to an unrelated criminal offense.

The scrupulously-honored test is subject to several criticisms. Clearly, the police were aware when they arrested Mosley that he possibly was involved in a killing, and the Court's holding invites the police to subject a defendant to a series of interrogations when they have evidence of the defendant's involvement in multiple crimes. What did the Supreme Court mean when it required that the second interrogation address a crime different in time, nature, and place? What about a bank robber who flees in a car and hits a pedestrian? Are the bank robbery and auto accident different in time, nature, and place?

An example of the application of *Mosley* is *United States v. Tyler.* Tyler was arrested for the murder of a government informant and, after being read his *Miranda* rights, invoked his right to silence. He was taken to a small room in the police barracks in which a timeline of the murder investigation and crime scene photographs were pasted to the wall. After several hours, Detective Ronald Egolf entered the room and engaged Tyler in a general discussion on his family, education, and hunting and, after roughly an hour, directed Tyler to "tell the truth." Tyler allegedly started to cry, Egolf again warned him of his *Miranda* rights, and Tyler confessed to involvement in the murder. The Third Circuit Court of Appeals held that Tyler's interrogation was inconsistent with "scrupulously honoring Tyler's assertion of silence." Can you explain the court's decision (*United States v. Tyler,* 164 F.3d 150, 155 [3d Cir. 1998]).

The Supreme Court, in *Edwards v. Arizona,* established a separate **initiation** test for determining whether a defendant who invokes his or her right to an attorney may be once again interrogated. Under what circumstances would a waiver and subsequent confession be considered voluntary, knowing, and intelligent? The facts in *Edwards* are remarkably similar to the facts in *Mosley.* Edwards was arrested for burglary, robbery, and murder and then waived his rights, agreed to talk, and later asserted his right to counsel. The next morning, two detectives approached Edwards and again read him his *Miranda* rights. Edwards agreed to talk to the police and confessed.

The confession obtained by the detectives to a crime to which Edwards earlier had invoked his right to counsel clearly would be inadmissible under the *Mosley* test. The U.S. Supreme Court, however, explained that a new test was required because an individual who invokes his or her right to counsel clearly lacks confidence in his or her ability to withstand the pressures of interrogation and desires the help of a lawyer. The Court held that Edwards "is not subject to further interrogation by the authorities until counsel has been made available to him, unless the accused himself *initiates* further communication, exchanges or conversations with the police." A confession obtained in the absence of counsel is presumed to be involuntary (*Edwards v. Arizona,* 451 U.S. 477, 484–485 [1981]).

In *Arizona v. Roberson,* the Supreme Court extended *Edwards,* which prohibits reinterrogation about the same crime, to prohibit the police from reinterrogating a suspect about a *different crime.* Justice Stevens explained that a suspect who requests a lawyer clearly believes that he or she is in need of legal assistance regardless of whether interrogated about the same offense or a different offense. Stevens reasoned that such a suspect who is again approached by the police will find it difficult to overcome the pressures of custodial interrogation and again assert his or her right to a lawyer. Justice Kennedy, in dissent, pointed out that the *Edwards–Roberson* rule will prevent the police from interrogating suspects based on newly discovered evidence or offenses (*Arizona v. Roberson,* 486 U.S. 675 [1988]).

Some of the difficulties with the initiation test are illustrated by *United States v. Green.* In *Green,* a defendant was arrested on a drug charge, was read his *Miranda* rights, invoked his right to an attorney, and pled guilty. Three months later, the police obtained an arrest warrant charging the defendant with an unrelated homicide that had taken place six months before he had been arrested on the drug charge. The defendant subsequently was interrogated on the homicide and, after being advised of his *Miranda* rights, confessed. Despite the fact that five months had passed between the time that the defendant invoked his right to counsel and the time that he confessed to the murder, the District of Columbia Court of Appeals ruled that a strict interpretation of the *Edwards* rule dictated that the confession should be suppressed (*United States v. Green,* 592 A.2d 985 [D.C. App. 1991]). The U.S. Supreme Court was in the process of considering this case when the defendant died, and as a result, no ruling was issued. How would you resolve the dilemma confronting the judge in *Green?*

The next issue confronting the U.S. Supreme Court was clarifying what the Court meant in *Edwards* when it wrote that a suspect is not subject to interrogation until a lawyer has been "made available to him." In *Minnick v. Mississippi,* Mississippi argued that once a defendant requests and meets with an attorney, "counsel has been made available to him." Following this meeting, Mississippi argued that the police are free to interrogate a suspect without a lawyer being present. The Supreme Court, however, held that a "fair reading of *Edwards*...demonstrates that we have interpreted the rule to bar police-initiated interrogation unless the accused has counsel with him at the time of questioning....When counsel is requested, interrogation must cease, and officials may not reinitiate interrogation without counsel present, whether or not the accused has consulted with his attorney" (*Minnick v. Mississippi,* 498 U.S. 146, 150 [1990]).

In summary, keep three points in mind when it comes to a suspect's invocation of the *Miranda* rights and waiver of the *Miranda* rights.

- ***Invocation of counsel.*** We saw in *Davis* that the invocation of a right to counsel and presumably the right to silence requires a *clear and unambiguous* statement.
- ***Scrupulously honored.*** Mosley taught us that the waiver of the right to silence following the assertion of this right is considered voluntary in those instances in which the police *scrupulously honored* the suspect's rights.
- ***Initiation.*** A waiver of the invocation of the right to an attorney following the assertion of this right is considered voluntary in those instances in which the defendant *initiates* contact with the police.

What do we mean by *initiation?* Must there be a clear and affirmative statement of waiver? The U.S. Supreme Court provided an answer to this question in *Oregon v. Bradshaw,* the next case on the study site. In reading *Bradshaw,* pay attention to the legal test for waiver of the right to a lawyer. The Supreme Court ruled that Bradshaw's question to a police officer, "Well, what is going to happen to me now?" constituted initiation and a waiver of Bradshaw's previous request for a lawyer. The Court reasoned that "[a]lthough ambiguous, the respondent's question in this case as to what was going to happen to him evinced a willingness and a desire for a generalized discussion about the investigation; it was not merely a necessary inquiry arising out of the incidents of the custodial relationship." Did Bradshaw intend to waive his right to an attorney? Ask yourself whether the law has made it difficult or easy for the police to obtain a waiver from an individual who has previously invoked his or her right to an attorney.

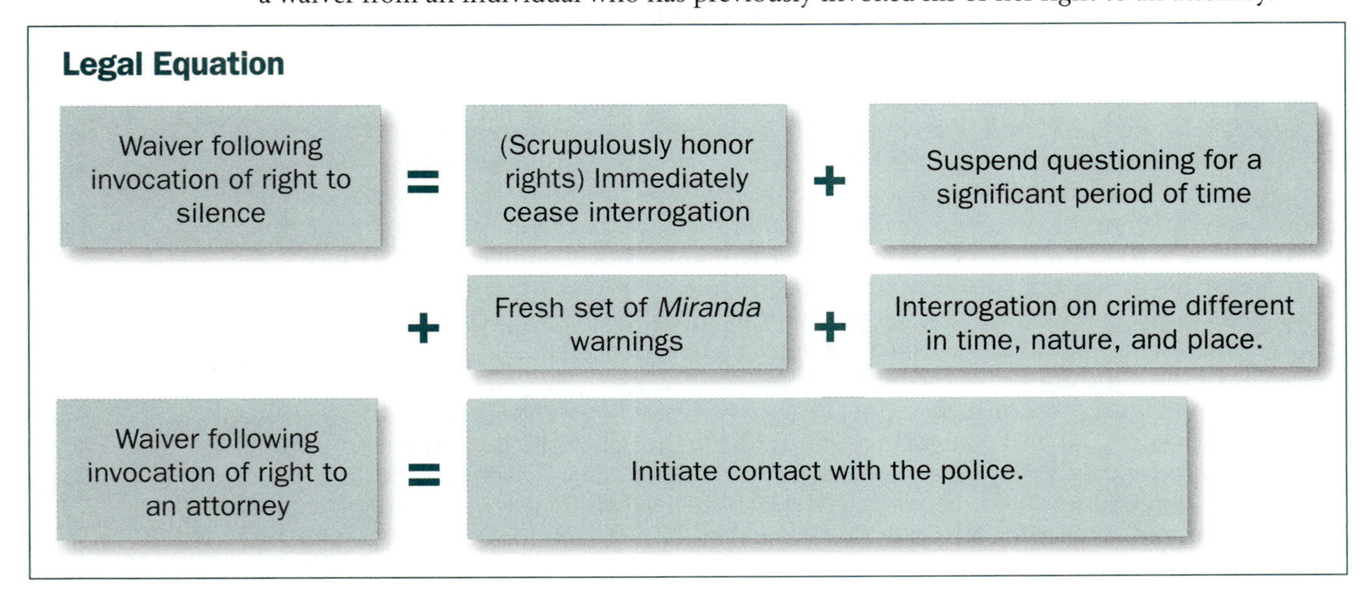

8.8 YOU DECIDE

Defendant Wayne Montgomery was convicted of possession of a sawed-off shotgun and three firearms. Montgomery asserted his right to an attorney. The federal agents then proceeded to photograph and fingerprint Montgomery. The following conversation then occurred.

Montgomery:	Am I being charged with each gun?
Agent Sherman:	You will probably be charged with two counts.
Montgomery:	Did all of the guns fire?
Agent Sherman:	Yes. Why do you want to know?
Montgomery:	The sawed-off was in pieces [in a duffel bag].
Agent Sherman:	That is right, but it only took a minute to put together.
Montgomery:	Ya, but it was missing a spring.
Agent Sherman:	Well, the State Police fired the gun and it worked. Did you have any problem firing the gun?
Montgomery:	I could not get it to work.

Montgomery then indicated that he did not want to talk any more about the firearms, and the conversation ended. His attorney unsuccessfully sought to suppress this statement, and it was introduced into evidence at trial as evidence that the defendant knowingly possessed the firearms. Did Montgomery initiate the conversation with Agent Sherman and waive his right to an attorney? *United States v. Montgomery,* 714 F.2d 201 (1st Cir. 1983).

You can find the answer by referring to the study site, http://www.sagepub.com/lippmancp.

Criminal Procedure in the News

In 2006, the United Nations Committee Against Torture called for an impartial national investigation of alleged "police brutality and torture in Chicago, about which nothing has been done for a long time." The report was issued by ten independent international experts charged with monitoring compliance with the international Convention Against Torture and Other Cruel, Inhuman or Degrading Treatment or Punishment (1984).

This echoed a 1990 report by the international human rights organization Amnesty International that called for an investigation into ongoing allegations of torture of individuals subjected to police interrogation in Chicago.

It is alleged that between 1973 and 1991, at least sixty-six individuals were tortured by Chicago Police Commander Jon Burge and by the officers under his supervision in the Area 2 police headquarters in Chicago. Burge and his fellow officers are accused of beating suspects, shocking them with electric wires and cattle prods, suffocating them using plastic bags, and jamming guns against their heads or in their mouths in order to extract confessions. The credibility of this charge is bolstered by a report by the Chicago Police Department's Office of Professional Standards (OPS), which, in 1990, listed the names of fifty alleged victims of police torture. The report determined that physical abuse "did occur and...it was systematic....[T]he type of abuse...was not limited to the usual beatings, but went into such areas as psychological techniques and planned torture." The OPS investigation also concluded that members of the police command were aware of the "systematic abuse" and either participated in the activity or failed to intervene to bring it to an end.

The case that first brought these charges to public attention involved Andrew Wilson, convicted of killing two police officers. Wilson ultimately won a civil judgment against the City of Chicago, which admitted that Wilson had been tortured and that Burge and others had acted in an "outrageous manner and utilized methods far beyond those...permitted and expected by the Police Department." Lawyers for the City also conceded that Burge and others had tortured another suspect nine days earlier. This led to Burge's termination in 1993 and to the suspension of two detectives. It later was revealed that Chicago had spent more than six million dollars in legal fees defending Burge and the police under his command against charges of torture.

There is no question that most of the individuals who were apparently tortured by Burge and his men, in fact, were guilty. Some innocent individuals, however, were convicted. In January 2003, Illinois Governor George Ryan granted four death row inmates pardons after concluding that their confessions had been obtained by Burge and his unit through torture.

The claims of torture have received support from a number of state and federal courts. In 1999, Federal District Court Judge Milton Shadur wrote that it is "now common knowledge that...Jon Burge and...officers working under him regularly engaged in the physical abuse and torture of prisoners to extract confessions...beatings and other means of torture occurred as an established practice, not just on an isolated basis"

(*United States ex rel. Maxwell v. Gilmore,* 37 F.2d 1078 [N.D. Ill. 1999] [Memorandum and order]).

Federal District Court Judge Diane Wood, in *Hinton v. Uchtman* (2005), wrote that the defendant's torture allegations were "reminiscent of the news reports of 2004 concerning the notorious Abu Ghraib facility in Iraq." She observed that this type of conduct "imposes a huge cost on society: it creates distrust of the police generally, despite the fact that most police officers would abhor such tactics, and it creates a cloud over even the valid convictions in which the problem officers played a role" (*Hinton v. Uchtman,* 395 F.3d 810, 833 [7th Cir. 2005]).

There is no doubt that the systematic use of torture has called into question the credibility of criminal convictions in Chicago. In 2006, two special prosecutors issued a 300-page report discussing 148 cases of alleged torture in Chicago. The report concluded that Burge and a dozen police officers abused suspects and that at least three former prosecutors failed to inquire into the condition of suspects. The same pattern of indifference was displayed by high-level police and prosecutorial officials in Chicago. The prosecution of individuals accused of torture, according to the report, likely is barred by the statute of limitations.

The special prosecutors' report concluded that there is firm evidence of the abuse of Andrew Wilson and two other individuals. The investigators "believed" but could not substantiate that torture took place in roughly one-half of the other cases in the study. Chicago police officials responded that this type of abuse could not occur today. They pointed to the video recording of interrogations in murder and sex-crime cases, databases that track the performance of police officers, and strong executive leadership in the department.

You can read more about the Andrew Wilson case in John Conroy, *Unspeakable Acts, Ordinary People: The Dynamics of Torture* (New York: Alfred A. Knopf, 2000).

The *Report of the Special State's Attorney* (2006) is available online at http://chicagotribune.com/burge.

Interrogation

You should have it firmly fixed in your mind that a defendant may not be interrogated by the police prior to the reading of the *Miranda* warnings. Following the reading of the *Miranda* rights, there also are firm limits on police **interrogation.** As we have seen, once a suspect invokes either the right to silence or the right to an attorney, he or she is not subject to interrogation. The police must *scrupulously honor* the right to silence and may interrogate a suspect only about a crime different in time, nature, and place after suspending interrogation for a period of time and issuing a fresh set of *Miranda* warnings. A suspect who invokes his or her right to an attorney may be interrogated only in the event that the suspect *initiates* contact with the police.

What is the definition of *police interrogation?* Does this mean that the police are prohibited from conversing with the suspect? Can the police let a suspect know that they found several hundred pounds of cocaine in his or her house or inform the suspect of the progress of the investigation or of the fact that a co-conspirator confessed?

In *Rhode Island v. Innis,* the U.S. Supreme Court defined *interrogation.* The Court explained that interrogation involves either **express questioning** or the **functional equivalent of express questioning.**

- ***Express questioning.*** Questions directed to a suspect by the police.
- ***Functional equivalent.*** Words or actions on the part of the police (other than those normally attendant to arrest and custody) that the police should know are reasonably likely to elicit an incriminating response from the suspect.

Express questioning entails a direct question. The test for the functional equivalent of questioning is whether the police should know that a practice is likely to elicit an incriminating statement from a suspect. The police are required to put themselves in the shoes of the suspect and ask themselves whether a statement or practice is likely to lead the suspect to incriminate himself or herself. For example, the police should anticipate that an appeal to religion may lead a suspect who is a member of the clergy to incriminate himself or herself.

In reading *Rhode Island v. Innis,* ask yourself whether the legal test for interrogation is clearly stated by the Court. Do you believe that the police unconstitutionally interrogated Innis?

Did the police interrogate Innis?

Rhode Island v. Innis, *446 U.S. 291 (1980), Stewart, J.*

Facts

On the night of January 12, 1975, John Mulvaney, a Providence, RI, taxicab driver, disappeared after being dispatched to pick up a customer. His body was discovered four days later buried in a shallow grave in Coventry, RI. He had died from a shotgun blast aimed at the back of his head.

On January 17, 1975, shortly after midnight, the Providence police received a telephone call from Gerald Aubin, also a taxicab driver, who reported that he had just been robbed by a man wielding a sawed-off shotgun. Aubin further reported that he had dropped off his assailant near Rhode Island College in a section of Providence known as Mount Pleasant. While at the Providence police station waiting to give a statement, Aubin noticed a picture of his assailant on a bulletin board. Aubin so informed one of the police officers present. The officer prepared a photo array, and again Aubin identified a picture of the same person. That person was the respondent. Shortly thereafter, the Providence police began a search of the Mount Pleasant area.

At approximately 4:30 A.M. on the same date, Patrolman Lovell, while cruising the streets of Mount Pleasant in a patrol car, spotted the respondent standing in the street facing him. When Patrolman Lovell stopped his car, the respondent walked towards it. Patrolman Lovell then arrested the respondent, who was unarmed, and advised him of his so-called *Miranda* rights. While the two men waited in the patrol car for other police officers to arrive, Patrolman Lovell did not converse with the respondent other than to respond to the latter's request for a cigarette.

Within minutes, Sergeant Sears arrived at the scene of the arrest, and he also gave the respondent the *Miranda* warnings. Immediately thereafter, Captain Leyden and other police officers arrived. Captain Leyden advised the respondent of his *Miranda* rights. The respondent stated that he understood those rights and wanted to speak with a lawyer. Captain Leyden then directed that the respondent be placed in a "caged wagon," a four-door police car with a wire screen mesh between the front and rear seats, and be driven to the central police station. Three officers, Patrolmen Gleckman, Williams, and McKenna, were assigned to accompany the respondent to the central station. They placed the respondent in the vehicle and shut the doors. Captain Leyden then instructed the officers not to question the respondent or intimidate or coerce him in any way. The three officers then entered the vehicle, and it departed.

While en route to the central station, Patrolman Gleckman initiated a conversation with Patrolman McKenna concerning the missing shotgun. As Patrolman Gleckman later testified:

> At this point, I was talking back and forth with Patrolman McKenna stating that I frequent this area while on patrol and [that because a school for handicapped children is located nearby] there's a lot of handicapped children running around in this area, and God forbid one of them might find a weapon with shells and they might hurt themselves.

Patrolman McKenna apparently shared his fellow officer's concern:

> I more or less concurred with him [Gleckman] that it was a safety factor and that we should, you know, continue to search for the weapon and try to find it.

While Patrolman Williams said nothing, he overheard the conversation between the two officers:

> He [Gleckman] said it would be too bad if the little—I believe he said a girl—would pick up the gun, maybe kill herself.

The respondent then interrupted the conversation, stating that the officers should turn the car around so he could show them where the gun was located. At this point, Patrolman McKenna radioed back to Captain Leyden that they were returning to the scene of the arrest, and that the respondent would inform them of the location of the gun. At the time the respondent indicated that the officers should turn back, they had traveled no more than a mile, a trip encompassing only a few minutes.

The police vehicle then returned to the scene of the arrest where a search for the shotgun was in progress. There, Captain Leyden again advised the respondent of his *Miranda* rights. The respondent replied that he understood those rights but that he "wanted to get the gun out of the way because of the kids in the area in the school." The respondent then led the police to a nearby field, where he pointed out the shotgun under some rocks by the side of the road.

The trial court sustained the admissibility of the shotgun and testimony related to its discovery. That evidence was later introduced at the respondent's trial, and the jury returned a verdict of guilty on all counts.

Issue

In *Miranda v. Arizona,* the Court held that once a defendant in custody asks to speak with a lawyer, all interrogation must cease until a lawyer is present. The issue, therefore, is whether the respondent was "interrogated" by the police officers in violation of the respondent's undisputed right under *Miranda* to remain silent until he had consulted with a lawyer. In resolving this issue, we first define the term *interrogation* under *Miranda* before turning to a consideration of the facts of this case.

Reasoning

The starting point for defining *interrogation* in this context is, of course, the Court's *Miranda* opinion. There, the Court observed that "[by] custodial interrogation, we mean questioning initiated by law enforcement officers after a person has been taken into custody or otherwise deprived of his freedom of action in any significant way." This passage and other references throughout the opinion to "questioning" might suggest that the *Miranda* rules were to apply only to those police interrogation practices that involve express questioning of a defendant while in custody. We do not, however, construe the *Miranda* opinion so narrowly. The concern of the Court in *Miranda* was that the "interrogation environment" created by the interplay of interrogation and custody would "subjugate the individual to the will of his examiner" and thereby undermine the privilege against compulsory self-incrimination. The police practices that evoked this concern included several that did not involve express questioning. For example, one of the practices discussed in *Miranda* was the use of lineups in which a coached witness would pick the defendant as the perpetrator. This was designed to establish that the defendant was in fact guilty as a predicate for further interrogation. A variation on this theme discussed in *Miranda* was the so-called "reverse lineup" in which a defendant would be identified by coached witnesses as the perpetrator of a fictitious crime, with the object of inducing him to confess to the actual crime of which he was suspected in order to escape the false prosecution. The Court in *Miranda* also included in its survey of interrogation practices the use of psychological ploys, such as to "[posit] the guilt of the subject," to "minimize the moral seriousness of the offense," and "to cast blame on the victim or on society." It is clear that these techniques of persuasion, no less than express questioning, were thought, in a custodial setting, to amount to interrogation.

We conclude that the *Miranda* safeguards come into play whenever a person in custody is subjected to either express questioning or its functional equivalent. That is to say, the term *interrogation* under *Miranda* refers not only to express questioning but also to any words or actions on the part of the police (other than those normally attendant to arrest and custody) that the police should know are reasonably likely to elicit an incriminating response from the suspect. The latter portion of this definition focuses primarily upon the perceptions of the suspect, rather than the intent of the police. This focus reflects the fact that the *Miranda* safeguards were designed to vest a suspect in custody with an added measure of protection against coercive police practices, without regard to objective proof of the underlying intent of the police. A practice that the police should know is reasonably likely to evoke an incriminating response from a suspect thus amounts to interrogation. But, since the police surely cannot be held accountable for the unforeseeable results of their words or actions, the definition of interrogation can extend only to words or actions on the part of police officers that they *should have known* were reasonably likely to elicit an incriminating response. By "incriminating response," we refer to any response—whether inculpatory or exculpatory—that the *prosecution* may seek to introduce at trial. As the Court observed in *Miranda:*

> This is not to say that the intent of the police is irrelevant, for it may well have a bearing on whether the police should have known that their words or actions were reasonably likely to evoke an incriminating response. In particular, where a police practice is designed to elicit an incriminating response from the accused, it is unlikely that the practice will not also be one which the police should have known was reasonably likely to have that effect.

Any knowledge the police may have had concerning the unusual susceptibility of a defendant to a particular form of persuasion might be an important factor in determining whether the police should have known that their words or actions were reasonably likely to elicit an incriminating response from the suspect.

Turning to the facts of the present case, we conclude that the respondent was not "interrogated" within the meaning of *Miranda*. It is undisputed that the first prong of the definition of *interrogation* was not satisfied, for the conversation between Patrolmen Gleckman and McKenna included no express questioning of the respondent. Rather, that conversation was, at least in form, nothing more than a dialogue between the two officers to which no response from the respondent was invited.

Moreover, it cannot be fairly concluded that the respondent was subjected to the "functional equivalent" of questioning. It cannot be said, in short, that Patrolmen Gleckman and McKenna should have known that their conversation was reasonably likely to elicit an incriminating response from the respondent. There is nothing in the record to suggest that the officers were aware that the respondent was peculiarly susceptible to an appeal to his conscience concerning the safety of handicapped children. Nor is there anything in the record to suggest that the police knew that the respondent was unusually disoriented or upset at the time of his arrest.

Holding

The case thus boils down to whether, in the context of a brief conversation, the officers should have known that the respondent would suddenly be moved to make a self-incriminating response. Given the fact that the entire conversation appears to have consisted of no more than a few offhand remarks, we cannot say that the officers should have known that it was reasonably likely that Innis would so respond. This is not a case where the police carried on a lengthy harangue in the presence of the suspect. Nor does the record support the respondent's contention that under the circumstances, the officers' comments were particularly "evocative." It is our view, therefore, that the respondent was not subjected by the police to words or actions that the police should have known were reasonably likely to elicit an incriminating response from him.

By way of example, if the police had done no more than to drive past the site of the concealed weapon while taking the most direct route to the police station, and if the respondent, upon noticing for the first time the proximity of the school for handicapped children, had blurted out that he would show the officers where the gun was located, it could not seriously be argued that this "subtle compulsion" would have constituted "interrogation" within the meaning of the *Miranda* opinion.

Dissenting, *Marshall, J.*, joined by *Brennan, J.*

One can scarcely imagine a stronger appeal to the conscience of a suspect—any suspect—than the assertion that if the weapon is not found, an innocent person will be hurt or killed. And not just any innocent person, but an innocent child—a little girl—a helpless, handicapped little girl on her way to school. The notion that such an appeal could not be expected to have any effect unless the suspect were known to have some special interest in handicapped children verges on the ludicrous. As a matter of fact, the appeal to a suspect to confess for the sake of others, to "display some evidence of decency and honor," is a classic interrogation technique.

Gleckman's remarks would obviously have constituted interrogation if they had been explicitly directed to respondent, and the result should not be different because they were nominally addressed to McKenna. This is not a case where police officers speaking among themselves are accidentally overheard by a suspect. These officers were "talking back and forth" in close quarters with the handcuffed suspect, traveling past the very place where they believed the weapon was located. They knew respondent would hear and attend to their conversation, and they are chargeable with knowledge and responsibility for the pressures to speak which they created. . . .

Dissenting, *White, J.*

As this example illustrates, the Court's test creates an incentive for police to ignore a suspect's invocation of his rights in order to make continued attempts to extract information from him. If a suspect does not appear to be susceptible to a particular type of psychological pressure, the police are apparently free to exert that pressure on him despite his request for counsel, so long as they are careful not to punctuate their statements with question marks. And if, contrary to all reasonable expectations, the suspect makes an incriminating statement, that statement can be used against him at trial. The Court thus turns *Miranda*'s unequivocal rule against any interrogation at all into a trap in which unwary suspects may be caught by police deception.

The Court's assumption that criminal suspects are not susceptible to appeals to conscience is directly contrary to the teachings of police interrogation manuals, which recommend appealing to a suspect's sense of morality as a standard and often successful interrogation technique. Surely, the practical experience embodied in such manuals should not be ignored in a case such as this in which the record is devoid of any evidence—one way or the other—as to the susceptibility of suspects in general or of Innis in particular.

Questions for Discussion

1. Why did Innis confess? Out of guilt or self-interest? Should the police have been aware that the discussion concerning handicapped children might elicit an incriminating response?
2. Was the shotgun important to the prosecution's case against Innis? Would the police likely have been successful in obtaining a confession once Innis met with a lawyer?
3. Can you give an example of actions that are likely to lead a suspect to self-incriminate? What about showing a suspect photos of a bloody crime scene?
4. The definition of *interrogation* in *Innis* must be applied to the facts in each case. As a police officer, would you be clear after reading *Innis* about what you can and cannot say to a suspect?
5. How would you rule in this case?
6. ***Problems in policing.*** Explain how the police can rely on the rule in *Innis* to elicit a confession from a suspect who has invoked his or her *Miranda* rights.

Cases and Comments

Taped Interrogations. Questions about what transpired during police interrogation often come down to a "swearing contest" at trial between the police and the defendant. The officer testifies that he or she respected the defendant's rights, and the defendant alleges that the confession was coerced or was the product of police manipulation and trickery.

Many legal scholars advocate the taping of interrogations to provide a record of what transpired in the interrogation room and to guard against psychologically and physically coercive interrogations. Various states, by statute or court decision, require taping of at least some serious felony cases. This has been required by the supreme courts of Alaska, Minnesota, and New Jersey and for certain offenses by the state legislatures of Illinois, Maine, New Mexico, Texas, and Wisconsin and by the District of Columbia. In 2004, the American Bar Association also endorsed the audio or video recording of interrogations. Australia, Canada, and England provide for the taping of confessions. At last count, 450 local police departments also require the videotaping of interrogations.

In 2004, in *Commonwealth v. DiGiambattista,* the Massachusetts Supreme Court ruled that "when there is not at least an audiotape recording of the complete interrogation, the defendant is entitled (on request) to a jury instruction advising that the State's highest court has expressed a preference that such interrogations be recorded whenever practicable, and cautioning the jury that because of the absence of any recording of the interrogation in the case before them, they should weigh evidence of the defendant's alleged statement with great caution and care."

Valero DiGiambattista was convicted of burning the home that he vacated following a dispute with his landlord. The police obtained a confession by suggesting that DiGiambattista had been caught on videotape and had been seen by a witness at the crime scene while minimizing the seriousness of the burning of the unoccupied dwelling and suggesting that DiGiambattista needed counseling to cure his alcoholism. The police seemingly disregarded the fact that DiGiambattista's description of how he set the fire by pouring gasoline throughout the house was at odds with the forensic evidence gathered at the crime scene. In addition, the stores where he claimed to have purchased the gasoline can and gasoline had no record of such purchases. At the urging of the police officers, DiGiambattista wrote a letter of apology to the landlord that repeated the information in the confession and explained that he had been stressed and drunk and that he was grateful that no one was injured. The Massachusetts Supreme Court ruled that DiGiambattista's confession was involuntary based on the police officers' reliance on trickery combined with minimization of the seriousness of the defendant's offense and references to counseling, which the court believed indicated that the suspect would receive a relatively light sentence.

The Massachusetts Supreme Court's opinion also included a number of observations concerning the desirability of recording interrogations. The court noted that the failure of the police to record DiGiambattista's interrogation meant that the court was forced to spend a significant amount of time reconstructing what had occurred several years ago. The court also observed that prosecutors should favor taping because it makes it easier for the government to demonstrate beyond a reasonable doubt that a suspect's confession was voluntary. A court, for example, might conclude after viewing DiGiambattista's interrogation that despite the tactics employed by the police, his confession was voluntary. Videotaping also would deter coercive police practices and inspire confidence in the police. The Massachusetts Supreme Court therefore held that based on these policy reasons, the jury in criminal prosecutions should be instructed that they are to weigh confessions that are not recorded with "great caution and care." The court explained that it was only fair to inform the jury that the party with the burden of proof has decided not to preserve "evidence of that interrogation in a more reliable form, and to tell them that they may consider that fact as part of their assessment."

The main objection to recording is that it will discourage suspects from making statements to the police because they may be reluctant to provide a permanent record of their admissions of guilt that may be used in a court of law. Other critics point to the financial cost of taping. Another criticism is that the police can conceal abuse by coercing suspects and then turning on the videotape and interrogating suspects in a calm and controlled fashion. What is your view? Should there be a requirement that interrogations be videotaped? You might be interested to know that the FBI generally does not tape confessions. What about only audiotaping confessions? See *Commonwealth v. Valerio DiGiambattista,* 813 N.E.2d 516 (Mass. 2004). See also *Stephan v. State,* 711 P.2d 1156 (Alaska 1985).

8.9 YOU DECIDE

Charles Sawyer was arrested for aggravated sexual battery at his home, and the officers informed him that they were taking him to the jail to "discuss what was going on." At the jail, Sawyer was taken to the office of Detective Clark. Clark was seated behind a desk and read Sawyer the arrest warrant and the affidavit of the complaint that detailed that Sawyer had rubbed the leg and vaginal area of a twelve-year-old girl. Sawyer then admitted rubbing the girl's leg while denying the other allegation. He then was read his *Miranda* rights. Was Detective Clark's statement the functional equivalent of interrogation? Was Clark merely fulfilling a legal responsibility to inform Sawyer of the charges against him? See *State v. Sawyer,* 156 S.W.3d 531 (Sup. Ct. Tenn. 2005).

In *Blake v. State,* a Maryland Appellate Court considered whether reading an arrest warrant and a statement of first-degree murder charges to seventeen-year-old Leeander Jerome Blake, after he had been arrested in his home, read his *Miranda* rights, and invoked his right to an attorney constituted the functional equivalent of interrogation. The statement of charges was handed to Blake in his cell by Detective Johns and by uniformed Officer Reese forty-five minutes following his arrest. Maryland law requires the serving of a warrant and charging document on a suspect. The charging document indicated that the penalty was "DEATH." This statement was false; Maryland law limits the death penalty to offenders who are at least eighteen. As the two left, Reese said to Blake in a loud voice, "I bet you want to talk now, huh!" Johns interjected, "No, he doesn't want to talk to us. He already asked for a lawyer. We cannot talk to him now." Thirty minutes later, Johns returned to the cell to give Blake his clothing, which had been brought to the police station by an officer. Blake, who was wearing his boxer shorts and T-shirt, asked the detective whether he could still talk to him. The detective responded, "Are you saying that you want to talk to me now?" Blake responded, "Yes." He was taken to a room where he was again advised of his *Miranda* rights and confessed. Was this the functional equivalent of interrogation? In the alternative, did Blake initiate the contact with the police under *Bradshaw?* See *Blake v. State,* 849 A.2d 410 (Md. Ct. App. 2004).

You can find the answer by referring to the study site, http://www.sagepub.com/lippmancp.

Sixth Amendment Right to Counsel: Police Interrogations

The Sixth Amendment provides for the right to a speedy and public trial before an impartial jury with the right to obtain witnesses and to confront your accusers. The Amendment further guarantees that an individual shall "have the assistance of counsel for his defense." The right to an attorney is crucial; without the skill and expertise of a lawyer, an individual may find himself or herself unable to meaningfully contest his or her guilt at trial. The U.S. Supreme Court, in a series of cases, extended the Sixth Amendment right to counsel beyond the criminal trial to provide protections to individuals subjected to interrogation in the postindictment phases of the criminal justice process. Keep two points in mind as we explore the Sixth Amendment right to counsel.

The Sixth Amendment right supplements the due process voluntariness and Fifth Amendment *Miranda* protections. The Sixth Amendment automatically attaches following the initiation of criminal proceedings. At this point, guilt or innocence is to be determined in a court of law.

The Sixth Amendment protection insures that the criminal justice process functions in a fair fashion. In contrast, the due process voluntariness test protects individuals against involuntary confessions, and *Miranda* is intended to safeguard the right against self-incrimination.

In 1964, in *Massiah v. United States,* as we have seen, the U.S. Supreme Court proclaimed that following indictment, individuals enjoy a *Sixth Amendment right to counsel* that provides protection against the police deliberately eliciting incriminating statements (*Massiah v. United States,* 377 U.S. 201, 206 [1964]). As you recall, the Sixth Amendment right to counsel also provided the basis for the Court's decision two years later in *Escobedo v. Illinois.* These two decisions were thereafter overshadowed by the Supreme Court's decision in *Miranda v. Arizona* recognizing that the Fifth Amendment provides protections for individuals subjected to custodial interrogation. The Sixth Amendment was not again employed to protect individuals from interrogation until 1977 when the Supreme Court applied the Sixth Amendment in *Brewer v. Williams* (430 U.S. 387 [1977]). *Brewer* was followed by a number of decisions that further defined the Sixth Amendment right to counsel.

As noted above, the Sixth Amendment provides protections to individuals confronting formal criminal proceedings.

In 2008, in *Rothergy v. Gillepsie County,* the U.S. Supreme Court clarified that the Sixth Amendment right attaches at a criminal defendant's "initial appearance before a judicial officer," where he or she learns the charge against him, a probable cause determination is made, and bail is set restricting the defendant's liberty (*Rothergy v. Gillepsie County,* 554 U.S. ___ [2008]). At this point, an individual's status has shifted from that of a criminal suspect to that of a criminally accused. As the Supreme Court observed in *Moran v. Burbine,* the Sixth Amendment's "intended function is not to wrap a protective cloak around the attorney–client relationship for its own sake.... [By] its very terms, [the Sixth Amendment] becomes applicable only when the government's role shifts from investigation to accusation.... [I]t is only then that the assistance of one versed in the intricacies of law is needed to assure the prosecution's case encounters the 'crucible of meaningful adversarial testing'" (*Moran v. Burbine,* 475 U.S. 412, 430 [1986]).

The philosophy underlying the Sixth Amendment protection from involuntary interrogation is that individuals against whom criminal proceedings have been initiated are entitled to have their guilt or innocence determined in a court of law before a judge and jury and that this process should not be short-circuited by permitting the police to elicit incriminating information from an individual in the absence of his or her lawyer.

Massiah provided the foundation for the development of the Sixth Amendment right to counsel. As you may recall, Massiah was indicted for federal narcotics violations, retained a lawyer, pled guilty, and was released on bail. Massiah's co-defendant, Colson, agreed to cooperate with the government and engaged Massiah in a conversation in Colson's car, which was equipped with a radio transmitter. A government agent overheard Massiah make several incriminating remarks. The Supreme Court ruled that although Massiah had made a voluntary admission, his statement was obtained in violation of Massiah's Sixth Amendment right to counsel. Justice Stewart explained that at a time when Massiah was entitled to have his guilt adjudicated in a courtroom presided over by a judge, Massiah had been subjected to police orchestrated extrajudicial interrogation in the absence of counsel. This denied Massiah a range of rights, including the opportunity to cross-examine the witnesses against him. In summary, Massiah had been denied his right to counsel "where there was used against him at his trial evidence of his own incriminating words, which federal agents had deliberately elicited from him after he had been indicted and in the absence of counsel" (*Massiah v. United States,* 377 U.S. 201, 204 [1964]).

The Supreme Court did not return to the **Sixth Amendment protection against the deliberate eliciting of a confession** until *Brewer v. Williams* in 1977. Williams had been arraigned for the murder of a ten-year-old child and was being transported to Des Moines, Iowa. The deeply religious, former mental patient confessed after one of the officers gave an emotional speech on the importance of providing the young woman with a "Christian burial." The Supreme Court concluded that Detective Leaming "deliberately and designedly set out to elicit information from Williams just as surely as and perhaps more effectively than if he had formally interrogated him." Detective Leaming was fully aware that Williams was represented by an attorney, and the Supreme Court stressed that in such circumstances, a heavy burden rests on the government to establish that Williams intentionally relinquished or abandoned his Sixth Amendment right to counsel. The Supreme Court concluded that Williams's Sixth Amendment rights had been violated and held that his confession had been improperly admitted into evidence. *Brewer* is important for extending the Sixth Amendment and Fourteenth Amendment right to a lawyer by holding that a person is "entitled to the help of a lawyer at or after the time that judicial proceedings have been initiated against him—'whether by way of formal charge, preliminary hearing, indictment, information or arraignment'" (*Brewer,* 430 U.S. at 398).

Would Brewer have been decided differently if Detective Leaming had asked Williams whether he wanted to waive his right to an attorney and to discuss the charges against him? In 2009, in *Montejo v. Louisiana,* the Supreme Court reversed a decision in *Michigan v. Jackson* (475 U.S. 625 [1986]) and held that the police are free to initiate contact with a defendant following a preliminary hearing in which the Sixth Amendment right to counsel has attached and that the defendant should be given the opportunity by the police to waive legal representation. It previously was assumed that any statements made by a defendant in response to police-initiated questioning following the attachment of a suspect's Sixth Amendment right to counsel were involuntary. Justice Scalia explained that in roughly twenty-four states including Louisiana, lawyers are appointed for defendants without requiring the defendants to request legal representation at a hearing and that defendants like Montejo may welcome the opportunity to cooperate with the police. Montejo clearly was aware of the consequences of talking to the police without his lawyer being present because he had been read his *Miranda* rights after being approached by the police following the hearing, had agreed to talk to law enforcement officials, and subsequently wrote a letter of apology to the victim's widow (*Montejo v. Louisiana,* 556 U.S. ___ [2009]).

The main importance of the Sixth Amendment is in providing defendants protection against interrogation by government informants. In 1980, in *United States v. Henry,* the Supreme Court held that the Sixth Amendment provided protections to prison inmates facing trial against unknowing interrogations by undercover government agents. The Court held that the government had contravened Henry's Sixth Amendment right when the FBI instructed Nichols, a paid government informant, to gather information on Henry's involvement in a bank robbery. Nichols was directed to engage Henry in discussions but not to directly question Henry about the crime. The Supreme Court nevertheless concluded that the informant was not a passive listener. He had engaged Henry in conversation and succeeded in eliciting a confession. Justice Burger noted that even if the government officials did not intend for the informant to take active steps to obtain a confession, the government must have anticipated that it had created a situation that was likely to "induce Henry to make incriminating statements without the assistance of counsel." Consider how the decision in *Henry* differs from the U.S. Supreme Court decision in the *Miranda* case of *Illinois v. Perkins* (*United States v. Henry,* 447 U.S. 264, 272–273 [1980]).

Six years later, in *Kuhlmann v. Wilson,* the Supreme Court seemingly reversed course and ruled that the government did not violate Wilson's Sixth Amendment rights. An informant was instructed not to ask questions concerning Wilson's pending murder and robbery prosecution and was advised to "keep his ears open" and to pay attention to any unsolicited admissions of guilt. The informant reportedly listened to Wilson's spontaneous statements of guilt and testified against Wilson at trial. The Supreme Court stressed that the Sixth Amendment is not violated when the government through "luck or happenstance" obtains incriminating statements from the accused after the right to counsel has attached. The defendant must demonstrate that the police and the informant did not merely listen but took some action that was "designed deliberately to elicit incriminating remarks" (*Kuhlmann v. Wilson,* 477 U.S. 436, 459 [1986]).

In summary, the Sixth Amendment right to counsel applies under certain conditions:

- ***Judicial proceedings.*** The Sixth Amendment applies to both federal and state government agents at or after the time that judicial proceedings have been initiated against an accused—whether by way of formal charge, preliminary hearing, indictment, information, or arraignment.
- ***Deliberately elicited.*** The government may not intentionally elicit information. This prohibits the use of informants to directly interrogate suspects as well as the creation of a situation likely to induce a defendant to make incriminating statements concerning a pending charge without the assistance of counsel.
- ***Waiver.*** The police may initiate contact with an individual whose Sixth Amendment right to counsel has attached following a preliminary hearing, and the individual is free to talk to the police. The suspect must voluntarily, knowingly, and intelligently relinquish his or her right to counsel prior to his or her interrogation.

Keep in mind that the Supreme Court held in *McNeil v. Wisconsin* that the Sixth Amendment is "offense specific." In *McNeil,* McNeil was considered to have automatically asserted his Sixth Amendment right to counsel when he appeared with a lawyer at a bail hearing for armed robbery. The U.S. Supreme Court ruled that this did not prohibit the deputy sheriff from later reading McNeil the *Miranda* rights and obtaining a confession about a factually *unrelated* murder, attempted murder, and armed burglary. Justice Scalia explained that the Sixth Amendment applies only to the specific offense that is the subject of criminal proceedings and that McNeil was required to affirmatively assert his desire to consult with an attorney under *Miranda* when questioned about the homicides (*McNeil v. Wisconsin,* 501 U.S. 171 [1991]). Note that at the time that *McNeil* was decided, the police would have been prohibited by the Sixth Amendment from questioning McNeil on the same offense that was the subject of the bail hearing (as you may recall, this rule was changed in 2009 in *Montejo v. Louisiana*). Another point to keep in mind is that the Sixth Amendment applies only to the specific offense for which you have been prosecuted. An indictment for murder does not protect you against being interrogated for a robbery that occurred during the murder (*Texas v. Cobb,* 532 U.S. 162 [2000]).

You likely are fairly confused at this point. The important point is that once proceedings have been initiated against a suspect and the suspect has requested or retained a lawyer, the police are prohibited from interrogating the suspect outside the presence of a lawyer. This is intended to insure that innocence or guilt is established at trial rather than through police questioning. Now that you understand the Sixth Amendment right to counsel, you might ask yourself why we need this protection. Why is *Miranda* not sufficient?

You can find Kuhlmann v. Wilson *on the study site, http://www.sagepub.com/lippmancp.*

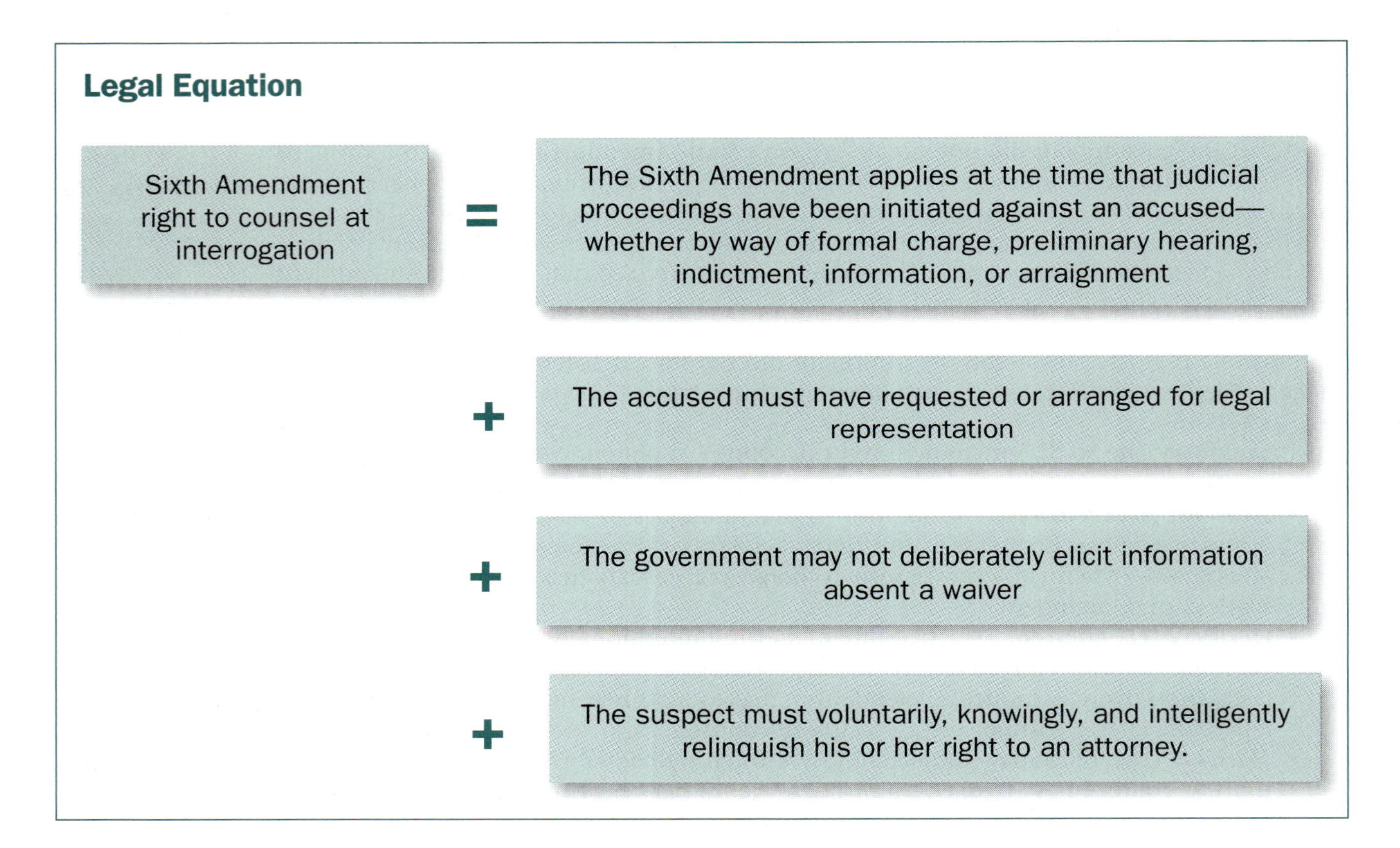

Chapter Summary

Confessions are essential in the investigation and detection of crime. The procedural standards governing confessions are based on the following:

- **Due Process Clause** of the Fourteenth Amendment.
- **Fifth Amendment** right against self-incrimination.
- **Sixth Amendment** right to counsel.

Together, these constitutional amendments have been interpreted to insure that confessions are the product of fair procedures:

- ***Voluntary.*** Are the product of voluntary choice and are not the result of psychologically or physically coercive interrogation tactics.
- ***Procedures***. Result from fair and uniform procedures.
- ***Reliable.*** May be relied on as a truthful account of the facts.
- ***Trials.*** Do not result in a defendant's guilt or innocence being determined by extrajudicial, police-orchestrated questioning rather than in an adversarial trial.

The three constitutional approaches to confessions are summarized below:

Due process. The due process voluntariness test was first articulated in *Brown v. Mississippi* in 1936. This requires that a confession be the result of a free and voluntary choice and not be the product of compulsion. Courts decide whether a confession is voluntary by analyzing the totality of the circumstances. This test is criticized for failing to provide law enforcement officials with clear standards to guide their decisions and is difficult for courts to apply. The Supreme Court attempted to provide greater clarity in *McNabb v. United States* (1943) and in *Mallory v. United States* (1957), which require the police to immediately bring suspects before a judicial officer for arraignment. Any confession obtained by unnecessarily delaying the presentation of a suspect before a judge is inadmissible. These rulings were limited by congressional legislation and proved to have limited impact on state criminal procedure.

In 1964, in *Escobedo v. Illinois,* the Supreme Court took an additional step to clarify the protections to be extended to suspects when the Court held that Escobedo was entitled to be informed of his rights to silence and counsel under the Sixth Amendment and that Escobedo's statement had been unconstitutionally obtained and improperly introduced into evidence.

Miranda. The Fifth Amendment right against self-incrimination was extended to the states in *Malloy v. Hogan* (1964). The Fifth Amendment provided the basis for *Miranda v. Arizona* (1966). *Miranda* established that individuals subjected to custodial interrogation are to be informed that anything they say may be used against them and that they have the right to silence and the right to an attorney, appointed or retained. The *Miranda* warning is intended to provide individuals with the necessary information to resist the inherent pressures of custodial interrogation. There are a number of central components of the *Miranda* rule.

Custodial interrogation. *Miranda* is triggered by *custodial interrogation*. This is the *threshold determination* and occurs when there is a custodial arrest or the functional equivalent of a custodial arrest. In determining whether there is the functional equivalent of custodial interrogation, judges ask whether a reasonable person, based on the totality of the circumstances, would believe that the individual is in police custody to a degree associated with a formal arrest. Courts typically ask whether a reasonable person would feel free to leave.

Public safety. In *New York v. Quarles,* the U.S. Supreme Court recognized a *public safety exception* to *Miranda*. This exception permits the police to ask questions reasonably prompted by a reasonable concern with public safety without first advising a suspect of his or her *Miranda* rights. The Supreme Court concluded that a reasonable concern with the safety of the police or the public outweighs the interest in protecting the suspect's right against self-incrimination.

***Miranda* warning.** The *three-part Miranda warning* is essential for informing suspects of their rights and of the consequences of waiving their rights. The *Miranda* judgment states that the warnings are to be recited in "clear and unequivocal terms" and that a suspect is to be "clearly informed" of his or her rights. The Supreme Court has provided broad guidance to the police on how to recite the *Miranda* rights. *Miranda* is a flexible formula. The test is whether the warnings viewed in their totality convey the essential information to the suspect.

Invocation of rights. Following the reading of the *Miranda* rights, a defendant has the opportunity to *assert his or her right to a lawyer or right to silence or to waive these rights*. In *Davis v. United States* (1994), the Supreme Court held that an individual is required to "articulate his desire to have counsel present... sufficiently clearly that a reasonable police officer in the circumstances would understand the statement to be a request for an attorney." The Court reasoned that a rule that required the police to cease questioning following an ambiguous statement by the accused would transform *Miranda* into a "wholly irrational obstacle to interrogations." A defendant also is required to invoke the right to silence in an unambiguous fashion.

Voluntary waiver. The Supreme Court stressed in *Miranda* that the government is required to meet a "heavy burden" in demonstrating that a suspect voluntarily, knowingly, and intelligently waived his or her rights. The *Miranda* decision noted that any evidence that an accused was threatened, tricked, or cajoled into a waiver is sufficient to demonstrate that a suspect did not *voluntarily waive* his or her rights. A waiver also will not be upheld if obtained under coercive circumstances such as a lengthy interrogation or a lengthy incarceration prior to a confession.

Knowing and intelligent waiver. We have seen that an individual must understand the *Miranda* rights as well as the consequences of waiving them. *Tague v. Louisiana* held that a police officer may not automatically conclude that an individual *knowingly and intelligently* waived his or her rights. What factors are relevant in determining whether a waiver of *Miranda* is knowing and intelligent? In *Fare v. Michael C.,* the Supreme Court indicated that the question whether a waiver is knowing and intelligent is determined on a case-by-case basis by the totality of the circumstances. In *Fare,* this analysis considered the "juvenile's age, experience, education, background, and intelligence and whether he [or she] has the capacity to understand the warnings given him [or her]...and the consequences of waiving those rights." Courts also will examine whether the defendant acted in a calm and rational fashion or in an emotional and incoherent manner. The Supreme Court stressed that the Constitution does not require that an individual should be informed of all the information that might prove useful in arriving at a decision whether to waive his or her rights, such as the strength of the prosecution's case.

Express and implied waiver. A waiver, as we have seen, must be voluntary, knowing, and intelligent. *Miranda* indicated that an "express statement that the individual is willing to make a statement and does not want an attorney followed closely by a statement could constitute a waiver." A waiver will not be presumed from an accused's silence. The Supreme Court has recognized implied as well as explicit waivers and ruled that "in some cases, a waiver can be clearly inferred from the actions and words of the person interrogated." In these instances, the prosecution is required to establish that although there was no affirmative waiver, the suspect engaged in a "course of conduct indicating waiver."

Question first and warn later. The U.S. Supreme Court was next asked to address whether a waiver is valid that is obtained through a *question first and warn later* tactic. In *Missouri v. Seibert,* the Supreme Court stated that the issue when the police question first and warn later is whether "it would be reasonable to find that in these circumstances the warnings could function 'effectively' to advise the suspect that he or she had a real choice about giving an admissible statement." In other words, when a suspect is warned that "anything you say may be used against you," will he or she understand that despite the initial confession, he or she need not speak to the police? The Supreme Court suggested in a footnote that this might require that the police inform a suspect that the first confession is inadmissible in evidence.

Interrogation following invocation of the *Miranda* rights. Once individuals invoke their *Miranda* rights, the Supreme Court has recognized that they still may be subjected to interrogations. The Court ruled that the admissibility of statements obtained after a person in custody had decided to remain silent depends on whether his or her right to silence had been *scrupulously honored.* The Court, in *Edwards v. Arizona,* established a separate *initiation test* for determining whether a defendant who invokes his or her right to an attorney may be once again interrogated. Initiation does not require a direct waiver of an individual's right to a lawyer. In *Oregon v. Bradshaw,* the Supreme Court held that the initiation standard is satisfied by a generalized discussion regarding the criminal investigation.

Interrogation. In *Rhode Island v. Innis,* the Supreme Court defined *interrogation.* The Court explained that interrogation entails *express questioning* or the *functional equivalent of direct questioning.* The test for the functional equivalent of direct questioning is whether the police should know that their words or actions are likely to elicit an incriminating statement from a suspect.

Sixth Amendment. In 1966, in *Massiah v. United States,* the U.S. Supreme Court proclaimed that following the initiation of criminal proceedings, individuals enjoy a *Sixth Amendment right to counsel* that protects them from the government's deliberately eliciting incriminating statements. The Sixth Amendment was not again applied to protect individuals from interrogation in the pretrial phase of the criminal justice process until 1977 when the Supreme Court applied the Sixth Amendment in *Brewer v. Williams. Brewer* was followed by a number of decisions that further defined the Sixth Amendment right to counsel.

As noted above, the Sixth Amendment provides protections to individuals *confronting formal criminal proceedings.* At this point, an individual's status has shifted from that of a criminal suspect to a criminally accused. The philosophy underlying the Sixth Amendment protection is that an individual against whom criminal proceedings have been initiated is entitled to have his or her guilt or innocence determined in a court of law before a judge and jury and that this process should not be short-circuited by permitting the police to elicit incriminating information from a defendant in the absence of his or her attorney or a waiver of the defendant's Sixth Amendment right.

In reviewing this chapter, be certain that you understand the three constitutional approaches to interrogations and the points in the criminal justice process in which each applies:

- **Fourteenth Amendment due process voluntariness test** prohibits involuntary confessions and applies at all stages of the criminal justice process. You always have this protection.
- **Fifth Amendment *Miranda* rights** provide protections during custodial interrogation. You only have this protection during custodial interrogation.
- **Sixth Amendment right to counsel** applies after the initiation of formal proceedings against an accused following a request or hiring of a lawyer. You have this protection once your status shifts from criminal suspect to criminal defendant.

In thinking about Chapter 8, consider how the U.S. Supreme Court has attempted to balance the rights of the defendant against the interests of society in interrogations. For example, the invocation of the right to an attorney insulates a suspect from police interrogation unless the suspect initiates contact with the police. However, invocation of the right to counsel under *United States v. Davis* requires an affirmative and clear statement by the accused. The invocation of the right to a lawyer provides a defendant with significant protection against police interrogation but is easily waived under *Oregon v. Bradshaw* by a statement that relates generally to the criminal justice process. An individual who invokes his or her right to silence may still be interrogated by the police about a crime different in time, nature, and place where the police scrupulously honor the suspect's rights (*Mosley v. Michigan*). Of course, the definition of *interrogation* is limited to express questioning or its functional equivalent, opening the door to the type of "subtle compulsion" that the police employed in *Rhode Island v. Innis*.

In Chapter 9, we turn our attention to other investigative mechanisms available to the police: lineups and identifications.

Chapter Review Questions

1. Why are confessions important tools in criminal investigation?
2. What are some of the dangers of relying on confessions to obtain criminal convictions?
3. Can you identify some of the reasons that suspects make false confessions?
4. Write a one-page response to the following quote. Supreme Court Justice Felix Frankfurter famously remarked, in regard to the due process test, that it is "impossible...to...precisely...delimit the power of interrogation allowed to state law enforcement officers in obtaining confessions. No single litmus-paper test...has...evolved" (*Columbine v. Connecticut,* 367 U.S. 568, 601–602 [1961]).
5. What is the significance of the *McNabb–Mallory* rule?
6. Summarize the holding in *Escobedo v. Illinois*. How did this set the stage for the Supreme Court's decision in *Miranda v. Arizona*?
7. Why was the right against self-incrimination included in the U.S. Constitution? Distinguish between testimonial and nontestimonial evidence.
8. What is the holding of the U.S. Supreme Court in *Miranda v. Arizona?* Explain how this decision is intended to counter the pressures inherent in incommunicado interrogation.
9. What is the test for custodial interrogation? Discuss the public safety exception.
10. How should the *Miranda* rights be read to a suspect?
11. Give an example of a statement that satisfies the legal test for invoking the right to a lawyer under *Miranda*. Provide an example of a statement that would not satisfy the standard for invoking the right to a lawyer under *Miranda*.
12. Distinguish between a voluntary and an involuntary waiver. What factors does a court consider in determining whether a waiver is knowing and intelligent? What is the difference between an express and an implied waiver?
13. Why is it important whether an individual is considered to be subject to custodial interrogation? List the factors that a court evaluates in determining whether a suspect is subjected to custodial interrogation.
14. What is the legal test for determining whether the police can interrogate a suspect who has invoked his or her right to silence? What is the legal test for determining whether the police can interrogate a suspect who has invoked his or her right to a lawyer?
15. What is the legal test determining whether an individual has initiated contact with the police?
16. Define *interrogation* as articulated by the U.S. Supreme Court. Distinguish between direct questioning and the functional equivalent of direct questioning. Why would it be helpful for the police to understand the concept of interrogation under *Miranda*?

17. How does the Sixth Amendment right to counsel protect individuals from interrogation by the police?
18. Does *Miranda* handcuff the ability of the police to rely on confessions, or does it favor the police?
19. Write a brief essay illustrating how the U.S. Supreme Court's decisions on police interrogation have balanced the interests of the suspect and the interests of society.

Legal Terminology

admissions
confessions
custodial interrogation
express questioning
express waiver
false confession
Fourteenth Amendment due process voluntariness test
functional equivalent of express questioning
fundamental fairness
implied waiver
incommunicado interrogation
initiation
interrogation
involuntary confessions
Miranda warnings
nontestimonial evidence
police methods test
public safety exception
question first and warn later
scrupulously honor
Sixth Amendment protection against the deliberate eliciting of a confession
Star Chamber
statements
testimonial evidence
third degree
voluntary, knowing, and intelligent waiver

Criminal Procedure on the Web

Log on to the Web-based student study site at **http://www.sagepub.com/lippmancp** to assist you in completing the Criminal Procedure on the Web exercises, as well as for additional features such as leading cases, podcasts, self-quizzes, and audio/video links.

1. Explore the debate over whether *Miranda* impedes the police.
2. Read about false confessions and the conviction of innocent individuals on the Web site of the Innocence Project.
3. Read about the psychology of confessions.

Bibliography

Liva Baker, *Miranda: Crime, Law, and Politics* (New York: Atheneum, 1983). A history of the *Miranda* decision.

Joshua Dressler and Alan C. Michaels, *Understanding Criminal Procedure: Investigation,* vol. 1, 4th ed. (Newark, NJ: LexisNexis, 2006), Chaps. 24–25. An easily understood discussion of the law on police interrogations and confessions.

Steven A. Drizen and Richard A. Leo, "The Problem of False Confessions in the Post-DNA World," *North Carolina Law Review* 82 (2004) 891–1007.

Joseph D. Grano, *Confessions, Truth and the Law* (Ann Arbor: University of Michigan Press, 1996). A criticism of the *Miranda* rule by a well-known conservative law professor.

Fred E. Inbau, "Police Interrogation—A Practical Necessity," *Journal of Criminal Law & Criminology & Police Science* 16 (1961) 16–19.

Saul M. Kassin and Gisli H. Gudjonsson, "True Crimes, False Confessions," *Scientific American Mind,* July (2005), pp. 24–31. A clear and understandable essay on the causes of false confessions by two leading psychological experts.

Wayne R. LaFave, Jerold H. Israel, and Nancy J. King, *Criminal Procedure,* 4th ed. (St. Paul, MN: Thomson/West, 2004), Chap. 6. A technical and fully footnoted discussion of the constitutional law regarding police interrogations.

Leonard W. Levy, *The Origins of the Fifth Amendment* (New York: Oxford University Press, 1968). The definitive historical account of the origins and meaning of the Fifth Amendment.

Stephen A. Saltzburg, Daniel J. Capra, and Angela Davis, *Basic Criminal Procedure,* 4th ed. (St. Paul, MN: Thomson/West, 2005), Chap. 7. A clear and concise outline of the law of interrogations.

David Simon, *Homicide: A Year on the Killing Streets* (New York: Random House, 1991), pp. 204–242. An interesting and informative journalistic account of the interrogation practices of the Baltimore police.

9 Eyewitness and Scientific Identifications

Was the police officer's identification of the suspect reliable?

Glover drove to headquarters where he described the seller to D'Onofrio and Gaffey. Glover at that time did not know the identity of the seller. He described him as being "a colored man, approximately five feet eleven inches tall, dark complexion, black hair, short Afro style, and having high cheekbones, and of heavy build. He was wearing at the time blue pants and a plaid shirt." D'Onofrio, suspecting from this description that respondent might be the seller, obtained a photograph of respondent from the Records Division of the Hartford Police Department. He left it at Glover's office. D'Onofrio was not acquainted with respondent personally but did know him by sight and had seen him "[s]everal times. . . ." Glover, when alone, viewed the photograph for the first time upon his return to headquarters on May 7; he identified the person shown as the one from whom he had purchased the narcotics.

Core Concepts and Summary Statements

Introduction

A. Identifications involve three procedures: lineups, showups, and photographic identifications.

B. Identification is a crucial step in the criminal justice system that may lead to a suspect's being charged with a crime. The challenge is to insure that the identification will be conducted in a reliable fashion.

C. Physical identifications, lineups, and showups are subject to constitutional limitations under the Sixth Amendment right to counsel and the Fifth and Fourteenth Amendments' Due Process Clause. Photographic identifications are subject to limitations under the Due Process Clause, and there is no right to the presence of an attorney.

Wrongful Convictions and Eyewitness Identification

A. Identification is not a science; it is an inexact process. Misidentifications are a leading cause of false convictions.

B. There are three steps involved, each of which involves the risk of error: perception, memory, and identification.

C. A number of steps have been proposed to improve the process of identifications, most notably, the double-blind, sequential lineup procedure.

The Sixth Amendment and Eyewitness Identifications

A. In 1967, the U.S. Supreme Court in *United States v. Wade* and in *Gilbert v. California* established that suspects have a Sixth Amendment constitutional right to a lawyer at all postindictment lineups and physical confrontations.

B. Absent the presence of a lawyer or waiver of a lawyer, a prosecutor may not introduce the results of a postindictment identification at trial.

C. The prosecutor may ask a witness for an in-court identification. In those instances in which the lineup was conducted in violation of the Sixth Amendment, the prosecution is required to establish by clear and convincing evidence that the in-court identification is not the product of a tainted identification procedure.

D. Appearance in a lineup or showup is not testimonial evidence protected under the Fifth Amendment right against self-incrimination.

E. The Sixth Amendment right to counsel is applicable at all critical stages of the criminal process. Critical stages are those procedures between arraignment and trial in which a failure to provide the defendant with a lawyer may prevent a fair trial.

F. The postarraignment lineup or showup, according to the majority of the Supreme Court, is a critical stage because individuals in police lineups or showups who are unrepresented by a lawyer are at risk of being falsely identified as the perpetrators of criminal acts.

G. Absent the presence of a defense lawyer, the Supreme Court observed, the individuals who conducted a lineup could not be subjected to effective cross-examination concerning the composition or conduct of the lineup.

The Sixth Amendment and Prearraignment Identifications

In 1972, in *Kirby v. Illinois,* the Supreme Court concluded that "a showup after arrest, but before the initiation of any adversary criminal proceedings (whether by way of formal charge, preliminary hearing, indictment, information, or arraignment), unlike the postindictment confrontations in *Wade* and in *Gilbert,* is not a critical stage of criminal prosecutions at which the accused . . . is entitled to counsel."

The Sixth Amendment and Photographic Displays

In 1973, in *United States v. Ash,* the Supreme Court held that the Sixth Amendment does not entitle the accused to the presence of a lawyer at a postindictment photographic display containing his or her photo.

The Due Process Test

On the same day that the Supreme Court decided *Wade* and *Gilbert,* the Court in *Stovall v. Denno* established a Fifth and Fourteenth Amendment due process test for the admission of the results of identification procedures. The judge is charged with the responsibility for determining by a totality of the circumstances whether the confrontation "was so unnecessarily suggestive and conducive to irreparable mistaken identification" that the defendant is denied due process of law.

Suggestiveness, Reliability, and the Totality of the Circumstances

A. In 1977, in *Manson v. Brathwaite,* the Supreme Court fully developed the due process test for the admissibility of the result of identifications. The Supreme Court adopted a totality-of-the-circumstances test in which the defendant must demonstrate that the procedure was suggestive. The burden then shifts to the prosecution to demonstrate that the procedure nevertheless was reliable, meaning that the result could be trusted.
B. In *Neil v. Biggers,* the Supreme Court affirmed that the standard for admitting an in-court identification in light of suggestive identification procedures is whether there is a "very substantial likelihood of irreparable misidentification." The question is whether the totality of the circumstances indicate that the identification at the showup is reliable.

State Law on Identifications

The Massachusetts Supreme Court and New York Court of Appeals have held that the due process clauses of their state constitutions provide greater protection than the Due Process Clause of the U.S. Constitution and require the per se (automatic) exclusion of unduly suggestive identifications from evidence, however reliable.

Scientific Identification

The traditional test for the admissibility of scientific evidence was articulated in 1923 in *Frye v. United States*. The *Frye* test asks whether a scientific technique is "sufficiently established to have gained general acceptance in the particular field in which it belongs." The U.S. Supreme Court developed an alternative to the *Frye* test for the federal courts in *Daubert v. Merrell Dow Pharmaceutical*. The *Daubert* test takes a broader view than *Frye* and holds that scientific evidence is required to be both relevant and reliable and is not limited to scientific techniques that are generally accepted by the scientific community.

DNA Evidence

A. DNA, or deoxyribonucleic acid, is a molecule that stores an individual's genetic code. Each individual has a distinct genetic code (other than identical twins).
B. DNA may be used to include or exclude an individual as a suspect during a police investigation. DNA also may be employed to establish guilt or innocence at trial.
C. State and federal courts almost without exception have admitted DNA evidence. DNA evidence has been excluded when the DNA sample has been contaminated or the evidence indicates that there has been a failure to follow accepted procedures.
D. The DNA Analysis Backlog Elimination Act provides that persons convicted of certain federal crimes who are incarcerated, or who are on parole, probation, or supervision must provide federal authorities with a tissue, fluid, or other bodily sample on which a DNA analysis can be performed.

Polygraph Evidence

A. The polygraph, or "lie detector," is a form of scientific identification. The test measures an individual's physiological responses (blood pressure, perspiration, and respiration) to questions asked by a trained examiner. The examiner evaluates whether the suspect's answers are "truthful" or "untruthful" based on his or her reaction.
B. The polygraph is not generally considered admissible into evidence. The lie detector is not generally accepted by the scientific community (*Frye*) and is not considered reliable (*Daubert*).

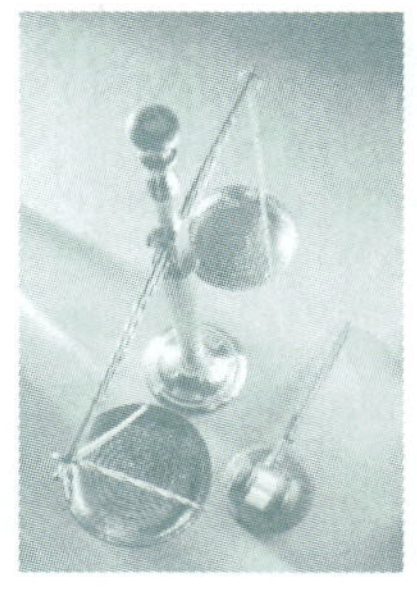

Introduction

You are confronted by a gun-waving assailant wearing a baseball hat in the early evening. She demands your wallet, and when you hesitate, she threatens you with a knife. You nervously hand over your wallet and, still shaking, call the police. The officer asks you to describe the robber. Would you be able to provide an accurate description of her height, weight, face structure, and voice? As you read this, you likely are already forming a vision of the robber in your mind.

The police move quickly to solve the crime and, the next day, arrange for you to view an individual that they have arrested for another armed robbery on the same day. The police want to determine whether this is the person who robbed you. They likely will make use of one of three forms of **eyewitness identification.**

1. ***Lineups.*** Victims or eyewitnesses view a group of individuals, typically six in number. They then are asked to identify the perpetrator from this "six pack." **Fillers**, **foils,** or **distractors** are people innocent of the particular offense who are recruited by the police to participate in the lineup. The police ask the victim or eyewitness, "Did any of these individuals commit the crime?"

2. ***Showups.*** The police may stage a **confrontation** between the victim or eyewitness and a single suspect. The police ask the victim or eyewitness, "Is this the man or woman who committed the crime?"

3. ***Photographic identifications.*** The victim or eyewitness is asked to determine whether the perpetrator is pictured in any of the photographs. In most cases, the photo array is composed of at least six photographs that are similar in size and shape. The police ask the victim or eyewitness, "Is the individual who committed the crime pictured in any of the photos?"

A fourth type of identification is **scientific identification**. This involves the use of scientific techniques such as fingerprints, DNA, or hair analysis to identify the perpetrator of a crime. A police investigation generally employs a combination of eyewitness identifications and scientific identifications.

These various types of identifications serve several functions in the criminal investigative process:

- ***Identification.*** Identifications may narrow the range of individuals under investigation.
- ***Exoneration.*** Identifications may eliminate suspects from the investigation.
- ***Indictment.*** Identifications may lead to charging an individual with a crime.
- ***Confidence in indictment and conviction.*** Identifications supplement the other evidence at trial and increase confidence that the defendant was properly indicted, prosecuted, and convicted.

Returning to our armed robbery case, your eyewitness identification of the perpetrator may lead to her being charged with a felony. At trial, when you take the stand, you likely will be asked whether you identified an individual as the robber at a lineup or showup or in a photographic identification. Your positive response will support the credibility of your **in-court identification** when you testify that the individual that you earlier identified as the robber is the defendant sitting at the defense table. There is little doubt that your testimony will have a powerful influence on the jury when they consider the defendant's guilt or innocence.

In this chapter, we will see that the U.S. Supreme Court has held that identification procedures must comply with the Sixth Amendment and with the Fifth and Fourteenth Amendments to the U.S. Constitution. These constitutional standards are intended to insure fair procedures that will prevent innocent individuals from being misidentified as the perpetrators of a crime.

Sixth Amendment. The Sixth Amendment provides, in part, that "[i]n all criminal prosecutions, the accused shall...have the assistance of counsel for his defense." The U.S. Supreme Court has held that an individual has the right to an attorney during lineups and showups that are conducted following the initiation of adversary criminal proceedings (whether by way of formal charge, preliminary hearing, indictment, information, or arraignment). There is no right to an attorney for photographic identifications. The defendant may file a motion to exclude the lineup identification from trial by demonstrating that the "government denied my right to an attorney."

Due process. Both the Fifth and the Fourteenth Amendments provide that an individual shall not be "deprived of life, liberty, or property without due process of law." Due process entitles individuals to reliable identification procedures prior to the initiation of criminal proceedings and throughout the criminal justice process. The results of identifications that run the risk of misidentifying innocent individuals are to be excluded from evidence at trial. The defendant has the burden of demonstrating that "yes, I was identified, but the procedure was so unfair that there is a substantial likelihood that I might have been misidentified." The prosecution may respond by establishing that the results of the identification are reliable or accurate.

You may recall from our discussion of interrogations that identification procedures do not violate the right against self-incrimination and that a suspect does not possess a Fifth Amendment right to refuse to participate. The Fifth Amendment protects individuals against being required to disclose information or what is termed *testimonial evidence*. This, as we have seen, involves words that communicate guilt. Identification procedures entail the display of an individual's physical characteristics, and scientific tests require the taking of physical material from the human body. The government may obtain a court order to compel a suspect's participation, and a refusal to cooperate may result in an individual's being held in contempt of court. A failure to participate also may be used as evidence of guilt at trial. In other words, you can be required to appear in a police lineup, to submit to a photograph, or to give a voice exemplar, fingerprint, or handwriting sample.

In this chapter, we will first briefly explore the *three stages of eyewitness identification* and the threats to the accuracy of identifications. These three stages are as follows:

- ***Perception.*** You view the crime.
- ***Memory.*** You remember what happened.
- ***Identification.*** You recall what happened and identify the perpetrator.

As you read this material, ask yourself whether we can completely eliminate the possibility of error or misidentifications. You also should consider whether this is "much ado about nothing." How important are eyewitness identifications in the determination of guilt and innocence? Following our overview of the psychology of identifications, we will outline some suggested procedures to insure accurate identifications. The bulk of the chapter will discuss the two constitutional tests for identifications.

- **Sixth Amendment** right to counsel
- **Fifth and Fourteenth Amendment** protection of due process of law

Consider whether these constitutional protections adequately protect individuals against the possibility of misidentification. We then will look at two scientific forms of identification.

- DNA
- Polygraphs

You should reflect on the implications of DNA evidence for the accuracy of verdicts in criminal cases. Another question to consider is whether the results of polygraphs should be admissible in court.

As you read this chapter, pay particular attention to the balance that is struck by the U.S. Supreme Court between the right of the individual to be protected against suggestive identification procedures and the societal interest in investigating crime and in identifying the perpetrators of crime. We certainly want to prosecute and to convict criminals. At the same time, these procedures must be viewed as fair and should not be so biased that we run the risk that innocent individuals will be prosecuted or convicted.

Wrongful Convictions and Eyewitness Identification

Misidentifications

Identification is an inexact process. Consider the experience of Jennifer Thompson. On June 18, 2006, Jennifer wrote an article in the *New York Times* recounting her devastating ordeal in 1984 when a male assailant broke into her locked apartment while she was asleep and raped her. Jennifer was determined not to be a passive victim and told herself that she would insure that her attacker was brought to justice. Her strategy was to maneuver the rapist into the dimly lighted areas of her otherwise dark apartment in order to observe his distinguishing features: height, weight, hair, clothing, scars, and tattoos.

Jennifer later provided the police with a detailed description of the crime and a composite sketch of her attacker. A few days later, Jennifer, who is Caucasian, identified her African American attacker from a catalog of photographs and subsequently identified him in a lineup. She explained in an interview that her memory was relatively fresh and that Ronald Cotton looked exactly like the man who raped her. She was even more confident in this conclusion after listening to her assailant's voice and observing his height and weight. It also turned out that Ronald's alibi was fabricated and that his family's explanation that he was asleep on the couch on the evening of the rape was contradicted by testimony that he was seen riding his bike late at night. The police subsequently searched Ronald's bedroom and seized a flashlight under his bed that was similar to the one used by the rapist. Tests indicated that the rubber on Cotton's shoes was consistent with rubber found at the crime scene. Ronald was the only suspect included in the identification parade: the other six individuals were government employees. Jennifer was confident that Ronald was her assailant and later recounted that following the lineup, the police told her that they had already identified Ronald as the chief suspect based on his prior conviction for a similar offense. Another woman was raped on the same evening in Jennifer's neighborhood by an assailant who followed the same pattern as the man who raped Jennifer. The second victim observed a lineup, passed over Ronald Cotton, and identified a different individual as her attacker.

In 1986, Jennifer took the stand at trial and identified Ronald Junior Cotton as the rapist. The jury convicted Ronald, and he was sentenced to life imprisonment. The conviction was overturned on appeal. In 1987, Ronald once again was brought to trial. This time, the second victim explained that she was too scared to have come forward during the first trial and now felt confident in identifying Ronald as her attacker. Ronald Cotton's lawyers alleged that their client was innocent and that another inmate, Bobby Poole, had bragged that he was responsible. Jennifer, however, strongly and confidently insisted that she had never encountered Poole in her life. Ronald was convicted of two acts of burglary and of two acts of rape and was sentenced to two life sentences plus fifty-four years. Jennifer recounted that she was relieved that Ronald would never hurt or rape another woman.

In 1995, Jennifer learned that DNA results indicated that her rapist indeed was Bobby Poole. Ronald Cotton was completely innocent and was released from prison. Bobby Poole had been arrested and convicted for two attempted sexual assaults that took place the same night that Ronald Cotton was arrested and now pled guilty to raping Jennifer. In July 1995, the governor of North Carolina pardoned Ronald resulting in his eligibility for $5,000 in compensation from the State. Jennifer admits that even today, when she thinks of her rapist, she sees the image of Ronald Cotton, despite the fact that she knows that he is innocent. How can this type of misidentification occur?

Perception

Most of us would share Jennifer's confidence in her ability to identify the perpetrator of the rape under similar circumstances. After all, who can forget such a frightening experience. You undoubtedly also are certain that you could identify the person who robbed you in our hypothetical example. There are three steps involved in identification:

- ***Perception.*** Observing the crime.
- ***Memory.*** Remembering the crime.
- ***Identification.*** Retrieving the information and identifying the perpetrator.

It may surprise you to learn that misidentification is the primary cause of false convictions. In other words, even under the best of conditions, there is the possibility that your faulty memory will lead you to select an innocent individual as your attacker. As early as 1932, Edwin Borchard studied sixty-five cases of wrongful convictions and found that twenty-nine of the individuals were convicted as a result of faulty eyewitness identifications. In eight of these cases, the wrongfully convicted person and the guilty criminal "bore not the slightest resemblance to each other," while in twelve other instances, the "resemblance, while fair, was still not at all close. In only two cases can the resemblance be called striking." In 1996, a National Institute of Justice study of twenty-eight wrongfully convicted individuals concluded that in the majority of the cases, the most "compelling evidence" was eyewitness testimony, which clearly was "wrong." In 2005, a study of 340 incarcerated individuals who later were exonerated determined that the "most common cause" of wrongful convictions is eyewitness misidentification. At least one misidentification was involved in sixty-four percent of the false convictions and in ninety percent of the false convictions for rape (Gross et al., 2005, p. 542).

Why does the identification of the perpetrator of a crime involve such a high degree of error? Psychologists previously thought that our minds were like video cameras that recorded every experience. We now are more sophisticated and realize that most crime victims are frightened and overwhelmed and are unable to accurately observe or recount the offender's age, dress, weight, height, facial features, voice, and other distinguishing characteristics. Psychologists identify three sets of factors that explain misidentifications.

Crime factors. Your ability to perceive what occurred may be limited when the crime is committed relatively quickly. The victim may explain to the police that "it happened so rapidly that I did not even know what hit me."

Victim factors. You may be too nervous to focus on the perpetrator or may find that you primarily concentrate on the weapon or on the offender's hat, clothes, shoes, voice, or physical build and overlook other factors. There also is a tendency to perceive "what we expect to see." Our biases, prejudices, and fears may lead us to identify a perpetrator as a member of a certain race, ethnic group, or religion. We simply are unaccustomed to paying close attention to the people we encounter. Individuals often are able to offer only a general description. We all have experienced the phenomenon of drawing a blank when asked to describe someone and have been able to recount only that he or she "was tall or short," "big and bulky," or "small and slim."

Offender factors. Studies indicate that people are unable to accurately identify the features of individuals of a different race. We all have heard victims report that an attacker was Asian, Latino, Caucasian, or African American and draw a blank concerning the perpetrator's features. This difficulty is compounded by a range of factors such as the facts that the perpetrator may hide his or her features under a hat, that the crime occurred at night, or that there are multiple offenders.

Memory

The second step is to store our *perception* in our *memory*. Memory is our personal diary of what happened. However, unlike a written diary, memories fade and change with the passage of time. We particularly want to forget painful events, and few of us can claim the capacity to remember the type of small details that may be crucial in a criminal case. Would you be able to recall the color of an assailant's eyes, hair texture, and style or shape of his or her face. In addition, the power of suggestion can lead us to unconsciously change our memory. We know that witnesses who view an individual in a photo array are likely to select the same individual in a lineup because they are drawn to a "familiar face." In the case of Dale Brison, discussed in the National Institute of Justice study, a Pennsylvania court observed that the victim was unable to describe her assailant to the police and may have selected Brison "merely because she remembered seeing him in the neighborhood." Another example of the modification of memory through the power of suggestion occurred in 2003 during the pursuit of the "Beltway snipers," who were responsible for killing ten people in the Washington, D.C., area. The media reported that a white van was at the scene of one of the initial shootings. Witnesses to other shootings all subsequently reported that they had spotted a white van. The police were surprised to find that the two killers were arrested while driving a blue Chevrolet Caprice and had never driven a white van.

Identifications

Assuming that you overcome the challenges of perception and memory, the third step is *identification,* or retrieval. Identification, like perception and memory, involves threats to accuracy.

Selection. Identification is like a multiple-choice test. Victims and eyewitnesses first mentally compare one person to another. They then typically select the individual in the lineup or photo display who most closely resembles their memory of the perpetrator, even in those instances in which none of the individuals seems to fit the witnesses' memory of the perpetrator.

Suggestiveness. The police examiner conducting the lineup or photo array may unintentionally or intentionally influence a witness's identification. This may occur as a result of the examiner's tone of voice, nod of approval, or body language.

Closure. A victim may become tired and exhausted and identify an individual as the perpetrator in order to "move on with his or her life."

These factors combine to create a risk of misidentification. The Innocence Project at Cardozo Law School in New York analyzed eighty-two cases of misidentification. Forty-five percent involved a photo display, thirty-seven percent a physical lineup, and twenty percent a one-person showup. Studies indicate that following an identification, a witness typically develops increasing confidence in his or her selection. This self-assurance, in turn, leads jurors to unquestioningly trust the accuracy of the victim's courtroom identification of the offender. We next outline several steps that might improve the accuracy of identifications.

The Identification Process

The federal government and each state and locality typically adopt their own procedures for identifications. The U.S. Justice Department and American Bar Association have suggested various modifications in the identification process to insure greater accuracy. Several states have adopted some or all of these procedures, including New Jersey, North Carolina, Virginia, and Wisconsin as well as cities such as Seattle and Boston. These procedures have three goals:

- ***Police influence.*** To eliminate the possibility that the police officer conducting the identification will intentionally or unintentionally influence the eyewitness.
- ***Pressure.*** To limit the pressure on the victim or eyewitness to select one of the individuals in the lineup or photo array.
- ***Accuracy.*** To increase the accuracy of identifications.

Consider whether these innovations would have prevented Jennifer Thompson from identifying Ronald Cotton as the man who raped her.

Blind administration. The individual administering the identification should not be informed which individual in the lineup is the suspect. This prevents the administrator from unintentionally or intentionally influencing the selection.

Double-blind. This means that neither the administrator of the identification process nor the eyewitness is aware of the identity of the suspect.

Instructions. The administrator instructs the eyewitness that the administrator does not know the identity of the suspect and that the suspect may not be in the lineup. This eliminates the possibility that the eyewitness will look to the administrator to guide his or her selection or will feel compelled to single out an individual as the perpetrator. Following the identification, the police should not indicate that the witness has selected the "right" person. These suggestive comments may unduly influence the suspect's future identifications.

Single eyewitness. One individual at a time should view the lineup, showup, or photo array, and eyewitnesses should not be permitted to confer with one another. This prevents witnesses from influencing one another. A witness also should not be told who was identified by other individuals. Witnesses, where possible, also should not be shown photographs of the suspect or permitted to view the suspect prior to the lineup.

Sequential presentation. The participants in the lineup or pictures in a photo array are presented to the victim or eyewitness one at a time. The witness is asked to make a decision about each person immediately following the confrontation. The witness also is asked to rank his or her degree of confidence in the decision. This differs from the typical **simultaneous lineup** in which all the lineup members are shown to the witness at the same time. The theory behind the sequential lineup is that the eyewitness will examine each suspect separately and determine whether he or she is the offender. This is thought to eliminate pressure on an eyewitness to select the person who most closely resembles the perpetrator. The vast majority of police departments continue to use simultaneous lineups.

In 2003, the National Institute of Justice published a manual for training in identifications for law enforcement officers. The manual discusses one of the most difficult issues: the composition of a lineup or photographic display.

Balance. Participants in the lineup should be similar in age, height, weight, and race and should be dressed in a similar fashion. There must be a balance. On the one hand, the suspect should not clearly stand out from the other participants. On the other hand, a close resemblance between all the individuals will make the identification difficult and may lead to misidentifications. Selection should be based on information provided to the police by the victim following the crime rather than the actual physical appearance of the individual whom the police believe committed the crime. Copies of the victim's initial description of the offender should be made available to the defense attorney.

Distinctive features. Fillers in the lineup should possess the offender's distinctive features mentioned by the victim or by an eyewitness to the police during the prelineup investigation. Courts have upheld the right of the police to order participants to shave or cut their hair or to alter their physical appearance. Individuals also may be required to speak or to make physical gestures.

Number. At a minimum, five fillers in photo arrays and four fillers in lineups are to be included to reduce the risk that an individual is selected as a result of a "guess" by a victim or by an eyewitness.

Preservation. Following a lineup or showup, the results should be recorded by the police on a standard form. This typically involves recording the number of the lineup member who was selected, the name of the eyewitness, the date, the investigator, and ideally, a statement describing the identification. The lineup or showup should be photographed or videotaped. Photograph lineups also should be preserved to defend against legal challenges. Each eyewitness should complete a form indicating the assigned number of the individual whom he or she selected. Eyewitnesses also may make comments on the form explaining the basis for their choice. The police officer conducting the lineup should compile his or her notes and the forms and photographs into a final report that should be made available to the prosecution and defense attorneys.

Photographs. The photographs in photo arrays should be uniform and neutral in appearance to avoid influencing the selection. The photos should not mingle color photographs with "black-and-white pictures," and there should be no visible identifying marks, such as writing on the back of a photo indicating that an individual has been indicted or imprisoned.

In addition to these suggested procedures, some judges have taken steps at trial to help jurors evaluate courtroom identifications. This is intended to assist jurors in understanding that courtroom identifications by witnesses on some occasions may be mistaken.

Jury instructions. Jurors are instructed to evaluate whether the witness who made a courtroom identification possessed the opportunity and ability to observe the offender at the crime scene and whether his or her identification was influenced by outside influences. Jurors also typically are instructed to consider the length of time between the crime and the identification as well as any past failures by the eyewitness or victim to identify the suspect (see *United States v. Telfaire*, 469 F.2d 552 [D.C. Cir. 1972]).

Expert witness. Judges have permitted the defense to present expert testimony educating jurors on the psychological barriers to eyewitness identification. In *United States v. Brownlee,* the Third Circuit Court of Appeals reversed the district court's refusal to permit expert testimony, ruling that the expert witness would have proven helpful to the jury in evaluating the reliability of the courtroom identification (*United States v. Brownlee,* 454 F.3d 131 [3d Cir. 2006]).

The suggested procedures sketched in this section of the text are intended to strengthen the constitutional protections accorded to defendants during criminal identifications. We next examine these two constitutional safeguards.

- ***Right to an attorney.*** The Sixth Amendment right to an attorney at lineups and showups applies once adversary proceedings have been initiated against the accused.
- ***Due process.*** The Fifth and Fourteenth Amendments' due process guarantee of reliable procedures applies at every stage of the criminal process.

The Sixth Amendment and Eyewitness Identifications

In 1967, the U.S. Supreme Court announced in *United States v. Wade* that the existing system in which suspects are unrepresented by a lawyer at lineups and showups violated the Sixth Amendment right to counsel (*United States v. Wade,* 388 U.S. 218 [1967]). The holding in *Wade* was affirmed and clarified by the Supreme Court in another case decided on the same day (*Gilbert v. California,* 388 U.S. 263 [1967)]).The **Wade–Gilbert rule** provides as follows:

Right to a lawyer. A suspect has a constitutional right to a lawyer at all postindictment lineups and confrontations.

Lineup results at trial. Absent the presence of a lawyer, or a suspect's waiver of a lawyer, at a postindictment lineup or showup, the results may not be introduced by the prosecutor at trial.

In-court identification. A prosecutor may not ask a witness for an in-court identification of the defendant unless the prosecutor establishes by clear and convincing evidence that the in-court identification is not the product of an identification at which the suspect was denied a lawyer in violation of the Sixth Amendment.

In the next sections, we outline the *Wade* decision. The first step is to explore why the Supreme Court ruled that Wade had the right to a lawyer at his postindictment identification.

The Sixth Amendment and Critical Stages of Criminal Prosecution

The U.S. Supreme Court held that Wade was entitled to the "guiding hand of counsel" at the lineup. The Sixth Amendment provides that "[i]n all criminal prosecutions, the accused shall enjoy the right... to have the Assistance of Counsel for his defense." The Supreme Court majority explained that the Sixth Amendment right to an attorney applies at **critical stages of a criminal proceeding.** *Critical stages* are those procedures following the initiation of criminal proceedings at which a failure to provide the defendant a lawyer may prevent him or her from obtaining a fair trial. The lineup according to the majority of the Court is a critical stage because the pretrial lineup may "well settle the accused's fate and reduce the trial itself to a mere formality" (*Wade,* 388 U.S. at 224).

Why is a lineup "critical"? We know that a victim or eyewitness who identifies an individual as the perpetrator in a lineup is likely to identify the same person as the offender when testifying at trial. These courtroom identifications tend to heavily influence jurors. A mistaken identification in a lineup or showup as a result may contribute to the conviction of an innocent individual. A lawyer at the lineup or showup provides a defendant with two levels of protection.

1. ***Protection at the identification.*** A lawyer's observation of a lineup provides an incentive for the police to insure that the identification process is fair and reliable and is not suggestive.
2. ***Protection at the trial.*** The lawyer at trial is able to point out to the jury that the lineup was unfair and argue that the jury should question the accuracy of the identification.

In the next section, we will examine some of the practices that the Supreme Court in *Wade* described as being used in lineups that made it important to provide suspects the protection of a lawyer.

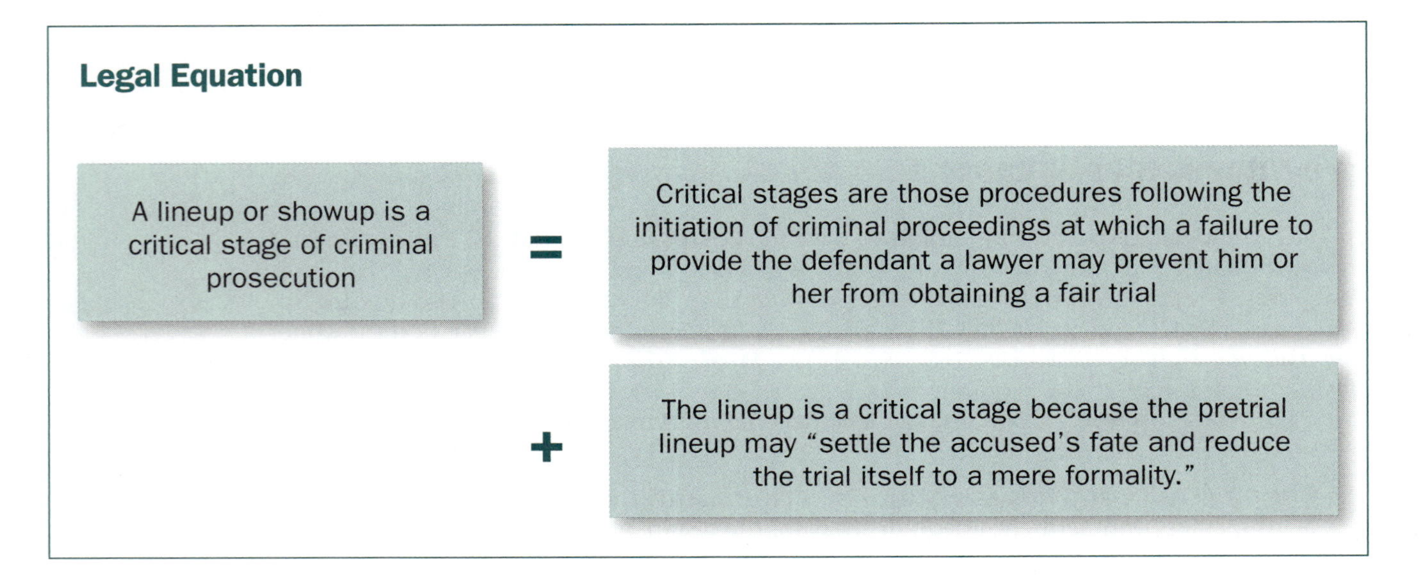

The Threat of Suggestive Lineups

The Supreme Court in *Wade* pointed to "numerous instances of **suggestive procedures**" to illustrate why defendants require the assistance of an attorney at a pretrial lineup or showup. The Court observed that the police typically believe that they have arrested the perpetrator of the crime and often unintentionally or intentionally communicate this to the victim or eyewitnesses. The Court highlighted several common practices (235):

- Everyone in the lineup other than the suspect is known to the victim.
- The suspect is the only person in the lineup whose physical appearance and dress matches the description of the perpetrator.
- The individuals in the lineup are asked to try on an item of clothing that fits only the suspect.
- The police point out the suspected perpetrator to the victim prior to the lineup.
- The victim is asked to identify whether an individual in a jail cell is the suspected perpetrator.

We next examine how the presence of defense lawyers can insure fair and reliable identification procedures.

The Role of the Defense Attorney

Remember that the failure to provide a defendant with a lawyer at a lineup or showup during a critical stage results in the exclusion at trial of the results of the confrontation. Individuals should be informed of their right to the presence and advice of an attorney of their choice and that a lawyer will be appointed at no expense in the event that they cannot afford legal representation. A defendant may knowingly, voluntarily, and intelligently waive his or her right to a lawyer.

A lawyer's role is to observe the lineup and to take note of how the police conduct the lineup. The lawyer's presence provides an incentive for the police to insure fair procedures. The U.S. Supreme Court explained that an attorney serves an important purpose because suspects are likely to be nervous and lack the training to detect improper influences and may be distracted by other individuals in the lineup and by the commotion and bright lights. There is disagreement among commentators, but most agree that the attorney should not object to or correct police procedures. The lawyer will have the opportunity to question the fairness and accuracy of the lineup on cross-examination at trial.

Law enforcement officers are required to notify the lawyer in advance of the lineup to insure his or her presence. In the event that the lawyer is unavailable, the lineup should be postponed or a substitute attorney appointed, or the suspect should be asked whether he or she is willing to waive representation by a lawyer. The next section discusses the consequences of failing to provide legal representation to a defendant at a postindictment lineup or showup.

Tainted Lineups and Courtroom Identifications

As you recall, the Supreme Court held in *Wade* and in *Gilbert* that a failure to provide a defendant with a lawyer results in the exclusion of the results of a postindictment identification from trial. The Supreme Court explained that "[o]nly a per se [automatic] exclusionary rule" can insure that law enforcement authorities will "respect the accused's constitutional right to the presence of his counsel at the critical lineup" (*Gilbert,* 388 U.S. at 272).

What is the impact of a failure to provide an attorney on courtroom identifications? In *Gilbert,* the Supreme Court held that a witness may still identify the offender where the prosecution establishes by clear and convincing evidence that the in-court identification is based on observations that are not derived from the lineup. The test to be applied is "[w]hether, granting establishment of the primary illegality, the evidence to which instant objection is made has been come at by exploitation of that illegality or instead by means sufficiently distinguishable to be purged of the primary taint." Application of this test requires the weighing and balancing of various factors. A judge is likely to permit a courtroom identification by a witness who had a clear view of the crime, whose description of the offender matched the individual he or she selected at the lineup, and for whom a short period elapsed between the identification and the crime. Several factors for judges to consider were identified in *Gilbert.*

- The witness's opportunity to observe the offender during the criminal act.
- The extent of the similarity between the prelineup description of the offender and the physical appearance of the individual identified in the lineup.
- The identification or failure to identify the defendant at a photographic array or at the lineup.
- Whether there was a brief or lengthy period between the criminal act and the lineup identification.

You will find both *United States v. Wade* and *Gilbert v. California* on the study site. In reading these cases, you should focus on three issues. First, does a lineup or showup violate a defendant's Fifth Amendment right against self-incrimination? Second, why did the Supreme Court recognize that a defendant has a right to a lawyer at a postindictment lineup or showup? Third, under what circumstances may a victim or eyewitness make an in-court identification of an offender who has been denied his or her right to an attorney? In considering the *Wade–Gilbert* rule, pay attention to how the Supreme Court balances the protections to be accorded to defendants against society's interest in criminal investigation and prosecution. You should also make note of the Supreme Court's concern with insuring that identifications are conducted in a fair fashion.

You can find United States v. Wade *and* Gilbert v. California *on the study site, http://www.sagepub.com/lippmancp.*

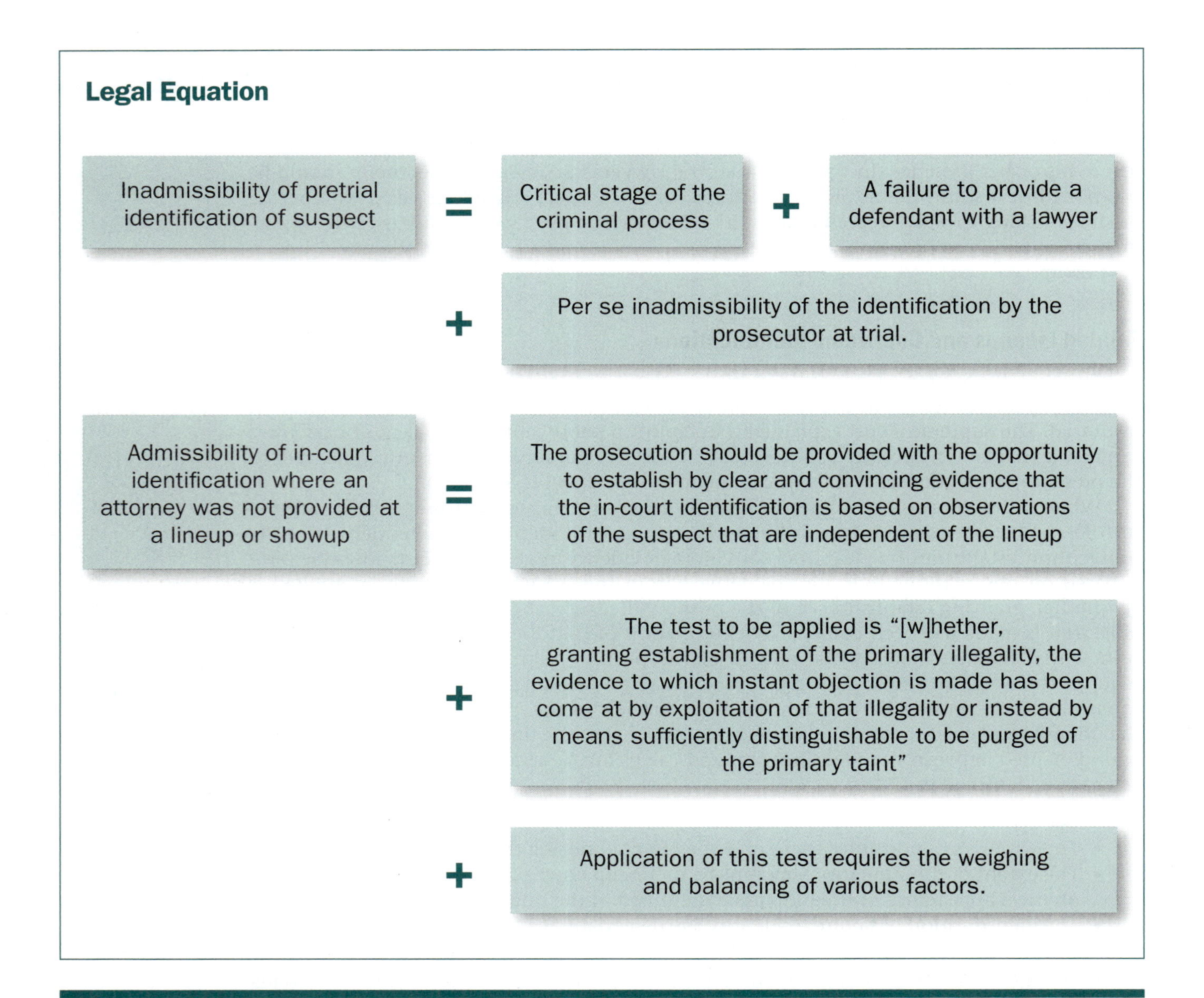

Cases and Comments

1. ***The Role of Counsel.*** The American Law Institute (ALI) is a private group of lawyers and judges who work for legal reform. In 1975, the ALI published the *Model Code of Pre-Arraignment Procedure* in which they discussed two different approaches to the role of the attorney at a lineup. The accepted view is that the lawyer is to observe police procedures to guard against unfairness. The alternative view is that the lawyer should make verbal objections and suggestions. The commentary observes that one problem with the second approach is that a court that adopts this perspective may prevent a lawyer from raising any issues that the attorney did not object to at the lineup. As a result, lawyers would feel compelled to raise every conceivable problem with the lineup and slow the procedure.

2. ***Congressional Legislation.*** Congress attempted to overturn the decision in *Wade* in the Omnibus Crime Control and Safe Streets Act of 1968. Section 3502 provides

that the "testimony of a witness that saw the accused commit or participate in the commission of the crime for which the accused is being tried shall be admissible in evidence in a criminal prosecution in any trial court ordained and established under Article III of the Constitution of the United States." Judges have tended to disregard this statute. How does this statute change the holdings in *Wade* and *Gilbert*? The question for constitutional scholars is whether Congress under the separation of powers doctrine may reverse through legislation a constitutional decision by the U.S. Supreme Court.

9.1 YOU DECIDE

Kare Asjernesen, a Norwegian seaman whose ship was docked at St. Thomas, Virgin Islands, was robbed as he was leaving the bathroom at Katie's Bar. A stranger approached him in the narrow corridor outside the bathroom and suddenly drew and held a knife to Asjernesen's neck. The assailant took eight dollars from Asjernesen and fled. The police arrived roughly thirty minutes later. Asjernesen described the robber as a dark brown African with prominent lips, five feet, ten inches tall, weighing 135 to 140 pounds, wearing pink pants and white shoes. Asjernesen's ship was scheduled to leave the next day at 1:00 P.M. The bartender stated that the robber was named "Al" or "Bomba." The police located and arrested Bomba at roughly 3:40 A.M. He was wearing pink pants and white shoes but was slightly over six feet tall and weighed 195 pounds.

Asjernesen went to the police station and identified Charles Callwood ("Bomba") as the robber. Callwood was seated next to one or two plainclothes police officers who bore no physical resemblance to the accused. Callwood claimed that the police pointed at him and asked Asjernesen whether Callwood was the robber. Following the identification, Asjernesen sat in the same room with Callwood filling in the details of his complaint.

Asjernesen made an in-court identification of Callwood and was asked on cross-examination about his identification in the police station. His testimony, perhaps due to Asjernesen's poor grasp of English, indicated that his identification was both immediate and influenced by the police identification of Callwood as the robber.

The Third Circuit Court of Appeals curiously affirmed the judgment of the trial court that the identification was conducted at a "critical stage" in the criminal justice process and that Callwood was improperly deprived of the representation of a lawyer. The Third Circuit Court of Appeals, however, also affirmed the ruling of District Court Judge A. Leon Higgenbotham that Asjernesen's in-court identification of Callwood was based on an observation of the suspect independent of the lineup. Callwood was found guilty of robbery at trial and was sentenced to prison for ten years.

Do you agree with the prosecutor's argument at trial that the government was justified in conducting the identification as a showup in the absence of Callwood's lawyer because Asjernesen's ship was departing the island at roughly 1:00 P.M. and that it was necessary to obtain an identification of Callwood as quickly as possible? As a judge, would you have permitted Asjernesen to make an in-court identification? See *Virgin Islands v. Callwood,* 440 F.2d 1206 (3d Cir. 1971).

You can find the answer by referring to the study site, http://www.sagepub.com/lippmancp.

The Sixth Amendment and Prearraignment Identifications

In *Kirby v. Illinois,* the U.S. Supreme Court held that a **showup** following arrest but before the initiation of adversary criminal proceedings (whether by way of formal charge, preliminary hearing, indictment, information, or arraignment) is not a critical stage of criminal prosecution at which the suspect is entitled to counsel (*Kirby v. Illinois,* 406 U.S. 682 [1972]).

Willie Shard reported to the Chicago police that two men had robbed him of his wallet containing traveler's checks and a Social Security card. The next day, two officers stopped Kirby and Bean, and when asked for identification, the two men produced three traveler's checks, a Social Security card, and other documents bearing the name Willie Shard. Kirby and Bean were arrested and taken to the police station where Shard positively identified them as the robbers. Six weeks later, Kirby and Bean were indicted for the robbery of Willie Shard. Shard testified that he had identified the two men at the police station, and he then identified them in the courtroom. Both Kirby and Bean were convicted and appealed on the grounds that they had been denied a lawyer at the showup (684).

The U.S. Supreme Court held that the defendants were not entitled to legal representation at the showup following their arrest. The Court explained that the Sixth Amendment right to counsel attaches following the commencement of criminal proceedings, which is the "starting point of our whole system of adversary criminal justice." The Supreme Court offered two reasons for the right to a lawyer attaching following the initiation of criminal proceedings:

1. ***Efficiency.*** During the investigative stage, the police should not be required to slow their investigation and to delay lineups and showups until the defendant hires a lawyer.
2. ***Prosecution.*** The initiation of criminal proceedings by the filing of a formal charge indicates that the Government has decided to prosecute the accused, and it is at this point that the accused is in need of legal protection, advice, and assistance (690).

Justices Brennan, Douglas, and Marshall, dissenting from the majority, argued that suspects should receive the assistance of a lawyer at all stages of the criminal justice process (698). Five years following *Kirby,* in *Moore v. Illinois,* the Supreme Court once again confronted the question at what point a suspect should be entitled to the assistance of an attorney.

In *Moore,* the victim was raped at knifepoint in her bedroom. She was able to view Moore's face for ten to fifteen seconds and provided the police with a description of the rapist along with a notebook that the assailant left behind. The police showed the victim two groups of photographs. She selected thirty suspects who resembled her attacker from the first group of 200 photos. The victim then selected two or three individuals from a second group of ten photographs. Defendant Moore was among this group. The police also found a letter in the notebook left behind by the perpetrator written by a woman with whom Moore had been staying (*Moore v. Illinois,* 434 U.S. 220, 222 [1977]).

Six days following the sexual assault, Moore was arrested for the crime, and the next morning, he appeared at a preliminary hearing to determine whether he should be bound over to a grand jury. Moore appeared before the judge and was charged with rape and deviate sexual behavior. The victim was asked by the judge whether she saw her assailant in the courtroom, and she pointed at Moore.

The victim testified at trial that she had identified Moore as her assailant in the preliminary hearing. She then proceeded to identify the defendant in the courtroom as the man who had raped her. Moore was convicted of rape, deviate sexual behavior, burglary, and robbery.

The Supreme Court had little difficulty in holding that Moore's Sixth Amendment rights were violated by his identification without legal representation at the preliminary hearing. The Supreme Court observed that it was difficult to conceive of a more suggestive identification. The victim viewed her assailant for only ten to fifteen seconds and later was asked to make an identification "after she was told she was going to view the suspect, after she was told his name and heard it called as he was led before the bench, and after she heard the prosecutor recite the evidence believed to implicate the petitioner" (229–230).

Why is the identification of Moore excluded from evidence while the identification of Kirby is admissible in evidence? An identification that is obtained prior to the initiation of a formal criminal prosecution (*Kirby*) is just as likely to influence the jury or to run the risk of misidentification as an identification that is obtained following the initiation of a formal criminal prosecution (*Moore*). On the other hand, providing a suspect an attorney prior to the initiation of criminal proceedings may prove burdensome to the police who require the flexibility and freedom to utilize lineups and confrontations as an investigative tool without being required to wait for the arrival of a lawyer. As noted in *Kirby,* the Court did not want to "import into a routine police investigation an absolute constitutional guarantee historically and rationally applicable only after the onset of formal prosecutorial proceedings" (690). As we shall see later in this chapter, a defendant subjected to a suggestive confrontation prior to the initiation of adversary proceedings always has a remedy under the Due Process Clause of the U.S. Constitution.

In the next section, we will explore whether defendants have a Sixth Amendment right to a lawyer during a photographic identification.

You can find Kirby v. Illinois *and* Moore v. Illinois *on the study site, http://www.sagepub.com/lippmancp.*

Legal Equation

Preindictment lineups and right to an attorney	=	A showup or lineup after arrest but before the initiation of adversary criminal proceedings (whether by way of formal charge, preliminary hearing, indictment, information, or arraignment) is not a critical stage of criminal prosecution at which the accused is entitled to counsel.

Cases and Comments

State Law. In *Blue v. State,* the Alaska Supreme Court ruled that an individual is entitled to legal representation at a preindictment lineup.

Three plainclothes officers located the individuals that they believed had robbed a bar within two and one-half hours of the crime. One of the officers telephoned Francis Nickens, the bartender in the tavern that had been robbed, and asked her to come to the Circle M. She arrived roughly twenty minutes later and was ushered into the poolroom. Nickens was confronted with three undercover police officers and three patrons along with the two suspects. Nickens identified Dennis Benefield as one of the robbers and, after some difficulty, also selected Clifton Blue. The two suspects were formally arrested and charged with armed robbery. A second preindictment lineup was conducted at which the accused were accompanied by a lawyer. Nickens identified Benefield but continued to have difficulty identifying Blue. The eyewitnesses to the robbery failed to identify either Benefield or Blue. The two were later indicted for armed robbery. Nickens identified both Benefield and Blue as the robbers at trial. She based her in-court identification of Blue on her prior identification at the Circle M Bar as well as having seen Blue during the robbery, although both robbers wore nylon stockings over their heads.

Blue appealed his conviction arguing that he possessed a right to an attorney at the identification at the Circle M lineup. He noted that Article I, Section 11 of the Alaska Constitution provides in part that "in all criminal prosecutions, the accused shall have the right... to have the assistance of counsel for his defense."

The Alaska Supreme Court recognized the interests of a suspect in having a lawyer present to observe the lineup. This would enable the attorney to point out any suggestive aspects of the lineup in his or her cross-examination of the police at trial. The Alaska Supreme Court accordingly held that in "balancing the need for prompt investigation against a suspect's right to fair procedures... a suspect who is in custody is entitled to have counsel present at a pre-indictment lineup unless exigent circumstances exist so that providing counsel would unduly interfere with prompt and purposeful investigation."

The Supreme Court ruled that Blue was properly provided with an attorney at the second preindictment lineup. As for the first identification in the Circle M, the Alaska Supreme Court found that the police "were making every effort to conduct a lineup while the memory of the witness was fresh.... [P]roviding a right to counsel at this late hour of the night might have postponed the lineup until the following day.... [P]roviding counsel could have precluded the State's diligent efforts to obtain an identification while the facts were still fresh in the eyewitness' mind." The Alaska Supreme Court concluded that providing a lawyer under these circumstances was neither "practical, reasonable or mandated by our constitution." See *Blue v. State,* 558 P.2d 636 (Alaska 1977).

In 1981, the California Supreme Court, in *People v. Bustamonte,* ruled that Article I, Section 15 of the California Constitution, which provides a defendant "the assistance of counsel," guarantees a lawyer at lineup. The California Supreme Court held that a pretrial lineup is a "critical stage in the prosecution of a criminal case." It is at this point that many innocent individuals are at risk of being swept up into the criminal justice system. The court characterized the rule in *Kirby* as "wholly unrealistic." The defendants who are most in need of protection from an erroneous identification are the defendants whose indictment primarily depends on identification by eyewitnesses. The *Kirby* rule "removes the protective effects of counsel's presence precisely when the danger of convicting an innocent defendant upon a mistaken identification is greatest." The California Supreme Court observed that the police can circumvent *Wade* and *Gilbert* by simply delaying a formal indictment and then conducting a lineup at which a lawyer is not required. Extending the right to counsel to preindictment lineups may burden the police and delay lineups, but this is not a sufficiently significant obstacle to justify denying suspects the protection of a lawyer. See *People v. Bustamonte,* 634 P.2d 927 (Cal. 1981).

In *Commonwealth v. Richman,* the Pennsylvania Supreme Court held that a suspect was entitled to representation by an attorney following an arrest based on a warrant as well as following a warrantless arrest. Judge Eagen, in his concurring opinion, observed that the "artificial distinction . . . between post-charge and precharge lineups is unwise and infringes upon the protections society should grant an accused. To force an accused to stand alone against the full force and investigative powers of organized society, until he is actually charged with the commission of the crime, is an outrageous injustice" (*Commonwealth v. Richman,* 320 A.2d 351, 352–353 [Pa. 1974]). Do you agree with the decisions of the Alaska, California, and Pennsylvania Supreme Courts or with the decision of the U.S. Supreme Court in *Kirby v. Illinois*?

The Sixth Amendment and Photographic Displays

In *United States v. Wade,* the U.S. Supreme Court held that an individual had no right to a lawyer to observe the taking of fingerprints, hair and blood samples, and other tests that relied on standard scientific techniques and procedures. The Court reasoned that the defense attorney and defense experts could easily examine the test results and procedures following the test and effectively cross-examine the police laboratory technicians at trial.

What about photographic identifications? **Photographic displays,** or **noncorporeal identifications,** pose a particular challenge. On one hand, the defense attorney typically is informed of the results of an identification and is able to examine the photographs to detect whether the suspect's photo was larger, more colorful, or distinguished in any fashion from the other photos. On the other hand, unless a lawyer is present, there is no way of knowing what occurred during the identification.

In 1973, in *United States v. Ash,* the U.S. Supreme Court held that a postindictment photographic display is not a "critical stage" of the prosecution and that the Sixth Amendment does not entitle the accused to the presence of a lawyer (*United States v. Ash,* 413 U.S. 300 [1973]).

Almost three years after being arrested for armed robbery and two years following their indictment, Charles Ash and John Bailey were brought to trial. On the eve of the trial, the prosecutor used an array of five color photographs to confirm that the eyewitnesses would be able to make in-court identifications. Three of the four witnesses selected the picture of Ash. None of the witnesses selected the photo of Bailey.

At trial, the three eyewitnesses who were in the bank at the time of the robbery identified Ash as the gunman but cautioned that they were uncertain of their identifications. None of the eyewitnesses made an in-court identification of Bailey. The fourth eyewitness who had seen the robbers remove their masks made positive in-court identifications of both Ash and Bailey. Ash was convicted and sentenced to a prison term of between eighty months and twelve years. Bailey was acquitted (301–305).

Ash claimed that he had been denied the right to counsel at the photo display, which constituted a "critical stage" of the criminal process. How could Ash's lawyer effectively challenge the fairness of the photographic display on cross-examination when he did not observe the identification?

The U.S. Supreme Court held that there was much less need for a lawyer at a photographic display than at a lineup. A lawyer must be present at a lineup to observe any bias and suggestiveness and to effectively cross-examine the police at trial (306–313). In contrast, in a photographic display, the accused is not present and has no need for a lawyer's assistance. The defense attorney is able to guard against suggestiveness by inspecting the size and format of the photographs and then has the opportunity to point out any bias to the jury (316–318).

Justices Brennan, Douglas, and Marshall challenged the reasoning of the majority, noting that a defense lawyer's access to a photo display cannot capture gestures, facial expressions, inflections, or comments by the police that may have intentionally or unintentionally influenced a witness. The dissenters argued that a fair trial could be guaranteed only by providing for the right to a lawyer at both a **corporeal identification** and a noncorporeal photographic display.

Justice Brennan pointed out that the fact that a witness identified a suspect in a photographic display is as potentially harmful to a defendant at trial as the fact that a witness identified a suspect at a lineup. He observed that there is "something ironic about the court's conclusion today that a pretrial lineup identification is a 'critical stage' of the prosecution because counsel's presence can help to compensate for the accused's deficiencies as an observer, but that a pretrial photographic identification is not a 'critical stage'... because the accused is not able to observe it at all.... [T]here simply is no meaningful difference... between corporeal and photographic identifications" (344).

The Supreme Court's ruling in *Ash* that a lawyer is not required at photo arrays, according to some commentators, has led the police to rely on photographic identifications rather than physical lineups. Do you agree with the Supreme Court's conclusion that "[w]e are not persuaded that the risks inherent in the use of photographic displays are so pernicious that an extraordinary system of safeguards is required" (320).

You can find United States v. Ash *on the study site, http://www.sagepub.com/lippmancp.*

Legal Equation

Photo display and Sixth Amendment right to counsel	=	The right to a lawyer historically is limited to a "trial-like adversary confrontation" in which a suspect is physically present and is being examined by governmental authorities
	+	These postindictment confrontations are considered critical only when the presence of a lawyer is necessary to protect the defendant and to guarantee the defendant a fair trial
	+	In a photographic display, the accused is not present, and therefore, there is no need for the lawyer to assist him or her. The photographic array can be re-created by the defense attorney prior to trial.

Cases and Comments

1. ***Photo of a Lineup.*** Defendant Gregory Richard Barker appealed his convictions on three counts of bank robbery. Barker contends that the district court should have granted his motion for a mistrial on the ground that his Sixth Amendment rights were violated when a prosecution witness, Tomory, was shown a photograph of a lineup and made a positive identification of Barker. Neither Barker nor his attorney had been notified, and neither was present at Tomory's postindictment identification. Tomory previously had been unable to pick Barker out of a "physical" lineup.

The circuit court of appeals held that the fact that the lineup is depicted in the photograph does not call into question the reasoning behind the decision in *Ash.* Counsel must be present where there is a potential "that the accused might be misled by his lack of familiarity with the law or overpowered by his professional adversary," or where counsel would "produce equality in a trial-like adversary confrontation." In this case, as in *Ash,* the defendant was not present when the photograph of the lineup was shown to the witnesses and thus could not be "misled" or "overpowered," during the identification process. The defense attorney is able to examine the photographs and to cross-examine the police, whether the photos portrayed a lineup or an array of suspects. The court concluded that a defendant has no right to have counsel present when a witness is shown a photograph of a lineup. Does this ruling undermine the protections provided in *Wade.* See *United States v. Barker,* 988 F.2d 77 (9th Cir. 1993). See also *United States v. Amrine,* 724 F.2d 84 (8th Cir. 1983) (defendant had no right to have counsel present when witnesses are shown a videotape of a lineup).

2. ***State Law.*** The Pennsylvania Supreme Court interpreted Article I, Section 9 of the Pennsylvania Constitution as requiring the presence of a lawyer during a postarrest photo array. There is no requirement of a lawyer prior to an arrest. William Pereau, a taxicab driver, was robbed at gunpoint on December 25, 1980. Pereau contacted the police and viewed one hundred slides, none of which apparently pictured the robbers. Nine days later, Pereau opened the newspaper and saw a picture of one of the robbers, John Ferguson, who had been arrested for the robbery-homicide of another cabdriver. On January 12, 1981, Pereau viewed a photo array and immediately identified Ferguson as the robber. Ferguson was arrested two days later for robbing Pereau. On March 4, 1981, Pereau failed to identify Ferguson in a lineup but, the next day, singled him out at a preliminary hearing. As Ferguson's trial approached, Pereau met with a prosecutor on March 25, 1982. The prosecutor presented Pereau with the same photo array that he had viewed on January 12, 1981, and Pereau once again selected Ferguson.

A Pennsylvania superior court ruled that the taxicab driver's identification of Ferguson on January 12, 1981, was admissible in evidence at trial. The March 25, 1982, identification, however, was held inadmissible at trial because Ferguson's lawyer was not present. Would Ferguson have benefited from the presence of a lawyer at both photo identifications? Is the Pennsylvania law on photo identifications a better approach than the Supreme Court holding in *United States v. Ash.* See *Commonwealth v. Ferguson,* 475 A.2d 810 (Pa. Super. Ct. 1984).

The Due Process Test

We have seen that suspects involved in lineups and showups following the initiation of criminal proceedings are entitled to representation by a lawyer. The dissenting judges pointed out that this left suspects in lineups or showups conducted prior to the initiation of criminal proceedings and in photo displays with little protection against suggestive identification procedures.

On the same day that the Supreme Court decided *Wade* and *Gilbert,* the Court responded in *Stovall v. Denno* to the concerns of the dissenting judges and held that suspects during the preindictment phase are protected by the Due Process Clauses of the Fifth and Fourteenth Amendments against identification procedures that create a likelihood that an innocent individual will be misidentified and deprived of life (the death penalty) or liberty (prison) without due process of law (unfairly).

The due process test applies throughout the criminal justice process. In other words, the due process test applies to lineups, showups, and photographic displays, whether preindictment or postindictment. Professor Joshua Dressler (Dressler & Michaels, 2006, p. 569) notes that the due process test "applies regardless of whether the identification was corporeal or noncorporeal, occurred before or after formal charges were initiated, and whether or not counsel was present." The next section examines the Fifth and Fourteenth Amendment due process test as explained in 1977 by the Supreme Court in *Manson v. Brathwaite* (432 U.S. 98 [1977]).

You can read Stovall v. Denno, *which is discussed later in the chapter, on the study site, http://www.sagepub.com/lippmancp.*

Suggestiveness, Reliability, and the Totality of the Circumstances

In *Manson,* Glover, a police undercover agent, and Henry Alton Brown, a police informant, went to an apartment in Hartford, Connecticut, to purchase narcotics from "Dickie Boy" Cicero. They knocked, and the door was opened twelve to eighteen inches. Glover observed a man and a woman, asked for "two things" of narcotics, and handed the man two ten-dollar bills. The door closed, and when the door reopened, the man handed Glover two glassine bags. Glover stood within two feet of "the seller" and observed his face. Glover immediately drove to police headquarters where he described the seller to Officer D'Onofrio, who concluded that the description fit Brathwaite. D'Onofrio then obtained a photo of Brathwaite that he left for Glover. Two days following the sale, Glover identified the photo as the individual who sold him narcotics, and Brathwaite accordingly was arrested and, eight months later, was brought to trial for the possession and sale of heroin. Glover testified that there was no doubt that the photograph pictured the man whom he had seen at the apartment and proceeded to make an in-court identification of Brathwaite. The jury rejected Brathwaite's alibi defense and convicted him of two counts of selling an illegal narcotic (*Manson v. Brathwaite,* 432 U.S. 98, 101–103 [1977]).

Brathwaite argued that Glover's testimony regarding his identification of Brathwaite in the photograph should have been excluded from evidence on the grounds that the identification was so suggestive that it created an unreasonable risk that Glover would make a false identification and select Brathwaite as the individual who had sold him drugs. After all, why was Glover not given the pictures of various individuals from which to choose rather than a single photograph? There also was a significant possibility that Glover was influenced by D'Onofrio's conclusion that Glover's description fit Brathwaite (110).

The U.S. Supreme Court recognized that Brathwaite was correct in arguing that the single photo identification was so suggestive that it ran an unreasonable risk that Glover would select Brathwaite as the individual who sold him drugs. This procedure also was unnecessary because D'Onofrio easily could have compiled an array of several photographs. The Court nevertheless rejected Brathwaite's argument that testimony regarding the identification process should have been automatically excluded from evidence (per se exclusion). The adoption of such an inflexible rule inevitably would "frustrate" rather than "promote" justice. The fact that a procedure is suggestive did not mean that the identification is inaccurate and should be automatically excluded from evidence. The Supreme Court adopted a "totality-of-the-circumstances" test to the admission of identifications under the due process test. There are four steps involved in determining whether to admit identification evidence under this test.

First, the defendant must establish by a preponderance of the evidence (fifty-one percent) that the procedure was suggestive. Second, the obligation shifts to the prosecution to demonstrate that the procedure nevertheless is reliable, meaning that the result can be trusted.

- ***Suggestive.*** The defendant must establish that the identification was impermissibly suggestive by a preponderance of the evidence.
- ***Reliable.*** The prosecution must demonstrate that the identification is reliable, meaning that the identification can be trusted.

Reliability is the central question in determining whether an identification violates due process of law. Reliability is determined by a totality of the circumstances considering various factors relating to the witness's observation of the offender. Third, the judge examines the following six factors to determine the reliability of the identification:

- ***Perception.*** Opportunity to view the offender at the time of the crime.
- ***Concentration.*** Ability to focus on the offender's appearance.
- ***Accuracy.*** Accuracy of the description of the suspect following the crime.
- ***Certainty.*** Certainty in the identification of the defendant.
- ***Time.*** Length of time that elapsed between the crime and the identification.
- ***Other evidence.*** Additional evidence that the defendant was involved in the crime.

These factors tell us that we should have confidence in the identification of an offender by a victim or eyewitness who closely observed an offender for a lengthy period of time. On the other hand, we may question the identification of an offender by a victim or eyewitness who does not have the opportunity to clearly view the offender.

Fourth, these factors are to be weighed against the fact that the witness may be influenced by the suggestiveness of the identification. *The court must determine whether, based on the totality of the circumstances, the suggestive procedures create a "very substantial likelihood of irreparable misidentification."* In other words, did the identification result from the observation of the suspect at the scene of the crime, or did the identification result from the suggestive identification (114–117)? The judge must now rule whether the identification is admissible or inadmissible.

- ***Admissible.*** The witness may testify at trial that he or she identified the defendant prior to the trial if the judge determines, based on the totality of the circumstances, that there is no substantial likelihood of irreparable misidentification.
- ***Inadmissible.*** The witness may not testify at trial that he or she identified the defendant prior to the trial if, based on the totality of the circumstances, there is a substantial likelihood of irreparable misidentification.

The Supreme Court in *Brathwaite* held that Glover's identification of Brathwaite was reliable and was not the product of the suggestiveness of the photograph. Glover was a trained observer who stood within two feet of Glover for two to three minutes. He provided D'Onofrio an accurate description within several minutes of having purchased the narcotics and viewed the photograph two days later. At trial, Glover indicated that there is "no question whatsoever" concerning the accuracy of his identification. The Supreme Court concluded that "[t]hese indicators of Glover's ability to make an accurate identification are hardly outweighed by the corrupting effect of the challenged identification itself. Although identifications arising from single-photograph displays may be viewed in general with suspicion, . . . [in this case] Glover examined the photograph alone, [and] there was no coercive pressure to make an identification arising from the presence of another. The identification was made in circumstances allowing care and reflection" (114–116).

Neil v. Biggers is an example of the Supreme Court's application of the totality-of-the-circumstances approach to a one-person showup. The victim was grabbed from behind in her kitchen by an assailant and then taken at knifepoint to the woods where she was raped. The entire incident lasted between fifteen and thirty minutes. The victim testified that she was able to see the perpetrator's face, which was illuminated by the light from the bedroom and by the full moon. As a result, she was able to provide the police with a general description of the assailant's age, height, complexion, skin texture, hair, and high-pitched voice (*Neil v. Biggers,* 409 U.S. 188 [1972]).

Over the course of the next seven months, the victim viewed lineups, showups, and thirty or forty photographs, none of which she believed included her assailant. The police then asked the victim to come to the police station to view a detainee. Two detectives walked the suspect past the victim, and at the victim's request, Biggers was directed to say, "Shut up or I'll kill you." The victim testified that she had "no doubt" that Biggers was her assailant (193).

The Supreme Court concluded that the victim's identification was reliable. She spent a significant amount of time with her assailant, was able to view his face, and provided a fairly complete description following the rape. As a nurse, she was accustomed to viewing people's physical characteristics and had an "unusual opportunity to observe and identify her assailant." The victim had viewed a number of individuals before singling out her assailant. The Court concluded that the victim's identification undoubtedly was reliable and more than likely was not influenced by the suggestiveness of the lineup. In addition, there was a compelling reason for accepting the identification because there "are rarely witnesses to a rape other than the victim, who often has a limited opportunity of observation" (200–201).

Manson v. Brathwaite is the next case in the text. Ask yourself whether the Supreme Court in *Manson* was correct in adopting the totality-of-the-circumstances approach rather than the per se approach in regard to the admissibility of identifications. Are courts engaging in the "fiction" that a suggestive identification is reliable because the victim or eyewitnesses had an opportunity to observe the offender at the scene of the crime?

You can find Neil v. Biggers *on the study site, http://www.sagepub.com/lippmancp.*

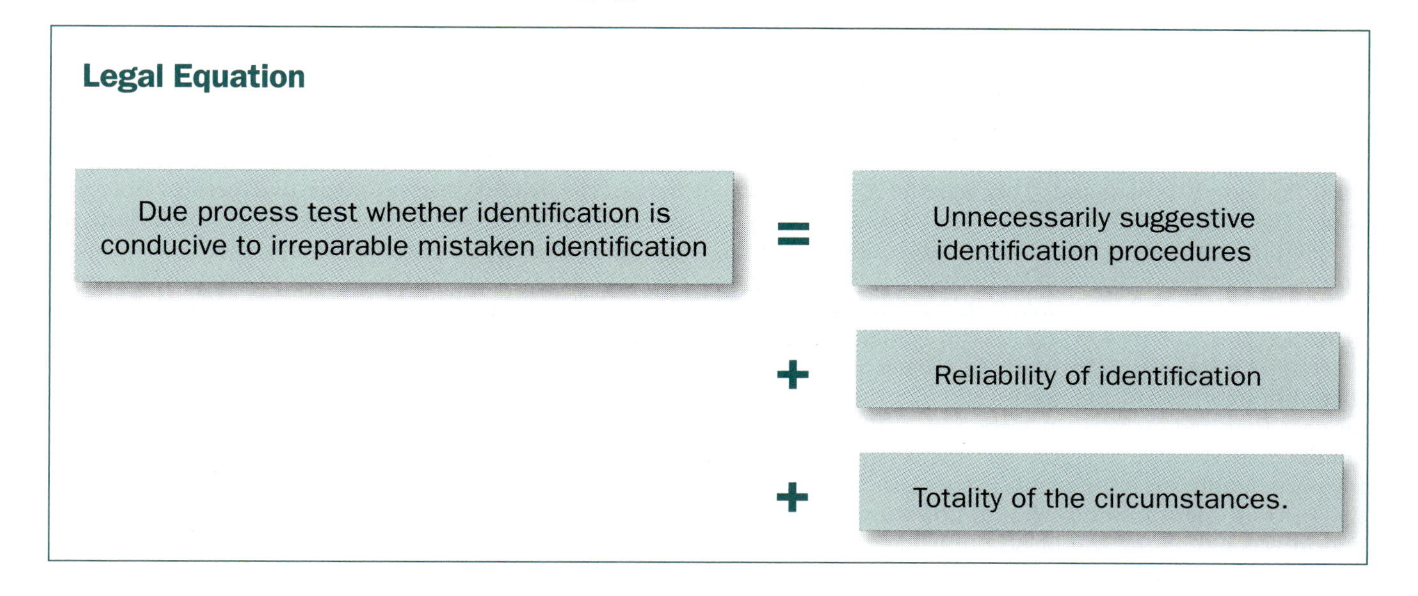

Was the identification in the photo display reliable?

Manson v. Brathwaite, 432 U.S. 98 (1977), *Blackmun, J.*

Facts

Jimmy D. Glover, a full-time trooper of the Connecticut State Police in 1970, was assigned to the Narcotics Division in an undercover capacity. On May 5 of that year, about 7:45 P.M., and while there was still daylight, Glover and Henry Alton Brown, an informant, went to an apartment building at 201 Westland, in Hartford, for the purpose of purchasing narcotics from "Dickie Boy" Cicero, a known narcotics dealer. Cicero, it was thought, lived on the third floor of that apartment building. Glover and Brown entered the building, observed by backup officers D'Onofrio and Gaffey, and proceeded by stairs to the third floor. Glover knocked at the door of one of the two apartments served by the stairway. The area was illuminated by natural light from a window in the third floor hallway. The door was opened twelve to eighteen inches in response to the knock. Glover observed a man standing at the door and, behind him, a woman. Brown identified himself. Glover then asked for "two things" of narcotics. The man at the door held out his hand, and Glover gave him two $10 bills. The door closed. Soon the man returned and handed Glover two glassine bags. While the door was open, Glover stood within two feet of the person from whom he made the purchase and observed his face. Five to seven minutes elapsed from the time the door first opened until it closed the second time.

Glover and Brown then left the building. This was about eight minutes after their arrival. Glover drove to headquarters where he described the seller to D'Onofrio and Gaffey. Glover at that time did not know the identity of the seller. He described him as being "a colored man, approximately five feet eleven inches tall, dark complexion, black hair, short Afro style, and having high cheekbones, and of heavy build. He was wearing at the time blue pants and a plaid shirt." D'Onofrio, suspecting from this description that respondent might be the seller, obtained a photograph of respondent from the Records Division of the Hartford Police Department. He left it at Glover's office. D'Onofrio was not acquainted with respondent personally but did know him by sight and had seen him "[s]everal times" prior to May 5. Glover, when alone, viewed the photograph for the first time upon his return to headquarters on May 7; he identified the person shown as the one from whom he had purchased the narcotics.

The toxicological report on the contents of the glassine bags revealed the presence of heroin. The report was dated July 16, 1970. Respondent was arrested on July 27 while visiting at the apartment of a Mrs. Ramsey on the third floor of 201 Westland. This was the apartment at which the narcotics sale had taken place on May 5.

Respondent was charged, in a two-count information, with possession and sale of heroin.... At his trial in January 1971, the photograph from which Glover had identified respondent was received in evidence without objection on the part of the defense. Glover also testified that although he had not seen respondent in the eight months that had elapsed since the sale, "there [was] no doubt whatsoever" in his mind that the person shown on the photograph was respondent. Glover also made a positive in-court identification without objection. No explanation was offered by the prosecution for the failure to utilize a photographic array or to conduct a lineup.

Respondent, who took the stand in his own defense, testified that on May 5, the day in question, he had been ill at his Albany Avenue apartment ("a lot of back pains, muscle spasms...a bad heart...high blood pressure...neuralgia in my face, and sinus") and that at no time on that particular day had he been at 201 Westland. His wife testified that she recalled, after her husband had refreshed her memory, that he was home all day on May 5. Doctor Wesley M. Vietzke, an internist and assistant professor of medicine at the University of Connecticut, testified that respondent had consulted him on April 15, 1970, and that he took a medical history from him, heard his complaints about his back and facial pain, and discovered that he had high blood pressure. The physician found respondent, subjectively, "in great discomfort." Respondent in fact underwent surgery for a herniated disc on August 17.

The jury found respondent guilty on both counts of the information. He received a sentence of not less than six nor more than nine years. His conviction was affirmed by the Supreme Court of Connecticut. That court noted the absence of an objection to Glover's in-court identification and concluded that respondent "has not shown that substantial injustice resulted from the admission of this evidence." Fourteen months later, respondent filed a petition for habeas corpus in the United States District Court for the District of Connecticut. He alleged that the admission of the identification testimony at his state trial deprived him of due process of law to which he was entitled under the Fourteenth Amendment. The district court...dismissed respondent's petition. On appeal, the United States Court of Appeals for the Second Circuit reversed....

In brief summary, the court felt that evidence as to the photograph should have been excluded, regardless of reliability, because the examination of the single photograph was unnecessary and suggestive. And, in the court's view, the evidence was unreliable in any event. We granted certiorari.

Issue

Petitioner at the outset acknowledges that "the procedure in the instant case was suggestive [because only one photograph was used] and unnecessary" [because there was no emergency or exigent circumstance]. The respondent, in agreement with the court of appeals, proposes a per se rule of exclusion that he claims is dictated by the demands of the Fourteenth Amendment's guarantee of due process.... [T]he courts of appeals appear to have developed at least two approaches to such evidence. The first, or per se approach, employed by the Second Circuit in the present case, focuses on the procedures employed and requires exclusion of the out-of-court identification evidence, without regard to reliability, whenever it has been obtained through unnecessarily suggested confrontation procedures. The justifications advanced are the elimination of evidence of uncertain reliability, deterrence of the police and prosecutors, and the stated "fair assurance against the awful risks of misidentification."

The second, or more lenient, approach is one that continues to rely on the totality of the circumstances. It permits the admission of the confrontation evidence if, despite the suggestive aspect, the out-of-court identification possesses certain features of reliability. Its adherents feel that the per se approach is not mandated by the Due Process Clause of the Fourteenth Amendment. This second approach, in contrast to the other, is ad hoc and serves to limit the societal costs imposed by a sanction that excludes relevant evidence from consideration and evaluation by the trier of fact.

Reasoning

Mr. Justice Stevens, in writing for the Seventh Circuit in *Kirby*, observed, "There is surprising unanimity among scholars in regarding such a rule [the per se approach] as essential to avoid serious risk of miscarriage of justice." He pointed out that well-known federal judges have taken the position that "evidence of, or derived from, a showup identification should be inadmissible unless the prosecutor can justify his failure to use a more reliable identification procedure." Indeed, the ALI *Model Code of Pre-Arraignment Procedure,* sections 160.1 and 160.2 (1975) (hereafter *Model Code*) frowns upon the use of a showup or the display of only a single photograph.

The respondent here stresses the same theme and the need for deterrence of improper identification practice, a factor he regards as preeminent. Photographic identification, it is said, continues to be needlessly employed.... He argues that a totality rule cannot be expected to have a significant deterrent impact; only a strict rule of exclusion will have direct and immediate impact on law enforcement agents. Identification evidence is so convincing to the jury that sweeping exclusionary rules are required. Fairness of the trial is threatened by suggestive confrontation evidence, and thus, it is said, an exclusionary rule has an established constitutional predicate.

There are, of course, several interests to be considered and taken into account.... Thus, *Wade* and its companion cases reflect the concern that the jury not hear eyewitness testimony unless that evidence has aspects of reliability. It must be observed that both approaches before us are responsive to this concern. The per se rule, however, goes too far since its application automatically and peremptorily, and without consideration of alleviating factors, keeps evidence from the jury that is reliable and relevant.

The second factor is deterrence. Although the per se approach has the more significant deterrent effect, the totality approach also has an influence on police behavior. The police will guard against unnecessarily suggestive procedures under the totality rule, as well as the per se one, for fear that their actions will lead to the exclusion of identifications as unreliable.

The third factor is the effect on the administration of justice. Here the per se approach suffers serious drawbacks. Since it denies the trier reliable evidence, it may result, on occasion, in the guilty going free. Also, because of its rigidity, the per se approach may make error by the trial judge more likely than the totality approach. And in those cases in which the admission of identification evidence is error under the per se approach but not under the totality approach—cases in which the identification is reliable despite an unnecessarily suggestive identification procedure—reversal is a Draconian sanction. Certainly, inflexible rules of exclusion that may frustrate rather than promote justice have not been viewed recently by this Court with unlimited enthusiasm.... Unlike a warrantless search, a suggestive preindictment identification procedure does not in itself intrude upon a constitutionally protected interest. Thus, considerations urging the exclusion of evidence deriving from a constitutional violation do not bear on the instant problem.

We therefore conclude that reliability is the linchpin in determining the admissibility of identification testimony for both pre- and post-*Stovall* confrontations. The factors to be considered... include the opportunity of the witness to view the criminal at the time of the crime, the witness's degree of attention, the accuracy of his prior description of the criminal, the level of certainty demonstrated at the confrontation, and the time between the crime and the confrontation. Against these factors is to be weighed the corrupting effect of the suggestive identification itself.

We turn, then, to the facts of this case and apply the analysis:

1. The opportunity to view. Glover testified that for two to three minutes, he stood at the apartment door, within two feet of the respondent. The door opened twice, and each time the man stood at the door. The moments passed, the conversation took place, and payment was made. Glover looked directly at his vendor. It was near sunset, to be sure, but the sun had not yet set, so it was not dark or even dusk or twilight. Natural light from outside entered the hallway through a window. There was natural light, as well, from inside the apartment.
2. The degree of attention. Glover was not a casual or passing observer, as is so often the case with eyewitness identification. Trooper Glover was a trained police officer on duty—and specialized in dangerous duty—when he called at the third floor of 201 Westland in Hartford on May 5, 1970. Glover himself was a Negro and unlikely to perceive only general features of "hundreds of Hartford black males," as the court of appeals stated. It is true that Glover's duty was that of ferreting out narcotics offenders and that he would be expected in his work to produce results. But it is also true that as a specially trained, assigned, and experienced officer, he could be expected to pay scrupulous attention to detail, for he knew that subsequently he would have to find and arrest his vendor. In addition, he knew that his claimed observations would be subject later to close scrutiny and examination at any trial.
3. The accuracy of the description. Glover's description was given to D'Onofrio within minutes after the transaction. It included the vendor's race, his height, his build, the color and style of his hair, and the high cheekbone facial feature. It also included clothing the vendor wore. No claim has been made that respondent did not possess the physical characteristics so described. D'Onofrio reacted positively at once. Two days later, when Glover was alone, he viewed the photograph D'Onofrio produced and identified its subject as the narcotics seller.
4. The witness's level of certainty. There is no dispute that the photograph in question was that of respondent. Glover, in response to a question

whether the photograph was that of the person from whom he made the purchase, testified, "There is no question whatsoever." This positive assurance was repeated.

5. The time between the crime and the confrontation. Glover's description of his vendor was given to D'Onofrio within minutes of the crime. The photographic identification took place only two days later. We do not have here the passage of weeks or months between the crime and the viewing of the photograph.

These indicators of Glover's ability to make an accurate identification are hardly outweighed by the corrupting effect of the challenged identification itself. Although identifications arising from single-photograph displays may be viewed in general with suspicion, we find in the instant case little pressure on the witness to acquiesce in the suggestion that such a display entails. D'Onofrio had left the photograph at Glover's office and was not present when Glover first viewed it two days after the event. There thus was little urgency, and Glover could view the photograph at his leisure. And since Glover examined the photograph alone, there was no coercive pressure to make an identification arising from the presence of another. The identification was made in circumstances allowing care and reflection.

Although it plays no part in our analysis, all this assurance as to the reliability of the identification is hardly undermined by the facts that respondent was arrested in the very apartment where the sale had taken place, and that he acknowledged his frequent visits to that apartment.

Holding

Surely, we cannot say that under all the circumstances of this case, there is "a very substantial likelihood of irreparable misidentification." Short of that point, such evidence is for the jury to weigh. We are content to rely upon the good sense and judgment of American juries, for evidence with some element of untrustworthiness is customary grist for the jury mill. Juries are not so susceptible that they cannot measure intelligently the weight of identification testimony that has some questionable feature.

Of course, it would have been better had D'Onofrio presented Glover with a photographic array including "so far as practicable...a reasonable number of persons similar to any person then suspected whose likeness is included in the array." *Model Code,* section 160.2(2). The use of that procedure would have enhanced the force of the identification at trial and would have avoided the risk that the evidence would be excluded as unreliable. But we are not disposed to view D'Onofrio's failure as one of constitutional dimension to be enforced by a rigorous and unbending exclusionary rule. The defect, if there be one, goes to weight and not to substance....

Dissenting, *Marshall, J.*, joined by *Brennan, J.*

Today's decision can come as no surprise to those who have been watching the Court dismantle the protections against mistaken eyewitness testimony erected a decade ago....But it is still distressing to see the Court virtually ignore the teaching of experience embodied in those decisions and blindly uphold the conviction of a defendant who may well be innocent.

The magnitude of the Court's error can be seen by analyzing...*Wade*...and the decisions following it. The foundation of...*Wade*...was the Court's recognition of the "high incidence of miscarriage of justice" resulting from the admission of mistaken eyewitness identification evidence at criminal trials. Relying on numerous studies made over many years by such scholars as Professor Wigmore and Mr. Justice Frankfurter, the Court concluded that "[t]he vagaries of eyewitness identification are well-known; the annals of criminal law are rife with instances of mistaken identification." It is, of course, impossible to control one source of such errors—the faulty perceptions and unreliable memories of witnesses—except through vigorously contested trials conducted by diligent counsel and judges. The Court in the *Wade* cases acted, however, to minimize the more preventable threat posed to accurate identification by "the degree of suggestion inherent in the manner in which the prosecution presents the suspect to witnesses for pretrial identification."...The crux of the *Wade* decisions...was the unusual threat to the truth-seeking process posed by the frequent untrustworthiness of eyewitness identification testimony. This, combined with the fact that juries unfortunately are often unduly receptive to such evidence, is the fundamental fact of judicial experience ignored by the Court today.

First, the per se rule...is not "inflexible." Where evidence is suppressed, for example, as the fruit of an unlawful search, it may well be forever lost to the prosecution. Identification evidence, however, can by its very nature be readily and effectively reproduced. The in-court identification, permitted under *Wade* and *Simmons* if it has a source independent of an uncounseled or suggestive procedure, is one example. Similarly, when a prosecuting attorney learns that there has been a suggestive confrontation, he can easily arrange another lineup conducted under scrupulously fair conditions. Since the same factors are evaluated in applying both the Court's totality test and the *Wade* independent-source inquiry, any identification which is "reliable" under the Court's test will support admission of evidence concerning such a fairly conducted lineup. The evidence of an additional, properly conducted confrontation will be more persuasive to a jury, thereby increasing the chance of a justified conviction where a reliable identification was tainted by a suggestive confrontation. At the same time, however, the effect of an unnecessarily suggestive identification—which has no value whatsoever in the law enforcement process—will be completely eliminated.

Second, other exclusionary rules have been criticized for preventing jury consideration of relevant and usually reliable evidence in order to serve interests unrelated to guilt or innocence, such as discouraging illegal searches or denial of counsel. Suggestively obtained eyewitness testimony is excluded, in contrast, precisely because of its unreliability and concomitant irrelevance. Its exclusion both protects the integrity of the truth-seeking function of the trial and discourages police use of needlessly inaccurate and ineffective investigatory methods.

Indeed, impermissibly suggestive identifications are not merely worthless law enforcement tools. They pose a grave threat to society at large in a more direct way than most governmental disobedience of the law.... For if the police and the public erroneously conclude, on the basis of an unnecessarily suggestive confrontation, that the right man has been caught and convicted, the real outlaw must still remain at large. Law enforcement has failed in its primary function and has left society unprotected from the depredations of an active criminal.

For these reasons, I conclude that adoption of the per se rule would enhance, rather than detract from, the effective administration of justice. In my view, the Court's totality test will allow seriously unreliable and misleading evidence to be put before juries. Equally important, it will allow dangerous criminals to remain on the streets while citizens assume that police action has given them protection. According to my calculus, all three of the factors upon which the Court relies point to acceptance of the per se approach.

Even more disturbing than the Court's reliance on the totality test, however, is the analysis it uses, which suggests a reinterpretation of the concept of due process of law in criminal cases. The decision suggests that due process violations in identification procedures may not be measured by whether the government employed procedures violating standards of fundamental fairness. By relying on the probable accuracy of a challenged identification, instead of the necessity for its use, the Court seems to be ascertaining whether the defendant was probably guilty. Until today, I had thought that "Equal justice under law" meant that the existence of constitutional violations did not depend on the race, sex, religion, nationality, or likely guilt of the accused. The Due Process Clause requires adherence to the same high standard of fundamental fairness in dealing with every criminal defendant, whatever his personal characteristics and irrespective of the strength of the State's case against him. Strong evidence that the defendant is guilty should be relevant only to the determination whether an error of constitutional magnitude was nevertheless harmless beyond a reasonable doubt. By importing the question of guilt into the initial determination of whether there was a constitutional violation, the apparent effect of the Court's decision is to undermine the protection afforded by the Due Process Clause. "It is therefore important to note that the state courts remain free, in interpreting state constitutions, to guard against the evil clearly identified by this case."

I consider first the opportunity that Officer Glover had to view the suspect. Careful review of the record shows that he could see the heroin seller only for the time it took to speak three sentences of four or five short words, to hand over some money, and later after the door reopened, to receive the drugs in return. The entire face-to-face transaction could have taken as little as fifteen or twenty seconds. But during this time, Glover's attention was not focused exclusively on the seller's face. He observed that the door was opened twelve to eighteen inches, that there was a window in the room behind the door, and most importantly, that there was a woman standing behind the man. Glover was, of course, also concentrating on the details of the transaction—he must have looked away from the seller's face to hand him the money and receive the drugs. The observation during the conversation thus may have been as brief as five or ten seconds.

As the Court notes, Glover was a police officer trained in and attentive to the need for making accurate identifications. Nevertheless, both common sense and scholarly study indicate that while a trained observer such as a police officer "is somewhat less likely to make an erroneous identification than the average untrained observer, the mere fact that he has been so trained is no guarantee that he is correct in a specific case. His identification testimony should be scrutinized just as carefully as that of the normal witness." Moreover, "identifications made by policemen in highly competitive activities, such as undercover narcotic agents... should be scrutinized with special care." Yet it is just such a searching inquiry that the Court fails to make here.

Another factor on which the Court relies—the witness's degree of certainty in making the identification—is worthless as an indicator that he is correct. Even if Glover had been unsure initially about his identification of respondent's picture, by the time he was called at trial to present a key piece of evidence for the State that paid his salary, it is impossible to imagine his responding negatively to such questions as, "Is there any doubt in your mind whatsoever" that the identification was correct? As the Court noted in *Wade*, "'It is a matter of common experience that, once a witness has picked out the accused at the [pretrial confrontation], he is not likely to go back on his word later on.'"

Finally, the Court makes much of the fact that Glover gave a description of the seller to D'Onofrio shortly after the incident. Despite the Court's assertion that because "Glover himself was a Negro and unlikely to perceive only general features of 'hundreds of Hartford black males,' as the Court of Appeals stated," the description given by Glover was actually no more than a general summary of the seller's appearance. We may discount entirely the seller's clothing, for that was of no significance later in the proceeding. Indeed, to the extent that Glover noticed clothes, his attention was diverted from the seller's face. Otherwise, Glover merely described vaguely the seller's height, skin color, hairstyle, and build. He did say that the seller had "high cheekbones," but there is no other mention of facial features, nor even an estimate of age. Conspicuously absent is any indication that the seller was a native of the West Indies, certainly something which a member of the black community could immediately recognize from both appearance and accent.

From all of this, I must conclude that the evidence of Glover's ability to make an accurate identification is far weaker than the Court finds it. In contrast, the procedure used to identify respondent was both extraordinarily suggestive and strongly conducive to error. In dismissing "the corrupting effect of the suggestive identification" procedure here, the Court virtually grants the police license to convict the innocent. By displaying a single photograph of respondent to the witness Glover, under the circumstances in this record, almost everything that could have been done wrong was done wrong.

In the first place, there was no need to use a photograph at all. Because photos are static, two-dimensional, and often outdated, they are "clearly inferior in reliability" to corporeal procedures. While the use of photographs is justifiable and often essential where the police have no knowledge of an offender's identity, the poor reliability of photos makes their use inexcusable where any other means of identification is available. Here, since Detective D'Onofrio believed that he knew the seller's identity, further investigation without resort to a photographic showup was easily possible. With little inconvenience, a corporeal lineup including Brathwaite might have been arranged. Properly conducted, such a procedure would have gone far to remove any doubt about the fairness and accuracy of the identification.

Worse still than the failure to use an easily available corporeal identification was the display to Glover of only a single picture, rather than a photo array. With good reason, such single-suspect procedures have "been widely condemned." They give no assurance that the witness can identify the criminal from among a number of persons of similar appearance, surely the strongest evidence that there was no misidentification. . . . The use of a single picture (or the display of a single live suspect, for that matter) is a grave error, of course, because it dramatically suggests to the witness that the person shown must be the culprit. Why else would the police choose the person? And it is deeply ingrained in human nature to agree with the expressed opinions of others—particularly others who should be more knowledgeable—when making a difficult decision. In this case, moreover, the pressure was not limited to that inherent in the display of a single photograph. Glover, the identifying witness, was a state police officer on special assignment. He knew that D'Onofrio, an experienced Hartford narcotics detective, presumably familiar with local drug operations, believed respondent to be the seller. There was at work, then, both loyalty to another police officer and deference to a better-informed colleague. Finally, of course, there was Glover's knowledge that without an identification and arrest, government funds used to buy heroin had been wasted.

The Court discounts this overwhelming evidence of suggestiveness, however. It reasons that because D'Onofrio was not present when Glover viewed the photograph, there was "little pressure on the witness to acquiesce in the suggestion." That conclusion blinks psychological reality. There is no doubt in my mind that even in D'Onofrio's absence, a clear and powerful message was telegraphed to Glover as he looked at respondent's photograph. He was emphatically told that "this is the man," and he responded by identifying respondent then and at trial "whether or not he was in fact 'the man.'"

I must conclude that this record presents compelling evidence that there was "a very substantial likelihood of misidentification" of respondent Brathwaite. The suggestive display of respondent's photograph to the witness Glover likely erased any independent memory that Glover had retained of the seller from his barely adequate opportunity to observe the criminal. . . . [T]he facts here reveal a substantial likelihood of misidentification in violation of respondent's right to due process of law. . . . I dissent from the Court's reinstatement of respondent's conviction.

Questions for Discussion

1. Was the identification in *Manson v. Brathwaite* impermissibly suggestive, and did it create a substantial likelihood of misidentification? Why did the Supreme Court rule that the use of Glover's photographic identification at trial did not violate due process?
2. What is the difference between the per se and the totality-of-the-circumstances approaches to the admissibility of identifications? Which approach do you favor?
3. Do you agree with the majority's conclusion that Glover's identification of Brathwaite was reliable? Summarize the argument of the dissent. Do you find the majority or the dissent more persuasive?
4. ***Problems in policing.*** In organizing a lineup, how would you avoid "suggestiveness"? Design a photo array that is not suggestive.

Cases and Comments

1. ***Single-Person Showups and Due Process.*** In *Stovall v. Denno,* as noted earlier, the Supreme Court analyzed the totality of the circumstances and affirmed the reliability of a single-person showup. Mrs. Behrendt, the victim of a brutal stabbing, identified her assailant and the killer of her husband from her hospital bed after having undergone an emergency surgery the previous day. Stovall was brought into the victim's hospital room while handcuffed to one of five police officers. He was the only African American in the room. Behrendt testified at trial that she identified Stovall as the perpetrator when he was presented to her, and she then proceeded to make an in-court identification. The defendant was convicted, sentenced to death, and appealed on the grounds that the victim's identification in the hospital room under suggestive circumstances violated due process of law.

The Supreme Court observed in *Stovall* that single-person showups have been "widely condemned" and observed that the confrontation in the hospital room was "unnecessarily suggestive and conducive to irreparable mistaken identification." The showup in this particular case, however, was not in violation of due process because the victim was the only person who could "exonerate Stovall." The hospital staff was uncertain how long Mrs. Behrendt might live, and the police wanted to learn as quickly as possible whether they had apprehended the correct suspect. The police, "[f]aced with the responsibility of identifying the attacker, with the need for immediate action and with the knowledge that Mrs. Behrendt could not visit the jail . . . followed the only feasible procedure and took Stovall to the hospital room. Under the circumstances, the usual police station line-up . . . was out of the question." See *Stovall v. Denno,* 388 U.S. 293 (1967).

The Supreme Court in *Stovall* held that due process is to be determined in light of the totality of the circumstances. Under this test, the suggestiveness of the identification was balanced against the fact that Mrs. Behrendt was able to see her assailant during the attack and was balanced against Mrs. Behrendt's severe medical condition. The police also needed to act quickly to determine whether the killer was still at large. You can read the decision for yourself on the Web site and determine whether you agree with the Supreme Court that the identification satisfied the demands of due process.

The Supreme Court in both *Biggers* and *Stovall* criticized single-person showups as suggestive but recognized that at times, this procedure is unavoidable. Single-person showups typically are conducted by the police in three instances.

- ***Crime scene.*** The police may apprehend a suspect immediately following a crime and present the suspect to the victim or to an eyewitness for identification. Showups that have been conducted immediately following a crime generally have been found to be reliable. The resort to this extraordinary procedure is justified by the need to protect the public against an offender who threatens the community.
- ***Courthouse.*** A victim or eyewitness may observe a suspect during an arraignment before a judge or inadvertently encounter the suspect in the courthouse. Courts will examine the impact of this encounter on the reliability of a witness's courtroom identification.
- ***Emergency.*** The police may face an emergency in which they are unable to rely on a lineup or photographic identification. Identifications under these circumstances are considered necessary to preserve identification evidence that otherwise may be lost. Courts balance the opportunity of the eyewitness or victim to view the crime against the suggestiveness of the identification and the risk of losing evidence.

You can find Stovall v. Denno *on the study site, http://www.sagepub.com/lippmancp.*

2. ***Lineups and Due Process.*** *Foster v. California* is an example of an identification tainted by "impermissible suggestiveness." Foster and Grice were prosecuted for the armed robbery of a Western Union office in violation of the California Penal Code. The only witness was Joseph David, the late-night manager of the Western Union office. David was called to the police station following Foster's arrest. There were three men in the lineup. Foster was close to six feet in height. The other men were short, and Foster was the only individual in the lineup who wore a leather jacket similar to the one worn by the robber. David "thought" that Foster was the robber but was not certain. He then asked to speak to Foster, and the two sat across from one another in an office. Following this meeting, David told the police that he remained uncertain as to whether Foster was the robber. A week later, the police arranged for a second five-person lineup; Foster was the only person who appeared in both lineups. David now was convinced that Foster was the robber and identified him as the offender.

The U.S. Supreme Court had little difficulty in reaching the conclusion based on the totality of the circumstances that the identification procedures were "unnecessarily suggestive and conducive to irreparable mistaken identification." Justice Abe Fortas concluded that *Foster* presents a "compelling example of unfair lineup procedures." First, Foster stood out from the other two men in the first lineup based on his height and his leather jacket. The police then resorted to a one-to-one confrontation. After failing to obtain an identification, another lineup was conducted, and Foster was the only individual who appeared in both the first and the second lineups. This finally yielded a definite identification. The "suggestive elements...made it all but inevitable that David would identify petitioner whether or not he was in fact 'the man.'" In effect, the police repeatedly said to the witness, "This is the man." The "pretrial confrontations" were "clearly so arranged as to make the resulting identifications virtually inevitable." Can you explain why the identifications in *Manson* and *Biggers* were considered reliable and the identification in *Foster* was considered unreliable? See *Foster v. California,* 394 U.S. 440, 441–444 (1969).

3. ***Photographic Identifications and Due Process.*** In 1968, in *Simmons v. United States,* the U.S. Supreme Court relied on the due process test to determine the admissibility of an in-court identification.

Three men robbed a savings and loan association in Chicago. Two of the men remained in the bank for roughly five minutes. The police were able to link the automobile used in the robbery to Andrews, Simmons, and Garrett. The police obtained six photos of Andrews and Simmons from Andrews's sister. These two individuals in most instances were pictured in a group along with various other individuals. A day following the robbery, the photos were separately shown to the five bank employees. Each witness identified Simmons as one of the robbers. A week or two later, three of the witnesses identified photographs of Garrett as the other robber; the other two stated that they did not have a clear view of the second robber. None identified Andrews. Simmons, Garrett, and Andrews were subsequently indicted. The FBI later showed the employees a series of photos, and they once again were able to identify Simmons.

The Government did not introduce the results of the photographic identification at trial and relied solely on the in-court identifications by the five bank employees. Each identified Simmons as one of the robbers at trial, and three identified Garrett. Simmons and Andrews subsequently were convicted of armed robbery. Andrews's conviction was reversed on appeal.

Simmons argued that the pretrial photographic identifications were unnecessarily suggestive and conducive to misidentification at trial, that the use of the photographs denied him due process of law, and that his conviction should be reversed. The Supreme Court declined to prohibit police reliance on photographs of suspects despite the risk of misidentification. The Court reasoned that photos can assist in "apprehending offenders and sparing innocent suspects...arrest by allowing eyewitnesses to exonerate them through scrutiny of photographs." The majority of the Court recognized the possibility that an eyewitness may make an error and select a photo of an individual who closely resembles the person who actually committed the crime or that a photograph may be displayed in suggestive fashion that draws the eyewitness's attention to a particular suspect. The Court majority conceded that in such cases, the photographic image is likely to remain fixed in the mind of the eyewitness when identifying the perpetrator at a lineup or when making an in-court identification. The Court nevertheless ruled that "each case must be considered on its own facts" and that "convictions based on eyewitness identification at trial following a pretrial identification by photograph will be set aside...only if the photographic identification procedure was so impermissibly suggestive as to give rise to a very substantial likelihood of irreparable misidentification."

In this instance, the Supreme Court stressed that the FBI had to act quickly. The suspects remained at large, and it was essential to determine whether the FBI was "on the right track, so that they could properly deploy their forces in Chicago and, if necessary, alert officials in other cities." Second, there was little likelihood of misidentification. The Court observed that the employees viewed the robbers, who did not wear masks, for five minutes in a well-lighted bank. The photo identification took place the following day when the employees' memories were fresh. The witnesses viewed the photos alone, and there is no indication that they were coached by the FBI.

The five eyewitnesses who identified Simmons in the photographic display again identified Simmons in the courtroom. They all affirmed their courtroom identifications under cross-examination. None identified Andrews, who was not as clearly presented in the photos. The Supreme Court concluded that "[t]aken together, these circumstances leave little room for doubt that the identification of Simmons was correct, even though the identification procedure employed may have in some respects fallen short of the ideal.... [T]he identification procedure...was not such as to deny Simmons due process of law." See *Simmons v. United States,* 390 U.S. 377 (1968).

Courts typically evaluate four areas in examining the suggestiveness of photographic identifications.

- ***Display.*** Whether the display of the photographs singled out a particular individual.
- ***Police.*** Whether the words, gestures, or actions of the police pointed to a particular photograph.
- ***Photo.*** Whether a particular photograph was sufficiently different in size, color, and the suspect's appearance to influence the selection of the eyewitness.
- ***Instructions.*** Whether the police indicated that the photograph of the offender may not be included in the photos.

You can find Simmons v. United States *on the study site, http://www.sagepub.com/lippmancp.*

9.2 YOU DECIDE

In December 2000, Theodore Rogers, a crack-cocaine addict living in Kentucky accompanied his supplier, James Moorman, to Merillville, Indiana. In return, Moorman gave Rogers some cocaine. The two left Kentucky in the morning and arrived at their destination in the afternoon. Rogers exited the vehicle, and Moorman drove off with an African American male who was waiting in the parking lot. Rogers returned after roughly twenty-five minutes, and Rogers took the wheel for the trip home. Rogers was pulled over for reckless driving, and the police uncovered a brick of cocaine in the glove compartment and $2,000 in cash hidden in the spare tire in the trunk. In September or October 2001, Rogers pled guilty. Shortly thereafter, Rogers agreed to assist the police but indicated that he did not believe that any of the photographs that he was shown pictured the African American male he had seen in the parking lot ten months earlier (it seems that the suspect's photo was in the array). Rogers did provide the police with a description of the man, which was not available to the Seventh Circuit Court of Appeals in its consideration of the case.

The police later arrested Winfred Owens, an African American male who the police believed had met with Moorman. Rogers testified that he immediately recognized Owens when the two briefly were cellmates in a lockup in a federal courthouse in late October 2001. Owens had just been arrested and was inexplicably placed in the same cell as Rogers, who was returning from a hearing before the federal district court, which was considering whether to accept his guilty plea. At trial, Rogers testified against Owens and identified him in court as the man he had seen in December 2000. Rogers admitted on cross-examination that he remembered Owens "better because he had spent time with him in the same cell." Asked to describe the man he had first seen in December 2000, Rogers, who is an African American, replied that the man "was a black guy" and that, to him, "most black guys look alike." Rogers pled guilty pursuant to a plea agreement to one count of possession with the intent to distribute cocaine and was sentenced to fifty-one months in prison. Owens was convicted and sentenced to ninety-seven months imprisonment. Owens appealed on the grounds that his identification had been unduly suggestive. Was Owens's identification "unnecessarily suggestive and conducive to irreparable mistaken identification"? See *United States v. Rogers*, 387 F.3d 925 (7th Cir. 2004).

You can find the answer by referring to the study site, http://www.sagepub.com/lippmancp.

State Law on Identifications

The Massachusetts Supreme Court and the New York Court of Appeals have held that the due process clauses of their state constitutions provide greater protection than the Due Process Clause of the U.S. Constitution and require the per se (automatic) exclusion of unduly suggestive identifications from evidence, however reliable. These two appellate courts have explained that their decisions to differ from their judicial brethren in virtually every other state are based on the fact that empirical studies indicate that suggestive identifications lead to mistaken identifications and increase the risk of wrongful convictions (*Commonwealth v. Johnson,* 650 N.E.2d 1257 [Mass. 1969]; *People v. Adams,* 423 N.E.2d 379 [N.Y. 1981]).

The Wisconsin Supreme Court has interpreted its state constitution to prohibit showups unless the police lacked probable cause for an arrest or the showup was necessitated by an emergency situation. The court advised that where showups are conducted, the police should avoid locations that may communicate that the suspect is guilty, such as squad cars or police stations. They also should insure that suspects are not visibly handcuffed. The police were further instructed to advise eyewitnesses that the "real suspect" may not be in the showup and that the investigation will continue regardless of the outcome of the identification. According to the Wisconsin Supreme Court, an eyewitness also should not participate in more than a single showup, lineup, or photographic identification (*Wisconsin v. Dubose,* 699 N.W.2d 582 [2005]).

The Georgia Supreme Court has held that the jury no longer should consider the confidence that a witness expresses in his or her identification in evaluating the reliability of an in-court identification (*Brodes v. State,* 614 S.E.2d 766 [Ga. 2006]).

In reading *Commonwealth v. Johnson,* pay particular attention to the reasons that the Massachusetts Supreme Court gives in deciding to follow the per se approach to identifications rather than the Supreme Court's "reliability" approach articulated in *Brathwaite.*

You can find People v. Adams *and* Wisconsin v. Dubose *on the study site, http://www.sagepub.com/lippmancp.*

Should Massachusetts follow a per se exclusion rather than a reliability approach to suggestive identifications?

Commonwealth v. Johnson, 650 N.E.2d 1265 (Mass. 1995), Liacos, C.J.

Issue

The defendant appeals from his conviction of larceny from a person after a trial by a jury of six in the Boston Municipal Court Department. The sole issue on appeal is whether the judge erred in denying the defendant's motion to suppress the victim's pretrial identification after concluding that the identification procedure was unnecessarily suggestive.

Facts

Leopoldino Goncalves was working at a parking lot on the corner of Traveler Street and Washington Street in Boston. After he finished work, at approximately 10:50 P.M., Goncalves walked across the street to use a public telephone that was located on Washington Street. Street lights provided the only illumination.

When Goncalves finished using the telephone, a white female with a limp approached him and asked him for a dollar. Goncalves told the woman that he did not have any money. A black male armed with a machete then approached. The man grabbed Goncalves's wallet and, at the same time, the woman snatched money from Goncalves's front pocket. The assailants discarded the wallet after removing the money. They left the area together in an automobile. Goncalves pursued them in his own automobile, but he lost sight of them in a public housing project. The entire incident described lasted only a few minutes.

Approximately forty-five minutes later, Goncalves went to the Area D-4 police station and reported the robbery. He described the male assailant as a twenty-seven to thirty-year-old black male, six feet tall with a medium build, weighing 170 pounds, and wearing a black cap, blue jeans, and a brown sweatshirt. Goncalves was shown about six books containing photographs of suspects but was unable to identify his assailants. Goncalves then accompanied a police officer to view a group of potential suspects. Once again, Goncalves did not make an identification.

The day following the incident, four police officers arrived at Goncalves's place of employment at approximately 5 P.M. They told Goncalves that they wanted him to view two suspects. Goncalves accompanied the officers. When they arrived at the location where the suspects were being held, Goncalves saw a group of six to eight people. Only one adult black male, the defendant, was present, and a female with a limp was the only adult white female present. The two suspects were being "detained" by police officers, but they were not handcuffed. The defendant and the woman were brought forward a few steps by the officers. Goncalves then identified the pair as his assailants. Goncalves based his identification in part on the fact that the clothing worn by the suspects was the same as that worn by his assailants.

The defendant possessed several characteristics that did not match Goncalves's initial description of the male assailant. A booking photograph taken of the defendant at the time of his arrest, the day after the incident, shows that the defendant had a moustache. Yet Goncalves had never mentioned that the male assailant had a moustache. The booking sheet indicates that the defendant is thirty-seven years old and weighs 220 pounds, whereas Goncalves had described a man of approximately twenty-seven years in age, weighing 170 pounds, with a medium build. Finally, at the time of the hearing on the motion to suppress, the defendant was missing several front teeth. When describing his assailants to the police, Goncalves did not tell them that the male assailant had missing teeth.

The judge ruled that Goncalves's identification of the defendant was tainted because it was made at an unnecessarily suggestive showup. The evidence presented at the motion hearing supports this conclusion. Although one-on-one confrontations are not per se excludable, they are disfavored because of their inherently suggestive nature. Showups have been permitted when conducted in the immediate aftermath of a crime and in exigent circumstances. The showup employed by the police in this case was conducted eighteen hours after the crime. It took place in the area of the housing project where Goncalves had seen his assailants drive the previous night; the defendant was brought forward from the group before Goncalves positively identified him; and the defendant was wearing clothes similar to those worn by the male assailant. Based on these facts, the judge was warranted in concluding that the identification procedure was unnecessarily suggestive.

Although the judge found the identification procedure unnecessarily suggestive, he found that the identification was admissible because it was reliable. In so doing, the judge relied on appeals court decisions which have adopted the "reliability test," set forth in *Manson v. Brathwaite,* regarding the admissibility of identifications obtained through unnecessarily suggestive procedures. This test . . . is sometimes also referred to as the "totality" test or the "totality of the circumstances" test.

This court, however, has never accepted the reasoning in *Brathwaite* as an accurate interpretation of the due process requirements of article 12 of the Declaration of Rights of the Massachusetts Constitution. Whether we should embrace *Brathwaite,* as have the majority of other States, is a question we have left open. In cases involving an unnecessarily suggestive identification, we have adhered to the stricter rule of per se exclusion. . . .

The rule of per se exclusion...states that the defendant bears the burden of demonstrating, by a preponderance of the evidence, that the "witness was subjected by the State to a confrontation that was unnecessarily suggestive and thus offensive to due process." If this is established, then the prosecution is barred from introducing that particular confrontation in evidence at trial. "The prosecution is limited to introducing at trial only such identifications by the witness as are shown at the suppression hearing not to be the product of the suggestive confrontation—the later identifications, to be usable, must have an independent source." The prosecution must demonstrate the existence of an independent source by "clear and convincing evidence."

The Commonwealth now urges us to abandon the per se rule of exclusion and...follow the reliability test of Brathwaite. Under the "reliability" test, if a defendant demonstrates that an identification was unnecessarily suggestive, evidence of that identification is not per se excluded. Instead, the court must determine whether the identification was, under the "totality of the circumstances," nevertheless reliable....

We have carefully considered the matter, and for the reasons set forth, we conclude that we cannot accept *Brathwaite* as satisfying the requirements of article 12. We conclude that article 12 requires the application of the stricter per se approach....

Our past resistance to the so-called reliability test reflects this court's concern that the dangers present whenever eyewitness evidence is introduced against an accused require the utmost protection against mistaken identifications. There is no question that the danger of mistaken identification by a victim or a witness poses a real threat to the truth-finding process of criminal trials. Indeed, mistaken identification is believed widely to be the primary cause of erroneous convictions....With the stakes so high, due process does not permit second best. Compounding this problem is the tendency of juries to be unduly receptive to eyewitness evidence. We have stated that "the law has not taken the position that a jury can be relied on to discount the value of an identification by a proper appraisal of the unsatisfactory circumstances in which it may have been made. On the contrary, this court, like others, has read the Constitution to require that where the conditions are shown to have been highly and unnecessarily suggestive, the identification should not be brought to the attention of the jury."...The "reliability test" is unacceptable because it provides little or no protection from unnecessarily suggestive identification procedures, from mistaken identifications and, ultimately, from wrongful convictions.

The *Brathwaite* Court examined three primary "interests" before holding that the per se rule should be abandoned in favor of the less protective "reliability" test. The first of these was the concern regarding the dangers presented by eyewitness evidence. The Court acknowledged that a witness's recollection "can be distorted easily by the circumstances or by later actions of the police." While the per se approach addresses this concern, the Court stated, it "goes too far since its application automatically and peremptorily, and without consideration of alleviating factors, keeps evidence from the jury that is reliable and relevant." We believe that Justice Marshall, dissenting in *Brathwaite,* had a more realistic view of the trial process when he stated that "this conclusion totally ignores the lessons of *Wade.* The dangers of mistaken identification are...simply too great to permit unnecessarily suggestive identifications."...

Indeed, studies conducted by psychologists and legal researchers since Brathwaite have confirmed that eyewitness testimony is often hopelessly unreliable. Permitting the admission of an identification obtained through unnecessarily suggestive procedures can serve only to exacerbate this problem. Furthermore, contrary to the *Brathwaite* Court's unsubstantiated claim, the per se approach does not keep relevant and reliable identification evidence from the jury. Subsequent identifications shown to come from a source independent of the suggestive identification remain admissible under the per se approach. The per se approach excludes only the unnecessarily suggestive identification and subsequent tainted identifications. As stated earlier, the court examines five factors in determining whether there was an independent source for subsequent identifications by the witness of the defendant. If, for example, the prosecution is able to demonstrate that the witness got a good look at his assailant and his initial description matches a description of the defendant, the court may conclude that there was an independent source and may admit evidence of any identification subsequent to the unnecessarily suggestive one.

The *Brathwaite* Court also discussed the public interest in deterring police from using identification procedures which are unnecessarily suggestive. The Court acknowledged that the per se rule is superior in promoting that interest because it provides greater deterrence against police misconduct. The Court nevertheless concluded, "The police will guard against unnecessarily suggestive procedures under the totality rule, as well as the per se one, for fear that their actions will lead to the exclusion of identifications as unreliable."

To the contrary, it appears clear to us that the reliability test does little or nothing to discourage police from using suggestive identification procedures. One commentator has noted that "under *Brathwaite,* the showup has flourished, because the totality approach has failed to discourage this practice. As a deterrent to suggestive police practices, the Federal standard is quite weak. Almost any suggestive lineup will still meet reliability standards." Indeed, an example of this result is seen in the instant case: The suggestion inherent in the showup procedure that was used to identify the defendant is plain. Furthermore, the showup was unnecessarily suggestive in that it was not conducted immediately after the crime or in exigent circumstances. Yet the motion judge permitted the introduction of the identification based on his opinion that the identification was reliable. Rather than deterring unreliable identification procedures, the effect of the...reliability test has been, and would be in this Commonwealth, a message to police that absent extremely aggravating circumstances, suggestive showups will not result in suppression. Whether or not to use a more fair and accurate identification procedure is, under that test, left to the officer's discretion.

Finally, the *Brathwaite* Court considered the impact of the two tests on the administration of justice. It was here that the Court found what it considered to be the most serious drawbacks of the per se approach. However, it is also here, in our view, that the Court erred most. The Court opined, "Since it denies the trier reliable evidence, [the per se approach] may result, on occasion, in the guilty going free." The inverse of this is probably more accurate: The admission of unnecessarily suggestive identification procedures under the reliability test would likely result in the innocent being jailed while the guilty remain free. The *Brathwaite* Court disregards the wisdom of Justice Harlan when he wrote, "It is far worse to convict an innocent man than to let a guilty man go free."

Holding

This case presents an example of why we should not abandon the per se rule of exclusion and replace it with the reliability test. There is absolutely no evidence that the in-court identification of the defendant was the result of anything independent of the unnecessarily suggestive showup. For example, Goncalves's description of his assailant, given to police just after the incident, did not match the defendant's appearance, in part because the defendant possessed the unique feature of several missing teeth. Regardless of this fact, following the showup, Goncalves was able to "remember" that his assailant had missing teeth. Such flimsy evidence should not be permitted at trial. Only a rule of per se exclusion can ensure the continued protection against the danger of mistaken identification and wrongful convictions. Accordingly, we reject *Brathwaite*.... The verdict of guilty is vacated. The judgment of conviction is reversed.

Dissenting, *Greaney, J.*, joined by *Lynch, J.*

What is important to me is the fact that forty-seven States have adopted the reliability test to govern the admissibility of identification evidence. The weight of this body of outside law should not be lightly disregarded. The highest court of each of these States was aware of its right to fashion a different test under its state constitution, but significantly, each chose not to do so, opting instead for the reliability test. Underlying the choice made by the forty-seven States is tacit recognition of at least the following principles:

First, a criminal trial is meant to be a search for the truth in which the people (as represented by the prosecution) have the right to present reliable evidence tending to prove a defendant's guilt.

Second, since reliability is the linchpin governing the admission of all evidence, identification evidence which is found reliable by a judge, after a careful pretrial inquiry, should not be withheld from the jury.

Third, the jury is capable of sorting out issues of suggestiveness and reliability. It is not logical to deprive them of the antecedents of an in-court identification and to allow speculation on how a victim or identifying witness came to make his or her in-court identification.

I conclude that the reliability test sufficiently protects a defendant's rights under article 12 and allows the prosecution, in the protection of society's interests, to present its case on a level playing field.

Questions for Discussion

1. Why does the Massachusetts Supreme Court conclude that the identifications in *Johnson* were suggestive? Do you believe that these identifications were reliable?
2. Distinguish between the reliability and per se approaches to identifications.
3. Why is the Massachusetts Supreme Court critical of the reliability test? Do you agree with this criticism?
4. ***Problems in policing.*** If you were a police officer in Massachusetts, would the decision in *Johnson* significantly affect your ability to conduct identifications?

9.3 YOU DECIDE

Theresa Ellen Barthel was in bed at about 10:00 P.M. on July 16, 1981, when she awoke to find a man standing next to her bed. The lights were on in the room, and she was able to see the intruder, who, after a brief struggle, began to rape her. During the rape, he placed a pillow over her face. Following the rape, she was able to see her assailant grab his clothes and run out of the apartment. She called her husband and reported that the rapist was five feet, eight inches to five feet, nine inches in height and weighed between 160 and 170 pounds with brown wavy or curly hair. Barthel stated that she did not know whether the assailant had tattoos on his body. Rosario Dispensa, who had recently moved into the apartment complex, was seen wearing only his pants at 3:00 A.M. heading toward his apartment. Dispensa explained that he typically returned from work as a restaurant manager at 2:00 A.M. and then frequently relaxed by taking a swim in the complex pool. His fingerprints were not found in Barthel's apartment, and a cigarette butt in the apartment was not the brand that Dispensa smoked. Although Dispensa has a great deal of body hair, only two hairs were on the sheets. A toxicologist testified that these were pubic hairs; one of the hairs possessed microscopic characteristics similar to the hair furnished by Dispensa. An alibi witness testified that Dispensa was asleep with her between 3:00 A.M. and 5:00 A.M. Dispensa was roughly six feet tall, weighed 180 to 185 pounds, wore glasses, and had straight hair, his body was marked by prominent tattoos on his arms and shoulders as well as by visible cuts and scabs, and he had a prominent moustache. His female alibi witness stated that his sexual organ was deformed.

Two Houston police detectives took Barthel to the restaurant where Dispensa worked. They reportedly did not disclose their purpose. Following lunch, one of the officers approached Dispensa in his office and told him that he was a suspect in a sex crime and directed him to walk through the restaurant so that the victim could observe him. Dispensa was warned that a refusal would result in his arrest and inclusion in a lineup. The first time Dispensa walked through the restaurant Barthel did not respond. He then was directed by Detective Yarborough who was standing next to the cashier to walk through the restaurant once again, and as he directly passed by Barthel, she identified him as the rapist, burst into tears, and fled the restaurant. Barthel testified that when Dispensa walked by, Detective Henning told her to "look." The first time that Dispensa passed, she did not see his face and identified him only the second time when he walked directly by the table. Barthel also testified that she did not see Detective Yarborough talking to Dispensa at the cash register between the first and the second times that Dispensa walked through the restaurant. Dispensa claimed that he was identified only on his third walk through the restaurant and that, during this walk, he was accompanied by Detective Yarborough. Barthel testified regarding her identification of Dispensa at trial and made an in-court identification. Was the evidence of Barthel's identification in the restaurant properly admitted into evidence? See *Dispensa v. Lynaugh*, 847 F.2d 211 (5th Cir. 1988).

You can find the answer by referring to the study site, http://www.sagepub.com/lippmancp.

9.4 YOU DECIDE

Defendant Joseph Arthur Emanuele was convicted of robbing both the Millvale Bank and the Waterworks Bank. Martha Hottel, a teller, observed the man who robbed the Millvale Bank before he approached her window. Five weeks later, she was shown a six-photo array and selected a photograph of the defendant but stated that she "wasn't one hundred percent sure." Several weeks later, Hottel was shown a second array and selected someone other than the defendant. The robber's image was not captured by the bank's security cameras, and the defendant's fingerprints were not detected in the bank. At the Waterworks Bank, a robber also demanded money from teller Lorraine Woessner. She first observed the man at close range for several minutes in the bank lobby. Woessner was unable to identify the robber's photograph from a six-photo array. His image was captured by the security camera in the bank.

The two tellers were waiting to testify when they saw defendant Emanuele escorted by two U.S. Marshals being led from the courtroom in shackles. The two tellers talked to one another, remarking that "it has to be him." Woessner allegedly stated that "'when she saw him she knew exactly that's who it was.'" The trial court permitted both witnesses to make courtroom identifications. The Third Circuit Court of Appeals held that the issue was whether this impermissibly suggestive confrontation created a substantial likelihood of misidentification in light of the totality of the circumstances. Was it an "abuse of discretion" for the trial court to permit Woessner to make a courtroom identification? What about Hottel? See *United States v. Emanuele*, 51 F.3d 1123 (3d Cir. 1993). See also *State v. Armlijo*, 549 P.2d 616 (Ariz. App. 1976).

You can find the answer by referring to the study site, http://www.sagepub.com/lippmancp.

You can find United States v. Emanuele *and* State v. Armlijo *on the study site, http://www.sagepub.com/lippmancp.*

Scientific Identification

Judges are gatekeepers who screen the evidence before it is presented to the jury. The criminal justice system relies on trained scientific experts to analyze clothing fibers, hair, blood, handwriting, voice patterns, ballistics, footprints, and fingerprints. There is a particular challenge to insure that the technical and often confusing scientific evidence that lawyers want to introduce at trial is based on recognized scientific procedures.

The traditional test for the admissibility of scientific evidence was articulated in 1923 in *Frye v. United States*. The ***Frye* test** asks whether a scientific technique or approach is "sufficiently established to have gained general acceptance in the particular field in which it belongs." In *Frye,* the District of Columbia Federal Court of Appeals determined that the polygraph did not enjoy professional acceptance and ruled that the results of a "lie detector" test were inadmissible at trial. By the 1970s, the *Frye* test for the admissibility of scientific evidence had been accepted by forty-three states (*Frye v. United States,* 293 F. 1013 [D.C. Cir. 1923]). A Florida court, for instance, ruled that expert testimony on "Shaken Baby Syndrome" was properly presented to the jury because this diagnosis had been fully accepted by the medical profession and by other courts (*Johnson v. Florida,* 933 So. 2d 568, 570 [Fla. App. 2006]). Two years earlier, the Illinois Supreme Court considered whether a convicted child molester who was about to be released from prison should be civilly committed as a sexually violent person. The Supreme Court reviewed the practice in other states and the academic literature and concluded that "risk assessment tables" that predict the possibility of a convicted child molester violating the law in the future have "gained general acceptance in the psychological and psychiatric communities" and were properly relied on by the lower court judge in making this determination (*In re Commitment of Stephen E. Simons,* 821 N.E.2d 1184 [Ill. 2004]).

In 1993, in *Daubert v. Merrell Dow Pharmaceutical,* the U.S. Supreme Court developed an alternative to the *Frye* test. The ***Daubert* test** is followed by judges in federal courts and takes a broader view than *Frye. Daubert* asks a judge to study the research and views of experts and to reach his or her own conclusion as to whether a scientific technique is reliable and will assist the "trier of fact to understand the evidence or to determine a fact in issue." Today, roughly twenty-three states accept the *Frye* standard and twenty-one accept *Daubert* (*Daubert v. Merrell Dow Pharmaceutical,* 509 U.S. 579 [1993]). In *United States v. Mahone,* the First Circuit Court of Appeals held that the ACE-V method for the analysis of footprints was admissible under the *Daubert* test. The appellate court noted that the ACE-V method is "tested in published studies and has been the subject of widespread publication, including books devoted to footwear impressions.... [There is a] potential error rate of zero.... Finally ACE-V is clearly highly accepted in the forensics field; the same method is used for latent impression analysis of fingerprints" (*United States v. Mahone,* 453 F.3d 68, 71–72 [1st Cir. 2006]).

In most cases, the two approaches will lead to the same result. For example, Astrology is not generally accepted by the scientific community (*Frye*), and a judge researching the topic would likely reach the conclusion that astrology has not been accepted as valid in scientific journals (*Daubert*).

You can find Frye v. United States *and* Daubert v. Merrell Dow Pharmaceutical *on the study site, http://www.sagepub.com/lippmancp.*

DNA Evidence

As the United States developed into a mobile and urban society, local law enforcement found that criminals avoided apprehension by moving from one town to the next or by fading into the urban landscape. Information about crimes was initially conveyed by telegraphic communication. In the 1870s, the police began to circulate photographs as a method of apprehending criminals. Another major innovation was the **Bertillon method.** This was named after Alphonse Bertillon, a Paris police officer who pioneered the identification of criminals through the precise physical measurement of eleven physical dimensions (such as the width of the head and length of the feet) and the charting of scars and unusual physical attributes. This system was gradually supplemented and later replaced by fingerprinting. Fingerprinting was a revolutionary development that was exhibited by a detective from Scotland Yard at the St. Louis World's Fair in 1904. St. Louis subsequently established the first fingerprint department in the United States (Friedman, 1993).

Today, **DNA** evidence has introduced yet another scientific advance in the investigation and detection of crime. DNA, or deoxyribonucleic acid, is a molecule that stores an individual's genetic code. An individual exhibits the same unique genetic code in each cell whether the cell is extracted from bones, teeth, saliva, semen, hair, or blood. Every individual has a distinct genetic code (other than identical twins).

DNA analysis can be compared to looking at the pages in a book. You can examine the first word in the first sentence on four pages of a book (a suspect's DNA) and compare this to the first word in the first sentence of four pages of another book (DNA at the crime scene). In the event that both patterns are the same, there is a genetic "match." At trial, the expert in DNA expresses this match in statistical terms and, for example, will testify that only 0.0015 of the population, or one in 100,000 people, will exhibit such a match. On the other hand, the DNA may exclude a match in those instances in which the patterns are not the same. DNA may be obtained from the saliva on a stamp, cigarette, or bite mark; fluids excreted in a rape; hair on a pillow; sweat from a glove; or blood at a crime scene.

DNA has a number of applications in the criminal process:

- ***Detection.*** DNA may be used to connect an individual or individuals to various criminal acts.
- ***Investigation.*** DNA includes or excludes an individual as a suspect.
- ***Guilt or innocence***. DNA may establish guilt or innocence at trial. Individuals who have been convicted may discover DNA evidence that establishes their innocence.

We have come to view DNA as the final word on guilt or innocence. In 2006, Virginia governor Mark Warner responded to claims that Virginia had executed an innocent man and ordered a DNA examination on the body of the deceased inmate, Roger Keith Coleman. The individuals who had unsuccessfully worked for twenty years for Coleman's release admitted that they had been wrong when the DNA indicated that Coleman, in fact, was guilty of the rape and murder of his nineteen-year-old sister-in-law.

DNA is not always a "magic bullet" that will reliably tell us whether an individual is guilty or innocent.

- ***Contamination.*** A defendant's DNA sample may become mixed up with another person's DNA. DNA also may deteriorate as a result of a failure to safeguard the sample.
- ***Laboratory procedures.*** The laboratory may make a mistake in analysis or in calculating statistical probabilities.
- ***Significance.*** There may be numerous explanations for the presence of a suspect's DNA at the crime scene, and this may lead to the prosecution and possible conviction of an innocent individual. In other instances, a jury may become so confused about DNA evidence that they either fail to take it into account or exaggerate its significance.
- ***Relevancy.*** DNA is not always relevant to the issue in a case. For instance, in a rape prosecution, the issue may be whether there was consent rather than whether the defendant was the perpetrator.

The Admissibility of DNA Evidence

DNA was first used in criminal cases in 1986 when Dr. Alec J. Jeffreys conducted a DNA analysis that indicated that a suspect had falsely confessed to two rape-murders. DNA next was employed in England in 1987 to convict Robert Melias of rape.

The West Virginia Supreme Court was the first to accept DNA analysis. The lower state court cautiously approached the scientific validity of DNA analysis and warned that "pseudoscience is more dangerous than no science at all." The West Virginia Supreme Court proceeded to affirm the appellant's rape conviction and held that the "reliability of these [DNA] tests is now generally accepted by geneticists, biochemists, and the like.... Thus no *Frye* hearing will be required in the future for judicial notice of reliability." The West Virginia Supreme Court noted that DNA evidence could be challenged at trial by calling into question the procedures used to collect, preserve, and analyze the DNA (*State v. Woodall,* 385 S.E.2d 253 [W. Va. 1989]). Three years later, the Second Circuit Court of Appeals in *United States v. Jakobetz* took the first step toward the admissibility of DNA evidence in federal courts by holding that the "general theories of genetics which support DNA profiling are unanimously accepted with the scientific community" (*United States v. Jakobetz,* 955 F.2d 784, 800 [2d Cir. 1992]).

DNA evidence now is considered admissible by virtually every state and federal court. This evidence has been excluded only when the DNA sample has been contaminated or when there has been a failure to follow accepted procedures. In 2006, the U.S. Supreme Court fully embraced DNA evidence in *House v. Bell* when it ruled that Paul House was entitled to a new trial in federal court based in large part on DNA evidence that was not available at his 1985 trial, which, together with other evidence, supported his "actual innocence." The Supreme Court majority found that the "central forensic proof connecting House to the crime—the blood and the semen—has been called into question [by the DNA], and House has put forward substantial evidence pointing to a different suspect. Accordingly, and although the issue is close, we conclude that this is the rare case where—had the jury heard all the conflicting testimony—it is more likely than not that no reasonable juror viewing the record as a whole would lack reasonable doubt" (*House v. Bell,* 547 U.S. 518 [2006]).

In 2009, in *District Attorney's Office v. Osborne,* the U.S. Supreme Court held that William G. Osborne, who had been convicted in 1994 of kidnapping and sexual assault, did not have a right under the Due Process Clause of the U.S. Constitution to be given access to evidence for the purpose of DNA testing. Justice Roberts recognized that DNA possessed an "unparalleled ability" to exonerate the innocent and to convict the guilty but stressed that the policy of permitting inmates following their conviction to gain access to DNA testing was a matter for the state legislatures. Alaska law did not leave Osborne without a remedy. Alaska permits inmates to obtain access to, or to test, any type of newly discovered or newly available evidence that the petitioner is able to demonstrate by "clear and convincing evidence" will establish his or her innocence. Other state statutes specifically provide convicted felons with access to DNA while prohibiting access to DNA by certain categories of felons, such as offenders who have confessed to a crime. Massachusetts and Oklahoma along with Alaska do not have laws that specifically address postconviction DNA testing. Alabama recently passed a law giving individuals on death row access to DNA evidence (*District Attorney's Office for the Thirteenth Judicial District v. Osborne,* ___ U.S. ___ [2009]).

DNA Databases

The **Combined DNA Index System** (CODIS) is an electronic database that integrates the DNA profiles contained in the criminal offender databases of the fifty states and the federal government. Each jurisdiction determines the individuals from whom DNA is collected. States typically include individuals convicted of rape, murder, and sexual offenses in the "offender index." A second category is collected in the "forensic index" and contains DNA collected at crime scenes. CODIS is modeled on the Automated Fingerprint Identification System, which provides a nationwide search of fingerprints.

In 2000, Congress facilitated the collection of DNA when it passed the DNA Analysis Backlog Elimination Act, which provides funds to state forensic laboratories confronting a backlog of DNA. California, Louisiana, New Mexico, Texas, and Virginia are among the states that have significantly expanded their databases. For example, in 2004, California voters adopted Proposition 69, which requires the collection of DNA samples from all felons and from adults and juveniles arrested for or charged with specified crimes. In the next few years, California will be required to expand its DNA-collection program to include adults arrested or charged with felonies. Law enforcement officials using CODIS can compare the DNA evidence they have collected to the DNA on the database. The police, for instance, can connect the DNA from a crime scene with the DNA of an offender in the database and identify a previously unknown suspect. A controversial technique approved by the FBI is "near-match" searching. A partial match between DNA at the crime scene and the DNA of an individual in CODIS is relied on to justify the investigation of the individual's relatives as possible perpetrators of the crime. The national DNA database at present contains roughly 6.7 million profiles.

Forty-six states and the federal government collect DNA from all felons. The federal government along with fifteen states also collects DNA from some arrestees. Sixteen states collect DNA from various categories of misdemeanor offenders, and thirty-five states collect DNA from some juveniles.

As of June 2006, CODIS had resulted in over 34,500 matches and had assisted in roughly 36,100 investigations. In 2006, Prince George's County, Maryland, police employed the federal database system to apprehend an individual who stabbed two grandmothers to death during a robbery of their flower shop in 2003. The suspect was already in jail on an unrelated charge and had a lengthy arrest record involving drugs, assault, theft, and auto theft.

Privacy advocates have voiced concern over proposals to expand the DNA database to include individuals who have been arrested or to collect DNA from all Americans at birth. Critics also point to the costs and resources required to compile a national database. There is the additional question whether expanding the DNA database will significantly increase the number of convictions because DNA is not always available at the crime scene. Of course, there would be a continuing necessity to protect the data in order to prevent the misuse of information by employers who, for instance, may desire to investigate the medical background of potential employees.

Collection of DNA

The DNA Analysis Backlog Elimination Act provides that persons convicted of certain federal crimes who are incarcerated, or who are on parole, probation, or supervision, must provide federal authorities with a tissue, fluid, or other bodily sample on which a DNA analysis can be performed. Virtually every federal court has upheld the constitutionality of this statute, while state courts have upheld the constitutionality of similar state statutes. These judgments have relied either on offenders' diminished expectation of privacy or on the "special needs" to solve past and future criminal cases. An Illinois court observed that "regardless of which analytic approach we follow, we see a common thread that leads to the conclusion that the Fourth Amendment is not offended by the statute" (*People v. Peppers,* 817 N.E.2d 1152, 1157 [Ill. App. 2004]).

In the leading case of *United States v. Kincade,* six judges of the Ninth Circuit Court of Appeals sitting en banc affirmed the constitutionality of the mandatory extraction of blood for DNA analysis from a recently released armed robber who was under supervised release and receiving treatment in a residential drug program. Five judges reasoned that the limited expectation of privacy of individuals who have committed a "qualifying offense" under the DNA Backlog Act is clearly outweighed by the "overwhelming interest" in insuring that individuals on conditional release comply with the conditions of their supervision and do not engage in further criminal activity. Judge Gould comprised the sixth vote in the majority opinion and reasoned that the DNA program is justified by a "special need" to deter recidivism, to arrest recidivists, and to return them to prison as soon as possible (*United States v. Kincade,* 379 F.3d 813, 838–840 [9th Cir. 2004]).

Judge Reinhardt, writing for five dissenting judges, warned that the appellate court's decision opened the door to the suspicionless extraction of DNA from high school and college students, applicants for driver's licenses or for federal employment, and individuals traveling on airplanes (844). Judge Hawkins, in a separate dissenting opinion, observed that although more criminals clearly would be apprehended in a world that is "unrestrained" by Fourth Amendment protection for DNA, this is not the "world that Mr. [James] Madison and the First Congress create[d] for us" (876).

In 2006, an amendment to the renewal of the federal Violence Against Women Act significantly expanded the federal DNA database by authorizing DNA collection from anyone arrested for a federal crime and from illegal immigrants detained by federal agents.

A particularly controversial police tactic is the employment of DNA dragnets to detect individuals responsible for high-profile crimes. At least twenty dragnets have been conducted in the United States over the past fifteen years in cities and regions including Truro, Massachusetts; Chicago; Miami; Prince George's County, Maryland; and Oklahoma City. During these dragnets, DNA has been collected from more than 5,000 people. Some of these dragnets have raised controversial questions of racial profiling. In 1994, police in Ann Arbor, Michigan, conducted a dragnet of more than 600 African American males. The perpetrator, whose DNA had not been collected, was later apprehended attacking a fourth victim.

Exonerating the Innocent

DNA has been used to exonerate the innocent as well as to convict the guilty. In 1998, the National Institute of Justice published a study documenting the cases of twenty-eight wrongfully incarcerated individuals who had been freed as a result of DNA testing. One of the most active organizations currently engaged in analyzing DNA evidence to free innocent individuals is the Innocence Project at Cardozo University Law School in New York. A fairly recent example of the work of the clinic is the case of Jimmy Ray Bromgard who, on October 1, 2002, became the 111th individual to be exonerated by postconviction DNA testing. Prior to his release, Bromgard had spent fifteen and a half years in a Montana prison for the rape of an eight-year-old girl, a crime he did not commit. The police developed a composite sketch of the alleged assailant based on the victim's account. A police officer, believing that Bromgard resembled the sketch, asked him to participate in a lineup. The victim selected Bromgard but cautioned that she was uncertain whether he was the perpetrator. After viewing a videotape of the lineup, she stated that her confidence level was "60%, 65% sure." At trial, the victim was asked to rate her confidence in the identification without percentages and replied that "I am not too sure." The judge nevertheless allowed her to identify Bromgard as her assailant in court. The police forensic expert testified that there was a less than one in ten thousand chance that the pubic hair discovered in the victim's bedroom did not belong to Bromgard. In addition, a checkbook belonging to the victim was found on the street where Bromgard lived. His only defense was that he claimed to have been at home asleep when the crime was committed and that a forensic analysis concluded that his fingerprints were not at the crime scene or on the checkbook. The eighteen-year-old Bromgard was convicted of three counts of sexual intercourse without consent and sentenced to three concurrent forty-year terms of imprisonment.

Bromgard's lawyer failed to prepare an opening or closing statement, made no effort to suppress the courtroom identification, neglected to retain an expert to challenge the forensics evidence, and did not file an appeal. An expert panel later concluded that the testimony concerning the hair evidence was "completely contrary to accepted scientific principles." The prosecutors responded to the report by agreeing to support a judicial motion by the Innocence Project to subject the victim's underwear to DNA analysis. The results indicated that Bromgard was not the source of the semen.

Bromgard's case is not unique. The Innocence Project presently lists over 232 postconviction DNA exonerations in the United States. The first took place in 1989, and inmates subsequently have been exonerated in thirty-two states. Seventeen of these individuals were on death row or had served time on death row, and the average length of time served by inmates who were exonerated was twelve years. Seventy percent of the exonerated were minorities, 138 of whom were African American. Texas, Illinois, and New York lead the country in exonerations, and as of 2007, seventeen exonerations have occurred in Dallas County, Texas, which is more than the number of exonerations in forty-seven of the fifty states.

The Innocence Project concludes that mistaken identifications are the primary cause of these false convictions in seventy-five percent of the cases. In more than a third of the cases, experts and prosecutors relied on fraudulent scientific evidence or exaggerated the statistical significance of evidence in obtaining convictions. Other important factors are false confessions, dishonest jailhouse informants, and incompetent defense attorneys.

The Congressional Innocence Protection Act of 2001 establishes procedures for inmates in the federal system to petition courts for DNA tests when the new evidence is central to a prisoner's claim of innocence. The law also prohibits the destruction of biological evidence related to a criminal case so long as a defendant remains incarcerated. The statute further provides that in the case of "unjust imprisonment," an individual may receive between $5,000 and $50,000 a year in a non–death penalty case or $100,000 a year in a death penalty case. States are encouraged to establish similar compensation schemes for unjust imprisonments. The 2004 Justice for All Act authorizes money for postconviction DNA testing in federal courts, provides funds to state crime laboratories to analyze the backlog of DNA evidence, and provides money to train technicians to conduct DNA analysis and to establish state agencies to monitor the performance of crime laboratories.

Compensation for the wrongfully convicted is increasingly being provided by state legislatures. Twenty-five states at present provide compensation. In states without statutes, individuals may sue for damages. The statutes typically require that an individual establish his or her "actual innocence" as a condition of payment, and the laws usually establish limits on the money that may be awarded. Maine requires that an individual receive a pardon from the governor and that the claim be filed within two years following the pardon. Recovery is limited to $300,000. State compensation schemes vary. Tennessee authorizes awards for as much as $1 million; Alabama, Michigan, Hawaii, and Vermont offer up to $50,000, while the Wisconsin Claims Board limits payments to $25,000. California restricts payments to $100 per day, and New Hampshire sets the limit at $20,000.

Barry Scheck and Peter Neufeld, the co-directors of the Cardozo Innocence Project, propose that states create innocence commissions to investigate miscarriages of justice and to suggest reforms in the criminal justice system. North Carolina has responded by establishing an Actual Innocence Commission to investigate and report on the "common causes of wrongful conviction of the innocent and to develop potential procedures to decrease the possibility of conviction of the innocent... thereby increasing conviction of the guilty." The commission's mission statement notes that DNA testing confirms that there is the very real possibility that individuals have been convicted of crimes they did not commit. The overall goal of the commission's efforts are to maintain public trust and confidence in the justice system.

Criminal Procedure in the News

On March 13, 2006, members of the second-ranked Duke lacrosse team held a team party in an off-campus house rented by the team's three co-captains. The evening entertainment featured two African American exotic dancers hired at a cost of $800 to entertain over thirty Caucasian members of the team. The facts are in dispute. One of the women was a former navy veteran, a mother of two, and a student at North Carolina Central University, a predominantly local African American institution. She alleged that one of the players called out, "Did you bring any sex toys?" The woman answered, "No," and a man proclaimed, "That's OK, we'll just use a broom." The two women allegedly were alarmed and ran out of the house. They were persuaded to return, and the young woman purportedly was held down in the bathroom while three of the players who called themselves Adam, Matt, and Brett forced her to engage in sexual acts. She alleged that they also robbed her and that in resisting her assailants, she broke several fake fingernails. The two women fled the house, and a neighbor reported hearing one of the players shouting, "Hey, b____, thank your grandpa for my nice cotton shirt." The party then apparently broke up. The police would later return with a search warrant and with the full cooperation of the three residents. The police found five fake fingernails, a makeup bag and ID, and $160 in cash. The three lacrosse players voluntarily accompanied the police to headquarters where they agreed to make statements without a lawyer.

The alleged rape had come to the attention of the police when they responded to a call and encountered a woman passed out in a Honda in a local shopping center. This may have resulted from alcohol or narcotics or the administration of a "date drug" that rendered her unconscious. The woman was taken to a medical facility where she reported to a nurse that she had been raped. The Durham prosecutor, Michael Nifong, subsequently indicted three players on first-degree rape, sexual assault, and kidnapping: Reade Seligmann, Collin Finnerty, and David Evans, who was to graduate the next day. Evans's lawyers alleged that Nifong had refused the defendants' offer to take a polygraph exam and to provide evidence that allegedly supported their claim of innocence. Nifong, who was facing reelection, pronounced that he had "no doubt" that the victim had been raped.

The case presents troubling issues of race, class, and gender. The largely privileged lacrosse players are predominantly drawn from private schools in the northeastern states, and the vast majority are able to afford the expensive tuition at Duke. The team had a reputation on campus for heavy drinking and wild behavior. In contrast, the victim represents that portion of Durham that does not enjoy the fruits of wealth and privilege. A number of aspects of the case kept the media fixated and led several local attorneys to call on Nifong not to proceed with the prosecution.

- Prosecutor Nifong obtained a court order to take the DNA of forty-five of the forty-six Duke players. None matched the fluids extracted from the alleged victim. Nifong later dismissed the importance of the lack of DNA, noting that the assailants might have been wearing condoms. The only DNA match was between the semen removed from the victim and the semen of her boyfriend.
- The DNA results from the state laboratory were confirmed by a private lab. Prosecutor Nifong improperly withheld the private laboratory results from the judge and from the defense attorneys. He later explained that this was an inadvertent error.
- The physical evidence did not necessarily support that the victim was raped. Swelling was evident, but this could have resulted from the fact that she had several customers that day, including entertaining a couple with a vibrator. There also was no tearing, bleeding, or abrasions. On the other hand, the nurse at the hospital found that the victim screamed uncontrollably, was in intense pain, and reported extreme muscle tenderness.
- Reade Seligmann was able to present time-stamped photographs that supported his claim that he was not at the house at the time of the alleged sexual molestation.
- The other dancer, Kim Roberts, initially supported the victim's story and later dismissed the allegations as "crock." In October 2006, Kim Roberts appeared on CBS television's *Sixty Minutes* and publicly questioned whether the other dancer had been raped.
- Defense attorneys released documents indicating that the victim had a record of petty crime and, at one point, had stolen a taxi and had made a false allegation of rape while a young woman. There also was evidence of mental and emotional instability.

Most troubling was the identification process.

- Two officers recorded the victim's descriptions of her attackers. Their notes differed on her description of their appearance.
- On March 16, 2006, the victim was shown the photos of four possible suspects on the lacrosse team named Adam, Matt, or Brett and of twenty other team members (Finnerty and Evans were not included). She did not identify any of the photos as her attackers, observing that "this is harder than I thought."
- Five days later, she viewed twelve photographs, including Evans. She stated that the photos all "looked the same" and was unable to identify any of the players.

On April 3, 2006, the victim was shown the photos of forty-six of the forty-seven lacrosse players taken twelve days earlier. Roughly thirty of the players had attended the party. She viewed each picture for one minute. The transcript indicates that she stated that the third photo was of a man who was "sitting on a couch in front of the TV." The fourth photo "looked like Brett but I'm not sure." The victim stated that the fifth photo "looks like one of the guys who assaulted me." She stated that he "looks just like him without the mustache . . . ninety percent sure." The fifth individual was Evans who subsequently revealed the he has never had a mustache. The victim was one hundred percent certain that the seventh photo of Reade Seligmann "looks like one of the guys who assaulted me." She later identified Finnerty and stated that she was one hundred percent certain that he was one of the assailants. The victim went on to identify other individuals who allegedly had been present at the party.

Defense lawyers moved to suppress the photographic identifications and to bar identifications at trial. They argued that the entire array was prejudicial because it was composed of lacrosse players. A failure to include nonsuspects, according to the research findings of Iowa State psychologist Gary Wells, results in an identification being a "multiple choice test without any wrong answers" or in the words of the defense lawyers "a pin-the-tail-on-the-donkey identification." There also was the added difficulty of the victim's making a cross-racial identification, which research indicates involves a high error rate.

The defense attorneys claimed that the limited pool of individuals included in the photo array indicated that the prosecution was out to get their clients. On the other hand, the array did represent individuals of the same age, sex, race, and physical stature. The identification process also met the standard of at least five nonsuspects for every suspect in the array.

On December 22, 2006, District Attorney Mike Nifong dismissed first-degree rape charges against the three former Duke University lacrosse players. He announced that he would pursue charges of kidnapping and of a first-degree sex offense. The court papers indicated that the dismissal stemmed from the fact that the victim told an investigator that she had been penetrated from behind and "while she initially believed that she had been vaginally penetrated by a male sex organ, she cannot at this time testify with certainty that a penis was the body part that penetrated her." The newly announced charges carried up to twenty-four years in prison, and the dropping of the rape charges meant that the lack of a DNA match with any of the three defendants would not pose a barrier to the prosecution. In mid-January 2007, the complainant told prosecutors that two rather than three Duke players assaulted her and that the third "stood by" during the attack. She also alleged that the assault took place earlier in the evening than she first reported. Records indicated that she was on her cell phone at the time.

The North Carolina Bar Association filed ethics charges against Michael Nifong, accusing him of misleading and inflammatory statements about the Duke rape case. This included calling the defendants "young hooligans" and explaining that the lack of DNA resulted from the defendants' use of condoms, a statement which had no evidentiary support. On January 24, 2007, a second set of ethics charges were brought against Nifong for "withholding DNA evidence from the defense." Several weeks later, Nifong removed himself from the prosecution and asked the North Carolina Attorney General to take over the case.

On April 11, 2007, the North Carolina Attorney General, Roy A. Cooper, declared that the players were innocent of all charges, claiming that the players had been wrongly accused by an "unchecked," "overreaching," and "rogue" prosecutor who relied on "faulty and unreliable" accusations. Mr. Cooper noted that "no DNA confirms the accuser's story. No other witness confirms her story. Other evidence contradicts her story. She contradicts herself." On June 15, 2007, Nifong announced his resignation at his ethics hearing, and roughly five weeks later, he was disbarred from the practice of law based on what the North Carolina Bar Association determined to be a pattern of "dishonest conduct."

Polygraph Evidence

The **polygraph,** or "lie detector," is a form of scientific identification. The test measures an individual's physiological responses (blood pressure, perspiration, and respiration) to questions asked by a trained examiner. The examiner evaluates whether a person's answers are "truthful" or "untruthful" based his or her reactions.

What about the admissibility of the results of a polygraph examination at trial? The polygraph is not generally considered admissible into evidence. The test is not viewed as generally accepted by the scientific community (*Frye*) and has not been established as reliable by federal courts (*Daubert*). The National Research Council of the National Academy of Sciences (2003), a prestigious government-sponsored organization of scientists, conducted a comprehensive study of lie detectors and concluded that there is "little basis for the expectation that a polygraph test could have extremely high accuracy" and that investments in "improving polygraph techniques and interpretation will bring only modest improvements in accuracy." The report identified a number of problems with polygraph examinations, including the lack of trained examiners, the ability to defeat the test through "countermeasures," the failure to determine whether the test has the same degree of accuracy for all ethnic and racial groups, and the fact that there are various innocent explanations for responses that are thought to indicate a lack of truthfulness.

In 1989, in *United States v. Scheffer,* the U.S. Supreme Court affirmed the constitutionality of the prohibition on the introduction of polygraph evidence at military courts-martial. Edward Scheffer, a member of the U.S. Air Force, was prosecuted and convicted for the use of methamphetamines and other offenses. Scheffer sought to enhance the credibility of his claim that he had not used drugs by taking a polygraph examination. The trial judge held that the lie-detector testimony was inadmissible under the military rules of evidence that explicitly prohibited the introduction of the results of polygraph examinations (*United States v. Scheffer,* 523 U.S. 303, 308–310 [1989]).

Justice Clarence Thomas, in his majority opinion, noted that the Congressional Office of Technology Assessment had concluded that there was "limited scientific evidence establishing the validity of polygraph testing." Judge Thomas explained that the exclusion of polygraph evidence was based on the legitimate governmental interest in prohibiting the introduction of unreliable evidence into a court of law. Permitting a jury to hear this evidence, according to Justice Thomas, also would interfere with the jury's evaluation of the facts presented at trial. The natural tendency would be for jurors to give significant weight to the views of expert polygraph witnesses as to whether the defendant was truthful or untruthful. The introduction of the polygraph evidence also would divert the jury from the question of a defendant's guilt or innocence to questions regarding whether the polygraph was properly administered (309–310).

Justice Thomas stressed that the scientific community "remains extremely polarized about the reliability of polygraph techniques" and that "state and federal courts continue to express doubt about whether such evidence is reliable." He concluded that "[w]e cannot say . . . that presented with such widespread uncertainty, [the military] acted arbitrarily or disproportionately in promulgating a per se rule excluding all polygraph evidence" (309–311).

You will not be surprised to learn that most state and federal courts follow the policy of the military in excluding polygraph examinations. The New Mexico Supreme Court is the only state supreme court that has ruled that polygraph evidence is admissible at trial. Several federal district courts have agreed to consider polygraph evidence under certain limited circumstances (*State v. Dorsey,* 539 P.2d 304 [N.M. 2004]). As a juror, would you want to consider for yourself whether polygraph evidence is helpful in evaluating Scheffer's claim that he had not used drugs? Researchers are busy developing new technologies to measure truthfulness, including voice-stress analysis, thermal facial imaging, and brain imaging.

You can find United States v. Scheffer *on the study site, http://www.sagepub.com/lippmancp.*

Chapter Summary

Identifications by eyewitnesses and victims are one of the primary investigative tools in the arsenal of law enforcement. A positive identification narrows an investigation and may lead to a formal criminal charge and to criminal prosecution. In other instances, law enforcement authorities may conduct identifications of individuals against whom criminal charges already have been filed in order to build or to strengthen their case. Following these pretrial identifications, the victims or eyewitnesses typically are asked to repeat their identifications at trial. Prosecutors have learned that jurors view these courtroom identifications as powerful and persuasive evidence of a defendant's guilt.

There are three primary forms of eyewitness identification: lineup, showup, and photographic identification. These typically are used in combination with one another and with scientific identifications.

Two constitutional provisions regulate eyewitness identifications. The Sixth Amendment guarantees the right to an attorney at lineups and showups following the initiation of proceedings against a defendant. Preindictment identifications and photographic identifications are regulated by the Fifth and Fourteenth Amendments' Due Process Clauses. Postindictment lineups also are subject to challenge on due process grounds.

Identifications are inherently subject to error and are the leading cause of false convictions. The question remains whether we can safeguard these procedures against the errors that inevitably occur in the process of perception, memory, and identification. Double-blind, sequential lineup procedures and other steps have been proposed to augment the constitutional protections surrounding identifications.

The Sixth Amendment right to counsel applies to all critical stages of the criminal process. Critical stages are those procedures following a formal charge at which representation by a lawyer is essential to a fair trial. The U.S. Supreme Court recognized in *Wade* and *Gilbert* that a lineup or showup is a critical stage because individuals who are unrepresented are at risk of being falsely identified. A defense attorney who observes a suggestive lineup is in a position to cross-examine the police who conducted the lineup or showup in order to call the identification into question in the minds of the jury.

The failure to permit a defendant to have access to a lawyer or to waive his or her right to a lawyer results in the exclusion from trial of the results of the identification. The prosecutor nevertheless may ask a witness for an in-court identification in those instances in which the prosecution is able to establish by clear and convincing evidence that the in-court identification is not the product of the tainted identification procedure.

In *Kirby v. Illinois,* the U.S. Supreme Court concluded that a showup after arrest but before "the initiation of any adversary criminal proceedings (whether by way of formal charge, preliminary hearing, indictment, information, or arraignment) is not a critical stage of criminal prosecution at which the accused is entitled to counsel."

In 1973, in *United States v. Ash,* the U.S. Supreme Court held that the Sixth Amendment does not entitle the accused to the presence of a lawyer at a postindictment photographic display. The Court reasoned that postindictment confrontations are considered critical only when the presence of a lawyer is essential to the protection of the defendant's ability to receive a fair trial. Photo arrays are easily re-created, and for this reason, there is no right for either the lawyer or the defendant to observe the identification.

In *Stovall v. Denno,* the U.S. Supreme Court held that all identification procedures, showups, and photo arrays are required to satisfy the standards of the Fifth and Fourteenth Amendments' Due Process Clauses. The due process test was fully elaborated in *Manson v. Brathwaite.* Identifications violate the Due Process Clause when they are unnecessarily suggestive and "conducive to irreparable mistaken identification." This is to be evaluated based on the totality of the circumstances.

The traditional test for the admissibility of scientific evidence was articulated in 1923 in *Frye v. United States. Frye* asks whether a scientific technique is "sufficiently established to have gained general acceptance in the particular field in which it belongs." *Frye* is gradually being replaced in the federal system by the test developed by the U.S. Supreme Court in *Daubert v. Merrell Dow Pharmaceutical. Daubert* requires a judge to determine whether a scientific test is both relevant and reliable. DNA, or deoxyribonucleic acid, has been recognized as admissible under both the *Frye* and the *Daubert* tests. DNA has revolutionized law enforcement by providing a scientific technique for identifying guilty individuals and for exonerating the innocent. On the other hand, polygraphs, or lie detectors, are not considered reliable and are inadmissible into evidence.

Chapter Review Questions

1. Distinguish lineups, showups, and photographic identifications.
2. Why do perception, memory, and identification create a risk of misidentification?
3. Discuss the procedures that have been proposed to insure more accurate identifications.
4. Why are lineups, showups, and photographic identifications not considered a violation of the Fifth Amendment right against self-incrimination?
5. Why are lineups and showups a critical stage of a criminal proceeding?
6. Summarize the Sixth Amendment *Wade–Gilbert* rule.

7. What is the role of defense counsel at lineups under the *Wade–Gilbert* rule?
8. Why did the Supreme Court not follow the *Wade–Gilbert* rule in *Kirby v. Illinois*?
9. What is the holding in *United States v. Ash?* Why did the Supreme Court not follow the *Wade–Gilbert* rule in *Ash*?
10. Discuss the Fifth and Fourteenth Amendments standard established in *Manson v. Brathwaite* for determining whether a witness may testify concerning the results of a suggestive identification procedure.
11. What is the difference between the *Frye* and *Daubert* tests? Discuss how DNA has impacted the criminal justice system.
12. Why are polygraph examinations generally inadmissible at trial?
13. How does the Supreme Court strike a balance between rights and liberties on one hand and the interest in criminal investigation and prosecution on the other in regard to eyewitness identification?

Legal Terminology

Bertillon method
Combined DNA Index System
confrontation
corporeal identification
critical stages of a criminal proceeding
Daubert test
distractors
DNA
double-blind
eyewitness identification
fillers
foils
Frye test
in-court identification
noncorporeal identification
photographic displays
polygraph
scientific identification
sequential presentation
showup
simultaneous lineup
suggestive procedures
Wade–Gilbert rule

Criminal Procedure on the Web

Log on to the Web-based student study site at **http://www.sagepub.com/lippmancp** to assist you in completing the Criminal Procedure on the Web exercises, as well as for additional features such as leading cases, podcasts, self-quizzes, and audio/video links.

1. Read about conducting physical confrontations and photo identifications.
2. Take a look at what a law enforcement officer should know about DNA. Explain DNA evidence. On what objects is DNA likely to be found during a crime scene investigation?
3. Examine cases of individuals who were falsely convicted and who have been exonerated by DNA evidence. Analyze the cases in which false identifications have led to wrongful convictions.
4. Review and discuss the Jennifer Thompson case.
5. Read the order of the North Carolina Bar Association disbarring Mike Nifong from the practice of law.

Bibliography

Edwin M. Borchard, *Convicting the Innocent: Sixty-five Actual Errors of Criminal Justice* (New York: Garden City Publishing, 1932). One of the first studies of wrongful convictions.

Joshua Dressler and Alan C. Michaels, *Understanding Criminal Procedure: Investigation,* vol. 1, 4th ed. (Newark, NJ: LexisNexis, 2006), Chap. 26. An accessible review of the psychology of identifications and of the law of eyewitness identifications.

Samuel R. Gross et al., "Exonerations in the United States 1989 Through 2001," *Journal of Criminal Law and Criminology* 95 (2) (2005) 523–555. A comprehensive study of wrongful convictions.

Jerald Israel and Wayne R. LaFave, *Criminal Procedure in a Nutshell,* 6th ed. (St. Paul, MN: West Publishing, 2001), Chap. 5. A concise summary of the law regulating eyewitness identifications.

Wayne R. LaFave, Jerold H. Israel, and Nancy J. King, *Criminal Procedure,* 4th ed. (St. Paul, MN: Thomson/West, 2004), pp. 380–402. A comprehensive discussion of eyewitness identification with citations to the relevant cases.

National Academy of Sciences, *The Polygraph and Lie Detection* (Washington, DC: National Academies Press, 2003). A scientific examination of the reliability and accuracy of polygraphs.

National Institute of Justice, *Convicted by Juries, Exonerated by Science: Case Studies in the Use of DNA Evidence to Establish Innocence After Trial* (Washington, DC: Author, 1966). An early study of wrongful convictions and the use of DNA evidence to establish innocence.

National Institute of Justice, *Eyewitness Evidence: A Trainer's Manual for Law Enforcement* (Washington, DC: Author, 2003). Guidelines for law enforcement in conducting identifications.

Stephen A. Saltzburg, Daniel J. Capra, and Angela J. Davis, *Basic Criminal Procedure,* 4th ed. (St. Paul, MN: Thomson/West, 2005), Chap. 8. A clear and well-organized presentation of the law of eyewitness identification featuring the holdings of the major U.S. Supreme Court cases.

10 The Exclusionary Rule and Entrapment

Is the evidence that was seized by the police admissible in evidence?

A paper, claimed to be a warrant, was held up by one of the officers. [Miss Mapp] grabbed the "warrant" and placed it in her bosom. A struggle ensued in which the officers recovered the piece of paper and as a result of which they handcuffed appellant, because she had been "belligerent" in resisting their official rescue of the "warrant" from her person. Running roughshod over appellant, a policeman "grabbed" her, "twisted [her] hand," and she "yelled [and] pleaded with him" because "it was hurting." Appellant, in handcuffs, was then forcibly taken upstairs to her bedroom where the officers searched a dresser, a chest of drawers, a closet, and some suitcases. They also looked into a photo album and through personal papers belonging to the appellant. The search spread to the rest of the second floor, including the child's bedroom, the living room, the kitchen, and a dinette. The basement of the building and a trunk found therein were also searched. The obscene materials for possession of which she was ultimately convicted were discovered in the course of that widespread search.

At the trial, no search warrant was produced by the prosecution, nor was the failure to produce one explained or accounted for. At best, "There is, in the record, considerable doubt as to whether there ever was any warrant for the search of defendant's home."

Core Concepts and Summary Statements

Introduction

A. Historically, federal agents and state police who engaged in unreasonable searches and seizures were subject to a civil suit by the victim for the return of property or damages or were subject to criminal prosecution as well as to disciplinary procedures.

B. In 1914, in *Weeks v. United States,* the U.S. Supreme Court ruled that the Fourth Amendment required that evidence seized in violation of the Amendment was to be excluded from evidence in federal courts. In 1961, in *Mapp v. Ohio,* the Supreme Court extended the exclusionary rule to criminal trials in state courts.

C. The entrapment defense can be used by defendants who can demonstrate that a government agent induced them to commit a crime.

The Exclusionary Rule

A. *Weeks v. United States* held that evidence seized in a search that violated the Fourth Amendment is to be excluded from use as evidence in federal courts.

B. In *Wolf v. Colorado,* the U.S. Supreme Court held that the requirements of the Fourth Amendment are incorporated into the Fourteenth Amendment and are applicable to the states.

C. The *silver platter doctrine* was declared unconstitutional in 1960 in *Elkins v. United States.* This involved federal officials evading the requirements of the Fourth Amendment exclusionary rule by introducing evidence at trial that had been seized by state officials in violation of the Fourth Amendment.

D. In 1961, in *Mapp v. Ohio,* the United States Supreme Court held that the Fourth Amendment exclusionary rule extended to the states.

Debating the Exclusionary Rule

A. There are several justifications for the exclusionary rule. First, the failure to exclude evidence seized as a result of an unreasonable search undermines the Fourth Amendment prohibition on unreasonable searches and seizures. The exclusionary rule also deters the police from carrying out illegal searches and seizures and safeguards the integrity of the courts.

B. The threat of the exclusion of evidence has led to increased police attention to the law of search and seizure, and studies indicate that the exclusionary rule is invoked in a limited number of cases and has not significantly impeded criminal prosecutions.

C. The exclusionary rule has been criticized for failing to deter unlawful searches and seizures and for resulting in the exclusion of reliable evidence from trial. The exclusionary rule imposes the cost of an unlawful search on society by impeding criminal prosecutions rather than on the police officer who is responsible for the unlawful search. A search that violates the Fourth Amendment also results in the exclusion of evidence, whether the constitutional violation is modest or significant.

D. A number of alternatives to the exclusionary rule have been proposed: civil suits, criminal prosecutions, civilian review boards, and internal administrative procedures.

Invoking the Exclusionary Rule

A. The reasonableness of a search and seizure may be challenged by filing a pretrial motion to suppress. Most state and the federal courts place the burden of proof on the defendant when the search or seizure is based on a warrant. The burden is placed on the prosecution when the police act without a warrant.

B. The defense may appeal following a criminal conviction on the grounds that the judge was in error in admitting the evidence at trial. In contrast, the prosecution is required to appeal a decision to admit the evidence immediately.

C. A defendant who has exhausted his or her state court appeals and has been unsuccessful in overturning his or her conviction may file a writ of habeas corpus.

Standing

A defendant has standing to challenge the introduction of evidence that is obtained through the violation of his or her personal Fourth Amendment rights. The legal test to be applied for standing in the case of an alleged violation of the Fourth Amendment prohibition on unreasonable searches and seizures is whether the defendant has a subjective and objectively reasonable expectation of privacy in the area that is subject to the search. The burden of proof customarily is placed on the defendant.

Exceptions to the Exclusionary Rule

A. The Supreme Court, in 1973 in *United States v. Calandra,* held that the exclusionary rule is a judge-made remedy whose primary purpose is to deter unreasonable searches and seizures. The Court adopted a balancing approach that resulted in recognition of exceptions to the exclusionary rule in those instances in which judges conclude that excluding the evidence would have little deterrent impact on the police and that this modest benefit is outweighed by the social cost of excluding the evidence from trial.

B. These exceptions include collateral proceedings, attenuation, good faith, independent source, inevitable discovery, and impeachment.

Does the Exclusionary Rule Deter Unreasonable Searches and Seizures?

A. A number of scholars have studied whether the exclusionary rule deters unconstitutional searches and seizures. Researchers have concluded that it is virtually impossible to answer the question of whether fewer unlawful searches have occurred as a result of the exclusionary rule.

B. Studies also indicate that the police, prosecutors, and judges dismiss relatively few cases because of the exclusionary rule.

Entrapment

A. Entrapment is a defense that may be invoked by a defendant who alleges that the government induced him or her to commit a crime.

B. The vast majority of states and the federal courts follow the subjective test. This asks whether the defendant has a predisposition to commit a crime and likely would have committed the crime absent the involvement of the government. A minority of jurisdictions follow the objective test, which focuses on the conduct of the government. Due Process is a third test. Defendants generally have been unsuccessful in arguing that the government's conduct is so outrageous that the prosecution is prohibited by the Due Process Clause of the U.S. Constitution.

C. Entrapment is an affirmative defense that must be raised by the defendant.

Introduction

At this point, we have fully discussed the Fourth Amendment prohibition on unreasonable searches and seizures. The text of the Fourth Amendment is silent on the consequences of an unreasonable search and seizure. Should the evidence be excluded from trial? What of imposing a penalty on the police officers or compensating the subject of the unlawful search?

Historically, federal agents and state police who carried out unconstitutional searches and seizures were subject to civil suits for the return of property or for damages or were criminally prosecuted or were subjected to internal administrative discipline. These procedures had the advantage of focusing responsibility on the police officers who failed to follow the law. Critics of these remedies, however, argued that that civil actions, criminal prosecutions, and disciplinary procedures were ineffective in controlling police practices and that an alternative approach was required. Civil actions, for example, were expensive and rarely resulted in significant monetary awards for victims. Prosecutors were reluctant to bring criminal actions against the police, and law enforcement officials were equally hesitant to pursue administrative complaints against officers who may have carried out an unlawful search that led to a criminal conviction.

In 1914, in *Weeks v. United States,* the U.S. Supreme Court ruled that the Fourth Amendment required that evidence seized in an unlawful search was to be excluded from use as evidence in federal courts. In 1961, in *Mapp v. Ohio,* the U.S. Supreme Court sent shockwaves through the criminal justice system by extending the federal exclusionary rule to criminal trials in state and local courts. The Court explained that the exclusionary rule was required to deter the police from disregarding constitutional standards and to maintain the integrity of the judiciary by excluding unlawfully seized evidence from trials. The Supreme Court shortly thereafter held that the exclusionary rule was a judge-made remedy rather than a remedy that was guaranteed by the Fourth Amendment to the U.S. Constitution. The sole purpose of this judge-made exclusionary rule was to deter unreasonable searches and seizures.

The exclusionary rule has been one of the primary flashpoints in the debate over whether the American criminal justice system has gone too far in protecting criminal perpetrators while disregarding the interests of victims and society. Critics ask whether it makes sense to exclude reliable evidence from trial and thereby to permit criminal defendants to walk out the courthouse door without having to confront all the evidence against them.

In the first portion of this chapter we trace the evolution of the exclusionary rule. Pay particular attention to development of the exclusionary rule following *Mapp v. Ohio.* Ask yourself whether the Supreme Court has unduly limited the exclusionary rule or has struck the proper balance. Keep in mind that the exclusionary rule applies to searches and seizures under the Fourth Amendment. As you may recall, evidence also may be excluded from trial based on the violation of other constitutional amendments. Two examples are the suppression of confessions and the suppression of in-court identifications.

- ***Interrogations and identifications and the Fifth, Sixth, and Fourteenth Amendments.*** Coerced confessions and confessions obtained in violation of *Miranda v. Arizona,* as well as confessions extracted in violation of the Sixth Amendment, are excluded from the prosecutor's case-in-chief.
- ***Sixth Amendment.*** A failure to provide an attorney at a lineup following the initiation of criminal proceedings results in the exclusion at trial of evidence from the lineup.

The second part of the chapter discusses entrapment. Entrapment is a defense to a criminal charge that is available to defendants who allege that they were induced to commit a crime by the government. We will first discuss the predisposition test that focuses on whether an individual's criminal conduct is the product of the creative activity of the government. The objective test, in contrast, is concerned with whether government conduct falls below the standard for the proper use of government power. Due Process is a third test that is applied in those instances in which the conduct of the government is so unfair and outrageous that it is in violation of the Due Process Clause of the U.S. Constitution. As you read the second half of the chapter, consider which test for entrapment you consider to be the most fair and effective and which best deters governmental misconduct.

It may strike you as unusual that so much time is spent discussing the exclusionary rule and entrapment, given that both are infrequently applied by judges and appellate courts. This is due to the fact that these two doctrines raise important issues regarding the balance between the prosecution and the defense in the criminal justice system and pose the challenge of how to control and to provide a remedy for the violation of constitutional rights by the police. As you read this chapter, consider whether you favor the exclusionary rule and whether we should have an entrapment defense. Are there better alternatives?

The Exclusionary Rule

As you have just read, the Supreme Court has extended the Fourth Amendment exclusionary rule to prosecutions in federal and state courts. The **exclusionary rule** provides that evidence that is obtained as a result of a violation of the Fourth Amendment prohibition on unreasonable searches and seizures is inadmissible in a criminal prosecution to establish a defendant's guilt. **Derivative evidence,** or evidence that is discovered as a result of the unlawfully seized items, is considered the **fruit of the poisonous tree** and also is excluded from evidence. For example, records of illegal drug transactions that are seized in the course of an unlawful search are excluded from evidence, because the records are the direct result of an illegal search. The confessions resulting from the interrogation of individuals whose names are listed as part of the drug transactions will be excluded from evidence as the fruit of the poisonous tree.

The exclusionary rule, in summary, excludes the following from trial:

- ***Direct evidence.*** Evidence that is directly derived from the unreasonable search
- ***Fruit of the poisonous tree.*** Evidence that is derived from the evidence that is directly seized

The exclusionary rule nevertheless remains controversial. Why the reluctance to exclude items that were unreasonably seized from evidence? The primary reason is that this might result in a guilty defendant being set free to rape, rob, and steal once again. What of the interests of victims and of society in the conviction of criminals? The next sections shed some light on why the Supreme Court embraced the exclusionary rule.

The Exclusionary Rule and Federal Courts

In *Weeks v. United States,* the Supreme Court held that evidence seized in the course of an unreasonable search that violates the Fourth Amendment is to be excluded from evidence in federal courts. The police arrested Weeks and searched his home without a warrant. They seized various personal papers that were turned over to the U.S. Marshal. Later that same day the police and U.S. Marshal searched Weeks's home a second time and seized various lottery tickets and letters that were used to convict Weeks for the use of the mails to transport lottery tickets in violation of federal law. Justice William R. Day ruled that the introduction of this evidence against the defendant violated the Fourth Amendment to the U.S. Constitution. He stressed that if letters and documents that are unlawfully seized from a defendant are introduced into evidence against that defendant at trial, the Fourth Amendment "is of no value" and "might as well be stricken from the Constitution." The efforts to bring the guilty to the bar of justice, "praiseworthy as they are, are not to be aided by the sacrifice of those great principles established by years of endeavor and suffering which have resulted in their embodiment in the fundamental law of the land" (*Weeks v. United States,* 232 U.S. 383, 392 [1914]). The question remained whether this same remedy was available against state law enforcement officers.

The Exclusionary Rule and State Courts

In 1949, in *Wolf v. Colorado,* the U.S. Supreme Court held that the requirements of the Fourth Amendment were incorporated into the Fourteenth Amendment and were applicable to the states. Justice Felix Frankfurter wrote that the "security of one's privacy against arbitrary intrusion by the police—which is the core of the Fourth Amendment—is basic to a free society... [and] is therefore implicit in the concept of ordered liberty" (*Wolf v. Colorado,* 338 U.S. 25, 27, 33 [1949]).

The Supreme Court, however, also ruled that states were not required to exclude from trial evidence obtained in violation of the Fourth and Fourteenth Amendments. The exclusionary rule, according to the opinion in *Wolf,* is not "an explicit requirement" of the Fourth Amendment and is a remedy created by the judiciary to maintain the integrity of the courtroom and to deter police disregard for the Fourth Amendment. In the words of Justice Frankfurter, "In a prosecution in a State court for a State crime, the Fourteenth Amendment does not forbid the admission of evidence obtained by an unreasonable search and seizure." The Court pointed to the fact that virtually none of the countries in the English-speaking world recognized the exclusionary rule and that thirty states rejected the *Weeks* doctrine, while only seventeen were in agreement with

Weeks. There was nothing in the U.S. Constitution to prevent these thirty states from continuing to rely on civil, criminal, and administrative remedies rather than the exclusionary rule to deter the police from engaging in unreasonable searches and seizures (30). Judge Benjamin Cardozo summarized the point of view in the thirty states that rejected the exclusionary rule when he wrote in a New York Court of Appeals decision that the "criminal [should not] go free because the constable has blundered" (*People v. Defore,* 150 N.E. 585, 587 [1926]).

Three Supreme Court judges dissented, including Justice Frank Murphy, who strongly criticized his judicial brethren and wrote that he did not believe that the requirements of the Fourth Amendment should be determined by counting how many states or countries rely on the exclusionary rule. Justice Murphy warned that the decision in *Weeks*

> will do inestimable harm to the cause of fair police methods in our cities and states.... It must have tragic effect upon public respect for our judiciary. For the Court now allows... shabby business: lawlessness by officers of the law. (46)

The Supreme Court, despite its decision in *Wolf,* was not prepared to hold that the Due Process Clause of the U.S. Constitution permitted state courts to admit evidence obtained in a blatantly unreasonable fashion. In the case at issue in *Rochin v. California,* the police, suspecting that Rochin had swallowed capsules containing illegal narcotics, directed a doctor to force a vomiting-inducing solution into Rochin's stomach. The police subsequently discovered two morphine tablets. The Supreme Court ruled that the police conduct "shocked the conscience and violated the Due Process Clause of the Fourteenth Amendment" and that the morphine tablets should have been excluded from evidence. The Court explained that

> illegally breaking into the privacy of the petitioner, the struggle to open his mouth and remove what was there, the forcible extraction of his stomach's contents... are methods too close to the rack and the screw to permit of constitutional differentiation. (*Rochin v. California,* 342 U.S. 165, 172 [1952])

The next important development following *Wolf* was a series of cases in which the Supreme Court limited the **silver platter doctrine**. This practice involved federal officials making an end run around the exclusionary rule by relying on evidence in federal prosecutions that had been seized by state officials in violation of the Fourth Amendment. The evidence was "served" by state law enforcement officers to federal prosecutors on a "silver platter." In 1960, the silver platter doctrine was ruled unconstitutional in *Elkins v. United States*. In *Elkins,* the Supreme Court proclaimed that the holding in *Wolf*—that the Fourteenth Amendment Due Process Clause prohibited unreasonable searches and seizures by state officials—marked the death knell for the silver platter doctrine.

> For sure no distinction can logically be drawn between evidence obtained in violation of the Fourth Amendment and that obtained in violation of the Fourteenth. The Constitution is flouted equally in either case. To the victim it matters not whether his constitutional right has been invaded by a federal agent or by a state officer. (*Elkins v. United States,* 364 U.S. 206, 215 [1960])

The Supreme Court now was ready to take the final step of extending the exclusionary rule to the states. What arguments persuaded the court to change course?

The Extension of the Exclusionary Rule to the State Courts

In 1961, in *Mapp v. Ohio,* the U.S. Supreme Court ruled that the Fourth Amendment right to privacy, which is applicable to the states through the Fourteenth Amendment Due Process Clause,

> is enforceable against [the states] by the same sanction of exclusion as is used against the Federal Government. Were it otherwise then... the assurance against unreasonable... searches and seizures would be "a form of words."

The Court observed that an increasing number of states had adopted the exclusionary rule after concluding that other remedies had proven ineffective in deterring unreasonable searches and seizures. The Supreme Court also stressed that the exclusionary rule insured judicial integrity by insuring that courts would not become accomplices to disobedience to the Constitution that judges were sworn to uphold. The three dissenting judges, however, objected that the Supreme Court was unjustifiably imposing the exclusionary rule on state criminal justice systems (*Mapp v. Ohio,* 367 U.S. 643 [1961]).

Mapp clearly stated that the exclusionary rule is "part and parcel" and is "an essential part" of the Fourth Amendment, which is to be applied in cases of unreasonable searches and seizures that violate the Fourth Amendment (655). In a series of decisions following *Mapp,* the Supreme Court retreated from this position and held that the exclusionary rule is not constitutionally required and is a judge-made remedy developed to deter police disregard for the Fourth Amendment. In 1974, in *United States v. Calandra,* the Supreme Court, in an often-quoted statement, proclaimed that the exclusionary rule is "a judicially created remedy designed to safeguard Fourth Amendment rights generally through its deterrent effect rather than a personal constitutional right of the party aggrieved" (*United States v. Calandra,* 414 U.S. 338, 347 [1974]).

Why is this significant? The view that the exclusionary rule is a judge-made remedy means that the doctrine is not an ironclad requirement of the Constitution that judges are compelled to apply in every circumstance.

Mapp v. Ohio is the next case in the textbook. What were the reasons that the Supreme Court offered to explain why it extended the exclusionary rule to the states? Should states be left free to follow the remedies for unreasonable searches and seizures that they consider appropriate?

Should the exclusionary rule be extended to criminal prosecutions in the states?

Mapp v. Ohio, 397 U.S. 643 (1961), Clark, J.

Facts

Appellant stands convicted of knowingly having had in her possession and under her control certain lewd and lascivious books, pictures, and photographs in violation of section 2905.34 of Ohio's Revised Code. This law provides that

> no person shall knowingly . . . have in his possession or under his control an obscene, lewd, or lascivious book [or] . . . picture. . . . Whoever violates this section shall be fined not less than two hundred nor more than two thousand dollars or imprisoned not less than one nor more than seven years, or both.

On May 23, 1957, three Cleveland police officers arrived at appellant's residence in that city pursuant to information that "a person [was] hiding out in the home, who was wanted for questioning in connection with a recent bombing, and that there was a large amount of policy paraphernalia being hidden in the home." Miss Mapp and her daughter by a former marriage lived on the top floor of the two-family dwelling. Upon their arrival at that house, the officers knocked on the door and demanded entrance, but appellant, after telephoning her attorney, refused to admit them without a search warrant. They advised their headquarters of the situation and undertook a surveillance of the house.

The officers again sought entrance some three hours later, when four or more additional officers arrived on the scene. When Miss Mapp did not come to the door immediately, at least one of the several doors to the house was forcibly opened, and the policemen gained admittance. Meanwhile Miss Mapp's attorney arrived, but the officers, having secured their own entry, and continuing in their defiance of the law, would permit him neither to see Miss Mapp nor to enter the house. It appears that Miss Mapp was halfway down the stairs from the upper floor to the front door when the officers, in this highhanded manner, broke into the hall. She demanded to see the search warrant. A paper, claimed to be a warrant, was held up by one of the officers.

Miss Mapp grabbed the "warrant" and placed it in her bosom. A struggle ensued in which the officers recovered the piece of paper and as a result of which they handcuffed appellant, because she had been "belligerent" in resisting their official rescue of the "warrant" from her person. Running roughshod over appellant, a policeman "grabbed" her and "twisted [her] hand," and she "yelled [and] pleaded with him" because "it was hurting." Appellant, in handcuffs, was then forcibly taken upstairs to her bedroom, where the officers searched a dresser, a chest of drawers, a closet, and some suitcases. They also looked into a photo album and through personal papers belonging to the appellant. The search spread to the rest of the second floor, including the child's bedroom, the living room, the kitchen, and a dinette. The basement of the building and a trunk found therein were also searched. The obscene materials for possession of which she was ultimately convicted were discovered in the course of that widespread search.

At the trial no search warrant was produced by the prosecution, nor was the failure to produce one explained or accounted for. At best, "There is, in the record, considerable doubt as to whether there ever was any warrant for the search of defendant's home." The Ohio Supreme Court believed a "reasonable argument" could be made that the conviction should be reversed "because the 'methods' employed to obtain the [evidence]...were such as to 'offend a sense of justice,'" but the court found determinative the fact that the evidence had not been taken "from defendant's person by the use of brutal or offensive physical force against defendant."

Issue

The State says that even if the search were made without authority, or otherwise unreasonably, it is not prevented from using the unconstitutionally seized evidence at trial. In *Wolf v. Colorado*...this Court did indeed hold "that in a prosecution in a State court for a State crime, the Fourteenth Amendment does not forbid the admission of evidence obtained by an unreasonable search and seizure." On this appeal, of which we have noted probable jurisdiction, it is urged once again that we review that holding.

Reasoning

Seventy-five years ago, in *Boyd v. United States* (116 U.S. 616, 630 [1886]), considering the Fourth and Fifth Amendments as running "almost into each other" on the facts before it, this Court held that the doctrines of those Amendments

> apply to all invasions on the part of the government and its employees of the sanctity of a man's home and the privacies of life. It is not the breaking of his doors, and the rummaging of his drawers, that constitutes the essence of the offence; but it is the invasion of his indefeasible right of personal security, personal liberty and private property....Breaking into a house and opening boxes and drawers are circumstances of aggravation; but any forcible and compulsory extortion of a man's own testimony or of his private papers to be used as evidence to convict him of crime or to forfeit his goods, is within the condemnation...[of those Amendments].

The Court noted that "constitutional provisions for the security of person and property should be liberally construed....It is the duty of courts to be watchful for the constitutional rights of the citizen, and against any stealthy encroachments thereon."

In this jealous regard for maintaining the integrity of individual rights, the Court gave life to Madison's prediction that "independent tribunals of justice...will be naturally led to resist every encroachment upon rights expressly stipulated for in the Constitution by the declaration of rights." Concluding, the Court specifically referred to the use of the evidence there seized as "unconstitutional."

Less than 30 years after *Boyd,* this Court, in *Weeks v. United States* (232 U.S. 383 [1914]), stated that

> the Fourth Amendment...put the courts of the United States and Federal officials, in the exercise of their power and authority, under limitations and restraints [and]...forever secure[d] the people, their persons, houses, papers and effects against all unreasonable searches and seizures under the guise of law...and the duty of giving to it force and effect is obligatory upon all entrusted under our Federal system with the enforcement of the laws.

Specifically dealing with the use of the evidence unconstitutionally seized, the Court concluded as follows:

> If letters and private documents can thus be seized and held and used in evidence against a citizen accused of an offense, the protection of the Fourth Amendment declaring his right to be secure against such searches and seizures is of no value, and, so far as those thus placed are concerned, might as well be stricken from the Constitution. The efforts of the courts and their officials to bring the guilty to punishment, praiseworthy as they are, are not to be aided by the sacrifice of those great principles established by years of endeavor and suffering which have resulted in their embodiment in the fundamental law of the land.

Finally, the Court in that case clearly stated that use of the seized evidence involved "a denial of the constitutional rights of the accused." Thus, in the year 1914, in the *Weeks* case, this Court "for the first time" held that "in a federal prosecution the Fourth Amendment barred the use of evidence secured through an illegal search and seizure." This Court has ever since required of federal law officers a strict adherence to that command that this Court has held to be a clear, specific, and constitutionally required—even if judicially implied—deterrent safeguard, without insistence upon which the Fourth Amendment would have been reduced to "a form of words." It meant, quite simply, that "conviction by means of unlawful seizures and enforced confessions...should find no sanction in the judgments of the courts...," and that such evidence "shall not be used at all."

The plain and unequivocal language of *Weeks*—and its later paraphrase in *Wolf*—to the effect that the *Weeks* rule is of constitutional origin, remains entirely undisturbed. In *Byars v. United States* (273 U.S. 28 [1927]), a unanimous Court declared that

> the doctrine [cannot]...be tolerated under our constitutional system, that evidence of a crime discovered by a federal officer in making a search without lawful warrant may be used against the victim of the unlawful search where a timely challenge has been interposed.

The Court, in *Olmstead v. United States* (277 U.S. 438 [1928]), in unmistakable language restated the *Weeks* rule "that the Fourth Amendment, although not referring to or limiting the use of evidence in courts, really forbade its introduction if obtained by government officers through a violation of the Amendment." In *McNabb v. United States* (318 U.S. 332 [1943]), we noted that "a conviction in the federal courts, the foundation of which is evidence obtained in disregard of liberties deemed fundamental by the Constitution, cannot stand."

In 1949, 35 years after *Weeks* was announced, this Court, in *Wolf v. Colorado,* again for the first time, discussed the effect of the Fourth Amendment upon the states through the operation of the Due Process Clause of the Fourteenth Amendment....After declaring that the "security of one's privacy against arbitrary intrusion by the police" is "implicit in 'the concept of ordered liberty' and as such enforceable against the States through the Due Process Clause," and announcing that it "stoutly adhere[d]" to the *Weeks* decision, the Court decided that the *Weeks* exclusionary rule would not then be imposed upon the states as "an essential ingredient of the right." The Court's reasons for not considering essential to the right to privacy, as a curb imposed upon the states by the Due Process Clause, that which decades before had been posited as part and parcel of the Fourth Amendment's limitation upon federal encroachment of individual privacy, were bottomed on factual considerations....

The Court in *Wolf* first stated that "the contrariety of views of the States" on the adoption of the exclusionary rule of *Weeks* was "particularly impressive," and, in this connection, that it could not "brush aside the experience of States which deem the incidence of such conduct by the police too slight to call for a deterrent remedy...by overriding the [States'] relevant rules of evidence." While in 1949, prior to the *Wolf* case, almost two-thirds of the states were opposed to the use of the exclusionary rule, now, despite the *Wolf* case, more than half of those since passing upon it, by their own legislative or judicial decision, have wholly or partly adopted or adhered to the *Weeks* rule. Significantly, among those now following the rule is California, which, according to its highest court, was "compelled to reach that conclusion because other remedies have completely failed to secure compliance with the constitutional provisions...." In connection with this California case, we note that the second basis elaborated in *Wolf* in support of its failure to enforce the exclusionary doctrine against the states was that "other means of protection" have been introduced to protect "the right to privacy." The experience of California that such other remedies have been worthless and futile is buttressed by the experience of other states. The obvious futility of relegating the Fourth Amendment to the protection of other remedies has, moreover, been recognized by this Court since *Wolf.*

It, therefore, plainly appears that the factual considerations supporting the failure of the *Wolf* Court to include the *Weeks* exclusionary rule when it recognized the enforceability of the right to privacy against the states in 1949, while not basically relevant to the constitutional consideration, could not, in any analysis, now be deemed controlling. Some five years after *Wolf,* in answer to a plea made here term after term that we overturn its doctrine on applicability of the *Weeks* exclusionary rule, this Court indicated that such should not be done until the states had "adequate opportunity to adopt or reject the [*Weeks*] rule."...Today we once again examine *Wolf*'s constitutional documentation of the right to privacy free from unreasonable State intrusion, and, after its dozen years on our books, are led by it to close the only courtroom door remaining open to evidence secured by official lawlessness in flagrant abuse of that basic right, reserved to all persons as a specific guarantee against that very same unlawful conduct. We hold that all evidence obtained by searches and seizures in violation of the Constitution is, by that same authority, inadmissible in a state court.

Since the Fourth Amendment's right of privacy has been declared enforceable against the states through the Due Process Clause of the Fourteenth [Amendment], it is enforceable against them by the same sanction of exclusion as is used against the federal government. Were it otherwise, then just as without the *Weeks* rule, the assurance against unreasonable federal searches and seizures would be "a form of words," valueless and undeserving of mention in a perpetual charter of inestimable human liberties. So too, without that rule, the freedom from State invasions of privacy would be so ephemeral and so neatly severed from its conceptual nexus with the freedom from all brutish means of coercing evidence as not to merit this Court's high regard as a freedom "implicit in the concept of ordered liberty."

At the time that the Court held in *Wolf* that the Amendment was applicable to the states through the Due

Process Clause, the cases of this Court, as we have seen, had steadfastly held that as to federal officers, the Fourth Amendment included the exclusion of the evidence seized in violation of its provisions. Even *Wolf* "stoutly adhered" to that proposition.... Therefore, in extending the substantive protections of due process to all constitutionally unreasonable searches—state or federal—it was logically and constitutionally necessary that the exclusion doctrine—an essential part of the right to privacy—be also insisted upon as an essential ingredient of the right newly recognized by the *Wolf* case. In short, the admission of the new constitutional right by *Wolf* could not consistently tolerate denial of its most important constitutional privilege, namely, the exclusion of the evidence that an accused had been forced to give by reason of the unlawful seizure. To hold otherwise is to grant the right but in reality to withhold its privilege and enjoyment. Only last year the Court itself recognized that the purpose of the exclusionary rule "is to deter—to compel respect for the constitutional guaranty in the only effectively available way—by removing the incentive to disregard it."

Moreover, our holding that the exclusionary rule is an essential part of both the Fourth and Fourteenth Amendments is not only the logical dictate of prior cases, but it also makes very good sense. There is no war between the Constitution and common sense. Presently, a federal prosecutor may make no use of evidence illegally seized, but a State's attorney across the street may, although he supposedly is operating under the enforceable prohibitions of the same Amendment. Thus the State, by admitting evidence unlawfully seized, serves to encourage disobedience to the federal Constitution which it is bound to uphold. Moreover... "the very essence of a healthy federalism depends upon the avoidance of needless conflict between state and federal courts."... In nonexclusionary states, federal officers, being human, were by it invited to and did, as our cases indicate, step across the street to the state's attorney with their unconstitutionally seized evidence. Prosecution on the basis of that evidence was then had in a state court in utter disregard of the enforceable Fourth Amendment. If the fruits of an unconstitutional search had been inadmissible in both state and federal courts, this inducement to evasion would have been sooner eliminated....

Federal-state cooperation in the solution of crime under constitutional standards will be promoted, if only by recognition of their now mutual obligation to respect the same fundamental criteria in their approaches:

> However much in a particular case insistence upon such rules may appear as a technicality that inures to the benefit of a guilty person, the history of the criminal law proves that tolerance of shortcut methods in law enforcement impairs its enduring effectiveness.

Denying shortcuts to only one of two cooperating law enforcement agencies tends naturally to breed legitimate suspicion of "working arrangements" whose results are equally tainted.

There are those who say, as did Justice (then Judge) Cardozo, that under our constitutional exclusionary doctrine "the criminal is to go free because the constable has blundered." In some cases this will undoubtedly be the result. But, ... "there is another consideration—the imperative of judicial integrity." The criminal goes free, if he must, but it is the law that sets him free. Nothing can destroy a government more quickly than its failure to observe its own laws, or worse, its disregard of the charter of its own existence. As Mr. Justice Brandeis, dissenting, said in *Olmstead v. United States* (277 U.S. 438, 485 [1928]),

> Our Government is the potent, the omnipresent teacher. For good or for ill, it teaches the whole people by its example.... If the Government becomes a lawbreaker, it breeds contempt for law; it invites every man to become a law unto himself; it invites anarchy.

Nor can it lightly be assumed that, as a practical matter, adoption of the exclusionary rule fetters law enforcement. Only last year this Court expressly considered that contention and found that "pragmatic evidence of a sort" to the contrary was not wanting. The Court noted that

> the federal courts themselves have operated under the exclusionary rule of *Weeks* for almost half a century; yet it has not been suggested either that the Federal Bureau of Investigation has thereby been rendered ineffective, or that the administration of criminal justice in the federal courts has thereby been disrupted. Moreover, the experience of the states is impressive.... The movement towards the rule of exclusion has been halting but seemingly inexorable.

Holding

The ignoble shortcut to conviction left open to the State tends to destroy the entire system of constitutional restraints on which the liberties of the people rest. Having once recognized that the right to privacy embodied in the Fourth Amendment is enforceable against the states, and that the right to be secure against rude invasions of privacy by state officers is, therefore, constitutional in origin, we can no longer permit that right to remain an empty promise. Because it is enforceable in the same manner and to like effect as other basic rights secured by the Due Process Clause, we can no longer permit it to be revocable at the whim of any police officer who, in the name of law enforcement itself, chooses to suspend its enjoyment. Our decision, founded on reason and truth, gives to the individual no more than that which the Constitution guarantees him, to the police officer no less than that to which honest law enforcement is entitled, and, to the courts, that judicial integrity so necessary in the true administration of justice.

The judgment of the Supreme Court of Ohio is reversed and the case remanded for further proceedings not inconsistent with this opinion.

Concurring, *Douglas, J.*

The Ohio Supreme Court sustained [Mapp's] conviction even though it was based on the documents obtained in the lawless search. For in Ohio evidence obtained by an unlawful search and seizure is admissible in a criminal prosecution at least where it was not taken from the "defendant's person by the use of brutal or offensive force against defendant." This evidence would have been inadmissible in a federal prosecution.... "The effect of the Fourth Amendment is to put the courts of the United States and Federal officials, in the exercise of their power and authority, under limitations and restraints...." It was therefore held that evidence obtained (which in that case was documents and correspondence) from a home without any warrant was not admissible in a federal prosecution.

We held in *Wolf v. Colorado* that the Fourth Amendment was applicable to the states by reason of the Due Process Clause of the Fourteenth Amendment. But a majority held that the exclusionary rule of the *Weeks* case was not required of the states, that they could apply such sanctions as they chose. That position had the necessary votes to carry the day. But with all respect, it was not the voice of reason or principle.... If evidence seized in violation of the Fourth Amendment can be used against an accused, "his right to be secure against such searches and seizures is of no value, and... might as well be stricken from the Constitution." When we allowed states to give constitutional sanction to the "shabby business" of unlawful entry into a home... we did indeed rob the Fourth Amendment of much meaningful force.

There are, of course, other theoretical remedies. One is disciplinary action within the hierarchy of the police system, including prosecution of the police officer for a crime. Yet as Mr. Justice Murphy said in *Wolf v. Colorado,*

> Self-scrutiny is a lofty ideal, but its exaltation reaches new heights if we expect a District Attorney to prosecute himself or his associates for well-meaning violations of the search and seizure clause during a raid the District Attorney or his associates have ordered.

The only remaining remedy, if exclusion of the evidence is not required, is an action of trespass by the homeowner against the offending officer. Mr. Justice Murphy showed how onerous and difficult it would be for the citizen to maintain that action and how meager the relief even if the citizen prevails. The truth is that trespass actions against officers who make unlawful searches and seizures are mainly illusory remedies.

Without judicial action making the exclusionary rule applicable to the states, *Wolf v. Colorado* in practical effect reduced the guarantee against unreasonable searches and seizures to "a dead letter," as Mr. Justice Rutledge said in his dissent.

Wolf v. Colorado was decided in 1949. The immediate result was a storm of constitutional controversy that only today finds its end. I believe that this is an appropriate case in which to put an end to the asymmetry that *Wolf* imported into the law. It is an appropriate case, because the facts it presents show—as would few other cases—the casual arrogance of those who have the untrammeled power to invade one's home and to seize one's person.

Dissenting, *Harlan, J.*, joined by *Frankfurter, J.*, and *Whittaker, J.*

I would not impose upon the states this federal exclusionary remedy. The reasons given by the majority for now suddenly turning its back on *Wolf* seem to me notably unconvincing.

First, it is said that "the factual grounds upon which *Wolf* was based" have since changed, in that more States now follow the *Weeks* exclusionary rule than was so at the time *Wolf* was decided. While that is true, a recent survey indicates that at present one-half of the states still adhere to the common law nonexclusionary rule, and one, Maryland, retains the rule as to felonies. But in any case surely all this is beside the point, as the majority itself indeed seems to recognize. Our concern here, as it was in *Wolf,* is not with the desirability of that rule but only with the question whether the states are constitutionally free to follow it or not....

The preservation of a proper balance between state and federal responsibility in the administration of criminal justice demands patience on the part of those who might like to see things move faster among the states in this respect. Problems of criminal law enforcement vary widely from state to state. One state, in considering the totality of its legal picture, may conclude that the need for embracing the *Weeks* rule is pressing, because other remedies are unavailable or inadequate to secure compliance with the substantive constitutional principle involved. Another, though equally solicitous of constitutional rights, may choose to pursue one purpose at a time, allowing all evidence relevant to guilt to be brought into a criminal trial and dealing with constitutional infractions by other means. Still another may consider the exclusionary rule too rough-and-ready a remedy in that it reaches only unconstitutional intrusions that eventuate in criminal prosecution of the victims. Further, a state after experimenting with the *Weeks* rule for a time may, because of unsatisfactory experience with it, decide to revert to a nonexclusionary rule.... For us the question remains, as it has always been, one of state power, not one of passing judgment on the wisdom of one state course or another. In my view this Court should continue to forbear from fettering the states with an adamant rule that may embarrass them in coping with their own peculiar problems in criminal law enforcement.

Further, we are told that imposition of the *Weeks* rule on the states makes "very good sense" in that it will promote recognition by state and federal officials of their "mutual obligation to respect the same fundamental criteria" in their approach to law enforcement and will avoid "needless conflict between state and federal courts." Indeed the majority now finds an incongruity in *Wolf*'s discriminating perception between the demands of "ordered liberty" as respects the basic right of "privacy" and the means of securing it among the states. . . . An approach that regards the issue as one of achieving procedural symmetry or of serving administrative convenience surely disfigures the boundaries of this Court's functions in relation to the state and federal courts. . . . I do not believe that the Fourteenth Amendment empowers this Court to mould state remedies effectuating the right to freedom from "arbitrary intrusion by the police" to suit its own notions of how things should be done. . . .

A state conviction comes to us as the complete product of a sovereign judicial system. Typically a case will have been tried in a trial court and tested in some final appellate court and will go no further. In the comparatively rare instance when a conviction is reviewed by us on due process grounds, we deal then with a finished product in the creation of which we are allowed no hand, and our task, far from being one of overall supervision, is, speaking generally, restricted to a determination of whether the prosecution was constitutionally fair. The specifics of trial procedure, which in every mature legal system will vary greatly in detail, are within the sole competence of the states. I do not see how it can be said that a trial becomes unfair simply because a state determines that evidence may be considered by the trier of fact, regardless of how it was obtained, if it is relevant to the one issue with which the trial is concerned, the guilt or innocence of the accused.

Of course, a court may use its procedures as an incidental means of pursuing other ends. . . . I regret that I find so unwise in principle and so inexpedient in policy a decision motivated by the high purpose of increasing respect for Constitutional rights. But in the last analysis I think this Court can increase respect for the Constitution only if it rigidly respects the limitations that the Constitution places upon it and respects as well the principles inherent in its own processes. In the present case I think we exceed both and that our voice becomes only a voice of power, not of reason.

Questions for Discussion

1. Trace the development of the exclusionary rule from *Weeks* to *Wolf* to *Mapp*.
2. What reasons did the Supreme Court offer for extending the exclusionary rule to the states in *Mapp*?
3. Is the exclusionary rule more effective than other remedies in protecting Fourth Amendment rights?
4. Summarize Justice Harlan's dissent. Do you agree with Justice Harlan?
5. ***Problems in policing.*** As a police officer, you may find that you are uncertain about the lawfulness of a search. Would you be deterred from carrying out a search by the exclusionary rule? Which threat is the greatest deterrent—being sued for damages, being criminally prosecuted, or being administratively punished by the police department?

Debating the Exclusionary Rule

The Justification for the Exclusionary Rule

A great deal of ink has been spilled by authors debating the merits of the exclusionary rule. Four arguments traditionally are offered in support of the exclusionary rule.

Constitutional rights. The Fourth Amendment protects individuals against unreasonable searches and seizures, and this safeguard would be seriously weakened if evidence seized in an unreasonable search is used against an accused at trial. Justice Tom Clark observed in *Mapp v. Ohio* that the exclusionary rule is an "essential ingredient" of the Fourth Amendment and that a failure to recognize the constitutional status of the exclusionary rule is to "grant the right but in reality to withhold its privilege and enjoyment" (655).

Deterrence. The exclusionary rule deters the police from disregarding constitutional procedures in future investigations. The Supreme Court noted in *Elkins v. United States* that the purpose of the exclusionary rule is to deter the police and to "compel respect for the constitutional guaranty in the only effectively available way...by removing the incentive to disregard it." The Court noted that the exclusionary "rule is calculated to prevent [future violations], not to repair [past violations]" (*Elkins v. United States,* 304 U.S. 206, 217 [1940]).

Judicial integrity. Judges are charged with interpreting and protecting the Constitution of the United States, and confidence in the rule of law is promoted by the fair and equal enforcement of the law. Courts, for this reason, must not be seen to be turning a blind eye to lawbreaking by governmental officials. This is what is referred to as the imperative of judicial integrity. Supreme Court Justice Louis Brandeis, dissenting in *Olmsted v. United States,* observed in an often-cited statement that

> the future of the government will be imperiled if it fails to observe the law scrupulously. Our Government is the potent, the omnipresent teacher. For good or for ill, it teaches the whole people by its example. Crime is contagious. If the Government becomes a lawbreaker, it breeds contempt for law; it invites every man to become a law unto himself; it invites anarchy. To declare that in the administration of the criminal law the end justifies the means—to declare that the Government may commit crimes in order to secure the conviction of a private criminal—would bring terrible retribution. Against that pernicious doctrine this Court should resolutely set its face. (*Olmsted v. United States,* 277 U.S. 438, 468 [1928])

Social cost. The cost of excluding evidence has led police departments to stress the importance of *police professionalism* and to introduce training programs to insure that law enforcement personnel follow Fourth Amendment procedures. The result is that a relatively small proportion of cases lead to the acquittal of defendants based on the exclusion of evidence. In those instances in which evidence is excluded and individuals are released, it is contended that it is better for society to bear this cost of governmental wrongdoing than to impose the cost on a defendant whose rights have been violated.

There are some equally strong arguments against the exclusionary rule. Examine the arguments presented in the next section and formulate your own opinion.

Arguments Against the Exclusionary Rule

There are a number of criticisms of the exclusionary rule. These criticisms taken together make the point that the exclusionary rule imposes a high cost on society in terms of the "loss" of evidence in criminal trials and thereby reduces rather than enhances respect for the criminal justice system.

Constitution. The Supreme Court has held that the exclusionary rule is a "judicially created remedy" that is intended to deter the police from engaging in unreasonable searches rather than a constitutionally required remedy that is "part and parcel" of the Fourth Amendment. This means that judges are free to limit or even abolish the exclusionary rule.

Deterrence. Former Chief Justice Warren Burger dismissed the notion that the exclusionary rule deters the police from violating Fourth Amendment rights as a "wistful dream." The police are concerned with gathering evidence and with making arrests and do not stop to analyze whether a search satisfies the ever-changing and complicated standards for searches and seizures established by the Supreme Court. The immediate impact of an unreasonable search is felt by the prosecutor who loses evidence rather than by the police officer. It may take several years and the exhaustion of appeals for the legality of a search to be finally decided (*Bivens v. Six Unknown Named Agents,* 403 U.S. 388 [1971]).

Judicial integrity. The exclusionary rule decreases respect for the judiciary by requiring courts to take the side of defendants rather than victims.

Truth seeking. The exclusionary rule undermines the purpose of a criminal trial, which is the determination of an individual's guilt or innocence based on available and reliable evidence.

Penalizing victims. The protection of criminal defendants undermines rather than promotes respect for the criminal justice system. This was articulated by the U.S. Supreme

Court in *Irvine v. California.* The Court noted that "rejection of the evidence does nothing to punish the wrong-doing official, while it may, and likely will, release the wrong-doing defendant. . . . It protects [the suspect] against whom incriminating evidence is discovered, but does nothing to protect innocent persons who are the victims of illegal but fruitless searches" (*Irvine v. California,* 347 U.S. 128, 136 [1954]).

Lack of flexibility. The exclusionary rule excludes evidence regardless of whether the police committed a technical violation of the law or engaged in a blatant and intentional violation of the Fourth Amendment. In both cases, the identical remedy is imposed: the exclusion of the evidence. As Chief Justice Burger observed, this equates the freeing of a tiger and a mouse in a schoolroom as equally serious offenses (*Bivens v. Six Unknown Named Agents,* 403 U.S. 388, 419 [1971]).

Limited application. The exclusionary rule has no impact on the police in those instances in which the police seize a gun or drugs in order to remove the contraband from the streets and have no intention of pursuing a criminal prosecution. In this instance there is "no evidence to exclude" and "no penalty paid by the police." The reasonableness of the search and seizure also often does not come to the attention of the courts when a defendant plea-bargains and enters a guilty plea in exchange for a lesser sentence or other consideration.

Alternative Remedies to the Exclusionary Rule

Critics of the exclusionary rule argue that deterrence may be more effectively achieved through various alternative procedures that do not require the exclusion of evidence from trial. Do you believe that any or all of the procedural mechanisms listed below will be more effective than the exclusionary rule in deterring unlawful Fourth Amendment searches?

Civil tort suits for damages against police officers who have engaged in unreasonable searches and seizures and the government: Civil actions against the police and state governments must overcome a number of difficult barriers to be successful. There also must be adequate monetary compensation provided to successful litigants to serve as an incentive for individuals to take the time and expense to file suit.

Criminal prosecution of the police for violation of civil liberties: Prosecutors may be reluctant to bring charges against police officers, particularly for relatively minor violations of the law.

Police administrative procedures subjecting officers to penalties that include demotions, fines, suspensions, and termination of employment: Police administrators may be hesitant to discipline officers and risk damaging morale, particularly when the evidence led to the arrest of dangerous criminals.

A civilian review board that examines cases of suspected abuse, which are referred to the board by defense lawyers and trial court judges: The panel would be composed of citizens, lawyers, judges, and police officials and would be authorized to impose penalties ranging from fines to termination from the police force. The police historically have been strongly opposed to outside review boards and complain that members of the board may not fully understand the demands and pressures of policing.

A judicial hearing conducted prior to the prosecution of the criminal charge: In the event that the judge concludes that a police officer carried out an unlawful search, the judge would be authorized to impose an appropriate penalty ranging from a fine or suspension to termination from the police force. A related proposal is to hold the hearing following the trial before the same judge and jury who heard the case. The judge would instruct the jury on the law, and they would decide whether the officer conducted an unlawful search. The judge then would impose an appropriate punishment. This approach saves the time and expense of gathering the facts. Critics point out that judges and juries will be influenced in their decision making by whether the trial ended in a conviction.

As we shall see later in the chapter, the Supreme Court has responded to criticisms of the exclusionary rule by creating various exceptions. The next section of the text discusses the process that a defense lawyer follows when seeking to suppress evidence under the exclusionary rule.

Invoking the Exclusionary Rule

The first step in challenging the reasonableness of a search is filing a pretrial motion to suppress. Most states and the federal courts place the burden of proof on the defendant when the search or seizure is based on a warrant. The burden of proof is reversed and is placed on the government when the police act without a warrant. Why? A warrant has been issued by a judge based on evidence presented by the government that meets the probable cause standard. The presumption is that the evidence on which the warrant is based satisfies the probable cause standard, and the defendant is assigned the heavy burden of demonstrating that the warrant is deficient. The defendant must demonstrate a lack of probable cause by clear and convincing evidence. In the case of a warrantless search, the police are aware of the evidence that constitutes probable cause and are in the best position to demonstrate the legality of the search. The government also bears the burden of proving that a search was justified as an exception to the warrant requirement.

A decision by the trial judge to admit the evidence results in the evidence being introduced at trial. Following a conviction, the defense may appeal and raise the issue of whether the judge made the correct decision in admitting the evidence. In contrast, the prosecution in most states is required to act immediately if it wishes to appeal a decision not to admit evidence. Why? Because the defendant may be acquitted at trial. At this point the prosecution is prevented from subjecting the defendant to the double jeopardy of an additional trial. The lengthy appeal process, of course, may persuade the prosecutor to take his or her chances at trial without the evidence.

A decision by a judge to admit evidence that was challenged by a defendant on a timely motion to suppress constitutes error when the judge's decision is held by an appellate court to have been based on an incorrect analysis of the law. This requires a reversal of the guilty verdict unless the judge's admission of the evidence is considered to be **harmless error**. The prosecution will want to preserve the guilty verdict and will argue on appeal that the trial judge's decision is correct and, in any event, constitutes harmless error. This requires that the prosecution establish beyond a reasonable doubt that there is no reasonable probability that the evidence influenced the outcome of the trial (*Chapman v. California,* 386 U.S. 18 [1967]).

A defendant who has exhausted his or her state court appeals and finds that the appellate courts have affirmed the ruling of the trial court judge can look to an additional avenue of relief by filing a writ of habeas corpus with a federal district court or by pursuing a similar remedy in the state court. Habeas corpus is a request to the court to require the government to bring an individual who is in custody before the court to determine the legality of his or her detention. Access to the federal courts requires an allegation that an individual's detention resulted from a violation of his or her constitutional rights before trial or during trial. A defendant in custody also may rely on federal habeas corpus in those instances in which new information comes to light that indicates that the conviction was based on a constitutional violation. Habeas corpus is a complicated topic that we will cover in depth when we turn our attention to judicial appeals in Chapter 14 (*Stone v. Powell,* 428 U.S. 465 [1976]).

Standing

A defendant is required to have **standing** to challenge the introduction of evidence at trial. In other words, a defendant may be surprised to learn that he or she may not be eligible to contest the legality of a search. In 1969, in *Alderman v. United States,* the U.S. Supreme Court held that Alderman did not have standing to suppress evidence obtained through an illegal wiretap of a codefendant's telephone conversation. The Supreme Court explained that the extension of standing to individuals whose personal rights have not been violated would significantly increase the costs of the exclusionary rule (*Alderman v. United States,* 394 U.S. 165, 175 [1969]). The legal test to be applied for standing in the case of an alleged violation of the Fourth Amendment prohibition on unreasonable searches and seizures is whether the defendant has both a subjective and an objectively reasonable expectation of privacy in the area that is subject to the search. The burden of proof typically is placed on the defendant.

Below are some other examples of instances in which petitioners have lacked standing to suppress evidence.

Automobile passengers. A police officer stopped an automobile that he believed was fleeing the scene of a robbery. A search uncovered a box of rifle shells and a sawed-off shotgun under the front seat. The two petitioners were passengers, neither of whom owned the automobile. The Supreme Court ruled that the petitioners lacked an expectation of privacy in the glove compartment and under the seat and held that they lacked standing to suppress the evidence (*Rakas v. Illinois,* 439 U.S. 128 [1978]).

Overnight guests. The police entered a home without a warrant or consent looking for Olson, an overnight guest, who was wanted for suspected involvement in a murder-robbery. Olson was found hiding in a closet. The Supreme Court held that an overnight guest such as Olson possessed a reasonable expectation of privacy in the home. The Court held that "to hold that an overnight guest has a legitimate expectation of privacy . . . merely recognizes everyday expectations of privacy that we all share" (*Minnesota v. Olson,* 495 U.S. 91, 98 [1990]).

Possessory interest in items that are seized. The police directed Cox to empty the contents of her purse. Rawlings admitted that he owned a jar that was found in the purse containing 1,800 capsules of LSD. The Supreme Court held that Rawlings's possession of the drugs did not provide standing to challenge the search and seizure and that he was required to possess an expectation of privacy in the "area of the search," that is, the purse. Rawlings had met Cox only a few days before the search and had never before placed any items in Cox's purse. The Supreme Court also found it significant that Rawlings had no right to exclude other individuals from access to the purse, and in fact other individuals had freely rummaged through the purse (*Rawlings v. Kentucky,* 448 U.S. 98 [1980]).

Commercial transactions. Carter and Johns traveled from Chicago to the Twin Cities to meet with Thompson at her apartment. They had never before been in Thompson's apartment. The three of them spent two and a half hours bagging cocaine. A search of the apartment uncovered cocaine residue and plastic baggies. The Supreme Court overturned the Minnesota Supreme Court's recognition of Carter and Johns's standing to seek to suppress the evidence seized in Thompson's apartment. The Court based its decision on the commercial nature of the relationship, the brief period of time the two had spent on the premises, and the lack of a previous connection between Carter, Johns, and Thompson (*Minnesota v. Carter,* 525 U.S. 83 [1998]).

The target of a police investigation. In *United States v. Payner,* the U.S. Supreme Court held that Payner lacked standing to challenge the introduction of documents against him at trial that had been stolen by a private investigator from the briefcase of another individual as part of an Internal Revenue Service investigation of Payner (*United States v. Payner,* 447 U.S. 727 [1980]).

The standing doctrine is a method of limiting the "cost" of the exclusionary rule by restricting the number of individuals who are eligible to challenge the introduction of the evidence. The Supreme Court also has limited the cost of the exclusionary rule by creating a number of exceptions to its application.

You can find Minnesota v. Carter *on the study site, http://www.sagepub.com/lippmancp.*

Exceptions to the Exclusionary Rule

We have seen that in *Mapp v. Ohio* the Supreme Court held that the exclusionary rule was a constitutional rule that was intended to deter the police and to protect the integrity of the courts. The U.S. Supreme Court, in 1973, in *United States v. Calandra,* modified this holding and held that the exclusionary rule is a judge-made remedy that is designed to deter unreasonable searches and seizures.

Calandra was followed by a number of cases in which the Supreme Court recognized exceptions to the exclusionary rule. These exceptions are based on a determination in each instance that the modest amount of additional deterrence to be gained from excluding the evidence from trial is outweighed by the cost to society of excluding the evidence from trial. As you read this section, pay particular attention to the Supreme Court's employment of this balancing test. Is the court's analysis based on hard facts or on speculation? Should the Supreme Court have recognized these exceptions to the exclusionary rule? The next section of this chapter discusses the following exceptions:

- Collateral proceedings
- Attenuation
- Good faith
- Independent source
- Inevitable discovery
- Impeachment

Collateral Proceedings

The **collateral proceedings** exception permits the use of unlawfully seized evidence in proceedings that are not part of the formal trial (literally "off to the side" or "loosely related" to the trial). This includes bail hearings, preliminary hearings, grand jury proceedings, sentencing hearings, and habeas corpus review. What is the explanation for this exception? In most of these collateral proceedings, there is an interest in a full presentation of the facts. The application of the exclusionary rule would deny judges evidence that might prove useful in determining whether to charge a defendant with a criminal offense, in setting bail, or in sentencing a defendant. Balancing citizen protection against this is the fact that the Supreme Court has concluded that excluding the fruits of an unlawful search from these proceedings would have little additional impact in deterring police violations of the Fourth Amendment. The police already are deterred by the prospect that unlawfully seized evidence will not be available to establish a defendant's criminal guilt at trial, and little additional deterrence will be achieved by excluding the evidence from collateral proceedings.

The Supreme Court also has ruled that evidence seized in an unreasonable search is admissible in *various noncriminal proceedings*. This includes parole revocation hearings, immigration hearings, and tax and other administrative proceedings. Unlawfully seized evidence also is admissible in forfeiture hearings, which are quasi-criminal proceedings in which the Court determines whether property is connected to certain specified crimes and therefore should be forfeited to the government. In each of these instances, the Supreme Court weighed the additional deterrence that would result from the exclusion of evidence against the costs of excluding the evidence and held that the price paid by society in excluding the evidence far outweighs the modest benefits in terms of deterrence.

Attenuation

In the typical case there is a direct causal connection between an unreasonable search and the seizure of evidence. The evidence is the product of an unlawful search and therefore is excluded from evidence. In other instances, however, the connection between the search and the seizure of the evidence is **attenuated** (weak), and the U.S. Supreme Court has held that the exclusionary rule does not apply. A weak connection between the unlawful search and the seizure of evidence also is referred to as *dissipating the taint* or as **purging the taint** of the illegality. As early as 1939, in *Nardone v. United States,* the Supreme Court recognized that evidence seized as a result of an illegal search may be admissible where the "connection [has]... become so attenuated as to dissipate the taint" (*Nardone v. United States,* 308 U.S. 338, 341 [1939]).

An example of attenuation is *United States v. Boone*. In *Boone,* Officer Phil Barney executed an unlawful search of a vehicle driven by defendant Boone. The search led to the discovery of illegal narcotics, and as Barney stepped away from the car, defendants Boone and Greenfield sped away at an excessive speed. Barney followed in hot pursuit, and the defendants, facing imminent apprehension, threw narcotics out the window. The discarded narcotics were subsequently seized by the police. Should the drugs be excluded as the product of Officer Barney's unreasonable search and seizure? The Tenth Circuit Court of Appeals ruled that the suspects' tossing the drugs out the window was a voluntary act that broke the connection between the unlawful search and the discovery of the narcotics. As a result, the Tenth Circuit held that the drugs were admissible in evidence. The court observed that

> Officer Barney's initial illegal search did not cause the defendants to flee at a high rate of speed or to throw [the drugs] onto the highway.... It would be nonsensical to hold that officer Barney had no right to collect the evidence of drug possession that defendants voluntarily discarded onto the highway. (*United States v. Boone,* 62 F.3d 323, 326 (10th Cir. 1995)

In *Brown v. Illinois,* the Supreme Court articulated three circumstances that determine whether there is an *attenuation of the taint* of an unlawful search (*Brown v. Illinois,* 422 U.S. 590, 603 [1975]. As you can see from these three factors, shown below, attenuation will be found when there is a significant passage of time between the initial illegality and the discovery of the evidence or where a number of factors intervene as well as in those instances in which the police mistakenly or unintentionally misinterpreted the law.

Temporal proximity. A lengthy period of time attenuates the taint. In *Ceccolini,* the police illegally seized evidence that led them to a witness who testified for the prosecution at trial. The Supreme Court ruled that the four-month period between the initial illegality and the interrogation of the witness attenuated the taint and that the testimony was properly admitted at trial (*United States v. Ceccolini,* 435 U.S. 268 [1978]).

Intervening circumstances. Intervening events that weaken the connection between the unlawful search and the evidence that is seized may attenuate the initial taint. Independent and voluntary acts of individuals, for instance, may break the chain of causation. This is illustrated in *Boone* by the intervening events of the suspects' fleeing from the scene of the initial search and by their throwing the drugs out the window. In contrast, reading the *Miranda* warnings to a suspect and brief visits by friends and family have not been found to break the chain of causation of an illegal arrest.

Intentional violation. Judges resist finding attenuation where the police intentionally violate the law. A finding of attenuation would reward a conscious disregard of legal standards. In *Brown,* the police broke into the defendant's apartment, illegally arrested him at gunpoint without probable cause, and obtained a confession after reading him his *Miranda* rights. The Supreme Court stressed that the

> illegality here...had a quality of purposefulness. The impropriety of the arrest was obvious....The manner in which Brown's arrest was effected gives the appearance of having been calculated to cause surprise, fright, and confusion....The deterrent purpose of the exclusionary rule would be well-served by excluding the subsequent confessions. (*Brown v. Illinois,* 322 U.S. 590, 592–595, 603–604 [1975])

In the recent case of *Hudson v. Michigan,* the U.S. Supreme Court articulated a *constitutional interest* test for attenuation. The Court stated that evidence is admissible at trial when the police fail to follow a constitutional requirement under the Fourth Amendment that serves to protect an individual's privacy in the home rather than to protect an individual against unreasonable searches and seizures.

Constitutional interest. In *Hudson,* the Supreme Court held that the requirement that the police knock and announce their presence and wait a reasonable period of time before executing a search warrant is intended to protect individuals against unannounced violations of the privacy of the home rather than to protect individuals against unreasonable searches and seizures. As a result, evidence seized following a failure to knock and announce should not be excluded from evidence. The Court stated that "even given a direct causal connection, the interest protected by the constitutional guarantee that has been violated would not be served by suppression of the evidence obtained" (*Hudson v. Michigan,* 547 U.S. 586 [2006]).

There is one last point to keep in mind: Courts are less inclined to find that a taint is attenuated in regard to a witness's testimony than in the case of physical evidence. Why? The cost of excluding a witness's testimony significantly harms the prosecution's case, and many witnesses undoubtedly would have voluntarily come forward and testified on behalf of the government after learning of the prosecution.

We now review the important and complicated 1963 case of *Wong Sun v. United States.* The U.S. Supreme Court in *Wong Sun* articulated the rule that has guided judicial decisions on attenuation: "whether, granting establishment of the primary illegality, the evidence by which instant objection is made has been come at by exploitation of that illegality or instead by means sufficiently distinguishable to be purged of the primary taint." This test asks whether the evidence was the direct result of an unlawful search and should be excluded from evidence or was so far removed from the unlawful search that it should be admitted into evidence (*Wong Sun v. United States,* 371 U.S. 471, 486 [1963]).

In the case at issue in *Wong Sun,* federal narcotic agents illegally arrested James Toy in the bedroom in the rear of his laundry. Toy, in turn, implicated Johnny Yee as a drug dealer; Yee was arrested, and several tubes of heroin were seized in his home. Yee, in turn, stated that he had obtained the drugs from Toy and Wong Sun. Wong Sun subsequently was arrested in the back room of his apartment by six officers. Yee, Toy, and Wong Sun all were charged with narcotics offenses, and Wong Sun was released on his own recognizance. Wong Sun later voluntarily returned, was interrogated, and provided statements to federal narcotics agents (473–478). The Supreme Court was asked to disentangle this knotty case and to rule on whether the narcotics and Wong Sun's confession were the fruits of the poisonous tree of what the defense alleged was Toy's illegal arrest.

Toy's statement. The Supreme Court ruled that the police lacked probable cause to enter Toy's laundry and to arrest him. The Government argued that Toy's statement implicating Yee was an "act of free will" that purged the taint of the unlawful invasion. The Supreme Court, however, rejected the Government's argument. Six or seven officers had broken down the door and followed Toy into the bedroom. He was immediately handcuffed and arrested. The Court held that "it is unreasonable to infer that Toy's response was sufficiently an act of free will to purge the primary taint of the unlawful invasion" (486).

Seizure of narcotics from Yee. Was there a direct relationship between Toy's statement and the seizure of the narcotics from Yee? The Supreme Court held that the police would not have seized the narcotics absent Toy's statement and that the drugs had been detected through the "exploitation of that illegality" (i.e., the illegal arrest of Toy) and accordingly should be excluded from evidence (487).

Wong Sun's statement. Wong Sun's unsigned confession was not considered to be the fruit of the poisonous tree and was properly admitted into evidence at trial. Wong Sun was released on his own recognizance after his arraignment and returned voluntarily several days later to make the statement. The Supreme Court held that the connection between the arrest and the statement was "so attenuated as to dissipate the taint"(491).

Hudson v. Michigan, in 2006, is the Supreme Court's most recent decision on attenuation. The police obtained a warrant to search Hudson's home for drugs and firearms. In executing the warrant, the police "announced their presence," but failed to comply with the constitutional requirement that they wait a reasonable period of time before opening the unlocked front door and seizing a large quantity of drugs and firearms. The Supreme Court held that the Fourth Amendment exclusionary rule was inapplicable, because the purpose of the knock and announce rule is to alert residents to a police search and "has nothing to do with the seizure of the evidence." In reading *Hudson,* pay attention to the Supreme Court's weighing of the benefits and costs of applying the exclusionary rule. What will be the impact of this decision on the protections afforded to individuals under the exclusionary rule?

You can find a fuller version of Hudson v. Michigan *on the study site, http://www.sagepub.com/lippmancp.*

Does violation of the knock and announce rule require suppression of evidence seized in the search?

Hudson v. Michigan, 547 U.S. 586 (2006), Scalia, J.

We decide whether violation of the knock and announce rule requires the suppression of all evidence found in the search.

Facts

Police obtained a warrant authorizing a search for drugs and firearms at the home of petitioner Booker Hudson. They discovered both. Large quantities of drugs were found, including cocaine rocks in Hudson's pocket. A loaded gun was lodged between the cushion and armrest of the chair in which he was sitting. Hudson was charged under Michigan law with unlawful drug and firearm possession.

This case is before us only because of the method of entry into the house. When the police arrived to execute the warrant, they announced their presence, but waited only a short time—perhaps "three to five seconds,"—before turning the knob of the unlocked front door and entering Hudson's home. Hudson moved to suppress all the inculpatory evidence, arguing that the premature entry violated his Fourth Amendment rights.

The Michigan trial court granted his motion.... The Michigan Court of Appeals reversed, relying on Michigan Supreme Court cases holding that suppression is inappropriate when entry is made pursuant to warrant but without proper knock and announce. The Michigan Supreme Court denied leave to appeal. Hudson was convicted of drug possession. He renewed his Fourth Amendment claim on appeal, but the Court of Appeals rejected it and affirmed the conviction. The Michigan Supreme Court again declined review. We granted certiorari.

Issue

The common law principle that law enforcement officers must announce their presence and provide residents an opportunity to open the door is an ancient one. Since 1917, when Congress passed the Espionage Act, this traditional protection has been part of federal statutory law.... We were asked in *Wilson v. Arkansas* (514 U.S. 927, 931–936 [1995]) whether the rule was also a command of the Fourth Amendment. Tracing its origins in our English legal heritage, we concluded that it was.... *Wilson* and cases following it have noted the many situations in which it is not necessary to knock and announce. It is not necessary when "circumstances present a threat of physical violence," or if there is "reason to believe that evidence would likely be destroyed if advance notice were given," or if knocking and announcing would be "futile" (*Richards v. Wisconsin,* 520 U.S. 385, 394 [1997]). We require only that police "have a reasonable suspicion... under the particular circumstances" that one of these grounds for failing to knock and announce exists, and we have acknowledged that "this showing is not high."

When the knock and announce rule does apply, it is not easy to determine precisely what officers must do. How many seconds' wait are too few? Our "reasonable wait time" standard is necessarily vague. *United States v. Banks* (a drug case, like this one) held that the proper measure was not how long it would take the resident to reach the door, but how long it would take to dispose of the suspected drugs—but that such a time (15 to 20 seconds in that case) would necessarily be extended when, for instance, the suspected contraband was not easily concealed (*United States v. Banks,* 540 U.S. 31, 40–41 [2003]). If our evaluation is subject to such calculations, it is unsurprising that... police officers about to encounter someone who may try to harm them will be uncertain how long to wait.

Happily, these issues do not confront us here. From the trial level onward, Michigan has conceded that the entry was a knock and announce violation. The issue here is remedy. The courts in which *Wilson* has been tried have specifically declined to decide whether the exclusionary rule is appropriate for violation of the knock and announce requirement. That issue is squarely before us now.

Reasoning

We adopted the federal exclusionary rule for evidence that was unlawfully seized from a home without a warrant in violation of the Fourth Amendment. We began applying the same rule to the states, through the Fourteenth Amendment, in *Mapp v. Ohio*. Suppression of evidence, however, has always been our last resort, not our first impulse. The exclusionary rule generates "substantial social costs," which sometimes include setting the guilty free and the dangerous at large. We have therefore been "cautio[us] against expanding" it, and "have repeatedly emphasized that the rule's 'costly toll' upon truth-seeking and law enforcement objectives presents a high obstacle for those urging [its] application." We have rejected "indiscriminate application" of the rule, and have held it to be applicable only "where its remedial objectives are thought most efficaciously served,"—that is, "where its deterrence benefits outweigh its 'substantial social costs.'" We have explained that "whether the exclusionary sanction is appropriately imposed in a particular case . . . is 'an issue separate from the question whether the Fourth Amendment rights of the party seeking to invoke the rule were violated by police conduct.'" In other words, exclusion may not be premised on the mere fact that a constitutional violation was a "but-for" cause of obtaining evidence. . . .

We did not always speak so guardedly. . . . *Mapp* . . . suggested wide scope for the exclusionary rule. . . . But we have long since rejected that approach. . . . In this case . . . the constitutional violation of an illegal manner of entry was not a but-for cause of obtaining the evidence. Whether that preliminary misstep had occurred or not, the police would have executed the warrant they had obtained, and would have discovered the gun and drugs inside the house. But even if the illegal entry here could be characterized as a but-for cause of discovering what was inside, we have "never held that evidence is 'fruit of the poisonous tree' simply 'because it would not have come to light but for the illegal actions of the police.'" . . . But-for cause . . . can be too attenuated to justify exclusion. . . .

Attenuation can occur, of course, when the causal connection is remote. Attenuation also occurs when, even given a direct causal connection, the interest protected by the constitutional guarantee that has been violated would not be served by suppression of the evidence obtained. . . . For this reason, cases excluding the fruits of unlawful warrantless searches say nothing about the appropriateness of exclusion to vindicate the interests protected by the knock and announce requirement. Until a valid warrant has issued, citizens are entitled to shield "their persons, houses, papers, and effects," from the government's scrutiny. Exclusion of the evidence obtained by a warrantless search vindicates that entitlement. The interests protected by the knock and announce requirement are quite different—and do not include the shielding of potential evidence from the government's eyes.

One of those interests is the protection of human life and limb, because an unannounced entry may provoke violence in supposed self-defense by the surprised resident. Another interest is the protection of property. Breaking a house (as the old cases typically put it) absent an announcement would penalize someone who "did not know of the process, of which, if he had notice, it is to be presumed that he would obey it ." . . . The knock and announce rule gives individuals "the opportunity to comply with the law and to avoid the destruction of property occasioned by a forcible entry." And third, the knock and announce rule protects those elements of privacy and dignity that can be destroyed by a sudden entrance. It gives residents the "opportunity to prepare themselves for" the entry of the police. "The brief interlude between announcement and entry with a warrant may be the opportunity that an individual has to pull on clothes or get out of bed." In other words, it assures the opportunity to collect oneself before answering the door.

What the knock and announce rule has never protected, however, is one's interest in preventing the government from seeing or taking evidence described in a warrant. Since the interests that were violated in this case have nothing to do with the seizure of the evidence, the exclusionary rule is inapplicable. . . .

Quite apart from the requirement of unattenuated causation, the exclusionary rule has never been applied except "where its deterrence benefits outweigh its 'substantial social costs.'" The costs here are considerable. In addition to the grave adverse consequence that exclusion of relevant incriminating evidence always entails (viz., the risk of releasing dangerous criminals into society), imposing that massive remedy for a knock and announce violation would generate a constant flood of alleged failures to observe the rule, and claims that any asserted . . . justification for a no knock entry had inadequate support. The cost of entering this lottery would be small, but the jackpot enormous: suppression of all evidence, amounting in many cases to a get-out-of-jail-free card. Courts would experience as never before the reality that "the exclusionary rule frequently requires extensive litigation to determine whether particular evidence must be excluded." Unlike the warrant or *Miranda* requirements, compliance with which is readily determined (either there was or was not a warrant; either the *Miranda* warning was given, or it was not), what constituted a "reasonable wait time" in a particular case (or for that matter, how many seconds the police in fact waited), or whether there was "reasonable suspicion" of the sort that would invoke the exceptions [to knock and announce], is difficult for the trial court to determine and even more difficult for an appellate court to review.

Another consequence of the incongruent remedy Hudson proposes would be police officers' refraining from timely entry after knocking and announcing. As we have observed, the amount of time they must wait is necessarily uncertain. If the consequences of running afoul of the rule were so massive, officers would be inclined to wait longer than the law requires—producing preventable violence against officers in some cases and the destruction of evidence in many others. We deemed these consequences severe enough to produce our unanimous agreement that a mere "reasonable suspicion" that knocking and announcing "under the particular circumstances, would be dangerous or futile, or that it would inhibit the effective investigation of the crime," will cause the requirement to yield.

Next to these "substantial social costs" we must consider the deterrence benefits, existence of which is a necessary condition for exclusion. (It is not, of course, a sufficient condition: "It does not follow that the Fourth

Amendment requires adoption of every proposal that might deter police misconduct.") To begin with, the value of deterrence depends upon the strength of the incentive to commit the forbidden act. Viewed from this perspective, deterrence of knock and announce violations is not worth a lot. Violation of the warrant requirement sometimes produces incriminating evidence that could not otherwise be obtained. But ignoring knock and announce can realistically be expected to achieve absolutely nothing except the prevention of destruction of evidence and the avoidance of life-threatening resistance by occupants of the premises—dangers which, if there is even "reasonable suspicion" of their existence, suspend the knock and announce requirement anyway. Massive deterrence is hardly required.

It seems to us not even true, as Hudson contends, that without suppression there will be no deterrence of knock and announce violations at all. Of course even if this assertion were accurate, it would not necessarily justify suppression. Assuming (as the assertion must) that civil suit is not an effective deterrent, one can think of many forms of police misconduct that are similarly "undeterred."... We cannot assume that exclusion in this context is necessary deterrence simply because we found that it was necessary deterrence in different contexts and long ago. That would be forcing the public today to pay for the sins and inadequacies of a legal regime that existed almost half a century ago....

Holding

In sum, the social costs of applying the exclusionary rule to knock and announce violations are considerable; the incentive to such violations is minimal to begin with, and the extant deterrences against them are substantial—incomparably greater than the factors deterring warrantless entries when *Mapp* was decided. Resort to the massive remedy of suppressing evidence of guilt is unjustified.

Dissenting, *Breyer, J.*, joined by *Stevens, J.*, *Souter, J.*, and *Ginsburg, J.*

The Court destroys the strongest legal incentive to comply with the Constitution's knock and announce requirement. And the Court does so without significant support in precedent.... In *Weeks, Silverthorne,* and *Mapp,* the Court based its holdings requiring suppression of unlawfully obtained evidence upon the recognition that admission of that evidence would seriously undermine the Fourth Amendment's promise. All three cases recognized that failure to apply the exclusionary rule would make that promise a hollow one, reducing it to "a form of words," "of no value" to those whom it seeks to protect. Indeed, this Court in *Mapp* held that the exclusionary rule applies to the states in large part due to its belief that alternative state mechanisms for enforcing the Fourth Amendment's guarantees had proved "worthless and futile."

Why is application of the exclusionary rule any the less necessary here? Without such a rule, as in *Mapp*, police know that they can ignore the Constitution's requirements without risking suppression of evidence discovered after an unreasonable entry. As in *Mapp*, some government officers will find it easier, or believe it less risky, to proceed with what they consider a necessary search immediately and without the requisite constitutional... compliance....

Questions for Discussion

1. Summarize the knock and announce rule.
2. What are the interests that the Supreme Court majority determines are protected by the knock and announce rule? Why does the Supreme Court hold that the evidence discovered as a result of the violation of the knock and announce rule is too attenuated to be subject to the exclusionary rule?
3. Explain why the Supreme Court concludes that the social costs of applying the exclusionary rule in regard to the knock and announce rule outweigh the benefits in terms of deterrence.
4. What developments does the Supreme Court majority argue make it unnecessary to rely on the exclusionary rule?
5. ***Problems in policing.*** As a police officer, would you view the decision in *Hudson* as favorable or unfavorable? Why?

Case and Comments

Miranda and Attenuation. Defendant Patane was arrested outside his home and handcuffed. A federal agent had been informed that the defendant, a convicted felon, possessed a Glock pistol. The agent began giving the *Miranda* warning and was interrupted by the defendant who stated that he knew the rights. The defendant then informed the officer that "the Glock is in my bedroom on a shelf.... The agent seized the pistol and the defendant was indicted and convicted for being a felon in possession of firearm in violation of federal law."

The government acknowledged on appeal that Patane had not been fully and effectively informed of his

Miranda rights, and the Tenth Circuit Court of Appeals held that the pistol and the defendant's statement were both inadmissible into evidence. Justice Clarence Thomas, writing for the Court majority, held that a failure to provide the *Miranda* warnings does not violate a suspect's constitutional rights. Violations occur only "upon the admission of unwarned statements into evidence at trial." Justice Thomas further ruled that the introduction into evidence of the "nontestimonial fruit" of a voluntary statement, such as Patane's Glock, does not violate the Self-Incrimination Clause. The Self-Incrimination Clause prohibits compelling a defendant to be a "witness against himself." The term "witness," according to Justice Thomas, restricts the right against self-incrimination to testimonial evidence. Nontestimonial evidence, such as a gun, is unable to "bear witness" against an accused.

Justice Souter, with whom Justices Stevens and Ginsburg joined in dissent, proclaimed that "in closing their eyes to the consequences of giving an evidentiary advantage to those who ignore *Miranda,* the majority adds an important inducement for interrogators to ignore the rule in that case." The dissenting judges argued that a failure to provide the *Miranda* warning raises a presumption that a confession is involuntary, and the confession as well as the fruits of the seizure of the evidence should be excluded from evidence. The dissenters concluded that the decision in *Patane* must be viewed as an "unjustifiable invitation to law enforcement to flaunt *Miranda* when there may be physical evidence to be gained."

How does *Patane* illustrate the attenuation doctrine? Do you agree with the decision? See *United States v. Patane,* 542 U.S. 630 (2004).

You can find United States v. Patane *on the study site, http://www.sagepub.com/lippmancp.*

Good Faith Exception

In 1976, Supreme Court Justice Byron White, in dissenting in *Stone v. Powell,* argued that the exclusionary rule should not be applied where evidence is unlawfully seized by an officer acting in the "good faith belief" that his or her conduct complies with the Fourth Amendment and the officer has reasonable grounds for his or her belief. Justice White explained that a police officer who believes that he or she is acting lawfully will not be deterred by the prospect that unlawfully seized evidence will be excluded from evidence at trial. He concluded the only thing that is accomplished by withholding the evidence from the jury is interference with the "truth-finding function" of the trial. Briefly stated, the exclusionary rule under these circumstances provides little benefit while exacting a significant cost (*Stone v. Powell,* 428 U.S. 465, 540 [1976]). In 1984, in *United States v. Leon,* the Supreme Court recognized the **good faith exception** to the exclusionary rule. In the last three decades, the Court has relied on the good faith exception to uphold the constitutionality of searches in five circumstances. In each of these cases, the police were found to have acted with an honest and objectively reasonable belief in the legality of the search.

- ***Reliance on a warrant.*** The police reasonably, but incorrectly, believed that the search warrant issued by the judge was based on probable cause (*United States v. Leon*).
- ***Reliance on assurance by a judge that a warrant meets Fourth Amendment standards.*** The police reasonably, but incorrectly, relied on the assurance of a judge that a warrant met the requirements of the Fourth Amendment (*Massachusetts v. Sheppard*).
- ***Reliance on legislation.*** The police reasonably relied on a statute that later was declared unconstitutional (*Illinois v. Krull*).
- ***Reliance on data entered into a computer by a court employee.*** A police officer reasonably relied on computer information that was incorrectly entered by a court employee (*Arizona v. Evans*).
- ***Reliance on apparent authority of a third party to consent.*** The police reasonably, but incorrectly, believed that an individual possessed the authority to consent to an entry of his or her home (*Illinois v. Rodriguez*).

Reliance on a warrant. In 1984, in *United States v. Leon* (468 U.S. 897 [1984]), Justice White along with five other members of the Supreme Court recognized the good faith exception to the exclusionary rule. In the incident at issue in *Leon,* an informant alerted the police that he had witnessed a drug sale at a home in Burbank, California, five months previously.

He reported that the suspects stored cash and narcotics in homes in Burbank. The police subsequently placed the residences and suspects under surveillance, and their observations appeared to corroborate the informant's information. They secured a warrant from a judge, searched the residences, seized drugs and a large amount of cash, and charged the defendants with conspiracy to possess and distribute cocaine as well as a variety of other criminal counts. A federal district court held a hearing and suppressed use of the narcotics as evidence. The judge ruled that the affidavit supporting the warrant failed to establish the informant's reliability and credibility and did not constitute probable cause (901–905).

The U.S. Supreme Court nevertheless held that the police had acted in objectively reasonable good faith reliance on the warrant and that application of the "extreme sanction of exclusion is inappropriate." The Court explained that "the marginal or nonexistent benefits produced by suppressing evidence obtained in objectively reasonable reliance on a subsequently invalidated search warrant cannot justify the substantial costs of exclusion" (922, 926).

What is the test for a good faith belief in the lawfulness of a search? In determining whether an officer acted in good faith, the Supreme Court instructed that courts should ask whether "a reasonably well trained officer would have known that the search was illegal" despite the warrant issued by a judge. The Court found that the police in *Leon* carried out a thorough and responsible investigation and obtained a warrant in good faith and, in the view of the Supreme Court, reasonably believed that their search of the homes was based on a warrant founded on probable cause.

Officers would not be acting in good faith, and suppression would be appropriate, in those instances in which

- the police clearly are aware or should be aware that the warrant lacks probable cause. This would arise in situations in which the police knew or should have known that the information in the affidavit was false or that the information did not meet the probable cause standard.
- the warrant is "fatally flawed." For instance, the warrant may not be specific in terms of the place to be searched or the items to be searched for.
- the judge issuing the warrant is not "neutral and detached" and acts as a "rubber stamp for the police" or as "an arm of the prosecution" (914–922).

Reliance on assurance by a judge that a warrant meets Fourth Amendment standards. In the companion case of *Massachusetts v. Sheppard,* the Supreme Court affirmed that the exclusionary rule should not be applied in those cases in which the police act in good faith reliance on the assurance of a judge that a warrant, which later is determined by an appellate court to be defective, constitutes sufficient authority to carry out a search (*Massachusetts v. Sheppard,* 468 U.S. 981 [1984]).

The officers sought an arrest warrant for the search and seizure of items in Sheppard's residence linking him to a homicide. Detective O'Malley was able to locate only a warrant form authorizing the seizure of a "controlled substance." The judge told the police that he would make the necessary changes to insure that the warrant authorized a search for evidence of a murder. However, the judge did not modify that portion of the warrant that authorized a search for controlled substances and failed to incorporate the police officer's affidavit listing the items that the police were seeking in the home. As a result, the warrant authorized the police to seize unspecified controlled substances and did not authorize the seizure of various items that linked Sheppard to the homicide. As a result, the homicide evidence was suppressed by the trial court judge. The Supreme Court held that although the warrant clearly authorized a search for narcotics, a police officer should not be expected to "disbelieve a judge who has just advised him . . . that the warrant he possesses authorized him to conduct the search he requested" (984–991).

Justices Brennan and Marshall objected in their dissent that the exclusionary rule was part of the protections included in the Fourth Amendment, and they called for a restoration of the principle recognized in *Weeks* that an individual whose privacy has been invaded in violation of the Fourth Amendment has a constitutional right to prevent the government from making use of any evidence obtained through illegal police conduct (928–941).

Reliance on legislation. The Supreme Court nevertheless continued to expand the application of the good faith exception. In 1987, in *Illinois v. Krull,* the Court held that evidence seized in objectively reasonable reliance on a statute later held to be unconstitutional was admissible at trial. The Court stated that "unless a statute is clearly unconstitutional, an officer cannot be expected to question the judgment of the legislature that passed the law" (*Illinois v. Krull,* 480 U.S. 340, 349–350 [1987]). The Court asked whether excluding the evidence from trial would deter the legislature from passing unconstitutional statutes in the future. The Supreme Court reasoned that legislatures are motivated by public opinion and politics and are relatively unconcerned about the fate of a statute in the courts. As a result, legislators are unlikely to be deterred from passing unconstitutional laws in the future by the court's exclusion of the evidence from trial. Balanced against this was the significant cost of excluding evidence that had been seized in good faith by the police (352).

Reliance on data entered into a computer by a court employee. In 1995, in *Arizona v. Evans,* the U.S. Supreme Court was asked to apply the good faith exception to an arrest executed by Phoenix police officer Bryan Sargent. Officer Sargent reasonably relied on information that he downloaded from the computer terminal in his squad car. The computer erroneously indicated that Isaac Evans, whom Officer Sargent had pulled over for driving the wrong way on a one-way street, was the subject of an outstanding misdemeanor arrest warrant. Evans was placed under arrest, and while he was being handcuffed, he dropped a marijuana cigarette. A search of Evans's automobile led to the seizure of a bag of marijuana that had been concealed under the front seat. It later was found that that the arrest warrant had been quashed roughly seventeen days prior to his arrest. The Supreme Court noted that these types of errors occur on isolated occasions and that suppressing the evidence will not deter court clerks from making similar mistakes in the future (*Arizona v. Evans,* 514 U.S. 1 [1995]).

Reliance on apparent authority of a third party to consent. In *Illinois v. Rodriguez,* (this case appears in Chapter 6 under consent searches) Gail Fischer reported to the police that she had been the victim of domestic violence by Edward Rodriguez. She told the officers that he was at "our" apartment, where she had clothes and furniture. Fischer took the police over to the apartment. She let them in with her key, and they subsequently seized narcotics that they spotted in plain view and arrested Rodriguez. The contraband was suppressed on the grounds that Fischer lacked "common access and control for most purposes," which is the requirement for a third party consent. Her name was not on the lease or mailbox, and she did not pay rent, only occasionally spent the night, and never entertained friends at the apartment. The Supreme Court reversed and held that the police "reasonably believed" that Fischer possessed authority to consent to a search of the apartment. See *Illinois v. Rodriguez,* 497 U.S. 177 (1990).

In summary, in each of the cases in which the Supreme Court recognized the good faith exception, the police reasonably believed that they were complying with the law. In both *Leon* and *Sheppard,* they acted in a diligent and responsible fashion based on warrants that later proved to be defective. In *Krull* the police relied in good faith on a state statute that later was ruled to be unconstitutional, and the police officer in *Evans* acted on the basis of inaccurate computer information. In any of these cases, would you have excluded the evidence from trial? In 2009, in *Herring v. United States,* the U.S. Supreme Court confronted the question of whether the good faith exception should be applied when a law enforcement officer makes an arrest based on an error in the police electronic database. The defense argued that the good faith exception should not be recognized when the police are responsible for the mistake.

You can find United States v. Leon *and* Arizona v. Evans *on the study site, http://www.sagepub.com/lippmancp.*

Did the officer act in good faith in relying on a police database that falsely indicated that there was an arrest warrant for the defendant?

Herring v. United States, 555 U.S. ___ (2009), Roberts, J.

Issue

The Fourth Amendment forbids "unreasonable searches and seizures," and this usually requires the police to have probable cause or a warrant before making an arrest. What if an officer reasonably believes there is an outstanding arrest warrant, but that belief turns out to be wrong because of a negligent bookkeeping error by another police employee? The parties here agree that the ensuing arrest is still a violation of the Fourth Amendment, but dispute whether contraband found during a search incident to that arrest must be excluded in a later prosecution. The issue is whether the exclusionary rule should be applied.

Facts

On July 7, 2004, Investigator Mark Anderson learned that Bennie Dean Herring had driven to the Coffee County Sheriff's Department to retrieve something from his impounded truck. Herring was no stranger to law enforcement, and Anderson asked the county's warrant clerk, Sandy Pope, to check for any outstanding warrants for Herring's arrest. When she found none, Anderson asked Pope to check with Sharon Morgan, her counterpart in neighboring Dale County. After checking Dale County's computer database, Morgan replied that there was an active arrest warrant for Herring's failure to appear on a felony charge. Pope relayed the information to Anderson and asked Morgan to fax over a copy of the warrant as confirmation. Anderson and a deputy followed Herring as he left the impound lot, pulled him over, and arrested him. A search incident to the arrest revealed methamphetamine in Herring's pocket and a pistol (which as a felon he could not possess) in his vehicle.

There had, however, been a mistake about the warrant. The Dale County sheriff's computer records are supposed to correspond to actual arrest warrants, which the office also maintains. But when Morgan went to the files to retrieve the actual warrant to fax to Pope, Morgan was unable to find it. She called a court clerk and learned that the warrant had been recalled five months earlier. Normally when a warrant is recalled, the court clerk's office or a judge's chambers calls Morgan, who enters the information in the sheriff's computer database and disposes of the physical copy. For whatever reason, the information about the recall of the warrant for Herring did not appear in the database. Morgan immediately called Pope to alert her to the mix-up, and Pope contacted Anderson over a secure radio. This all unfolded in 10 to 15 minutes, but Herring had already been arrested and found with the gun and drugs, just a few hundred yards from the sheriff's office.

Herring was indicted in the District Court for the Middle District of Alabama for illegally possessing the gun and drugs violations. He moved to suppress the evidence on the ground that his initial arrest had been illegal, because the warrant had been rescinded. The magistrate judge recommended denying the motion, because the arresting officers had acted in a good faith belief that the warrant was still outstanding. Thus, even if there were a violation, there was "no reason to believe that application of the exclusionary rule here would deter the occurrence of any future mistakes." The Court of Appeals for the Eleventh Circuit affirmed. The Eleventh Circuit found that the arresting officers in Coffee County "were entirely innocent of any wrongdoing or carelessness." The court assumed that whoever failed to update the Dale County sheriff's records was also a law enforcement official but noted that "the conduct in question [wa]s a negligent failure to act, not a deliberate or tactical choice to act." Because the error was merely negligent and attenuated from the arrest, the Eleventh Circuit concluded that the benefit of suppressing the evidence "would be marginal or nonexistent."

Reasoning

The Fourth Amendment protects "the right of the people to be secure in their persons, houses, papers, and effects, against unreasonable searches and seizures," but it "contains no provision expressly precluding the use of evidence obtained in violation of its commands." Nonetheless, our decisions establish an exclusionary rule that, when applicable, forbids the use of improperly obtained evidence at trial. We have stated that this judicially created rule is "designed to safeguard rights generally through its deterrent effect."

The fact that a violation occurred—that is, that a search or arrest was unreasonable—does not necessarily mean that the exclusionary rule applies. Indeed, exclusion "has always been our last resort, not our first impulse," and our precedents establish important principles that constrain application of the exclusionary rule.

First, the exclusionary rule is not an individual right and applies only where it "result[s] in appreciable deterrence." We have repeatedly rejected the argument that exclusion is a necessary consequence of a violation. Instead we have focused on the efficacy of the rule in deterring violations in the future.

In addition, the benefits of deterrence must outweigh the costs. "We have never suggested that the exclusionary rule must apply in every circumstance in which it might provide marginal deterrence." "To the extent that application of the exclusionary rule could provide some incremental deterrent, that possible benefit must be weighed against [its] substantial social costs." The principal cost of applying the rule is, of course, letting guilty and possibly dangerous defendants go free—something that "offends basic concepts of the criminal justice system." "The rule's costly toll upon truth-seeking and law enforcement objectives presents a high obstacle for those urging [its] application."

These principles are reflected in the holding of *Leon:* When police act under a warrant that is invalid for lack of probable cause, the exclusionary rule does not apply if the police acted "in objectively reasonable reliance" on the subsequently invalidated search warrant. We (perhaps confusingly) called this objectively reasonable reliance "good faith." In a companion case, *Massachusetts v. Sheppard,* we held that the exclusionary rule did not apply when a warrant was invalid because a judge forgot to make "clerical corrections" to it.

Shortly thereafter, in *Krull,* we extended these holdings to warrantless administrative searches performed in good faith reliance on a statute later declared unconstitutional. Finally, in *Evans,* we applied this good faith rule to police who reasonably relied on mistaken information in a court's database that an arrest warrant was outstanding. We held that a mistake made by a judicial employee could not give rise to exclusion for three reasons: The exclusionary rule was crafted to curb police rather than judicial misconduct, court employees were unlikely to try to subvert the Fourth Amendment, and "most important, there [was] no basis for believing that application of the exclusionary rule in [those] circumstances" would have any significant effect in deterring the errors. *Evans* left unresolved "whether the evidence should be suppressed if police personnel were responsible for the error," an issue not argued by the State in that case, but one that we now confront.

The extent to which the exclusionary rule is justified by these deterrence principles varies with the culpability of the law enforcement conduct. As we said in *Leon,* "An assessment of the flagrancy of the police misconduct constitutes an important step in the calculus" of applying the exclusionary rule. Similarly, in *Krull* we elaborated that "evidence should be suppressed 'only if it can be said that the law enforcement officer had knowledge, or may properly be charged with knowledge, that the search was unconstitutional under the Fourth Amendment.'"

Anticipating the good faith exception to the exclusionary rule, Judge Friendly wrote that "the beneficent aim of the exclusionary rule to deter police misconduct can be sufficiently accomplished by a practice . . . outlawing evidence obtained by flagrant or deliberate violation of rights. . . . The deterrent value of the exclusionary rule is most likely to be effective" when "official conduct was flagrantly abusive of rights."

Indeed, the abuses that gave rise to the exclusionary rule featured intentional conduct that was patently unconstitutional. In *Mapp v. Ohio,* which extended the exclusionary rule to the states, officers forced open a door to Ms. Mapp's house, kept her lawyer from entering, brandished what the court concluded was a false warrant, and then forced her into handcuffs and canvassed the house for obscenity. "The situation in *Mapp*" featured a "flagrant or deliberate violation of rights." An error that arises from nonrecurring and attenuated negligence is thus far removed from the core concerns that led us to adopt the rule in the first place. And in fact since *Leon,* we have never applied the rule to exclude evidence obtained in violation of the Fourth Amendment, where the police conduct was no more intentional or culpable than this.

To trigger the exclusionary rule, police conduct must be sufficiently deliberate that exclusion can meaningfully deter it and sufficiently culpable that such deterrence is worth the price paid by the justice system. As laid out in our cases, the exclusionary rule serves to deter deliberate, reckless, or grossly negligent conduct or in some circumstances recurring or systemic negligence. The error in this case does not rise to that level. The pertinent analysis of deterrence and culpability is objective, not an "inquiry into the subjective awareness of arresting officers." We have already held that "our good-faith inquiry is confined to the objectively ascertainable question whether a reasonably well trained officer would have known that the search was illegal" in light of "all of the circumstances." These circumstances frequently include a particular officer's knowledge and experience, but that does not make the test any more subjective than the one for probable cause, which looks to an officer's knowledge and experience but not his subjective intent. We do not suggest that all recordkeeping errors by the police are immune from the exclusionary rule. In this case, however, the conduct at issue was not so objectively culpable as to require exclusion. In *Leon* we held that "the marginal or nonexistent benefits produced by suppressing evidence obtained in objectively reasonable reliance on a subsequently invalidated search warrant cannot justify the substantial costs of exclusion." The same is true when evidence is obtained in objectively reasonable reliance on a subsequently recalled warrant.

If the police have been shown to be reckless in maintaining a warrant system, or to have knowingly made false entries to lay the groundwork for future false arrests, exclusion would certainly be justified under our cases should such misconduct cause a violation. . . . In a case where systemic errors were demonstrated, it might be reckless for officers to rely on an unreliable warrant system.... But there is no evidence that errors in Dale County's system are routine or widespread. Officer Anderson testified that he had never had reason to question information about a Dale County warrant, and both Sandy Pope and Sharon Morgan testified that they could remember no similar miscommunication ever happening on their watch. That is even less error than in the database at issue in *Evans,* where we also found reliance on the database to be objectively reasonable. Because no such showings were made here, the Eleventh Circuit was correct to affirm the denial of the motion to suppress.

Holding

Petitioner's claim that police negligence automatically triggers suppression cannot be squared with the principles underlying the exclusionary rule as they have been explained in our cases. In light of our repeated holdings that the deterrent effect of suppression must be substantial and outweigh any harm to the justice system, we conclude that when police mistakes are the result of negligence such as that described here, rather than systemic error or reckless disregard of constitutional requirements, any marginal deterrence does not "pay its way." In such a case, the criminal should not "go free because the constable has blundered." The judgment of the Court of Appeals for the Eleventh Circuit is affirmed.

Dissenting, *Ginsburg, J.,* joined by *Stevens, J., Souter, J.,* and *Breyer, J.*

Electronic databases form the nervous system of contemporary criminal justice operations. In recent years, their breadth and influence have dramatically expanded. Police today can access databases that include not only data from the updated National Crime Information Center (NCIC), but also terrorist watch lists, the federal government's employee eligibility system, and various commercial databases. As a result, law enforcement has an increasing supply of information within its easy electronic reach. The risk of error stemming from these databases is not slim.... Law enforcement databases are insufficiently monitored and often out of date. Government reports describe, for example, flaws in NCIC databases, terrorist watch list databases, and databases associated with the federal government's employment eligibility verification system.

Inaccuracies in expansive, interconnected collections of electronic information raise grave concerns for individual liberty. "The offense to the dignity of the citizen who is arrested, handcuffed, and searched on a public street simply because some bureaucrat has failed to maintain an accurate computer data base" is evocative of the use of general warrants that so outraged the authors of our Bill of Rights. Negligent recordkeeping errors by law enforcement threaten individual liberty, are susceptible to deterrence by the exclusionary rule, and cannot be remedied effectively through other means. Such errors present no occasion to further erode the exclusionary rule. The rule "is needed to make the Fourth Amendment something real; a guarantee that does not carry with it the exclusion of evidence obtained by its violation is a chimera." In keeping with the rule's "core concerns," suppression should have attended the unconstitutional search in this case.

Dissenting, *Souter, J.*

In *Arizona v. Evans,* we held that recordkeeping errors made by a court clerk do not trigger the exclusionary rule, so long as the police reasonably relied upon the court clerk's recordkeeping. The rationale for our decision was premised on a distinction between judicial errors and police errors. Distinguishing between police recordkeeping errors and judicial ones not only is consistent with our precedent, but also is far easier for courts to administer than the Chief Justice's case-by-case, multifactored inquiry into the degree of police culpability. I therefore would apply the exclusionary rule when police personnel are responsible for a recordkeeping error that results in a violation of the Fourth Amendment.

Questions for Discussion

1. Summarize the facts in *Herring*.
2. Describe the balancing test that judges are to apply in evaluating whether to apply the exclusionary rule. Give some examples of cases in which the Supreme Court has held that the exclusionary rule does not apply.
3. Chief Justice Roberts bases the decision on the deterrence function of the exclusionary rule. Explain why he argues that to trigger the exclusionary rule, the police conduct must be "sufficiently deliberate that exclusion can meaningfully deter it, and sufficiently culpable that such deterrence is worth the price paid by the justice system." Why does the conduct of Investigator Anderson not meet this legal standard?
4. Are there some situations in which Justice Roberts would apply the exclusionary rule to an arrest and search and seizure based on what later proved to be an error in police recordkeeping? In your answer, pay attention the distinction between a subjective belief and an objective belief in the accuracy of a database.
5. Can you explain why Justice Roberts writes that the error in recordkeeping was "nonrecurring and attenuated" and "far removed" from the "core concerns" that led to the

(Continued)

(Continued)

adoption of the exclusionary rule? Would the exclusionary rule apply to a situation in which Investigator Anderson had arrested Herring based on his own belief that there was an outstanding arrest warrant for Herring?

6. Why does the dissent argue that the application of the exclusionary rule in *Herring* may serve a beneficial deterrent function? Is Justice Ginsburg right to be concerned about the consequences of a failure to apply the exclusionary rule for the civil liberties of Americans? Should the exclusionary rule apply to violations of the Fourth Amendment regardless of the police officer's good faith belief that he or she is acting lawfully?

7. ***Problems in policing.*** Summarize the good faith exception to the exclusionary rule.

Cases and Comments

State Law. A number of state courts have ruled that their constitutions require that searches be carried out only on probable cause and accordingly have rejected the good faith exception established in *Leon*. These include Connecticut, Delaware, Georgia, Idaho, Iowa, Montana, New Hampshire, New Jersey, Pennsylvania, South Carolina, and Vermont.

In 1988, in *State v. Carter,* the North Carolina Supreme Court rejected the good faith exception. The defendant, Robert Lee Carter, was convicted of first-degree rape and first-degree kidnapping as well as an assault inflicting serious bodily injury on the seventy-eight-year-old victim. Carter was on work release during the day from the Orange County prison unit. At 4:30 P.M., he failed to report to the van to be taken back to the prison unit. He was found by a search party at 6:15 P.M., roughly thirty-three yards from where the victim was lying unconscious and beaten. Carter smelled of alcohol and was dirty and disheveled. His shovel and a roll of toilet paper that he had removed from the work site were found adjacent to the victim's body. The following day, the victim's eyeglasses were found under Carter's hat. The victim's identification of her assailant generally fit Carter. The central evidence at Carter's trial was a blood smear on the defendant's clothing that was consistent with the victim's blood type. A serologist testified over the defendant's objection that a blood smear on underwear seized from defendant after he was returned to the Orange County prison unit was consistent with the victim's blood type but definitely was not defendant's blood type.

The trial court admitted the evidence of the defendant's blood type based on a good faith belief by the police that the seizure of the blood was constitutional. The drawing of the blood from Carter was based on a nontestimonial identification order issued by a judge. An identification order in North Carolina is a court order authorizing the seizure of an item that will be of "material aid in determining whether the person named in the affidavit committed the offense." This is commonly employed by the prosecution to gather evidence that does not intrude on an individual's right to privacy and may involve fingerprints, hair samples, urine and saliva samples, and shoe impressions. There must be "reasonable grounds to suspect" that the person named in the identification order committed the offense. In North Carolina an identification order is used to compel persons to appear to provide evidence who are suspects and who are not under arrest as well as to gather evidence from persons formally charged and arrested who have been released from custody pending trial.

The North Carolina Supreme Court held that Article 1, Section 20 of the North Carolina constitution prohibiting unreasonable searches and seizures requires a search warrant based on probable cause to draw a blood sample from an individual in custody and that the judge should not have ordered the drawing of blood based on an identification order. A warrant is based on probable cause to believe that the item to be seized constitutes evidence of an offense or of the identity of the person who participated in the crime.

The North Carolina Supreme Court held that the state constitution, like the U.S. Constitution, requires the exclusion of evidence obtained by an unreasonable search and seizure. The North Carolina court stressed that it was free to construe its own state constitution differently than it construed the federal Constitution "as long as our citizens are thereby accorded no lesser rights than they are guaranteed by the parallel federal provision." The Supreme Court observed that North Carolina constitution Article 1, Section 20, prohibiting unreasonable searches and seizures requires that warrants shall be issued only on probable cause identifying the persons, places, and items to be searched or seized. A state statute, section 15A-974, provides that evidence must be suppressed if "its exclusion is required by either the United States or North Carolina Constitutions."

State policy is to exclude evidence seized as a result of an unreasonable search and seizure. The state supreme court explained that this is based on the belief that the exclusionary rule is "the only effective bulwark against governmental disregard for constitutionally protected privacy rights." The exclusion of evidence that is the product of an unreasonable search also is vital for "maintaining the integrity of the judicial branch of government" and deterring police misconduct. The court stressed that "it can be no part of our constitutional duties to signal a retreat from these salutary advances in constitutional compliance which have guided police practices in this state since 1937." The fact that the guilty, at times, will escape punishment is tolerable according to the court "because the constitutional values thereby safeguarded are so precious." The North Carolina Supreme Court refused to apply the good faith exception, concluding that the application of this doctrine was a decision that should be made by the state legislature rather than by the courts.

The North Carolina Supreme Court also concluded that an action for civil damages against the police does not provide an adequate alternative to the exclusionary rule. Juries are reluctant to bring verdicts against the police who, for the most part, lack sufficient money to compensate victims. Victims typically also lack funds to pursue civil actions, and suits against the local governments who employ the police officers typically are barred by the doctrine of sovereign immunity.

Justice Mitchell, in dissent, pointed out that the police relied in good faith on an order issued by a judge. He noted that the failure of the majority to adopt the good faith exception will only advantage the guilty and harm society. Unlike "punishment of intentionally unlawful conduct by officers, which the exclusionary rule arguably deters, punishment of an officer's good faith reliance on a judicial order cannot deter future similar conduct." There certainly was probable cause to believe that Carter committed the assault-rape, and the police could have easily obtained a search warrant. They instead mistakenly applied for a nontestimonial identification procedure, which was granted by a judge.

How would the U.S. Supreme Court rule in *Carter?* See *United States v. Carter,* 370 S.E.2d 553, N.C. 1988).

10.1 YOU DECIDE

Baltimore police officers obtained and executed a warrant to search the person of Lawrence McWebb and the "premises known as 2036 Park Avenue third floor apartment." The police reasonably believed that there was only a single apartment on the third floor. This was based on information provided by a reliable informant, by visually examining the building, and by checking with the utility company. The third floor in fact was divided into two apartments, one occupied by McWebb and one occupied by Garrison. Six Baltimore police officers executed the warrant; they encountered McWebb in the front of the building and used his key to enter the building. As they entered the vestibule on the third floor, they encountered Garrison. The doors to both apartments were open, and they could see into the interior of both McWebb's apartment to the left and Garrison's apartment to the right. It was only after entering Garrison's apartment and seizing heroin, cash, and drug paraphernalia that the police realized that the third floor contained two apartments and that they were searching the "wrong unit."

Was the search and seizure of Garrison's apartment lawful based on the police officers' reasonable belief that the third floor was one large unit? See *Maryland v. Garrison,* 480 U.S. 79 (1987).

You can learn what the court decided by referring to the study site, http://www.sagepub.com/lippmancp.

Independent Source

We have seen that evidence that is directly obtained as a result of an unconstitutional search is excluded from evidence at trial. The **independent source doctrine** provides that evidence that is unlawfully seized nevertheless is admissible where the police are able to demonstrate that the evidence was *also* obtained through *independent* and *lawful* means. In *Silverthorne Lumber Company v. United States,* the U.S. Supreme Court held that facts obtained through a constitutional violation are not "inaccessible. If knowledge of them [also] is gained from an independent source they may be proved like any others, but the knowledge gained by the Government's own wrong cannot be used by it" (*Silverthorne Lumber Company v. United States,* 251 U.S. 385, 392 [1920]). Supreme Court Justice Antonin Scalia explained the independent source doctrine as follows: "Where an unlawful entry has given investigators knowledge of facts x and y [and z], but fact z [also] has been learned by other [lawful] means, fact z can be said to be admissible because [it is] derived from an 'independent source'" (*Murray v. State,* 487 U.S. 533, 538 [1988]).

In 1984, in *Nix v. Williams,* the U.S. Supreme Court stated that

> the interest of society in deterring unlawful police conduct and the public interest in having juries receive all probative evidence of a crime are properly balanced by putting the police in the same, not a worse, position than they would have been had no police error or misconduct...occurred. (*Nix v. Williams,* 467 U.S. 431, 444 [1984])

In other words, while the government is prohibited from using evidence obtained from the illegal search, this should not deprive the jury of hearing the same evidence so long as it can be demonstrated that the evidence also was obtained as a result of an independent and legal search.

The leading case on the independent source doctrine is *Murray v. State*. In the case at issue in *Murray*, federal agents received information that a warehouse was being used for illegal drug activities. Law enforcement agents placed the warehouse under surveillance, developed probable cause, unlawfully entered the premises without a warrant, and observed bales of marijuana. The agents then left and applied for a warrant. The warrant application did not refer to the illegal entry or rely on information obtained during the illegal entry. The police then entered the warehouse with a warrant and seized the marijuana based on the information provided by the informant (535–546).

Justice Antonin Scalia observed that the agents' "lawful search appeared to be genuinely independent of the earlier tainted one." He remanded the case to clarify whether the two searches were truly independent and posed two questions to the lower court: whether the decision to seek a warrant was "prompted" by what they had seen during the initial entry, and whether information obtained during that entry was "presented to the Magistrate and affected his decision to issue the warrant" (543). Can you explain why Justice Scalia wanted the appellate court judge to address these two questions?

You can find Murray v. State *on the study site, http://www.sagepub.com/lippmancp.*

Inevitable Discovery Rule

The **inevitable discovery rule** provides that evidence that is seized as the result of an unconstitutional search is admissible where the government can prove by the preponderance of the evidence that the evidence would have been inevitably discovered in the same condition in a lawful fashion. In *Nix v. Williams*, the Supreme Court explained that the independent source doctrine and the inevitable discovery rule both are based on the proposition that the police would have lawfully obtained the evidence had the police misconduct not taken place and that the government should not be punished by the exclusion of the evidence. In both instances, the government has not benefited by its wrongful behavior, and the defendant has not suffered any harm.

The inevitable discovery rule was first fully articulated by the Supreme Court in *Nix v. Williams*. In *Nix*, the defendant Williams was interrogated by Officer Leaming in violation of Williams's Sixth Amendment right to counsel and subsequently led the police to the location of the body of his ten-year-old victim, Pamela Powers. The police called off their 200-person search for Pamela's body following Williams's promise to cooperate with the police. At the time, the Supreme Court observed that

> one search team...was only two and one-half miles from where Williams soon guided Leaming and his party to the body....It is clear that the search parties were approaching the actual location of the body and we are satisfied...that the volunteer search teams would have resumed the search had Williams not...led the police to the body and the body inevitably would have been found [within an estimated three to five hours]. (436, 448)

Justices Brennan and Marshall in dissent noted that the independent source doctrine was distinguished from the inevitable discovery rule by the fact that the evidence introduced at trial because of the independent source exception is in fact obtained by lawful means, while the evidence introduced at trial because of the inevitable discovery rule has not yet been discovered. The dissenters noted that the inevitable discovery exception "necessarily implicates a hypothetical finding that differs in kind from the factual finding that precedes application of the independent source rule." Justices Brennan and Marshall would require the government to satisfy a high standard of proof before admitting evidence under the inevitable discovery rule in order to "impress the fact finder with the importance of the decision and thereby reduce the risk that illegally obtained evidence will be admitted" (459–460).

Courts have divided over whether a legal search must already have been under way at the time of the unlawful police behavior in order to establish that evidence inevitably would have been discovered. In *U.S. v. Pardue,* the First Circuit Court of Appeals determined that an officer had exceeded the scope of a *Terry* frisk when he discovered two boxes of ammunition in Pardue's backpack. The officer then arrested Pardue for misdemeanor domestic violence. The court held that the ammunition inevitably would have been discovered during a standard inventory search of the backpack at police headquarters. The question arises whether courts should extend inevitable discovery to searches that have not yet been initiated based on police testimony that such a search definitely would have been undertaken (*U.S. v. Pardue,* 385 F.3d 101 [1st Cir. 2004]).

You can read Nix v. Williams *on the study site, http://www.sagepub.com/lippmancp.*

10.2 YOU DECIDE

Los Angeles Police Officer Juan Torres received reports from merchants that they had seen suspicious activity near a red and white van parked in front of the Central Market. They observed various people entering and exiting the van around 6:00 P.M., when Torres was known to be off duty. The occupants were described as "male Hispanics." Torres had been assigned to foot patrol in the area for five years and knew that heroin dealers typically worked out of parked vans. On July 22, 1987, Torres encountered the van while on patrol. He ordered two men sitting in front to exit the vehicle.

Torres looked into the van and noticed that the sun visor on the driver's side was "hanging low." He touched the visor and several pieces of paper fell to the floor. He picked up one of the pieces of paper and found a list of names and numbers. He read one of the names out loud and a man in the back of the van responded. Torres engaged the man in conversation in Spanish and the man explained that he and the others had recently crossed into the United States from Mexico. The number next to each name was the amount of money each of the men had paid to be illegally brought into the United States. Torres questioned several other men, detained the occupants, and contacted the Immigration and Naturalization Service. He did not find either narcotics or weapons.

The two men who had been sitting in front, Ramirez-Sandoval and Maravi-Hospinal, were arrested and charged with offenses involving transporting and harboring illegal aliens. They moved to suppress the evidence. The district court held that although Torres had lawfully detained the occupants of the automobile, he also had illegally reached into the van and knocked the papers from the sun visor. The interrogation was the "fruit of the poisonous tree." The government argued that the "testimony of the alien" was admissible under either the attenuation or inevitable discovery exceptions.

Would Torres inevitably have questioned the men in the van concerning their immigration status? How should the appellate court rule? See *United States v. Jesus Ramirez-Sandoval,* 872 F.2d 1392 (9th Cir. 1989).

You can learn what the court decided by referring to the study site, http://www.sagepub.com/lippmancp.

Impeachment

Evidence that is seized in an unlawful search may be used for the **impeachment** of a defendant who takes the stand. Impeachment is defined as an opposing lawyer's attack on a witness's *credibility* during cross-examination. Credibility means whether a witness is to be believed. For example, if a defendant charged with the possession of illegal child pornography states that he or she has never possessed child pornography, this statement may be challenged on cross-examination by introducing at trial child pornography that was unlawfully seized from his or her house. The jury is instructed that they may consider such evidence that is *inconsistent* with the defendant's testimony in evaluating the defendant's credibility. The judge also instructs the jury that it may not consider this evidence in evaluating whether the defendant is guilty of the possession of child pornography.

What is the reason for the impeachment exception to the exclusionary rule? The U.S. Supreme Court has reasoned that the jury is entitled to hear all the information that may assist in deciding the case and that a defendant should not be permitted to offer testimony that may be false (perjured) without being challenged.

The Supreme Court reasons that the police are deterred from unconstitutional conduct by the exclusion of unlawfully seized evidence from the prosecutor's case-in-chief. The fact that illegally obtained evidence may be used for impeachment purposes does not significantly limit the deterrent value of the exclusionary rule. All witnesses whose statements or actions are inconsistent leave their credibility open to question during cross-examination, and the fact that the evidence has been obtained in an illegal fashion should not prohibit its use at trial when the defendant takes the stand and "opens the door" to cross-examination. Keep in mind that the defendant is not required to testify in his or her own defense and that if the defendant does not takes the stand, the jury will not hear the evidence.

The leading case on the impeachment exception is *Walder v. United States*. Walder was charged with the sale of illegal narcotics. Two years earlier he had been indicted for purchasing narcotics, but the indictment was dismissed after the narcotics had been suppressed as the fruit of an illegal search. Two witnesses testified at Walder's trial that they had purchased narcotics from Walder. Walder took the stand and testified on direct questioning that he had never sold, given, or transmitted narcotics to anyone. On cross-examination, Walder repeated that he had never "purchased, sold or sent" narcotics, and he denied that the government had ever seized narcotics from his home. A police officer then took the stand and testified that narcotics had been seized in an earlier unlawful search of Walder's home (*Walder v. United States,* 347 U.S. 62 [1954]).

The U.S. Supreme Court, in affirming the use of unlawfully seized evidence for impeachment purposes, held that

> it is one thing to say that the Government cannot make any affirmative use of evidence unlawfully obtained. It is quite another to say that the defendant can turn the illegal method by which evidence was obtained to his advantage and provide himself with a shield against the contradiction of his untruths.

The majority stressed that the defendant was free to deny the charges when he took the stand. In this case, however, the defendant offered a "sweeping claim" that he had never trafficked in or possessed narcotics (63–64).

In *Walder,* the defendant's statement on *direct testimony* led to the prosecutor's introduction of the fact that drugs were uncovered in the earlier search. In *United States v. Havens,* the Supreme Court held that a statement by a defendant on *cross-examination* was subject to impeachment. The Supreme Court rejected the court of appeals ruling that only a defendant's statements on direct testimony were subject to impeachment by the fruits of an illegal search. The Court proclaimed that

> it is essential . . . to the proper functioning of the adversary system that when a defendant takes the stand, the government be permitted proper and effective cross-examination in an attempt to elicit the truth. The defendant's obligation to testify truthfully is fully binding . . . when . . . cross-examined. (*United States v. Havens,* 446 U.S. 620, 622–626 [1980])

Justices Brennan and Marshall, in dissent, were critical of the Supreme Court majority's "disregard" of their obligation to enforce the Bill of Rights as a "bulwark of our national unity." They asked whether the Court would be prepared to

> acquiesce in torture . . . if it demonstrably advanced the fact finding process. . . . [T]he Constitution does not countenance police misbehavior, even in the pursuit of truth. The processes of our judicial system may not be fueled by the illegalities of government authorities. (633–634)

Defendants also may be impeached by confessions that were unlawfully obtained by the police in violation of *Miranda:*

Inconsistent statements. In *Harris v. New York,* the Supreme Court held that a defendant's testimony denying that he had sold narcotics may be impeached on cross-examination by the prosecutor through the use of the defendant's confession that had been suppressed by the judge. The Supreme Court explained that *Miranda* cannot be "perverted into a shield" that permits a defendant to "use perjury" without the "risk of confrontation with prior inconsistent utterances" (*Harris v. New York,* 401 U.S. 222, 226 [1971]). In 2009, the Supreme Court held in *Kansas v. Ventris* that confessions obtained by a jailhouse informant in violation of the Sixth Amendment also could be used to impeach a defendant's testimony at trial (*Kansas v. Ventris,* __ U.S. __ [2009]).

Defense witnesses. In *James v. Illinois,* the Supreme Court refused to extend the impeachment exception to include the impeachment of defense witnesses by statements unlawfully obtained from the defendant. Why? The interest in "discouraging or disclosing perjured testimony" by defense witnesses is outweighed by the fact that the police would have an added incentive to disregard legal rules knowing that defense witnesses as well as the defendant himself or herself would be subject to impeachment. Defendants also would be reluctant to call defense witnesses knowing that the witnesses may be subject to impeachment, effectively limiting their ability to mount a defense. Defense witnesses, in turn, would be reluctant to testify, knowing that they may be impeached and possibly charged with perjury (*James v. Illinois,* 493 U.S. 307, 317, 319 [1990]).

You can find Walder v. United States *and* Harris v. New York *on the study site, http://www.sagepub.com/lippmancp.*

In this chapter, we have seen that the exclusionary rule is based on the proposition that the rule deters police disregard of the Fourth Amendment. The exceptions to the exclusionary rule such as good faith are justified on the grounds that excluding the evidence would not greatly contribute to deterrence. The concluding section asks whether the empirical evidence supports the argument that the exclusionary rule deters the police. We also examine the contention that the exclusionary rule results in the guilty escaping punishment.

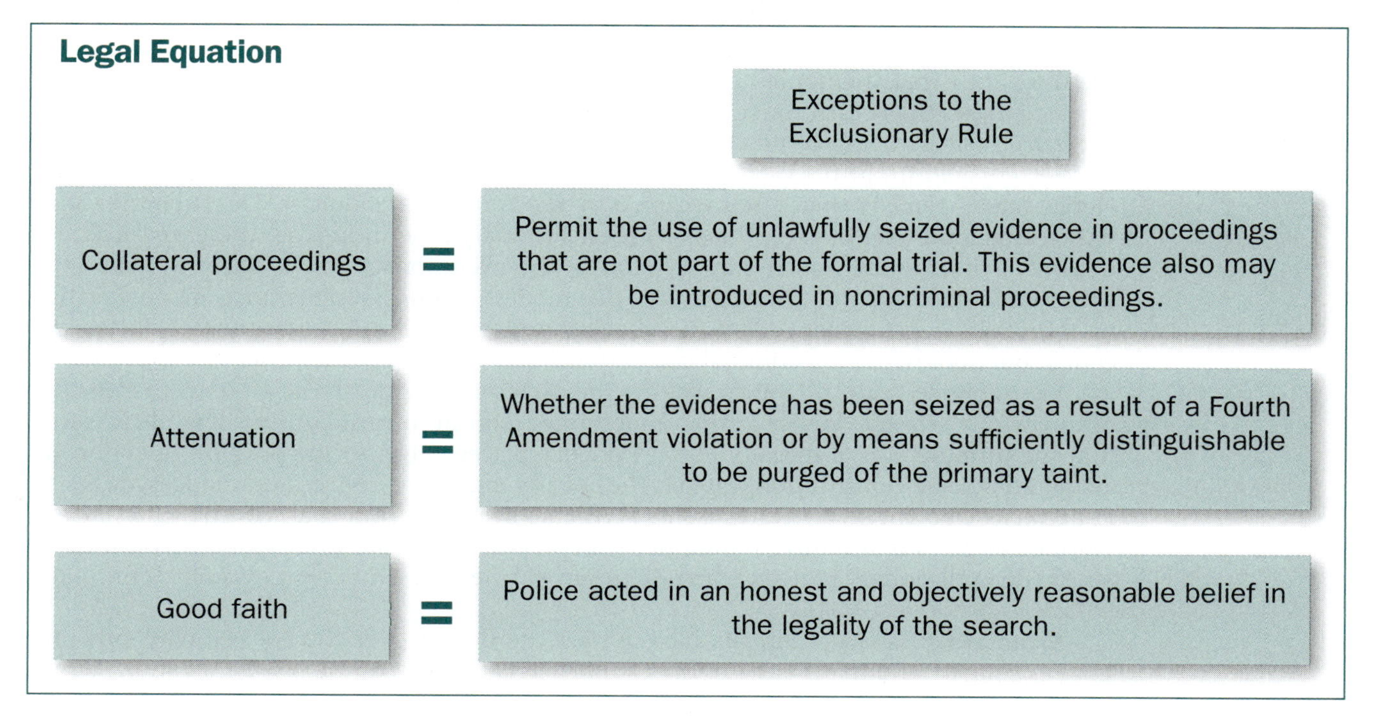

(Continued)

(Continued)

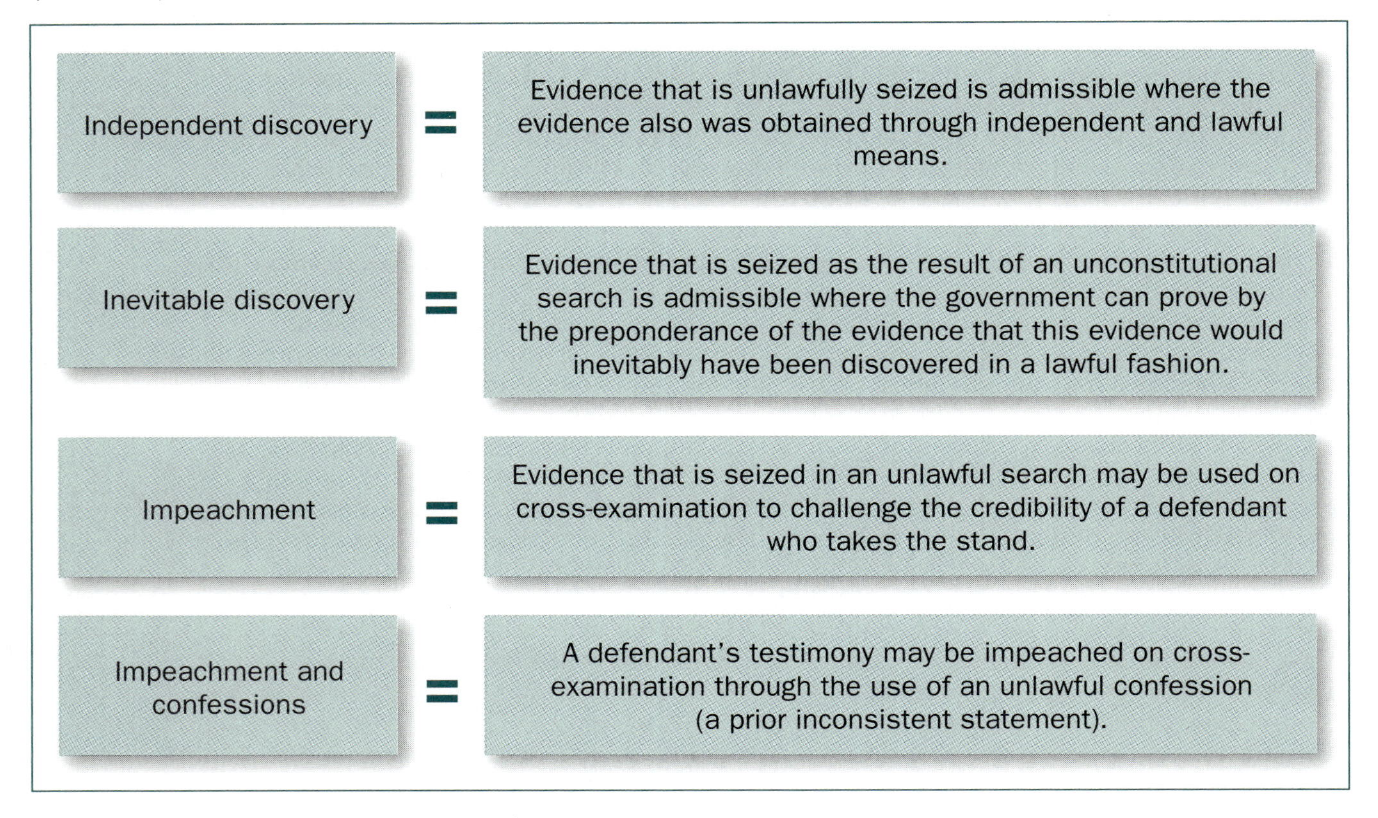

Does the Exclusionary Rule Deter Unreasonable Searches and Seizures?

We have seen that the Supreme Court held in *Mapp v. Ohio* that the exclusionary rule is required under the Fourth Amendment to enforce the prohibition on unreasonable searches and seizures and to protect judicial integrity. A majority of the Supreme Court almost immediately retreated from this view and in a series of cases held that the exclusionary rule is a "judge-made" remedy that is not required by the Fourth Amendment. The Supreme Court has created a number of exceptions to the exclusionary rule. In most of these instances the Court has determined that the application of the exclusionary rule is likely to have little deterrent impact and that the benefits of this modest amount of deterrence are outweighed by the costs of lost evidence and the possibility that a guilty defendant will walk out the courtroom door without a criminal conviction.

The Supreme Court no longer justifies the exclusionary rule on the grounds that the use of unlawfully seized evidence at trial undermines judicial integrity. After all, while it is true that the introduction of illegally seized evidence places judges in the position of endorsing a violation of the Constitution, there is the equally important concern that judges are assisting guilty defendants when they exclude reliable evidence from trial. Former Chief Justice Warren Burger, for instance, questioned whether the Supreme Court should continue to apply the exclusionary remedy when the result is "the release of countless guilty criminals" (403 U.S. 383, 416 [1971]).

A number of social scientists have joined the debate over the exclusionary rule and have examined whether the exclusionary rule deters unconstitutional searches and seizures. Researchers concede that it is virtually impossible to answer the question of whether fewer illegal searches are carried out as a result of the exclusionary rule and have concluded that the data neither support nor refute the deterrent value of the exclusionary rule. Supreme Court Justice Harry Blackmun, after providing a detailed review of social science research in his opinion in *United States v. Janis,* concludes that "no empirical researcher, proponent or opponent of the [exclusionary] rule has yet been able to establish with any assurance whether the rule has a deterrent effect." The result according to Justice Blackmun is to call into question the argument that the exclusionary rule protects our Fourth Amendment rights (*United States v. Janis,* 428 U.S. 433, 450, n.22 [1976]).

We can only conclude that the benefits of the exclusionary rule in terms of deterring Fourth Amendment violations are uncertain. What of the costs? Does the exclusionary rule result in the exclusion of evidence that is required to convict defendants? Should we consider a less costly alternative? Thomas Davies, in an important essay, reviews a number of studies and concludes that the "nonprosecution and/or nonconviction" of cases by the police, prosecutors, and judges based on the illegal seizure of evidence is "in the range of 0.6% to 2.35%" of all felony arrests. Davies concludes that while these "loss rates" are not "trivial," they do not amount to a "major impact" on the criminal justice system, "particularly in light of the fact that some of these charges likely would have been dropped or downgraded to misdemeanors or would not have resulted in prison sentences." In Davies's study of the California justice system, he finds that the highest percentage of cases lost due to the exclusionary rule involve drug charges (7.1%). In other areas, the exclusionary rule had almost no impact whatsoever (Davies, 1983).

Davies's findings are reinforced by Peter Nardulli. Nardulli conducted a three-county study of 7,500 cases in three states. Motions to suppress physical evidence were filed in roughly 5% of cases, most of which involved narcotics or weapons violations. These motions were successful in only 0.56% of all cases, meaning that forty cases (0.56%) were lost as a result of the exclusionary rule. Nardulli observes that only eight of the forty cases involved crimes of violence and that some of the cases may not have resulted in convictions at trial in any event. The highest percentage of "lost cases" were for narcotics offenses. Nine of the forty defendants would have received less than one month in jail; fifteen would have received less than two months. Only one defendant could have expected a sentence of more than one year. Nardulli concedes that his study may not be representative of every jurisdiction, but that based on his data, the exclusionary rule has a "truly marginal effect on the criminal court system."

These data suggest that despite the heated debate and lengthy academic commentaries on the exclusionary rule, we are unable to draw a firm conclusion regarding the impact of the rule on the police. We also have seen that lawyers file motions to suppress physical evidence in a relatively small number of cases. In addition, few "criminals" escape punishment as a result of these motions to suppress physical evidence. This may indicate that the police may be adhering to legal standards or that defense lawyers simply do not believe that motions to suppress physical evidence will be successful in most instances. Critics may justifiably argue that even one "lost" case is too high a price to pay for the exclusionary rule. On the other hand, defenders of the exclusionary rule may credibly contend that the rule highlights the importance of police respect for the prohibition on unreasonable searches and seizures and that the rule serves to reinforce the commitment of the judicial branch to civil liberties (Nardulli, 1983).

The next part of the chapter discusses the affirmative defense of entrapment. Entrapment, like the exclusionary rule, provides defendants with legal protection against police practices. This defense protects defendants in those instances in which police tactics may induce otherwise innocent individuals to engage in criminal conduct.

Entrapment

American common law did not recognize the defense of **entrapment.** The fact that the government entrapped or induced a defendant to commit a crime was irrelevant in evaluating a defendant's guilt or innocence.

The development of the defense is traced to the U.S. Supreme Court's 1932 decision in *Sorrells v. United States.* In *Sorrells,* an undercover prohibition agent posing as a "thirsty tourist" struck up a friendship with Sorrells and was able to overcome Sorrells's resistance and persuade him to locate some illegal alcohol. Sorrells's conviction for illegally selling alcohol was reversed by the U.S. Supreme Court (*Sorrells v. United States,* 287 U.S. 435 [1932]).

The decision defined entrapment as the "conception and planning of an offense by an officer, and his procurement of its commission by one who would not have perpetrated it except for the trickery, persuasion, or fraud of the officer." The essence of entrapment is the government's inducement of an otherwise innocent individual to commit a crime. Decisions have clarified that the prohibition on entrapment extends to the activities of undercover agents, confidential informants, and private citizens acting under the direction of law enforcement personnel. The defense has been raised in cases ranging from prostitution to the illegal sale of alcohol, cigarettes, firearms, and narcotics and to public corruption. There is some indication that the defense may not be relied on to excuse a crime of severe violence.

There are good reasons for the government to rely on undercover strategies:

- Certain crimes are difficult to investigate and to prevent without using informants. These include prostitution, public corruption, and crimes related to the illegal sale of narcotics.
- Undercover techniques, such as posing as a buyer of stolen goods, can result in a large number of arrests without the expenditure of substantial resources.
- Individuals will be deterred from criminal activity by the threat of government involvement in the crime.

Entrapment also is subject to criticism:

- The government may "manufacture crime" by individuals who otherwise may not engage in criminal activity.
- The government may lose respect by engaging in lawbreaking.
- The informants who are employed by the government to infiltrate criminal organizations may be criminals whose own illicit activity often is overlooked in exchange for their assistance.
- Innocent individuals are approached in order to test their moral virtue by determining whether they will engage in criminal activity.

The Law of Entrapment

In developing a legal test to regulate entrapment, judges and legislators have attempted to balance the need of law enforcement to rely on undercover techniques against the interest in ensuring that innocent individuals are not pressured or tricked into illegal activity. As noted by U.S. Supreme Court Chief Justice Earl Warren in 1958, "A line must be drawn between the trap for the unwary innocent and the trap for the unwary criminal" (*Sherman v. United States,* 356 U.S. 369, 372 [1958]).

Two competing legal tests for entrapment were nicely articulated by the U.S. Supreme Court in *Sherman v. United States* in 1958. Sherman's conviction on three counts of selling illegal narcotics was overturned by the Supreme Court, and the facts, in many respects, illustrate the perils of government undercover tactics. Kalchinian, a government informant facing criminal charges, struck up a friendship with defendant Sherman. They met and regularly talked during their visits to a doctor who was assisting both of them to end their dependence on drugs. Kalchinian was able to overcome Sherman's resistance and persuade him to obtain and to split the cost of illegal narcotics.

Members of the Supreme Court unanimously agreed that Sherman had been entrapped. Five judges supported a subjective approach to entrapment and four an objective test. The federal government and a majority of states follow a subjective test, while the Model Penal Code and a minority of states rely on the objective approach. Keep in mind that the legal concept of entrapment was developed by judges, and the availability of this defense has not been recognized as part of a defendant's constitutional right to due process of law. Entrapment in many states is an affirmative defense that places the burden on the defendant to meet a preponderance of the evidence standard. Other states require the defendant to produce some evidence and then place the burden on the government to prove the absence of entrapment (LaFave, 2000).

The Subjective Test

The **subjective test for entrapment** focuses on the defendant and asks whether the accused possessed the criminal intent or "predisposition" to commit the crime or whether the government "created" the crime. In other words, "but for" the actions of the government, would the accused have broken the law? Was the crime the "product of the creative activity of the government" or a result of the defendant's own criminal design?

The first step is to determine whether the government induced the crime. This requires that the undercover agent or informant persuade or pressure the accused. A simple offer to sell or to purchase drugs is a "mere offer" and does not constitute an "inducement." Rather, inducement requires appeals to friendship, compassion, promises of extraordinary economic or material gain or sexual favors, or assistance in carrying out the crime.

The second step is the most important and involves evaluating whether the defendant possessed a "predisposition" or readiness to commit the crime with which he or she is charged. The law assumes that a defendant who is predisposed is ready and willing to engage in criminal conduct in the absence of inducements and for this reason is not entitled to rely on the defense of entrapment. In other words, the government must direct its undercover strategy against the unwary criminal rather than the unwary innocent.

How is predisposition established? A number of factors are considered (*United States v. Fusko,* 869 F.2d 1048 [7th Cir. 1989]).

- The character or reputation of the defendant, including prior criminal arrests and convictions for the type of crime involved
- Whether the government or the accused suggest the criminal activity
- Whether the defendant was engaged in criminal activity for profit
- Whether the defendant was reluctant to commit the offense
- The attractiveness of the inducement

In *Sherman* the purchase of the drugs was initiated by the informant, Kalchinian, who overcame Sherman's initial resistance and persuaded him to obtain drugs. Kalchinian, in fact, had instigated two previous arrests and himself was facing sentencing for a drug offense. The two split the costs. There is no indication that Sherman was otherwise involved in the drug trade, and a search failed to find drugs in his home. Sherman's nine-year-old sales conviction and five-year-old possession conviction did not indicate that he was ready and willing to sell narcotics. In other words, before Kalchinian induced Sherman to purchase drugs, he seemed to be genuinely motivated to overcome his addiction.

The underlying theory is that the judge is carrying out the intent of the legislature and that these elected representatives did not intend that the law would be used to punish otherwise innocent individuals who were induced to commit crimes by government trickery and pressure. The issue of entrapment under the subjective test is to be decided by the jury in determining the guilt or innocence of the accused.

The Objective Test

The **objective test for entrapment** focuses on the conduct of the government rather than on the character of the individual. Justice Felix Frankfurter in his dissenting opinion in *Sherman* stated that the crucial question is "whether police conduct revealed in the particular case falls below standards to which common feelings respond, for the proper use of governmental power." The police, of course, must rely on undercover work, and the test for entrapment is whether in offering inducements the government is likely to attract those "ready and willing" to commit crimes "should the occasion arise" or is relying on tactics and strategies that are likely to attract those who "normally avoid crime and through self-struggle resist ordinary temptations." Under the subjective approach, if an informant makes persistent appeals to compassion and friendship and then asks a defendant to sell narcotics, the defendant has no defense if he is predisposed to selling narcotics. Under the objective approach, there would be a defense, because the police conduct rather than the defendant's predisposition is the central consideration (LaFave, 2000, p. 458).

Frankfurter wrote that public confidence in the integrity and fairness of the government must be preserved and that government power is "abused and directed to an end for which it was not constituted when employed to promote rather than detect crime and to bring about the downfall of those who, left to themselves, might well have obeyed the law." These unacceptable methods lead to a lack of respect for the law and encourage criminality. Frankfurter argued that judges accordingly must condemn corrupt and uncivilized methods of law enforcement even where this results in the acquittal of the accused. Frankfurter criticized the predisposition test for providing protection for "innocent defendants" while permitting the government to subject defendants who are predisposed to commit crimes to all varieties of unethical strategies and schemes.

In *Sherman,* Frankfurter condemned Kalchinian's repeated requests to the accused to obtain drugs. He pointed out that Kalchinian took advantage of the fact that Sherman was struggling to overcome his addiction and that Sherman possessed a natural sympathy for the pain suffered by Kalchinian in withdrawing from narcotics. *Sherman* and *Sorrells* suggest that practices prohibited under the objective test include the following:

- Taking advantage of weaknesses
- Repeated appeals to friendship, sympathy
- Promising substantial economic gain
- Pressure or threats
- Providing the equipment required for carrying out a crime
- False representations designed to induce a belief that solicited criminal conduct is not prohibited by law

Critics nevertheless complain that the objective test has not resulted in clear and definite standards to guide law enforcement. Can you determine at what point Kalchinian crossed the line? Critics also charge that it makes little sense to acquit defendants who are "predisposed" based on the fact that an "innocent" individual may have been tricked into criminal activity by the government. The determination of entrapment under the objective test is a question for the judge rather than the jury. Justice Frankfurter reasoned that the judge is the guardian of the integrity of the courtroom and is responsible for insuring that the police have not employed impermissible investigative techniques. The judge also is in a position to articulate general principles to guide the police in the future.

The Due Process Test

The **due process test for entrapment** is a constitutionally based entrapment defense. A defendant may rely on the entrapment defense in those instances in which the government's conduct was so unfair and outrageous that it violates the Due Process Clause of the Fifth and Fourteenth Amendments to the U.S. Constitution, and it therefore would be unjust to convict the defendant. This theory proves particularly useful to defendants in jurisdictions that follow the subjective test who possess a predisposition and are otherwise precluded from invoking the entrapment defense.

The U.S. Supreme Court rejected due process tests in *United States v. Russell.* In the situation at issue in this case, Joe Shapiro, an undercover agent for the Federal Bureau of Narcotics and Dangerous Drugs, met with Richard Russell and his codefendants John and Patrick Connolly. Shapiro offered to provide them with the chemical phenyl-2-propanone, an essential element in the manufacture of methamphetamine, in return for one-half of the drug produced. The three provided Shapiro with a sample of their most recent batch and showed him their laboratory, where Shapiro observed an empty bottle of phenyl-2-propanone. The next day Shapiro delivered one hundred grams of propanone and observed two of the defendants begin to manufacture methamphetamine. Shapiro later was given one-half the drug and purchased a portion of the remainder. A warrant was obtained, and a search revealed two bottles of propanone, neither of which had been provided by Shapiro (*United States v. Russell,* 411 U.S. 423 [1973]).

The defendants certainly were predisposed to manufacture and sell narcotics, but creatively claimed that the government violated due process by prosecuting them for a crime in which the government had been intimately involved. The U.S. Supreme Court, in rejecting this argument, stressed that while propanone was "difficult to obtain, it was by no means impossible" as indicated by the fact that the defendants had been manufacturing "speed" without the propanone provided by Shapiro. The Court concluded that

> while we may some day be presented with a situation in which the conduct of law enforcement agents is so outrageous that due process principles would absolutely bar the government from invoking judicial process to obtain a conviction... the instant case is distinctly not of that breed.

The Supreme Court stressed that the investigation of drug-related offenses often requires infiltration into and cooperation with narcotics rings and that the law enforcement tactics employed in *Russell* "can hardly be said to violate fundamental fairness" or to be "shocking to the universal sense of justice."

Invoking the Entrapment Defense

Entrapment is an *affirmative defense,* meaning that it must be raised by the defendant. In jurisdictions following the subjective approach, the defendant generally is required to establish the fact of inducement by a government agent. The burden then shifts to the government to counter the defense by establishing the defendant's "predisposition" beyond a reasonable doubt. In contrast, jurisdictions that have adopted the objective test generally place both the burden of production of evidence and persuasion on the defendant. The defendant under the objective test must convince the jury that he or she was entrapped by a predominance of the evidence, which is a balance of probabilities, or slightly over fifty percent.

Can you both deny that you committed a criminal offense and also claim that you were entrapped? In *Matthews v. United States,* the U.S. Supreme Court held that a defendant was entitled to deny committing a criminal offense while also relying on the "inconsistent defense" of entrapment. In *Matthews,* the Court upheld the defendant's right both to deny that he had intended as a federal official to engage in bribery and to contend that he had been entrapped (*Matthews v. United States,* 485 U.S. 58 [1988]).

We might question whether courts should be involved in evaluating law enforcement tactics and in acquitting individuals who are otherwise clearly guilty of criminal conduct. Can innocent individuals really be pressured into criminal activity? Do we want to limit the ability of the police to use the techniques they believe are required to investigate and punish crime? There also appear to be no clear judicial standards for determining predisposition under the subjective test and for evaluating acceptable law enforcement tactics under the objective approach. On the other hand, there clearly should be a mechanism for limiting abusive investigative practices by the police.

The next case in the text is *Jacobson v. United States. Jacobson* is a leading Supreme Court case that raises the question of whether Jacobson was predisposed to purchase child pornography or whether his predisposition was the product of the creative activity of the government. *Jacobson* also raises the issue of whether predisposition should be measured at the time that the government first approached Jacobson or at the time that that the government offered to sell Jacobson illegal child pornography. You will find two cases on the Web site that raise the question of identifying the circumstances under which the requirements of the due process test are satisfied: *United States v. Hampton,* decided by the U.S. Supreme Court in 1976, and the 1996 Florida decision in *Madera v. State.*

You will find United States v. Hampton *and* Madera v. State *on the study site, http://www.sagepub.com/lippmancp.*

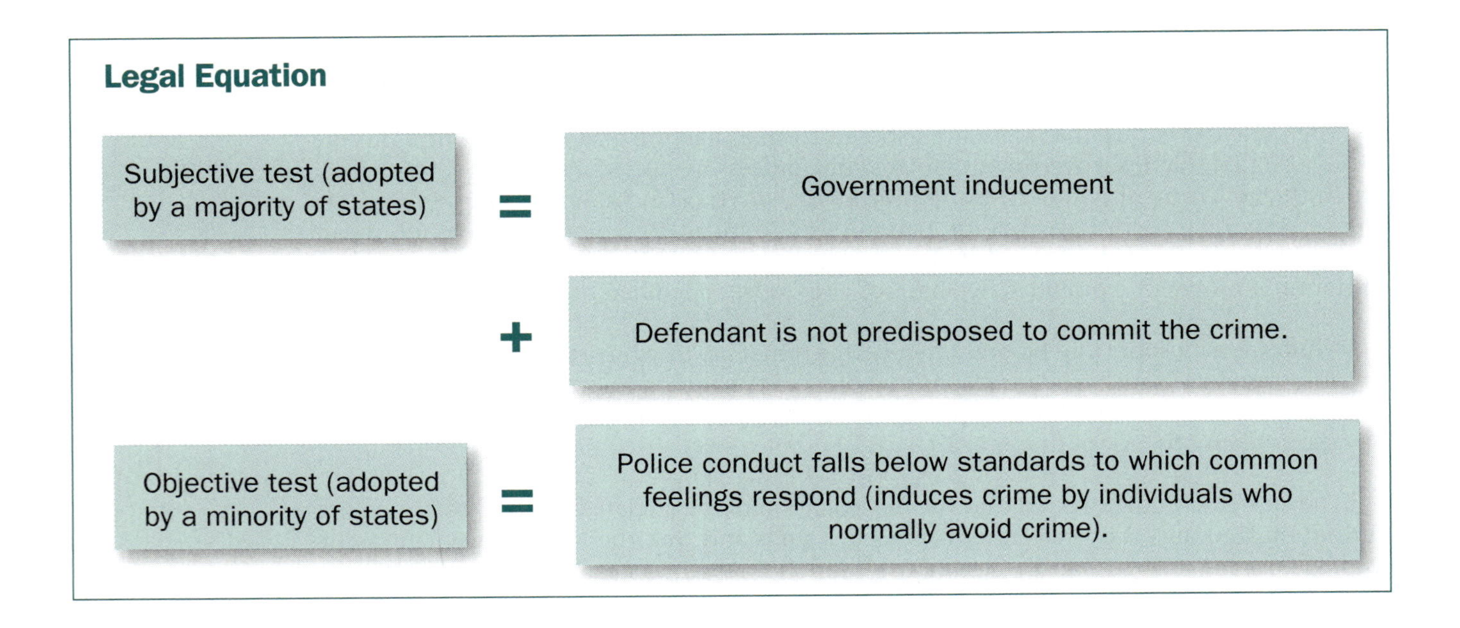

Criminal Procedure in the News

The investigation of domestic terrorism typically involves surveillance and infiltration of suspect terrorist groups. The use of informants allows law enforcement to identify members of terrorist cells, to gather intelligence, and to prevent planned terrorist attacks. In the past several years, a number of individuals brought to trial on terrorism charges or who currently face terrorism charges have alleged that they were entrapped, contending that undercover government informants encouraged them to enter into a terrorist conspiracy. Several of these cases are summarized below.

Illinois mall bombing. Derrick Shareef, twenty-two, was arrested in December 2007 for the attempted use of a weapon of mass destruction against persons and property in the Cherryvale Shopping Center in Rockford, Illinois, and for the attempted malicious damage and destruction of property by fire and explosion. A confidential FBI informant allegedly suggested that Shareef bomb a mall, helped him select the target, and arranged for Shareef to "trade" two stereo speakers for (nonfunctioning) grenades, a handgun, and (nonfunctioning) ammunition.

Albany money laundering. Yassin M. Aref, thirty-three, and Muhammed M. Hossain, fifty-one, were convicted in October 2006 of money laundering and conspiracy to support terrorism. They each were sentenced to fifteen years in prison. FBI informant Shaheed "Malik" Hussein recorded conversations with Aref and Hossain for over a year in which the two agreed to launder $50,000 that Hussein represented he was to receive from the sale of a shoulder-fired missile to a terrorist group that planned to assassinate Pakistan's Ambassador to the United Nations. Shaheed Hussein previously had worked as a translator for the New York Department of Motor Vehicles and had falsified answers on driver's examinations that had enabled eighty people to fraudulently receive driver's licenses.

Miami bombing plot. Seven men were arrested in June 2006 and were accused of conspiring to bomb various government buildings in Miami as well as the Sears Tower in Chicago. The men were part of the Seas of David religious cult that had been infiltrated by two FBI informants, including one who posed as a member of al-Qaeda. The seven men were recorded swearing oaths of allegiance to al-Qaeda, and the informant provided them with video cameras to photograph targets. The leader of the group reportedly stated that his goal was to form an Islamic army and to launch a ground war that was "as good or greater than 9/11." The two informants were each paid over $15,000 by the government, and one was given permanent residence in the United States.

Lodi conspiracy. A suspected al-Qaeda terrorist cell in Lodi, California, was identified by a government informant. Two Islamic clerics were deported, and in June 2005, Hamid Hyatt, age twenty-two, and his father, age forty-seven, were arrested. Hamid was convicted of one count of material support for a terrorist organization based on his attendance at a terrorist training camp and also was convicted of three counts of lying to the FBI. His father, a taxi driver, was acquitted of providing false information to the FBI. The informant, Nassem Khan, was a fast-food worker who allegedly was paid $250,000 for infiltrating the Islamic community in Lodi. His credibility was called into question by his previous allegations that various al-Qaeda leaders, including Osama Bin Laden, had visited Lodi.

Detroit terrorist plot. Three Moroccan immigrants were arrested in September 2001; two of the defendants were convicted of providing material support to terrorists, and the third was convicted of document fraud. The government later asked the judge to withdraw the convictions when it was disclosed that the prosecution had withheld favorable evidence from the defense attorneys. Yousef Hmimssa, who briefly lived with the three defendants, agreed to testify for the government at a time when he was facing criminal charges that conceivably could have resulted in eighty-one years in prison, including a charge for the fraudulent use of credit cards to make purchases totaling over $250,000. Several of the documents withheld by the government suggested that Hmimssa may have fabricated his testimony about the Moroccan immigrants.

On August 27, 2004, several days before the opening of the Republican Convention in New York, Shahwar Matin Siraj, age twenty-two, and James Elshafay, nineteen, were arrested for conspiracy to bomb the Herald Square subway station, a transportation stop serving a busy shopping district in the heart of New York City. The defendants were both found to be in possession of a crude diagram of the subway station. Siraj received the maximum thirty-year sentence in January 2007, and Elshafay, in return for his testimony against Siraj, was sentenced to five years in prison.

Their conversations had been recorded by Osama Eldawoody, a fifty-year-old Egyptian immigrant, who had been paid over $100,000 by the New York City Police Department in return for monitoring activities in mosques. It was reported that he had visited the three mosques to which he was assigned roughly 570 times each. Eldawoody also regularly stopped by the Islamic bookstore owned by Siraj's uncle, where he met and began to mentor Siraj and Elshafay in their study of the Koran and Islam. He recorded his conversations with the two men over a period of roughly a year.

The police had received tips that Siraj was a volatile personality who regularly denounced the U.S. and praised Osama Bin Laden. He had entered the United States illegally from Pakistan in 1999. Reportedly he was angered over American policy in Iraq and allegedly possessed CDs containing instructions on bomb construction. The tapes of his conversations with Eldawoody recorded him expressing a desire for "1,000 to 2,000 to die in one day." He added that "I'm ready to do anything, I don't care about my life." Siraj insisted at his trial that he would not have entered into the bombing plot had Eldawoody not shown him photos of the abuse at Abu Ghraib and told him that it was a religious duty to kill Americans. The tape indicates that as the day of the planned bombing grew near, Siraj developed cold feet and told Eldawoody and Elshafay that he did not want to handle any explosives.

Elshafay, in contrast, was eager to ignite a bomb and proposed that he dress like an Orthodox Jew to lessen the chance that he would be detected. Elshafay first met Siraj in 2002 at the Islamic bookstore, and their conversations led to discussions about bombing prominent sites in New York. Elshafay went so far as to compile a list of possible targets, including various bridges.

Elshafay was raised by an Irish mother and an abusive and largely absent Egyptian father. He flunked the ninth grade three times and ultimately received a G.E.D. Elshafay revealed on cross-examination that he was on medication for depression and schizophrenia, had suffered from substance abuse, and recently had been institutionalized. He testified that the backlash against Muslims following 9/11 had inspired him to ask Eldawoody to instruct him on the beliefs and principles of Islam.

Did Siraj and Elshafay pose a threat? They were not affiliated with a terrorist group, had no knowledge of explosives, and had not fully developed a plan of attack. The government was able to obtain a conviction by demonstrating that they had entered into a conspiratorial agreement and had taken an affirmative act in furtherance of the agreement. They had been given backpacks to carry the explosives by Eldawoody and had visited the Herald Square stop with Eldawoody three days before their arrest. Eldawoody clearly assumed the role of a father figure to the two young men and encouraged their militancy by criticizing U.S. policy in Iraq and by instructing them that there was a religious duty to conduct Jihad against the United States. He also had told the young men that there was a shadowy terrorist group, The Brotherhood, that would provide them with explosives and financial support.

On the other hand, Siraj had a reputation for incendiary rhetoric and was listening to tapes denouncing U.S. policy in the Middle East long before he met Eldawoody. Elshafay had been angered by the anti-Islamic rhetoric following the attacks on September 11, 2001, and had compiled a list of possible targets. The use of informants is vital to identifying "lone wolf" terrorists who may pose a future threat. The penetration of terrorist cells sends a strong message that the government is able to detect and to break up terrorist plots and prevent attacks. Eldawoody may have encouraged the alienation of these two young defendants, but they clearly were receptive to the message that they possessed a religious duty to kill Americans.

Should the government have targeted Siraj and Elshafay for investigation and prosecution? Were the young men entrapped?

Was Jacobson predisposed to order child pornography through the mail?

Jacobson v. United States, 503 U.S. 540 (1992), White, J.

Issue

On September 24, 1987, petitioner Keith Jacobson was indicted for violating a provision of the Child Protection Act of 1984, which criminalizes the knowing receipt through the mails of a "visual depiction [that] involves the use of a minor engaging in sexually explicit conduct...." Petitioner defended on the ground that the Government entrapped him into committing the crime through a series of communications from undercover agents that spanned the twenty-six months preceding his arrest. Petitioner was found guilty after a jury trial. The court of appeals affirmed his conviction, holding that the Government had carried its burden of proving beyond reasonable doubt that petitioner was predisposed to break the law and hence was not entrapped. The central issue is whether...the Government overstepped the line between setting a trap for the "unwary innocent" and the "unwary criminal" and as a matter of law failed to establish that petitioner was independently predisposed to commit the crime for which he was arrested....

Facts

In February 1984, petitioner, a fifty-six-year-old veteran-turned-farmer who supported his elderly father in Nebraska, ordered two magazines and a brochure from a California adult bookstore. The magazines, titled *Bare Boys I* and *Bare Boys II,* contained photographs of nude preteen and teenage boys. The contents of the magazines startled petitioner, who testified that he had expected to receive photographs of "young men eighteen years or older."

The young men depicted in the magazines were not engaged in sexual activity, and petitioner's receipt of the magazines was legal [at the time he received them] under both federal and Nebraska law. Within three months, the law with respect to child pornography changed; Congress passed the act illegalizing the receipt through the mails of sexually explicit depictions of children. In the very month that the new provision became law, postal inspectors found petitioner's name on the mailing list of the California bookstore that had mailed him *Bare Boys I* and *II.* There followed over the next two and one-half years repeated efforts by two Government agencies, through five fictitious organizations and a bogus pen pal, to explore petitioner's willingness to break the new law by ordering sexually explicit photographs of children through the mail.

The Government began its efforts in January 1985 when a postal inspector sent petitioner a letter supposedly from the American Hedonist Society, which in fact was a fictitious organization. The letter included a membership application and stated the society's doctrine: that members had the "right to read what we desire, the right to discuss similar interests with those who share our philosophy, and finally that we have the right to seek pleasure without restrictions being placed on us by outdated puritan morality." Petitioner enrolled in the organization and returned a sexual attitude questionnaire that asked him to rank on a scale of one to four his enjoyment of various sexual materials, with one being "really enjoy," two being "enjoy," three being "somewhat enjoy," and four being "do not enjoy." Petitioner ranked the entry "pre-teen sex" as a two, but indicated that he was opposed to pedophilia.

For a time, the Government left petitioner alone. But then a new "prohibited mailing specialist" in the postal service found petitioner's name in a file, and in May 1986, petitioner received a solicitation from a second fictitious consumer research company, Midlands Data Research, seeking a response from those who "believe in the joys of sex and the complete awareness of those lusty and youthful lads and lasses of the neophite *[sic]* age." The letter never explained whether "neophite" referred to minors or to young adults. Petitioner responded: "Please feel free to send me more information, I am interested in teenage sexuality. Please keep my name confidential."

Petitioner then heard from yet another Government creation, Heartland Institute for a New Tomorrow (HINT), which proclaimed that it was "an organization founded to protect and promote sexual freedom and freedom of choice. We believe that arbitrarily imposed legislative sanctions restricting *your* sexual freedom should be rescinded through the legislative process." The letter also enclosed a second survey. Petitioner indicated that his interest in "preteen sex–homosexual" material was above average, but not high. In response to another question, petitioner wrote: "Not only sexual expression but freedom of the press is under attack. We must be ever vigilant to counter attack right wing fundamentalists who are determined to curtail our freedoms."

HINT replied, portraying itself as a lobbying organization seeking to repeal "all statutes which regulate sexual activities, except those laws which deal with violent behavior, such as rape. HINT is also lobbying to eliminate any legal definition of 'the age of consent.'" These lobbying efforts were to be funded by sales from a catalog to be published in the future "offering the sale of various items which we believe you will find to be both interesting and stimulating." HINT also provided computer matching of group members with similar survey responses, and, although petitioner was supplied with a list of potential "pen pals," he did not initiate any correspondence.

Nevertheless, the Government's "prohibited mailing specialist" began writing to petitioner, using the pseudonym "Carl Long." The letters employed a tactic known as "mirroring," which the inspector described as "reflecting whatever the interests are of the person we are writing to." Petitioner responded at first, indicating that his interest was primarily in "male-male items." Inspector "Long" wrote back,

> My interests too are primarily male-male items. Are you satisfied with the type of VCR tapes available? Personally, I like the amateur stuff better if its *[sic]* well produced as it can get more kinky and also seems more real. I think the actors enjoy it more.

Petitioner responded, "As far as my likes are concerned, I like good looking young guys (in their late teens and early twenties) doing their thing together." Petitioner's letters to "Long" made no reference to child pornography. After writing two letters, petitioner discontinued the correspondence.

By March 1987, thirty-four months had passed since the Government had obtained petitioner's name from the mailing list of the California bookstore, and twenty-six months had passed since the postal service had commenced its mailings to petitioner. Although petitioner had responded to surveys and letters, the Government had no evidence that petitioner had ever intentionally possessed or been exposed to child pornography. The postal service had not checked petitioner's mail to determine whether he was receiving questionable mailings from persons—other than the Government—involved in the child pornography industry.

At this point, a second Government agency, the customs service, included petitioner in its own child pornography sting, Operation Borderline, after finding his name on lists submitted by the postal service. Using the name of a fictitious Canadian company called Produit Outaouais, the customs service mailed petitioner a brochure advertising photographs of young boys engaging in sex. Petitioner placed an order that was never filled.

The postal service also continued its efforts in the Jacobson case, writing to petitioner as the [fictitious company] Far Eastern Trading Company Ltd. The letter began,

> As many of you know, much hysterical nonsense has appeared in the American media concerning "pornography" and what must be done to stop it from coming across your borders. This brief letter does not allow us to give much comments; however, why is your government spending millions of dollars to exercise international censorship while tons of drugs, which makes yours the world's most crime ridden country are passed through easily.

The letter went on to say:

> We have devised a method of getting these to you without prying eyes of U. S. Customs seizing your.... After consultations with American solicitors, we have been advised that once we have posted our material through your system, it cannot be opened for any inspection without authorization of a judge.

The letter invited petitioner to send for more information. It also asked petitioner to sign an affirmation that he was "not a law enforcement officer or agent of the U.S. Government acting in an undercover capacity for the purpose of entrapping Far Eastern Trading Company, its agents or customers." Petitioner responded. A catalog was sent, and petitioner ordered *Boys Who Love Boys,* a pornographic magazine depicting young boys engaged in various sexual activities. Petitioner was arrested after a controlled delivery of a photocopy of the magazine.

When petitioner was asked at trial why he placed such an order, he explained that the Government had succeeded in piquing his curiosity:

> Well, the statement was made of all the trouble and the hysteria over pornography and I wanted to see what the material was. It didn't describe the—I didn't know for sure what kind of sexual action they were referring to in the Canadian letter.

In petitioner's home, the Government found the *Bare Boys* magazines and materials that the Government had sent to him in the course of its protracted investigation, but no other materials that would indicate that petitioner collected, or was actively interested in, child pornography.

Reasoning

There can be no dispute about the evils of child pornography or the difficulties that laws and law enforcement have encountered in eliminating it.... Likewise, there can be no dispute that the Government may use undercover agents to enforce the law:

> It is well settled that the fact that officers or employees of the Government merely afford opportunities or facilities for the commission of the offense does not defeat the prosecution. Artifice and stratagem may be employed to catch those engaged in criminal enterprises.

In their zeal to enforce the law, however, Government agents may not originate a criminal design, that is, they may not implant in an innocent person's mind the disposition to commit a criminal act and then induce commission of the crime so that the Government may prosecute. Where the Government has induced an individual to break the law and the defense of entrapment is at issue, as it was in this case, the prosecution must prove beyond reasonable doubt that the defendant was disposed to commit the criminal act prior to first being approached by Government agents.

Inducement is not at issue in this case. The Government does not dispute that it induced petitioner to commit the crime. The sole issue is whether the Government carried its burden of proving that petitioner was predisposed to violate the law before the Government intervened. By the time petitioner finally placed his order, he had already been the target of twenty-six months of repeated mailings and communications from Government agents and fictitious organizations. Therefore, although he had become predisposed to break the law by May 1987, it is our view that the Government did not prove that this predisposition was independent and not the product of the attention that the Government had directed at petitioner since January 1985.

The prosecution's evidence of predisposition falls into two categories: evidence developed prior to the postal service's mail campaign, and that developed during the course of the investigation. The sole piece of preinvestigation evidence is petitioner's 1984 order and receipt of the *Bare Boys* magazines. But this is scant if any proof of petitioner's predisposition to commit an illegal act, the criminal character of which a defendant is presumed to know. It may indicate a predisposition to view sexually oriented photographs that are responsive to his sexual tastes, but evidence that merely indicates a generic inclination to act within a broad range, not all of which is criminal, is of little probative value in establishing predisposition.

Furthermore, petitioner was acting within the law at the time he received these magazines. Receipt through the mails of sexually explicit depictions of children for noncommercial use did not become illegal under federal law until May 1984, and Nebraska had no law that forbade petitioner's possession of such material until 1988. Evidence of predisposition to do what once was lawful is not, by itself, sufficient to show predisposition to do what is now illegal, for there is a common understanding that most people obey the law even when they disapprove of it. This obedience may reflect a generalized respect for legality or the fear of prosecution, but for whatever reason, the law's prohibitions are matters of consequence. Hence, the fact that petitioner legally ordered and received the *Bare Boys* magazines does little to further the Government's burden of proving that petitioner was predisposed to commit a criminal act. This is particularly true given petitioner's unchallenged testimony that he did not know until they arrived that the magazines would depict minors.

The prosecution's evidence gathered during the investigation also fails to carry the Government's burden. Petitioner's responses to the many communications prior to the ultimate criminal act were at most indicative of certain personal inclinations, including a predisposition to view photographs of preteen sex and a willingness to promote a given agenda by supporting lobbying organizations. Even so, petitioner's responses hardly support an inference that he would commit the crime of receiving child pornography through the mails. Furthermore, a person's inclinations and "fantasies... are his own and beyond the reach of government...."

On the other hand, the strong arguable inference is that, by waving the banner of individual rights and disparaging the legitimacy and constitutionality of efforts to restrict the availability of sexually explicit materials, the Government not only excited petitioner's interest in sexually explicit materials banned by law but also exerted substantial pressure on petitioner to obtain and read such material as part of a fight against censorship and the infringement of individual rights. For instance, HINT described itself as "an organization founded to protect and promote sexual freedom and freedom of choice" and stated that "the most appropriate means to accomplish [its] objectives is to promote honest dialogue among concerned individuals and to continue its lobbying efforts with State Legislators." These lobbying efforts were to be financed through catalog sales. Mailings from the equally fictitious American Hedonist Society and the correspondence from the nonexistent Carl Long continue these themes.

Similarly, the two solicitations in the spring of 1987 raised the specter of censorship while suggesting that petitioner ought to be allowed to do what he had been solicited to do. The mailing from the customs service referred to "the worldwide ban and intense enforcement on this type of material," observed that "what was legal and commonplace is now an 'underground' and secretive service," and emphasized that "this environment forces us to take extreme measures" to ensure delivery. The postal service solicitation described the concern about child pornography as "hysterical nonsense," decried "international censorship," and assured petitioner, based on consultation with "American solicitors," that an order that had been posted could not be opened for inspection without authorization of a judge. It further asked petitioner to affirm that he was not a Government agent attempting to entrap the mail order company or its customers. In these particulars, both Government solicitations suggested that receiving this material was something that petitioner ought to be allowed to do.

Petitioner's ready response to these solicitations cannot be enough to establish beyond reasonable doubt that he was predisposed, prior to the Government acts intended to create predisposition, to commit the crime of receiving child pornography through the mails. The evidence that petitioner was ready and willing to commit the offense came only after the Government had devoted two and one-half years to convincing him that he had or should have the right to engage in the very behavior proscribed by law. Rational jurors could not say beyond a reasonable doubt that petitioner possessed the requisite predisposition prior to the Government's investigation and that it existed independent of the Government's many and varied approaches to petitioner. Where entrapment was found as a matter of law, "the Government [may not] play on the weaknesses of an innocent party and beguile him into committing crimes which he otherwise would not have attempted."

Law enforcement officials go too far when they "implant in the mind of an innocent person the disposition to commit the alleged offense and induce its commission in order that they may prosecute." Like the *Sorrells* Court, we are

> unable to conclude that it was the intention of the Congress in enacting this statute that its processes of detection and enforcement should be abused by the instigation by government officials of an act on the part of persons otherwise innocent in order to lure them to its commission and to punish them.

When the Government's quest for convictions leads to the apprehension of an otherwise law-abiding citizen who, if left to his own devices, likely would have never run afoul of the law, the courts should intervene.

Holding

Because we conclude that this is such a case and that the prosecution failed, as a matter of law, to adduce evidence to support the jury verdict that petitioner was predisposed, independent of the Government's acts and beyond a reasonable doubt, to violate the law by receiving child pornography through the mails, we reverse the court of appeals judgment affirming the conviction of Keith Jacobson.

Dissenting, *O'Connor, J.,* joined by *Rehnquist, C.J.,* and *Kennedy, J.,* and joined in part by *Scalia, J.*

Keith Jacobson was offered only two opportunities to buy child pornography through the mail. Both times, he ordered. Both times, he asked for opportunities to buy more. He needed no Government agent to coax, threaten, or persuade him; no one played on his sympathies or friendship or suggested that his committing the crime would further a greater good. In fact, no Government agent even contacted him face to face. The Government contends that from the enthusiasm with which Mr. Jacobson responded to the chance to commit a crime, a reasonable jury could permissibly infer beyond a reasonable doubt that he was predisposed to commit the crime. I agree. The first time the Government sent Mr. Jacobson a catalog of illegal materials, he ordered a set of photographs advertised as picturing "young boys in sex action fun." He enclosed the following note with his order: "I received your brochure and decided to place an order. If I like your product, I will order more later." For reasons undisclosed in the record, Mr. Jacobson's order was never delivered.

The second time the Government sent a catalog of illegal materials, Mr. Jacobson ordered a magazine called *Boys Who Love Boys,* described as: "11 year old and 14 year old boys get it on in every way possible. Oral, anal sex and heavy masturbation. If you love boys, you will be delighted with this." Along with his order, Mr. Jacobson sent the following note: "Will order other items later. I want to be discreet in order to protect you and me."

Government agents admittedly did not offer Mr. Jacobson the chance to buy child pornography right away. Instead, they first sent questionnaires in order to make sure that he was generally interested in the subject matter. Indeed, a "cold call" in such a business would not only risk rebuff and suspicion, but might also shock and offend the uninitiated, or expose minors to suggestive materials. Mr. Jacobson's responses to the questionnaires gave the investigators reason to think he would be interested in photographs depicting preteen sex.

The Court, however, concludes that a reasonable jury could not have found Mr. Jacobson to be predisposed beyond a reasonable doubt on the basis of his responses to the Government's catalogs, even though it admits that, by that time, he was predisposed to commit the crime. The Government, the Court holds, failed to provide evidence that Mr. Jacobson's obvious predisposition at the time of the crime "was independent and not the product of the attention that the Government had directed at petitioner." In so holding, I believe the Court fails to acknowledge the reasonableness of the jury's inference from the evidence, redefines "predisposition," and introduces a new requirement that Government sting operations have a reasonable suspicion of illegal activity before contacting a suspect....

Today, the Court holds that Government conduct may be considered to create a predisposition to commit a crime, even before any Government action to induce the commission of the crime. In my view, this holding changes entrapment doctrine. Generally, the inquiry is whether a suspect is predisposed before the Government induces the commission of the crime, not before the Government makes initial contact with him. There is no dispute here that the Government's questionnaires and letters were not sufficient to establish inducement; they did not even suggest that Mr. Jacobson should engage in any illegal activity. If all the Government had done was to send these materials, Mr. Jacobson's entrapment defense would fail. Yet the Court holds that the Government must prove not only that a suspect was predisposed to commit the crime before the opportunity to commit it arose but also before the Government came on the scene.

...After this case, every defendant will claim that something the Government agent did before soliciting the crime "created" a predisposition that was not there before. For example, a bribe taker will claim that the description of the amount of money available was so enticing that it implanted a disposition to accept the bribe later offered. A drug buyer will claim that the description of the drug's purity and effects was so tempting that it created the urge to try it for the first time. In short, the Court's opinion could be read to prohibit the Government from advertising the seductions of criminal activity as part of its sting operation, for fear of creating a predisposition in its suspects. That limitation would be especially likely to hamper sting operations such as this one, which mimic the advertising done by genuine purveyors of pornography. No doubt the Court would protest that its opinion does not stand for so broad a proposition, but the apparent lack of a principled basis for distinguishing these scenarios exposes a flaw in the more limited rule the Court today adopts.... The Government conduct in this case is not comparable. While the Court states that the Government "exerted substantial pressure on petitioner to obtain and read such material as part of a fight against censorship and the infringement of individual rights," one looks at the record in vain for evidence of such "substantial pressure."

...The second puzzling thing about the Court's opinion is its redefinition of predisposition. The Court acknowledges that "petitioner's responses to the many communications prior to the ultimate criminal act were...indicative of certain personal inclinations, including a predisposition to view photographs of preteen sex...." If true, this should have settled the matter; Mr. Jacobson was predisposed to engage in the illegal conduct. Yet, the Court concludes, "Petitioner's responses hardly support an inference that he would commit the crime of receiving child pornography through the mails."

...Because I believe there was sufficient evidence to uphold the jury's verdict, I respectfully dissent.

Questions for Discussion

1. What is the issue in *Jacobson*? Why is this an important question for the Supreme Court to decide?
2. Summarize the majority and dissenting decisions. Which judgment do you find more persuasive?
3. Do you believe that the government should have devoted time and resources to pursuing and prosecuting Jacobson?
4. This was a 5-to-4 decision. Do you believe that the Supreme Court's judgment in *Jacobson* interferes with law enforcement's ability to investigate crimes?

Chapter Summary

In 1914, in *Weeks v. United States,* the U.S. Supreme Court ruled that evidence seized in violation of the Fourth Amendment is to be excluded from evidence in federal prosecutions. Thirty-five years later, in *Wolf v. Colorado,* the Court held that the requirements of the Fourth Amendment are incorporated into the Fourteenth Amendment and are applicable to proceedings in state and local courts. In 1961, in *Mapp v. Ohio,* the Supreme Court held that the Fourth Amendment exclusionary rule also applied to prosecutions in state courts. The Court explained that the exclusionary rule is "part and parcel" of the Fourth Amendment, provides a deterrent to police disregard for the Fourth Amendment, and protects the integrity of the judicial process by excluding tainted evidence from trial. These twin goals, according to the majority of the justices on the Court at that time, could not be accomplished through civil remedies, criminal prosecution, or disciplinary proceedings. Subsequently, in a series of judgments, the Court shifted its position and ruled that the exclusionary rule is a "judge-made" remedy that is not required by the Fourth Amendment, whose sole purpose is to deter unreasonable searches and seizures.

The typical avenue for challenging the reasonableness of a search and seizure is the filing of a pretrial motion to suppress. Most states and the federal courts place the burden of proof on the defendant when the search or seizure is based on a warrant. The burden is reversed and is placed on the government when the police act without a warrant. The legal test to be applied for standing to file a motion to suppress an alleged violation of the Fourth Amendment prohibition on unreasonable searches and seizures is whether an individual has a subjective and reasonable expectation of privacy in the area that was searched. The burden of proof for demonstrating standing customarily is placed on the defendant.

The Supreme Court has created a number of exceptions to the exclusionary rule in those instances in which the Court has concluded that the limited deterrent value of excluding the evidence is outweighed by the costs of excluding the evidence from the trial. In other words, in these cases the Court found that there was "too much pain for too little gain." These exceptions are as follows:

- ***Collateral proceedings.*** The evidence is admissible in criminal proceedings that are not part of the formal trial as well as in certain civil proceedings.
- ***Attenuation.*** There is a weak connection between the unlawful search and the seizure of the evidence.
- ***Good faith.*** The police acted in an objectively reasonable fashion in seizing the evidence.
- ***Independent source.*** The evidence was also discovered through lawful means that are separate and distinct from the unlawful seizure of the evidence.
- ***Inevitable discovery.*** The evidence eventually would have been lawfully discovered.
- ***Impeachment.*** Unlawfully seized items may be introduced on cross-examination to attack the defendant's credibility.

Entrapment provides an affirmative defense when the government has relied on tactics and strategies that are likely to induce an otherwise innocent individual to commit a crime. The development of the defense is traced to the U.S. Supreme Court's 1932 decision in *Sorrells v. United States*. The decision defines entrapment as the "conception and planning of an offense by an officer, and his procurement of its commission by one who would not have perpetrated it except for the trickery, persuasion, or fraud of the officer." The subjective and objective tests are the two major competing approaches to entrapment. Defendants also have argued that unfair and outrageous police strategies violate the Due Process Clause of the U.S. Constitution.

The subjective test for entrapment *focuses on the defendant* and asks whether the accused possessed the criminal intent or "predisposition" to commit the crime or whether the government "created" the crime.

The objective test for entrapment *focuses on the conduct of the government rather than on the character of the individual.*

The due process test for entrapment permits a defendant to rely on the entrapment defense in those instances in which the government's conduct is so unfair and outrageous that it violates the Due Process Clause of the Fifth and Fourteenth Amendments and therefore it would be unfair to convict the defendant.

The next chapter discusses other remedies that are available to defendants whose constitutional rights have been violated.

Chapter Review Questions

1. Trace the development of the exclusionary rule from *Weeks* to *Mapp* and *Calandra*.
2. Outline the arguments for and against the exclusionary rule. What alternative procedural mechanisms to the exclusionary rule have been proposed? Will these procedures deter police violations of the Fourth Amendment?
3. Outline the steps involved in filing a motion to suppress evidence.
4. Who has standing to file a motion to suppress?
5. List and discuss the exceptions to the exclusionary rule.
6. Why did the judiciary develop a good faith exception to the exclusionary rule?
7. What do the empirical data indicate in regard to whether the exclusionary rule deters the police from engaging in unreasonable searches and seizures? What about the data concerning the costs of the exclusionary rule?
8. Does the interest in judicial integrity justify the application of the exclusionary rule?
9. Define entrapment. What is the purpose of the entrapment defense?
10. Describe the objective, subjective, and due process tests for entrapment.
11. Outline the arguments for and against the entrapment defense.
12. Should there be an entrapment defense?

Legal Terminology

attenuated
collateral proceedings
derivative evidence
due process test for entrapment
entrapment
exclusionary rule
fruit of the poisonous tree
good faith exception
harmless error
impeachment
independent source doctrine
inevitable discovery rule
objective test for entrapment
purging the taint
silver platter doctrine
standing
subjective test for entrapment

Criminal Procedure on the Web

Log on to the Web-based student study site at **http://www.sagepub.com/lippmancp** to assist you in completing the Criminal Procedure on the Web exercises, as well as for additional features such as leading cases, podcasts, self-quizzes, and audio/video links.

1. Take a test on the Supreme Court opinion in *Mapp v. Ohio,* and review the arguments for and against the exclusionary rule.
2. Read a defense of the exclusionary rule by the Cato Institute, a conservative, libertarian organization.
3. The *Christian Science Monitor* offers a view on the use of confidential informants in investigating terrorism.
4. Consider the use of informants and allegations of entrapment in the prosecution of the conspiracy to bomb the subway stop at Herald Square in New York City and in the case of Derrick Shareef in Rockford, Illinois.

Bibliography

Thomas A. Davies, "A Hard Look at What We Know (and Still Need to Learn) About the 'Social Costs' of the Exclusionary Rule: The NIJ Study and Other Studies of 'Lost' Arrests," *American Bar Foundation Research Journal* 8 (Summer, 1983), pp. 611–690. A review and analysis of the empirical research on the exclusionary rule.

Joshua Dressler and Alan C. Michaels, *Understanding Criminal Procedure: Investigation,* vol. 1, 4th ed. (Newark, NJ: LexisNexis, 2006), pp. 365–409, 571–585. An accessible overview of the law and policy of the exclusionary rule and of entrapment.

Yale Kamisar, "*Mapp v. Ohio:* The First Shot Fired in the Warren Court's Criminal Procedure 'Revolution.'" In *Criminal Procedure Stories,* Carol S. Steiker, ed. (New York: Foundation Press, 2006), pp. 45–100. A history of *Mapp v. Ohio* and of legal developments following the decision.

Wayne R. LaFave, Jerald H. Israel, and Nancy J. King, *Criminal Procedure,* 4th ed. (St. Paul, MN: West Publishing, 2000), pp. 104–141, 298–310. A detailed legal discussion of the law of the exclusionary rule and entrapment.

Gary T. Marx, *Undercover: Police Surveillance in America* (Berkeley: University of California Press, 1988). A socio-historical study and commentary on the use of undercover police surveillance.

Peter Nardulli, "The Societal Cost of the Exclusionary Rule: An Empirical Assessment," *American Bar Foundation Research Journal* 8 (Summer, 1983), pp. 600–602. A large-scale empirical study of the impact of the exclusionary rule in nine counties that concludes that the exclusionary rule does not impede criminal prosecutions.

Dallin Oaks, "Studying the Exclusionary Rule in Search and Seizure," *University of Chicago Law Review* 37 (Summer, 1970), pp. 665–757. The definitive study arguing that the exclusionary rule frustrates the prosecution of defendants and interferes with the prevention and punishment of crime.

11 Civil and Criminal Remedies for Constitutional Violations

Is the police officer liable for employing excessive force?

Brosseau repeated her commands and hit the driver's side window several times with her handgun, which failed to deter Haugen. On the third or fourth try, the window shattered. Brosseau unsuccessfully attempted to grab the keys and struck Haugen on the head with the barrel and butt of her gun. Haugen, still undeterred, succeeded in starting the Jeep. As the Jeep started or shortly after it began to move, Brosseau jumped back and to the left. She fired one shot through the rear driver's side window at a forward angle, hitting Haugen in the back.

Core Concepts and Summary Statements

Introduction

A. The exclusionary rule does not provide individuals with an adequate remedy in every instance in which their constitutional rights have been violated. Individuals who claim to have been deprived of their constitutional rights also may file civil actions in state or federal court for damages.

B. Police officers may be criminally prosecuted before a state as well as before a federal court.

Civil Remedies

A. Individuals who claim that they have been deprived of their constitutional rights by the police or another public official may file a civil action and ask for damages as well as an injunction.

B. 42 U.S.C. § 1983 provides a remedy against state and local officials. A *Bivens* action may be filed against federal officials.

Section 1983 Legal Actions Against Local and State Law Enforcement Officials

A. The U.S. Supreme Court interpreted the "Ku Klux Klan Act" of 1871, 42 U.S.C. § 1983, to apply to police officers and other representatives of the State who deprive individuals of their constitutional rights.

B. A plaintiff must establish by a preponderance of the evidence three elements: (1) that the defendant acted under the color of state law and (2) violated an individual's constitutional rights and (3) that a constitutional right was "clearly established."

C. The Supreme Court has held that this test is not mandatory. A court may simply examine whether an individual acted under the color of state law and violated a constitutional right that is clearly established.

Color of State Law

A. An individual acts under the color of state law when he or she acts under the authority of state law. A wrongdoer is considered to act under the color of state law even when he or she goes beyond the limits of his or her lawful authority.

B. In determining whether off-duty police officers were acting under the color of state law, judges look at the totality of the circumstance and ask whether the off-duty police officer's acts were undertaken in furtherance of his or her responsibilities as a police officer or were undertaken as a private citizen.

Violation of Federal Constitutional and Statutory Rights

The second step in a § 1983 legal action is to establish that the defendant violated a right guaranteed by the U.S. Constitution or federal law.

Individual Liability Under § 1983

Liability under § 1983 may be imposed on the officer who is directly responsible for violating an individual's constitutional rights as well as on his or her commanding officer. A supervisor may be held liable where there is an "affirmative link" between the supervisor and the misconduct of police officers.

Absolute and Qualified Immunity

A. Judges, prosecutors, witnesses, jurors, and other individuals have absolute immunity for decisions in the courtroom and may not be sued under § 1983.

B. The police and other criminal justice professionals have qualified immunity. They may be sued and held civilly liable only for the violation of clearly established constitutional rights.

The Affirmative Duty to Protect

A. The police have no legal obligation to protect the public and are not civilly liable for failing to protect members of the public from crime. They are legally responsible only for harm to an individual over whom they have custody.

B. Courts have developed a "state-created danger" exception to the rule that a government official will not be held liable for a failure to intervene to protect the public. This arises where state action creates or exposes an individual to danger that he or she would not otherwise confront.

The Liability of Local Government Entities Under § 1983

A. States and state agencies cannot be sued under § 1983. The Eleventh Amendment to the U.S. Constitution provides for the sovereign immunity of states from prosecution.

B. This immunity does not extend to cities, towns, counties, and local governmental agencies. The Supreme Court in *Monnell v. Department of Social Services* interpreted the term individual in § 1983 to permit plaintiffs to sue local cities, counties, and agencies.

Injunctions

Section 1983 also allows for injunctions against a local government or government agency. A violation of an injunction is punishable by contempt, which may result in a fine or imprisonment.

Pattern and Practice of the Deprivation of Constitutional Rights

The federal Police Misconduct Statute, 42 U.S.C. § 14141, provides that it is unlawful for state or local law enforcement officers or law enforcement agencies to "engage in a pattern or practice of conduct" that deprives individuals of a constitutional right or of a right guaranteed by the laws of the United States. The U.S. Attorney General, when he or she has "reasonable cause" to believe that such a pattern of violations exists, may ask a court to direct a police department to correct the practice.

State Tort Remedies Against Law Enforcement Officers

State law enforcement officers may be sued in state court for torts. Towns, counties, and states under some circumstances may be held financially liable under state law.

Remedies for Constitutional Violations by Federal Law Enforcement Officers

In 1971, in *Bivens v. Six Unknown Named Agents,* the U.S. Supreme Court held that federal law enforcement officers are responsible for violating individuals' Fourth Amendment rights. Federal officers have been held legally liable under *Bivens* actions for violations of other constitutional rights, including the Fifth Amendment right against self-incrimination and the Eighth Amendment right against cruel and unusual punishment.

Criminal Prosecutions

A. State and local police officers who commit common crimes may be prosecuted in state court.

B. Criminal charges also may be brought by the Department of Justice against state and federal criminal justice officials for the violation of U.S. statutes, including laws protecting individuals' constitutional rights. In terms of federal constitutional rights, prosecutions typically are based on an 1866 civil rights law, 18 U.S.C. § 242, that authorizes the prosecution of state or federal officials who act under the "color" of a local or state law or custom with the specific intent of depriving an individual of a constitutional right or of a right protected under federal law.

Administrative Remedies

A. There are two major approaches to enforcing police department internal regulations. Internal affairs divisions of the police department investigate misconduct. The punishment for violations of police regulations typically is imposed by an officer's commanding officer with the agreement of the chief of police.

B. Civilian review boards and agencies are composed of private citizens with authority to investigate and, in some instances, to discipline the police.

Internal Affairs

The internal affairs division of the police department is charged with investigating misconduct by police department employees.

External Review

Civilian review boards and agencies typically are appointed by the mayor or city council and, in most cases, are composed of a cross-section of the community. The boards typically apply a preponderance-of-the-evidence standard requiring that the weight of credible evidence establish that the officer engaged in misconduct. Civilian boards have different powers in various cities.

Introduction

We have seen that the exclusionary rule is intended to deter police violations of the Fourth Amendment. The violation of other constitutional amendments also may result in the exclusion of unlawfully obtained evidence from trial. A central criticism of the exclusionary rule is that the exclusion of evidence from trial punishes the prosecutor who litigates the case rather than the police officer responsible for the constitutional violation. The educational impact of the exclusionary rule on the police at times is diminished by the fact that the admissibility of evidence seized by the police may be definitively decided only on appeal long after the police conducted the search. Defense attorneys also complain that the exceptions to the exclusionary rule have considerably limited the circumstances in which the exclusionary rule is applied (*Bivens v. Six Unknown Named Agents,* 403 U.S. 388, 416–418 [1971]).

The exclusionary rule has the additional limitation of not providing a remedy for every constitutional violation. For example, a defendant who is unlawfully arrested and searched and whose case is not brought to trial will not be able to rely on the exclusionary rule to deter future police misconduct. Defendants who plea-bargain and plead guilty also will not be able to bring the alleged misconduct of the police to the attention of a court. Defendants fortunately are able to rely on remedies other than the exclusionary rule.

There are three categories of additional remedies available to deter police violation of constitutional rights. The focus of these remedies is on the legal responsibility and guilt of the police officers alleged to have engaged in the unlawful conduct rather than on the exclusion of evidence from a criminal trial.

- ***Civil remedies.*** Legal actions may be filed against individual officers, their supervisors, and local governments for money damages. Injunctions and "pattern-or-practice" suits may be filed asking a court to order that the police stop enforcing a policy that violates individuals' constitutional rights.
- ***Criminal remedies.*** State and federal police officers may be criminally prosecuted and punished.
- ***Administrative remedies.*** Police officers may be subjected to internal administrative procedures for violating departmental regulations. Officers who are found guilty may be subjected to discipline ranging from fines and suspensions to termination.

A police officer may be subject to one or all of these remedies. An officer may be named as a defendant in a civil suit seeking money damages and as a defendant in a criminal prosecution and also may be required to appear before an administrative hearing to determine whether internal disciplinary punishment should be imposed. This is not "double jeopardy," because the rule against two prosecutions for the same offense applies only to criminal proceedings. Another important point is that an individual may be criminally prosecuted before a state as well as before a federal court. This is the so-called **dual sovereignty doctrine.** The state and federal governments are separate entities, and each has an interest in punishing the criminal offense.

A well-known example of the application of these various remedies is the Rodney King incident in Los Angeles. Three police officers were exonerated on state charges of assault with a deadly weapon and excessive force by a Los Angeles jury. Two of the officers then were convicted in a federal criminal proceeding of violating King's civil rights. King later won a $3.8 million verdict against the City of Los Angeles.

In this chapter, we primarily focus on the liability of the police and law enforcement officials. We will first examine civil remedies against state and federal officials, then briefly discuss criminal prosecutions, and conclude the chapter with administrative procedures. A number of influential legal commentators argue that we should rely on these remedies rather than on the exclusionary rule to deter police misconduct. As you read the chapter, consider whether the remedies discussed are effective in protecting individual rights. Keep the following chapter outline in mind as you read through the text, and be certain that you understand each of these topics.

- Federal civil law remedies against state and local police under Section 1983
- Pattern-or-practice decrees
- State civil law remedies against state and local police (tort suits)
- Federal civil remedies against federal law enforcement agents
- Criminal prosecutions
- State prosecutions
- Federal prosecutions
- Administrative remedies
- Internal affairs divisions
- External review

Civil Remedies

Individuals who have been harmed by another person may file a civil suit for money damages. This type of *tort* action, unlike a criminal case, primarily is intended to compensate the victim rather than to punish the "tortfeasor."

The police or other public officials may be sued for damages by individuals who believe that they have been deprived of their constitutional rights. The judge or jury in these damage actions may award *compensatory damages,* or money that pays for the actual expenses and harm suffered by the plaintiff. In exceptional cases of extreme and intentional abuse, *punitive damages*, or money to deter other police officers or public officials from committing similar constitutional violations, also may be awarded.

The primary goal of this chapter is to acquaint you with the requirements for suing local, state, and federal officers and police departments. We will devote most of the chapter to two types of constitutional tort actions.

State officers. State law enforcement officers who violate federal constitutional rights or a right under federal law may be sued in a state or federal court under **Title 42, Section 1983 of the U.S. Code,** along with a town, city, or county. Plaintiffs also may seek injunctive relief to halt an unconstitutional practice by the police.

Federal officers. Federal law enforcement officers who violate constitutional rights may be sued in federal courts in a ***Bivens* legal suit.**

Two other civil remedies are available. Police officers may be sued under state law for committing a tort (civil wrong) against an individual. These legal actions typically claim damages for torts such as assault and battery, false arrest and imprisonment, and the intentional infliction of emotional distress. The U.S. Department of Justice also may seek a court order prohibiting a local police agency from engaging in a pattern or practice of conduct that deprives persons of constitutional rights.

In this chapter, we will first look at federal civil remedies and state civil remedies against state officials and then turn our attention to federal civil remedies against federal officials. We then will briefly discuss criminal prosecutions and administrative disciplinary procedures.

Section 1983 Legal Actions Against Local and State Law Enforcement Officers

The Civil Rights Act of 1871 was adopted by Congress following the Civil War to enable former African American slaves and Union sympathizers living in the South to seek damages against members of the "white supremacist" Ku Klux Klan, who were working for local governments that deprived African Americans of their federal constitutional rights. The statute was rarely invoked in the almost one hundred years that it was on the books. In 1961, in *Monroe v. Pape,* the U.S. Supreme Court considered whether the "Ku Klux Act" protected Monroe, an African American whose home had been unlawfully entered by thirteen Chicago police officers. The officers, although lacking a warrant, required Monroe, his wife, and their six children to stand naked as the officers ransacked the house, emptied drawers, and ripped mattresses. Monroe was taken to the police station, interrogated for ten hours in regard to a two-day-old murder, and was not permitted to call his family, friends, or an attorney and was not brought before a judge. He subsequently was released without being formally charged. Monroe sued the officers under the Ku Klux Klan Act (42 U.S.C. § 1983) for violating his Fourth Amendment rights. Section 1983 reads as follows:

> Every person who, under color of any statute, ordinance, regulation, custom or usage of any State or Territory, subjects or causes to be subjected any citizen of the United States or other person within the jurisdiction thereof to the deprivation of any rights, privileges, or immunities secured by the Constitution and laws, shall be liable to the party injured....

The U.S. Supreme Court breathed new life into the Ku Klux Klan Act by holding that § 1983 applied to police officers and other representatives of the government who abused their official authority by depriving individuals of their constitutional rights (*Monroe v. Pape,* 365 U.S. 167 [1961]). The judgment in *Monroe v. Pape* opened the door to individuals suing state officials for damages in federal or in state court. Individuals were free to file a civil rights action in federal court without first going through the state court system. Plaintiffs also were assisted by the Attorneys Fee Act of 1976, which authorizes courts to award attorneys' fees as well as damages to individuals who succeed in winning § 1983 legal actions (42 U.S.C. § 1988[b]).

There are three elements to a § 1983 legal action that a plaintiff must establish by a preponderance of the evidence. In the next sections, we will look at each of these elements.

- ***Color of law.*** The defendant must have acted under the "color of state law."
- ***Constitutional rights.*** The defendant's act must have violated a plaintiff's constitutional rights or a right provided by a federal law.
- ***Immunity.*** A police officer possesses qualified immunity and is liable only when he or she violates a "well-established constitutional right." Judges, prosecutors, witnesses, and jurors are entitled to absolute immunity for acts at trial.

Color of State Law

An individual acts under the **color of state law** when he or she acts under the authority of state law. A defendant is considered to act under the color of state law even when he or she goes beyond the limits of lawful authority. The U.S. Supreme Court has explained that color of law requires that the defendant exercise power that he or she "possessed by virtue of state law and made possible only because the wrongdoer is clothed with the authority of state law" (*West v. Atkins,* 487 U.S. 42, 48 [1988]). For example, a police officer may illegally stop an individual based on his or her authority and then conduct an unlawful search or interrogation. These unlawful acts were made possible by the fact that the officer acted under the color of state law (*United States v. Classic,* 313 U.S. 299 [1941]).

In most instances, there is little question that officers who are sued under § 1983 are carrying out their professional responsibilities and are acting under the color of state law. This determination, however, in some cases may prove somewhat more complicated. What about an off-duty police officer who gets involved in a fight in a bar or an off-duty police officer who "moonlights" as a security guard? Are they acting under the color of state law? In determining whether an off-duty police officer has acted under the color of state law, courts look at the totality of the circumstances and ask whether the individual's acts were undertaken in furtherance of his or her responsibilities as a police officer or were undertaken as a private citizen. Some judges, in asking whether a defendant acted under the color of state law, look to see whether an off-duty officer used police-issued firearms, equipment, and squad cars and identified himself or herself as a police officer. Another consideration is whether police regulations require officers to enforce the law against wrongdoers even when off-duty. Consider the following examples.

Private activity. The Ninth Circuit Court of Appeals held that an off-duty officer who killed an individual in a bar fight did not act under color of state law. The officer did not identify himself as a sheriff's deputy or make an effort to arrest the victim and used his own weapon, although loaded with ammunition from the police department (*Huffman v. County of Los Angeles,* 147 F.3d 1054 [9th Cir. 1998]). In another case, the defendant failed to identify himself as a police officer in a fight in a restaurant, and the Sixth Circuit Court of Appeals stressed that the defendant had driven to the restaurant in his own automobile (*Neuens v. City of Columbus,* 303 F.3d 667 (6th Cir. 2002). An off-duty officer who used a police-issued firearm to kill his wife and to commit suicide was not held to have acted in his professional capacity and was not considered to have acted under color of state law (*Bonsignore v. City of New York,* 683 F.2d 635 [2d Cir. 1982]).

Security guard. An off-duty police officer working as a security guard at a mall was considered to be acting under the color of law when she shot a shoplifter with a weapon issued by the police department while wearing her police uniform and attempted to arrest the perpetrator (*Abraham. v. Raso,* 183 F.3d 279 [3d Cir. 1999]). A police officer serving as a bank teller as part of a police department hiring program approached a customer who was causing a commotion, flashed his police identification, and displayed his firearm and was determined to have acted under color of state law. The appellate court noted that the officer considered that his primary responsibility while working in the bank was to the police department rather than to the bank (*Traver v. Meshriy,* 627 F.2d 934 [9th Cir. 1979]). A deputy sheriff who while acting as a security guard at an amusement park wore his badge, identified himself as a police officer, and arrested the plaintiff for trespassing was held to have acted under the color of state law (*Griffin v. Maryland,* 378 U.S. 130 [1964]).

Police function. An off-duty police officer was determined to have acted under color of law when he physically grabbed one of three men who were causing a disturbance in a restaurant and, during the ensuing struggle, shot and killed two of the individuals and severely injured the third. The officer used police-issued mace and a firearm. Police regulations required him to carry the firearm at all times and to intervene to arrest individuals involved in criminal activity "twenty-four hours a day" (*Stengal v. Belcher,* 522 F.2d 438 [6th Cir. 1975]).

We next turn our attention to the constitutional and federal rights protected under § 1983.

Violation of Federal Constitutional and Statutory Rights

The second step for a plaintiff is establishing that the defendant violated a right guaranteed by the U.S. Constitution or federal law. The violation of a right guaranteed by a state constitution but not guaranteed by the U.S. Constitution may not be the subject of a legal suit under § 1983.

A § 1983 action, for example, may be based on an alleged violation of the Fourth Amendment. This might involve a claim that the police carried out an unlawful arrest or unconstitutional search and seizure or used unreasonable force in detaining a suspect. Civil rights actions also may allege that the police coerced a plaintiff to confess in violation of the Fifth Amendment or a claim that a confession was obtained in violation of a plaintiff's Sixth Amendment right to counsel. A § 1983 action for "wrongful death" also may be filed by a family that claims that the police use of deadly force violated the right to life of a deceased family member. Prisoners have relied on § 1983 in claims that they have been subjected to conditions constituting cruel and unusual punishment in violation of the Eighth Amendment. The following are examples of some § 1983 cases filed against police officers in recent years.

Excessive force. A police officer fired a rubber projectile at the head of an individual who was threatening to kill himself with a knife, causing serious brain injury, and was alleged to have unreasonably seized the victim. See *Mercado v. City of Orlando,* 407 F.3d 11152 (11th Cir. 2005).

Search and seizure. An individual arrested for a misdemeanor narcotics charge was subjected to a strip search and visual cavity search during the booking process and alleged that the jail's blanket strip search policy violated the Fourth Amendment prohibition on unreasonable searches and seizures. See *Way v. County of Ventura,* 445 F.3d 808 (9th Cir. 2006).

Fabrication of evidence. The plaintiff was sentenced to death and later exonerated when his DNA did not match the DNA at the crime scene. The police report allegedly misrepresented that the plaintiff had revealed information that was not known to the general public. See *Washington v. Wilmore,* 407 F.3d 274 (4th Cir. 2005).

False arrest and malicious prosecution. District of Columbia police officers Adams and Baxter filed an arrest report and submitted an affidavit to prosecutors that omitted important facts. The affidavit signed by Officer Adams, which was based on Officer Baxter's arrest report, did not mention that the two robbery victims, when confronted with the defendant, stated that he was not the individual who had carried out the theft. The affidavit also alleged that the police observed the defendant getting into his automobile "within seconds" after a building employee saw the robber leave the building. However, between eight and ten minutes had passed when the police spotted the defendant getting into his automobile. See *Pitt v. District of Columbia,* 491 F.3d 494 (D.C. Ct. App. 2007).

A police officer who is sued under § 1983 may offer the defense that even accepting all of the defendant's allegations as true, the officer did not violate the plaintiff's constitutional rights. In the event that the judge agrees, the case will be dismissed before trial. A good example is *Chavez v. Martinez.* Martinez was left partially blinded and paralyzed following a gun battle with the police. Officer Chavez accompanied Martinez to the hospital, interrogated him, and obtained a confession while Martinez was receiving medical treatment. Martinez claimed that his right against self-incrimination had been violated and brought a § 1983 suit against Chavez. The U.S. Supreme Court noted that Martinez had never been criminally charged and therefore held that Martinez's statements had not been used in evidence against him at a criminal trial. As a result, Martinez's Fifth Amendment right not to be "compelled to be a witness" against himself had not been violated by Officer Martinez (*Chavez v. Martinez,* 538 U.S. 760 [2003]).

Town of Castle Rock v. Gonzales is another recent example of a case in which the U.S. Supreme Court failed to find a constitutional violation. In *Town of Castle Rock,* Gonzales's husband defied a court-ordered restraining order that prohibited him from approaching his wife and daughters and abducted and murdered the couple's three young daughters. Gonzales claimed that the failure of the police to respond to her pleas for assistance reflected the police department's "official policy or custom" of refusing to respond to violations of restraining orders and nonenforcement of restraining orders. The Supreme Court held that Gonzales had not suffered a deprivation of her constitutional rights. The Court reasoned that Gonzales did not have a due process right to require the police to enforce the restraining order against her husband and that recognition of an obligation on the police to enforce the restraining order would be contrary to the discretion inherent in law enforcement (*Town of Castle Rock v. Gonzales,* 545 U.S. 748 [2005]).

In the next section, we discuss the circumstances under which a police officer and other police and public officials may be held liable under § 1983.

You can read Town of Castle Rock v. Gonzales *on the study site, http://www.sagepub.com/lippmancp.*

Individual Liability Under Section 1983

Liability under § 1983 may be imposed on a police officer who is directly responsible for violating an individual's constitutional rights as well as on his or her commanding officer and, in some cases, city officials. In *Rizzo v. Goode,* the plaintiffs sued the mayor of Philadelphia as well as the City's managing director and two supervising police officers for a persistent pattern of police abuse. The U.S. Supreme Court stated that standard for supervisory liability is proof of an "affirmative link" between the actions or orders of the supervisors and the allegations of police misconduct (*Rizzo v. Goode,* 423 U.S. 362 [1976]).

The required affirmative link was found in *Shaw v. Stroud* where Sergeant Stroud possessed "direct responsibility" for supervising Officer Morris and was determined by the Fourth Circuit Court of Appeals to have been aware of Morris's "frequent use of excessive force." Stroud failed to investigate or to take action to prevent recurrence of this "constant and dangerous threat to the welfare of arrestees," and as a consequence, the appellate court concluded that Morris's shooting and killing of a suspect in the course of executing an arrest was a "natural and foreseeable consequence of Stroud's failure to investigate" (*Shaw v. Stroud,* 13 F.3d 791, 800 [4th Cir. 1994]).

In *Holland v. Harrington,* a sheriff and two of his deputies employed a heavily armed SWAT team to arrest a suspect in his home who was wanted for misdemeanor assault and reckless endangerment. The court determined that there was an "affirmative link" between the sheriff and his deputies and the acts of their subordinate officers. The appellate court, however, refused to hold the defendants liable for employing excessive force on the grounds that it could not be said that the supervisors "lacked any plausible basis for believing that 'dynamic entry' was warranted in this situation" (*Holland v. Harrington,* 268 F.3d 1179, 1181, 1191 [10th Cir. 2001]).

The next sections discuss the defenses of absolute and qualified immunity that may be raised by criminal justice professionals who are sued under § 1983.

Absolute and Qualified Immunity

The U.S. Supreme Court stressed in *Harlow v. Fitzgerald* that § 1983 suits are intended to compensate individuals who have been harmed by a violation of their federal constitutional rights and rights under federal statutes. On the other hand, the Court also recognized that § 1983 suits impose a burden on government officials, some of whom may prove to be completely innocent. Litigation involves considerable financial expenditures, diverts officials from their jobs, deters individuals from public service, and inhibits officials from aggressively enforcing the law (*Harlow v. Fitzgerald,* 457 U.S. 800, 814 [1982]).

The U.S. Supreme Court has attempted to strike a balance between the costs and the benefits of § 1983 suits and has held that judges, prosecutors, witnesses, and jurors enjoy **absolute immunity** from suit. This immunity helps to insure that the judicial process functions efficiently and smoothly because individuals are completely protected against a § 1983 suit for acts undertaken during the judicial process. Other public officials are provided with **qualified immunity** and are subject to legal actions when they violate clearly established legal rules. The absolute and qualified immunities are summarized below.

Absolute immunity. Judges, prosecutors, witnesses, jurors, and other individuals involved in the trial process are provided with complete immunity from § 1983 civil suits for statements and actions during the judicial process. The explanation is that during a trial, individuals are asked to make difficult choices and should not be in fear of being sued. In *Pierson v. Ray,* the U.S. Supreme Court held that a judge who unconstitutionally convicted a group of African American civil rights activists was immune from a § 1983 suit. The Court reasoned that judges should not be placed in the position of being fearful that a controversial decision to convict or to severely sentence a defendant will lead to the judge's being sued. Defendants who are unhappy with a decision always have the option of appealing a judge's decision (*Pierson v. Ray,* 386 U.S. 547 [1967]).

Police officers, prison officials, correctional officers, probation officers, and other criminal justice practitioners are provided with qualified immunity.

Qualified immunity. Individuals with qualified immunity are liable under § 1983 for the violation of a "clearly established right." The test for the police is whether an objectively reasonable officer would be aware that his or her conduct is unlawful. This insures that police officers will be held liable only when the officer knows or should have known that he or she is violating the law. In those instances in which the law is uncertain, individuals with qualified immunity are immune from prosecution for violating an individual's constitutional rights because the government official was unable to look to clear legal principles to guide his or her conduct. Qualified immunity recognizes that the police and other criminal justice professionals work under enormous pressures and that the line between unlawful and lawful conduct often is unclear. Qualified immunity allows the police to enforce the law without fear that they will be held legally liable. The first step is to ask whether these individuals violated the plaintiff's constitutional rights. The second step is to ask whether the right was clearly established. The third step is that an officer is legally responsible only for violating a clearly established constitutional or federal right.

Couden v. Duffy illustrates a federal court of appeals application of qualified immunity in evaluating the actions of police officers. Members of the Delaware Joint Violent Crime Fugitive Task Force established surveillance on a house based on a tip that a fugitive wanted for drug and weapons-related charges might be at the address. At roughly 8:30 P.M., Pamelia Couden, along with her five children, drove up to a house two doors from the home that was under surveillance. She kept the engine running as fourteen-year-old Adam put his skateboard in the garage and went inside to tell his sister Tiffany that the family was going out to dinner. Couden turned on her "brights" and honked the horn to hurry Adam along.

Plainclothes officer Armstrong approached the car with his gun removed from his holster without identifying himself and attempted to open the front door to the car. As Couden began to drive away, a second officer, Freebery, shattered the front window with a flashlight. Three officers entered the house, arrested Adam, and "threw him on the floor, pushed his head down, pointed guns at him and sprayed him with mace." They asked for Adam's driver's license, and he told them that he was too young to drive. The officers left him on the floor and returned twenty minutes later to remove the handcuffs. Judge Fuentes, in his opinion, held that the officers employed unnecessary and excessive force against Adam. The judge stressed that there was no indication that Adam resisted arrest or attempted to flee and that there was no reason to believe that he was armed. The Fourth Amendment standard for excessive force was clearly established, and a reasonable officer would not have believed under the circumstances that the level of force used against Adam Couden was lawful. In his dissenting opinion, Judge Weiss noted that the police did not have the luxury of "20/20 hindsight" and may have reasonably believed that the 200-pound, six-foot-tall Adam was an armed burglar or fugitive (*Couden v. Duffy,* 446 F.3d 583 [3d Cir. 2005]).

In 2009, in *Pearson v. Callahan,* Supreme Court Justice Samuel Alito held that courts possess the discretion to first determine whether the constitutional right that a plaintiff alleges was violated by government officials was clearly established before determining whether the police violated the plaintiff's constitutional rights. In a lengthy and complicated judgment, Justice Alito pointed out that where a court finds that the police did not disregard a clearly established constitutional right, there is no necessity for the court to undertake a time-consuming and detailed analysis of whether the police violated an individual's constitutional rights. Alito disposed of Callahan's § 1983 action against the police by noting that in conducting a warrantless search, the police had reasonably relied on the decisions of various appellate courts that had held that the police are authorized to conduct a warrantless search and seizure based on the fact that an occupant had consented for an undercover informant to enter a home ("consent-once-removed" doctrine). Justice Alito concluded that "[b]ecause the unlawfulness of the officers' conduct...was not clearly established, petitioners are entitled to qualified immunity" (*Pearson v. Callahan,* 555 U.S. ___ [2009]).

The next case in the textbook is *Brosseau v. Haugen.* Officer Rochelle Brosseau, a member of the Puyallup, Washington, Police Department, shot Kenneth Haugen as he attempted to flee in his vehicle. Brosseau later explained that she feared that Haugen posed a threat to other officers as well as to individuals in the area. The U.S. Supreme Court did not question the appellate court's determination that Brosseau violated Haugen's Fourth Amendment rights by employing excessive force. The question before the Supreme Court was whether Brosseau was entitled to qualified immunity. In other words, is the legal standard governing the employment of deadly force under these circumstances well established? Pay particular attention to the evidence that the majority of the Court relies on in reaching its decision (*Brosseau v. Haugen,* 543 U.S. 194 [2004]).

You can find Pearson v. Callahan *on the study site, http://www.sagepub.com/lippmancp.*

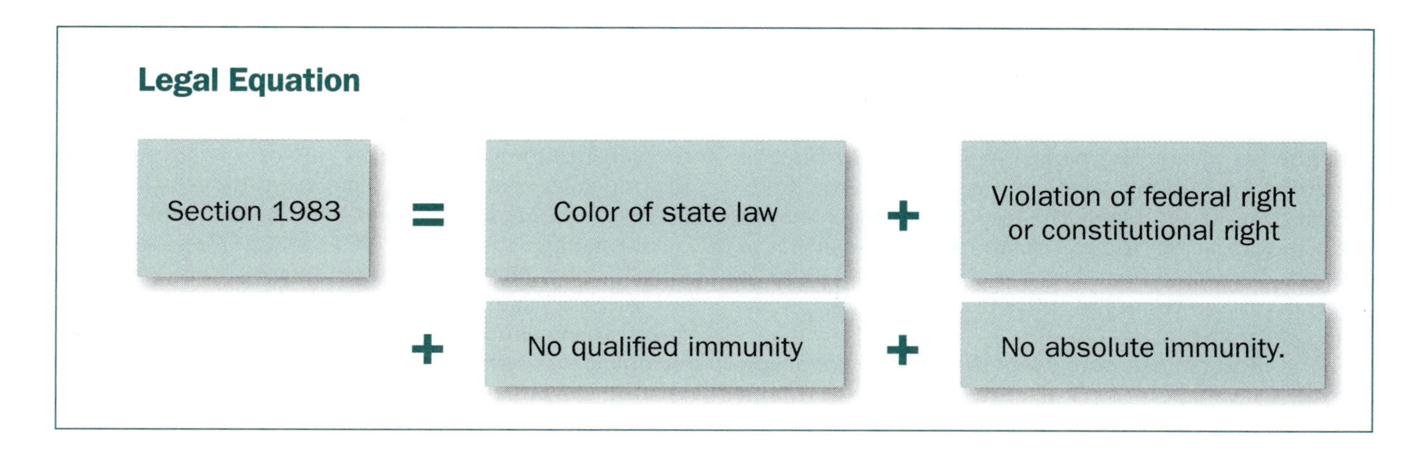

Is Officer Brosseau entitled to qualified immunity for the use of excessive force?

Brosseau v. Haugen, 543 U.S. 194 (2004), Per curiam

Issue

Officer Rochelle Brosseau, a member of the Puyallup, Washington, Police Department, shot Kenneth Haugen in the back as he attempted to flee from law enforcement authorities in his vehicle. Haugen subsequently filed this action in the United States District Court for the Western District of Washington pursuant to 42 U.S.C. § 1983. He alleged that the shot fired by Brosseau constituted excessive force and violated his federal constitutional rights. The district court granted . . . judgment to Brosseau after finding she was entitled to qualified immunity. The Court of Appeals for the Ninth Circuit reversed.

Facts

The material facts, construed in a light most favorable to Haugen, are as follows. On the day before the fracas, Glen Tamburello went to the police station and reported to Brosseau that Haugen, a former crime partner of his, had stolen tools from his shop. Brosseau later learned that there was a felony no-bail warrant out for Haugen's arrest on drug and other offenses. The next morning, Haugen was spray-painting his Jeep Cherokee in his mother's driveway. Tamburello learned of Haugen's whereabouts, and he and cohort Matt Atwood drove a pickup truck to Haugen's mother's house to pay Haugen a visit. A fight ensued, which was witnessed by a neighbor who called 911.

Brosseau heard a report that the men were fighting in Haugen's mother's yard and responded. When she arrived, Tamburello and Atwood were attempting to get Haugen into Tamburello's pickup. Brosseau's arrival created a distraction, which provided Haugen the opportunity to get away. Haugen ran through his mother's yard and hid in the neighborhood. Brosseau requested assistance, and shortly thereafter, two officers arrived with a K–9 to help track Haugen down. During the search, which lasted about thirty to forty-five minutes, officers instructed Tamburello and Atwood to remain in Tamburello's pickup. They instructed Deanna Nocera, Haugen's girlfriend who was also present with her three-year-old daughter, to remain in her small car with her daughter. Tamburello's pickup was parked in the street in front of the driveway; Nocera's small car was parked in the driveway in front of and facing the Jeep; and the Jeep was in the driveway facing Nocera's car and angled somewhat to the left. The Jeep was parked about four feet away from Nocera's car and twenty to thirty feet away from Tamburello's pickup.

An officer radioed from down the street that a neighbor had seen a man in her backyard. Brosseau ran in that direction, and Haugen appeared. He ran past the front of his mother's house and then turned and ran into the driveway. With Brosseau still in pursuit, he jumped into the driver's side of the Jeep and closed and locked the door. Brosseau believed that he was running to the Jeep to retrieve a weapon.

Brosseau arrived at the Jeep, pointed her gun at Haugen, and ordered him to get out of the vehicle. Haugen ignored her command and continued to look for the keys so he could get the Jeep started. Brosseau repeated her commands and hit the driver's side window several times with her handgun, which failed to deter Haugen. On the third or fourth try, the window shattered. Brosseau unsuccessfully attempted to grab the keys and struck Haugen on the head with the barrel and butt of her gun. Haugen, still undeterred, succeeded in starting the Jeep. As the Jeep started or shortly after it began to move, Brosseau jumped back and to the left. She fired one shot through the rear driver's side window at a forward angle, hitting Haugen in the back. She later explained that she shot Haugen because she was "'fearful for the other officers on foot who [she] believed were in the immediate area, [and] for the occupied vehicles in [Haugen's] path and for any other citizens who might be in the area.'"

Despite being hit, Haugen, in his words, "'st[ood] on the gas'"; navigated the "'small, tight space'" to avoid the other vehicles; swerved across the neighbor's lawn; and continued down the street. After about a half block, Haugen realized that he had been shot and brought the Jeep to a halt. He suffered a collapsed lung and was airlifted to a hospital. He survived the shooting and subsequently pleaded guilty to the felony of "eluding." By so pleading, he admitted that he drove his Jeep in a manner indicating "a wanton or willful disregard for the lives . . . of others." He subsequently brought this § 1983 action against Brosseau.

Reasoning

When confronted with a claim of qualified immunity, a court must ask first the following question: "Taken in the light most favorable to the party asserting the injury, do the facts alleged show the officer's conduct violated a constitutional right?" As the court of appeals recognized, the constitutional question in this case is governed by the principles enunciated in *Tennessee v. Garner,* 471 U.S. 1 (1985), and *Graham v. Connor,* 490 U.S. 386 (1989). These cases establish that claims of excessive force are to be judged under the Fourth Amendment's "'objective reasonableness'" standard. Specifically with regard to deadly force, we explained in *Garner* that it is unreasonable for an officer to "seize an unarmed, nondangerous suspect by shooting him dead." But "[w]here the officer has probable cause to believe that the suspect poses a threat of serious physical harm, either to the officer or to others, it is not constitutionally unreasonable to prevent escape by using deadly force."

We express no view as to the correctness of the court of appeals' decision on the constitutional question itself. We believe that, however that question is decided, the court of appeals was wrong on the issue of qualified immunity.

Qualified immunity shields an officer from suit when she makes a decision that, even if constitutionally deficient, reasonably misapprehends the law governing the circumstances she confronted. Because the focus is on whether the officer had fair notice that her conduct was unlawful, reasonableness is judged against the backdrop of the law at the time of the conduct. If the law at that time did not clearly establish that the officer's conduct would violate the Constitution, the officer should not be subject to liability or, indeed, even the burdens of litigation.

It is important to emphasize that this inquiry "must be undertaken in light of the specific context of the case, not as a broad general proposition." As we previously said, "[T]here is no doubt that...that use of force is contrary to the Fourth Amendment if it is excessive under objective standards of reasonableness. Yet that is not enough. Rather...the right the official is alleged to have violated must have been clearly established in a more particularized...sense. The contours of the right must be sufficiently clear that a reasonable official would understand that what he is doing violates that right." The relevant, dispositive inquiry in determining whether a right is clearly established is whether it would be clear to a reasonable officer that his conduct was unlawful in the situation he confronted.

The court of appeals acknowledged this statement of law but then proceeded to find fair warning in the general tests set out in *Graham* and *Garner.* In so doing, it was mistaken. *Graham* and *Garner,* following the lead of the Fourth Amendment's text, are cast at a high level of generality. Of course, in an obvious case, these standards can "clearly establish" the answer, even without a body of relevant case law. The present case is far from the obvious one where *Graham* and *Garner* alone offer a basis for decision.

We therefore turn to ask whether, at the time of Brosseau's actions, it was "clearly established" in this more "particularized" sense that she was violating Haugen's Fourth Amendment right. The parties point us to only a handful of cases relevant to the "situation [Brosseau] confronted": whether to shoot a disturbed felon, set on avoiding capture through vehicular flight, when persons in the immediate area are at risk from that flight. Specifically, Brosseau points us to *Cole v. Bone,* 993 F.2d 1328 (CA8 1993), and *Smith v. Freland,* 954 F.2d 343 (CA6 1992).

In these cases, the courts found no Fourth Amendment violation when an officer shot a fleeing suspect who presented a risk to others. *Cole v. Bone* (holding the officer "had probable cause to believe that the truck posed an imminent threat of serious physical harm to innocent motorists as well as to the officers themselves"); *Smith v. Freland* (noting "a car can be a deadly weapon" and holding the officer's decision to stop the car from possibly injuring others was reasonable). *Smith* is closer to this case. There, the officer and suspect engaged in a car chase, which appeared to be at an end when the officer cornered the suspect at the back of a dead-end residential street. The suspect, however, freed his car and began speeding down the street. At this point, the officer fired a shot, which killed the suspect. The court held the officer's decision was reasonable and thus did not violate the Fourth Amendment. It noted that the suspect, like Haugen here, "had proven he would do almost anything to avoid capture" and that he posed a major threat to, among others, the officers at the end of the street.

Haugen points us to *Estate of Starks v. Enyart,* 5 F.3d 230 (CA7 1993)...involving a fleeing suspect. There, the court concluded that the threat created by the fleeing suspect's failure to brake when an officer suddenly stepped in front of his just-started car was not a sufficiently grave threat to justify the use of deadly force.

These three cases taken together undoubtedly show that this area is one in which the result depends very much on the facts of each case. None of them squarely governs the case here; they do suggest that Brosseau's actions fell in the "'hazy border between excessive and acceptable force.'" The cases by no means "clearly establish" that Brosseau's conduct violated the Fourth Amendment.

The judgment of the United States Court of Appeals for the Ninth Circuit is therefore reversed, and the case is remanded for further proceedings consistent with this opinion.

Questions for Discussion

1. Summarize the facts in *Brosseau v. Haugen.*
2. Why did the Supreme Court hold that Brosseau violated Haugen's constitutional rights?
3. Discuss the reasons why the Supreme Court concluded that the law was "hazy" in regard to whether Officer Brosseau lawfully employed deadly force under the circumstances. Should the police be expected to keep informed of the judicial decisions of federal courts of appeals?
4. The Supreme Court suggests that Brosseau might have reasonably believed that she was legally authorized to employ deadly force to prevent Haugen's flight on the grounds that Haugen posed a threat to the public. Was it reasonable to believe that Haugen posed a threat to other officers or to the public?

Criminal Procedure in the News

We all have found ourselves absorbed by high-speed police vehicle pursuits broadcast on the television news or on "reality TV" programs. These exciting chases typically end with the apprehension of the suspect. We rarely witness what critics contend are the dangers of pursuits. Consider the following.

Seventeen percent of pursuits are intended to apprehend an individual suspected of committing a serious felony. In most cases, motorists who defy the police have committed misdemeanors and flee because they do not have a current driver's license or car registration, are drunk, or possess narcotics.

Roughly forty percent of automobile pursuits result in a crash, twenty percent in physical injury, and one percent in death.

Over 300 individuals die in these crashes each year. Two-thirds of the (non–law enforcement) victims are suspects or passengers, and one-third are innocent motorists or bystanders. Approximately one percent of all police officers killed in the line of duty die as a result of a high-speed pursuit. An officer dies in a high-speed chase every eleven weeks.

We lack an accurate system of recording the number of police pursuits. The National Highway Traffic Administration has a voluntary state Fatality Analysis Reporting System (FARS). Individuals who study pursuits speculate that the number of pursuits may be two or three times greater than the figures reported by FARS.

A number of major urban police departments have limited pursuits to dangerous felonies. These departments have concluded that apprehending individuals suspected of less severe offenses is not worth the possible loss of life. The general standard adopted by these departments is that a pursuit is to be authorized only in those instances in which the benefit to be gained from the pursuit clearly outweighs the threat of injury or death to the police or to the public. This has drastically cut down on the number of pursuits and has significantly reduced the resulting injuries and fatalities. There also is an effort to further limit pursuits by developing technological devices that are able to disable vehicles and to improve the technological capacity to track the movements of vehicles through aerial and electronic surveillance.

Most departments continue to provide police officers with the discretion to initiate a high-speed pursuit. This unlimited pursuit policy appears to have the support of most police officers who understandably find it difficult to accept that they must watch a suspected criminal flee without responding. The police persuasively argue that an individual suspected of a misdemeanor who flees may pose the same threat on the road as an individual who is suspected of a felony. Once having apprehended these misdemeanants, the police may find that they are engaged in serious criminal activity ranging from hostage taking to drug possession. Police officers also point out that individuals who know that they can escape apprehension will be tempted to flee. This will increase rather than decrease the number of individuals who flee at high speeds. Defenders of police pursuits argue that fatalities can be reduced by additional training and that the blame for injuries and fatalities from high-speed pursuits should be directed at the suspects rather than at the officers who are protecting the public. A number of police officers contend that the solution lies in subjecting individuals who flee to harsh penalties (sixteen states have statutes imposing heavy penalties) and in authorizing the police to employ deadly force.

The U.S. Supreme Court found itself in the middle of this debate in 1998 when it issued a judgment in the case of *County of Sacramento v. Lewis*. Two Sacramento police officers observed a motorcycle traveling at a high speed. The motorcycle was operated by eighteen-year-old Brian Willard, and the passenger on the backseat was sixteen-year-old Philip Lewis. Officer James Smith, a Sacramento County Sheriff's Department deputy, turned on his emergency lights and siren and pursued the motorcycle. The motorcycle wove in and out of traffic through a residential area for 1.3 miles, forcing two cars and a bicycle to swerve off the road. The motorcycle reached speeds of up to 100 miles per hour with Smith following at a distance of 100 feet. At this speed, Smith required 650 feet to stop his cruiser. The motorcycle tipped over as Willard attempted to execute a sharp left turn. Smith slammed on his brakes, and his squad car skidded into Lewis, propelling him some 70 feet down the road, inflicting massive injuries and killing Lewis. Smith's pursuit was against the department policy of the Sacramento California Sheriff's Department, which required an officer to communicate his or her intention to pursue a vehicle to the sheriff's dispatch center. The policy also required the officer to evaluate whether the seriousness of the offense merited a chase at speeds in excess of the speed limit and to consider whether the pursuit entailed an unreasonable risk to life and property. The pursuit must be discontinued when the hazards of persisting in the pursuit are determined to outweigh the benefits.

The § 1983 legal action alleged that Lewis had been deprived of his life without due process of law. The Supreme Court held that in order to establish the claim, the plaintiffs were required to demonstrate that Smith's conduct "shocks the conscience." In the context of a high-speed chase, Justice Souter held that this requires proof that Smith intentionally deprived Lewis of his life. Why this high standard? Justice Souter explained that police officers should not be placed in the position of fearing that an unreasonable or risky decision may result in legal liability. The police in deciding whether to initiate a pursuit must make a difficult and split-second decision that balances the need to apprehend a suspect against the safety of innocent individuals on the highway. In the case before the Supreme Court, Smith acted instinctively to enforce the law in response to Willard's "outrageous behavior," and there was no indication that Smith possessed an intent to "terrorize," to "cause harm," or to "kill" Willard. Justice Souter concluded that the fact that Smith may have exercised bad judgment in initiating or in executing the pursuit should not result in legal liability (*County of Sacramento v. Lewis,* 523 U.S. 813 [1998]).

In 2007, in *Scott v. Harris,* the U.S. Supreme Court held that Officer Timothy Scott's ramming of Victor Harris's vehicle constituted a Fourth Amendment seizure. Harris was severely injured and was left a quadriplegic. The Supreme Court stressed that Officer Scott's decision, although it placed Harris at risk, was reasonable given that Harris had intentionally created a threat to a significant number of innocent individuals. Justice Scalia seemingly came down on the side of those departments and police officers that advocated an aggressive pursuit policy. He stressed that there was nothing unreasonable about initiating the pursuit and disabling Harris's vehicle. There was no guarantee that had Scott abandoned the pursuit, Harris would have reduced his speed. Justice Scalia explained that he was reluctant to require the police to call off a pursuit whenever the pursuit may threaten the public safety. This would result in motorists concluding that they would be able to escape apprehension by fleeing from the police at a rapid rate of speed. Justice Scalia concluded his decision by noting that the Supreme Court majority had reached the sensible conclusion that an officer's effort to "terminate a dangerous high-speed car chase that threatens the lives of innocent bystanders does not violate the Fourth Amendment, even when it places the fleeing motorist at risk of serious injury or death" (*Scott v. Harris,* 550 U.S. 372 [2007]). What is your view of high-speed police pursuits? Should § 1983 provide a remedy for individuals whose conduct provokes a deadly high-speed chase?

Immunity of Judges and Prosecutors

As we noted, judges, prosecutors, witnesses, and jurors are immune from being sued under § 1983 for acts undertaken as part of the judicial process. This means that a court will immediately dismiss a case filed against a judge, prosecutor, witness, or juror for acts during trial. Keep in mind that officials still may be criminally prosecuted for penal offenses such as corruption, bribery, or conspiracy to deprive an individual of his or her civil rights.

The immunity of judges for decisions made as part of their judicial function originated in medieval times. The U.S. Supreme Court observed in *Mireles v. Waco* that "[a]lthough unfairness and injustice to a litigant may result on occasion, it is a general principle of the highest importance of the proper administration of justice that a judicial officer, in exercising the authority vested in him, shall be free to act upon his convictions without apprehension of personal consequences to himself" (*Mireles v. Waco,* 502 U.S. 9, 10 [1991]). The immunity of judges is based on several considerations.

- ***Resources.*** Decisions at trial inevitably will disappoint people, and without immunity, judges constantly will be subject to legal suits. These cases will consume the time, energy, and resources of judges.
- ***Decisions.*** Judges will avoid difficult decisions to prevent being sued.
- ***Correcting errors.*** Judicial errors can be corrected by criminal appeals rather than by bringing civil suits against judges.

The immunity of judges covers decisions made during the trial process, even where the decision is in error, corrupt, or motivated by bias or prejudice. The Supreme Court, for example, held in *Mireles v. Waco* that a judge who directed the police to use physical force to bring a lawyer into the courtroom was immune from a § 1983 suit. The Court explained that it is a normal function of a judge to order that individuals should be brought into court. In this instance, the judge was entitled to immunity despite the fact that he lacked authority to order the police to employ physical force. On the other hand, the U.S. Supreme Court held that a judge was not immune from a § 1983 suit based on his firing of a probation officer who was in charge of writing sentencing reports for the judge. The Court explained that this was an administrative rather than a judicial matter (*Forrester v. White,* 484 U.S. 219 [1984]).

Prosecutors also enjoy absolute immunity for decisions relating to the judicial process. In *Imbler v. Pachtman,* the U.S. Supreme Court held that District Attorney Richard Pachtman was immune from a § 1983 suit that alleged that he had knowingly used false testimony and suppressed evidence during Paul Imbler's trial for armed robbery and murder. The U.S. Supreme Court explained in *Imbler* that the basis of immunity for prosecutors is similar to the reason why immunity is recognized for judges. The "public trust of the prosecutor's office would suffer if he were constrained in making every decision by the consequences in terms of his own potential liability in a suit for damages.... [I]f the prosecutor could be made to answer... each time... a person charged him with wrongdoing, his energy and attention would be diverted from the... duty of enforcing the criminal law" (*Imbler v. Pachtman,* 424 U.S. 409, 426–427 [1976]).

Imbler held that a prosecutor enjoys immunity for his or her role in "initiating a prosecution and in presenting the State's case." In 2009, in *Van De Kamp et al. v. Goldstein,* Thomas Goldstein was convicted of murder. His conviction was based to a large extent on the testimony of Edward Fink, a jailhouse informant. A federal district court found that Fink had not been truthful in his testimony and that the Los Angeles County District Attorney's Office had failed to inform Goldstein's lawyer that Fink had received reductions in his sentence in the past for providing prosecutors in other cases with testimony that supported the Government's case. The district court found that the prosecutor had an obligation to communicate this information to the defendant and that, had this information been revealed to Goldstein's attorneys, this might have made a difference at Goldstein's criminal trial. The district court ordered that California should either release Goldstein or provide him with a new trial. Goldstein filed a § 1983 suit that alleged the prosecutor's office had failed to provide proper "training and supervision" to the trial attorneys who had neglected to reveal the information regarding Fink's continuing collaboration with the prosecutor's office. The U.S. Supreme Court held that the prosecutor's office was entitled to absolute immunity because the allegation that the prosecutor's office had failed to train and to supervise attorneys is "directly connected" with the performance of prosecutors during a criminal trial (*Van De Kamp et al. v. Goldstein,* 555 U.S. ___ [2009]).

In *Burns v. Reed,* the next case in the text, the U.S. Supreme Court was asked to determine whether prosecutors are entitled to absolute immunity for legal advice given to the police and for statements made during a pretrial probable cause hearing.

You can find Van De Kamp et al. v. Goldstein *on the study site, http://www.sagepub.com/lippmancp.*

Is the prosecutor entitled to immunity for giving legal advice to the police and for falsifying evidence in a probable cause hearing?

Burns v. Reed, 500 U.S. 478 (1991), White, J.

Issue

The issue in this case is whether a state prosecuting attorney is absolutely immune from liability for damages under 42 U.S.C. § 1983 for giving legal advice to the police and for participating in a probable-cause hearing. The Court of Appeals for the Seventh Circuit held that he is.

Facts

The relevant facts are not in dispute. On the evening of September 2, 1982, petitioner Cathy Burns called the Muncie, Indiana, police and reported that an unknown assailant had entered her house, knocked her unconscious, and shot and wounded her two sons while they slept. Two police officers, Paul Cox and Donald Scroggins, were assigned to investigate the incident. The officers came to view petitioner as their primary suspect, even though she passed a polygraph examination and a voice stress test, submitted exculpatory handwriting samples, and repeatedly denied shooting her sons.

Speculating that petitioner had multiple personalities, one of which was responsible for the shootings, the officers decided to interview petitioner under hypnosis. They became concerned, however, that hypnosis might be an unacceptable investigative technique, and therefore sought the advice of the Chief Deputy Prosecutor, respondent Richard Reed. Respondent told the officers that they could proceed with the hypnosis.

While under hypnosis, petitioner referred to the assailant as "Katie" and also referred to herself by that name. The officers interpreted that reference as supporting their multiple-personality theory. As a result, they detained petitioner at the police station and sought respondent's advice about whether there was probable cause to arrest petitioner. After hearing about the statements that petitioner had made while under hypnosis, respondent told the officers that they "probably had probable cause" to arrest petitioner. Based on that assurance, the officers placed petitioner under arrest.

The next day, respondent and Officer Scroggins appeared before a county court judge in a probable-cause hearing, seeking to obtain a warrant to search petitioner's house and car. During that hearing, Scroggins testified, in response to respondent's questioning, that petitioner had confessed to shooting her children. Neither the officer nor respondent informed the judge that the "confession" was obtained under hypnosis or that petitioner had otherwise consistently denied shooting her sons. On the basis of the misleading presentation, the judge issued a search warrant.

Petitioner was charged under Indiana law with attempted murder of her sons. Before trial, however, the trial judge granted petitioner's motion to suppress the statements given under hypnosis. As a result, the prosecutor's office dropped all charges against petitioner.

On January 31, 1985, petitioner filed an action in the United States District Court for the Southern District of Indiana against respondent, Officers Cox and Scroggins, and others. She alleged that the defendants were liable under 42 U.S.C. § 1983 for violating her rights under the Fourth, Fifth, and Fourteenth Amendments to the United States Constitution, and she sought compensatory and punitive damages.... After petitioner presented her case, the district court granted respondent a directed verdict, finding that respondent was absolutely immune from liability for his conduct.

Petitioner appealed to the United States Court of Appeals for the Seventh Circuit. That court affirmed. It held that "a prosecutor should be afforded absolute immunity for giving legal advice to police officers about the legality of their prospective investigative conduct." In a brief footnote, the court also held that respondent was absolutely immune from liability for his role in the probable-cause hearing. Because the courts of appeals are divided regarding the scope of absolute prosecutorial immunity, we granted certiorari.

Title 42 U.S.C. § 1983 is written in broad terms. It purports to subject "every person" acting under color of state law to liability for depriving any other person in the United States of "rights, privileges, or immunities secured by the Constitution and laws."

The Court has consistently recognized, however, that § 1983 was not meant "to abolish wholesale all common-law immunities." The section is to be read "in harmony with general principles of tort immunities and defenses rather than in derogation of them." In addition, we have acknowledged that for some "special functions," it is "'better to leave unredressed the wrongs done by dishonest officers than to subject those who try to do their duty to the constant dread of retaliation.'"

Imbler was the first case in which the Court addressed the immunity of state prosecutors from suits under § 1983. Noting that prior immunity decisions were "predicated upon a considered inquiry into the immunity historically accorded the relevant official at common law and interests behind it," the Court stated that the "liability of a state prosecutor under § 1983 must be determined in the same manner." The Court observed that at common law, prosecutors were immune from suits for malicious prosecution and for defamation and that this immunity extended to the knowing use of false testimony before the grand jury and at trial.

The interests supporting the common-law immunity were held to be equally applicable to suits under § 1983. That common-law immunity, like the common-law immunity for judges and grand jurors, was viewed as necessary to protect the judicial process. Specifically, there was "concern that harassment by unfounded litigation would cause a deflection of the prosecutor's energies from his public duties, and the possibility that he would shade his decisions instead of exercising the independence of judgment required by his public trust."

The Court in *Imbler* declined to accord prosecutors only qualified immunity because, among other things, suits against prosecutors for initiating and conducting prosecutions "could be expected with some frequency, for a defendant often will transform his resentment at being prosecuted into the ascription of improper and malicious actions to the State's advocate"; lawsuits would divert prosecutors' attention and energy away from their important duty of enforcing the criminal law; prosecutors would have more difficulty than other officials in meeting the standards for qualified immunity; and potential liability "would prevent the vigorous and fearless performance of the prosecutor's duty that is essential to the proper functioning of the criminal justice system." The Court also noted that there are other checks on prosecutorial misconduct, including the criminal law and professional discipline.

The Court therefore held that prosecutors are absolutely immune from liability under § 1983 for their conduct in "initiating a prosecution and in presenting the State's case," insofar as that conduct is "intimately associated with the judicial phase of the criminal process." Each of the charges against the prosecutor in *Imbler* involved conduct having that association, including the alleged knowing use of false testimony at trial and the alleged deliberate suppression of exculpatory evidence. The Court expressly declined to decide whether absolute immunity extends to "those aspects of the prosecutor's responsibility that cast him in the role of an administrator or investigative officer rather than that of an advocate." It was recognized, though, that "the duties of the prosecutor in his role as advocate for the State involve actions preliminary to the initiation of a prosecution and actions apart from the courtroom."

Decisions in later cases are consistent with the functional approach to immunity employed in *Imbler.* These decisions have also emphasized that the official seeking absolute immunity bears the burden of showing that such immunity is justified for the function in question. The presumption is that qualified rather than absolute immunity is sufficient to protect government officials in the exercise of their duties. We have been "quite sparing" in our recognition of absolute immunity and have refused to extend it any "further than its justification would warrant."

We now consider whether the absolute prosecutorial immunity recognized in *Imbler* is applicable to (a) respondent's participation in a probable-cause hearing, which led to the issuance of a search warrant, and (b) respondent's legal advice to the police regarding the use of hypnosis and the existence of probable cause to arrest petitioner.

We address first respondent's appearance as a lawyer for the State in the probable-cause hearing, where he examined a witness and successfully supported the application for a search warrant. The decision in *Imbler* leads to the conclusion that respondent is absolutely immune from liability in a § 1983 suit for that conduct.... [P]etitioner has challenged only respondent's participation in the hearing and not his motivation in seeking the search warrant or his conduct outside of the courtroom relating to the warrant. Petitioner's complaint alleged only "Deputy Prosecutor Reed asked of police officer Donald Scroggins various questions and in doing so and in concert with other Defendants deliberately misled the Court into believing that the Plaintiff had confessed to the shooting of her children."

Like witnesses, prosecutors and other lawyers were absolutely immune from damages liability at common law for making false or defamatory statements in judicial proceedings (at least so long as the statements were related to the proceeding) and also for eliciting false and defamatory testimony from witnesses. This immunity extended to "any hearing before a tribunal which performed a judicial function."

The prosecutor's actions at issue here—appearing before a judge and presenting evidence in support of a motion for a search warrant—clearly involve the prosecutor's "role as advocate for the State," rather than his role as "administrator or investigative officer," the protection for which we reserved judgment in *Imbler.* Moreover, since the issuance of a search warrant is unquestionably a judicial act, appearing at a probable-cause hearing is "intimately associated with the judicial phase of the criminal process." It is also connected with the initiation and conduct of a prosecution, particularly where the hearing occurs after arrest, as was the case here.

Holding

Pretrial court appearances by the prosecutor in support of taking criminal action against a suspect present a substantial likelihood of vexatious litigation that might have an untoward effect on the independence of the prosecutor. Therefore, absolute immunity for this function serves the policy of protecting the judicial process, which underlies much of the Court's decision in *Imbler.* Furthermore, the judicial process is available as a check on prosecutorial actions at a probable-cause hearing. The safeguards built into the judicial system tend to reduce the need for private damages actions as a means of controlling unconstitutional conduct. Accordingly, we hold that respondent's appearance in court in support of an application for a search warrant and the presentation of evidence at that hearing are protected by absolute immunity.

Reasoning

Turning to respondent's acts of providing legal advice to the police, we note first that neither respondent nor the court below has identified any historical or common-law support for extending absolute immunity to such actions by prosecutors. Indeed, the court of appeals stated that its "review of the historical or common law basis for the immunity in question does not yield any direct support for the conclusion that a prosecutor's immunity from suit extends to the act of giving legal advice to police officers."

We do not believe...that advising the police in the investigative phase of a criminal case is so "intimately associated with the judicial phase of the criminal process," that it qualifies for absolute immunity. Absent a tradition of immunity comparable to the common-law immunity from malicious prosecution, which formed the basis for the decision in *Imbler,* we have not been inclined to extend absolute immunity from liability under § 1983. The United States...argues that the absence of common-law support here should not be determinative, because the office of public prosecutor was largely unknown at English common law, and prosecutors in the eighteenth and nineteenth centuries did not have an investigatory role, as they do today. We are not persuaded. First, it is American common law that is determinative, and the office of public prosecutor was known to American common law. Second, although "the precise contours of official immunity" need not mirror the immunity at common law, we look to the common law and other history for guidance because our role is "not to make a freewheeling policy choice," but rather to discern Congress' likely intent in enacting § 1983. "We do not have a license to establish immunities from § 1983 actions in the interests of what we judge to be sound public policy."

The next factor to be considered—risk of vexatious litigation—also does not support absolute immunity for giving legal advice. The court of appeals asserted that absolute immunity was justified because "a prosecutor's risk of becoming entangled in litigation based on his or her role as a legal advisor to police officer is as likely as the risks associated with initiating and prosecuting a case." We disagree. In the first place, a suspect or defendant is not likely to be as aware of a prosecutor's role in giving advice as a prosecutor's role in initiating and conducting a prosecution. But even if a prosecutor's role in giving advice to the police does carry with it some risk of burdensome litigation, the concern with litigation in our immunity cases is not merely a generalized concern with interference with an official's duties but rather is a concern with interference with the conduct closely related to the judicial process. Absolute immunity is designed to free the judicial process from the harassment and intimidation associated with litigation. That concern therefore justifies absolute prosecutorial immunity only for actions that are connected with the prosecutor's role in judicial proceedings, not for every litigation-inducing conduct.

The court of appeals speculated that anything short of absolute immunity would discourage prosecutors from performing their "vital obligation" of giving legal advice to the police. But the qualified immunity standard is today more protective of officials than it was at the time that *Imbler* was decided. "As the qualified immunity defense has evolved, it provides ample protection to all but the plainly incompetent or those who knowingly violate the law." Although the absence of absolute immunity for the act of giving legal advice may cause prosecutors to consider their advice more carefully, "'where an official could be expected to know that his conduct would violate statutory or constitutional rights, he should be made to hesitate.'" It is incongruous to allow prosecutors to be absolutely immune from liability for giving advice to the police but to allow police officers only qualified immunity for following the advice. Ironically, it would mean that the police, who do not ordinarily hold law degrees, would be required to know the clearly established law, but prosecutors would not.

The United States argues that giving legal advice is related to a prosecutor's roles in screening cases for prosecution and in safeguarding the fairness of the criminal judicial process. That argument, however, proves too much. Almost any action by a prosecutor, including his or her direct participation in purely investigative activity, could be said to be in some way related to the ultimate decision whether to prosecute, but we have never indicated that absolute immunity is that expansive. Rather, as in *Imbler,* we inquire whether the prosecutor's actions are closely associated with the judicial process. Indeed, we implicitly rejected the United States' argument when we held that the Attorney General was not absolutely immune from liability for authorizing a warrantless wiretap. Even though the wiretap was arguably related to a potential prosecution, we found that the Attorney General "was not acting in a prosecutorial capacity" and thus was not entitled to the immunity recognized in *Imbler.*

As a final basis for allowing absolute immunity for legal advice, the court of appeals observed that there are several checks other than civil litigation to prevent abuses of authority by prosecutors. Although we agree, we note that one of the most important checks, the judicial process, will not necessarily restrain out-of-court activities by a prosecutor that occur prior to the initiation of a prosecution, such as providing legal advice to the police. This is particularly true if a suspect is not eventually prosecuted. In those circumstances, the prosecutor's action is not subjected to the "crucible of the judicial process."

Holding

In sum, we conclude that respondent has not met his burden of showing that the relevant factors justify an extension of absolute immunity to the prosecutorial function of giving legal advice to the police. For the foregoing reasons, we affirm in part and reverse in part the judgment of the court of appeals.

Questions for Discussion

1. What is the holding in *Burns v. Reed?*
2. Why does the Supreme Court distinguish in its judgment between Burns's participation in the probable cause hearing and Burns's legal advice to the police?
3. What are the reasons that the Supreme Court gives for recognizing the immunity of prosecutors?

11.1 YOU DECIDE

How does the precedent established in *Burns v. Reed* explain the Supreme Court's decision in *Buckley v. Fitzsimmons.* In *Buckley,* the Supreme Court held that a prosecutor possessed qualified immunity rather than absolute immunity for fabricating evidence that falsely linked Buckley to the killing of an eleven-year-old child and for making false statements to the media in regard to Buckley's involvement in the murder. See *Buckley v. Fitzsimmons,* 509 U.S. 259 (1993).

You can find the answer by referring to the study site, http://www.sagepub.com/lippmancp.

11.2 YOU DECIDE

Briscoe was convicted in state court of burglarizing a house trailer. He filed a § 1983 action against LaHue, a member of the Bloomington, Indiana, police force, alleging that LaHue had violated Briscoe's constitutional right to due process by committing perjury in the criminal proceedings leading to his conviction. LaHue testified that Briscoe was one of no more than 50 to 100 people in the town whose fingerprints might match a partial thumbprint discovered at the crime scene. Briscoe contended that LaHue was aware that the FBI and the state police had concluded that the partial print was too incomplete to be of significance and that there was no evidence connecting him to the burglary. Briscoe sought $100,000 in damages. The U.S. Supreme Court considered Briscoe's appeal along with a companion case brought by Vickers and Ballard. Vickers and Ballard alleged that Hunley, a member of the Cedar Lake, Indiana, police force, had deprived them of their right to due process and to a fair trial. Vickers and Ballard contended that Hunley had falsely testified that they had the opportunity to meet and coordinate their statements in which they denied responsibility for a sexual assault. They argued that Hunley's testimony had called the credibility of their statements into question and had led to their conviction for sexual assault. Were Officers LaHue and Hunley entitled to absolute or qualified immunity? See *Briscoe v. LaHue*, 460 U.S. 325 (1983).

You can find the answer by referring to the study site, http://www.sagepub.com/lippmancp.

The Affirmative Duty to Protect

We have seen that police officers are liable under § 1983 when their acts result in a violation of individuals' clearly established constitutional rights or rights clearly established under federal law. On the other hand, judges, prosecutors, and other participants in the trial process have absolute immunity for acts undertaken as part of the judicial function.

A question that continues to be a topic of debate is whether the police, correctional officers, or other government officials are civilly liable for failing to protect an individual or the public from a criminal act. Should a police officer be held legally responsible for failing to respond to a report of domestic violence that leads to the injury or death of the victim? What about a parole board that releases an individual who shortly thereafter commits a heinous murder? The victims in these instances have suffered harm to their life, liberty, and perhaps property. Is there a clear difference between a police officer who directly harms an individual and a police officer whose failure to act results in an individual's being victimized by a crime? The "clearly established" legal principle is that the police and other government officials have no legal obligation to intervene to protect the general public. This constitutional principle is based on several considerations.

- ***Legal claims.*** Every crime victim could sue the police and overwhelm the judicial process.
- ***Causality.*** The government should not be held responsible for the acts of private individuals over whom the government has no control.
- ***Discretion.*** The police have limited time and resources and are in the best position to decide what complaints require an immediate response.

The U.S. Supreme Court in *DeShaney v. Winnebago County Social Services Department* held that governmental employees have no duty to intervene to prevent a criminal offense. In *DeShaney*, the Winnebago County Department of Social Services received reports that four-year-old Joshua DeShaney was being abused by his father. Joshua was twice admitted to the local hospital with multiple bruises and abrasions. On the second occasion, he was placed under the temporary custody of the hospital by the juvenile court. The hospital nonetheless decided to return Joshua to his home. The caseworker made monthly visits and observed that Joshua had a number of suspicious injuries. Joshua shortly thereafter was once again beaten and returned home by the hospital. Four months later, Joshua was severely beaten, suffered massive brain injuries, fell into a coma, and was confined to a medical treatment institution for the remainder of his life (*DeShaney v. Winnebago County Social Services Department,* 489 U.S. 189, 192 [1989]).

The U.S. Supreme Court held that the Fourteenth Amendment Due Process Clause does not impose an affirmative duty on the government to intervene to protect life, liberty, or property from the acts of private individuals. The Court explained that the purpose of due process is to protect the people from the government, and the Due Process Clause does not require the government to protect citizens from one another. The Supreme Court recognized that the government has an affirmative duty to protect individuals such as prisoners over whom it exercises physical control and with whom it has a "special relationship." The affirmative duty to protect in these instances "arises not from the State's knowledge of the individual's predicament or from its expressions of intent to help him, but from the limitation which it has imposed on his freedom to act on his own behalf. There, however, is no such responsibility towards the 'public at large.'"

The holding in *Winnebago* has been relied on by federal and state courts to dismiss claims against the police that allege that law enforcement officers have failed to protect citizens from crime. In *Pinder v. Johnson,* Officer Johnson arrested Don Pittman, a violent domestic batterer and former felon who had terrorized his former girlfriend, Carol Pinder. Pittman subsequently was released and was warned to stay away from Pinder. He almost immediately set fire to Carol Pinder's home, killing her three children by smoke inhalation. The Fourth Circuit Court of Appeals held that based on *Deshaney,* Officer Johnson had no duty to protect Pinder and her children because the children had not been confined by the State (*Pinder v. Johnson,* 54 F.3d 1169 [4th Cir. 1994]).

Courts have developed a "state-created danger" exception to the rule that a government official does not have civil liability for a failure to intervene. This arises where state action creates or exposes an individual to a danger that he or she would not otherwise confront. For example, the police let a violent and dangerous inmate who was on "trustee status" drive a marked patrol car. The inmate stopped and murdered a young woman. In this example, although the killing was committed by the inmate, the action of the police officer in giving the informant the patrol car "exposed the victim to a danger which she would not otherwise confront" (*Nishiyami v. Dickinson County,* 814 F.2d 277 [6th Cir. 1987]).

In *Kennedy v. Ridgefield City,* Kimberley Kennedy reported to Officer Noel Shields that a thirteen-year-old neighbor, Michael Burns, had molested Kennedy's nine-year-old daughter. She related that Michael had a pattern of extreme and frightening violence and requested that Officer Shields tell her before he contacted the Burns family. Kennedy explained that this would enable her family to take protective measures. Shields assured Kennedy that he would contact her before talking to the family. Shields nonetheless contacted Michael's mother and shortly thereafter informed Kimberley Kennedy that he had approached the Burns family. It was early evening, and the fearful Kennedy family made plans to leave the neighborhood the next morning. Shields promised that the police would patrol the neighborhood to insure the Kennedys' safety. Michael broke into the Kennedys' home later that night and shot and seriously wounded Kennedy and killed her husband. The Fourth Circuit held that Shields had placed the Kennedys in danger by his failure to inform Kimberley before he talked to the Burns family and by the failure to patrol the neighborhood. The Fourth Circuit stressed that under the "state-created danger doctrine, a police officer may be liable for actions that create or increase a known or obvious danger to an individual that he or she would otherwise not face.... Shields' actions both created and aggravated the risk plaintiff faced from Burns" (*Kennedy v. Ridgefield City,* 439 F.3d 1055, 1067 [9th Cir. 2004]).

In the next case in the text, *Commonwealth Bank & Trust Company v. Russell,* the Fourth Circuit Court of Appeals confronts the question whether a sheriff should be held legally responsible for an escaped prisoner who murders two individuals. The case asks you to consider at what point a law enforcement official should be legally liable for the criminal conduct of an inmate. Following this case, we will discuss the circumstances under which legal responsibility may be imposed on the local government under § 1983.

Are county officials legally liable for a killing committed by an escaped inmate?

Commonwealth Bank & Trust Company v. Russell, 825 F.2d 12 (4th Cir. 1987), Sloviter, C.J.

Issue

Commonwealth Bank & Trust Company, N.A., the executor of the estate of Frank and Betty Lent, appeals from the order of the district court dismissing its claim brought under 42 U.S.C. § 1983 alleging that the Lents, who were murdered by an escaped prisoner, were deprived of their constitutional rights through the actions of the defendant prison and county officials.

Facts

The complaint alleges that the Lents were residents of Potter County; that Elmer Slingerland, a prisoner, was confined in the Potter County Jail on July 22, 1985, on charges of homicide, burglary, robbery, and theft in the April 15, 1985, murder of a Potter County resident who had been shot several times; that Slingerland was being held on $250,000 bail; that sometime in the evening on July 24, 1985, two turnkeys and other agents of the Potter County jail supervised recreation in the jail yard and that when the prisoners were returned to their cells, no head count was conducted; that it was the policy of the jail not to take counts because of a series of inoperable locks in the cell block area; and that on the morning of July 25, 1985, employees of the jail discovered that Slingerland had escaped.

A ladder from the recreation yard had been placed inside one of the exterior walls of the jail. The complaint alleges that Slingerland used the ladder "as well as the deteriorating condition of the wall," trees outside the wall, and horseshoes from the recreation yard to scale the wall and descend to the street outside the jail or in the alternative that he used unsecured access to windows and the roof of the jail and then scaled the interior aspect and top of the jail wall to escape. According to the complaint, after escaping, Slingerland stole a handgun from a Potter County farm home and used that handgun in the shooting deaths of the Lents.

The complaint alleges that defendants Dale "Bill" Russell, the Potter County sheriff, and the Potter County commissioners knew or should have known that deficiencies in the internal locking mechanisms of the jail, deficiencies in other portions of the jail including the jail wall and adjacent trees external to the wall, and deficiencies in the training and supervision of the jail's turnkeys could lead to the injuries suffered by the Lents; that "municipal officials did have knowledge of inadequate jail conditions and security since Pennsylvania Department of Corrections Reports regularly faulted the facility and procedures at the Potter County Jail"; that defendants failed to remedy the deficiencies, institute proper correctional procedures, and train and supervise jail employees; and that defendants' failure to act constituted "gross negligence, reckless indifference, and willful neglect" of the rights of the Lents. The complaint alleges that the acts or omissions of the defendants who are supervisory municipal officials constituted an official policy which resulted in the Lents' deaths and that, since Slingerland, the person whose affirmative conduct caused the harm, was under the direct control or supervision of the defendants, the Lents' death can be attributed to them.

Count I of the complaint alleges a claim under § 1983 for loss of the Lents' "liberty interest in their expectation of continuing life and property interest in the ownership, use and continued enjoyment of their real and personal property" in violation of their rights under the Fourteenth Amendment.

The district court dismissed the § 1983 claim for failure to state a claim upon which relief can be granted. The court, relying on *Martinez v. California,* 444 U.S. 277 (1980), held that Slingerland was not an agent of the state, that the defendants had no reason to believe that the Lents were in any greater danger than the public at large, and that there was no "special relationship" between Potter County and the Lents which created an affirmative duty of care and protection. Plaintiff appeals.

Reasoning

The complaint adequately alleges that the defendants were acting under color of state law, that the Lents were deprived of interests in life and property, and that the defendants acted with the reckless indifference or callous disregard that will support a claim of violation of the Fourteenth Amendment under § 1983. The facts alleged, however, implicate yet another requirement of § 1983, i.e., that the constitutional deprivation alleged be fairly attributable to defendants' conduct. As the district court recognized, the starting point for consideration of this issue is the Supreme Court's decision in *Martinez v. California*. In *Martinez,* a fifteen-year-old girl was tortured and then murdered by a parolee five months after his release from prison. The parolee, who had been convicted of rape, was committed initially to a state mental hospital as a "Mentally Disordered Sex Offender not amenable to treatment" and thereafter sentenced to a term of imprisonment of one to twenty years, with a recommendation that he not be paroled. He was paroled five years later notwithstanding that according to the complaint, parole officials were fully informed of his dangerous propensities and the likelihood that he would commit another violent crime. The complaint was dismissed.

The Supreme Court affirmed, holding that the plaintiffs "have not alleged a claim for relief under Federal law." The Court concluded that "taking these particular allegations as true, the [State officials] did not deprive [plaintiffs'] decedent of life within the meaning of the Fourteenth Amendment." The Court reasoned that the young woman's life was taken by the parolee five months after his release. He was in no sense an agent of the parole board. Further, the parole board was not aware that [plaintiffs'] decedent, as distinguished from the public at large, faced any special danger. We need not and do not decide that a parole officer could never be deemed to "deprive" someone of life by action taken in connection with the release of a prisoner on parole. But we do hold that at least under the particular circumstances of this parole decision, [plaintiffs'] decedent's death is too remote a consequence of the parole officers' action to hold them responsible under the federal civil rights law.... [I]t is perfectly clear that not every injury in which a State official has played some part is actionable under that statute.

Since *Martinez,* the courts have dismissed § 1983 claims against State officials for injuries or deaths caused by parolees or released criminals. For example, *Fox v. Custis,* 712 F.2d 84 (4th Cir. 1983), involved a § 1983 suit by three female plaintiffs who were raped, beaten, shot, stabbed, and set on fire by a parolee. The complaint alleged that the parole board and parole officers continued the parolee on parole despite their knowledge that the parolee was convicted for defrauding an innkeeper three weeks after his release and despite their suspicion that shortly after the parolee's release, he had committed an act of arson which resulted in a woman's death. The dismissal of the complaint was affirmed on the ground that no special relationship existed between the plaintiffs and the State officials which gave rise to an affirmative duty of protection. The court found that "the claimants here were simply members of the general public, living in the free society, and having no special custodial or other relationship with the State.... The State agent defendants here were 'unaware that the [claimants] as distinguished from the public at large faced any special danger.'"

In a recent case presenting facts similar to this one, an inmate of a minimum security facility who was being held for an alleged parole violation and was awaiting trial on burglary escaped from the facility and, two months later, raped the plaintiff. Her § 1983 suit against the county, the county board of supervisors, and other county officials was dismissed because the court found that no special relationship existed between plaintiff and the officials. The *Bowers* court accurately summarized the general state of the applicable law when it stated that there was no deprivation actionable under § 1983 because "The defendants in this case did not place [plaintiff's decedent] in a place or position of danger; they simply failed adequately to protect her, as a member of the public, from a dangerous man."

Some courts have held that even where the defendants are aware of a risk of harm to a particular individual, no § 1983 claim is stated against the officials if the released prisoner caused that harm. *Estate of Gilmore v. Buckley,* 787 F.2d 714, 721 (1st Cir. 1986) (plaintiff's decedent was murdered by a man who had previously threatened her life and had been hospitalized for mental evaluation as a result of her complaints). We need not decide whether we would adopt a similarly restrictive view when there is knowledge of potential harm by a parolee to a particular individual. Here, the defendants had no knowledge of danger peculiar to the Lents, as distinguished from other members of the general public. Moreover, since the prisoner escaped, the causal nexus to defendants' actions is even more attenuated than in cases where the perpetrator of the subsequent crime has been intentionally released.

Plaintiff argues that defendants' maintenance of the jail in a condition which made escape likely and the placement of Slingerland, a particularly dangerous prisoner, in that jail when it was in an unsafe condition created a situation that posed an immediate threat to the life and safety of individuals, such as the Lents, who resided in the community surrounding the jail. Plaintiff makes a sympathetic argument. It must fail because the residents in the communities surrounding the jail are part of the "public at large," referred to in *Martinez.* They cannot reasonably be characterized as individuals who defendants knew "faced any special danger." Nor do we believe that the brief interval between the escape and the crime in this case is sufficient to distinguish it from *Martinez* where five months elapsed after release before the crime was committed. We read *Martinez* as holding that the key element that was missing was a causal nexus, the same element we find missing here.

Of course, as the Supreme Court itself noted in *Martinez,* cases "where local law enforcement officials themselves beat a citizen to death" are not comparable to the situation presented here. Cases where the harm is directly inflicted by officials acting under color of state law present the archetypical circumstances for which § 1983 was enacted. It is clear, however, that § 1983 is not limited to cases of direct harm inflicted by state officials. This is suggested by the distinction made in *Martinez* between that victim there and those who the authorities knew face a "special danger."

None of the categories of cases finding a "special danger" or "special relationship" since the *Martinez* decision is relevant here. A prisoner is, by virtue of his or her custody, in a special relationship with the custodial authorities and dependent upon them for protection. If the authorities recklessly disregard the prisoner's safety, they may be liable under § 1983 for acts performed by another inmate. Patients committed to a public hospital are in a comparable special relationship.

We have also held that yet another special relationship arises between a state agency having responsibility to protect abused children and those children. See *Estate of Bailey v. County of York,* 768 F.2d 503, 508–511 (3d Cir. 1985). Plaintiff relies on *Bailey,* arguing that the facts here are comparable. We do not agree. In *Bailey,* the complaint alleged that the agency, which had notice of child abuse, took the child in its custody, received information confirming the child abuse, was aware of the source of the abuse, temporarily placed the child in protective custody, and returned her to her mother's care without adequately investigating the whereabouts of the child, her mother, or the mother's paramour who had previously abused the child. This case is distinguishable from *Bailey* in the significant fact that defendants here were unaware of any particular threat to the Lents such as was posed to the child in *Bailey,* who had actually been in the custody of the county officials and replaced by them in a position of danger.

No authority supports extending § 1983 as far as plaintiff seeks. The recent case referred to us by plaintiff, *Nishiyama v. Dickson County, Tennessee,* 814 F.2d 277 (6th Cir. 1987), is not comparable. In that case, the murder on which the § 1983 suit was based was committed by a convicted felon who was put on "trusty" status by the sheriff and his deputies and was permitted to use a sheriff's department patrol car without supervision. Furthermore, the sheriff's department officials were advised that the felon was using the car to stop people and did nothing for ten hours to prevent these actions. While driving that patrol car, the felon directed the victim to pull over to the side of the road and, when she obeyed, beat her to death. In that case, because the officials gave the felon the instrumentality of law enforcement which enabled him to commit the offense, the Sixth Circuit held the complaint stated a claim. The court found that the cases we cite above were inapplicable because "in none of [those] cases did the state officers by their acts facilitate the crime by providing the criminal with the necessary means and the specific opportunity to commit his crime."

Holding

In this case, the tragic consequences of Slingerland's escape cannot reasonably be attributed to the county officials. Although one might argue that the county officials' gross negligence or reckless indifference with respect to the conditions of the jail were a contributing factor in the eventual murder of the Lents, they were too remote a cause to permit maintenance of this § 1983 lawsuit. For the foregoing reasons, we will affirm the order of the district court dismissing the complaint.

Questions for Discussion

1. Explain why the Fourth Circuit decided not to hold Sheriff Russell liable under § 1983.
2. Are the precedents cited in the Court's opinion similar or different from *Russell*?
3. Would you hold Sheriff Russell liable on a state-created-danger theory? What of the argument that Sheriff Russell has a "special relationship" and duty of care to citizens who lived nearby to the jail?

11.3 YOU DECIDE

Hilliard was a passenger in an automobile driven by her male friend. The car was involved in a minor traffic accident, and the driver was arrested for driving under the influence of alcohol and taken into custody. The automobile was impounded. The police concluded that Hilliard also was inebriated and ordered her not to drive. The police left Hilliard in what the defendant terms a "high-crime area." She unsuccessfully attempted to telephone for help at a convenience store and later was robbed and sexually assaulted and was discovered bleeding, bruised, naked, and barely conscious the next morning. Did the police have an obligation to protect Hilliard? Will Hilliard's § 1983 action prove successful? See *Hilliard v. City and County of Denver,* 930 F.2d 1516 (10th Cir. 1991).

You can find the answer by referring to the study site, http://www.sagepub.com/lippmancp.

The Liability of Local Government Entities Under Section 1983

State governments and state agencies cannot be sued under § 1983. The Eleventh Amendment to the U.S. Constitution provides for sovereign immunity from prosecution.

This immunity does not extend to cities, towns, counties, and local governmental agencies. The U.S. Supreme Court in *Monell v. Department of Social Services* interpreted the term *individual* in § 1983 to permit plaintiffs to sue local cities, counties, and local governmental agencies (*Monell v. Department of Social Services,* 436 U.S. 658 [1978]).

Cities, counties, and local governmental agencies are liable when police officials or other employees inflict an injury while carrying out an official governmental "policy" (an officially adopted local law or regulation adopted by the police department) or custom (a long-standing, unwritten, and widely recognized practice by police officers).

Liability. A local government is not liable when a police officer takes the law into his or her own hands. A town or county is not liable merely because an employee violates an individual's rights.

Causality. The police officer or governmental employee must be shown to have violated an individual's constitutional or federal rights as a result of following governmental policy. A single violation of an individual's rights is sufficient to impose liability on a municipality (*Pembauer v. City of Cincinnati,* 475 U.S. 469 [1969]).

The Supreme Court explained that there were three policy reasons behind the decision by Congress in drafting § 1983 to impose liability on towns and counties.

Accountability. In a democracy, we look to local governments to protect our rights and liberties, and local governments should be held accountable and compensate people when governmental policies result in a violation of individuals' rights.

Resources. Police officers and local officials in most cases lack the money to adequately compensate individuals whose rights are violated. Local governments typically have "deep pockets" and therefore should compensate individuals for injuries caused by government officials in carrying out municipal policies.

Local budgets. Taxpayers likely will react angrily to the fact that damage awards against a city, town, or county are paid out of the local budget. Officials as a result will make a special effort to insure that the police and other local officials follow the requirements of the U.S. Constitution and federal law (*Owen v. City of Independence,* 445 U.S. 622 [1980]).

As illustrated by the two examples summarized below, plaintiffs suing a town or city have a steep road to climb. The U.S. Supreme Court requires a close causal relationship between local policies and the injuries suffered by an individual seeking damages. The plaintiff must demonstrate a link between a government policy or decision and the acts of the police or other government officials.

Hiring. In *Board of the County Commissioners of Bryan County v. Brown,* Reserve Deputy Sheriff Stacy Burns employed excessive force in removing Jill Brown from her automobile, severely injuring her knees. It later emerged that Sheriff Robert Moore in hiring Burns had not closely reviewed Burns's arrest record, which showed arrests for various misdemeanors including assault and battery, resisting arrest, and public drunkenness. Brown argued that the Board of the County Commissioners of Bryan County had approved the hiring of Burns and therefore should be held liable for her injury. The U.S. Supreme Court held that in order to recover damages from the county, Brown was required to demonstrate that the sheriff in hiring Burns had consciously disregarded the high likelihood and "plainly obvious" fact that Burns would commit this precise constitutional violation. Was it predictable from Burns's arrest record that he would assault a citizen? (*Board of the County Commissioners of Bryan County v. Brown,* 520 U.S. 397 [1997]).

Training. Geraldine Harris was arrested and twice collapsed at the police station. The second time she was left lying on the floor, and the police neglected to call an ambulance. On her release, Harris was hospitalized for two weeks for emotional disabilities. The U.S. Supreme Court held that the failure of the City of Canton, Ohio, to train the police to identify the symptoms of mental disability did not necessarily mean that the City is legally responsible under § 1983 for what happened to Harris. The Court stated that there must be a demonstration that Canton officials had been deliberately indifferent to the constitutional rights of its citizens. A City is deliberately indifferent when officials ignore a known risk. In this instance, Harris had not demonstrated that there was an "obvious need" for the training of law enforcement officers in the identification of detainees suffering from emotional disabilities and, in addition, that had such a training program been provided, Harris's injury would have been avoided by a "hypothetical officer" under similar circumstances (*City of Canton v. Harris,* 489 U.S. 378 [1989]).

In summary, it is difficult to hold a city, town, or county liable under § 1983. In the two cases discussed in this section, the plaintiff was required to establish an intentional disregard of a known risk and that this "deliberate indifference" caused the harm suffered by the plaintiff. In the next sections, we will look at two other legal steps that may be taken against a governmental agency that is alleged to be responsible for violating constitutional rights: injunctions and pattern-or-practice lawsuits by the U.S. Department of Justice.

11.4 YOU DECIDE

Eric Jordan, a violent, twenty-three-year-old paranoid schizophrenic, was committed to the city hospital psychiatric unit and was treated with twice the normal dosage of the tranquilizer Haldol. He then was placed in an unlocked area while he waited to be processed for admission. There was only a single employee supervising the area who was concentrating on completing paperwork. Jordan walked out of the hospital and, a "few minutes" following his escape, "initiated a series of brutal, random assaults on people in the neighborhood of the hospital, killing an elderly woman and injuring several others before he could be apprehended." A number of hospital memorandums had expressed concern over the lack of security during the processing of patients and noted that in the past, several individuals had walked out of the hospital. The staff was aware or should have been aware from hospital records that Jordan might prove dangerous. One staff member, rather than calming Jordan down, engaged in a shouting match and increased Jordan's agitation. The impact of Haldol can be unpredictable and can cause "restlessness in schizophrenics." Jordan, however, was left without supervision or restraints. One doctor conceded that Jordan would not have gone on a rampage had he not been given an overdose of Haldol. The City and County of San Francisco's protocol for treatment of patients does not require or recommend doses of Haldol beyond that recommended by the manufacturer, and there is no indication that the hospital had administered overdoses of the drug in the past. Can the City and County of San Francisco and its employees be held liable under § 1983 for failing to protect Jordan's victims against the violation of their due process rights to life and liberty? See *Buenavista v. City and County of San Francisco,* 255 Cal. Rptr. 329 (1989).

You can find the answer by referring to the study site, http://www.sagepub.com/lippmancp.

Injunctions

Section 1983 also allows plaintiffs to ask for injunctive relief against a local government or governmental agency. An **injunction** is a court order that directs an individual or government to stop an unlawful activity. A violation of an injunction is punishable by contempt, which results in a fine or imprisonment. Several federal courts have employed injunctive relief in the past to halt patterns of unconstitutional conduct in state prison systems.

Judges have proven reluctant to tell the police how to run their department and prefer to leave these decisions to local officials. Injunctions typically have been issued only where there is evidence that police officials have resisted demands to change discriminatory or harmful police department policies that present a clear and immediate threat of harm. In most cases, plaintiffs have not been able to demonstrate that they are likely to be victimized by a department policy, and courts have reasoned that in the event of injury, individuals can bring a § 1983 claim for damages.

In *Los Angeles v. Lyons,* the U.S. Supreme Court held that the use of potentially lethal carotid and bar holds by Los Angeles police officers, although having resulted in the death of ten civilians, did not pose a sufficient threat of future harm to justify an injunction. The Court recognized that in the countless encounters between the police and citizens, there undoubtedly will be "instances in which strangleholds will be illegally applied and injury and death unconstitutionally inflicted on the victim.... [H]owever, it is no more than conjecture to suggest that in every instance of a traffic stop, arrest, or other encounter between the police and a citizen, the police will act unconstitutionally and inflict injury without provocation or legal excuse." The Court also concluded that it is sheer speculation to assert that "Lyons himself will again be involved in one of those unfortunate instances, or that he will be arrested in the future and provoke the use of a chokehold by resisting arrest, attempting to escape, or threatening deadly force or serious bodily injury" (*Los Angeles v. Lyons,* 461 U.S. 95, 107 [1981]).

In *Rizzo v. Goode,* the Supreme Court refused to order Philadelphia to revise its police department complaint and disciplinary procedures and to order Philadelphia to incorporate a discussion in the departmental manual on the limits on police powers. The Court explained that only a few officers were responsible for the mistreatment of citizens and that there was no evidence that the police department had encouraged police abuse. The appropriate remedy is to impose an injunction on the "problem officers" rather than for the federal courts to intervene in the administration of the Philadelphia police department (*Rizzo v. Goode,* 423 U.S. 362 [1976]).

Lankford v. Gelston is one of the handful of cases in which an injunction has been issued. The Fourth Circuit Court of Appeals issued an injunction against the Baltimore Police Department, which had conducted dragnet searches of 300 homes during a three-week hunt for two individuals suspected of killing one police officer and wounding another. The appellate court held that "[t]he character of the department's conduct places a strong obligation on the court to make sure that similar conduct will not recur. Police protestations of repentance and reform...offer insufficient assurance that similar raids will not ensue when another aggravated crime occurs" (*Lankford v. Gelston,* 364 F.2d 197, 203 [4th Cir. 1966]). Another legal remedy that is available to modify police department policies is the pattern-or-practice suit, which can be brought by the U.S. Attorney General.

Pattern and Practice of the Deprivation of Constitutional Rights

The federal Police Misconduct Statute, 42 U.S.C. § 14141, provides that it is unlawful for law enforcement officers or law enforcement agencies to "engage in a pattern or practice of conduct" that deprives individuals of a constitutional right or right guaranteed by the laws of the United States. The U.S. Attorney General, when he or she has "reasonable cause" to believe that such a pattern or practice of violations has occurred, may ask a court to direct a police department to correct the practice. This request for a **pattern-or-practice decree** is a mechanism to address a widespread practice rather than an isolated incident. In recent years, police departments in Cincinnati; Detroit; Los Angeles; Montgomery County and Prince George's County, Maryland; New York City; Pittsburg; Providence, Rhode Island; Steubenville, Ohio; and Tulsa have voluntarily entered into arrangements (consent decrees) pledging to improve training, increase monitoring of police misconduct, investigate excessive and deadly force, and reform citizen complaint procedures and internal disciplinary mechanisms. Progress is monitored by officials in Washington, D.C.

States also provide tort remedies to individuals who claim to have been deprived of their constitutional rights. In the next section, we outline state tort remedies.

State Tort Remedies Against Law Enforcement Officers

State law enforcement officers may be sued in state court for torts or acts that harm another individual. Towns, counties, and states under some circumstances also may be held liable for torts under state law.

A law enforcement officer may be held responsible for the torts such as assault and battery, wrongful death, false arrest and imprisonment, trespass, destruction of property, and breaking and entering. Arresting an individual without probable cause and taking him or her to the station house for processing may constitute false arrest, false imprisonment, and the intentional infliction of emotional distress, along with other torts. A jury may award compensatory damages to compensate an individual for the harm that he or she has suffered as well as punitive damages. Punitive or exemplary damages are damages beyond the amount required to compensate the victim and are intended to deter the tortfeasor and other individuals from acting in such a grossly reckless fashion in the future.

Tort actions are difficult to win because the police possess the defense of *official immunity.* This provides that a law enforcement official is not liable for his or her tortious acts unless there is a demonstration that the officer committed the tort in a "willful or malicious fashion." This requires proof by a preponderance of the evidence (fifty-one percent) that the officer acted purposely or with disregard for the risk of harm to the plaintiff. Courts reason that the police must make difficult decisions and should be provided with a wide latitude in making decisions. A plaintiff in a tort suit for excessive use of force must establish that the police intentionally injured him or her or acted without reasonable grounds to believe that the plaintiff posed a threat to the officer.

A legal action also may be brought in some states against the police department or local town or county that employed the police officer. The principle of *respondeat superior* holds an agency liable for the willful or malicious acts of their employees taken in the course of their employment. Keep in mind that this is an enormously complicated area of the law and that state statues widely differ on the circumstances in which a local or state government may be held liable in tort.

In *Leonzal v. Grogan,* David and Sharon Leonzal sued the City of Duluth, Minnesota, for assault and battery and for intentional infliction of emotional distress. The Leonzals were involved in a series of heated arguments with their neighbors that led to a number of calls to 911 and complaints to the city attorney. In August 1989, a neighbor called 911 and reported that Leonzal was waiving a shotgun and allegedly threatening the neighbor and her dog. Several officers positioned themselves outside Leonzal's house with weapons drawn. The police called Leonzal and asked him to step outside to speak with them. Leonzal denied the neighbor's story and, as he stepped outside, began shouting at the officers. He was told to "freeze and put his hand above his head." Leonzal continued shouting and was ordered to lie facedown. He refused and was forced to his knees, handcuffed, and placed in the squad car. Leonzal conceded that he owned guns and told the officers where the three hunting rifles were located in his home. The police seized the weapons and released Leonzal, who had been bruised during the encounter. Leonzal insisted that the police knew that his neighbor was emotionally unstable, that the allegation was untrue, and that he posed no threat.

A Minnesota appellate court determined that an officer responding to a 911 call is a prime example of a situation requiring the exercise of judgment. The officers in this instance confronted an individual who reportedly had a shotgun in his house who was threatening his neighbors. The Minnesota court noted that the police must consider a range of factors in determining how to respond. The factors include the potential danger posed by the individual to the neighbors and the credibility of the complaint. These considerations must be weighed and balanced by the police with little time for reflection based on incomplete information. This discretion "compels application of official immunity." Under the circumstances, the police clearly acted with care rather than with a willful and malicious intent to harm Leonzal. The Minnesota court also held that the City of Duluth was entitled to legal immunity. The appellate court noted that imposing liability on Duluth for any mistakes made by the officers would encourage police administrators to direct officers to respond with extreme caution to 911 calls and create a potential threat to the public safety (*Leonzal v. Grogan,* 516 N.W.2d 210 [Minn. App. 1999]).

We now turn our attention to available legal remedies against federal law enforcement officers and against federal employees for the violation of constitutional rights and federal rights.

Remedies for Constitutional Violations by Federal Law Enforcement Officers

In 1971, in *Bivens v. Six Unknown Named Agents,* the U.S. Supreme Court held that federal law enforcement officers are responsible for *constitutional torts* that violate individuals' Fourth

Amendment rights. This was a significant step because § 1983, the federal statute that provides a civil remedy for the violation of constitutional rights, covers state rather than federal officials.

In *Bivens,* six FBI agents conducted a warrantless search of Webster Bivens's apartment. Bivens was arrested for violating federal drug laws and was manacled in front of his family. He was taken to the federal courthouse in Brooklyn, New York, where he was interrogated, booked, and subjected to a visual strip search and eventually released. Bivens filed a tort action in federal court against the police officers who arrested him without probable cause. He claimed that the events surrounding his unlawful arrest subjected him to "humiliation, embarrassment and mental suffering" and asked for $15,000 in damages from each of the six law enforcement officers. The U.S. Supreme Court held that although there was no specific federal statute that provides a remedy against federal agents, "'[t]he very essence of civil liberty certainly consists in the right of every individual to claim the protection of the laws, whenever he receives an injury.'... [P]etitioner is entitled to recovery money damages for any injuries he has suffered as a result of the agents' violation of the [Fourth] Amendment" (*Bivens v. Six Unknown Named Agents,* 403 U.S. 388, 396 [1971]). So-called *Bivens* legal actions have been extended to cover the Fifth Amendment right against self-incrimination and the Eighth Amendment prohibition on cruel and unusual punishments.

Most *Bivens* legal actions are brought against federal law enforcement officers and correctional officials. The requirements for a *Bivens* suit are essentially the same as the requirements for a § 1983 suit. Federal judges and prosecutors enjoy *absolute immunity,* meaning that they cannot be sued. On the other hand, law enforcement and correctional officers, the heads of federal agencies, and presidential aides are provided *qualified immunity* for violating constitutional rights that are not clearly established. The question is whether the defendant "could have reasonably believed that his or her actions were legally consistent with legal rules that were clearly established at the time." *Bivens* suits may not be brought against the federal government or federal government agencies. The elements of a *Bivens* action are as follows.

Color of law. The official's actions must be undertaken in the exercise of his or her official duties.

Constitutional right. The official's actions must have violated the plaintiff's constitutional rights.

Reasonableness. As noted, individuals involved in a "judicial function" have absolute immunity. Other defendants possess qualified immunity. The defendant is liable when he or she violates a clearly established right and a reasonable individual would be aware that his or her acts are unlawful in the circumstances that he or she confronts. A defendant may not be held liable for violating a right in which the law is uncertain and is not clearly established. The U.S. Supreme Court ruling in *Pearson v. Callahan,* discussed earlier in the chapter, provides judges with the discretion to decide whether the official is alleged to have violated a clearly established right before undertaking a constitutional analysis.

The Supreme Court explained that in *Bivens,* it balanced two considerations. On one hand, individuals are entitled to monetary damages to compensate for injuries caused by the federal government. In cases in which the government does not pursue a prosecution, this becomes particularly important because the victim will be unable to look to the exclusionary rule to deter the police from future legal violations. On the other hand, it seems only fair to protect government officers by recognizing qualified immunity where the law is unclear. In *Anderson v. Creighton,* the U.S. Supreme Court majority explained that providing the qualified immunity defense to law enforcement officials who reasonably believe that their actions are lawful allows federal agents to act without fear that they will later be sued by an individual who claims that they violated his or her constitutional rights (*Anderson v. Creighton,* 483 U.S. 635 [1987]). There also is the consideration that legal suits divert police officers' attention from the protection of the public, discourage individuals from public service, and may deter the police from acting aggressively against crime (*Harlow v. Fitzgerald,* 457 U.S. 800, 814 [1982]).

The Supreme Court has decided a number of important cases under *Bivens,* four of which are summarized bellow.

Excessive force. In *Saucier v. Katz,* military police officers forcibly removed Elliot Katz from a public outdoor gathering to be addressed by Vice President Al Gore after Katz unfurled a protest banner. Katz alleged that he was shoved or thrown into a police van and filed suit against Officer Don Saucier for violating his Fourth Amendment rights. The U.S. Supreme Court held that Saucier was entitled to qualified immunity based on the fact that Saucier was under the duty to protect the safety and security of Vice President Gore and that there was no clearly established legal rule at the time prohibiting Saucier from acting as he did (*Saucier v. Katz,* 533 U.S. 194 [2001]).

Journalists. In *Wilson v. Layne,* the U.S. Marshals invited a *Washington Post* reporter and photographer to accompany them on raids to arrest armed individuals against whom there were outstanding warrants. The U.S. Supreme Court held that the journalists' entry into Wilson's house to observe the arrest violated the sanctity of his home. The warrant permitted the limited entry by the police to arrest Wilson inside his dwelling and did not authorize the presence of journalists. Were the marshals aware that their conduct was unlawful? The Court held that the marshals were entitled to qualified immunity because at the time there was no judicial decision holding that the participation of a journalist is unconstitutional. In the seven years between the entry into Wilson's home and the Supreme Court judgment in *Layne,* the Supreme Court noted that courts divided on the constitutionality of the presence of journalists. Justice Rehnquist noted that it would be unfair to hold the defendants liable when the judges themselves disagreed (*Wilson v. Layne,* 526 U.S. 603 [1999]).

False arrest. Secret Service agents were entitled to qualified immunity because their decision to arrest James Bryant, who they believed posed a threat to President Ronald Reagan, was reasonable although mistaken, and as a result, the agents did not violate Bryant's Fourth Amendment right against unreasonable search and seizure. The agents possessed trustworthy information that Bryant had written a letter referring to an assassination scheme that might be carried out during President Reagan's forthcoming visit to Germany. He made oral statements regretting that President Reagan had not been assassinated and refused to talk to Secret Service agents about the plot to kill the president. The Supreme Court stressed that qualified immunity is intended to insure that federal agents will not assume a cautious attitude because they fear being sued. This is "nowhere more important than when the specter of Presidential assassination is raised" (*Hunter v. Bryant,* 502 U.S. 224 [1991]).

Search warrant. In *Groh v. Ramirez,* Jeff Groh, an agent for the Bureau of Alcohol, Tobacco and Firearms, received a tip from an informant that visitors to Joseph Ramirez's ranch had seen a large stock of weaponry. Groh prepared an application for a warrant to search for and to seize automatic firearms and destructive devices including grenades, grenade launchers, rocket launchers, and other listed items. In the portion of the warrant specifying the place to be searched and the contraband that Groh expected to find, Groh typed a description of Ramirez's "blue home" and made no mention of the items listed on the application. The U.S. Supreme Court held that the warrant failed to specify the items to be seized, and as a result, the warrant was characterized by a "glaring" and "fatal deficiency." The Court concluded that Groh had violated Ramirez's Fourth Amendment rights and held that the particularity requirement is well established and that no reasonable officer could believe that Officer Groh's search was constitutional under the Fourth Amendment (*Groh v. Ramirez,* 540 U.S. 531 [2001]).

Bivens actions are brought against individuals. What about suing the federal government? The common law rule is that the "king can do no wrong," enjoys sovereign immunity, and may not be sued. The **Federal Tort Claim Act,** 28 U.S.C. § 1346(b), is a partial waiver of the federal government's sovereign immunity. The government under this statute is liable if a law enforcement officer commits assault and battery, false imprisonment, false arrest, abuse of process, or malicious prosecution. The government is not legally responsible for acts of libel, slander, misrepresentation, deceit, or interference with a contract between individuals (28 U.S.C. § 268[h]). The next section discusses the criminal prosecution of state and federal law enforcement officers.

You can find Anderson v. Creighton *and* Saucier v. Katz *on the study site, http://www.sagepub.com/lippmancp.*

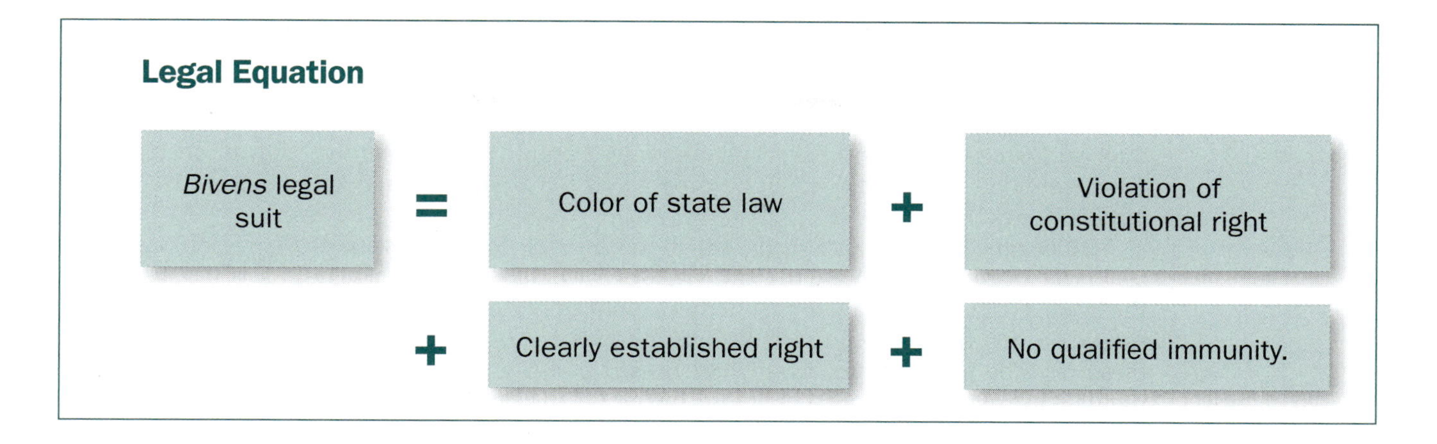

Criminal Prosecutions

State Criminal Prosecutions

State and local police officers who commit crimes may be prosecuted in state and in federal courts. Prosecutions, however, are rarely brought by state prosecutors. Prosecutors depend on the cooperation of the local police and are reluctant to bring charges. Jurors also are hesitant to convict police officers. Prosecutors confront the additional problem of finding credible witnesses. In trials of police officers, prosecutors typically are forced to rely on the testimony of officers who themselves conspired in the criminal activity and who have agreed to testify in return for a lesser sentence. In other instances, prosecutors may have to rely on the testimony of drug dealers and convicted criminals who have been victimized by police criminality. Prosecutors confronting these challenges understandably may encourage an individual to seek a civil remedy rather than look to the government to initiate a criminal prosecution. In a civil suit, the standard to prove guilt is much lower than in a criminal case, and the individual bringing a civil suit may receive monetary compensation. There are obvious advantages to bringing a civil case as opposed to relying on a criminal prosecution. Some of the considerations that an individual must weigh and balance are set forth below.

- ***Remedy.*** A civil case may lead to monetary compensation and a criminal case to the incarceration and fine of the defendant.
- ***Conviction.*** Guilt in a civil case is based on preponderance of the evidence (fifty-one percent), while a criminal case demands guilt beyond a reasonable doubt (guilt to a moral certainty).
- ***Jury.*** A unanimous verdict is not required in most state civil cases; unanimity or near unanimity is required in a criminal case.
- ***Costs.*** Some states and the federal government may provide attorneys' fees for lawyers bringing successful civil suits that vindicate an individual's constitutional rights. In a criminal case, the government brings the action, and there is no cost to the individual.

Police officers typically are prosecuted for felony offenses (punishable by more than a year in prison) that are defined in a state's criminal codes. These are the same laws that apply to citizens. Felony charges that typically are brought against the police include homicide, serious assault and battery, sexual offenses, robbery, burglary, bribery, extortion of money and drugs, trespass on private property, and hate crimes. A 1988 report by the U.S. Government's General Accounting Office reported drug-related police corruption in Chicago, Cleveland, Detroit, Los Angeles, Miami, New Orleans, New York, Philadelphia, Savannah, and Washington, D.C. The findings of the report are echoed by the 1994 Mollen Commission in New York City that found that a number of drug crimes had been carried out by small, organized groups of police officers who engaged in acts such as the unconstitutional search and seizure of the homes of known drug dealers. The drugs were then seized and sold by the officers on the street or sold back to the drug dealers. These crimes both harm victims and lower confidence in the integrity of the police.

State criminal codes also often include specific provisions punishing official misconduct and obstruction of justice by government employees. Remember that under the *dual sovereignty rule,* a defendant may be prosecuted for a crime by a state as well as the federal government.

Police officers are in an unusual situation. They use force and seize property from individuals in the process of enforcing the law. These acts would be considered criminal if engaged in by the average citizen. In evaluating whether an officer is guilty of a crime, the law takes into consideration that the police must make difficult decisions in a short period of time under extreme pressures. The U.S. Supreme Court has stressed that the police must make "split-second judgments...in circumstances that are tense, uncertain and rapidly evolving." For instance, in evaluating whether a police officer used excessive force, the Supreme Court standard is whether the officer's actions are objectively reasonable in light of the facts and circumstances. Courts have held that this must be judged from the perspective of a reasonable police officer rather than with the "20/20 vision of hindsight" (*Graham v. Connor,* 490 U.S. 386, 396 [1989]).

You only have to open a newspaper or watch the evening news to find coverage of confrontations between police and citizens. In a controversial case, two Detroit police officers were convicted of involuntary manslaughter for the 1995 killing of Malice Green, who had been taken into custody after a traffic stop. Three years later, Pittsburgh officers were acquitted of the involuntary manslaughter of motorist Johnny Gammage. In 1999, Los Angeles Police Officer Rafael Perez, assigned to the department's Rampart Division, was arrested for stealing cocaine from the L.A.P.D. property room. In exchange for a reduced sentence of five years in prison, Perez admitted to stealing a million dollars worth of cocaine and implicated more than seventy members of CRASH (Community Resources Against Street Hoodlums) in criminal activity. This included covering up three unjustified shootings by officers, one of which involved allowing the victim to bleed to death to prevent him from testifying. The police involved also reportedly planted evidence and framed innocent individuals, falsely arrested individuals, committed perjury, physically abused and humiliated suspects, engaged in drug dealing and the extortion of money from drug dealers, and carried out a bank robbery. Perez's partner Nino Durden was charged with attempted murder and, in exchange for confirming much of Perez's testimony, received a five-year prison sentence. Roughly a hundred criminal convictions in Los Angeles have been overturned on the grounds that the arrests and convictions were based on fabricated evidence or on unconstitutionally seized evidence. Professor Erwin Chemerinsky, in introducing the report of the Board of Inquiry appointed to investigate Perez's allegations, observed that "[n]othing is more inimical to the rule of law than police officers...flouting it and using their authority to convict innocent people....This is conduct associated with the most repressive dictators and police states." In the next section, we will see that criminal prosecutions also may be brought by federal prosecutors.

Federal Criminal Prosecutions

Criminal charges may be brought by the U.S. Department of Justice against state as well as federal criminal justice officials for the violation of U.S. statutes, including laws protecting individuals' constitutional rights. In terms of constitutional rights, prosecutions typically are based on an 1866 civil rights law (18 U.S.C. § 242) that authorizes the prosecution of state or federal officials who act under the color of law or custom with the specific intent to deprive an individual of a constitutional right or right protected under federal law. The leading case interpreting § 242 is *Screws v. United States,* in which a Georgia sheriff and two deputies were convicted of beating to death a handcuffed African American detainee (*Screws v. United States,* 325 U.S. 91 [1945]).

Section 242 is one of three color-of-law federal criminal statutes that provide a legal basis for the U.S. Justice Department's prosecution of state and federal officials.

- ***Title 18, Section 242 of the U.S. Code.*** Acts under color of any law, statute, ordinance, regulation, or custom that willfully subject an individual to deprivation of right protected by the U.S. Constitution or by a federal statute.

- ***Title 18, Section 241 of the U.S. Code.*** Participation in a conspiracy to act under color of state law to deprive an individual of a constitutional right or right guaranteed under a federal statute.
- ***Title 18, Section 245 of the U.S. Code.*** Interference, intimidation, or injury to an individual because of involvement in a federally protected activity, including a federal program or employment, service as a juror, or receipt of a federal benefit.

In 2005, the FBI investigated more than 1,100 allegations that officers acted under the color of law to deprive an individual of a constitutional right or right protected under U.S. law. The FBI records that these investigations fall under five broad areas:

- Excessive force
- Sexual assault
- False arrest and fabrication of evidence
- Deprivation of property
- Failure to protect an individual from harm

In *Lynch v. United States,* a Georgia sheriff and one of his deputies appealed their convictions for depriving several African American detainees of equal protection of the laws, unlawfully detaining them without due process of law, and subjecting them to assault and battery and to torture and cruel and unusual punishment. The sheriff and his deputies, after attending a Ku Klux Klan cross burning and rally, arrested a number of African Americans for public drunkenness, only one of whom apparently was inebriated. The individuals arrested then were handed over to hooded and robed members of the white supremacist Ku Klux Klan who subjected the detainees to abuse and beatings. The Fifth Circuit concluded that the sheriff and his deputy "willfully failed to accord these victims the opportunity for . . . a trial, and . . . turned them over to [the] mob to suffer trial by ordeal, with the conscious purpose and willful intent of depriving them of their constitutional right to a legal trial" (*Lynch v. United States,* 189 F.2d 476, 481 [5th Cir. 1951]).

One of the most shocking incidents of police brutality in recent years involved Brooklyn Police Officer Justin Volpe, who pled guilty and received a thirty-year sentence in 1999 for sodomizing Abner Louima with a baton in the bathroom of the precinct house. Louima subsequently settled his civil suit for over eight million dollars.

The last section of the chapter outlines police department procedures for disciplining police officers who violate internal police department regulations.

Administrative Remedies

We now turn our attention to remedies that do not involve the courts, or what are called *nonjudicial remedies*. These nonjudicial administrative procedures are carried out by the police department or by agencies independent of the police department. There are two major approaches to enforcing police department regulations.

Internal affairs. This is a unit of the police department that investigates misconduct. The punishment for violations of police regulations are typically imposed by the officer's commanding officer with the agreement of the police chief.

Civilian review. These agencies are composed of private citizens with authority to investigate and, in some instances, to discipline the police.

Internal Affairs

The *internal affairs division* of the police department is charged with investigating improper conduct by police department employees. Internal affairs maintains the reputation and public respect for the police by demonstrating that misconduct will not be tolerated. Fair and objective investigations also serve to protect police officers against false allegations of misconduct. The type of misconduct investigated may range from insulting a motorist to bribery and theft. Some sense of the types of investigations carried out by internal affairs divisions is indicated by looking at the authority to investigate of the St. Petersburg, Florida, Police Department's Internal Affairs Division.

- An allegation of misconduct against an employee of the department
- The discharge of a firearm by an employee, other than for training, practice, or sports hunting
- Any vehicle pursuit
- Suicides or deaths while in custody
- An investigation authorized by the Chief of Police

Misconduct under the regulations of most police departments may include the following types of behavior:

- Crime
- Excessive force
- False arrest
- Illegal search
- Harassment
- Conduct unbecoming an officer, including drinking on duty and neglect of duty
- Minor uniform and disciplinary violations

An internal affairs investigation may be initiated by a citizen complaint, by a referral from other police officers, or by information uncovered by internal affairs. Following the investigation, the record is reviewed by the commander of internal affairs, who may reach one of various conclusions.

- ***Unfounded.*** The evidence does not support the allegations.
- ***Exonerated.*** The incident occurred, but the officer's conduct was consistent with police department policy.
- ***Not sustained.*** The evidence is not sufficient to "clearly prove or disprove" the allegation.
- ***Sustained.*** The investigation indicates that the complaint is valid.

A case that is unfounded, exonerated, or not sustained is closed. A case that is sustained results in a recommendation for disciplinary action.

A sustained case typically is sent to the officer's commanding officer and then is transmitted up the chain of the command to the police chief for the final decision. In setting the appropriate penalty, various factors are considered including the resulting harm to the public, whether the officer's violation occurred while he or she was attempting to protect the public, the officer's past record, and whether the violation is partially explained by the officer's lack of experience. Public controversy has erupted in cities such as Seattle in cases in which the police chief has acted in his or her view of the public interest and has refused to follow the recommendation that an officer should be subjected to harsh punishment. There are various disciplinary punishments that may be imposed by the Chief of Police:

- Counseling
- Training
- Verbal reprimand
- Written reprimand
- Fine
- Suspension without pay
- Demotion
- Termination

A national sample indicates that roughly ten percent of cases are sustained and that approximately three-quarters of these cases result in reprimands or suspensions. In serious cases, the department may initiate procedures to decertify an officer to prevent him or her from ever again serving as a police officer in the state. The complaint also may be referred to the local prosecutor for criminal prosecution. A citizen who is the victim of police misconduct also may decide to file a tort claim or to seek a remedy under § 1983.

Reports in several major cities have concluded that departments at times have overlooked police misconduct and that the "blue wall of silence" has frustrated investigations. On the other hand, there are numerous examples of departments vigorously enforcing the law. In 2005, four Chicago Police tactical officers assigned to Special Operations Section pled guilty to stealing narcotics and cash from drug dealers. The department subsequently announced that it was disbanding Special Operations. In 2003, a police department gang specialist was sentenced to life in prison for operating a Chicago-to-Miami drug ring with gang members. Prosecutors called him the "most corrupt cop in Chicago history." Two years earlier, a former Chicago police deputy pled guilty to involvement in a jewelry theft ring and was sentenced to thirteen years in prison. Keep in mind that studies indicate that a small number of police officers engage in misconduct and that departments have developed various programs to identify and to monitor the conduct of these "rogue police officers." Monitoring and investigations also have been improved by mounting surveillance cameras on police squad cars.

External Review

The obvious objection to leaving the investigation of misconduct to Internal Affairs is that the police are no different than other organizations in preferring to simply overlook rather than to punish misconduct. This is the familiar tendency to "circle the wagons" and to protect your fellow workers and your department's reputation. Several towns and cities have attempted to assert effective control over the police by creating review boards composed of ordinary citizens. These boards may investigate and, in some cases, recommend discipline for police officers.

The police historically have resisted and resented external or **civilian review.** The police confront danger on a daily basis and understandably may believe that the public does not understand the challenges that they confront. Law enforcement officers caution that the "second-guessing" of their decisions by the public lowers morale and diverts attention from their primary mission, which is to control crime and to insure safe and secure communities. Police administrators complain that involving citizens in disciplining officers undermines the administrators' respect and authority.

The police were able to resist civilian review for many years, and civilian review was limited to a small number of modest-sized cities. The notion that the public should be involved in police oversight gradually developed momentum, and by 1994, roughly eighty percent of police departments with over 1,000 officers had adopted some form of civilian review. The argument in favor of citizen involvement is that it improves community relations and enables ordinary citizens to communicate with the police.

Civilian review boards typically are appointed by the mayor or city council and, in most instances, are composed of a cross-section of the community. In some cities, nonuniformed police officers also sit on the board. The boards typically apply a preponderance-of-the-evidence standard requiring that the weight of credible evidence must indicate that the officer engaged in misconduct. Civilian boards have different powers in different cities and follow several general patterns that are listed below.

- ***Civilian review.*** The civilian review board has full powers to hire professionals to investigate police misconduct. The board recommends punishment to the police chief.
- ***Civilian investigation.*** The review board investigates complaints while the police department is in charge of evaluating the evidence and disciplining officers.

- ***Civilian oversight.*** The review board or a single auditor monitors police investigations for objectivity and fairness. The investigation, the evaluation of the evidence, and the punishment are left to the police.
- ***Civilian mediation.*** Review boards mediate or attempt to resolve some less serious disputes between the citizen and the police officer.

Each civilian review board tends to be somewhat different, and you should read about the police disciplinary procedures in your area. In Oakland, California, the civilian board holds open hearings on cases, and discipline is imposed by the city manager rather than by the police chief. Flint, Michigan, has a city ombudsman who investigates and disciplines misconduct by employees throughout the city government. Rochester, New York, has introduced mediation (negotiation) between police officers and citizens in an effort to resolve disputes. In Berkeley, California, the civilian review board and the police conduct simultaneous investigations and send their separate recommendations to the city manager. The civilian board also makes recommendations on police policies and investigative practices and invites civilians to offer suggestions.

The New York City Civilian Complaint Review Board has a budget of over ten million dollars and subpoena power, or the authority to compel people to testify or to hand over evidence. It is interesting that less than ten percent of the complaints in New York City are substantiated. A significant percentage of these substantiated charges, however, result in some form of discipline. This is not unusual. The data indicate that civilian panels tend to support the police in most instances. This may indicate either that the boards are effective in limiting police misconduct or, in the alternative, that a large number of serious incidents are either going unreported or being held to be unfounded.

It is inevitable in a large organization that some people will give in to the temptations of power or money or find themselves overwhelmed by the stresses and strains of the street. There is no magic formula to solve police misconduct. The effective redress of citizen grievances and police accountability requires a combination of approaches ranging from training and monitoring of "problem" officers to legal and administrative remedies.

Chapter Summary

The exclusionary rule does not always provide an adequate remedy to deter police misconduct. An individual may be unlawfully searched, and the issue of the search may not be raised by the defense because the charges are dropped. The exclusionary rule also will not assist a victim of excessive force who is not charged with a crime. There are three remedies in addition to the exclusionary rule available to deter and to punish police violation of constitutional rights.

Civil remedies. Civil suits may be brought against individual police officers, their supervisors, and local governments for money damages. Injunctions may be filed requesting a court to order that the police stop enforcing a policy that violates individuals' constitutional rights or rights protected under federal law. The Department of Justice also may bring a "pattern-or-practice" legal action requiring a police department to halt a persistent pattern of violating constitutional rights.

Criminal remedies. State prosecutors may bring criminal charges against state and local police officers for the violation of state criminal statutes. U.S. prosecutors also may file charges under federal law against state and federal officers for the violation of individuals' constitutional rights.

Administrative remedies. Police officers may be subjected to internal administrative procedures for violating departmental regulations. These investigations may be conducted by internal affairs divisions or by external civilian review boards. Complaints that are sustained may result in penalties ranging from fines and suspensions to termination.

The primary mechanism for bringing a civil suit against a state or local police officer is § 1983. There are three steps in a § 1983 action.

Color of law. The defendant must have acted under the "color of state law."

Constitutional rights. The defendant must have violated a constitutional right or a right provided by a federal law. The U.S. Supreme Court declared that this step was not "mandatory" in *Herring v. United States*. *Herring* held that a judge may first determine whether a right was clearly established before turning his or her attention to the question whether the defendant's constitutional rights were violated.

Liability under § 1983 may be imposed on a police officer who is directly responsible for violating an individual's constitutional rights as well as on the officer's commanding officer and, in some cases, city officials. The standard for supervisory liability is proof of an "affirmative link" between the actions or orders of supervisors and the allegations of police misconduct.

The next step is to determine whether the § 1983 suit is barred by absolute or by qualified immunity.

Absolute immunity. Judges, prosecutors, witnesses, jurors, and other individuals possess absolute immunity for acts undertaken as part of the judicial function. This is based on the interest in insuring that decisions in the judicial process are not being influenced by the threat of a legal suit. Errors at trial always may be corrected on appeal.

Qualified immunity. Police officers and other governmental officials may be sued only for violation of clearly established constitutional rights or rights clearly established by federal law. This permits the police to enforce the law with confidence that they will be held liable only in the event that they disregard clearly established legal principles.

A question that continues to be debated is whether the police or other government officials are civilly liable for failing to protect an individual from a criminal act. The rule is that the police and other government officials do not have an affirmative legal duty to protect the general public. Courts have developed a "state-created danger" exception that applies in circumstances in which state action creates or exposes an individual to danger that he or she would not otherwise have confronted.

States and state agencies cannot be sued under § 1983. This immunity, however, does not extend to cities, towns, counties, and local governmental agencies. Cities, counties, and local governmental agencies are liable when police officials or other employees inflict an injury while carrying out a governmental "policy" (an officially adopted local law or regulation adopted by the police department) or custom (a long-standing, unwritten, and widely recognized practice by police officers). Section 1983 also allows for injunctive relief against a local government or governmental agency. A violation of an injunction is punishable by contempt and may result in a fine or imprisonment.

The federal Police Misconduct Statute provides that it is unlawful for law enforcement officers or law enforcement agencies to "engage in a pattern or practice of conduct" that deprives individuals of a constitutional right or right guaranteed by the laws of the United States. The U.S. Attorney General, when he or she has "reasonable cause" to believe that such a pattern of violations has occurred, may ask a court to direct a police department to correct the practice. This is a mechanism to address a widespread practice rather than an isolated incident. Departments confronting pattern-or-practice suits in a number of cases have voluntarily entered into consent decrees with the Department of Justice.

State and local law enforcement officers also may be sued in state court for committing a tort. A law enforcement officer may be held liable for the torts such as assault and battery, wrongful death, false arrest and imprisonment, trespass, destruction of property, and breaking and entering. These legal actions are difficult to bring because the police possess the defense of official immunity. A legal action also may be brought in some states against the police department or local town or county that employed the police officer. The principle of *respondeat superior* holds a government agency liable for the acts of employees undertaken in the course of their employment.

What about the liability of federal law enforcement officers and federal employees? In 1971, in *Bivens v. Six Unknown Named Agents*, the U.S. Supreme Court held that federal law enforcement officers are civilly liable for the violations of individuals' Fourth Amendment rights. This was a significant step because § 1983 covers state rather than federal officials. The Federal Tort Claim Act is a partial waiver of the federal government's sovereign immunity. The government is liable if a law enforcement officer commits assault and battery, false imprisonment, false arrest, abuse of process, or malicious prosecution.

State and local police officers who commit crimes are subject to criminal prosecution in state and federal court. Criminal charges also may be brought by the U.S. Department of Justice against state and federal criminal justice officials for the violation of U.S. statutes, including laws protecting individuals' constitutional rights. These prosecutions typically are based on an 1866 civil rights law (18 U.S.C. § 242) that authorizes the prosecution of state or federal officials who act under the color of a local or state law or custom with the specific intent of depriving an individual of a constitutional right or of a right protected under federal law.

There also are administrative procedures for enforcing internal police department regulations. These investigations are carried out by the internal affairs division within the police department and by external civilian review boards composed of private citizens with authority to investigate and, in some instances, to discipline the police.

The question is whether those judges, legal scholars, and commentators who argue that the exclusionary rule exacts too high a price are correct in the view that the civil, criminal, and administrative remedies discussed in this chapter can adequately protect individuals' constitutional rights. Consider your view of this question as you review the material in the chapter.

Chapter Review Questions

1. How do the remedies discussed in this chapter differ from the exclusionary rule?
2. Discuss the "color of state law" requirement for a § 1983 action.
3. Explain absolute immunity and qualified immunity. How does qualified immunity balance the interests of a defendant who is a police officer and the interests of the plaintiff bringing the case?
4. Under what circumstances may a local town, city, or county be held liable under § 1983?
5. What is the purpose of an injunction? When will the U.S. Department of Justice bring a "pattern-or-practice" action against a law enforcement agency?
6. Explain the purpose and requirements of a *Bivens* action. Is the federal government subject to a civil suit?
7. Distinguish between state tort and criminal remedies. What is the role of the U.S. Department of Justice in criminal prosecutions?
8. Outline the role of the internal affairs divisions and civilian review boards in monitoring, investigating, and disciplining the police.
9. Summarize the various remedies discussed in this chapter.

Legal Terminology

absolute immunity
Bivens legal suit
civilian review
color of state law
dual sovereignty doctrine
Federal Tort Claim Act
injunction
pattern-or-practice decree
qualified immunity
Title 42, Section 1983 of the U.S. Code
tort actions

Criminal Procedure on the Web

Log on to the Web-based student study site at **http://www.sagepub.com/lippmancp** to assist you in completing the Criminal Procedure on the Web exercises, as well as for additional features such as leading cases, podcasts, self-quizzes, and audio/video links.

1. Read about police training in high-speed pursuits and the debate over high-speed pursuits.
2. View the video that the U.S. Supreme Court watched in deciding *Scott v. Harris*.
3. Consult resources on police ethics and misconduct.

Bibliography

Michael G. Collins, *Section 1983 Litigation in a Nutshell,* 3rd ed. (St. Paul, MN: West Publishing, 2005). An accessible and clear explanation of judicial decisions interpreting § 1983.

John C. Jeffries Jr., Pamela S. Karlan, Peter W. Low, and George A. Rutherglen, *Civil Rights Actions: Enforcing the Constitution,* 2nd ed. (New York: Foundation, 2007). A comprehensive and sophisticated discussion of legal remedies for constitutional violations.

12 The Initiation of the Legal Process, Bail, and the Right to Counsel

Did Clarence Gideon have the right to a lawyer at his trial?

[Clarence Gideon] was charged in a Florida state court with having broken and entered a poolroom with intent to commit a misdemeanor. This offense is a felony under Florida law. Appearing in court without funds and without a lawyer, petitioner asked the court to appoint counsel for him. . . . [The judge replied,] "Mr. Gideon, I am sorry, but I cannot appoint Counsel to represent you in this case. Under the laws of the State of Florida, the only time the Court can appoint Counsel to represent a Defendant is when that person is charged with a capital offense. I am sorry, but I will have to deny your request to appoint Counsel to defend you in this case." . . . Put to trial before a jury, Gideon conducted his defense about as well as could be expected from a layman. He made an opening statement to the jury, cross-examined the State's witnesses, presented witnesses in his own defense, declined to testify himself, and made a short argument "emphasizing his innocence to the charge contained in the Information filed in this case." The jury returned a verdict of guilty, and petitioner was sentenced to serve five years in the state prison.

Core Concepts and Summary Statements

Introduction

This chapter discusses the prosecutor's discretion to bring a criminal charge and the defendant's first appearance before a magistrate or judge. The text focuses on two aspects of the first appearance: first, pretrial release, bail, and the conditions of pretrial confinement; and second, the right to an appointed lawyer for indigents and the right to effective legal representation.

The Prosecutorial Discretion to Charge

A. Prosecutors retain "broad discretion" over whether to file a criminal charge and over which criminal charge to file. There is a presumption of regularity. Courts presume that in the absence of clear evidence to the contrary, prosecutors honestly, fairly, and responsibly exercise their authority.

B. Prosecutors may not engage in selective prosecution or vindictive prosecution.

Probable Cause to Detain a Suspect

A. In *Gerstein v. Pugh,* the U.S. Supreme Court held that the Constitution requires a judicial determination of probable cause as a condition of a suspect's "extended restraint of liberty." This "nonadversarial" probable cause hearing must be held "promptly" following an arrest.

B. In *County of Riverside v. McLaughlin,* the Supreme Court defined "promptly" and held that a forty-eight-hour period of delay is a presumptively reasonable period of time within which to hold the hearing.

First Appearance

A. The first appearance is triggered by the prosecutor's filing of a complaint.

B. At the first appearance, a suspect is informed of the criminal charges and of his or her rights, the conditions for pretrial release are established, and a lawyer is appointed for indigent defendants.

Pretrial Release

A. The Eighth Amendment to the U.S. Constitution provides that "excessive bail shall not be required." The bail provision has not been incorporated into the Due Process Clause of the Fourteenth Amendment. Most state constitutions, however, create a right to bail in all but capital cases.

B. The Bail Clause has "never been thought to accord a right to bail in all cases, but merely . . . provide[s] that bail should not be excessive in those cases where it is appropriate to grant bail. Bail is not compulsory where the punishment may be death."

C. Bail is excessive where the bail figure is more than is required to guarantee that a suspect will appear for trial.

D. In 1987, in *United States v. Salerno,* the U.S. Supreme Court affirmed the constitutionality of preventive detention.

Pretrial Detention

An individual who is not released prior to trial typically is detained in a short-term correctional facility. In *Bell v. Wolfish,* the Supreme Court held that while these detainees retain their constitutional rights, they are subject to reasonable regulations adopted to insure order and security in the institution. The Court cautioned that detainees have not been convicted of a crime and may not be subjected to "arbitrary or purposeless" conditions that constitute punishment.

Indigency and the Right to Counsel

In 1963, in *Gideon v. Wainwright,* the U.S. Supreme held that the Fourteenth Amendment incorporated the Sixth Amendment right to counsel and that indigent individuals charged with felonies in state courts are entitled to an appointed counsel.

Right to Counsel and Critical Stages of the Prosecution

A. The U.S. Supreme Court has held that individuals are entitled to a lawyer when formal adversarial criminal proceedings are initiated against them.

B. Following the initiation of formal criminal proceedings, the right to counsel attaches at critical stages of the prosecution. A critical stage is considered to be any phase of the prosecution that may negatively impact the defendant's ability to present a defense at trial and at which the presence of an attorney would safeguard the defendant.

The Meaning of "All Criminal Prosecutions"

A. In *Argersinger v. Hamlin,* the U.S. Supreme Court held that "absent a knowing and intelligent waiver, no person may be imprisoned for any offense, whether classified as petty, misdemeanor, or felony, unless he was represented by counsel."

B. In *Scott v. Illinois,* the justices held that unless a defendant is provided with a lawyer, a court may not sentence him or her to imprisonment.

Determining Indigency

The Supreme Court has not defined the standards for determining whether an individual is indigent and therefore entitled to the appointment of a lawyer in a criminal prosecution. States have different standards for indigency and, in many cases, the standard is set forth in a state legislative statute.

The Right to Select an Appointed Counsel

A. Where the state appoints a lawyer, a defendant has no right to be represented by a specific lawyer, although a court may take the defendant's preference into consideration.

B. A nonindigent defendant possesses the Sixth Amendment right to be represented by the lawyer of his or her choice. A defendant does not have the right to be represented by an individual who is not a member of the bar, who has a conflict of interest, or whom he or she cannot afford.

The Right to Effective Legal Representation

A. The U.S. Supreme Court has held that there is a two-prong test for ineffective assistance of counsel.

B. To pass the first test, the defendant is required to identify specific aspects of the lawyer's performance that fall below the range of reasonably effective competence demanded by an attorney in a criminal case.

C. The second question is whether there is a "reasonable probability that the result would have been different."

D. In *United States v. Cronic,* the Court indicated that there are cases in which a lawyer's conduct falls dramatically below the expected standard and that therefore prejudice will be automatically presumed.

The Right to Self-Representation

In 1975, in *Faretta v. California,* the U.S. Supreme Court held that the Sixth Amendment provides an accused with a "constitutionally protected right" of self-representation.

Introduction

In earlier chapters, we discussed the investigation and detection of crime by the police through searches and seizures and through the interrogation and identification of suspects. Once the police have completed their investigation, they must decide whether to formally arrest a suspect and to turn the case over to the prosecutor. They may decide to drop the case and to continue the investigation because of a belief that a suspect is not guilty, because they lack evidence, or because they consider the crime to be a fairly minor violation of the law. The police also may decide to continue the investigation and to focus on other suspects. In some instances, the police may conclude that a warning will deter an individual from violating the law in the future or that a defendant already has spent enough time in jail to provide adequate punishment.

In the next three chapters, we will examine the pretrial, trial, and appeal stages of the criminal justice process. This chapter covers the early steps in the pretrial process. We first discuss prosecutorial discretion and the filing of criminal charges. Then we turn our attention to the initial stages of the pretrial process: the determination of probable cause to detain a suspect and the defendant's first appearance before a magistrate or judge. The remainder of the chapter discusses two central aspects of the first appearance:

- Pretrial release and bail and the conditions of pretrial confinement
- The right of an indigent to be represented by a lawyer

As you read the chapter, pay particular attention to the protections accorded to individuals in the pretrial process and to how the Supreme Court balances these safeguards against the social interest in the criminal prosecution of offenders.

The Prosecutorial Discretion to Charge

Following a suspect's arrest, responsibility for the case shifts to the prosecutor, who is the government official responsible for enforcing the criminal law through the prosecution of criminal offenses. U.S. Supreme Court Justice Robert Jackson famously observed that the prosecutor is perhaps the most powerful person in the criminal justice system. Courts have recognized the authority of prosecutors to decide who is to be charged with a crime, what crime to charge, and whether to plea-bargain a case. The prosecutor also has discretion over whether to refer a defendant to a diversion program for substance abuse or psychological counseling or for some other purpose rather than to prosecute the individual.

In *Wayte v. United States,* the U.S. Supreme Court observed that prosecutors retain "broad discretion" as to whether to prosecute. "So long as the prosecution has probable cause to believe that the accused has committed an offense defined by statutes, the decision whether or not to prosecute, and what charge . . . generally rests entirely in his discretion" (*Wayte v. United States,* 470 U.S. 598, 607 [1985]). There is a **presumption of regularity**: Courts presume that in the absence of clear evidence to the contrary, prosecutors honestly, fairly, and responsibly exercise their authority.

An example of the prosecutor's exercise of discretion is *United States v. Batchelder.* Two identical federal statutes applied in this case; each punished a felon who takes possession of a firearm transported across state lines. The prosecutor charged and convicted Batchelder under the statute that carried a penalty of five years rather than under the statute that carried a penalty of two years. The U.S. Supreme Court upheld the prosecutor's exercise of discretion, explaining that "there is no appreciable difference between the discretion a prosecutor exercises when deciding whether to charge under one of two statutes with different elements and the discretion he exercises when choosing one of two statutes with identical elements." Consider that the end result of the decision in *Batchelder* was that the prosecutor was able to determine the amount of time that Batchelder potentially would spend in prison without having to explain or defend his decision (*United States v. Batchelder,* 442 U.S. 113, 125 [1979]).

Why have courts recognized the discretion of prosecutors to prosecute or not to prosecute a case and to decide what criminal charges to bring against a defendant rather than to subject these decisions to review by a judge? There are several reasons listed below why courts have adopted the view that prosecutors' charging decisions are "ill-suited for judicial review" (*Wayte v. United States,* 470 U.S. 598, 607 [1985]).

Separation of powers. The prosecutor is a member of the executive branch and is charged with responsibility for insuring that the "laws are faithfully executed." Judges are members of the judicial branch and are reluctant to interfere with the daily decisions of the executive unless the prosecutor violates the state constitution or U.S. Constitution.

Discretionary judgment. A prosecutor considers a range of factors and information in deciding whether to prosecute a case. Courts lack the expertise to evaluate the prosecutor's weighing and balancing of factors such as the strength of evidence, the impact of the prosecution in deterring other crimes, the government's priorities for enforcement, the circumstances of the case, and the defendant's personal character and background.

Resources. A review of the prosecutor's decisions would delay prosecutions and consume considerable time and energy.

The U.S. Supreme Court has observed that although "prosecutorial discretion is broad," it is not "unlimited." Courts will step in and review a prosecutor's decisions where there is an allegation that the prosecutor engaged in either selective prosecution in violation of the Equal Protection Clause of the Fifth and Fourteenth Amendments or **vindictive prosecutions** in violation of the Due Process Clause of the Fifth and Fourteenth Amendments.

Selective prosecution. The Equal Protection Clause of the Fifth and Fourteenth Amendments prohibits a prosecutor from prosecuting an individual because of the individual's race, gender, religion, or exercise of his or her fundamental rights. (You may recall this was discussed in Chapter 2.) A leading example of this protection comes from *Wayte v. United States*. Wayte protested the Vietnam War and wrote government officials stating that he had no intention of registering for the military draft. Wayte's name, along with the names of 133 other individuals who wrote the government refusing to register for the military draft, was sent to the U.S. Department of Justice for prosecution. In each case, these individuals were warned by the FBI that they were required to register or would be subject to prosecution. Wayte nevertheless continued to resist the draft and was prosecuted for draft evasion. He argued that this so-called passive enforcement system violated the First Amendment to the U.S. Constitution by targeting vocal opponents of the war for prosecution while the government took no action against the other 674,000 nonregistrants who had not written the government.

The U.S. Supreme Court held that in order for Wayte to succeed in his claim of selective prosecution, he was required to demonstrate that the prosecutor's decision had a "discriminatory effect" and that "it was motivated by a discriminatory purpose." What precisely is required under this two-prong test? The first question is whether individuals are singled out for prosecution who are members of a particular race, gender, or religion or who have engaged in the exercise of a fundamental freedom while other "similarly situated" individuals who do not fall within the group are not prosecuted. The second question is whether the prosecutorial policy is based on an intent to discriminate against the members of the group. Wayte failed to satisfy this burden. He was unable to demonstrate that the government prosecution policy was based on an intent to punish individuals who protested the draft. Individuals were not prosecuted who initially expressed an intent to refuse to register for the draft and who later registered after meeting with the FBI. The Supreme Court found that the purpose in relying on the passive enforcement system was to enable the government efficiently and easily to identify individuals who were subject to prosecution for draft resistance rather than to spend the time and resources required to locate all nonregistrants (*Wayte v. United States,* 470 U.S. 598, 606 [1985]).

Defendants have a heavy burden in overcoming the presumption of regularity and establishing a discriminatory intent. In *United States v. Turner,* the African American defendants were indicted on one count of distributing cocaine and contended that they had been selected for prosecution because of their race. They submitted a memorandum documenting that between 1991 and 1993, the Office of the Federal Public Defender for the Central District of California had defended crack cocaine cases involving forty-seven African American and five Hispanic defendants and that no Caucasians had been indicted for an offense involving crack cocaine. This pattern of selective prosecution was corroborated by newspaper articles and an academic study. The Ninth Circuit Court of Appeals rejected the claim of racial discrimination and held that the defendants had failed to produce evidence that individuals arrested for the same offense belonging to "other races had been left unprosecuted." The appellate court, instead, concluded that the statistics reflected the fact that the distribution of crack cocaine is dominated by violent African American street gangs. The data failed to establish that the government had failed to pursue similarly situated Caucasian or Hispanic individuals. What other data could the defendants have submitted to strengthen their claim? (*United States v. Turner,* 104 F.3d 1180, 1185 [1997]).

Vindictive prosecutions. In a vindictive prosecution, a prosecutor retaliates against a defendant who asserts his or her rights by bringing a more serious charge against the defendant. Courts have held that this vindictive prosecution is "patently unconstitutional," violates an individual's right to due process of law, and risks deterring other individuals from asserting their rights.

In *Blackledge v. Perry,* Perry was convicted of the misdemeanor of assault with a deadly weapon. Perry then filed a notice of appeal to a superior court in which, under North Carolina law, he was entitled to a new trial before a jury. In other words, in this second stage, the slate is wiped clean and the prior conviction no longer is recognized. The prosecutor responded by filing a new indictment charging Perry with the felony of assault with a deadly weapon with the intent to kill and to inflict serious bodily injury. Perry subsequently entered a guilty plea to the felony charge.

The U.S. Supreme Court held that an individual convicted of an offense is

> entitled to pursue his statutory right to a trial *de novo* [new trial] without apprehension that the State will retaliate by substituting a more serous charge from the original one, thus subjecting him to a significantly increased potential period of incarceration.

The Court held that under these circumstances, there is a "realistic likelihood of vindictiveness" on the part of the prosecutor and that the prosecutor had improperly filed a felony charge against Perry (*Blackledge v. Perry,* 417 U.S. 21 [1974]).

The U.S. Supreme Court has not presumed vindictiveness on the part of a prosecutor who brings more serious charges against a defendant who, prior to trial, refuses to plead guilty and announces that he or she plans to proceed to trial. In *United States v. Goodwin,* Goodwin was arrested and arraigned before a U.S. magistrate for various misdemeanors. He opened plea negotiations with the government but later informed the prosecutor that he did not plan to plead guilty and wanted a jury trial. Another prosecutor then obtained a four-count indictment charging Goodwin with a felony along with several misdemeanors. Goodwin was convicted and moved to set aside the verdict on the grounds of prosecutorial vindictiveness.

The Supreme Court rejected Goodwin's claim, explaining that it is natural for a prosecutor to continue to assess the strength of his or her case prior to trial and that a prosecutor may conclude in good faith that a more severe charge is justified. A change in a prosecutor's charging decision made after the initial trial is completed is "much more likely to be improperly motivated than is a pretrial decision." A prosecutor should

> remain free before trial to exercise the broad discretion entrusted to him to determine the extent of the societal interest in prosecution. An initial decision should not freeze future conduct.... The initial charges filed by a prosecutor may not reflect the extent to which an individual is legitimately subject to prosecution. (*United States v. Goodwin,* 457 U.S. 368, 381–382 [1962])

We now turn our attention to the initial steps in the criminal justice process that follow a decision by the police to arrest an individual for a criminal offense.

Probable Cause to Detain a Suspect

The first step for a prosecutor following the arrest of an individual without an arrest warrant or formal indictment by a grand jury is a judicial determination of whether there is probable cause to detain the suspect for an extended period. In *Gerstein v. Pugh* (discussed in Chapters 5 and 12), the U.S. Supreme Court held that a Florida law that permitted a suspect to be held for a month or more before being taken before a judge to determine whether there is probable cause constituted an unreasonable restraint on liberty in violation of the Fourth Amendment. The U.S. Supreme Court stated that the Constitution requires a judicial determination of probable cause as a condition for an "extended restraint of liberty." This "nonadversarial" **probable cause hearing** must be held "promptly" following an arrest. In *County of Riverside v. McLaughlin,* the U.S. Supreme Court defined "promptly" and held that a forty-eight-hour period of delay is a presumptively reasonable period of time within which to conduct the hearing. The forty-eigh-hour requirement balances the interest in protecting society by detaining a suspect against the risk that an overly lengthy detention will unduly interfere with a suspect's job, income, and personal life and freedom. The probable cause standard to detain a suspect is the same as the probable cause standard to arrest a suspect.

The time between the arrest and the probable cause hearing allows the police to undertake "administrative steps incident to arrest." This includes "completing paperwork, searching the suspect, inventorying property, fingerprinting, photographing, checking for a prior record, laboratory testing, and conducting line-ups" (*Sanders v. City of Houston,* 543 F. Supp. 694, 701 [1982]). The *Gerstein* hearing often is combined with the *first appearance* (discussed below).

In *County of Riverside v. McLaughlin,* the next case in the text, the U.S. Supreme Court discusses the requirement that a suspect is to be brought "promptly" before a magistrate following his or her arrest for a determination of whether there is probable cause. Pay attention to how the U.S. Supreme Court balances various interests and determines that a forty-eight-hour period between arrest and the *Gerstein* hearing is reasonable under the Fourth Amendment. Is this too lengthy a period to detain an individual without a determination that there is probable cause to detain the suspect?

How long may the police detain a suspect before obtaining a probable cause determination before a magistrate?

County of Riverside v. McLaughlin, 500 U.S. 44 (1991), O'Connor, J.

Issue

This is a class action brought under 42 U.S.C. § 1983 challenging the manner in which the County of Riverside, California, provides probable cause determinations to persons arrested without a warrant....Under county policy...arraignments must be conducted without unnecessary delay and, in any event, within two days of arrest. This two-day requirement excludes from computation weekends and holidays. Thus, an individual arrested without a warrant late in the week may in some cases be held for as long as five days before receiving a probable cause determination. Over the Thanksgiving holiday, a seven-day delay is possible.

Facts

In August 1987, Donald Lee McLaughlin filed a complaint in the U.S. District Court for the Central District of California, seeking injunctive and declaratory relief on behalf of himself and "all others similarly situated." The complaint alleged that McLaughlin was then currently incarcerated in the Riverside County Jail and had not received a probable cause determination. He requested "an order and judgment requiring that the defendants and the County of Riverside provide in-custody arrestees, arrested without warrants, prompt probable cause, bail and arraignment hearings."...The second amended complaint named three additional plaintiffs—Johnny E. James, Diana Ray Simon, and Michael Scott Hyde.... The...complaint alleged that each of the named plaintiffs had been arrested without a warrant, had received neither a prompt probable cause nor a bail hearing, and was still in custody....

In March 1989, plaintiffs asked the district court to issue a preliminary injunction requiring the county to provide all persons arrested without a warrant a judicial determination of probable cause within thirty-six hours of arrest. The district court issued the injunction, holding that the county's existing practice violated this Court's decision in *Gerstein.* Without discussion, the district court adopted a rule that the county provide probable cause determinations within thirty-six hours of arrest, except in exigent circumstances.

Reasoning

In *Gerstein,* this Court held as unconstitutional Florida procedures under which persons arrested without a warrant could remain in police custody for thirty days or more without a judicial determination of probable cause. In reaching this conclusion, we attempted to reconcile important competing interests. On the one hand, states have a strong interest in protecting public safety by taking into custody those persons who are reasonably suspected of having engaged in criminal activity, even where there has been no opportunity for a prior judicial determination of probable cause. On the other hand, prolonged detention based on incorrect or unfounded suspicion may unjustly "imperil [a] suspect's job, interrupt his source of income, and impair his family relationships." We sought to balance these competing concerns by holding that states "must provide a fair and reliable determination of probable cause as a condition for any significant pretrial restraint of liberty, and this determination must be made by a judicial officer either before or promptly after arrest."...

Inherent in *Gerstein*'s invitation to the states to experiment and adapt was the recognition that the Fourth Amendment does not compel an immediate determination of probable cause upon completing the administrative steps incident to arrest. Plainly, if a probable cause hearing is constitutionally compelled the moment a suspect is finished being booked, there is no room whatsoever for "flexibility and experimentation by the states." Incorporating probable cause determinations "into the procedure for setting bail or fixing other conditions of pretrial release"—which *Gerstein* explicitly contemplated—would be impossible. Waiting even a few hours so that a bail hearing or arraignment could take place at the same time as the probable cause determination would amount to a constitutional violation. Clearly, *Gerstein* is not that inflexible....

But flexibility has its limits; *Gerstein* is not a blank check. A state has no legitimate interest in detaining for extended periods individuals who have been arrested without probable cause. The Court recognized in *Gerstein* that a person arrested without a warrant is entitled to a fair and reliable determination of probable cause and that this determination of probable cause must be made promptly. Unfortunately, as lower court decisions applying *Gerstein* have demonstrated, it is not enough to say that probable cause determinations must be "prompt." This vague standard simply has not provided sufficient guidance. Instead, it has led to a flurry of systematic challenges to city and country practices, putting federal judges in the role of making legislative judgments and overseeing local jail house operations.

Our task in this case is to articulate more clearly the boundaries of what is permissible under the Fourth Amendment. Although we hesitate to announce that the Constitution compels a specific time limit, it is important to provide some degree of certainty so that states and counties may establish procedures with confidence that they fall within constitutional bounds. Taking into account the competing interests articulated in *Gerstein,* we believe that a jurisdiction that provides judicial determinations of probable cause within forty-eight hours of arrest will, as a general matter, comply with the promptness requirement of *Gerstein.* For this reason, such jurisdictions will be immune from systemic challenges.

This is not to say that the probable cause determination in a particular case passes constitutional muster simply because it is provided within forty-eight hours. Such a hearing may nonetheless violate *Gerstein* if the arrested individual can prove that his or her probable cause determination was delayed unreasonably. Examples of unreasonable delay are delays for the purpose of gathering additional evidence to justify the arrest, a delay motivated by ill will against the arrested individual, or delay for delay's sake. In evaluating whether the delay in a particular case is unreasonable, however, courts must allow a substantial degree of flexibility. Courts cannot ignore the often unavoidable delays in transporting arrested persons from one facility to another, handling late-night bookings where no magistrate is readily available, obtaining the presence of an arresting officer who may be busy processing other suspects or securing the premises of an arrest, and other practical realities.

Where an arrested individual does not receive a probable cause determination within forty-eight hours, the calculus changes. In such a case, the arrested individual does not bear the burden of proving an unreasonable delay. Rather, the burden shifts to the Government to demonstrate the existence of a bona fide emergency or other extraordinary circumstance. The fact that in a particular case it may take longer than forty-eight hours to consolidate pretrial proceedings does not qualify as an extraordinary circumstance. Nor, for that matter, do intervening weekends. A jurisdiction that chooses to combine probable cause determinations with arraignments must do so as soon as is reasonably feasible, but in no event later than forty-eight hours after arrest.

Holding

For the reasons we have articulated, we conclude that Riverside County is entitled to combine probable cause determinations with arraignments. The record indicates, however, that the county's current policy and practice do not comport fully with the principles we have outlined. The county's current policy is to offer combined proceedings within two days, exclusive of Saturdays, Sundays, and holidays. As a result, persons arrested on Thursdays may have to wait until the following Monday before they receive a probable cause determination. The delay is even longer if there is an intervening holiday. Thus, the county's regular practice exceeds the forty-eight-hour period we deem constitutionally permissible, meaning that the county is not immune from systemic challenges, such as this class action.

As to arrests that occur early in the week, the county's practice is that "arraignment[s] usually take place on the last day" possible. There may well be legitimate reasons for this practice; alternatively, this may constitute delay for delay's sake. We leave it to the court of appeals and the district court, on remand, to make this determination. The judgment of the court of appeals is vacated, and the case is remanded for further proceedings consistent with this opinion.

Dissenting, *Scalia, J.*

We said that "the Fourth Amendment requires a judicial determination of probable cause as a prerequisite to extended restraint of liberty...either before or promptly after arrest." Though how "promptly" we did not say, it was plain enough that the requirement left no room for intentional delay unrelated to the completion of "the administrative steps incident to arrest." Plain enough, at least, that all but one federal court considering the question understood *Gerstein* that way. Today, however, the Court discerns something quite different in *Gerstein*. It finds that the plain statements set forth above (not to mention the common law tradition of liberty upon which they were based) were trumped by the implication of a later dictum in the case which, according to the Court, manifests a "recognition that the Fourth Amendment does not compel an immediate determination of probable cause upon completing the administrative steps incident to arrest."

Determining the outer boundary of reasonableness is a more objective and more manageable task. We were asked to undertake it in *Gerstein,* but declined—wisely, I think, since we had before us little data to support any figure we might choose. As the Court notes, however, *Gerstein* has engendered a number of cases addressing not only the scope of the procedures "incident to arrest," but also their duration. The conclusions reached by the judges in those cases, and by others who have addressed the question, are surprisingly similar. I frankly would prefer even more information, and for that purpose would have supported reargument on the single question of an outer time limit. The data available are enough to convince me, however, that certainly no more than twenty-four hours is needed.

A few weeks before issuance of today's opinion, there appeared in *The Washington Post* the story of protracted litigation arising from the arrest of a student who entered a restaurant in Charlottesville, Virginia, one evening, to look for some friends. Failing to find them, he tried to leave—but refused to pay a $5 fee (required by the restaurant's posted rules) for failing to return a red tab he had been issued to keep track of his orders. According to the story, he "was taken by police to the Charlottesville jail" at the restaurant's request. "There, a magistrate refused to issue an arrest warrant," and he was released. That is how it used to be, but not, according to today's decision, how it must be in the future. If the Fourth Amendment meant then what the Court says it does now, the student could lawfully have been held for as long as it would have taken to arrange for his arraignment, up to a maximum of forty-eight hours.

Justice Story wrote that the Fourth Amendment "is little more than the affirmance of a great constitutional doctrine of the common law." It should not become less than that. One hears the complaint, nowadays, that the Fourth Amendment has become constitutional law for the guilty, that it benefits the career criminal (through the exclusionary rule) often and directly but the ordinary citizen remotely if at all. By failing to protect the innocent arrestee, today's opinion reinforces that view. The common law rule of *prompt* hearing had as its primary beneficiaries the innocent—not those whose fully justified convictions must be overturned to scold the police; nor those who avoid conviction because the evidence, while convincing, does not establish guilt beyond a reasonable doubt; but those so blameless that there was not even good reason to arrest them. While in recent years we have invented novel applications of the Fourth Amendment to release the unquestionably guilty, we today repudiate one of its core applications so that the presumptively innocent may be left in jail. Hereafter a law-abiding citizen wrongfully arrested may be compelled to await the grace of a Dickensian bureaucratic machine as it churns its cycle for up to two days—never once given the opportunity to show a judge that there is absolutely no reason to hold him, that a mistake has been made. In my view, this is the image of a system of justice that has lost its ancient sense of priority, a system that few Americans would recognize as our own.

Questions for Discussion

1. Explain the holding in *McLaughlin*. How does this modify the rule established in *Gerstein*?
2. Discuss the interests that the Supreme Court balances in reaching its decision.
3. Summarize the court's discussion regarding "unreasonable delay."
4. How should Riverside County modify its procedures to meet the constitutional standard established in *McLaughlin*?
5. Outline the argument in Justice Scalia's dissent. As a Supreme Court justice, would you support the majority or dissenting opinion?

First Appearance

The next step following an arrest is the **first appearance** or the *initial appearance*. The first appearance is triggered by the filing of a **complaint,** which is a sworn statement by the prosecutor charging the defendant with a specific offense. The federal rules of criminal procedure and most states specify that a defendant is to be brought before a magistrate or judge "without unnecessary delay." States differ on the permissible time between the arrest and the first appearance. The Supreme Court has set the outside limit at forty-eight hours (*County of Riverside v. McLaughlin,* 500 U.S. 44 [1991]). The Court has held that a confession obtained after failing to promptly present a defendant to a magistrate is inadmissible in evidence (*McNabb v. United States,* 318 U.S. 332 [1943]; *Mallory v. United States,* 354 U.S. 449 [1957]). The initial appearance has four primary purposes.

- ***Criminal charges.*** The defendant is informed of the precise charges against him or her.
- ***Constitutional rights.*** The defendant is informed of his or her rights. This includes the *Miranda* warnings, the entitlement to a lawyer and the right to consult with a lawyer, the availability of pretrial release and bail, the right to a preliminary hearing and speedy trial, the right against self-incrimination, and the right to exclude unlawfully obtained evidence.
- ***Pretrial release.*** A determination is made whether to release the defendant from custody prior to trial. The judge will fix the amount of bail or establish the conditions of the defendant's pretrial release.
- ***Attorney.*** A lawyer is appointed for indigent defendants.

In some jurisdictions, a defendant is provided the opportunity to enter a plea of guilty or not guilty at the first appearance; in others, a defendant may be required to enter a plea to the criminal charges. In the case of misdemeanors punishable by a modest fine, defendants typically plead guilty in order to dispose of the matter.

Criminal Procedure in the News

Jena, Louisiana, is a rural town with a population of 3,000, eighty-five percent of whom are Caucasian. In 2006 and 2007, events in the town and at Jena High School sparked a national debate on whether the American criminal justice system is biased against African Americans.

Twenty percent of Jena High School's students are African American. During the school day, Caucasian students typically gathered under a shady "White tree," while African Americans congregated on bleachers near the auditorium. In September 2006, an African American student asked a school official for permission to sit under the "White tree" and was told that he was free to sit wherever he wanted.

The next day, three nooses were found dangling from the "White tree." The nooses were a stark reminder of the days in which African Americans were discriminated against and lynched. The three students responsible for hanging the nooses were sent to an alternative school for a month and were required to serve Saturday detentions and to meet other requirements before returning to school. Superintendent Roy Breithaupt reportedly commented that "adolescents play pranks. I don't think it was a threat against anybody."

There was unhappiness among African American students and parents over what they viewed as a "slap on the wrist" for this "hate crime." The district attorney, Reed Walters, then visited Jena High School and addressed a racially divided school assembly in an effort to calm the atmosphere. He reportedly grew frustrated over the students' lack of attentiveness, advised the African American students to disregard the "innocent prank," and warned that he could "take their lives away with a stroke of his pen." As tensions mounted, the police were called in to patrol the halls, and the school was placed on total lockdown during the week of September 8, 2006.

On November 30, 2006, a fire burned down the main building of the high school. The situation escalated on December first, when an African American student was attacked by Caucasian students as he attempted to enter a party with six of his friends. A

Caucasian male was charged with battery stemming from his involvement in the fight. The next day there was a heated exchange between a Caucasian student and African American students at a local convenience store. The African American students managed to grab a shotgun from the Caucasian student, and as a result one of the African American students was charged with theft of a firearm, second-degree robbery, and disturbing the peace.

On December 4, a Caucasian student, Justin Barker, allegedly belittled an African American student and was attacked outside the school auditorium. He was knocked out with a single punch and kicked in the head. He reportedly suffered a concussion, a swollen eye, and injuries to his face, ears, and hand but was treated and released from the hospital and was sufficiently recovered to attend a party later that night. Barker subsequently denied having made the belittling comments. Superintendent Breithaupt described the fight as a "premeditated ambush and attack by six students against one" in which the "victim . . . was beaten and kicked into a state of bloody unconsciousness."

In connection with this attack, six African American students were removed from class and arrested, one of whom was an unnamed fourteen-year-old juvenile. The five older students were charged as adults with attempted second-degree murder and conspiracy to commit second-degree murder and were expelled from school. Bail was set at between $70,000 and $138,000 for each student.

One of these students, sixteen-year-old Michael Bell, a star football player, had his bail fixed at $90,000 and was the only defendant who failed to obtain pretrial release. The judge explained that this high bail was based on Bell's record of four juvenile offenses, including two battery charges. Bell's charges were reduced on the day of the trial, and he was convicted of aggravated battery and conspiracy to commit aggravated battery before an all-White jury. There were several aspects of the trial that were considered unfair by Bell's supporters.

Aggravated assault. The prosecutor alleged that Bell's tennis shoe constituted a "deadly weapon" and that his kicking of Barker merited a conviction for aggravated battery. Aggravated battery in Louisiana is the infliction of serious bodily harm with a dangerous weapon.

Evidence. A number of witnesses testified that Bell had beaten Barker, while other witnesses were unable to determine whether Bell was involved.

Jury. Bell's conviction was tainted by the fact that several members of the jury were alleged to be friends of the prosecuting attorney and of other individuals involved in Bell's prosecution.

Public defender. The public defender, Blane Williams, an African American, urged Bell to accept a plea bargain, did not challenge the all-White composition of the jury, and failed to call witnesses in Bell's defense.

On appeal, Bell's convictions were overturned on the grounds that the charges should have been brought in juvenile court. Louisiana announced that it would not appeal the decision, and Bell was released. In December 2007, Bell pled guilty to a simple battery charge, was sentenced to eighteen months in a juvenile institution, and agreed to cooperate with the prosecution. Charges against the other defendants subsequently were reduced, and they were charged as adults (because they were over seventeen at the time of the incident) with second-degree battery and conspiracy.

On September 20, 2007, an estimated 20,000 demonstrators gathered in Jena to protest the prosecution of the "Jena Six." The rally was led by the Reverends Al Sharpton and Jesse Jackson and drew support from hip-hop artists Mos Def, Salt-N-Pepa, and Ice Cube and popular singers David Bowie and John Mellencamp. Protestors called for equal treatment for African Americans in the criminal justice system.

On September 26, 2007, prosecutor Reed Walters wrote a commentary in the *New York Times* in which he explained that he had served as district attorney for sixteen years and that he had always acted in good faith to "match the facts to any applicable laws and to seek justice for those who have been harmed." Prosecutor Walters stated that while the placing of nooses on the schoolyard tree constituted a "mean-spirited" act that deserved the "condemnation of all civilized peoples," it was neither a state nor a federal crime. He justified the charges against the African American students on the grounds that Justin Barker had not been involved in hanging the nooses, had been "blindsided and knocked unconscious by a vicious blow to the head," and had been "brutally kicked by at least six people" while on the ground. Walters alleged that Michael Bell initially had been justifiably charged as an adult based on his role as the "instigator of the attack" and on "the seriousness of the charge and his prior criminal record." He concluded by reminding readers that as a prosecutor, he was "bound to enforce the laws of Louisiana as they exist today, not as they might in [his critics'] vision of a perfect world."

On July 31, 2007, in an effort to end racial controversy in Jena, the "White tree" was cut down. In June 2009, the five defendants pled no contest to misdemeanor simple battery and were sentenced to seven days' probation and were fined $500.

What evidence supports the contention that the criminal charges brought against the Jena Six were racially motivated? Are you persuaded that Reed Walters merely was enforcing the law in a neutral and objective fashion? What would have been the fate of the Jena Six had there not been national attention focused on the story?

Pretrial Release

In England, the practice at the time of the drafting of the U.S. Constitution was that individuals who had been arrested and who were awaiting trial could be released from detention by depositing money or title to property with the court. A failure to appear for trial resulted in the forfeiture of the money or property. The thinking was that an individual should not be detained without a finding of guilt.

This philosophy has led to the modern court practice known as *posting bail.* The U.S. Constitution provides for **bail** in the Eighth Amendment, which states that "excessive bail shall not be required." This bail provision has not been incorporated into the Due Process Clause of the Fourteenth Amendment. Most state constitutions, however, create a right to bail in all but capital cases. The fundamental nature of bail was recognized by the U.S. Supreme Court in *Schlib v. Kuebel,* in which the Court observed that "bail, of course, is basic to our system of law, and the Eighth Amendment's proscription of excessive bail has been assumed to have application to the States through the Fourteenth Amendment" (*Schlib v. Kuebel,* 404 U.S. 357, 365 [1971]).

The U.S. Supreme Court declared in *Stack v. Boyle* that the primary purpose of bail is to insure that the defendant appears for trial. An amount of bail beyond that required to guarantee the defendant's appearance for trial is "excessive" under the Eighth Amendment. The Court noted that

> the modern practice of requiring a bail bond or the deposit of a sum of money subject to forfeiture serves as . . . assurance of the presence of an accused. Bail set at a figure higher than an amount reasonably calculated to fulfill this purpose is "excessive" under the Eighth Amendment. (*Stack v. Boyle,* 342 U.S. 1, 4–5 [1951])

Despite the fundamental nature of individual access to bail, the **Bail Clause** has

> never been thought to accord a right to bail in all cases, but merely to provide that bail should not be excessive in those cases where it is proper to grant bail. . . . The Eighth Amendment has not prevented Congress from defining the classes of cases in which bail shall be allowed in this country. Thus, in criminal cases, bail is not compulsory where the punishment may be death. (*Carlson v. Landon,* 342 U.S. 524,545 [1952])

Forty state constitutions deny bail to individuals charged with capital offenses. The U.S. Department of Justice, Bureau of Justice Statistics reports that in 2002, sixty-two percent of individuals arrested for felonies were released on bail prior to trial. The number of individuals released varied by the offenses. Eight percent of murder defendants were released as compared with forty-two percent of individuals charged with robbery, forty-four percent of individuals charged with motor vehicle theft, forty-nine percent of individuals charged with burglary, and fifty-five percent of individuals charged with rape. Defendants with an "active criminal justice status," such as those on parole or probation at the time of their arrest, are released on bail less than one-half of the time.

There are several reasons why bail is viewed as important to a defendant.

- ***Detention.*** An individual may spend several months in jail waiting for his or her trial.
- ***Personal hardship.*** A failure to make bail strains family life and likely will result in a loss of employment and income.
- ***Preparation for trial.*** A defendant who is released is able to help his or her lawyer prepare for trial. There is some evidence that individuals who do not make bail are more likely to be convicted and are more likely to be sentenced to jail.

Balanced against the importance of bail to the individual is the fact that society has an interest in detaining individuals who may engage in criminal conduct.

The cash bond historically has been the principle form of bail in the United States. This **money bail** system requires that defendants deposit an amount of money with the court as a condition of release. The money is returned when the individual appears for trial. In most instances, individuals are unable to deposit the full amount of bail. They turn to a bail bondsman for a **surety bond.** The defendant is required to deposit ten percent of the bond with the bondsman, and the bondsman deposits the money with the court. The bondsman retains the ten percent amount as a fee for posting the bail and forfeits the entire amount of the money bail if the defendant fails to appear for trial. Bondsmen have been known to hire "bounty hunters" to track down individuals who fail to appear for trial.

Justice William Douglas observed that the system of money bail may result in the release of wealthy individuals who have sufficient money to pledge for their freedom, while indigents find themselves lacking the resources to post a deposit and are detained (*Bandy v. United States,* 81 S. Ct. 197, 5 L. Ed. 2d 218 [1960]).

In 1967, the President's Commission on Law Enforcement and Administration of Justice published a report titled *The Challenge of Crime in a Free Society* that concludes that the money bail system discriminates against the poor who are unable to meet bail. The taxpayers also are placed in the position of paying the costs of detaining those individuals who are unable to make bail and are incarcerated. The commission found that the amount of bail typically is fixed by a schedule based on the nature of the defendant's criminal offense and has little relationship to whether a defendant is likely to appear for trial. The report recommends the pretrial release without financial conditions of all but a small percentage of defendants and would deny release to defendants who present a high risk of flight or dangerous acts prior to trial (131–132).

One of the first reform efforts was sponsored by the Vera Institute, a research organization that sponsored the Manhattan Bail Project in New York City. The program evaluated the background of indigent defendants and determined whether an individual would appear for trial if provided **release on recognizance**. The factors evaluated included prior convictions, the nature of the offense, whether the accused was employed, and whether the accused had roots in the community. The result was that only 1.6% of the individuals recommended for release failed to appear for trial.

Despite the criticism of the commercial bail bond system, most states primarily rely on this mechanism. Illinois, Kentucky, Oregon, and Wisconsin have abolished private bail bondsmen and have substituted a system based on release on personal recognizance or on the requirement of a money deposit with the court, most of which is returned when the defendant appears for trial. The model for bail reform efforts is the federal Bail Reform Act of 1984 (18 U.S.C. §§ 3141–3150), which has largely abandoned the system of money bail. A judicial official is to order the pretrial release of an individual on personal recognizance or upon execution of an unsecured appearance bond (a promise to pay in the event of nonappearance) "unless the judicial officer determines that such release will not reasonably assure the appearance of the individual . . . or will endanger the safety of any other person or the community." In the event that the judicial officer determines that these forms of pretrial release will not "reasonably assure the appearance of the person . . . or will endanger the safety of any other person or the community," the judicial officer shall order the individual's release subject to various conditions listed in the statute, including the posting of money bail or property.

The Bail Reform Act also makes provision for the **preventive detention** of individuals who pose a risk of flight or a risk to the community. Preventive detention permits the government to obtain a court order providing for the pretrial confinement of an individual who is awaiting trial. Roughly seventeen state constitutions also provide for preventive detention of offenders.

The federal Bail Reform Act provides that a pretrial detention hearing is to be held on the motion of a prosecutor in those instances in which a defendant is charged with a crime of violence, an offense with a maximum penalty of death or life imprisonment, designated drug offenses, or any felony in the event that the individual has two or more convictions for one of the listed offenses. A hearing also may be held on the motion of a prosecutor or judge on the grounds that there is a serious risk that the defendant will flee, obstruct justice, or interfere with a witness or juror. Detention is ordered in the event that a judicial official finds by clear and convincing evidence that "no condition or combination of conditions will reasonably assure the appearance of the person as required and the safety of any other person and the community."

In 1987, in *United States v. Salerno,* the U.S. Supreme Court affirmed the constitutionality of preventive detention. Defendants Salerno and Cafaro were alleged to be high-ranking organized crime figures and were charged with thirty-five acts of racketeering activity, including fraud, extortion, gambling, and conspiracy to commit murder. The U.S. government successfully petitioned the federal district court to order the defendants' detention under the federal Bail Reform Act of 1984. Salerno and Cafaro argued that they were being detained without having been convicted of a crime in violation of the Due Process Clause and that they were being denied access to bail guaranteed under the Eighth Amendment. As you read *Salerno,* you will want to pay attention to the somewhat technical reasoning of the U.S. Supreme Court. The decision rests on several legal conclusions that are outlined below.

Substantive due process. The act does not constitute impermissible punishment before trial. The U.S. Congress did not intend preventive detention to serve as punishment. It instead is an administrative procedure to protect the community. This interest strongly outweighs the individual's interest in liberty. Detention is limited to the "most serious crimes," detention hearings are promptly conducted, and there are limits on the length of detentions. The judge is required to issue a written order explaining the reasons for the detention.

Procedural due process. The defendant is permitted representation by an attorney, the right to present evidence, and the right to cross-examine witnesses. The government must satisfy the standards set forth in the act by clear and convincing evidence, and the defendant has the right to an immediate appeal.

Eighth Amendment. The Bail Clause does not provide a right to bail in every instance and does not prohibit the detention of an individual prior to trial. The only limitation is that the government may not employ excessive means to achieve its goal. The government is not employing excessive means when it detains an individual awaiting trial to prevent him or her from committing additional crimes.

As you read *United States v. Salerno,* consider whether preventive detention strikes an appropriate balance between the protection of society and the rights of the defendant. Does preventive detention constitute the punishment of an individual who has yet to be convicted of a crime?

May defendants be detained without bail to prevent them from engaging in additional criminal activity?

United States v. Salerno, 481 U.S. 739 (1987), Rehnquist, C.J.

Issue

The Bail Reform Act of 1984 (the act) allows a federal court to detain an arrestee pending trial if the Government demonstrates by clear and convincing evidence after an adversary hearing that no release conditions "will reasonably assure . . . the safety of any other person and the community." The U.S. Court of Appeals for the Second Circuit struck down this provision of the act as facially unconstitutional. . . . We granted certiorari because of a conflict among the courts of appeals regarding the validity of the act. We [now examine whether] the act fully comports with constitutional requirements.

Facts

Responding to "the alarming problem of crimes committed by persons on release," Congress formulated the Bail Reform Act of 1984 as the solution to a bail crisis in the federal courts. The act represents the national legislature's considered response to numerous perceived deficiencies in the federal bail process. By providing for sweeping changes in both the way federal courts consider bail applications and the circumstances under which bail is granted, Congress hoped to "give the courts adequate authority to make release decisions that give appropriate recognition to the danger a person may pose to others if released."

To this end, Section 3141(a) of the act requires a judicial officer to determine whether an arrestee shall be detained. Section 3142(e) provides that

> if, after a hearing pursuant to the provisions of subsection (f), the judicial officer finds that no condition or combination of conditions will reasonably assure the appearance of the person as required and the safety of any other person and the community, he shall order the detention of the person prior to trial.

Section 3142(f) provides the arrestee with a number of procedural safeguards. He may request the presence of counsel at the detention hearing, he may testify and present witnesses in his behalf as well as proffer evidence, and he may cross-examine other witnesses appearing at the hearing. If the judicial officer finds that no conditions of pretrial release can reasonably assure the safety of other persons and the community, he must state his findings of fact in writing (3142(i)) and support his conclusion with "clear and convincing evidence" (3142(f)).

The judicial officer is not given unbridled discretion in making the detention determination. Congress has specified the considerations relevant to that decision. These factors include the nature and seriousness of the charges, the substantiality of the Government's evidence against the arrestee, the arrestee's background and characteristics, and the nature and seriousness of the danger posed by the suspect's release. Should a judicial officer order detention, the detainee is entitled to expedited appellate review of the detention order.

Respondents Anthony Salerno and Vincent Cafaro were arrested on March 21, 1986, after being charged in a 29-count indictment alleging various violations of the Racketeer Influenced and Corrupt Organizations (RICO) Act, mail and wire fraud offenses, extortion, and various criminal gambling violations. The RICO counts alleged thirty-five acts of racketeering activity, including fraud, extortion, gambling, and conspiracy to commit murder.

At respondents' arraignment, the Government moved to have Salerno and Cafaro detained on the ground that no condition of release would assure the safety of the community or any person. The district court held a hearing at which the Government made a detailed proffer of evidence. The Government's case showed that Salerno was the "boss" of the Genovese crime family of La Cosa Nostra and that Cafaro was a "captain" in the Genovese family. According to the Government's proffer, based in large part on conversations intercepted by a court-ordered wiretap, the two respondents had participated in wide-ranging conspiracies to aid their illegitimate enterprises through violent means. The Government also offered the testimony of two of its trial witnesses, who were prepared to assert at trial that Salerno personally participated in two murder conspiracies. Salerno opposed the motion for detention, challenging the credibility of the Government's witnesses. He offered the testimony of several character witnesses as well as a letter from his doctor stating that he was suffering from a serious medical condition. Cafaro presented no evidence at the hearing but instead characterized the wiretap conversations as merely "tough talk."

The district court granted the Government's detention motion, concluding that the Government had established by clear and convincing evidence that no condition or combination of conditions of release would ensure the safety of the community or any person:

> The activities of a criminal organization such as the Genovese Family do not cease with the arrest of its principals and their release on even the most stringent of bail conditions. The illegal businesses, in place for many years, require constant attention and protection, or they will fail.... When business as usual involves threats, beatings, and murder, the present danger such people pose in the community is self-evident.

Respondents appealed, contending that to the extent that the Bail Reform Act permits pretrial detention on the ground that the arrestee is likely to commit future crimes, it is unconstitutional.... The U.S. Court of Appeals for the Second Circuit agreed.... The court concluded that the Government could not, consistent with due process, detain persons who had not been accused of any crime merely because they were thought to present a danger to the community. It reasoned that our criminal law system holds persons accountable for past actions, not anticipated future actions.

Reasoning

A facial challenge to a legislative act is, of course, the most difficult challenge to mount successfully, since the challenger must establish that no set of circumstances exists under which the act would be valid.... We think respondents have failed to shoulder their heavy burden to demonstrate that the act is "facially" unconstitutional. Respondents present two grounds for invalidating the Bail Reform Act's provisions permitting pretrial detention on the basis of future dangerousness. First, they rely upon the conclusion of the court of appeals that the act exceeds the limitations placed upon the federal government by the Due Process Clause of the Fifth Amendment. Second, they contend that the act contravenes the Eighth Amendment's proscription against excessive bail. We treat these contentions in turn.

The Due Process Clause of the Fifth Amendment provides that "No person shall...be deprived of life, liberty, or property, without due process of law...." This Court has held that the Due Process Clause protects individuals against two types of government action. So-called substantive due process prevents the government from engaging in conduct that "shocks the conscience," or interferes with rights "implicit in the concept of ordered liberty." When government action depriving a person of life, liberty, or property survives substantive due process scrutiny, it must still be implemented in a fair manner. This requirement has traditionally been referred to as procedural due process.

Respondents first argue that the act violates substantive due process, because the pretrial detention it authorizes constitutes impermissible punishment before trial. The Government, however, has never argued that pretrial detention could be upheld if it were "punishment." The court of appeals assumed that pretrial detention under the Bail Reform Act is regulatory, not penal, and we agree that it is. As an initial matter, the mere fact that a person is detained does not inexorably lead to the conclusion that the government has imposed punishment.

To determine whether a restriction on liberty constitutes impermissible punishment or permissible regulation, we first look to legislative intent. Unless Congress expressly intended to impose punitive restrictions, the punitive/regulatory distinction turns on "whether an alternative purpose to which [the restriction] may rationally be connected is assignable for it, and whether it appears excessive in relation to the alternative purpose assigned [to it]." We conclude that the detention imposed by the act falls on the regulatory side of the dichotomy. The legislative history of the Bail Reform Act clearly indicates that Congress did not formulate the pretrial detention provisions as punishment for dangerous individuals. Congress instead perceived pretrial detention as a potential solution to a pressing societal problem. There is no doubt that preventing danger to the community is a legitimate regulatory goal.

Nor are the incidents of pretrial detention excessive in relation to the regulatory goal Congress sought to achieve. The Bail Reform Act carefully limits the circumstances under which detention may be sought to the most serious of crimes. See 18 U.S.C. § 3142(f) (detention hearings available if case involves crimes of violence, offenses for which the sentence is life imprisonment or death, serious drug offenses, or certain repeat offenders). The arrestee is entitled to a prompt detention hearing, and the maximum length of pretrial detention is limited by the stringent time limitations of the Speedy Trial Act. Moreover...the conditions of confinement envisioned by the act appear to reflect the regulatory purposes relied upon by the Government. The statute at issue here requires that detainees be housed in a "facility separate, to the extent practicable, from persons awaiting or serving sentences or being held in custody pending appeal" (18 U.S.C. § 3142(i)(2)). We conclude, therefore, that the pretrial detention contemplated by the Bail Reform Act is regulatory in nature and does not constitute punishment before trial in violation of the Due Process Clause.

The court of appeals nevertheless concluded that "the Due Process Clause prohibits pretrial detention on the ground of danger to the community as a regulatory measure, without regard to the duration of the detention." Respondents characterize the Due Process Clause as erecting an impenetrable "wall" in this area that "no governmental interest—rational, important, compelling or otherwise—may surmount."

We do not think the clause lays down any such categorical imperative. We have repeatedly held that the Government's regulatory interest in community safety can, in appropriate circumstances, outweigh an individual's liberty interest....We have also held that the government may detain mentally unstable individuals who present a danger to the public and dangerous defendants who become incompetent to stand trial. We have approved of postarrest regulatory detention of juveniles when they present a continuing danger to the community. Even competent adults may face substantial liberty restrictions as a result of the operation of our criminal justice system. If the police suspect an individual of a crime, they may arrest and hold him until a neutral magistrate determines whether probable cause exists. Finally, respondents concede and the court of appeals noted that an arrestee may be incarcerated until trial if he presents a risk of flight or a danger to witnesses....We think that these cases show a sufficient number of exceptions to the rule that the congressional action challenged here can hardly be characterized as totally novel. Given the well-established authority of the government, in special circumstances, to restrain individuals' liberty prior to or even without criminal trial and conviction, we think that the present statute providing for pretrial detention on the basis of dangerousness must be evaluated in precisely the same manner that we evaluated the laws in the cases discussed above.

The Bail Reform Act of 1984 responds to an even more particularized governmental interest than the interest we sustained in *Schall v. Martin* (467 U.S. 253, 1984). The statute we upheld in *Schall* permitted pretrial detention of any juvenile arrested on any charge after a showing that the individual might commit some undefined further crimes. The Bail Reform Act, in contrast, narrowly focuses on a particularly acute problem in which the Government interests are overwhelming. The Act operates only on individuals who have been arrested for a specific category of extremely serious offenses (18 U.S.C. § 3142(f)). Congress specifically found that these individuals are far more likely to be responsible for dangerous acts in the community after arrest. Nor is the Act by any means a scattershot attempt to incapacitate those who are merely suspected of these serious crimes. The Government must first of all demonstrate probable cause to believe that the charged crime has been committed by the arrestee, but that is not enough. In a full blown adversary hearing, the Government must convince a neutral decision maker by clear and convincing evidence that no conditions of release can reasonably assure the safety of the community or any person (18 U.S.C. § 3142(f)). While the Government's general interest in preventing crime is compelling, even this interest is heightened when the Government musters convincing proof that the arrestee, already indicted or held to answer for a serious crime, presents a demonstrable danger to the community. Under these narrow circumstances, society's interest in crime prevention is at its greatest.

On the other side of the scale, of course, is the individual's strong interest in liberty. We do not minimize the importance and fundamental nature of this right. But, as our cases hold, this right may, in circumstances where the government's interest is sufficiently weighty, be subordinated to the greater needs of society. We think that Congress's careful delineation of the circumstances under which detention will be permitted satisfies this standard. When the Government proves by clear and convincing evidence that an arrestee presents an identified and articulable threat to an individual or the community, we believe that, consistent with the Due Process Clause, a court may disable the arrestee from executing that threat. Under these circumstances, we cannot categorically state that pretrial detention "offends some principle of justice so rooted in the traditions and conscience of our people as to be ranked as fundamental."

Finally, we may dispose briefly of respondents' facial challenge to the procedures of the Bail Reform Act. To sustain them against such a challenge, we need only find them "adequate to authorize the pretrial detention of at least some [persons] charged with crimes," whether or not they might be insufficient in some particular circumstances. We think they pass that test. As we stated in *Schall,* "There is nothing inherently unattainable about a prediction of future criminal conduct."

Under the Bail Reform Act, the procedures by which a judicial officer evaluates the likelihood of future dangerousness are specifically designed to further the accuracy of that determination. Detainees have a right to counsel at the detention hearing (18 U.S.C. § 3142(f)). They may testify in their own behalf, present information by proffer or otherwise, and cross-examine witnesses who appear at the hearing.... The judicial officer charged with the responsibility of determining the appropriateness of detention is guided by statutorily enumerated factors, which include the nature and the circumstances of the charges, the weight of the evidence, the history and characteristics of the putative offender, and the danger to the community (§ 3142(g)). The Government must prove its case by clear and convincing evidence (§ 3142(f)). Finally, the judicial officer must include written findings of fact and a written statement of reasons for a decision to detain (§ 3142(i)). The act's review provisions, § 3145(c), provide for immediate appellate review of the detention decision.

We think these extensive safeguards suffice to repel a facial challenge. The protections are more exacting than those we found sufficient in the juvenile context... and they far exceed what we found necessary to effect limited postarrest detention in *Gerstein v. Pugh.* Given the legitimate and compelling regulatory purpose of the act and the procedural protections it offers, we conclude that the act is not facially invalid under the Due Process Clause of the Fifth Amendment.

Respondents also contend that the Bail Reform Act violates the Excessive Bail Clause of the Eighth Amendment. The court of appeals did not address this issue because it found that the Act violates the Due Process Clause. We think that the Act survives a challenge founded upon the Eighth Amendment. The Eighth Amendment addresses pretrial release by providing merely that "[e]xcessive bail shall not be required." This Clause, of course, says nothing about whether bail shall be available at all. Respondents nevertheless contend that this Clause grants them a right to bail calculated solely upon considerations of flight. They rely on *Stack v. Boyle,* in which the Court stated that "[b]ail set at a figure higher than an amount reasonably calculated [to ensure the defendant's presence at trial] is 'excessive' under the Eighth Amendment." In respondents' view, since the Bail Reform Act allows a court essentially to set bail at an infinite amount for reasons not related to the risk of flight, it violates the Excessive Bail Clause. Respondents concede that the right to bail they have discovered in the Eighth Amendment is not absolute. A court may, for example, refuse bail in capital cases. And, as the court of appeals noted and respondents admit, a court may refuse bail when the defendant presents a threat to the judicial process by intimidating witnesses. Respondents characterize these exceptions as consistent with what they claim to be the sole purpose of bail—to ensure the integrity of the judicial process.

While we agree that a primary function of bail is to safeguard the courts' role in adjudicating the guilt or innocence of defendants, we reject the proposition that the Eighth Amendment categorically prohibits the government from pursuing other admittedly compelling interests through regulation of pretrial release. The above quoted dictum in *Stack v. Boyle* is far too slender a reed on which to rest this argument. The Court in *Stack* had no occasion to consider whether the Excessive Bail Clause requires courts to admit all defendants to bail, because the statute before the Court in that case in fact allowed the defendants to be bailed. Thus, the Court had to determine only whether bail, admittedly available in that case, was excessive if set at a sum greater than that necessary to ensure the arrestees' presence at trial.

We need not decide today whether the Excessive Bail Clause speaks at all to Congress's power to define the classes of criminal arrestees who shall be admitted to bail. For even if we were to conclude that the Eighth Amendment imposes some substantive limitations on the national legislature's powers in this area, we would still hold that the Bail Reform Act is valid. Nothing in the text of the Excessive Bail Clause limits permissible Government considerations solely to questions of flight. The only arguable substantive limitation of the Bail Clause is that the Government's proposed conditions of release or detention not be "excessive" in light of the perceived evil. Of course, to determine whether the Government's response is excessive, we must compare that response against the interest the Government seeks to protect by means of that response. Thus, when the Government has admitted that its only interest is in preventing flight, bail must be set by a court at a sum designed to ensure that goal, and no more. We believe that when Congress has mandated detention on the basis of a compelling interest other than prevention of flight, as it has here, the Eighth Amendment does not require release on bail.

Holding

In our society liberty is the norm, and detention prior to trial or without trial is the carefully limited exception. We hold that the provisions for pretrial detention in the Bail Reform Act of 1984 fall within that carefully limited exception. The act authorizes the detention prior to trial of arrestees charged with serious felonies who are found after an adversary hearing to pose a threat to the safety of individuals or to the community which no condition of release can dispel. The numerous procedural safeguards detailed above must attend this adversary hearing. We are unwilling to say that this congressional determination, based as it is upon that primary concern of every government—a concern for the safety and indeed the lives of its citizens—on its face violates either the Due Process Clause of the Fifth Amendment or the Excessive Bail Clause of the Eighth Amendment.

Dissenting, *Marshall, J.*, joined by *Brennan, J.*

This case brings before the Court for the first time a statute in which Congress declares that a person innocent of any crime may be jailed indefinitely, pending the trial of allegations that are legally presumed to be untrue, if the Government shows to the satisfaction of a judge that the accused is likely to commit crimes, unrelated to the pending charges, at any time in the future. Such statutes, consistent with the usages of tyranny and the excesses of what bitter experience teaches us to call the police state, have long been thought incompatible with the fundamental human rights protected by our Constitution.

Today a majority of this Court holds otherwise. Its decision disregards basic principles of justice established centuries ago and enshrined beyond the reach of governmental interference in the Bill of Rights. The essence of this case may be found, ironically enough, in a provision of the act to which the majority does not refer. Title 18 U.S.C. § 3142(j)(II) provides that "nothing in this section shall be construed as modifying or limiting the presumption of innocence." But the very pith and purpose of this statute is an abhorrent limitation of the presumption of innocence. The majority's untenable conclusion that the present act is constitutional arises from a specious denial of the role of the Bail Clause and the Due Process Clause in protecting the invaluable guarantee afforded by the presumption of innocence.

The statute now before us declares that persons who have been indicted may be detained if a judicial officer finds clear and convincing evidence that they pose a danger to individuals or to the community. The statute does not authorize the Government to imprison anyone it has evidence is dangerous; indictment is necessary. But let us suppose that a defendant is indicted and the Government shows by clear and convincing evidence that he is dangerous and should be detained pending a trial, at which trial the defendant is acquitted. May the Government continue to hold the defendant in detention based upon its showing that he is dangerous? The answer cannot be yes, for that would allow the Government to imprison someone for uncommitted crimes based upon "proof" not beyond a reasonable doubt. The result must therefore be that once the indictment has failed, detention cannot continue. But our fundamental principles of justice declare that the defendant is as innocent on the day before his trial as he is on the morning after his acquittal. Under this statute an untried indictment somehow acts to permit a detention, based on other charges, which after an acquittal would be unconstitutional. The conclusion is inescapable that the indictment has been turned into evidence, if not that the defendant is guilty of the crime charged, and that left to his own devices he will soon be guilty of something else. "If it suffices to accuse, what will become of the innocent?"

To be sure, an indictment is not without legal consequences. It establishes that there is probable cause to believe that an offense was committed and that the defendant committed it. Upon probable cause, a warrant for the defendant's arrest may issue; a period of administrative detention may occur before the evidence of probable cause is presented to a neutral magistrate. Once a defendant has been committed for trial, he may be detained in custody if the magistrate finds that no conditions of release will prevent him from becoming a fugitive. But in this connection the charging instrument is evidence of nothing more than the fact that there will be a trial.

It is not a novel proposition that the Bail Clause plays a vital role in protecting the presumption of innocence. Reviewing the application for bail pending appeal by members of the American Communist Party, . . . Justice Jackson wrote,

> If I assume that defendants are disposed to commit every opportune disloyal act helpful to Communist countries, it is still difficult to reconcile with traditional American law the jailing of persons by the courts because of anticipated but as yet uncommitted crimes. Imprisonment to protect society from predicted but unconsummated offenses is . . . unprecedented in this country and . . . fraught with danger of excesses and injustice.

As Chief Justice Vinson wrote for the Court in *Stack v. Boyle,* "Unless th[e] right to bail before trial is preserved, the presumption of innocence, secured only after centuries of struggle, would lose its meaning."

Throughout the world today there are men, women, and children interned indefinitely, awaiting trials that may never come or that may be a mockery of the word, because their governments believe them to be "dangerous." Our Constitution, whose construction began two centuries ago, can shelter us forever from the evils of such unchecked power. Over 200 years it has slowly, through our efforts, grown more durable, more expansive, and more just. But it cannot protect us if we lack the courage, and the self-restraint, to protect ourselves. Today a majority of the Court applies itself to an ominous exercise in demolition. Theirs is truly a decision that will go forth without authority and come back without respect.

Questions for Discussion

1. Why were Salerno and Cafaro subjected to preventive detention? What are the procedures that the government is required to follow to detain an individual under the Bail Reform Act?
2. Summarize the Supreme Court's discussion of procedural and substantive due process.
3. How did the Supreme Court respond to the claim that preventive detention violates the Bail Clause of the Eighth Amendment?
4. Do you agree with the majority or with the dissent?
5. Are you confident in the ability of courts to predict whether an individual will prove to be a threat to the community if released prior to trial?

12.1 YOU DECIDE

Jovanda Blackson was arrested in August 2005 and charged with corruptly obstructing the administration of justice in an official proceeding. She was detained without bail pursuant to a provision in the law of the District of Columbia that permits pretrial detention in a case that involves a charge of obstruction of justice or "a serious risk that the person will obstruct or attempt to obstruct justice, or threaten, injure, or intimidate or attempt to threaten, injure, or intimidate a prospective witness or juror."

Blackson's arrest stemmed from her service as a juror in a first-degree murder trial in which she apparently was acquainted with one of the defendants. During the deliberations, she insisted that the other jurors vote to acquit the accused and his codefendant. Blackson allegedly argued that "it did not matter what the other jurors may think," cursed at them several times, and hit her hand into her palm while speaking to the other jurors. The other jurors did not report any specific overt threats or violent acts by Blackson, but they did state that they felt "threatened" by her. Blackson contacted the defendant's wife during the jury deliberations to help shape her arguments to the other jurors.

Pursuant to her arrest, the prosecutor asserted that there were no conditions on Blackson's release that would protect the public safety. The judge issued an order detaining Blackson and explained that Blackson had demonstrated that she was willing to obstruct justice for a casual acquaintance. Blackson was aware of the identity of the jurors from the first trial who would be witnesses at her trial for the obstruction of justice. The court concluded that there was a serious risk that Blackson would obstruct or attempt to obstruct justice; or threaten, injure, or intimidate; or attempt to threaten, injure, or intimidate a prospective witness or juror.

As a judge, would you deny Blackson bail and order her pretrial detention? See *Blackson v. United States*, 897 A.2d 187 (D.C. App. 2006).

12.2 YOU DECIDE

In 1990, Nelson Mantecon-Zayas was indicted on federal drug charges in Florida. A magistrate judge ordered him released on a $200,000 bond. Roughly one year later, he was indicted on another drug charge in Puerto Rico and ordered to post an additional $50,000 in bail. This amount later was increased to $200,000. Nelson Mantecon-Zayas challenged the financial condition of his release, contending that he did not possess properties or assets valued at $400,000. He accordingly requested a reduction in the bail established in Puerto Rico. The district court held that bail was set at the figure that was required to assure that Mantecon-Zayas appeared for trial.

Does a defendant have a right to a bail amount that is within his or her financial capabilities? Should Mantecon-Zayas's bail be reduced? How would you rule in this case? See *United States v. Mantecon-Zayas*, 949 F.3d 548 (1st Circ. 1991).

You can learn what the court decided by referring to the study site, http://www.sagepub.com/lippmancp.

Pretrial Detention

An individual who is not released prior to trial typically is detained in a short-term correctional facility. In *Bell v. Wolfish,* the Supreme Court held that while these detainees retain their constitutional rights, they are subject to reasonable regulations intended to insure order and security in the institution. The Court cautioned that detainees have not been convicted of a crime and may not be subjected to "arbitrary or purposeless" conditions that constitute punishment. In *Wolfish,* the U.S. Supreme Court reviewed various practices in the Metropolitan Correctional Center in New York City in an effort to clarify the dividing line between reasonable detention policies and punishment. In reading the Supreme Court's opinion, ask yourself whether the Court has struck the proper balance between the interests of detainees and the interests in institutional security.

Were the pretrial detainees subjected to unconstitutional punishment?

Bell v. Wolfish, 441 U.S. 520 (1979), Rehnquist, C.J.

Issue

This case requires us to examine the constitutional rights of pretrial detainees—those persons who have been charged with a crime but who have not yet been tried on the charge. The parties concede that to ensure their presence at trial, these persons legitimately may be incarcerated by the Government prior to a determination of their guilt or innocence, and it is the scope of their rights during this period of confinement prior to trial that is the primary focus of this case.

Facts

The MCC was constructed in 1975 to replace the converted waterfront garage on West Street that had served as New York City's federal jail since 1928. It is located adjacent to the Foley Square federal courthouse and has as its primary objective the housing of persons who are being detained in custody prior to trial for federal criminal offenses in the U.S. District Courts for the Southern and Eastern Districts of New York and for the District of New Jersey. Under the Bail Reform Act, 18 U.S.C. § 3146, a person in the federal system is committed to a detention facility only because no other less drastic means can reasonably ensure his presence at trial. In addition to pretrial detainees, the MCC also houses some convicted inmates who are awaiting sentencing or transportation to federal prison or who are serving generally relatively short sentences in a service capacity at the MCC, convicted prisoners who have been lodged at the facility under writs of habeas corpus issued to ensure their presence at upcoming trials, witnesses in protective custody, and persons incarcerated for contempt.

The MCC differs markedly from the familiar image of a jail; there are no barred cells, dank, colorless corridors, or clanging steel gates. It was intended to include the most advanced and innovative features of modern design of detention facilities. As the court of appeals stated, it "represented the architectural embodiment of the best and most progressive penological planning." The key design element of the 12-story structure is the "modular" or "unit" concept, whereby each floor designed to house inmates has one or two largely self-contained residential units that replace the traditional cellblock jail construction. Each unit in turn has several clusters or corridors of private rooms or dormitories radiating from a central two-story multipurpose or common room, to which each inmate has free access approximately sixteen hours a day. Because our analysis does not turn on the particulars of the MCC concept or design, we need not discuss them further.

When the MCC opened in August 1975, the planned capacity was 449 inmates, an increase of fifty percent over that of the former West Street facility. Despite some dormitory accommodations, the MCC was designed primarily to house these inmates in 389 rooms, which originally were intended for single occupancy. While the MCC was under construction, however, the number of persons committed to pretrial detention began to rise at an "unprecedented" rate. The Bureau of Prisons took several steps to accommodate this unexpected flow of persons assigned to the facility, but despite these efforts, the inmate population at the MCC rose above its planned capacity within a short time after its opening. To provide sleeping space for this increased population, the MCC replaced the single bunks in many of the individual rooms and dormitories with double bunks. Also, each week some newly arrived inmates had to sleep on cots in the common areas until they could be transferred to residential rooms as space became available.

On November 28, 1975, less than four months after the MCC had opened, the named respondents initiated this action . . . in the district court. . . . The petition served up a veritable potpourri of complaints that implicated virtually every facet of the institution's conditions and practices. Respondents charged, in part, that they had been deprived of their statutory and constitutional rights because of overcrowded conditions; undue length of confinement; improper searches; inadequate recreational, educational, and employment opportunities; insufficient staff; and objectionable restrictions on the purchase and receipt of personal items and books. We granted certiorari to consider the important constitutional questions raised by these decisions and to resolve an apparent conflict among the circuits. We now reverse.

Reasoning

We are not concerned with the initial decision to detain an accused and the curtailment of liberty that such a decision implies. Neither respondents nor the courts below question that the Government may permissibly detain a person suspected of committing a crime prior to a formal adjudication of guilt. Nor do they doubt that the Government has a substantial interest in ensuring that persons accused of crimes are available for trials and, ultimately, for service of their sentences, or that confinement of such persons pending trial is a legitimate means of furthering that interest. Instead, what is at issue when an aspect of pretrial detention that is not alleged to violate any express guarantee of the Constitution is challenged is the detainee's right to be free from punishment. . . . In evaluating the constitutionality of conditions or restrictions of pretrial detention that implicate only the protection against deprivation of liberty without due process of law, we think that the proper inquiry is whether those conditions amount to punishment of the detainee. Under such circumstances, the Government concededly may detain him to ensure his presence at trial and may subject him to the restrictions and conditions of the detention facility so long as those conditions and restrictions do not amount to punishment or otherwise violate the Constitution.

Not every disability imposed during pretrial detention amounts to "punishment" in the constitutional sense, however. Once the Government has exercised its conceded authority to detain a person pending trial, it obviously is entitled to employ devices that are calculated to effectuate this detention. Traditionally, this has meant confinement in a facility, which, no matter how modern or how antiquated, results in restricting the movement of a detainee in a manner in which he would not be restricted if he simply were free to walk the streets pending trial. Whether it be called a jail, a prison, or a custodial center, the purpose of the facility is to detain. Loss of freedom of choice and privacy are inherent incidents of confinement in such a facility. The fact that such detention interferes with the detainee's understandable desire to live as comfortably as possible and with as little restraint as possible during confinement does not convert the conditions or restrictions of detention into "punishment."

A court must decide whether the disability is imposed for the purpose of punishment or whether it is but an incident of some other legitimate governmental purpose. Absent a showing of an expressed intent to punish on the part of detention facility officials, that determination generally will turn on "whether an alternative purpose to which [the restriction] may rationally be connected is assignable for it, and whether it appears excessive in relation to the alternative purpose assigned [to it]." Thus, if a particular condition or restriction of pretrial detention is reasonably related to a legitimate governmental objective, it does not, without more, amount to "punishment." Conversely, if a restriction or condition is not reasonably related to a legitimate goal—if it is arbitrary or purposeless—a court permissibly may infer that the purpose of the governmental action is punishment that may not constitutionally be inflicted upon detainees qua detainees.

One further point requires discussion. The petitioners assert, and respondents concede, that the "essential objective of pretrial confinement is to ensure the detainees' presence at trial." While this interest undoubtedly justifies the original decision to confine an individual in some manner, we do not accept respondents' argument that the Government's interest in ensuring a detainee's presence at trial is the only objective that may justify restraints and conditions once the decision is lawfully made to confine a person. "If the government could confine or otherwise infringe the liberty of detainees only to the extent necessary to ensure their presence at trial, house arrest would in the end be the only constitutionally justified form of detention." The Government also has legitimate interests that stem from its need to manage the facility in which the individual is detained. These legitimate operational concerns may require administrative measures that go beyond those that are, strictly speaking, necessary to ensure that the detainee shows up at trial. For example, the Government must be able to take steps to maintain security and order at the institution and make certain no weapons or illicit drugs reach detainees. Restraints that are reasonably related to the institution's interest in maintaining jail security do not, without more, constitute unconstitutional punishment, even if they are discomforting and are restrictions that the detainee would not have experienced had he been released while awaiting trial.

Judged by this analysis, respondents' claim that double-bunking violated their due process rights fails. . . . On this record, we are convinced as a matter of law that double-bunking as practiced at the MCC did not amount to punishment and did not, therefore, violate respondents' rights under the Due Process Clause of the Fifth Amendment. Each of the rooms at the MCC that house pretrial detainees has a total floor space of approximately seventy-five square feet. Each of them designated for double-bunking contains a double bunk bed, certain other items of furniture, a wash basin, and an uncovered toilet. Inmates generally are locked into their rooms from 11 P.M. to 6:30 A.M. and for brief periods during the afternoon and evening head counts. During the rest of the day, they may move about freely between their rooms and the common areas.

We disagree with both the district court and the court of appeals that there is some sort of "one man, one cell" principle lurking in the Due Process Clause of the Fifth Amendment. While confining a given number of people in a given amount of space in such a manner as to cause them to endure genuine privations and hardship over an extended period of time might raise serious questions under the Due Process Clause as to whether those conditions amounted to punishment, nothing even approaching such hardship is shown by this record.

Detainees are required to spend only seven or eight hours each day in their rooms, during most or all of which they presumably are sleeping. The rooms provide more than adequate space for sleeping. During the remainder of the time, the detainees are free to move between their rooms and the common area. While double-bunking may have taxed some of the equipment or particular facilities in certain of the common areas, this does not mean that the conditions at the MCC failed to meet the standards required by the Constitution. Our conclusion in this regard is further buttressed by the detainees' length of stay at the MCC. Nearly all of the detainees are released within sixty days. We simply do not believe that requiring a detainee to share toilet facilities and this admittedly rather small sleeping place with another person for generally a maximum period of sixty days violates the Constitution.

Respondents also challenged certain MCC restrictions and practices that were designed to promote security and order at the facility on the ground that these restrictions violated the Due Process Clause of the Fifth Amendment and certain other constitutional guarantees, such as those within the First and Fourth Amendments.... In our view, the court of appeals failed to heed its own admonition not to second-guess prison administrators.... Our cases have established several general principles that inform our evaluation of the constitutionality of the restrictions at issue. First, we have held that convicted prisoners do not forfeit all constitutional protections by reason of their conviction and confinement in prison.... "There is no iron curtain drawn between the Constitution and the prisons of this country." So, for example, our cases have held that sentenced prisoners enjoy freedom of speech and religion under the First and Fourteenth Amendments; that they are protected against invidious discrimination on the basis of race under the Equal Protection Clause of the Fourteenth Amendment; and that they may claim the protection of the Due Process Clause to prevent additional deprivation of life, liberty, or property without due process of law. Pretrial detainees, who have not been convicted of any crimes, retain at least those constitutional rights that we have held are enjoyed by convicted prisoners.

Our cases also have insisted on a second proposition: Simply because prison inmates retain certain constitutional rights does not mean that these rights are not subject to restrictions and limitations. Lawful incarceration brings about the necessary withdrawal or limitation of many privileges and rights, a retraction justified by the considerations underlying our penal system. The fact of confinement as well as the legitimate goals and policies of the penal institution limit these retained constitutional rights. There must be a "mutual accommodation between institutional needs and objectives and the provisions of the Constitution that are of general application." This principle applies equally to pretrial detainees and convicted prisoners. A detainee simply does not possess the full range of freedoms of an unincarcerated individual.

Third, maintaining institutional security and preserving internal order and discipline are essential goals that may require limitation or retraction of the retained constitutional rights of both convicted prisoners and pretrial detainees.... Prison officials must be free to take appropriate action to ensure the safety of inmates and corrections personnel and to prevent escape or unauthorized entry.

Finally, as the court of appeals correctly acknowledged, the problems that arise in the day-to-day operation of a corrections facility are not susceptible of easy solutions. Prison administrators therefore should be accorded wide-ranging deference in the adoption and execution of policies and practices that in their judgment are needed to preserve internal order and discipline and to maintain institutional security.... Judicial deference is accorded not merely because the administrator ordinarily will, as a matter of fact in a particular case, have a better grasp of his domain than the reviewing judge but also because the operation of our correctional facilities is peculiarly the province of the legislative and executive branches of our government, not the judicial. With these teachings of our cases in mind, we turn to an examination of the MCC security practices that are alleged to violate the Constitution.

At the time of the lower courts' decisions, the Bureau of Prisons' "publisher-only" rule, which applies to all bureau facilities, permitted inmates to receive books and magazines from outside the institution only if the materials were mailed directly from the publisher or a book club. The warden of the MCC stated in an affidavit that "serious" security and administrative problems were caused when bound items were received by inmates from unidentified sources outside the facility. He noted that in order to make a "proper and thorough" inspection of such items, prison officials would have to remove the covers of hardback books and to leaf through every page of all books and magazines to ensure that drugs, money, weapons, or other contraband were not secreted in the material. "This search process would take a substantial and inordinate amount of available staff time." However, "there is relatively little risk that material received directly from a publisher or book club would contain contraband, and therefore, the security problems are significantly reduced without a drastic drain on staff resources."

It is desirable at this point to place in focus the precise question that now is before this Court. Subsequent to the decision of the Court of Appeals, the Bureau of Prisons amended its publisher-only rule to permit the receipt of books and magazines from bookstores as well as publishers and book clubs. In addition, petitioners have informed the Court that the bureau proposes to amend the rule further to allow receipt of paperback books, magazines, and other soft-covered materials from any source. The bureau regards hardback books as the "more dangerous source of risk to institutional security," however, and intends to retain the prohibition against receipt of hardback books unless they are mailed directly from publishers, book clubs, or bookstores. Accordingly, petitioners request this Court to review the district court's injunction only to the extent it enjoins petitioners from prohibiting receipt of hard-cover books that are not mailed directly from publishers, book clubs, or bookstores.

We conclude that a prohibition against receipt of hardback books unless mailed directly from publishers, book clubs, or bookstores does not violate the First Amendment rights of MCC inmates. That limited restriction is a rational response by prison officials to an obvious security problem. It hardly needs to be emphasized that hardback books are especially serviceable for smuggling contraband into an institution; money, drugs, and weapons easily may be secreted in the bindings. They also are difficult to search effectively. There is simply no evidence in the record to indicate that MCC officials have exaggerated their response to this security problem and to the administrative difficulties posed by the necessity of carefully inspecting each book mailed from unidentified sources.

The restriction, as it is now before us, allows softbound books and magazines to be received from any source and hardback books to be received from publishers, bookstores, and book clubs. In addition, the MCC has a "relatively large" library for use by inmates. To the limited extent the rule might possibly increase the cost of obtaining published materials, this Court has held that where "other avenues" remain available for the receipt of materials by inmates, the loss of "cost advantages does not fundamentally implicate free speech values." We are also influenced in our decision by the fact that the rule's impact on pretrial detainees is limited to a maximum period of approximately sixty days.

Inmates at the MCC were not permitted to receive packages from outside the facility containing items of food or personal property except for one package of food at Christmas. This rule was justified by MCC officials on three grounds. First, officials testified to "serious" security problems that arise from the introduction of such packages into the institution, the "traditional file in the cake kind of situation" as well as the concealment of drugs "in heels of shoes [and] seams of clothing." As in the case of the publisher-only rule, the warden testified that if such packages were allowed, the inspection process necessary to ensure the security of the institution would require a "substantial and inordinate amount of available staff time." Second, officials were concerned that the introduction of personal property into the facility would increase the risk of thefts, gambling, and inmate conflicts, the "age-old problem of you have it and I don't." Finally, they noted storage and sanitary problems that would result from inmates' receipt of food packages. Inmates are permitted, however, to purchase certain items of food and personal property from the MCC commissary. Neither the district court nor the court of appeals identified which provision of the Constitution was violated by this MCC restriction. We assume, for present purposes, that their decisions were based on the Due Process Clause of the Fifth Amendment, which provides protection for convicted prisoners and pretrial detainees alike against the deprivation of their property without due process of law. But as we have stated, these due process rights of prisoners and pretrial detainees are not absolute; they are subject to reasonable limitation or retraction in light of the legitimate security concerns of the institution.

Corrections officials concluded that permitting the introduction of packages of personal property and food would increase the risks of gambling, theft, and inmate fights over that which the institution already experienced by permitting certain items to be purchased from its commissary. "It is enough to say that they have not been conclusively shown to be wrong in this view." It is also all too obvious that such packages are handy devices for the smuggling of contraband.... It does not therefore deprive the convicted inmates or pretrial detainees of the MCC of their property without due process of law in contravention of the Fifth Amendment.

The MCC staff conducts unannounced searches of inmate living areas at irregular intervals. These searches generally are formal unit shakedowns during which all inmates are cleared of the residential units, and a team of guards searches each room. Prior to the district court's order, inmates were not permitted to watch the searches. Officials testified that permitting inmates to observe room inspections would lead to friction between the inmates and security guards and would allow the inmates to attempt to frustrate the search by distracting personnel and moving contraband from one room to another ahead of the search team.

It may well be argued that a person confined in a detention facility has no reasonable expectation of privacy with respect to his room or cell and that therefore the Fourth Amendment provides no protection for such a person. In any case, given the realities of institutional confinement, any reasonable expectation of privacy that a detainee retained necessarily would be of a diminished scope. Assuming that a pretrial detainee retains such a diminished expectation of privacy after commitment to a custodial facility, we nonetheless find that the room-search rule does not violate the Fourth Amendment.

It is difficult to see how the detainee's interest in privacy is infringed by the room-search rule.... Permitting detainees to observe the searches does not lessen the invasion of their privacy; its only conceivable beneficial effect would be to prevent theft or misuse by those conducting the search. The room-search rule simply facilitates the safe and effective performance of the search which all concede may be conducted. The rule itself, then, does not render the searches "unreasonable" within the meaning of the Fourth Amendment.

Inmates at all Bureau of Prisons facilities, including the MCC, are required to expose their body cavities for visual inspection as a part of a strip search conducted after every contact visit with a person from outside the institution. Corrections officials testified that visual cavity searches were necessary not only to discover but also to deter the smuggling of weapons, drugs, and other contraband into the institution.... Admittedly, this practice instinctively gives us the most pause. However, assuming for present purposes that inmates, both convicted prisoners and pretrial detainees, retain some Fourth Amendment rights upon commitment to a corrections facility, we nonetheless conclude that these searches do not violate that Amendment. The Fourth Amendment prohibits only unreasonable searches, and under the circumstances, we do not believe that these searches are unreasonable.

The test of reasonableness under the Fourth Amendment is not capable of precise definition or mechanical application. In each case it requires a balancing of the need for the particular search against the invasion of personal rights that the search entails. Courts must consider the scope of the particular intrusion, the manner in which it is conducted, the justification for initiating it, and the place in which it is conducted. A detention facility is a unique place fraught with serious security dangers. Smuggling of money, drugs, weapons, and other contraband is all too common an occurrence, and inmate attempts to secrete these items into the facility by concealing them in body cavities are documented in this record. That there has been only one instance where an MCC inmate was discovered attempting to smuggle contraband into the institution on his person may be more a testament to the effectiveness of this search technique as a deterrent than to any lack of interest on the part of the inmates to secrete and import such items when the opportunity arises. We do not underestimate the degree to which these searches may invade the personal privacy of inmates. Nor do we doubt, as the district court noted, that on occasion a security guard may conduct the search in an abusive fashion. Such abuse cannot be condoned. The searches must be conducted in a reasonable manner. But we deal here with the question of whether visual body cavity inspections as contemplated by the MCC rules can ever be conducted on less than probable cause. Balancing the significant and legitimate security interests of the institution against the privacy interests of the inmates, we conclude that they can.

Holding

We do not think that the four MCC security restrictions and practices constitute "punishment" in violation of the rights of pretrial detainees under the Due Process Clause of the Fifth Amendment. Respondents do not even make such a suggestion; they simply argue that the restrictions were greater than necessary to satisfy petitioners' legitimate interest in maintaining security. Therefore, the determination whether these restrictions and practices constitute punishment in the constitutional sense depends on whether they are rationally related to a legitimate nonpunitive governmental purpose and whether they appear excessive in relation to that purpose. Ensuring security and order at the institution is a permissible nonpunitive objective, whether the facility houses pretrial detainees, convicted inmates, or both. For the reasons previously set forth, we conclude that these particular restrictions and practices were reasonable responses by MCC officials to legitimate security concerns. Respondents simply have not met their heavy burden of showing that these officials have exaggerated their response to the genuine security considerations that actuated these restrictions and practices. And as might be expected of restrictions applicable to pretrial detainees, these restrictions were of only limited duration so far as the MCC pretrial detainees were concerned.

There was a time not too long ago when the federal judiciary took a completely hands-off approach to the problem of prison administration. In recent years, however, these courts largely have discarded this hands-off attitude and have waded into this complex arena. The deplorable conditions and Draconian restrictions of some of our nation's prisons are too well known to require recounting here, and the federal courts rightly have condemned these sordid aspects of our prison systems. But many of these same courts have, in the name of the Constitution, become increasingly enmeshed in the minutiae of prison operations. Judges, after all, are human. They, no less than others in our society, have a natural tendency to believe that their individual solutions to often intractable problems are better and more workable than those of the persons who are actually charged with and trained in the running of the particular institution under examination. But under the Constitution, the first question to be answered is not whose plan is best, but in what branch of the Government is lodged the authority to initially devise the plan. This does not mean that constitutional rights are not to be scrupulously observed. It does mean, however, that the inquiry of federal courts into prison management must be limited to the issue of whether a particular system violates any prohibition of the Constitution or, in the case of a federal prison, a statute. The wide range of "judgment calls" that meet constitutional and statutory requirements are confided to officials outside of the judicial branch of government.

Dissenting, *Marshall, J.*

The Court holds that the Government may burden pretrial detainees with almost any restriction, provided detention officials do not proclaim a punitive intent or impose conditions that are "arbitrary or purposeless." As if this standard were not sufficiently ineffectual, the Court dilutes it further by according virtually unlimited deference to detention officials' justifications for particular impositions. Conspicuously lacking from this analysis is any meaningful consideration of the most relevant factor, the impact that restrictions may have on inmates. Such an approach is unsupportable, given that all of these detainees are presumptively innocent and many are confined solely because they cannot afford bail. I believe the proper inquiry in this context is not whether a particular restraint can be labeled "punishment." Rather, as with other due process challenges, the inquiry should be whether the governmental interests served by any given restriction outweigh the individual deprivations suffered.

To make detention officials' intent the critical factor in assessing the constitutionality of impositions on detainees is unrealistic.... It will often be the case that officials believe, erroneously but in good faith, that a specific restriction is necessary for institutional security. As the district court noted, "zeal for security is among the most common varieties of official excess," and the litigation in this area corroborates that conclusion. A standard that focuses on punitive intent cannot effectively eliminate this excess. Indeed, the Court does not even attempt to "detail the precise extent of the legitimate governmental interests that may justify conditions or restrictions of pretrial detention." Rather, it is content merely to recognize that "the effective management of the detention facility... is a valid objective that may justify imposition of conditions and restrictions of pretrial detention and dispel any inference that such restrictions are intended as punishment."

Although the Court professes to go beyond the direct inquiry regarding intent and to determine whether a particular imposition is rationally related to a nonpunitive purpose, this exercise is at best a formality. Almost any restriction on detainees, including, as the Court concedes, chains and shackles, can be found to have some rational relation to institutional security, or more broadly, to "the effective management of the detention facility." Yet this toothless standard applies irrespective of the excessiveness of the restraint or the nature of the rights infringed. Moreover, the Court has not in fact reviewed the rationality of detention officials' decisions. Instead, the majority affords "wide-ranging" deference to those officials "in the adoption and execution of policies and practices that in their judgment are needed to preserve internal order and discipline and to maintain institutional security." Reasoning that security considerations in jails are little different than in prisons, the Court concludes that cases requiring substantial deference to prison administrators' determinations on security-related issues are equally applicable in the present context.

Yet as the Court implicitly acknowledges, the rights of detainees, who have not been adjudicated guilty of a crime, are necessarily more extensive than those of prisoners "who have been found to have violated one or more of the criminal laws established by society for its orderly governance." Judicial tolerance of substantial impositions on detainees must be concomitantly less. However, by blindly deferring to administrative judgments on the rational basis for particular restrictions, the Court effectively delegates to detention officials the decision whether pretrial detainees have been punished. This, in my view, is an abdication of an unquestionably judicial function.

When assessing the restrictions on detainees, we must consider the cumulative impact of restraints imposed during confinement. Incarceration of itself clearly represents a profound infringement of liberty, and each additional imposition increases the severity of that initial deprivation. Since any restraint thus has a serious effect on detainees, I believe the Government must bear a more rigorous burden of justification than the rational-basis standard mandates. At a minimum, I would require a showing that a restriction is substantially necessary to jail administration. Where the imposition is of particular gravity, that is, where it implicates interests of fundamental importance or inflicts significant harms, the Government should demonstrate that the restriction serves a compelling necessity of jail administration.

Simply stated, the approach I advocate here weighs the detainees' interests implicated by a particular restriction against the governmental interests the restriction serves. As the substantiality of the intrusion on detainees' rights increases, so must the significance of the countervailing governmental objectives.

To conclude, as the Court does here, that double-bunking has not inflicted "genuine privations and hardship over an extended period of time," is inappropriate where respondents have not had an adequate opportunity to produce evidence suggesting otherwise.... I would leave to the district court in the first instance the sensitive balancing inquiry that the Due Process Clause dictates.

In support of its restriction, the Government presented the affidavit of the MCC warden, who averred without elaboration that a proper and thorough search of incoming hardback books might require removal of the covers. Further, the warden asserted, "in the case of all books and magazines," it would be necessary to leaf through every page to ascertain that there was no contraband. The warden offered no reasons why the institution could not place reasonable limitations on the number of books inmates could receive or use electronic devices and fluoroscopes to detect contraband rather than requiring inmates to purchase hardback books directly from publishers or stores. As the court of appeals noted, "Other institutions have not recorded untoward experiences with far less restrictive rules."

As for the prohibition on the receipt of outside packages, the asserted interest in ameliorating sanitation and storage problems and avoiding thefts, gambling, and inmate conflicts over personal property is belied, as the Court seems to recognize, by the policy of permitting inmate purchases of up to $15 a week from the prison commissary. Detention officials doubtless have a legitimate interest in preventing introduction of drugs or weapons into the facility. But as both the district court and the court of appeals observed, other detention institutions have adopted much less restrictive regulations than the MCC's governing receipt of packages. Inmates in New York state institutions, for example, may receive a thirty-five-pound package each month, as well as clothing and magazines.

I would also affirm the ruling of the courts below that inmates must be permitted to observe searches of their cells. Routine searches such as those at issue here may be an unavoidable incident of incarceration. Nonetheless, the protections of the Fourth Amendment do not lapse at the jailhouse door. Detention officials must therefore conduct such searches in a reasonable manner, avoiding needless intrusions on inmates' privacy. Because unobserved searches may invite official disrespect for detainees' few possessions and generate fears that guards will steal personal property or plant contraband, the inmates' interests are significant.

In my view, the body cavity searches of MCC inmates represent one of the most grievous offenses against personal dignity and common decency. After every contact visit with someone from outside the facility, including defense attorneys, an inmate must remove all of his or her clothing, bend over, spread the buttocks, and display the anal cavity for inspection by a correctional officer. Women inmates must assume a suitable posture for vaginal inspection, while men must raise their genitals. And, as the Court neglects to note, because of time pressures, this humiliating spectacle is frequently conducted in the presence of other inmates.

Not surprisingly, the Government asserts a security justification for such inspections. These searches are necessary, it argues, to prevent inmates from smuggling contraband into the facility. In crediting this justification despite the contrary findings of the two courts below, the Court overlooks the critical facts. As respondents point out, inmates are required to wear one-piece jumpsuits with zippers in the front. To insert an object into the vaginal or anal cavity, an inmate would have to remove the jumpsuit, at least from the upper torso.... There was medical testimony, moreover, that inserting an object into the rectum is painful and "would require time and opportunity which is not available in the visiting areas," and that visual inspection would probably not detect an object once inserted. Additionally, before entering the visiting room, visitors and their packages are searched thoroughly by a metal detector, fluoroscope, and by hand. Correction officers may require that visitors leave packages or handbags with guards until the visit is over. Only by blinding itself to the facts presented on this record can the Court accept the Government's security rationale.

Without question, these searches are an imposition of sufficient gravity to invoke the compelling-necessity standard. It is equally indisputable that they cannot meet that standard. Indeed, the procedure is so unnecessarily degrading that it "shocks the conscience." Here, the searches are employed absent any suspicion of wrongdoing. It was this aspect of the MCC practice that the court of appeals redressed, requiring that searches be conducted only when there is probable cause to believe that the inmate is concealing contraband.

That the Court can uphold these indiscriminate searches highlights the bankruptcy of its basic analysis. Under the test adopted today, the rights of detainees apparently extend only so far as detention officials decide that cost and security will permit. Such unthinking deference to administrative convenience cannot be justified where the interests at stake are those of presumptively innocent individuals, many of whose only proven offense is the inability to afford bail. I dissent.

Dissenting, *Stevens J.*, joined by *Brennan, J.*

An empirical judgment that most persons formally accused of criminal conduct are probably guilty would provide a rational basis for a set of rules that treat them like convicts until they establish their innocence. No matter how rational such an approach might be—no matter how acceptable in a community where equality of status is the dominant goal—it is obnoxious to the concept of individual freedom protected by the Due Process Clause. If ever accepted in this country, it would work a fundamental change in the character of our free society.

Some of the individuals housed in the MCC are convicted criminals. As to them, detention may legitimately serve a punitive goal, and there is strong reason, even apart from the rules challenged here, to suggest that it does. But the same is not true of the detainees who are also housed there and whose rights we are called upon to address. Notwithstanding the impression created by the Court's opinion, these people are not "prisoners," they have not been convicted of any crimes, and their detention may serve only a more limited, regulatory purpose. Prior to conviction every individual is entitled to the benefit of a presumption both that he is innocent of prior criminal conduct and that he has no present intention to commit any offense in the immediate future. That presumption does not imply that he may not be detained or otherwise subjected to restraints on the basis of an individual showing of probable cause that he poses relevant risks to the community. For our system of justice has always and quite properly functioned on the assumption that when there is probable cause to believe (1) that a person has committed a crime, and (2) that absent the posting of bail he poses at least some risk of flight, there is justification for pretrial detention to ensure his presence at trial.

The fact that an individual may be unable to pay for a bail bond, however, is an insufficient reason for subjecting him to indignities that would be appropriate punishment for convicted felons. Nor can he be subject on that basis to onerous restraints that might properly be considered regulatory with respect to particularly obstreperous or dangerous arrestees. An innocent man who has no propensity toward immediate violence, escape, or subversion may not be dumped into a pool of second-class citizens and subjected to restraints designed to regulate others who have. For him, such treatment amounts to punishment. And because the due process guarantee is individual and personal, it mandates that an innocent person be treated as an individual human being and be free of treatment that, as to him, is punishment.

Questions for Discussion

1. What is the purpose of confining pretrial detainees?
2. How does the Supreme Court define punishment? Note the importance of intent and effective correctional management in evaluating whether a policy constitutes punishment. Distinguish punishment from detention.
3. Discuss the court's holdings in regard to the receipt of books and packages, the searches of cells and body cavities, and double-bunking.
4. Why do the dissenting judges emphasize that some of the detainees in the MCC have not been convicted of a crime?
5. Why is the dissent critical of the reliance on the intent of correctional officials to determine whether a policy constitutes punishment?
6. Compare and contrast the conclusions of the majority and dissent in regard to the correctional policies discussed in *Bell v. Wolfish*.
7. Should judges defer to the judgment of correctional officials?

Indigency and the Right to Counsel

The remainder of the chapter focuses on a second important aspect of the first appearance: the provision of an appointed counsel for an indigent defendant.

The Sixth Amendment provides that "in all criminal prosecutions, the accused shall enjoy the right...to have the assistance of counsel for his defense." In England under the common law, defendants charged with misdemeanors were entitled to the assistance of a lawyer at trial. Individuals charged with felonies, on the other hand, were denied the assistance of a lawyer at trial. Lawyers were thought to impede the prosecution of these more serious offenses. The American colonists wanted to protect individuals against the power of prosecutors and judges. At the time of the adaptation of the Bill of Rights in 1791, the constitutions of twelve of the thirteen American colonies provided for the right to counsel, and this protection subsequently was included in the Sixth Amendment of the U.S. Constitution.

The first major U.S. Supreme Court judgment addressing the right to counsel was the famous case of *Powell v. Alabama*. As you may recall from reading about *Powell* in Chapter 2, the Supreme Court relied on the Due Process Clause of the Fourteenth Amendment in holding that the "Scottsboro Boys" had been denied their fundamental right to legal representation. The Supreme Court overturned the defendants' convictions. During the pretrial phase, the trial judge in *Powell* appointed "all members of the bar" to represent the defendants. This was "little more than an expansive gesture, imposing no definite obligation upon any one." On the day of the trial, the judge named two unqualified lawyers to represent the defendants and provided the lawyers with a limited time to prepare their defense. The Supreme Court concluded that the trial court judge denied the defendants their Sixth Amendment right to a lawyer. The Court stressed that legal representation is crucial to a fair hearing and that absent the appointment of effective counsel, innocent defendants are at risk of criminal conviction. The right to the appointment of effective legal representation is particularly vital in a capital case such as *Powell:*

> Where the defendant is unable to employ counsel and is incapable of making his own defense because of ignorance, feeble mindedness, [or] illiteracy...it is the duty of the court...to assign counsel....for [the defendant] as a necessary requisite of due process of law. (*Powell v. Alabama,* 287 U.S. 45, 53,71 [1932])

The decision in *Powell* established a limited right to appointed counsel for indigents who were "incapable" of representing themselves and who were facing the death penalty. The Supreme Court demonstrated little hesitancy six years later, in *Johnson v. Zerbst,* in holding that in federal criminal prosecutions, an accused may not be deprived of his "life or liberty unless he has or waives the assistance of counsel." The Court stressed that even the

> intelligent and educated layman...left without the aid of counsel...may be put on trial without a proper charge, and convicted upon incompetent evidence, or evidence irrelevant to the issue or otherwise inadmissible. He lacks both the skill and knowledge adequately to prepare his defense...[and] requires the guiding hand of counsel at every step in the proceedings against him. (*Johnson v. Zerbst,* 304 U.S. 458, 463 [1938])

The Supreme Court was not ready to extend the Sixth Amendment protection to defendants in state criminal prosecutions. In *Betts v. Brady,* the Court refused to hold that the Due Process Clause incorporated the Sixth Amendment and required the appointment of a lawyer to represent the accused in every state criminal case. Justice Roberts held that the right to an attorney is not fundamental to the justice process and that Maryland had no constitutional obligation to appoint a lawyer to represent the indigent Betts, who was convicted of robbery and sentenced to eight years in prison. The Due Process Clause requires a state only to appoint a lawyer in special circumstances where the

> trial is offensive to the common and fundamental ideas of fairness and right.... We cannot say that the Amendment embodies...[a] command that no trial for any offense, or in any court, can be fairly conducted and justice accorded a defendant who is not represented by counsel. (*Betts v. Brady,* 316 U.S. 455 [1942])

In this instance, Betts claimed that he had an alibi and therefore could not have committed the robbery with which he was charged. The Supreme Court concluded that he was not "helpless." Betts was forty-three and intelligent and had experience as a defendant in the criminal justice system, and he was "fully able to examine witnesses to support the claim that he was at another location at the time of the robbery" (473). The Court did recognize that "special circumstances" might require that a state appoint a defense lawyer to represent young offenders with little education or mentally challenged defendants who confront a prosecution for complicated crimes involving technical defenses (*Uveges v. Pennsylvania,* 335 U.S. 437, 441 [1948]).

Justices Black, Douglas, and Murphy dissented in *Betts* and argued that the right to a lawyer in a criminal case is fundamental to liberty and that the Sixth Amendment is incorporated into the Due Process Clause. The dissenters insisted that it is "shocking to the conscience" to subject innocent individuals to "increased dangers of conviction merely because of their poverty." It is nearly impossible to determine whether a defendant such as Betts would be able to adequately represent himself or herself at trial in the absence of a defense attorney (476).

In 1963, in the famous case of *Gideon v. Wainwright,* the U.S. Supreme abandoned the "special circumstances" test established in *Betts v. Brady* and held that the Fourteenth Amendment incorporated the Sixth Amendment right to counsel and that indigent individuals charged with felonies in state courts are entitled to an appointed counsel. This decision established that indigent defendants confronting state as well as federal prosecutions are entitled to legal representation.

Clarence Gideon was convicted and sentenced to five years in prison for breaking into and entering a poolroom. His request for an attorney had been denied, and despite the fact that he had conducted an adequate defense for a "layman," the Supreme Court held that Gideon had been denied due process of law. Justice Black stressed that "any person haled into court, who is too poor to hire a lawyer, cannot be assured a fair trial unless counsel is provided for him. This seems to us to be an obvious truth." The "noble ideal" that all individuals are equal before the law cannot be realized if the ability of an individual to present a defense is based on an individual's personal wealth or income (344).

It is interesting as you read *Gideon v. Wainwright* to note how the Supreme Court justifies overturning the precedent in *Betts v. Brady*. Do you believe that indigent individuals have a fundamental right to have the government provide them with a lawyer in a felony prosecution?

Was the trial judge constitutionally required to appoint a lawyer to represent Gideon?

Gideon v. Wainwright, 372 U.S. 335 (1963), Black, J.

Facts

Petitioner was charged in a Florida state court with having broken into and entered a poolroom with intent to commit a misdemeanor. This offense is a felony under Florida law. Appearing in court without funds and without a lawyer, petitioner asked the court to appoint counsel for him, whereupon the following colloquy took place:

> The COURT: Mr. Gideon, I am sorry, but I cannot appoint Counsel to represent you in this case. Under the laws of the State of Florida, the only time the Court can appoint Counsel to represent a Defendant is when that person is charged with a capital offense. I am sorry, but I will have to deny your request to appoint Counsel to defend you in this case.
>
> The DEFENDANT: The United States Supreme Court says I am entitled to be represented by Counsel.

Put to trial before a jury, Gideon conducted his defense about as well as could be expected from a layman. He made an opening statement to the jury, cross-examined the State's witnesses, presented witnesses in his own defense, declined to testify himself, and made a short argument "emphasizing his innocence to the charge contained in the Information filed in this case." The jury returned a verdict of guilty, and petitioner was sentenced to serve five years in the state prison. Later, petitioner filed in the Florida Supreme Court this habeas corpus petition attacking his conviction and sentence on the ground that the trial court's refusal to appoint counsel for him denied him rights "guaranteed by the Constitution and the Bill of Rights by the United States Government." Treating the petition for habeas corpus as properly before it, the State Supreme Court, "upon consideration thereof" but without an opinion, denied all relief.

Issue

Since 1942, when *Betts v. Brady* was decided by a divided Court, the problem of a defendant's federal constitutional right to counsel in a state court has been a continuing source of controversy and litigation in both state and federal courts. To give this problem another review here, we granted certiorari. Since Gideon was proceeding *in forma pauperis,* we appointed counsel to represent him and requested both sides to discuss in their briefs and oral arguments the following: "Should this Court's holding in *Betts v. Brady* be reconsidered?"

Reasoning

The facts upon which Betts claimed that he had been unconstitutionally denied the right to have counsel appointed to assist him are strikingly like the facts upon which Gideon here bases his federal constitutional claim. Betts was indicted for robbery in a Maryland state court. On arraignment, he told the trial judge of his lack of funds to hire a lawyer and asked the court to appoint one for him. Betts was advised that it was not the practice in that county to appoint counsel for indigent defendants except in murder and rape cases. He then pleaded not guilty, had witnesses summoned, cross-examined the State's witnesses, examined his own, and chose not to testify himself. He was found guilty by the judge, sitting without a jury, and sentenced to eight years in prison.

Like Gideon, Betts sought release by habeas corpus, alleging that he had been denied the right to assistance of counsel in violation of the Fourteenth Amendment. Betts was denied any relief, and on review this Court affirmed. It was held that a refusal to appoint counsel for an indigent defendant charged with a felony did not necessarily violate the Due Process Clause of the Fourteenth Amendment, which for reasons given the Court deemed to be the only applicable federal constitutional provision. The Court...

held that refusal to appoint counsel under the particular facts and circumstances in the *Betts* case was not so "offensive to the common and fundamental ideas of fairness" as to amount to a denial of due process. Since the facts and circumstances of the two cases are so nearly indistinguishable, we think the *Betts v. Brady* holding if left standing would require us to reject Gideon's claim that the Constitution guarantees him the assistance of counsel. Upon full reconsideration we conclude that *Betts v. Brady* should be overruled.

The Sixth Amendment provides, "In all criminal prosecutions, the accused shall enjoy the right... to have the Assistance of Counsel for his defense." We have construed this to mean that in federal courts counsel must be provided for defendants unable to employ counsel, unless the right is competently and intelligently waived. Betts argued that this right is extended to indigent defendants in state courts by the Fourteenth Amendment. In response, the Court stated that while the Sixth Amendment laid down

> no rule for the conduct of the States, the question recurs whether the constraint laid by the Amendment upon the national courts expresses a rule so fundamental and essential to a fair trial, and so, to due process of law, that it is made obligatory upon the States by the Fourteenth Amendment.

We think the Court in *Betts* was wrong... in concluding that the Sixth Amendment's guarantee of counsel is not one of these fundamental rights. Ten years before *Betts v. Brady,* this Court, after full consideration of all the historical data examined in *Betts,* had unequivocally declared that "the right to the aid of counsel is of this fundamental character" in *Powell v. Alabama*. While the Court, at the close of its *Powell* opinion, did by its language, as this Court frequently does, limit its holding to the particular facts and circumstances of that case, its conclusions about the fundamental nature of the right to counsel are unmistakable.... In our adversary system of criminal justice, any person haled into court, who is too poor to hire a lawyer, cannot be assured a fair trial unless counsel is provided for him. This seems to us to be an obvious truth.

Governments, both state and federal, quite properly spend vast sums of money to establish machinery to try defendants accused of crime. Lawyers to prosecute are everywhere deemed essential to protect the public's interest in an orderly society. Similarly, there are few defendants charged with crime, few indeed, who fail to hire the best lawyers they can get to prepare and present their defenses. That government hires lawyers to prosecute and defendants who have the money hire lawyers to defend are the strongest indications of the widespread belief that lawyers in criminal courts are necessities, not luxuries. The right of one charged with crime to counsel may not be deemed fundamental and essential to fair trials in some countries, but it is in ours. From the very beginning, our state and national constitutions and laws have laid great emphasis on procedural and substantive safeguards designed to assure fair trials before impartial tribunals in which every defendant stands equal before the law. This noble ideal cannot be realized if the poor man charged with crime has to face his accusers without a lawyer to assist him. A defendant's need for a lawyer is nowhere better stated than in the moving words of Mr. Justice Sutherland in *Powell v. Alabama:*

> The right to be heard would be, in many cases, of little avail if it did not comprehend the right to be heard by counsel. Even the intelligent and educated layman has small and sometimes no skill in the science of law. If charged with crime, he is incapable, generally, of determining for himself whether the indictment is good or bad. He is unfamiliar with the rules of evidence. Left without the aid of counsel, he may be put on trial without a proper charge, and convicted upon incompetent evidence, or evidence irrelevant to the issue or otherwise inadmissible. He lacks both the skill and knowledge adequately to prepare his defense, even though he have a perfect one. He requires the guiding hand of counsel at every step in the proceedings against him. Without it, though he be not guilty, he faces the danger of conviction because he does not know how to establish his innocence. (287 U.S. 45, 69 [1932]).

Holding

The Court in *Betts v. Brady* departed from the sound wisdom upon which the Court's holding in *Powell v. Alabama* rested. Florida, supported by two other states, has asked that *Betts v. Brady* be left intact. Twenty-two states, as friends of the Court, argue that *Betts* was "an anachronism when handed down" and that it should now be overruled. We agree. The judgment is reversed, and the cause is remanded to the Supreme Court of Florida for further action not inconsistent with this opinion.

Questions for Discussion

1. What is the holding in *Gideon v. Wainwright?*
2. Explain in your own words why Gideon has a fundamental right to be represented by a lawyer at trial.
3. Why did the Supreme Court overturn *Betts?*

Right to Counsel and Critical Stages of Prosecution

The Sixth Amendment right to counsel and right of an indigent to appointed counsel is not limited to the criminal trial. The right to a lawyer would provide little protection if individuals were denied assistance when subjected to custodial interrogation, when negotiating a plea bargain, or when determining whether to enter a guilty plea or a not guilty plea prior to trial. The U.S. Supreme Court has established a two-part test to determine when the Sixth Amendment right to counsel attaches.

The Sixth Amendment provides that in "all criminal prosecutions" the accused is entitled to have the "Assistance of Counsel" for his or her defense. The Supreme Court has held that an individual is entitled to a lawyer when formal adversarial criminal proceedings are initiated. Formal adversarial criminal proceedings begin when a formal charge is issued by an indictment or by information filed by a prosecutor, or when a charge is brought against the accused at an arraignment or preliminary hearing. It is commonly observed that at this point, an individual confronts the full force of the prosecution and is transformed from a suspect into a defendant (*Kirby v. Illinois,* 406 U.S. 682, 689 [1972]).

Following the initiation of formal criminal proceedings, the right to counsel attaches at **critical stages of the prosecution.** A critical stage is considered any phase of the prosecution that may negatively impact the defendant's ability to present a defense at trial and at which the presence of an attorney would safeguard the defendant. In *Gerstein,* a critical stage is described as "those pretrial procedures that would impair a defense on the merits if the accused is required to proceed without counsel" (*Gerstein v. Pugh,* 420 U.S. 102, 122 [1973]), and in *United States v. Wade* (discussed in Chapter 9), the Supreme Court described a critical stage as "any stage of the prosecution.... in court or out, where Counsel's absence might derogate from the right to a fair trial" (*United States v. Wade,* 388 U.S. 218, 226 [1967]). In *United States v. Gouveia,* the Court stressed that a critical stage is a "situation" where the results "might well settle the accused's fate and reduce the trial itself to a mere formality" (*United States v. Gouveia,* 467 U.S. 180, 189 [1984]).

Courts have not found a procedure to be critical where a lawyer is able later to reconstruct whether the procedure was carried out in a fair fashion. For example, a lawyer can determine the accuracy of a DNA test following the test. You should be aware that some states more broadly interpret the right to a lawyer and provide individuals with legal representation at "important points in the criminal process," such as when bail is being set, while other state statutes provide that the right to counsel attaches as "soon as feasible" after an individual is taken into custody. The Wisconsin state statutes, in section 967.06(1), provide that "[as] soon as practicable after a person has been detained or arrested in connection with any offense that is punishable by incarceration...the person shall be informed of his or her right to counsel."

You can find a list of some critical and noncritical stages of criminal prosecution in Chart 12.1. In the next section, we discuss whether an indigent defendant is entitled to an appointed counsel during "all criminal prosecutions" or only during "some criminal prosecutions."

Chart 12.1 Critical Stages and the Right to Legal Representation

Stage of Criminal Process	*Prosecution Right to a Lawyer*
Arraignment	Yes
Preliminary hearing	Yes
Postindictment lineup	Yes
Custodial interrogation	Yes
Plea bargaining negotiations	Yes
Trial	Yes
Sentencing	Yes
Photographic array	No
Handwriting exemplar	No
DNA swab	No
Preindictment lineup	No
Bail	No

The Meaning of "All Criminal Prosecutions"

The Sixth Amendment provides that "in all criminal prosecutions, the accused shall enjoy the right... to have the Assistance of Counsel for his defense." In *Gideon v. Wainwright,* the U.S. Supreme Court interpreted this clause to provide Clarence Gideon with the right to an attorney in his felony trial. Gideon's conviction and five-year prison sentence accordingly were reversed by the Court. The Court expanded the right to counsel at trial in *Argersinger v. Hamlin.* In *Argersinger,* the Court held that "absent a knowing and intelligent waiver, no person may be imprisoned for any offense, whether classified as petty, misdemeanor, or felony, unless he was represented by counsel." In other words, an individual who if convicted confronts imprisonment for even a single day is entitled to be represented by a lawyer (*Argersinger v. Hamlin,* 407 U.S. 25 [1972]).

Why did the Supreme Court draw the line at this point rather than distinguish between petty misdemeanors (punishable by less than six months) and felonies? The Court observed that a trial for an offense punishable by less than six months in jail is likely to be as complex as a case involving a crime punishable by one year or more in jail. A defendant confronting incarceration, however brief, is in need of legal assistance to understand the consequences of decisions such as whether to take the stand at trial. In the absence of legal representation, the temptation will be for prosecutors and judges to encourage defendants to plead guilty in order to dispose of misdemeanor prosecutions as quickly as possible.

In *Scott v. Illinois,* the U.S. Supreme Court was asked to expand the right to counsel to cover criminal prosecutions that do not result in imprisonment. Scott was convicted of the shoplifting of goods valued at $150. The Illinois statute provided for punishment by a $500 fine or by a year in prison or both, and Scott was punished by a $50 fine. Scott appealed on the grounds that the Sixth and Fourteenth Amendments required Illinois to provide him with an appointed lawyer. The U.S. Supreme Court affirmed Scott's conviction and fine and held that the Constitution provides that "no indigent criminal defendant [is to] be sentenced to a term of imprisonment unless the State has afforded him the right to assistance of appointed counsel in his defense" (*Scott v. Illinois,* 440 U.S. 367 [1979]). There is no right to a counsel in the event that a fine is imposed.

The decision in *Scott* means that unless a defendant is provided with a lawyer, a judge may not sentence him or her to imprisonment. In *Alabama v. Shelton,* Shelton was accused of the misdemeanor of third-degree assault, a charge that carried penalties of one year in prison and a $2,000 fine. Shelton was not provided with a lawyer at trial; he was convicted, received a thirty-day suspended sentence, and was placed on unsupervised probation for two years. The Supreme Court overturned Shelton's conviction and held that a suspended sentence that may result in imprisonment in the future may not be imposed where a defendant has not been provided with an attorney at trial. Do you agree that the Alabama court should be required to provide Shelton with a lawyer at trial based on the speculative possibility that he may be incarcerated in the future? See *Alabama v. Shelton,* 534 U.S. 654 (2002).

In reading the next case, *Scott v. Illinois,* consider whether the U.S. Supreme Court has struck the proper balance in determining when a defendant is entitled to an appointed attorney.

Did Scott have a right to a lawyer in his trial for shoplifting?

Scott v. Illinois, *440 U.S. 367 (1979), Rehnquist, J.*

Issue

Petitioner Aubrey Scott was convicted of shoplifting merchandise valued at less than $150. The applicable Illinois statute set the maximum penalty for such an offense at a $500 fine or one year in jail, or both. The petitioner argues that a line of this Court's cases culminating in *Argersinger v. Hamlin* requires state provision of counsel whenever imprisonment is an authorized penalty.

Facts

The Supreme Court of Illinois rejected Scott's contention, quoting the following language from *Argersinger:*

> We hold, therefore, that absent a knowing and intelligent waiver, no person may be imprisoned for any offense, whether classified as petty, misdemeanor, or felony, unless he was represented by counsel at his trial.... Under the rule we announce today, every judge will know when the trial of a misdemeanor starts that no imprisonment may be imposed, even though local law permits it, unless the accused is represented by counsel. He will have a measure of the seriousness and gravity of the offense and therefore know when to name a lawyer to represent the accused before the trial starts.

The Supreme Court of Illinois went on to state that it was "not inclined to extend *Argersinger*" to the case where a defendant is charged with a statutory offense for which imprisonment upon conviction is authorized but not actually imposed upon the defendant.

Reasoning

We agree with the Supreme Court of Illinois that the federal Constitution does not require a state trial court to appoint counsel for a criminal defendant such as petitioner, and we therefore affirm its judgment.... The Supreme Court of Illinois, in quoting the above language from *Argersinger,* clearly viewed the latter as *Argersinger's* holding. Additional support for this proposition may be derived from the concluding paragraph of the opinion in that case:

> The run of misdemeanors will not be affected by today's ruling. But in those that end up in the actual deprivation of a person's liberty, the accused will receive the benefit of "the guiding hand of counsel" so necessary where one's liberty is in jeopardy.

> There is considerable doubt that the Sixth Amendment itself, as originally drafted by the framers of the Bill of Rights, contemplated any guarantee other than the right of an accused in a criminal prosecution in a federal court to employ a lawyer to assist in his defense.... In *Argersinger,* the State of Florida urged that... any offense punishable by less than six months in jail should not require appointment of counsel for an indigent defendant.... The Court rejected arguments that social cost or a lack of available lawyers militated against its holding, in some part because it thought these arguments were factually incorrect. But they were rejected in much larger part because of the Court's conclusion that incarceration was so severe a sanction that it should not be imposed as a result of a criminal trial unless an indigent defendant had been offered appointed counsel to assist in his defense, regardless of the cost to the states implicit in such a rule. The Court in its opinion repeatedly referred to trials "where an accused is deprived of his liberty," and to "a case that actually leads to imprisonment even for a brief period." The chief justice in his opinion concurring in the result also observed that "any deprivation of liberty is a serious matter."

Holding

Although the intentions of the *Argersinger* Court are not unmistakably clear from its opinion, we conclude today that *Argersinger* did indeed delimit the constitutional right to appointed counsel in state criminal proceedings.... We believe that the central premise of *Argersinger*—that actual imprisonment is a penalty different in kind from fines or the mere threat of imprisonment—is eminently sound and warrants adoption of actual imprisonment as the line defining the constitutional right to appointment of counsel. *Argersinger* has proved reasonably workable, whereas any extension would create confusion and impose unpredictable, but necessarily substantial, costs on fifty quite diverse states.

We therefore hold that the Sixth and Fourteenth Amendments to the U.S. Constitution require only that no indigent criminal defendant be sentenced to a term of imprisonment unless the State has afforded him the right to assistance of appointed counsel in his defense. The judgment of the Supreme Court of Illinois is accordingly affirmed.

Dissenting, *Brennan, J.,* joined by *Marshall, J.,* and *Stevens, J.*

The Court today retreats to the indefensible position that the *Argersinger* "actual imprisonment" standard is the only test for determining the boundary of the Sixth Amendment right to appointed counsel in state misdemeanor cases, thus necessarily deciding that in many cases (such as this one) a defendant will have no right to appointed counsel even when he has a constitutional right to a jury trial. This is simply an intolerable result. Not only is the "actual imprisonment" standard unprecedented as the exclusive test, but also the problems inherent in its application demonstrate the superiority of an "authorized imprisonment" standard that would require the appointment of counsel for indigents accused of any offense for which imprisonment for any time is authorized.

First, the authorized imprisonment standard more faithfully implements the principles of the Sixth Amendment identified in *Gideon.* The procedural rules established by state statutes are geared to the nature of the potential penalty for an offense, not to the actual penalty imposed in particular cases. The authorized penalty is also a better predictor of the stigma and other collateral consequences that attach to conviction of an offense. With the exception of *Argersinger,* authorized penalties have been used consistently by this Court as the true measures of the seriousness of offenses. Imprisonment is a sanction particularly associated with criminal offenses; trials of offenses punishable by imprisonment accordingly possess the characteristics found by *Gideon* to require the appointment of counsel. By contrast, the actual imprisonment standard, as the Court's opinion in this case demonstrates, denies the right to counsel in criminal prosecutions to accuseds who suffer the severe consequences of prosecution other than imprisonment.

Second, the authorized imprisonment test presents no problems of administration. It avoids the necessity for time-consuming consideration of the likely sentence in each individual case before trial and the attendant problems of inaccurate predictions, unequal treatment, and apparent and actual bias....

Finally, the authorized imprisonment test ensures that courts will not abrogate legislative judgments concerning the appropriate range of penalties to be considered for each offense. Under the actual imprisonment standard,

> [the] judge will...be forced to decide in advance of trial—and without hearing the evidence—whether he will forgo entirely his judicial discretion to impose some sentence of imprisonment and abandon his responsibility to consider the full range of punishments established by the legislature. His alternatives, assuming the availability of counsel, will be to appoint counsel and retain the discretion vested in him by law, or to abandon this discretion in advance and proceed without counsel.

The authorized imprisonment standard, on the other hand, respects the allocation of functions between legislatures and courts in the administration of the criminal justice system.

The apparent reason for the Court's adoption of the actual imprisonment standard for all misdemeanors is concern for the economic burden that an authorized imprisonment standard might place on the states. But, with all respect, that concern is both irrelevant and speculative.

This Court's role in enforcing constitutional guarantees for criminal defendants cannot be made dependent on the budgetary decisions of state governments. A unanimous Court made that clear in *Mayer v. Chicago* (404 U.S. 189 [1971]), in rejecting a proposed fiscal justification for providing free transcripts for appeals only when the appellant was subject to imprisonment:

> The invidiousness of the discrimination that exists where criminal procedures are made available only to those who can pay is not erased by any differences in the sentences that may be imposed. The State's fiscal interest is, therefore, irrelevant.

In any event, the extent of the alleged burden on the states is, as the Court admits, speculative. Although more persons are charged with misdemeanors punishable by incarceration than are charged with felonies, a smaller percentage of persons charged with misdemeanors qualify as indigent, and misdemeanor cases as a rule require far less attorney time.

Furthermore, public defender systems have proved economically feasible, and the establishment of such systems to replace appointment of private attorneys can keep costs at acceptable levels even when the number of cases requiring appointment of counsel increases dramatically. The public defender system alternative also answers the argument that an authorized imprisonment standard would clog the courts with inexperienced appointed counsel.

Perhaps the strongest refutation of respondent's alarmist prophecies that an authorized imprisonment standard would wreak havoc on the states is that the standard has not produced that result in the substantial number of states that already provide counsel in all cases where imprisonment is authorized—states that include a large majority of the country's population and a great diversity of urban and rural environments. Moreover, of those states that do not yet provide counsel in all cases where any imprisonment is authorized, many provide counsel when periods of imprisonment longer than thirty days, three months, or six months are authorized. In fact, Scott would be entitled to appointed counsel under the current laws of at least 33 states.

It may well be that adoption by this Court of an authorized imprisonment standard would lead state and local governments to re-examine their criminal statutes. A state legislature or local government might determine that it no longer desired to authorize incarceration for certain minor offenses in light of the expense of meeting the requirements of the Constitution. In my view this re-examination is long overdue. In any event, the Court's actual imprisonment standard must inevitably lead the courts to make this re-examination, which plainly should more properly be a legislative responsibility.

Dissenting, *Blackmun, J.*

I would hold that the right to counsel secured by the Sixth and Fourteenth Amendments extends at least as far as the right to jury trial secured by those Amendments. Accordingly, I would hold that an indigent defendant in a state criminal case must be afforded appointed counsel whenever the defendant is prosecuted for a nonpetty criminal offense, that is, one punishable by more than six months' imprisonment, whenever the defendant is convicted of an offense and is actually subjected to a term of imprisonment. This resolution, I feel, would provide the bright line that defendants, prosecutors, and trial and appellate courts all deserve.... On this approach, of course, the judgment of the Supreme Court of Illinois upholding petitioner Scott's conviction should be reversed, since he was convicted of an offense for which he was constitutionally entitled to a jury trial. I, therefore, dissent.

Questions for Discussion

1. What is the holding of the Supreme Court in *Scott v. Illinois*?
2. Why did the Court hold that an appointed attorney was constitutionally required in *Argersinger* and not in *Scott?* Do you agree that the two situations are significantly different?
3. Summarize Justice Brennan's criticisms of the actual imprisonment standard.
4. What is Justice Blackmun's view?
5. Do you believe that the Supreme Court considered the economic costs of providing an appointed attorney for indigents in all criminal trials?

12.3 YOU DECIDE

In 1990, Nichols pled guilty to conspiracy to possess cocaine with intent to distribute. A prior state misdemeanor conviction for Driving Under the Influence (DUI), for which Nichols was fined $250 and was not incarcerated, was factored into his sentence under the U.S. Sentencing Commission Guidelines. This resulted in Nichols's sentence for drug possession being increased from Category I (168–210 months) to Category II (188–235 months). Nichols objected to the inclusion of his DUI misdemeanor conviction in his criminal history, because he was not represented by counsel at that proceeding. He maintained that consideration of his misdemeanor conviction in establishing his sentence for the drug crimes violated the Sixth Amendment. See *Nichols v. United States*, 511 U.S. 738 (1994).

Should Nichols have been provided with counsel at his first hearing? Is his lack of counsel at that hearing sufficient justification not to include his DUI conviction in consideration of his sentence for drug possession?

You can learn what the court decided by referring to the study site, http://www.sagepub.com/lippmancp.

Determining Indigency

The U.S. Supreme Court has not defined the standard for determining whether an individual is an **indigent** who is entitled to be represented by an appointed counsel in a criminal prosecution. Georgia defines an indigent as an individual "who is arrested or charged with a crime punishable by imprisonment who lacks sufficient income or other resources to employ a qualified lawyer to defend him or her without hardship on the individual or his or her dependents." States have different standards for indigency, and in many cases, the standard is set forth in a state legislative statute. The standard followed in Washington State, which is outlined below, is typical of the types of considerations that are employed for determining indigency (RCW 10.101.010 (1)).

- ***Public assistance.*** Receiving one of various types of public assistance, for example, Temporary Assistance for Needy Families, poverty-related veteran's benefits, food stamps, refugee resettlement benefits, Medicaid, or supplemental security income; or
- ***Income.*** Receiving an annual income, after taxes, of 125% or less of the current federally established poverty level; or
- ***Available funds.*** Inability to pay the anticipated cost of a lawyer for the case before the court as a result of insufficient available funds.

Individuals who do not meet these standards may apply to the court to be recognized as an indigent on the grounds that they have significant health costs, child support, or other extraordinary financial circumstances. The next section discusses whether an indigent defendant has the right to select a lawyer or whether he or she must accept the defense attorney assigned to the case.

The Right to Select an Appointed Counsel

A defendant has no right to be represented by a specific appointed counsel, although a court may take the defendant's preference into consideration. In *Morris v. Slappy,* the public defender assigned to represent Morris was hospitalized. The U.S. Supreme Court upheld the trial court's refusal to grant Morris a continuance and decision to assign a new lawyer to represent Morris. The Court reasoned that there is no right to a "meaningful attorney-client relationship" and explained that a court cannot guarantee that an attorney and his or her client share a close working relationship or that the defendant has trust and confidence in his or her assigned attorney (*Morris v. Slappy,* 461 U.S. 1, 13–14 [1983]).

A nonindigent defendant possesses the Sixth Amendment right to be represented by the lawyer of his or her choice. A defendant, however, does not have the right to be represented by an individual who is not a member of the bar, by a lawyer who has a conflict of interest, or by a lawyer whom he or she cannot afford to hire. The U.S. Supreme Court has held that a trial judge's wrongful rejection of a defendant's "first choice" of an attorney results in an automatic reversal of a defendant's conviction (*United States v. Gonzalez-Lopez,* 548 U.S. __ [2008]). In the next section, we will see that both indigent and nonindigent defendants have the right to effective legal representation.

The Right to Effective Legal Representation

The adversary process in a criminal trial involves a contest between zealous advocates: A prosecutor who represents the interests of the government and a defense attorney who represents the defendant. As noted by the U.S. Supreme Court, a defense attorney possesses the "overarching duty to advocate the defendant's cause" as well as the duty to "bring to bear such skill and knowledge as will render the trial a reliable adversarial testing process." The assumption is that this process will result in a clear and comprehensive presentation of the facts and allow the jury to make an informed determination of the defendant's guilt or innocence (*Strickland v. Washington,* 466 U.S. 668 [1984]).

The Supreme Court has recognized that the adversary process functions effectively when both the defense and prosecution are represented by competent and skilled lawyers. The Court accordingly held in *Strickland v. Washington* that the Sixth Amendment guarantees an indigent as well as a nonindigent defendant representation by an "effective counsel." The right to the effective assistance of a lawyer is crucial to a defendant receiving a fair trial; a lawyer who is "ineffective" deprives a defendant of the competent representation expected of a lawyer under the Sixth Amendment. The right to an "effective counsel" applies at the "guilt or innocence" phase of trial as well as at sentencing and at a defendant's first appeal of his or her conviction. The U.S. Supreme Court has held that there is a two-prong test for an **ineffective assistance of counsel**.

Deficient performance. The defendant is required to identify specific aspects of the lawyer's performance that fall below the range of reasonably effective competence expected of an attorney in a criminal case. In making this determination, judges look at the "totality of the circumstances" that confronted the lawyer at the time, and there is a presumption that the lawyer acted in an effective fashion. This means that an appellate court examines the entire situation that confronted an attorney and requires that the lawyer made a reasonable decision rather than the best or most intelligent decision.

Prejudice. Absent the lawyer's error, the question is whether there is a "reasonable probability that the result would have been different." A "reasonable probability" is a probability sufficient to undermine confidence in the outcome.

In *Strickland,* Washington pled guilty to three murders, torture, kidnapping, and theft. Washington's attorney concluded that it would be difficult to overcome his client's confession and to avoid the death penalty and decided that the best course was to argue that the defendant's sense of remorse and acceptance of responsibility justified sparing him from the death penalty. The judge in reviewing the record found several aggravating circumstances that outweighed these mitigating factors and imposed the death penalty. Washington contended that his attorney was ineffective in six different respects and, in particular, that he did not seek out character witnesses or request a psychiatric examination to demonstrate that the defendant was a nonviolent individual who was devoted to his family. The U.S. Supreme Court held that the lawyer's decision was "well within the range of professionally reasonable judgments," and given the

> overwhelming aggravating factors that there is no reasonable probability that the omitted evidence would have changed the conclusion that the aggravating circumstances outweighed the mitigating circumstances and, hence, the sentence imposed. (699–700)

Several of the Supreme Court's important ineffective counsel decisions are outlined below.

Lack of knowledge of the law. A lawyer is considered ineffective whose ignorance of the law affected the outcome of the trial. For example, the defense attorney in a rape prosecution was unaware that he was required to file a motion for pretrial discovery to determine the evidence that the prosecution planned to introduce at trial, and as a result, he failed to file a pretrial motion to suppress bedsheets, hairs, and fibers that had been seized by the government. The evidence was admitted at trial, and the defendant was convicted. The lawyer incorrectly believed that the government was obligated to inform him that the sheets had been seized; he claimed that he had been told that the victim was reluctant to testify and that the case would not go forward. The U.S. Supreme Court held that the lawyer displayed a "shocking ignorance of the law" that fell below professional norms (*Kimmelman v. Morrison,* 477 U.S. 365 [1986]). In *Glover v. United States,* the Supreme Court held that a defense attorney's failure to object to the judge's error in calculating the defendant's sentence that resulted in an increase in the length of the sentence of at least six months constituted ineffective assistance of counsel (*Glover v. United States,* 531 U.S. 198 [2001]).

Duty to investigate. The U.S. Supreme Court requires lawyers in death penalty cases to conduct an investigation into possible mitigating circumstances. The lawyer is not required to continue to carry on an investigation where it does not appear that his or her investigation will lead to useful information. In *Wiggins v. Smith,* Wiggins was convicted of first-degree murder. The public defenders argued at the capital punishment hearing that Wiggins was not a direct participant in the homicide and should not be sentenced to death. The Supreme Court noted that the defense lawyers had information that Wiggins's mother was an alcoholic who on at least one occasion had left her children without food and that he had spent time in foster care and had been severely abused. The Supreme Court found that the public defenders had failed to pursue this mitigating evidence and that a "reasonably competent attorney would have realized that pursuing the leads in these records was necessary in making an informed choice among possible defenses" (*Wiggins v. Smith,* 539 U.S. 510 [2003]). In 2005, in *Rompilla v. Beard,* the Supreme Court held that the public defenders' conduct fell below the level of reasonable performance when they failed to examine a file that included mitigating evidence regarding Rompilla's childhood and, instead, relied on interviews with Rompilla's family and health professionals that indicated that there were no mitigating factors that could be presented at the death penalty sentencing stage (*Rompilla v. Beard,* 545 U.S. 374 [2005]). In *Burger v. Kemp,* the Supreme Court held that an attorney acted reasonably in interviewing all the witnesses brought to his attention before deciding to terminate the investigation. The Court noted that the lawyer had discovered "little that was helpful and much that was harmful," and his decision "not to mount an all-out investigation was supported by reasonable professional judgment" (*Burger v. Kemp,* 483 U.S. 776 [1987]).

Perjury. A lawyer is not required to break legal rules to assist his or her client. In *Nix v. Whiteside,* the lawyer told Whiteside that if Whiteside committed perjury, the lawyer was obligated to report this misconduct to the judge, highlight the defendant's perjury at trial, and withdraw from the case. Whiteside decided to testify truthfully and was convicted. The U.S. Supreme Court held that the lawyer had acted properly in accordance with codes of professional conduct (*Nix v. Whiteside,* 475 U.S. 157 [1986]).

Closing argument. In *Yarborough v. Gentry,* the U.S. Supreme Court held that a lawyer's closing argument is subject to review for ineffective assistance of counsel. The defense counsel in *Yarborough* offered a "relatively brief" nine-paragraph closing argument that failed to mention various aspects of a stabbing that indicated that it might have been accidental. The Supreme Court held that there are various approaches to a closing argument, that "which issues to sharpen and how best to clarify them are questions with many reasonable answers," and that when a lawyer "focuses on some issues to the exclusion of others, there is a strong presumption that he did so for tactical reasons rather than through sheer neglect" (*Yarborough v. Gentry,* 540 U.S. 1 [2003]).

Consultation with defendant. In *Florida v. Nixon,* the public defender Michael Corin unsuccessfully attempted to persuade the prosecutor to drop the capital punishment charge against Nixon in exchange for Nixon's guilty plea. Corin decided that based on the overwhelming evidence of Nixon's guilt, the best course was for Nixon to "concede guilt, thereby preserving...credibility in urging leniency during the penalty stage of the proceedings." Nixon was unresponsive and "never verbally approved or protested" Corin's proposed strategy. The jury recommended the death penalty despite the fact that Corin presented eight witnesses who testified that Nixon suffered from a personality disorder and brain damage. The U.S. Supreme Court held that Corin fulfilled his duty to consult with Nixon and to explain the costs and benefits of the proposed trial strategy. The fact that Nixon remained "unresponsive" did not make Corin's proposed course of action "unreasonable." Death penalty cases present unique challenges, because the defendant's life is at stake, and a lawyer may reasonably decide to focus on the penalty stage in an effort to spare his or her client's life. The question is whether the lawyer's strategy satisfied the requirements of the *Strickland* test (*Florida v. Nixon,* 543 U.S. 175 [2004]).

On the same day that the Supreme Court issued a judgment in *Strickland,* the Court handed down a decision in *United States v. Cronic.* The Supreme Court held that a defendant convicted of a check-kiting scheme was not denied effective assistance of counsel when the young real estate lawyer who was assigned to represent him was given only twenty-five days to prepare for a trial and to review thousands of documents. The importance of *Cronic* is that the Court indicated that there are cases in which a lawyer's conduct so dramatically falls below the expected standard that prejudice will be automatically presumed and the defendant's conviction reversed. This arises where the defense lawyer "entirely fails to subject the prosecution's case to meaningful adversarial testing" and makes no meaningful effort to represent the defendant at trial. The Court also observed that there are some instances, such as *Powell v. Alabama,* in which the "likelihood that any lawyer...could provide effective assistance is so small" that there is a "presumption of prejudice" and that the court is not required to examine the "actual conduct of the trial" (*United States v. Cronic,* 466 U.S. 648 [1984]).

An example of a presumption of prejudice is *Holloway v. Arkansas.* In *Holloway,* the Supreme Court relied on this "automatic reversal" rule to overturn the conviction of three individuals who were represented by the same appointed attorney. The defendants' lawyer claimed that he had a conflict of interest and unsuccessfully requested the trial court to appoint additional lawyers. The defense attorney pointed out that by claiming that one of the defendants was innocent, he would be placing the burden of guilt on one of the other two defendants whom he was representing. The Supreme Court held that the trial court was required either to appoint separate counsel or to satisfy itself that the conflict would not interfere with the defense (*Holloway v. Arkansas,* 435 U.S. 475 [1978]). A court may refuse to permit a defendant to waive a conflict of interest that it views as preventing a defendant from receiving adequate representation and may require the defendant to be represented by a different attorney at trial (*Wheat v. United States,* 486 U.S. 153 [1988]).

Critics claim that the test for ineffectiveness of counsel is too demanding and that defendants have little chance to succeed in challenging their conviction. The Center for Capital Litigators in Columbia, South Carolina, has compiled data that indicate that courts have held that lawyers acted in a constitutionally competent fashion in approximately ninety-seven percent of the cases in which their conduct was challenged. In the next case in the text, *People v. York,* ask yourself whether the defense counsel's failure to introduce DNA evidence in his client's rape prosecution constituted "ineffective assistance of counsel." Do you agree with the decision of the Illinois court?

Was the failure to introduce evidence of the DNA test ineffective representation?

People v. York, 727 N.E.2d 674 (Ill. Dist. 2000), Galasso, J.

Facts

At trial, Karen Johnson-Stewart, the victim's mother, testified that on December 13, 1996, the victim visited a friend's house. When the victim returned home, she immediately went to her bedroom. The next day, an ambulance transported the victim to the hospital, because she was complaining of abdominal pain. The victim underwent surgery and was hospitalized for four to seven days. Colleen Cruse, a registered nurse who treated the victim, testified that she prepared a "sexual assault kit" after the victim revealed that she had been assaulted.

The victim testified that at 4:30 P.M. on December 13, 1996, she left her home to visit a friend. As the victim walked toward her friend's home, defendant drove by with two other men. Someone in the car offered the victim a ride. The victim knew defendant, because he was a family friend, but she did not know the men riding with defendant. The victim later learned that defendant was traveling with Thomas Best and Brandon Gaston, the codefendants. The group drove to see the victim's friend and the victim's cousin, but neither was home. The group eventually went to Best's home, where they listened to music in a bedroom. A man in a wheelchair was also in the room. The victim testified that defendant, Best, and Gaston waited for the man to leave, and then "they shut the door, turned off the lights and locked the door." Best removed the victim's pants and underwear. Best, Gaston, and defendant took turns engaging in sexual intercourse with the victim. Two men restrained the victim while the third assaulted her. The victim did not want to have sex with any of them, and she told each to stop. She recalled that defendant was on top of her for a shorter time than the others. The men promised the victim that they would buy her a pair of shoes if she did not tell anyone about the incident. When the victim returned home, she did not report the incident, because she was scared. The victim eventually underwent surgery at the hospital because she "had got something torn up inside" her. The victim later identified her attackers in a photographic lineup.

The victim denied that anyone in the bedroom was smoking cannabis or drinking alcohol. She acknowledged that a girl was in a bedroom across the hall during the attack. Although she thought the girl might help her, the victim did not call out or scream.

Defendant testified that he knew the victim before the attack and that he was with Gaston and Best on December 13, 1996. The three saw the victim walking, and either Gaston or Best offered her a ride. The victim accepted, and the group eventually arrived at the house where defendant, Best, and Gaston were residing. Defendant left to visit his girlfriend and returned to find the group in an upstairs bedroom. After everyone smoked cannabis, defendant helped the man in the wheelchair get into his car. When defendant returned, he saw the victim lying on her back on the bed, and it appeared that her clothing had been "fumbled with." She did not appear to be upset.

Defendant left to answer the front door to complete a drug transaction. When he returned to the bedroom, defendant saw Best and Gaston assaulting the victim. He asked them "what the hell" they were doing. Defendant stated that he would have intervened if the victim had requested assistance. He asked Best and Gaston to leave and told them, "You all going to catch some cases." Defendant went downstairs and played a video game. Gaston, Best, and the victim walked downstairs approximately ten to twenty minutes later. Defendant denied committing the acts that the victim described.

Defense counsel then attempted to introduce the results of DNA testing by asking defendant whether he received a report of the results while he was awaiting trial. The trial court sustained the prosecutor's objection that defendant's testimony was inadmissible hearsay. The record reveals that DNA samples were recovered from the victim at the time she was hospitalized. Testing revealed that Best and Gaston deposited semen on the victim and that defendant did not. Although the jury learned that defendant submitted to DNA testing, defense counsel failed to introduce the test results.

During closing argument, the prosecutor stated, "it would have been nice to have DNA evidence if we would have had some semen present or something like that, but gee." Defense counsel did not argue that the State failed to introduce forensic evidence linking defendant to the crime. A jury found defendant guilty, and the trial court sentenced him to sixteen years' imprisonment.

On appeal, the State abandons the accountability theory that it introduced at trial. The State does not assert that the jury found that defendant aided and abetted Gaston and Best. Instead, the State merely asserts that the evidence was sufficient to prove that defendant actually assaulted the victim.

Issue

Defendant argues that his trial counsel rendered ineffective assistance by failing to introduce the exculpatory DNA test results. The State responds that counsel was effective, because DNA evidence is not required to convict a defendant of aggravated criminal sexual assault, and the jury heard sufficient evidence to find defendant guilty.

Reasoning

Under *Strickland v. Washington,* defense counsel is ineffective only if (1) counsel's representation fell below an objective standard of reasonableness and the shortcomings of counsel were so severe as to deprive defendant of a fair trial, and (2) there is a reasonable probability that but for counsel's unprofessional errors, the result of the proceedings would have been different. Decisions about which witnesses to call and which evidence to present ultimately rest with defense counsel. Courts have long viewed these decisions as matters of trial strategy that are generally immune from ineffective assistance claims. However, a defendant will succeed on a valid claim of ineffective assistance when counsel's strategy is so unsound that he or she fails to conduct any meaningful adversarial testing.

Furthermore, defense counsel's failure to present available evidence to support a defense constitutes ineffective assistance of counsel. In *People v. Gunnart* (578 N.E.2d 1081 [1996]), defense counsel was ineffective for failing to investigate and present information that could have been used to corroborate the defendant's trial testimony. Counsel did not subpoena emergency 911 recordings or defendant's criminal record. Counsel also failed to interview witnesses before they testified at trial.

In this case, defendant's story was that he did not participate in the assault and that he attempted to intervene. Defendant testified that during the assault, he asked Best and Gaston to leave the house. When they ignored his request, defendant went to a different part of the house and played a video game. The DNA testing revealed that defendant did not deposit semen on the victim. However, defense counsel failed to present the available test results to corroborate defendant's trial testimony. The DNA evidence would have supported defendant's story, and the State concedes that the evidence was available and conclusive. Defense counsel recognized that the test results were important exculpatory evidence. Her failure to introduce the evidence properly was the result of incompetence, not trial strategy.

At a minimum, defense counsel could have offered to stipulate that defendant did not deposit semen on the victim. When counsel attempted to improperly use defendant's testimony to introduce the test results, the prosecutor acknowledged that the test results were exculpatory. In fact, the prosecutor suggested that he would have stipulated to the results if defense counsel had made such a request before trial.

Defendant correctly argues that this case resembles *People v. Popoca* (615 N.E.2d 778 [1993]), where the defendant was found guilty of several offenses, including the attempted murder of his wife and daughter. At trial, defense counsel argued that the defendant's voluntary intoxication prevented him from forming the mental state required to commit the offenses. However, counsel did not introduce expert testimony to support the theory. This court affirmed the defendant's convictions and sentences on direct appeal, and defendant filed a postconviction petition alleging ineffective assistance of trial counsel. At the postconviction hearing, defendant presented expert testimony that he claimed his counsel should have presented at trial. The expert testified that defendant had a family history of substance abuse and that his blood alcohol concentration was 0.20 at the time of the incident. The expert classified the defendant as a "severe alcohol dependent," because the defendant suffered from blackouts, used alcohol excessively, abused several substances, and drank in the morning. The defendant also suffered from a "neurophysical depressive disorder." The expert concluded that the combination of low intelligence and alcohol abuse drastically limited the defendant's ability to make appropriate decisions on the date of the incident. We concluded that trial counsel rendered ineffective assistance by failing to present an expert to explain the effects that alcohol had on the defendant. We reversed the trial court's dismissal of the postconviction petition and remanded the cause. As in *Popoca,* this defendant would have greatly benefited from expert testimony that supported the defense theory. The conclusive forensic evidence would have substantially improved defendant's claim of innocence.

In *People v. West* (719 N.E.2d 664 [1994]), the murder defendant appealed the denial of his postconviction petition, alleging that his trial counsel was ineffective for failing to retain a forensic expert. The defendant's theory at trial was that the victim's mother murdered the victim. To advance his theory, the defendant claimed that it was essential to show that the victim's external injuries predated the time when the victim began living with the defendant. Rather than retaining his own forensic expert, defense counsel cross-examined the State's expert to prove the defendant's theory.

Our supreme court concluded that defense counsel was not ineffective in *West.* On cross-examination, the State's expert testified that the victim suffered some of her external injuries while she was living with her mother. The supreme court concluded that a second forensic expert would have merely offered cumulative evidence. Therefore, the defendant failed to show how the testimony of a second expert would have affected the outcome of the trial.

The current case is distinguishable from *West.* The prosecutor declined to introduce the results of the DNA testing, because he knew it supported the defense story. Although defense counsel could not introduce the test results without calling her own expert, she chose to question defendant about the results. The trial court predictably sustained the State's objection to defendant's testimony. If defense counsel had introduced the DNA evidence, the outcome of the trial likely would have been different. The evidence would not have been cumulative.

In *People v. Todd,* the defendant claimed his trial counsel was ineffective for failing to call an independent forensic expert. The defendant noted that the State's experts could not link the defendant to any of the hairs discovered at the crime scene, and the defendant believed that an additional expert would have undermined the State's theory that he removed the victim's clothing and strangled her without depositing any of his own hair. . . . The supreme court concluded that defense counsel was not ineffective for failing to present an additional expert on the subject. The court noted that the defendant's argument was speculative, because he could not show whether any expert could state the claim in scientific terms (*People v. Todd,* 687 N.E.2d 998 [1997]). In contrast, expert testimony concerning the DNA evidence would not be speculative in the current case. There is no question that the tests revealed that defendant did not deposit semen on the victim. Defendant could use the results to support his theory that he did not have intercourse with the victim.

In *People v. Mehlberg* (618 N.E.2d 1168 [1993]), DNA evidence was the key to the State's evidence against the defendant in an aggravated criminal sexual assault prosecution. The Appellate Court, Fifth District, held that defense counsel's failure to call a DNA expert did not constitute ineffective assistance, because counsel cross-examined the State's experts and challenged the evidence in his closing argument. Such tactics were considered "within the wide range of reasonable professional conduct." The court held that although the testimony of a defense expert may be more effective than a defense counsel's cross-examination and closing argument challenging DNA test results, counsel's failure to produce such an expert does not render his or her assistance ineffective. In the current case, defense counsel could not cross-examine the prosecution's experts, because the State did not call any experts. To introduce the exculpatory DNA evidence, defense counsel had to call her own expert witness or offer to stipulate to the test results.

Finally, the State argues that counsel's failure to introduce the evidence was harmless. During closing argument, the prosecutor stated, "It would have been nice to have DNA evidence." The State contends that, by this statement, the prosecutor informed the jury that forensic testing revealed that defendant's DNA was not found on the victim. We disagree. The jury could have inferred that the tests were inconclusive.

Holding

We note that medical evidence is not necessary to prove a defendant guilty of aggravated criminal sexual assault. At a new trial on remand, the State need not prove that defendant deposited semen on the victim. Nevertheless, to ensure that defendant receives a fair trial, defense counsel should introduce the exculpatory DNA evidence for the trier of fact to consider. For these reasons, the judgment of the circuit court of Stephenson County is reversed, and the cause is remanded for a new trial.

Questions for Discussion

1. Discuss the Illinois District Court's application of the two-prong *Strickland* test for ineffectiveness of counsel to the facts in *People v. York*.
2. How does the lawyer's performance in *York* compare with the lawyer's performance in the five cases relied on as precedent by the District Court?
3. As judge, would you have reversed the verdict of the trial court? Why did the lawyer fail to make an effort to raise the lack of DNA evidence at trial?

12.4 YOU DECIDE

William Mitchell, a "borderline mentally retarded" defendant, was sentenced to eighty years in prison for aggravated robbery with a deadly weapon. He previously had been incarcerated in a maximum security state hospital for nineteen years. Mitchell appeared before the jury during *voir dire* (selection of jurors) in the same T-shirt that the jury would later learn had been worn by the suspect two years earlier in carrying out the offense. Mitchell was arrested the day following the robbery wearing a T-shirt "identical to the one worn by the robbery suspect captured on the store's video camera." The investigating detective described the shirt as "blue colored" with writing that said "Cameron Elementary Scotties" and a photo of a Scottish terrier. He was photographed in the shirt, and the store clerk later identified him as the perpetrator. The photo was shown to the jury prior to viewing the videotape. Mitchell was brought from the jail to the courthouse in the blue T-shirt. His lawyer did not raise the issue of the shirt until prior to the closing arguments. The victim identified Mitchell from a photo spread the day after the robbery and identified him again at trial, and the jury viewed a video of the robbery.

Was the defendant deprived of effective representation of counsel? See *Mitchell v. State*, 23 S.W.3d 582 (Tex. App. 2000).

12.5 YOU DECIDE

Defense counsel represented an African American defendant charged with the murder of a Caucasian female. During *voir dire,* the defense attorney told the prospective jurors that he was a southern white male, that he did not like African Americans, and that he was ashamed of his prejudice. At the penalty phase, he urged the white jurors not to let race become a factor in their decision and to resist any prejudicial feelings that they had. The lawyer failed to call various witnesses and to cross-examine a key prosecution witness.

Were the defense lawyer's remarks a reasonable strategic approach to the trial? See *State v. Davis,* 872 So. 2d 250 (Fla. 2004).

You can learn what the court decided by referring to the study site, http://www.sagepub.com/lippmancp.

The Right to Self-Representation

What if a defendant insists on representing himself or herself at trial? This is termed acting ***pro se*** (on his or her own). Recognition of a right to self-representation would seem at odds with the U.S. Supreme Court's conclusion in *Gideon* that individuals who represent themselves are unable to present an effective defense to a criminal charge.

In 1975, in *Faretta v. California,* the Supreme Court held that the trial court had unlawfully refused to permit Anthony Faretta to represent himself in a prosecution for grand theft. Justice Stewart reviewed the history of self-representation in England and in the American colonies and states, and he concluded that the Sixth Amendment provides a "constitutionally protected right" to the accused to represent himself or herself. A refusal to permit a defendant to represent himself or herself will result in a reversal on appeal of the verdict in the trial court (*Faretta v. California,* 422 U.S. 806, 816–832 [1975]). This decision was based on several policy considerations:

- ***Personal choice.*** The right to make an individual choice as to how to conduct a defense is a fundamental constitutional principle.
- ***Consequences.*** The defendant "suffers the consequences if the defense fails."
- ***Respect for the law.*** Compelling a defendant to accept a lawyer will lead the accused to question the fairness of the justice system and may result in the reluctance of the accused to cooperate with his or her attorney.
- ***Strategy.*** There may be instances in which self-representation benefits the accused by eliciting sympathy from the jury.

Justice Blackmun, in dissent, objected that the decision in *Faretta* formally recognized the constitutional right of an individual to "make a fool of himself" (852).

A judge is not obligated to warn defendants of the risks of representing themselves. The Supreme Court requires judges only to inform defendants of the charges against them, of their right to a lawyer, and of the possible punishment. To relinquish their right to appointed counsel, defendants must unequivocally waive their right to counsel and invoke the right to self-representation (*Iowa v. Tovar,* 541 U.S. 77 [2004]). The decision in *Faretta* suggests that there are three limitations on self-representation.

- ***Notice.*** A defendant must inform the court in advance and not interfere with the schedule of the trial by making the request for self-representation at the last minute.
- ***Competence.*** Defendants must be competent to stand trial and to represent themselves and must knowingly and intelligently waive their right to an attorney. They are not required to be aware of the law or the rules of evidence (see *Indiana v. Edwards* discussed below).
- ***Disruptive.*** Defendants who interfere with the conduct of the trial forfeit the right to self-representation.

In *McKaskle v. Wiggins,* the U.S. Supreme Court upheld the practice of appointing a "standby counsel" to assist a defendant with his or her defense. The "standby lawyer" may not interfere with the defendant's decisions at trial or "overshadow the defendant" by actively participating in the trial. There is no constitutional right to a "hybrid representation" in which the defendant and the lawyer divide responsibilities at trial (*McKaskle v. Wiggins,* 465 U.S. 168 [1984]). There also is no right to self-representation on an appeal (*Martinez v. Court of Appeal of California* (528 U.S. 152 [2000]).

Several Supreme Court justices in *Martinez v. Court of Appeal of California* expressed doubts about the wisdom of the decision in *Faretta* and suggested that recognition of the right of self-representation interferes with the smooth functioning of trials. The justices also expressed concern that defendants lacked the knowledge and expertise required to present an effective defense.

In 2008, in *Indiana v. Edwards,* the U.S. Supreme Court responded to this criticism of *Faretta,* holding that the right of self-representation "is not absolute." Defendant Ahmad Edwards was charged with attempted murder, battery, and other crimes stemming from an attempt to steal a pair of shoes from a department store. Edwards suffered from schizophrenia, but because he had had a number of years of treatment, he was found competent to stand trial. (Competency requires that defendants have the capacity to understand the nature of the charges against them and that they have sufficient ability to consult with their lawyers.) The trial court ruled that even though Edwards had been found competent to stand trial, he lacked the mental capacity to represent himself, and the trial court appointed a lawyer to represent him. Edwards subsequently was convicted of murder and battery; he appealed based on the trial court's refusal to permit him to represent himself at trial.

The U.S. Supreme Court affirmed the denial of Edwards's request for self-representation, holding that the

> Constitution permits states to insist upon representation by counsel for those competent enough to stand trial . . . but who still suffer from severe mental illness to the point where they are not competent to conduct trial proceedings by themselves.

The Supreme Court explained that by upholding the right of a trial court judge to deny a mentally challenged defendant the right of self-representation, it hoped to lessen the concerns of critics who claimed that *Faretta* resulted in unfairness to defendants who represented themselves (*Indiana v. Edwards,* 554 U.S. __ [2008]).

Chapter Summary

The prosecutor has been called one of the most powerful persons in the criminal justice system. He or she possesses broad discretion to charge an individual with a crime as well as broad discretion to determine what crime is charged. Courts take the position that prosecutors' exercise of authority is ill-suited for judicial review and adhere to a presumption of regularity. The presumption is that prosecutors honestly, fairly, and responsibly exercise their authority. Two constitutional limitations on prosecutorial discretion are discussed in the chapter:

Selective prosecution. The Equal Protection Clause of the Fifth and Fourteenth Amendments prohibits prosecution of individuals because of their race, gender, or exercise of fundamental rights.

Vindictive prosecution. In a vindictive prosecution, a prosecutor retaliates against a defendant who asserts his or her constitutional or statutory rights by bringing a more serious charge against the defendant.

When an individual is arrested without an arrest warrant or formal indictment by a grand jury, the first step for the prosecutor is a determination that there is probable cause to detain the suspect. In *Gerstein v. Pugh,* the U.S. Supreme Court held that the Constitution requires a judicial determination of probable cause as a condition for an "extended restraint of liberty." This "nonadversarial" probable cause hearing must be held "promptly" following an arrest. In *County of Riverside v. McLaughlin,* the U.S. Supreme Court defined "promptly" and held that a forty-eight-hour period of delay is a presumptively reasonable period of time within which to hold the hearing.

The next step is the first appearance. The first appearance has four major purposes.

- ***Criminal charges.*** The defendant is informed of the precise charges against him or her.
- ***Constitutional rights.*** The defendant is informed of his or her rights.
- ***Pretrial release.*** A determination is made as to whether the defendant is to be released from custody prior to trial. The judge will fix the amount of bail or the conditions of the defendant's pretrial release.
- ***Attorney.*** A lawyer is appointed for indigent defendants.

The U.S. Constitution provides for bail in the Eighth Amendment, which states that "excessive bail shall not be required." The bail provision has not been incorporated into the Due Process Clause of the Fourteenth

Amendment. Most state constitutions, however, create a right to bail in all but capital cases. Despite the fundamental nature of individual access to bail, the Bail Clause has

> never been thought to accord a right to bail in all cases, but merely to provide that bail should not be excessive in those cases where it is proper to grant bail. . . . Thus, in criminal cases, bail is not compulsory where the punishment may be death.

A bail amount is constitutionally excessive that is more than the amount required for a defendant to appear for trial. In 1987, in *United States v. Salerno,* the U.S. Supreme Court affirmed the constitutionality of the preventive detention of individuals whose appearance at trial cannot be guaranteed and who pose a threat to other individuals or to the community.

An individual who is not released prior to trial typically is detained in a short-term correctional facility. In *Bell v. Wolfish,* the Supreme Court held that while detainees retain their constitutional rights in such facilities, they are subject to reasonable regulations adopted to insure order and security in the institution. The Court cautioned that detainees have not been convicted of a crime and may not be subjected to "arbitrary or purposeless" conditions that constitute punishment.

An indigent defendant is entitled to legal representation. In 1963, in *Gideon v. Wainwright,* the U.S. Supreme held that the Fourteenth Amendment incorporates the Sixth Amendment right to counsel and held that indigent individuals charged with felonies in state courts are entitled to an appointed counsel. The Court has held that an individual has the right to representation by a lawyer when formal adversarial criminal proceedings are initiated against him or her. Following the initiation of formal criminal proceedings, the right to counsel attaches at a "critical stage" of the prosecution. A critical stage is considered any phase of the prosecution that may negatively impact the defendant's ability to present a defense at trial and at which the presence of an attorney would safeguard the defendant.

Are defendants entitled to a lawyer in all criminal trials? In *Argersinger v. Hamlin,* the U.S. Supreme Court held that "absent a knowing and intelligent waiver, no person may be imprisoned for any offense, whether classified as petty, misdemeanor, or felony, unless he was represented by counsel." In *Illinois v. Scott,* the Supreme Court held that there is no right to counsel when a monetary fine is imposed.

The Supreme Court has not defined the standards for determining whether a defendant is an indigent who is entitled to the appointment of a lawyer in a criminal prosecution. States have varying standards for indigency, and in many states, the standard is defined in a state legislative statute.

A defendant has no right to be represented by a specific appointed counsel, although a court may take the defendant's preference into consideration. A nonindigent defendant possesses the Sixth Amendment right to be represented by the lawyer of his or her choice. A defendant does not have the right to be represented by an individual who is not a member of the bar, who has a conflict of interest, or whom he or she cannot afford.

The Court held in *Strickland v. Washington* that the Sixth Amendment guarantees an indigent as well as a nonindigent defendant representation by "effective counsel." The U.S. Supreme Court has held that there is a two-prong test for ineffective assistance of counsel.

Deficient performance. The defendant is required to identify specific aspects of the lawyer's performance that fall below the range of reasonably effective competence demanded by an attorney in a criminal case.

Prejudice. If counsel had not made errors in the defense, is there a "reasonable probability that the result would have been different"? A "reasonable probability" is probability sufficient to undermine confidence in the outcome.

The Court has indicated that there are cases in which the lawyer's conduct so dramatically falls below the expected standard that prejudice will be automatically presumed.

In 1975, in *Faretta v. California,* Justice Stewart reviewed the history of self-representation in England and in the American colonies and states, and he concluded that the Sixth Amendment proves a "constitutionally protected right" of defendants to represent themselves. Individuals who lack the requisite mental capacity do not possess a right of self-representation.

Chapter Review Questions

1. Discuss the presumption of regularity regarding a prosecutor's filing of criminal charges. Why is the exercise of prosecutorial discretion in bringing criminal charges considered to be ill-suited for judicial review? What is the legal test for selective prosecutions and vindictive prosecutions?
2. What is the significance of *Gerstein v. Pugh* and of *County of Riverside v. McLaughlin*?
3. Outline the purpose of the first appearance.
4. Discuss the law and purpose of bail. When is the preventive detention of a defendant legally justified?
5. Outline the Supreme Court's decisions leading to the judgment in *Gideon v. Wainwright*. What is the holding in *Gideon*?
6. An individual has the right to legal representation in all criminal prosecutions. What is the dividing line between the cases in which an indigent has the right to the appointment of a lawyer and the cases in which an indigent does not have the right to the appointment of a lawyer? How does this distinction affect a judge's sentencing of a defendant?
7. Discuss the legal test for determining a significant stage of prosecution.
8. What factors are considered in determining indigency?
9. Does an individual have an absolute right to a lawyer of his or her choice?
10. Outline the legal test for effective representation of counsel.
11. What are the limitations on the right of self-representation?

Legal Terminology

bail
Bail Clause
complaint
critical stages of the prosecution
first appearance
indigent
ineffective assistance of counsel
money bail
presumption of regularity
preventive detention
pro se
probable cause hearing
release on recognizance
surety bond
vindictive prosecution

Criminal Procedure on the Web

Log on to the Web-based student study site at **http://www.sagepub.com/lippmancp** to assist you in completing the Criminal Procedure on the Web exercises, as well as for additional features such as leading cases, podcasts, self-quizzes, and audio/video links.

1. Read about Clarence Gideon and the history of the litigation in *Gideon v. Wainwright.*
2. Explore the strange case of John Mark Karr and the investigation into the murder of JonBenét Ramsey.
3. Watch a video and read about public defenders.
4. Read a report about the inadequate representation of indigent defendants.

Bibliography

David Cole, "*Gideon v. Wainwright* and *Strickland v. Washington,* Broken Promises." In *Criminal Procedure Stories,* Carol S. Steiker, ed. (New York: Foundation Press, 2006), pp. 101–128. A history of *Gideon v. Wainwright* and the contemporary impact of the decision.

Joshua Dressler and Alan C. Michaels, *Understanding Criminal Procedure: Investigation,* vol. 1, 4th ed. (Newark, NJ: LexisNexis, 2006), pp. 587–637. A comprehensive and concise discussion of the Sixth and Fourteenth Amendment right to counsel.

Wayne R. LaFave, Jerold H. Israel, and Nancy J. King, *Principles of Criminal Procedure: Post-Investigation* (St. Paul, MN: West Publishing, 2004), pp. 73–152. A detailed discussion of the right to counsel.

Stephen A. Saltzburg, Daniel J. Capra, and Angela J. Davis, *Basic Criminal Procedure,* 4th ed. (St. Paul, MN: West Publishing, 2003), pp. 565–594. An easily understood discussion of the leading cases on right to counsel.

13 The Courtroom

The Pretrial and Trial Process

Is a five-person jury constitutional?

The Fourteenth Amendment guarantees the right of trial by jury in all state nonpetty criminal cases. The Court in Duncan applied this Sixth Amendment right to the States because "trial by jury in criminal cases is fundamental to the American scheme of justice." . . . When the Court . . . permitted the reduction in jury size—or, to put it another way, when it held that a jury of six was not unconstitutional—it expressly reserved ruling on the issue whether a number smaller than six passed constitutional scrutiny. The Court refused to speculate when this so-called slippery slope would become too steep. We face now, however, the twofold question whether a further reduction in the size of the state criminal trial jury does make the grade too dangerous, that is, whether it inhibits the functioning of the jury as an institution to a significant degree, and, if so, whether any State interest counterbalances and justifies the disruption so as to preserve its constitutionality.

Core Concepts and Summary Statements

Introduction

The pretrial and trial phases of the criminal justice system strike a balance between the efficient prosecution of criminal offenders on one hand and democratic participation in the criminal justice system and the protection of defendants against unfair and arbitrary prosecutions on the other hand.

Preliminary Hearing

A. The preliminary hearing is a "mini-trial" in which a magistrate or judge determines whether there is sufficient evidence to bind over the defendant for trial or whether the defendant should be released.

B. A preliminary hearing is not constitutionally required. In indictment states, the prosecutor may bypass the preliminary hearing by taking the case immediately to the grand jury. In information states, the prosecutor may file an information and may bring a charge either before a preliminary hearing or before a grand jury.

Grand Jury

A. The grand jury is charged with responsibility for determining whether to indict an individual for a crime. The grand jury may agree that an individual has committed a crime and return a "true bill" or determine that evidence does not support the criminal charge and return a "no bill." The grand jury may decide to undertake an independent investigation and may issue a presentment or report.

B. The grand jury is technically independent of the prosecution. In practice, the grand jury possesses several powers that make it a particularly powerful arm of the prosecutor.

Arraignment

Once a decision is made to indict an individual or to bind him or her over for trial, the individual is brought before a judge, informed of the charges filed against him or her, and asked to enter a plea of guilty, not guilty, not guilty by reason of insanity, or nolo contendere.

Pretrial Motions

A defense attorney may file various pretrial motions: double jeopardy, speedy trial, change of venue, discovery, and suppression of evidence.

Constitutional Right to a Jury Trial

The Sixth Amendment provides that in all criminal prosecutions, the accused shall enjoy the right to a public trial. In 1969, in *Duncan v. Louisiana,* the U.S. Supreme Court held that the right to a jury trial is fundamental to the American scheme of justice and is protected under the Due Process Clause of the Fourteenth Amendment. A jury trial is required for a serious crime that carries a sentence of more than six months.

The Twelve-Member Jury Requirement

The twelve-member jury is not required by the Sixth Amendment. In 1970, in *Williams v. Florida,* the Court approved the constitutionality of a six-person jury.

Jury Selection

A. The selection of the jury pool from which the jury is drawn typically is based on names drawn from voter registration lists or lists of licensed drivers. Several states rely on the key-man system in which community leaders select individuals from a list.
B. Individuals are examined by the lawyers in a process termed *voir dire.* They may be struck from the jury based on challenges for cause when they are unable to make an impartial decision as to guilt or innocence or based on peremptory challenges in which the lawyers are not required to offer any reason whatsoever.
C. The Equal Protection Clause prohibits intentional discrimination against individuals in the selection of the jury. The Sixth Amendment requires that the jury represent a fair cross-section of the community.
D. The questions that may be asked on voir dire depend on the nature of the charge. In capital punishment cases, individuals may be asked whether they are willing to impose the death penalty.

Peremptory Challenges

Each attorney may reject a limited number of potential jurors without providing a reason. Peremptory challenges may not be used to challenge potential jurors solely on account of their race or gender.

Challenge to Judges

Judges are required to remove, or recuse, themselves from a case or may be removed based on their inability to function in a neutral and impartial fashion.

Public Trial

The Sixth Amendment provides that in "all criminal prosecutions, the accused shall enjoy the right to a . . . public trial." An unruly defendant may be removed from the courtroom, and there is no absolute right of the public or of the media to have access to the trial.

The Trial

The defendant now enters the formal trial stage of the criminal justice system.

Opening Statement

Prosecutors and defense lawyers may make brief opening statements.

Presentation of Evidence

A. The prosecution presents the case-in-chief. The defense attorney may then cross-examine the witnesses, and the prosecutor has the opportunity to rehabilitate the witness. The defense attorney next presents the rebuttal.
B. The defense counsel may make a motion for a judgment of acquittal. In the event that the motion is not granted, the defense may present various legal defenses. The defense may renew the motion for a judgment of acquittal. The prosecution then may present rebuttal evidence.

Confrontation

The Sixth Amendment provides that in all criminal prosecutions, the accused shall enjoy the right to be confronted with the witnesses against him. This applies to all phases of the pretrial and trial phases and sentencing.

Cross-Examination

A. The cross-examination of witnesses is central to the Confrontation Clause.
B. Hearsay is testimony that repeats a statement made by another person that is offered into evidence to "prove the truth of the matter asserted."
C. Hearsay violates the Confrontation Clause because the person who made the statement is not subject to cross-examination. The U.S. Supreme Court nevertheless has held that the Confrontation Clause permits the use of hearsay under certain limited circumstances.

Hearsay

Hearsay involves a witness testifying as to what someone else said outside the courtroom, which is introduced to prove a fact that is involved in the case. Hearsay evidence violates the Confrontation Clause because the person who made the original statement is not subject to immediate cross-examination, and there is no way to test the accuracy of the statement. The U.S. Supreme Court nevertheless has held that the Confrontation Clause permits the use of hearsay under certain limited circumstances.

Compulsory Process

The Sixth Amendment Compulsory Process Clause provides defendants with the right to obtain witnesses, documents, and other evidence required to challenge the prosecutor's case and to present the defendant's case.

Burden of Proof

The adversarial system places on the prosecution both the burden of going forward and the burden of persuasion to establish a defendant's guilt.

Reasonable Doubt

The jury is required to find the defendant guilty beyond a responsible doubt.

Closing Arguments

Following the presentation of evidence, the prosecutor and defense lawyers summarize their cases.

Jury Instructions

The judge issues instructions to the jury before they adjourn to discuss the defendant's guilt or innocence.

Jury Deliberations

During the jury deliberations, jurors ordinarily may have a copy of the charges and the judge's jury instructions.

Jury Unanimity

In 1972, in *Apocaca v. Oregon,* the U.S. Supreme Court held that the Sixth Amendment requirement of jury unanimity is not incorporated into the Fourteenth Amendment. In the companion case of *Johnson v. Louisiana,* the Court upheld a 9-to-3 verdict.

Jury Nullification

A jury may disregard the law and facts and acquit a defendant.

Guilty Pleas

A. The majority of criminal cases are not brought to trial and instead are disposed of by guilty pleas. Individuals agree to plead guilty in return for dropping the charges, for a lesser sentence, or for a sentencing recommendation.
B. The U.S. Supreme Court has upheld the constitutionality of plea bargaining. The trial judge is required to insure that the defendant entering a guilty plea understands the elements of the criminal charge, the facts required to establish the criminal charge, and that the plea is entered voluntarily.

Introduction

In this chapter, we examine the pretrial and trial phases of the criminal justice process. During this portion of the criminal justice process, there is an effort to strike a balance between the interest in convicting the guilty and the fact that defendants are presumed innocent until proven guilty. The procedures during this phase of the criminal justice process also reflect the interest in public participation in the criminal justice system.

The government is required to establish that there is probable cause to bring the case to trial. There are two procedures that are relied on to determine whether the government may proceed to trial.

1. ***Preliminary hearing.*** The prosecutor files an information or written formal charge that is reviewed by a judge at the preliminary hearing.
2. ***Grand jury.*** The prosecutor files a criminal complaint, and a grand jury composed of ordinary citizens decides whether to issue an indictment.

This is followed by the formal charging of a criminal offense at the arraignment and the defendant's entry of a formal plea.

Prior to trial, the defendant may file pretrial motions challenging violations of his or her constitutional rights. These motions include double jeopardy, speedy trial, and improper venue; the discovery of potentially exonerating evidence in the possession of the prosecution; and the filing of motions to suppress unlawfully obtained evidence. The next step is the selection of the jury. Due process procedures are designed to insure that the jury-selection process is free from discrimination and that the jury reflects a cross-section of the community. Keep in mind the important role played by the jury in protecting defendants against unfair prosecution and prosecutorial abuse.

The next phase of the process is the trial itself. As you read about opening statements, presenting evidence, closing arguments, and jury decision making, pay attention to how trial procedures are organized to strike a balance between the efficient criminal prosecution of offenders and the interest in insuring that defendants are treated in accordance with due process of law and that their guilt or innocence is determined by the evidence rather than on the basis of unfounded accusations. The last section of the chapter discusses guilty pleas, plea bargaining, and determining guilt without a formal trial. The vast majority of criminal cases are decided by a defendant's plea of guilty, and the question arises whether this is desirable.

We first turn to a discussion of the preliminary hearing and the grand jury.

Preliminary Hearing

Following the *first appearance,* both the U.S. Magistrate's Act, 18 U.S.C. § 3060, and Rule 5.1 of the Federal Rules of Criminal Procedure provide that a **preliminary hearing** should be held within ten days to determine whether the defendant should be *bound over* for trial or *bound over* to a grand jury. Most States require that a preliminary hearing is to be held within a reasonable period of time. The purpose of the preliminary hearing is to determine whether there is sufficient evidence to subject the defendant to criminal prosecution. This is different than the first appearance at which a magistrate determines whether there is probable cause to justify the defendant's "prolonged detention."

The preliminary hearing is conducted as a "mini-trial" in which the defendant has a right to representation by a lawyer. The prosecutor presents witnesses. These witnesses may be cross-examined by the defense attorney, who also has the right to present witnesses in an effort to highlight "fatal weaknesses" in the prosecution's case (*Coleman v. Alabama,* 309 U.S. 1 [1970]). The magistrate then determines whether there is sufficient evidence to bind over the defendant for trial or whether the defendant should be released. As observed by the Wisconsin Supreme Court, the purpose of the preliminary hearing is to prevent "hasty, malicious, improvident, and oppressive prosecutions" that subject individuals to the "humiliation and anxiety involved in public prosecution" and to "avoid the [unnecessary] expense of a public trial" (*Thies v. State,* 189 N.W. 539, 541 [Wis. 1922]).

Courts follow one of two standards in determining whether to bind over a defendant for trial. The basic question is whether a crime was committed and whether the defendant committed the crime. Most states adhere to the probable cause standard, while a minority of states adhere to the prima facie approach.

Probable cause. The judge determines whether there is a "fair probability" based on the evidence presented during the preliminary hearing that the Government will succeed in convicting the defendant at trial. The issue is whether there is probable cause to believe that a defendant may be convicted.

Prima facie. The judge determines whether the prosecution's evidence, if believed by the jury, is sufficient to convict the defendant at trial.

The U.S. Supreme Court has held that a preliminary hearing is not required by the U.S. Constitution. States are categorized as either indictment states, **information** states, or **modified indictment states** based on the role of the preliminary hearing.

Indictment states. The eighteen indictment states, the District of Columbia, and the federal government provide that following the preliminary hearing, a felony charge is to be brought before a grand jury. A prosecutor may "bypass" the preliminary hearing by immediately taking a charge before a grand jury.

Information states. Prosecutors in twenty-eight states may bring a felony charge based on a "sworn statement" (information) and then may bring a charge either before a preliminary hearing or before a grand jury.

Modified indictment states. Four states require indictments for felonies punishable by capital punishment and life imprisonment.

A preliminary hearing is not required where the defendant waives the preliminary hearing, where the defendant is charged with a misdemeanor, or where the grand jury has issued an indictment before the preliminary hearing is conducted.

The preliminary hearing was developed because prosecutors would delay bringing defendants before a grand jury and because the judiciary wanted to insure that defendants were not being detained without sufficient evidence to bring them to trial. The preliminary hearing also is less time-consuming and is viewed as fairer to defendants than is the grand jury. We now turn our attention to the grand jury.

Grand Jury

The grand jury is thought to have originated in 1166 in the Assize of Clarendon. The assize was composed of twelve "good and lawful" men who were appointed in each community and who were responsible for apprehending and presenting individuals responsible for the commission of crimes to royal courts. As the grand jury evolved, it was authorized to take the initiative in investigating criminal activity and to issue criminal charges against individuals at the request of the Crown. In 1681, the English grand jury established a reputation as the protector of individual rights when two London grand juries refused to indict two political enemies of King Charles II: the Earl of Shaftesbury and Stephen College.

The institution of what became known as the grand jury was brought to the American Colonies where it served as both a sword to investigate crime and a shield to resist what was viewed as the unjust indictment of individuals critical of British colonial authorities. In 1734, three colonial grand juries refused to indict newspaper publisher Peter Zenger for "seditious libel" for criticizing the colonial government. This was followed by a series of cases in which American grand juries refused to bring charges against political dissidents accused of calling for an end to colonial rule. In the language of the U.S. Supreme Court, the grand jury came to be regarded as an institution that provides "primary security to the innocent against hasty, malicious and oppressive persecution; it serves the invaluable function...of standing between the accuser and the accused...to determine whether a charge is founded upon reason or was dictated by an intimidating power or by malice and personal ill will" (*Wood v. Georgia,* 370 U.S. 375 [1962]).

The importance of the grand jury in the political philosophy of the drafters of the U.S. Constitution is indicated by the fact that the Fifth Amendment provides that "no person shall be held to answer for a capital, or otherwise infamous crime, unless on a presentment or indictment of a Grand Jury." Rule 7 of the Federal Rules of Criminal Procedure requires indictment by a grand jury for federal offenses punishable by death or for crimes punishable by more than one year in prison.

At the time of the adoption of the Fifth Amendment, every state required indictment for felonies before a grand jury. As we have seen, twenty-two states at present require a grand jury indictment for at least some criminal offenses. The movement away from the grand jury was initiated by Michigan in 1859. The thinking was that the election of prosecutors would insure a popular check on the power of prosecutors and that indictment by grand juries no longer was required to restrain governmental power and abuse. Several states, including California, followed the lead of Michigan and authorized prosecutors to file an information and then to exercise the option of submitting the case either to a preliminary hearing or to a grand jury.

In 1984, in *Hurtado v. California,* the U.S. Supreme Court addressed whether states are required to provide a grand jury indictment. In *Hurtado,* the U.S. Supreme Court upheld a murder conviction that had been brought as a result of an information filed by the prosecutor that had been found to be based on probable cause at a preliminary hearing and that had not been brought before a grand jury. The Court stressed that it was concerned with insuring "fundamental fairness" and that this "principle of liberty and justice" was adequately protected by subjecting a defendant to either a preliminary hearing or a grand jury (*Hurtado v. California,* 110 U.S. 516, 537–538 [1884]).

Selecting a Grand Jury

The grand jury was abolished in England in 1933 and is not used in any country other than the United States. The grand jury at common law was composed of twenty-three persons, twelve of whom were required to support issuing an indictment. Rule 6 of the Federal Rules of Criminal Procedure provides that a grand jury should be constituted by between sixteen and twenty-three persons. States differ in the required size of the grand jury, although all require a majority vote. Qualifications also vary for service on a grand jury. In general, a member of the grand jury must be a resident of the relevant jurisdiction, must be at least eighteen years of age, and must not have been convicted of a felony. Individuals are required to have the capacity to speak, write, read, and understand English and are to exhibit honesty, intelligence, and good character.

The process of selecting the grand jury from the pool of individuals called to serve is termed **purging the grand jury.** In most states, the pool is randomly selected from the list employed to select the **petit jury** (the jury at trial). The list must represent a "fair cross-section of the community" and may be based on licensed drivers, taxpayers, voter lists, or other sources. The selection of the members of the grand jury is carried out by the prosecutor in the presence of a judge. A few states continue to use the **key-man** system in which the grand jury is selected by a group of influential members of the community.

Individuals may not be intentionally excluded from a grand jury because of race, gender, or national origin. A defense attorney prior to trial may challenge the composition of a grand jury, and a successful challenge results in the dismissal of the indictment. In those instances in which a trial court judge improperly denies the motion to dismiss an indictment, a guilty verdict at trial will be automatically reversed where an appeals court determines that individuals were intentionally excluded from the grand jury. In *Vazquez v. Hillery,* the Supreme Court reversed a guilty verdict that the Court found was tainted by the discriminatory selection of members of the grand jury (*Vazquez v. Hillery,* 474 U.S. 254 [1986]).

Why this *automatic reversal rule?* The U.S. Supreme Court has reasoned that discrimination in the selection of the grand jury "destroys the appearance of justice and thereby casts doubt on the integrity of the judicial process" and "impairs the confidence of the public in the administration of justice" (*Rose v. Mitchell,* 443 U.S. 545, 556 [1979]). Automatic reversal deters prosecutors from discriminating in the selection of grand jurors. Another reason for automatic reversal is that it cannot be assumed that a grand jury that is untainted by discrimination would have brought the same charges against the defendant.

Keep in mind that a grand jury does not merely determine whether there is probable cause to proceed to trial. The grand jury has the discretion to charge a defendant with a "greater offense or a lesser offense," may charge a defendant with one or multiple criminal offenses, may charge a capital offense or a noncapital offense, and is not required to "indict in every case where a conviction can be obtained" (*United States v. Ciambrone,* 601 F.2d 616, 629 [2d Cir. 1979]) (Friendly, J., dissenting).

Duration

The term of a federal grand jury is eighteen months with the possibility of a six-month extension. The time required for a grand jury to complete its task depends on the function of a particular jury. For example, a prosecutor may call a grand jury to indict for a common crime such as a bank robbery and quickly obtain an indictment by presenting videotapes of the robbery, asking bank employees to identify the suspect, and showing the jurors marked bills that were found in the defendant's automobile. In other instances, the grand jury may be asked to investigate a complicated white-collar crime and may be requested to hear the testimony of numerous witnesses and to examine a large number of documents.

Grand Jury Indictment

Following the selection and empanelment of the grand jury, the judge explains the role of the jury to the jurors. The judge then releases the jury to carry out their responsibilities and does not participate in the deliberations. The grand jury, in theory, is an independent body that may pursue its own investigation. The reality of the grand jury is that the prosecutor exercises almost complete control over the deliberations. The prosecutor typically submits an **indictment** or a written accusation that an individual or individuals have committed a crime. Rule 7 of the Federal Rules of Criminal Procedure provides that an indictment "must be a plain, concise, and definite written statement of the essential facts constituting the offense charged and must be signed by an attorney for the government" along with the foreperson of the grand jury. The prosecutor then presents the witnesses and other evidence that the jury should consider in determining whether the individual who is the subject of the indictment should be brought to trial. The grand jury does not depend entirely on the prosecutor and retains the authority to call witnesses and to ask their own questions of witnesses. This is a nonadversarial procedure in which defense lawyers and defendants are not present. During the jury's discussion and vote whether to indict, the prosecutor is not present. The grand jury, at the conclusion of the investigation, may take several courses of action.

True bill. The grand jury agrees that an individual has committed a criminal offense and returns a **true bill** that indicates the vote of the grand jurors supporting the indictment. The indictment is signed by the prosecutor and filed with the court.

No bill. The grand jury decides that the evidence does not support that an individual should be brought to trial and issues a **no bill.** The prosecutor may seek an indictment before another grand jury for the same offenses.

Presentment. A grand jury votes to undertake an investigation that goes beyond the indictment and may issue a **presentment.** This often is termed a *runaway grand jury.* The presentment is a report filed with the court that may name the individuals that the jury finds engaged in criminal activity.

Grand juries apply the probable cause and prima facie tests discussed in the previous section. In the vast majority of cases, juries issue a true bill. It has been remarked that a prosecutor could persuade a grand jury to "indict a ham sandwich." An indictment is required to possess two features.

- ***Essential elements.*** The essential legal elements of the crime. This includes the required criminal intent and criminal act.
- ***Factual specificity.*** The defendant's intent and acts that constitute the crime.

Grand Jury Investigations

The grand jury possesses several powers that make it a particularly powerful arm of the prosecutor in investigating criminal activity.

Defense attorney. An individual called to testify may not bring an attorney into the hearing. He or she may consult with a lawyer who is required to stand outside the hearing.

Right against self-incrimination. The grand jury may prevent an individual called to testify from relying on his or her Fifth Amendment rights by obtaining a judicial order granting the individual immunity from prosecution. This may be **transactional immunity** that immunizes an individual from prosecution regarding any events about which he or she testifies. In **use and derivative use immunity,** the prosecution is prohibited from relying on an individual's testimony or any material derived from the testimony to prosecute the individual.

Testimony. An individual has no right to testify before the grand jury, and there is no provision for the individual's lawyer to cross-examine witnesses appearing before the grand jury.

Law of evidence. In the federal system and in most states, the laws of evidence generally are not applied. Grand juries may rely on hearsay evidence and unlawfully seized evidence.

Exculpatory evidence. In many states, a prosecutor is under no obligation to present evidence favorable to the accused in his or her possession.

Subpoena. The grand jury may compel an individual to testify by issuing a **subpoena ad testificandum** and may compel an individual to submit documents or tangible evidence (e.g., clothing) by issuing a **subpoena duces tecum.** A failure to comply may result in criminal contempt and jail.

Secrecy. Grand jury proceedings are conducted in secret. The secrecy requirement is intended to prevent individuals who are indicted from fleeing, to insure freedom in grand jury deliberations, to enable individuals to testify without fear of retribution, to prevent tampering with witnesses, and to protect the identity of suspects who are not found to be involved in criminal activity. In several states, a defendant may have limited access to the transcript of the grand jury proceedings prior to his or her criminal trial (*United States v. Procter & Gamble,* 356 U.S. 677 [1958]).

The grand jury is in theory independent of prosecutors and judges and possesses significant powers that it exercises behind closed doors. The general rule is that the jury's decision to indict or refuse to indict may not be challenged by a prosecutor or by a defense attorney. The basis for this rule is that challenges would lead to burdensome delays. The defendant can take comfort in the fact that despite the indictment, the prosecutor still is required to establish the defendant's guilt beyond a **reasonable doubt** at trial (*Costello v. United States,* 350 U.S. 359 [1956]). What is the future of the unique American institution of the grand jury?

The Future of the Grand Jury

The grand jury remains a controversial institution, and there continues to be a debate over whether states and the federal government should continue to rely on this institution. Defenders of the grand jury argue that whatever its flaws, the jury is a mechanism for popular participation in deciding whether to prosecute an individual for a crime. This enhances public confidence in the criminal justice system and protects "citizens [defendants] against unfounded accusation, whether it comes from the government or be prompted by partisan passion" (*Hurtado v. California,* 110 U.S. 516, 556 [1884]). The high percentage of cases in which the jury returns a true bill according to supporters of the grand jury does not necessarily mean that the jury is a "rubber stamp." The explanation may lie in the fact that prosecutors are aware that to obtain a true bill from the grand jury, a case must be thoroughly documented. The strength of the cases that are endorsed by the grand jury is indicated by the fact that a high percentage of these cases result in criminal convictions.

The trend nonetheless is against reliance on the grand jury. There is a lack of faith in the capacity of the grand jury to meaningfully review the decisions of prosecutors to indict individuals. Some of the central criticisms of the grand jury are listed below.

Ineffective check. Critics observe that the grand jury works closely with the prosecutor and rarely refuses to indict a suspect. In the words of former U.S. District Court Judge William Campbell, the grand jury is the "total captive of the prosecutor" who "can indict anybody, at any time, for almost anything before any grand jury" (*Hawkins v. Superior Court,* 586 P.2d 916 [Cal. 1978]).

Unqualified. The existence of probable cause to bring an indictment is a legal question, and laypersons lack the expertise to make this determination. Grand jurors, as a result, tend to follow the prosecutor rather than exercise independent judgment.

Nonadversarial. The defendant has no ability to challenge the facts presented by the prosecutor. The defendant's lawyer is not present, and the defendant is not provided with the opportunity to address the grand jury.

Resources. The grand jury is a lengthy process. Jurors must be notified and selected, witnesses examined, and the grand jury must deliberate over whether to indict. This involves significant financial costs.

The grand jury stands in stark contrast to the preliminary hearing, which involves a public and adversarial hearing in which probable cause is determined by a legally trained magistrate or judge. The grand jury and preliminary hearing are compared in Chart 13.1. The next step before trial is the arraignment.

Chart 13.1 A Comparison Between the Preliminary Hearing and the Grand Jury

	Preliminary Hearing	*Grand Jury*
Defendant present	Yes	No
Represented by a lawyer	Yes	No
Right to testify	Yes	No
Presiding officer	Yes (magistrate)	No (foreman)
Public attendance	Yes	No
Standard of proof	Probable cause	Probable cause
Decision regarding probable cause	Magistrate (binds over)	Grand jury (indictment)
Power to undertake own investigation	No	Yes

Arraignment

Once the decision is made to indict an individual or to bind him or her over for trial, the next step is an **arraignment.** At the arraignment, a defendant is brought before a judge, is informed of the charges filed against him or her, and is required to enter one of four possible pleas.

- ***Not guilty.*** "I did not commit the crime."
- ***Not guilty by reason of insanity.*** "I did not know the nature and quality of my act."
- ***Nolo contendere.*** "I do not want to contest the criminal charge."
- ***Guilty.*** "I committed the crime and let me describe the facts of my crime."

A plea of **nolo contendere,** or "no contest," requires the permission of the court. This plea is used when a defendant while not admitting guilt does not dispute the charge. The plea carries all the consequences of a guilty plea with one exception. The exception is that unlike a guilty plea or criminal conviction, a plea of nolo contendere may not be admitted into evidence in a civil trial to establish that the defendant committed an act that injured the victim and therefore is civilly liable to pay damages to the victim. Ordinarily, a criminal conviction for a crime like aggravated assault can be introduced in a civil trial to prove that the defendant injured the plaintiff and now should be held liable for medical expenses and monetary damages. A plea of nolo contendere prevents the plaintiff at a civil trial from pointing to the criminal conviction as evidence that he or she was assaulted by the defendant.

The judge at the arraignment is responsible for insuring that a plea of nolo contendere or guilty is voluntary. In the event that the defendant pleads not guilty at the arraignment and indicates the he or she plans to proceed to trial, the defense lawyers may file various pretrial motions that are discussed in the next section of the chapter.

Pretrial Motions

There are several **pretrial motions** that may be filed by a defense attorney. These requests can profoundly impact the outcome of a defendant's case. We will briefly examine five important aspects of what is known as "motion practice."

- Double jeopardy
- Speedy trial
- Change of venue
- Discovery
- Suppression of evidence

Double Jeopardy

The Fifth Amendment to the U.S. Constitution provides that "[n]o person...shall...be subject for the same offence to be twice put in jeopardy of life or limb...." This clause appears in most state constitutions and has been incorporated by the U.S. Supreme Court into the Fourteenth Amendment Due Process Clause (*Benton v. Maryland,* 395 U.S. 784 [1969]). The meaning of this clause is far from clear, and the Supreme Court has handed down a number of decisions explaining the prohibition against **double jeopardy.**

The notion that an individual may not be prosecuted more than once for the same offense or punished more than once for the same crime has been a feature of the legal systems that form the foundation of modern American law. The ancient Greek philosopher Demosthenes proclaimed in 353 B.C. that "the laws forbid the same man to be tried twice on the same issue." Double jeopardy also appears in the Roman Digest of Justinian in 533 A.D. The prohibition on double jeopardy also has been a guiding principle of English court decisions as early as 1200. The famous English eighteenth-century legal commentator William Blackstone referred to the "[u]niversal maxim of the Common Law of England that no man is to be brought into jeopardy of his life more than once for the same offence."

The U.S. Supreme Court has held that the prohibition against double jeopardy involves three constitutional protections:

1. protection against a second prosecution for the same offense following an acquittal,
2. protection against a second prosecution for the same offense following a conviction, and
3. protection against multiple punishments for the same offense.

Why is the prohibition against double jeopardy considered fundamental to the concept of justice? A good argument can be made that there is nothing unfair about subjecting a person to multiple trials in an effort to obtain a criminal conviction in order to remove a dangerous individual from society. In *United States v. Difrancesco,* the U.S. Supreme Court discussed various interests protected by the prohibition against double jeopardy (*United States v. Difrancesco,* 449 U.S. 117 [1980]).

Finality of judgments. A trial court verdict of not guilty should be respected and should not be modified in a second trial.

Prosecutorial abuse. The government, with its substantial resources, should not subject an individual to a series of prosecutions in order to obtain a conviction. There is a danger that the government will use the first trial to identify weaknesses in its case and then correct these problems and obtain a conviction in the second prosecution.

Individual security. An individual should not be subjected to the anxiety, stress, and economic costs of multiple prosecutions.

Punishment. An individual who is convicted and sentenced should not be punished a second time for the same act.

What types of cases are subject to the prohibition against double jeopardy? The Double Jeopardy Clause applies when there is a second criminal prosecution, whether the charges are felonies or misdemeanors or involve juvenile justice. This means that an individual may be criminally prosecuted for motor vehicular homicide and civilly sued for injuring the occupants of the other vehicle. You should keep in mind that it is not always an easy question whether a second trial is civil or criminal, and the Supreme Court has developed a lengthy list of factors to be considered in making this determination (*Hudson v. United States,* 522 U.S. 93 [1997]). In *Kansas v. Hendricks,* the Kansas Sexually Violent Predator Act provided for the civil commitment of persons who, due to a "mental abnormality," "personality abnormality," or "personality disorder," are likely to engage in "predatory acts of sexual violence." Leroy Hendricks was committed to a mental institution under this Kansas statute after having served ten years in prison for taking "indecent liberties" with two juveniles. The U.S. Supreme Court found that the purpose of the Kansas statute was civil treatment rather than criminal punishment and that, as a result, Hendricks had not been subjected to double jeopardy (*Kansas v. Hendricks,* 521 U.S. 346 [1997]).

The Double Jeopardy Clause prohibits a second prosecution only in those instances in which "jeopardy attached" in the first proceeding. The U.S. Supreme Court has adopted three rules to determine the point at which jeopardy attaches and a second criminal prosecution is prohibited.

- ***Jury trial.*** Jeopardy attaches when the jury is impaneled and sworn in to uphold the U.S. Constitution.
- ***Judge.*** In a bench trial before a judge, jeopardy attaches when the first witness is sworn in to testify.
- ***Plea of guilty.*** Jeopardy attaches when the judge accepts the defendant's plea and enters a conviction.

In other words, double jeopardy is not triggered by a pretrial motion or by a prosecutor's or defense attorney's opening argument in a bench trial before a judge. There are various exceptions that are discussed in the next six sections of the chapter to the rule that the attachment of jeopardy bars a second trial or additional punishment.

Mistrials

In some instances, a court may grant a **mistrial,** and a second prosecution may be instituted despite the fact that jeopardy has attached. A mistrial is a fundamental error that causes a cancellation of the trial. The basic law regarding mistrials is outlined below.

Mistrial on motion or with consent of defendant. A retrial for the same offense is permitted where a mistrial is ordered in response to a motion by a defendant or with the defendant's consent. The defendant's request for a mistrial or consent to a mistrial results in a waiver of double jeopardy, and the defendant may be retried for the same offense. This is a "deliberate election" by the defendant to "forgo his or her valued right" to have his or her guilt or innocence determined by the jury that has been impaneled or by the judge who is presiding over the case. A defendant who believes that he or she is prejudiced by judicial or prosecutorial error may conclude that he or she likely will be convicted and that he or she stands a better chance of acquittal at a second trial. On the other hand, the defendant may decide to continue with his or her present trial and avoid the anxiety, expense, and delay of multiple prosecutions.

The U.S. Supreme Court has stressed that the important consideration is that it is the defendant's decision whether to accept a mistrial or whether to continue with the trial. In *United States v. Dinitz,* the U.S. Supreme Court concluded that a retrial was not prohibited by the Double Jeopardy Clause where the judge excluded the defense counsel from the trial because of misconduct, and the defendant, rather than appeal the decision or continue with the case, requested a mistrial. The Supreme Court held that Dinitz's motion for a mistrial removed "any barrier to re-prosecution" (*United States v. Dinitz,* 424 U.S. 600 [1976]).

There is a "narrow exception" in the case of "prosecutorial overreaching" to the rule that a defendant's request for a mistrial does not prohibit a second prosecution. A second trial violates the Double Jeopardy Clause in those instances in which a prosecutor "goad[s] a defendant into requesting a mistrial." In *Oregon v. Kennedy,* the prosecutor asked a witness whether he had not "done business" with the defendant because "he is a crook." The defendant, fearful that he was tainted in the eyes of the jury, asked for and was granted a mistrial. The U.S. Supreme Court held that the defendant's "valued right to complete his trial before the first jury would be a hollow shell if the inevitable motion for mistrial was held to prevent a later invocation of the bar of double jeopardy in all circumstances" (*Oregon v. Kennedy,* 456 U.S. 667, 673 [1982]).

Mistrial over defendant's objection. A mistrial that is declared by a judge despite the objection of the defendant ordinarily bars the defendant's retrial. The exception is when the mistrial is based on **manifest necessity** (*United States v. Perez,* 434 U.S. 497 [1978]). Manifest necessity arises in those instances in which the judge concludes that justice would not be served by continuing the trial (*Illinois v. Somerville,* 410 U.S. 458 [1973]). In these situations, the defendant's interest in his or her trial being completed by a particular tribunal is subordinated to the public interest in a fair trial. In *Wade v. Hunter,* the U.S. Supreme Court set forth two general categories of manifest necessity outlined below in which a judge properly exercises his or her discretion to declare a mistrial and a second trial is not barred by the Double Jeopardy Clause.

An impartial verdict cannot be reached. In the case of a hung jury or a deadlocked jury, there is the risk that any verdict that may be reached will be the product of impatience or frustration (*United States v. Perez,* 22 U.S. 579 [1824]). Another instance in which an impartial verdict may be difficult to reach is a prosecution in which a juror turns out to be acquainted with the defendant and therefore may be biased against the Government. An additional example is the death of the judge during the trial, which prevents the case from proceeding (*Simmons v. United States,* 142 U.S. 148 [1891]).

A conviction could be reached, but an error makes a reversal on appeal a certainty. An example is a situation in which one of the jurors at trial is discovered to have served on the grand jury that indicted the defendant and presumably already has reached a conclusion regarding the defendant's guilt. Any conviction would likely be reversed on appeal and the government would be compelled to reprosecute the defendant (*Thompson v. United States,* 155 U.S. 271 [1894]). In *Illinois v. Somerville,* the trial court granted a mistrial on the motion of the Government and over the defendant's objection when it was discovered on the first day of the trial that the indictment had failed to allege that the defendant had acted with the criminal intent required for the crime of theft. State law prohibited an amendment of the indictment. This defect, without question, would result in a guilty verdict being overturned on appeal. The U.S. Supreme Court held that continuing the trial would not serve the ends of public justice and ruled that a second trial was not barred by the prohibition on double jeopardy (*Illinois v. Somerville,* 410 U.S. 458 [1973]).

The Supreme Court is reluctant to recognize manifest necessity where there is a risk that the prosecutor is intentionally creating the conditions for a mistrial in order to strengthen the Government's case and bring a second trial. In *Downum v. United States,* a mistrial was declared when the prosecution declared that a crucial witness had not yet been located. The Supreme Court concluded that the mistrial had been requested by the prosecutor in order to terminate the trial in hopes of strengthening the Government's case in a future trial and that, under these circumstances, a second prosecution was barred by double jeopardy (*Downum v. United States,* 372 U.S. 734 [1963]).

Appeals

A defendant who appeals and whose conviction is overturned may be retried without violating the prohibition on double jeopardy. The reason why a second trial is permitted is that a defendant who appeals is considered to have waived the right to claim double jeopardy if he or she is again prosecuted for the same criminal offense. An exception is where an appeals court determines that the evidence at trial was insufficient to establish the defendant's guilt. In this instance, the Government has been provided the opportunity to establish the defendant's guilt and has failed to present facts to establish the defendant's guilt beyond a reasonable doubt, and a retrial is barred by double jeopardy (*Green v. United States,* 355 U.S. 184 [1957]).

Punishment

A defendant may not be punished twice for the same offense. The prosecution, however, may appeal a trial judge's failure to follow the law in sentencing a defendant. An appellate court may instruct the trial court to impose a harsher sentence without violating the Double Jeopardy Clause (*United States v. DiFrancesco,* 449 U.S. 117 [1980]).

Same Offense

Double jeopardy prohibits prosecuting a defendant more than once for the same offense. What is considered the "same offense"? Two issues arise in defining *same offense.*

Same transaction. Double jeopardy is not violated by prosecuting an individual for separate crimes committed during a single transaction. A defendant may be prosecuted for the homicide of each person who is killed during a crime. Killing three persons during the robbery of a fast-food restaurant may result in prosecution for three homicide counts. In *Ciucci v. Illinois,* the defendant was brought to trial and convicted in a separate trial for each homicide. The first two trials resulted in a term of imprisonment, and the third and last trial led to the imposition of the death penalty (*Ciucci v. Illinois,* 356 U.S. 571 [1969]).

Same offense. An individual who commits a criminal act that violates two criminal statutes may be charged with a violation of each law. The fact that there is *some overlap* in the evidence that is relied on during a trial to establish a violation of each offense does not violate double jeopardy. An individual may be convicted of conspiracy to commit a premeditated murder and of the premeditated killing of another person despite the fact that *some* of the evidence that establishes the conspiracy or agreement to kill also may be relied on to establish a premeditated intent to kill. The key point is that these are separate offenses. A conspiracy to murder requires an agreement to kill, and first-degree murder requires a killing. On the other hand, under the so-called ***Blockburger* test** established in *Blockburger v. United States,* it is a violation of double jeopardy to prosecute a defendant who commits a criminal act for violating two statutes that rely on the same evidence (*Blockburger v. United States,* 284 U.S. 299 [1932]). Examples include prosecuting a defendant for both auto theft and joyriding and prosecuting a defendant for both selling cocaine and selling a controlled substance (*Brown v. United States,* 432 U.S. 161, 167–168 [1977]).

Next, we discuss the **dual sovereignty doctrine,** which permits prosecution for the same offense by two states or by a state and the federal government.

Dual Sovereignty Doctrine

In 1959, in *Heath v. Alabama,* the U.S. Supreme Court held that double jeopardy did not prohibit Alabama and Georgia from each prosecuting a defendant for murder. The Court explained that the two states are independent sovereign entities, each of which possessed an interest in enforcing its own law (*Heath v. Alabama,* 474 U.S. 82 [1985]). The Court earlier had held in *Bartkus v. Illinois* that double jeopardy did not bar a state and federal prosecution of an individual for bank robbery (*Bartkus v. Illinois,* 359 U.S. 121 [1959]). These two cases are the foundation of the dual sovereignty doctrine. The dual sovereignty doctrine provides that double jeopardy does not prohibit successive prosecutions for the same criminal act by a state government and by the federal government or by two state governments. Roughly twenty-five states prohibit state prosecutions following a federal prosecution for the same act. The federal government follows a policy of bringing a federal prosecution following a state prosecution only where there are "compelling reasons." In *Waller v. Florida,* the Supreme Court held that a state government and local municipalities within the state are not "separate entities" and that double jeopardy prohibits prosecutions by the state government and by a city, county, or local government or prosecutions by two local governments (*Waller v. Florida,* 397 U.S. 387 [1970]).

Collateral Estoppel

The **collateral estoppel** doctrine provides that an "ultimate fact" that is established in a criminal prosecution may not again be litigated in a second prosecution involving the same parties. In *Ashe v. Swenson,* Ashe was suspected of having robbed six individuals during a poker game. He was acquitted of having robbed Knight. Following his acquittal, Ashe was indicted for robbing Roberts, another of the participants in the poker game. The U.S. Supreme Court held that collateral estoppel is embodied in the Fifth Amendment guarantee against double jeopardy and is applicable to the states. The Court explained that once there is at least reasonable doubt that Ashe was one of the robbers, the state could not "present the same or different identification evidence in a second prosecution for the robbery of Knight in the hope that a different jury might find that evidence more convincing." The Supreme Court observed that the prosecutor was using the first trial as a "dry run" in hopes of strengthening its case in the second trial, which is precisely what is prohibited under double jeopardy (*Ashe v. Swenson,* 397 U.S. 436 [1970]).

The next pretrial motion is the claim that a defendant has not been provided with a speedy trial.

Speedy Trial

The Sixth Amendment to the U.S. Constitution provides that "[i]n all criminal prosecutions, the accused shall enjoy the right to a speedy... trial." The Fourteenth Amendment Due Process Clause incorporates the right to **speedy trial,** which also is guaranteed by law in each of the fifty states. Scholars point to the English Magna Carta of 1215, one of the most famous human rights documents in history, as the first clear statement of the right to a speedy trial. The U.S. Supreme Court has recognized that the "history of the right to a speedy trial and its reception in this country clearly establish that it is one of the basic rights preserved by our Constitution" (*Klopfer v. North Carolina,* 386 U.S. 213, 223, 226 [1967]).

In *Smith v. Hooey,* the U.S. Supreme Court identified three *individual interests* protected by the right to a speedy trial, which are summarized below (*Smith v. Hooey,* 393 U.S. 374, 393 [1969]).

Incarceration. A lengthy incarceration prior to trial results in unnecessary hardship, may lead to the loss of a job or educational opportunity, disrupts family life, and interferes with preparation for trial.

Public accusation. An individual who is released on bail for a lengthy period while waiting for trial may be the subject of public criticism and isolation and suffer psychological anxiety and stress.

Preparation for trial. Incarceration interferes with an individual's ability to prepare for trial. A lengthy delay may result in witnesses dying or disappearing and may make it difficult for witnesses to recollect events.

In *Barker v. Wingo,* the U.S. Supreme Court argued that there is a *societal interest* in speedy trials. The Court identified several societal interests (*Barker v. Wingo,* 407 U.S. 514 [1972]).

Backlog. The failure to provide for swift trials leads to a backlog of cases and places pressure on prosecutors to drop charges or to reduce the sentences of defendants who agree to plead guilty.

Bail. The longer an individual must wait to stand trial, the greater the possibility that an individual who is released on bail my "jump bail" and not report for trial.

Crime. An individual who is released for a lengthy period prior to trial may commit additional crimes.

Incarceration. Individuals who are incarcerated for a lengthy period prior to trial may deteriorate psychologically and develop resentments that may interfere with their rehabilitation. The family of an individual who is detained for a lengthy period may have to be supported from public funds.

The right to a speedy trial attaches when an individual finds himself or herself "accused" of a crime. An individual is considered accused following either the filing of a formal indictment or information or the "actual restraints imposed by arrest." The right to a speedy trial also may arise when a detainer (criminal charge) is filed against an accused who already is serving a sentence on other charges. A defendant in addition to a right to a speedy trial has a constitutional right to a speedy sentencing hearing and to a speedy appeal (*United States v. Marion,* 404 U.S. 307, 321 [1971]). In *United States v. Lovasco,* the government waited more than eighteen months to file an indictment against Lovasco for possessing stolen firearms and for dealing in firearms without a license. The U.S. Supreme Court held that this delay did not violate the Speedy Trial Clause. The Court explained that there is a strong interest in prosecutors delaying an indictment until they are persuaded that there is sufficient evidence to believe that the Government will be able to establish an individual's guilt beyond a reasonable doubt at trial and that there is a societal interest in pursuing prosecutions for firearms offenses (*United States v. Lovasco,* 431 U.S. 783 [1977]).

In *United States v. Strunk,* the Supreme Court stressed that the remedy for a violation of the right to a speedy trial is dismissal of the charges. This drastic result has made courts reluctant to hold that the defendant's right to a speedy trial has been violated. A defendant may waive a speedy trial. A speedy trial claim generally must be raised at the trial phase or else the claim is waived (*United States v. Strunk,* 412 U.S. 434 [1973]).

We now come to the essential question that the text of the Sixth Amendment does not answer. What is the standard to determine whether a trial is speedy or whether a trial is unreasonably delayed? *Barker v. Wingo* established the prevailing standard for a speedy trial. In *Barker,* Manning and Barker were arrested in July 1958 for the murder of an elderly couple. Barker obtained his release from prison after ten months. As a result of a number of continuances, the Government did not prosecute and convict Barker for five years following his indictment. The Supreme Court held that Barker had not been prejudiced by the delay, because none of his witnesses had died or had become unavailable. The Court also noted that Barker's lawyer did not object to the continuance of the case, because the defendant apparently was hoping that Manning would be acquitted and would have no reason to assist the Government and to testify against Barker. The Supreme Court expressed doubt whether Barker, in fact, "want[ed] a speedy trial" (*Barker v. Wingo,* 407 U.S. 514, 536–538 [1972]).

The Supreme Court noted in *Barker* that the right to a speedy trial is a "vague concept" and that it is "impossible to determine with precision when the right has been denied." The Court declined to undertake the difficult task of establishing a specified time period in which a trial must be held and adopted a "balancing test." The Court identified "some of the factors" that a judge should "assess in determining" whether a defendant has been deprived of a speedy trial. The determination whether the defendant's right to a speedy trial has been violated should be based on an analysis of the totality of the circumstances. These circumstances include the following considerations (525–531).

Length. The length of the delay is the "triggering mechanism." A lengthy delay is presumptively prejudicial to the defendant. The delay must be evaluated in light of the complexity of the case against the accused. A conspiracy to commit a white-collar crime clearly requires more trial preparation for the prosecution than a street crime.

Reason for the delay. "[D]ifferent weights should be assigned to different reasons." An intentional effort to delay the trial is weighed against the Government. A more neutral reason such as a crowded judicial docket or a negligent failure by the prosecutor to conduct forensic tests is to be weighed to some degree against the Government. A delay is justified when based on a reason that is beyond the prosecutor's control such as a missing witness. A delay caused by the defendant weighs against the defendant and is viewed as a "waiver of the right to a speedy trial."

Assertion of the right. The defendant is responsible for raising the right to a speedy trial. A failure to assert delay during a lengthy period prior to trial or to wait to assert delay until trial counts against a defendant who claims to have been prejudiced. As noted, a failure to raise delay at trial results in a waiver of a speedy-trial claim.

Prejudice. Courts are reluctant to find unreasonable delay in the absence of prejudice. Examples of prejudice include a lengthy pretrial incarceration that interferes with the defendant's ability to work on his or her defense and the death or disappearance of witnesses.

In *Dogett v. United States,* Dogett left the United States before being indicted in 1980 on federal drug charges, and a warrant was issued for his arrest. The Drug Enforcement Administration (DEA) was aware that Dogett had been imprisoned in Panama and requested that he be returned to stand trial in the United States. The DEA neglected to pursue the matter and was aware that following Doggett's prison term in Panama, he had moved to Colombia in 1981. In 1982, Doggett reentered the United States, married, earned a college degree, was steadily employed, and lived openly under his own name. He was arrested in September 1988 when his name appeared during a search of a database for names of individuals against whom there were outstanding arrest warrants. Doggett moved to dismiss the indictment on the grounds that his right to a speedy trial had been violated.

The Supreme Court found that Doggett had not been informed of the indictment against him in the United States and had filed the speedy trial claim following his arrest. The Court held that Doggett had been denied a speedy trial and concluded that "[c]ondoning prolonged and unjustifiable delays in prosecution would...penalize many defendants for the State's failure....The Government...can hardly complain too loudly, for [its] persistent neglect in concluding a criminal prosecution indicates an uncommonly feeble interest in bringing an accused to justice; the more weight the Government attaches to securing a conviction, the harder it will try to get it" (*Doggett v. United States,* 505 U.S. 647, 657 [1992]).

In 2009, the Supreme Court reached a different result in *Vermont v. Brillon*. Brillon was arrested in July 2001 on felony domestic assault and for being a habitual offender. In June 2004, he was convicted and sentenced to twelve to twenty years in prison. The Vermont Supreme Court held that the three-year delay had violated Brillon's right to a speedy trial and that the delay had been caused by Brillon's assigned counsel and therefore was attributable to Vermont. The U.S. Supreme Court reversed this judgment and held that while the Vermont Public Defender is part of the criminal justice system, for purposes of speedy trial, assigned lawyers are not considered "state actors." The Court explained that a "contrary conclusion" would encourage appointed lawyers to "delay proceedings by seeking unreasonable continuances, hoping thereby to obtain a dismissal of the indictment on speedy trial grounds." On the other hand, the Court recognized that a delay that results from the "breakdown" in the public defender system caused by a lack of funding or a shortage of available lawyers could be charged to the State (*Vermont v. Brillon,* ___ U.S. ___ [2009]).

Most states have speedy trial acts. Congress passed the Speedy Trial Act of 1974, 18 U.S.C. §§ 361, 362, two years following the decision in *Barker v. Wingo.* The Act singles out time as the crucial determining factor in evaluating whether a defendant has received a speedy trial. The Act requires that an information or indictment charging an individual with a criminal offense shall be filed within thirty days from the date of the arrest or service of a summons. This period may be extended for thirty days in the event that a grand jury is not in session. An arraignment is to be conducted within ten days of the filing of an indictment and information. A trial is to be held within seventy days of the filing of the information or indictment or within seventy days of the date that the defendant first appears before a judicial officer, whichever is later. A judge, in the event that the Government fails to provide a speedy trial, may dismiss the charges with or without prejudice depending on the interest in bringing the defendant to trial. Factors to be considered in evaluating whether the prosecutor should be permitted to bring a case to trial despite a violation of the speedy trial requirements include the seriousness of the offense and the societal interest in prosecuting the crime. The Act is full of qualifications and exceptions, and several types of delays do not count against the limits established by the Speedy Trial Act. These include a delay created by the unavailability of the defendant or a delay resulting from the absence of an essential witness, delays caused by a co-defendant, transportation delays, delays caused by other proceedings, and delays stemming from the filing of pretrial motions. Lawyers who intentionally create unnecessary delays are subject to a fine. The average time from the filing of a federal criminal offense to trial today is roughly one year. We now turn to a pretrial motion regarding the location of the trial.

Change of Venue

Article III, Section 2 of the U.S. Constitution originally required that jury trials for federal criminal cases are to be held "in the State where said Crimes shall have been committed." This clause was a response to the British practice of forcing American colonists to stand trial in England or in some other location far from the place where the crime was committed. During the debates over the ratification of the Constitution, Article III, Section 2 was criticized on the grounds that the text did not guarantee that the accused would be provided a trial by jury of the **vicinage.** Vicinage refers to the selection of a jury from the community in which the crime was committed. As a result, the Sixth Amendment was amended to require a trial "by an impartial jury of the State and *district* wherein the crime shall have been committed." Rule 18 of the Federal Rules of Criminal Procedure is followed by most state statutes and rules of state courts in requiring that a "prosecution shall be had in a district in which the offense was committed." The physical location of the judicial district in which the prosecution is to occur is termed the **venue.**

What if a defendant believes that he or she cannot obtain a fair trial in the venue of the trial? In *Groppi v. Wisconsin,* the U.S. Supreme Court held that a state is required to allow a change of venue in those instances in which a defendant demonstrates that a fair trial cannot be achieved in the district (*Groppi v. Wisconsin,* 400 U.S. 505 [1971]). A majority of state statutes and rules of state courts have adopted the change-of-venue standard of Rule 21(a) of the Federal Rules of Criminal Procedure. Rule 21(a) requires that the court, on the motion of the defendant, shall transfer the trial to another district in the event that the court is "satisfied" that there exists "so great a prejudice against the defendant that the defendant cannot obtain a fair and impartial trial." California requires a change of venue whenever the dissemination of potentially prejudicial material results in a "reasonable likelihood" that a fair trial cannot be obtained (*Powell v. Superior Court,* 283 Cal. Rptr. 777 [Cal. App. 1991]). In other words, a defendant in the federal criminal justice system and in state criminal justice systems may file a pretrial motion to change the venue of a prosecution in those instances in which the defendant satisfies the trial court judge that the jurors are so biased that a fair trial is impossible. Courts understandably are reluctant to change the venue of a trial. This may require witnesses and the lawyers to travel to distant locations and is contrary to the interest in selecting a jury from the area in which the crime has been committed. An effort generally is made to find a nearby district that is not exposed to the prejudicial material. This process can be further complicated where the defense argues that the district should reflect a particular racial or ethnic balance.

The issue of pretrial prejudice and fair trials most clearly arises in criminal cases that receive widespread media coverage. This may prove to be a particular problem in a small community where a sensational crime dominates the news or in a larger community where a case attracts national media attention. The most famous example of pretrial publicity and prejudice is the prosecution in Cleveland, Ohio, in 1954, of Dr. Sam Sheppard for bludgeoning to death his pregnant, socialite wife. The *Sheppard* case was the topic of so much interest that it later formed the basis for a popular television program called *The Fugitive* (*Sheppard v. Maxwell,* 384 U.S. 333, 363 [1966]).

The pretrial coverage of the trial was "massive and pervasive.... For months the virulent publicity about Sheppard and the murder made the case notorious," and "bedlam reigned at the courthouse during the trial." The news media was described as having "inflamed and prejudiced" the public, witnesses, and jurors and as having created a "carnival atmosphere."

The U.S. Supreme Court held that due process "requires that the accused receive a trial before an impartial jury free from outside influences." The Court recognized the difficulty of eliminating the impact of prejudicial publicity from the minds of jurors given the "pervasiveness of modern communication" and held that in those instances in which there is a "reasonable likelihood" that prejudicial news coverage will prevent a fair trial, courts should grant a continuance (suspension) of the trial until the "threat abates" or should transfer the trial to another county "not so permeated with publicity." In the event that the trial is not transferred, courts also can limit the impact of publicity by placing "gag orders" on statements by lawyers to the media, sequestering the jury to prevent jurors from being exposed to the media, advising the jury to remain impartial, and prohibiting the media from interviewing witnesses. A more drastic approach adopted by a small number of states is to keep the trial in the judicial district and to select a jury from another location (363).

The U.S. Supreme Court in *Sheppard* presumed that the widespread, detailed, and long-lasting publicity accompanying Sheppard's murder case prejudiced the jury. This same *presumption-of-prejudice approach* was adopted in *Rideau v. Louisiana.* In *Rideau,* two months prior to trial, a local television station broadcast Rideau's twenty-minute confession to the police on three occasions over a three-day period. In the confession, Rideau admitted the commission of the crimes for which he subsequently was tried and convicted. It was estimated that roughly two-thirds of the 150,000 people in the Louisiana parish had viewed the confession. The Supreme Court held that the trial court's denial of Rideau's motion for a change of venue denied Rideau due process of law. Despite the fact that the three jurors who had watched the confession testified that they were capable of objectively weighing the evidence and of maintaining a presumption of innocence, the Supreme Court held that the broadcast of the confession had reduced the trial to a "hollow formality." The Court did not explain its decision but appears to have adopted the view that in the case of pervasive and detailed publicity in a relatively small community, it is unlikely that jurors will be able to avoid being influenced by the publicity or avoid being affected by the hostile atmosphere created in the community toward the defendant (*Rideau v. Louisiana,* 373 U.S. 723 [1963]).

The recent trend is toward an *actual-prejudice standard* in deciding whether a change of venue is required. The trial court judge, before granting a change of venue under this standard, is to determine whether the jurors are able to act in an objective and fair fashion. The fact that a juror is exposed to prejudicial publicity is not the test. In fact, it is desirable that jurors should be interested in the news and well informed. The question is whether a juror is able to make a decision based solely on the evidence presented in court and "can lay aside his impression or opinion." The burden is on the defendant to demonstrate "the actual existence of such an opinion in the mind of the juror [jurors] as will raise the presumption of partiality." In other words, the defendant must demonstrate that based on the totality of circumstances, the jurors are predisposed to find the defendant guilty (*Irvin v. Dowd,* 366 U.S. 717 [1961]).

In *Irvin,* headline stories in Vanderburgh County, Indiana, proclaimed that Irvin had confessed to six murders and to twenty-four burglaries and that he had offered to plead guilty in exchange for a ninety-nine-year sentence. Ninety percent of prospective jurors at Irvin's murder trial who were examined expressed a fixed opinion as to Irvin's guilt ranging from mere suspicion to absolute certainty. The U.S. Supreme Court found a "pattern of deep and bitter prejudice" based on the fact that eight of the twelve jurors selected thought that Irvin was guilty. Several jurors stated that it "would take evidence to overcome their belief" in the defendant's guilt. The Court questioned whether the jurors had been able to "exclude this preconception of guilt from [their] deliberation" and had been able to reach an impartial verdict. The trial court, by accepting these jurors, had denied Irvin due process of law (727–728).

In 1975, in *Murphy v. Florida,* the U.S. Supreme Court held that the infamous and colorful "Murph the Surf" had not been denied due process of law when a Dade County Criminal Court failed to move the venue of his murder trial. Murphy's arrest was the subject of intense media attention. He was known for his role in the notorious 1964 theft of the Star of India sapphire from a museum in New York and was legendary in Miami for his colorful lifestyle. The U.S. Supreme Court stressed that most of the publicity in the case appeared seven months prior to the selection of the jury. Only twenty of the seventy-eight persons had an opinion regarding Murphy's guilt, and there was no indication that the individuals selected to serve on the jury had an opinion regarding the defendant's guilt or innocence (*Murphy v. Florida,* 421 U.S. 794 [1975]).

The passage of time was found by the U.S. Supreme Court to have been significant in reducing community bias in *Patton v. Young.* In *Patton,* the defendant's 1966 conviction for murdering a fellow high school student was overturned. He was retried in 1970, and all but 2 of the 163 veniremen, or individuals in the jury pool, had heard of the case. In fact, 126 of these individuals indicated that in the past, they had had an opinion regarding the case. The four years that elapsed between the first and the second trial, in the view of the Court, had eliminated any threat that the jury had been biased against Young. Community interest in the case had faded, newspaper coverage between the two trials had been extremely limited and generally was neutral in tone, and there appeared to be little current community interest in the case (*Patton v. Young,* 467 U.S. 1025 [1984]).

In summary, the Supreme Court has held that a change of venue is required where the totality of the circumstances indicates that jurors are so influenced by pretrial publicity that they are not able to act in an impartial fashion and to decide the case based on the evidence presented in court. The factors considered by courts in making this determination include the following:

- There is persistent and widespread publicity regarding the case immediately prior to the trial and during the selection of the jury.
- The publicity describes the crime in detail and assumes the defendant's guilt.
- A significant percentage of the community is exposed to the publicity.
- A high percentage of the jury pool is aware of the case and possesses an opinion.
- Individuals selected for the jury express an inability to objectively evaluate the case, or the publicity must be so persistent and widespread that the court is unwilling to accept that the individuals are able to objectively evaluate the case.

Rule 21(b) of the Federal Rules of Criminal Procedure and the venue provisions of a significant number of states provide that a change of venue also is available based on "the convenience of the parties." In *Platt v. Minnesota Mining and Manufacturing Co.,* the U.S. Supreme Court listed a number of factors to be considered in determining the convenience of the parties including the location of witnesses, documents, and lawyers and the expense and ease of travel to the site of the trial. In other words, an individual may be prosecuted for mailing a letter bomb to an address in a distant rural part of the state. It might be fairer and more practical to prosecute the individual at the site from which the bomb was mailed rather than at the location to which the bomb was delivered to the intended victim (*Platt v. Minnesota Mining and Manufacturing Co.,* 376 U.S. 240 [1964]). The next pretrial motion is discovery.

You can find Murphy v. Florida *on the study site, http://www.sagepub.com/lippmancp.*

Discovery

Trials in the United States until the late twentieth century were conducted based on "ambush" and "surprise." The prosecution and defense entered the courtroom with a limited ability to predict the evidence that the other side might present at trial. In 1985, in *Brady v. Maryland,* the U.S. Supreme Court held that the Due Process Clause requires prosecutors, when requested by the defense, to disclose exculpatory (exonerating) evidence within their possession that is relevant to the innocence, guilt, or sentence of the accused. The purpose of the ***Brady* rule** is to prevent miscarriages of justice by requiring the disclosure of evidence that may prevent the conviction of an innocent individual or that may result in a reduction in the defendant's sentence (*Brady v. Maryland,* 373 U.S. 83 [1963]).

In *Brady,* the prosecution withheld a co-conspirator's admission that he had committed the actual killing. This information would not have led to Brady's acquittal, but the Court determined that he was treated unfairly because the evidence might have been used by Brady's attorney to argue that he did not deserve the death penalty. The U.S. Supreme Court, in other cases, has found an obligation on the part of the government to turn over statements to the defense that raise questions regarding the truthfulness of the witnesses' testimony. In 1985, in *United States v. Bagley,* Bagley was indicted for narcotics and firearms violations. The defense attorney requested the names and addresses of prosecution witnesses and any "deals, promises or inducements made to witnesses in exchange for their testimony." The Government turned over affidavits from its two central witnesses indicating that they had not been offered any "rewards," and the two testified against Bagley at trial. Following Bagley's conviction, it was discovered that the two witnesses had been paid for assisting the Government. Bagley's attorney might have attacked the credibility of the two witnesses when they were on the stand had this information been provided by the Government. The Supreme Court remanded the case for a "determination whether there is reasonable probability that, had the inducement offered by the Government... been disclosed to the defense, the result of the trial would have been different" (*United States v. Bagley,* 473 U.S. 667 [1985]).

The constitutional requirement to hand over exculpatory information is binding on both state and federal prosecutors. State statutes and state rules of procedure take varying positions on disclosure of other evidence ranging from virtually no disclosure to complete disclosure. Rule 16 of the Federal Rules of Criminal Procedure addresses disclosure in federal courts. Several examples of state and federal approaches to discovery are outlined below.

Names and addresses of witnesses. One-half of the states provide for discovery of the names and addresses of all persons known to have relevant information. A number of other jurisdictions and the federal government do not make this information available, because of a fear of intimidation of witnesses. A third group requires disclosure only of individuals "intended" to be called at trial.

Witness statements. A majority of states either do not permit discovery of the statements of interviewed witnesses or leave this to the discretion of the judge. Roughly fourteen states and the federal government do not require pretrial disclosure of the statements of witnesses. The federal policy is based on the interest in protecting witnesses from harassment.

Police officers. Police personnel records generally are not discoverable. Some states require disclosure in the event that the records are likely to contain information relevant to the officer's credibility.

Most jurisdictions provide for the disclosure of medical and physical examinations and scientific tests, documents and tangible objects, and statements made by the accused. A codefendant's statements that are to be introduced into evidence generally are not discoverable, because this might lead to the intimidation of a witness.

The last pretrial motion is the motion to suppress unconstitutionally obtained evidence.

Motion to Suppress

As previously discussed, evidence obtained in violation of the Fourth Amendment may be suppressed and excluded from evidence (Chapter 10). Confessions that are obtained in violation of the Fifth Amendment *Miranda* requirement (Chapter 8) and identifications that are obtained in violation of the Fifth or Sixth Amendment (Chapter 9) also may be suppressed. We now turn our attention to the trial process and to the right to a jury trial.

Criminal Procedure in the News

The law recognizes an attorney–client privilege. This means that an attorney may not reveal information that his or her client shares regarding past criminal activity. The thinking is that this allows a defendant in a criminal case to be open and honest with his or her lawyer. The attorney–client privilege creates various ethical dilemmas. For example, what if the defendant takes the stand and denies that he or she committed a crime after admitting to the lawyer that he or she in fact did commit the crime? Should a lawyer remain silent despite the fact that his or her client is committing perjury?

Two fairly recent cases raise yet another problem, a lawyer whose client admits that he committed a crime for which another individual was charged and convicted. Virginia lawyer Leslie P. Smith represented William Jones who was prosecuted along with Daryl R. Atkins for killing Eric Nesbitt during a robbery. In Virginia, only the "triggerman" is eligible for the death penalty. During a debriefing session with prosecutors on August 6, 1997, Jones described the robbery and the killing. His account did not match the prosecutor's theory of the case, and the prosecutor turned to Smith and remarked, "Do you see we have a problem here?" The prosecutor noted that "[t]his isn't going to do us any good" and turned off the tape recorder and spent fifteen minutes persuading Jones to name Atkins as the shooter. The tape was turned back on, and Jones "improved" his story to support that Atkins was the shooter. Jones entered into a plea bargain in exchange for testifying against Atkins and ultimately received a life sentence while Atkins was sentenced to death. Atkins's lawyers did not know that Jones's testimony was untrue. They did file an appeal on Atkins's behalf to the U.S. Supreme Court, which, in 2002, ruled that the Constitution prohibits the execution of mentally retarded individuals such as Atkins. Virginia nonetheless continued to argue after the Supreme Court decision that Atkins was not sufficiently mentally retarded to prevent his execution and continued to seek a death sentence against Atkins.

Leslie Smith believed that the prosecutors had committed clear misconduct by coaching a witness and concealing from the defense that Jones was the "shooter." He prepared a memorandum following the interrogation session that he submitted to the Virginia State Bar Association. The Virginia State Bar counseled that Smith had an ethical obligation based on attorney–client privilege not to reveal this information to Atkins's defense team. The bar association stressed that the client is the "holder of privilege," and only the client can waive the privilege. In 2008, the Virginia State Bar changed its view and advised Smith that he was free to reveal this information. The Commonwealth's prosecuting attorney dismissed Smith's account as "false and libelous" and "adamantly" denied Smith's allegations.

There was only roughly an hour and three-quarters of material on the audiotape of Jones's interrogation despite the fact that a detective testified that the questioning lasted two hours. In January 2008, a Virginia state court judge listened to Smith's testimony and commuted the death sentence of Daryl R. Atkins to life on the grounds of prosecutorial misconduct.

Defendants in Virginia typically are executed within seven years of the jury verdict, and had Atkins's death sentence not been delayed by the decision of the U.S. Supreme Court, Atkins likely would have been executed before Smith was granted permission to disclose what transpired. Ethics experts questioned the original position of the Virginia State Bar and objected to allowing an individual to die in order to uphold the attorney–client privilege. Roxie Bacon, a former president of the State Bar of Arizona, asked, "What in the world can explain any ethics rule, and any state bar advice, that allows a prosecutor to grossly abuse her power and force a defense attorney to remain quiet about it for 10 years, during which the harmed defendant could have been executed?"

In April 2008, in a similar case, Cook County, Illinois, Judge James Schreier vacated the conviction of Alton Logan for the January 1982 robbery-murder of a security guard at a McDonald's restaurant and ordered a new trial. Public Defender Marc Miller had represented Edgar Hope, who also was accused of the January 1982 McDonald's holdup. Hope told Miller that Logan had nothing to do with the robbery and that the other shooter during the robbery was Andrew Wilson. Wilson was facing prosecution for the February 1982 murder of two police officers and was represented by Public Defenders Dale Coventry and Jamie Kunz. Miller talked to Coventry and Kunz, who, in turn, talked to Wilson. Wilson admitted that he was with Hope at the McDonald's during the killing and stated that the truth could be revealed only following his death. The lawyers all executed an affidavit that was stored in a metal box for twenty-six years, which stated that they had been informed that Logan was not responsible for the murder of security guard Lloyd Wicklife. They did not name the identity of the true shooter. Wilson's story was supported by the fact that when Wilson was arrested, the police did not reveal that they had seized a shotgun that ballistics tests indicated had been used in the McDonald's murder.

In November 2007, Wilson passed away in prison, and the lawyers now were free to share their story before a judge. They claimed that had Logan been sentenced to death, they would have violated the attorney–client privilege to save his life, even at the risk of losing their licenses to practice law. The public defenders who came forward noted that without the attorney–client privilege, Wilson likely never would have admitted that he was involved in the killings and that he would have taken this secret to his grave. Logan's uncle observed that justice "had to be done. . . . But to lay him there for 26 years . . . it makes me a little bitter." Logan now is a free man.

Constitutional Right to a Jury Trial

Article III, Section 2 of the U.S. Constitution provides that "[t]he Trial of all Crimes, except in Cases of Impeachment, shall be by Jury; and such Trial shall be held in the State where the said Crimes shall have been committed." The Sixth Amendment to the U.S. Constitution provides that "in all criminal prosecutions, the accused shall enjoy the right to a speedy and public trial by an impartial jury of the State and District wherein the crime shall have been committed." The right to a jury trial is guaranteed by law in all fifty states, and ten state constitutions guarantee a trial by jury for *all* criminal offenses.

In 1968, in *Duncan v. Louisiana,* the U.S. Supreme Court held that the right to a jury trial in "serious criminal cases" is "fundamental to the American scheme of justice," is protected under the Due Process Clause of the Fourteenth Amendment, and "must therefore be respected by the States" (*Duncan v. Louisiana,* 391 U.S. 145, 149 [1968]). The Supreme Court explained that the constitutional guarantee of a jury trial reflects a recognition that "community participation" in the criminal justice system provides a safeguard against the "unchecked power" of a "corrupt or overzealous prosecutor" as well as against the "compliant, biased or eccentric judge" and government officials who seek to "eliminate enemies" by bringing "unfounded criminal charges" (156).

The conviction of nineteen-year-old Gary Duncan illustrates why the right to a jury trial is so important. Duncan, an African American, had been arrested for touching the arm of a Caucasian student, who, along with three of his friends, was attempting to intimidate two African American students.

Duncan was sentenced to sixty days in jail and received a $150 fine for a simple battery, a criminal offense that was punishable by imprisonment for up to two years and a $300 fine. His request for a jury trial was denied on the grounds that the Louisiana Constitution provided for jury trials only for offenses that were punishable by capital punishment or imprisonment at hard labor. The Supreme Court followed the common law practice in England and in the American colonies and held that a jury trial is required for a "serious crime" that carries a sentence of more than six months in prison. Jury trials, on the other hand, are not required for crimes that are punishable by six months in prison or less. The Supreme Court clarified that the distinction between "serious" and "petty" offenses is based on the sentence that may be imposed under the criminal statute under which a defendant is charged rather than on the penalty that the judge actually imposes on the defendant at trial.

In *Baldwin v. New York,* the U.S. Supreme Court held that a New York City ordinance that prohibited jury trials in crimes with penalties punishable by up to one year in prison was unconstitutional. The Court ruled that "no offense can be deemed 'petty' for purposes of the right to a trial by jury where imprisonment for more than six months is authorized." The Supreme Court noted that New York City was the only jurisdiction that denied a jury trial to an individual charged with a crime carrying a prison term of over six months (*Baldwin v. New York,* 399 U.S. 66 [1970]).

The U.S. Supreme Court carved out a special rule for jury trials for criminal contempt. Individuals who do not comply with court orders may be charged with criminal contempt, and contempt statutes generally do not carry a fixed penalty. In *Codispoti v. Pennsylvania,* the Supreme Court held that an individual charged with contempt must be provided with a jury trial as a condition for imposing a punishment of more than six months in prison. In other words, in the case of contempt, the actual punishment dictates whether a jury trial is required (*Codispoti v. Pennsylvania,* 418 U.S. 506 [1974]).

In *Blanton v. City of North Las Vegas,* the U.S. Supreme Court affirmed that the Sixth Amendment does not guarantee a jury trial for "petty crimes or offenses" and that a jury trial accordingly is not required for the prosecution of these crimes under the Fourteenth Amendment. The Court, however, held that a defendant charged with an offense carrying a maximum prison term of six months or less may be entitled to a jury trial "if he can demonstrate" that the statute punishes the offense with additional penalties that "clearly reflect a legislative determination that the offense in question is a 'serious one.'" The Court applied this test and held that a defendant charged with driving under the influence (DUI) in Nevada is not entitled to a jury trial. The maximum prison sentence did not exceed six months, and the mandatory ninety-day license suspension ran concurrently with the prison sentence. The alternative sentence of forty-eight hours of community service while dressed in clothing identifying the individual as a DUI offender is less oppressive than a prison sentence. The possible $1,000 fine is below the $5,000 level established by the U.S. Congress in its definition of the statutory limit for a petty offense (*Blanton v. City of North Las Vegas,* 489 U.S. 538 [1989]). The Court later held that a DUI charge carrying a maximum penalty of six months in prison, a $5,000 fine, a five-year term of probation, and other penalties did not require a jury trial (*United States v. Nachtigal,* 507 U.S. 1 [1993]).

The last issue confronting the Supreme Court was whether a defendant is entitled to a jury trial in the event that he or she is charged with several counts of a crime that carries a statutory criminal penalty of six months or less. In *Lewis v. United States,* Lewis was charged with two counts of obstructing the mail, each charge carrying a criminal sentence of six months. The Supreme Court reasoned that the legislature categorized obstructing the mail as a petty offense and the fact that an individual is charged with two counts of a petty offense does not revise the legislative judgment that obstructing the mail is not a serious crime. The fact that an individual is charged with two or more counts does not transform obstructing the mail into a serious offense. The next issue is whether the traditional twelve-person jury is constitutionally required.

You can find Duncan v. Louisiana *under Chapter 2 on the study site, http://www.sagepub.com/lippmancp.*

The Twelve-Member Jury Requirement

In 1898, in *Thompson v. Utah,* the U.S. Supreme Court held that the Sixth Amendment follows the common law and guarantees an individual a jury composed of twelve persons, "neither more nor less" (*Thompson v. Utah,* 170 U.S. 343, 349 [1898]). Rule 23 of the Federal Rules of Criminal Procedure accordingly requires that a jury shall consist of twelve individuals. A majority of states follow the federal government in requiring twelve-person juries. In 1970, in *Williams v. Florida,* the Supreme Court reversed direction and held that the twelve-person requirement "cannot be regarded as an indispensable component of the Sixth Amendment" that is incorporated into the Due Process Clause of the Fourteenth Amendment. Justice White found little evidence in the history and language of the U.S. Constitution to support the view that the Framers intended to require juries to be composed of twelve individuals. White explained that Florida's six-person jury is able to perform the same functions as the common law twelve-person jury. The six-person jury is sufficiently large to represent a cross-section of the community and to insure a lively debate among competing points of view and to resist outside influences. This insures that a defendant's guilt or innocence will be fully considered by a cross-section of the community. The Court reviewed social science research and concluded that the decisions reached by twelve-person and six-person juries are not significantly different and that the size of the jury has little impact on the outcome of a case. The Court also noted that it is less time-consuming and less expensive to conduct trials with smaller juries (*Williams v. Florida,* 399 U.S. 78, 99–102 [1970]).

In 1978, in *Ballew v. Georgia,* the Supreme Court considered whether Georgia could constitutionally conduct criminal trials with juries of fewer than six persons. The Court concluded that a jury of fewer than six is less likely to represent the diversity of the community and is less likely to engage in vigorous debate and discussion than a six-person jury. Individuals in a smaller group who disagree with the majority may find themselves isolated and pressured into adopting the majority viewpoint. This may lead to inaccurate fact-finding and to inaccurate verdicts and risks convicting innocent individuals. Are you persuaded by the Supreme Court decision in *Ballew v. Georgia* that the five-person jury is constitutionally unacceptable while the six-person jury is acceptable? What is the basis for setting the bar at six rather than five persons? Following the decision in *Ballew,* we explore the process of selecting a jury.

Is it constitutional for Georgia to prosecute Ballew before a five-person jury?

Ballew v. Georgia, 435 U.S. 223 (1978), Blackmun, J.

Issue

This case presents the issue whether a state criminal trial to a jury of only five persons deprives the accused of the right to trial by jury guaranteed to him by the Sixth and Fourteenth Amendments. Our resolution of the issue requires an application of principles enunciated in *Williams v. Florida* where the use of a six-person jury in a state criminal trial was upheld against similar constitutional attack.

Facts

In November 1973, petitioner Claude Davis Ballew was the manager of the Paris Adult Theatre at 320 Peachtree Street, Atlanta, GA. On November 9, two investigators from the Fulton County Solicitor General's office viewed at the theater a motion picture film entitled *Behind the Green Door.* After they had seen the film, they obtained a warrant for its seizure, returned to the theater, viewed the film once again, and seized it. Petitioner and a cashier were arrested. Investigators returned to the theater on November 26, viewed the film in its entirety, secured still another warrant, and on November 27, once again viewed the motion picture and seized a second copy of the film. On September 14, 1974, petitioner was charged in a two-count misdemeanor accusation with "distributing obscene materials in violation of Georgia Code section 26-2101 in that the said accused did, knowing the obscene nature thereof, exhibit a motion picture film entitled 'Behind the Green Door' that contained obscene and indecent scenes...."

Petitioner was brought to trial in the Criminal Court of Fulton County. After a jury of five persons had been selected and sworn, petitioner moved that the court impanel a jury of twelve persons. That court, however, tried its misdemeanor cases before juries of five persons pursuant to Ga. Const., Art. 6, paragraph 16, section 1. Ballew contended that for an obscenity trial, a jury of only five was constitutionally inadequate to assess the contemporary standards of the community. He also argued that the Sixth and Fourteenth Amendments required a jury of at least six members in criminal cases. The motion for a twelve-person jury was overruled, and the trial went on to its conclusion before the five-person jury that had been impaneled. At the conclusion of the trial, the jury deliberated for thirty-eight minutes and returned a verdict of guilty on both counts of the accusation. The court imposed a sentence of one year and a $1,000 fine on each count, the periods of incarceration to run concurrently and to be suspended upon payment of the fines.

Petitioner took an appeal to the Court of Appeals of the State of Georgia....The court found no errors in the instructions, in the issuance of the warrants, or in the presence of the two convictions. In its consideration of the five-person-jury issue, the court noted that *Williams v. Florida* had not established a constitutional minimum number of jurors.

The Supreme Court of Georgia denied certiorari.

Reasoning

The Fourteenth Amendment guarantees the right of trial by jury in all state nonpetty criminal cases. The Court in *Duncan* applied this Sixth Amendment right to the States because "trial by jury in criminal cases is fundamental to the American scheme of justice." The right attaches in the present case because the maximum penalty...as it existed at the time of the alleged offenses, exceeded six months' imprisonment.

In *Williams v. Florida,* the Court reaffirmed that the "purpose of the jury trial, as we noted in *Duncan,* is to prevent oppression by the Government. 'Providing an accused with the right to be tried by a jury of his peers gave him an inestimable safeguard against the corrupt or overzealous prosecutor and against the compliant, biased, or eccentric judge.'" This purpose is attained by the participation of the community in determinations of guilt and by the application of the common sense of laymen who, as jurors, consider the case. Williams held that these functions and this purpose could be fulfilled by a jury of six members. As the Court's opinion in that case explained at some length, common law juries included twelve members by historical accident, "unrelated to the great purposes which gave rise to the jury in the first place." The Court's earlier cases that had assumed the number twelve to be constitutionally compelled were set to one side because they had not considered history and the function of the jury. Rather than requiring twelve members, then, the Sixth Amendment mandated a jury only of sufficient size to promote group deliberation, to insulate members from outside intimidation, and to provide a representative cross-section of the community. Although recognizing that by 1970, little empirical research had evaluated jury performance, the Court found no evidence that the reliability of jury verdicts diminished with six-member panels. Nor did the Court anticipate significant differences in result, including the frequency of "hung" juries. Because the reduction in size did not threaten exclusion of any particular class from jury roles, concern that the representative or cross-section character of the jury would suffer with a decrease to six members seemed "an unrealistic one." As a consequence, the six-person jury was held not to violate the Sixth and Fourteenth Amendments.

When the Court in *Williams* permitted the reduction in jury size—or, to put it another way, when it held that a jury of six was not unconstitutional—it expressly reserved ruling on the issue whether a number smaller than six passed constitutional scrutiny. The Court refused to speculate when this so-called "slippery slope" would become too steep. We face now, however, the twofold question whether a further reduction in the size of the state criminal trial jury does make the grade too dangerous, that is, whether it inhibits the functioning of the jury as an institution to a significant degree and, if so, whether any state interest counterbalances and justifies the disruption so as to preserve its constitutionality.

First, recent empirical data suggest that progressively smaller juries are less likely to foster effective group deliberation. At some point, this decline leads to inaccurate fact finding and incorrect application of the common sense of the community to the facts. Generally, a positive correlation exists between group size and the quality of both group performance and group productivity. A variety of explanations has been offered for this conclusion. Several are particularly applicable in the jury setting. The smaller the group, the less likely are members to make critical contributions necessary for the solution of a given problem. Because most juries are not permitted to take notes, memory is important for accurate jury deliberations. As juries decrease in size, then, they are less likely to have members who remember each of the important pieces of evidence or argument. Furthermore, the smaller the group, the less likely it is to overcome the biases of its members to obtain an accurate result. When individual and group decision making were compared, it was seen that groups performed better because prejudices of individuals were frequently counterbalanced, and objectivity resulted. Groups also exhibited increased motivation and self-criticism. All these advantages, except, perhaps, self-motivation, tend to diminish as the size of the group diminishes. Because juries frequently face complex problems laden with value choices, the benefits are important and should be retained. In particular, the counterbalancing of various biases is critical to the accurate application of the common sense of the community to the facts of any given case.

Second, the data now raise doubts about the accuracy of the results achieved by smaller and smaller panels. Statistical studies suggest that the risk of convicting an innocent person rises as the size of the jury diminishes.... As the size diminishes to five and below...there is an enlarged risk of the conviction of innocent defendants.

Another doubt about progressively smaller juries arises from the increasing inconsistency that results from the decreases. Third, the data suggest that the verdicts of jury deliberation in criminal cases will vary as juries become smaller and that the variance amounts to an imbalance to the detriment of one side, the defense....Fourth, what has just been said about the presence of minority viewpoint[s] as juries decrease in size foretells problems not only for jury decision making but also for the representation of minority groups in the community. The Court repeatedly has held that meaningful community participation cannot be attained with the exclusion of minorities or other identifiable groups from jury service. "It is part of the established tradition in the use of juries as instruments of public justice that the jury be a body truly representative of the community." The exclusion of elements of the community from participation "contravenes the very idea of a jury...composed of 'the peers or equals of the person whose rights it is selected or summoned to determine.'" Although the Court in *Williams* concluded that the six-person jury did not fail to represent adequately a cross-section of the community, the opportunity for meaningful and appropriate representation does decrease with the size of the panels. Thus, if a minority group constitutes 10 percent of the community, 53.1 percent of randomly selected six-member juries could be expected to have no minority representative among their members, and 89 percent not to have two. Further reduction in size will erect additional barriers to representation.

Fifth, several authors have identified in jury research methodological problems tending to mask differences in the operation of smaller and larger juries. For example, because the judicial system handles so many clear cases, decision makers will reach similar results through similar analyses most of the time. One study concluded that smaller and larger juries could disagree in their verdicts in no more than 14 percent of the cases. Disparities, therefore, appear in only small percentages. Nationwide, however, these small percentages will represent a large number of cases. And it is with respect to those cases that the jury trial right has its greatest value. When the case is close, and the guilt or innocence of the defendant is not readily apparent, a properly functioning jury system will insure evaluation by the sense of the community and will also tend to insure accurate fact finding.

While we adhere to, and reaffirm our holding in, *Williams v. Florida,* these studies, most of which have been made since *Williams* was decided in 1970, lead us to conclude that the purpose and functioning of the jury in a criminal trial is seriously impaired, and to a constitutional degree, by a reduction in size to below six members. We readily admit that we do not pretend to discern a clear line between six members and five. But the assembled data raise substantial doubt about the reliability and appropriate representation of panels smaller than six. Because of the fundamental importance of the jury trial to the American system of criminal justice, any further reduction that promotes inaccurate and possibly biased decision making, that causes untoward differences in verdicts, and that prevents juries from truly representing their communities, attains constitutional significance.

Georgia here presents no persuasive argument that a reduction to five does not offend important Sixth Amendment interests....Georgia argues that its use of five-member juries does not violate the Sixth and Fourteenth Amendments because they are used only in misdemeanor cases. . . . The problem with this argument is that the purpose and functions of the jury do not vary significantly with the importance of the crime. . . . In the present case, the possible deprivation of liberty is substantial. The State charged petitioner with misdemeanors, and he has been given concurrent sentences of imprisonment, each for one year, and fines totaling $2,000 have been imposed. We cannot conclude that there is less need for the imposition and the direction of the sense of the community in this case than when the State has chosen to label an offense a felony. The need for an effective jury here must be judged by the same standards announced and applied in *Williams v. Florida*. . . . Georgia submits that the five-person jury adequately represents the community because there is no arbitrary exclusion of any particular class. . . . But the data outlined above raise substantial doubt about the ability of juries truly to represent the community as membership decreases below six. If the smaller and smaller juries will lack consistency, as the cited studies suggest, then the sense of the community will not be applied equally in like cases. Not only is the representation of racial minorities threatened in such circumstances, but also majority attitude or various minority positions may be misconstrued or misapplied by the smaller groups.

The States utilize juries of less than twelve primarily for administrative reasons. Savings in court time and in financial costs are claimed to justify the reductions. The financial benefits of the reduction from twelve to six are substantial; this is mainly because fewer jurors draw daily allowances as they hear cases. On the other hand, the asserted saving in judicial time is not so clear. . . . If little time is gained by the reduction from twelve to six, less will be gained with a reduction from six to five. Perhaps this explains why only two States, Georgia and Virginia, have reduced the size of juries in certain nonpetty criminal cases to five. Other States appear content with six members or more. In short, the State has offered little or no justification for its reduction to five members.

Holding

Petitioner, therefore, has established that his trial on criminal charges before a five-member jury deprived him of the right to trial by jury guaranteed by the Sixth and Fourteenth Amendments.

Questions for Discussion

1. What criminal charge was brought against Ballew? Why did Ballew object to a five-person jury? Summarize the holding of the U.S. Supreme Court in *Ballew*.
2. Why did the U.S. Supreme Court approve of a six-person jury in *Williams* and disapprove of a five-person jury in *Ballew*?
3. The Supreme Court judgment in *Ballew* relies heavily on social science studies. How does this differ from the type of evidence that the Court relies on in other cases that you have read? Should the Court employ this type of data to reach a decision? Why did the Court decide not to base its decision in *Ballew* solely on the intent of the Framers of the Constitution and on the history of the jury trials in the United States?

Jury Selection

The jury pool, or **venire** (i.e., master list or jury list), from which a petit panel is selected typically is based on names drawn from voter registration lists or lists of taxpayers or lists of licensed drivers over eighteen years of age. Several states continue to rely on the key-man system. Under the key-man system, the individuals who serve on juries are drawn from a master list compiled by community notables. Individuals who are to serve on juries typically receive a summons directing them to appear at a designated time and place for jury service. In most jurisdictions, individuals will be asked to complete an information form that will help to determine their eligibility for jury service.

The Federal Jury Selection and Service Act of 1968, 28 U.S.C. §§ 1861–1862, 1865–1867, regulates the selection of grand juries and petit juries in the federal courts. Most state statutes follow this federal statute in proclaiming that all eligible individuals are to have the opportunity to be considered for jury service and have the obligation to serve when summoned for service. Several principles guide selection of the jury pool. The jury pool in the federal courts is drawn from the district in which the crime is committed, and within states, the jury pool is drawn from the geographic area in which the crime is committed. The following are some other basic guidelines for the selection of the jury venire.

Random selection. Individuals are to be selected in a random fashion.

Discrimination. Individuals shall not be excluded from service based on race, color, religion, sex, national origin, or economic status.

Fair cross-section. The individuals who are called to serve on the jury should reflect a cross-section of the community.

Exemption. Various individuals are ineligible to serve on a petit jury. This includes non-citizens; individuals less than eighteen years of age; individuals who are unable to read, write, and understand or speak English; individuals whose mental or physical condition prevents their service; and convicted felons. Various states exempt law enforcement officers, firefighters, and other individuals who serve a vital public function. Individuals may be temporarily excused as a result of illness or personal obligations.

Individuals who are called for jury service appear at the courthouse and are randomly assigned to courtrooms. The questioning of individuals to determine who is to serve on the jury is called **voir dire,** or "to speak the truth." The prosecutor and defense attorney may remove individuals from the jury pool based on a **peremptory challenge** (without offering a reason) or based on a **challenge for cause** (based on bias or prejudice). A lawyer is not required to offer a reason for exercising a peremptory challenge. A challenge for cause requires a reason. The grounds for a challenge for cause typically are stated in a statute. This ordinarily includes a prohibition against individuals serving on the jury who sat on the grand jury, who are acquainted with an individual involved in the case, or who are related to an individual in the case. A defense attorney or prosecutor also may strike an individual for cause when the lawyer satisfies the judge that the individual cannot be fair (actual bias) or when an individual's background or experience indicates that he or she likely will not be impartial (implied bias). An example of actual bias is an individual who states on voir dire that he or she cannot be fair to a defendant. Implied bias may arise in a criminal case when a potential juror recently has been the victim of the same crime with which the defendant is charged.

The next sections discuss the prohibition against discrimination in the selection of jurors. We first discuss the protections provided by the Equal Protection Clause and then examine the Sixth Amendment cross-section requirement and outline the constitutional protections surrounding voir dire.

Equal Protection Clause

The Equal Protection Clause of the Fourteenth Amendment provides that "[n]o State shall...deny to any person within its jurisdiction the equal protection of the law." The U.S. Supreme Court has interpreted the Equal Protection Clause as prohibiting the intentional exclusion of individuals from jury service because of their race, ethnicity, gender, or religion. In *Strauder v. West Virginia,* the Supreme Court held a statute unconstitutional that limited jury service to "white male persons." The Court, however, also held that the diversity of the American population made it unrealistic to obligate the State to take affirmative steps to insure that each jury is composed of members of various racial, religious, ethnic, or gender groups (*Strauder v. West Virginia,* 100 U.S. 303 [1879]). In 1881, the Supreme Court held that the Equal Protection Clause was violated by a Delaware County jury-selection system that, although not listing race as a criterion for jury service, was administered in a discriminatory fashion and resulted in only Caucasian citizens being called to serve on local juries (*Neal v. Delaware,* 143 U.S. 370 [1881]).

The impact of these two decisions in insuring that juries are selected in a fair and impartial fashion is limited by the requirement that defendants alleging discrimination in the jury-selection process demonstrate an intent to discriminate. In *Norris v. Alabama,* the U.S. Supreme Court recognized that a prima facie (presumptive) case of purposeful discrimination may be established by the **rule of exclusion,** the substantial underrepresentation of a group in the jury venire as compared with the percentage of the group in the community.

An inference of discrimination is strengthened by a finding that the locality employs a jury-selection system that may be easily manipulated so as to exclude members of a particular group. Once a prima facie case is established, the burden shifts to the State or locality to offer concrete facts to support the claim that the government did not discriminate and that the underrepresentation is due to factors such as the failure of individuals to register to vote or the failure of individuals to obtain driver's licenses (*Norris,* 294 U.S. 587 [1935]).

In *Turner v. Fouche,* the U.S. Supreme Court held that a prima facie case of discrimination was established in a Georgia county in which sixty percent of the population was African American and only thirty-seven percent of the jury list was African American. The Court was particularly troubled by the fact that 171 of the 178 persons disqualified for lack of "intelligence" or "uprightness" were African Americans, indicating that the underrepresentation of African Americans at least in part resulted from the "subjective" process employed to compile the jury list (*Turner v. Fouche,* 396 U.S. 346 [1970]).

As the Supreme Court noted in *Casteneda v. Partida* in finding a prima facie case of discrimination against Hispanics in Texas, it is unlikely that a large disparity in the racial representation of a group resulted from chance or from an accident. The Supreme Court concluded in *Partida* that in the absence of an explanation by the Government for the underrepresentation of Hispanics, the only conclusion that reasonably can be reached is that the disparity resulted from intentional discrimination by governmental officials (*Castaneda v. Partido,* 430 U.S. 482 [1977]).

Cross-Section of the Community

The U.S. Supreme Court, in *Glasser v. United States,* held that the Sixth Amendment requires that a federal jury be drawn from a fair cross-section of the community in which the crime has been committed (*Glasser v. United States,* 315 U.S. 60 [1942]). The Federal Jury Selection and Service Act of 1968, 28 U.S.C. §§ 1861–1869, repeats the requirement that a jury is to be drawn from a "fair cross-section of the community." There are at least four reasons for this requirement.

Decision making. The jury should represent the commonsense judgment of a cross-section of the community. This protects the defendant from the "overzealous or mistaken prosecutor" and "biased" judge.

Impartial jury. The **fair cross-section requirement** prevents the Government from "packing" the jury with pro-prosecution jurors and insures that neither the prosecution nor the defense has an advantage.

Unfairness. The appearance of unfairness should be avoided at trial.

Civil rights. The right of historically disadvantaged groups to exercise their political rights and to serve on juries should be safeguarded.

In 1975, in *Taylor v. Louisiana,* the U.S. Supreme Court held that the Sixth Amendment fair cross-section requirement is explicitly incorporated into the Fourteenth Amendment and is applicable to the States (*Taylor v. Louisiana,* 419 U.S. 522 [1975]). In *Taylor,* the Supreme Court struck down a Louisiana law that stated that in order to be eligible for jury service, a woman was required to file a declaration stating that she was willing to serve. Men were not required to file a similar declaration. This procedure resulted in the exclusion of fifty-three percent of eligible voters. In practice, very few women were available for jury service, and in Taylor's case, no women were among the 175 persons in the jury pool. The Supreme Court stated that a primary purpose of a jury is to represent the "commonsense judgment of the community." The Court concluded that Taylor's Sixth Amendment right had been violated and held that a defendant may challenge the selection of a jury on the grounds that the venire does not include a cross-section of the community despite the fact that the defendant is not a member of the group that is excluded or underrepresented (*Taylor v. Louisiana,* 419 U.S. 522 [1975]).

The U.S. Supreme Court articulated the test for Sixth Amendment cross-section challenges in *Duren v. Missouri.* The Court held that there are three criteria for a fair cross-section challenge to the jury venire.

Group. The group to be excluded is a "distinctive" group in the community. Large and distinctive groups are to be represented in the jury venire.

Representation. The representation of the group in the venire from which the jury is selected is "not fair and reasonable in relation to the number of such persons in the community."

Systematic exclusion. The underrepresentation is a result of the systematic exclusion of the group from the jury-selection process. The flawed selection process has resulted in underrepresentation of a group for a number of months and not merely in a single trial.

The burden shifts to the prosecution once the defendant establishes a prima facie case. The prosecution is required to demonstrate that a "significant state interest is manifestly and primarily advanced by those aspects of the jury selection process, such as exemption criteria, that result in the disproportionate exclusion of a distinctive group" (367). In other words, the Government must establish that there is a persuasive reason for relying on a selection process that consistently excludes a group from jury service.

In *Duren,* Missouri law permitted women to exempt themselves from jury service. As a result, women comprised fifty-four percent of the local community and constituted only fifteen percent of individuals eligible to serve on juries. The Supreme Court held that this underrepresentation could not be justified on the grounds that jury service would take women from their household responsibilities and impose a hardship on their families. The Court stressed that the administrative convenience in "dealing with women as a class is insufficient justification for diluting the quality of community judgment represented by the jury in criminal trials." A woman that has responsibilities at home can always apply for an individual exemption from jury service and should not be able to exempt herself automatically from jury service by filing a declaration (*Duren v. Missouri,* 439 U.S. 367 [1979]).

The Sixth Amendment cross-section requirement protects distinctive groups, and courts thus far have limited this protection to women and racial and ethnic minorities. Efforts to provide for a broader representation of college students, young people, factory workers, and the less educated generally have proven unsuccessful.

Most courts have held that a disparity of at least ten percent or more between the percentage of a group in the population and the percentage of a group in the jury pool is required to meet the underrepresentation requirement.

Keep in mind that there are several major differences between a claim of a violation of the Equal Protection Clause and a claim under the Sixth Amendment that a jury is drawn from a venire that does not represent a cross-section of the community.

Group membership. A defendant relying on the Equal Protection Clause is required to establish that members of a racial, ethnic, religious, or gender group of which they are a member are underrepresented on the jury venire. A defendant relying on the Sixth Amendment may appeal on the grounds that a jury does not represent a cross-section of the community despite the fact that the defendant is not a member of the underrepresented group.

Intent to discriminate. The defendant in an action based on the Equal Protection Clause is required to establish a prima facie case based on an intent to discriminate and the exclusion of a group from the jury pool. The defendant in a motion for a failure to represent a cross-section of the community is required to demonstrate a prima facie case based on the systematic exclusion of a fair and reasonable number of members of a group over a period of several months from the jury pool.

Legal actions based on a violation of the Equal Protection Clause and legal actions based on the Sixth Amendment are directed at the venires from which the members of a jury are selected. A defendant is not guaranteed the representation of particular groups on the petit jury at trial. We next turn to the selection of the individuals who will serve on the petit jury at trial.

Voir Dire

The fact that a jury pool is created in a nondiscriminatory fashion and reflects a cross-section of the community does not guarantee that every member of the venire is willing and able to fairly and objectively weigh and balance the evidence at trial. The Supreme Court has recognized that voir dire is of the utmost importance in insuring the protection of a criminal defendant's Sixth Amendment right to an impartial jury. The voir dire involves questioning the potential jurors to determine whether they should be excluded for cause or whether the lawyer should exercise a peremptory challenge and exclude the juror "without cause." Keep in mind that lawyers also use voir dire to establish a personal connection with potential jurors who will be asked to weigh and to evaluate the evidence presented by the lawyer during the trial.

Rule 24 of the Federal Rules of Criminal Procedure provides that a judge may examine prospective jurors or may permit the lawyers to conduct the voir dire. In the event that the judge conducts the voir dire, he or she may permit the lawyers to ask additional questions or to submit questions. States adopt various approaches to the role of judges and lawyers during voir dire. It is argued that lawyers are so concerned about the impartiality of jurors that they ask more questions than is necessary and consume valuable time selecting the jury. Lawyers, on the other hand, typically argue that judges do not take the time required to fully explore a potential juror's background and attitudes.

The courts, other than in cases in which race or ethnicity is a prominent part of a trial, have established very few legal rules regarding the questions that may be asked on voir dire. This is based on the belief that the trial court judge is in the best position to evaluate the questions that are required to reveal whether a juror is fair and impartial and that the lawyers or judge should be free to ask whatever questions the judge believes will be helpful in revealing the jurors' attitudes and beliefs.

The most important U.S. Supreme Court case regarding racial prejudice and voir dire is *Ham v. South Carolina*. In *Ham,* an African American civil rights worker was convicted of possessing marijuana. The trial judge conducted the voir dire and asked general questions concerning whether jurors were able to maintain fairness and objectivity and to remain impartial. The judge refused to ask the specific questions proposed by the defense attorney regarding whether the jurors were prejudiced against the defendant because of his race or because he wore a beard. Chief Justice Rehnquist held that a central purpose of the Due Process Clause of the Fourteenth Amendment is to insure that trials are conducted in accordance with the "essential demands of fairness" and to prohibit States from "invidiously discriminating on the basis of race." Justice Rehnquist accordingly ruled that the Fourteenth Amendment required the trial judge in *Ham* to question the jurors on the subject of racial prejudice. Justice Rehnquist stated that the judge was not required to "put the questions in any particular form, or to ask any particular number of questions on the subject." On the other hand, there is no requirement to inquire into the prospective jurors' bias against beards. Facial hair is one of a number of possible biases that a juror may possess, and there is no constitutional requirement that a court explore every possible prejudice (*Ham v. South Carolina,* 409 U.S. 524, 526 [1973]).

Ham has been narrowly interpreted by the U.S. Supreme Court. In *Ristaino v. Ross,* an African American defendant was charged with armed robbery, assault with a dangerous weapon, and assault with the intent to murder a Caucasian victim. Justice Powell held that *Ham* did not announce a rule of "universal applicability," and the fact that the defendant and victim were of different races did not require that questions should be posed to potential jurors regarding race. Race in *Ristaino* was not at the center of the trial and was unlikely to "distort the verdict." A crucial fact in *Ham* was that the defendant was a controversial community activist who claimed that white jurors would not afford him a fair trial (*Ristaino v. Ross,* 424 U.S. 589, 596 [1976]).

At least four Supreme Court judges have endorsed the view that where a violent crime involves individuals of different racial and ethnic groups, there is a "reasonable probability" that racial or ethnic prejudice will infect the trial and that the trial court judge should pose questions regarding racial prejudice (*Rosales-Lopez v. United States,* 451 U.S. 182, 192 [1981]). In *Turner v. Murray,* the U.S. Supreme Court held that a defendant accused of an interracial crime carrying the death penalty is entitled to have prospective jurors informed of the victim's race and to have prospective jurors questioned regarding racial bias. The Supreme Court judges noted that the "risk of racial prejudice infecting a capital sentencing proceeding is especially serious" in light of the "discretion given the jury at the death-penalty hearing" and the "complete finality of the death sentence" (*Turner v. Murray,* 476 U.S. 28, 35 [1986]).

The selection of jurors in death penalty cases has been of particular concern to the U.S. Supreme Court. As you may recall, the jury first determines whether an individual is guilty or not guilty of the criminal charge. The next step is the sentencing phase at which the jury determines whether to impose a sentence of death or to impose a sentence of life imprisonment. The Court has held that potential jurors may be excluded *for cause* who during voir dire state that they are unwilling to vote for the death penalty. These jurors, according to the Supreme Court, have indicated that they are unwilling to follow the judge's instructions to impose capital punishment in those cases in which the statutory standard is satisfied (*Witherspoon v. Illinois,* 391 U.S. 510 [1968]). The Supreme Court later broadened the grounds for excluding jurors for cause and authorized the exclusion of individuals whose views would "prevent or substantially impair" their willingness to impose capital punishment (*Wainwright v. Witt,* 469 U.S. 412 [1985]). In 2007, in *Uttecht v. Brown,* the Supreme Court upheld a Washington court's granting of a prosecution motion to exclude a juror for cause who indicated that while he did not categorically oppose the death penalty, he could not impose the death penalty unless he was persuaded beyond a "shadow of a doubt" that the offender would kill once again if released. The Supreme Court concluded that the trial court reasonably concluded that the juror would be "substantially impaired" in imposing the death penalty and that the juror was properly removed for cause. Justice Stevens, in his dissent, argued that the juror only expressed the intelligent view that he could impose the death penalty only under certain specific circumstances and had never indicated that he was incapable of following the state laws regarding the death penalty (*Uttecht v. Brown,* 551 U.S. 1 [2007]).

In the next case in the text, *Lockhart v. McCree,* the U.S. Supreme Court considers whether individuals who state that they are unwilling to impose the death penalty may be excluded from the jury at the "guilt phase" of the trial or whether these jurors are required to be excluded only from the sentencing phase of the trial. What is your view regarding "death-qualified juries" in capital punishment cases?

Are death-qualified juries required at the guilt phase of capital punishment cases?

Lockhart v. McCree, 476 U.S. 162 (1986), Rehnquist, C.J.

Issue

In this case, we address the question left open by our decision nearly eighteen years ago in *Witherspoon v. Illinois:* Does the Constitution prohibit the removal for cause, prior to the guilt phase of a bifurcated capital trial, of prospective jurors whose opposition to the death penalty is so strong that it would prevent or substantially impair the performance of their duties as jurors at the sentencing phase of the trial? We hold that it does not.

Facts

On the morning of February 14, 1978, a combination gift shop and service station in Camden, Arkansas, was robbed, and Evelyn Boughton, the owner, was shot and killed. That afternoon, Ardia McCree was arrested in Hot Springs, Arkansas, after a police officer saw him driving a maroon and white Lincoln Continental matching an eyewitness's description of the getaway car used by Boughton's killer. The next evening, McCree admitted to police that he had been at Boughton's shop at the time of the murder. He claimed, however, that a tall black stranger wearing an overcoat first asked him for a ride, then took McCree's rifle out of the back of the car and used it to kill Boughton. McCree also claimed that, after the murder, the stranger rode with McCree to a nearby dirt road, got out of the car, and walked away with the rifle. McCree's story was contradicted by two eyewitnesses who saw McCree's car between the time of the murder and the time when McCree said the stranger got out and walked away, and who stated that they saw only one person in the car. The police found McCree's rifle and a bank bag from Boughton's shop alongside the dirt road. Based on ballistics tests, a Federal Bureau of Investigation officer testified that the bullet that killed Boughton had been fired from McCree's rifle.

McCree was charged with capital felony murder. In accordance with Arkansas law, the trial judge at voir dire removed for cause, over McCree's objections, those prospective jurors who stated that they could not under any circumstances vote for the imposition of the death penalty. Eight prospective jurors were excluded for this reason. The jury convicted McCree of capital felony murder, but rejected the State's request for the death penalty, instead setting McCree's punishment at life imprisonment without parole.

The district court held a hearing on the "death qualification" issue in July 1981, receiving in evidence numerous social science studies concerning the attitudes and beliefs of "*Witherspoon*-excludables," along with the potential effects of excluding them from the jury prior to the guilt phase of a bifurcated capital trial. In August 1983, the court concluded, based on the social science evidence, that "death qualification" produced juries that "were more prone to convict" capital defendants than "non-death-qualified" juries. The court ruled that "death qualification" thus violated both the fair-cross-section and impartiality requirements of the Sixth and Fourteenth Amendments, and granted McCree habeas relief. The Eighth Circuit found "substantial evidentiary support" for the district court's conclusion that the removal for cause of "*Witherspoon*-excludables" resulted in "conviction-prone" juries, and affirmed the grant of habeas relief on the ground that such removal for cause violated McCree's constitutional right to a jury selected from a fair cross-section of the community.

Reasoning

Of the six studies introduced by McCree that at least purported to deal with the central issue in this case, namely, the potential effects on the determination of guilt or innocence of excluding "*Witherspoon* excludables" from the jury, three were also before this Court when it decided *Witherspoon*. There, this Court reviewed the studies and concluded:

> The data adduced by the petitioner...are too tentative and fragmentary to establish that jurors not opposed to the death penalty tend to favor the prosecution in the determination of guilt. We simply cannot conclude, either on the basis of the record now before us or as a matter of judicial notice, that the exclusion of jurors opposed to capital punishment results in an unrepresentative jury on the issue of guilt or substantially increases the risk of conviction.

The Court accordingly concluded that in "light of the presently available information, we are not prepared to announce a per se constitutional rule requiring the reversal of every conviction returned by a jury selected as this one was."

It goes almost without saying that if these studies were "too tentative and fragmentary" to make out a claim of constitutional error in 1968, the same studies, unchanged but for having aged some eighteen years, are still insufficient to make out such a claim in this case.

Nor do the three post-*Witherspoon* studies introduced by McCree on the "death qualification" issue provide substantial support for the "per se constitutional rule" McCree asks this Court to adopt. All three of the "new" studies were based on the responses of individuals randomly selected from some segment of the population but who were not actual jurors sworn under oath to apply the law to the facts of an actual case involving the fate of an actual capital defendant. We have serious doubts about the value of these studies in predicting the behavior of actual jurors. In addition, two of the three "new" studies did not even attempt to simulate the process of jury deliberation, and none of the "new" studies was able to predict to what extent, if any, the presence of one or more "*Witherspoon* excludables" on a guilt-phase jury would have altered the outcome of the guilt determination.

Finally, and most importantly, only one of the six "death qualification" studies introduced by McCree even attempted to identify and account for the presence of so-called "nullifiers," or individuals who, because of their deep-seated opposition to the death penalty, would be unable to decide a capital defendant's guilt or innocence fairly and impartially. McCree concedes...that studies that fail to take into account the presence of such "nullifiers" thus are fatally flawed. Surely, a "per se constitutional rule" as far reaching as the one McCree proposes should not be based on the results of the lone study that avoids this fundamental flaw.

Having identified some of the more serious problems with McCree's studies, however, we will assume for purposes of this opinion that the studies are both methodologically valid and adequate to establish that "death qualification" in fact produces juries somewhat more "conviction-prone" than "non-death-qualified" juries. We hold, nonetheless, that the Constitution does not prohibit the States from "death qualifying" juries in capital cases.

The Eighth Circuit ruled that "death qualification" violated McCree's right under the Sixth Amendment, as applied to the States via incorporation through the Fourteenth Amendment, to a jury selected from a representative cross-section of the community. But we do not believe that the fair-cross-section requirement can, or should, be applied as broadly as that court attempted to apply it. We have never invoked the fair-cross-section principle to invalidate the use of either for-cause or peremptory challenges to prospective jurors, or to require petit juries, as opposed to jury panels or venires, to reflect the composition of the community at large. The limited scope of the fair-cross-section requirement is a direct and inevitable consequence of the practical impossibility of providing each criminal defendant with a truly "representative" petit jury. We remain convinced that an extension of the fair-cross-section requirement to petit juries would be unworkable and unsound, and we decline McCree's invitation to adopt such an extension.

But even if we were willing to extend the fair-cross-section requirement to petit juries, we would still reject the Eighth Circuit's conclusion that "death qualification" violates that requirement. The essence of a "fair-cross-section" claim is the systematic exclusion of "a 'distinctive' group in the community." In our view, groups defined solely in terms of shared attitudes that would prevent or substantially impair members of the group from performing one of their duties as jurors, such as the "*Witherspoon* excludables" at issue here, are not "distinctive groups" for fair-cross-section purposes.

Our prior jury-representativeness cases, whether based on the fair-cross-section component of the Sixth Amendment or the Equal Protection Clause of the Fourteenth Amendment, have involved such groups as blacks, women, and Mexican Americans. The wholesale exclusion of these large groups from jury service clearly contravened all three of the aforementioned purposes of the fair-cross-section requirement. Because these groups were excluded for reasons completely unrelated to the ability of members of the group to serve as jurors in a particular case, the exclusion raised at least the possibility that the composition of juries would be arbitrarily skewed in such a way as to deny criminal defendants the benefit of the commonsense judgment of the community. In addition, the exclusion from jury service of large groups of individuals not on the basis of their inability to serve as jurors, but on the basis of some immutable characteristic such as race, gender, or ethnic background, undeniably gave rise to an "appearance of unfairness." Finally, such exclusion improperly deprived members of these often historically disadvantaged groups of their right as citizens to serve on juries in criminal cases.

The group of "*Witherspoon* excludables" involved in the case at bar differs significantly from the groups we have previously recognized as "distinctive." "Death qualification," unlike the wholesale exclusion of blacks, women, or Mexican Americans from jury service, is carefully designed to serve the State's concededly legitimate interest in obtaining a single jury that can properly and impartially apply the law to the facts of the case at both the guilt and sentencing phases of a capital trial. There is very little danger, therefore, and McCree does not even argue, that "death qualification" was instituted as a means for the State to arbitrarily skew the composition of capital-case juries.

Furthermore, unlike blacks, women, and Mexican Americans, "*Witherspoon* excludables" are singled out for exclusion in capital cases on the basis of an attribute that is within the individual's control. It is important to remember that not all who oppose the death penalty are subject to removal for cause in capital cases; those who firmly believe that the death penalty is unjust may nevertheless serve as jurors in capital cases so long as they state clearly that they are willing to temporarily set aside their own beliefs in deference to the rule of law. Because the group of "*Witherspoon* excludables" includes only those who cannot and will not conscientiously obey the law with respect to one of the issues in a capital case, "death qualification" hardly can be said to create an "appearance of unfairness."

Finally, the removal for cause of "*Witherspoon* excludables" in capital cases does not prevent them from serving as jurors in other criminal cases, and thus leads to no substantial deprivation of their basic rights of citizenship. They are treated no differently than any juror who expresses the view that he would be unable to follow the law in a particular case. "*Witherspoon* excludables," or for that matter any other group defined solely in terms of shared attitudes that render members of the group unable to serve as jurors in a particular case, may be excluded from jury service without contravening any of the basic objectives of the fair-cross-section requirement. It is for this reason that we conclude that "*Witherspoon* excludables" do not constitute a "distinctive group" for fair-cross-section purposes, and hold that "death qualification" does not violate the fair-cross-section requirement.

McCree argues that even if we reject the Eighth Circuit's fair-cross-section holding, we should affirm the judgment below on the alternative ground, adopted by the district court, that "death qualification" violated his constitutional right to an impartial jury. McCree concedes that the individual jurors who served at his trial were impartial, as that term was defined by this Court. In short, McCree does not claim that his conviction was tainted by any of the kinds of jury bias or partiality that we have previously recognized as violative of the Constitution. Instead, McCree argues that his jury lacked impartiality because the absence of "*Witherspoon* excludables" "slanted" the jury in favor of conviction.

We do not agree. McCree's "impartiality" argument apparently is based on the theory that because all individual jurors are to some extent predisposed towards one result or another, a constitutionally impartial *jury* can be constructed only by "balancing" the various predispositions of the individual *jurors*. Thus, according to McCree, when the State "tips the scales" by excluding prospective jurors with a particular viewpoint, an impermissibly partial jury results. We have consistently rejected this view of jury impartiality, including as recently as last term when we squarely held that an impartial jury consists of nothing more than "jurors who will conscientiously apply the law and find the facts."

The view of jury impartiality urged upon us by McCree is both illogical and hopelessly impractical. On a more practical level, if it were true that the Constitution required a certain mix of individual viewpoints on the jury, then trial judges would be required to undertake the Sisyphean task of "balancing" juries, making sure that each contains the proper number of Democrats and Republicans, young persons and old persons, white-collar executives and blue-collar laborers, and so on. Adopting McCree's concept of jury impartiality would also likely require the elimination of peremptory challenges, which are commonly used by both the State and the defendant to attempt to produce a jury favorable to the challenger.

Holding

In our view, it is simply not possible to define jury impartiality, for constitutional purposes, by reference to some hypothetical mix of individual viewpoints. Prospective jurors come from many different backgrounds, and have many different attitudes and predispositions. But the Constitution presupposes that a jury selected from a fair cross-section of the community is impartial, regardless of the mix of individual viewpoints actually represented on the jury, so long as the jurors can conscientiously and properly carry out their sworn duty to apply the law to the facts of the particular case. We hold that McCree's jury satisfied both aspects of this constitutional standard.

Dissenting, *Marshall, J.*, joined by *Brennan, J.*, and *Stevens, J.*

Respondent contends here that the "death-qualified" jury that convicted him, from which the State, as authorized by *Witherspoon,* had excluded all venirepersons unwilling to consider imposing the death penalty, was in effect "organized to return a verdict" of guilty. In support of this claim, he has presented overwhelming evidence that death-qualified juries are substantially more likely to convict or to convict on more serious charges than juries on which unalterable opponents of capital punishment are permitted to serve. Respondent does not challenge the application of *Witherspoon* to the jury in the sentencing stage of bifurcated capital cases. Neither does he demand that individuals unable to assess culpability impartially ("nullifiers") be permitted to sit on capital juries. All he asks is the chance to have his guilt or innocence determined by a jury like those that sit in noncapital cases—one whose composition has not been tilted in favor of the prosecution by the exclusion of a group of prospective jurors uncommonly aware of an accused's constitutional rights but quite capable of determining his culpability without favor or bias.

The data strongly suggest that death qualification excludes a significantly large subset—at least 11 percent to 17 percent—of potential jurors who could be impartial during the guilt phase of trial. Among the members of this excludable class are a disproportionate number of blacks and women.

The perspectives on the criminal justice system of jurors who survive death qualification are systematically different from those of the excluded jurors. Death-qualified jurors are, for example, more likely to believe that a defendant's failure to testify is indicative of his guilt, more hostile to the insanity defense, more mistrustful of defense attorneys, and less concerned about the danger of erroneous convictions. This pro-prosecution bias is reflected in the greater readiness of death-qualified jurors to convict or to convict on more serious charges. And, finally, the very process of death qualification—which focuses attention on the death penalty before the trial has even begun—has been found to predispose the jurors that survive it to believe that the defendant is guilty.

The evidence thus confirms, and is itself corroborated by, the more intuitive judgments of scholars and of so many of the participants in capital trials—judges, defense attorneys, and prosecutors. The chief strength of respondent's evidence lies in the essential unanimity of the results obtained by researchers using diverse subjects and varied methodologies. Even the Court's haphazard jabs cannot obscure the power of the array. The true impact of death qualification on the fairness of a trial is likely even more devastating than the studies show.

Faced with the near unanimity of authority supporting respondent's claim that death qualification gives the prosecution a particular advantage in the guilt phase of capital trials, the majority here makes but a weak effort to contest that proposition. Instead, it merely assumes for the purposes of this opinion "that 'death qualification' in fact produces juries somewhat more 'conviction-prone' than 'non-death-qualified' juries," and then holds that this result does not offend the Constitution. This disregard for the clear import of the evidence tragically misconstrues the settled constitutional principles that guarantee a defendant the right to a fair trial and an impartial jury whose composition is not biased toward the prosecution.

Questions for Discussion

1. Explain the reason that McCree appealed his conviction for capital felony murder. What was the holding of the U.S. Supreme Court in *McCree*?
2. What did McCree hope to establish by introducing social science studies of jury decision making?
3. Why did the Supreme Court reject McCree's argument that the jury did not represent a fair cross-section of the community?
4. How did the majority of the Supreme Court respond to McCree's argument that the jury was not impartial?
5. Summarize the views of the dissenting judges. Do you agree with the dissent or with the majority?

Peremptory Challenges

The exclusion of individuals who state that they are unwilling to impose the death penalty is only one example of the exclusion of individuals for cause. The thinking is that a juror who has his or her "mind made up" cannot fairly and impartially weigh the evidence, should not serve on the jury, and should be struck for cause. In other cases, an individual's background and personal relationships may lead a judge to agree with a lawyer that a potential juror cannot be fair. This may arise when an individual is married to a police officer, has a child who is a police officer, or has been the victim of the same crime with which the defendant is charged. Once individuals have been removed for cause, the lawyers may exercise their peremptory challenges. A peremptory challenge is a challenge that is "exercised without a reason stated, without inquiry, and without being subject to the court's control." Peremptory challenges, although not required by the U.S. Constitution, historically have been considered fundamental to a fair trial and "one of the most important of the rights secured to the accused" (*Swain v. Alabama,* 380 U.S. 202, 219, 220 [1965]).

Rule 24(b) of the Federal Rules of Criminal Procedure provides both the prosecution and the defense with twenty peremptory challenges in a death-penalty case. In a trial for an offense punishable by imprisonment for more than one year, the government may exercise six peremptory challenges, and the defendant or defendants may exercise ten peremptory challenges. The defense and prosecution each are provided with three peremptory challenges in the case of an offense punishable by no more than one year or by a fine or both. State statutes and state rules of procedure generally provide both the defense and the prosecution with an equal number of peremptory challenges. Why are peremptory challenges viewed as essential to a fair trial?

Impartial trial. Both the defense and prosecution should be permitted to exclude people who they believe will be unfair despite the fact that they cannot point to specific facts and circumstances to support this conclusion. Peremptory challenges also promote the perception that the jury is fair.

Voir dire. A lawyer or judge may closely question a juror who, in the end, is not excluded for cause. This may lead the juror to become irritated or frustrated, and the lawyer may conclude that the best course is to remove the individual from the jury panel.

Judges historically placed very few limitations on peremptory challenges by lawyers. In 1965, in *Swain v. Alabama,* Swain challenged the selection of the jury in Talladega County, Alabama, that sentenced him to death. He alleged that peremptory challenges had been used in the county to exclude every African American called for jury service since 1950. The Supreme Court held that lawyers were free to exclude jurors based on race, religion, gender, ethnicity, or hair or eye color. The belief was that a lawyer had the right to act in the "best interest" of his or her client and that the lawyer properly may conclude that minorities would be unsympathetic to his or her client and exclude them from the jury. The only limitation was that the Equal Protection Clause prohibited excluding jurors based on an intent to discriminate on account of race, gender, or ethnicity. In the case of Talledega County, there simply was not enough information to determine the reason for excluding African Americans from jury service. Do you agree with the decision in *Swain* that the Equal Protection Clause does not prohibit a prosecutor from relying on peremptory challenges to strike African Americans or Hispanics from a jury? (*Swain v. Alabama,* 380 U.S. 202 [1965]).

In 1986, in *Batson v. Kentucky,* the Supreme Court reconsidered its decision in *Swain* and changed course. In *Batson,* the prosecutor used his peremptory challenges to remove all four African Americans from the jury venire, and Batson was convicted by an "all-white jury" of second-degree burglary and of receipt of stolen goods. The Supreme Court held that the Equal Protection Clause prohibits a prosecutor from challenging potential jurors "solely on account of their race...on the assumption that black jurors as a group will be unable to impartially consider the State's case against a black defendant." In other words, a peremptory challenge must be based on a factor other than race, and a lawyer may not exclude potential jurors on account of their race (*Batson v. Kentucky,* 476 U.S. 79 [1986]).

Batson established a three-part approach to be followed by a defendant claiming that peremptory challenges were used in discriminatory fashion.

Defendant. The defendant first is required to demonstrate facts or circumstances from which it may be inferred that potential jurors have been excluded based on race. This includes an analysis of the race of the jurors who are struck and of the race of the jurors who remain on the venire as well as an analysis of the types of questions that were asked by the prosecutor.

Prosecutor. In the event that the defendant establishes a prima facie case of discrimination, the prosecutor must provide a "race-neutral explanation" for the exercise of his or her peremptory challenges. This requires an explanation that each potential minority juror was removed based on some factor or factors that the prosecutor believes will interfere with the individual's fair and impartial evaluation of the evidence and that the removal was not based on race. In *Purkett v. Elm,* the Supreme Court upheld a prosecutor's exclusion of two African American jurors based on the fact that one juror had long hair and the other facial hair. The Court stressed that this is a characteristic that may be equally applicable to Caucasian as well as to African American jurors and does not indicate a racially discriminatory motive. It is not a defense for the prosecutor merely to deny that his or her actions were based on a discriminatory motive (*Purkett v. Elm,* 514 U.S. 765 [1995]).

Judge. The judge determines whether the prosecutor's explanation is the real reason for exercising the "strikes" or whether the exclusion of jurors was racially motivated. The judge may find that a "fantastic explanation" is a "pretext" or "mask" for racial discrimination.

In *Powers v. Ohio,* the Supreme Court ruled that a defendant of one race may file an appeal based on the exclusion of individuals of a different race from the jury. The Court reasoned that the defendant's appeal served the public interest in the integrity of the criminal justice system by protecting the right of all individuals to serve on juries (*Powers v. Ohio,* 499 U.S. 400 [1991]). In 1995, in *Georgia v. McCollum,* the Supreme Court held that a prosecutor as well as a defense attorney may challenge the exercise of peremptory challenges on the grounds that the challenges were racially motivated (*Georgia v. McCollum,* 505 U.S. 42 [1992]).

In 1994, in *J.E.B. v. Alabama ex rel.,* the Supreme Court held that lawyers are prohibited from using peremptory challenges to exclude jurors based on gender. The Court reasoned that the Equal Protection Clause "prohibits discrimination in jury selection on the basis of gender...on the assumption that an individual will be biased in a particular case for no reason other than the fact that the person happens to be a woman or happens to be a man." As with race, the "'core guarantee of equal protection ensuring citizens that their State will not discriminate...would be meaningless were we to approve the exclusion of jurors on the basis of such assumptions, which arise solely from the jurors' gender'" (*J.E.B. v. Alabama ex rel.,* 511 U.S. 127, 146 [1994]).

In 2008, Supreme Court Justice Samuel J. Alito held that Michael Brooks, a college-age senior, had been struck from a capital punishment case in Louisiana because he is an African American. The prosecutor dismissed Brooks based on the fact that Brooks, who was pursuing a degree in education, expressed concern and appeared to be "nervous" about losing his required "student teaching time" and that, as a result, Brooks might be inclined to find the defendant guilty of a lesser offense in order to avoid spending time considering whether the defendant deserved the death penalty. Judge Alito observed that Brooks did not seem concerned once the college administrators stated that they would insure that Brooks did not lose teaching time. Caucasian members of the venire were not struck who expressed concern that the jury's sequestration would interfere with work, school, family, or other obligations. Judge Alito noted that the prosecutor was speculating in regard to Brooks's behavior on the jury and that, in any event, a single juror could not persuade an entire jury to convict a defendant of a lesser offense. The prosecutor accurately had predicted that the trial and sentencing phase would last only two days, and the argument that Brooks would seek to end the trial as quickly as possible was unpersuasive. Judge Alito questioned whether the prosecutor challenged Brooks because he appeared to be nervous and concluded that Brooks's exclusion had been motivated in "substantial part by a discriminatory intent" (*Snyder v. Louisiana,* 552 U.S. ___ [2008]).

As you reflect on peremptory challenges, ask yourself whether you would agree with commentators who argue that despite the rule established in *Batson v. Kentucky,* peremptory challenges continue to be used to exclude members of minority groups from juries.

Judges as well as jurors can be excluded from trial. The next section discusses the ability of lawyers to file a motion asking a judge to remove himself or herself from a case based on the judge's alleged bias or conflict of interest.

You can find Snyder v. Louisiana *on the study site, http://www.sagepub.com/lippmancp.*

13.1 YOU DECIDE

Thaddeus Jimenez was convicted of first-degree murder in an apparent gang-related homicide. He appealed the verdict based on the trial judge's refusal to ask potential jurors, "Would the fact that an accused is allegedly a member of a street gang, prevent you from giving him a fair and impartial trial?" Jimenez argued that this question was crucial to determining whether to strike jurors "for cause." How would you rule? See *People v. Jimenez,* 672 N.E.2d 914 (Ill. App. 1996).

You can find the answer by referring to the study site, http://www.sagepub.com/lippmancp.

13.2 YOU DECIDE

Roy Neal Shelling was convicted of the murder of Carlos McMahon, whom he suspected of being involved romantically with his wife, Lisa Robinson. Shelling was extremely jealous and had a history of threatening individuals whom he suspected of dating his estranged wife. Shelling claimed on appeal that the prosecutor had improperly exercised his peremptory challenges in excluding four African American jurors who in response to a question on voir dire stated that they agreed with the verdict in the O.J. Simpson case. The prosecutor claimed that the case had some similarities to the trial of O.J. Simpson, and the question was intended to determine whether potential jurors would be willing to convict the defendant on the basis of circumstantial evidence. The prosecutor argued that he had no reason to exclude African American jurors because the defendant, the victim, and the witnesses were all African Americans. See *Shelling v. State,* 52 S.W.2d 213 (Tex. App. 2001).

You can find the answer by referring to the study site, http://www.sagepub.com/lippmancp.

Challenges to Judges

The Fifth and Fourteenth Amendments' Due Process Clauses guarantee that a defendant will be tried before a neutral and impartial judge. The federal "challenge-for-cause" statute as well as state statutes and rules of criminal procedure typically permit a lawyer to file a motion to remove a judge from a case based on a demonstration that the judge is "biased." This may arise where there is a close friendship between the judge and a lawyer or between the judge and a defendant. A judge also may have a financial interest in the outcome of a case. An example is a judge who has money invested in a corporation that is being charged with criminal activity (28 U.S.C. § 144). A judge should not wait for a lawyer to file a motion to remove the judge from a case. Members of the judiciary have an ethical responsibility to uphold the "appearance of justice" and should recuse, or remove, themselves from a case where there may be a perception that the process is unfair or biased. In general, the fact that a judge has expressed an opinion on a case is not sufficient cause for a judge's **recusal.** Roughly one-third of the states permit both the defense and the prosecution to file a peremptory challenge and to remove a judge from a case. This permits the removal of a judge where the lawyers believe, but cannot establish, that a judge will be unfair.

In 2009, in *Caperton v. A.T. Massey,* the U.S. Supreme Court held that an elected judge was required by the Due Process Clause of the Constitution to recuse himself or herself from a case involving a litigant who had contributed an "extraordinary" amount of money to the judge's campaign. The Court proceeded to rule that the chief judge of the West Virginia Supreme Court should have removed himself from a case involving a coal company whose chief executive had donated three million dollars to the judge's campaign because the "disproportionate influence" of the contribution created a "serious risk" of "actual bias." Thirty-nine states elect some or all of their judges (*Caperton v. A.T. Massey,* ___ U.S. ___ [2009]).

We now turn our attention to the trial process and to guilty pleas. The constitutional right to a public trial, which is discussed in the next section, is intended to guarantee that a defendant's guilt is determined in a trial open to the public rather than behind closed doors. This is based on the belief that "sunlight" is the best protection against a defendant's being "railroaded" and unjustifiably convicted of a criminal offense.

Public Trial

The Sixth Amendment to the U.S. Constitution provides that "[i]n all criminal prosecutions, the accused shall enjoy the right to a . . . public trial." This right is recognized as a central component of due process and was one of the first rights incorporated into the Fourteenth Amendment. The right to a public trial applies to all hearings related to the trial including preliminary hearings, pretrial suppression hearings, jury selection, the issuing of **jury instructions,** and sentencing hearings and to all phases of the trial that have a "reasonably substantial" relationship to the defendant's defense against the criminal charges. A defendant may be excluded from "bench conferences" between the lawyers and the judge during the trial or other conferences that address points of law (*In re Oliver,* 333 U.S. 257 [1948]). For example, the Supreme Court held that a defendant had no right to attend a hearing in which a judge made a determination that the two alleged child victims whom the defendant allegedly sodomized were capable of understanding basic facts and comprehending their obligation to testify truthfully and were competent to testify at trial. The Court explained that the defendant's presence would not have contributed to his ability to defend himself and noted that the defendant had the opportunity at trial to assist his lawyer in cross-examining the two children (*Kentucky v. Stincer,* 482 U.S. 730 [1987]).

The requirement of a public trial is designed to protect defendants from being subjected to secret trials in which the government takes advantage of the lack of public scrutiny to railroad the accused. In *Waller v. Georgia,* the Supreme Court listed several other benefits of public trials for the accused (*Waller v. Georgia,* 467 U.S. 39, 46 [1984]).

Fairness. Public attention on the trial insures that the accused is fairly treated by the judge, prosecutor, and jury and is not unjustly condemned.

Witnesses. A public trial draws attention to the case and may result in witnesses coming forward to offer evidence.

Truthfulness. Witnesses are aware that the truthfulness of their testimony will be evaluated by the public.

The right to a public trial requires that there be public access to the trial and that the trial be conducted in a location that is reasonably accessible to the public.

The defendant does not have an absolute right to attend his or her trial. In *Illinois v. Allen,* Allen engaged in unruly and abusive behavior and disrupted his trial for armed robbery. He was removed from the courtroom during the prosecution's presentation of evidence and was returned to the courtroom when he promised to act in a respectful fashion. The U.S. Supreme Court upheld the trial judge's exclusion of Allen and held that there are at least three constitutionally permissible methods with which a trial court judge may respond to a disruptive defendant like Allen: "(1) bind and gag him, thereby keeping him present; (2) cite him for contempt; (3) take him out of the courtroom until he promises to conduct himself properly" (*Illinois v. Allen,* 397 U.S. 337 [1970]). The Supreme Court advised that removal should be employed before resorting to binding and gagging a defendant. Binding and gagging run the risk of prejudicing the jury against a defendant, interfere with the ability of the defendant to communicate with his or her lawyer, and undermine the decorum of the trial and, for these reasons, should be used only as a "last resort" (*Illinois v. Allen,* 397 U.S. 337 [1970]). Various state statutes and state rules of trial procedure prohibit beginning a trial without the defendant being present. The U.S. Supreme Court interpreted Rule 43 of the Federal Rules of Criminal Procedure to prohibit the trial of a defendant who is not present at the beginning of the trial. At this point, the trial may continue in the event that the defendant chooses to be absent (*Crosby v. United States,* 506 U.S. 255 [1993]). The Supreme Court held that a defendant may forfeit the right to be present at a trial by failing to attend the trial after having been warned that his or her continued absence would "effectively foreclose his right to testify and to confront personally the witnesses against him" (*Taylor v. United States,* 414 U.S. 17 [1973]).

The surrounding circumstance of the trial also may be so prejudicial to the defendant that there is a violation of the defendant's right to due process of law. In 1976, in *Estelle v. Williams,* the U.S. Supreme Court held that requiring the defendant to stand trial in prison or in jail clothing may prejudice the jurors against the defendant and violates due process of law. Defendants who pose a danger may be required to stand trial while shackled or restrained where there is a strong need to prevent violence or to prevent escape (*Estelle v. Williams,* 425 U.S. 501 [1976]). The Supreme Court has held that a judge may order the shackling of a defendant during the penalty phase of a death-penalty trial to protect safety, to prevent escape, and to prevent disruptions (*Deck v. Missouri,* 544 U.S. 622 [2005]). The Government does not have to make a special showing of the need for security officers in the courtroom. The Supreme Court has held that this is not "inherently prejudicial," because most people will interpret the presence of the security guards as a safeguard against outside disruption rather than as a response to the defendant's violent tendencies (*Holbrook v. Flynn,* 475 U.S. 560 [1986]).

Members of the public generally do not attend criminal trials and depend on the media to inform them of developments. The right of the press to attend a trial is based on the First Amendment right to freedom of expression rather than on the Sixth Amendment right to a public trial (*Gannett Co. v. DePasquale,* 443 U.S. 368 [1979]; *Waller v. Georgia,* 467 U.S. 39, 46 [1984]). The public and press historically have been free to attend criminal proceedings and trials, and their presence helps to monitor the fairness of hearings, provides a sense of confidence in the integrity of the proceedings, and promotes public awareness and discussion of the justice process (*Globe Newspaper Co. v. Superior Court,* 457 U.S. 596 [1982]). The Supreme Court has extended the right of the media to attend criminal trials to include preliminary hearings, the pretrial suppression of evidence hearings, and the process of jury selection and sentencing. The Court has stated that the presumption of openness may be "overcome only by an overriding interest based on a finding that closure is essential to preserve higher values and is narrowly tailored to serve that interest." The narrowly-tailored-language standard means that a court should make an effort to close a portion of a trial rather than the entire hearing. For example, a portion of jury selection in a case involving the rape of a young girl might be closed to protect the privacy of several prospective jurors (*Press Enterprise Co. v. Superior Court I,* 464 U.S. 501 [1984]). The circumstances under which the media may be excluded from portions of a trial are "rare," and the balance should be struck with "special care" so as to preserve the First Amendment rights of the press and of the public (*Waller v. Georgia,* 467 U.S. 39, 45 [1984]). Closure as outlined below has been upheld to prevent pretrial prejudice, to preserve the defendant's right to a fair trial, and to protect the privacy of minors who are alleged to have been victims of sexual abuse.

Prejudicial publicity. The press and public may be excluded from a preliminary hearing where there is a substantial probability that the publicity will prejudice the defendant's right to a fair trial and there are no reasonable alternatives to closing the hearing (*Press Enterprise Co. v. Superior Court II,* 478 U.S. 1 [1986]).

Juveniles. Criminal proceedings may be closed to protect juveniles alleged to have been the victims of sexual abuse. There must be a factual demonstration that closure will serve this compelling governmental interest and that the denial of access is narrowly tailored to serve this interest. In other words, the Government must demonstrate that a public hearing is reasonably likely to cause a juvenile to suffer trauma or public embarrassment that will have a negative impact and that the restriction on the press is no greater than is required to protect the juvenile (*Globe Newspaper Co. v. Superior Court,* 457 U.S. 596 [1982]).

Judicial proceedings also may be closed in the interests of national security when sensitive intelligence information may be discussed in the courtroom.

The Trial

The defendant now enters the formal trial stage of the criminal justice process. The same theme of balancing the societal interest in criminal prosecutions against the interest in protecting the rights of the defendant is evident in the procedures at trial. We will examine the following phases of the trial.

- ***Opening statement.*** The prosecution and the defense each outline their case.
- ***Evidence.*** The prosecution and the defense present their cases, and the witnesses are subject to cross-examination. The defendant's right to cross-examine witnesses is protected by the Confrontation Clause of the U.S. Constitution, and the defendant's right to present a defense is protected by the Compulsory Process Clause of the U.S. Constitution.
- ***Closing argument.*** The prosecution and the defense summarize their cases.
- ***Jury instructions.*** The judge instructs the jury in regard to the law that is to be followed.
- ***Jury deliberations.*** The jury evaluates the facts and returns a verdict.

Opening Statement

Prosecutors and defense lawyers may make brief **opening statements.** The prosecutor's opening statement generally is followed by the defense attorney's statement. In some jurisdictions, the defense attorney has the option of making his or her statement following the prosecutor's presentation of evidence.

The opening statement is a brief verbal presentation of the evidence that a lawyer plans to present. Think about the opening statement as a "road map." The purpose is to outline the evidence that will be introduced at trial and to explain the significance of the evidence and to demonstrate how the accumulated evidence establishes either the defendant's innocence or guilt. It is unethical for a lawyer to refer to evidence in the opening statement unless he or she has a good faith basis for believing that the evidence will be presented by a witness and will be admitted into evidence by the judge. The opening statement also should not be used to make an impassioned argument or emotional appeal. The judge typically responds to any improprieties in the opening statement by instructing the jury to disregard the lawyer's statements. Gross impropriety may result in a judge's declaring a mistrial.

Presentation of Evidence

The prosecution now presents the **case-in-chief.** The prosecution has the burden of proving every element of the crime with which the defendant is charged beyond a reasonable doubt. The prosecutor, in an effort to establish the defendant's guilt beyond a reasonable doubt, may present the direct testimony of witnesses and may introduce documents, scientific tests, and tangible (physical) evidence. The prosecutor on direct examination is not permitted to ask witnesses leading questions (questions that suggest the answer to the question). The defense attorney then may subject the prosecution's witnesses to **cross-examination.** This involves asking the witness questions about his or her direct examination. The purpose is to raise questions about the accuracy of the direct testimony or about the credibility (believability) of the witness. Leading questions may be employed during cross-examination. The judge has the authority to step in and to limit questions that are confusing, that attack the witness, or that are repetitious. Following cross-examination, the prosecutor may *rehabilitate* the witness, or repair the damage to the witness through *redirect examination.* The defense may be permitted an additional opportunity to question the witness on *recross-examination.*

The defense counsel at this point may make a **motion for a judgment of acquittal** based on the claim that "no reasonable juror could conclude that that guilt was proven beyond a reasonable doubt." Assuming the motion is not granted, the defense phase of the process now begins. The first step is the defense attorney's case-in-chief, or what is often termed the **rebuttal** phase of the trial. This involves the direct testimony of defense witnesses who then are subject to cross-examination by the prosecutor. During this portion of the trial, the defense lawyer has the opportunity to present various defenses including self-defense, necessity, duress, or alibi. The defense attorney may make yet another motion for a judgment of acquittal following the presentation of the defense case. Motions for acquittal are rarely granted, and the prosecution at this point may present rebuttal evidence designed to attack any defenses that were presented by the defense.

The prosecutor may agree to allow the defense to stipulate certain facts, or in other words to agree to certain facts. This relieves the prosecution of the burden of establishing an element of the offense. The defendant, for example, may stipulate the fact that the victim was killed in order to insure that the prosecution does not introduce into evidence photos picturing a bloody body.

There are several interesting aspects of the presentation of witnesses. First, as you undoubtedly recall, objects excluded pursuant to the exclusionary rule may not be used at trial. Second, individuals who hold a privilege may not be required to testify without the approval of the "holder of the privilege." A defendant typically must waive his or her privilege before testimony may be heard from clergy, doctors, or lawyers. Third, the prosecutor or defense attorney may ask the judge to inform the jury that the fact that a witness is unavailable should not be interpreted in a negative fashion. In the alternative, the prosecutor or defense can request the judge to issue a "missing witness instruction to the jury" that tells the jurors that they may infer that the absence of a witness is to be interpreted in a "negative fashion." In a New York case, the defendant failed to produce an employee who allegedly could support his claim that his sexual relations with the complainant were consensual and that he had not raped her. The judge held that the jury could draw a negative inference from the defendant's failure to produce the witness: The "defendant was on trial for uncommonly heinous crimes. He testified that complainant's accusation was a lie. If (as defendant swore) his version was true, his friend Camacho was the only person in the world who could rescue him from the prospect of a lengthy prison term. Under these circumstances one would expect an accused to go to Herculean lengths to get Camacho before the jury" (*People v. Savinon,* 100 N.Y.2d 193 [N.Y. 2003]). Last, the defendant may choose to testify or to assert his or her constitutional right against self-incrimination and remain silent. The prosecutor may not comment on the defendant's failure to testify.

The next section discusses the constitutional basis of a defendant's right to cross-examine the prosecution's witnesses. We then discuss the constitutional basis for a defendant's right to present witnesses in his or her own defense.

Confrontation

The Sixth Amendment provides that "[i]n all criminal prosecutions, the accused shall enjoy the right...to be confronted with the witnesses against him." In 1965, in *Pointer v. Texas,* the **Confrontation Clause** was incorporated into the Fourteenth Amendment (*Pointer v. Texas,* 380 U.S. 400 [1965]). The clause guarantees a defendant the right to be present in the courtroom and to confront the witnesses and evidence against him or her. The U.S. Supreme

Court has extended the Sixth Amendment to all phases of the pretrial proceedings and the trial "substantially related" to the defendant's ability to defend against the charges or that affect the defendant's defense at trial. This includes pretrial hearings to suppress, jury selection, jury instructions, sentencing, and discussions in the judge's chambers that involve the facts of the case.

The Confrontation Clause is closely related to the right to a public trial and is based on a concern with insuring the accuracy of trials by requiring witnesses to testify under oath and to submit to cross-examination. The requirement of sworn testimony is intended to stress the seriousness of the testimony and helps to insure truthfulness and to guard against perjury. The defendant has the opportunity to cross-examine witnesses and to test their recollection and accuracy. This allows the jury to evaluate a witness's believability and personal demeanor.

Two of the most interesting Confrontation Clause cases involve juveniles alleged to have been sexually molested. The issue was whether the defendants had an absolute right to confront "face-to-face" the witnesses against them. In *Coy v. Iowa,* the Supreme Court held that the defendant's ability to confront witnesses face-to-face was violated when a state court placed a screen in front of the juveniles that blocked their view of the defendant. The defendant could barely see the witnesses through the screen. The Supreme Court criticized the trial court for acting on a general legislative presumption regarding the trauma experienced by juvenile victims who testify at trial rather than engaging in an individualized analysis as to whether testifying in front of the defendant would upset the juvenile (*Coy v. Iowa,* 487 U.S. 1012 [1988]).

In *Maryland v. Craig,* the U.S. Supreme Court upheld the constitutionality of permitting a juvenile alleged to have been the victim of a sexual offense to testify through the use of a one-way closed-circuit television. The statute required a finding that the closed-circuit television was necessary to advance the important state interest in preventing the victim from suffering the type of extreme emotional trauma that likely would result from confronting the defendant and that would leave the alleged victim incapable of "reasonably communicating." The Supreme Court reasoned that the defendant would not be prejudiced by the use of the television, because the jury likely would conclude that the closed-circuit television was being used because the victim was fearful of testifying in the courtroom rather than because the victim was fearful of the defendant (*Maryland v. Craig,* 497 U.S. 836 [1990]). The next section discusses the right to cross-examine witnesses, which is the core of the Confrontation Clause.

Cross-Examination

John Henry Wigmore, the famous scholar of the law of evidence, called cross-examination the "greatest" contribution of the common law and characterized cross-examination as the "greatest legal engine ever invented for the discovery of the truth." The U.S. Supreme Court has held that cross-examination is the essential right protected by the Confrontation Clause. The purpose of cross-examination is to determine whether a witness's testimony can withstand questioning that probes the witness's accuracy, consistency, and objectivity. The Supreme Court held in *Davis v. Alaska* that the defendant's right to confrontation was violated when the trial judge prohibited the defense attorney from cross-examining a key prosecution witness who testified that he saw the defendant along with other men in possession of a safe stolen in a robbery. The defendant's lawyer had sought unsuccessfully to call attention to the fact that the witness's juvenile probation could have been revoked had he failed to testify on behalf of the prosecution (*Davis v. Alaska,* 415 U.S. 308 [1974]). In 1988, in *Olden v. Kentucky,* the Supreme Court held that the defendant's rights had been violated by the trial court's refusal to permit the defense attorney to question the victim of an alleged rape regarding her extramarital relationship that the defendant contended provided the victim with a motive to fabricate the rape charge (*Olden v. Kentucky,* 488 U.S. 227 [1988]). The next section examines the admissibility at trial of hearsay evidence.

Hearsay

Rule 801 of the Federal Rules of Evidence defines **hearsay** as a "statement, other than one made by the declarant while testifying at the trial or hearing, offered in evidence to prove the truth of the matter asserted." In other words, hearsay involves a witness testifying as to what someone else said outside the courtroom, which is introduced to prove a fact that is involved in the case. Hearsay evidence violates the Confrontation Clause because the person who made the original statement is not subject to immediate cross-examination, and there is no way to test the accuracy of the statement. The U.S. Supreme Court nevertheless has held that the Confrontation Clause permits the use of hearsay under certain limited circumstances.

Let me caution that hearsay is one of the most complicated and confusing areas of the law of evidence and that this section merely provides an introduction to the topic. In *Ohio v. Roberts,* the Supreme Court held that hearsay evidence may be used in those instances in which the declarant whose statements are to be used against the defendant is unavailable. In other words, it is necessary to rely on a witness's testimony regarding the content of another individual's statement because the declarant is unavailable. Second, the hearsay statement must have been made under circumstances providing sufficient "indicia of reliability" that the statement actually was made. The Supreme Court in *Roberts* held that the trial court had properly permitted the prosecution to introduce the statement of an unavailable witness at trial. The witness had testified at the preliminary hearing and had been cross-examined at the hearing by the defense counsel, and the statement was found to carry the indicia of reliability (*Ohio v. Roberts,* 448 U.S. 56, 66 [1980]).

The Supreme Court also held that hearsay meets the indicia of reliability in those instances in which a statement is within one of twenty "firmly rooted" categories of hearsay testimony that historically have been recognized as reliable by the common law. Some of these exceptions seem to make little sense in light of modern science but continue to be recognized by the courts. For example, a witness may testify as to a statement made by a homicide victim confronting imminent and immediate death regarding the identity of the killer. The thinking is that there is no motive for an individual who is confronting death to misrepresent the truth.

The Supreme Court in *Crawford v. Washington* held that the essence of the Confrontation Clause is the prohibition on the use of testimony by an unavailable declarant who is not subject to cross-examination. The Supreme Court accordingly held that out-of-court statements that are "testimonial" are inadmissible unless the declarant has been cross-examined earlier by a lawyer representing the defendant. The Court did not define *testimonial* and merely noted that examples of testimonial statements are statements made at a preliminary hearing or before a grand jury or statements made during a previous trial or during police interrogations (*Crawford v. Washington,* 541 U.S. 36, 51 [2004]).

In 2006, in *Davis v. Washington,* the U.S. Supreme Court held that statements made in response to police interrogation that are intended to gather information as part of a response to an ongoing emergency are "nontestimonial" and admissible in a prosecution against the accused. The declarant in this situation is not a "witness" and is not "testifying" against the accused. The Supreme Court held in *Davis* that the victim's statements made during a 911 emergency call were nontestimonial and admissible as evidence that the accused had violated an order of protection (*Davis v. Washington,* 547 U.S. 813 [2006]).

In 2009, the U.S. Supreme Court held that analysts who create crime laboratory reports that are used at trial are required to testify and to subject themselves to cross-examination. This provides the defense with the opportunity to probe whether the test was conducted in accordance with established procedures and whether the test results support the analyst's conclusion. In the past, a sworn affidavit recording the results of the test was considered sufficient in most state and federal courts. Defendants could challenge the test results through their own experts or by conducting their own test and could ask the judge to subpoena (order) the analyst to testify. The dissenting opinion warned that requiring analysts to testify will create a "crushing burden," and defense attorneys will request that analysts testify in the hope that the analysts will be unable to appear and that the case will be dismissed. Justice

Scalia dismissed this alarmist conclusion and noted that the Confrontation Clause may "make the prosecution of criminals more burdensome, but that is equally true of the right to trial by jury and the privilege against self-incrimination" (*Melendez-Diaz v. Massachusetts,* 557 U.S. ___ [2009]).

In summary, testimonial hearsay is not admissible unless the declarant is unavailable and, at an earlier time, was subject to cross-examination by the accused. Nontestimonial hearsay does not fall within the protection of the Confrontation Clause and is admissible despite the fact that the declarant was not subject to cross-examination so long as the statement carries the indicia of reliability. The defendant in addition to the constitutional right to confront the prosecution's witnesses has the constitutional right to present witnesses and evidence in his or her own defense.

You can find Melendez-Diaz v. Massachusetts *on the study site, http://www.sagepub.com/lippmancp.*

Compulsory Process

The Sixth Amendment provides that an individual shall have "compulsory process for obtaining witnesses in his favor." The **Compulsory Process Clause** is incorporated into the Fourteenth Amendment Due Process Clause. This right has two components. First, the defendant has the right to obtain witnesses, documents, and other evidence that are required to defend himself or herself. For example, Rule 17 of the Federal Rules of Criminal Procedure provides that the court at the request of a defendant shall issue subpoenas at no cost to an indigent defendant to compel the appearance of witnesses to testify on the defendant's behalf and shall issue subpoenas to compel the production of books, papers, and documents. The right to compulsory process is based on the belief that it would be contrary to the constitutional values that constitute the foundation of the criminal justice system to convict an individual who has limited access to the witnesses and to the evidence necessary to defend himself or herself (*Taylor v. Illinois,* 484 U.S. 400 [1988]).

The second aspect of the Compulsory Process Clause is the right to present witnesses, documents, and other evidence at trial and to present a criminal defense. The Supreme Court in several cases has been asked to determine whether a trial court judge has interfered with a defendant's right to present a defense. In 1987, in *Rock v. Arkansas,* the U.S. Supreme Court held that a rule automatically excluding all hypnotically refreshed testimony impermissibly interferes with the defendant's right to testify in his or her own behalf (*Rock v. Arkansas,* 483 U.S. 44, 61 [1987]). The Court observed that Arkansas "has not shown that hypnotically enhanced testimony is always so untrustworthy and so immune to the traditional means of evaluating credibility that it should disable a defendant from presenting her version of the events for which she is on trial" (*Rock v. Arkansas,* 483 U.S. 44, 61 [1987]).

In *Chambers v. Mississippi,* the U.S. Supreme Court held that the trial court's refusal to permit three witnesses to testify that another individual had told each of them that he had committed the crime with which Chambers was charged violated Chambers's right to due process. The Court explained that the statements appeared trustworthy and that a local court's application of the hearsay rule should not be permitted to interfere with a defendant's right to present a defense. The Supreme Court explained that the testimony of the three witnesses was "critical to Chambers' defense" and that in "these circumstances, where constitutional rights directly affecting the ascertainment of guilt are implicated, the hearsay rule may not be applied mechanistically to defeat the ends of justice" (*Chambers v. Mississippi,* 410 U.S. 284, 302 [1973]).

In *Webb v. Texas,* the trial court judge announced that he expected the witness to perjure himself and warned that this would lead him to increase the prison sentence that the witness already was serving. The witness refused to testify, and the U.S. Supreme Court held that the judge had intimidated the witness and, as a result, had prevented the defendant from presenting a defense. The Court concluded that the "judge's threatening remarks, directed only at the single witness for the defense, effectively drove that witness off the stand, and thus deprived the petitioner of due process of law under the Fourteenth Amendment" (*Webb v. Texas,* 409 U.S. 95, 98 [1972]).

In *Washington v. Texas,* the Supreme Court held that a statute providing that an accomplice to a crime may not testify as a defense witness violated the defendant's right to compulsory process. This law "rested on the unstated premises that the right to present witnesses was subordinate to the court's interest in preventing perjury, and that erroneous decisions were best avoided by preventing the jury from hearing any testimony that might be perjured, even if it were the only testimony available on a crucial issue." The Court held that the statute unconstitutionally prevented the defendant from presenting "relevant and material testimony." Chief Justice Warren noted that Texas permitted accomplices to testify on behalf of the prosecution, testimony that presented an even greater threat of perjury than did testimony on behalf of the defense (*Washington v. Texas,* 388 U.S. 14, 21 [1967]).

Burden of Proof

Trials in the American criminal justice system are adversarial. The adversarial process involves a courtroom clash between a prosecutor representing the Government and a defense attorney representing the defendant. Each lawyer is expected to zealously represent his or her client and is responsible for presenting the law and the facts that favor his or her side.

The **burden of proof** is the standard that must be satisfied for a criminal conviction. The burden of proof has two components: first, the *burden of going forward* (or the burden of production) and, second, the *burden of persuasion.* The burden of going forward involves responsibility for presenting evidence to establish guilt. The burden of persuasion belongs to the party at the trial who is required to persuade the jury. In the American legal system, the prosecution is responsible for the burden of going forward with the evidence as well as for the burden of persuasion. The burden of persuasion requires proving the defendant's guilt beyond a reasonable doubt. Why are these burdens placed on the prosecution? The theory is that a criminal conviction carries serious consequences and that the Government must bear the burden of criminally convicting a defendant and depriving a defendant of his or her liberty. We do not place the burden of proof on the defendant to establish innocence; the burden is on the Government to establish guilt.

The defendant is not required to assist the Government in establishing the defendant's guilt at trial. The Fifth Amendment provides that "no person . . . shall be compelled in any criminal case to be a witness against himself." The defendant has a Fifth Amendment right to refuse to testify in his or her own defense. The defendant is not required to take stand, and the prosecutor may not comment to the jury on the defendant's refusal to testify. The defendant also may ask the judge to tell the jurors that they should not conclude that the defendant is guilty based on his or her failure to testify. A defendant may decide to testify to present a defense such as self-defense, necessity, or duress. The defendant also may testify in an effort to present facts that reduce the seriousness of the criminal charge (e.g., voluntary manslaughter or murder in the heat of passion rather than intentional murder or the intentional and premeditated killing of another) or to contest the prosecution's case (e.g., to establish an alibi). A defendant who takes the stand, of course, is subject to cross-examination. The next section discusses the reasonable doubt standard.

Reasonable Doubt

Conviction for a crime requires that the jury find the defendant guilty **beyond a reasonable doubt**. In *In re Winship,* the U.S. Supreme Court held that the beyond-a-reasonable-doubt standard has been a requirement of the common law at least since 1798 and is part of the defendant's right to due process of law. The Court proclaimed that the Due Process

Clause "protects the accused from conviction except upon proof beyond a reasonable doubt of every fact necessary to constitute the crime with which he is charged." There are several reasons for requiring this "higher degree of persuasion in criminal cases" (*In re Winship,* 397 U.S. 358, 364 [1970]).

Presumption of innocence. Defendants are presumed to be innocent. The prosecution must meet a high standard to justify a criminal conviction that may result in depriving a defendant of his or her liberty and freedom.

False convictions. Placing a heavy burden on the government guards against false convictions.

Seriousness of criminal conviction. The reasonable doubt standard impresses jurors with the seriousness of their task and emphasizes that defendants should not be lightly convicted of a crime.

Community confidence. The reasonable doubt standard assures the public that innocent individuals are not being convicted and assures innocent individuals going about their ordinary business that they will not be subjected to criminal prosecution and conviction absent strong evidence of guilt.

The U.S. Constitution does not require that the judge use any specific words or expressions in explaining the beyond-a-reasonable-doubt standard of proof to the jury. The requirement is that the instructions as a whole convey the reasonable doubt standard. The question is "not whether the instruction 'could have' been applied in an unconstitutional manner, but whether there is a reasonable likelihood that the jury did so apply it" (*Victor v. Nebraska,* 511 U.S. 1, 5–6 [1993]).

In *Cage v. Louisiana,* a judge's instructions to a jury equated reasonable doubt with a "grave uncertainty" and with an "actual substantial doubt." The U.S. Supreme Court rejected this formula and held that the jury could have interpreted the instruction to allow a finding of guilt based on a degree of proof below that required by the Due Process Clause (*Cage v. Louisiana,* 498 U.S. 39, 42 [1990]). On the other hand, in *Victor v. Nebraska,* the Supreme Court approved a trial court's instruction that a jury must reach "an abiding conviction to a moral certainty of the truth of the charge" to explain reasonable doubt because the instruction as a whole adequately informed the jury of the need to achieve a "subjective state of near certitude of...guilt" (*Victor v. Nebraska,* 511 U.S. 1, 15 [1993]). Phrases that are commonly used to communicate the reasonable doubt standard include "satisfies the reason and judgment of those who are bound to act conscientiously" and "a doubt that would cause prudent people to hesitate before acting in a matter of importance to themselves."

A failure to adequately describe the reasonable doubt standard to the jury will result in an appellate court's overturning a defendant's conviction. The central point is that the instructions should stress that beyond a reasonable doubt is a high standard of proof.

At the conclusion of the prosecution and defense cases, the lawyers have the opportunity to summarize their cases to the jury in their closing arguments.

Closing Arguments

Following the presentation of evidence by the prosecutor and the defense, the lawyers make their **closing arguments.** The prosecutor goes first, and the defense then replies. The prosecutor is permitted to respond to the defense. The thinking behind this arrangement is that the prosecutor bears the burden of proving guilt beyond reasonable doubt and should be provided with the opportunity to rebut the defendant's closing arguments.

In *Herring v. New York,* U.S. Supreme Court Justice Potter Stewart noted that the closing argument is a vital part of the adversarial process because it permits both sides to submit their complete case to the jury (*Herring v. New York,* 422 U.S. 853 [1975]).

The prosecutor and defense attorney are expected to adhere to the same standard of conduct in their closing statements. Trial courts tend to be more concerned about the conduct of prosecutors, who possess a special responsibility as representatives of the Government to insure that their authority is exercised in a fair and just fashion and is not employed to abuse and to convict the innocent (*Berger v. United States,* 295 U.S. 78 [1935]). The U.S. Supreme Court has stressed that while the lawyers should be given significant freedom in making their closing arguments, these arguments may be limited to insure that a trial is orderly and fair. The American Bar Association Standards for Criminal Justice (1980), section 3.5, sets forth several types of prohibited arguments.

- Intentional misstatement of evidence or misleading of the jury
- Arguments that are not supported by the evidence that was introduced at trial
- Expressions of personal beliefs or opinions in regard to the truth or falsity of the evidence or in regard to the defendant's guilt
- Reference to issues beyond the trial itself or speculation on the social consequences of a conviction or of an acquittal
- Appeals that are calculated to inflame emotions and prejudices
- Comments that draw negative inferences from the defendant's assertion of his constitutional rights including a failure to testify or to consent to a search

The U.S. Supreme Court has recognized that in the heat of a trial, lawyers occasionally may breach these standards (*Dunlop v. United States,* 165 U.S. 486 [1897]). The Court has held that a prosecutor's argument violates due process in those instances that the argument "so infected the trial with unfairness as to make the resulting conviction a denial of due process" (*Donnelly v. DeChristoforo,* 416 U.S. 637 [1974]). In other words, courts require that the defense demonstrate that the remark likely prejudiced or had an impact on the verdict. Professors LaFave, Israel, and King list various factors that are considered by courts in evaluating the impact of a closing argument. This analysis is based on the totality of the circumstances and considers the following:

- Whether the remarks are particularly inflammatory or likely to incite the jury
- Whether the remarks are isolated or extensive
- Whether the remarks were provoked by the closing argument of the other side
- Whether the defense lawyer made an objection to the remarks thereby indicating a fear of prejudice
- Whether the trial court judge issued instructions to the jury in an effort to limit the prejudice
- Whether the remarks are combined with other errors at trial
- Whether there is overwhelming evidence of guilt

The **invited response** doctrine is used by courts to evaluate the impact of a prosecutor's remarks. In those cases in which the prosecutor's closing argument is a response to the arguments made by the defense attorney, courts are inclined to rule that the prosecutor's remarks were balanced by the defense lawyer's closing argument and were an effort to "right the scale" and thereby were not prejudicial to the defendant (*United States v. Young,* 470 U.S. 1 [1985]). Appellate courts increasingly have expressed frustration over the trend toward the abuse of the closing argument and have hinted that lawyers who persist in such conduct risk a suspension of their licenses to practice law (*United States v. Modica,* 663 F.2d 1173 [2d Cir. 1981]).

Courts rarely reverse a conviction based on a prosecutor's closing argument. In *Darden v. Wainwright,* the prosecutor in seeking the death penalty blamed the Department of Corrections in Florida for granting the defendant a weekend furlough and referred to him as an "animal" who should not have been permitted to leave his cell without a "leash." The prosecutor, in his closing argument, expressed regret that the victim had not been armed so that she could have "blown" the defendant's "face off." The prosecutor also stated he regretted that when the defendant changed his appearance following the killing that he had not "cut his throat." The Supreme Court held that the prosecutor's argument did not "manipulate" or "misstate" the evidence, and the trial court judge had instructed the jurors that their decision should be made on the basis of the evidence. The weight of the evidence against the defendant was "heavy" and "overwhelming," and much of the "objectionable content" was "invited by or was responsive" to the defense attorney's summation (*Darden v. Wainwright,* 477 U.S. 168 [1986]).

Jury Instructions

The judge issues instructions to the jury before they begin to discuss the defendant's guilt or innocence. These instructions typically are given following the closing arguments, but the judge usually gives a copy of the instructions to the lawyers beforehand to enable them to refer to the instructions during their closing arguments. A judge's instructions usually include the following.

- The judge decides the law, and the jury is the finder of fact.
- The defendant is presumed innocent until proven guilty beyond a reasonable doubt.
- The burden is on the prosecution to establish guilt beyond a reasonable doubt.
- The elements of the crime with which the defendant is charged.
- The procedures to be followed by the jury.

In most jurisdictions, there are standard **pattern jury instructions** that a judge follows. The lawyers are permitted to ask the judge to submit particular instructions and may object to a judge's instructions and appeal the verdict in those instances in which the judge's instructions are alleged to be in error. Jury instructions are a controversial area. The instructions often are given in technical legal language. Studies indicate that jurors understandably have a difficult time fully understanding instructions in complex areas of the criminal law such as the insanity defense or white-collar crime.

Jury Deliberations

During the jury deliberations, jurors ordinarily are provided with copies of the charges and of the judge's jury instructions. The judge also may allow the jurors to view the exhibits that were introduced into evidence. Judges have the discretion to permit jurors to take notes during the trial and to bring the notes into the jury room during their deliberations. In most jurisdictions, the jury may ask to examine specific portions of the trial testimony. The jury, at the end of their deliberations, may return a verdict of guilty or not guilty and, where relevant, not guilty by reason of insanity.

In those instances in which a jury is unable to reach a verdict and is "deadlocked," the judge may order the jurors to deliberate for a reasonable period of time before dismissing the **hung jury.** The U.S. Supreme Court has approved of a trial court judge issuing a so-called *Allen* or **dynamite charge** when a jury is deadlocked. This charge is named after the judge's instruction in *Allen v. United States* in which the judge instructed the jury that if a significant number of jurors favor a conviction, the dissenting juror or jurors "ought to reconsider whether your doubt is a reasonable one." On the other hand, "if a majority or even a lesser number...favor...an acquittal, the rest of you should ask...whether you should accept the weight and sufficiency of evidence which fails to convince your fellow jurors beyond a reasonable doubt" (*Allen v. United States,* 164 U.S. 492 [1896]).

Following the verdict, the defense and prosecution may request that the judge poll the jury. This **jury poll** involves asking each juror whether he or she agrees with the verdict. In the event that the poll reveals that the jury in fact has failed to reach a verdict, the judge may order the jurors to continue their deliberations or may dismiss the jury. A defendant's ability to attack a jury verdict on the grounds of juror misconduct is limited by the fact that jurors are prohibited by law in most jurisdictions from testifying regarding jury deliberations. For example, the U.S. Supreme Court prohibited a defense attorney from interrogating jurors regarding the consumption of alcohol and unlawful narcotics during the trial (*Tanner* *v. United States,* 484 U.S. 107, 121 [1987]). There are two situations in which a juror may testify as to what occurred during jury deliberations.

1. ***Prejudicial information.*** Prejudicial information was improperly brought to the attention of a juror or jurors.
2. ***Outside influences.*** Outside influences and pressures were brought to bear on a juror.

The information must be demonstrated to have had an impact on the jury verdict. The next issue to be examined is jury decision making on the verdict.

Jury Unanimity

The requirement that juries consist of twelve individuals became accepted practice in England in the fourteenth century. The origins of this rule are unclear, but it appears to be based on the notion that an individual should not be held criminally liable unless twelve of his or her neighbors are all persuaded of his or her guilt. The unanimity requirement, by the eighteenth century, had been firmly established as the practice in the American colonies and was subsequently enshrined in the Sixth Amendment to the U.S. Constitution.

Today, forty-eight states follow the requirement in Rule 31 of the Federal Rules of Criminal Procedure and require that a "verdict shall be unanimous." In *Apodaca v. Oregon,* the U.S. Supreme Court held that the Sixth Amendment requirement of unanimity is not incorporated into the Fourteenth Amendment and upheld the constitutionality of an Oregon statute that provided that a verdict of guilty may be based on the vote of ten out of twelve jurors. Justice White explained that permitting a conviction to be based on ten or eleven votes rather than on unanimity does not interfere with the jury's ability to reflect the "commonsense judgment of the community" and to safeguard the defendant against prosecutorial abuse. The Supreme Court also dismissed the notion that a conviction based on less than a unanimous verdict will allow the majority of jurors to disregard the views of "minority elements" and thereby undermine the requirement that the jury verdict reflect a cross-section of the community. The Court noted that the Constitution requires that diverse groups be provided with the opportunity to be represented on juries and that there is no evidence that nonunanimous verdicts result in the views of "minority jurors" being ignored or overlooked (*Apodaca v. Oregon,* 406 U.S. 404 [1972]).

In *Johnson v. Louisiana,* decided the same day as *Apodaca,* the Supreme Court upheld a 9-to-3 guilty verdict in a robbery case. The Court rejected the contention that the fact that Johnson was convicted on a less-than-unanimous vote indicated that the jury had failed to find the defendant guilty beyond a reasonable doubt. The fact that three jurors did not agree with the majority did not establish the existence of reasonable doubt regarding the defendant's guilt, "particularly when such a heavy majority of the jury... remains convinced of guilt. That rational men disagree... is not... equivalent to a failure of proof... nor does it indicate infidelity to the reasonable doubt standard." Justice Douglas, in his dissenting opinion, questioned whether due process permits states to apply a "watered-down" version of the Sixth Amendment and pointed out that research indicates that in roughly ten percent of cases requiring a unanimous verdict, the minority of jurors succeed in changing the minds of the majority. Justice Douglas concluded that the decision in *Johnson* undermines an essential safeguard of individual freedom and liberty. Do you agree? (*Johnson v. Louisiana,* 406 U.S. 456, 361–362, 383, 387 [1972]).

The question remained at what point a majority vote is not sufficiently strong to meet the requirements of due process. Justice Blackmun, for example, noted that a "system employing a 7–5 standard, rather than a 9–3 or a 75% minimum, would afford me the greatest difficulty" (366). In *Burch v. Louisiana,* the U.S. Supreme Court was confronted with a Louisiana statute that provided that misdemeanors punishable by imprisonment of more than six months are to be tried by a jury of six persons, five of whom "must concur to enter a verdict." The Court announced without a lengthy explanation that "lines must be drawn somewhere if the substance of the jury trial right is to be preserved" and that permitting six-person juries to reach nonunanimous verdicts threatens the ability of the jury to represent the community and to safeguard defendants. The Court noted that Louisiana was one of two states that permitted six-person juries to decide cases based on nonunanimous verdicts and that Louisiana's interest in saving time and money by providing for nonunanimous verdicts is outbalanced by the need to protect the constitutional role of the jury and due process of law (*Burch v. Louisiana,* 441 U.S. 130, 138–139 [1979]).

Jury Nullification

A jury verdict acquitting a defendant cannot be appealed. An acquittal ordinarily is based on the decision of a jury that the prosecutor failed to present facts that established the defendant's guilt beyond a reasonable doubt. In some isolated instances, a jury may find that the prosecutor proved a defendant guilty beyond a reasonable doubt but nonetheless may refuse to return a guilty verdict. This situation may arise where the jury believes that a law is unfair or that it is unfair under the circumstances to convict a defendant. A jury's disregard of the law and acquittal of a defendant is termed **jury nullification.** An example would be a jury's decision to acquit a husband or wife who killed a dying, elderly spouse or parent who is in extreme pain.

There is a rich tradition in the United States of jury nullification in which juries have followed their own conscience rather than the law. The most famous American example is a colonial jury's refusal to convict newspaper publisher Peter Zenger for the seditious libel of British authorities. Northern juries in the nineteenth century acquitted individuals who broke the law by assisting fugitive slaves.

The prevailing view in most state courts and in the federal courts is that the judge instructs the jury as to the law and that the jury is limited to determining whether the facts establish an individual's guilt. Most trial court judges accordingly instruct jurors that they have a duty to enforce the law and do not inform jurors of their ability to nullify the law. As observed by the U.S. Supreme Court in *Sparf and Hansen* in 1895, "it is the duty of juries in criminal cases to take the law from the court, and apply that law to the facts as they find them to be from the evidence (*Sparf and Hansen v. United States,* 156 U.S. 51, 102 [1895]). In 1983, a federal circuit court condemned jury nullification as "lawless, a denial of due process" and as "an exercise of erroneously seized power" (*United States v. Washington,* 705 F.2d 489, 494 [D.C. Cir. 1983]).

As a practical matter, a jury is free to disregard the law because a jury verdict is not subject to appeal. Defense lawyers, during their closing arguments, may suggest to jurors that they disregard the law. In *United States v. Dougherty,* the District of Columbia Court of Appeals held that jurors should not be instructed that they have the authority to disregard the law. "The fact that there is widespread existence of the jury's prerogative, and approval of its existence as a 'necessary counter to case-hardened judges and arbitrary prosecutors,' does not establish as an imperative that the jury must be informed by the judge of that power. . . . An explicit instruction to a jury conveys an implied approval that runs the risk of degrading the legal structure requisite for true freedom, for an ordered liberty that protects against anarchy as well as tyranny" (*United States v. Dougherty,* 473 F.2d 1113, 1136 [D.C. Cir. 1972]). In 1997, in *United States v. Thomas,* the Second Circuit Court of Appeals held that jury nullification is a violation of a juror's sworn oath to follow the law as instructed by the court and that a trial court judge has the duty to discourage a jury's resort to nullification and is required to remove an individual from the venire or jury who refuses to follow the law (*United States v. Thomas,* 116 F.3d 606 [1997]).

The question in the last analysis is whether jury nullification is an essential safeguard against unjust laws and overly aggressive prosecutors or whether jury nullification promotes disregard for the law. Keep in mind that although jury nullification may protect individuals against oppressive governments, it also was employed in some instances by southern juries in the 1960s to prevent the conviction of individuals accused of murdering civil rights workers. Should juries be explicitly instructed that they have the power to disregard the law? The next section of the chapter discusses waiving a trial and entering a plea of guilty.

You can find United States v. Dougherty *on the study site, http://www.sagepub.com/lippmancp.*

13.3 YOU DECIDE

Hemant Lakhani was convicted for his role in the attempted unlawful importation of shoulder-fired missiles into the United States and was sentenced to forty-seven years in prison. Lakhani was unaware that the individual with whom he was negotiating the sale, Muhammad Habib Ur Rehman, was an FBI informant. The jury rejected Lakhani's plea of entrapment. Following the trial, one of the jurors was interviewed on the radio and claimed that she had been pressured by the other jurors into rejecting the plea of entrapment and into convicting Lakhani. The juror had recently purchased a new house that she was eager to move into, and she was told that in the event that she held out for an acquittal, the jury deliberations would extend several months. The juror stated that she regretted her decision. "Yeah, yeah, I really do. Because as far as I'm concerned the man was entrapped. I shoulda held out." Lakhani appealed his conviction on the grounds of juror misconduct. How would you rule? See *United States v. Lakhani*, 480 F.3d 171 (3d Cir. 2007).

You can find the answer by referring to the study site, http://www.sagepub.com/lippmancp.

Guilty Pleas

You undoubtedly are aware that the vast majority of criminal cases are not brought to trial and instead are disposed of by guilty pleas. In a **plea bargain,** the defendant agrees to plead guilty (or, in some instances, nolo contendere) in return for a "benefit" from the prosecution. The Federal Rules of Criminal Procedure identify three types of plea bargains.

Charges. The prosecutor dismisses some of the charges against the defendant or charges the defendant with a less serious offense. This results in a less severe prison sentence, and the defendant avoids a conviction for a more serious offense.

Sentence. The prosecutor agrees to request the judge to issue a specific sentence. This may involve the length of the sentence, a request that sentences for multiple crimes run concurrently rather than consecutively, or a request that the defendant be given probation rather than a prison sentence.

Sentence recommendation. The prosecutor agrees not to oppose the defendant's request for a specific sentence with the understanding that the judge is free to impose whatever sentence he or she views as appropriate.

The American Bar Association Standards for Criminal Justice, section 14-1.8 (3rd ed., 1997), lists four considerations that explain why it is good social policy for prosecutors to offer a benefit to defendants who plead guilty.

Responsibility. The guilty plea indicates that a defendant is taking responsibility for his or her actions and is expressing regret for the crime.

Flexibility. The guilty plea creates the opportunity for the judge to engage in creative sentencing alternatives such as drug treatment or probation.

Victims. The defendant's guilty plea avoids subjecting victims to the painful experience of a trial.

Cooperation. The defendant may agree to cooperate with the police or prosecutor in other investigations and prosecutions.

Plea bargaining also permits the prosecution to focus resources on those cases in which there is a strong public interest in bringing a defendant to trial or in which a defendant refuses to enter into a plea bargain. Critics, however, point to several troubling aspects of plea bargaining.

Disparity. Defendants who plead guilty typically receive less severe sentences than defendants who are convicted at trial. The result is that individuals are perceived to be punished for exercising the constitutional right to a public trial. There also may be a disparity between the sentences handed out to individuals who enter into plea bargains. This means that the penalty that is imposed on individuals as a result of the plea-bargaining process may not fit the crime.

Innocent defendants. There is a risk that innocent individuals will plead guilty to avoid the uncertainty of trial.

Administrative convenience. A defense lawyer may persuade a defendant to bargain because the lawyer wants to avoid taking the time to prepare the case for a criminal trial. There also is the temptation for defense lawyers to persuade clients to plead guilty in an effort to maintain a good working relationship with the prosecutors' office in hopes of being offered attractive bargains in future cases.

Should plea bargaining be abolished? Would the criminal justice system be overwhelmed by the number of criminal trials? It is possible that prohibiting plea bargaining merely would result in bargains being informally entered into by lawyers behind the scenes rather than bargains being openly presented to a judge. On the other hand, plea bargaining has been successfully eliminated in Alaska and in some counties in Arizona, Iowa, Louisiana, Michigan, Oregon, and Texas.

The Constitutionality of Plea Bargaining

A defendant who enters into a plea bargain waives three very important constitutional rights:

- The Fifth Amendment right against self-incrimination
- The Sixth Amendment right to a criminal trial
- The Sixth Amendment right of a defendant to confront the witnesses against him or her

The U.S. Supreme Court has upheld the constitutionality of plea bargains entered into by defendants and by prosecutors who are seeking the "mutuality of advantage" of avoiding trial. The Court noted that the Constitution does not prohibit a defendant from waiving his or her rights when motivated by a "desire to accept the certainty or probability of a lesser penalty rather than face a wider range of possibilities extending from acquittal to conviction and a higher penalty authorized by law for the crime charged" (*Brady v. United States,* 397 U.S. 742, 751–752 [1970]). In *Santobello v. New York,* the U.S. Supreme Court observed that plea bargaining is "essential to the administration of justice," and "[p]roperly administered, it is to be encouraged" (*Santobello v. New York,* 404 U.S. 257, 260 [1970]).

There are a number of steps that must be satisfied as a condition for a court's accepting a guilty plea. In *Brady v. United States,* the U.S. Supreme Court held that "[w]aivers of constitutional rights not only must be voluntary but must be knowing, intelligent acts done with sufficient awareness of the relevant circumstances and likely consequences" (*Brady v. United States,* 397 U.S. 742, 748 [1970]). The Court ruled that it is unconstitutional for a judge to accept a guilty plea without an affirmative statement by a defendant indicating that he or she has met the constitutional standard for waiver (*Boykin v. United States,* 395 U.S. 238, 242 [1969]).

The constitutional standard is fully articulated in Rule 11 of the Federal Rules of Criminal Procedure. Rule 11 requires that before accepting a plea of guilty or a plea of nolo contendere, the judge must address the defendant personally in open court and insure that the defendant understands the consequences of a guilty plea. The judge is required to cover the following points.

Nature of the criminal charges. The judge is required to explain the charges to which the defendant is pleading guilty and the possible criminal sentence (*McCarthy v. United States,* 394 U.S. 454, 467 [1969]). In *Henderson v. Morgan,* the Supreme Court held that Morgan's guilty plea to second-degree murder was not an intelligent and voluntary admission of guilt because the court never explained to Morgan that second-degree murder required a specific intent to kill and Morgan's guilty plea to second-degree murder was inconsistent with his statement that he had not intended to kill the victim (*Henderson v. Morgan,* 426 U.S. 637 [1976]).

Factual basis of the plea. The judge should explain how the specific facts of the defendant's case fit the requirements of the criminal charge to which the defendant is pleading guilty. This is intended to insure that the defendant does not plead guilty to a criminal charge that does not fit the facts of the case. In *North Carolina v. Alford,* Alford was indicted for first-degree murder and pled guilty to second-degree murder in order to avoid the possibility of receiving the death penalty. Alford insisted that he was innocent and was sentenced to thirty years in prison. The U.S. Supreme Court held that the trial court judge had properly accepted Alford's guilty plea in light of the "strong factual" support from witnesses that Alford had killed the victim (*North Carolina v. Alford,* 400 U.S. 25 [1970]).

Voluntary. Courts may not accept a plea of guilty without first determining that the plea is voluntary and is not the result of force or threats or of promises that are not explicitly set forth in the plea bargain. A prosecutor that offers a defendant a choice between alternatives that the defendant is free to accept or to reject is not considered to have coerced a guilty plea. In *Bordenkircher v. Hayes,* Hayes was indicted for attempting to cash a forged check in the amount of $88.30, an offense punishable by a term of from two to ten years in prison. The prosecutor offered to recommend a sentence of five years in prison in exchange for Hayes pleading guilty. He warned that in the event that Hayes refused to plead guilty and save the court the inconvenience and necessity of a trial, he would return to the grand jury and seek an indictment under the Kentucky Habitual Criminal Act based on Hayes's two prior felony convictions. Hayes chose to stand trial and was sentenced under the habitual offender law to life in prison. Hayes contended that the prosecutor had acted vindictively in an effort to force him to plead guilty. The U.S. Supreme Court held that the "course of conduct engaged in by the prosecutor...which no more than openly presented the defendant with the unpleasant alternatives of forgoing trial or facing charges on which he was plainly subject to prosecution, did not violate the Due Process Clause of the Fourteenth Amendment" (*Bordenkircher v. Hayes,* 434 U.S. 357, 365 [1978]).

The trial court judge also is required to inform the defendant that a guilty plea will result in the waiver of a defendant's right to raise constitutional violations committed prior to the entry of the plea. This includes challenges based on the lawfulness of arrest, unlawful searches and seizures, coerced confessions, denial of a speedy trial, and entrapment.

Can a defendant change his or her mind and withdraw a guilty plea or plea of nolo contendere?

Prior to acceptance of the plea. A defendant may withdraw a guilty plea prior to a judge's acceptance of the plea.

Acceptance of the plea. Once a plea is accepted, the federal courts and most state courts provide that a defendant may withdraw a guilty plea prior to sentencing based on any "fair and just reason."

Sentencing. Following the imposition of the sentence, a defendant typically must meet a more demanding "**miscarriage** of justice" or "manifest injustice" standard.

In *Hyde v. United States,* the U.S. Supreme Court explained that the high standard that is required for withdrawing a guilty plea reflects the fact that a guilty plea is a "grave and solemn act," which is "accepted only with care and discernment." Permitting defendants to automatically withdraw a guilty plea would reduce guilty pleas to a "mere gesture, a temporary and meaningless formality reversible at the defendant's whim."

In evaluating whether a defendant possesses a "fair and just reason" to withdraw a guilty plea, judges ask why the defendant wants to change his or her plea. A defendant is in a strong position to withdraw a plea in those cases in which the defendant asserted his or her innocence when pleading guilty, in which the court failed to explain the nature of the charges, or in which the defendant's lawyer did not fully inform the defendant of the significance of a guilty plea. In most cases, courts are willing to recognize that a defendant has a "fair and just reason" so long as the withdrawal of the plea will not work a hardship on the prosecutor and on the judge, both of whom now confront the prospect of preparing for trial.

Courts are particularly reluctant to recognize a withdrawal of a plea after a judge hands down a sentence. Following sentencing, a defendant is likely to question whether it was wise to plead guilty, and permitting a defendant to withdraw a plea would undermine the interest in maintaining the integrity of a defendant's decision to plead guilty or nolo contendere (*Hyde v. United States,* 520 U.S. 670, 677 [1997]).

What if the prosecutor does not follow the plea agreement with the defendant? Courts have recognized that a defendant may withdraw his or her plea in those instances in which a prosecutor fails to follow an agreement. In *Santobello v. New York,* the prosecutor reduced two gambling charges to a lesser charge in exchange for a guilty plea. At sentencing, a new prosecutor recommended a one-year sentence, the maximum under the statute. The defense attorney objected that the prosecutor who had entered into the agreement had agreed to make no sentencing recommendation. The U.S. Supreme Court returned the case to the state court to determine whether the best course was to permit the defendant to withdraw his plea or whether the best course was to order the prosecutor to enforce the original plea agreement (*Santobello v. New York,* 404 U.S. 257 [1971]).

In *United States v. Benchimol,* the defendant agreed to plead guilty to mail fraud in exchange for a recommendation of probation. The sentencing report to the judge incorrectly indicated that the prosecutor was not making a sentencing recommendation, and the defendant's lawyer informed the court that, in fact, the government recommended probation. The prosecutor replied, "That is an accurate representation," and the defendant was sentenced to six years in prison. The Supreme Court rejected the defendant's effort to withdraw his plea and held that the Government had not agreed to "enthusiastically" make a recommendation (*United States v. Benchimol,* 471 U.S. 453 [1985]). The Government is not obligated to fulfill a plea agreement in those instances in which a defendant fails to meet his or her end of the bargain and, for example, refuses to testify against the other individuals involved in a bank robbery (*United States v. Simmons,* 390 U.S. 377 [1968]).

In reading *North Carolina v. Alford,* consider whether the trial court should have accepted Alford's plea of guilty. Did Alford voluntarily enter a guilty plea?

You can find Bordenkircher v. Hayes *on the study site, http://www.sagepub.com/lippmancp.*

Did the prosecutor coerce Alford into pleading guilty?

North Carolina v. Alford, *400 U.S. 25 (1970), White, J.*

Facts

On December 2, 1963, Alford was indicted for first-degree murder, a capital offense under North Carolina. The court appointed an attorney to represent him, and this attorney questioned all but one of the various witnesses who appellee said would substantiate his claim of innocence. The witnesses, however, did not support Alford's story but gave statements that strongly indicated his guilt. Faced with strong evidence of guilt and no substantial evidentiary support for the claim of innocence, Alford's attorney recommended that he plead guilty but left the ultimate decision to Alford himself. The prosecutor agreed to accept a plea of guilty to a charge of second-degree murder, and on December 10, 1963, Alford pleaded guilty to the reduced charge.

Before the plea was finally accepted by the trial court, the court heard the sworn testimony of a police officer who summarized the State's case. Two other witnesses besides Alford were also heard. Although there was no eyewitness to the crime, the testimony indicated that shortly before the killing, Alford took his gun from his house, stated his intention to kill the victim, and returned home with the declaration that he had carried out the killing. After the summary presentation of the State's case, Alford took the stand and testified that he had not committed the murder but that he was pleading guilty because he faced the threat of the death penalty if he did not do so. In response to the questions of his counsel, he acknowledged that his counsel had informed him of the difference between second- and first-degree murder and of his rights in case he chose to go to trial. The trial court then asked appellee if, in light of his denial of guilt, he still desired to plead guilty to second-degree murder and appellee answered, "Yes, sir. I plead guilty on—from the circumstances that he [Alford's attorney] told me." After eliciting information about Alford's prior criminal record, which was a long one, the trial court sentenced him to thirty years' imprisonment, the maximum penalty for second-degree murder.

Issue

Alford sought postconviction relief in the state court. Among the claims raised was the claim that his plea of guilty was invalid because it was the product of fear and coercion. After a hearing, the state court found that the plea was "willingly, knowingly, and understandingly" made on the advice of competent counsel and in the face of a strong prosecution case. Subsequently... on appeal, a divided panel of the Court of Appeals for the Fourth Circuit reversed on the ground that Alford's guilty plea was made involuntarily.... We vacate the judgment of the court of appeals and remand the case for further proceedings.

Reasoning

We held in *Brady v. United States* that a plea of guilty which would not have been entered except for the defendant's desire to avoid a possible death penalty and to limit the maximum penalty to life imprisonment or a term of years was not for that reason compelled within the meaning of the Fifth Amendment.... The standard was and remains whether the plea represents a voluntary and intelligent choice among the alternative courses of action open to the defendant. That he would not have pleaded except for the opportunity to limit the possible penalty does not necessarily demonstrate that the plea of guilty was not the product of a free and rational choice, especially where the defendant was represented by competent counsel whose advice was that the plea would be to the defendant's advantage.... As previously recounted, after Alford's plea of guilty was offered and the State's case was placed before the judge, Alford denied that he had committed the murder but reaffirmed his desire to plead guilty to avoid a possible death sentence and to limit the penalty to the thirty-year maximum provided for second-degree murder. Ordinarily, a judgment of conviction resting on a plea of guilty is justified by the defendant's admission that he committed the crime charged against him and his consent that judgment be entered without a trial of any kind. The plea usually subsumes both elements, and justifiably so, even though there is no separate, express admission by the defendant that he committed the particular acts claimed to constitute the crime charged in the indictment. Here, Alford entered his plea but accompanied it with the statement that he had not shot the victim.

If Alford's statements were to be credited as sincere assertions of his innocence, there obviously existed a factual and legal dispute between him and the State. Without more, it might be argued that the conviction entered on his guilty plea was invalid, since his assertion of innocence negatived any admission of guilt, which, as we observed last term in *Brady*, is normally "central to the plea and the foundation for entering judgment against the defendant...." In addition to Alford's statement, however, the court had heard an account of the events on the night of the murder, including information from Alford's acquaintances that he had departed from his home with his gun stating his intention to kill and that he had later declared that he had carried out his intention. Nor had Alford wavered in his desire to have the trial court determine his guilt without a jury trial. Although denying the charge against him, he nevertheless preferred the dispute between him and the State to be settled by the judge in the context of a guilty plea proceeding rather than by a formal trial. Thereupon, with the State's telling evidence and Alford's denial before it, the trial court proceeded to convict and sentence Alford for second-degree murder.

[W]hile most pleas of guilty consist of both a waiver of trial and an express admission of guilt, the latter element is not a constitutional requisite to the imposition of criminal penalty. An individual accused of crime may voluntarily, knowingly, and understandingly consent to the imposition of a prison sentence even if he is unwilling or unable to admit his participation in the acts constituting the crime. Nor can we perceive any material difference between a plea that refuses to admit commission of the criminal act and a plea containing a protestation of innocence when, as in the instant case, a defendant intelligently concludes that his interests require entry of a guilty plea, and the record before the judge contains strong evidence of actual guilt. Here, the State had a strong case of first-degree murder against Alford. Whether he realized or disbelieved his guilt, he insisted on his plea because in his view he had absolutely nothing to gain by a trial and much to gain by pleading. Because of the overwhelming evidence against him, a trial was precisely what neither Alford nor his attorney desired. Confronted with the choice between a trial for first-degree murder, on the one hand, and a plea of guilty to second-degree murder, on the other, Alford quite reasonably chose the latter and thereby limited the maximum penalty to a thirty-year term. When his plea is viewed in light of the evidence against him, which substantially negated his claim of innocence and which further provided a means by which the judge could test whether the plea was being intelligently entered, its validity cannot be seriously questioned. In view of the strong factual basis for the plea demonstrated by the State and Alford's clearly expressed desire to enter it despite his professed belief in his innocence, we hold that the trial judge did not commit constitutional error in accepting it.... Alford now argues in effect that the State should not have allowed him this choice but should have insisted on proving him guilty of murder in the first degree. The States in their wisdom may take this course by statute or otherwise and may prohibit the practice of accepting pleas to lesser included offenses under any circumstances. But this is not the mandate of the Fourteenth Amendment and the Bill of Rights. The prohibitions against involuntary or unintelligent pleas should not be relaxed, but neither should an exercise in arid logic render those constitutional guarantees counterproductive and put in jeopardy the very human values they were meant to preserve.

Holding

The Court of Appeals for the Fourth Circuit was in error to find Alford's plea of guilty invalid because it was made to avoid the possibility of the death penalty. That court's judgment . . . is vacated, and the case is remanded to the court of appeals for further proceedings consistent with this opinion.

Dissenting, *Brennan, J.*, joined by *Douglas, J.*, and *Marshall, J.*

Last term, this Court held, over my dissent, that a plea of guilty may validly be induced by an unconstitutional threat to subject the defendant to the risk of death, so long as the plea is entered in open court and the defendant is represented by competent counsel who is aware of the threat, albeit not of its unconstitutionality. The record demonstrates that the actual effect of the unconstitutional threat was to induce a guilty plea from a defendant who was unwilling to admit his guilt.

I adhere to the view that, in any given case, the influence of such an unconstitutional threat "must necessarily be given weight in determining the voluntariness of a plea." And, without reaching the question whether due process permits the entry of judgment upon a plea of guilty accompanied by a contemporaneous denial of acts constituting the crime, I believe that at the very least such a denial of guilt is also a relevant factor in determining whether the plea was voluntarily and intelligently made. With these factors in mind, it is sufficient in my view to state that his decision to plead guilty was not voluntary but was "the product of duress as much so as choice reflecting physical constraint."

Questions for Discussion

1. Why does Alford argue that the trial court judge should have refused to accept his guilty plea?
2. What is the holding of the Supreme Court in *Alford*?
3. Did the Supreme Court find it significant that there was a factual basis for Alford's plea?
4. Was Alford's guilty plea coerced? Should a defendant be permitted to assert his or her innocence and plead guilty?
5. Would the criminal justice system have been better served by bringing Alford to trial rather than by accepting a guilty plea?

13.4 YOU DECIDE

Mosher and two co-defendants were indicted for armed robbery. Mosher withdrew his not-guilty plea and, in June 1964, pled guilty to armed robbery. On July 9, 1965, he was sentenced to a minimum of forty years and to a maximum of sixty years in prison. Mosher moved to vacate his guilty plea on the grounds that it was involuntary. His lawyer had met with the judge, had incorrectly interpreted the judge's remarks, and had misinformed Mosher that he would receive a sentence of between fifteen and sixteen years in jail in return for a guilty plea. The trial court judge conducted an evidentiary hearing and concluded that Mosher was induced to plead guilty by statements made by his counsel, Morahan. Mosher was told by Morahan that Judge Trainor had promised to give him a minimum sentence of fifteen to sixteen years of prison if he pled guilty.

Judge Trainor made no such promise. Morahan's representations and assurances to Mosher that such a promise had been made by the judge were untrue. Mosher's prison sentence was contrary to the assurances given by Morahan to Mosher regarding the sentence that would be imposed.

Was Mosher's guilty plea involuntary? See *Mosher v. LaValle*, 491 F.2d 1346 (2d Cir. 1973). What if Mosher had misinterpreted Morahan's statement and had erroneously concluded that the judge had promised a more lenient sentence? See *United States ex rel. LaFay v. Fritz*, 455 F.2d 297 (2d Cir. 1972); *United States ex rel. Curtis v. Zelker*, 466 F.2d 1092 (2d Cir. 1972).

You can find the answer by referring to the study site, http://www.sagepub.com/lippmancp.

13.5 YOU DECIDE

Charles Jideonwo is a citizen of Nigeria who entered the United States on a student visa in 1980. In 1981, he was granted residency status based on his marriage to an American citizen with whom he had one child. In 1994, Jideonwo pled guilty to one count of conspiracy to possess with intent to distribute heroin. Jideonwo was sentenced to four years and eleven months in exchange for a guilty plea and a promise to cooperate in future narcotics investigations. Jideonwo specifically negotiated a sentence of under five years because individuals sentenced to prison for less than five years were eligible to request the Immigration and Naturalization Service to waive their deportation to their country of citizenship. In 1996, the law was changed to make an individual convicted of an aggravated felony ineligible for a waiver. Jideonwo received notice that he was to be deported and asked the Seventh Circuit Court of Appeals to order the Immigration and Naturalization Service to halt his deportation. Would Jideonwo's deportation violate the plea agreement that he entered into with the U.S. Government? See *Jideonwo v. INS*, 224 F.3d 692 (7th Cir. 2007). What if the prosecutor exceeded his authority and guaranteed that the defendant would not be deported in the event that he pled guilty? See *Pedro v. United States*, 79 F.3d 1065 (11th Cir. 1990).

You can find the answer by referring to the study site, http://www.sagepub.com/lippmancp.

Chapter Summary

Following the first appearance, the next step typically is the preliminary hearing. The purpose of the preliminary hearing is to determine whether there is sufficient evidence to bind the defendant over for trial or, in the alternative, whether there is sufficient evidence to send the case to a grand jury. The preliminary hearing is conducted as a "mini-trial" in which the defendant has a right to be represented by a lawyer. The basic question is whether a crime was committed and whether the defendant committed the crime. Most states adhere to the probable cause standard, while a minority of jurisdictions adhere to the prima facie approach. A preliminary hearing is not constitutionally required. In indictment states, the prosecutor may bypass the preliminary hearing by taking the case immediately to the grand jury. In information states, the prosecutor may file an information and may bring a charge either before a preliminary hearing or before a grand jury.

The grand jury is constituted of between sixteen and twenty-three persons who provide a check on the prosecutor and determine whether there is sufficient evidence to proceed to trial. At the conclusion of the grand jury's investigation, the grand jury may return a true bill and issue an indictment or refuse to indict and return a no bill, or the grand jury may decide to undertake an independent investigation of criminal activity and file a presentment with the court. The grand jury is, in theory, independent of prosecutors and judges but, in practice, possesses several powers that make it a particularly powerful arm of the prosecutor in investigating criminal activity.

Once the decision is made by the grand jury to indict an individual or by a preliminary hearing to bind a defendant over for trial, the next step is an arraignment. At the arraignment, a defendant is brought before a trial court judge and is informed of the charges filed against him or her and is asked to enter one of four possible pleas: guilty, not guilty, nolo contendere, or not guilty by reason of insanity.

Prior to trial, the defense attorney may file a number of pretrial motions.

Double jeopardy. A defendant may not be prosecuted or punished more than once for the same offense. Despite the fact that jeopardy has attached, a second trial may be conducted in the case of a mistrial granted on the defendant's motion or with the defendant's consent or based on manifest necessity. Separate trials may be conducted by "dual sovereigns."

Speedy trial. The federal government and the states require speedy trials for individuals accused of crimes. The question whether a trial is "speedy" primarily is based on the time that has elapsed between the accusation against the defendant and the defendant's trial, taking into consideration the totality of the circumstances, including the complexity of the case.

Venue. A trial may be transferred to another district in the event that the court is satisfied that the prejudice against a defendant is so great that the defendant cannot obtain a fair and impartial trial.

Discovery. The prosecution is required to provide exculpatory material to the defense. Several states also require the disclosure of information such as the names of witnesses and the statements of witnesses.

Motion to suppress. Evidence seized in violation of the Fourth Amendment as well as unconstitutionally obtained confessions and identifications may be excluded from evidence.

The Sixth Amendment provides that "in all criminal prosecutions, the accused shall enjoy the right to a . . . public trial by an impartial jury." In 1968, in *Duncan v. Louisiana,* the U.S. Supreme Court held that the right of a jury trial in "serious criminal cases" is "fundamental to the American scheme of justice" and is protected under the Due Process Clause of the Fourteenth Amendment and "must therefore be respected by the States." The Court held that a jury trial is required for "serious crimes" that carry a sentence of more than six months. The federal government and a majority of states require twelve-person juries. In 1970, in *Williams v. Florida,* the U.S. Supreme Court held that the twelve-person requirement is not an indispensable component of the Sixth Amendment as incorporated into the Due Process Clause of the Fourteenth Amendment. Eight years later, in *Ballew v. Georgia,* the Supreme Court held that Georgia could not constitutionally conduct criminal trials with juries of fewer than six persons.

The jury pool, or venire from which a petit panel is drawn, typically is based on names drawn from voter registration lists or lists of licensed drivers, and several states rely on the key-man system. Individuals in the jury venire are subject to voir dire and may be struck from the jury based on a challenge for cause or based on a peremptory challenge. The Fifth Amendment Equal Protection Clause prohibits intentional discrimination based on race, ethnicity, gender, or religion in the jury-selection process. The Sixth Amendment requires that a jury should be drawn from a fair cross-section of the community. Individuals may be excluded during voir dire for cause based on an inability to fairly and impartially weigh the evidence. A peremptory challenge is a challenge that is exercised "without a reason." In 1986, in *Batson v. Kentucky,* the U.S. Supreme Court held that the Equal Protection Clause prohibits a prosecutor from challenging potential jurors "solely on account of their race . . . on the assumption that black jurors as a group will be unable to impartially consider the State's case against a black defendant." In 1994, the U.S. Supreme Court held in *J.E.B. v. Alabama ex rel.* that lawyers also are prohibited from using peremptory challenges to exclude jurors based on gender. Judges with a conflict of interest should remove themselves from a case (or recuse themselves), and a defendant may file a motion requesting that a judge remove himself or herself from the case on the grounds that the judge is unable to be fair and impartial.

The Sixth Amendment provides that in all criminal prosecutions, the accused shall enjoy the right to a "public trial." This is intended to protect individuals from secret prosecutions. A defendant does not have an absolute right to attend his or her trial. In *Illinois v. Allen,* the U.S. Supreme Court held that an unruly defendant may be removed from the courtroom during his or her trial.

The trial has a number of phases.

Opening statement. The lawyers may make brief opening statements.

Presentation of evidence. The prosecution presents the case-in-chief and the defense responds with a rebuttal. Witnesses may be cross-examined, and both the defense and the prosecution may introduce testimonial hearsay where a witness is unavailable and was subject to cross-examination. Nontestimonial hearsay is admissible where the statement is considered to satisfy the indicia of reliability. The defendant has a Sixth Amendment right to confront the witnesses against him or her and to cross-examine these individuals. The Compulsory Process Clause guarantees a suspect the ability to obtain witnesses in his or her favor and to obtain documents required for presenting a defense.

Burden of proof. The accusatorial system places the burden of going forward (or the burden of production) and the burden of proof on the prosecution.

Reasonable doubt. Each element of the offense must be established beyond a reasonable doubt, or by a "near certitude" of guilt.

Closing argument. The prosecution and the defense have the opportunity to summarize their cases.

Jury instructions. The judge instructs the jury on the law, and the jury must apply the law to the facts in deciding whether the defendant is guilty beyond a reasonable doubt.

Jury deliberations. The jury generally is permitted to examine a copy of the charges and the judge's instructions, and in most cases, the jurors may view items introduced into evidence. The U.S. Supreme Court has approved nonunanimous verdicts based on a 9-to-3 vote on the grounds that a "heavy majority" of the jury remains "convinced of guilt." The jury possesses the power of nullification: the ability to disregard the law and to acquit a defendant despite overwhelming evidence of guilt.

The vast majority of criminal cases do not reach trial and are disposed of by guilty pleas. These cases typically are plea-bargained. The U.S. Supreme Court has upheld this practice, although it has required that a guilty plea should be knowing, intelligent, and voluntary. A defendant may withdraw a plea prior to a judge's acceptance of the plea. Once the plea is accepted, it may be withdrawn for a "fair and just reason." Following the imposition of a sentence, a plea may be withdrawn only on a "miscarriage of justice" or "manifest injustice" standard.

This chapter illustrates the detailed steps that must be followed under the U.S. Constitution during the pretrial and trial phases of the criminal justice system. Consider how these rules strike a balance between the efficient prosecution of crime and the interest in protecting defendants against unfair and discriminatory prosecutions. In Chapter 14, we turn our attention to sentencing and to criminal appeals.

Chapter Review Questions

1. What is the purpose of a preliminary hearing?
2. Discuss the role of the grand jury. Why is the grand jury such a powerful institution?
3. Describe the function of an arraignment.
4. Outline the purpose of the pretrial motions raising issues of double jeopardy, speedy trial, change of venue, discovery, and the suppression of evidence.
5. When is a defendant entitled to a jury trial?
6. Discuss the constitutional requirements regarding the size of the jury.
7. What are the limitations on the selection of jurors imposed by the Equal Protection Clause and the Sixth Amendment cross-section-of-the-community requirement?
8. What is voir dire? Discuss challenges for cause and death-qualified juries. Describe the *Batson* requirement and peremptory challenges.
9. Why does the Sixth Amendment guarantee public trials? When may a defendant be excluded from his or her trial? Discuss the tension between a free press and a free trial.
10. What is the purpose of the opening statement?
11. Discuss the Confrontation Clause and discuss cross-examination. When may hearsay evidence be relied on at trial? What is required under the Sixth Amendment Compulsory Process Clause?
12. What is the significance of the burden of proof? Why is the prosecution required to prove guilt beyond a reasonable doubt? In your own words, describe the beyond-a-reasonable-doubt standard.
13. What information is included in a judge's instructions to the jury? What are the limitations on the closing arguments at trial?
14. Discuss whether jury unanimity is required. When may a jury engage in jury nullification?
15. What are the policy arguments for and against plea bargaining and the disposing of a defendant's criminal charges through a guilty plea? What constitutional issues are presented by the plea-bargaining process? Describe the conditions that must be satisfied before a trial court judge may accept a defendant's guilty plea.

Legal Terminology

arraignment
beyond a reasonable doubt
Blockburger test
Brady rule
burden of proof
case-in-chief
challenge for cause
closing argument
collateral estoppel
Compulsory Process Clause
Confrontation Clause
cross-examination
double jeopardy
dual sovereignty doctrine
dynamite charge
fair cross-section requirement
hearsay
hung jury
indictment
information
invited response
jury instructions
jury nullification
jury poll
key man
manifest necessity
miscarriage
mistrial
modified indictment states
motion for a judgment of acquittal
no bill
opening statement
pattern jury instructions
peremptory challenge
petit jury
plea bargain
preliminary hearing
presentment
pretrial motions
purging the grand jury
reasonable doubt
rebuttal
recusal
rule of exclusion
speedy trial
subpoena ad testificandum
subpoena duces tecum
transactional immunity
true bill
use and derivative use immunity
venire
venue
vicinage
voir dire

Criminal Procedure on the Web

Log on to the Web-based student study site at **http://www.sagepub.com/lippmancp** to assist you in completing the Criminal Procedure on the Web exercises, as well as for additional features such as leading cases, podcasts, self-quizzes, and audio/video links.

1. Watch a Public Broadcasting program on guilty pleas and plea bargaining and read interviews and articles on plea bargaining.
2. Read about the moral dilemmas confronting defense attorneys, including whether to represent a client who the attorney knows is guilty of the criminal charge.
3. Watch dramatic moments from current criminal trials.
4. Learn about famous murder trials.

Bibliography

Mark E. Cammack and Norman M. Garland, *Advanced Criminal Procedure in a Nutshell,* 2nd ed. (St. Paul, MN: Thomson/West, 2006), pp. 60–436. A straightforward introduction to pretrial, trial, and conviction.

Pamela S. Karlan, *"Batson v. Kentucky:* The Constitutional Challenges of Peremptory Challenges," *Criminal Procedure Stories,* ed. Carol S. Steiker (New York: Foundation Press, 2006), pp. 381–412. A history and discussion of the prohibition against the reliance on race in peremptory challenges.

Nancy J. King, *"Duncan v. Louisiana:* How Bigotry in the Bayou Led to the Federal Regulation of State Juries," *Criminal Procedure Stories,* ed. Carol S. Steiker (New York: Foundation Press, 2006), pp. 261–294. A history of the incorporation of the right to a jury trial into the Fourteenth Amendment Due Process Clause.

Wayne R. LaFave, Jerald H. Israel, and Nancy J. King, *Criminal Procedure,* 4th ed. (St. Paul, MN: Thomson/West, 2004), pp. 714–881, 966–1208. A detailed and exhaustive discussion of pretrial, trial, and conviction.

William J. Stuntz, *"Bordenkircher v. Hayes:* Plea Bargaining and the Decline of the Rule of Law," *Criminal Procedure Stories,* ed. Carol S. Steiker (New York: Foundation Press, 2006), pp. 351–379. A legal history of *Bordenkircher v. Hayes* and the impact of plea bargaining on the American criminal justice system.

14 Sentencing and Appeals

Is it cruel and unusual punishment to execute an individual by lethal injection?

Kentucky's execution facilities consist of the execution chamber, a control room separated by a one-way window, and a witness room. The warden and deputy warden remain in the execution chamber with the prisoner, who is strapped to a gurney. The execution team administers the drugs remotely from the control room through five feet of IV tubing. If, as determined by the warden and deputy warden through visual inspection, the prisoner is not unconscious within sixty seconds following the delivery of the sodium thiopental to the primary IV site, a new three-gram dose of thiopental is administered to the secondary site before injecting the pancuronium and potassium chloride.... A physician is present to assist in any effort to revive the prisoner in the event of a last-minute stay of execution.

Core Concepts and Summary Statements

Introduction

The chapter covers sentencing, appeals, and habeas corpus.

A Brief History of Sentencing in the United States

A. The English system of harsh criminal punishments was brought to the United States.
B. In the United States in the nineteenth century, emphasis was placed on incarceration, rehabilitation, and indeterminate sentences. In the twentieth century, there was a shift to determinate sentences.
C. In the last several years, there has been a modest movement toward community-based services for offenders.

Criminal Punishment

A. A penalty does not necessarily constitute a *criminal punishment*.
B. A criminal punishment triggers various constitutional rights and protections.

Purposes of Punishment

There are several purposes of punishment: retribution, deterrence, incapacitation, restitution, and restoration.

Types of Punishment

Criminal punishments include imprisonment, fines, probation, intermediate sanctions, and capital punishment.

Approaches to Sentencing

There are various approaches to sentencing: determinate sentences, mandatory minimum sentences, indeterminate sentences, and presumptive sentences.

The Judicial Sentencing Process

A. In most jurisdictions a judge is required to request a presentence report from a probation officer.
B. The judge conducts a sentencing hearing at which the defense attorney and prosecutor argue for a favorable sentence.
C. The defendant has the right to make a statement at the sentencing hearing.

Sentencing Guidelines

A. The Federal Sentencing Reform Act of 1984 established the U.S. Sentencing Commission. The commission drafted guidelines to be followed by judges in sentencing offenders.
B. Sentences under the federal guidelines are based on a formula that reflects the seriousness and characteristics of the offense and the criminal history of the offender. The judge employs a sentencing grid and is required to sentence the defendant within the narrow range where the offender's criminal offense and criminal history intersect on the grid.
C. Judges are required to document the reasons for criminal sentences and are obligated to provide a specific

reason for any upward or downward departure.

D. Several recent U.S. Supreme Court decisions have held that it is unconstitutional to enhance a sentence based on facts found to exist by the judge by a preponderance of the evidence rather than by a jury beyond a reasonable doubt.

E. The U.S. Supreme Court also has ruled that the sentencing guidelines are advisory. An appellate court should examine whether a judge's sentencing decision is reasonable, whether it is inside or outside the guidelines.

Determinate Sentences

A. Determinate sentences possess the advantage of providing for predictable, definite, and uniform sentences.

B. The federal government introduced mandatory minimum sentences in the Anti–Drug Abuse Act of 1986 and its 1988 amendments.

Cruel and Unusual Punishment

A. The Eighth Amendment to the U.S. Constitution is the primary constitutional check on criminal punishments.

B. The U.S. Supreme Court has ruled that the prohibition against cruel and unusual punishment applies to the states as well as to the federal government, and virtually every state constitution contains similar language.

Methods of Punishment

A. Courts have not limited the prohibition on cruel and unusual punishment to acts condemned at the time of passage of the Eighth Amendment. "Cruel and unusual punishment" is an evolving concept.

B. The death penalty historically has been viewed as a constitutionally acceptable form of punishment. Cruelty requires the intentional infliction of unnecessary pain.

Capital Punishment

A. Judges have been particularly concerned with the proportionality of the death penalty.

B. In *Gregg v. Georgia,* in 1976, the U.S. Supreme Court approved a Georgia statute designed to insure the proportionate application of capital punishment.

C. In weighing states, the jury is required to find that the aggravating circumstances outweigh the mitigating circumstances. Nonweighing states provide that the death penalty may be imposed once the jury finds an aggravating circumstance. The aggravating circumstance is to be evaluated in light of the totality of evidence.

D. The death penalty may not be imposed for rape or robbery, and juveniles and mentally challenged individuals may not be subjected to the death penalty.

The Eighth Amendment and Sentences for a Term of Years

The U.S. Supreme Court appears to have accepted that the length of a criminal sentence is the province of elected state legislators and that judicial intervention should be "extremely rare" and limited to sentences that are "grossly disproportionate" to the seriousness of the offense.

Equal Protection

A. Judicial decisions have consistently held that it is unconstitutional for a judge to base a sentence on a defendant's race, gender, ethnicity, or nationality.

B. In regard to laws that do not discriminate on their face, a defendant claiming that his or her sentence is discriminatory in violation of the Equal Protection Clause must demonstrate both a discriminatory impact and a discriminatory intent.

Criminal Appeals

A. The federal government and all fifty states accordingly provide an appeal as a matter of right for felony convictions. This appeal generally is to an intermediate appellate court. A second, discretionary appeal (optional) may be filed with the state supreme court.

B. The U.S. Supreme Court has held that during an appeal, as a matter of right, an individual possesses constitutional rights.

C. In general, an appeal may be filed only following a final judgment. In some isolated instances, an interlocutory appeal may be filed prior to the final judgment where it would be too late to wait for the final judgment.

D. Appellate courts examine whether an error is harmless. "Plain errors" are so serious that they are reviewed despite the fact that the defense attorney did not raise the issue at trial.

E. The violation of fundamental constitutional rights results in the automatic reversal of a verdict.

F. A new legal rule that is established on appeal is "fully retroactive" to all cases that have yet to be filed and to all cases or appeals that have been filed.

Habeas Corpus

A. An application for habeas corpus is a noncriminal (civil) lawsuit in which the defendant (now called the petitioner or plaintiff) asks the court for a *writ of habeas corpus* on the grounds that he or she is being unlawfully detained. In the event that the court finds that the plaintiff is unlawfully convicted or is being held without justification, the judge will order the individual to be released from custody.

B. An individual filing a habeas corpus petition must be in custody and is required to file a claim within one year of having exhausted his or her state appeals.

C. Federal appellate courts determine whether the state court judgment is reasonable. Appellate courts rarely conduct a hearing on the facts. An appellate court will not retroactively apply the law, and habeas corpus generally is not available to individuals who have failed to follow the rules for filing appeals in their state.

D. An individual generally may not file a habeas petition that raises an issue that already has been included in a prior habeas petition and may not file a second habeas petition that raises an issue that could have been (but was not) included in a prior habeas petition.

Introduction

Following a criminal conviction, the attention of the defendant, the lawyers, and the judge shifts to the sentencing phase of the trial. The sentencing decision will determine the nature and length of the defendant's punishment.

Despite the fact that every effort is made to insure that a defendant is fairly treated throughout the pretrial and trial phases of the criminal justice system, there always is the possibility that a defendant's conviction has been significantly influenced by an error. This might involve a judge's mistake in admitting unlawfully obtained evidence or a judge's failure to tell the jury to disregard a prosecutor's improper and inflammatory remarks during the closing argument. As a result, the federal government and the states provide individuals with an appeal to review the lawfulness of their convictions. Defendants who have exhausted their appeals are provided with yet another safeguard in the writ of habeas corpus. This civil action permits a defendant to petition federal courts to examine whether the trial court and appellate courts have reasonably interpreted the law in upholding his or her conviction.

The rights accorded to defendants during sentencing and appeal and in petitioning for a writ of habeas corpus are yet another example of the effort to strike a balance between the societal interest in criminal convictions and the protection of individual rights. In summary, this chapter covers sentencing, appeals, and habeas corpus.

A Brief History of Sentencing in the United States

The English common law punished felonies with the death penalty. The infliction of death could be barbaric. Beheading and hanging were the most humane of the punishments, which also included breaking on the wheel, drawing and quartering, and burning at the stake. Misdemeanants were punished by public floggings. These punishments were staged in public to deter crime. Economic offenses resulted in fines, and offenders were expected to provide restitution. Destitute petty criminals in some instances were transported to distant English colonies in order to remove them from society.

The English system of harsh punishment was brought to the newly established American colonies. Here again, felonies resulted in the death penalty. Minor offenses were punished by flogging or by confinement in the stocks or the pillory. Economic offenders who were unable to pay fines or restitution were subjected to forced labor or flogging, confined in the stocks, or branded. The strong religious tradition of the American colonies led to a focus on crimes against "public morality." The Massachusetts Criminal Code of 1648 punished witchcraft, sodomy, adultery, and various religious crimes. One innovation was to "warn out" offenders and to exclude them from towns. Imprisonment largely was unknown.

The Bill of Rights ratified in 1791 prohibited cruel and unusual punishment. The English system of harsh punishment gradually came to be replaced by a somewhat more humane approach to punishment that eventually led to limitations on the death penalty; abolition of floggings, whipping, and branding; and a prohibition on corporal punishment. Serious offenses continued to result in death before a firing squad or in a gas chamber and later the electric chair.

In 1787, Quaker Benjamin Rush proposed a "house of reform" in which prisoners would be incarcerated and rehabilitated and come to abandon their criminal careers. In 1790, Pennsylvania became the first state to follow Rush's ambitious plans and introduced the penitentiary ("a place to do penance") system. The advocates of imprisonment believed that offenders could be reformed and rehabilitated through personal contemplation, bible study, and hard work.

These early penal institutions quickly became overcrowded and understaffed, and they were criticized as incubators of crime that warehoused prisoners. Reformers argued that personal transformation could best be achieved by adopting a system of indeterminate punishments. In 1870, the National Prison Congress endorsed a system of "sentences of indeterminate duration." This resolution was sponsored by Zebulon Brockway, the superintendent of the Elmira Reformatory in New York. Brockway persuaded Michigan to adopt the first indeterminate sentence law, which provided for a three-year term for "common prostitutes." This sentence could be terminated at the discretion of the warden of the Detroit House of Corrections in the event that the inmate was determined to have been rehabilitated.

New York adopted a modified form of indeterminate sentencing. Its statute established a maximum prison term. Judges were to fix a prison term within this limit. The term of imprisonment that the defendant actually served was left to the discretion of prison administrators. The stress was on "individualized sentencing" and on reforming the offender rather than on punishing the crime. By 1922, thirty-seven states had adopted statutes modeled on the New York law. States gradually began to rely on the evaluation of psychiatrists, social workers, and parole boards to determine an inmate's fitness for release.

Indeterminate sentences and rehabilitation were criticized as placing too much control in unelected judges and correctional officials. In the 1970s, there was a backlash against indeterminate sentencing, and critics declared it to have been a failure. Legislators responded by taking the power to fix sentences from judges.

The stage now was set for a movement toward determinate or fixed-time sentencing. The emphasis under this "just deserts" model was on incarcerating defendants for definite terms in order to incapacitate them and to deter them from engaging in crime. In 1976, California introduced a new determinate sentencing law that proclaimed that the purpose of imprisonment is punishment and that this purpose is best served by "terms proportionate to the seriousness of the offense." The law provided for uniformity in the sentences of offenders committing the same offense under similar circumstances. In 1980, Minnesota introduced a system of sentencing guidelines. A similar system was adopted by the federal government in 1984.

By 2005, the system of determinate punishment was beginning to lose steam. The prison population in most states outpaced available prison space, and state budgets increasingly were threatened by the need to build additional penitentiaries. Roughly half of the states reduced the length of criminal sentences, thirteen states repealed harsh sentences for drug crimes, and other states introduced counseling and drug treatment as alternatives to incarceration. Nine states modified correctional policies to enable inmates to gain an early release from prison. There also was a commitment to providing inmates re-entering society with drug counseling and other services thought to be required to enable them to take advantage of their new-won freedom. President George W. Bush signed the Second Chance Act of 2007 (18 U.S.C. § 3621(e)), which provided grants to states to ease the adjustment of individuals released from prison.

Criminal Punishment

Professor George P. Fletcher, in his book *Rethinking Criminal Law,* writes that the central characteristic of a criminal law is that a violation of the rule results in the imposition of punishment by a court. This issue is important, because a criminal charge triggers various constitutional rights, such as the right not to be subjected to double jeopardy, the right to a lawyer, and the right to a trial by a jury. Would the quarantine of individuals during a flu pandemic be considered a civil disability or a criminal penalty? The Supreme Court, in *Kennedy v. Mendoza-Martinez* (377 U.S. 144, 168–169 [1963]), has listed various considerations that determine whether a law is criminal:

- Does the legislature characterize the penalty as civil or criminal?
- Has the type of penalty imposed historically been viewed as criminal?
- Does the penalty involve a significant disability or restraint on personal freedom?
- Does the penalty promote a purpose traditionally associated with criminal punishment?
- Is the imposition of the penalty based on an individual's intentional wrongdoing?
- Has the prohibited conduct traditionally been viewed as criminal?

Whether a law is considered to impose criminal punishment may have important consequences for a defendant. For instance, in *Smith v. Doe,* the U.S. Supreme Court was asked to decide whether Alaska's sex offender registration law constituted *ex post facto* criminal punishment. In 1994, the U.S. Congress passed the Jacob Wetterling Crimes Against Children and Sexually Violent Offender Registration Act that makes certain federal criminal justice funding dependent on a state's adoption of a sex offender registration law. By 1996, every state, the District of Columbia, and the federal government had enacted some type of "Megan's Law." These statutes were named in memory and honor of Megan Kanka, a seven-year-old New Jersey child who had been sexually assaulted and murdered in 1994 by a neighbor who, unknown to Megan's family, had prior convictions for sexual offenses against children.

Alaska adopted a retroactive law that required both convicted sex offenders and child kidnappers to register and keep in contact with local law enforcement authorities. Alaska provided nonconfidential information to the public on the Internet, including an offender's crime, address, place of employment, and photograph. Supreme Court Justice Anthony Kennedy, in his majority opinion in *Smith v. Doe,* agreed with Alaska that this statute is intended to protect the public from the danger posed by sexual offenders through the dissemination of information and that the law is not intended to constitute and did not constitute unconstitutional ex post facto (retroactive) criminal punishment (*Smith v. Doe,* 528 U.S. 846 [1997]).

The issue of whether a law imposes criminal punishment also was important to Leroy Hendricks, an inmate with a long history of sexually molesting children, who was scheduled for release from a Kansas prison. As Hendricks was to be released, Kansas invoked the state's Sexually Violent Predator Act (Kan. State. Ann. § 59-29a01), which establishes procedures for the indefinite civil commitment in a wing of the penitentiary of persons who are likely to engage in repeated "predatory acts of sexual violence." The U.S. Supreme Court ruled that the law did not subject Hendricks to double jeopardy, because the confinement of "mentally unstable individuals who present a danger to the public... [is a] classic example of nonpunitive detention." The aim was to treat individuals and to release them when they no longer pose a threat (*Hendricks v. Kansas,* 521 U.S. 348 [1997]).

The next section briefly outlines the purposes or goals that form the basis of sentencing in the criminal justice system. These purposes include the following:

- Retribution
- Deterrence
- Rehabilitation
- Incapacitation
- Restoration

Purposes of Punishment

The United States, as indicated in our earlier discussion, has gone through various approaches to criminal punishment. We continue to debate whether the primary goal of punishment should be to assist offenders to turn their lives around or to safeguard society by locking up offenders. Others rightly point out that we should not lose sight of the need to require offenders to compensate crime victims. In considering the various approaches to punishment listed below, ask yourself what goals should guide our criminal justice system.

Retribution. Retribution imposes punishment based on just deserts. Offenders should receive the punishment that they deserve based on the seriousness of their criminal acts. The retributive philosophy is based on the familiar biblical injunction of "an eye for an eye, a tooth for a tooth." Retribution assumes that we all know right from wrong, are morally responsible for our conduct, and should be held accountable.

Deterrence. The theory of **specific deterrence** imposes punishment to deter or discourage a defendant from committing a crime in the future. **General deterrence** punishes an offender as an example to deter others from violating the law.

Rehabilitation. Punishment is intended to reform the offender and to transform him or her into a law-abiding and productive member of society. **Rehabilitation** appeals to the idealistic notion that people are essentially good and can transform their lives when encouraged and given support.

Incapacitation. The aim of **incapacitation** is to remove offenders from society to prevent them from continuing to menace others. This approach accepts that there are criminally inclined individuals who cannot be deterred or rehabilitated. **Selective incapacitation** singles out offenders who have committed certain serious offenses for lengthy incarceration. In many states, a conviction for a drug offense or a second or third felony under a "three strikes and you're out" law results in a lengthy prison sentence or life imprisonment.

Restoration. Restoration stresses the harm caused to victims of crime and requires offenders to engage in financial restitution and community service to compensate the victim and the community and to "make them whole once again." The restorative justice approach recognizes that the needs of victims often are overlooked in the criminal justice system. This approach also is designed to encourage offenders to develop a sense of individual responsibility and to become responsible members of society.

This discussion of the purposes of punishment is no mere academic theorizing. Judges, when provided with the opportunity to exercise discretion, are guided by these purposes in determining the appropriate punishment. For example, in a New York case, the court described Dr. Bernard Bergman as a man of "unimpeachably high character, attainments and distinction" who is "respected by people around the world for his work in religion, charity and education." Bergman's desire for money apparently drove him to fraudulently request payment from the U.S. government for medical treatments that, in fact, he had not provided to nursing home patients. He entered guilty pleas to fraud charges in both New York and federal courts, and he argued that he should not be imprisoned, because he did not require "specific deterrence."

Judge Marvin Frankel, in his judgment in *United States v. Bergman,* recognized that there was little need for incapacitation and doubted whether imprisonment would provide rehabilitation. He nevertheless imposed a four-month prison sentence, explaining that this "stern sentence" should be "sufficiently frightening" to deter other white-collar professionals who may be tempted to break the law. Judge Frankel also explained that the four-month sentence served the retributive interest in punishing Bergman for the harm he caused to society (*United States v. Bergman,* 416 F. Supp. 496 [S.D.N.Y. 1976]).

Types of Punishment

Various types of punishments are available to judges. These punishments often are used in combination with one another:

- ***Imprisonment.*** Individuals sentenced to a year or less generally are sentenced to local jails. Sentences for longer periods typically are served in state or federal prisons.
- ***Fines.*** State statutes usually provide for fines as an alternative to incarceration or in addition to incarceration.
- ***Probation.*** Probation involves the suspension of a prison sentence so long as an individual continues to report to a probation officer and to follow certain standards of personal conduct. This may involve psychiatric treatment or a program of counseling for alcohol or drug abuse. The conditions of probation are required to be reasonably related to the rehabilitation of the offender and to the protection of the public.
- ***Intermediate sanctions.*** These include house arrest with electronic monitoring, short-term "shock" incarceration, community service, and restitution. Intermediate sanctions may be imposed as a criminal sentence, as a condition of probation, following imprisonment, or in combination with a fine.
- ***Death.*** Thirty-five states and the federal government provide for the death penalty for homicide. The other states provide for life without parole.

The federal government and most states also provide for *assets forfeiture* or the seizure pursuant to a court order of the "fruits" of illegal narcotics transactions (along with certain other crimes) or of the "instrumentalities" that were used in such activity. The burden rests on the government to establish by a preponderance of the evidence that instrumentalities (vehicles), profits (money), or property are linked to an illegal transaction. In *United States v. Ursery,* the U.S. Supreme Court held that the seizure of money and property did not qualify as double jeopardy, because forfeitures do not constitute punishment (*United States v. Ursery,* 518 U.S. 267 [1996]).

Approaches to Sentencing

The approach to sentencing historically has shifted in response to the prevailing criminal justice thinking and philosophy. The states and the federal government generally follow four different approaches to sentencing offenders. Criminal codes may incorporate more than a single approach.

- ***Determinate sentences.*** The state legislature provides judges with little discretion in sentencing and specifies that the offender is to receive a specific sentence. A shorter or longer sentence may be given to an offender, but this must be justified by the judge. Recent Supreme Court decisions indicate that the facts on which the enhancement of a sentence is based must be found by the jury to exist beyond a reasonable doubt.
- ***Mandatory minimum sentences.*** The legislature requires judges to sentence an offender to a mandatory minimum sentence, regardless of mitigating factors. Prison sentences in some jurisdictions may be reduced by good-time credits earned by the individual while incarcerated.
- ***Indeterminate sentences.*** The state legislature gives judges discretion within defined limits to set a minimum and maximum sentence. In some jurisdictions, the judge possesses only the discretion to establish a maximum sentence. The decision to release an inmate prior to fully serving his or her sentence is vested in a parole board.
- ***Presumptive sentencing guidelines.*** The legislature establishes a commission that develops a sentencing formula based on various factors, stressing the nature of the crime and the offender's criminal history. Judges may be strictly limited in terms of discretion or may be provided with some flexibility within established limits. The judge must justify departures from the presumptive sentence on the basis of various aggravating and mitigating factors that are listed in the guidelines. Appeals are provided in order to maintain "reasonable sentencing practices" in those instances in which a judge departs from the presumptive sentence in the guidelines. Recent U.S. Supreme Court decisions have held that guidelines should be considered advisory rather than binding on a judge.

The Judicial Sentencing Process

The judge in most jurisdictions is required to order a probation officer to conduct a presentence investigation and to compile a report. The **presentence report** contains information regarding the defendant, including his or her criminal record and financial condition and other circumstances that may influence the defendant's future behavior. The report addresses aggravating and mitigating circumstances, including the impact of the crime on the victim. The document concludes by providing the judge with the types of sentences that are available. A report typically is required in most jurisdictions in the cases of first offenders, for offenders under twenty-one years old, and for felonies. The judge in various jurisdictions may waive the report in the event that the trial record contains enough information on which to base the sentence. In the federal system and in most states, the defendant has a right to inspect the sentencing report to insure accuracy. A defendant in a capital case has a constitutional right to inspect the presentence report (*Gardner v. Florida,* 430 U.S. 349 [1977]). Portions of the report that are considered sensitive may be withheld from the defendant. This includes information that might disrupt the defendant's rehabilitation program or lead to the physical harm of defendants or other persons as well as the name of and impact of the crime on a juvenile victim and information provided upon a promise of confidentiality (*Williams v. New York,* 337 U.S. 241 [1949]).

Following the preparation of the presentence report, the judge conducts a **sentencing hearing**. In 1967, in *Mempa v. Rhay* (389 U.S. 128 [1967]), the U.S. Supreme Court held that a sentencing hearing is a "critical stage" of the criminal justice process and that a defendant at this point in the process has a Sixth Amendment right to a lawyer. The lawyers are given the opportunity to describe aggravating or mitigating circumstances and to make arguments in support of one of the various sentencing alternatives that are available (e.g., probation as opposed to incarceration). The defendant also is provided the opportunity to make a statement. This is called the **right of allocution**. The U.S. Supreme Court has recognized that a defendant at sentencing may assert the right to remain silent and that no negative inference may be drawn from his or her silence (*Mitchell v. United States,* 526 U.S. 314 [1999]). The federal courts and most state courts also allow victim impact statements. The purpose is to provide the judge with information on the impact of the crime on the victim and the victim's family (*Payne v. Tennessee,* 501 U.S. 808 [1991]). The judge considers the presentence report and other relevant information and pronounces the sentence in open court. In the case of misdemeanors, sentences typically are announced immediately following the sentencing hearing. Felony sentencing typically is delayed until the judge has had the opportunity to consider all relevant information.

The judge in most jurisdictions is entitled to consider a broad range of information in setting the sentence (*Williams v. New York,* 337 U.S. 241 [1949]). For example, the Constitution protects only the right of a defendant to testify truthfully (*United States v. Grayson,* 438 U.S. 41 [1978]), and a judge may consider the fact that a defendant testified falsely during the trial as indicating that the defendant possesses an antisocial attitude that will interfere with his or her rehabilitation. In some states the judge is obligated to provide a written statement of the reasons for the sentence. Federal court judges are required to advise the defendant of his or her right to an appeal.

An individual convicted of multiple crimes may be given **consecutive sentences,** meaning that the sentences for each criminal act are served one after another. In the alternative, an individual may be subjected to **concurrent sentences,** meaning that the sentences for all criminal acts are served at the same time.

Governors and the president of the United States, in the case of federal offenses, may grant an offender **clemency,** resulting in a reduction of the individual's sentence or in the *commutation* of a death sentence to life in prison. A **pardon** exempts an individual from additional punishment. The U.S. Constitution, in Article II, Section 2, authorizes the president to pardon "offenses against the United States." Former Illinois governor George Ryan, in 2004, concluded that the problems in the administration of the death penalty risked the execution of an innocent, and he responded by pardoning four individuals on death row and commuting the sentences of over 100 individuals to life in prison.

In the next sections, we will examine two of the more important and controversial types of sentencing schemes: sentencing guidelines and determinate sentencing.

Sentencing Guidelines

As we have seen, at the turn of the twentieth century, most states and the federal government employed indeterminate sentencing. The legislature established the outer limits of sentences, and parole boards were provided with the authority to release individuals prior to the completion of their sentences in the event that they demonstrated that they had been rehabilitated. This approach is based on the belief that an individual who is incarcerated will be inspired to demonstrate that he or she no longer poses a threat to society and deserves an early release. Disillusionment with the notion of rehabilitation and the uncertain length and extreme variation in the time served by different offenders for similar crimes led to the introduction of determinate sentencing.

In 1980, Minnesota adopted **sentencing guidelines** in an effort to provide for uniform proportionate and predictable sentences. Currently over a dozen states employ guidelines. In 1984, the U.S. Congress responded to this movement by passing the Sentencing Reform Act. The law went into effect in 1987 and established the U.S. Sentencing Commission, which drafted binding guidelines to be followed by federal judges in sentencing offenders. The Sentencing Commission is composed of seven members appointed by the president with the approval of the U.S. Senate. At least three of the members must be federal judges. The Sentencing Commission monitors the impact of the guidelines on sentencing and proposes needed modifications (18 U.S.C. §§ 3531–3626, 28 U.S.C. §§ 991–998).

The Sentencing Reform Act abandoned rehabilitation as a primary purpose of imprisonment. The goals are retribution, deterrence, incapacitation, and the education and treatment of offenders. All sentences are determinate, and an offender's term of imprisonment may be reduced only by credit for good behavior earned while in custody.

Sentences under the federal guidelines are based on a complicated formula that reflects the seriousness and characteristics of the offense and the criminal history of the offender. The judge employs a sentencing grid and must sentence an offender within the narrow range where the offender's criminal offense and criminal history intersect. In formulating the appropriate sentence within the range authorized under the guidelines, a judge is to consider a number of factors, including the basic aims of sentencing and the need to avoid unwarranted disparities. The commission, in developing the guidelines, examined tens of thousands of sentencing decisions and enlisted the assistance of law enforcement.

Judges are required to document the reasons for criminal sentences and are obligated to provide a specific reason for an upward or downward departure from the sentence authorized by the guidelines. The prosecution may appeal a sentence below the presumed range and the defense may appeal any sentence above the presumed range. The process of applying the guidelines can be incredibly complicated and may require a judge to undertake as many as seven separate steps. The federal guidelines also specify that a judge must approve plea bargains or negotiated agreements between defense and prosecuting attorneys to insure that any sentence agreed upon is within the range established by the guidelines. The impact of the guidelines is difficult to measure, but studies suggest that the guidelines have increased the percentage of defendants who receive prison terms.

The federal guidelines are much more complicated than most state guidelines and provide judges with much less discretion in sentencing. A number of federal judges have publicly criticized the guidelines as unduly complicated and as limiting their discretion to impose more lenient sentences on deserving defendants. Judge Harry T. Edwards has noted that the guidelines do not introduce uniformity, because they are easily manipulated by the charge that is lodged by the prosecutor or by whether the prosecutor includes aggravating factors (e.g., possession of a firearm) in the indictment. Judge Edwards also noted that despite the guidelines, plea bargaining has led to disparities in sentencing (*United States v. Harrington,* 947 F.2d 956 [1991]). Judges who have been critical of the guidelines undoubtedly silently rejoiced over a series of recent U.S. Supreme Court decisions that have held that the federal as well as state sentencing guidelines should be regarded as advisory rather than binding on judges.

Several Supreme Court decisions have held that it is unconstitutional to enhance a sentence based on facts found to exist by the judge by a preponderance of the evidence (a probability) rather than by a jury beyond a reasonable doubt. According to the Supreme Court, excluding the jury from the fact-finding process constitutes a violation of a defendant's Sixth Amendment right to trial by a jury of his or her peers. The result is that any enhancement of a sentence is to be determined by the jury rather than by a judge. In *Apprendi v. New Jersey,* the U.S. Supreme Court explained that to

> guard against . . . oppression and tyranny on the part of rulers, and as the great bulwark of [our] . . . liberties, trial by jury has been understood to require that "the truth of every accusation . . . should . . . be confirmed by the unanimous suffrage of twelve of [the defendant's] equals and neighbors." (*Apprendi v. New Jersey,* 530 U.S. 466, 477 [2000])

In *Blakely v. Washington,* decided in 2004, Blakely pled guilty to kidnapping his wife. The judge followed Washington's sentencing guidelines and determined that Blakely had acted with "deliberate cruelty" and imposed an "exceptional" sentence of ninety months rather than the standard sentence of fifty-three months. The U.S. Supreme Court ruled that a judge's sentence is required to be based on "the facts reflected in the jury verdict or admitted by the defendant" and that a judge may not enhance a sentence based on facts that a jury did not find beyond a reasonable doubt to exist (*Blakely v. Washington,* 542 U.S. 296 [2004]). The Court later held that the question of whether a consecutive rather than a concurrent sentence should be imposed historically had been a question for the judge rather than for the jury (*Oregon v. Ice,* 555 U.S. __ [2009]).

In a third case, *United States v. Booker,* the U.S. Supreme Court held that the enhancement of sentences by a judge under the Federal Sentencing Guidelines unconstitutionally deprives defendants of their right to have facts determined by a jury of their peers. Booker was convicted of possession with intent to distribute at least fifty grams of crack cocaine. His criminal history and the quantity of drugs in his possession required a sentence of between 210 and 262 months in prison. The judge, however, concluded that a preponderance of the evidence showed that Booker had possessed an additional 556 grams of cocaine and that he also was guilty of obstructing justice. These findings required the judge to select a sentence of between 360 months and life, and the judge sentenced Booker to thirty years in prison. The Supreme Court ruled that the trial judge had acted unconstitutionally and explained that Booker, in effect, had been convicted of possessing a greater quantity of drugs than was charged in the indictment and that the determination of facts was a matter for the jury rather than for the judge.

Justice Breyer concluded that the best course under the circumstances was for judges to view the guidelines as advisory and to use their own judgment in sentencing a defendant. Why? An advisory system enables judges to formulate a sentence without consulting the jury. On the other hand, mandatory guidelines under the Supreme Court decisions require the jury to find each fact on which a sentence enhancement is based beyond a reasonable doubt. A judge under advisory guidelines is unrestricted by the guidelines, which merely constitute one factor among many to be considered by the judge (*United States v. Booker,* 543 U.S. 220 [2005]).

The Supreme Court recently once again addressed the federal guidelines and explicitly held that the guidelines are advisory. In these judgments, the Court held that an appellate court should examine whether a judge's sentencing decision is reasonable, whether it is inside or outside the sentencing range in the guidelines. In other words, a trial court judge does not have to satisfy an extraordinarily high burden on appeal to justify a sentence that departs from the guidelines.

In *Rita v. United States,* Rita was convicted of perjury, making false statements, and obstructing justice. The judge rejected the claim that Rita's "special circumstances" regarding his health, fear of retaliation, and military record were "special enough" to require a sentence lower than the one established in the guidelines, and the judge sentenced Rita to thirty-three months, the shortest sentence allowable under the guidelines. Rita appealed, and the Supreme Court held that appellate courts should consider sentences that are within the guidelines range as presumptively reasonable. Justice Breyer noted that a sentence within the designated range is properly assumed reasonable, because this indicates an agreement between the judge and the Sentencing Commission in regard to the appropriate punishment. In this instance, the sentencing judge reasonably concluded that the circumstances were insufficient to justify a sentence lower than that provided in the guidelines (*Rita v. United States,* 551 U.S. ___ [2006]).

Gall v. United States provides another example of a downward departure from the guidelines. Brian Gall was arrested for taking part some years earlier in a conspiracy to distribute ecstasy while at the University of Iowa. Three and one-half years after withdrawing from the conspiracy, Gall pled guilty. The presentence report recommended a sentence of thirty to thirty-seven months in prison. The district court sentenced Gall to thirty-six months probation. The district court reasoned that his voluntary withdrawal from the conspiracy and the fact that he "turned his life around" indicated that it was unlikely that Gall would return to a life of crime and that he did not pose a danger to society. The trial court judge also recognized that Gall had committed the drug crimes at an "immature age." The case was appealed, and the Eighth Circuit Court of Appeals struck down the sentence, indicating that the trial court must demonstrate "extraordinary circumstances" to justify a significant "downward departure" from the sentence specified in the guidelines.

The Supreme Court held that the Eighth Circuit Court of Appeals had applied an incorrect standard in requiring extraordinary circumstances. Justice John Paul Stevens held that all sentences, whether inside or outside the guidelines, are to be reviewed based on the reasonableness of the trial judge's decision. The reviewing court should consider the totality of the circumstances, including the extent of variance from the guidelines. The appellate court in this review process should give "due deference" to the sentencing court, and the fact that the appellate court might reasonably have reached a different conclusion did not justify a reversal of the sentence. The Supreme Court stressed that the trial court judge is in the best position to sentence the defendant. The judge is able to observe the witnesses, examine the evidence, and obtain full knowledge of the facts (*Gall v. United States* 552 U.S. ___ [2007].

In summary, in the past several years, the U.S. Supreme Court has firmly established that federal and state sentencing guidelines are advisory rather than mandatory. An appellate court, in reviewing the sentence, is to ask whether the sentence is reasonable under the circumstances. In 2007, Justice Ruth Bader Ginsburg, in her majority opinion in *Kimbrough v. United States,* wrote that the guidelines, "formerly mandatory," now are "one of many factors" that a court may consider in establishing an appropriate sentence. The judge may determine in a particular case that a within-guidelines sentence is "greater than necessary" to serve the objectives of sentencing or, alternatively, that it is "less than is required." In other words, a judge should start by calculating the sentence under the guidelines and then may consider other factors that may justify departing from the sentence under the guidelines. Justice Ginsburg affirmed that reasonablenesss is the standard to be applied on appellate review (*Kimbrough v. United States,* 552 U.S. ___ [2007]). In 2009, in *Nelson v. United States,* the Supreme Court once again stressed that a sentencing court is not required to follow the guidelines. The Court stressed that the trial court should not presume that the guidelines provide the sentence that the defendant "reasonably" should receive. An appellate court in reviewing the sentence is to ask whether the sentence handed out by the trial court judge is "reasonable" (*Nelson v. United States,* 555 U.S. ___ [2009]).

The significance of recent developments is that the U.S. Supreme Court has resisted imposing a straightjacket on sentencing decisions and has returned sentencing decisions to the authority of judges. All sentences, whether inside or outside the guidelines, are to be reviewed by appellate courts based on whether they are "reasonable."

Determinate Sentences

Determinate sentences have the advantage of being predictable, definite, and uniform. On the other hand, this "one size fits all" approach may prevent judges from tailoring sentences to the circumstances of a specific case. A particularly controversial area of determinative sentencing is mandatory minimum drug offenses. In 1975, New York governor Nelson Rockefeller initiated the controversial "Rockefeller drug laws" that required that an individual convicted of selling two ounces of a narcotic substance or of possessing eight ounces of a narcotic substance receive a sentence of between eight and twenty years, regardless of the individual's criminal history. The New York model in which a judge must sentence a defendant to a minimum sentence was followed by other states. The federal government joined this trend and introduced mandatory minimum sentences in the Anti–Drug Abuse Act of 1986 and its 1988 amendments. The most debated aspect of federal law is the punishment of an individual based on the type and amount of drugs in his or her possession, regardless of the individual's criminal history. The following quantities are punishable by five years in prison under federal law:

- 100 grams of heroin
- 500 grams of powder cocaine
- 5 grams of crack cocaine
- 100 kilograms of marijuana

The following quantities are punishable by ten years in prison under federal law:

- 1 kilogram of heroin
- 5 kilograms of powder cocaine
- 50 grams of crack cocaine
- 1,000 kilograms of marijuana

Congress softened the impact of the mandatory minimum drug sentences by providing that a judge may issue a lesser sentence in those instances in which prosecutors certify that a defendant has provided "substantial assistance" in convicting other drug offenders. There also is a safety valve that permits a reduced sentence for defendants determined by the judge to be low-level, nonviolent, first-time offenders.

Prosecutors argue that the mandatory minimum sentences are required to deter individuals from entering into the lucrative drug trade. The threat of a lengthy sentence also is necessary in order to encourage the cooperation of defendants. Prosecutors stress that individuals who are convicted and sentenced were fully aware of the consequences of their criminal actions.

These mandatory minimum laws nevertheless have come under attack by both conservative and liberal politicians, by the American Bar Association, and by the Judicial Conference, which is the organization of federal judges. An estimated twenty-two states, including Connecticut, Louisiana, Michigan, North Dakota, and Pennsylvania, have recently modified or are considering amending their mandatory minimum narcotics laws. New York also modified the Rockefeller drug laws in 2004 when Governor George Pataki signed the Drug Law Reform Act, and its legislators are contemplating abandoning determinate sentences for drug offenders. This trend is encouraged by studies that indicate that these laws have the following problems:

- ***Inflexibility.*** They fail to take into account the differences between defendants.
- ***Plea bargaining.*** Drug kingpins are able to trade information for reduced sentences.
- ***Prosecutorial discretion.*** Some prosecutors who object to the laws charge defendants with the possession of a lesser quantity of drugs to avoid the mandatory sentencing provisions.
- ***Increase in prison population.*** The laws are thought to be responsible for the growth of the state and federal prison population.
- ***Disparate effects.*** A significant percentage of individuals sentenced under these laws are African Americans or Hispanics involved in street-level drug activity. The increase in the number of women who are incarcerated is attributed to the fact that females find themselves arrested for assisting their husbands or lovers who are involved in the drug trade.

In *Hutto v. Davis,* the U.S. Supreme Court upheld the constitutionality of mandatory minimum state drug laws. The Court reasoned that Hutto's forty-year prison sentence and $20,000 fine was not disproportionate to his conviction on two counts of possession with intent to distribute and the distribution of a total of nine ounces of marijuana with a street value of roughly $200. The Court held that the determination of the proper sentence for this offense was a matter that was appropriately determined by the Virginia legislature (*Hutto v. Davis,* 454 U.S. 370 [1982]).

In 2007, in *Cunningham v. California,* the U.S. Supreme Court held unconstitutional California's sentencing scheme, in which the judge rather than the jury is authorized to find aggravating circumstances that enhance a defendant's sentence. In reading *Cunningham,* pay particular attention to the reasoning of the Supreme Court.

Does California's determinate sentencing law violate the Sixth Amendment?

Cunningham v. California, 549 U.S. 270 (2007), Ginsburg, J.

Issue

California's determinate sentencing law (DSL) assigns to the trial judge, not to the jury, authority to find the facts that expose a defendant to an elevated "upper-term" sentence. The facts so found are neither inherent in the jury's verdict nor embraced by the defendant's plea, and they need only be established by a preponderance of the evidence, not beyond a reasonable doubt. The question presented is whether the DSL, by placing sentence-elevating fact finding within the judge's province, violates a defendant's right to trial by jury safeguarded by the Sixth and Fourteenth Amendments.

Facts

Petitioner John Cunningham was tried and convicted of continuous sexual abuse of a child under the age of fourteen. Under the DSL, that offense is punishable by imprisonment for a lower-term sentence of six years, a middle-term sentence of twelve years, or an upper-term sentence of sixteen years (Cal. Penal Code Ann. § 288.5(a) [West 1999]). As further explained below, the DSL obliged the trial judge to sentence Cunningham to the twelve-year middle term unless the judge found one or more additional facts in aggravation. Based on a post-trial sentencing hearing, the trial judge found by a preponderance of the evidence six aggravating circumstances, among them the particular vulnerability of Cunningham's victim and Cunningham's violent conduct, which indicated a serious danger to the community. In mitigation, the judge found one fact: Cunningham had no record of prior criminal conduct. Concluding that the aggravators outweighed the sole mitigator, the judge sentenced Cunningham to the upper term of sixteen years.

A panel of the California Court of Appeal affirmed the conviction and sentence; one judge dissented in part, urging that this Court's precedent precluded the judge-determined four-year increase in Cunningham's sentence. The California Supreme Court,...in a reasoned decision...considered the question here presented and held that the DSL survived Sixth Amendment inspection.

Enacted in 1977, the DSL replaced an indeterminate sentencing regime that had been in force in California for some sixty years. Under the prior regime, courts imposed open-ended prison terms (often one year to life), and the parole board—the Adult Authority—determined the amount of time a felon would ultimately spend in prison. In contrast, the DSL fixed the terms of imprisonment for most offenses and eliminated the possibility of early release on parole. Through the DSL, California's lawmakers aimed to promote uniform and proportionate punishment. Murder and certain other grave offenses still carry lengthy indeterminate terms with the possibility of early release on parole.

For most offenses, including Cunningham's, the DSL regime is implemented in the following manner. The statute defining the offense prescribes three precise terms of imprisonment—a lower-, a middle-, and an upper-term sentence. For example, Penal Code section 288.5(a) (West 1999) indicates that a person convicted of continuous sexual abuse of a child "shall be punished by imprisonment in the state prison for a term of 6, 12, or 16 years." Penal Code section 1170(b) (Supp. 2006) controls the trial judge's choice; it provides that "the court shall order imposition of the middle term, unless there are circumstances in aggravation or mitigation of the crime." "Circumstances in aggravation or mitigation" are to be determined by the court after consideration of several items: the trial record; the probation officer's report; statements in aggravation or mitigation submitted by the parties, the victim, or the victim's family; and "any further evidence introduced at the sentencing hearing."

The DSL directed the state's Judicial Council (the voting members consist of the chief justice of the California Supreme Court and other judges) to adopt rules guiding the sentencing judge's decision as to whether to "impose the lower or upper prison term" (Penal Code § 1170.3(a)(2) [West 2004]). Restating section 1170(b), the council's rules provide that "the middle term shall be selected unless imposition of the upper or lower term is justified by circumstances in aggravation or mitigation" (rule 4.420(a)). "Circumstances in aggravation," as crisply defined by the Judicial Council, means "facts which justify the imposition of the upper prison term" (rule 4.405(d)). Facts aggravating an offense, the rules instruct, "shall be established by a preponderance of the evidence" (rule 4.420(b)), and must be "stated orally on the record" (rule 4.420(e)). The judge must provide a statement of reasons for a sentence only when a lower- or upper-term sentence is imposed (rules 4.406(b), 4.420(e)).

The rules provide a nonexhaustive list of aggravating circumstances, including "facts relating to the crime" (rule 4.421(a), e.g., the crime involved great violence, great bodily harm, threat of great bodily harm, or other acts disclosing a high degree of cruelty, viciousness, or callousness), "facts relating to the defendant," (rule 4.421(b)), e.g., the defendant has engaged in violent conduct that indicates a serious danger to society, and "any other facts statutorily declared to be circumstances in aggravation" (rule 4.421(c)). Beyond the enumerated circumstances, the judge is free to consider any "additional criteria reasonably related to the decision being made" (rule 4.408(a)). "A fact that is an element of the crime," however, "shall not be used to impose the upper term" (rule 4.420(d)). In sum, California's DSL, and the rules governing its application, direct the sentencing court to start with the middle term and to move from that term only when the court itself finds and places on the record facts—whether related to the offense or the offender—beyond the elements of the charged offense.

Justice Alito maintains, however, that a circumstance in aggravation need not be a fact at all. In his view, a policy judgment, or even a judge's "subjective belief" regarding the appropriate sentence, qualifies as an aggravating circumstance. California's rules, however, constantly refer to "facts." As just noted, the rules define "circumstances in aggravation" as "facts which justify the imposition of the upper prison term" (rule 4.405(d)). And "circumstances in aggravation," the rules unambiguously declare, "shall be established by a preponderance of the evidence" (rule 4.420(b)), a clear fact-finding directive to which there is no exception. It is unsurprising, then, that State's counsel, at oral argument, acknowledged that he knew of no case in which a California trial judge had gone beyond the middle term based not on any fact the judge found, but solely on the basis of a policy judgment or subjective belief.

Notably, the penal code permits elevation of a sentence above the upper term based on specified statutory enhancements relating to the defendant's criminal history or circumstances of the crime (e.g., Penal Code § 667 et seq. [West Supp. 2006]), § 12022 et seq.). Unlike aggravating circumstances, statutory enhancements must be charged in the indictment, and the underlying facts must be proved to the jury beyond a reasonable doubt (Penal Code § 1170.1(e)). A fact underlying an enhancement cannot do double duty; it cannot be used to impose an upper-term sentence and, on top of that, an enhanced term (Penal Code § 1170(b)). Where permitted by statute, however, a judge may use a fact qualifying as an enhancer to impose an upper-term rather than an enhanced sentence.

Reasoning

This Court has repeatedly held that under the Sixth Amendment, any fact that exposes a defendant to a greater potential sentence must be found by a jury, not a judge, and established beyond a reasonable doubt, not merely by a preponderance of the evidence. While this rule is rooted in longstanding common law practice, its explicit statement in our decisions is recent.... Charles Apprendi was convicted of possession of a firearm for an unlawful purpose, a second-degree offense under New Jersey law punishable by five to ten years imprisonment. A separate hate crime statute authorized an "extended term" of imprisonment: Ten to twenty years could be imposed if the trial judge found, by a preponderance of the evidence, that "the defendant in committing the crime acted with a purpose to intimidate an individual or group of individuals because of race, color, gender, handicap, religion, sexual orientation or ethnicity." The judge in Apprendi's case so found and therefore sentenced the defendant to twelve years' imprisonment. This Court held that the Sixth Amendment proscribed the enhanced sentence. We held, in *Apprendi,* that "any fact that increases the penalty for a crime beyond the prescribed statutory maximum must be submitted to a jury, and proved beyond a reasonable doubt."

We have since reaffirmed the rule of *Apprendi,* applying it to facts subjecting a defendant to the death penalty (*Ring v. Arizona,* 536 U.S. 584 [2002]), facts permitting a sentence in excess of the "standard range" under Washington's Sentencing Reform Act (*Blakely v. Washington,* 542 U.S. 296 [2004]), and facts triggering a sentence range elevation under the then-mandatory Federal Sentencing Guidelines (*United States v. Booker,* 543 U.S. 220 [2005]). *Blakely* and *Booker* bear most closely on the question presented in this case.

Applying the rule of *Apprendi,* this Court held Blakely's sentence unconstitutional. The State in *Blakely* had endeavored to distinguish *Apprendi* on the ground that "under the Washington guidelines, an exceptional sentence is within the court's discretion as a result of a guilty verdict." We rejected that argument. The judge could not have sentenced Blakely above the standard range without finding the additional fact of deliberate cruelty. Consequently, that fact was subject to the Sixth Amendment's jury-trial guarantee. It did not matter, we explained, that Blakely's sentence, though outside the standard range, was within the ten-year maximum for class B felonies:

> Our precedents make clear... that the "statutory maximum" for *Apprendi* purposes the maximum sentence a judge may impose solely on the basis of the facts reflected in the jury verdict or admitted by the defendant.... In other words, the relevant "statutory maximum" is not the maximum sentence a judge may impose after finding additional facts, but the maximum he may impose without any additional findings. When a judge inflicts punishment that the jury's verdict alone does not allow, the jury has not found all the facts "which the law makes essential to the punishment,"... and the judge exceeds his proper authority."

Freddie Booker was convicted of possession with intent to distribute crack cocaine and was sentenced under the Federal Sentencing Guidelines. The facts found by Booker's jury yielded a base guidelines range of 210 to 262 months' imprisonment, a range the judge could not exceed without undertaking additional fact finding. The judge did so, finding by a preponderance of the evidence that Booker possessed an amount of drugs in excess of the amount determined by the jury's verdict. That finding boosted Booker into a higher guidelines range. Booker was sentenced at the bottom of the higher range, to 360 months in prison.

In an opinion written by Justice Stevens for a five-member majority, the Court held Booker's sentence impermissible under the Sixth Amendment. In the majority's judgment, there was "no distinction of constitutional significance between the Federal Sentencing Guidelines and the Washington procedures at issue in [*Blakely*]." Both systems were "mandatory and impose[d] binding requirements on all sentencing judges." Justice Stevens's opinion for the Court, it bears emphasis, next expressed a view on which there was no disagreement among the justices. He acknowledged that the Federal Sentencing Guidelines would not implicate the Sixth Amendment were they advisory:

> We have never doubted the authority of a judge to exercise broad discretion in imposing a sentence within a statutory range. Indeed, everyone agrees that the constitutional issues presented by [this case] would have been avoided entirely if Congress had omitted from the [federal Sentencing Reform Act] the provisions that make the Guidelines binding on district judges.... For when a trial judge exercises his discretion to select a specific sentence within a defined range, the defendant has no right to a jury determination of the facts that the judge deems relevant.... The Guidelines as written, however, are not advisory; they are mandatory and binding on all judges.

Under California's DSL, an upper-term sentence may be imposed only when the trial judge finds an aggravating circumstance. An element of the charged offense, essential to a jury's determination of guilt or admitted in a defendant's guilty plea, does not qualify as such a circumstance. Instead, aggravating circumstances depend on facts found discretely and solely by the judge. In accord with *Blakely,* therefore, the middle term prescribed in California's statutes, not the upper term, is the relevant statutory maximum. "The 'statutory maximum' *Apprendi* purposes is the maximum sentence a judge may impose solely on the basis of the facts reflected in the jury verdict or admitted by the defendant." Circumstances in aggravation are found by the judge, not the jury, and need only be established by a preponderance of the evidence, not beyond a reasonable doubt; this violates *Apprendi*'s bright-line rule: Except for a prior conviction, "any fact that increases the penalty for a crime beyond the prescribed statutory maximum must be submitted to a jury, and proved beyond a reasonable doubt."

While "that should be the end of the matter," in *People v. Black,* (113 P.3d 534 [2005]) the California Supreme Court held otherwise. In that court's view, the DSL survived examination under our precedent intact. The *Black* court acknowledged that California's system appears on surface inspection to be in tension with the rule of *Apprendi.* But in "operation and effect," the court said, the DSL "simply authorize[s] a sentencing court to engage in the type of fact finding that traditionally has been incident to the judge's selection of an appropriate sentence within a statutorily prescribed sentencing range." Therefore, the court concluded, "the upper term is the 'statutory maximum' and a trial court's imposition of an upper term sentence does not violate a defendant's right to a jury trial under the principles set forth in *Apprendi, Blakely,* and *Booker.*" The *Black* court's conclusion that the upper term, and not the middle term, qualifies as the relevant statutory maximum, rested on several considerations. First, the court reasoned that, given the ample discretion afforded trial judges to identify aggravating facts warranting an upper term sentence, the DSL

> does not represent a legislative effort to shift the elements of a crime (to be proved by the judge) to sentencing factors (to be decided by the judge). Instead, it affords the sentencing judge discretion to decide, with the guidance of rules and statutes, whether the facts of the case and the history of the defendant justify the higher sentence. Such a system does not diminish the power of the jury.

We cautioned in *Blakely,* however, that broad discretion to decide what facts may support an enhanced sentence, or to determine whether an enhanced sentence is warranted in any particular case, does not shield a sentencing system from the force of our decisions. If the jury's verdict alone does not authorize the sentence—if, instead, the judge must find an additional fact to impose the longer term, the Sixth Amendment requirement is not satisfied.

The *Black* court also urged that the DSL is not cause for concern, because it reduced the penalties for most crimes over the prior indeterminate sentencing regime. Furthermore, California's system is not unfair to defendants, for they "cannot reasonably expect a guarantee that the upper term will not be imposed" given judges' broad discretion to impose an upper-term sentence or to keep their punishment at the middle term. The *Black* court additionally noted that the DSL requires statutory enhancements (as distinguished from aggravators)—for example, the use of a firearm or other dangerous weapon, or infliction of great bodily injury (Penal Code §§ 12022, 12022.7–12022.8 [West 2000 and Supp. 2006])—to be charged in the indictment and proved to a jury beyond a reasonable doubt.

The *Black* court's examination of the DSL, in short, satisfied it that California's sentencing system does not implicate significantly the concerns underlying the Sixth Amendment's jury-trial guarantee. Our decisions, however, leave no room for such an examination. Asking whether a defendant's basic jury-trial right is preserved, though some facts essential to punishment are reserved for determination by the judge, we have said, is the very inquiry *Apprendi*'s bright-line rule was designed to exclude.

California's DSL does not resemble the advisory system the *Booker* Court had in view. Under California's system, judges are not free to exercise their "discretion to select a specific sentence within a defined range." California's legislature has adopted sentencing triads, three fixed sentences with no ranges between them. Cunningham's sentencing judge had no discretion to select a sentence within a range of six to sixteen years. His instruction was to select twelve years, nothing less and nothing more, unless he found facts allowing the imposition of a sentence of six or sixteen years. Fact finding to elevate a sentence from twelve to sixteen years, our decisions make plain, falls within the province of the jury employing a beyond-a-reasonable-doubt standard, not the bailiwick of a judge determining where the preponderance of the evidence lies. Because the DSL allocates to judges sole authority to find facts permitting the imposition of an upper-term sentence, the system violates the Sixth Amendment.

Holding

To summarize: Contrary to the *Black* court's holding, our decisions from *Apprendi* to *Booker* point to the middle term specified in California's statutes, not the upper term, as the relevant statutory maximum. Because the DSL authorizes the judge, not the jury, to find the facts permitting an upper-term sentence, the system cannot withstand measurement against our Sixth Amendment precedent.

As to the adjustment of California's sentencing system in light of our decision, "the ball . . . lies in [California's] court." We note that several states have modified their systems in the wake of *Apprendi* and *Blakely* to retain determinate sentencing. They have done so by calling upon the jury—either at trial or in a separate sentencing proceeding—to find any fact necessary to the imposition of an elevated sentence. As earlier noted, California already employs juries in this manner to determine statutory sentencing enhancements. Other states have chosen to permit judges genuinely "to exercise broad discretion . . . within a statutory range," which, "everyone agrees," encounters no Sixth Amendment issue. California may follow the paths taken by its sister states or otherwise alter its system, so long as the state observes Sixth Amendment limitations declared in this Court's decisions. States that have altered their statutes include Alaska, Arizona, Indiana, Kansas, Minnesota, North Carolina, Tennessee, Oregon, and Washington.

For the reasons stated, the judgment of the California Court of Appeal is reversed in part, and the case is remanded for further proceedings not inconsistent with this opinion.

Questions for Discussion

1. Describe California's determinate sentencing scheme. Summarize the ruling of the California Supreme Court in *Black*.
2. Why does the U.S. Supreme Court hold California's statutory sentencing scheme unconstitutional?
3. Is the holding in *Cunningham* consistent with the holdings in *Apprendi, Blakely,* and *Booker*?
4. What is the significance of the distinction between a "sentence enhancement" and aggravating circumstances that elevate a criminal sentence?
5. As a legislator, how would you amend the California sentencing scheme to satisfy the requirements of the Sixth Amendment to the U.S. Constitution?
6. As a matter of social policy, should the legislature or judges have the primary role in criminal sentencing? What should be the role of juries?

Cruel and Unusual Punishment

The **Eighth Amendment** to the U.S. Constitution is the primary constitutional provision that regulates the imposition of capital punishment. The Eighth Amendment states, "Excessive bail shall not be required, nor excessive fines imposed, nor cruel and unusual punishments inflicted." The prohibition on cruel and unusual punishment received widespread acceptance in the new American nation. In fact, the language in the U.S. Bill of Rights is taken directly from the Virginia Declaration of Rights of 1776 which, in turn, was inspired by the English Bill of Rights of 1689. The English document significantly limited the powers and prerogatives of the British monarchy and recognized certain basic rights of the English people (*Harmelin v. Michigan,* 501 U.S. 957, 961 [1991]).

The U.S. Supreme Court has ruled that the prohibition against cruel and unusual punishment applies to the states as well as to the federal government, and virtually every state constitution contains similar language. The following sections of the text discuss three aspects of the clause: (1) methods of punishment, (2) death sentences or **capital punishment**, and (3) sentences for a term of years.

Methods of Punishment

Patrick Henry expressed concern during Virginia's consideration of the proposed federal constitution that the absence of a prohibition on cruel and unusual punishment would open the door to the use of torture to extract confessions. In fact, during the debate in the first Congress on the adoption of a Bill of Rights, one representative objected to the Eighth Amendment on the grounds that "villains often deserve whipping, and perhaps having their ears cut off" (*Rummel v. Estelle,* 445 U.S. 263, 288 [1980]).

There is agreement that the Eighth Amendment prohibits punishments that were considered cruel at the time of the amendment's ratification, including burning at the stake, crucifixion, breaking on the wheel, drawing and quartering, and use of the rack and thumbscrew. The Supreme Court observed as early as 1890 that "if the punishment prescribed for an offense against the laws of the state were manifestly cruel and unusual as burning at the stake, crucifixion, breaking on the wheel, or the like, it would be the duty of the courts to adjudge such penalties to be within the constitutional prohibition" (*In re Kemmler,* 136 U.S. 436, 446 [1890]). The Delaware Supreme Court, in 1963, held that whipping was constitutionally permissible on the grounds that the practice was recognized in the state in 1776 (*Delaware v. Cannon,* 190 A.2d 514 [Del. 1963]).

The vast majority of courts have not limited cruel and unusual punishment to acts condemned at the time of passage of the Eighth Amendment and have viewed this as an evolving concept. The U.S. Supreme Court has stressed that the Eighth Amendment "must draw its meaning from the evolving standards of decency that mark the progress of a maturing society." An example of the application of the prohibition on cruel and unusual punishment to a new situation is *Trop v. Dulles*. In *Trop,* the U.S. Supreme Court held that it was unconstitutional to deprive Trop, and roughly 7,000 others convicted of military desertion, of their American citizenship. Chief Justice Earl Warren wrote that depriving deserters of citizenship, while involving "no physical mistreatment," was more "primitive than torture" in that individuals are transformed into "stateless persons without the right to live, work or enjoy the freedoms accorded to citizens in the United States or in any other nation" (*Trop v. Dulles,* 356 U.S. 86, 101 [1958]).

The death penalty historically has been viewed as a constitutionally acceptable form of punishment (*Furman v. Georgia,* 408 U.S. 238 [1972]). The Supreme Court noted in *In re Kemmler* that punishments are

> cruel when they involve torture or a lingering death; but the punishment of death is not cruel within the meaning of that word as used in the constitution. [Cruelty] implies there is something inhuman and barbarous—something more than the mere extinguishment of life. (447)

The Supreme Court has rejected the contention that death by shooting (*Wilkerson v. Utah,* 99 U.S. 130 [1978]) and electrocution are cruel and barbarous, noting in 1890 that the newly developed technique of electrocution is a "more humane method of reaching the result." In the case at issue in *Louisiana ex rel. Francis v. Resweber,* Francis was strapped in the electric chair and received a bolt of electricity before the machine malfunctioned. The U.S. Supreme Court rejected the claim that subjecting the petitioner to the electric chair a second time constituted cruel and unusual punishment. The Court observed that there was no intent to inflict unnecessary pain, and the fact that "an unforeseeable accident prevented the prompt consummation of the sentence cannot . . . add an element of cruelty to a subsequent execution" (*Louisiana ex rel. Francis v. Resweber,* 329 U.S. 459, 464 [1974]).

In 2008, the U.S. Supreme Court addressed the constitutionality of the execution of individuals through the use of lethal injection. In *Baze v. Rees,* the Court upheld the constitutionality of Kentucky's lethal injection protocol. In 1977, Oklahoma passed the first lethal injection law. The law was motivated by the desire to find a less expensive and more humane method of execution. The thirty-five death penalty states, along with the federal government, presently provide for lethal injection. The trend is for states to provide that lethal injection is the only method of execution. Between 1976 and 2006, 838 of the 1,016 executions in the United States were carried out by lethal injection. Three executions were conducted by the federal government and the remainder by the states. Roughly thirty state correctional agencies employ the identical three-drug sequence of sodium thiopental, pancuronium bromide, and potassium chloride used by Oklahoma.

Opponents of lethal injection claim that the individuals who administer the protocol lack the training to safely administer the drugs. The anesthesia level from sodium thiopental at times fails to sufficiently insulate the inmate from pain, and inmates may experience suffocation from the pancuronium bromide (which causes death by asphyxiation) and excruciating pain from the potassium chloride (which results in cardiac arrest), and the equipment on some occasions has malfunctioned. Pancuronium bromide also can prevent an inmate from indicating that he or she is suffering pain. There are stories of veins collapsing, needles popping out of an inmate's arm, and blocked tubes preventing the administration of the anesthesia.

In December 2006, Florida executed Nieves Diaz for murder. Diaz remained alive in obvious pain for twenty minutes following the administration of the first dose, and after thirty-five minutes a second lethal dose was administered. The medical examiner determined that the chemicals accidentally had been injected into soft tissue rather than into the vein. Governor Jeb Bush temporarily suspended executions in the state and appointed a commission to evaluate the humanity and legality of lethal injections. Florida reintroduced lethal injection eighteen months later. In June 2008, an Ohio lower court judge held that the state's three-drug protocol ran the risk of causing unnecessary pain and is unconstitutional in light of the Ohio statute that "death by lethal injection must be caused quickly and painlessly." In reading *Baze v. Rees,* ask yourself whether lethal injection constitutes cruel and unusual punishment.

Does lethal injection constitute cruel and unusual punishment?

Baze v. Rees, ___ U.S. ___ (2008), Roberts, J.

Facts

Like thirty-five other states and the federal government, Kentucky has chosen to impose capital punishment for certain crimes. As is true with respect to each of these states and the federal government, Kentucky has altered its method of execution over time to more humane means of carrying out the sentence. That progress has led to the use of lethal injection by every jurisdiction that imposes the death penalty.

Petitioners in this case—each convicted of double homicide—acknowledge that the lethal injection procedure, if applied as intended, will result in a humane death. They nevertheless contend that the lethal injection protocol is unconstitutional under the Eighth Amendment's ban on "cruel and unusual punishment," because of the risk that the protocol's terms might not be properly followed, resulting in significant pain. They propose an alternative protocol, one that they concede has not been adopted by any state and has never been tried.

By the middle of the nineteenth century, "hanging was the 'nearly universal form of execution' in the United States." In 1888, following the recommendation of a commission empanelled by the governor of New York to find "the most humane and practical method known to modern science of carrying into effect the sentence of death," New York became the first state to authorize electrocution as a form of capital punishment. By 1915, eleven other states had followed suit, motivated by the "well-grounded belief that electrocution is less painful and more humane than hanging."

Electrocution remained the predominant mode of execution for nearly a century, although several methods, including hanging, shooting, and lethal gas were in use at one time. Following the nine-year hiatus in executions that ended with our decision in *Gregg v. Georgia,* however, state legislatures began responding to public calls to reexamine electrocution as a means of assuring a humane death. In 1977, legislators in Oklahoma, after consulting with the head of the anesthesiology department at the University of Oklahoma College of Medicine, introduced the first bill proposing lethal injection as the state's method of execution. A total of thirty-six states have now adopted lethal injection as the exclusive or primary means of implementing the death penalty, making it by far the most prevalent method of execution in the United States. In twenty-six states, it is the exclusive method of execution. It is also the method used by the federal government.

Of these thirty-six states, at least thirty (including Kentucky) use the same combination of three drugs in their lethal injection protocol. The first drug, sodium thiopental (also known as Pentothal), is a fast-acting barbiturate sedative that induces a deep, coma-like unconsciousness when given in the amounts used for lethal injection. The second drug, pancuronium bromide (also known as Pavulon), is a paralytic agent that inhibits all muscular-skeletal movements and, by paralyzing the diaphragm, stops respiration. Potassium chloride, the third drug, interferes with the electrical signals that stimulate the contractions of the heart, inducing cardiac arrest. The proper administration of the first drug ensures that the prisoner does not experience any pain associated with the paralysis and cardiac arrest caused by the second and third drugs.

Kentucky replaced electrocution with lethal injection in 1998. The Kentucky statute does not specify the drugs or categories of drugs to be used during an execution, instead mandating that "every death sentence shall be executed by continuous intravenous injection of a substance or combination of substances sufficient to cause death." Prisoners sentenced before 1998 have the option of electing either electrocution or lethal injection, but lethal injection is the default if—as is the case with petitioners—the prisoner refuses to make a choice at least twenty days before the scheduled execution. If a court invalidates Kentucky's lethal injection method, Kentucky law provides that the method of execution will revert to electrocution.

Shortly after the adoption of lethal injection, officials working for the Kentucky Department of Corrections set about developing a written protocol to comply with the requirements of the law. Kentucky's protocol called for the injection of two grams of sodium thiopental, fifty milligrams of pancuronium bromide, and 240 milliequivalents of potassium chloride. In 2004, as a result of this litigation, the department chose to increase the amount of sodium thiopental from two grams to three grams. Between injections, members of the execution team flush the intravenous (IV) lines with twenty-five milligrams of saline to prevent clogging of the lines by precipitates that may form when residual sodium thiopental comes into contact with pancuronium bromide. The protocol reserves responsibility for inserting the IV catheters to qualified personnel having at least one year of professional experience. Currently, Kentucky uses a certified phlebotomist and an emergency medical technician (EMT) to perform the venipunctures necessary for the catheters. They have up to one hour to establish both primary and secondary peripheral intravenous sites in the arm, hand, leg, or foot of the inmate. Other personnel are responsible for mixing the solutions containing the three drugs and loading them into syringes.

Kentucky's execution facilities consist of the execution chamber, a control room separated from the chamber by a one-way window, and a witness room. The warden and deputy warden remain in the execution chamber with the prisoner, who is strapped to a gurney. The execution team administers the drugs remotely from the control room through five feet of IV tubing. If, as determined by the warden and deputy warden through visual inspection, the prisoner is not unconscious within sixty seconds following the delivery of the sodium thiopental to the primary IV site, a new three-gram dose of thiopental is administered to the secondary site before injecting the pancuronium and potassium chloride. In addition to assuring that the first dose of thiopental is successfully administered, the warden and deputy warden also watch for any problems with the IV catheters and tubing.

A physician is present to assist in any effort to revive the prisoner in the event of a last-minute stay of execution. By statute, however, the physician is prohibited from participating in the "conduct of an execution," except to certify the cause of death. An electrocardiogram verifies the death of the prisoner. Only one Kentucky prisoner, Eddie Lee Harper, has been executed since the commonwealth adopted lethal injection. There were no reported problems at Harper's execution.

Petitioners Ralph Baze and Thomas C. Bowling were each convicted of two counts of capital murder and sentenced to death. The Supreme Court of Kentucky upheld their convictions and sentences on direct appeal. After exhausting their state and federal collateral remedies, Baze and Bowling sued three state officials in the Franklin Circuit Court for the Commonwealth of Kentucky, seeking to have Kentucky's lethal injection protocol declared unconstitutional. After a seven-day bench trial, during which the trial court received the testimony of approximately twenty witnesses, including numerous experts, the court upheld the protocol, finding there to be minimal risk of various claims of improper administration of the protocol. On appeal, the Supreme Court of Kentucky stated that a method of execution violates the Eighth Amendment when it "creates a substantial risk of wanton and unnecessary infliction of pain, torture or lingering death." Applying that standard, the court affirmed.

Issue

We granted certiorari to determine whether Kentucky's lethal injection protocol satisfies the Eighth Amendment....

Reasoning

The Eighth Amendment to the Constitution, applicable to the states through the Due Process Clause of the Fourteenth Amendment, provides that "excessive bail shall not be required, nor excessive fines imposed, nor cruel and unusual punishments inflicted." We begin with the principle, settled by *Gregg,* that capital punishment is constitutional. It necessarily follows that there must be a means of carrying it out. Some risk of pain is inherent in any method of execution—no matter how humane—if only from the prospect of error in following the required procedure. It is clear, then, that the Constitution does not demand the avoidance of all risk of pain in carrying out executions.

Petitioners do not claim that it does. Rather, they contend that the Eighth Amendment prohibits procedures that create an "unnecessary risk" of pain. Specifically, they argue that courts must evaluate "(a) the severity of pain risked, (b) the likelihood of that pain occurring, and (c) the extent to which alternative means are feasible, either by modifying existing execution procedures or adopting alternative procedures." Petitioners envision that the quantum of risk necessary to make out an Eighth Amendment claim will vary according to the severity of the pain and the availability of alternatives but that the risk must be "significant" to trigger Eighth Amendment scrutiny.

Kentucky responds that this "unnecessary risk" standard is tantamount to a requirement that states adopt the "least risk" alternative in carrying out an execution, a standard the commonwealth contends will cast recurring constitutional doubt on any procedure adopted by the states. Instead, Kentucky urges the Court to approve the "substantial risk" test used by courts as described below.

This Court has never invalidated a state's chosen procedure for carrying out a sentence of death as the infliction of cruel and unusual punishment. In *Wilkerson v. Utah* (99 U.S. 130 [1878]), we upheld a sentence to death by firing squad imposed by a territorial court, rejecting the argument that such a sentence constituted cruel and unusual punishment. We noted there the difficulty of "defin[ing] with exactness the extent of the constitutional provision which provides that cruel and unusual punishments shall not be inflicted." Rather than undertake such an effort, the *Wilkerson* Court simply noted that "it is safe to affirm that punishments of torture,...and all others in the same line of unnecessary cruelty, are forbidden" by the Eighth Amendment. By way of example, the Court cited cases from England in which "terror, pain, or disgrace were sometimes superadded" to the sentence, such as where the condemned was "emboweled alive, beheaded, and quartered," or instances of "public dissection in murder, and burning alive." In contrast, we observed that the firing squad was routinely used as a method of execution for military officers. What each of the forbidden punishments had in common was the deliberate infliction of pain for the sake of pain—"superadd[ing]" pain to the death sentence through torture and the like.

We carried these principles further in *In re Kemmler* (136 U.S. 436 [1889]). There we rejected an opportunity to incorporate the Eighth Amendment against the states in a challenge to the first execution by electrocution, to be carried out by the State of New York. In passing over that question, however, we observed that

> punishments are cruel when they involve torture or a lingering death; but the punishment of death is not cruel within the meaning of that word as used in the Constitution. It implies there something inhuman and barbarous, something more than the mere extinguishment of life.

We noted that the New York statute adopting electrocution as a method of execution "was passed in the effort to devise a more humane method of reaching the result."

Petitioners do not claim that lethal injection or the proper administration of the particular protocol adopted by Kentucky by themselves constitute the cruel or wanton infliction of pain. Quite the contrary, they concede that "if performed properly," an execution carried out under Kentucky's procedures would be "humane and constitutional." That is because, as counsel for petitioners admitted at oral argument, proper administration of the first drug, sodium thiopental, eliminates any meaningful risk that a prisoner would experience pain from the subsequent injections of pancuronium and potassium chloride.

Instead, petitioners claim that there is a significant risk that the procedures will not be properly followed—in particular, that the sodium thiopental will not be properly administered to achieve its intended effect—resulting in severe pain when the other chemicals are administered. Our cases recognize that subjecting individuals to a risk of future harm—not simply actually inflicting pain—can qualify as cruel and unusual punishment. To establish that such exposure violates the Eighth Amendment, however, the conditions presenting the risk must be "sure or very likely to cause serious illness and needless suffering," and give rise to "sufficiently imminent dangers." We have explained that to prevail on such a claim there must be a "substantial risk of serious harm," an "objectively intolerable risk of harm" that prevents prison officials from pleading that they were "subjectively blameless for purposes of the Eighth Amendment."

Simply because an execution method may result in pain, either by accident or as an inescapable consequence of death, does not establish the sort of "objectively intolerable risk of harm" that qualifies as cruel and unusual. In *Louisiana ex rel. Francis v. Resweber,* (329 U.S. 459 [1947]), a plurality of the Court upheld a second attempt at executing a prisoner by electrocution after a mechanical malfunction had interfered with the first attempt. The principal opinion noted that "accidents happen for which no man is to blame" and concluded that such an accident, with "no suggestion of malevolence," did not give rise to an Eighth Amendment violation.

As Justice Frankfurter noted in a separate opinion based on the Due Process Clause, however, "a hypothetical situation" involving "a series of abortive attempts at electrocution" would present a different case. In terms of our present Eighth Amendment analysis, such a situation—unlike an "innocent misadventure"—would demonstrate an "objectively intolerable risk of harm" that officials may not ignore. In other words, an isolated mishap alone does not give rise to an Eighth Amendment violation, precisely because such an event, while regrettable, does not suggest cruelty, or that the procedure at issue gives rise to a "substantial risk of serious harm."

Much of petitioners' case rests on the contention that they have identified a significant risk of harm that can be eliminated by adopting alternative procedures, such as a one-drug protocol that dispenses with the use of pancuronium and potassium chloride, and additional monitoring by trained personnel to ensure that the first dose of sodium thiopental has been adequately delivered. Given what our cases have said about the nature of the risk of harm that is actionable under the Eighth Amendment, a condemned prisoner cannot successfully challenge a state's method of execution merely by showing a slightly or marginally safer alternative.

Permitting an Eighth Amendment violation to be established on such a showing would threaten to transform courts into boards of inquiry charged with determining "best practices" for executions, with each ruling supplanted by another round of litigation touting a new and improved methodology. Such an approach finds no support in our cases, would embroil the courts in ongoing scientific controversies beyond their expertise, and would substantially intrude on the role of state legislatures in implementing their execution procedures—a role that by all accounts the states have fulfilled with an earnest desire to provide for a progressively more humane manner of death. Accordingly, we reject petitioners' proposed "unnecessary risk" standard as well as the dissent's "untoward" risk variation.

Instead, the proffered alternatives must effectively address a "substantial risk of serious harm." To qualify, the alternative procedure must be feasible, readily implemented, and in fact significantly reduce a substantial risk of severe pain. If a state refuses to adopt such an alternative in the face of these documented advantages, without a legitimate penological justification for adhering to its current method of execution, then a state's refusal to change its method can be viewed as "cruel and unusual" under the Eighth Amendment.

In applying these standards to the facts of this case, we note at the outset that it is difficult to regard a practice as "objectively intolerable" when it is in fact widely tolerated. The thirty-six states that sanction capital punishment have adopted lethal injection as the preferred method of execution. The federal government uses lethal injection as well. This broad consensus goes not just to the method of execution, but also to the specific three-drug combination used by Kentucky. Thirty states, as well as the federal government, use a series of sodium thiopental, pancuronium bromide, and potassium chloride, in varying amounts. No state uses or has ever used the alternative one-drug protocol belatedly urged by petitioners. This consensus is probative but not conclusive with respect to that aspect of the alternatives proposed by petitioners.

In order to meet their "heavy burden" of showing that Kentucky's procedure is "cruelly inhumane," petitioners point to numerous aspects of the protocol that they contend create opportunities for error. Their claim hinges on the improper administration of the first drug, sodium thiopental. It is uncontested that, failing a proper dose of sodium thiopental that would render the prisoner unconscious, there is a substantial, constitutionally unacceptable risk of suffocation from the administration of pancuronium bromide and pain from the injection of potassium chloride. We agree with the state trial court and state supreme court, however, that petitioners have not shown that the risk of an inadequate dose of the first drug is substantial. And we reject the argument that the Eighth Amendment requires Kentucky to adopt the untested alternative procedures petitioners have identified.

Petitioners contend that there is a risk of improper administration of sodium thiopental, because the doses are difficult to mix into solution form and load into syringes; because the protocol fails to establish a rate of injection, which could lead to a failure of the IV; because it is possible that the IV catheters will infiltrate into surrounding tissue, causing an inadequate dose to be delivered to the vein; because of inadequate facilities and training; and because Kentucky has no reliable means of monitoring the anesthetic depth of the prisoner after the sodium thiopental has been administered.

As for the risk that the sodium thiopental would be improperly prepared, petitioners contend that Kentucky employs untrained personnel who are unqualified to calculate and mix an adequate dose, especially in light of the omission of volume and concentration amounts from the written protocol. The state trial court, however, specifically found that "if the manufacturers' instructions for reconstitution of Sodium Thiopental are followed, . . . there would be minimal risk of improper mixing, despite converse testimony that a layperson would have difficulty performing this task." We cannot say that this finding is clearly erroneous, particularly when that finding is substantiated by expert testimony describing the task of reconstituting powder sodium thiopental into solution form as "not difficult at all.... You take a liquid, you inject it into a vial with the powder, then you shake it up until the powder dissolves and, you're done. The instructions are on the package insert."

Likewise, the asserted problems related to the IV lines do not establish a sufficiently substantial risk of harm to meet the requirements of the Eighth Amendment. Kentucky has put in place several important safeguards to ensure that an adequate dose of sodium thiopental is delivered to the condemned prisoner. The most significant of these is the written protocol's requirement that members of the IV team must have at least one year of professional experience as a certified medical assistant, phlebotomist, EMT, paramedic, or military corpsman. Kentucky currently uses a phlebotomist and an EMT, personnel who have daily experience establishing IV catheters for inmates in Kentucky's prison population. Moreover, these IV team members, along with the rest of the execution team, participate in at least ten practice sessions per year. These sessions, required by the written protocol, encompass a complete walk-through of the execution procedures, including the siting of IV catheters into volunteers. In addition, the protocol calls for the IV team to establish both primary and backup lines and to prepare two sets of the lethal injection drugs before the execution commences. These redundant measures ensure that if an insufficient dose of sodium thiopental is initially administered through the primary line, an additional dose can be given through the backup line before the last two drugs are injected.

The IV team has one hour to establish both the primary and backup IVs, a length of time the trial court found to be "not excessive but rather necessary," contrary to petitioners' claim that using an IV inserted after any "more than ten or fifteen minutes of unsuccessful attempts is dangerous because the IV is almost certain to be unreliable." And, in any event, the mere fact that the protocol gives the IV team one hour to establish intravenous access does not mean that team members are required to spend the entire hour in a futile attempt to do so. The qualifications of the IV team also substantially reduce the risk of IV infiltration.

In addition, the presence of the warden and deputy warden in the execution chamber with the prisoner allows them to watch for signs of IV problems, including infiltration. Three of the commonwealth's medical experts testified that signs of infiltration would be "very obvious," even to the average person, because of the swelling that would result. Kentucky's protocol specifically requires the warden to redirect the flow of chemicals to the backup IV site if the prisoner does not lose consciousness within sixty seconds. In light of these safeguards, we cannot say that the risks identified by petitioners are so substantial or imminent as to amount to an Eighth Amendment violation.

Nor does Kentucky's failure to adopt petitioners' proposed alternatives demonstrate that the commonwealth's execution procedure is cruel and unusual. First, petitioners contend that Kentucky could switch from a three-drug protocol to a one-drug protocol by using a single dose of sodium thiopental or other barbiturate. That alternative was not proposed to the state courts below. As a result, we are left without any findings on the effectiveness of petitioners' barbiturate-only protocol, despite scattered references in the trial testimony to the sole use of sodium thiopental or pentobarbital as a preferred method of execution.

In any event, the commonwealth's continued use of the three-drug protocol cannot be viewed as posing an "objectively intolerable risk" when no other state has adopted the one-drug method, and petitioners proffered no study showing that it is an equally effective manner of imposing a death sentence. Indeed, the State of Tennessee, after reviewing its execution procedures, rejected a proposal to adopt a one-drug protocol using sodium thiopental. The state concluded that the one-drug alternative would take longer than the three-drug method and that the "required dosage of sodium thiopental would be less predictable and more variable when it is used as the sole mechanism for producing death." ...We need not endorse the accuracy of those conclusions to note simply that the comparative efficacy of a one-drug method of execution is not so well established that Kentucky's failure to adopt it constitutes a violation of the Eighth Amendment.

Petitioners also contend that Kentucky should omit the second drug, pancuronium bromide, because it serves no therapeutic purpose while suppressing muscle movements that could reveal an inadequate administration of the first drug. The state trial court, however, specifically found that pancuronium serves two purposes. First, it prevents involuntary physical movements during unconsciousness that may accompany the injection of potassium chloride. The commonwealth has an interest in preserving the dignity of the procedure, especially where convulsions or seizures could be misperceived as signs of consciousness or distress. Second, pancuronium stops respiration, hastening death. Kentucky's decision to include the drug does not offend the Eighth Amendment.

Petitioners' barbiturate-only protocol, they contend, is not untested; it is used routinely by veterinarians in putting animals to sleep. Moreover, twenty-three states, including Kentucky, bar veterinarians from using a neuromuscular paralytic agent like pancuronium bromide, either expressly or, like Kentucky, by specifically directing the use of a drug like sodium pentobarbital. If pancuronium is too cruel for animals, the argument goes, then it must be too cruel for the condemned inmate. Whatever rhetorical force the argument carries, it overlooks the states' legitimate interest in providing for a quick, certain death. In the Netherlands, for example, where physician-assisted euthanasia is permitted, the Royal Dutch Society for the Advancement of Pharmacy recommends the use of a muscle relaxant (such as pancuronium dibromide) in addition to thiopental in order to prevent a prolonged, undignified death. That concern may be less compelling in the veterinary context, and in any event other methods approved by veterinarians—such as stunning the animal or severing its spinal cord—make clear that veterinary practice for animals is not an appropriate guide to humane practices for humans.

Petitioners also fault the Kentucky protocol for lacking a systematic mechanism for monitoring the "anesthetic depth" of the prisoner. Under petitioners' scheme, qualified personnel would employ monitoring equipment, such as a bispectral index (BIS) monitor, blood pressure cuff, or EKG to verify that a prisoner has achieved sufficient unconsciousness before injecting the final two drugs. The visual inspection performed by the warden and deputy warden, they maintain, is an inadequate substitute for the more sophisticated procedures they envision.

At the outset, it is important to re-emphasize that a proper dose of thiopental obviates the concern that a prisoner will not be sufficiently sedated. All the experts who testified at trial agreed on this point. The risks of failing to adopt additional monitoring procedures are thus even more "remote" and attenuated than the risks posed by the alleged inadequacies of Kentucky's procedures designed to ensure the delivery of thiopental.

But more than this, Kentucky's expert testified that a blood pressure cuff would have no utility in assessing the level of the prisoner's unconsciousness following the introduction of sodium thiopental, which depresses circulation. Furthermore, the medical community has yet to endorse the use of a BIS monitor, which measures brain function, as an indication of anesthetic awareness. The asserted need for a professional anesthesiologist to interpret the BIS monitor readings is nothing more than an argument against the entire procedure, given that both Kentucky law and the American Society of Anesthesiologists' own ethical guidelines prohibit anesthesiologists from participating in capital punishment. Nor is it pertinent that the use of a blood pressure cuff and EKG is "the standard of care in surgery requiring anesthesia," as the dissent points out. Petitioners have not shown that these supplementary procedures, drawn from a different context, are necessary to avoid a substantial risk of suffering.

The dissent believes that rough-and-ready tests for checking consciousness—calling the inmate's name, brushing his eyelashes, or presenting him with strong, noxious odors—could materially decrease the risk of administering the second and third drugs before the sodium thiopental has taken effect. Again, the risk at issue is already attenuated, given the steps Kentucky has taken to ensure the proper administration of the first drug. Moreover, the scenario the dissent posits involves a level of unconsciousness allegedly sufficient to avoid detection of improper administration of the anesthesia under Kentucky's procedure, but not sufficient to prevent pain. There is no indication that the basic tests the dissent advocates can make such fine distinctions. If these tests are effective only in determining whether the sodium thiopental has entered the inmate's bloodstream, the record confirms that the visual inspection of the IV site under Kentucky's procedure achieves that objective.

Reasonable people of good faith disagree on the morality and efficacy of capital punishment, and for many who oppose it, no method of execution would ever be acceptable. But as Justice Frankfurter stressed in *Resweber,* "One must be on guard against finding in personal disapproval a reflection of more or less prevailing condemnation." This Court has ruled that capital punishment is not prohibited under our Constitution, and that the states may enact laws specifying that sanction. "The power of a State to pass laws means little if the State cannot enforce them." State efforts to implement capital punishment must certainly comply with the Eighth Amendment, but what that Amendment prohibits is wanton exposure to "objectively intolerable risk," not simply the possibility of pain.

Holding

Kentucky has adopted a method of execution believed to be the most humane available, one it shares with 35 other states. Petitioners agree that, if administered as intended, that procedure will result in a painless death. The risks of maladministration they have suggested—such as improper mixing of chemicals and improper setting of IVs by trained and experienced personnel—cannot remotely be characterized as "objectively intolerable." Kentucky's decision to adhere to its protocol despite these asserted risks, while adopting safeguards to protect against them, cannot be viewed as probative of the wanton infliction of pain under the Eighth Amendment. Finally, the alternative that petitioners belatedly propose has problems of its own and has never been tried by a single state.

Throughout our history, whenever a method of execution has been challenged in this Court as cruel and unusual, the Court has rejected the challenge. Our society has nonetheless steadily moved to more humane methods of carrying out capital punishment. The firing squad, hanging, the electric chair, and the gas chamber have each in turn given way to more humane methods, culminating in today's consensus on lethal injection. The broad framework of the Eighth Amendment has accommodated this progress toward more humane methods of execution, and our approval of a particular method in the past has not precluded legislatures from taking the steps they deem appropriate, in light of new developments, to ensure humane capital punishment. There is no reason to suppose that today's decision will be any different. The judgment below concluding that Kentucky's procedure is consistent with the Eighth Amendment is, accordingly, affirmed.

Concurring, *Stevens, J.*

When we granted certiorari in this case, I assumed that our decision would bring the debate about lethal injection as a method of execution to a close. It now seems clear that it will not. The question of whether a similar three-drug protocol may be used in other states remains open and may well be answered differently in a future case on the basis of a more complete record. Instead of ending the controversy, I am now convinced that this case will generate debate not only about the constitutionality of the three-drug protocol, and specifically about the justification for the use of the paralytic agent, pancuronium bromide, but also about the justification for the death penalty itself.

Because it masks any outward sign of distress, pancuronium bromide creates a risk that the inmate will suffer excruciating pain before death occurs. There is a general understanding among veterinarians that the risk of pain is sufficiently serious that the use of the drug should be proscribed when an animal's life is being terminated. As a result of this understanding among knowledgeable professionals, several states—including Kentucky—have enacted legislation prohibiting use of the drug in animal euthanasia. It is unseemly—to say the least—that Kentucky may well kill petitioners using a drug that it would not permit to be used on their pets. Use of pancuronium bromide is particularly disturbing because—as the trial court specifically found in this case—it serves "no therapeutic purpose." The drug's primary use is to prevent involuntary muscle movements, and its secondary use is to stop respiration. In my view, neither of these purposes is sufficient to justify the risk inherent in the use of the drug.

The plurality believes that preventing involuntary movement is a legitimate justification for using pancuronium bromide because "the Commonwealth has an interest in preserving the dignity of the procedure, especially where convulsions or seizures could be misperceived as signs of consciousness or distress." This is a woefully inadequate justification. Whatever minimal interest there may be in ensuring that a condemned inmate dies a dignified death, and that witnesses to the execution are not made uncomfortable by an incorrect belief (which could easily be corrected) that the inmate is in pain, is vastly outweighed by the risk that the inmate is actually experiencing excruciating pain that no one can detect. Nor is there any necessity for pancuronium bromide to be included in the cocktail to inhibit respiration when it is immediately followed by potassium chloride, which causes death quickly by stopping the inmate's heart.

Moreover, there is no nationwide endorsement of the use of pancuronium bromide that merits any special presumption of respect. While state legislatures have approved lethal injection as a humane method of execution, the majority have not enacted legislation specifically approving the use of pancuronium bromide, or any given combination of drugs. And when the Colorado legislature focused on the issue, it specified a one-drug protocol consisting solely of sodium thiopental. In the majority of states that use the three-drug protocol, the drugs were selected by unelected department of correction officials with no specialized medical knowledge and without the benefit of expert assistance or guidance. As such, their drug selections are not entitled to the kind of deference afforded legislative decisions.

Nor should the failure of other state legislatures, or of Congress, to outlaw the use of the drug on condemned prisoners be viewed as a nationwide endorsement of an unnecessarily dangerous practice. Even in those states where the legislature specifically approved the use of a paralytic agent, review of the decisions that led to the adoption of the three-drug protocol has persuaded me that they are the product of "administrative convenience" and a "stereotyped reaction" to an issue, rather than a careful analysis of relevant considerations favoring or disfavoring a conclusion. Indeed, the trial court found that "the various States simply fell in line" behind Oklahoma, adopting the protocol without any critical analysis of whether it was the best available alternative. In my view, therefore, states wishing to decrease the risk that future litigation will delay executions or invalidate their protocols would do well to reconsider their continued use of pancuronium bromide.

The thoughtful opinions written in this case have persuaded me that current decisions by state legislatures, by the Congress of the United States, and by this Court to retain the death penalty as a part of our law are the product of habit and inattention rather than an acceptable deliberative process that weighs the costs and risks of administering that penalty against its identifiable benefits, and that rests in part on a faulty assumption about the retributive force of the death penalty.

We... [have] identified three societal purposes for death as a sanction: incapacitation, deterrence, and retribution. In the past three decades, however, each of these rationales has been called into question.

While incapacitation may have been a legitimate rationale in 1976, the recent rise in statutes providing for life imprisonment without the possibility of parole in forty-eight states demonstrates that incapacitation is neither a necessary nor a sufficient justification for the death penalty. Moreover, a recent poll indicates that support for the death penalty drops significantly when life without the possibility of parole is presented as an alternative option. And the available sociological evidence suggests that juries are less likely to impose the death penalty when life without parole is available as a sentence.

The legitimacy of deterrence as an acceptable justification for the death penalty is also questionable, at best. Despite thirty years of empirical research in the area, there remains no reliable statistical evidence that capital punishment in fact deters potential offenders. In the absence of such evidence, deterrence cannot serve as a sufficient penological justification for this uniquely severe and irrevocable punishment.

We are left, then, with retribution as the primary rationale for imposing the death penalty. And indeed, it is the retribution rationale that animates much of the remaining enthusiasm for the death penalty....Our Eighth Amendment jurisprudence has narrowed the class of offenders eligible for the death penalty to include only those who have committed outrageous crimes defined by specific aggravating factors. It is the cruel treatment of victims that provides the most persuasive arguments for prosecutors seeking the death penalty. A natural response to such heinous crimes is a thirst for vengeance.

At the same time, however...our society has moved away from public and painful retribution toward ever more humane forms of punishment. State-sanctioned killing is therefore becoming more and more anachronistic. In an attempt to bring executions in line with our evolving standards of decency, we have adopted increasingly less painful methods of execution, and then declared previous methods barbaric and archaic. But by requiring that an execution be relatively painless, we necessarily protect the inmate from enduring any punishment that is comparable to the suffering inflicted on his victim. This trend, while appropriate and required by the Eighth Amendment's prohibition on cruel and unusual punishment, actually undermines the very premise on which public approval of the retribution rationale is based.

Full recognition of the diminishing force of the principal rationales for retaining the death penalty should lead this Court and legislatures to reexamine the question, "Is it time to kill the death penalty?" The time for a dispassionate, impartial comparison of the enormous costs that death penalty litigation imposes on society with the benefits that it produces has surely arrived.

A penalty may be cruel and unusual because it is excessive and serves no valid legislative purpose. Our cases holding that certain sanctions are "excessive," and therefore prohibited by the Eighth Amendment, have relied heavily on "objective criteria," such as legislative enactments. In those opinions we acknowledged that "objective evidence, though of great importance, did not 'wholly determine' the controversy, 'for the Constitution contemplates that in the end our own judgment will be brought to bear on the question of the acceptability of the death.'"

Our decisions in 1976 upholding the constitutionality of the death penalty relied heavily on our belief that adequate procedures were in place that would avoid the danger of discriminatory application identified by Justice Douglas's opinion in *Furman* and of excessiveness identified by Justices Brennan and Marshall. In subsequent years a number of our decisions relied on the premise that "death is different" from every other form of punishment to justify rules minimizing the risk of error in capital cases. Ironically, however, more recent cases have endorsed procedures that provide fewer protections to capital defendants than to ordinary offenders.

Of special concern to me are rules that deprive the defendant of a trial by jurors representing a fair cross section of the community. Litigation involving both challenges for cause and peremptory challenges has persuaded me that the process of obtaining a "death qualified jury" is really a procedure that has the purpose and effect of obtaining a jury that is biased in favor of conviction. The prosecutorial concern that death verdicts would rarely be returned by twelve randomly selected jurors should be viewed as objective evidence supporting the conclusion that the penalty is excessive.

Another serious concern is that the risk of error in capital cases may be greater than in other cases, because the facts are often so disturbing that the interest in making sure the crime does not go unpunished may overcome residual doubt concerning the identity of the offender. Our former emphasis on the importance of ensuring that decisions in death cases be adequately supported by reason rather than emotion has been undercut by more recent decisions placing a thumb on the prosecutor's side of the scales. Thus, in *Payne v. Tennessee* (501 U.S. 808 [1991]), the Court overruled earlier cases and held that "victim impact" evidence relating to the personal characteristics of the victim and the emotional impact of the crime on the victim's family is admissible, despite the fact that it sheds no light on the question of guilt or innocence or on the moral culpability of the defendant, and thus serves no purpose other than to encourage jurors to make life or death decisions on the basis of emotion rather than reason.

A third significant concern is the risk of discriminatory application of the death penalty. While that risk has been dramatically reduced, the Court has allowed it to continue to play an unacceptable role in capital cases. (See also *Evans v. State,* 914 A.2d 25, 64 [2006], affirming a death sentence despite the existence of a study showing that "the death penalty is statistically more likely to be pursued against a black person who murders a white victim than against a defendant in any other racial combination.")

Finally, given the real risk of error in this class of cases, the irrevocable nature of the consequences is of decisive importance to me. Whether or not any innocent defendants have actually been executed, abundant evidence accumulated in recent years has resulted in the exoneration of an unacceptable number of defendants found guilty of capital offenses. The risk of executing innocent defendants can be entirely eliminated by treating any penalty more severe than life imprisonment without the possibility of parole as constitutionally excessive.

In sum, just as Justice White ultimately based his conclusion in *Furman* on his extensive exposure to countless cases for which death is the authorized penalty, I have relied on my own experience in reaching the conclusion that the imposition of the death penalty represents

> the pointless and needless extinction of life with only marginal contributions to any discernible social or public purposes. A penalty with such negligible returns to the State [is] patently excessive and cruel and unusual punishment violative of the Eighth Amendment.

The conclusion that I have reached with regard to the constitutionality of the death penalty itself makes my decision in this case particularly difficult. It does not, however, justify a refusal to respect precedents that remain a part of our law. This Court has held that the death penalty is constitutional and has established a framework for evaluating the constitutionality of particular methods of execution. Under those precedents...I am persuaded that the evidence adduced by petitioners fails to prove that Kentucky's lethal injection protocol violates the Eighth Amendment. Accordingly, I join the Court's judgment.

Concurring, *Scalia, J.,* joined by *Thomas, J.*

Consistent with the original understanding of the Cruel and Unusual Punishments Clause, this Court's cases have repeatedly taken the view that the framers intended to prohibit torturous modes of punishment akin to those that formed the historical backdrop of the Eighth Amendment....We have never suggested that a method of execution is "cruel and unusual" within the meaning of the Eighth Amendment simply because it involves a risk of pain—whether "substantial," "unnecessary," or "untoward"—that could be reduced by adopting alternative procedures....It strains credulity to suggest that the defining characteristic of burning at the stake, disemboweling, drawing and quartering, beheading, and the like was that they involved risks of pain that could be eliminated by using alternative methods of execution. Quite plainly, what defined these punishments was that they were designed to inflict torture as a way of enhancing a death sentence; they were intended to produce a penalty worse than death, to accomplish something "more than the mere extinguishment of life." The evil the Eighth Amendment targets is intentional infliction of gratuitous pain, and that is the standard our method-of-execution cases have explicitly or implicitly invoked.

It is not a little ironic—and telling—that lethal injection, hailed just a few years ago as the humane alternative in light of which every other method of execution was deemed an unconstitutional relic of the past, is the subject of today's challenge. It appears the Constitution is "evolving" even faster than I suspected. And it is obvious that, for some who oppose capital punishment on policy grounds, the only acceptable end point of the evolution is for this Court, in an exercise of raw judicial power unsupported by the text or history of the Constitution, or even by a contemporary moral consensus, to strike down the death penalty as cruel and unusual in all circumstances. In the meantime, though, the next best option for those seeking to abolish the death penalty is to embroil the states in never-ending litigation concerning the adequacy of their execution procedures. But far from putting an end to abusive litigation in this area, and thereby vindicating in some small measure the states' "significant interest in meting out a sentence of death in a timely fashion," today's decision is sure to engender more litigation. At what point does a risk become "substantial"? Which alternative procedures are "feasible" and "readily implemented"? When is a reduction in risk "significant"? What penological justifications are "legitimate"? Such are the questions the lower courts will have to grapple with in the wake of today's decision. Needless to say, we have left the states with nothing resembling a bright-line rule.

Which brings me to yet a further problem with comparative-risk standards: They require courts to resolve medical and scientific controversies that are largely beyond judicial ken....We have neither the authority nor the expertise to micromanage the states' administration of the death penalty in this manner. There is simply no reason to believe that "unelected" judges without scientific, medical, or penological training are any better suited to resolve the delicate issues surrounding the administration of the death penalty than are state administrative personnel specifically charged with the task....To the extent that there is any comparative element to the inquiry, it should be limited to whether the challenged method inherently inflicts pain.

> The fact that [lethal gas] is less painful and more humane than hanging is all that is required to refute completely the charge that it constitutes cruel and unusual punishment within the meaning of this expression as used in [the Eighth Amendment].

Judged under the proper standard, this is an easy case. It is undisputed that Kentucky adopted its lethal injection protocol in an effort to make capital punishment more humane, not to add elements of terror, pain, or disgrace to the death penalty. And it is undisputed that, if administered properly, Kentucky's lethal injection protocol will result in a swift and painless death.... The risk of negligence in implementing a death penalty procedure...does not establish a cognizable Eighth Amendment claim. Because Kentucky's lethal injection protocol is designed to eliminate pain rather than to inflict it, petitioners' challenge must fail. I accordingly concur in the Court's judgment affirming the decision below.

Dissenting, *Ginsburg, J.,* joined by *Souter, J.*

It is undisputed that the second and third drugs used in Kentucky's three-drug lethal injection protocol, pancuronium bromide and potassium chloride, would cause a conscious inmate to suffer excruciating pain. Pancuronium bromide paralyzes the lung muscles and results in slow asphyxiation. Potassium chloride causes burning and intense pain as it circulates throughout the body. Use of pancuronium bromide and potassium chloride on a conscious inmate, the plurality recognizes, would be "constitutionally unacceptable."

The constitutionality of Kentucky's protocol . . . turns on whether inmates are adequately anesthetized by the first drug in the protocol, sodium thiopental. Kentucky's system is constitutional, the plurality states, because "petitioners have not shown that the risk of an inadequate dose of the first drug is substantial." I would not dispose of the case so swiftly given the character of the risk at stake. Kentucky's protocol lacks basic safeguards used by other states to confirm that an inmate is unconscious before injection of the second and third drugs. I would vacate and remand with instructions to consider whether Kentucky's omission of those safeguards poses an untoward, readily avoidable risk of inflicting severe and unnecessary pain.

Rare though errors may be, the consequences of a mistake about the condemned inmate's consciousness are horrendous and effectively undetectable after injection of the second drug. Given the opposing tugs of the degree of risk and magnitude of pain, the critical question here, as I see it, is whether a feasible alternative exists. Proof of "a slightly or marginally safer alternative" is, as the plurality notes, insufficient. But if readily available measures can materially increase the likelihood that the protocol will cause no pain, a state fails to adhere to contemporary standards of decency if it declines to employ those measures.

Other than using qualified and trained personnel to establish IV access, however, Kentucky does little to ensure that the inmate receives an effective dose of sodium thiopental. After siting the catheters, the IV team leaves the execution chamber. From that point forward, only the warden and deputy warden remain with the inmate. Neither the warden nor the deputy warden has any medical training. The warden relies on visual observation to determine whether the inmate "appears" unconscious. In Kentucky's only previous execution by lethal injection, the warden's position allowed him to see the inmate best from the waist down, with only a peripheral view of the inmate's face. No other check for consciousness occurs before injection of pancuronium bromide. Kentucky's protocol does not include an automatic pause in the "rapid flow" of the drugs or any of the most basic tests to determine whether the sodium thiopental has worked. No one calls the inmate's name, shakes him, brushes his eyelashes to test for a reflex, or applies a noxious stimulus to gauge his response.

Nor does Kentucky monitor the effectiveness of the sodium thiopental using readily available equipment, even though the inmate is already connected to an electrocardiogram (EKG). A drop in blood pressure or heart rate after injection of sodium thiopental would not prove that the inmate is unconscious but would signal that the drug has entered the inmate's bloodstream. Kentucky's own expert testified that the sodium thiopental should "cause the inmate's blood pressure to become very, very low," and that a precipitous drop in blood pressure would "confir[m]" that the drug was having its expected effect. Use of a blood pressure cuff and EKG, the record shows, is the standard of care in surgery requiring anesthesia.

A consciousness check supplementing the warden's visual observation before injection of the second drug is easily implemented and can reduce a risk of dreadful pain. Pancuronium bromide is a powerful paralytic that prevents all voluntary muscle movement. Once it is injected, further monitoring of the inmate's consciousness becomes impractical without sophisticated equipment and training. Even if the inmate were conscious and in excruciating pain, there would be no visible indication.

Recognizing the importance of a window between the first and second drugs, other states have adopted safeguards not contained in Kentucky's protocol. Florida pauses between injection of the first and second drugs so the warden can "determine, after consultation, that the inmate is indeed unconscious." The warden does so by touching the inmate's eyelashes, calling his name, and shaking him. If the inmate's consciousness remains in doubt in Florida, "the medical team members will come out from the chemical room and consult in the assessment of the inmate." During the entire execution, the person who inserted the IV line monitors the IV access point and the inmate's face on closed circuit television. . . . In California, a member of the IV team brushes the inmate's eyelashes, speaks to him, and shakes him at the halfway point and, again, at the completion of the sodium thiopental injection. These checks provide a degree of assurance—missing from Kentucky's protocol—that the first drug has been properly administered. They are simple and essentially costless to employ, yet work to lower the risk that the inmate will be subjected to the agony of conscious suffocation caused by pancuronium bromide and the searing pain caused by potassium chloride. The record contains no explanation why Kentucky does not take any of these elementary measures.

The risk that an error administering sodium thiopental would go undetected is minimal, Kentucky urges, because if the drug were mistakenly injected into the inmate's tissue, not a vein, he "would be awake and screaming." That argument ignores aspects of Kentucky's protocol that render passive reliance on obvious signs of consciousness, such as screaming, inadequate to determine whether the inmate is experiencing pain.

First, Kentucky's use of pancuronium bromide to paralyze the inmate means he will not be able to scream after the second drug is injected, no matter how much pain he is experiencing. . . . Second, the inmate may receive enough sodium thiopental to mask the most obvious signs of consciousness without receiving a dose sufficient to achieve a surgical plane of anesthesia. If the drug is injected too quickly, the increase in blood pressure can cause the inmate's veins to burst after a small amount of sodium thiopental has been administered. Kentucky's protocol does not specify the rate at which sodium thiopental should be injected. The executioner, who does not have any medical training, pushes the drug "by feel" through five feet of tubing. In practice sessions, unlike in an actual execution, there is no resistance on the catheter; thus the executioner's training may lead him to push the drugs too fast.

"The easiest and most obvious way to ensure that an inmate is unconscious during an execution," petitioners argued to the Kentucky Supreme Court, "is to check for consciousness prior to injecting pancuronium [bromide]." The court did not address petitioners' argument. I would therefore remand with instructions to consider whether the failure to include readily available safeguards to confirm that the inmate is unconscious after injection of sodium thiopental, in combination with the other elements of Kentucky's protocol, creates an untoward, readily avoidable risk of inflicting severe and unnecessary pain.

Questions for Discussion

1. Why was lethal injection introduced? Describe the three drugs that are employed for lethal injection in Kentucky.
2. Explain why the petitioners argue that the drugs that are employed in Kentucky and the procedures followed in Kentucky constitute cruel and unusual punishment. Discuss the contention of Justice Stevens that pancuronium bromide poses a particular danger.
3. What is the legal standard that is employed by Justice Roberts in holding that the Kentucky lethal injection procedure does not constitute cruel and unusual punishment? Do you agree with this legal test?
4. Is it significant that virtually all states use the same three drugs as Kentucky in their lethal injection protocol? Does Justice Stevens believe that this should be a determining factor in the Supreme Court's decision?
5. Do Justices Thomas and Scalia believe that judges are equipped to evaluate whether lethal injection constitutes cruel and unusual punishment?
6. What is the basis of Justice Ginsburg's dissent? How does Justice Ginsburg differ from Justice Roberts in the legal standard that she employs to determine whether Kentucky's lethal injection protocol constitutes cruel and unusual punishment? Should Kentucky be required to take every possible step to safeguard individuals being subjected to lethal injection? Do all types of execution involve a measure of pain?
7. Would it have been important for the petitioners to present statistics and information on the number of improperly administered lethal injections using the three-drug protocol?
8. What is the legal standard proposed by Justices Thomas and Scalia for determining that a punishment is cruel and unusual?

As you read the next section on capital punishment, consider the consequences for capital punishment of a Supreme Court ruling that lethal injection constitutes cruel and unusual punishment. Keep Justice Stevens's argument in mind that capital punishment is unconstitutional.

Capital Punishment

The prohibition on cruel and unusual punishment also has been interpreted to require that punishment be proportionate to the crime. In other words, the "punishment must not be excessive"; it must "fit the crime." Judges have been particularly concerned with the proportionality of the death penalty. This reflects an understandable concern that a penalty that is so "unusual in its pain, in its finality and in its enormity" is imposed in an "evenhanded, nonselective, and nonarbitrary" manner against individuals who have committed crimes deserving of death (*Furman v. Georgia,* 408 U.S. 238, 256, 289 [1972]).

In *Furman v. Georgia,* five Supreme Court judges wrote separate opinions condemning the cruel and unusual application of the death penalty against some defendants, while others convicted of equally serious homicides were sentenced to life imprisonment. Justice Byron White concluded that there is "no meaningful basis for distinguishing the few cases in which [the death penalty] is imposed from the many cases in which it is not." Justice Potter Stewart observed in a concurring opinion that

> these death sentences are cruel and unusual in the same way that being struck by lightning is cruel and unusual.... The Eighth and Fourteenth Amendments cannot tolerate the infliction of a sentence of death under legal systems that permit this unique penalty to be so wantonly and so freakishly imposed. (*Furman v. Georgia,* 408 U.S. 238, 309, 313 [1972])

Justice Douglas controversially concluded in *Furman* that the death penalty was being selectively applied against the poor, minorities, and uneducated, while privileged individuals convicted of comparable crimes were sentenced to life in prison. Justice Douglas argued that the United States' system of capital punishment operated in practice to exempt anyone making over $50,000 from execution, while "blacks, those who never went beyond the fifth grade in school, those who make less than $3,000 a year or those who were unpopular or unstable [were] the only people executed." States reacted to this criticism by adopting mandatory death penalty laws that required that defendants convicted of intentional homicide receive the death penalty (256).

The U.S. Supreme Court ruled in *Woodson v. North Carolina* that treating all homicides alike resulted in the cruel infliction of death on undeserving defendants. The Court held that a jury "fitting the punishment to the crime" must consider the "character and record of the individual offender" as well as the "circumstances of the particular offense." The uniform system adopted in North Carolina treated "all persons convicted of a designated offense not as uniquely individual human beings, but as members of a faceless, undifferentiated mass to be subject to the blind infliction of the penalty of death" (*Woodson v. North Carolina,* 428 U.S. 280, 303 [1976]).

In 1976, in *Gregg v. Georgia,* the U.S. Supreme Court approved a Georgia statute designed to insure the proportionate application of capital punishment. The Georgia law limited the discretion of jurors to impose the death penalty by requiring jurors to find that a murder had been accompanied by one of several aggravating circumstances. This evidence was to be presented at a separate sentencing hearing and was to be weighed against any and all mitigating considerations. Death sentences were to be automatically reviewed by the state supreme court, which was charged with insuring that the verdict was supported by the facts and that capital punishment was imposed in a consistent fashion. This system was intended to insure that the death penalty was reserved for the most severe homicides and was not "cruelly imposed on undeserving defendants" (*Gregg v. Georgia,* 428 U.S. 153 [1976]).

Under Georgia's statute and others similar to it, the jury in the separate sentencing hearing or bifurcated sentencing hearing must find at least one aggravating circumstance beyond a reasonable doubt in order to impose capital punishment. These circumstances must be clearly stated. The *aggravated circumstances* listed in statutes typically include the following:

- The defendant previously has been convicted of a capital offense.
- The defendant committed the murder while engaged in the commission of a dangerous felony such as arson, rape, robbery, or burglary.
- The defendant intentionally killed a state or local public official or law enforcement officer who was engaged in the lawful performance of his or her duties.
- The murder was carried out for hire (money).

A defendant is not limited to the mitigating circumstances set forth in the statute, and the jury is entitled to consider any relevant mitigating circumstance. These *mitigating circumstances* typically include the following:

- The defendant was subject to duress or necessity under which he felt compelled to act to protect himself.
- The defendant was young or easily influenced.
- The defendant had no prior criminal record.
- The victim provoked the killing.
- The defendant's role was relatively minor, and he did not personally carry out the killing.

A judge's instructions must clearly inform the jury of the weight to be accorded to aggravating and mitigating circumstances (*Mills v. Maryland,* 486 U.S. 367 [1988]). These factors also must be clearly defined. A state law that provided for the death penalty for a killing that is "outrageously or wantonly vile, horrible, or inhuman in that it involved torture, aggravated battery or battery" was held to be unconstitutionally vague, and the inclusion of a vague factor, under some circumstances, may result in the reversal of a death sentence (*Godfrey v. Georgia,* 446 U.S. 420 [1980]).

There are two approaches to the consideration of aggravating and mitigating circumstances in the sentencing stage of death penalty trials. In **weighing states,** the jury is required to find that the aggravating circumstances outweigh the mitigating circumstances. **Nonweighing states** provide that the death penalty may be imposed once the jury finds an aggravating circumstance. The jury then considers the totality of the circumstances in determining whether to impose the death penalty. In *Ring v. Arizona,* a jury found the defendant guilty. The trial judge, following a sentencing hearing, concluded that the murder had been committed "in an especially heinous, cruel or depraved manner" in pursuit of an item of "pecuniary value." The U.S. Supreme court held that the determination of this fact, which increases the defendant's statutory maximum sentence from life in prison to death, should have been made by the jury rather than by the judge (*Ring v. Arizona,* 536 U.S. 584 [2004]).

The Supreme Court has held that in those jurisdictions in which the alternative to capital punishment is life in prison without the possibility of parole, the jury should be explicitly informed of the unavailability of parole (*Kelly v. South Carolina,* 534 U.S. 246 [2002]). The Supreme Court also has ruled that it is improper for a prosecutor to comment that a jury's verdict is not the final word and that the jury's verdict automatically will be reviewed by the state supreme court, because these comments relieve the jury of the "awesome responsibility" that they should feel in determining whether to impose the death penalty (*Caldwell v. Mississippi,* 472 U.S. 320 [1985]).

Are there offenses other than aggravated and intentional murder that the Supreme Court has held merit the death penalty? What of aggravated rape of an adult? In *Coker v. Georgia,* in 1977, the U.S. Supreme Court ruled that death is a grossly disproportionate and excessive punishment for aggravated rape and constitutes cruel and unusual punishment (*Coker v. Georgia,* 433 U.S. 584 [1977]). The Court also held that the death penalty is disproportionate punishment for robbery (*Enmund v. Florida,* 458 U.S. 782, 797 [1982]).

The possibility of death as the penalty for rape of a child, however, has instigated more dissent. In 2008, in *Kennedy v. Louisiana,* the U.S. Supreme Court held unconstitutional a Louisiana statute that imposed the death penalty on Kennedy for raping his eight-year-old stepdaughter. Justice Anthony Kennedy, writing for a five-judge majority, noted that only six of the thirty-six jurisdictions that at the time allowed for capital punishment imposed the death penalty for the rape of a child and that there was no national consensus that death was an appropriate punishment. (Justice Kennedy was in error in indicating that the federal government did not provide for the death penalty for the rape of a juvenile.) The Supreme Court in the past had limited capital punishment to cases of aggravated intentional homicide; this provided a bright-line rule and a clear and manageable standard for imposing a death sentence. The integrity of the death penalty process would be jeopardized by the imposition of death for the rape of a child, because children were easily influenced and unreliable witnesses, and families might be reluctant to report rapes committed by relatives if the punishment for such crimes included the possibility of the death penalty. Perpetrators facing death also would have little incentive to avoid killing childhood victims of rape. Judge Samuel J. Alito, in dissent, argued that the "worst childhood rapists" are the "epitome of moral depravity" and that the penalty of death was appropriate for serial child rapists and other dangerous offenders (*Kennedy v. Louisiana,* 554 U.S. ___ [2008]).

In 2005, in *Roper v. Simmons,* the Supreme Court held that the execution of individuals younger than eighteen offends contemporary standards of decency and violates the Eighth Amendment (*Roper v. Simmons,* 543 U.S. 551, 578 [2005]). The Eighth Amendment also prohibits the execution of "mentally retarded individuals" (*Atkins v. Virginia,* 536 U.S. 304 [2002]) and prohibits the execution of individuals who become insane while awaiting execution (*Ford v. Wainwright,* 477 U.S. 299 [1986]). In 1987, in *Tison v. Arizona,* the U.S. Supreme Court held that the death penalty was not disproportionate punishment for an individual who played a significant role in a felony murder and who exhibited a "reckless disregard for human life" (*Tison v. Arizona,* 481 U.S. 137 [1987]).

You can find Kennedy v. Louisiana *on the study site, http://www.sagepub.com/lippmancp.*

The Eighth Amendment and Sentences for a Term of Years

The U.S. Supreme Court has held that the length of a criminal sentence is the province of elected state legislators and that judicial intervention to review the "proportionality" of a sentence for a term of years should be "extremely rare" and should be limited to criminal sentences that are "grossly disproportionate" to the seriousness of the offense. Excessively severe sentences are not considered to advance any of the accepted goals of criminal punishment and constitute the purposeless and needless imposition of pain and suffering.

The implications of this approach are illustrated by Justice Sandra Day O'Connor's opinion in *Lockyer v. Andrade* in 2003. In *Lockyer,* the Supreme Court affirmed two consecutive twenty-five-year-to-life sentences for a defendant who on two occasions in 1995 stole videotapes with an aggregate value of roughly $150 from two stores. Each of these convictions, when combined with Andrade's arrest thirteen years earlier for three counts of residential burglary, triggered a separate mandatory sentence under California's **Three Strikes and You're Out law.** This statute provides for a mandatory sentence for individuals who commit a third felony after being previously convicted for two serious or violent felonies. Stringent penalties also are provided for a second felony. Justice O'Connor held that the sentence in *Andrade* was not grossly disproportionate and was not "an unreasonable application of our clearly established law" (*Lockyer v. Andrade,* 583 U.S. 63 [2003]).

In *Ewing v. California,* decided on the same day as *Lockyer,* Justice O'Connor affirmed a twenty-five-year sentence for Daniel Ewing under California's Three Strikes and You're Out law. Ewing was adjudged guilty of the grand theft of nearly $1,200 of merchandise and previously had been convicted of several violent or serious felonies. Justice Sandra Day O'Connor ruled that the Supreme Court was required to respect California's determination that it possessed a public safety interest in incapacitating and deterring recidivist felons like Ewing whose previous offenses included robbery and three residential burglaries (*Ewing v. California,* 538 U.S. 11 [2003]).

Weems v. United States is an example of the rare case in which the Supreme Court has ruled that a punishment is grossly disproportionate to the crime and is unconstitutional. Weems was convicted under the local criminal law in the Philippines of forging a public document. He was sentenced to twelve years at hard labor as well as to manacling at the wrist and ankle. During Weems's twelve-year imprisonment he was deprived of all legal rights, and upon his release, he lost all political rights (such as the right to vote) and was monitored by the court. The U.S. Supreme Court ruled that Weems's sentence was "cruel in its excess of imprisonment and that which accompanies and follows imprisonment. It is unusual in its character. Its punishments come under the condemnation of the Bill of Rights, both on account of their degree and kind" (*Weems v. United States,* 217 U.S. 349 [1910]).

You can find People v. Carmony, *a case involving the California Three Strikes and You're Out law, on the study site, http://www.sagepub.com/lippmancp.*

Criminal Procedure in the News

There currently are roughly 2,225 inmates in the United States sentenced to life in prison without the possibility of parole for crimes they committed as juveniles. Forty-two states and the federal government provide that a child under eighteen who commits certain serious crimes may be prosecuted as an adult and, if convicted, may be sentenced to life imprisonment without parole (LWOP).

In 2005, two nongovernmental organizations, Human Rights Watch and Amnesty International, compiled a comprehensive study of individuals serving life imprisonment for crimes committed as juveniles. In the volume, *The Rest of Their Lives: Life Without Parole for Child Offenders in the United States* (2005), the two organizations report that fifty-nine percent of juveniles serving LWOP are first offenders. Roughly ninety-three percent have been convicted of murder; twenty-six percent of these have been convicted of felony murder. The report notes that these felony murders typically involved a robbery or a burglary in which a co-felon killed the victim. The authors observe that a juvenile convicted of felony murder may not have known that a co-felon had a weapon or may not have anticipated that the victim of the felony would be killed. In twenty-seven of the forty-two states, LWOP is mandatory for an adult or for a child convicted of certain offenses, which in most instances include felony murder. Various statutes also authorize life imprisonment without parole for armed robbery, aggravated assault, certain drug offenses, and rape.

The eight states with the highest rates of LWOP for juveniles all provide for mandatory sentences for a range of offenses. Virginia, Louisiana, and Michigan have rates of LWOP for juveniles that are three to seven and a half times higher than the national average of 1.77 per 100,000 children. New Jersey and Utah permit LWOP for child offenders but have no child offenders currently serving LWOP. The District of Columbia, Alaska, Kansas, Kentucky, Maine, New Mexico, New York, and West Virginia all prohibit LWOP for juvenile offenders.

Observers attribute the trend toward LWOP for juveniles to a get-tough attitude toward crime. This has led many states to lower the age at which juveniles may be treated as adult offenders and has led to the introduction of pretrial procedures that permit prosecutors to automatically shift juveniles to the adult system without having to go through a hearing before a juvenile court judge (automatic transfer). Laws also have been introduced that authorize prosecutors to file charges against juveniles for certain offenses in adult criminal court without first filing a charge in juvenile court.

In 1990 there were 2,234 juveniles convicted of murder in the United States, 2.9 percent of whom were sentenced to LWOP. In 2000, the number of juveniles convicted of murder dropped to 1,006, but 9.1 percent were sentenced to LWOP. The Amnesty International and Human Rights Watch report notes that in four out of the seventeen years between 1985 and 2000, juveniles were more likely than adult offenders to receive either a death sentence or LWOP. These conviction rates are not only the result of a get-tough attitude toward juvenile crime. Juveniles, according to the report, are more likely than adult offenders to lack a familiarity with the technicalities of the criminal justice system and may be easily persuaded to confess or to plead guilty at trial. Juveniles also often are ill-equipped to meaningfully contribute to their defense.

Who are the juvenile offenders sentenced to LWOP? Sixteen percent of the youthful offenders incarcerated for LWOP were between thirteen and fifteen years old at the time that they committed their crimes. The estimated rate at which African American juveniles receive LWOP (6.6 per 10,000) is ten times greater than the rate for Caucasian juveniles (0.6% per 10,000). The average age of a juvenile who received LWOP is sixteen. The six youngest were thirteen years old at the time of their offenses. Sixteen percent were imprisoned for crimes committed at age fifteen or younger, while 354 confronted life imprisonment for offenses committed prior to their sixteenth birthday.

Human Rights Watch and Amnesty International point out that once condemned to an adult penitentiary, young people are at risk from other inmates and often do not have access to educational resources, positive role models, and support services. Human Rights Watch and Amnesty report that of the 54 countries surveyed in their study, only the United States and three other countries continue to sentence juveniles to LWOP.

A central function of the criminal law is to protect society. Some commentators argue that the law should punish criminal acts and should not be concerned with the age of the offender. Many of the juveniles sentenced to LWOP have engaged in particularly vicious criminal acts and undoubtedly were well aware of the consequences of their actions. On the other hand, in *Roper v. Simmons,* the U.S. Supreme Court stressed that juveniles are susceptible to "immature and irresponsible behavior," are vulnerable to "negative influences and outside pressures," are "categorically less culpable" than adults, and are less likely to be deterred by criminal punishment (*Roper v. Simmons,* 543 U.S. 551 [2005]).

In 1995, in *Harris v. Wright,* the Ninth Circuit Court of Appeals held that the nature of the crime rather than an offender's age is the crucial consideration in evaluating the proportionality of a sentence. The federal appellate court held that there is no clear distinction between a sentence of life imprisonment and a lengthy prison sentence and that "life imprisonment without parole is, for young and old alike, only an outlying point on the continuum of prison sentences" (*Harris v. Wright,* 93 F.3d 581 [9th Cir. 1996]). In 1989, in *Naovarath v. State,* the Nevada Supreme Court took an opposite point of view and held that sentencing a "child of this age [thirteen] to hopeless, life-long punishment and segregation is not a usual or acceptable response to childhood criminality, even where criminality amounts to murder." The Nevada judges were unwilling to accept that the youthful offender was "forever irredeemable" (*Naovarath v. State,* 779 P.2d 944, 947 [Nev. 1989]).

What is your view? Do you believe that LWOP for youthful offenders constitutes cruel and unusual punishment?

Equal Protection

Judicial decisions have consistently held that it is unconstitutional for a judge to base a sentence on a defendant's race, gender, ethnicity, or nationality. In other words, a sentence should be based on defendant's *act* rather than on a defendant's *identity.* A federal district court judge's sentence of thirty years in prison and lifetime supervision for two first-time offenders convicted of narcotics and weapons offenses was rejected by the federal Second Circuit Court of Appeals based on the trial court judge's observation that the South American defendants "should have stayed where they were.... Nobody tells them to come and get involved in cocaine.... My father came over with $3 in his pocket." The appellate court noted that it appeared that "ethnic prejudice somehow had infected the judicial process in the instant case." The appellate court observed that one of the defendant's "request that she be sentenced 'as for my person, not for my nationality,' was completely understandable under the circumstances" (*United States v. Edwardo-Franco,* 885 F.2d 1002 [2nd Cir. 1989]).

Statutes also have been held to be in violation of the Equal Protection Clause if they provide different sentences based on gender. In *State v. Chambers,* the New Jersey Supreme Court struck down a complicated statutory scheme that resulted in men receiving significantly shorter prison sentences than women convicted of the same crime. For instance, a female might be held on a gambling conviction "for as long as five years... [whereas a] first offender male, convicted of the same crime, would likely receive a state prison sentence of not less than one or more than two years." The female offender was required to serve the complete sentence, while the male would "quite likely" receive parole in four months and twenty-eight days. The New Jersey Supreme Court dismissed the argument that the "potentially longer period of detention" for females is justified on the grounds that women are good candidates for rehabilitation who could turn their lives around in prison. The court pointed out that there "are no innate differences [between men and women] in capacity for intellectual achievement, self-perception or self-control or the ability to change attitude and behavior, adjust to social norms and accept responsibility" (*State v. Chambers,* 307 A.2d 78 [1973]).

What of seemingly neutral laws that possess a discriminatory impact? The general rule is that a defendant must demonstrate both a discriminatory impact and a discriminatory intent. The difficulty of this task is illustrated by the Supreme Court's consideration of the discriminatory application of the death penalty in *McCleskey v. Kemp* (481 U.S. 279 [1987]).

Warren McCleskey, an African American, was convicted of two counts of armed robbery and one count of the murder of a white police officer. He was sentenced to death on the homicide count and to consecutive life sentences on the robbery counts. McCleskey claimed that the Georgia capital punishment statute violated the Equal Protection Clause in that under this statute, the death penalty was more likely to be imposed on African American defendants found guilty of murdering Caucasians than when either the defendants or the victims were of other races. McCleskey relied on a sophisticated statistical study of 2,000 Georgia murder cases involving 230 variables that had been conducted by Professors David C. Baldus, Charles Pulaski, and George Woodworth. This led to a number of important findings, including that defendants charged with killing Caucasians were over four times as likely to receive the death penalty as defendants charged with killing African Americans, and that African American defendants were one and one-tenth times as likely to receive the death sentence as other defendants.

The U.S. Supreme Court ruled that McCleskey had failed to meet the burden of clearly establishing that the decision makers in his specific case acted with a discriminatory intent to disadvantage McCleskey on account of his race. What of McCleskey's statistical evidence? The Supreme Court majority observed that the statistical pattern in Georgia reflected the decisions of a number of prosecutors in cases with different fact patterns, various defense counsels, and different jurors and did not establish that the prosecutor or jury in McCleskey's specific case or in any other specific case was biased. McCleskey killed a police officer, a charge that clearly permitted the imposition of capital punishment under Georgia law.

Criminal Appeals

The U.S. Supreme Court has followed the common law rule and has held that there is no due process right to a criminal appeal, and the decision as to whether to provide defendants a right to an appeal is a question to be decided by the legislative branch. Despite the fact that there is no requirement that an individual be provided any appeal whatsoever, various justices have expressed the belief that a defendant who is convicted of a crime should have the opportunity to have the judgment reviewed by an appellate court (*Ross v. Moffitt,* 417 U.S. 600, 609 [1974]). The consequences of a criminal conviction are too serious to have an individual's fate decided by a single judge and jury (*Jones v. Barnes,* 463 U.S. 745 [1983]). The federal government and all fifty states accordingly provide an appeal as a matter of right for a felony conviction. This appeal in most cases is to an intermediate appellate court. A discretionary appeal (optional) to state supreme court also is available. An appeal of a conviction for a misdemeanor usually involves a new trial (trial *de novo*) before an intermediate court. A number of claims may be raised on the appeal of a felony conviction. These issues typically include one or more of the following:

- ***Motion to suppress.*** The trial court improperly permitted the prosecution at trial to introduce a coerced or involuntary confession or evidence seized as a result of an unlawful search.
- ***Self-incrimination.*** There was a violation of the defendant's right against self-incrimination.
- ***Exonerating evidence.*** The prosecutor failed to disclose exculpatory evidence to the defense.
- ***Double jeopardy.*** The defendant was previously tried for the same crime.
- ***Speedy trial.*** The defendant was not provided with a speedy trial.
- ***Jury.*** The petit jury selection process was discriminatory.
- ***Judge.*** The judge's instructions to the jury were wrong.
- ***Defense attorney.*** The defendant was represented by an ineffective counsel.
- ***Prosecutor.*** The judge improperly permitted the prosecutor to introduce prejudicial evidence at trial or to engage in an inflammatory closing argument to the jury.
- ***Verdict.*** The facts at trial were insufficient to establish the defendant's criminal conviction.

The U.S. Supreme Court has held that a defendant who files an appeal as a matter of right possesses various constitutional rights. In 1956, in *Griffin v. Illinois,* the Supreme Court held that although Illinois is not required to provide an appeal as a matter of right, once it has provided the opportunity for an appeal, it is required to provide a free transcript of the criminal trial to indigents to avoid discriminating against individuals based on their economic status (*Griffin v. Illinois,* 351 U.S. 12 [1956]). Seven years later, the Supreme Court condemned the denial of legal representation to an indigent defendant who had filed an appeal as a matter of right. The Court held that the equality of treatment required by the Fourteenth Amendment is lacking where the "rich man" enjoys the benefit of a lawyer and a "meaningful appeal" while the "indigent" is forced to "shift for himself" and has an appeal that is little more than a "meaningless ritual." The right to "effective legal representation" does not extend to the discretionary appeal (*Wainwright v. Torna,* 455 U.S. 585 [1982]). An individual who files a successful appeal also may not be subjected to a vindictive prosecution (more serious charges) on retrial or vindictive sentencing (a longer sentence) following a reconviction (*North Carolina v. Pearce,* 395 U.S. 711 [1969]). One limitation on an appeal is that courts will not review a case that is **moot.** An example is the death of a defendant that makes it unnecessary for an appellate court to decide an appeal.

May a defendant file an appeal at any point during the trial when he or she believes that the judge has committed an error? The **final judgment rule** provides that a defendant ordinarily may appeal only following a guilty verdict and sentencing. There are several reasons for the final judgment rule:

- ***Respect.*** An appeals court should not interfere with the trial process by deciding questions in the middle of the trial.
- ***Delay.*** An appeal during the trial will delay the proceedings.
- ***Efficiency.*** Delaying an appeal until the end of the trial allows the appeals court to issue a single judgment that addresses all of the errors alleged to have been committed at trial.

The federal and state courts recognize an **interlocutory appeal** exception. This is limited to issues that cannot be effectively corrected by waiting until the final judgment and do not affect the determination of a defendant's guilt or innocence at trial (*Cohen v. Beneficial Industrial Loan Corporation,* 337 U.S. 541 [1941]). The U.S. Supreme Court has recognized four situations in which a defendant may file an interlocutory appeal.

Bail. In *Stack v. Boyle,* the Court recognized that a defendant may appeal excessive bail. A judgment following trial that an individual has been subjected to excessive bail would not provide remedy for a defendant who has not met bail and who has been incarcerated for many months (*Stack v. Boyle,* 342 U.S. 1 [1951]).

Double jeopardy. The proscription against double jeopardy protects individuals against being convicted more than once for the same crime as well as being subjected to a second trial for the same crime. The defendant who is required to wait for a final judgment to appeal already would have been subjected to a second trial in violation of the right not to be subjected to double jeopardy (*Abney v. United States,* 431 U.S. 651 [1977]).

Competency. An individual who is to be forcibly medicated in order to be competent to stand trial may file an interlocutory appeal (*Sell v. United States,* 539 U.S. 166 [2003]).

Speech or Debate Clause. The Speech or Debate Clause of the U.S. Constitution protects a member of Congress from standing trial and being held legally responsible for statements made in Congress (*Helstoski v. Meanor,* 442 U.S. 500 [1979]).

The general rule is that in order to appeal, an individual must first raise an objection at trial. The reason for the "raise or waive" rule is that this provides the trial court judge with the opportunity to correct an error and to avoid a reversal of a trial verdict on appeal. A reversal may lead to a second trial and result in considerable time and expense. The federal courts and most state courts provide for a **plain error exception.** Federal Rule of Criminal Procedure 52(b) states that there are plain errors "affecting substantial rights" that may be reviewed by an appellate court although not raised in the trial court. The purpose of the plain error exception is to prevent a miscarriage of justice. The U.S. Supreme Court defined a plain error as a clear error under existing law that "affects substantial rights" and that "seriously affects the fairness, integrity, or public reputation of judicial proceedings" (*United States v. Olano,* 507 U.S. 725 [1993]; *Johnson v. United States,* 520 U.S. 461 [1997]). An example of plain error may be a prosecutor's inflammatory and potentially prejudicial closing argument to the jury (*United States v. Young,* 470 U.S. 1 [1985]).

What is the standard of review on appeal? The fact that the trial court committed an error does not necessarily mean that the verdict will be reversed. Trial errors are reviewed under a **harmless error** standard. The appellate court must be convinced "beyond a reasonable doubt that the error complained of did not contribute to the conviction obtained." In other words, is the court convinced that the error did not influence the jury's guilty verdict? In *Chapman v. United States,* the U.S. Supreme Court concluded that it was "impossible" to conclude beyond a reasonable doubt that the prosecutor's and trial judge's comments to the jury that they could infer that the defendant was guilty from the fact the defendant did not take the stand in his or her own defense "did not contribute to petitioner's convictions." In other words, this was "a case in which, absent the constitutionally forbidden comments, honest, fair-minded jurors might very well have brought in not-guilty verdicts" (*Chapman v. United States,* 386 U.S. 18 [1967]).

The Supreme Court decision in *Chapman* recognized that there are some constitutional errors that are so serious that they cannot be considered harmless under any circumstances. The **automatic reversal rule** is limited to what the Supreme Court has described as "structural defects" that are fundamental to a fair trial. These constitutional errors are restricted to a "very limited class of cases" and include the denial of a lawyer at trial, a biased judge, racial discrimination in the selection of a jury, a rejection of the right to self-representation, denial of a public trial, inaccurate reasonable-doubt instruction to a jury, denial of a speedy trial, and a violation of double jeopardy (*Neder v. United States,* 527 U.S. 1 [1999]).

The Supreme Court has been concerned that permitting prosecutors to appeal will subject defendants to costly and lengthy appeals and may violate the defendants' rights against double jeopardy. The Double Jeopardy Clause was thought to prohibit appeals by the prosecution until the Supreme Court held in 1892 that the Congress and state legislatures might provide for limited categories of government appeals (*United States v. Sanges,* 354 U.S. 394 [1892]). Federal and state statutes accordingly recognize a narrow set of instances in which the prosecutor may file an appeal. The U.S. Supreme Court has characterized these situations as "something unusual, exceptional," and "not favored" (*Carroll v. United States,* 354 U.S. 394, 400 [1957]). For example, a prosecutor may file an interlocutory appeal contesting a pretrial order to suppress evidence and to exclude the evidence from trial. The reason is that at this point, the defendant's double jeopardy rights have not yet "attached," and the Double Jeopardy Clause would prohibit a second trial if the appeal were taken after the case proceeded to trial and the defendant was acquitted. The prohibition on a second trial would be particularly harmful in those instances in which the trial judge's exclusion of the evidence has resulted in the acquittal of a defendant who should have been convicted (18 U.S.C. § 3731).

The last issue in regard to criminal appeals is the **retroactivity of judicial decisions**. A U.S. Supreme Court ruling that breaks new constitutional ground, such as the right of a defendant to be represented at trial by a lawyer, applies to all other defendants with cases on appeal as well as to defendants whose cases are in "midstream," and to all cases that are brought to trial following the judgment. The reason for "retroactivity" is that the fact that a defendant's case was selected for review and that the appeal proved successful should not mean that this particular defendant should benefit while other defendants should not benefit from the decision (*Griffith v. Kentucky,* 479 U.S. 314 [1987]) (Chapter 2).

In the next section, we discuss habeas corpus. Habeas is a collateral remedy or an appeal that is available after a defendant has exhausted his or her direct state and federal appeals.

Habeas Corpus

State and federal judicial systems all provide for so-called **collateral remedies** or appeals that are available following the exhaustion of *direct appeals* or in some instances are available following a failure to take advantage of direct appeals. Federal **habeas corpus** review is the most important collateral remedy for both federal and state inmates.

An application for habeas corpus is a noncriminal (civil) lawsuit in which the defendant (now called the petitioner or plaintiff) asks the court for a writ on the grounds that he or she is being unlawfully detained. The writ of habeas corpus (literally "you have the body") is an order issued by a judge to a government official (usually the warden of a correctional institution) who has a person in custody to bring the person to court and to explain why the individual is in detention. In the event that the court finds that the plaintiff was unlawfully convicted or is being held without justification, the judge will order the individual released from custody.

The famous English jurist William Blackstone termed the writ of habeas corpus "the most celebrated writ in the English law." The "Great Writ of Liberty" has an important place in English and American history as a mechanism to protect individual rights. In 1677, in *Bushell's Case,* the writ was used to release a juror who was imprisoned for refusing to convict William Penn (discussed in Chapter 13). In 1867, the U.S. Supreme Court held that President Abraham Lincoln improperly suspended habeas corpus without the approval of Congress and had unlawfully established military courts with jurisdiction over civilians (*Ex parte, Milligan,* 71 U.S. 2 [1867]). In recent years, habeas corpus has been relied on by individuals who claim that they have been improperly detained as part of the "war on terror" (*Hamdi v. Rumsfeld,* 542 U.S. 507 [2004]).

The importance of the writ of habeas corpus is apparent from the fact that Article I, Section 9, Paragraph 2 of the U.S. Constitution provides that "[t]he Privilege of the Writ of Habeas Corpus shall not be suspended, unless when in Cases of Rebellion or Invasion the Public Safety may require it." In 1789, the First Judiciary Act authorized federal courts to grant writs of habeas corpus to federal prisoners. The Habeas Corpus Act of 1867 extended federal habeas review to state inmates. This law was intended to protect former African American slaves and northern activists who found themselves harassed by local law enforcement officials in the post–Civil War American South. In 1996, the U.S. Congress significantly limited the availability of habeas corpus in the Antiterrorism and Effective Death Penalty Act (AEDPA). This legislation was a response to the Oklahoma City terrorist bombing and was an effort to combat domestic terrorism by limiting the ability of individuals to challenge their death sentences. The basic language of the 1867 Act was incorporated into the AEDPA, which authorizes federal courts to issue a writ of habeas corpus when a prisoner is in custody pursuant to the judgment of a state or federal court "in violation of the Constitution or laws or treaties of the United States" (28 U.S.C. §§ 2241–2266). An application for a writ of habeas corpus customarily is filed with the federal district court in which an individual is incarcerated or convicted. There is provision for an additional appeal to a court of appeals and a discretionary appeal to the U.S. Supreme Court. Keep in mind that in a habeas petition filed by a state prisoner, a federal court reviews the judgment of a state trial court and of state courts of appeals, including the state supreme court.

The writ of habeas corpus is a topic of intense debate among judges and legal commentators and is a complicated and technical area of the law that even most lawyers do not fully understand. The Warren Court (1953–1969) in the 1960s viewed the writ as a mechanism for federal courts to insure that state courts protected the criminal procedural rights that the Warren Court had incorporated into the Fourteenth Amendment. The next two chief justices, Warren Burger (1969–1986) and his successor, William Rehnquist (1986–2005), headed courts that adopted a more limited view of federal habeas review of state court judgments.

Fay v. Noia is the most frequently cited example of the Warren Court's view that habeas review is required to insure that the constitutional rights of defendants are being protected by state courts. The U.S. Supreme Court ruled that Noia's failure to exhaust his appellate remedies in New York did not prevent federal courts from examining the voluntariness of his confession. Justice Brennan wrote that the history of the writ of habeas corpus is

> inextricably intertwined with the growth of fundamental rights of personal liberty. . . . Its root principle is that, in a civilized society, government must always be accountable to the judiciary for a man's imprisonment: if the imprisonment cannot be shown to conform with the fundamental requirements of law, the individual is entitled to his immediate release. (*Fay v. Noia,* 372 U.S. 391, 401–402 [1963])

Brennan later stressed that "conventional notions of finality of litigation have no place where life or liberty is at stake and infringement of constitutional rights is alleged" (*Sanders v. United States,* 373 U.S. 1, 7 [1963]).

The majority of judges on the Burger and Rehnquist Courts questioned whether federal courts should actively intervene in state court decision making. A particular concern was whether the federal courts should review a case like *Noia,* in which the defendant had not exhausted his state remedies. Justice Powell, in *Schneckloth v. Bustamonte,* pointed to the costs of federal courts engaging in active habeas corpus review:

- ***Limited judicial resources.*** Federal court dockets are flooded with petitions from prisoners, very few of which possess legal merit.
- ***Finality.*** The determination of a defendant's guilt in state court should be final and should not be subject to judicial reconsideration in federal courts.
- ***Federalism.*** State court decisions and procedures should be respected by the federal courts.
- ***Deterrence.*** Defendants should accept legal responsibility for their crimes and should not spend time and energy on continuing to claim their innocence or unconstitutional treatment.

Justice Powell stressed that habeas corpus review was undermining the deterrent and rehabilitative purposes of the criminal law and that

> at some point the law must convey to those in custody that a wrong has been committed, that...punishment has been imposed, that one should no longer look back with the view to resurrecting every imaginable basis for further litigation but rather should look forward to rehabilitation and to becoming a constructive citizen.

He noted that by subjecting state court judgments to "repetitive federal oversight, we render the actions of state courts a serious disrespect in derogation of the constitutional balance between the two systems." In Justice Powell's view, there is no reason to believe that state court judges are any less committed to protecting the rights of defendants than are federal judges. The question is whether the resources devoted to habeas review really advance the cause of justice. "Perhaps the single most disquieting consequence of open-ended habeas review is reflected in the [perceptiveness] of Mr. Justice Jackson's warning that 'it must prejudice the occasional meritorious application to be buried in a flood of worthless ones'" (*Schneckloth v. Bustamonte,* 412 U.S. 218, 259, 261, 274 [1973]).

Justice Robert Jackson criticized his Supreme Court colleagues for giving the federal courts a veto over state court decisions with which they disagreed. Jackson made the famous observation that "if there were a super–Supreme Court, a substantial proportion of our reversals of state courts would be reversed. We are not final because we are infallible, but we are infallible only because we are final" (*Brown v. Allen,* 344 U.S. 443, 534, 540 [1953]).

The Supreme Court's desire to limit the growth of habeas is illustrated by the Court's judgment in 1976 in *Stone v. Powell.* The Court majority held that where a state has provided an opportunity for "full and fair litigation of a Fourth Amendment claim," the Constitution does not require federal habeas corpus relief on the grounds that evidence obtained from an unconstitutional search and seizure was introduced at the individual's trial. Justice Powell explained that the deterrent effect of the exclusionary rule is achieved by the threat that evidence will be excluded from trial and that little additional deterrent effect is provided by the possibility that the evidence will be excluded on habeas review. He argued that

> the view that the deterrence of Fourth Amendment violations would be furthered rests on the dubious assumption that law enforcement authorities would fear that federal *habeas* review might reveal flaws in a search or seizure that went undetected at trial and on appeal. Even if one rationally could assume that some additional

> incremental deterrent effect would be present in isolated cases, the resulting advance of the legitimate goal of furthering Fourth Amendment rights would be outweighed by the acknowledged costs to other values vital to a rational system of criminal justice. (*Stone v. Powell,* 428 U.S. 465, 493, 494 [1976])

The AEDPA and the U.S. Supreme Court in recent years have combined to restrict the access of state prisoners to federal habeas corpus review. In developing the law of habeas corpus, the Supreme Court has employed the familiar balancing approach, in which the Court has attempted to strike a balance between the interest in finality of judgments and respect for state judges ("comity") on the one hand and the protection of the rights of the accused on the other hand. The federal courts now play the role of "quality control" and review habeas petitions to insure that the state trial and appeal courts provide defendants with a fair and reasonable consideration of their claims. Federal courts will intervene where there is clear evidence that the defendant's rights have been disregarded or where there is new evidence that the defendant is innocent. The following are the basic requirements for bringing a habeas claim in federal court.

Federal claim. The plaintiff must allege a violation of a federal constitutional right or a violation of federal law. A defendant who merely claims that newly discovered evidence indicates he or she is innocent, without tying the claim to the violation of a constitutional right, does not qualify for review. A violation of state law is not reviewable in a federal habeas review (*Herrera v. Collins,* 506 U.S. 390 [1993]).

Custody. A habeas petition challenges the lawfulness of an individual's detention, and the individual on whose behalf the petition is filed must be in custody. The custody may involve incarceration, probation, parole, or bail. An individual who has served a sentence may be regarded as in custody if there are continuing collateral consequences (e.g., loss of the right to vote).

Finality. The AEDPA requires that a state prisoner file a petition in federal district court "within a year of the final State court review of the conviction and sentence... or the expiration of the time for seeking such review" (28 U.S.C. § 2244(d)(1)).

Exhaustion. The plaintiff must exhaust state remedies before filing a petition for habeas corpus. A habeas review typically involves a limited review of the legal and factual determination of state courts.

Reasonableness of legal and factual determination. A federal court, in reviewing a state court decision, examines whether a state court decision directly disregarded a Supreme Court ruling, or unreasonably interpreted a Supreme Court ruling, or unreasonably interpreted the facts of a case. In other words, the question on habeas corpus review is whether the state court decision on the law and the facts is reasonable, not whether the state court decision is correct (*Williams v. Taylor,* 529 U.S. 362 [2000]). In *Bell v. Cone,* the Supreme Court held that the Tennessee court reasonably rejected a claim that a defense attorney had not provided effective representation by failing to present mitigating circumstances or a closing argument during the death penalty sentencing phase of the defendant's capital punishment trial. The Supreme Court noted that the available defense witnesses were unimpressive and that the defense attorney feared that the prosecution would bring out his client's criminal record if the defendant took the stand. The Court also noted that by waiving his closing argument, the defense attorney prevented the prosecutor from responding with a closing argument that might have highlighted the vicious nature of the defendant's offense (*Bell v. Cone,* 535 U.S. 685 [2002]).

Hearing on the facts. In most habeas cases, a district court decides the case based on the written trial record and on the written judgments of the state appellate courts. In certain limited circumstances, a federal district court will conduct a hearing in which witnesses will testify and the court will make factual determinations. There are six instances in which a district court will conduct a new hearing. The most frequent instance is when a defendant makes a claim of new evidence that supports a claim of "actual innocence" (*Townsend v. Sain,* 372 U.S. 293 [1963]).

Burden of proof. The basic rule is that the petitioner must demonstrate by a preponderance of the evidence that the constitutional error had a substantial and injurious impact or influence on the jury's guilty verdict (*Calderon v. Coleman,* 525 U.S. 141 [1993]). In other words, the defendant carries the burden of proof and must demonstrate actual prejudice (*Brecht v. Abrahamson,* 507 U.S. 619 [1993]).

There is no right to be represented by an attorney in the filing of a habeas corpus petition (*Murray v. Giarratano,* 492 U.S. 1 [1989]). However, states are required to provide prisoners with access to a law library or legal assistance in preparing habeas petitions (*Bounds v. Smith,* 430 U.S. 817 [1977]). The states may not prevent inmates from assisting one another in preparing petitions (*Johnson v. Avery,* 393 U.S. 483 [1969]).

There are several significant limitations on the ability of federal courts to grant habeas corpus review; these are outlined below.

Retroactivity. An individual filing a petition for habeas corpus may not rely on a new rule of law announced by the Supreme Court following the exhaustion of his or her direct state appeals. In other words, federal courts review whether a state court judge complied with existing law, not whether a different result would have been reached had the state courts applied the new rule. In *Teague v. Lane,* the Supreme Court held that Teague could not benefit from the court's decision in *Batson v. Kentucky* regarding peremptory challenges against African Americans that was handed down after Teague exhausted his appeals. There are various exceptions to this rule. For example, a "watershed" constitutional ruling (e.g., the right to counsel in a criminal trial) will be applied retroactively on habeas review (*Teague v. Lane,* 489 U.S. 288 [1989]).

Procedural default. In general, a federal court will not hear a habeas corpus petition in those instances in which a defendant failed to follow state procedures and did not raise an objection at trial and exhaust state appeals. In *Estelle v. Williams,* the U.S. Supreme Court held that Williams's failure to object to wearing prison clothes at trial resulted in a waiver of his due process claim (*Estelle v. Williams,* 425 U.S. 501, 513 [1976]). However, there are two exceptions that are relied on by defendants. The first is **cause and prejudice,** in which the defendant is required to demonstrate that the state caused the default by, for example, withholding information or some other misconduct. In *Banks v. Dretke,* the Supreme Court reversed the defendant's conviction based on the facts that the prosecution had failed to reveal that one of its chief witnesses was a government informant and that the other had been "extensively coached" on his testimony (*Banks v. Dretke,* 540 U.S. 668 [2004]). The defendant also can demonstrate that the procedural default was caused by ineffective assistance of counsel. The burden is on the defendant to demonstrate prejudice, which means that the defendant must demonstrate a reasonable probability that the error impacted the jury verdict. A second exception to the prohibition on habeas review of defaulted appeals is **actual innocence,** for which the defendant can establish "factual innocence" or "actual innocence" using new evidence. The standard is whether it is more likely than not, based on the new evidence, that no reasonable juror would have convicted the defendant (*Wainwright v. Sykes,* 433 U.S. 72 [1977]).

Successive petitions. The **successive petition doctrine** prohibits a second petition that raises a claim that has been presented in a prior habeas petition. The **abuse of writ doctrine** prohibits raising an issue that a defendant did not raise in the first petition, but could have raised. The AEDPA creates several exceptions. For example, a defendant may raise a new claim based on facts that previously could not have been discovered through the "exercise of due diligence." The court of appeals must approve district court consideration of a second petition (28 U.S.C. § 2244).

The U.S. Supreme Court has recognized that habeas corpus may be relied on to remedy a number of constitutional violations. Various examples are listed below.

- ***Evidence at trial.*** A defendant was denied due process of law by being convicted based insufficient evidence (*Jackson v. Virginia,* 443 U.S. 307 [1979]).
- ***Confessions.*** A defendant's conviction was based on statements obtained in violation of *Miranda v. Arizona* (*Withrow v. Williams,* 507 U.S. 680 [1993]).
- ***Ineffective assistance of counsel.*** Claims were made of racial discrimination in the selection of a grand jury (*Rose v. Mitchell,* 443 U.S. 545 [1979]).

- ***Jury instructions.*** Faulty jury instructions relieved the prosecution of proving elements of a crime or improperly placed the burden of proof on the defendant (*Engle v. Isaac,* 456 U.S. 152 [1982], *United States v. Frady,* 456 U.S. 132 [1982]).
- ***Prosecutorial misconduct.*** It was alleged that prosecutors withheld exculpatory evidence or made prejudicial comments during the trial (*Kyle v. Whitley,* 514 U.S. 419 [1995]).
- ***Actual innocence.*** A defendant claims that newly discovered evidence supports his or her clam of "actual innocence" (*Schlup v. Delo,* 513 U.S. 298 [1995]).

In the U.S. Supreme Court's habeas rulings, the Court has attempted to balance the interests in finality of state court judgments and comity (respect) toward state court judges against the interest in insuring that criminal convictions have not resulted from a disregard for constitutional rights. It certainly is the case that courts are overwhelmed with habeas petitions from imprisoned individuals, only a very small percentage of which result in an individual's release from prison. The Congressional Research Service, in 2006, reported that since 1997 an average of roughly 18,600 noncapital petitions were filed with federal courts, each of which required an average of five to seven months to consider. An average of 198 habeas petitions regarding capital punishment cases were filed each year. On the other hand, every judge would agree that there is an interest in reviewing claims of actual innocence based on new evidence.

In 2006, in *House v. Bell,* defendant Paul Gregory House was convicted and sentenced to death for the murder of Carolyn Muncey. House filed a habeas corpus petition based on new evidence that the victim's blood on his pants had resulted from vials of blood accidentally spilled on the pants by forensic examiners and that the semen found on the victim's clothing belonged to her husband. Witnesses also came forward who reported that Muncey's husband had confessed to the crime and that he had a history of abusing his wife and had offered the police a false alibi. The U.S. Supreme Court concluded that

> the central forensic proof connecting House to the crime—the blood and the semen—had been called into question, and that House has put forward substantial evidence pointing to a different suspect. Accordingly, and although the issue is close, we conclude that this is the rare case where—had the jury heard all the conflicting testimony—it is more likely than not that no reasonable juror viewing the record as a whole would find House guilty beyond a reasonable doubt. (*House v. Bell,* 547 U.S. 518 [2006])

On the other hand, there clearly are cases involving an abuse of habeas corpus. In *Calderon v. Thompson,* the U.S. Supreme Court rejected Thompson's habeas petition challenging his death sentence for rape and murder. The Supreme Court noted that Thompson had been given the benefit of almost thirteen years of state and federal review, including a consideration of his case by the governor of California. The Court concluded that Thompson's habeas corpus petition provided little new evidence beyond what had been presented at his original trial. He continued to claim that following consensual sexual contact with the victim, he had fallen asleep, and that an intruder had stabbed the victim five times in the head, wrapped her body in a sheet, removed it from the apartment, and scrubbed the carpet to remove her blood. Thompson's new evidence did not enhance the credibility of his "fantastic account of the events of the night of the murder," and the Supreme Court was unable to conclude that "no reasonable juror would have convicted Thompson" (*Calderon v. Thompson,* 523 U.S. 538 [1998]).

In summary, habeas corpus historically has protected individuals against unfair and arbitrary criminal convictions. Federal courts employ habeas today to insure that criminal convictions have not resulted from constitutional errors. Habeas also is available to review newly discovered or newly available evidence to guard against miscarriages of justice that result in the criminal conviction of the innocent. The question remains whether the benefits of habeas review are outweighed by the resources required to protect the rights of individuals.

Chapter Summary

The distinguishing characteristic of a criminal offense is that it is subject to punishment. Categorizing a law as criminal or civil has consequences for the protections afforded to a defendant, such as the prohibition against double jeopardy. Punishment is intended to accomplish various goals, including retribution, deterrence, rehabilitation, incapacitation, and restoration. Judges seek to accomplish the purposes of punishment through penalties ranging from imprisonment, fines, probation, and intermediate sanctions to capital punishment. Assets forfeiture may be pursued in a separate proceeding.

The federal government and the states have initiated a major shift in their approach to sentencing. The historical commitment to indeterminate sentencing and to the rehabilitation of offenders has been replaced by an emphasis on deterrence, retribution, and incapacitation. This primarily involves presumptive sentencing guidelines and mandatory minimum sentences. Several recent U.S. Supreme Court cases have resulted in sentencing guidelines that are advisory rather than binding on judges. An appellate court is required to find only that a sentence, whether inside or outside the guidelines, is "reasonable."

Constitutional attacks on sentences are typically based on the Eighth Amendment prohibition on the imposition of cruel and unusual punishment. The U.S. Supreme Court has ruled that the prohibition against cruel and unusual punishment applies to the federal government as well as to the states, and virtually every state constitution contains similar language. Three aspects of the clause were discussed: (1) it limits the *methods* employed to inflict punishment, (2) it restricts the *amount of punishment* that may be imposed, and (3) it regulates criminal punishment for a *term of years*. The Equal Protection Clause provides an avenue to challenge statutes and sentencing practices that result in different penalties for individuals based on their race, religion, gender, or ethnicity.

The effort to insure uniform approaches to sentencing is exemplified by the procedural protections that surround the death penalty. Legal rulings under the Eighth Amendment have limited the application of capital punishment to a narrow range of aggravated homicides committed by adult offenders. Constitutional challenges under the Eighth Amendment have proven unsuccessful against mandatory minimum sentences, as illustrated by the federal court's upholding of Three Strikes and You're Out laws and determinate penalties for drug possession. Judges have generally deferred to the decisions of legislators and have ruled that penalties for terms of years are proportionate to the offenders' criminal acts. The U.S. Supreme Court has stressed that such challenges should be upheld on "extremely rare" occasions where the sentence is "grossly disproportionate" to the seriousness of the offense.

Criminal sentences may not be based on the "suspect categories" of race, gender, religion, ethnicity, and nationality. Despite the condemnation of racial practices in the criminal justice system, the due process procedures surrounding the death penalty do not appear to have eliminated racial disparities in capital punishment. An equal protection challenge to the application of capital punishment, however, proved unsuccessful in *McCleskey v. Kemp*.

The U.S. Supreme Court has followed the common law rule and has held that there is no due process right to a criminal appeal, and the decision whether to provide defendants a right to an appeal is to be decided by the legislative branch. The federal government and all fifty states provide an appeal as a matter of right for a felony conviction. This appeal in most cases is to an intermediate appellate court. A discretionary appeal (optional) to the U.S. Supreme Court and to state supreme courts also is available. An appeal of a conviction for a misdemeanor usually involves a new trial (trial *de novo*) before an intermediate court. A number of claims may be raised on the appeal of a felony conviction. These issues typically include issues such as the denial of a motion to suppress, a prejudicial process of jury selection, double jeopardy, ineffectiveness of counsel, and a judicial error in the instructions to the jury.

There are several points to keep in mind in regard to criminal appeals.

Interlocutory appeal. The federal and state courts recognize an interlocutory appeal exception in the case of issues that cannot be effectively corrected by waiting until the final judgment and that do not affect the determination of a defendant's guilt or innocence at trial.

Plain error rule. The general rule is that in order to file an appeal, an individual must first raise an objection at trial. The federal courts and most state courts recognize a plain error exception that allows appellate courts to review an error that was not raised in the trial court. The purpose of the plain error exception is to prevent a miscarriage of justice. The U.S. Supreme Court defined a plain error as a clear error under existing law that "affects substantial rights" and that "seriously affects the fairness, integrity, or public reputation of judicial proceedings."

Harmless error standard. Trial errors are reviewed under a harmless error standard. The appellate court asks whether the court is convinced "beyond a reasonable doubt that the error complained of did not contribute to the conviction obtained." The question is whether the court is convinced that the error did not influence the jury's guilty verdict.

Automatic reversal rule. The Supreme Court has recognized that there are some constitutional errors that are so serious that they cannot be considered harmless under any circumstances. The automatic reversal rule is limited to what the Supreme Court has described as "structural defects" that are fundamental to a fair trial. These constitutional errors are restricted to a "very limited class of cases" and include the denial of a lawyer at trial, a biased judge, racial discrimination in the selection of a jury, a rejection of the right to self-representation, denial of a public trial, inaccurate reasonable-doubt instruction to a jury, denial of a speedy trial, and violation of double jeopardy.

Retroactivity of judicial decisions. The last issue in regard to criminal appeals is the retroactivity of judicial decisions. A U.S. Supreme Court ruling that breaks new constitutional ground, such as the right of a defendant to be represented at trial by a lawyer, applies to all other defendants with cases on appeal as well as to defendants whose cases are in "midstream" and to all cases that are brought to trial following the judgment.

A writ of habeas corpus is a noncriminal (civil) lawsuit in which the plaintiff asks the court for a writ on the grounds that he or she is being unlawfully detained. The importance of the writ of habeas corpus is apparent from the fact that Article I, Section 9, Paragraph 2 of the U.S. Constitution provides that "the Privilege of the Writ of Habeas Corpus shall not be suspended, unless when in Cases of Rebellion or Invasion the Public Safety may require." In 1996, the U.S. Congress significantly limited the availability of habeas corpus in the Antiterrorism and Effective Death Penalty Act (AEDPA). This legislation was a response to the Oklahoma City terrorist bombing and was an effort to combat domestic terrorism by limiting the ability of individuals to challenge their death sentences.

There are several requirements that must be satisfied by a defendant seeking a writ of habeas corpus:

- ***Federal claim.*** The plaintiff must allege a violation of a federal constitutional right or a violation of federal law.
- ***Custody.*** The individual on whose behalf the petition is filed must be in custody.
- ***Finality.*** The AEDPA requires that a state prisoner file a petition in federal district court "within a year of the final State court review of the conviction and sentence... or the expiration of the time for seeking such review (28 U.S.C. § 2244(d)(1)).
- ***Exhaustion.*** The plaintiff must exhaust state remedies before filing a petition for habeas corpus.

A habeas review typically involves a limited review of the legal and factual determination of state courts:

- ***Reasonableness of legal and factual determination.*** A federal court, in reviewing a state court decision, examines whether a state court decision directly disregarded a Supreme Court ruling, unreasonably interpreted a Supreme Court ruling, or unreasonably interpreted the facts of a case.
- ***Hearing on the facts.*** In most habeas cases, a district court decides the case based on the written trial record and on the written judgments of the state appellate courts.
- ***Burden of proof.*** The basic rule is that the petitioner must demonstrate by a preponderance of the evidence that the constitutional error had a substantial and injurious impact or influence on the jury's guilty verdict (*Calderon v. Coleman,* 525 U.S. 141 [1993]).

There are several significant limitations on the ability of federal courts to grant habeas corpus review, which are outlined below:

- ***Retroactivity.*** An individual filing a petition for habeas corpus may not rely on a new rule of law announced by the Supreme Court following the exhaustion of his or her direct state appeals.
- ***Procedural default.*** A federal court will not hear a habeas corpus petition in those instances that a defendant failed to follow state procedures and did not raise an objection at trial and exhaust state appeals. There are two exceptions that are relied on by defendants. The first is cause and prejudice, and the second is actual innocence.
- ***Successive petitions.*** The successive petition doctrine prohibits a second petition that raises a claim that has been presented in a prior habeas petition.

As you review criminal sentencing, appeals, and habeas corpus, consider how the U.S. Supreme Court has attempted to balance the efficient prosecution of criminal cases against the protection of individual rights and liberties.

Chapter Review Questions

1. Describe the general historical trend in sentencing in the United States.
2. What is the definition of criminal punishment? Why is it significant whether a penalty constitutes criminal punishment or a civil punishment?
3. Discuss the goals of criminal punishment. In your view, which is most important, and which is least important?
4. What punishments are available to a judge?
5. Summarize the types of criminal sentences and the process of judicial sentencing.
6. Describe sentencing guidelines. How do recent U.S. Supreme Court decisions modify the role of state and federal sentencing guidelines in judicial sentencing practices?
7. Outline the arguments for and against mandatory minimum sentences. Are mandatory minimum sentences constitutional?
8. Discuss the prohibition on cruel and unusual punishment and the U.S. Supreme Court ruling in *Baze v. Kentucky.*
9. Outline the sentencing phase in capital punishment cases.
10. What is the role of the Eighth Amendment in appellate court review of sentences for a term of years?
11. Discuss the role of the Equal Protection Clause in criminal sentencing.
12. Why are defendants provided with criminal appeals? Define and discuss the final judgment rule and interlocutory appeals. What is the importance of the plain error exception, the harmless error exception, and the automatic reversal rule?
13. Describe the importance of the writ of habeas corpus for the protection of rights and liberties. What are the requirements for filing a petition for a writ of habeas corpus? Outline the judicial debate over the role of habeas corpus.

Legal Terminology

abuse of writ doctrine
actual innocence
automatic reversal rule
capital punishment
cause and prejudice
clemency
collateral remedies
concurrent sentences
consecutive sentences
determinate sentencing
Eighth Amendment
final judgment rule
general deterrence
habeas corpus
harmless error
incapacitation
interlocutory appeal
moot
nonweighing states
pardon
plain error exception
presentence report
rehabilitation
restoration
retribution
retroactivity of judicial decisions
right of allocution
selective incapacitation
sentencing guidelines
sentencing hearing
specific deterrence
successive petition doctrine
Three Strikes and You're Out law
weighing states

Criminal Procedure on the Web

Log on to the Web-based student study site at **http://www.sagepub.com/lippmancp** to assist you in completing the Criminal Procedure on the Web exercises, as well as for additional features such as leading cases, podcasts, self-quizzes, and audio/video links.

1. Read about lethal injections and statistics on executions in the United States.
2. Learn about the debate over crack cocaine and powder cocaine and about public policy issues involved in sentencing.
3. Find out more about habeas corpus.

Bibliography

Mark E. Cammack and Norman M. Garland, *Advanced Criminal Procedure,* 2nd ed. (St. Paul, MN: West Publishing, 2006), pp. 437–505. A straightforward discussion of sentencing, appeals, and habeas corpus.

George P. Fletcher, *Rethinking Criminal Law* (New York: Oxford University Press, 2000), pp. 408–420. A discussion of the concept of criminal punishment and of the purposes of punishment.

Wayne R. LaFave, Jerald H. Israel, and Nancy J. King, *Criminal Procedure,* 4th ed. (St. Paul, MN: West Publishing, 2004), pp. 1209–1368. A detailed and technical legal discussion of sentencing, appeals, and habeas corpus.

Kate Stith, "*United States v. Mistretta:* The Constitution and the Sentencing Guidelines." In *Criminal Procedure Stories,* Carol S. Steiker, ed. (New York: Foundation Press, 2006), pp. 455–495. A legal history of sentencing guidelines.

Russell L. Weaver, Leslie W. Abramson, John M. Burkoff, and Catherine Hancock, *Principles of Criminal Procedure* (St. Paul, MN: West Publishing, 2004), pp. 376–411. A clear description of the law of sentencing, appeals, and habeas corpus.

15 Counterterrorism

May a United States citizen apprehended in the United States be detained as an enemy combatant?

Once in Pakistan, Padilla met with Khalid Sheikh Mohammad, a senior al-Qaeda operations planner, who directed Padilla to travel to the United States for the purpose of blowing up apartment buildings, in continued prosecution of al-Qaeda's war of terror against the United States. After receiving further training, as well as cash, travel documents, and communication devices, Padilla flew to the United States in order to carry out his accepted assignment. . . . Upon arrival at Chicago's O'Hare International Airport on May 8, 2002, Padilla was detained by FBI agents, who interviewed and eventually arrested him pursuant to a material witness warrant.

Core Concepts and Summary Statements

Introduction

In October 2001, the U.S. Congress passed and President George W. Bush signed the USA PATRIOT Act. This law was amended by the Patriot Act Improvement Act which was signed by President Bush in 2006.

Electronic Surveillance

A. In 1987, the U.S. Congress enacted the Foreign Intelligence Surveillance Act (FISA). The purpose of this legislation is to provide procedures for electronic surveillance and physical searches undertaken to protect the national security of the United States and to combat international terrorism.
B. FISA establishes the Foreign Intelligence Surveillance Court.
C. The government, in order to obtain a FISA warrant, is required to demonstrate probable cause that the "target" is the agent of a foreign power, is affiliated with an international terrorist group, or is engaged in international terrorism.
D. FISA warrants are based on a less demanding probable cause standard than ordinary criminal investigations.
E. The primary purpose of the surveillance is required to be the investigation of a threat to national security or the threat of terrorism. This language is intended to eliminate the wall between terrorism investigations and criminal investigations and to permit the sharing of information.
F. The place to be targeted by the surveillance must be used or about to be used by the agent of a foreign power or international terrorist.
G. Pen registers are employed to record telephone numbers dialed from a phone, and trap-and-trace devices record the numbers of incoming calls. An application to install a pen register is approved when the investigator certifies to a court that the information likely to be obtained is relevant to the investigation of a threat to national security or to the threat of terrorism.
H. Access to voice mail and to e-mail requires a search warrant issued by a judge based on probable cause.
I. Roving wiretaps permit the electronic surveillance of all telephones or computers or other electronic devices utilized by an individual without requiring that law enforcement obtain a separate warrant to monitor every phone or computer account or other electronic device that a "target" may utilize.
J. Electronic service providers are authorized to voluntarily disclose stored electronic communications in an emergency situation.

Sneak-and-Peek Warrants

A. Section 213 of the PATRIOT Act provides for sneak-and-peek searches. A sneak-and-peek warrant authorizes law enforcement to delay notifying an individual that they have conducted a search.
B. The government may conduct covert searches to investigate federal crimes when there is reasonable cause to believe that providing notice may result in an adverse result.
C. Section 219 of the PATRIOT Act authorizes a federal court with jurisdiction over an offense involving international or domestic terrorism to issue a nationwide search warrant.

Information and Records

A. Section 505 of the PATRIOT Act expands the authority of the FBI to issue national security letters and permits the FBI to obtain access to information when the information is relevant to the investigation of terrorism or secret intelligence activities.
B. The FISA court, under section 215 of the PATRIOT Act, may issue orders granting the government access to any "tangible" item (including books, records, or other documents) in a foreign intelligence investigation or in an international terrorism investigation. A request may be made for a tax return; education or medical records; or records from a library, bookstore, or firearm sale.

Detention of Noncitizens

A. The PATRIOT Act provides that a noncitizen may be detained for seven days without being charged with a criminal or immigration violation. The U.S. attorney general must certify that there are "reasonable grounds" to believe that an immigrant is a terrorist or has engaged in terrorist activities.
B. An individual may be held an additional six months if the individual is unlikely to be deported in the near future and the attorney general determines that the individual's release threatens national security or public safety. This certification may be renewed every six months.

Material Witness Warrants

The U.S. Congress enacted a material witness law in 1984 to enable the government to arrest a witness whose testimony is material to a criminal case and who may be unavailable to testify before a grand jury or in a criminal prosecution or who may flee in order to avoid testifying.

Monitoring of Attorney–Client Communications

In October 2001, U.S. Attorney General John Ashcroft issued an order permitting the Federal Bureau of Prisons to monitor attorney–client communications where the attorney general certifies that "reasonable suspicion exists to believe that a pre-trial detainee or an inmate may use communications with attorneys... to further or facilitate acts of terrorism."

Interrogations

A. The Bush administration determined that al-Qaeda was a terrorist organization and that apprehended members of al-Qaeda and of the Taliban in Afghanistan are not protected under the Geneva Conventions regulating the treatment of civilians and prisoners of war. As a result, the Department of Justice and Pentagon agreed that various enhanced interrogation techniques may be employed to obtain information that is vital to the protection of the national security of the United States.
B. The U.S. Congress formally put a halt to these interrogation techniques in the Detainee Treatment Act of 2005. Section 1001 provides that no person in the custody or under the effective control of the Department of Defense or under detention in a Department of Defense facility shall be subjected to any treatment or technique of interrogation that is not authorized in the *U.S. Army Field Manual on Intelligence Interrogation.*

Military Commissions and Combat Status Review Tribunals

A. On November 13, 2001, President George Bush, as commander in chief of the U.S. military, issued a military order establishing military commissions that were to conduct the trials of noncitizens who are members of al-Qaeda and who have engaged in international terrorism or who have assisted acts of terrorism against the United States.
B. In *Rasul v. Bush,* the U.S. Supreme Court held that federal courts possess jurisdiction to consider applications for habeas corpus from individuals detained at Guantanamo who were captured abroad during hostilities between the United States and the Taliban.
C. In *Hamdi v. Rumsfeld,* the Supreme Court held that an American citizen who had been detained in Afghanistan was entitled to a hearing to determine whether he was an unlawful combatant.
D. The U.S. Congress passed the Detainee Treatment Act, which among other provisions establishes combatant status review tribunals (CSRTs) to determine whether an individual is an unlawful enemy combatant. An individual's status then regularly is reviewed by administrative review boards that determine whether an individual should remain in custody.
E. In 2006, in *Hamdan v. Rumsfeld,* the U.S. Supreme Court held that the military commissions established by President George W. Bush possessed several fatal flaws.
F. President Bush responded by consulting with Congress. The Congress passed and President Bush then signed the Military Commissions Act of 2006, which reorganized military commissions and provided greater protections to defendants.
G. In 2008, in *Boumediene v. Bush,* the U.S. Supreme Court reviewed procedures of the CSRTs. The Court noted that Congress had suspended the writ of habeas corpus in the Military Commission Act but had failed to provide an adequate substitute procedure, and the suspension of the writ therefore was held to be unconstitutional.

Introduction

In October 2001, the U.S. Congress passed and President George W. Bush signed a new law to assist in combating the threat of terrorism titled the United and Strengthening America by Providing Appropriate Tools Required to Intercept and Obstruct Terrorism Act of 2001. This law is popularly known as the **USA PATRIOT Act.** Various amendments to the law later were incorporated into the PATRIOT Act Improvement Act that was signed by President Bush on March 9, 2006. The PATRIOT Act includes over one thousand counterterrorism measures; it is divided into ten sections and modifies over nine existing laws that address terrorism and related criminal activity. The two main purposes of the law are to define new federal criminal offenses relating to terrorism and to introduce reforms to criminal procedure to make it easier to investigate and detect acts of terrorism.

There are a wide variety of definitions of terrorism. The U.S. Department of State follows U.S. statutes and defines terrorism as "premeditated, politically motivated violence perpetrated against noncombatant targets by sub-national groups or clandestine agents, usually intended to influence an audience." International terrorism is terrorism involving individuals from more than one country or terrorism that involves the territory of more than one country. The key components of the State Department's definition of terrorism are the targeting of civilians to achieve a political objective that is carried out by individuals who are not part of an organized government (22 U.S.C. § 2656(d)).

The first part of this chapter outlines several provisions of the PATRIOT Act that are relevant to criminal procedure. The following topics are discussed:

- Electronic surveillance
- Sneak-and-peek warrants
- Information and records
- Detentions of noncitizens

The PATRIOT Act is only one of a number of procedural tools that are relied on to combat the international terrorist threat. The second portion of this chapter examines several additional counterterrorism mechanisms:

- Material witness warrants
- Monitoring of attorney–client communications
- Interrogations
- Military commissions and combat status review tribunals

The United States is a government and country based on the rule of law. In war or in times of national emergency, legal standards historically have been loosened in order to combat the threat confronting the nation. A number of judges and legal scholars have noted that the Constitution is not a "suicide pact" and that the first priority of government must be to protect the American people. This may involve a temporary limitation on civil rights and liberties. On the other hand, there is a danger that fear and insecurity may lead government officials to overreact and to sacrifice the very liberties that are at the core of our democracy. The challenge is to strike the appropriate balance between combating the threat to national security and protecting civil liberties. In striking this balance in times of war and national emergency, courts consistently have held that the protection of the country must take precedence over individual rights. As you read this chapter, consider whether the United States has struck the proper balance in the "war on terror."

Electronic Surveillance

In 1976, the Senate Select Committee to Study Government Operations with Respect to Intelligence Activities headed by Senator Frank Church of Idaho issued a report that documented widespread warrantless spying on Americans by U.S. intelligence agencies. This surveillance activity was based on the claim of various Democrat as well as Republican presidents that the president possessed the inherent power as commander in chief to protect the national security, and therefore the president was not required to obtain a court order or warrant. This claim was rejected by the U.S. Supreme Court in *United States v. United States District Court (Keith)* (407 U.S. 297 [1972]). The Court in *Keith* recognized that surveillance intended to protect the national security may be conducted on less than probable cause, but it held that the protection of individual privacy required judicial supervision of this surveillance activity. In 1987, in reaction to this ruling, the U.S. Congress enacted the **Foreign Intelligence Surveillance Act** (FISA, rhymes with Eliza) to provide procedures for electronic surveillance of threats to national security. In 1994, FISA was extended to cover physical searches of dwellings and other structures.

Keep in mind that FISA regulates surveillance within the United States of international threats to national security and of international terrorist activities. FISA also addresses the surveillance of Americans and American residents abroad. It does not regulate the surveillance of non–U.S. citizens and of non–U.S. residents outside of the United States (50 U.S.C. §§ 1801–1862).

FISA established the **Foreign Intelligence Surveillance Court** (FISC), which is comprised of eleven federal district court judges selected by the chief justice of the United States and by three other federal judges. Requests for a warrant to conduct surveillance of a threat to national security or for a warrant to conduct surveillance involving international terrorism are filed before a single judge. In the event that the request is turned down, the application is reviewed by the entire court. The proceedings and orders of FISC are secret, and the "target" of the warrant is not represented at the hearing. Government lawyers are required to satisfy four conditions to obtain a FISA warrant.

Target. The government must demonstrate probable cause that the target is the agent of a foreign power or a member of an international terrorist organization. The target may be a U.S. citizen, resident, or foreign national. The so-called lone wolf terrorism provision was added by the PATRIOT Act and authorizes the surveillance of non–U.S. residents who are not agents of a foreign power or affiliated with an international terrorist organization who are engaged in international terrorism or in activities in preparation for international terrorism.

Probable cause. The government is required to meet a lower probable cause standard than that used in ordinary criminal investigations. FISA orders are based on the "probability of a possibility" that the target of the order "may engage" in activities threatening the national security or "may engage" in terrorism.

Purpose. The primary purpose must be to investigate a threat to national security or threat of terrorism.

Place. The place or communication device targeted for surveillance must be being used or about to be used by a foreign power or terrorist organization to carry out activities that threaten the national security.

FISA is concerned with international threats to the United States. Domestic terrorism is covered by the wiretapping laws (Chapter 6). The individuals who may be a target of a FISA warrant for surveillance are individuals who work for a foreign organization or government (e.g., diplomats), foreign agents (e.g., persons involved in espionage), individuals affiliated with foreign terrorist groups, or individuals engaged in international terrorism.

FISA warrants are necessary for both electronic surveillance (e.g., wiretapping) and physical searches that are directed against foreign threats to national security and international terrorism. The government is required, if possible, to provide the FISA court with the identity of the individual to be targeted for surveillance as well as with the facts and circumstances that justify the surveillance. An American citizen or resident of the United States may not be singled out for surveillance based on the exercise of his or her First Amendment rights.

The standard is whether there is probable cause to believe that the target is an agent of a foreign power, is affiliated with a terrorist group, or is engaged in terrorism. The government must demonstrate the "probability of a possibility" that the target of the warrant "may engage" in activities that threaten the national security or "may engage" in terrorism, rather than probable cause that he or she is actually engaged in conduct threatening the national security or is engaged in terrorism. In other words, FISA warrants generally are easier to obtain than warrants for ordinary criminal investigations, which require probable cause that an individual is engaged in unlawful behavior. The reason for the more relaxed FISA standard is that the safety and security of the United States would be placed at risk by demanding that the government, before initiating surveillance, establish that there is probable cause that an individual is engaged in espionage or terrorism. On the other hand, there is a risk that FISA warrants may target individuals who later prove to be loyal and law-abiding Americans.

Originally, the FISA statute required that the sole purpose of the investigation was to protect national security or to combat terrorism. This standard was adopted, because there was a fear that the government would seek to use the relaxed standard for FISA warrants to pursue criminal investigations in those circumstances in which probable cause was lacking that the individual was engaged in criminal conduct. The government, in order to guard against this possibility, erected a "wall" between individuals investigating threats to national security and individuals engaged in criminal investigations. These two groups generally were prohibited from communicating and sharing information with one another. **The wall** came in for a great deal of criticism when it was revealed that information may not have been shared between government agencies regarding the presence in the United States of several of the individuals who later participated in the 9/11 attacks. The Congress responded in section 218 of the PATRIOT Act by requiring that a significant purpose (rather than the sole purpose) of surveillance under FISA must be national security or international terrorism. This language has been interpreted as opening the door to the sharing of information and coordination between national security officials and criminal investigators. The FISC has issued a judgment that so long as a "significant purpose" of the surveillance is to gain foreign intelligence information or information regarding terrorism, the government also may have the simultaneous objective of investigating the individual for a criminal activity. As a result of the breakdown of the wall, an investigator who is conducting a national security investigation who overhears information regarding credit card fraud now is free to communicate this information to federal investigators (*In re Sealed Case No. 02-001, 02-002,* 310 F.3d 717 [2002]).

FISA warrants for electronic surveillance and for physical searches authorize government investigations for 120 days and may be renewed for up to a year. This lengthy period of surveillance is considered necessary, because it may take a significant period of time to detect whether an individual is engaged in espionage or terrorism. The FISA law also recognizes that there is not always time to obtain a warrant for electronic surveillance. For example, an individual previously unknown to the government may receive a call from a known terrorist, and this individual, in turn, may place a call to yet another previously unknown telephone number. The FISA statute addresses this problem by authorizing the U.S. attorney general to conduct the emergency surveillance of U.S. citizens and residents for seven days before obtaining a warrant. There also is provision for the warrantless surveillance of non–U.S. citizens for a lengthier period of time.

In 2005, it was disclosed that the U.S. government was engaged in extensive warrantless surveillance of conversations between individuals in other countries and individuals in the United States. The domestic phone conversations of these American citizens and residents in many cases then also were monitored without a warrant. President George W. Bush claimed that this "terrorist surveillance program" was part of his responsibility as commander in chief to protect the United States. The disclosure of the warrantless surveillance program led Congress to revise FISA. FISA now is recognized as the sole mechanism regulating electronic surveillance. The attorney general and the director of national intelligence (head of all U.S. intelligence agencies) may continue to engage in warrantless electronic surveillance on individuals abroad and in each instance must specify how they will avoid collecting personal information without a warrant on Americans who may be involved in the phone conversation or electronic communications. American citizens and residents located at home or abroad may be placed under surveillance only in the event that they are demonstrated to be agents of a foreign power engaged in activities threatening the national security or are engaged in international terrorism, and a warrant must be issued by the FISC for this surveillance. FISA previously did not protect Americans located abroad from warrantless surveillance. The new law grants immunity from being sued to phone companies that cooperated in President Bush's surveillance program.

The 2006 amendments to FISA also expand the number of crimes for which Title III warrants (discussed in Chapter 6) for electronic surveillance in criminal investigations may be issued; these now include twenty federal offenses, including crimes involving biological weapons, violence at international airports, production of nuclear and other weapons of mass destruction, possession of explosive materials, receiving terrorist training, terrorist attacks against mass transit, arson, torture, firearm attacks in federal facilities, killing federal employees, aggravated identity theft, and the killing of foreign officials.

The next section discusses FISA's regulation of the collection of so-called transactional data, or information that records the addresses of communications rather than the content of communications.

Pen Registers and Trap-and-Trace Devices

Pen registers are employed to record telephone numbers dialed from a phone, and **trap-and-trace devices** record the numbers of incoming calls. Section 214 of the PATRIOT Act states that an application to install one of these devices requires an investigator to certify to a court that the information likely to be obtained is relevant for "any investigation to obtain foreign intelligence information . . . or to protect against international terrorism or clandestine intelligence activities." The target of the surveillance is not required to be a suspect in an investigation of national security or terrorism. The investigation may not be conducted solely on the basis of activities protected by the First Amendment to the Constitution.

Section 216 of the PATRIOT Act extends the standard for the use of pen registers and trap-and-trace devices to include the capturing of e-mail addresses and the addresses of Web pages downloaded during Internet browsing. The contents of the communication or Web page may not be examined under this provision. Recent amendments closely regulate the surveillance of e-mail and require the agency obtaining the order to inform the court of the name of the agent or agents who installed and monitored the device; the dates and times that the device was installed, monitored, and uninstalled; and the information obtained by the device. The PATRIOT Act extends surveillance powers by authorizing courts to issue an order for pen registers and trap-and-trace devices that applies throughout the United States. In the past, federal courts only were permitted to issue an order within the court's own district (18 U.S.C. §§ 3121–3127).

E-Mail and Voice Mail

The PATRIOT Act also addresses search warrants for the search of the content of stored voice mail and e-mail. The government may delay notification of the search of e-mail and voice mail in the event that notification is likely to have an adverse impact on the investigation. Section 220 authorizes a federal court to issue a nationwide search warrant for this type of "stored data."

Roving Wiretaps

Section 206 of the PATRIOT Act authorizes courts to issue warrants for **roving wiretaps,** or for what is termed "multi-point surveillance." This provision permits the electronic surveillance of all telephones or computers or other devices utilized by an individual without requiring that law enforcement obtain a separate warrant to monitor each phone or computer account or other electronic device that is utilized by the individual who is the target of the investigation. This provision is a response to the fact that terrorists regularly discard cell phones or switch between various devices to avoid surveillance. In 2006, section 206 was amended to require that the government provide details regarding the identity of the person to be placed under surveillance and to require law enforcement to notify the court when the surveillance shifts to a new communication device that was unknown at the time that the warrant was issued.

Emergency Electronic Surveillance

Electronic service providers (e.g., Internet service providers), when contacted by law enforcement, may voluntarily disclose stored electronic communications in an emergency situation involving the risk of danger or death or the immediate risk of serious physical harm.

Sneak-and-Peek Searches

Section 213 of the PATRIOT Act provides for what is termed anticipatory or **sneak-and-peek searches** (18 U.S.C. § 3103). A sneak-and-peek warrant authorizes law enforcement to delay notifying an individual that they have conducted a search. Law enforcement officers carrying out sneak-and-peek searches do not leave a copy of the warrant or a receipt indicating the material that they have examined in the dwelling. Where there is evidence of criminal activity, the police typically then return with a warrant and execute a search and a formal arrest. These types of searches have been conducted in isolated instances in the past, primarily for narcotics offenses (*United States v. Freitas,* 800 F.2d 1425 [9th Cir. 1986]); *United States v. Villegas,* 899 F.2d 1324 [2nd Cir. 1990]).

Section 213 for the first time creates specific statutory authorization for sneak-and-peek warrants. These searches are not limited to terrorism investigations and apply to all types of criminal investigations. The thinking is that there are certain circumstances in which notifying an individual of a search may jeopardize an investigation by alerting other members of a terrorist cell or criminal conspiracy that their organization is under investigation.

Section 213 states that the government may conduct covert searches in regard to federal crimes when there is reasonable cause to believe that providing notice may result in an "adverse result." An adverse result is defined as endangering an individual's life or physical safety, facilitating a flight from prosecution, risking destruction of or tampering with evidence, risking intimidation of potential witnesses, or seriously jeopardizing an investigation.

The initial version of section 213 provided that notice was to be provided to the subject of the search within a reasonable time. The 2006 amendment to the PATRIOT Act limits the delay in notification to thirty days, unless "the facts of the case justify a longer period of delay." The thirty-day delay may be extended for ninety days for "good cause shown." The ninety-day delay, in turn, may be extended by a judge if "the facts of the case justify a longer period of delay."

Sneak-and-peek searches in the past were limited to "intangible property." This might involve inspecting a computer file or documents or taking a photograph of a drug laboratory. Section 213 expands the scope of sneak-and-peek searches by authorizing the seizure of tangible (personal) property where a court finds a reasonable necessity for such seizure.

Law enforcement officials point out that section 213 merely imposes definite standards for searches that regularly have been conducted in the past. These types of searches are likely to be minimally intrusive into individuals' privacy, because law enforcement will not want to reveal the fact that they conducted a search by disrupting the dwelling. Critics of sneak-and-peek, on the other hand, make several points:

- ***Probable cause.*** A serious violation of the notice provision of the Fourth Amendment should be based on a strict probable cause standard rather than on reasonable cause.
- ***Terrorism.*** Sneak-and-peek searches should be limited to investigations of terrorism.
- ***Notice.*** Thirty days is too lengthy a period to delay notice, and the notice provision should not be subject to extensions.

- ***Accountability.*** Absent notification there is a no way to insure that the police entered the right home or limited their search and seizure to items listed in the warrant.
- ***Judicial review.*** There is little likelihood that a court will find that a prosecutor has failed to establish grounds to conduct a sneak-and-peek search given the broad basis for approving such searches.

Section 219 of the PATRIOT Act authorizes a federal court with jurisdiction over an offense involving international or domestic terrorism to issue a nationwide search warrant. Courts previously could issue warrants for use only within their own jurisdictions. The next section discusses how the PATRIOT Act has expanded the ability of federal law enforcement officers to gain access to business records and other information.

Information and Records

National Security Letters

In 1979, in *United States v. Miller,* the U.S. Supreme Court upheld the seizure of bank records by the police, reasoning that individuals do not possess a privacy interest in checks, deposit slips, and other financial information that a depositor voluntarily transmits to the bank. The Court reasoned that the "depositor takes the risk, in revealing his affairs to another, that the information will be conveyed... to the Government" (*United States v. Miller,* 425 U.S. 435, 443 [1976]). The *Miller* decision provided the basis for Congress to pass various statutes authorizing the FBI to obtain access to customer records from telephone companies and from financial, Internet, medical, educational, banking, credit card, and travel businesses and other related enterprises. Section 505 of the PATRIOT Act expands the authority of the FBI to issue **national security letters** (NSLs) to obtain access to information without a court order that is "relevant to an... investigation to protect against international terrorism or [secret] intelligence activities." The individual whose records are sought is not required to be the target of an investigation.

The PATRIOT Act Improvement Act allows recipients to challenge an NSL on the grounds that there is no reasonable possibility that the material that the government seeks will produce information relevant to the investigation. The FBI is authorized to impose a gag order on the recipient of an NSL. An intentional violation of a gag order with the intent to jeopardize an investigation is punishable by five years in prison. The thinking is that discussing the letter may jeopardize a national security investigation. An individual may petition to lift a gag order. The order generally will not be set aside if the FBI asserts that revealing the request for information will threaten the national security of the United States, impede a counterterrorism or counterintelligence investigation, interfere with diplomatic relations, or jeopardize the life or safety of an individual. Noncompliance with an NSL is punishable as contempt of court. The U.S. Congress, in order to guard against abuse of NSLs, now requires semiannual reports on the impact of these requests.

Seizure of Business Records

The director of the FBI or another FBI official may apply to the FISA court to issue orders granting the government access to any "tangible" item (including books, records, or other documents). These records may be requested from a library, bookstore, firearms sale, taxing authority, educational institution, or medical facility. An application is required to include a "statement of facts" demonstrating that there are reasonable grounds to believe that the tangible items that are sought are "relevant to an authorized or preliminary investigation to protect against international espionage or terrorism" or are "directed to obtain foreign intelligence information." The request for documents under section 215 must be accompanied by a statement of procedures that will be followed to protect against unauthorized individuals gaining access to the information. The "relevance standard" for these requests, although less than probable cause, has been held to be sufficient to seize information from a "third party." Probable cause is required when information that is to be seized is in the possession of the target of the investigation. Federal investigators are required to provide a description of the tangible thing that is sought. The attorney general is to submit an annual report on the use of section 215.

Individuals are prohibited from revealing that a request for information has been made. The recipient may petition for a modification or for a lifting of the gag order after one year. The standard to be used in evaluating whether to modify or to amend the gag order is similar to the standard for lifting a gag order for an NSL as discussed in the previous section.

Detention of Noncitizens

Section 412 of the PATRIOT Act provides that a noncitizen may be detained for seven days without being charged with a criminal or immigration violation. The attorney general of the United States must certify that there are "reasonable grounds to believe" that an immigrant is a terrorist or has engaged in terrorist activities. Immigration removal proceedings or criminal charges must be filed after seven days, or the individual must be released. Individuals may be held an additional six months if they are unlikely to be deported in the near future and the attorney general determines that their release threatens national security or public safety. This certification may be renewed every six months. A detainee may contest the certification by filing a writ of habeas corpus.

The next section discusses various counterterrorism procedures that are not addressed in the PATRIOT Act.

Material Witness Warrants

The federal government enacted a material witness law in 1984 to enable the government to arrest a witness whose testimony is material to a grand jury investigation or to a criminal prosecution and who may be unavailable at a later date to testify or who may flee in order to avoid testifying. Individuals are to be released following their testimony (18 U.S.C. § 3144).

The Department of Justice has reported that every individual detained under a **material witness warrant** has been found to have relevant information. The allegation is made that material witness warrants have been used in terrorist investigations to detain individuals who themselves are being investigated for terrorism. It is true that a number of individuals who ultimately were prosecuted or detained on charges of terrorism initially were detained as material witnesses. This is not surprising, because individuals detained on material witness warrants often are themselves engaged in terrorist activity.

Material witness warrants have been subject to criticism, and several reforms have been proposed:

- ***Detention.*** There should be limits on the length of detention. Individuals arrested on material witness warrants should be detained in separate facilities from individuals convicted of criminal activity.
- ***Flight.*** The government should be required to establish with a near certainty that unless detained, an individual is likely to flee or to be unavailable to testify.
- ***Information.*** Individuals detained should be informed of the reason for their detention and should be informed of their right to an attorney to challenge their arrests.

The government also has claimed the right to monitor the attorney–client communications between individuals arrested for terrorism and their lawyers.

Monitoring of Attorney–Client Communications

In October 2001, Attorney General John Ashcroft issued an order permitting the Federal Bureau of Prisons to monitor attorney–client communications when the U.S. attorney general certifies that "reasonable suspicion exits to believe that a pre-trial detainee or an inmate may use communications with attorneys . . . to further or facilitate acts of terrorism." This monitoring may be undertaken without a warrant. The government is required to notify the lawyer and the client that their communications "may be monitored" where reasonably necessary to deter "future acts of violence or terrorism." The thinking behind the order is that the attorney–client privilege to keep communications confidential does not apply where communications are intended to "facilitate criminal acts or a conspiracy to commit criminal acts" and are not related to "seeking or providing legal advice" (*Prevention of Acts of Violence and Terrorism,* § 28 C.F.R. 501.3 [2003]).

Defense attorneys have argued that the decision to monitor conversations should be based on a judicial warrant founded on probable cause rather than on the decision of the U.S. attorney general. There is a fear that the monitoring will interfere with the Sixth Amendment lawyer–client privilege by discouraging clients from freely communicating with their lawyers. In 2005, sixty-five-year-old defense attorney Lynne Stewart was convicted of material assistance to terrorism for assisting her client Omar Rahman, who was serving a life sentence for conspiracy to bomb various sites in New York City. Stewart was determined to have helped Rahman communicate with the terrorist Islamic Group in Egypt; she was sentenced to twenty-eight months in prison and lost her license to practice law. The government introduced surveillance tapes that, according to the prosecutor, demonstrated that Stewart conspired with Rahman and one of his followers to "get his message of violence out to the world" (*United States v. Sattar,* 272 F. Supp. 2d 348 [S.D.N.Y. 2002]).

Criminal Procedure in the News

In the course of roughly thirteen months, Great Britain was shaken by three terrorist plots by young "homegrown terrorists." The perpetrators all appear to have been ideologically driven Muslim youth, most of whom were citizens or longtime residents of Great Britain. On July 7, 2005, three bombs were exploded on a London subway within fifty seconds of one another. A fourth ripped the roof off a double-decker bus and shredded the back of the vehicle. The four suicide bombers killed fifty-six people and wounded another 700. A message on an al-Qaeda Web site warned that the attacks would continue as long as British troops remained in Afghanistan and Iraq. A tape produced by one of the bombers, Mohammad Sidique Khan, was broadcast on the Arab television station Al Jazeera on September 2, 2005, and warned that "we are at war and I am a soldier. Now you too will taste the reality of this situation." This was the deadliest attack in the city of London since a German V2 rocket killed 131 people during World War II.

The events of July 7 were followed two weeks later by an unsuccessful effort by four individuals to simultaneously explode bombs on the London public transport system. A fifth bomber apparently experienced problems in igniting his bomb and fled. As of August 2006, close to thirty individuals had been arrested for involvement in the plot. The media reported that the bombers had prepared themselves for the attacks by watching videos of English and American troops' alleged killing of women and children in Iraq.

On August 10, 2006, British authorities foiled a conspiracy inspired by al-Qaeda to kill thousands of people. The terrorists planned to detonate explosives simultaneously on as many as ten transatlantic flights originating from airports in the United Kingdom. The scheme called for members of the conspiracy to board flights on American carriers bound for the United States and to use cell phones to ignite a combination of various liquid chemicals that were to be stored in bottles placed in carry-on luggage. The explosions were to be detonated while the planes were over Los Angeles, New York, Washington, D.C., and other urban areas in the United States and in the United Kingdom. Pat Stevenson, the deputy commissioner of the London Metropolitan Police Service, stressed that the plot could have resulted in "mass murder" on an "unimaginable scale." President George W. Bush announced that this was a "stark reminder" that the United States was at "war with . . . fascists who will use any means to destroy those of us who love freedom [and] to hurt our nation."

The disclosure of the plot led to the virtual shutdown of air traffic in the United Kingdom and inconvenienced as many as 400,000 passengers. In anticipation of a second planned terrorist assault, the terror-alert status in the United Kingdom was raised from "high" to "critical," meaning that the public was warned of an imminent attack.

British intelligence had placed many of the suspects in the Heathrow plot under surveillance for as long as several months. Twenty-four individuals were arrested, and as many as fifty people spread across three continents may have been involved to some extent in the conspiracy. Virtually none of the young suspects had a record of terrorist activity that would have attracted the attention of intelligence services. Three of the men were converts to Islam, and one was only seventeen. It later was revealed that several of the men had met with al-Qaeda operatives in Pakistan who likely provided funding, planning, and training in bomb-making techniques. Several of the attackers had prepared martyrdom videos for television broadcast following the planned assaults. Italy, fearing that she was the next country to be targeted, responded by arresting forty people in raids on Muslim gathering places across the country.

British authorities responded by prohibiting carry-on luggage, and they searched every passenger, reducing the speed of travel through England's main airports to virtual gridlock. A number of commentators argued that the only tactic to guarantee the safety of passengers was to begin the racial profiling of Muslims. It was argued that most terrorist acts had been undertaken by young male Muslims from South Asia and that it made no sense to search grandmothers with walkers and little children on their way to holiday in Spain. (Excluding people from the security process is termed *positive profiling.*) Commentators pointed to the flawless safety record of Israel's El Al Airlines, which relies on the profiling of passengers. Lord John Stevens, former commissioner of the Metropolitan Police Service, added fuel to the fire when he endorsed racial profiling and wrote that "I'm a white, 62-year-old, suit-wearing ex-cop—I fly often, but do I really fit the profile of a suicide bomber?"

Superintendent Ali Dizael, the highest ranking Muslim on the London police force, responded that profiling would prove ineffective in detecting terrorists and would alienate the Muslim community, whose assistance was vital in the war on terror. Muslim leaders condemned the effort to create what they termed the offense of "traveling while Asian" and argued that any policy must be "intelligence-led and not bearded-led." Superintendent Dizael pointed out that terrorists come in every "size, shape, color and creed" and that the most effective approach was *behavior profiling,* the profiling of people based on their actions and reactions such as nervousness, sweating, and walking in a manner that may indicate that they are wearing a suicide belt. Investigating passengers before they arrive at the airport also may reveal suspicious patterns of activity, such as the use of a false address, the transfer of bank funds into an account, or a stolen credit card.

Muslim commentators pointed to various terrorists who did not fit the profile. The Israelis, for example, prevented the bombing of one of their planes in 1986 when they discovered that a young pregnant Irish woman, Anne Marie Murphy, was carrying a bomb that had been placed in her handbag by her Jordanian boyfriend. Oklahoma City bomber Timothy McVeigh, who was responsible for hundreds of deaths, also did not fit a profile. Superintendent Dizael urged British officials to appreciate that Muslims, like other English citizens, had been the victims of terrorism and shared the desire to see terrorists brought to the bar of justice. European countries have adopted a system of advanced passenger screening that analyzes passenger information prior to boarding. Several European states also are using racial profiling to single out Muslims, and enhanced security checks are being conducted on individuals from "high-risk" countries or who are traveling on "high-risk routes." There is evidence that that individuals of South Asian origin continue to be removed from aircraft in Great Britain, because their behavior or dress has created apprehension among the other passengers.

What is your view of the racial profiling of suspected terrorists? Consider the following incident. In November 2006, six Muslim imams (religious leaders) were removed from a flight in Minneapolis prior to its departure for Phoenix, Arizona. The men were handcuffed and led off the flight, questioned for thirty minutes, and then detained for several hours. Their money was refunded and they left the next day on another airline.

The six men had been attending a North American Imam Federation conference. Passengers and crew members complained that the men had engaged in "unsettling" behavior, allegedly making anti-American remarks and chanting "Allah" as they boarded. The men reportedly asked for seat belt extensions once on board, although they did not appear to require longer seat belts, and a ticket agent said that some of the men were praying in Arabic in the gate area prior to boarding the aircraft. One of the imams called the entire affair a "humiliation." The imams have filed a civil suit for damages. Was this a case of racial profiling?

Interrogations

One of the most controversial aspects of U.S. counterterrorism policy has been the use of enhanced interrogation techniques to question so-called high-value detainees. Article III of the Geneva Conventions on the law of war applies to what are termed "non-international conflicts" between a country and an insurgent or terrorist group. This article provides that detainees should be treated "humanely" and prohibits "violence to life and person, in particular... cruel treatment and torture.... [and] outrages upon personal dignity, in particular, humiliating and degrading treatment." The U.S. War Crimes Act of 1996 declares that it is a crime punishable by a fine and up to life imprisonment or death to intentionally violate Article III (18 U.S.C. § 2441).

The United States also is a signatory to the International Convention Against Torture and Other Cruel, Inhuman or Degrading Treatment or Punishment (1984) which prohibits "any act by which severe pain or suffering, whether physical or mental, is intentionally inflicted on a person." The treaty provides that "no exceptional circumstances" justify torture. Countries that sign the convention also are required to prevent acts of cruel, inhuman, or degrading treatment or punishment that do not amount to torture. U.S. federal courts have held that the torture convention is binding on the United States and that freedom from torture is a fundamental right of all people (*Filartiga v. Pena-Irala,* 630 F.2d 876 [2nd Cir. 1979]). The federal U.S. Torture Convention Implementation Act makes it a crime punishable by up to twenty years in prison to commit an act of torture "outside the United States." Torture is punishable by life in prison or death if death results from an act of torture (18 U.S.C. § 2340).

We need to take a brief detour in our discussion before proceeding. President Bush made the crucial determination that members of al-Qaeda who were apprehended by American forces in Iraq and Afghanistan were not entitled to any of the protections provided by the Geneva Conventions, which are the international treaties that virtually all countries, including the United States, accept as regulating the conduct of military conflicts. Instead, these individuals were to be regarded as unlawful **enemy combatants** who were to be treated humanely but were not entitled to the rights guaranteed to prisoners of war or to the protections guaranteed to ordinary civilians. President Bush's decision received some support from a federal district court, which held that John Walker Lindh, the so-called American Taliban, could be held criminally liable for assisting al-Qaeda in Afghanistan and that he was not entitled to be treated as a prisoner of war who had engaged in lawful armed combat (*United States v. Lindh,* 212 F. Supp. 2d 541 [E.D. Va. 2002]). As a result of President Bush's decision to deny protection under the Geneva Conventions to individuals affiliated with al-Qaeda and the Taliban, the Department of Justice and Department of Defense agreed that various enhanced interrogation techniques might be used to obtain information from detainees that was vital to the protection of the national security of the United States.

The Bush administration denied that the enhanced interrogation techniques employed against enemy combatants constituted torture or cruel treatment. A memorandum drafted by the Office of Legal Counsel of the U.S. Department of Justice (OLC) in August 2002 stated that to constitute torture under U.S. law, a practice must be "equivalent in intensity to the pain accompanying serious physical injury, such as organ failure, impairment of bodily function, or even death." Two years later, this statement was withdrawn by the Department of Justice, which explained that acts that did not meet the OLC standard still might constitute torture. A second point made by the Bush administration was that the president, as commander in chief, was charged with protecting the national security and safety of the United States and that individuals acting in response to his orders were not bound by the U.S. War Crimes Act and Torture Convention Implementation Act. According to this administration, the United States confronted a "ticking time bomb" of terrorist threats, and the president had to be free to employ whatever techniques were required to gather evidence to combat impending attacks.

The argument that President Bush was empowered to take whatever steps were required to gather information to protect the country was strengthened by the fact that in the aftermath of the September 11, 2001, attack on the United States, Congress authorized President Bush to wage war on anyone who had "planned, authorized, committed or aided" the attacks (Joint Resolution to authorize the use of United States Armed Forces against those responsible for the recent attacks launched against the United States, Pub. L. 107-40,.115 Stat. 224 [S.J. Res. 23, Sept. 18, 2001]).

The debate over enhanced interrogation continues to center on the questioning of several high-ranking al-Qaeda operatives, several of whom were integrally involved in planning the 9/11 attacks against the World Trade Center and the Pentagon. Military interrogators following these terrorist attacks were under pressure to collect intelligence on al-Qaeda's plans. Interrogators were authorized by officials in the Bush administration to use various coercive techniques; the most controversial involved "round the clock" interrogations, stress positions, the use of dogs, isolation for up to thirty days, and sensory deprivation. Even more coercive techniques could be employed with the approval of high-ranking government officials. These practices included threats of violence, pushing and shoving, and "exposure to cold weather or water." The use of water refers to waterboarding, which entails pouring water over an individual's face to simulate drowning. A number of these techniques were employed in combination with one another, along with other measures such as the continual playing of loud music. In some cases, suspected members of al-Qaeda were subjected to extraordinary rendition. This involved "abducting" suspected al-Qaeda terrorists living abroad or transferring alleged terrorists in U.S. custody and transporting them to countries supporting the war on terror, where they were secretly incarcerated, subjected to abusive interrogation, and held for lengthy periods without trial. A number of these individuals then were transported to the U.S. naval base at Guantanamo.

There was disagreement within the government over the effectiveness of enhanced interrogation techniques. Critics contended that these techniques strengthened the resolve of detainees to resist and that establishing trusting relationships with detainees had proven to be more effective than physical coercion in eliciting information. The information provided by detainees subjected to coercive questioning was thought to be unreliable, because they would tell interrogators "whatever they wanted to hear" in order to end their often painful interrogation. There also was the risk of retribution against American soldiers captured by countries whose nationals had been subjected to enhanced interrogation by the United States. On the other hand, a number of interrogators and members of the Bush administration contended that harsh techniques had resulted in obtaining information that had foiled terrorist plots and led to the arrest of several high-ranking members of al-Qaeda. The imminent threat of terrorist violence also did not allow interrogators the luxury of taking the time to develop a trusting relationship with detainees.

In 2006, the U.S. Supreme Court, in *Hamdan v. Rumsfeld,* held that members of al-Qaeda who were being detained at Guantanamo were protected under Article III of the Geneva Conventions (*Hamdan v. Rumsfeld,* 548 U.S. ___ [2006]). The U.S. Congress put a halt to enhanced interrogation techniques in the **Detainee Treatment Act of 2005** (DTA). Section 1001 of this act provides that no person in the custody or under the effective control of the Department of Defense or under detention in a Department of Defense facility shall be subjected to any treatment or technique of interrogation not authorized in the *U.S. Army Field Manual on Intelligence Interrogation*. Section 1003 prohibits "cruel, inhuman, or degrading treatment or punishment against any individual." This section did not extend to interrogations conducted by the Central Intelligence Agency (CIA).

Section 1004 of the DTA provides that in any civil action or criminal prosecution against a member of the U.S. armed forces or U.S. government resulting from the interrogation of an individual believed to be associated with international terrorist activity, a defense shall be that the individual did not know and a reasonable person would not have known that the interrogation techniques were unlawful. This section provides legal protection to individuals who carried out what they believed were legally authorized interrogation techniques. President Bush indicated when he signed the DTA that he did not interpret the statute as limiting his authority as commander in chief to order interrogation techniques required to protect national security.

In January 2009, President Barack Obama announced that the detainees no longer were to be referred to as enemy combatants and that detainees were to be treated in accordance with the Geneva Conventions. President Obama also ordered that both the military and the CIA conduct interrogations in accordance with the *Army Field Manual* and not engage in enhanced interrogation techniques such as waterboarding. A study was to be undertaken of the circumstances in which enhanced interrogation techniques might be required.

The debate over interrogation techniques took on added intensity in May 2009, when the Obama administration released four memorandums authored by the OLC in the U.S.

Department of Justice in 2002 and 2005 . These documents argued that various harsh interrogation techniques had been carefully limited to "further the Government's paramount interest in protecting the nation while avoiding unnecessary or serious harm" and could not be said to "shock the conscience." In contrast to these memos supporting the legality of enhanced interrogation, a confidential memorandum authored by the International Red Cross, which is charged with inspecting the detention of prisoners of war and other detainees, concluded that the United States had subjected fourteen high-value detainees to torture and to cruel and inhuman and degrading treatment.

The controversy over interrogation techniques escalated in August 2009, when the CIA released a document drafted in 2004 detailing abuse of detainees by agency employees and private contractors that took place primarily in Iraq and in Afghanistan. Attorney General Eric Holder responded by announcing that based on the recommendation of the Office of Professional Responsibility of the Department of Justice, he was appointing a career prosecutor to determine whether a full criminal investigation should be initiated of roughly a dozen interrogators who allegedly went beyond interrogation techniques authorized under American law. Attorney General Holder's decision was criticized, because career prosecutors in the Department of Justice during the Bush administration had decided against bringing prosecutions. Defenders of harsh interrogation methods also argued that the use of these techniques had led detainees to reveal information that had prevented terrorist attacks against the United States. Prosecutors in the Office of Professional Responsibility earlier also had conducted an internal review of the conduct of the lawyers responsible for drafting the legal opinions justifying the use of enhanced interrogation techniques and concluded that the lawyers "committed serious lapses in judgment." The report did not recommend criminal prosecution but indicated that state bar associations should consider disciplinary action against the lawyers.

President Obama continued to question the legality and necessity for the use of enhanced interrogation, but he publicly opposed subjecting individuals to criminal prosecution who had followed orders in conducting enhanced interrogation. Following Attorney General Eric Holder's decision to appoint a career prosecutor to determine whether a criminal investigation should be initiated of alleged unlawful interrogations, the White House announced that a new multiagency interrogation unit would be formed within the FBI. This High Value Interrogation Group would have members from various national security agencies and would develop and employ scientific and sophisticated noncoercive interrogation techniques. President Obama also announced that while detainees would continue to be sent abroad for interrogation by foreign countries, this questioning would be closely monitored to insure that detainees were not subject to abuse while in foreign custody.

A second controversial area concerns prosecution of enemy combatants before military commissions.

Military Commissions and Combat Status Review Tribunals

On November 13, 2001, President George Bush as commander in chief of the U.S. armed forces issued a military order regulating the detention and trial of noncitizens who are members of al-Qaeda and who have engaged in international terrorism or who have assisted acts of terrorism (Detention, Treatment, and Trial of Certain non-Citizens in the War Against Terrorism [Military Order of November 13, 2001]). President Bush's order provided that these unlawful enemy combatants were to be prosecuted before **military commissions.** The president claimed the authority to create military commissions without consulting with Congress based on the **Authorization for Use of Military Force** (AUMF) adopted by Congress following the September 11, 2001, terrorist attacks. This congressional resolution, as discussed in the previous section, authorized the president to "use all necessary and appropriate force against those nations, organizations, or persons" responsible for attacking the

United States "in order to prevent any future acts of international terrorism." This language, according to President Bush, authorized him to detain and to punish those responsible for attacking the United States.

A military commission is a court, composed of members of the military, that is used to prosecute captured enemy soldiers in the field of battle. Commissions also have been used to prosecute individuals when the military occupies another country or during a period of martial law when the normal courts are not functioning. These tribunals have been used by American armed forces from the first days of the republic; they were relied on by President Abraham Lincoln during the Civil War and were used to prosecute Nazi spies and captured Japanese war criminals during World War II. Commissions historically have been criticized for failing to provide the full rights and protections available in civilian courts or in American military courts-martial. Questions regarding the fairness of military commissions during World War II led Congress to require that military commissions when possible should provide the same protections to detainees that are accorded to U.S. soldiers in a court-martial.

Military commissions have the advantage of providing most of the basic rights that are considered important to a fair trial while possessing the flexibility to limit these rights in the interest of protecting national security. The Bush administration argued that court-martial procedures could not be fully followed by military commissions. The prosecution of terrorists required flexible procedures that permitted the introduction of hearsay evidence from unnamed informants and reliance on classified information that could not be revealed to the accused. Keep in mind that the military commission has jurisdiction over crimes against the law of war and does not have jurisdiction over domestic criminal offenses.

The precise procedures to be followed in the prosecution of individuals detained during the war on terror were spelled out in a military order issued by the Department of Defense (Department of Defense, Military Commission Order No. 1 [March 21, 2002]). A defendant under the military commissions established by President Bush could be excluded from trial to protect national security information and was not to be informed of evidence against him or her that might jeopardize national security. The commissions also were not required to follow the rules of evidence. The thinking was that the government may find it necessary to protect the identity of informants by relying on hearsay (e.g., information told by an informant to an FBI agent) and that the government should be able to rely on confessions obtained under pressure or coercion that the court nevertheless found to be reliable. A vote of two-thirds of the commission was sufficient to convict individuals of offenses that did not carry the death penalty. Appeals were to be taken to a panel consisting of three military officers appointed by the Secretary of Defense rather than to civilian tribunals. Lawyers for detainees at Guantanamo confronting prosecution before military commissions challenged the legality of their detentions before the U.S. Supreme Court.

The Supreme Court and Enemy Combatants

In 2004, the U.S. Supreme Court issued two important decisions regarding President Bush's designation of Guantanamo detainees as unlawful enemy combatants. The Bush Administration claimed that the federal courts had no jurisdiction to review the treatment of detainees at Guantanamo naval base, territory that the United States leased from Cuba. In *Rasul v. Bush,* the U.S. Supreme Court held that federal courts had jurisdiction to consider applications for habeas corpus from two Australian citizens and twelve Kuwaiti citizens detained at Guantanamo who had been captured in Afghanistan during hostilities between the United States and the Taliban and al-Qaeda. The Court held that although Guantanamo was located in Cuba, the naval base was situated in territory over which the United States exercised "jurisdiction and control." The Supreme Court clearly was influenced by the fact that the detainees had not been charged or convicted of any criminal offenses, claimed to be innocent of any wrongdoing, and were nationals of countries that were not at war with the United States (*Rasul v. Bush,* 542 U.S. 466 [2004]).

The next question was whether the detainees had rights that the Supreme Court was willing to enforce against the U.S. government. In the companion case of *Hamdi v. Rumsfeld,* the

Supreme Court held that Esam Fouad Hamdi, an American citizen who had been detained in Afghanistan while allegedly fighting for the Taliban, was entitled to a hearing to determine whether he was an enemy combatant. Hamdi, following his capture, was classified as an enemy combatant and transferred to a military prison in the United States. He claimed that he had not been involved in the armed struggle against the United States and that he had only recently arrived in Afghanistan to work for a humanitarian relief organization. Hamdi filed a writ of habeas corpus challenging the decision to detain him without a formal charge or a hearing.

The Supreme Court held that a U.S. citizen who has been detained abroad possessed the right to challenge his or her classification as an enemy combatant in a formal hearing. On the one hand, the government possessed an interest in removing enemy combatants from the battlefield as quickly and as efficiently as possible. This interest was outweighed in Hamdi's case by the threat posed to the liberty of an American citizen who had found himself mistakenly detained until the "cessation of hostilities." The decision in *Hamdi,* in essence, held that the status of detainees was to be determined based on evidence presented in a hearing (*Hamdi v. Rumsfeld,* 542 U.S. 507 [2004]).

The U.S. Congress responded to the decision in *Hamdi* by passing the Detainee Treatment Act (DTA), which among other provisions establishes **combat status review tribunals** (CSRTs) to evaluate whether detainees are enemy combatants. The decisions were subject to review by **administrative review boards.** There is some uncertainty, but it appears that an individual who is determined to be an enemy combatant may be detained without trial until the end of the war on terror; individuals who are not found to be enemy combatants are to be released.

An enemy combatant for purposes of the CSRT process is defined as an individual who is affiliated with or who supports the Taliban or al-Qaeda or associated forces that are engaged in hostilities against the United States or its coalition partners. A personal representative who is a military officer is to be appointed to represent each detainee. The CSRT is to be composed of three neutral commissioned officers of the U.S. armed forces who are appointed by the secretary of defense of the United States. The detainee has the right to attend all meetings other than those in which the tribunal deliberates and votes on the detainee's fate or meetings in which national security information is presented. The tribunal is not required to follow the law of evidence and is authorized to consider hearsay. Habeas corpus petitions challenging the result of a CSRT may be filed only with the U.S. Court of Appeals for the District of Columbia and are limited to determining whether the appropriate standard and procedures have been followed. The same U.S. Court of Appeals has similar jurisdiction to review the final decisions of military tribunals (Detainee Treatment Act of 2005, § 1005).

After the passage of the DTA, lawyers who had volunteered to represent several of the Guantanamo detainees petitioned the Supreme Court to examine whether the CSRTs and military commissions provided adequate due process protections.

The Supreme Court and Military Commissions

In 2006, in *Hamdan v. Rumsfeld,* the U.S. Supreme Court considered a challenge to military commissions filed by Salim Ahmed Hamdan, a Yemeni national detained at Guantanamo. Hamdan had served as a bodyguard and personal driver for Osama bin Laden and was charged with transporting weapons as part of an al-Qaeda conspiracy to commit acts of terrorism. He was indicted and scheduled to stand trial before a military commission and claimed the military commission procedures failed to satisfy the requirements of due process (*Hamdan v. Rumsfeld,* 548 U.S. ___ [2006]).

The Supreme Court approvingly noted that President Bush's order establishing military commissions provided for a number of protections for the accused. The Court, however, held that these military commissions possessed several fatal flaws.

Exclusion from trial. The accused and his or her civilian counsel may be excluded from the trial and denied knowledge of the evidence against him or her when the information may jeopardize the safety of witnesses, result in disclosure of the identity of informants, or jeopardize national security. The accused also may be denied access to sensitive information so long as the judge concludes that this will not deprive the defendant of a full and fair trial.

Failure to follow rules of evidence. Evidence may be admitted that "would have probative value to a reasonable person." This may result in the admission of hearsay and evidence obtained through coercion.

Jury verdicts. A guilty verdict for any offense and for any sentence not resulting in death may be based on a two-thirds vote.

Limited appeals. An appeal may be taken to a three-member review panel appointed by the secretary of defense, but only one panel member is required to have experience as a judge. The review panel makes a recommendation to the Secretary of Defense who, in turn refers the case to the president for final decision.

The Supreme Court held that the conflict with al-Qaeda was regulated by Article III of the Geneva Conventions, which requires that prosecutions should be conducted by a "regularly constituted court" that provides all the procedural protections to defendants that are recognized as "indispensable by civilized peoples." These guarantees are listed in Article 75 of the First Protocol Additional to the Geneva Conventions (1977) and encompass the fundamental protections provided by the American system of criminal justice, including the right to an impartial trial, the right to be present at a criminal trial, and the right to obtain and to cross-examine witnesses.

President Bush responded to the Supreme Court decision in *Hamdan* by consulting with Congress, which passed the **Military Commissions Act of 2006** (MCA). The act provides military commissions with jurisdiction over any foreign unlawful combatant who has engaged in hostilities against the United States or who has intentionally and materially supported hostilities against the United States. A military commission under the act is to consist of a military judge and at least five members (jurors). In a prosecution in which a defendant may be sentenced to death, a minimum of twelve jurors are required to unanimously support the verdict. Any commissioned officer of the armed forces on active duty may serve on the commission.

The commission system provides for a number of due process protections:

- The defendant is presumed innocent until proven guilty.
- The defendant is represented by an independent, appointed military counsel. The defendant also may retain private civilian counsel.
- Guilt is to be determined beyond a reasonable doubt.
- The defendant has a right to be present at all proceedings other than when the commission is discussing the verdict and voting on the verdict. A defendant may be excluded only for being disruptive or threatening the physical safety of individuals.
- The defendant may present evidence, call witnesses, and cross-examine witnesses.
- The defendant must be presented with the evidence against him or her. Evidence that involves national security may be summarized to avoid disclosing information.
- The defendant is protected against self-incrimination. An adverse inference may not be drawn from a failure to testify.
- The defendant has a right to self-representation.
- A finding of guilt and subsequent sentencing requires a two-thirds vote of the military commission. Sentences that involve confinement for ten years or more require a three-fourths vote of the commission. A sentence of death requires a unanimous vote of at least twelve members.
- Hearsay evidence is admissible so long as the evidence would have "probative value to a reasonable person." Evidence may not be excluded on the grounds that it was not seized based on a search warrant.
- Statements resulting from torture or in violation of the DTA may not be introduced into evidence. A statement obtained prior to the enactment of the DTA that violates the statute may be admitted if considered reliable and in "the interests of justice."

- Appeals may be taken to the Court of Military Commission Review, which is to be composed of three military judges. A further appeal may be taken to the U.S. Court of Appeals for the District of Columbia, which is limited to determining whether the final decision is consistent with the standards and procedures specified in the MCA and the U.S. Constitution.

President Barack Obama, almost immediately after being sworn into office, suspended prosecutions before military commissions "to permit the...administration time to review the military commission process...and the cases currently pending before the military commissions." This resulted in a temporary halt in the prosecution of five detainees charged with involvement in the September 11, 2001, attacks along with the suspension of the prosecution of roughly seventeen other detainees. President Obama announced his intention to further reform the military commission system to provide additional due process protections and where possible prosecute terrorists before civilian federal courts. The Obama administration as previously mentioned also announced that it would no longer use the term *unlawful enemy combatant* in order to highlight that terrorists captured and detained on the battlefield were protected under the Geneva Conventions.

The Supreme Court and Combat Status Review Tribunals

In 2008, in *Boumediene v. Bush,* Guantanamo detainees challenged the constitutionality of the MCA's suspension of the writ of habeas corpus for detainees at Guantanamo. The MCA provided for a limited right to appeal decisions of a CSRT to the U.S. Court of Appeals for the District of Columbia. The Court of Appeals was authorized only to consider whether the CSRT followed the required procedures and whether the procedures were consistent with the U.S. Constitution. There was no right to request the District of Columbia Court of Appeals to review the factual findings of the CSRTs.

The U.S. Supreme Court in *Boumediene* held that the detainees at Guantanamo had the right to habeas corpus review. Congress, although it lawfully had suspended the writ, was required to provide an adequate substitute procedure. The Court found that the MCA, however, had not provided an adequate substitute and that the MCA therefore constituted an unconstitutional suspension of the writ.

The need for an adequate substitute to review the determination that an individual was an unlawful enemy combatant, according to the Court, was particularly important, because the CSRT was an imperfect process that presented the risk of error. The Supreme Court noted that the CSRTs did not provide for the right to counsel, permitted evidence to be withheld from a detainee, and limited a detainee's ability to confront the witnesses against him or her in admitting hearsay evidence.

The specific shortcomings of the review procedure before the District of Columbia Court of Appeals included the failure to provide the petitioner with the ability to challenge findings of fact and to supplement the record with newly obtained or available evidence that established his or her innocence. The District of Columbia Court of Appeals also was not provided with explicit authority to release a detainee or to consider a constitutional challenge to the president's claim that he was authorized under the AUMF to detain individuals at Guantanamo indefinitely.

The decision in *Boumediene* opened the floodgates for the filing of over 200 habeas corpus petitions by Guantanamo detainees. Twenty-six individuals had been ordered by federal courts to be released from custody by July 2009, and the government has been successful in the continued detention of three individuals. The question for the court on habeas review is whether the "lawfulness of the detention is supported by a preponderance of the evidence." Mohammed el-Gharani was detained at age fourteen, and he was determined to be an enemy combatant based on inconsistent statements by two fellow detainees. The District of Columbia federal court questioned the reliability of the statements that alleged that el-Gharani, "a [then eleven-year-old] minor from a very poor family could have...become a member of a London based cell." Haji Bismullah, a former official of the Afghan government, was released when it was determined that he had been improperly detained as a result of questionable testimony by members of a rival clan in Afghanistan who had been refused a job by Bismullah. On the other hand, the District of Columbia Court of Appeals determined that Ghaleb al-Bihani was lawfully detained, because he had "directly supported" forces fighting against the United States in Afghanistan by training in an al-Qaeda military camp and serving as a cook for Taliban forces.

In February 2009, President Barack Obama announced that he planned to close the detention center at Guantanamo Bay as well as all "secret Central Intelligence Agency detention facilities located abroad" within a year. The thinking on closing Guantanamo was that although the facility was found to be "well run," the prison had come to be perceived by much of the international community as a site in which detainees were tortured and abused. The closing of Guantanamo has sparked opposition by members of Congress, who argue that the facilities where these detainees would be held in the United States will become targets for terrorist attacks. A review procedure was established to evaluate the status of the roughly 226 detainees who remained in the prison. The detainees either were to be prosecuted for war crimes before military or civilian courts or sent abroad to countries that were willing to accept them. The Obama administration also announced that, in those instances in which there was insufficient evidence to bring the individuals before a criminal tribunal, it would seek to detain individuals who "substantially supported" terrorism and who posed a threat to the United States. The Obama administration also asked the D.C. federal courts to suspend hearing habeas corpus petitions until it had completed its review of the status of individuals detained in Guantanamo.

Prosecutions at Guantanamo

Following almost seven years of legal conflict over the fate of detainees at Guantanamo, the first full-scale trial was conducted before a military tribunal. This resulted in the conviction of Osama bin Laden's former driver Salim Hamdan for material support for terrorism. The evidence indicated that Hamdan had served as a bodyguard for Osama bin Laden, driven him to various meetings, and transported firearms and munitions. The defense argued that Hamdan had been arrested far from the field of battle, had never engaged in armed conflict, and was an uneducated low-level employee with no direct involvement in terrorism. The commission convicted Hamdan of the material assistance of terrorism and acquitted him of conspiracy to engage in terrorism. The military officers who sat on the commission apparently were persuaded by defense evidence that Hamdan did not participate in the planning of terrorist attacks and was no more than a "paid employee" of Osama bin Laden. Hamdan was sentenced to the relatively light sentence of sixty-six months with credit for the five years that he had already served. David Hicks, an Australian Islamic convert, earlier had pled guilty to providing material aid for terrorism and had been transferred to Australia, where he was released after having spent nine months in prison.

Other alleged terrorists have been charged and convicted in civilian criminal courts. Both shoe bomber Richard Reid and Zacarias Moussaoui, the suspected twentieth 9/11 hijacker, pled guilty. Ramzi Yousef, the mastermind of a 1993 attack on the World Trade Center, and other individuals involved in the 1998 bombings of U.S. embassies in Africa were convicted in jury trials in federal courts. In May 2009, Ali al-Marri, who had been detained without trial on suspicion of being an al-Qaeda "sleeper agent," pled guilty in federal court to conspiracy to provide material support or resources to a foreign terrorist organization and was sentenced to fifteen years in prison.

The debate continues over whether terrorism should be treated as an act of war and prosecuted before a military commission or should be treated as a common crime and prosecuted before civilian criminal courts. The Bush administration tended to view the struggle against terrorism as war and favored prosecution before military courts. The Obama administration, while embracing many of the policies of the Bush administration, seems to view terrorism as an "international crime" that is best addressed where possible within the existing federal court system. The new president somewhat surprisingly announced that the high-value detainees at Guantanamo in some cases would be brought before military tribunals that provided detainees with additional due process protections. President Obama distanced his administration from the philosophy of the Bush administration when he announced that the terms *war on terror* and *long war* no longer would be used and would be replaced by the phrase "overseas contingency operation."

In the case of Jose Padilla, described below, the Fourth Circuit Court of Appeals was asked to decide whether a U.S. citizen affiliated with al-Qaeda who is detained on American territory may be treated as an unlawful enemy combatant and prosecuted before a military commission, or whether he should be considered a common criminal and criminally prosecuted before a civilian court. The Fourth Circuit Court of Appeals addressed this issue in 2005 in *Padilla v. Hanft*. What is your view?

May a United States citizen apprehended in the United States be detained as an enemy combatant?

Padilla v. Hanft, 423 F.3d 386 (4th Cir. 2005), Luttig, J.

Facts

Appellee Jose Padilla, a U.S. citizen, associated with forces hostile to the United States in Afghanistan and took up arms against U.S. forces in that country in our war against al-Qaeda. Upon his escape to Pakistan from the battlefield in Afghanistan, Padilla was recruited, trained, funded, and equipped by al-Qaeda leaders to continue prosecution of the war in the United States by blowing up apartment buildings in this country. Padilla flew to the United States on May 8, 2002, to begin carrying out his assignment, but he was arrested by civilian law enforcement authorities upon his arrival at O'Hare International Airport in Chicago.

Thereafter, in a letter to the secretary of defense, the president of the United States personally designated Padilla an enemy combatant against this country, stating that the United States is "at war" with al-Qaeda; that "Mr. Padilla engaged in conduct that constituted hostile and war-like acts, including conduct in preparation for acts of international terrorism that had the aim to cause injury to or adverse effects on the United States"; and that "Mr. Padilla represents a continuing, present and grave danger to the national security of the United States." Having determined that "detention of Mr. Padilla is necessary to prevent him from aiding al-Qaeda in its efforts to attack the United States or its armed forces, other governmental personnel, or citizens," the president directed the secretary of defense to take Padilla into military custody, in which custody Padilla has remained ever since. The full text of the president's memorandum to the Secretary of Defense reads as follows:

> In accordance with the Constitution and consistent with the laws of the United States, including the Authorization for Use of Military Force Joint Resolution (Public Law 107-40);
>
> I, GEORGE BUSH, as President of the United States and Commander in Chief of the U.S. armed forces, hereby DETERMINE for the United States of America that:
>
> (1) Jose Padilla, who is under the control of the Department of Justice and who is a U.S. citizen, is, and at the time he entered the United States in May 2002 was, an enemy combatant;
>
> (2) Mr. Padilla is closely associated with al Qaeda, an international terrorist organization with which the United States is at war;
>
> (3) Mr. Padilla engaged in conduct that constituted hostile and war-like acts, including conduct in preparation for acts of international terrorism that had the aim to cause injury to or adverse effects on the United States;
>
> (4) Mr. Padilla possesses intelligence, including intelligence about personnel and activities of al Qaeda, that, if communicated to the U.S., would aid U.S. efforts to prevent attacks by al Qaeda on the United States or its armed forces, other governmental personnel, or citizens;
>
> (5) Mr. Padilla represents a continuing, present and grave danger to the national security of the United States, and detention of Mr. Padilla is necessary to prevent him from aiding al Qaeda in its efforts to attack the United States or its armed forces, other governmental personnel, or citizens;
>
> (6) it is in the interest of the United States that the Secretary of Defense detain Mr. Padilla as an enemy combatant; and

(7) it is consistent with U.S. law and the laws of war for the Secretary of Defense to detain Mr. Padilla as enemy combatant.

Accordingly, you are directed to receive Mr. Padilla from the Department of Justice and to detain him as an enemy combatant.

DATE: June 9, 2002
Signature
/George Bush/

Al-Qaeda operatives recruited Jose Padilla, a U.S. citizen, to train for jihad in Afghanistan in February 2000, while Padilla was on a religious pilgrimage to Saudi Arabia. Subsequently, Padilla met with al-Qaeda operatives in Afghanistan, received explosives training in an al-Qaeda affiliated camp, and served as an armed guard at what he understood to be a Taliban outpost. When U.S. military operations began in Afghanistan, Padilla and other al-Qaeda operatives moved from safe house to safe house to evade bombing or capture. Padilla was, based on the facts with which we are presented, "armed and present in a combat zone during armed conflict between al Qaeda/Taliban forces and the armed forces of the United States."

Padilla eventually escaped to Pakistan, armed with an assault rifle. Once in Pakistan, Padilla met with Khalid Sheikh Mohammad, a senior al-Qaeda operations planner, who directed Padilla to travel to the United States for the purpose of blowing up apartment buildings, in continued prosecution of al-Qaeda's war of terror against the United States. After receiving further training, as well as cash, travel documents, and communication devices, Padilla flew to the United States in order to carry out his accepted assignment.

Upon arrival at Chicago's O'Hare International Airport on May 8, 2002, Padilla was detained by FBI agents, who interviewed and eventually arrested him pursuant to a material witness warrant issued by the District Court for the Southern District of New York in conjunction with a grand jury investigation of the September 11 attacks. Padilla was transported to New York, where he was held at a civilian correctional facility until, on June 9, 2002, the president designated him an enemy combatant against the United States and directed the secretary of defense to take him into military custody. Since his delivery into the custody of military authorities, Padilla has been detained at a naval brig in South Carolina.

On June 11, 2002, Padilla filed a petition for a writ of habeas corpus in the Southern District of New York, claiming that his detention violated the Constitution. The Supreme Court of the United States ultimately ordered Padilla's petition dismissed without prejudice, holding that his petition was improperly filed in the Southern District of New York (*Rumsfeld v. Padilla,* 542 U.S. 426 [2004]). On July 2, 2004, Padilla filed the present petition for a writ of habeas corpus in the District of South Carolina.

The district court subsequently held that the president lacks the authority to detain Padilla, that Padilla's detention is in violation of the Constitution and laws of the United States, and that Padilla therefore must either be criminally charged or released. This appeal followed.

Issue

The exceedingly important question before us is whether the president of the United States possesses the authority to detain militarily a citizen of this country who is closely associated with al-Qaeda, an entity with which the United States is at war; who took up arms on behalf of that enemy and against our country in a foreign combat zone of that war; and who thereafter traveled to the United States for the avowed purpose of further prosecuting that war on American soil, against American citizens and targets.

Reasoning

The Authorization for Use of Military Force (AUMF) joint resolution, upon which the president explicitly relied in his order that Padilla be detained by the military and upon which the Government chiefly relies in support of the president's authority to detain Padilla, was enacted by Congress in the immediate aftermath of the September 11, 2001, terrorist attacks on the United States. It provides as follows:

> The President is authorized to use all necessary and appropriate force against those nations, organizations, or persons he determines planned, authorized, committed, or aided the terrorist attacks that occurred on September 11, 2001, or harbored such organizations or persons, in order to prevent any future acts of international terrorism against the United States by such nations, organizations or persons.

The Supreme Court has already once interpreted this joint resolution in the context of a military detention by the president. In *Hamdi v. Rumsfeld* (542 U.S. 507 [2004]), the Supreme Court held, on the facts alleged by the Government, that the AUMF authorized the military detention of Yaser Esam Hamdi, an American citizen who fought alongside Taliban forces in Afghanistan, was captured by U.S. allies on a battlefield there, and was detained in the United States by the military. The "narrow question" addressed by the Court in *Hamdi* was "whether the Executive has the authority to detain citizens who qualify as 'enemy combatants,'" defined for purposes of that case as "individuals who... [were] part of or supporting forces hostile to the United States or coalition partners in Afghanistan and who engaged in an armed conflict against the United States there." The controlling plurality of the Court answered that narrow question in the affirmative, concluding, based upon "longstanding law-of-war principles," that Hamdi's detention was "necessary and appropriate" within the meaning of the AUMF, because "the capture and detention of lawful combatants and the capture, detention, and trial of unlawful combatants, by universal agreement and practice, are important incidents of war." The rationale for this law-of-war principle, Justice O'Connor explained for the plurality, is that "detention to prevent a combatant's return to the battlefield is a fundamental incident of waging war."

As the AUMF authorized Hamdi's detention by the president, so also does it authorize Padilla's detention. Under the facts as presented here, Padilla unquestionably qualifies as an enemy combatant as that term was defined for purposes of the controlling opinion in *Hamdi.* Indeed, under the definition of *enemy combatant* employed in *Hamdi,* we can discern no difference in principle between Hamdi and Padilla. Like Hamdi, Padilla associated with forces hostile to the United States in Afghanistan. And, like Hamdi, Padilla took up arms against U.S. forces in that country in the same way and to the same extent as did Hamdi. Because, like Hamdi, Padilla is an enemy combatant, and because his detention is no less necessary than was Hamdi's in order to prevent his return to the battlefield, the president is authorized by the AUMF to detain Padilla as a fundamental incident to the conduct of war.

Our conclusion that the AUMF as interpreted by the Supreme Court in *Hamdi* authorizes the president's detention of Padilla as an enemy combatant is reinforced by the Supreme Court's decision in *Ex parte Quirin* (317 U.S. 1 [1942]), on which the plurality in *Hamdi* itself heavily relied. In *Quirin,* the Court held that Congress had authorized the military trial of Haupt, a U.S. citizen who entered the country with orders from the Nazis to blow up domestic war facilities but was captured before he could execute those orders. The Court reasoned that Haupt's citizenship was no bar to his military trial as an unlawful enemy belligerent, concluding that

> citizens who associate themselves with the military arm of the enemy government, and with its aid, guidance and direction enter this country bent on hostile acts, are enemy belligerents within the meaning of . . . the law of war.

Like Haupt, Padilla associated with the military arm of the enemy, and with its aid, guidance, and direction entered this country bent on committing hostile acts on American soil. Padilla thus falls within *Quirin*'s definition of enemy belligerent as well as within the definition of the equivalent term accepted by the plurality in *Hamdi.* We understand the plurality's reasoning in *Hamdi* to be that the AUMF authorizes the president to detain all those who qualify as enemy combatants within the meaning of the laws of war, such power being universally accepted under the laws of war as necessary in order to prevent the return of combatants to the battlefield during conflict. Given that Padilla qualifies as an enemy combatant under both the definition adopted by the Court in *Quirin* and the definition accepted by the controlling opinion in *Hamdi,* his military detention as an enemy combatant by the president is unquestionably authorized by the AUMF as a fundamental incident to the president's prosecution of the war against al-Qaeda in Afghanistan.

Padilla marshals essentially four arguments for the conclusion that his detention is unlawful. None of them ultimately is persuasive.

Recognizing the hurdle to his position represented by the Supreme Court's decision in *Hamdi,* Padilla principally argues that his case does not fall within the "narrow circumstances" considered by the Court in that case, because, although he too stood alongside Taliban forces in Afghanistan, he was seized on American soil, whereas Hamdi was captured on a foreign battlefield. In other words, Padilla maintains that capture on a foreign battlefield was one of the "narrow circumstances" to which the plurality in *Hamdi* confined its opinion. We disagree. When the plurality articulated the "narrow question" before it, it referred simply to the permissibility of detaining "an individual who . . . was part of or supporting forces hostile to the United States or coalition partners" in Afghanistan and who "engaged in an armed conflict against the United States there." Nowhere in its framing of the "narrow question" presented did the plurality even mention the locus of capture.

The actual reasoning that the plurality thereafter employed is consistent with the question having been framed so as to render locus of capture irrelevant. That reasoning was that Hamdi's detention was an exercise of "necessary and appropriate force" within the meaning of the AUMF, because "detention to prevent a combatant's return to the battlefield is a fundamental incident of waging war." This reasoning simply does not admit of a distinction between an enemy combatant captured abroad and detained in the United States, such as Hamdi, and an enemy combatant who escaped capture abroad but was ultimately captured domestically and detained in the United States, such as Padilla. As we previously explained, Padilla poses the same threat of returning to the battlefield as Hamdi posed at the time of the Supreme Court's adjudication of Hamdi's petition. Padilla's detention is thus "necessary and appropriate" to the same extent as was Hamdi's.

Padilla directs us to a passage from the plurality's opinion in *Hamdi* in which, when responding to the dissent, the plurality charged that the dissent "ignored the context of the case: a United States citizen captured in a foreign combat zone." Padilla argues that this passage proves that capture on a foreign battlefield was one of the factual circumstances by which the Court's opinion was limited. If this language stood alone, Padilla's argument as to the limitation of *Hamdi* at least would have more force, though to acknowledge that foreign battlefield capture was part of the context of the case still is not to say (at least not necessarily) that the locus of capture was essential to the Court's reasoning. However, this language simply cannot bear the weight that Padilla would have it bear when it is considered against the backdrop of both the quite different limitations that were expressly imposed by the Court through its framing of the question presented, and the actual reasoning that was employed by the Court in reaching its conclusion, which reasoning was consistent with the question having been framed so as to render an enemy combatant's point of capture irrelevant to the president's power to detain. In short, the plurality carefully limited its opinion, but not in a way that leaves room for argument that the president's power to detain one who has associated with the enemy and taken up arms against the United States in a foreign combat zone varies depending upon the geographic location where that enemy combatant happens to have been captured.

Padilla also argues, and the district court held, that Padilla's military detention is "neither necessary nor appropriate," because he is amenable to criminal prosecution. Related to this argument, Padilla attempts to distinguish *Quirin* from his case on the grounds that he has simply been detained, unlike Haupt who was charged and tried in *Quirin*. Neither the argument nor the attempted distinction is convincing.

As to the fact that Padilla can be prosecuted, the availability of criminal process does not distinguish him from Hamdi. If the mere availability of criminal prosecution rendered detention unnecessary within the meaning of the AUMF, then Hamdi's detention would have been unnecessary and therefore unauthorized, since he too was detained in the United States and amenable to criminal prosecution. We are convinced, in any event, that the availability of criminal process cannot be determinative of the power to detain, if for no other reason than that criminal prosecution may well not achieve the very purpose for which detention is authorized in the first place—the prevention of return to the field of battle. Equally important, in many instances criminal prosecution would impede the Executive in its efforts to gather intelligence from the detainee and to restrict the detainee's communication with confederates so as to ensure that the detainee does not pose a continuing threat to national security even as he is confined—impediments that would render military detention not only an appropriate, but also the necessary, course of action to be taken in the interest of national security.

The district court acknowledged the need to defer to the president's determination that Padilla's detention is necessary and appropriate in the interest of national security. However, we believe that the district court ultimately accorded insufficient deference to that determination, effectively imposing upon the president the equivalent of a least-restrictive-means test. To subject to such exacting scrutiny the president's determination that criminal prosecution would not adequately protect the nation's security at a very minimum fails to accord the president the deference that is his when he acts pursuant to a broad delegation of authority from Congress, such as the AUMF.

As for Padilla's attempted distinction of *Quirin* on the grounds that, unlike Haupt, he has never been charged and tried by the military, the plurality in *Hamdi* rejected as immaterial the distinction between detention and trial (apparently regarding the former as a lesser imposition than the latter), noting that "nothing in *Quirin* suggests that [Haupt's U.S.] citizenship would have precluded his mere detention for the duration of the relevant hostilities."

Padilla . . . next argues that only a clear statement from Congress can authorize his detention, and that the AUMF is not itself, and does not contain, such a clear statement.

Padilla contends that *Quirin* . . . supports the existence of a clear statement rule. However, in no place in *Quirin* did the Court even purport to establish a clear statement rule. In its opinion, the Court did note that Congress had "explicitly" authorized Haupt's military trial. But to conclude from this passing note that the Court required a clear statement as a matter of law would be unwarranted. In fact, to the extent that *Quirin* can be understood to have addressed the need for a clear statement of authority from Congress at all, the rule would appear the opposite:

> The detention and trial of petitioners—ordered by the President in the declared exercise of his powers as Commander in Chief of the Army in time of war and of grave public danger—are not to be set aside by the courts without the clear conviction that they are in conflict with the Constitution or laws of Congress constitutionally enacted.

Of course, even were a clear statement by Congress required, the AUMF constitutes such a clear statement according to the Supreme Court. In Hamdi, stating that "it [was] of no moment that the AUMF does not use specific language of detention," the plurality held that the AUMF "clearly and unmistakably authorized" Hamdi's detention. Nothing in the AUMF permits us to conclude that the joint resolution clearly and unmistakably authorized Hamdi's detention but not Padilla's. To the contrary, read in light of its purpose clause ("in order to prevent any future acts of international terrorism against the United States") and its preamble (stating that the acts of 9/11 "render it both necessary and appropriate . . . to protect United States citizens both at home and abroad"), the AUMF applies even more clearly and unmistakably to Padilla than to Hamdi. Padilla, after all, in addition to supporting hostile forces in Afghanistan and taking up arms against our troops on a battlefield in that country as Hamdi did, also came to the United States in order to commit future acts of terrorism against American citizens and targets.

These facts unquestionably establish that Padilla poses the requisite threat of return to battle in the ongoing armed conflict between the United States and al-Qaeda in Afghanistan, and that his detention is authorized as a "fundamental incident of waging war" in order "to prevent a combatant's return to the battlefield." Congress "clearly and unmistakably" authorized such detention when, in the AUMF, it "permitted the use of 'necessary and appropriate force'" to prevent other attacks like those of September 11, 2001.

Finally, Padilla argues that even if his detention is authorized by the AUMF, it is unlawful under *Ex parte Milligan* (71 U.S. 2 [1866]). In *Milligan,* the Supreme Court held that a U.S. citizen associated with an anti-Union secret society but unaffiliated with the Confederate Army could not be tried by a military tribunal while access to civilian courts was open and unobstructed. *Milligan* purported to restrict the power of Congress as well as the power of the president. ("No usage of war could sanction a military trial...for any offence whatever of a citizen in civil life, in nowise connected with the military service. Congress could grant no such power...."). The *Milligan* Court's reasoning had "particular reference to the facts before it," namely, that Milligan was not "a part of or associated with the armed forces of the enemy." *Milligan* is inapposite here, because Padilla, unlike Milligan, associated with and has taken up arms against the forces of the United States on behalf of an enemy of the United States.

Holding

The Congress of the United States, in the Authorization for Use of Military Force joint resolution, provided the president all powers necessary and appropriate to protect American citizens from terrorist acts by those who attacked the United States on September 11, 2001. As would be expected, and as the Supreme Court has held, those powers include the power to detain identified and committed enemies such as Padilla, who associated with al-Qaeda and the Taliban regime, who took up arms against this nation in its war against these enemies, and who entered the United States for the avowed purpose of further prosecuting that war by attacking American citizens and targets on our own soil—a power without which, Congress understood, the president could well be unable to protect American citizens from the very kind of savage attack that occurred four years ago almost to the day. The detention of petitioner being fully authorized by act of Congress, the judgment of the district court that the detention of petitioner by the president of the United States is without support in law is hereby reversed.

Questions for Discussion

1. The issue in *Padilla* is whether a U.S. citizen arrested on U.S. territory may be detained as an enemy combatant. What is the holding of the Fourth Circuit Court of Appeals?
2. Explain why the court of appeals held that Padilla is not required to be prosecuted before a civilian criminal tribunal.
3. Why was Padilla not provided with a review before a CSRT?
4. Do you agree with the decision of the Fourth Circuit Court of Appeals?
5. What is your reaction to the following facts in regard to Padilla? Before the U.S. Supreme Court could rule on Padilla's petition for habeas corpus, President Bush ordered that Padilla be released from military custody and face criminal charges (*Padilla v. Hanft,* 547 U.S. 1062 [2006]). Padilla subsequently was convicted of conspiracy to murder, kidnap, and maim overseas. Prior to trial, Padilla's attorney filed a Motion to Dismiss for Outrageous Government Conduct, alleging that Padilla had been subjected to sensory and sleep deprivation, stress positions, and other indignities over the course of three years and seven months in detention.
6. In 2008, the Fourth Circuit Court of Appeals in *Ali Al-Marri* followed *Padilla* and held that a U.S. resident who is not a citizen who is apprehended on American territory and who has never taken up arms against the United States may be detained as an enemy combatant and is not entitled to be prosecuted before a civilian criminal court (*Ali Al-Marri v. Pucciarelli,* 534 F.3d 213 [4th Cir. 2008]). The U.S. Supreme Court granted certiorari. The Obama administration successfully petitioned the court to dismiss the case after releasing al-Marri from custody and transferring him into the criminal justice system for prosecution for providing material assistance to a terrorist group. Al-Marri pled guilty to conspiring to provide material support or resources to a foreign terrorist organization and was sentenced to fifteen years in federal prison. The question remains whether individuals who have provided substantial assistance to terrorist groups may be detained indefinitely without trial.
7. A Pentagon report made public in May 2009 found that of the 534 individuals released from Guantanamo under the Bush administration, roughly one in seven had become involved in terrorist activity. Does this suggest that the best course is to detain individuals suspected of involvement in terrorism rather than risk releasing individuals who later may engage in terrorist activities?

Chapter Summary

The Foreign Intelligence Surveillance Act provides procedures for national security electronic surveillance. In 1994, FISA was extended to cover physical searches of dwellings and other structures. FISA regulates surveillance within the United States of international threats to national security and international terrorist activities. FISA also addresses the surveillance of Americans and American residents abroad.

FISA establishes the Foreign Intelligence Surveillance Court, which is composed of eleven federal district court judges selected by the chief justice of the United States and by three other federal judges. FISA warrants are necessary for both electronic surveillance (e.g., wiretapping) and physical searches that are directed against foreign threats to national security or international terrorism. The proceedings and orders of FISC are secret, and the target of the warrant is not represented at the hearing. Government lawyers are required to satisfy four conditions to obtain a FISA warrant.

Target. The government must demonstrate probable cause that the "target" is the agent of a foreign power or a member of an international terrorist organization. The so-called lone wolf terrorism provision was added by the PATRIOT Act and authorizes the surveillance of non–U.S. residents who are not agents of a foreign power or affiliated with an international terrorist organization but who are engaged in international terrorism or in activities in preparation for international terrorism.

Probable cause. The government is required to meet a lower probable cause standard than in ordinary criminal investigations. FISA orders are based on the "probability of a possibility" that the target of the order "may engage" in activities threatening the national security or "may engage" in international terrorism.

Purpose. The primary purpose must be to investigate a threat to national security or a threat of terrorism.

Place. The place targeted for surveillance must be being used or about to be used by a foreign power or terrorist organization to carry out activities that threaten the national security.

A significant purpose of the surveillance must be to protect national security or to combat terrorism. This provision is intended to eliminate "the wall" between intelligence investigations and criminal investigations. Keep in mind that FISA regulates surveillance within the United States of international threats to national security and international terrorist activities. FISA also addresses the surveillance of Americans and American residents abroad. It does not regulate the surveillance of non–U.S. citizens and of non–U.S. residents outside of the United States.

The PATRIOT ACT provides for additional electronic surveillance techniques.

Pen registers and trap-and-trace devices. Pen registers are employed to record telephone numbers dialed from a phone, and trap-and-trace devices record the numbers of incoming calls. Section 214 of the PATRIOT Act states that an application to install one of these devices requires an investigator to certify to a court that the information likely to be obtained is relevant for any investigation "to obtain foreign intelligence information... or to protect against international terrorism or clandestine intelligence activities." The target of the surveillance is not required to be a suspect in the investigation of national security or terrorism.

Voice mail and e-mail. Section 204 of the PATRIOT Act provides that access to both voice mail and the contents of e-mail requires a search warrant issued by a judge based on probable cause.

Roving wiretaps. Section 206 of the PATRIOT Act authorizes courts to issue warrants for roving wiretaps or for what is termed "multi-point surveillance." This provision permits the electronic surveillance of all telephones or computers or other devices utilized by an individual without requiring that law enforcement obtain a separate warrant to monitor every phone or computer account or other electronic device that is utilized by the individual who is the target of the investigation.

Emergency electronic surveillance. Electronic service providers, when contacted by law enforcement, may voluntarily disclose stored electronic communications in an emergency situation involving the risk of danger or death or the immediate risk of serious physical harm.

Section 213 of the PATRIOT Act also provides for sneak-and-peek warrants. These searches are not limited to terrorism investigations and apply to all types of criminal investigations. The government may conduct "covert searches" in regard to federal crimes when there is reasonable cause to believe that providing notice may result in an "adverse result." Section 219 of the PATRIOT Act authorizes federal courts to issue nationwide search warrants for cases involving international or domestic terrorism.

The government also has authority to seize various documents and records relevant to investigations involving national security or terrorism.

National security letters. An FBI official, pursuant to section 505 of the PATRIOT Act, may request access to information that is relevant to an investigation of national security or terrorism. The individual whose records are sought is not required to be the target of an investigation.

Business records. Section 215 of the PATRIOT Act authorizes the director of the FBI or another FBI official to apply to the FISA court to issue orders granting the government access to any "relevant" "tangible" item (including books, records, or other documents). Records that may be requested include tax returns; education or medical records; and records from a library, bookstore, or firearm sale.

The PATRIOT Act also provides for the detention of noncitizens in section 412. A noncitizen may be detained for seven days without being charged with a criminal or immigration violation. The detention may be extended for six months where an individual is not immediately deported or charged with a criminal offense. The federal government enacted a material witness law in 1984 to enable the government to arrest a witness whose testimony is material to a grand jury investigation or criminal prosecution and who may be unavailable to testify or may flee in order to avoid testifying.

In October 2001, the U.S. attorney general issued an order permitting the Federal Bureau of Prisons to monitor, without a warrant, attorney–client communications where the attorney general certifies "reasonable suspicion exists to believe that a pre-trial detainee or an inmate may use communications with attorneys... to further or facilitate acts of terrorism."

As a result of President Bush's decision to deny protection under the Geneva Conventions to individuals affiliated with al-Qaeda, the Department of Justice and Department of Defense agreed that various enhanced interrogation techniques might be used to obtain information from detainees that is vital to the protection of the national security of the United States. The Bush administration denied that the enhanced interrogation techniques employed against enemy combatants constituted torture or cruel treatment. The U.S. Congress put a halt to enhanced interrogation techniques by the military in the Detainee Treatment Act of 2005 (DTA). Section 1001 of this act provides that no person in the custody or under the effective control of the Department of Defense or under detention in a Department of Defense facility shall be subjected to any treatment or technique of interrogation not authorized in the *U.S. Army Field Manual on Intelligence Interrogation.* Section 1003 prohibits "cruel, inhuman, or degrading treatment or punishment against any individual." This section does not extend to interrogations conducted by the Central Intelligence Agency.

In January 2009, President Barack Obama announced that the detainees no longer were to be referred to as enemy combatants and were to be treated in accordance with the Geneva Conventions. President Obama also ordered that both the military and the CIA follow the *Army Field Manual* and not engage in enhanced interrogation techniques, including waterboarding.

On November 13, 2001, President George Bush, as commander in chief of the U.S. armed forces, issued a military order regulating the detention and trial of noncitizens who are members of al-Qaeda and who have engaged in international terrorism or assisted acts of terrorism. President Bush's order provided that these unlawful enemy combatants were to be prosecuted before military commissions. In 2004, in *Rasul v. Bush,* the U.S. Supreme Court held that federal courts had jurisdiction to consider applications for habeas corpus from two Australian citizens and twelve Kuwaiti citizens detained at Guantanamo who had been captured in Afghanistan during hostilities between the United States and the Taliban and al-Qaeda. In the companion case of *Hamdi v. Rumsfeld,* the Supreme Court held that Esam Fouad Hamdi, an American citizen who had been detained in Afghanistan while allegedly fighting for the Taliban, was entitled to a hearing to determine whether he was an enemy combatant. The U.S. Congress responded to the decision in *Hamdi* by passing the Detainee Treatment Act, which among other provisions established combat status review tribunals (CSRTs) to evaluate whether detainees were enemy combatants. The decisions were subject to review by administrative review boards.

In 2006, in *Hamdan v. Rumsfeld,* the U.S. Supreme Court held that military commissions had failed to provide detainees with protections required under the Geneva Conventions. President Bush responded to the Supreme Court decision in *Hamdan* by consulting with Congress, which passed the Military Commissions Act of 2006. In 2008, in *Boumediene v. Bush,* the Supreme Court held that Congress had failed to provide detainees at Guantanamo an adequate substitute procedure when it suspended the writ of habeas corpus in the Military Commissions Act and that detainees had the legal right to file claims for habeas corpus challenging the legality of their detentions.

President Barack Obama has continued many of the Bush administration's counterterrorism policies. President Obama, however, has prohibited enhanced interrogation procedures, proclaimed that detainees are protected under the Geneva Conventions, and announced that the military prison at Guantanamo Bay would be closed and the detainees sent abroad or incarcerated in the United States. The Obama administration has symbolically distanced itself from the Bush administration's view that the struggle against terrorism is a war by announcing that the terms *enemy combatant, war on terror,* and *the long war* would no longer be used. A number of high value detainees were to be prosecuted in civilian courts. The question that continues to be debated is the appropriate balance between the need to investigate, detain, and punish terrorists against the U.S. historic commitment to the rule of law.

Chapter Review Questions

1. Discuss the purpose and operation of the Foreign Intelligence Surveillance Act. What is the legal standard for use of pen registers and trap-and-trace devices? Discuss the legal standard for e-mail and voice mail. How did "the wall" interfere with the ability of the government to combat terrorism?
2. What is a sneak-and-peek search? Why are these searches helpful in counterterrorism investigations?
3. Discuss national security letters and the process for obtaining "tangible items" under the PATRIOT Act.
4. Why did Congress provide for material witness warrants?
5. Do you agree that the government should monitor lawyer–client communications in terrorism cases without a warrant?
6. Discuss the debate over the enhanced interrogation of detainees.
7. Outline the basic features of combat status review tribunals and military commissions.
8. What protections are provided to individuals in prosecutions before military commissions? Should terrorist suspects be prosecuted before criminal courts or before military tribunals?
9. Summarize the holding in the major Supreme Court cases addressing the treatment of detainees at Guantanamo. Should the Supreme Court interfere with the president's authority as commander in chief to direct the war on terror?

Legal Terminology

administrative review board

Authorization for Use of Military Force (AUMF)

combat status review tribunal (CSRT)

Detainee Treatment Act of 2005

enemy combatant

Foreign Intelligence Surveillance Act (FISA)

Foreign Intelligence Surveillance Court (FISC)

material witness warrant

military commissions

Military Commissions Act of 2006 (MCA)

national security letter (NSL)

PATRIOT Act

pen register

roving wiretap

sneak-and-peek search

trap-and-trace device

wall, the

Criminal Procedure on the Web

Log on to the Web-based student study site at **http://www.sagepub.com/lippmancp** to assist you in completing the Criminal Procedure on the Web exercises, as well as for additional features such as leading cases, podcasts, self-quizzes, and audio/video links.

1. Read a speech by John Walker Lindh's father defending his son.
2. Learn about the trial of Zacarias Moussaoui.
3. Watch a video of the interrogation of Omar Khadar, a juvenile detainee at Guantanamo.
4. Review news coverage on the prosecution of Salim Hamdan.

Bibliography

Stephen Dycus, Arthur L. Berney, William C. Banks, and Peter Raven-Hansen, *National Security Law,* 4th ed. (New York: Wolters Kluwer, 2007). A comprehensive casebook on the technical aspects of international and domestic law on counterterrorism.

Louis Fisher, *Military Tribunals & Presidential Power* (Lawrence: University of Kansas Press, 2005). A history of the use of military tribunals in the United States.

Jack Goldsmith, *The Terror Presidency* (New York: Norton, 2007). An account of the debate over counterterrorism policy in the Bush administration by a former official in the Department of Justice.

Eric Lichtblau, *Bush's Law: The Remaking of American Justice* (New York: Pantheon, 2008). A journalist's account of the controversy surrounding President Bush's terrorist surveillance program.

Jane Mayer, *The Dark Side* (Doubleday: New York, 2008). An account of the debate over interrogation policy within the Bush administration.

Benjamin Wittes, *Law and the Long War: Justice in the Age of Terrorism* (New York: Penguin, 2008). A balanced discussion of the legal issues involved in U.S. counterterrorism policies.

Glossary

abandoned property property intentionally discarded by the owner.

absolute immunity judges, prosecutors, witnesses, and jurors may not be sued for acts undertaken as part of the judicial function.

abuse of writ doctrine prohibition on filing successive writs of habeas corpus raising the same issue.

actual innocence a claim on a petition for a writ of habeas corpus that the defendant did not commit a crime.

administrative inspections government agencies conduct searches to determine whether businesses, factories, apartments, and homes are conforming to a broad range of regulations.

administrative review board military officers who review decisions of combat status review tribunals.

admission an individual admits a fact that tends to establish guilt, such as his or her presence at the shooting scene. An admission, when combined with other facts, may lead to a criminal conviction.

affiant individual who swears to a warrant.

affidavit sworn statement setting forth facts constituting probable cause that an individual has committed a criminal offense.

***Aguilar–Spinelli* test** affidavit must detail informant's credibility and basis of knowledge.

airport screening passengers and their bags are subjected to an examination before boarding aircraft.

anonymous tip information from an unidentified informant.

appellant party appealing.

appellate courts courts of appeals.

appellee party against whom an appeal is filed.

arraignment the defendant is informed of the charges against him or her and is required to enter a plea.

arrest police custody of an individual based on probable cause that he or she committed a crime.

arrest warrant judicial finding that there is probable cause to arrest an individual.

articulable suspicion a police officer in justifying an intrusion must present *specific and articulable facts* that together with rational inferences drawn from those facts reasonably suggest that an individual has committed a crime or is about to commit a crime.

attenuated term used to describe a weak link between an unreasonable search and the resulting seizure of evidence; the exclusionary rule does not apply where evidence is attenuated.

Authorization for Use of Military Force (AUMF) congressional authorization for the use of force.

automatic reversal rule requirement that violation of a fundamental constitutional right during trial results in the reversal of a conviction on appeal.

automobile exception exception to requirement that police obtain a warrant before conducting a search; a warrant is not required for an automobile.

bail release prior to trial typically based on the payment of ten percent of a fixed bail amount.

Bail Clause clause in the Eighth Amendment that prohibits the requirement of excessive bail.

bench trial a trial in which a judge sits without a jury.

Bertillon method Alphonse Bertillon, a French police officer, pioneered the identification of criminals through precise physical measurements.

beyond a reasonable doubt each element of a criminal offense must be established beyond a reasonable doubt.

Bill of Rights first ten amendments to the U.S. Constitution.

binding authority a decision that establishes a precedent.

***Bivens* legal suit** federal law enforcement officers and other federal employees may be sued for violating an individual's constitutional rights or a right under federal law.

***Blockburger* test** double jeopardy prohibits prosecuting individuals for criminal offenses that have the same elements.

border exception seizures and/or searches at the U.S. border may be undertaken without articulable suspicion.

***Brady* rule** the prosecution is required to turn over exculpatory information to the accused.

brief a written legal argument submitted to an appellate court; also, to write a summary of a case.

bright-line rule a clear and unambiguous rule set by judicial precedent.

burden of proof prosecution must prove every element of a criminal charge beyond a reasonable doubt.

capital punishment a death sentence.

case-by-case determination the facts of each situation are evaluated to determine whether a police officer's conduct meets the applicable legal standard. An example is the standard for a reasonable suspicion stop in accordance with *Terry v. Ohio.*

case-in-chief the presentation of the prosecution's evidence at trial.

cause and prejudice exception that allows a defendant who defaulted on his or her appeal to file a writ of habeas corpus if he or she is able to demonstrate that the state caused the default by withholding information or by some other misconduct or that the default resulted from ineffective assistance of counsel.

certiorari a decision to hear an appeal.

challenge for cause a juror may be excluded from the jury based on an actual or presumed inability to impartially evaluate the evidence.

citation notice to an individual to appear for trial at a later date.

civilian review civilian review boards in most large cities investigate and recommend punishments for police found to have engaged in misconduct.

clemency a reduction in a criminal punishment.

closely regulated business a warrantless probable cause search is permitted for a heavily regulated business.

closing argument summary of the evidence by the prosecutor and defense.

collateral attack a constitutional challenge by an individual who has been convicted and incarcerated and has exhausted his or her state appeals.

collateral estoppel a fact established in a trial is assumed to be established in other prosecutions.

collateral proceedings permits the use of unlawfully seized evidence in proceedings that are not part of a formal trial.

collateral remedies remedies that are available following the exhaustion of direct appeals.

color of state law an act under the authority of state or federal law.

combat status review tribunal (CSRT) a group of three neutral commissioned officers of the U.S. armed forces who are appointed by the secretary of defense of the United States to determine whether a detainee is an unlawful combatant.

Combined DNA Index System CODIS is an electronic database that integrates DNA profiles contained in the criminal offender databases of the fifty states and the federal government.

common law judge-made law brought from England to the United States.

complaint a prosecutor's filing of a sworn statement charging a defendant with a specific offense or offenses.

Compulsory Process Clause Sixth Amendment right to compel the appearance of witnesses.

concurrent jurisdiction joint authority of federal and state courts over certain areas of criminal justice.

concurrent sentences criminal sentences served at the same time.

concurring opinion an opinion by a judge supporting a majority or dissenting opinion, typically based on other grounds.

confession an individual admits the commission of a crime in response to police questioning.

confrontation physical presentation of a suspect to a witness or victim.

Confrontation Clause Sixth Amendment right of a defendant to confront his or her accusers.

consecutive sentences criminal sentences served one after another.

consent search a search based on an individual's waiver of his or her Fourth Amendment rights.

constitutional political system political system in which the powers of the various branches of government are defined by a constitution. In the United States, the rights and liberties of the people also are set forth in the Bill of Rights to the U.S. Constitution.

constitutionalization extension of the rights and freedoms in the Bill of Rights relevant to criminal procedure to the fifty states.

contemporaneous with respect to searches, a requirement that the search must be undertaken immediately before the arrest, at the same time as the arrest, or immediately after the arrest.

contextualism a broad approach to interpreting constitutional texts that focuses on interpreting the document in light of current developments.

corporeal identification identification of an individual who is physically present.

courts of general jurisdiction courts that hear more serious criminal and civil cases.

courts of limited jurisdiction courts with jurisdiction over a narrow range of cases.

courts of original jurisdiction courts with jurisdiction over a broad range of cases.

critical stages of a criminal proceeding procedures between arraignment and trial at which a failure to provide the defendant a lawyer may prevent the defendant from obtaining a fair trial.

critical stages of the prosecution those phases of the prosecution that may negatively impact the defendant's ability to present a defense at trial and at which the presence of an attorney would safeguard the defendant.

cross-examination questions regarding the direct testimony of a witness.

curtilage the area immediately surrounding the home, considered part of the home.

custodial interrogation questioning initiated by law enforcement officers after a person has been taken into custody or otherwise deprived of his or her freedom of action in any significant way.

***Daubert* test** test for the admissibility of scientific evidence based on the relevance and reliability of the evidence.

derivative evidence evidence that is discovered as a result of unlawful seizure.

Detainee Treatment Act of 2005 (DTA) congressional act that provides that no person in the custody or under the effective control of the Department of Defense shall be subjected to any treatment or technique of interrogation not authorized in the *U.S. Army Field Manual on Intelligence Interrogation.*

determinate sentence a fixed and certain criminal punishment.

discretion the exercise of judgment by a decision maker in the criminal justice system.

discretionary appeal an appeal that an appellate court may review or decline to review at its discretion.

dissenting opinion an opinion by a judge disagreeing with the majority of judges.

distractors individuals in a lineup who are not suspects.

DNA deoxyribonucleic acid is a molecule that stores an individual's genetic code and is found in the cells of the human body.

double-blind the police and the witness do not know who is the suspect at a lineup or photograph parade.

double jeopardy prosecuting a defendant in the same jurisdiction on two occasions for the same offense.

drug courier profile a profile developed based on experience that isolates characteristics of a drug trafficker.

dual sovereignty doctrine an individual may be prosecuted twice for the same offense by different jurisdictions.

Due Process Clause Fifth and Fourteenth Amendments to the U.S. Constitution guarantee individuals due process of law. The Fourteenth Amendment Due Process Clause incorporates most of the protections of the Bill of Rights.

due process test for entrapment an entrapment defense that relies on the Due Process Clause's prohibition against the government engaging in outrageous conduct that induces an individual to commit a crime.

dynamite charge the judge instructs jurors who are in the minority to reconsider the reasonableness of their views.

Eighth Amendment amendment to the U.S. Constitution that includes a prohibition on cruel and unusual punishment.

emergency-aid doctrine warrantless entry by the police into the home to provide assistance to an individual.

en banc the entire court.

encounters informal police stops of individuals.

enemy combatant an individual who, if captured in battle by U.S. military forces, does not qualify as a prisoner of war.

entrapment situation in which the government entraps or induces an individual to commit a crime.

exclusionary rule rule that evidence that is obtained as a result of a violation of the Fourth Amendment prohibition on unreasonable searches and seizures is inadmissible in a criminal prosecution to establish a defendant's guilt.

exigent circumstances emergency circumstances justifying warrantless entry into the home.

expectation of privacy protection from government intrusion; areas with a high expectation of privacy may generally not be searched without a warrant.

express questioning a direct question.

express waiver an affirmative relinquishment of a right.

eyewitness identification identification of a suspect by a victim or witness.

fair cross-section requirement the jury must be selected from a group of individuals that fairly represent the community.

false confession an innocent individual confesses to a crime that he or she did not commit.

Federal Rules of Criminal Procedure detailed rules for criminal procedure drafted by federal judges and approved by Congress.

Federal Tort Claim Act a federal statute that authorizes an individual to sue the federal government for various torts.

fillers individuals in a lineup who are not suspects.

final judgment rule rule that an appeal may be taken only following a verdict.

first appearance following an arrest, a suspect's initial appearance before a judge for the determination of probable cause, to be informed of his or her rights, for decisions to be made on pretrial release and bail, and for the appointment of an attorney (for indigents).

first impression an issue that has never before been decided by a court.

fleeing-felon rule common law doctrine that police may use deadly force to apprehend a suspected felon who is fleeing the police.

foils individuals in a lineup who are not suspects.

Foreign Intelligence Surveillance Act (FISA) congressional act that establishes procedures for national security electronic surveillance and searches.

Foreign Intelligence Surveillance Court (FISC) special court that issues warrants for electronic surveillance and physical searches to investigate issues involving national security and terrorism.

Fourteenth Amendment amendment to the U.S. Constitution passed in 1868 in order to provide equal rights and opportunity to newly free African American slaves.

Fourteenth Amendment due process voluntariness test confessions may not be obtained through psychological or physical coercion that overcomes the will of the individual to resist.

frisk a police officer may pat down a suspect's outer clothing.

fruit of the poisonous tree evidence derived from unlawfully seized evidence.

***Frye* test** requires that a scientific technique be sufficiently established to have gained general acceptance in the particular field in which it belongs.

functional equivalent of express questioning words or actions on the part of the police that the police should know are reasonably likely to lead a defendant to incriminate himself or herself.

fundamental fairness Fourteenth Amendment Due Process Clause prohibits states from criminal procedures that are fundamentally unfair. States are otherwise free to structure their criminal justice systems.

general deterrence criminal penalty intended to discourage individuals from committing a crime.

general warrants warrants allowing colonial authorities to search anytime and anywhere.

***Gerstein* hearing** hearing to determine whether police possessed probable cause for an arrest.

good faith exception an exception to the exclusion of illegally seized evidence in situations where an officer has acted in the good faith belief that his or her conduct complies with the Fourth Amendment.

grab area the area within a suspect's immediate control that may be searched incident to an arrest.

habeas corpus Latin for "you have the body"; a writ of habeas corpus is an order issued by a judge to a government official (usually the warden of a correctional institution) to bring an imprisoned individual to court and explain why the individual is in detention.

harmless error an error made in admission of evidence that does not contribute to the conviction obtained. An appellate court must be convinced beyond a reasonable doubt that the error is harmless.

head notes short statements of the important points included in a legal decision.

hearsay a witness's testimony about what someone else said that is introduced to prove the "truth" of a fact or facts.

holding the conclusions reached by a judge in a case.

hung jury a jury unable to reach a verdict.

impeachment cross-examination that is intended to call into question a witness's credibility.

implied waiver the waiver of a right as indicated by an individual's words and actions and the totality of the circumstances.

incapacitation punishment intended to isolate an offender from society.

incommunicado interrogation law enforcement questioning of individuals in the isolation of a police station.

in-court identification a witness identifies the perpetrator of a criminal act in court.

independent source doctrine principle that provides that evidence that is unlawfully seized nevertheless is admissible where the police are able to demonstrate that the same evidence was also obtained through independent and lawful means.

indictment an accusation of criminal activity returned by a grand jury.

indigent an individual who is unable to afford a lawyer and who is entitled to the appointment of a lawyer at public cost.

ineffective assistance of counsel term to describe a lawyer's performance that falls below the range of reasonably effective competence and affects the outcome of the trial.

inevitable discovery rule rule providing that evidence seized as the result of an unconstitutional search is admissible where the government can prove that it would inevitably have been discovered in a lawful fashion.

informant an individual who provides information about criminal activity to law enforcement.

informant privilege an informant may not be required to testify.

information a document signed by a prosecutor charging an individual with a crime.

initiation the test for waiving a prior invocation of counsel under *Miranda*.

injunction a judicial order directing a halt to a harmful act or policy.

interlocutory appeal an appeal taken prior to the final verdict.

intermediate appeal courts courts between municipal courts and the supreme court.

interrogation words or actions on the part of the police that are likely to lead a suspect to incriminate himself or herself.

inventory an administrative procedure recording the possessions of an arrestee and the content of impounded automobiles.

invited response a prosecutor's closing statement that responds to a statement by the defense attorney.

involuntary confessions confessions that result from coercion, drugs, or a mental disability rather than free will.

judicial activism the philosophy that courts should play a role in creating social policy.

judicial restraint the philosophy that elected officials rather than courts should make social policy.

judicial review the U.S. Supreme Court reviews the decisions of the legislative and executive branches of government to determine whether they are consistent with the U.S. Constitution. The Court is the "final arbiter" of the meaning of the Constitution.

jury instructions a judge's direction to the jury regarding the law.

jury nullification a jury's refusal to follow the law and acquittal of a defendant.

jury poll a questioning of individual jurors regarding whether they support the jury verdict.

key man potential jurors are selected by a small group of individuals.

knock and announce refers to a requirement that police knock and announce their presence when serving a search warrant.

legal reporter book containing the written opinions of judges.

magistrate a lawyer who serves an eight-year term in a U.S. district court to issue search warrants, conduct preliminary hearings, and rule on pretrial motions.

majority opinion the decision of a majority of the judges on a court.

manifest necessity a mistrial based on the conclusion that public justice will not be served by continuing with the trial.

material witness warrant warrant allowing the government to arrest a witness whose testimony is material to a case and who may flee in order to avoid testifying.

military commissions tribunals composed of military officers that are convened to prosecute noncitizen, unlawful combatants accused of terrorism.

Military Commissions Act of 2006 congressional act establishing military commissions that are provided with jurisdiction over any alien unlawful combatant who has engaged in hostilities or has intentionally and materially supported hostilities against the United States.

***Miranda* warnings** the police are required to inform individuals of the right to remain silent, that anything they say may be used against them, and of the right to an attorney, retained or appointed.

miscarriage an individual may be subjected to a second trial despite the fact that jeopardy has attached.

misdemeanant individual arrested for a misdemeanor.

misdemeanor a crime carrying a criminal penalty of less than a year in prison.

mistrial a fundamental error that causes cancellation of a trial.

modified indictment states four states require indictments for felonies punishable by capital punishment and life imprisonment.

modified probable cause administrative searches may be based on a broad probable cause standard rather than on probable cause to search a specific structure.

money bail pretrial release of a defendant based on payment of a fixed amount of money.

moot an issue that it is unnecessary for an appellate court to address.

motion for a judgment of acquittal motion based on contention that "no reasonable juror could conclude that guilt was proven beyond a reasonable doubt."

motor vehicle checkpoint fixed point at which motor vehicles are stopped without articulable suspicion.

national security letter (NSL) letter issued by the attorney general of the United States requesting information relevant to an investigation of terrorism or secret foreign intelligence activities.

new judicial federalism state supreme courts interpreting state court constitutions often provide defendants with more rights than have been required by the U.S. Supreme Court in interpreting a similar clause in the U.S. Constitution.

no bill the grand jury refuses to indict an individual.

noncorporeal identification identification of the perpetrator of a crime who is not present by viewing photographs.

nonroutine border searches intrusive border searches that require reasonable suspicion.

nontestimonial evidence evidence that is noncommunicative in character.

nonweighing states states in which the death penalty may be imposed once the jury finds an aggravating circumstance and that the death penalty is justified based on the totality of the circumstances.

obiter dicta observations from the bench.

objective test for entrapment test for entrapment that focuses on the conduct of the government rather than on the character of the individual.

open fields areas distant from the home that lack an expectation of privacy.

opening statement the prosecutor and defense attorney each indicate at the beginning of the trial the evidence that they plan to introduce during the trial.

original jurisdiction the first court to hear a case.

originalist a judge who follows the intent of the framers of the U.S. Constitution.

pardon a release from additional criminal punishment.

particularity requirement requirement that a warrant be specific in regard to the objects to be seized and the place to be searched.

pattern jury instructions standard jury instructions.

pattern-or-practice decree a judicial order requiring a police department to adopt various reforms.

pen register device that records the numbers of outgoing calls from an individual telephone.

per curiam opinion an opinion of an entire court without any single judge being identified as the author.

peremptory challenge removal of jurors without an obligation to state a reason.

persuasive authority a decision that does not constitute a binding authority but that a court may consult to assist in making a judgment.

petit jury the jury.

petitioner an individual filing a collateral attack on a verdict following the exhaustion of direct appeals.

photographic displays witness identification of the perpetrator of a crime through the use of photographs.

physical seizure an act in which a law enforcement officer takes hold of a suspect with the intent to prevent the individual from leaving.

plain error exception exception that permits an appellate court to review an error that was not raised in the trial court.

plain-feel doctrine a police officer who pats down a suspect's outer clothing and feels an object whose contour or mass makes its identity immediately apparent may lawfully seize the item under the plain-feel doctrine.

plain view an exception to the Fourth Amendment warrant requirement that allows a police officer to seize an item without a search warrant when (1) the officer is lawfully positioned, and (2) there is probable cause to seize the object.

plea bargain agreement to plead guilty in return for a reduction in charges or other considerations.

plurality opinion a judicial opinion that represents the views of the largest number of judges on a court, although short of a majority.

police methods test due process test intended to regulate police interrogation techniques.

polygraph an instrument used to determine whether a person is telling the truth.

precedent a judicial opinion that controls the decisions of a court presented with the same issue.

preliminary hearing determination whether a defendant should be bound over for trial.

presentence report report submitted to a judge by a probation officer containing factors that are relevant for establishing a defendant's criminal sentence.

presentment a report filed by a grand jury with the court on criminal activity.

presumption of regularity a court's assumption that criminal justice decision makers acted in good faith rather than out of a discriminatory intent.

pretext arrest an arrest that is motivated by the intent to investigate law violations for which no probable cause or even articulable suspicion exists.

pretrial motions motions filed before the beginning of a criminal trial.

preventive detention the holding of an individual without the option to post bail, used where defendants pose a flight risk or a risk to the community.

pro se Latin for "on his or her own"; individuals act *pro se* who represent themselves at trial.

probable cause facts and circumstances within officers' knowledge, and of which they have reasonably trustworthy information, that would warrant a person of reasonable caution to believe that an offense has been or is being committed.

probable cause hearing a hearing to determine whether there is probable cause to detain a suspect.

property rights approach an approach to Fourth Amendment protection that assumes such protection is limited to physical intrusions of the home, comparable to trespassory approach.

public safety exception police may ask questions reasonably prompted by a reasonable concern with public safety without first advising a suspect of his or her *Miranda* rights.

purging the grand jury selecting the grand jury.

purging the taint the effect of an attenuated connection between an illegal search and evidence seized in such a search; if the connection is attenuated, it is said to purge the taint of the illegal search.

qualified immunity police officers, correctional officials, and other criminal justice professionals may be sued only for violating "well-established" constitutional rights.

question first and warn later police may question an individual without reading *Miranda,* obtain a confession, and then read the *Miranda* rights and reinterrogate the suspect. The confession is admissible so long the *Miranda* warnings function effectively to advise suspects of their rights.

racial profiling stopping or arresting individuals because of their race, ethnicity, religion, or other characteristic rather than because of their actions.

reasonable doubt the standard for a criminal conviction.

reasonable suspicion a police officer may undertake an investigative stop of a suspect where the officer has an objective, factual basis to suspect that "crime is afoot"—that is, the suspect has engaged in, is about to engage in, or is engaging in criminal activity.

reasoning an explanation of a judge's thinking in reaching a decision.

rebuttal the defense case at trial.

recusal judge should remove himself or herself from a case based on a conflict of interest or bias.

rehabilitation punishment that is designed to assist an individual who is criminally convicted to become a law-abiding and productive member of society.

release on recognizance pretrial release based on a promise to appear for trial.

respondent an individual against whom a collateral attack is directed.

restoration punishment that compensates the victim for the losses resulting from crime.

retribution punishment that is intended to exact vengeance or revenge.

retroactivity of judicial decisions principle that a U.S. Supreme Court judgment should be retroactively applied to all cases that are yet to be filed and cases that already have been filed.

right of allocution right of a defendant to address the judge at a sentencing hearing.

routine border searches unintrusive searches that do not require articulable suspicion.

roving wiretap electronic surveillance authorized for any device used by the target of the investigation.

rule of exclusion substantial underrepresentation of a group on the jury venire.

rule of four four Supreme Court judges are required to vote to hear a case.

scientific identification identification of a suspect through scientific procedures.

scrupulously honor police may question an individual who has invoked his or her right to silence about a crime different in time, nature, and place after waiting a significant period of time and giving a fresh set of *Miranda* warnings.

search governmental intrusion on an individual's expectation of privacy.

search incident to an arrest a search that is authorized by the fact of an arrest; it includes a search of the person arrested and the area within his or her immediate control.

search warrant authorization from a magistrate to search for and seize specified objects.

seizure a reasonable person would not believe himself or herself to be free to leave or to otherwise terminate the encounter.

selective incapacitation punishment that singles out offenders who have committed designated offenses for lengthy incarceration.

selective incorporation Fourteenth Amendment Due Process Clause incorporates only selected provisions of the Bill of Rights.

selective incorporation plus Fourteenth Amendment Due Process Clause incorporates selected portions of the Bill of Rights along with other rights.

selective prosecution prosecution in violation of the Equal Protection Clause of the Fifth and Fourteenth Amendments, which protect individuals from prosecution because of their race or their gender or the exercise of their fundamental rights.

sentencing guidelines a formula established by a state legislature for determining criminal sentences.

sentencing hearing a judicial hearing to determine a defendant's criminal sentence.

sequential presentation presentation of individuals in a lineup one after another.

show of authority seizure demonstration of authority by law enforcement officers in which they direct a suspect to halt, display their weapons, block the suspect's movement, or otherwise conduct themselves in a manner that would result in a reasonable person not feeling free to leave or otherwise terminate the encounter. The suspect must actually submit to the demonstration of authority.

showup a victim or eyewitness is confronted with a single suspect.

silver platter doctrine practice, ruled unconstitutional in 1960, in which federal officials relied on evidence in federal prosecutions that had been seized by state officials in violation of the Fourth Amendment.

simultaneous lineup a victim or eyewitness confronts all the participants in the lineup at the same time.

Sixth Amendment protection against the deliberate eliciting of a confession right to counsel that attaches after proceedings are brought against an individual.

sneak-and-peek search a search that is not disclosed to the subject of the search.

Socratic method use of question and answer technique in teaching.

special-needs searches searches that do not serve the normal needs of law enforcement.

specific deterrence punishment that is intended to deter a specific individual from committing additional crimes.

speedy trial Sixth Amendment right to a trial without unreasonable delay.

standing a defendant's eligibility to contest the legality of a search.

Star Chamber a special court that was established by the English king in the fifteenth century and that was charged with prosecuting and punishing political and religious dissidents.

stare decisis the practice of following the precedent set by previous court decisions.

statements an oral or written declaration to the police that may constitute an assertion of innocence.

stop and frisk the police may stop an individual in those instances in which they have a reasonable basis to believe that crime may be afoot. The police may conduct a frisk for weapons where the individual fails to dispel the officer's fear that the individual is armed and presently dangerous.

stop-and-identify statutes state laws that authorize the police to require a citizen subjected to a stop and frisk to present identification.

subjective test for entrapment test that asks whether the accused possessed the criminal intent or predisposition to commit the crime or whether the government created the crime.

subpoena ad testificandum a court order to produce a tangible object.

subpoena duces tecum a court order to produce documents.

successive petition doctrine rule prohibiting the filing of a second habeas petition that raises a claim that has been presented in a prior petition.

suggestive procedures identifications that influence the result by highlighting one of the participants.

supervisory authority the Supreme Court has the authority to direct lower federal courts to follow rules that are not based on the U.S. Constitution.

Supremacy Clause Article VI, Section 2 of the U.S. Constitution provides that the Constitution, the laws of the United States, and treaties shall be the "supreme Law of the Land." This gives the federal government priority over the state government when there is a conflict between federal and state laws.

surety bond bond posted by a bail bondsman indicating his or her promise to pay a defendant's bail in the event that the defendant does not appear for trial.

testimonial evidence evidence that is communicative in character.

third degree the use of coercion and violence by the police to extract confessions.

third party consent consent to a search provided by an individual with common authority who exercises mutual use of property and has joint access or control for most purposes.

Three Strikes and You're Out law law requiring that three felonies result in lengthy imprisonment or life in prison.

Title 42, Section 1983 of the U.S. Code individuals may be sued for acting under the color of state law for violating an individual's constitutional rights or a federal right.

tort actions a state court suit for damages to compensate individuals who have suffered harm.

total incorporation entire Bill of Rights is incorporated into the Fourteenth Amendment Due Process Clause.

total incorporation plus entire Bill of Rights along with other rights not contained in the Bill of Rights are incorporated into the Fourteenth Amendment Due Process Clause.

transactional immunity exemption from prosecution for any offense arising out of the act or transaction that is the subject of a witness's testimony.

trap-and-trace device a device that records the numbers of calls coming in to a telephone.

trespassory approach approach to Fourth Amendment protection that assumes such protection is limited to physical intrusions of the home, comparable to property rights approach.

trial *de novo* a new trial before a different court.

true bill records the names of the grand jurors issuing an indictment.

USA PATRIOT Act congressional act passed in October 2001 that provides procedures to combat terrorism.

use and derivative use immunity a witness may not be prosecuted based on information derived from his or her testimony.

venire group of individuals from which a jury is selected.

venue location of the trial.

vicinage selection of the jury from the area in which the crime is committed.

vindictive prosecution prosecution in violation of the Due Process Clause of the Fifth and Fourteenth Amendments, which protect individuals who assert their constitutional or statutory rights from retaliation in the form of having more serious charges brought against them.

voir dire examination of potential jurors.

voluntary, knowing, and intelligent waiver a relinquishment of *Miranda* rights must be the product of a free and deliberate choice and with full awareness of the nature of the right being abandoned and the consequences of the decision to abandon it.

***Wade–Gilbert* rule** the suspect has a constitutional right to a lawyer at all postindictment lineups and confrontations. Absent the presence or waiver of a lawyer, the results may not be introduced by the prosecutor at trial. A prosecutor may not ask a witness for an in-court identification unless the prosecution establishes by clear and convincing evidence that the in-court identification is not the product of a tainted identification procedure.

wall, the a policy that prohibited communication between the FBI and CIA in regard to national security and terrorism.

weighing states states in which a sentence of death is based on balancing aggravating and mitigating circumstances.

writs of assistance documents used by eighteenth-century American colonial authorities to compel individuals to assist in carrying out a search.

Case Index

Subject Index

About the Author

Matthew Lippman has taught criminal law and criminal procedure in the Department of Criminology, Law, and Justice at the University of Illinois at Chicago (UIC) for more than twenty years. He has also taught courses on civil liberties, law and society, and terrorism and teaches international criminal law at John Marshall Law School in Chicago. He earned a doctorate in political science from Northwestern University and a master of law from Harvard Law School, and he is a member of the Pennsylvania Bar.

He has been voted by the graduating seniors at UIC to receive the Silver Circle Award for outstanding teaching on six separate occasions and has also received the UIC Flame Award from the University of Illinois Alumni Association, as well as the Excellence in Teaching Award, the Teaching Recognition (Portfolio) Award, and the Honors College Fellow of the Year Award. The UIC chapter of Alpha Phi Sigma, the criminal justice honors society, named him "criminal justice professor of the year" on three occasions. He is also recognized in *Who's Who Among America's Teachers*. In 2008, he was recognized as College of Liberal Arts and Sciences Master Teacher. He has served in every major administrative position in the Department of Criminology, Law, and Justice, including department head, director of undergraduate studies, and director of graduate studies.

Professor Lippman is author of 100 articles and three books. These publications focus on criminal law and criminal procedure, international human rights, and comparative law. He also is author of *Contemporary Criminal Law Concepts, Cases, and Controversies* (2nd ed., 2010). His work is cited in hundreds of academic publications and by international courts and organizations.

He has also served on legal teams appearing before the International Court of Justice in The Hague, has testified as an expert witness on international law before numerous state and federal courts, and has consulted with both private organizations and branches of the U.S. government. He regularly appears as a radio and television commentator and is frequently quoted in leading newspapers.

SAGE

PINE
FORGE

CORWIN

CQ PRESS